S0-BBA-753

Principles of
MARKETING

THIRD EDITION

Principles of MARKETING

THIRD EDITION

THOMAS C. KINNEAR
University of Michigan

KENNETH L. BERNHARDT
Georgia State University

SCOTT, FORESMAN/LITTLE, BROWN HIGHER EDUCATION
A Division of Scott, Foresman and Company
Glenview, Illinois   London, England

To Connie, Maggie, and Jamie
Kathy and Karen

Scott, Foresman Series in Marketing
Thomas C. Kinnear, Consulting Editor

Acknowledgments

Acknowledgments appear on pp. A–33 through A–36, which are legal extensions of the copyright page.

The cover illustration shows the areas of the earth for which various Sprint satellites are responsible.

Illustration by Earl Gee; Art Directors, Tony Milner/Mark Anderson

Library of Congress Cataloging-in-Publication Data

Kinnear, Thomas C., 1943–
Principles of marketing / Thomas C. Kinnear, Kenneth L. Bernhardt.
— 3rd ed.
p. cm.
Includes bibliographical references.
ISBN 0-673-38565-5 : $32.00
1. Marketing. I. Title.
HF5415.K5227 1990
658.8—dc20 89-27719
ISBN: 0-673-38565-5 CIP

Printed in the United States of America.
2 3 4 5 6-RRW-94 93 92 91 90

Preface

Marketing is constantly affected by the economic, social, technological, and political environments in which we live. In the 1990s organizations confront a marketplace that will continue breaking down into an increasing array of consumer groups, each with its own special needs and interests. But these organizations also face a greatly expanded marketplace, one encompassing most of the nations of the world. Because change in the marketing environment seems to be accelerating, today's marketers and organizational decision makers increasingly view the **marketing concept** as the key to success.

In the third edition, we continue to organize *Principles of Marketing* around the theme of the marketing concept, emphasizing that the basic function of marketing is to identify and satisfy consumer needs. The book introduces future decision makers to the fundamentals of marketing. Using contemporary applications, it helps students gain sound insights into a dynamic world involving product, distribution (place), promotion, and price decisions for organizational and consumer products, physical products, intangible services, and profit and not-for-profit organizations. Significant issues of marketing are illustrated with current data. Topics are covered step-by-step to lead the reader through these challenging areas and yet extensively enough to allow depth of understanding.

What's New in the Third Edition

This edition has been informed not only by changes in the marketing environment, but also by the latest thinking of marketing professionals and by marketing practice appropriate to the 1990s. For example, we have added discussion of topics as broad as the **quality movement** in industry and the role marketing plays in it; but we have also added discussion of topics as particular but important as the recently developed practice of **slotting allowances** in retail distribution. A new chapter, "Public Policy, Regulation, and Ethical Marketing," draws together related subjects of great importance to marketers today. We now have separate chapters on "Wholesalers" and "Retailers." The changing nature of **global competition** is emphasized throughout the text and especially in the perspective brought to the chapter "International Marketing: A Global Approach."

Every chapter has current, new applications and examples presented with supporting color photographs and illustrations. And to help students apply their knowledge in some new ways, we have added *PC Exercises* (a disk accompanies each book) for each chapter and *Review Your Marketing Knowledge* questions at strategic points within chapters.

Emphasis on Practical Applications

There is a link between marketing theory and marketing practice that students will find increasingly important as they understand more about the field. In presenting key concepts and approaches, we emphasize their practical applications. Each chapter opens with a *Marketing Profile* that introduces the chapter's issues by describing a real situation in which marketing decisions were made. There are at least two *Marketing in Action* features per chapter that provide concise illustrations of selected concepts. Two *Case Applications* close each chapter; these open-ended problem-solving situations focus on specific marketing problems and solutions and can form the basis for active discussion in the classroom.

Features to Facilitate Learning

We have added two new features to this edition to facilitate learning:

1. Each chapter contains a *Personal Computer Exercise* to allow students to explore issues in the chapter in more depth. The exercise is explained in the chapter and implemented on a self-contained computer disk that is included with the text.
2. *Review Your Marketing Knowledge* questions appear at least twice in each chapter to challenge students to think about and review the material they have been reading.

Other features have been revised to conform to the changes in the third edition:

3. *Learning objectives* are stated for each chapter.
4. *Key points* presented at the end of each chapter reinforce learning.
5. Key terms are defined after each chapter in a *Glossary* and appear in boldface in the text where introduced.
6. *Issues for Discussion* at the close of every chapter help students think through the implications of the concepts introduced in the chapter.
7. *Figures* and *tables* are generously used to "graph out" important text explanations. Current *color photos* depict the world of marketing through advertisements and everyday marketing situations.
8. Appendix A, *Careers in Marketing,* provides guidance to students in their search for jobs. Appendix B, *Financial Concepts,* outlines information on costs, margin analysis, breakeven analysis, and profitability calculation.
9. *Name/Subject* and *Product/Company* indexes allow access to specific items.
10. *Full color* throughout brightens and opens up the material, making it more inviting for the student.

The Ancillary Package

Ancillary materials have become very important in the study of marketing. They provide options to instructors and students who wish to supplement and enhance sections of the text. We have provided ancillaries that should be useful in a wide range of courses and instructional settings:

Instructor's Manual

Study Guide

Test Bank

TextMaster operates on IBM PC and compatible microcomputers to provide the printed Test Bank's questions in a computerized format. In addition to allowing you to develop, maintain, and revise the Test Bank, TestMaster enables you to add your own questions or even create your own test bank. This test generator has been designed for easy use.

Marketing Casebook

150 Color Teaching Transparencies

PharmaSim: a Computerized Marketing Simulation enables students to use and refine their marketing knowledge and skills in either an individual or a team environment.

Videotapes

Acknowledgments

We want to acknowledge the contributions of Hiram Barksdale, Gloria Barczak, Cathy Goodwin, and Vicki Einhorn of Georgia State University. We thank Michael R. Pearce of the University of Western Ontario for permission to reproduce and modify the materials that form the basis of the first part of Chapter 8. We also thank Jane Monto, Catherine Minnick, and Beth Thompson for helping develop case materials and profiles.

We acknowledge the contributions of those colleagues who reviewed earlier editions:

C. L. Abercrombie	*Memphis State University*
Gerald S. Albaum	*University of Oregon*
Les R. Dlaby	*Lake Forest College*
Michael J. Etzell	*University of Notre Dame*
Kathleen A. Krentler	*San Diego State University*
Duncan G. LaBay	*University of Lowell*
Marilyn Liebrenz-Himes	*George Washington University*
Jill Long	*Valparaiso University*
Lynn J. Loudenback	*New Mexico State University*
Karen MacDonnel Christensen	*University of South Florida*
Donald G. Norris	*Miami University*
Terry Paul	*The Ohio State University*
Judith Powell	*University of Richmond*
Robert Reuchert	*University of Minnesota*
Edward A. Riodan	*Wayne State University*
Donald L. Shawver	*University of Missouri, Columbia*

And we also acknowledge the comments and guidance of our colleagues on the reviewing panel for the third edition:

Joe Cantrell	*De Anza College*
William Carner	*SW Missouri State University*
Wayne Chandler	*Eastern Illinois University*
Kent Claussen	*Parkland College*
William Curtis	*University of Nebraska*
Cynthia Forbes	*Golden Gate University*
Peggy Gilbert	*SW Missouri State University*
Marlene Katz	*Canada College*
Stephen P. King	*Keene State College*
R. Eugene Klippel	*Grand Valley State College*
Ross Lanser	*University of California Santa Cruz*
Ford Laumer	*Auburn University*
Marilyn Liebrenz-Himes	*George Washington University*
Michael Mayo	*Kent State University*
Martin Meyers	*University of Wisconsin—Stevens Point*
Ronald Michaels	*University of Kansas*
Keith Murray	*Northeastern University*
Joseph Myslivec	*Central Michigan University*
Allan V. Palmer	*University of North Carolina*
Bruce Seaton	*Florida International University*
Bill Tadlock	*University of Arkansas—Little Rock*
Burk C. Tower	*University of Wisconsin—Oshkosh*
Judy Wilkinson	*University of Akron*

The editorial staff at Scott, Foresman/Little, Brown provided sound counsel and handled a million details. Special thanks must be given to Melissa Rosati, Jane Steinmann, Andrea Coens, Jacqueline Kolb, Brett Spalding, and Karen Koblik.

Thomas C. Kinnear
Kenneth L. Bernhardt

Overview

PART FOUR

Distribution

PART FIVE

Promotion

PART SIX

Pricing

PART SEVEN

Marketing Applications: Situations, Trends, and Issues

Contents

PART ONE

Marketing and the Environment

1

2

PART TWO

The Marketplace

4

Market Analysis: Segmentation and Targeting 98

5

Consumer Buying Behavior 132

10

Product Development and Management 294

PART FOUR

Distribution

11

Channels of Distribution 334

12

Wholesalers 372

13

Retailers 394

PART FIVE

Promotion

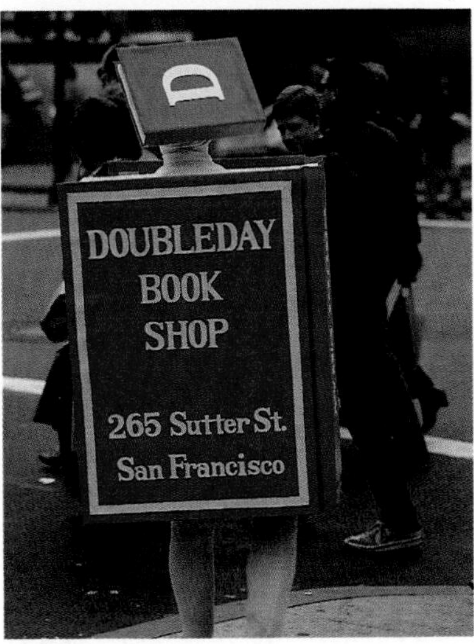

PART SIX

Pricing

19

Pricing Procedures 606

PART SEVEN

Marketing Applications: Situations, Trends, and Issues

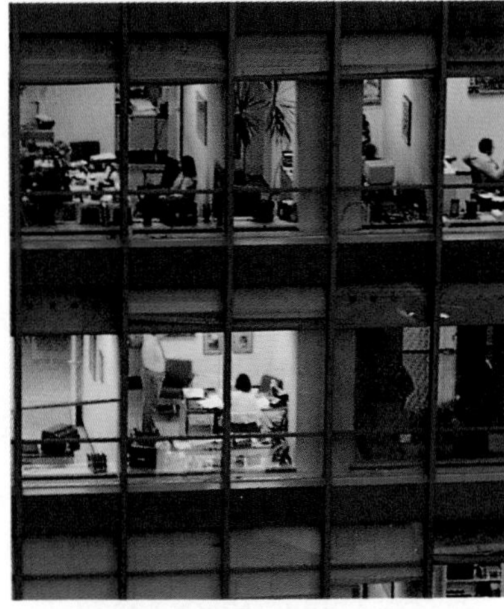

Principles of MARKETING

THIRD EDITION

PART ONE

Marketing and the Environment

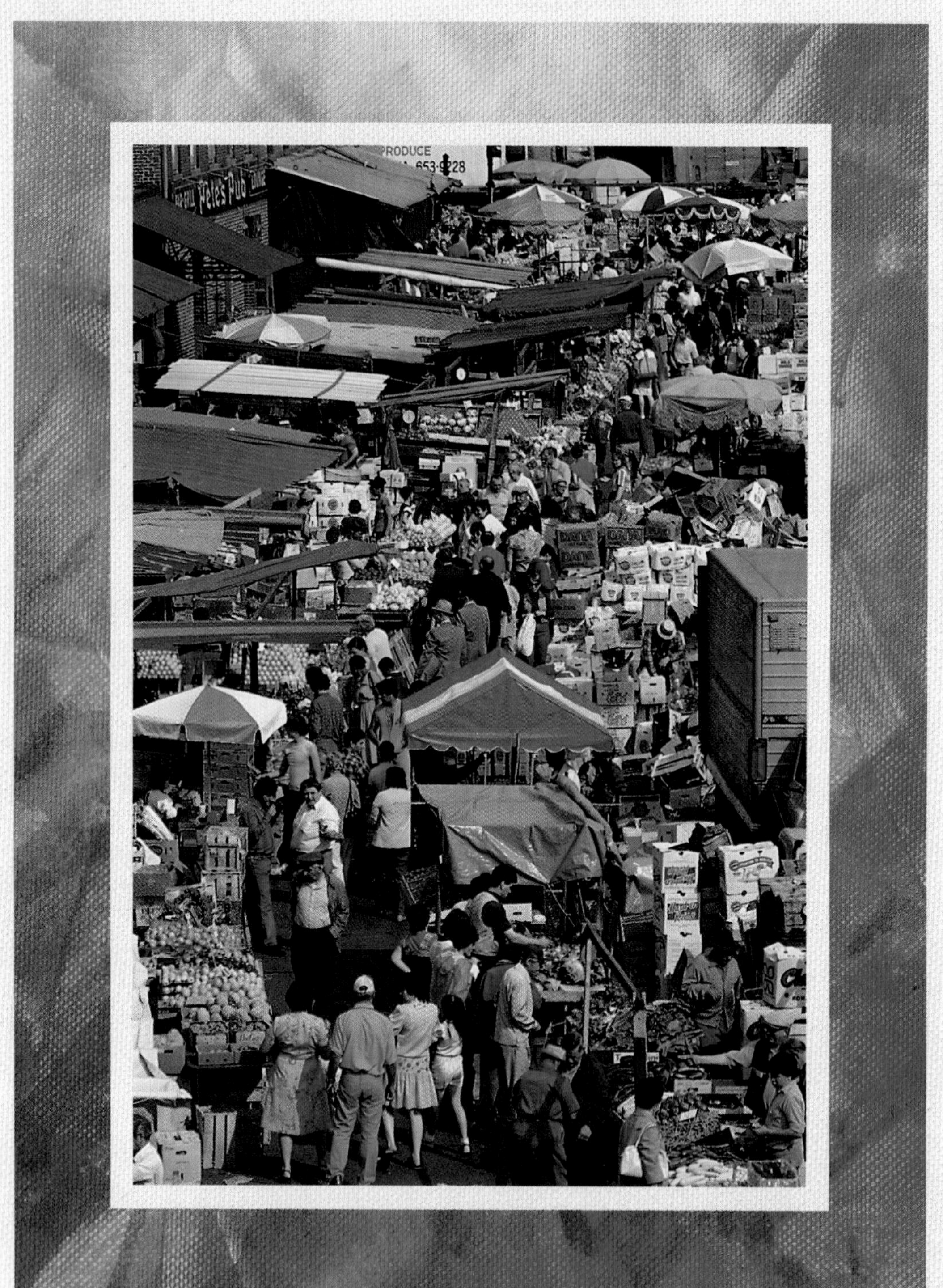
PRODUCE
Pete's Pub

1

Marketing: An Introduction

Learning Objectives

Upon completing this chapter, you will be able to do the following:

DEFINE
marketing and the marketing concept.

DESCRIBE
the marketing functions that benefit the economy and organizations.

DISCUSS
the development of marketing in organizations.

COMPARE
the production, sales, and marketing concepts of organizational operations.

UNDERSTAND
the importance of marketing to you, to the economy as a whole, and to business and not-for-profit organizations.

IDENTIFY
different approaches to the study of marketing.

LIST
numerous examples of marketing activity.

MARKETING PROFILE

White Castle Looks to Marketing to Build for the Future

For years the family-owned White Castle Restaurant chain has operated in a traditional fashion with little emphasis on marketing—whether in advertising, franchising to aid in expansion, or expanding product lines to attract new consumers. Sales for the Columbus, Ohio-based firm were $268.5 million in 1986. McDonald's is estimated to equal that sales level every eight days. White Castle is a small player in the fast-food industry, with sales comprising only .5% of the $56 billion industry total. However, competitors are now taking note of the changes at the firm because of White Castle's new aggressiveness in marketing. The only area where White Castle had not historically fully developed its business skills is marketing. As E. W. Ingram III, grandson of the company's co-founder said, "We've realized for a long time that we were not strong marketers. Now we're looking to the outside (to use marketing) for a new direction and new ideas."

White Castle has begun to work with its existing product line to build awareness among young consumers:

• A packaged children's meal has been developed and advertised extensively in an effort to reach an age group often neglected by other chains.

• Test marketing of chicken nuggets and a breakfast sandwich has begun. Previously, White Castle had not expanded its product line since the late 1960s, when a fish sandwich was introduced.

Market research has been utilized to help define consumer purchase trends:

• For years White Castle has received requests for shipments of frozen hamburgers from loyal customers who had moved away from the firm's Midwest and East marketing area. An 800 phone number has been established to allow customers to order their burgers in bulk.

• Customers in areas where White Castle has stores were found to be purchasing in quantity, freezing the hamburgers, and microwaving them later. To capitalize on this trend, packaged frozen hamburgers are being test marketed in grocery stores in five cities, mainly in the Midwest, with limited advertising support.

All White Castle stores are company owned, except for several stores in Japan. Steps are being taken to increase market penetration:

• Thirteen stores were added in 1987 and twenty were opened in 1988, giving White Castle a total of 228 outlets in ten eastern and midwestern states.

• An additional twenty outlets are planned for 1989, with potential sites being examined in Dallas-Fort Worth, Denver, Atlanta, Baltimore, Washington, Philadelphia, and Florida.

• Older restaurants are slated for remodeling, while new stores will reflect changing customer needs such as drive-in service and expanded seating.

White Castle once relied on repeat business to maintain market share. With the aging of its traditional customer base, a change in focus was necessary. Fred P. Schindler, the chain's director of advertising, has said, "We need a new generation of customer." Marketing is a key to White Castle's efforts to expand its presence in the highly competitive fast food industry.

The profile describes the struggle of one company to stay competitive by using what we call *marketing*. The exact meaning of this term will become clear as you read this book; for now, just note that marketing has a major role in the success or failure of organizations. It impinges on product, distribution, promotion, and price decisions, while staying responsive to an ever-changing environment. This chapter presents some marketing basics and shows their influence in society and in our lives.

SOURCES: Scott Hume, "White Castle builds savvy in marketing," *Advertising Age*, November 2, 1987, pp. 6, 108; "White Castle extends its marketing, not product line," *Marketing News*, January 17, 1986, pp. 16; Julia Flynn Siler, *The New York Times* in the *Ann Arbor News*, May 8, 1988, pp. C10.

Marketing is an important, dynamic, fascinating, and sometimes frustrating subject area. It is important because it affects our daily lives, the society we live in, and the success and failure of all organizations. It is dynamic because it operates in the real world, which is constantly changing. It is fascinating: examples of marketing successes and failures form the folklore of American business. It can also be frustrating because its ever-changing nature makes it impossible to reduce it to a set of equations that yield right answers. It is part science and part art. In short, it is an important and intriguing area to work in and study.

This book is designed to introduce marketing to those who have not studied it before. Thus, it contains the basic vocabulary and concepts of the field. In presenting this material, we use many real examples of marketing in action; we want it to come alive for you. Think of yourself as being part of the management at White Castle. Put yourself in the position of having to apply marketing principles to White Castle's weakening position in the fast food industry. It would be a bit scary, but also exciting, to have this responsibility, wouldn't it? The White Castle example is but one of hundreds of actual marketing contexts in this book; we want you to place yourself in these real-world situations as you read this book. In the end we hope you will have a good basic understanding of the field of marketing.

In this chapter, we will develop definitions for *marketing* and *the marketing concept*; discuss the importance of marketing to you, to the economy, and to business and not-for-profit organizations; describe what marketing does and how this benefits the economy; examine how we now think of marketing in contrast to earlier views; and explore different approaches to the study of marketing. Finally, we will present an overview of the rest of this book.

Defining Marketing

The situation you just read about at White Castle illustrates the activity of marketing in various ways. Before looking at more examples, we need to develop a formal definition.

In 1960, the American Marketing Association provided a now outdated definition of *marketing* as follows:

> *Marketing is the performance of business activities that direct the flow of goods and services to the customer or user.*[1]

This definition was consistent with the marketing thought of its day, but we now recognize that it is too narrow on many counts. Marketing is performed not only in business but also in not-for-profit organizations and in situations outside the business world. Illustrations of this will be presented later in this chapter.

Indeed, marketing involves more than just physical goods and services. Figure 1–1 shows that ideas are marketed as well. Additionally, marketing impact is felt long before goods and services begin to flow from producer to consumer. Marketing contributes to the makeup and design of a physical good, service, or idea that is directed to the consumer by providing inputs about *consumer needs.* As the president of Casio, Inc. (a watchmaker) noted, "[We] set out to fill the customer's wants."[2] Marketing is relevant long before production occurs.

We need a definition that captures the common denominator of all marketing activity. This common denominator is the concept of exchange. **Exchange** involves all the activities associated with receiving something from someone by giving something in return. Figure 1–1 illustrates the different types of things that may be exchanged.

Figure 1–1 Examples of Marketing Exchanges

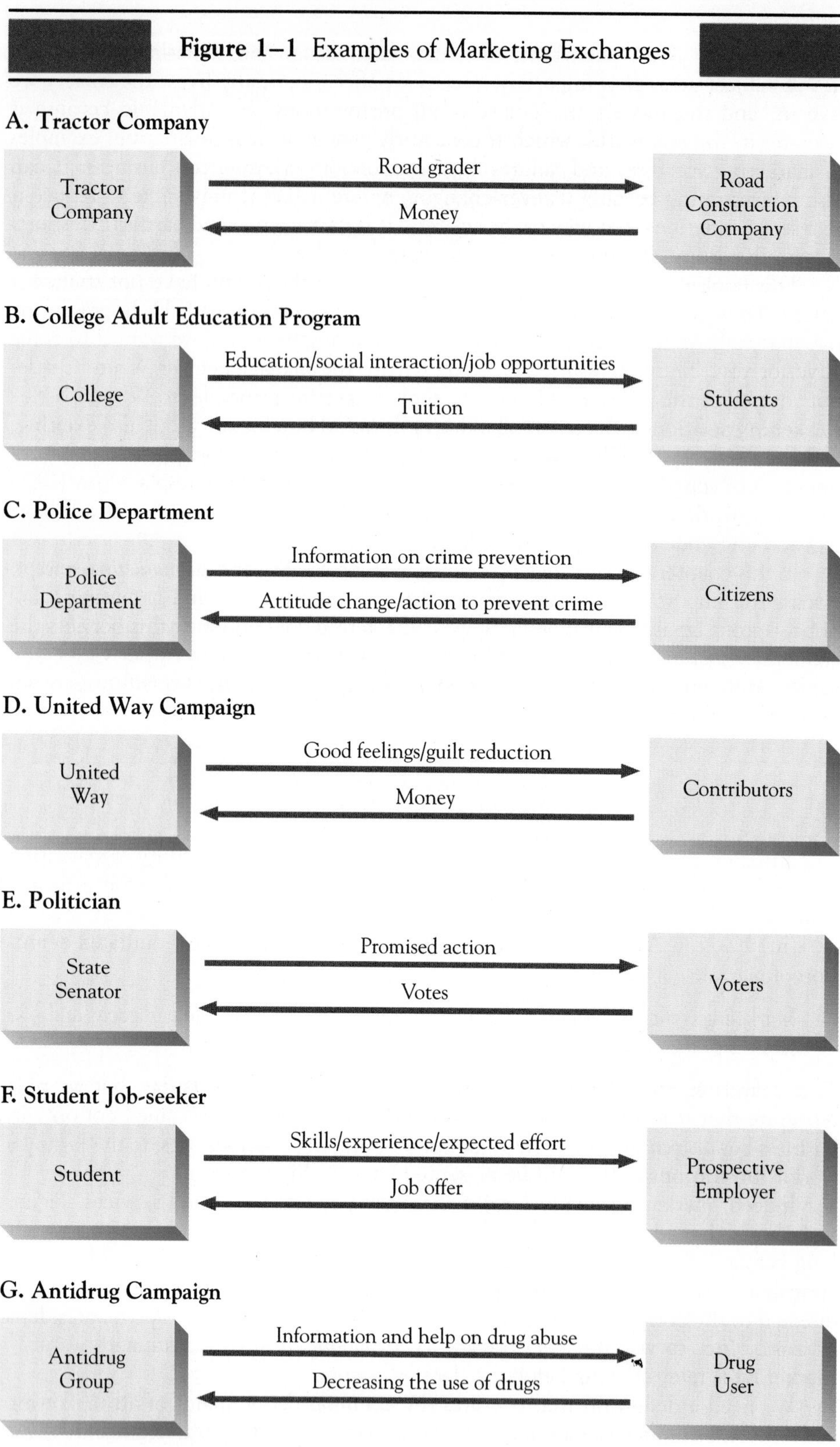
A. Tractor Company
Tractor Company
Road grader
Money
Road Construction Company
B. College Adult Education Program
College
Education/social interaction/job opportunities
Tuition
Students
C. Police Department
Police Department
Information on crime prevention
Attitude change/action to prevent crime
Citizens
D. United Way Campaign
United Way
Good feelings/guilt reduction
Money
Contributors
E. Politician
State Senator
Promised action
Votes
Voters
F. Student Job-seeker
Student
Skills/experience/expected effort
Job offer
Prospective Employer
G. Antidrug Campaign
Antidrug Group
Information and help on drug abuse
Decreasing the use of drugs
Drug User

Figure 1–2 Exchanges Involving Intermediaries

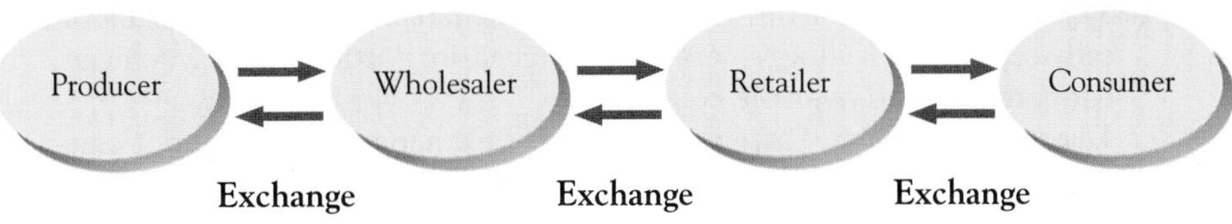

What is given or received need not be a physical product or money (A), but can be the acceptance of an idea (C), a gift to charity (D), attendance at a school (B), or even a job offer (F). Indeed, students looking for jobs are involved in marketing—the marketing of themselves.

All that is necessary is that *something of value be exchanged.* For example, in a United Way campaign, contributors of money gain good feelings and reduce their guilt in return for their money; in an election campaign, a political candidate gains votes in exchange for promised action. Note that the intent of the exchange may not be the increased consumption of something. In an antidrug campaign (see part G of Figure 1–1), a decrease in the usage of drugs is exchanged for information and help on drug abuse. When the objective of an exchange is to decrease consumption, it is commonly called **demarketing.**

Recently, the American Marketing Association redefined **marketing** to be consistent with this approach.

> *Marketing is the process of planning and executing the conception, pricing, promotion, and distribution of ideas, goods, and services to create exchanges that satisfy individual and organizational objectives.*[3]

Historically, the exchanges of physical products for money or other products took place in a central marketplace in a town or city. Hence, *marketing* took its name from the market where these exchanges were made. The name remains, even though the applications have extended well beyond the historical origins.

Often the process of exchange is more complex than in Figure 1–1. The producer of a product may be so far removed from the consumer that it would be impossible or prohibitively expensive to complete exchanges for many products without the presence of intermediaries. Wholesalers and retailers play this role for many products. Thus, instead of one exchange, a series of exchanges are involved in getting products from producers to consumers, as Figure 1–2 illustrates.

The Need for Marketing

As soon as organizations or people consider the possibility of creating a good, service, or idea, they are in the market for a consumer and must seek to understand consumer needs. Alternatively, as soon as organizations or people develop the ability to consume goods, services, or ideas, they are in the market for a product. In these circumstances, the basis for a satisfactory exchange seems to be in place. Unfortunately, the exchange may not take place, because there are usually *gaps* or *separations* between producers and consumers of goods, services, and ideas.

The most important of these separations are the following:[4]

1. *Spatial Separation.* Parties to a potential exchange are usually geographically separated. Kellogg's cereal is produced in Battle Creek, Michigan, but consumed all over the country.
2. *Temporal Separation.* Parties to a potential exchange usually cannot complete an exchange at the *time* products are produced. The products must be moved from producer to the location of consumers, which takes time. Also, consumers want the goods available at their convenience. For example, most toy sales occur in November and December, but production occurs throughout the year.
3. *Perceptual Separation.* Both producers and consumers may be unaware or uninterested in each others' offerings. There is thus a need for producers to obtain information about consumers, and for consumers to know about product availability and price. Producers also need information about consumers to guide the production of goods, services, and ideas.
4. *Separation of Ownership.* There is an inherent separation of ownership between producers and consumers. The marketing system strives to allow title for goods to pass from producers to consumers.
5. *Separation of Values.* Producers and consumers place different values on products. The producer looks at value in terms of costs and competitive prices, while the consumer values the product in terms of its utility and his or her ability to pay for it. IBM placed high values on its PS/2 computers, based upon cost and competitive activity. Unfortunately for IBM, many American businesses have placed much lower values on these machines, basing their judgments upon both the expected utility (office productivity, repair costs, software availability, current stock of old PCs) the PCs will give them and their ability to pay.

Marketing Fills Exchange Gaps

The force or activity that overcomes these separations is called *marketing.* The greater the separation preventing exchange from occurring, the greater the role of marketing in realizing market potentials.

Marketing bridges these separations by performing certain basic functions, discussed in more detail in Chapters 12, 13, and 14. For now, note that **functions of marketing** are divided into three types: *transactional, logistical,* and *facilitating.*

Transactional functions are the actual *buying* and *selling* of products. Selling involves the promotion of products with advertising and personal selling, while buying involves seeking and evaluating of alternative products. *Logistical functions* are the *storage* and *transportation* of products. *Facilitating functions* include *financing* products, *risk-taking* by holding ownership, *providing market information, developing standards,* and *grading* products against these standards. These marketing activities bridge the gap between producers and consumers so that exchange can occur.

Marketing Creates Utility

By bridging the market separations, marketing creates **utility** or value for the parties in the exchange. In general, human and organizational needs are satisfied by the creation of four separate utilities: *form, place, time,* and *possession.*

Table 1–1 Market Separations, Functions Performed, and Utility Created

Market Separations	Functions Performed to Bridge Separation	Utility Created
Spatial	Transportation Storage	Place
Temporal	Storage	Financing Risk-taking Time
Perceptual	Selling Provision of market information	Form, plus facilitates all other utilities
Ownership	Buying Selling Risk-taking financing	Possession
Values	Buying Selling Standards and grading Provision of market information	Possession, Form

Form utility is provided by the production of the good, service, or idea itself. To the extent that marketing input affects this production, marketing helps create form utility. A successful product can best fit a market if marketing input is involved during this utility formation. *Place utility* means having your product at the place where consumers need it. *Time utility* is having it available when it is needed, and *possession utility* means getting the product to the consumer so that he or she can use it. Put simply, the objective is to have the right product at the right place, at the right time, for the right person. There is value to the consumer in all these utilities.

Only marketing creates place, time, and possession utility. Additionally, it can have a major impact on form utility. Thus, marketing creates real value. For example, a bushel of wheat offers little utility to a hungry person, but, after it is made into bread, delivered to a place near the consumer's home, at the time the consumer is hungry, then it has much more utility. Table 1–1 summarizes the relationships among market separations, functions performed, and utilities created. It is because the market separations exist between sellers and buyers that marketing functions must be performed, thus creating utilities.

Marketing Within the Organization

Because gaps exist between producers of goods, services, and ideas, and their potential customers, certain transactional, logistical, and facilitating functions must be performed. The decisions made within an organization as to *which functions* it should perform and the *way to perform them* are important factors in the success or failure of that organization. Marketing management deals with both of these types of decisions, as well as the process by which these decisions are made. The way marketing management has been perceived within organizations has changed dramatically over the years. A brief review will help us understand the current position.

The Production Concept

In his book *The Wealth of Nations,* published in 1776, Adam Smith wrote:

> *Consumption is the sole end and purpose of all production, and the interest of the producers ought to be attended to only so far as it may be necessary for promoting that of the consumer.*[5]

Unfortunately, it was almost two hundred years before this philosophy attained wide acceptance in organizations. Instead, through the eighteenth and nineteenth centuries, and until about 1930, organizations pursued a **production concept.** They produced and distributed those products they were able to provide most efficiently, and they presumed there would be a market for them. The economic guideline of the times was that supply created its own demand. To some extent this was true, because production emphasis was on basic products such as food, shelter, and clothing. Consumers had little discretionary income and purchased what basic products were available. The mass-production concept for mass markets was not developed until the end of this period. The production orientation describes many countries' economies even today. Indeed, it can make sense when supply of a good is less than demand, especially in rural economies where no competition is present.

The Sales Concept

By the 1920s, improved manufacturing technology had given rise to mass production and a rising standard of living in the United States. The associated increase in discretionary income had created a mass market. But producers could produce more than markets would accept, so they decided "to get out there and sell," again paying little attention to identifying and satisfying consumer needs. The "hard sell" became

Once almost synonymous with "marketing," the "hard sell" approach is now only a small part of marketing philosophy.

almost synonymous with marketing. This philosophy is still at work today in many car dealerships and in door-to-door selling of products. The objective of the sales concept viewpoint is to sell what is available, using all the advertising and personal selling skills one has, with little concern for postpurchase satisfaction.

Robert Keith, the former chief executive officer of Pillsbury, described his company before it adopted the marketing concept:

> *We are professional flour millers. Blessed with a supply of the finest North American wheat, plenty of water power, and excellent milling machinery, we produce flour of the highest quality. Our basic function is to mill quality flour, and of course . . . we must hire salespersons to sell it just as we hire accountants to keep our books.*[6]

The Marketing Concept

In the early 1950s a new philosophy began to emerge. It was one that reflected Adam Smith's words. The idea was that producers should do an analysis of the needs of potential customers and then make decisions designed to satisfy these needs. One of the first corporations to adopt what was called the **marketing concept** was General Electric. Its 1952 Annual Report stated:

> *It [the marketing concept] introduces the marketing person at the beginning rather than at the end of the production cycle and integrates marketing into each phase of the business. Thus, marketing, through its studies and research, will establish for the engineer, the design and manufacturing person, what the customer wants in a given product, what price he or she is willing to pay, and where and when it will be wanted. Marketing will have authority in product planning, production scheduling, and inventory control, as well as sales, distribution, and servicing of the product.*[7]

Many successful companies such as Procter & Gamble, General Mills, and DuPont have adopted the marketing concept, and are referred to as *marketing-oriented companies.* To them, the marketing concept involves:

- **focusing on consumer needs;**
- **integrating all activities of the organization, including production, to satisfy these needs;**
- **achieving long-run profits through satisfaction of consumer needs.**

The failure (or lack of great success) of many other companies has at least partially been attributed to their failure to adopt this concept. Recall, in the *Marketing Profile* at the beginning of this chapter, the weak position that White Castle held before developing an emphasis on marketing.

In the 1970s and 1980s the marketing concept has been increasingly adopted by not-for-profit organizations.[8] Here the same focus on consumer needs and integrated effort exists, but the objective is to attain some measure of success other than profits. Museums, hospitals, churches, schools, and police departments have all benefited from the application of the marketing concept.

Making the marketing concept within an organization operational on a day-to-day basis is difficult, and few organizations are able to implement it completely on this basis. It is, however, a useful philosophy for guiding organizations, and a goal worth striving for. At its most basic level, the marketing concept is a philosophy that guides a firm in all its activities. It is an attitude, an approach to doing business.

Marketing Management

An organization can take action to perform marketing functions by deciding the specific *product* offered, *distribution* system used, *promotional* campaign adopted, and *price* charged. More formally:

> ***Marketing management*** *is the analysis, planning, implementation, and control of marketing decisions in the areas of product offering, distribution, promotion and pricing. Its purpose is to encourage and facilitate mutually satisfactory exchanges that meet organizational objectives.*

The marketing manager must make decisions in these areas, as illustrated by the examples in Figure 1–1:

- The marketing manager for a tractor company must decide what new products to offer, what price to charge for them, and which tractor dealers to use.
- The marketing manager at a college must decide how to advertise and determine the exact components of the school's program.
- A student (you as a marketing manager) must decide what to put on his or her resumé and what to wear to the interview.
- A director of an antidrug campaign must decide whether to use social workers, community leaders, or school personnel to give help on drug abuse.

Organizing for the Marketing Concept

Adoption of the marketing concept has important implications for the way one organizes the reporting relationships within an organization. In general terms, all marketing activities must be integrated to satisfy customer needs. The designation of one person as vice-president of marketing, or marketing manager, is one way this integrated effort is assured. A detailed discussion of how organizations may be structured for this purpose is presented in Chapter 20.

A Societal Marketing Concept

Recently, it has been suggested that there are possible negative consequences for society that result from the use of the marketing concept. That is, by focusing on the needs of a specific group of consumers, broader interests are ignored.

- Certain hospitals may dump charity patients because of intensive competition for the health-care dollar by health-care providers and because of tightening reimbursement conditions by both government and private insurance organizations.
- Products with high sugar content are promoted to children who like them, but these products contribute to their tooth decay.
- Consumers do not want antipollution devices or seat belts and other safety equipment in their cars. However, these devices improve air quality, save lives, and reduce hospital costs.

The societal marketing concept adds to the marketing concept by focusing the decision-maker's attention not only on consumer satisfaction, but also on the broader societal consequences of satisfying these consumer needs. Specifically:

> *The* **societal marketing concept** *is a decision-making approach that focuses on consumer needs and their societal consequences. It integrates all activities of the organization to satisfy these consumer needs, in a way that is consistent with concern for broader societal consequences. The purpose of this approach is to achieve long-run objectives (profit or others) through the satisfaction of these consumer needs, which must be balanced against the needs of society as a whole.*

This is a difficult standard to implement, and not all marketers agree that it should be undertaken. It implies that one might give up some profits or market share to avoid a broader societal concern. As a company manager or owner, would you be willing to use only returnable bottles if it cost you some sales? Would you stop marketing high-sugar cereals and candy to children if your whole profitability depended on it? Would you voluntarily put seat belts and antipollution devices on cars if they raised your costs and didn't help your sales? These are difficult decisions. Additionally, the societal marketing concept places the manager in the role of a moral or social judge who must decide what is good or bad for society. Some people question whether this is a legitimate role for managers to play. Although the focus of this book is on the marketing concept, we also discuss the broader societal consequences in Chapter 8.

Review Your Marketing Knowledge

- Regarding the White Castle profile that began this chapter, describe the types of separations that exist, the marketing functions performed by White Castle, and the utility created.
- In your search for a job after graduation, describe the separations that exist, the marketing functions that you will need to perform, and the utility you will create.

Applying Marketing Principles

So far we have examined the marketing role in exchanges, noted the functions that are performed in these exchanges, and examined marketing's role within the organization. Now let us expand our understanding of these marketing principles by noting a number of real-world applications. These examples include a consumer product (Helene Curtis), an industrial product (Supreme Truck Bodies), financial services (Chase Manhattan Bank), an educational institution (St. Mary's College), an idea (Dallas Police Department), and government activities (Michigan Tourism). All these organizations use marketing to facilitate exchanges. All attempt to apply the marketing concept in their own way.

Helene Curtis[9]

Marketing is extremely important for a successful introduction of a new product in the haircare industry. Helene Curtis' Salon Selectives line, introduced in mid-1987, has been lauded for the timing of the introduction, the brand positioning, and overall

You don't always need a salon to look salon beautiful. You've got Salon Selectives from Helene Curtis.
1 3 5 7
4 levels of salon Shampoos.
B H S P
4 types of salon Conditioners. Select the special combination that makes your hair so salon beautiful, they'll want to know, "Who does your hair?"
3 H
If your hair is dry and you want to make it softer and shinier, your Salon Selectives combination is Level 3 Shampoo for gentle cleansing; Type H Conditioner to bring out your natural highlights.
"Who does your hair?"
SALON SELECTIVES
FROM HELENE CURTIS
Feel salon beautiful every day.

Salon Selectives is a value-priced line with an upscale image.

marketing implementation. Curtis provided heavy advertising support to generate brand awareness during the introductory phase. Specifically:

- $14 million was spent on a TV campaign, and another $26 million was spent on consumer and trade promotions for Salon Selectives.
- Coupons were used, including a direct mailing of a 30-cents-off coupon to 70 million households. Two 1-dollar-off coupons were distributed in June, while a special retail price was offered on full size bottles of Salon Selectives.

Salon Selectives was presented to the consumer as a "value-priced" line with an upscale image. "The positioning is terrific. Curtis is sure to pull business from both the upper end, dominated by (Procter & Gamble Company's) Vidal Sassoon and (International Playtex's) Jhirmack and the lower end, including its own Suave customers and (Revlon Group's) Flex," said Suzanne Grayson, president of Grayson & Associates, a cosmetics and fragrance consultant.

Helene Curtis has segmented the Salon Selectives shampoo by cleaning levels rather than the traditional normal, oily, and dry. Conditioners are segmented by "types" such as Type B for body building and texture and type H for highlights. With such a complex product line, industry analysts point out that Helene Curtis must be careful to address the benefits of the eight-part product line in its advertising.

With the introduction of the Salon Selectives line, Helene Curtis executives are being careful to avoid the mistakes made when the Curtis product Atune was introduced. Launched with only a $15 million support budget, Atune was positioned ambiguously as both a permed and color-treated hair product, making it an easy target for many competitors' products with heavier advertising budgets. The attention placed on product positioning and the $40 million dollar advertising and promotion budget backing Salon Selectives demonstrate Helene Curtis' desire to strengthen its position in the haircare industry. President Ronald J. Gidwitz said he is counting on the Salon Selectives line "to add to our leadership shares in both (the shampoo and conditioner) categories."

Supreme Truck Bodies[10]

Supreme, a manufacturer of specialty truck bodies in Goshen, Indiana, has managed to achieve a 700 percent increase in sales over the last five years in what is considered a low growth industry. Rick Horn, sales and marketing vice-president, described the marketing plan that facilitated this impressive sales growth as controlled chaos reflecting the nature of the business. "Not only do I have different competitors within different areas, but within a particular product line, depending on where we are. It's a highly segmented market, both geographically and by product line." With such a high degree of segmentation, flexibility must be built into a marketing plan.

Horn developed a three-tier selling plan consisting of distributors, a company sales force, and mounting stations. Mounting stations, company stores that sell and service truck bodies, had never been utilized by Supreme and were designed to help gain market penetration where company presence was weak. A tiered system provides flexibility by allowing Supreme to adapt selling techniques for each market.

Direct selling efforts were increased by Horn as a means of maintaining competitive prices and eliminating ineffectual distributors. Direct sales also provided Supreme with the opportunity to pursue larger customers and fleet buyers who could be better served by Supreme.

Company owned monitoring stations have contributed to direct sales efforts. Regions that had weak market share were targeted by Horn. Supreme maintains a strong commitment to its distributors—as long as they produce the expected sales. Horn said, "What we have found is that a good, aggressive, independent distributor does the best job for us, if we can find one in that market. In some markets we have, in others, we haven't. All we are trying to do is stay flexible." Industry analysts agree that Supreme has been able to develop a strong, flexible distributor network.

Growth has also been fueled by the expansion of the product line, making Supreme one of the few full-line manufacturers in the field. Supreme began an advertising program in trade publications directed toward end users to aid in the product-introduction phase. General advertising levels were also increased to aid in corporate awareness on the national level. Previously, Supreme used little to no advertising.

Horn feels Supreme is not only a market-driven company but also a profit-driven company. Supreme's marketing philosophy is to keep accounts relatively small and to be sure they are all profitable. Flexibility in all phases of marketing will help meet the challenges of maintaining Supreme's growth.

Chase Manhattan Bank[11]

With the expected repeal of the Glass-Steagall Act limiting the securities power of banks and prohibiting them from selling their own mutual funds, Chase Manhattan Bank is beginning a national marketing campaign touting expanded services. Vista Mutual Funds and other investment products are supported with a $4 million campaign that began in January 1988. Leigh Dance, Chase's marketing manager for investment products, said, "Our long-term strategy is that Glass-Steagall will fade away, so we're developing an advance strategy of how to market mutual funds while building an image."

Market research was used to help determine consumer acceptance for investment products offered by banks, particularly Chase. Survey results demonstrated the large potential market for such financial products. Specific research methods and results included:

- Focus groups and over 600 individual interviews.
- A 1987 survey by the Financial Services Group of Market Facts, Chicago. It found the market for mutual funds to be maturing. 90 percent of the U.S. population do not invest in mutual funds, with only 30 percent of this group deemed rejectors. 32 percent of this group said that if they did invest in mutual funds, they would do so through a savings and loan, not a broker.

With the Glass-Steagall Act still in effect, funds are sponsored and distributed through MFS Financial Services, Boston. MFS "took a silent role in order for the funds to have the look and feel of Chase. Although the funds have the security of Chase behind them, they're not Chase-sponsored," according to Dance. Dance feels that this strategy will help build an image of Chase as a marketer of mutual funds. Chase is using its member bank network to offer the funds nationwide, providing convenient service for consumers.

Advertising is being placed in seventeen major daily newspapers and will be expanded to include full-color ads in national business and personal finance publications. Regional business, upscale lifestyle, professional, and entertainment magazines will be added to the existing media schedule. Copy will focus on Chase's reputation, the convenience of investing at a bank, and the features and advantages associated with the Vista Funds.

- An image ad states, "A Proud Heritage. A Bold Image," and focuses on Chase's experience in financial services.
- A direct response ad proclaims, "A Proud Heritage. A Strong Family," and highlights the Vista Funds and customer convenience and service. The ad also contains a coupon and an 800 telephone number for consumer response.

With deregulation and the change in consumer attitudes toward investing, marketing will play a critical role in attracting new customers. Chase Manhattan has recognized this fact and moved quickly to become a player in the field.

St. Mary's College[12]

"We just had to face the facts," said Michael Vernetti, an administrator for St. Mary's College outside San Francisco. "The baby boom was over, and undergraduate enrollment had started to be a problem. We had to do something to stop losing money." To dig itself out of the $1 million deficit it had accumulated during the previous three years, St. Mary's established a self-supporting part-time program aimed at luring working adults to the campus. Backed by a yearly advertising and marketing budget of $20,000, the adult division thrived. The part-time enrollment tripled, and the school doubled its enrollment by 1990. In fact, while St. Mary's estimates that its 1550-student undergraduate division will lose $200,000, the college, as a whole, will more than cover all costs. "The new adult programs are helping to carry the school financially," says Vernetti. "It's very profitable."

Many other colleges have been discovering the advantages of adult education lately. In fact, most colleges have quietly been running adult degree programs at night for years. But now soaring administrative costs, shrinking federal support for fulltime graduate programs, and a dwindling undergraduate base have forced schools to focus sharply and competitively on the adult student. Colleges are creating special programs—both degree-oriented and generalized—for the working adult, and they are painfully learning how to promote them. The potential market is huge: It ranges from adults returning to acquire a new degree, to professionals seeking certification or licensing renewals, to those interested in brushing up on new theories.

"Colleges are amateurs at selling themselves," said Peter C. Tolos, a marketing consultant who has helped California state colleges and Drexel University set up their adult divisions. "You have to push the idea that there is a customer and the program is a product that has to be marketed," he says. And Rosalind K. Loring, dean of the University of Southern California's Continuing Education program, which opened a $2.5 million center recently, agrees. "A degree program has a target audience that's easy to locate," she says. "But establishing noncredit general courses takes time, different skills, and money."

Dallas Police Department[13]

Some marketing applications utilize one marketing variable over others. Using the promotional techniques of soap and soft-drink makers, the Dallas Police Department launched a drive to "sell" citizens on crime prevention. Funds totaling $787,205, with $336,000 allowed for a January-through-October ad campaign, were provided by a grant from the Texas Criminal Justice Department. A nine-member review committee, comprised mainly of police department administrative personnel, selected Rominger Advertising Agency to handle the campaign. Rominger's proposal was selected out of seventeen submitted to the committee. Requests for proposals stressed that "the results should maximize citizens' participation in eliminating the opportunity for crimes to be committed in Dallas." President Bart Rominger said that his proposal definitely included input from minority leadership; the black head of the Dallas Urban League and a prominent Mexican-American surgeon have been designated consultants. "Crime. Don't ask for it." was the theme of the campaign used in newspaper ads, radio, and TV.

The remainder of the $787,205 grant was used for administration, overhead, and additional personnel expense. Over a twenty-month period, specially trained crews of parapolice visited high-crime neighborhoods to explain to residents how they could prevent various crimes. Also in the plans was a ten-month public service ad program to follow the paid ad campaign.

Michigan Tourism[14]

The Michigan Travel Bureau is heavily marketing tourism in the state. Competition in the travel industry is fierce; states in the Great Lakes region that had ignored

Michigan keeps its tourism business booming by constantly updating and refocusing its Travel Bureau ads.

tourism are now spending heavily to attract visitors. Michigan ranks third in spending for the Great Lakes area behind the province of Ontario ($24.3 million) and the state of Illinois ($15.5 million). Michigan's budget is about $10.0 million. John Savich, director of the Bureau, said that, in order to sustain the momentum of the tourism industry, two things are needed: more sophisticated marketing and better cooperation between government and business. "Successful marketing, I think, in many respects means looking at opportunities and making them go further than they would if you didn't help them along. The product we have to offer, a vacation experience in Michigan, is continuing to improve. . . . Our task is to promote them (products) so people take full advantage of them."

The Bureau's primary method of promotion is TV advertising. $4.5 million was spent on TV, for coverage that was mainly out of state. Phone inquiries, generated by the advertising, increased 8 percent over the previous year to 328,000. New ads in the campaign focused on people instead of scenery. As Savich explained, "This is a consumer industry. And you don't succeed in a consumer industry in the 1980s by keeping things the same."

State government is making an effort to focus on long-term planning for the tourism industry. A Task Force on the Future of Tourism in Michigan was formed to plan for industry development. Recommendations included: a focus on the needs of travel operators, a shift in promotional emphasis to growing segments of the travel industry rather than the maturing segments now doing well, and adequate funding from the state to achieve these goals. For example, Michigan has always been known for its camping, hunting, and fishing resources. Now, as Savich pointed out, the Michigan Travel Bureau is promoting the upper income recreational activities that can be found in the state such as golf, skiing, and fine dining. "We're filling in with those more sophisticated forms of entertainment so that now we've got it all. The higher end is where most of the investment has taken place. Because people of the '80s are willing to spend a little bit more on themselves if the value is there."

Importance of Marketing

Perhaps when you began reading this book you asked, "Why should I be concerned about studying marketing?" Indeed, it is a question that must be answered about any discipline. Marketing is an important area to learn about for three basic reasons: (1) it has a direct impact on you personally; (2) it is a major component of all economic activity; and (3) it is critical to the success and failure of all organizations.

Importance to You

In the past day or two, you may have listened to a radio ad, seen a television ad, or read a newspaper or magazine ad; stopped by some stores to buy food, books, or clothing; complained about the price of a textbook you had to purchase; attempted to sell your old books or stereo system by placing a flyer on bulletin boards; or contributed blood at a Red Cross blood drive on campus. These are but a few of the direct ways in which marketing affects you on a daily basis. We all either react to marketing activity (seeing ads, buying goods at a store, or giving blood), or we make use of it ourselves (selling books and stereo equipment). All these activities encourage and facilitate exchange.

There are two other major dimensions of marketing that influence you directly: career possibilities in marketing, and your need to market yourself for the job you want. Career opportunities in marketing include retail merchandising and store management, brand management, advertising media buying or account management, marketing research, sales, public relations, and physical distribution management. These careers need people of different interests and skills. By the time you finish this book you will understand the nature of these careers. Additionally, at the end of this book, the *Careers in Marketing* Appendix contains a more detailed description of career opportunities in marketing. Even if your career interest is not in marketing, you will interact on the job with marketing people and probably will work in an organization that is trying hard to be marketing oriented. Either way, it is important to have knowledge and skills in marketing.

One final point: when you seek a job upon graduation, you will have a marketing problem. The courses you have taken in school, your experience in jobs or activities, your resumé, and your personal style and appearance are all part of the *you* that will need to find a job. Marketing thinking can guide the formation of your product and facilitate the exchange that will lead to the right job for you. See the *Careers In Marketing* Appendix.

Importance to the Economy

Marketing is important to the economy as a whole. It helps support the high level of economic activity that we have in the United States. Without the encouragement and facilitating of exchanges that marketing provides, the high level of economic activity could not exist.

Some additional facts will also help point out marketing's importance to the economy:

- Approximately 25 to 35 percent of employed people in the United States are engaged in jobs that are either directly or indirectly related to marketing.[15]
- On average, approximately 50 percent of every consumer dollar spent is related to marketing activity.[16] This value varies by product type. For example, in the marketing of cookies, marketing costs as a percentage of retail

sales are broken down approximately as follows: advertising, 5 percent; shipping and distribution, 5 percent; packaging, 7 percent; manufacturer's sales force, 20 percent; and retail expenses and profit, 16 percent. This totals 53 percent.

- About 45 percent of American family expenditures are spent on services such as transportation, health care, education, recreation, and shelter. Here marketing's importance relative to other activities is enhanced. Peter Drucker, a well-known general management writer, has said, "Any enterprise has two—and only two—basic functions: marketing and innovation.[17] This is especially true of service organizations, where "production" plays less of a role.

Importance to Organizations

The success or failure of specific products, or even of whole organizations, is dependent on many factors, including management skills, production capabilities, financial resources and management, and marketing skills and programs. To say which is most important in a given situation is difficult. However, *Business Week,* in a bold cover story, did describe marketing as the new priority for business.[18] The section on applying marketing principles vividly points out the negative consequences of ineffective marketing and points out the positive benefits of an effective marketing program.

Drucker said it well when he noted that:

> *Marketing is so basic that it cannot be considered a separate function. . . . It is the whole business seen from the point of view of its final results, that is, from the customer's point of view. Concern and responsibility for marketing must therefore permeate all areas of the enterprise.*[19]

REVIEW YOUR MARKETING KNOWLEDGE

- The level of retail sales in the post-Thanksgiving to December 24 time frame is considered critical to the success of specific retailers. How might this also be critical to the economy as a whole?
- North American Honda has been extremely successful in the U.S. automobile market without the designation of someone as Vice President of Marketing. How is this possible?

The Study of Marketing

Table 1–2 shows five possible approaches to the study of marketing. These views are like those of five blindfolded people describing an elephant on the basis of touching some part of it. The descriptions will be very different, depending on what part the person is touching—the trunk, ears, sides, or legs. So it is with marketing. All of the approaches give different perspectives, but each has its merits. In this book we shall draw upon each of them to some degree, although our main thrust will be on the *managerial* or *micro* approach. The managerial approach puts emphasis on making marketing decisions within an organization and is based solidly on the marketing concept. This concept is also the cornerstone of this book.

Table 1–2 Approaches to the Study of Marketing

Approach	Description
1. Managerial or Micro	The focus is on the way decisions are made. The emphasis is on the actual product, distribution, promotion, and pricing decisions made by marketers in carrying out the marketing functions. The marketing concept guides all activities.
2. Commodity	Marketers study the movement of specific goods from producer to end consumers. All institutions involved and functions performed are described.
3. Functional	The basic functions of marketing are described and their performance by various institutions is evaluated in terms of cost and effectiveness.
4. Institutional	The organizations that perform the functions are studied. Included are wholesalers and retailers, the transportation and warehouse systems, and other agencies.
5. Societal or Macro	This view focuses on marketing's impact on societal groups such as children, on the economy, or on society as a whole. It is thus concerned with legal and public policy issues, economic development, aggregate consumption patterns, and marketing cost/benefit.

Overview of the Book

This chapter has explained the basics of marketing: what it is and how it can benefit all types of organizations, society as a whole, and you as an individual. The rest of the book presents a more detailed look at the various aspects of marketing.

Chapter 2 focuses on the *managerial* approach by looking at marketing management, while Chapter 3 examines the marketing environment faced by a marketing decision maker. The study of the consumer—the heart of marketing analysis—is discussed in Chapters 4, 5, and 6. Chapter 7 looks at marketing research as a means of obtaining the necessary information to allow better decision making. Chapter 8 draws upon the *societal* approach to discuss marketing and public policy, a topic that is also very relevant to marketing managers.

Chapters 9 through 19 discuss specific marketing management decision areas. Chapters 9 and 10 focus on product aspects, and Chapters 11, 12, 13, and 14 deal with distribution decisions. Chapter 11 presents a *functional* view of marketing channels, while Chapter 12 focuses on an *institutional* look at marketing wholesalers, and Chapter 13 on marketing retailers. Chapter 14 integrates the *functional* and *institutional* approaches in its look at physical distribution. Chapter 15 examines promotional procedures in marketing, while Chapters 16 and 17 explore advertising and personal selling. Chapters 18 and 19 discuss pricing decisions.

The last part of the book discusses certain specific marketing situations, trends, and issues. Chapter 20 discusses the organization of the marketing function within organizations. Since we believe that marketing of services, not-for-profit organizations, and marketing in the international environment are all part of the mainstream of marketing, these topics are integrated throughout this book. But we also believe that these topics deserve special attention. Chapters 21 and 22 explore marketing services and not-for-profit organizations, while Chapter 23 is devoted to international marketing. In the last chapter, we discuss the integration of all aspects of the marketing plan.

The text presents relevant concepts along with real-world applications of these concepts within each chapter through textual examples and the longer "Marketing in Action," and, at the end of the chapter, through the two cases. In addition, twice within each chapter you are given a chance to think about what you are learning in the "Review Your Marketing Knowledge" sections. One other feature designed to help you develop a deeper understanding of the material in the text is the "personal computer exercise" at the end of most chapters. These exercises give you a chance to explore marketing concepts in depth using marketing data. These exercises are contained in the computer disk attached to this text.

KEY POINTS

• Exchange involves all the activities associated with receiving something from someone by giving something in return. This activity is an essential function of all aspects of our society.

• Marketing includes all the activities designed to make exchange occur and work better. It thus affects each of us in our daily lives, the economy and society in which we live, and the success or failure of organizations.

• The application of the marketing concept is a key factor in the performance of organizations. This concept focuses on consumer needs and integrates all activities of the organization to satisfy these needs while achieving long-run profits or other objectives.

• In applying the marketing concept, a manager needs to be concerned about the broader societal consequences of satisfying consumer needs.

• About half of the GNP comes from marketing; 25 to 35 percent of all jobs in the United States are directly or indirectly related to marketing.

• Marketing is involved in the exchanges of physical goods, services, and ideas.

• Marketing functions are designed to fill the gaps or separations that exist between producers of goods, services, and ideas and the consumers.

• In performing these functions, marketing creates time, place, and possession utility, and to some degree it contributes to form utility.

• Specific decisions related to these functions fall within the domain of marketing management. Thus, the marketing manager makes decisions about products, distribution, promotion, and price.

ISSUES FOR DISCUSSION

1. For each of the marketing examples discussed in this chapter, indicate what you believe is being exchanged.

2. For each of the marketing examples in this chapter, indicate what separations exist between producers and consumers, and indicate what utility is created by marketing.

3. In your search for a job upon graduation, what market separations will exist?

4. A social critic commented: "Marketing . . . something like three-quarters to nine-tenths of it is idle waste." Discuss.

5. How has marketing's failure to have an influence on form utility at White Castle contributed to this company's problems? (See the Marketing Profile.)

6. What is the difference between (a) marketing and personal selling, (b) marketing and advertising, (c) marketing and marketing management?

7. Do accounting firms like Arthur Young and Price Waterhouse practice marketing? Explain. Do theater groups and hospitals need marketing?

8. Give examples from your own experience of the marketing concept, the sales concept, and the production concept in action.

9. Why can the adoption of the marketing concept and the growth in the consumer movement occur at the same time?

10. Should marketing managers make judgments about the broader societal implications of their marketing decisions? Why or why not?

GLOSSARY

Demarketing: term used to describe an exchange when the objective is to decrease the consumption of a product.

Exchange: all the activities associated with receiving something from someone by giving something in return.

Functions of marketing: activities that bridge the separations between producers (of goods, services, and ideas) and consumers.

Marketing: the process of planning and executing the conception, pricing, promotion, and distribution of ideas, goods, and services to create exchanges that satisfy individual and organizational objectives.

Marketing concept: the view that organizations should identify and satisfy consumer needs through an integrated effort; the idea that organizations can best meet their objectives by satisfying consumer needs.

Marketing management: the analysis, planning, implementation, and control of marketing decisions in the area of product offering, distribution, promotion, and pricing. The purpose of these activities is to encourage and facilitate mutually satisfactory exchanges that meet organizational objectives.

Production concept: the idea that organizations produce and distribute those products they are able to provide most efficiently, while presuming that a market exists for them.

Sales concept: the idea that organizations should aggressively sell those products they want to produce.

Societal marketing concept: a view that focuses the organization's attention on the broader societal consequences of its marketing actions.

Utility: value created by satisfying human and organizational needs in terms of form, place, time, and possession.

NOTES

1. Committee on Definitions, American Marketing Association, *Marketing Definitions: A Glossary of Marketing Terms* (American Marketing Association, 1960), p. 15.

2. "When Marketing Failed at Texas Instruments," *Business Week,* June 22, 1981, pp. 91–94.

3. Peter D. Bennett, *Dictionary of Marketing Terms,* (American Marketing Association, 1988), p. 115.

4. William McInnes, "A Conceptual Approach to Marketing," in Reavis Cox, Wroe Alderson, and Stanley J. Shapiro, eds., *Theory in Marketing* (Irwin, 1964), p. 56.

5. Adam Smith, *The Wealth of Nations,* Book IV (Modern Library, 1937), p. 625.

6. Robert F. Keith, "The Marketing Revolution," *Journal of Marketing,* January 1960, pp. 35–38.

7. 1952 Annual Report of the General Electric Company, p. 21. (Note: Certain language in the original, now considered sexist, has been changed.)

8. The first formal argument for this appeared in Philip Kotler and Sidney I. Levy, "Broadening the Concept of Marketing," *Journal of Marketing,* Vol. 33, January, 1969, pp. 10–15.

9. Laurie Freeman, "Curtis' Salon Selectives Shakes Haircare Market," *Advertising Age,* March 23, 1987, p. 22.

10. Bill Kelley, "Supreme Brings High-Growth to Low-Tech," *Sales & Marketing Management,* September 1986, pp. 66–70.

11. "Bank Invests in Marketing Campaign for Its Mutual Funds," *Marketing News,* February 29, 1988, p. 24.

12. Based on "Colleges Learn the Hard Sell," *Business Week,* February 14, 1977, pp. 92–94; personal conversation with St. Mary's personnel, April, 1989.

13. Based on "Dallas Readies Anti-Crime Ads," *Advertising Age,* December 23, 1978, p. 25.

14. Eric Whisenhunt, "Travel and Tourism," *Michigan Business,* March 1987, pp. 28–31; Ron Garbinski, "FYI (top secret)," *Michigan Business,* March 1987, pp. 31–33.

15. U.S. Department of Labor, Bureau of Labor Statistics, *Survey of Current Business* (at various dates).

16. This is a difficult number to estimate. Reavis Cox in *Distribution in a High-Level Economy* (Prentice-Hall, 1965), p. 149, put this value at 41.7 percent. I. Fredrick Dewhurst in *Does Distribution Cost Too Much?* (Twentieth Century Fund, 1963), pp. 117–18, estimated this value at 58.9 percent.

17. Peter Drucker, *The Practice of Management* (Harper & Row, 1954), p. 38.

18. See "Marketing The New Priority," *Business Week* (November 21, 1983), pp. 96–106.

19. Drucker, p. 38.

CASE APPLICATION 1–1

Anheuser-Busch and a Total Marketing Approach

"Our philosophy is to be marketing driven in every aspect of our business," says Michael J. Roarty, executive vice president and director of marketing at Anheuser-Busch, Inc. (A-B). "Whether we are selling beer, introducing new products, or educating consumers about responsible consumption, we rely on a total marketing approach." Although the beer industry has been relatively flat in terms of growth, Anheuser-Busch has achieved significant sales growth, particularly with Budweiser and Bud Light, the Nos. 1 and 3 best-selling beer brands, respectively, in the country. Jerry Steinman, publisher of *Beer Marketer's Insights*, remarked, "To keep Budweiser growing in the face of the flat market is an amazing development. They are taking it out of the hides of the competition." The company's continued success can be attributed to the total marketing approach pursued by A-B.

Flagship brand Budweiser is positioned as an All-American beer that is a reward for a hard day's work. The slogan, "For All You Do, This Bud's For You," developed in 1978, is still being utilized with great success. Tom Sharbaugh, group brand director of Budweiser and Bud Light, attributes A-B's performance to the firm's "ability to take an old brand name and constantly refresh what that brand name stands for in the minds of the under 35 crowd."

Another contribution to Budweiser's strong performance is the ability to successfully target different market segments. Using the national advertising campaign as a starting point, spot market advertising can be tailored to reflect the local population. Additionally, the "This Bud's For You" reward statement can be seen on print ads targeting Blacks and Hispanics, white collar and blue collar workers, and even hockey fans and hunters.

Sales promotions are heavily employed by A-B, particularly on the local level. Sports events are a favorite sponsorship choice serving as an efficient way to reach the target audience of young men. Currently, Anheuser-Busch is a sponsor of 80 percent of all major-league sports broadcasts in the United States and hundreds of college sports broadcasts, according to Mark Lamping, director of the company's sports marketing division.

Unlike competitors, A-B does not rely on extensive use of price promotions to gain market share for Budweiser or Bud Light. Although competitive brands often feature discount prices that undercut the Budweiser brands, A-B has been able to increase market share with heavy advertising support and promotional activities.

Merchandising for both Budweiser and Bud Light plays an integral role in marketing plans. "We work very hard to link together all pieces of the marketing mix, as opposed to putting a commercial on TV and expecting great things to happen," Sharbaugh explains. Bud Light's popular figure of Spuds MacKenzie can be found on neon bar lights, key chains, towels and golf shirts, as well as point-of-sale displays.

Distribution is another strong point for A-B. There are more than 900 A-B wholesalers who are well trained, financed and committed to selling Budweiser beer. "Busch insists on excellence in personnel, delivery, warehousing, and community involvement," says Troy LaGrone, president of one of A-B's largest wholesalers.

A-B's marketing skills were in evidence with the 1982 introduction of Bud Light, which amazingly has not cannibalized Budweiser sales. Bud Light's highly successful "Gimme a Light" campaign helped build brand awareness and consumption levels. This long-running advertising campaign has been kept fresh with new adaptations through the years. With the addition of the Spuds campaign in 1987, Bud Light has gained considerable exposure. Spuds even made *People* magazine's best dressed list! A-B executives can point to the Spuds campaign as another example of the firm's creative marketing abilities.

SOURCES: "Anheuser-Busch Relies on 'Total Marketing,' " *Marketing News*, February 28, 1986, pp. 22, 31; Anitra S. Brown, "Barrelling Through," *Marketing & Media Decisions*, March 1988, pp. 91–98; Russ Bowman, "Sales Promotion: Strategic Arrows," *Marketing & Media Decisions*, March 1988, pp. 138.

Questions

1. Evaluate Michael Roarty's description of A-B: "Marketing driven in every aspect of our business."

2. What separations exist between A-B and its distributors and between A-B and its end customers?

3. What intermediate exchanges are involved in getting A-B's products to the end consumer? What is exchanged in each instance?

4. What functions does A-B perform in the marketing of its products?

Borden's Regional Marketing Flexibility

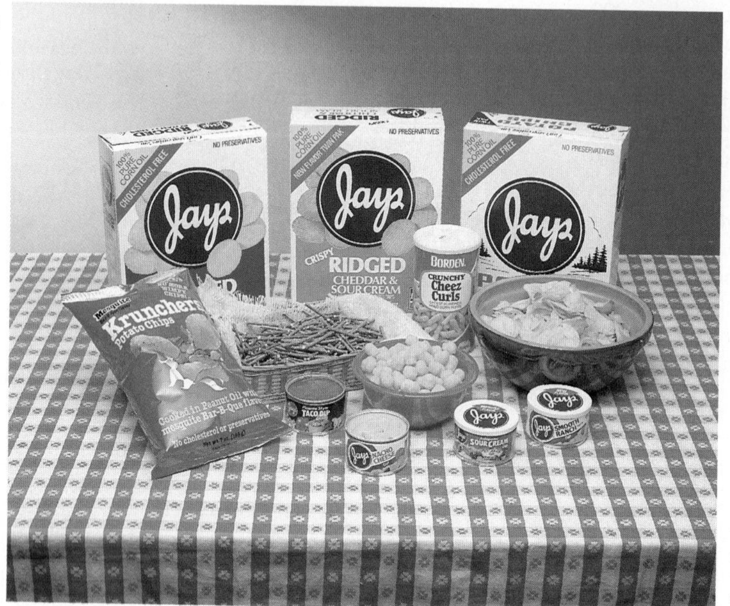

Many food companies have spent the last few years acquiring a wide range of businesses, some quite different from the parent firm in product lines and areas of expertise. Borden went through a phase of diversification, buying firms with a range of products from women's apparel to fertilizer. Today, Borden has sold off many of these firms to pursue a strategy designed to make it a consumer-products giant in dairy products, salty snack foods, pasta, and specialty groceries.

Borden has become one of the food industry's most successful consolidators by building a regional network of companies. Regional marketing strategies are being utilized by several major food companies, including Campbell Soup Company. By bringing together regional pasta, dairy, and snack food operations, Borden can achieve efficiencies of scale in manufacturing and gain regional marketing flexibility.

The regional network facilitates national introductions of popular local products because distribution systems are already in place. For example:

• Creamette Pasta was expanded from its Midwest base through the acquisitions of regional companies to become the first national pasta brand. Borden bought regional pasta manufacturers such as Gioia in Buffalo, Viviano in Pittsburgh, Anthony's in Los Angeles, and Prince in Boston. Borden teams Creamette with the appropriate regional brand and sells both labels against the competition through the local sales distribution network. Creamette can be found in 46 states today.

• In its snack food business, Borden has utilized a similar strategy. Snacktime, Jays, and Laura Scudder's were purchased to give Borden national coverage and have added more than $250 million to the company's sales base. Plants that covered the same market area were closed to help achieve economies of scale in manufacturing.

Borden has worked to fill regional companies' product lines in order to increase sales.

• In Chicago, Jays is the leading potato chip but once had less than 5 percent of the cheese puff market. Borden brought Wise's Cheez Doodles into Chicago through the existing Jays distribution network and used some of Jays' advertising budget to support the new product. Jays' sales increased 22 percent and share in cheese puffs increased to 8.5 percent.

Regional companies have helped develop new products as well as borrow products from one another.

• Snacktime created Krunchers!, a kettle-cooked potato chip that is very popular, generating sales of $17 million in its markets. Wise introduced a kettle-cooked chip in its New York market with great success.

Borden has maintained its leading status in dairy products. Through the use of heavy brand name awareness campaigns, Borden has been able to charge more for its milk. Borden uses radio advertising to position itself as the dairy farmer just down the road, rushing to get the milk to market. With thousands of radio stations to choose from, Borden can place radio spots that emphasize the local angle, quality, and a specific product pitch in virtually every market.

In groceries, Borden has concentrated on developing small segments of the market with products such as NoneSuch mincemeat and Cremora non-dairy creamer. Brands directed at small parts of the market make Borden less susceptible to competition and require little advertising. Jon Hettenger, executive vice president for the grocery division, said, "A lot of these businesses aren't big enough to attract attention. No one cares about displacing Snow's (clam products) market share. It would cost too much." Small brands have been quite profitable for Borden with the grocery group, including pasta, contributing $169 million toward income.

Borden is still a conglomerate and is expanding its business in wall coverings, chemical industrial specialties, and do-it-yourself consumer goods. Any new additions to the firm must fall into one of the six categories Chairman and CEO Romero Ventres has defined: dairy, pasta, snacks, niche grocery products, consumer do-it-yourself goods, and specialty industrial chemicals. Growth is occurring in conjunction with a well-defined strategy and an emphasis on regional marketing.

SOURCE: Bill Saporito, "How Borden Milks Packaged Goods," *Fortune,* December 14, 1987, pp. 139–144.

Questions

1. What are the advantages/disadvantages of a regional marketing strategy?

2. How does a regional approach affect distribution strategies?

3. How did Borden create a national pasta with Creamette?

4. What has Borden done to maintain its mature dairy business?

2

Marketing Management and Strategic Planning

Learning Objectives

Upon completing this chapter, you will be able to do the following:

DEFINE
the key concepts of *marketing mix*, *marketing strategy*, *marketing tactics*, and *strategic marketing planning*.

UNDERSTAND
the nature of marketing management decision making and its importance to the organization.

LIST
the internal organizational constraints and the environmental constraints that influence marketing management.

DESCRIBE
the role of business definition, objectives, and target markets in the formulation of marketing plans.

DISCUSS
the components of a short-run marketing plan.

IDENTIFY
strategic options available to marketers as they plan for long-term growth.

MARKETING PROFILE

Marketing Orientation and Skills Lead Merck to Prominence

In 1987, Merck & Company displaced IBM as America's most admired company, according to *Fortune*'s annual survey of top business executives. Again in 1988 and 1989, the New Jersey pharmaceutical firm was ranked first on the prestigious *Fortune* list. In addition to receiving this important accolade, Merck also garnered an impressive array of other kudos in 1987 and 1988. For instance, *Business Week* named Merck as one of the nation's five best-managed companies in 1987. *Forbes* rated Merck as the most innovative company in the pharmaceutical industry. *Sales and Marketing Management* judged Merck's sales force the best in the pharmaceutical industry, and *Fortune* selected Merck's new cholesterol-lowering drug, Mevacor, as one of its thirteen "products of the year." Several factors have contributed to the development of Merck's outstanding reputation and the company's excellent financial position. Among these factors is a strong marketing orientation from product inception to distribution.

Merck's marketing orientation has changed the way Research and Development is done in the pharmaceutical industry. Before 1975, Merck and the rest of the industry generally used a hit-or-miss method of developing drugs. According to this practice, chemical compounds were unsystematically created and later tested for potential medical efficacy—in other words, the possible applications of a new compound were not known in advance. Not surprisingly, this method sometimes resulted in long discovery droughts. The early 1970s was one of those periods for Merck. In 1975, Roy Vagelos, Merck's current CEO, came to the company to direct its research labs. His goal was to revitalize Merck's R&D process and generate new products.

Vagelos, a physician and biochemist, jettisoned Merck's former method of drug development. Instead, he

encouraged Merck's scientists to target the specific biochemical reactions associated with a given disease and then try to devise a "chemical bullet" to combat them. As a result, scientists began to take a more systematic aim at disease, especially those diseases for which a good potential drug market existed. This new strategy was associated with strong financial support for R&D. By the mid-1980s, Merck's R&D investment began to pay off with the introduction of several important new drugs, including an anti-hypertensive, two potent antibiotics, a genetically engineered hepatitis B vaccine, and the cholesterol-lowering agent Mevacor. These product introductions have translated into strong financial results for the company and a larger contribution to R&D (11 percent of sales in 1987).

Although this market orientation has been an important engine for the company's activities, it has also played a key role in insuring the success of Merck's drugs after they are on the market. Merck understands that developing useful drugs is only half of the marketing process. Convincing physicians and pharmacists of a drug's value, accurately answering their questions, and engendering their trust are equally vital to company success. As a result of this philosophy, Merck maintains a top-notch, highly trained sales force. According to Jerry Keller, vice president of sales for Merck's pharmaceutical division, having a highly trained sales force that can build relationships of trust with customers is the "absolute key" to marketing prescription drugs. For this reason, all Merck salespeople undergo an extensive three-phase training program, which ranges from anatomy and physiology to sales presentation methods to the study of specific diseases and maladies treated with Merck products. In addition, Merck salespeople receive individual training from a physician/mentor as well as updates on new medical and pharmaceutical developments.

Though it remains to be seen if Merck can hold on to its new marketing orientation and remain successful in the long run, we see in this profile how critical decisions made by marketing management can be to the overall success of a major corporation. The marketing managers formulated two plans. The first, over a one-year period, introduced specific new products and developed the particular sales training used. The second concerned commitment to specifically targeted customer groups and the overall way Merck chose to compete. Both types of decisions will be discussed.

SOURCES: *1987 Annual Report*, Merck & Company. John A. Byrne, "The Miracle Company," *Business Week*, October 19, 1987, pp. 84–88. Stuart Gannes, "Merck Has Made Biotech Work," *Fortune*, January 19, 1987, pp. 58–64. "Merck's Grand Obsession," *Sales and Marketing Management*," June, 1987.

In this chapter we discuss marketing decision making in the organization. We will examine the *types* of decisions that are made, and look at the marketing decision-making process. The domain of marketing management is an exciting and difficult area. Imagine yourself being in charge of Merck and having to make the decisions presented in the *Marketing Profile.* Or imagine being responsible for marketing at St. Mary's College, or the Dallas Police Department, or any of the other organizations presented in Chapter 1.

More specifically, in this chapter we examine the environmental factors that affect marketing management, including consumers, competition, technology, government, and economic conditions. We explore the impact of internal organizational constraints on marketing management, including level of financial resources and skills and weaknesses of an organization. Marketing management objectives and business definition, and the importance of target markets are also discussed. In addition, we compare one-year marketing plans to multiyear plans, and look at the planning approaches that aid these activities. Finally, we define *marketing strategy, marketing tactics, marketing mix,* and *strategic marketing planning.*

Marketing Management Decisions

In Chapter 1 marketing management is defined as marketing decisions in the areas of product offerings, distribution, promotion, and pricing—those activities over which the marketing manager has control. These activities are referred to as the **marketing mix** of the organization, or the organization's *controllables,* because the manager decides exactly what the organization should do about product, distribution, promotion, and price. Some authors have referred to the marketing mix as the *4 Ps: product, place (distribution), promotion,* and *price.*[1]

Table 2–1 presents a more detailed view of the types of decisions that must be made for each of the marketing mix variables. Figure 2–1 illustrates the marketing decision maker's role in relation to these controllables.

Much of the rest of this book is concerned with decisions in each of the marketing mix components. Of course, the marketing manager cannot control everything. Indeed, the manager makes decisions within the context of *constraints* that operate both inside and outside the organization. These are *existing factors* that the manager must consider when making marketing-mix decisions.

Internal Constraints

Internal constraints include organizational objectives, financial resources, organizational strengths or skills, business definition, organizational weaknesses, and cost structure. The manager must make decisions that are consistent with these internal existing factors.

The last internal constraint that the marketing manager needs to consider is the *cost structure* of the product being marketed, the amount and composition of the additional cost of supplying increased output. The lower these costs, the easier it may be to cover the costs of a marketing program. For example, an airline or telephone company can handle additional customers at almost no additional costs because their costs are predominantly fixed in the short run. The airplanes fly and the phone lines are there no matter what. Fixed costs are high relative to variable costs here.

Alternatively, in the production and marketing of clothes, variable costs are high relative to fixed costs. Materials and labor costs are a major proportion of total cost

Table 2–1 The Marketing Mix

Product: Product planning; product research and development; product testing; and the service accompanying the product	
Activities	1. Market research on product planning, development, and product testing 2. Technical research, development, and laboratory testing of new products; improvements on existing products 3. Product research on the development of product styling and fashions 4. Presale service—product application engineering 5. Postsale service—product installation, maintenance, and guarantee service
Distribution (Place): The selection, coordination, and evaluation of channels; transportation; warehousing; and inventory control	
Activities	1. Transportation 2. Warehousing and inventory control 3. Determination of the basic channels of distribution 4. Selection of individual establishments within the basic channels 5. Manufacturers' efforts to develop and assist the channel of distribution
Promotion: Sales management; personal selling; advertising; sales promotional programs; and all other forms of marketing communications	
Activities	1. Product branding and promotional packaging 2. Printed media advertising (newspapers, magazines, and brochures) 3. Broadcast media advertising (radio and television) 4. Sales management and personal selling, including training, and supervision and the sales efforts of company management personnel 5. Special promotional activities—promotional warranties, trade shows, dealer aids, and product displays
Price: Price determination; pricing policies; and specific pricing strategies	
Activities	1. Determining list price of products given demand, cost, and competitive constraints 2. Determining volume and channel member discounts 3. Setting overall strategy on pricing above or below competitors' prices 4. Dealing with legal constraints on prices

SOURCE: Based on Clyde E. Harris, Jr., Richard R. Still, and Melvin R. Crask, "Stability or Change in Marketing Methods," *Business Horizons* (October 1978), p. 33.

in the production of additional pieces of clothing. This leaves only a small amount of money per unit of clothing for marketing. The organization's ability to support a marketing program is, thus, limited. Indeed, most clothing manufacturers undertake no consumer advertising and have small sales forces and warehouse facilities. Only those with a large enough market share of larger markets, such as Levi Strauss and Haggar, can support large marketing programs.

External Constraints

External constraints such as consumer demand, competition, economic conditions, the political and legal environment, the social environment, technology, and existence of marketing intermediaries must also be considered in making marketing mix decisions. They make up the **marketing environment,** the existing environment

Figure 2–1 The Marketing Decision Maker and the Marketing Mix

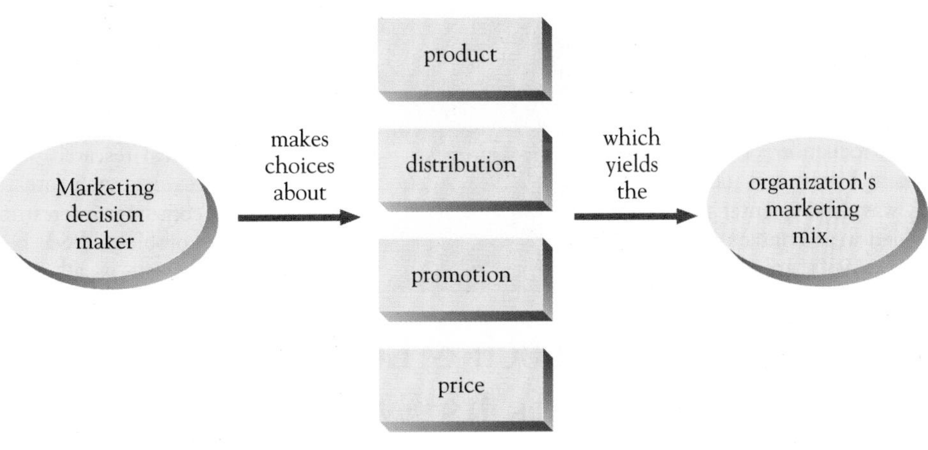

within which the manager makes marketing decisions. Marketing environment is discussed in detail in Chapter 3.

Managers do not control either the internal or external constraints as they do the marketing mix, but these factors are not totally uncontrollable. Within the firm, managers can try to influence corporate objectives, raise more funds, overcome lack of skills, or even change the cost structure. Outside the firm, they can try to influence consumer demand, competitive conditions, technology, or even political and legal factors. However, in the short run, all these constraints are beyond the marketer's control. The importance of monitoring and responding to internal and external constraints is shown in the Bausch & Lomb *Marketing in Action* in this section.

The Process of Marketing Decision Making

Figure 2–2 presents an overview of the marketing decision-making process. In order to make effective marketing mix decisions, the marketing manager first *analyzes* both internal and external constraints. This activity is called a **situation analysis.** As its name implies, it defines the circumstances that the marketer confronts as he or she prepares to develop a marketing mix. From this analysis the manager will define *problems* and *opportunities* that confront the organization. Problems must be dealt with if the organization is to improve its performance, and opportunities form the basis of the future success of the organization. Table 2–2 gives illustrations of selected constraints and shows how they have caused problems or created opportunities for certain organizations.

Organizational objectives guide the marketing mix that an individual manager selects. If top management has set high short-run profitability objectives for a firm, this will prevent a marketing manager from utilizing an aggressive marketing mix that would sacrifice short-run profits in order to gain sales or market share. If a motion picture company sets its objectives in terms of the revenues earned from the production of movies, a marketer would have difficulty pursuing product offerings in other entertainment areas such as television or concerts.

Financial resources also affect marketing mix decisions. The organization may not have the funds to support its own sales force or a large advertising program. Or, the organization may have considerable financial resources, but top management may

MARKETING IN ACTION

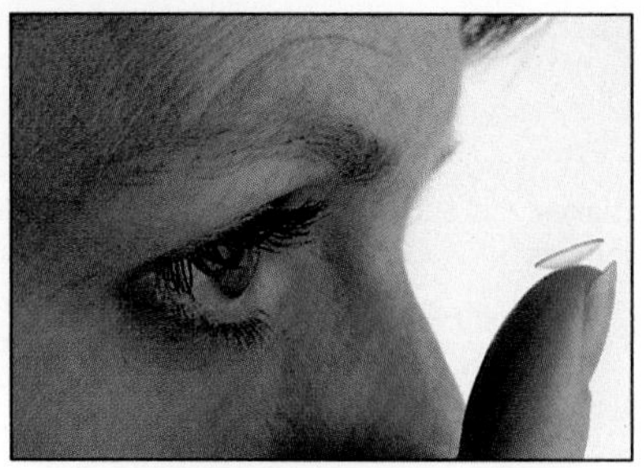

Bausch & Lomb Keeps Its Eye on Constraints

After nearly losing pace with the rest of the contact lens industry a few years ago, Bausch & Lomb Inc. (B&L) has regained its strong competitive position with the introduction of some advanced contact lenses and other products. B&L was slow to enter the booming extended-wear contact lens market in the early 1980s. It had been paying more attention to improving old products than developing new ones when the first extended-wear lenses came out in 1981. Shaken by its sudden competitive disadvantage, however, B&L revised its marketing strategy to mesh better with its internal and external constraints. As a result, B&L finally entered the market and ultimately surpassed its competitors.

In terms of internal constraints, B&L reevaluated its strengths as a company and sought to better use those strengths. For instance, B&L had been a pioneer in contact lenses. As part of its new strategy, B&L decided to expand on its traditional strength in R&D. From 1982–1986, B&L increased its R&D spending by an average of 15 percent each year, reaching $26 million in 1986. In addition, the company also invested $25 million in a new R&D center, which was started in 1986. B&L also formed groups of specialists from various fields into "tiger teams" whose task was to develop new product ideas. B&L's renewed dedication to R&D has already yielded results. B&L introduced a line of bifocal contact lenses in May 1987 as well as a rigid gas-permeable lens which is three times more oxygen-permeable than current soft extended-wear lenses. In addition, B&L has recently introduced a number of other products, including a collagen eye bandage and an enzymatic lens cleaner.

Assessing its external constraints, B&L realized that the company had greatly lost touch with consumers' tastes. Besides not perceiving the demand for extended-wear lenses, B&L had also misjudged consumer demand in other ways. For example, the company had occasionally done extensive technical research on a product only to realize much later that there was no consumer interest in it. To remedy this problem, B&L began to involve marketers at all stages of product development.

B&L's shift in marketing strategy was also related to a positive reassessment of another external constraint—the company's distribution network. With an extensive distribution network of drugstores already in place for lens care products, B&L was well-prepared to expand its product line to include eye-care items and cosmetics. Given declining margins for contact lenses and the slow growth of that market, B&L is eager to continue to diversify beyond lenses.

After having briefly lost sight of its key external and internal constraints, B&L has gotten back on track. It now has a marketing strategy which clearly reflects its constraints and is much better prepared to tackle its ambitious sales goal of $1.2 billion in 1990.

SOURCE: Lois Therrien, "Bausch & Lomb Is Correcting Its Vision of Research," *Business Week*, March 30, 1987, p. 91.

---

differentially allocate funds to different groups. In this situation one marketer may have the money to aggressively market his or her product, while another in the same organization may have such limited funds that only a small marketing program is possible. Firms such as General Foods and General Electric allot funds this way.

As a manager makes marketing mix decisions within the constraints of organizational objectives and financial resources available, he or she must also consider the organization's *strengths,* or *skills,* and its *weaknesses.* This assessment of the capabilities of the organization includes marketing, production, management, research and development, and finances.

The marketing manager should not reach beyond the capabilities of the organization in formulating a marketing mix. The idea is to develop a marketing mix that utilizes the distinctive skills of the organization. We saw in the Bausch & Lomb

Figure 2–2 The Process of Marketing Decision Making

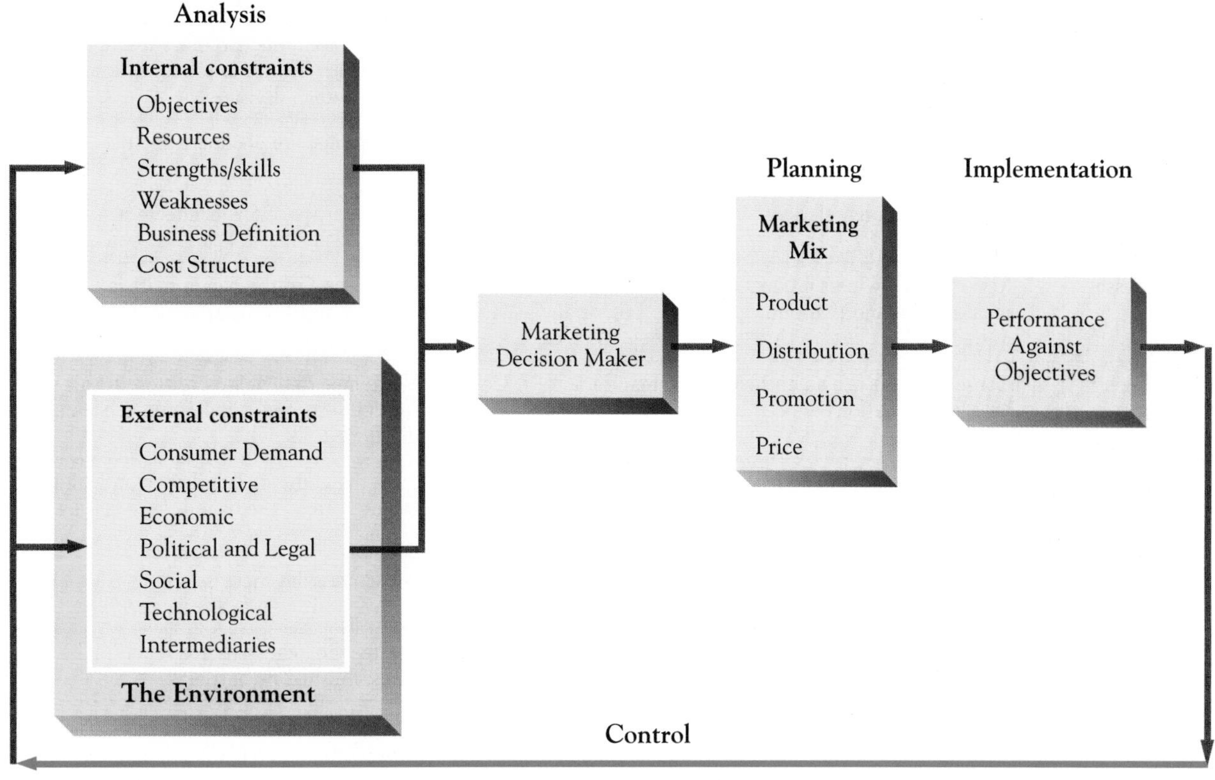

example that management struggled to make decisions that were consistent with its skills.

After assessing skills, the marketer can then *plan* a marketing mix consistent with the situation analysis. This plan is then *implemented* in detail, and the results are monitored. Results are compared to objectives, thus helping the marketer *control* the marketing plan. Feedback from the control system forms the basis for another situation analysis. As the results of the situation analysis change, so should the marketing plan.

We see that this process of making marketing management decisions follows the definition of marketing management—it involves the analysis, planning, implementation, and control of the market mix. However, the cornerstone of the marketing plan is marketing strategy.

Marketing Strategy

Marketing strategy is best introduced with a few examples:[2]

Pocket Books, Inc., revolutionized the book business in the United States about thirty years ago. After the failure of many of its predecessors, the company successfully launched a mass distribution of the now-familiar paperback book. The initial strategy was as follows:

Table 2–2 The Impact of Selected Constraint Factors on Organizations

Factor	Situation	Impact
Objectives	General Motors tries to become a significant competitor in the subcompact car market in the United States.	Top management commits corporate resources to a joint venture with Toyota to produce Novas and to create a new Saturn division.
Resources	Pillsbury hasn't sufficient funds to properly support Godfather's Pizza chain.	Godfather's market share declines, and it is sold by Pillsbury.
Strengths/Skills	Kraft has a strong relationship with distribution channel.	Holds prime freezer space for its cheese in supermarkets.
Weaknesses	Xerox lacks low-cost production capability in small copiers and is also myopic to the potential in this market.	Leaves the small end of the copier market open for Japanese firms and loses market share.
Consumer Demand	Consumer tastes change; there is a demand for lighter formulations of beer and caffeine-free products.	Companies attempt to develop position in this segment—Bud Light, and caffeine-free Coke and Pepsi are developed.
Competition from Other Firms	IBM enters the home computer market.	Apple expects the computer market to grow faster than before but is concerned about long-run loss of share.
Economic	Interest rates in 1984–1988 are far below 1981 and 1982 levels.	New home and car sales increase.
Political	Michigan law bans nonreturnable bottles and cans for soft drinks and beer.	Channels for recyling cans and recirculating bottles must be established by bottlers.
Technological	The 32-bit microcomputer chip is invented.	The complex operating system that makes the Macintosh computer so easy to use is made possible.

- Well-known best sellers and generically popular themes (westerns, detective stories) were reprinted in convenient size, in soft covers, in visually attractive and reasonably sturdy formats.
- The target audience consisted of people of all ages and interests who bought on impulse.
- The prices were considerably cheaper than those for hard-cover books. They were competitive with magazine and lending library alternatives and were conducive to impulse purchase.
- Books were distributed to all levels of traffic outlets through magazine and newspaper jobbers.
- Point-of-sale display was the major communication mechanism.

McDonald's revolutionized the fast-food business.

- It concentrated on the highly popular hamburger.
- A delivery system was designed that provided immediate service (pre-cooked food stored in warming bins).
- "Perfection" was insured for french fries.

McDonald's marketing strategy revolutionized the fast-food industry.

- Prices were at a bargain, impulse level, but allowed for trade-ups to bigger hamburgers.
- Outlets were established at high-traffic locations.
- McDonald's aimed for the target markets of the traveling public and young people.

Acura became the number one car in the United States in consumer satisfaction.

- They built a high-quality, fuel-efficient, sporty car.
- These cars were targeted to upper-middle-class people who were willing to pay a premium for quality and handling.
- A completely new, competent, and aggressive dealer network was established, separate from the Honda network.
- Dealers charged a premium price above that of competitive American and European cars.
- Acura advertised heavily.

The Common Thread

The common thread about these statements of **marketing strategy** is that each sets down the basic logic, but not the specific details, of how the organization intends to compete. The strategy statement is a long-term one that guides more short-run marketing activity.

Each strategy statement provides guidelines about the *target market* that will be served and the marketing mix to be used.

1. *The Target Market.* What is the intended audience of the marketing mix, and what are its basic requirements? This topic is the main thrust of

Chapters 4 and 5. Note that every marketing strategy is directed toward a specific group of consumers. We see this in the *Pocket Books*, *McDonald's*, and *Acura* examples, in all the examples in Chapter 1, and in the Merck profile that began this chapter. A strategy that is not directed toward a specified target market or group of markets does not provide the needed direction for developing the marketing mix.

2. *The Product.* What is its definition, its positioning? What are its dimensions? (See Chapters 9 and 10.)
3. *The Distribution System.* How will the product be brought to the user? (See Chapters 11, 12, 13, and 14.)
4. *The Promotional System.* How will the potential buyer be made aware, persuaded to buy, and persuaded to rebuy? (See Chapters 15, 16, and 17.)
5. *The Price.* What is the relative value of the offer *vis-a-vis* alternatives? (See Chapters 18 and 19.)

All components of the strategy are interrelated. All the elements of the marketing mix must be integrated to serve the needs of the target market.

Organizations without a well thought-out marketing strategy can easily flip-flop in their marketing actions. This does not mean that an organization's marketing strategy should be set in stone for all time. Indeed, as the internal and external constraints change, so too must strategy. For example, Tylenol, an aspirin substitute, was sold only in drug stores, with little advertising, and at a premium price. It had small sales but high profits. This strategy worked well for about fifteen years. However, a major competitor, Datril, entered the market at a lower price and used heavy advertising. A situation analysis by Tylenol's management showed that they had the required skills and resources for a strategic change. Their new strategy included supermarket distribution, a low price, and heavy advertising. The result was that Tylenol not only easily outdistanced Datril, but also outsold all aspirin products.

Sometimes changes in the internal and external constraints occur very quickly. Recent examples include oil surpluses and technological advances in computer chips. A good strategy must be prepared for these types of changes through the use of *contingency planning*. Changes in strategy are developed in advance of possible changes in environmental and internal factors. If these changes then occur, the changed strategy is implemented. For example:

- What should Hertz do if another oil shortage occurs?
- What should Coke do if a national law is passed banning nonreturnable bottles?
- What should colleges and universities do if federal aid for student loans is cut back?

Marketing Tactics

Having a marketing strategy provides no guarantee of success. The strategy itself may be ill conceived, and there are many possible ways to implement it. Specific decisions have to be made about each of the marketing mix elements. These implementation decisions are called **marketing tactics.** The details of these tactics form the heart of the organization's **short-term marketing plan** (often called the *one-year marketing plan*). This plan takes the long-term marketing strategy—the *strategic marketing plan*—as a given and develops detailed executions on each market mix element.

Tactical decisions include the following:

- *Product*—number of items in the product line; styling; color; functional features
- *Place*—choice of specific wholesalers and retailers; programs to motivate the channel members
- *Promotion*—which creative presentation to use in ads; choice of media (TV versus magazine); choice of media vehicle (which TV programs); timing of ads; monies to be expended; sales force selection, assignment, and compensation procedures
- *Price*—specific price for an item; quantity discounts; special sales

Note that these decisions deal with the details and short-run aspects of a marketing program. An advertising campaign can be changed in the short run; so can the price or color of a product. All of these types of changes can take place within a given marketing strategy.

In the *Marketing Profile* that began this chapter, Merck's new success in the pharmaceutical market is based upon (1) a long-term marketing strategy directing it to compete in certain segments of the market (target market) and outlining the overall way in which it will compete (strategy); and (2) the effectiveness of the tactics used to implement this strategy, including advertising budgets, media, marketing research, sales force, and product offerings.

Hewlett-Packard (H-P) illustrates well the efforts of one company to set a marketing strategy and to effectively implement that strategy through the tactics that it uses. In the past few years, H-P was not noted for pursuing a particularly aggressive marketing campaign. Because of the lack of new product introduction, H-P's market share in minicomputers had dropped from 7.3 percent in 1982 to only 5.9 percent in 1986. In order to counter these troubling developments, H-P has undergone a major reorganization designed to instill a marketing emphasis throughout the company. Specifically:

- H-P has been revamped into an organization built around market areas: business systems, engineering systems, manufacturing systems, test and measurement instruments, and medical and analytical instruments.
- New marketing projects have been instituted, including: a market research information center; direct marketing; stronger third party vendor relationships to facilitate entry into new markets; increasing awareness of marketing among all H-P employees.
- An increased emphasis has been placed on developing detailed annual marketing plans. Richard Alberding, executive vice president of marketing and international said, "We now have H-P management convinced that it must spend as much time reviewing marketing strategy as [it spends on] R&D and manufacturing."
- Marketing efforts have been centralized. The field sales force has been combined into one marketing group with a well defined chain of command. All telephone inquiries are received at one site with leads then transmitted to the appropriate sales representative before the next day.

The primary goal of H-P's restructuring has been to instill a company-wide focus on understanding customers' needs. Alberding said, "We found pretty quickly in the international arena that being closer to our users really would be one of the keys to

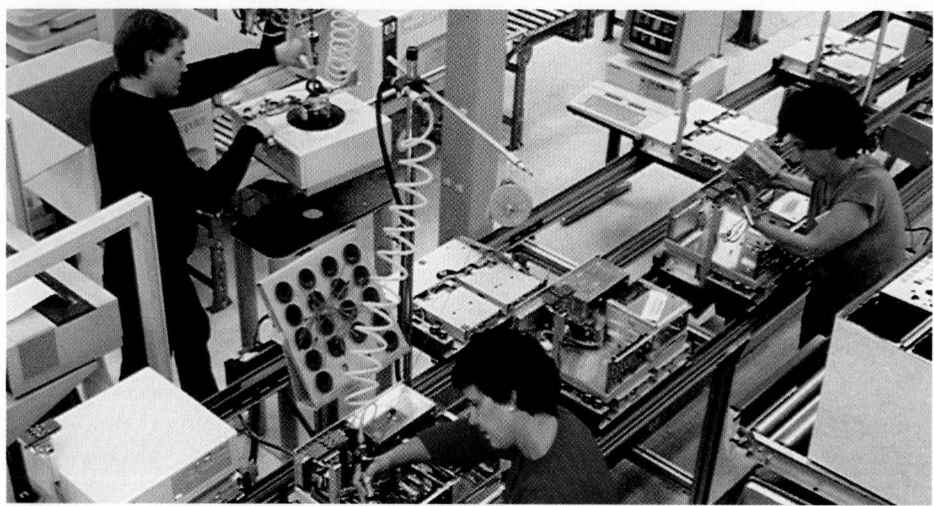

Hewlett Packard is becoming more marketing and customer driven.

our success. And, of course, today we're finding that as a company bent on becoming more marketing and customer driven, that all begins with understanding the users more specifically." The company has learned to "focus on market segments with a package that includes careful product positioning, channel selection, and service." In addition:

- Most of the product line has been reworked to better serve customers' needs for computers that are compatible. Spectrum, introduced in 1986, runs most of customers' existing software and facilitates quick adaptations by H-P as technologies and market demands change.
- Sales channels are being expanded. H-P began working with outside software houses and specialty retailers to gain entrance into new markets.
- Efforts to build retail dealer sales are being stressed so that H-P can gain market presence in the PC field.

Marketing has paid off for H-P in many areas. Market share has increased in the midrange computer market. Earnings have grown consistently. Craig S. Symons, vice president at Gartner Group, sums up H-P's progress saying, "Clearly, H-P is now the only midrange company that has a legitimate shot at Digital and IBM."[3]

The importance of effective marketing tactics should not be underestimated. The chapters on the marketing mix elements deal with the proper development of these marketing tactics. These tactical decisions are themselves based upon the situation analysis (see Figure 2–2), which would be included in an annual marketing plan.

The distinction between strategy and tactics is illustrated by the following questions:

- Are we doing the right things? (Strategy)
- Are we doing things right? (Tactics)

Marketing Control

Implemented marketing plans need to be controlled by the marketing manager. The function of **marketing control** is to provide the manager with feedback on how the plans are progressing. With this feedback, the manager is in a position to know whether adjustments are needed in the short-run marketing plan or even in the guiding, long-run marketing strategy.

Short-Run Control

Short-run control involves comparing actual results to those budgeted in the marketing plan. Typical measures compared include (1) sales levels in units and dollars, (2) market share, (3) marketing cost levels, and (4) profits. These comparisons are made not only on a companywide level, but also at the level of geographic region (states, cities, salesperson territories), product line or item, customer type (steel industry, etc.), level of trade (retail versus wholesale), order size, and financial arrangement of sale (cash versus charge, and commission rate). These results are usually available on monthly, or at least quarterly, bases to the manager.

For example, a marketing manager for Honeywell computers may receive a report that directly compares the sales and profit level budgeted in the Denver territory for its new computer terminal. If sales or profits are either lower or higher than expected, the manager can investigate the causes further. In this process, called **management by exception,** the manager focuses control-related attention on those areas where major differences exist between budget levels and actual performance, investigates them, and takes corrective action if needed or possible. Thus, if terminal sales are below expectation in Honeywell Computer's Denver operation because of poor account coverage, the marketing manager can rearrange sales territories to attain better account coverage. Control helps identify appropriate courses of action.

Note that the sign for this problem comes from the control system. Also note that effective control requires that a plan be in place to provide a budget level for comparison with actual results. Without marketing planning, there can be no effective marketing control.

Strategic Control

Periodically, the marketing manager must also appraise the effectiveness of the long-term marketing strategy. The fundamental method for doing this is the **marketing audit,** a systematic, unbiased, and comprehensive appraisal of the organization's marketing environment, organizational capabilities, objectives, and strategy.

An audit must be undertaken because the marketing environment is almost always changing. Basically, a marketing audit examines the firm's environmental and internal constraints and determines whether current objectives and strategies are appropriate in light of these assessments (see Figure 2–2). The audit is often done by personnel other than those currently responsible for marketing strategy to ensure that a fresh and unbiased appraisal will be made. Consultants are often used.

Our understanding of strategy and control will be developed further by discussing the process in which they take place. This process is called strategic marketing planning.

Review Your Marketing Knowledge

- For the Merck profile that began this chapter, describe the internal and external constraints that might have an impact upon the company's marketing decisions.
- What are the components of Merck's marketing strategy and tactics? How should marketing control be exercised?
- For your job search, what is your overall strategy and what tactics will you use?

Strategic Marketing Planning

Strategic marketing planning involves three interrelated decisions: (1) determining the business definition, (2) setting objectives for the business, and (3) determining the marketing strategy. These decisions are based on a thorough analysis of both internal and external constraints (see Figure 2–2). The analysis and the resulting decisions constitute **strategic marketing planning.** The *Marketing in Action* feature in this section presents a partial description of Bic's approach to strategic marketing planning.

Business Definition

Notice in the *Marketing in Action* feature that the starting point for Bic's strategic marketing planning is setting objectives. The company can start with this because it is operating within the context of an already agreed upon business definition, a step which must precede objective-setting. (We should note that the use of *business* in this section includes all organizations, whether profit-oriented or not.)

Every successful organization, whether profit or not-for-profit, has a vision of what it is all about. The answer to the question "What business are we in?" gives the definition that provides the organization with its thrust and direction, and is the cornerstone of its marketing strategy. Consider some examples:[4]

- Xerox Corporation recently redefined itself from "a copier manufacturer" to a "supplier of automated office systems."
- Black and Decker expanded its business definition beyond "tools for skilled hands" to include small appliances with its acquisition of General Electric housewares (toasters, mixers, etc.).
- After successfully assisting in fund-raising to find a vaccine for polio, the March of Dimes redefined its business as the elimination of birth defects.

Clearly, these changes affect the strategic thrust of the organization. Table 2–3 gives a more detailed example, showing how business definition directs marketing strategy. It considers the position of Owens-Corning when it initially introduced Fiberglas as a new product:

> *Had the company taken the position that it was in the business of supplying a raw material to processors, its strategy would have differed enormously from the actual strategy based on the concept of "bringing better end products to the ultimate user." Because Owens-Corning put the ultimate user first, it manufactured the first Fiberglas fishing rods and luggage when the traditional manufacturers delayed adopting the new material. It launched consumer marketing programs to establish the new applications and then "gave" the business back to the normal suppliers. DuPont, with its nylon, used a similar philosophy, which also affected both strategy and employee behavior. Returning to Owens-Corning, it is evident that several business definitions might have been selected by the firm, each of which would have called for a different strategy.*[5]

Components of a Good Business Definition. Having noted the great importance of business definition for marketing strategy, we must now consider what constitutes a good business definition. Theodore Levitt, in his classic article "Marketing Myopia,"[6] sounded a warning about having too narrow a business definition. Concerning the railroads he noted:

MARKETING IN ACTION

Bic's Strategy for Growth

Introducing the Mini-Bic.
So advanced, it goes where no lighter has gone before.
Mini
BiC

"I think it's important that I take a minute to define *strategy* in general. Basically, *strategy* is a means to an end. It's an overall plan of action developed to meet a specific objective or set of objectives. Thus, the first element in developing a strategy is to establish objectives. Without a clear, concise statement of objectives, there can be no viable strategy.

"At Bic, specific objectives are set before a project is undertaken. This holds true for something as inexpensive as the development of a selling sheet all the way up to the major launch of a new product. If we spend money, we know what we want for it—and this has been the case since the first Bic stick pen went into production. At Bic, we feel that it's important to set objectives, develop strategies, and put them to work quickly.

"We do not plan for small growth. In other words, we don't sit down and say let's grow 8 percent next year. We plan for the big idea—the idea that will give us fast growth and make us a major factor in any market we enter.

"The disposable 'crystal' stick pen, still our largest seller, was regionally launched in 1959 and nationally launched with a retail price of nineteen cents in 1964. The company's objective was clear and concise—*dominate the ball point pen market.* The strategy that was developed to meet this objective was simple—*produce a product that draws a line as well or better than anything on the market, price it significantly lower than the competition, make it available almost universally, and let consumers know about it.* I don't have to tell you the rest of the story. Today, Bic accounts for about two of every three ball pens sold at retail. Additionally, we have a substantial commercial and industrial business.

"The corporation's growth strategy called for a new product outside the writing-instrument field. It was felt that for the product to be a success it would have to (1) be sold through essentially the same distribution channels as our pens; (2) have the capability to be mass-produced at a low cost while maintaining high-quality standards; and (3) compete in a market that showed tremendous growth potential. The disposable butane lighter market fit these criteria; so, we launched the Bic Lighter. There were a couple of distinct differences in our marketing strategy for lighters versus our strategy when we launched ball pens:

1. Bic Lighter carried a suggested retail price equivalent to the major competition, not below it. This allowed us to recoup initial investment more rapidly.
2. There was a great deal more trade promotion emphasis placed on chain stores (particularly food) than on wholesalers because it was felt that chain stores represented the greatest growth opportunity.

"Our latest new venture is the Bic Shaver. It's a business that's even more dependent on the high volume, promotion-minded food chains than the lighter business."

SOURCE: Based on a talk given by Donald M. Wilchek, "Bic's Strategy for Growth." Mr. Wilchek is a marketing manager for Bic.

They let others take customers away from them because they assumed themselves to be in the railway business rather than in the transportation business.[7]

Additionally, he noted that movie companies are in the entertainment business, not just in film-making, and that oil companies are in the energy business, not just the oil business.

The **business definition,** then, should give the *core* of what customer needs an organization satisfies rather than describe a particular product, process, or set of procedures. Marketing-oriented organizations are more likely to have broad definitions of their businesses.

Table 2–3 Fiberglas: Alternative Business Definitions

Possible Definition	Strategic Implications
Supplier of a raw material	Concentration on production, contract selling, extraction development, long-term contracts
Mining	Similar to above
Bringing greater efficiency and profits to the manufacturers who elect to adopt Fiberglas in their finished products	Interfacing of seller's technical expert with customer's technical expert; trial installations, industrial marketing, processing research
Better end products for consumer	Consumer marketing programs, joint ventures, manufacturing of final products

SOURCE: Robert T. Davis, *Marketing Strategy (A): A Note* (Graduate School of Business, Stanford University, 1975), p. 3.

There is also some risk of defining a business so broadly that the organization moves beyond its skill level or out of an area where it has a competitive advantage. This has happened to many organizations. For example:

- The Quaker Oats Company in the 1970s recast itself from a marketer of such staple foods as oatmeal, pancake mix, and dry cereals into a marketer of toys (Fisher-Price and Marx) and theme restaurants (Magic Pan). In the mid-1980s, it retrenched to its core business of staple foods.
- National Can Corp. recast itself from a producer of metal containers, bottles, and plastic containers into a firm that processed fruits and vegetables, marketed pet food (Skippy and Laddie Boy dog food) and protein products. The mid-1980s found it retrenching also.
- Gillette in the 1970s and early 1980s had ventured into such product areas as digital watches, calculators, and smoke alarms. Gillette has now returned to developing products for markets that it knows best: men's and women's grooming and cosmetic products.

Thus, business definition is a trade-off between being so narrow that you miss market changes, and being so broad that you go beyond an organization's skill base. One author suggests that a good business definition should be:[8]

1. specific enough to have impact upon the behavior of the organization
2. focused more upon the satisfaction of customer needs than the characteristics of the product being produced
3. able to reflect the essential skills of the organization
4. attainable
5. flexible

Multibusiness Organizations. Of course, it is possible for an organization to be in more than one business. Companies such as General Electric, DuPont, B. F. Goodrich, Exxon, and Sears are diversified into many different businesses, each business with a separate marketing strategy. For these types of organizations, two questions must be asked concerning business definition:

1. What businesses are we in?
2. How do these businesses relate to each other in (a) their ability to supply financial resources *to* the organization, or (b) their need for financial resources *from* the organization?

Several approaches have been developed to deal with these questions, but only two will be discussed here: portfolio analysis and market attractiveness-business strength analysis. For these procedures, it is first necessary to divide the organization into separate **strategic business units (SBUs).** An SBU should have a distinct set of customers, a distinct set of competitors, separate costs from other SBUs, and must be able to have a separate strategy. Thus an SBU can be one or more divisions of an organization, a product line in a single division, or even a single product.

Portfolio Analysis. Portfolio analysis was developed by the Boston Consulting Group (BCG) in the 1960s. In its scheme, Strategic Business Units (SBUs) are displayed on a two-dimensional grid, a *portfolio matrix,* as shown in Figure 2–3. The horizontal axis gives market share relative to the industry's largest competitor. The vertical axis is the growth rate of the market. The size of the circles drawn on the portfolio matrix represent the sales level of the SBU. BCG noted that the cash flow generated by an SBU was affected by its position on this *growth-share matrix.* To add flair to their scheme, they gave names to these positions in the portfolio: cash cows, dogs, question marks, and stars.[9]

Cash Cows (lower-left quadrant) are high share-low growth SBUs. They tend to have a lower cost position relative to competitors due to having more experience at producing and marketing their product. This experience comes from their high market share. With slow market growth, major investment in plants, equipment, and working capital are not needed. As a result of both these factors, these SBUs generate cash beyond their needs, which is then available for use by other SBUs.

Figure 2–3 Product Categories in the Product Portfolio Matrix

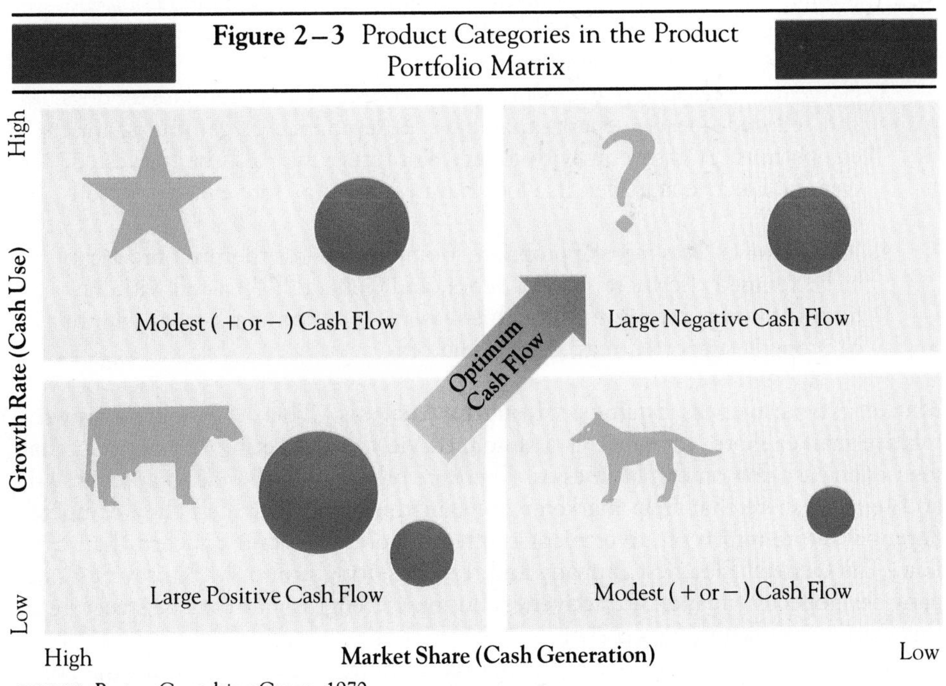

SOURCE: Boston Consulting Group, 1970

Dogs (lower-right quadrant) are low share-low growth SBUs. They neither generate nor require large amounts of cash, but often have poor profitability.

Question marks (upper-right quadrant), sometimes called *problem children*, are SBUs with a low share of a high-growth market. They usually cannot generate enough cash to support the investment needed to either maintain their current market share (since they have to grow with the market to do so), or to gain market share. The market growth is an opportunity, but a large cash inflow will be needed if the SBU is ever to gain sufficient share to become a star.

Stars (upper-left quadrant) are high-share SBUs in high-growth markets. They are often approximately in balance in terms of cash generation and cash needs. As the market growth rate slows, they will become the cash cows of the future.

If SBUs were left on their own to use their cash as they wish, then cash cows would likely overspend to gain more share, and question marks would be starved for cash. Thus, cash from cash-cow SBUs is used to support question marks in their quest to become stars. We define a *success sequence* as the movement of a question mark to a star and then to a cash cow. Alternatively, a *disaster sequence* is the movement of a star to a question mark to a dog, or the movement of a cash cow to dog status.

Market growth rate is generally beyond the control of the decision maker. Marketers, of course, try to make markets grow faster, but there is a limit to their ability to do this, and as a result, they cannot completely control growth. Getting mature markets—such as commodities, paper, steel, or radios—to grow faster is not generally considered to be worth the probable cost of trying to do so. To BCG, then, strategic options available to marketers are related to the stance one takes relative to market share. Marketers can take four actions to directly affect their market share:

1. *Building market share* is usually for question marks and requires cash support beyond that which these SBUs can generate themselves. Honda's building of its American car business is an example.
2. *Holding market share* is usually for mature businesses with strong shares (cows) or for stars deemed worthy of continued support. Honda's motorcycle cash cow in the United States was managed in this way, with the cash used to support its auto business.
3. *Harvesting or reducing market share* will yield cash. It is appropriate for dogs and selected question marks that have little chance of gaining against competitors. A cash cow with a very dim future may also be harvested. General Electric managed its clock business this way for years before selling it.
4. *Withdrawal or divesting* is appropriate for many dogs, as their resources can be better used elsewhere. RCA, Xerox, and General Electric all withdrew from the computer business for this reason. Question marks that cannot be properly supported may also be sold off.

Market Attractiveness-Business Strengths Analysis. The BCG, market growth-relative market share, approach is a simplified view of marketing competition that focuses on cash flow among businesses. There are other factors besides market growth and relative share that help marketers explain the world in which they compete. Potential future return on investment is often a more important concern than cash flow. The General Electric Company and the consulting firm of McKinsey & Company developed the market attractiveness-business strengths matrix. The structure of this matrix is shown in Figure 2–4.

Each of the two dimensions of the matrix is an index that summarizes the combined impact of a number of factors. The market-attractiveness axis is related to such

Figure 2–4 Industry Attractiveness-Business Strengths Matrix

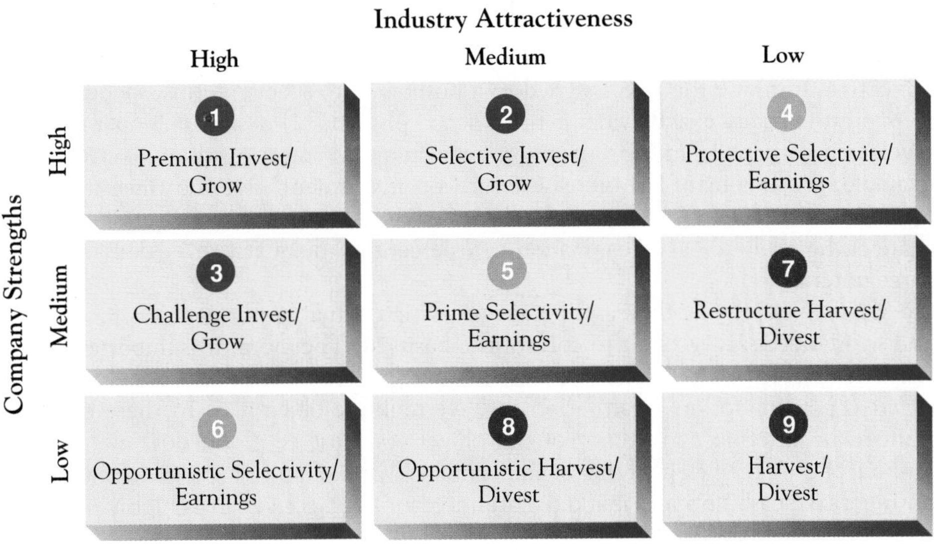

factors as size of the market, growth rate of the market, cyclicality and seasonality of the market, the nature of competitors and their competitive behavior, technological developments, government regulation, profit margins, and sensitivity to economic fluctuations. In order to form the index, the marketing manager of a business must select the relevant factors, rate the business on the factors, weight each of the factors, and then combine the weights and ratings to form the index. This combining procedure can be a simple weighted average or some more complex operation, depending on the judgment of the manager.

Industry Attractiveness
High
Medium
Low
Company Strengths
High
Medium
Low
1
Premium Invest/ Grow
2
Selective Invest/ Grow
4
Protective Selectivity/ Earnings
3
Challenge Invest/ Grow
5
Prime Selectivity/ Earnings
7
Restructure Harvest/ Divest
6
Opportunistic Selectivity/ Earnings
8
Opportunistic Harvest/ Divest
9
Harvest/ Divest

The business-strengths axis is a similarly combined summary of such factors as company market share, sales growth rate, customer loyalty, marketing skills relevant to the business, fit with distribution structure, technological capabilities, financial resources, product differentiation, and cost position relative to competitors. The emphasis for the ratings on both dimensions is on the potential return on investment in the business.

The two axes are combined to form the nine-block matrix shown in Figure 2–4. The cells in the matrix define the role that a business will have in the organization and the amount of resources that will be available for marketing. Cells 1, 2, and 3 define the businesses that will receive the resources to grow, the so-called "green light" businesses. The market is high or medium in attractiveness and the organization has high enough skills and resources to take advantage of the market. Cells 7, 8, and 9 define the businesses that lack opportunity in terms of market and/or company capabilities. These "red light" businesses are managed to harvest their resources or are just divested. The cells on the diagonal (4, 5, and 6) define businesses that are to receive selective investment, and where caution (the yellow light) is the operating style.

Of course, an overall SBU strategy of either building, or holding, or reducing market share will have a major impact on that SBU's marketing strategy and plan. Share gains are obtained by increases in marketing activity and vice versa. Thus, the critical importance of business definition within the product portfolio becomes clear. It outlines the role marketing will play for each business.

Objectives

The second step in strategic marketing planning is to set *objectives* for the business. Objectives translate the role assigned to a business into specific terms. Good objectives must (1) state exactly what is to be accomplished, (2) designate a quantitative level to be attained, and (3) specify a time frame for meeting the objective. For example, the statement "to increase return on investment" does not meet the last two criteria of level and time. But this statement—"to increase Cheerios' market share of the ready-to-eat cereal market to 7 percent in the next year"—does meet all three criteria.

Objectives provide the baseline against which actual performance is measured, and so are necessary in order to control the business. Therefore, it is important that these objectives be attainable.

It is possible for an organization to have multiple objectives. In these circumstances the internal consistency of the objectives must be a concern, along with ranking the objectives in terms of importance. For example, a business may have both positive cash flow and market-share increase as objectives. It is highly unlikely that both objectives can be reached simultaneously.

Finally, overall business objectives must be factored into appropriate subfunction objectives. Thus, the marketing, production, and finance departments will each have objectives to meet. Within marketing, each component of the marketing mix will also be assigned specific objectives. For example, sales' objectives may be to open 20 percent more accounts, and advertising's to increase awareness by 40 percent. This set of objectives at each level of the organization is called the *hierarchy of objectives;* it determines the targets that the marketing strategy is intended to reach.

With the business defined, its role designated, and objectives set, the marketing strategy can be determined; then the tactical details of the marketing plan can be developed. Figure 2–5 summarizes these steps, which are based upon an analysis of constraint factors—a situation analysis.

The whole strategic marketing planning process can be neatly summarized on the following four dimensions.[10] Each organization combines these four into its own individual format:

1. What the firm *must* do—in terms of the outside environment
2. What the firm *can* do—in terms of ability and competence
3. What the top management *wants* to do—as individuals
4. What the firm *should* do—given societal and ethical constraints

Figure 2–5 Marketing Planning Sequence

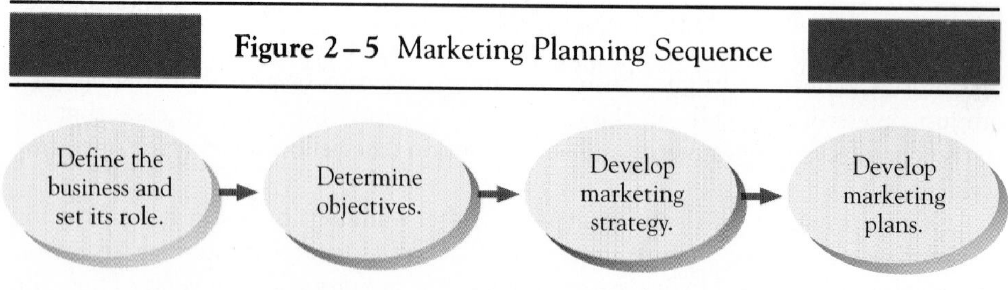
Define the business and set its role.
Determine objectives.
Develop marketing strategy.
Develop marketing plans.

Figure 2–6 Alternative Growth Strategies

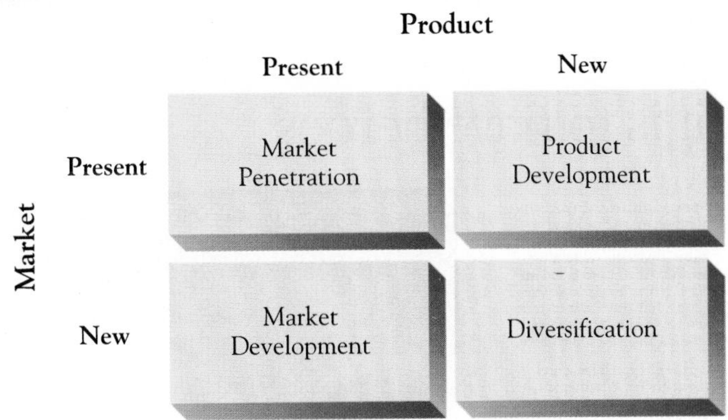

Growth Strategies

We have already noted that growth is only one of the many possible roles one may assign to a business. However, it is an extremely important one and is essential to the long-run prosperity of the organization.

Figure 2–6 presents a classification scheme for alternative strategies for growth. The key dimensions of choice are product-market relationships. There are four choices:

1. *Market Penetration*—gaining increased sales by getting greater market share with present products in current markets. For example, Crest toothpaste attempts to increase its market share by more effective advertising.
2. *Market Development*—gaining increased sales by taking present products to new markets (segments, other countries). Japanese electronics companies, like Panasonic, have moved aggressively into Europe.
3. *Product Development*—gaining increased sales by introducing new products in present markets. This is the main thrust of Merck, as described at the beginning of this chapter.
4. *Diversification*—gaining increases in sales by introducing new products into new markets. For example, Ford Motor Company moved into the aerospace business.

Diversification can be accomplished in many ways, depending on (1) whether the technology of the new products is related to technology currently used in the organization, and (2) the nature of the new market entered (see Figure 2–7).

1. *Vertical Integration.* The firm moves *forward* to own or control the channel of distribution (IBM opens some retail computer stores), or *backward* to own or control sources of supply (*The New York Times* owns a paper mill). Here, the firm becomes its own customer.
2. *Horizontal Diversification.* This option involves adding to a product line items that are targeted for the same type of markets. The new items may be related to current technology, such as the National Cash Register (NCR) Company's calculating machines were when they were added to its regular cash register line; or they may be unrelated, as NCR's computers were.

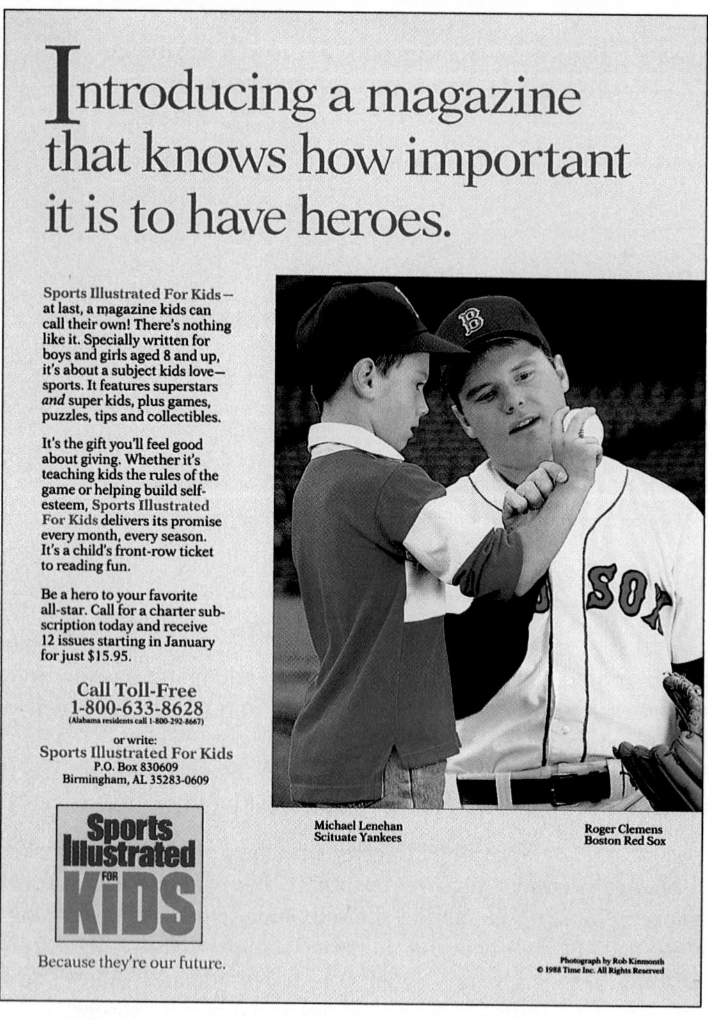

Sports Illustrated **targets a customer group similar to its current market.**

3. *Concentric Diversification.* Here related technology is taken to customer groups similar to current customers (marketing- and technology-related concentric diversification). Or related technology is taken to new customer groups (technology-related concentric diversification). Or unrelated technology is taken to customer groups similar to current customers (marketing-related concentric diversification). An example of the latter type would be Seagram's acquisition of Taylor wines from Coca-Cola.
4. *Conglomerate Diversification.* New products that are technologically unrelated to current products are taken to new classes of customers. For example, IT&T, which originally operated telephone systems, moved into the hotel, motel, car rental, and heating and air-conditioning businesses.

There are many approaches to growth. For example, Pepperidge Farm's strategy for growth in the 1980s and 1990s is presented in the *Marketing in Action* in this section. Pepperidge Farm has changed its overall strategy from product development to market penetration.

Pepperidge Farm's Three-Step Marketing Strategy for Growth

Pepperidge Farms, the dean of America's upper-crust baked goods marketers, has returned its focus to the products it knows best, and business is booming. After branching out into a broad line of frozen foods in the 1970s, Pepperidge didn't pay much strategic attention to its flagship cookie and bread lines. When its frozen food products failed to be as convenient or popular as competitors' entries, however, Pepperidge found itself in a bind. In response, the Campbell Soup Company, Pepperidge's parent firm, selected a new CEO for the troubled bakery company. In 1984, Richard Shea, a former food engineer with extensive product knowledge and a clear sense of business and marketing priorities, moved into Pepperidge's top spot.

Shea brought to the job his experience of launching many new products for Pillsbury, Green Giant, Borden's, and Campbell. Shea didn't intend to use his experience to continue Pepperidge's policy of broad, unfocused product introduction, however. Instead, his aim has been to make a more select—yet consistently top-quality and top-priced—line of products. This goal is part of Shea's simple three-step strategy for Pepperidge: According to Shea, "You have to have a crystal-clear product strategy and a religious appreciation for quality. Once you get that right, you get on to production; and once you get that right, you get a big ad budget and blow the product out of there."

As part of Shea's strategy, Pepperidge has focused again on its core cookie business with the introduction of a popular line of "lumpy bumpy" cookies. At the same time, frozen food items have been cut back. Shea has also modernized Pepperidge's production facilities to improve quality.

As part of Shea's marketing thrust, the delivery time for cookies has been cut to less than five days and for bread to less than three. These figures compare with an industry average of five to ten days for such baked goods. Shea aims to shave the delivery time for cookies still further to 72 hours in order to offer retailers maximum flexibility and insure product freshness. Finally, Pepperidge is not lacking commitment to advertising as it did before. In one quarter alone the company spent $14 million on advertising, ranking it the fifth largest food advertiser.

Pepperidge has found new success by adhering to a simple but sensible marketing strategy. Pepperidge realized that breadth of product line is not necessarily the key to growth. Instead, a marketing strategy that emphasizes the strengths of the company and the wants of consumers is a better basis for success.

SOURCES: Bill Saporito, "A Smart Cookie at Pepperidge," *Fortune*, December 22, 1986, pp. 67–74; Judann Dagnoli, "Campbell Takes Stock in Soup," *Advertising Age*, September 28, 1987, p. 26.

Review Your Marketing Knowledge

- The typical university is made up of diverse units (literature, science, engineering, law, business, etc.), with each expected to play a role in the university community. For your university, what role is assigned to each unit, how does this affect the resources each receives, and how is each evaluated?
- Pillsbury operates in the food business with Green Giant vegetables, Pillsbury cake mixes, etc., and it also owns Burger King and other businesses. How should Pillsbury management assign the role of marketing for each of these businesses?

Figure 2–7 A Diversification Matrix

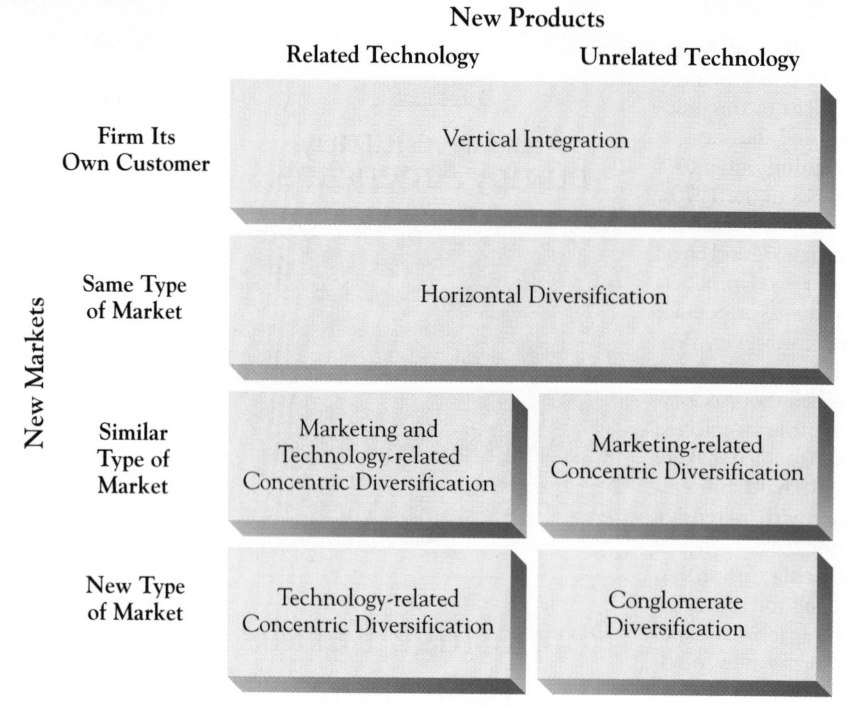

A Final Word About Marketing Strategy

Just what are the effects of various environmental situations and marketing activities on an organization's performance? Recently, the Strategic Planning Institute has provided data, from the PIMS (*P*rofit *I*mpact of *M*arketing *S*trategy) program, which are based on results in more than 2,000 businesses.

Table 2–4 Selected PIMS Findings

ROI increases when	**ROI decreases when**	**Cash flow increases when**	**Cash flow decreases when**
• relative market share increases • there are high-quality products and services • a heavy fixed capital base is highly utilized • there is a broad product line • medium-level R&D is directed at product quality	• there are high rates of new product introduction in fast-growing markets • there are high marketing expenditures • there are high inventories and high fixed capital	• there is low industry growth • there are low marketing expenditures • there is high market share (even when expenditures are high) • the market share is decreased	• there is long-run industry growth • there is new-product introduction • there are high marketing expenditures • there is low market share • the market share is increased

In this program, a company submits separate data for each of its businesses. Companies pay about $20,000 to $40,000 per year and agree to make their data available on a confidential basis in order to have access to the PIMS data base. The data base contains successes, failures, and also-rans; data are aggregated so that individual businesses cannot be identified. The data provided by a business cover the market environment, competition, strategy pursued, and financial performance results, plus projections of future sales, prices, and costs. The individual business may obtain insights on its own strategy from PIMS results tailored to its needs. However, our concern here is with broader generalizations to all marketing. Selected PIMS findings on return on investment (ROI) and cash flow are in Table 2–4.[11]

Personal Computer Exercise

Marketing's role in a business with a portfolio involves analyzing data related to many factors. This PC exercise allows you to prepare a product portfolio and an industry attractiveness/business strengths matrix. From this you should be able to determine the appropriate marketing role for each business.

KEY POINTS

- The marketing mix is composed of those factors over which the marketing manager has control. They are product, distribution, promotion, and price.
- In making marketing mix decisions, the marketer analyzes constraining factors. The first group of these factors is internal to the organization: objectives, financial resources, strengths, skills, weaknesses, and cost structure of the firm. The second group of constraints is external (outside the firm): consumer demand, competition, economic conditions, political and legal environment, social environment, technology, and the existence of marketing intermediaries.
- Marketing managers do an analysis of constraints, called a situation analysis, and then plan a marketing mix that will actualize opportunities and solve problems arising from this analysis. They implement this plan and monitor the results through the organization's control system.
- Marketing strategy establishes the basic logic, but not the specific details, of how the organization intends to compete. It identifies the target market and presents an overview of each element of the marketing mix.
- Marketing tactics set down the specific details of each element of the marketing mix, taking the marketing strategy as a given. These form the heart of the organization's one-year marketing plan.
- Strategic marketing planning involves three interrelated decisions: determining business definition, setting objectives, and establishing marketing strategy.
- Business definition identifies the customer needs that an organization satisfies, while keeping them consistent with its organization's skills.
- Firms involved in multiple businesses must not only develop a definition for each business, but must also determine how these businesses relate to each other. The BCG portfolio approach and market attractiveness-business strengths analysis aid in this process.
- Objectives set the standard against which an implemented strategy will be judged.
- Growth strategies are very important to the long-run prosperity of the organization. These include market penetration, market development, product development, and various types of diversification.

ISSUES FOR DISCUSSION

1. Thinking back to Chapter 1, what business definitions do you believe are being used by (a) Helene Curtis, (b) Supreme Truck Bodies, (c) Chase Manhattan Bank, (d) St. Mary's College, (e) Dallas Police Department, and (f) Michigan Tourism?

2. What appears to be the marketing strategy used by each of the organizations listed above?

3. Cite an example of one tactical marketing decision that is being made by each of these organizations.

4. Pick one important factor from the marketing environment that affects Helene Curtis' marketing strategy. Note how this factor might change and how Helene Curtis' strategy might be affected. Do the same for the rest of those organizations used as examples in Chapter 1, using a factor that is important to each.

5. In the mid-1980s, Levi Strauss found itself with falling sales in its mainstay product, jeans. What alternative opportunities for growth could Levi have pursued at this time? Cite a specific example of each and speculate about the outcomes.

6. General Mills was a conglomerate composed of many divisions, including cereals, toys, Lacoste clothes, wallpaper, and other food products. On what basis might management assign a role to each of these businesses? In the mid-1980s, General Mills sold off all but its food businesses. Why might it do this?

7. The medical systems products division of General Electric in the mid-1980s was given the "green light" as an investment receiver within GE. At that time it held a moderate position in the imaging world market (X-ray, scanners, etc.). What are the implications for the marketing of GE imaging products, given this new designation? How would a manager be evaluated before and after this designation?

8. Are the PIMS results for cash flow consistent with those that the BCG product portfolio matrix would predict?

9. "Some firms with very small market shares earn a high return on investment. This negates the PIMS results that market share and ROI are positively related." Discuss why such ROIs for firms with small market shares are earned and the implication for the summary results from PIMS.

10. Prepare a situation analysis for your job search. What implications does this have for your marketing plan to find a job?

GLOSSARY

Business definition: identifying the customer needs an organization satisfies. These must be consistent with its organizational skills.

Management by exception: a process in which a manager focuses attention on those areas where major differences exist between budget levels and actual performance. This process is part of the short-run control function.

Market attractiveness-business strengths: a way of classifying businesses in terms of their potential for return on investment on the indexed dimensions of market attractiveness and the strengths the organization has to compete in that business.

Marketing audit: a systematic, unbiased, and comprehensive appraisal of the organization's marketing environment, organizational capabilities, objectives, and strategy. This process is part of the strategic control function.

Marketing control: a system that provides feedback to the manager on the progress of short-run plans and the effectiveness of the long-term marketing strategy.

Marketing environment: factors outside the organization that the marketing manager cannot control.

Marketing mix: the elements under the control of marketing managers: product, distribution, promotion, and price.

Marketing plan: a blueprint for the firm's activities in the short run, including a situation analysis and details of the organization's marketing mix.

Marketing strategy: a plan of action that establishes the basic logic, but not the specific details of how the firm intends to compete in the long run.

Marketing tactics: the specific details of each element of the marketing mix.

Portfolio analysis: a way of classifying businesses using the dimensions of market growth and market share relative to the industry's largest competitor.

Situation analysis: an analysis of internal and external constraint factors.

Strategic business unit (SBU): a unit within an organization that includes a distinct set of customers and competitors, has separate costs, and has the ability to undertake a separate strategy.

Strategic marketing planning: a managerial function that involves determining business definition, setting objectives, and establishing marketing strategy for the long run.

NOTES

1. E. Jerome McCarthy was the first to popularize this in E. Jerome McCarthy and William Perreault, *Basic Marketing: A Managerial Approach,* 9th ed. (Irwin, 1987). The first edition was published in 1960.

2. The first two of these examples are quoted from Robert T. Davis, *Marketing Strategy (A): A Note* (Graduate School of Business, Stanford University, 1975), p. 1. The remainder of this section follows the approach used by Davis.

3. Jonathan Levine, "Mild-Mannered Hewlett-Packard Is Making Like Superman," *Business Week,* March 7, 1988, pp. 110–117; Jonathan Goodspeed, "H-P's Alberding: Hanging Tough in Palo Alto," *High-Tech Marketing,* March 1987, pp. 11–14.

4. The basic structure of these examples is from Derek F. Abell, *Defining The Business: The Starting Point of Strategic Planning.* (Prentice-Hall, 1980), pp. 4–6.

5. See Davis, p. 3.

6. Theodore Levitt, "Marketing Myopia," *Harvard Business Review,* September-October 1975.

7. See Levitt.

8. Davis, p. 3.

9. This section follows Derek F. Abell and John S. Hammond, *Strategic Market Planning* (Prentice-Hall, 1979), pp. 173–80.

10. Davis, p. 41.

11. Robert D. Buzzell and Bradley T. Gale, *The PIMS Principles: Linking Strategy to Performance* (New York: The Free Press, 1988).

Cummins Engine Company

Cummins Engine Company is one of a rare breed of U.S. companies—it has faced the challenge of low-priced Japanese competitors and, so far, has won. Surviving the Japanese threat has been anything but easy for the premier diesel engine manufacturer, however. It has entailed an important redefinition of Cummins' business goals as well as major changes in the company's marketing strategy.

Cummins is the world industry leader in heavy-duty diesel engines. It maintains a leadership position in diesel technology and a commanding share (55–60 percent) of the heavy-duty diesel engine market in the U.S. Traditionally, Cummins focused almost exclusively on the heavy-duty engine market. In the early 1980s, however, it modernized its engine line. As part of this process, it introduced advanced products in the medium-duty class and hoped to break into this market.

Just as Cummins was beginning to make this strategic shift, however, Nissan and Komatsu also began to try to break into the U.S. market for medium-duty engines. Although these Japanese firms were not yet challengers in the heavy-duty end of the market, they were poised to make a rapid advance into the market for medium-duty engines since the Japanese products were priced about 10–40 percent below the U.S. market price.

Carefully controlling costs and underpricing competitors to gain market share are mainstays of Nissan's and Komatsu's competitive strategies. Several American industries and product lines have lost significant market share in the face of this type of strategy. The steel, automobile, camera, and electronics industries are notable examples. Therefore, Cummins realized the threat it faced if it ceded any market share to the Japanese, even in a secondary product category such as medium-duty engines. Its worries were also aggravated in 1984 by poor demand for large diesel engines, which still constituted Cummins' main source of profit.

In face of the Japanese challenge, Cummins' CEO, Henry B. Schacht, immediately lowered prices on medium-duty engines to the Japanese level. As Schacht said, "If you don't give the Japanese a major price advantage, they can't get in." So started a dramatic shift in Cummins' business strategy.

Since Cummins, by its own standards, had maintained tight cost controls even before the Japanese threat, it faced an immense challenge in trying to lower its costs even more. Additional cost-cutting was inescapable, though, if it hoped to continue pricing on a par with the Japanese. Although traditional cost-cutting was fundamental to Cummins' new strategy, it was also complemented by other features:

- the acceleration of technical effort
- the move to restructure relations with customers
- the intense drive to improve substantially quality and delivery (as well as cost)
- the plan to expand into engine-related products and services

The elements of Cummins' new strategy are described below:

Technical Activity

The heart of Cummins' technical effort is to design and manufacture products that offer the customer the best value in reliability, durability, and, especially, fuel economy. Marketing research had determined that these factors were the most important ones to the customer. As part of this effort, Cummins has placed special emphasis on the development of electronic engine controls to control fuel use, for example. In addition, it has also become active in total vehicle electronics. Recently, the company established a subsidiary, Cummins Electronics Co., Inc., to develop and manufacture electronic products such as an on-board truck computer that records trip, load, and vehicle maintenance information.

Customer Relations

Cummins has also made strategic changes in its relations with its customers. Noting that customer satisfaction is the key to its success, it has begun to work closely with its truck-manufacturing customers. It is now involved in joint product planning of the customer's truck or equipment. By sharing its technical expertise, Cummins can help customers produce better-performing equipment. It has also helped its customers establish "Just in Time" (JIT) inventory systems. By making frequent and timely deliveries of products to customers, it has helped customers reduce costly supplies of inventory. Cummins has also established similar relationships with its own suppliers in order to reduce its own materials inventories.

Cost, Quality, and Delivery

Cummins has made extensive capital investments in tooling to lower manufacturing costs. It has emphasized acquiring flexible machine systems that are capable of performing a variety of operations, in contrast with the highly specialized tooling usually associated with automation. From the standpoint of human resources, Cummins has cut redundant layers of management and expanded the job functions of individual workers to improve productivity and lower costs. In addition, it has instituted a profit-sharing plan to give employees a personal stake in the company's performance and encourage superior productivity.

New Products and Services

As productivity at Cummins has increased and the company has downsized, talented personnel have become available within the company. In order to use this valuable resource and also reduce the company's dependence on a narrow line of products, it has branched out into a broader range of products and services. Cummins has acquired an interest in a number of firms that manufacture engine components and related products such as piston rings, cooling systems, generator sets, etc. It has also aggressively expanded its service activities. For instance, it has established domestic and international financial services subsidiaries to meet the credit needs of customers and distributors. Cummins Cash & Information Services, Inc., another new subsidiary, handles cash transfers and enables truckers to pay for fuel, repairs, and other travel-related expenses through a large network of truckstops and Cummins distributors. Furthermore, it has also invested in selected high-tech ventures that promise benefits to the company.

Cummins' expanded business definition—to be a provider of products and services to the trucking industry and other users of diesel engines—and its new marketing strategy have begun to show positive results for the firm. After sizable losses in 1986, which were largely associated with downsizing the firm, the company posted a small profit in 1987. It seems to be on the right track with its new strategy, as costs move more closely in line with product prices. Still, Cummins has a way to go before it meets its cost goals. Furthermore, additional cost reductions will be more difficult to achieve than initial ones were.

As difficult as such cost reductions are, however, they are a necessary move to keep in step with a changing competitive environment. Based on its past record, at least, Cummins is attuned to its environment and unafraid to make difficult adjustments. As Schacht has noted, "The fact is that the Japanese have established a new world price for our product. Face that fact. Don't pretend that it's not there. Operate in the world the way it is, not the way you wish it were." Cummins' realistic and flexible attitude has certainly been a key factor in Cummins' ability to overcome competitive challenges. This attitude will continue to be vital to the company's long-term survival.

SOURCES: *1985 Annual Report,* Cummins Engine Company. *1987 Annual Report,* Cummins Engine Company, April 1988. Geoffrey N. Smith, "The Yankee Samurai," *Forbes,* July 14, 1986, pp. 82–83.

Questions

1. What is Cummins' business definition? Has it changed?

2. What are the key elements of Cummins' marketing strategy?

3. What constraints precipitated a change in Cummins' marketing strategy? In general, should external or internal constraints be more important in determining a company's marketing strategy?

4. What growth strategies is Cummins following?

General Electric

After his appointment as CEO of the General Electric Company in 1981, Jack Welch defined a clear and formidable new business objective for the aging manufacturing company. Welch's goal was no less than to turn GE into "the most competitive business enterprise in the world." By many financial standards, Welch has moved GE much closer to that goal than it was before. For instance, Welch boosted company earnings 92 percent from 1980 to 1987. GE's stock price has also risen more than twice as fast as the Standard & Poor's index of 400 industrial stocks. In addition, the company-wide profit margin has increased about two percentage points to 10.4 percent.

How to tell if you have a fork stuck in your arm.
Nothing is more frustrating than finding out your dishes aren't clean because something jammed the dishwasher arm.
When our engineers thought about it, a light went on. And so a warning light went on our dishwashers.
It says Blocked Wash Arm. And it's a feature of an ingenious diagnostic system that monitors the dishwasher performance throughout the cycle.
It's also part of the system of electronics that makes the GE dishwasher the most advanced in the industry.
BLOCKED WASH ARM
The GE 2800 boasts more combinations of cleaning cycles. So it can tackle anything from the pâté on your delicate china to the melted macaroni on your casserole.
A Delay Start option even lets you begin doing the dishes when the water's hot but the utility rates are not.
It's all backed by our 90-day money-back Satisfaction Guaranteed program.* And the GE Answer Center* service can answer all your questions at 800-626-2000. Plus give you the name of your local GE dealer.
All of which helps make dishwashing something it always should have been.
Painless.
We bring good things to life.

Welch has accomplished these changes by implementing a strategic marketing orientation and restructuring GE to better suit this orientation. A key to the CEO's new strategy is that GE should operate only in those markets in which the company clearly offers the customer special value. Specifically, Welch aims for GE to be first or second in any market in which it competes—otherwise, it should get out of that market. As a result, from 1982 to 1989, GE abandoned 232 product lines in which it was not a leader. At the same time, GE has also made several acquisitions—most notably, RCA in 1986—in order to increase its strength in high technology (medical imaging systems, aircraft engines, plastics), services (GE Credit Corp., NBC) and core manufacturing businesses (appliances, lighting), which are the three areas set for strategic emphasis. The table on the next page shows GE's position in a dozen of its businesses.

In support of Welch's new strategy, GE has made extensive capital investments in certain key areas. For example, GE invested $1 billion to automate its major appliances plant. As a result of this massive investment, earnings for major home appliances tripled between 1981 and 1985. GE also invested $350 million to modernize its locomotive plant. Since this modernization, GE has moved from being a distant second in the U.S. locomotive industry to becoming a close competitor of General Motors, which holds first place.

Besides implementing massive structural changes in the company and undertaking huge capital investments, GE has also tried to revamp employee thinking to accord with the company's marketing emphasis. For instance, Jack Welch has declared that marketing is no longer just an organizational function of the firm but must be an *attitude* which permeates the entire company. In line with this all-pervasive marketing orientation, Welch has also stated that the design of GE as an industrial enterprise should begin with the customer—not with the production process.

Since 1981, GE has become a sleeker, more efficient, creative, and responsive company, as well as a better financial performer by most measures. The centrality of marketing to the company's entire business strategy has been a key to this transformation and should help GE move even closer to Welch's competitive goal.

SOURCES: Aaron Bernstein, "A Demanding Year for Labor," *Business Week* (Industrial/Technology Edition), Jan. 11, 1988, pp. 34–35; Marilyn A. Harris, with Zachary Schiller, Russell Mitchell and Christopher Power, "Can Jack Welch Reinvent GE?" *Business Week,* June 30, 1986, pp. 62–67; Russell Mitchell, "Jack Welch: How Good A Manager?" *Business Week,* December 14, 1987, pp. 92–103; Resa W. King, "25 Executives to Watch," *Business Week,* April 17, 1987, p. 240; Peter Petre, "What Welch Has Wrought at GE," *Fortune,* July 7, 1986, pp. 42–47; "The Mind of Jack Welch," *Fortune,* March 27, 1989, pp. 38–50.

Questions

1. How has GE marketing strategy changed under Welch?

2. How did internal constraints affect the development of a new marketing strategy? External constraints?

3. Looking at the BCG portfolio matrix, indicate which GE businesses fit in each quadrant (e.g., cash cow, star, etc.).

4. What changes in marketing tactics would logically flow from Welch's directive for GE to become more marketing oriented?

How a Dozen GE Businesses Rank . . .

	. . . In the U.S.	. . . And in the World
Aircraft engines	First	First
Broadcasting (NBC)	First	Not applicable
Circuit breakers	First *tied with Square D and Westinghouse*	First *tied with Merlin Gerin, Siemens, Westinghouse*
Defense electronics	Second *behind GM's Hughes Electronics*	Second *behind GM's Hughes Electronics*
Electric motors	First	First
Engineering plastics	First	First
Factory automation	Second *behind Allen-Bradley*	Third *behind Siemens and Allen-Bradley*
Industrial and power systems *turbines, meters, drive systems, power transmission controls*	First	First
Lighting	First	Second *behind Philips*
Locomotives	First	First *tied with GM's Electro-Motive*
Major appliances	First	Second *behind Whirlpool tied with Electrolux*
Medical diagnostic imaging	First	First

SOURCE: *Fortune,* March 27, 1989, p. 4.

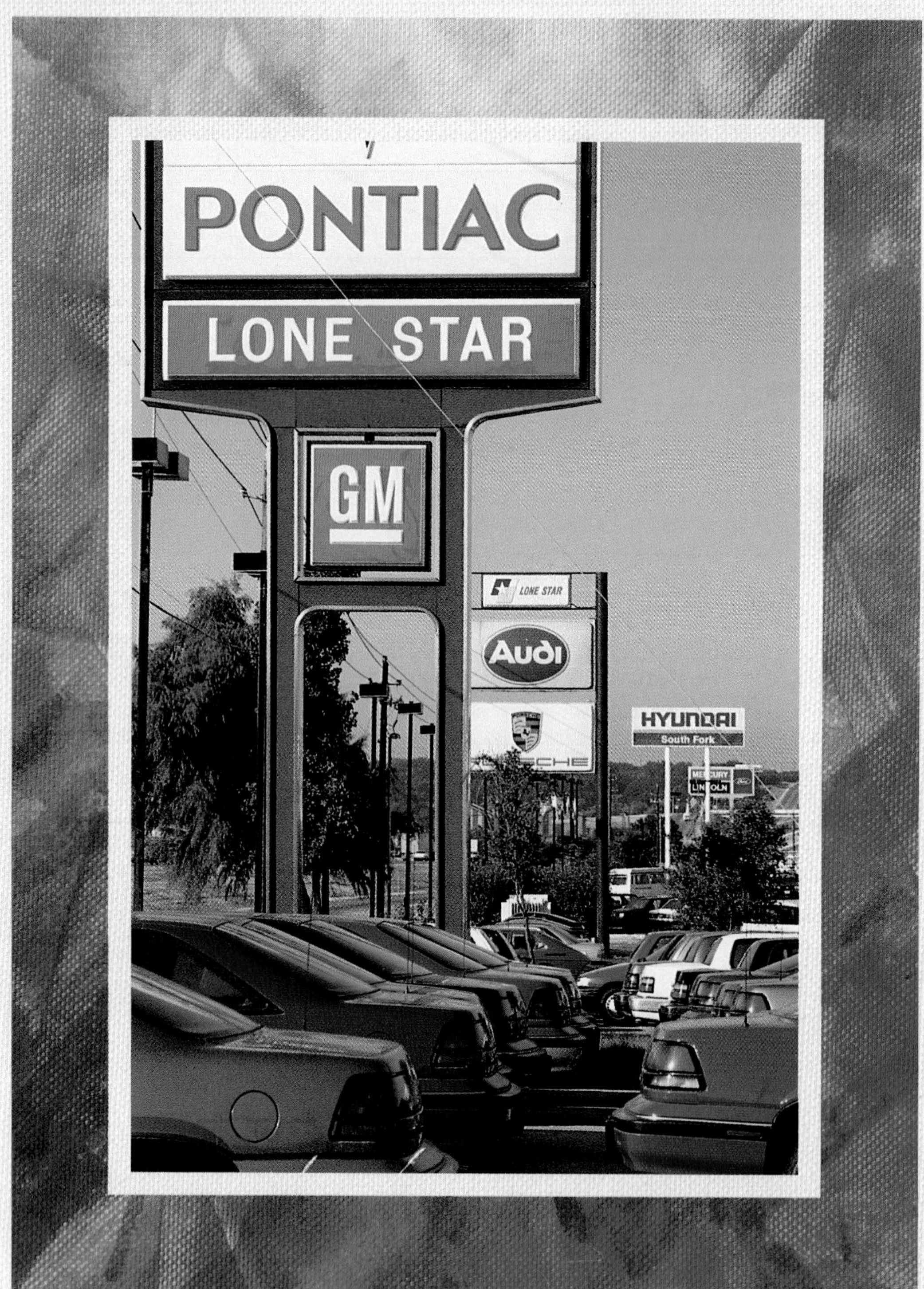
PONTIAC
LONE STAR
GM
LONE STAR
Audi
HYUNDAI
South Fork

3

The Marketing Environment

Learning Objectives

Upon completing this chapter, you will be able to do the following:

DEFINE
the terms *environmental change* and *environmental scanning.*

DESCRIBE
questions that a marketing manager should ask to acquire a picture of the environment.

DISCUSS
why environmental change is inevitable.

ILLUSTRATE
the eight stages in the process of technological innovation.

LIST
the main differences among the four kinds of competitive environments: absolute monopoly, oligopoly, monopolistic competition, and pure competition.

MARKETING PROFILE

The Environment Is Powerful

The events in an organization's environment are sometimes static, occasionally dynamic, and sometimes even tragic. When events are tragic, they can affect the image, sales, and marketing strategies of an organization.

Injuries or deaths to product users. Fraud. Price-gouging. Pollution. All these problems have plagued organizations. At Chrysler there was the spinning back of odometers on cars used by executives and later sold to consumers. Hertz has admitted overcharging motorists and insurers $13 million for repairs. As much as 80 percent of the $13 million in overcharges resulted from charging the retail cost of fixing cars—though Hertz received volume discounts on the repairs. Of those events in recent memory, however, the one that best captures the powerful influence tragedy can have on marketing strategy is the 1982 Tylenol incident.

On September 29, 1982, Mary Kellerman and Adam and Steven Janus, all of suburban Chicago, died from taking Extra-Strength Tylenol capsules into which cyanide had been injected. In the next weeks, five more deaths were linked directly to cyanide-laced Tylenol capsules. Johnson & Johnson Products, Inc. (J&J), the parent company of McNeil, the maker of Tylenol, then recalled over 31 million bottles of the product with a retail value of over $100 million. As a consequence, J&J third-quarter earnings dropped from 78 cents a share in 1981 to 51 cents in 1982. The company's marketing projections prior to the tragedy predicted 1983 sales for Tylenol to be over $1 billion. Of course, the environmental tragedy stopped J&J from achieving even half of the predicted sales.

Johnson & Johnson has always been very concerned about environmental events and its image, and developed its Credo to reflect these concerns. The J&J Credo addresses the need for business to make a profit while also acknowledging the need to respect employees as individuals and to make high-quality products. The Credo helped guide J&J through the product-tampering crisis with Tylenol.

Morton Thiokol, Inc., has also suffered dramatic environmental setbacks. On January 28, 1986, the space shuttle Challenger exploded 74 seconds after launch because of faults in Morton Thiokol's booster rockets. Besides killing seven astronauts, the disaster dealt a crushing blow to Thiokol's reputation as a dependable supplier of technology. Since then, a former Thiokol purchasing agent was indicted for allegedly operating a kickback scheme at the company, a fire at Thiokol's MX missile plant killed 5 employees in December 1987, and tests of Thiokol's redesigned booster rockets have turned up new flaws. Should those who need aerospace technology and expertise be doing business with Thiokol? The reputation Thiokol took years to build has been tarnished by one crisis after another. The environment has had a unique influence on this firm, and Thiokol knows that it has a long uphill battle to rebuild its name and image.

Whether the discussion revolves around Chrysler, Hertz, Johnson & Johnson, or Morton Thiokol, one point is certain: the environment affects the kind of decisions managers make about products or services. Today's managers must contend with the impact of forces more volatile and unpredictable than ever before. These forces, called *stakeholders,* include government regulatory agencies, competitors, international cartels, environmentalist groups, consumer interest groups, and demographic shifts. Any one of them can exert a tremendous influence on the marketing activities of a specific organization.

This growth in the number of stakeholders has affected marketing and made marketing decision making unpredictable and uncertain. It has become harder to anticipate the attack of an environmental force and to predict its consequences. This chapter illustrates the necessity for environmental scanning mechanisms that monitor major environmental forces for competitive activities, opportunities, consumer needs, and even bizarre acts.

SOURCE: Adapted from Judith Dobrzynski, "Morton Thiokol: Reflections On The Shuttle Disaster," *Business Week,* March 14, 1988, pp. 82–83, 86, 91; John A. Byrne, "Businesses are Signing Up for Ethics 101," *Business Week,* February 15, 1988, pp. 56–57; Gladiorn Hill, "The Shifting Sands of Public Consent," *New Management,* Spring 1987, pp. 47–50; and Ian Mitroff and Ralph H. Kilman, "Corporate Tragedies: Teaching Companies To Cope With Evil," *New Management,* Spring 1984, pp. 48–53.

Marketers must be aware of the key environmental forces that affect a firm's market opportunities, capabilities, and resources match. This chapter specifically deals with six of the most important external environmental forces facing marketing managers: social-cultural, economic, technological, political, ecological, and competitive. Marketers must analyze and diagnose each of them in order to fully utilize data and information in a timely manner. The record of business failures that have resulted entirely or partially from ignoring these forces—from not scanning the environment and taking informed action—could fill this entire book. Instead of dwelling solely on failure, however, our chapter offers a balance of actual company actions in environmental scanning—some successful, some unsuccessful.

It is impossible in a single chapter to adequately cover every important aspect of the external environment, but we will acquaint readers with the realities of environmental scanning faced by marketing managers. The extreme difficulty of matching market opportunities to organizational capabilities and resources—and the enormous skill required to pull it off—will become clear. This match is difficult to make, because the external environment, or some part of it, is always changing. Indeed, the firm's own actions help bring about some of these changes.

Environmental Change Is Inevitable

Change is perhaps the most powerful force of present-day life. In the past, change often came at a much more leisurely pace; yet even then, the inability of individuals, cities, and nation-states to adapt to evolving trends resulted in a loss of power or even destruction. We have become familiar with the historical accounts of the impact of sweeping changes in technology, the economy, and social organization on society and empires.

Historically, decision makers have been unable to foresee change and understand its significance. The Athenians did not understand why their city-state declined; the same was true of leaders in the crumbling Turkish empire many centuries later. More recently, American automobile manufacturers missed changes in the public's preference for smaller fuel-efficient cars. Their failure to understand customer needs (the marketing concept) is part of the reason for some of the lost market share. However, objective evidence gleaned from surveys of owners, records of problems reported, and internal audits—mostly proprietary information only circulated within the auto industry—shows improvements in the Big Three in the United States: General Motors, Ford, and Chrysler. Quality, fuel efficiency, car handling, and overall satisfaction are much better today than in 1980.[1] There is still room for improvement, but now marketing executives at the Big Three are picking up on environmental signals so they don't fall further behind foreign imports.

However, the marketing manager does not have the luxury of ignoring or disregarding these forces and institutions of change. He or she must make decisions about product, promotion, place, and price in an environment engulfed by continual change, uncertainty, and varying degrees of turbulence. Sudden shifts and totally unexpected events affect the marketing manager's decision choices. Drucker has called this era of rapid change *The Age of Discontinuity*,[2] while Toffler calls the present *Future Shock.*[3]

The **marketing environment** of an organization includes all those factors that may affect the organization directly or indirectly in any perceptible way.[4] Environmental factors affect organizations from two directions—input and output. The environment influences what goes into an organization, since environmental factors (people with values, needs, and goals), limited natural resources, and technology (equipment and procedures) are major parts of its input.

The organization then does something to the input, producing an output. The output (Macintosh personal computers, Alphabits cereal, Awake frozen orange drink, a room at the Hilton hotel) goes back into the environment, again affecting the organization as the output is consumed, utilized, and evaluated. Thus, organizations and their environments are inseparable, each affecting the other. This inseparability will be highlighted throughout the chapter. It will also become apparent that marketing *managerial skills* in observing, analyzing, and forecasting the environment may mean the difference between success, failure, or survival.

How many of you remember businesses with names like Robert Hall, W. T. Grant, Woolco, Studebaker, Daniel Boone Fried Chicken, The World Football League (WFL), and Korvette? These were once prospering businesses that eventually failed. A major contributing cause in each of these was management's inability to correctly and promptly observe, analyze, and forecast changes in the environment—that is, a failure in environmental analysis and diagnosis.[5]

Environmental Analysis and Diagnosis

Environmental analysis is the monitoring of external environmental forces. It is designed to determine the source of a firm's opportunities and threats. **Environmental diagnosis** is the process of making marketing decisions by assessing the significance of the data (opportunities and threats) in the environmental analysis.[6] The diagnosis is an opinion resulting from an evaluation of the available facts. The marketing decision maker must consider the strategy of the firm and the environmental forces.

The interrelationships of society and organizations were dramatically spelled out by Talcott H. Parsons, the American sociologist.[7] Parsons proposed four functions for society. First, in order to survive, a society must adapt itself to changing conditions in the environment. The adaptive part of society is the economy, which is supported, perpetuated, and reinforced by technological development. Second, a society must maintain its own basic patterns so that, in the future, the social system is still recognizable and in charge of its own actions. Third, society must integrate its different tasks and functions. The integrative part consists mainly of culture, which includes education, religion, art, mass communications, and philosophy. Last, society must move beyond adaptation, maintenance, and integration to attain worthwhile goals. The goal-attaining parts of society are the organizations and institutions that exist. In other words, society attains its goals through organizations; government, business firms, and educational institutions are the goal-attaining systems.[8]

Figure 3–1 shows the relationship of an organization to the major forces of society, which we will refer to as the external environment. The importance of this figure will become more clear as each force is clarified in the chapter. For the time being, think of every marketing manager as being in the middle of the figure. The immediate environmental forces—suppliers, customers, intermediaries, employees, creditors, and shareholders—are certainly important. However, just as important are the external environmental forces. Changes in the external environment affect the immediate environmental forces and the manager. For example, changes in the social-cultural environment can affect the number of customers available for a product and the marketing manager's decisions about new product development or advertising expenditures. The promoting of Pampers seemed to demonstrate what Procter & Gamble

Figure 3–1 The Environment Facing the Marketing Manager

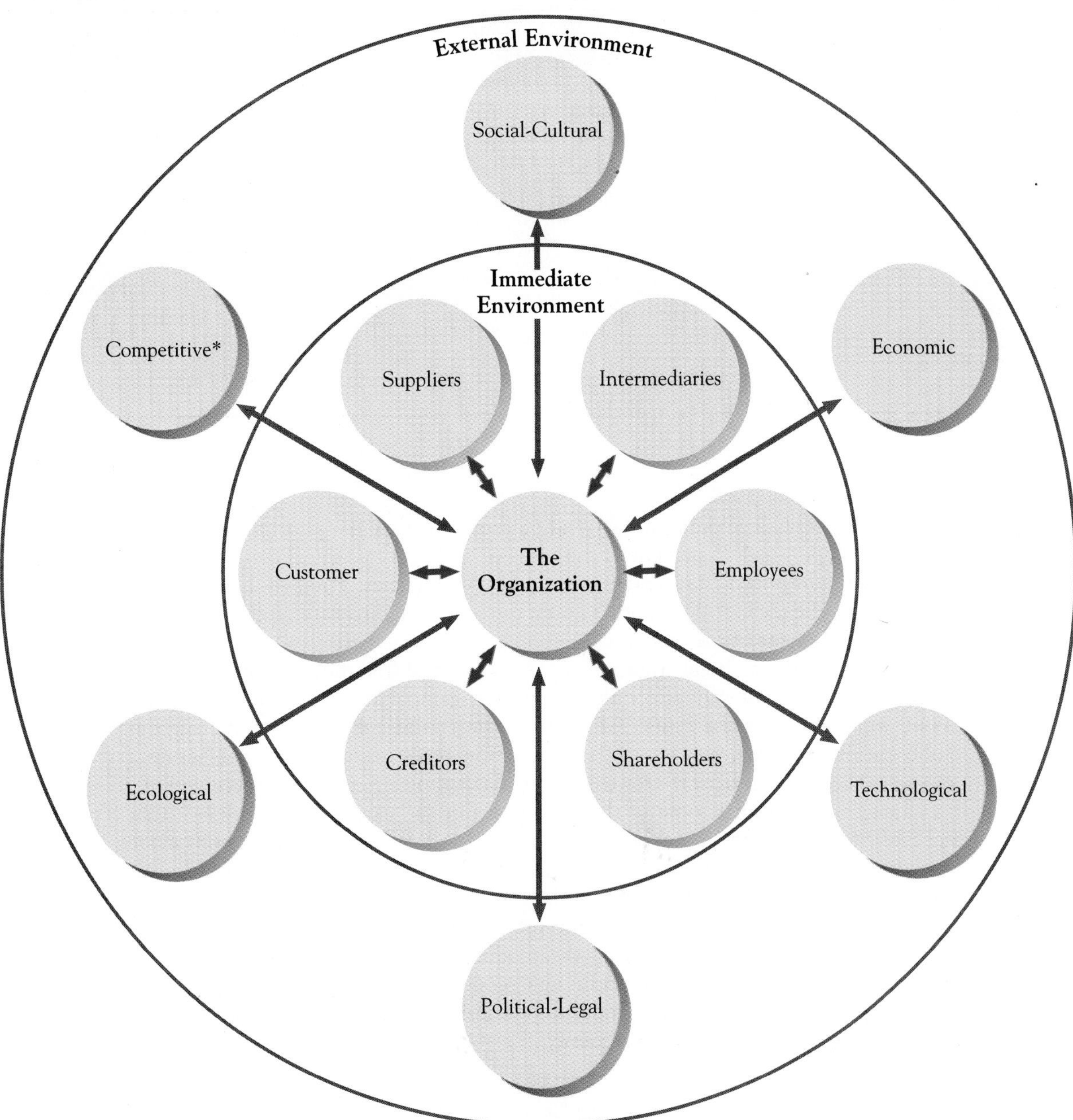

*Domestic and international competitors make up this environmental force.

Table 3–1 Some Important External Environmental Factors: A Marketing Perspective

Social-Cultural	Economic	Technological	Political-Legal	Ecological	Competitive
Life-style Changes	Interest Rates	New Products	Antitrust Laws	Environmental Protection	Number of Competitors
Life Expectancies	Deficit	Patent Laws	Product Liability Laws	Waste Management	Strengths of Competitors
Birthrate	Gross National Product	Productivity Measurement and Growth	Tax Laws	Public Image	Market Entry
Growth Rate (Immigration included)	Unemployment Levels	Industry R&D	Import/Export Trade	Safety of Products	Market Exit
Family Arrangements	Energy Sources and Costs	Federal Support of R&D	Trade Regulations	Packaging Procedures	Market Growth
Consumer Activism	Inflation Rates	Robotics	Investment Tax Credits		Market Share
Shifts in Population	Money Supply	Computer Technology			Foreign Competition
Changing Women's Roles					

(P&G) does best: develop a product and market it so that few can live without it. In 1975, Pampers had 75 percent of the disposable-diaper market. Then along came P&G's premium-priced Luvs and Kimberly-Clark's Huggies. Pampers has not only suffered from the competition, but also from the declining birthrate, and it now holds less than 36 percent of the market.[9]

Changes in the political environment, such as restriction requirements on advertising claims, can directly affect the promotion campaign selected for cigarettes, mouthwash, or headache relief. Changes in the ecological environment, such as pollution-control laws, can affect the production processes used to manufacture a product, like Monsanto's low-cost recyclable plastic bottle, and its marketing plan.

Table 3–1 identifies some of the key factors in the external environment that are likely to be of strategic importance to marketing managers. Any decisions made concerning the market mix will have to be made after carefully weighing and evaluating the factors identified in Table 3–1.

As you can see, the organization also influences the environment. For example, customers are directly influenced by the products or services offered; competitors respond to or take notice of a successful new product; and the rivers and streams can be affected by the waste products emitted in industrial production. The organization and its environmental forces are certainly in a state of constant give-and-take.

Review Your Marketing Knowledge

• Could the use of a valid organizational environment analysis have tipped Johnson & Johnson off and prevented the Tylenol tragedy?

• Where are you as a customer or client in terms of being a part of the environment for a law firm, a store such as J.C. Penney, or a fast food restaurant like Wendy's?

Environmental Scanning

Without taking into account the relevant environmental influences, a firm cannot expect to develop good strategic plans. *Environmental constraints* emerging out of the energy crisis were responsible for more fuel-efficient J-Cars and K-Cars. The environmental influence of a coffee-bean shortage and the ensuing rapid price increases spawned the "coffee maker" technological modification for Mr. Coffee automatic-drip coffee makers, hastened the development of a ground tea for automatic coffee machines and even produced a coffee substitute, Bravo. Pressures from the competition prompted Coca-Cola to change the formula for the taste of Coke. Likewise, health conscious Americans discovered the perils of plaque and Oral Research Laboratories provided their sole product Plax, a prebrushing rinse that removes bacterial plaque.

Business, in general, and marketing, specifically, derive their existence from the external environment. Thus, knowing what is going on in the environment is a continual process:

> *Perceiving in the environment needs and opportunities for adaptation even before they actually materialize—and designing and seeing through a continuous procession of actions to carry out adaptive innovation, these are the essence of business strategy. . . . The environment represents an everchanging sum total of the "facts of life" with which the corporation has come to terms.*[10]

Marketing Opportunities

Since change is inevitable in all parts of an organization's environment, marketing managers must be able to observe, analyze, and forecast events and shifts. Environmental analysis involves scanning the changing environmental forces that may affect a company's products and markets.[11] Failure to read, interpret, and take action in a changing situation means that marketing opportunities will probably be missed. A **marketing opportunity** is "a challenge to specific marketing action that is characterized by a generally favorable set of environmental circumstances and an acceptable probability of success."[12]

There are no guarantees that marketing managers will do a good job of observing, analyzing, and forecasting environmental forces. However, monitoring environmental forces is necessary to seize the best marketing opportunities available.[13] Without some form of environmental scanning program, the organization is not likely to adopt timely, efficient, and profitable marketing strategies.

Opportunities: Few or Many?

Some organizations have a significant number of opportunities. Others do not have many opportunities, or assume they have opportunities when they do not, or are not able to sense when opportunities present themselves. For years the main product of Hershey Foods Corporation was the chocolate candy bar. Hershey did not seek other opportunities; in fact, it refused to advertise. It was quite satisfied with having its candy bars sold by over one million retail stores. However, inflation, shortages, competition, and other environmental changes forced Hershey to search out opportunities through surveys, interviews, reviews of financial data, and discussions with investment bankers. The result has been a diversified company. Today Hershey still makes four of the top ten chocolate candies (Reese's peanut butter cups—third; Kit

Kat wafer bars—fifth; Hershey's milk chocolate with almonds–seventh; and the original chocolate bar—tenth), but they also make pasta products (Skinner, San Giorgio, Delmonico, and P&R) and New Trail granola bars for health conscious consumers. They also operate the 600-unit Friendly restaurant chain.[14]

W. T. Grant's experience stands in contrast to Hershey's. Grant's management sensed many opportunities. Thus, W. T. Grant entered the early 1970s with plans to expand operations. They felt that direct competition with Sears and Montgomery Ward would permit them to seize opportunities. The plan failed because Grant didn't have enough managerial talent to run the new stores, didn't have a distinct image (was Grant a variety chain, a discounter, or general-merchandise chain?), and wasn't competitive with the "big guys" like Sears and Wards in offering service or established brands. Grant did scan the environment, but the information they gathered and the use they made of it were inadequate.[15]

The W. T. Grant failure suggests how the marketing manager must respond to market opportunities. There are two crucial factors that must be weighed: the kind and quality of information reaching the marketing decision makers and the interpretation and use of that information. How the information is interpreted and used depends, in turn, on the goals and attitudes of the decision maker, which are also influenced by environmental forces.

The marketing manager has to weigh the environment's control over the organization and the organization's control over the environment. There is a mutual pressure system in the exchange of "benefits" and "costs." Most organizations (for example, Hershey's) find that they are largely controlled by environmental forces. However, some firms (Rockwell International and Coca-Cola) have a relative parity with their environment. In their cases, there is an even exchange of benefits and costs. Only a few firms, like IBM, are able to dominate their environments. Only a few can secure inputs from the environment and export outputs largely on the organization's terms (benefits). These firms are able to create their own marketing opportunities.

Scanning the environment requires the realistic assessment of a firm's position. Some questions to help a marketing manager gain a better picture of the environment are the following:

1. What is the nature of the industry the organization is operating in? Is there much innovation taking place? Is the technology employed sophisticated? Is it subject to legal constraints? Is the industry marked by great diversity in the demands or needs of the customers?
2. Are we a powerless organization within the industry or a dominant member of it? Do we use our power efficiently or do we flounder around? Does the organization have some special advantages in the industry—managerial talent, location, experience with markets, reputation?
3. What is the mix of attributes of the environment? How much turbulence exists? Is it dynamic, unpredictable, expanding, fluctuating? How much *hostility* exists? How much risk, stress, and dominance is there? How much *diversity* exists? What is the range of characteristics and needs of the markets? How much *technical complexity* exists? How sophisticated are the information, equipment, and processes needed to make and carry out strategic decisions? How much *restriction* exists? What are the legal and political constraints?

These and other similar questions have to be continually asked and answered by marketing managers so that they can observe, analyze, and forecast shifting environmental forces. Managers are not machines who automatically "check in" and respond.

They perceive, feel, think, problem solve, as well as distort, misinterpret, become frustrated, and react emotionally. Any organization's environmental scanning approach and its accuracy is a reflection of the marketing managers involved. In fact, the timeliness, thoroughness, and style of seizing marketing opportunities is largely dictated by top-level marketing decision makers.

The Response Continuum: Adjusting to the Environment

The organizational styles used to assess environmental forces and marketing opportunities can be described in terms of a continuum. At one pole (end point) is the reactive or passive organization. This type of firm primarily reacts to innovations and is reluctant to try something new. The philosophy here is that environmental forces are so unpredictable that the organization has little control or effect on them. In the early 1970s, Ford, GM, Chrysler, and American Motors certainly fit the description of being reactive and passive in the down-sized car market.

On the opposite end of the response continuum are firms that are aggressive and forceful in pursuing their objectives and plans. Toyota, Nissan, and Honda responded this way in the small-car market in the 1970s. These foreign car manufacturers believed that they could influence environmental forces by making sound and timely small-car decisions. This style is typical of marketing managers in the Merck example; aggressive and forceful organization takes purposeful action to meet challenges or create marketing opportunities. Lee Iacocca of Chrysler, Jack Welch, and John Reed of Citicorp are not only managers, but are also leaders. They are leaders who can envision the future and inspire others to join them. These leaders did not fear change, they embraced it and created it.[16]

Today a number of organizations would be classified by most observers as aggressive and forceful. A sample of these firms includes Apple Computer, Intel, American Express, Burger King, McDonald's, Wells Fargo Bank, General Electric, and 3M.

An aggressive company, American Express allows consumers to charge movie tickets at some theaters.

Table 3–2 Environmental Scanning at General Electric

General Electric (GE) operates one of the most sophisticated environmental forecasting departments of any major company. It has abandoned the extrapolation methods of the past and, instead, views the future as probabilistic. In January of each year, the forecasters prepare three different scenarios of the environment:

- A benchmark scenario
- A "best-of-all-possible-worlds" scenario
- A "worst-of-all-possible-worlds" scenario

General Electric uses a four-sided forecasting model. *Economic forecasting* (future gross national product, consumption, and productivity projections), technological forecasting (state-of-the-art-developments); political environment forecasting (government-business relations); and social environment forecasting (demographic trends, value changes).

Each scenario is a self-contained picture of relevant trends, events, and discontinuities that are selected for their occurrence probability and their potential impact on the business. For example, the forecasters see a substantially different consumer market in the 1990–1995 period, with a different age distribution, racial and ethnic makeup, birthrate, consumer lifestyle, and attitude toward business. To GE, forecasting is the business of managing uncertainty by anticipating possible scenarios and preparing contingency plans.

SOURCE: 1986 Annual Report, Rogene Bucholz, "General Electric Environmental Forecasting," In Rogene Bucholz, et al. (ed.) *Management Response To Public Issues* (Prentice-Hall, 1985) , pp. 112–125.

These and other organizations on the aggressive side of the continuum apply environmental scanning techniques and then make the necessary adaptations to meet the changes. An example of environmental scanning at General Electric is presented in Table 3–2.

The passive, reactive tendencies of some firms and the forceful, active tendencies of others are not presented as correct or incorrect. Instead we use the continuum to illustrate differences in managerial decision-making styles. Of course, most firms are not completely reactive or completely aggressive. The response mode of most marketing managers lies somewhere between the two poles. For example, Wells Fargo Bank is not always aggressive, but seems to be more forceful, on the average, than most banks. Wells Fargo managers seem to address shifts in the environment before many others in the banking industry sense various social, cultural, political, and technological environmental changes.[17]

To illustrate the difference between passive-reactive and forceful-active, let us look at the American railroad industry. In the early 1970s, records were set for freight tonnage, but earnings did not keep pace. The heavy usage resulted in bottlenecks, lost customers, car shortages, and equipment breakdown. Tonnage doubled in the 1980s. The passive firms waited until it was a *fait accompli* before dealing with equipment, plant, and personnel needs. The forceful, active firms recognized the environmental shifts and initiated plans to cope with changes in technology, regulations, competition, and demand.[18]

Marketing decisions about price, place, product, and promotion take place in an environment that is continually changing. We considered six major segments of the external environment. Certainly there are more, but we believe that most of these other forces can be placed into one of the six categories. As Drucker aptly states, "Results are obtained by exploiting opportunities, not by solving problems. All one can hope to get by solving a problem is to restore normalcy."[19] To exploit opportunities, marketing managers must have an appreciation of the forces outside the organization. This is what the remainder of the chapter will explore.

In some cases, opportunities may even seize organizations. Borg-Warner went into the dealer inventory finance business, developing the Borg-Warner Acceptance Corporation (B-WAC) as a last ditch attempt to stem the outflow of dealers and distributors.[20] B-WAC financed dealers' inventories, providing the dealers with both a service and an incentive not offered by competitors. The company actually stumbled into the service industry, since most managers resisted such a move. From this beginning, Borg-Warner now has service-industry earnings almost equal to their manufacturing-industry earnings.

The Social-Cultural Environment

The social-cultural environment consists of institutions, people and their values, and the norms of behavior that are learned and shared. It is the people—who they are, where they are, how they live, what they think, and what values they hold—that make up the social-cultural fabric of society. Values are defined as the likes, dislikes, beliefs, and prejudices that determine a person's view of the world.

The social-cultural environment affects marketing decisions about product, price, place, and promotion because it establishes what is an acceptable and equitable decision. Consider how important the following dimensions of the social-cultural environment have been in the marketing of goods and services.

- *Change in population trends.* For years it was thought that a family should have two to four children. Today this view is changing. It has had a significant effect on firms like Stouffer's (TV dinners), Levi Strauss (jeans), Gerber (baby food), Mattel (toys), and Carnation (milk).[21]
- *Increased number of homebased workers.* For at least eight million Americans, the journey to work consists of walking from one part of their house to another. No riding a bus, finding a babysitter, or having a boss looking over their shoulders. Professionals, service workers, and retailers in growing numbers are staying home and working.
- *Advance of the computer.* In a short time, the vacuum tube was replaced by the transistor. Silicon chips appeared in the 1970s, with magnetic disks replacing punch cards.
- *Commercial applications of genetic engineering.* Newly engineered genetic substances are increasing farm yields in arid climates, making plastics derived not from petroleum, but from vegetable fiber.
- *Fast-moving society.* Microwave ovens are becoming common household appliances. Now even turkeys are cooked in microwaves. Brother has a model that will calculate the weight, temperature, and cooking time for any dish, even a twenty-two pound turkey.
- *Increased number of married women in the work force.* At one time, most married women stayed home. Now, over 50 percent work. This has had a significant impact on firms that sell door-to-door, like Avon, Fuller Brush, and Electrolux. It has also created a need for child care, a change in product preferences, a focus on business fashion, and the substitution of teenagers and males as shoppers.
- *Increased interest in working a schedule that is not five days per week, eight hours per day.* Shorter workweeks and flextime schedules have been instituted by many companies for the benefit of their employees.

The marketing manager must monitor the social-cultural environment to develop clear ideas about the future. The behavior of significant groups of people in key locations, the bellwether (leading) states of Florida, California, Washington, Colorado, and Connecticut, may indicate new trends, consumer demands, consumer complaints, and consumer growth.[22] Early innovators in these locations adopt new products, ideas, and fashions. For example, imports made up 50 percent of automobile sales in California, and Colorado passed laws limiting shopping-center growth.

These examples indicate that social-cultural forces can and do affect marketing decision making. Three major classes, in particular, are extremely important for marketing managers to monitor—population trends, social structure, and cultural patterns. Each of these classes will be discussed in detail in Chapter 4.

The Economic Environment

Economic changes pose both problems and opportunities for marketing managers. An expanding economy has a direct effect on the demands for a company's product or service; it also facilitates the establishment of new companies. As growth continues, however, the mix of consumer demand shifts from food and shelter to consumer durables and to purchases like home computers, a second color-television set, or a vacation in Cancún, Mexico. Increased spending for recreational activities and goods that offer ego satisfaction become more common in a growth economy.

A major slowdown in economic growth can bring business failure, as was common in the early 1970s and early 1980s. But some companies offering lower priced goods can do well during slow periods. During the 1969–70 recession, retailers such as Kresge, Penney's, and Woolworth had sales gains, as did sellers of used automobiles, rental equipment services, and fabrics for making one's own clothes.[23]

Today the economic forecast for some industries is good. In the clothing industry, style is back in vogue. The baby-boomers are buying separate, up-to-the-minute wardrobes for work, play, and special occasions. The paper industry is operating at capacity; personal computer printers and their thick, how-to manuals are fueling the demand for paper. Like the trucking industry, airlines have, and can, expect more traffic. The biotechnology industry is ripe for growth as products for treating genetic disorder, AIDS, and various forms of carriers are being tested.

Other industries, because of economic factors, are stymied in terms of growth and opportunities. Interest rates are nipping any growth opportunities in the housing industry. Housing starts and sales were down in the 1987–1989 period. The steel industry has not recovered from its $6.7 billion losses in 1982–84. Imports now claim 30 percent of the American market. The oil industry is holding its breath. What will happen in the Middle East? What role will government play in tax changes, regulations, and investment credits?

The three most persistent economic problems in the early 1980s were inflation, sluggish productivity, and energy shortages. Although all three are related, the relentless increase in the price of everything, from hamburgers to a college education, still remains the great economic agony now that we are in the 1990s.

Inflation: Down But Still a Force

Inflation is a problem that involves everyone. **Inflation** is fairly easy to define: It is a general rise in the prices that people must pay for goods and services. Since the Great Depression of the 1930s, average prices in the United States have moved

Figure 3–2 The Result of Moderate Inflation in Next Five Years

steadily upward, almost never downward. The rate of inflation was relatively modest during the 1940s and '50s, but in the 1960s and '70s prices increased at a faster rate. The cost of most goods and services today is about ten times higher than it was during the 1930s and '40s. Then a haircut cost about 75 cents and a dime tip was sufficient; a meal in a comfortable restaurant cost 50 cents; a pair of durable and stylish shoes cost about $4.95. Inflation in 1988 was about 4.5 percent, which is down significantly from the double-digit rate of 12 percent in 1981.[24] But even at a 6 percent inflation rate, higher prices, represented in Figure 3–2, will become a reality by 1995.

The income earned by workers in the 1930s and 1940s, however, was not what it is today. The disposable income per capita, the money earned divided by a country's population, was about $500 then, compared to approximately $1,600 in 1987.[25]

Marketing managers are more concerned with the **disposable personal income (DPI),** a consumer's total aftertax income to be used for spending and savings. This income, available to individuals and families, provides a marketing manager with information on the general health and potential of markets. They attempt to determine how income is divided among families—the income distribution of a market. More discussion of income distribution is found in Chapter 4.

Are Americans better off economically today than thirty years ago? The *Marketing in Action* on the "good old days" indicates that the answer is yes.

MARKETING IN ACTION

"Life was better in the old days. It would really be great to turn the clock back." These are statements one hears about the past. But as the late comedian Jackie Gleason said, "The past remembers better than it lived." The average American has never had it so good economically. By almost any measure of health and wealth, Americans are better off today than in the 1950s, 1960s, and 1970s.

Despite oil shortages, inflation, stagnating productivity, more governmental red tape, and a Dow Jones Industrial average that crashed 508 points on October 19, 1987, economic gains came in the 1980s. In the 1990s, incomes are up, and so is our net worth. There are more opportunities to go to college, start a new business, and land a job. There are also more goods and services to purchase.

Since our economic well being is better, are we more satisfied? According to pollster Louis Harris, fewer Americans were satisfied with their economic lot in life in 1986 than in 1956. One reason for this dissatisfaction is that pay has been rising more slowly than during the boom times of

Were The Old Days Really So Good?

the sixties. Prices have nearly quadrupled, and taxes have been taking more of our income since the 1950s. However, the average American's buying power is two times greater than in the 1950s.

Americans are not the only citizens of the world now living better and buying more with their earnings. West Germany and Japan have made astounding progress, and the United States no longer has indisputably the highest standard of living among major industrialized nations. Germans have slightly fewer cars than Americans (42 for every 100 persons vs. 48 in the U.S.). However, they do not need as many since Germans are more likely to live in cities and Americans in suburbs. And in Japan today, 57 percent of the people have air conditioners, 71 percent have cars, and 99 percent have color television sets.

The nostalgia to bring back the "old economic times" in the United States and in other industrialized nations is not supported by facts and statistics. Are we living better economically today? The answer should be an unqualified *yes*.

SOURCES: Karen Pennar and G. David Wallace, "The Economy: Uncertainty Isn't About To Go Away," *Business Week*, February 22, 1988, pp. 52–53 and Sylvia Nason, "Do We Live As Well As We Used To?" *Fortune*, September 14, 1987, pp. 32–46.

Productivity

Most economists generally agree that inflation is worsened by decreasing productivity. A sluggish, or flat, productivity rate can slow the growth of the entire economy. During most of the 1960s, the American economy grew rapidly, with low unemployment and low inflation. But in the 1970s, and 1980s, the economy grew much less rapidly, with high unemployment and inflation; in 1988 productivity grew at a rate of only about 1.8 percent annually.

Productivity is an estimate of output per labor-hour worked. Certainly it is a crude measure, subject to short-term error. However, over the long term, productivity measures can clearly show trends. For years, productivity in the United States was increasing at an annual rate of 2.5 to 3.0 percent. However, the rate of productivity growth slid to an anemic 2.0 percent from 1970–1978 and was virtually flat from 1978 through 1985. Productivity in durable goods industries has started to rise at an annual rate of 2 percent.[26]

The implications of sluggish, or flat, productivity growth concern marketers. When workers produce more, total output grows, and employers can increase wages without raising prices; the rise in revenue from increased output will offset the higher wage costs. If productivity is flat, almost every dollar of wage gains is translated into price boosts. Goods and services that cost more will not be purchased, because consumers do not have the dollars to purchase them.

Four major reasons have been suggested for the slow growth of productivity in the United States from 1970 to 1985—a changing work force, reduced research and development expenditures, inadequate investment, and excessive government regulations.[27] Little can be done about the labor force. Beginning in the mid-1960s, many workers were employed who lacked the training and experience to become highly productive in their first few years; the result was lower productivity. Also, the work force contained a higher proportion of service and information workers. It seems harder for doctors, lawyers, accountants, teachers, and credit counselors to raise, or even measure, their productivity than for steelworkers and machine operators to do so.

The other three causes of sluggish productivity can be improved. However, solutions are not easy. For example, caution must be used in analyzing the trade-off between productivity increases and the quality of life if government regulations in some areas are eased or eliminated. Changing government regulations, increasing research and development expenditures, and increasing business investments are good news-bad news situations. The good news is that they can increase productivity. The bad news is that making these things happen will require coordination and cooperation among business, government, labor, and society.

Concern About Energy

The energy crisis certainly caught the attention of marketing managers. Since 1973, when the Organization of Petroleum Exporting Countries (OPEC) grabbed control of the world market and began to exact the wages of a monopoly, marketing managers in many industries have faced difficult, uncertain times.[28] OPEC raised the price from $7 a barrel in 1973 to $40 a barrel in 1980, surpassing the value of oil to buyers. Consumption dropped. (At the middle of 1989, oil was priced on the world market at around $19 a barrel.)

Currently, there is no *energy crisis*. We are not actually running out of energy—we are running out of cheap energy. We are also running out of the money to pay for doubling the supply of needed energy and to pay for higher-priced products and services that are related to energy.

Energy will have to be viewed as a means rather than an end if marketing managers and society are to win the battle. No one wants a kilowatt hour; the objective is to light a room. No one wants a gallon of gasoline; the object is to travel at a reasonable price from one place to another.

There is no "quick fix" for any new energy crisis that may occur in the 1990s. The highest priority in the United States still should be conservation. Investment in saving energy is the responsibility of all citizens, including those involved in marketing.

Energy conservation in the short run and long run will require creative solutions in all areas of business. A few innovative solutions have already surfaced which indicate that business understands the importance of saving energy. The makers of Maxwell House coffee developed a method to save natural gas. The first step in making instant coffee is to brew the coffee just as people do at home, except in 1000-gallon containers. The heat to brew the coffee had come from burning natural gas, and the process left Maxwell House with tons of coffee grounds. The company then had to use trucks (that burned gasoline) to cart the coffee grounds away. Maxwell House realized it could save most of the cost of the natural gas (and the gasoline cost) by burning the grounds to set the heat to brew subsequent batches of coffee. Natural gas is now used only to start the coffee grounds burning.

Conservation can come from technical solutions, like the Maxwell House example, or from social solutions. It is in these social solutions—which influence the way we live and act and how we satisfy needs—that marketing can have the biggest influence. It will mean "belt tightening" in a number of marketing areas. The degree of control displayed will clearly reflect marketing's commitment to alleviating the energy crisis. One thing is fairly certain about marketing's role—failure to practice energy conservation will lead to a consumer backlash.

Energy shortages strongly suggest that *demarketing* may become an even more significant marketing strategy in the future. *Demarketing* is a term used to describe the process of reducing consumer demand for goods and services to a level that can be supplied by a firm.

The signs of demarketing are already actively appearing in various industries. Firms like General Electric, Carnation, Campbell, and Armour are narrowing their product lines. Exxon, Shell, Texaco, and Gulf all have advertised ways of conserving gasoline. Public utilities now regularly advertise ways to make homes more energy-efficient. But demarketing doesn't mean *no marketing,* as one nonexpert indicated:

> *There is little doubt that the energy crisis will force an alteration in the role of the marketing man. In some industries, it may alter him out of existence. . . . When demand exceeds supply, marketing men can be replaced by order takers. The art of selling is unnecessary. There also is no need for advertising, sales promotion, incentives, sweepstakes, trading stamps, free road maps, or even windshield cleaning.*[29]

This view is too pessimistic in our opinion. However, it does point out correctly the concern about the energy crisis and its impact on marketing. Marketing managers in some industries will have to learn to deal with shortages. On the other hand, the energy crisis offers some opportunities. Bicycle and motorcycle manufacturers (for example, Schwinn and Honda) will have some good years ahead. Neighborhood "mom and pop" stores could enjoy a comeback as people try to conserve gas by driving fewer miles. Recorded home entertainment, via satellite dish, cable television, and vest-pocket size tape recorders will be even more important and curtail travel to entertainment.

The Technological Environment

Perhaps technological changes are the most visible of all the environmental changes, but public pride in controlled progress in the early 1900s appears to have changed to apprehension, or even fear, as we enter the 1990s. After two World Wars, a depression, and many unresolved economic and energy problems, there are few who believe that all change is positive and that increasing technical knowledge will produce still better technology that will undoubtedly improve the human condition.

Technology has touched almost every aspect of life in industrialized Western nations. In the process it has made widespread affluence possible. The Brookings Institute estimated that nearly half of the increase in American national income between 1929 and 1969 came from advances in *knowledge,* or what is referred to as technology.

Technology is a nation's accumulated competence to provide goods and services for people. Technology follows no course, seeks no ends, holds to no values. It is quite neutral and very natural. It is a part of nature, given meaning, substance, and

Table 3–3 Stages in the Technological Innovation Process

Stage	Characteristics	Comment
Research, Basic	1. Scientific suggestion, discovery, recognition of need or opportunity	The latter source seems to be the origin of the majority of contemporary innovations.
	2. Proposal of theory or design concept	The crystallization of the theory or design concept that is ultimately successful is usually the culmination of much trial and error.
Research, Applied	3. Laboratory verification of theory or design concept	The existence or the operational validity of the concept suggested in the previous stage is verified. The concept may be difficult for the forecaster to assess, since the thing demonstrated usually is a phenomenon rather than an application.
	4. Laboratory demonstration of application	The principle is embodied in a laboratory "breadboard" model of the device (or sample material or its process equivalent), which shows the theory of Stage 2 applied to perform a desired function or purpose.
Development	5. Full-scale or field trial	The concept moves from the laboratory bench into its first trial on a large scale. A succession of prototypes follows, leading eventually to a salable model.
	6. Commercial introduction or first operational use	The first sale of an operational system may be a deliberate or unconscious premature application of the previous stage and thus be replete with debugging problems.
Production and Marketing	7. Widespread adoption as indicated by substantial profits, common usage, significant impact	This stage is not sharply defined. An individual firm might choose to classify this as recovering its R&D investment through profits on the sale of the innovation or simply the achievement of profitability.
	8. Proliferation	The technical device is applied to other uses (e.g., the adapting of radar to police highway patrol work), or the principle is adapted to different purposes (e.g., radar microwave technology is adapted to cooking ovens).

SOURCE: J. R. Bright, *A Guide to Practical Technological Forecasting* (Prentice-Hall, 1973), pp. 3, 12.

function by people. So it is hardly valid to think of technology itself as being a problem, or the reason for problems occurring. People provide the impetus for technology to evolve. As vividly stated by the cartoon character Pogo, "We have met the enemy, and he is us." And we will almost certainly continue to expand our technology. The available technology has permitted organizations to meet the needs of consumers. Peter Drucker notes that three great industries and their technology—agriculture, steel, and automobiles—have powered the growth of the Western world. Drucker believes that the industries that will serve the future needs of society will be information, oceans, and the megalopolis.[30]

Technological Innovation: The Current Scorecard

Technological innovation involves all those activities translating technical knowledge into a physical reality that can be used on a societal scale. The process of technological innovation progresses from basic research to marketing.[31] Table 3–3 shows the stages in the cycle of innovation. The automobile was a technological innovation that had a long-term effect on the mobility of society and the purchasing patterns of consumers. The telephone, airplane, radio, television, computers, and various medical

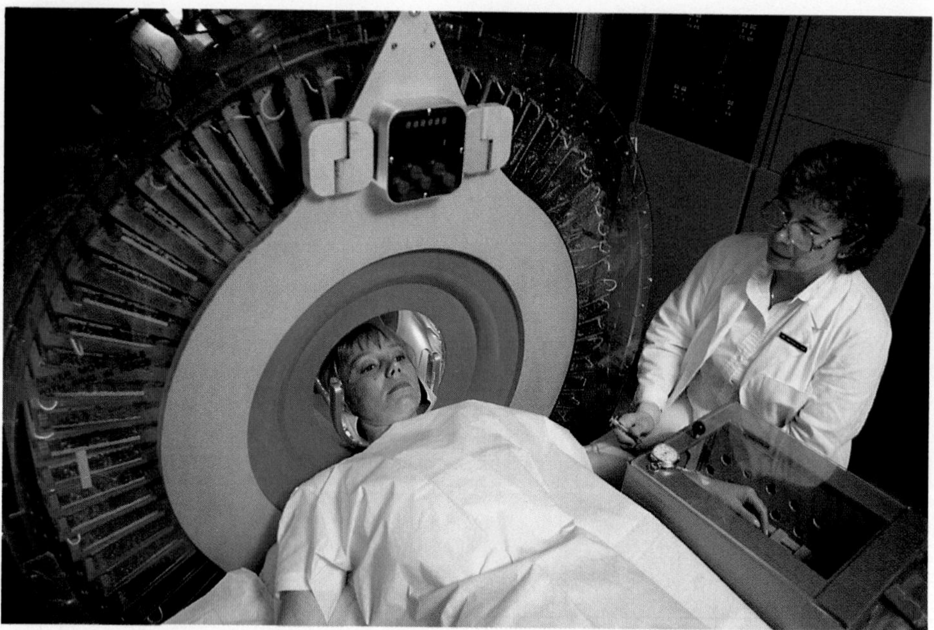

Technological innovations, such as this PETT scanner at NYU, have had a significant influence on society.

technologies have also had a significant influence on society. Recently, there has been a noticeable stagnation in technological innovations.

The lack of technological innovation and the potential impact on the economy have not gone unnoticed by policymakers. President Bush, even in a time of tight federal budgets, has supported outlays for research and development projects.

In 1987 American firms spent close to $60 billion on industrial research and development.[32] There is also an increase in group efforts to tackle problems too large for any single company. There is, however, a growing concern over what is being called techno-nationalism.

On October 23, 1986, Fujitsu, Ltd., the large Japanese electronics firm, announced that it would buy Fairchild Semiconductor Corporation, a Silicon Valley firm. This announcement was greeted with some concern in Washington.[33] Fairchild produces high-speed electronic circuits on tiny chips of silicon. Between 30 and 50 percent of Fairchild's products are sold to American defense contractors. Would the proposed sale put critical technology into the hands of the Japanese? Defense products, automobiles, and telecommunications equipment could all be affected by Fujitsu control of the technology. These concerns resulted in pressure on Fujitsu, and they decided to withdraw their offer to purchase.

Technologically it is meaningless to speak of America's discoveries and breakthroughs relative to those of Japan, West Germany, or any friendly nation. Technological development has become a joint product of multinational institutions—universities, research laboratories, corporations, even defense programs—that link skilled people through computers, satellite communications, and jet airplanes.

Technological information is disseminated in blueprints, codes, and institutions that reach Tokyo and West Berlin almost as soon as they reach Cleveland or Boston. Techno-nationalism (attempting to totally control a nation's technology) is almost impossible in today's world. This is a principle that American firms are beginning to realize as they form more technology partnerships with multinational firms. For example, Motorola, the number two United States chipmaker after Texas Instruments, Inc., (with a global market share of over 6 percent), found that it couldn't effectively penetrate the Japanese market. It solved its problem by joining Toshiba in exchanging important technology and getting help in acquiring a foothold in the Japanese market.[34]

It takes time and money to carry out the eight stages of technological innovation and marketing presented in Table 3–3. Before biomedicine, energy, or any innovation reaches the marketing stage, years may have passed. For example, Xerography took about eighteen years to move from the base research stage to the development stage, and another five to produce and market an office copier. The Kodak disc film represents eight years of product development, ultimately involving 15,000 employees. Product advertising alone cost $34 million—a mere pittance compared to the basic and applied research costs.[35] Furthermore, other environmental forces influence the innovation process. For example, the political and ecological environment certainly dampened the future and marketability of the SST, high-speed passenger trains, DDT, and cyclamates.

A new technology that has been worked on for fifteen years is high-definition television (HDTV).[36] This is a technology that promises to bring wide, crisp, cinema-like pictures and compact-disk digital sound to television with a worldwide market of over $40 billion by the year 2010. The initial HDTV sets will cost about $3,000 or more. Today, Zenith is the only United States producer that seems to be investing the time and money to be a world class player in this high promise and costly race.

The importance of the technological environment and technological innovation for marketing managers is aptly captured in the following statement:

> *Businesses that have been slow to react when major innovations have invaded their industry have often relinquished hard-won positions in a very few years, while companies that have successfully exploited the technological and business opportunities such innovations posed have rapidly become industry leaders. Yet even when recognizing the major strategic implications of technology for their companies, general managers have too often evaded the obligation to exercise their managerial skills. They have left the sophistication of technology and the complexity of converting it to business success convince them that technological innovation is a treacherous area that is best left to experts.*[37]

Marketing managers must be able to interpret technological changes and innovations in the environment. They must work closely with technological experts to translate knowledge competence into marketable products and services. They must be aware of the interrelatedness of the technological environment and other environments. The potential problems of technological innovations such as the commercial application of discoveries in superconductivity need to be evaluated and understood. The *Marketing in Action* on superconductivity presents some of the applications and problems in the technological area.

The Political-Legal Environment

The **political-legal environment** consists of the government rules and regulations that apply to organizations. The very words *rules and regulations* often make marketing and other executives uneasy and resentful. No one likes being regulated. The American manager, for years, has been a staunch theoretical supporter of a "hands-off" government policy—that is, not interfering in any way with business activity. Yet

MARKETING IN ACTION

Superconductivity: A Challenge for Marketing

An important series of technological discoveries in New York, Chicago, Houston, and Los Angeles has put superconductivity on the map. More than forty scientific meetings have been held and some 3,000 technical articles have been published. Researchers at more than thirty U.S. companies as well as at several dozen universities and national laboratories are working practically around the clock. Superconductivity enables some materials to carry electricity at low temperatures with virtually no loss of current, an achievement comparable to a person's shouting in Boston and being heard in London. However, to date most superconductors cannot carry enough current to make them useful in many applications. That is the cautious side of the superconductivity story.

The upbeat side of superconductivity is that there is every indication that in a year or two many applications will be available. Squadrons of scientists and engineers are at work to speed the commercial applications of superconductors. Three specific areas of application are the following:

- *Power systems*—if electricity can be transmitted without much loss, the country's electric demands could be met by burning less fuel. Power plants will become more efficient by using generators made with superconductivity electromagnets.
- *Electronics*—nothing since the transistor promises to overhaul computer science as drastically as superconductivity. Electronic systems will pack 100 or more times as much information-crunching power in smaller boxes. With powerful magnets and more sensitive detectors, medical imaging systems will give doctors dramatically sharper pictures.
- *Transportation*—"flying" trains that move at 300 mph because of inexpensive and lightweight superconducting magnets and motors will become commonplace. Also smaller, more efficient superconducting motors could power ships and electric cars.

These examples indicate that many products, from electricity to automobiles to medical services, will be affected by technological advances in superconductivity. The potential economic and market impact of superconductivity is enormous. Some believe that superconductivity will be much bigger than the invention of the transistor. Eventually, marketing experts will be faced with making decisions about how to profitably market products that use superconductors.

SOURCES: Emily T. Smith, Neil Gross, Evert Clark, and Jo Ellen Daws, "Superconductors: The All-Out Pursuit of Zero Resistance," *Business Week*, March 14, 1988, pp. 56–59; Anthony Ramirez, "Superconductors Get Into Business," *Fortune*, June 22, 1987; Emily T. Smith, Michael Oneal, and Randy Welch, "Putting Superconductors To Work-Superfast," *Business Week*, May 18, 1987, pp. 124–126; and John W. Wilson and Otis Port, "Our Life Has Changed," *Business Week*, April 6, 1987, pp. 94–100.

---

most managers know that the business system cannot work without some government rules and regulations to organize and monitor the marketplace.

The government has been an active regulator in the past decade. Some of the headline stories clearly display this increased government role:

- After several highly publicized commuter airline crashes, 177 pilots from 16 different airlines were withdrawn from service after the Department of Transportation determined that they were not properly certified.
- The Consumer Product Safety Commission banned the use of a flame-retardant called Tris-BP used in children's sleepwear. Sears had to remove thousands of garments with Tris-BP from its shelves.

Table 3–4 Airlines Before and After Deregulation

	1978	1983	1986
Number of airlines	36	98	74
Passengers (millions)	275	318	419
Total miles (billions)	2.5	2.8	3.7
Revenues (billions)	$22.9	$38.4	$41.5
Net income (billions)	$1.2	($0.2)	($0.1)
Employment (thousands)	333,000	328,000	362,000
Average annual pay and benefits per employee	$28,058	$42,000	$40,956

SOURCE: Civil Aeronautic Board, Air Transport Association, Airline Economics, Inc., 1987.

- In 1977 the Food and Drug Administration (FDA) proposed to ban the use of Saccharin, a noncaloric artificial sweetener, from any product. Tab, Diet Dr. Pepper, and Diet Pepsi all suffered lost sales. Soft-drink manufacturers and consumers complained so strongly that Congress delayed the ruling for years. In 1985, Congress, for the fourth time, extended the moratorium. NutraSweet, a highly concentrated sweetener 200 times sweeter than sugar, was approved by the FDA in 1981.
- The Federal Trade Commission continues to investigate the damaging effects of cigarettes. Laws regulating cigarette advertising were passed as a result of these investigations.
- The National Academy of Sciences found that chlorofluorocarbons, the propellents for aerosol sprays, posed a threat to consumers and to the earth's protective ozone layer. Companies like S. C. Johnson & Co. and DuPont switched to hydrocarbon propellents and took the banned sprays out of the market.
- The government has not only been an active regulator of the marketplace and business activities, it has also deregulated the airline, trucking, and railroad industries. There were many prohibitions against free pricing and the entry of competitors into the newly deregulated industries. While each industry responded somewhat differently, all three groups were faced with an environment that would only allow for the survival of the fittest.

An example of deregulation in the airline industry is presented in Table 3–4. There has been an increase in airline travelers from 25 million passengers in 1978 to 419 million in 1986.[38] There are 600 million passengers expected in 1990.

Government and Business

The number and variety of programs affecting business is huge. They are directed toward goals as disparate as economic growth, job security, and environmental pollution control. These programs can be divided into those that are designed specifically to support business and those intended to control various business activities.

Government Support. The business support programs can be divided into classifications such as subsidies, promotion, contracts, and research. Subsidy once meant directing the flow of resources to preferred users and was provided to stimulate agriculture and commerce. Today a *subsidy* involves the flow of money to politically determined programs. The government provides subsidies in the form of guaranteed and insured loans, funds to keep the maritime industry afloat and the airlines in the air, and money for the construction of highways to move people and products. The loans in 1971 to Lockheed, in 1979 to Chrysler, and in 1984 to Continental Illinois, were three of the most publicized subsidies to business. The government's $4.5 billion loan to Continental Illinois National Bank was the largest ever to a private firm.

The government is actively involved in *promoting* business through such devices as protecting home industries from foreign competition. The promotion effort has involved placing tariffs on imports and also providing support through the Small Business Administration for the small business owner.

A third type of support takes the form of government *contracts* for construction, production service, or analysis. This type of contract support is directed toward the stimulation of business. Today it takes over 60,000 full-time government employees to administer the billions of dollars spent annually on government contracts.

The federal government supports nearly one-fourth of all industrial scientists and engineers. In addition, it provides over half of all money spent annually for research and development. Much of the research output is of potential use by the business system. The future development and overall health of the nation's security and economy depend on adequate government support for *research.*

Government Control. There are four distinct areas of government control: investigation, antitrust, price control, and direct regulation. By means of hearings, reports, and news conferences, the government attempts to apply pressure to the behavior and attitudes of managers. For example, by *investigating* and *publicizing* the findings about Tris-BP, aerosol sprays, and cigarettes, the government has influenced public opinion about an industry or a company.

Unlike investigation control procedures, the second type of government control is based on law. The philosophy behind the antitrust laws is the belief in free and open competition. They are designed to protect the small business from the large business in the marketplace. Bigness, if it reduces competition, is considered undesirable. Justice Department threats to break up General Foods, IBM, General Motors, and Xerox reflect this government antitrust opinion. During its eight years, the Reagan administration showed less concern about bigness. The impact of various antitrust laws on business is more thoroughly discussed in Chapter 8, *Marketing and Public Policy.*[39]

Government played a role in breaking up the largest company in the United States, AT&T. The firm was broken up so that no one company would control the $75 billion-a-year telecommunications industry. The early results of the breakup indicate that customer complaints about poor service are likely to remain high, while the new competition has lowered prices for equipment and services.[40] Whether customer service will ever reach the level achieved before the breakup is now only speculation. However, some experts predict that customers will have to live with service inconveniences when the telephone stops working. The old AT&T was an excellent provider of services, and the new, leaner organization that replaced it may never be able to perform as well.[41]

In efforts to stop or slow down inflation, the government has options for controlling prices. The mildest form of this control is to ask business and labor to exercise

Figure 3–3 Government Interaction with Business

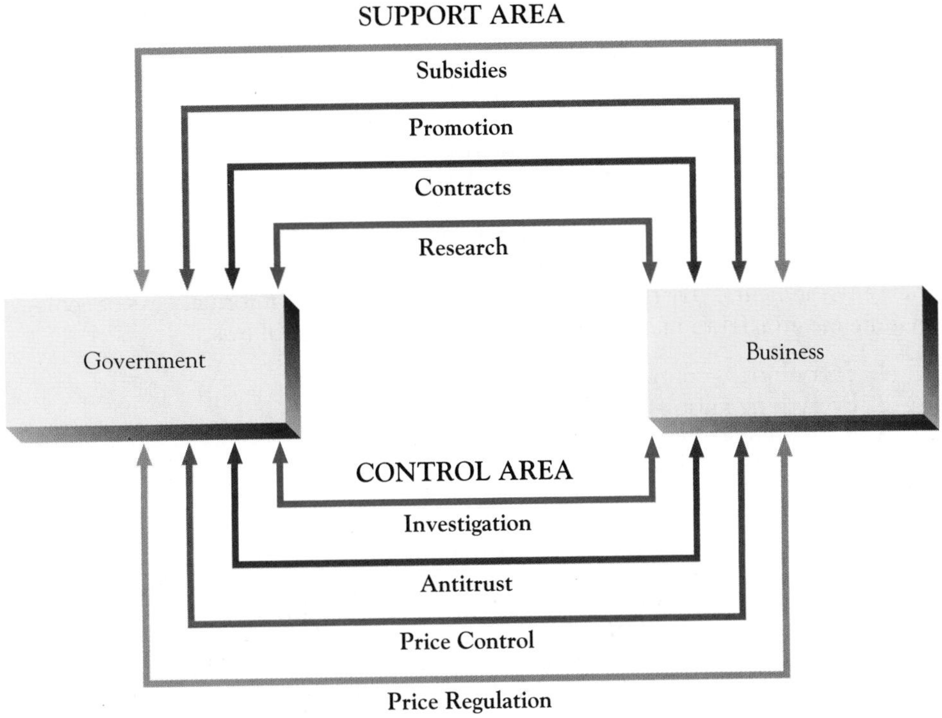

SOURCE: Based on G. Starling, *The Changing Environment of Business* (Kent, 1984), p. 197.

restraint in increasing wages and prices. The government can also set voluntary standards or guidelines for wage and price control. Finally, government can either limit increases in wages and prices or absolutely freeze them for a specified period of time.[42]

The fourth type of control, regulation, refers to the prescription of standards of business conduct, operation, or service. Regulations are designed to (1) protect the interests of consumers and employees from business exploitation, (2) protect health, morals, and safety, (3) protect the interests of inventors and competitors, or (4) control the entry into certain markets like transportation or broadcasting.

As changes in the technological, social-cultural, and economic environment occur, they set off reactions. These reactions have brought us to our present state of government involvement through supports and controls in business and society. Once an opinion gains political support, it can become law or public policy. The public has demanded that the government, to some extent, be involved in business activities. The government has complied with this opinion and has established the support-control framework presented in Figure 3-3.

The government is an active political force in the environment, affecting product, price, place, and promotion decisions. It offers support and control. Through its antitrust legislation, consumer protection legislation, and agencies it has a significant impact on marketing. This will be made even clearer in Chapter 8.

Review Your Marketing Knowledge

- What role does a marketing leader play with regard to environmental change?
- How does government control the marketing programs of business firms?

The Ecological Environment

The **ecological environment** consists of our natural surroundings. *Ecology* is the branch of natural science devoted to the study of the relationship between living things and their environment.[43] Barry Commoner has established four informal laws of ecology that are meaningful to marketing managers.[44] They are as follows:

1. Everything is connected to everything else.
2. Everything must go somewhere.
3. Nature knows best.
4. There is no such thing as a free lunch. Anything of importance has a cost.

These laws, when translated into marketing language, suggest that every company has pollution problems that must be assessed and controlled. The marketing managers and other executives must minimize the negative impact of business operations on the natural environment (water, air, plants, and wildlife).

Wastes, shortages, and other abuses to the natural environment are generated as a by-product of producing goods and services. Rachel Carson, in her best-selling book *Silent Spring* (1962), first alerted the world to the dangers of widely used chemical pesticides, particularly the organochlorine types of DDT and its related DDE and dieldrin. These agents interfere with life processes. She maintained that their uncontrolled use, without concern for harmful effects, promised future soil, water, and human health problems.

The tragic impact of chemicals on the ecological environment and to human life was brought into focus when a cloud of poisonous methyl isocyanate gas was accidentally released from the Union Carbide Company plant in Bhopal, India. Over 2,000 people were killed and 200,000 were injured. The methyl isocyanate was used to manufacture Sevin, a plant pesticide that was distributed widely throughout India for use on that country's corn, rice, soybean, cotton, and alfalfa crops.[45]

The ecological problems of energy shortages, pollution, and poor planning did not happen overnight. They are the result of years of economic growth, affluent lifestyles, urbanization, and technological development without concern for ecological consequences. We are all responsible, because we consume too much energy and are polluters. The Union Carbide Company discovered the importance of its responsibilities, especially since the Bhopal plant tragedy.[46]

In addition, marketing managers must be aware of regulations and public concern relating to the natural environment. Unfortunately, awareness is not enough. Marketing managers have to think in terms of producing goods and services, packaging goods, and promoting goods that will not permanently damage the natural environment. This type of action-oriented thinking will require much creativity, since the survival of the firm must be matched with the survival of the natural environment. Creativity is already apparent in the form of returnable bottles, recycled paper, and phosphate-free detergents. Because existing utility systems couldn't keep up with the

Table 3–5 Possible Competitive Situations

	Absolute Monopoly	Oligopoly	Monopolistic Competition	Pure Competition
Number of Sellers	One	Few	Many	A very large number
Concentration of Total Sales	100 percent of sales by one seller	High percentage by each seller	Small percentage by each seller	Very small percentage by each seller
Buyers' View of Product Differences	Unique product (no substitutes)	Highly differentiated	Few differences	No difference
Importance of Promotion	Low level of importance	Very important part of marketing mix	Less important	No importance
Importance of Price Competition	Not important	Avoid price competition	Very important	Unimportant
Relations with Distribution Channel	May be able to dictate terms	Considerable influence	Less influence	Very little influence

SOURCE: Based on D. Robin, *Marketing* (Harper & Row, 1978), p. 137.

growth, the Environmental Marketing Group of Boca Raton, Florida, took a creative approach to the state's tremendous growth by developing turnkey water and waste treatment plants for private housing developments. Sales have increased 669 percent in just four years.[47]

The Competitive Environment

Competition—domestically and internationally—is another important part of the external environment. Three factors of the **competitive environment** are the nature of competition, the entry and exit of competitors, and major strategy changes by competitors.

The Nature of Competition

There are four widely described competitive environments—the absolute monopoly, oligopoly, monopolistic competition, and pure competition. Table 3–5 presents some of the main features of each of these environments. At one extreme is the *absolute monopoly* (public utilities, telephone companies, and cable TV firms), with only one seller. In this market, there is little concern about promotion or price competition. Having control over a needed and unique product, this seller has considerable influence over other members of the distribution channel.

At the other extreme is the *purely competitive* environment (General Foods, Kelloggs, Post, General Mills), with a large number of sellers. Price competition is not possible, because all sellers have the same product and must keep their prices at the level of the others. If one seller raises prices, buyers will purchase from another seller who has not. If this seller reduced prices below the level of competition, it would be swamped with orders that produced little or no profit. The seller in the purely competitive environment is not able to influence the distribution channel members, because each seller sells only a small percentage of the total.

The two mid-range environments, *oligopoly* and *monopolistic competition*, are the most common forms in the United States. In the oligopolistic environment, a few large sellers account for a high percentage of the market. Promotion is a very important part of the marketing mix. Buyers typically view the products of oligopolists as having important differences. General Motors, Ford, and Chrysler are oligopolists. Their products have important differences to consumers. The airline, oil, computer, and chemical processing industries are controlled largely by oligopolists.

In the monopolistically competitive environment, there are many sellers who account for smaller percentages of total sales. The differences that exist in product are not that crucial to consumers. The monopolistically competitive firm (for example, Ethan Allen furniture) tends not to concentrate on sales promotion, but is very aware and concerned about sales competition.

Marketing managers must carefully examine the nature of domestic and foreign competition. Specifically, they need to determine what kind of market exists. For example, the domestic automotive industry must consider not only the few competitors in the United States, but also foreign competitors who are very active in the small-car market (Toyota, Nissan, Honda).

Entry and Exit of Competing Firms

One of the first factors a marketing manager examines in the competitive environment is how the competition has changed. That is, what new competitors are entering our business and which ones are leaving? If competitors leave, the probability of accomplishing corporate objectives increases.[48] When RCA and GE left the computer business, IBM's and Control Data's chances of success increased. However, when GAF left the amateur photography business, Kodak wasn't completely happy. This left an industry consisting only of Kodak, Berkey Photo, 3M, and Japanese firms making film and print paper. The move by GAF left Kodak in a vulnerable position, inviting closer government scrutiny on charges of having a monopoly.

When new competitors enter, the opposite effect occurs, since the new competitor makes it tougher to accomplish objectives. The National Football League (NFL) wasn't excited when the United States Football League (USFL) was formed. Watch companies like Bulova and Timex weren't pleased when Texas Instruments entered their business. Other significant entries were Citicorp challenging American Express in the traveler's-check business, and Procter & Gamble and Johnson & Johnson competing with Tampax in the tampon business.

Whether a firm enters a market depends on the ease of entry. Firms are reluctant to enter a market if there is a scarcity of raw materials or if the structural barriers are high. There are several entry barriers, including the following:

- *Product Differentiation.* There is strong customer loyalty to existing brands. The costs of getting customers to switch from Coca-Cola, Pepsi, IBM computers, Sears' children's clothes, and Crest toothpaste are high.
- *Economies of Scale.* The proportional unit costs of production, distribution, selling, advertising, R&D, and financing decline as more units are sold. If economies of scale exist (IBM has it in the computer business), then a firm that wishes to enter must do so at a unit-cost disadvantage or must enter the industry at the scale of the existing competitors.
- *Absolute Cost Advantages.* There are cost advantages deriving from patents, control of proprietary technology, and control of superior raw material resources.

- *Access to Marketing Channels.* If the present firms own or have strong influence over the major channels (Ford and General Motors), it can be very costly to enter a business.
- *Reaction of Current Firms.* If current firms will "live and let live," a proposed entry may be possible. If they "fight every inch of the way," it may be too costly.

Major Strategic Changes by Competitors

Marketing managers want to know what major competitors are doing. GE became quite concerned when Westinghouse introduced an unconditional guarantee that its electric light bulb would last either 2500 hours or for two years of normal use. And Xerox had to pay attention to the aggressive competition of IBM, Savin, Kodak, and SCM in the copier business. McDonald's watches Burger King and Wendy's to see what they are up to. Instead of only talking and being concerned with competitiveness across companies, there is now a growing interest in what is called a *nation's competitiveness.* The *Marketing in Action* on competitiveness captures some thoughts and views of business leaders on competitiveness in the United States.

The amount of concern varies with the economic structure of the industry. The industry can be a monopoly (as nickel used to be), oligopoly (like autos and oil), monopolistic competition (like furniture), or pure competition (like corn production). Large firms, like those in *Fortune*'s 500, might gain some advantage by closely examining the industry's structure and the strategic moves of competitors.

To be successful, a company must pay attention to its competition and look for their mistakes, weaknesses, and problems. Then it must launch programs and make decisions that hit those weak points, such as flawed product design, limited channels of distribution, and overpriced products. In 1980 and 1981, Apple attacked the home computer field, which was a weak point in the IBM line. The 1987 sales of Apple were over $2.6 billion (in 1977 sales were $2.7 million). Steven Jobs, Apple's former chairman, saw and seized the opportunity to market a computer that could help people keep track of their personal finances in their homes.[49] In 1987, Apple had about 12 percent of the $21 billion personal computer market, compared to IBM's 30 percent.

Companies have always kept a close watch on what competitors were doing. Some of the main collectors of competitive information and intelligence are Ford Motor Co., Rockwell International, Celanese, Union Carbide, Gillette, Revlon, Kraft, J.C. Penney, Digital Equipment Corporation, and Wang Laboratories. These firms are known to have batteries of competitor analysts.[50] How much of what these analysts learn is worth their salaries?

In some organizations, gathering information on competitors is starting to sound like CIA data gathering. An insider at one major equipment company stated that his company sends scouts to count smokestacks, delivery trucks, and employee's cars at rival factories. This intelligence data is used to determine production and staffing levels.[51] Data is also gathered from competitors' in-house telephone directories. The directory is used to reconstruct the organization chart.

Following are a few other examples of companies' gathering information about competitors:

Kraft, Inc. Analyzes point-of-purchase scanner data, which provides not only price information but also product features and promotional programs.

MARKETING IN ACTION

The Nation's Competitiveness Needs to Be Considered

What is the problem with the product performance of the United States world markets? A competitive nation raises its standard of living through trading with other nations and makes provisions to continue to do so. The key measure here is standard of living or income, not trade, and the competitiveness of a country is an important environmental concern that most of us are not familiar with. A few leaders have articulately expressed the importance of understanding and respecting national competitiveness. Here are a few insightful comments:

• Global competitiveness problems are serious. . . . U.S. industry must intensify efforts to be cost effective and focus on customers and markets. It must achieve, maintain, or surpass state-of-the-art technology. And it must keep the pressure on because foreign competitors are taking similar steps. (Richard E. Heckert, Chairman, E.I. du Pont de Nemours & Co., Inc.)

• Many of this generation of American business executives view the U.S. market as being so vast that it obviates the need to enter international markets. These companies design for domestic users and ignore overseas opportunities. U.S. businesspeople need to wake up. We live in a world economy and we must compete internationally. (Stephen A. Barre, President, Servco Corporation of America)

• Market differentiation can make up for a multitude of sins. There are no substitutes for a low-cost position and top technology. Up-to-date manufacturing and technology are critical, but niche market positioning, attention to the details of customers' needs, and playing from one's strengths can improve the competitiveness of any business. (Robert L. Yohe, President, Chemicals Group, Olin Corporation)

The competitiveness issue, as indicated by recent events such as lost international markets, trade deficits, and declining industries, is now a serious concern. Ignoring the decline of competitiveness in the United States will not make the problem go away. This point is vividly made by 4,000 *Harvard Business Review* readers who participated in a survey that indicated that 92 percent of them believe that U.S. competitiveness is deteriorating.

Despite the public doom and gloom about the competitiveness of U.S. industry, there are signs of hope. Many U.S. industries have become the world's low-cost producers. Japan's tremendous price advantage all but disappeared in the late 1980s. There are many large and small market-driven manufacturers who are already serving notice to the world that they intend to be and remain competitive in the marketplace.

SOURCES: Sylvia Nasar, "America's Competitive Revival," *Fortune*, January 4, 1988, pp. 44–52; Bruce R. Scott, "Competitiveness: 23 Leaders Speak Out," *Harvard Business Review*, July-August, 1987, pp. 106–123; "Competitiveness Survey: HBR Readers Respond," *Harvard Business Review*, September-October 1987, pp. 8–12.

Motorola, Inc.	Uses a computerized data base to monitor almost everything published by or about its competitors. With this data, Motorola's sales personnel can make point-by-point comparisons and upgrade their bids to customers.
AT&T	Has an 800-person worldwide network of employees who monitor competitors' sales teams, trade publications, and research papers for the latest developments. These bits of information are fed into a data base that is distilled into an electronic competitive digest. The digest is sent to 50 key managers around the globe.

Putting It All Together

Can you now picture yourself as a marketing manager who has to take the pulse of environmental forces? This is really a challenging, time-consuming, frustrating, but very necessary job. As discussed, scanning the environment is needed both to trace the opportunities and threats to the firm's marketing programs and to keep market surprises to a minimum. Some firms use formal methods to analyze the environment. Such techniques as economic forecasting, multivariate interaction analysis, mapping, and management information systems (MIS) are used to make forecasts. Unfortunately, these techniques are not yet used by most firms.

Perhaps, instead of recommending that all firms use sophisticated forecasting or MIS techniques to do a complete environmental analysis and diagnosis, we can suggest that marketers take more interest in "verbal and written information." Some firms may not have the resources or talent to employ sophisticated techniques.

Verbal and written information is simply what we learn by hearing or reading. These sources include the following:

- Radio and television
- Employees of the firm—peers, colleagues, and superiors
- Others outside the business—customers, persons in the marketing channels of distribution (wholesalers, retailers), competitors and their employees, financial executives, consultants, and government and university employees
- Newspapers, trade journals, industry newsletters, annual reports and 10Ks (The 10K is a very detailed annual report that all firms listed on the Stock Exchange must submit to the Securities and Exchange Commission.)

If marketing managers systematically examine these verbal and written sources of environmental information, they will be better prepared to cope with environmental changes. Armed with information about the environmental forces presented in Figure 3–1 on page 65, they can make better price, product, place, and promotion decisions. In short, if marketing managers are to make successful decisions, they must invest time and effort to understand environmental forces. The history of business failures—from the Edsel to the DeLorean —provides testimony that environmental forces can't be ignored.

Personal Computer Exercise

The use of economic and socio-cultural databases to acquire a profile of the environment can be very useful to a marketing manager. The PC Exercise allows you to examine a database of consumer information so that today's customer and potential customers are evaluated in terms of the firm's products/services. What type of demographic information would a food products firm such as Kellogg's use to make predictions of sales for the year 2010?

KEY POINTS

• Change in an organization's environment is inevitable. Surprises and sudden shifts in events will affect product, promotion, price, and place decisions.

• Environmental analysis is the process of monitoring external environmental forces. Environmental diagnosis is the assessment of data (opportunities and threats) in the environmental analysis.

• Environmental analysis provides an early warning system for the firm and is designed to pick out marketing opportunities. An opportunity is a "challenge to specific marketing action that is characterized by a generally favorable set of environmental circumstances and an acceptable probability of success."

• The social-cultural environment consists of people, institutions, and their values, and the norms of behavior that are learned and shared.

• Competition—both from domestic and international firms—is another environmental consideration. Marketers need to determine the nature of competition—whether monopoly, oligopoly, monopolistic competition, or pure competition. They need to monitor the entry, exit, and major strategic changes of competing firms.

• The economic environment is a major force in marketing. Three persistent and important economic factors in marketing are inflation, sluggish or flat productivity, and energy shortages.

• Technology is a nation's accumulated competence to provide goods and services for people. A major technological force that has affected the way we work, shop, and spend our leisure time is the automobile.

• The political-legal environment consists of the government rules and regulations that apply to organizations.

• The ecological environment includes our natural environment and the way we affect it.

• Some firms' responses to the environment are reactive or passive: they merely react to innovations in the market. On the other hand, some firms are active or aggressive in pursuing marketing opportunities: they make things happen.

ISSUES FOR DISCUSSION

1. What kind of skills does an environmental monitor (person) need to do an excellent job?
2. What changes in automobile safety have occurred since Ralph Nader published his book, *Unsafe at Any Speed?*
3. Explain why the marketing manager needs to understand how sluggish productivity affects the sales of goods and services.
4. Why did the government deregulate the airlines industry? What would be some of the problems of again regulating airlines?
5. Is technological innovation to improve quality of life still possible in the United States?
6. What are the sources of technological changes?
7. When analyzing the competitive environment, why is it necessary to use economic analysis?
8. What role did environmental forces play in convincing the Big Three U.S. automakers that quality is important to customers?
9. How have economies of scale influenced the price of television sets and small personal computers?
10. Suppose that the electric car is mass-produced and consumed in the 1990s. How would this change the economy, culture, and mobility patterns in society?

GLOSSARY

Disposable personal income (DPI): a consumer's total income minus taxes paid to all levels of government.

Ecological environment: the natural surroundings in which we live. Ecology is the study of the relationship between living things and their environment.

Environmental analysis: the process of monitoring external environmental forces.

Environmental diagnosis: the process of making marketing decisions by assessing the significance of the data of the environmental analysis.

External environment: all forces and events *outside* an organization that can influence it. Everything "outside" the organization is considered a part of the external environment.)

Marketing environment: all factors that may affect an organization directly or indirectly.

Marketing opportunity: a "challenge to specific marketing action that is characterized by a generally favorable set of environmental circumstances and an acceptable probability of success."

Monopolistic competition: many sellers account for smaller percentages of total sales.

Oligopolistic environment: a few large sellers account for a large percentage of the market.

Political-legal environment: the government rules and regulations that apply to an organization.

Productivity: an estimate of output per labor hour worked.

Social-cultural environment: institutions, people and their values, and the norms of behavior that are learned and shared.

Technology: a nation's accumulated competence to provide goods and services for people.

NOTES

1. Jeremy Main, "Detroit's Cars Really Are Getting Better," *Fortune,* February 2, 1987, pp. 90–98.

2. Peter Drucker, *The Age of Discontinuity* (Harper & Row, 1969).

3. Alvin Toffler, *Future Shock* (Bantam, 1970).

4. S.C. Jain, *Marketing Planning and Strategy* (South-Western, 1981), p. 69.

5. William F. Glueck, *Business Policy and Strategic Management* (McGraw-Hill, 1980), p. 88.

6. Glueck, *Business Policy,* p. 88.

7. Grover Starling, *The Changing Environment of Business* (Kent, 1988), pp. 7–9.

8. Starling, *The Changing Environment of Business,* p. 9.

9. "Trouble at Procter & Gamble," *Fortune,* March 5, 1984, p. 70.

10. J. D. Glover, "Rise and Fall of Corporations: Challenge and Response" (Harvard Business School Paper, Number 9–367–017, 1967), p. 4.

11. Glover, "Rise and Fall of Corporations, p. 4.

12. Martin L. Bell, *Marketing Concepts and Strategy* (Houghton Mifflin, 1972), p. 18.

13. Carolyn Y. Woo, "Market Share Leadership—Not Always So Good," *Harvard Business Review,* January-February 1984, pp. 50–54.

14. Francine Schwadel, "Hershey Cuts Its Reliance on Chocolate," *The Wall Street Journal* (July 11, 1984), p. 27.

15. Robert F. Hartley, *Marketing Mistakes* (Grid, 1976), pp. 45–58.

16. Jeremy Main, "Wanted: Leaders Who Can Make A Difference," *Fortune,* September 28, 1987, pp. 92–102.

17. Danny Miller and Peter H. Friesen, "Archetypes of Strategy Formulation," *Management Science,* May 1978, pp. 21–33.

18. Donald F. Harvey, *Business Policy and Strategic Management* (Charles E. Merrill, 1982), p. 80

19. Peter Drucker, *Management: Tasks, Responsibilities, Practices* (Harper & Row, 1974).

20. Irving D. Canton, "Learning to Love the Service Economy," *Harvard Business Review,* May-June 1984, pp. 89–97.

21. "Baby Boomers Push For Power," *Business Week,* July 2, 1984, pp. 52–62.

22. John Naisbitt, *Megatrends* (Warner, 1982), p. 74.

23. Starling, *Changing Environment of Business,* p. 64.

24. Based on U.S. Department of Commerce reports, estimates, and evaluations.

25. Michael Brody, "The 1990s," *Fortune,* February 2, 1987, pp. 22–24.

26. Norman Jones, "No Pain, No Gain: How America Can Grow Again," *Business Week,* April 20, 1987, pp. 68–69.

27. Todd May, Jr., "Surprising Help From the Crash," *Fortune,* January 18, 1988, pp. 68–76.

28. Philip Kotler and Sidney J. Levy, "Demarketing, Yes, Demarketing," *Harvard Business Review,* November-December 1971, pp. 74–80; and David W. Cravens, "Marketing Management In An Era of Shortages," *Business Horizons,* February 1974, pp. 79–85.

29. Joe Cappo, "Will Marketing Run Out of Energy?" *Chicago Daily News,* November 27, 1973, p. 34.

30. Drucker, *The Age of Discontinuity,* p. 12.

31. Ian M. Ross, "R & D: How To Stay Ahead in Technology," *Across the Board,* May 1987, pp. 8–15.

32. Otis Port and John W. Wilson, "America's R & D Performance: A Mixed Review," *Business Week,* April 20, 1987, pp. 59–60.

33. Robert B. Reich, "The Rise of Techno-Nationalism," *The Atlantic Monthly,* May 1987, pp. 63–69.

34. Robert Neff, John W. Wilson, and Michael Berger, "Making Deals That Won't Give Technology Away," *Business Week,* April 20, 1987, pp. 62–63.

35. Vincent P. Barabba, "How Kodak's Market Intelligence System Cuts Risk, Speeds Decisions," *Management Review,* August, 1984, pp. 8–13.

36. "Supertelevision," *Business Week,* January 30, 1989, pp. 56–63.

37. George R. Whie and Margaret B. W. Graham, "How To Spot a Technological Winner," *Harvard Business Review,* March-April 1978, pp. 146–52.

38. Margaret E. Kriz, "Winging It," *National Journal,* June 20, 1987, pp. 1584–1587.

39. Fred Luthans, Richard M. Hodgetts, and Kenneth R. Thompson, *Social Issues in Business* (Macmillan, 1987), pp. 232–234.

40. Gwen Kinkead, "Can AT&T Compete in Long Distance," *Fortune,* April 16, 1984, pp. 112–16.

41. Brian O'Reilley, "AT&T: What Was It We Were Trying To Fix?" *Fortune,* June 11, 1984, pp. 30–36.

42. John D. Aram, *Managing Business and Public Policy* (Marshfield, MA: Pitman Publishing, 1986), p. 8.

43. Frederick D. Sturdivant, *Business and Society,* (Irwin, 1981), p. 119.

44. Barry Commoner, *The Closing Circle* (Knopf, 1971), p. 33.

45. LaRue Tove Hosmer, *The Ethics of Management* (Irwin, 1987), pp. 54–57.

46. Al Ries and Jack Trout, *Bottom-Up Marketing* (McGraw-Hill, 1989), p. 127.

47. Derek F. Abell and John S. Hammond, *Strategic Market Planning* (Prentice-Hall, 1979), p. 53.

48. Al Ries and Jack Trout, *Bottom-Up Marketing.* (McGraw-Hill, 1989), p. 127.

49. "The Largest U.S. Corporations," *Fortune,* April 25, 1988, p. D17.

50. Steven Flax, 'How To Snoop on Your Competitors," *Fortune,* May 14, 1984, pp. 28–33.

51. "Never Mind MIS: Consider MI5," *Business Month,* February 1989, p. 15.

CASE APPLICATION 3–1

The Corporate Raiders Are Now Paying Attention To Walt Disney Company

Recently, Walt Disney Company has become aggressive marketing leaders. They have:

- Syndicated a business show for network affiliates.
- Outfitted Minnie Mouse in Madonna-type gloves and sunglasses.
- Provided a variety of programs to adults over 40 on the pay television Disney channel.
- Given away a gift every 15 seconds at Walt Disney World.
- More than $1 billion worth of projects under construction at Walt Disney World.

After years of simply rolling along, Walt Disney Co. came up with two of the top-grossing movies of 1986, *Down and Out In Beverly Hills* (which grossed an impressive $62 million) and *Ruthless People,* both from its new, adult label, Touchstone Films.

Michael D. Eisner, the Walt Disney Co. chief executive officer, has definitely made an impact on the firm. Under his leadership, company profits have doubled and the price of company stock has tripled. One of Eisner's goals is to broaden the Disney name into all segments of the entertainment industry. He took a step in this direction by selling films from the Disney film and television library to the domestic syndication market.

In the fall of 1985, Disney approached independent and affiliate television stations with Disney-Magic-1, a collection of 25 film titles, including *Dumbo* and *Splash,* as well as episodes from the *Wonderful World of Disney,* which ran on network television from 1954 to 1983.

The Disney Television Channel is one of the fastest growing on cable television. It has overtaken Time Inc. and Viacom, the perceived industry leaders, in setting new cable standards for marketing and pay services. The Disney Channel has 3 million subscribers and threatens to surpass both The Movie Channel and Cinemax.

Eisner, an idea-filled and creative executive, believes that the Disney Channel both sells merchandise based on Disney characters and promotes Disneyland and Walt Disney World. The theme parks stoke up enthusiasm for the movies and the inventiveness that goes into the movies can be diverted to keep the parks fresh. Most observers believe that Eisner has put some of founder Walt Disney's magic back into the company. Eisner, like Walt Disney, is known for being active and seizing opportunities before they pass. Before Eisner arrived, Walt Disney Co. put out three movies a year. Now his proactive, seize-the-opportunity approach is the reason for fifteen Walt Disney Co. movies in 1987 and 1988. *Good Morning, Vietnam* grossed a staggering $11.7 million in a single weekend.

Too Much, Too Fast?

There are some who wonder whether Eisner's aggressive marketing style may be too much, too fast and might tarnish the image of the Mickey Mouse factory. Minnie Mouse in Madonna-like clothing, licensing new apparel products, new Swatch-type Minnie watches, R-rated movies, licensing new characters, and other aggressive marketing moves are being questioned by some critics. Walt Disney took risks, but not at the pace that Eisner and his team are setting. Despite what critics are saying about the pace at Walt Disney Co., the Eisner philosophy remains the same: "As long as you act as if you're coming from behind, you have a shot at staying ahead."

SOURCES: Jay Clarke, "Disney World Grows Like Pinocchio's Nose," *Houston Chronicle,* March 6, 1988, p. 9; John Taylor, *Storming the Magic Kingdom: Wall Street, The Raiders and The Battle for Disney.* (Knopf, 1987); Myron Magnet, "Putting Magic Back In The Magic Kingdom," *Fortune,* January 5, 1987, p. 65; Pamela Ellis-Simons, "Hi Ho, Hi Ho," *Marketing & Media Decisions,* September 1986, pp. 52–64.

Questions

1. Why would critics be questioning the aggressive moves being made by Walt Disney Co.?

2. What environmental consideration do you feel played a major role in Eisner's making the type of marketing decisions he has made?

3. Why would Walt Disney Co. be attractive to other firms who would like to purchase a controlling interest in the firm?

CASE APPLICATION 3–2

Frito-Lay: Attacking the Problem and Reaching the Top Again

Competition, changes in customer preference and tastes, changing demographics, and contribution to the company's profit margin are top priority concerns at Frito-Lay, Inc., the Dallas-based snack food subsidiary of PepsiCo, Inc. The success stories about Frito-Lay have been presented in such major business books as *In Search of Excellence* and *A Passion for Excellence.* Frito-Lay's awesome store/door delivery system included 9,400 route salespersons and was considered a formidable force for competitors such as Nabisco, Eagle Snacks, and Wise Foods/Borden. Year after year, Frito-Lay brought in record sales and earnings, dominating the snack food industry with such brand favorites as FRITOS®, DORITOS®, TOSTITOS®, LAY'S®, and RUFFLES®. However, earnings eventually flattened, new products failed, and the marketing strategy was questioned.

© Frito-Lay, Inc. Printed with permission.

Michael Jordan, installed from PepsiCo as the president and chief executive officer, declared that Frito-Lay had to move away from "junk food" snacks to "healthier" fruit and granola based products. Publicly, Frito-Lay did not talk about what went wrong, but a picture unfolded about incorrect interpretation of the environment resulting in mistakes. Frito-Lay had unleashed new product after new product without sufficient advertising support. Previously, developing, testing, and modifying a product to meet customer preferences and tastes could take as long as ten years. However, new products had begun to appear in just six months. As many as 80 new items or packages were launched without proper preparation, planning, and testing. But Frito-Lay found that simply introducing products with their name and logo was not enough to assure success.

There has always been pressure at Frito-Lay to perform, to be first in the market. Frito-Lay is PepsiCo's largest division, accounting for nearly 40 percent of its earnings in 1986—$343 million of the parent's $902 million. The parent always pointed to Frito-Lay as the king of snack formula, a fact supported by $3.2 billion of Frito-Lay's $4 billion annual sales being mostly snacks. But with the American consumer asking more questions about healthier eating habits, the trend was toward reading labels, reducing salt intake, and generally eating healthier. The annual $20 billion snack-food industry saw a shift in consumer preferences away from "munchies" loaded with salt to healthier sounding alternative items such as granola bars.

The demand for healthier food snacks hit Frito-Lay especially hard in 1986. The company marketed TOPPELS®, a corn cracker with cheese toppings; Stuffers, corn or wheat shells filled with cheese, sour cream, or peanut butter; and Kincaid's, a homestyle, kettle-cooked potato chip. By October 1987, most of these new products had been yanked off supermarket shelves. Jordan didn't want to repeat the 1986 move into the market with salt and fat-based snacks.

The decisions made before the launching of TOPPELS®, Stuffers, and Kincaid's indicate that environmental concerns were not given serious consideration. Frito-Lay's research-and-development arm had wrestled with the problem of how hard the bite should be for the kettle-cooked, Kincaid's potato chip. Finally, a Cape Cod replicate was selected—a favorite of the vice president of marketing and sales. The mistake, however, was marketing the Kincaid's potato chip in pockets of the Midwest and the Southwest where the Cape Cod styled chip is not favored. The issue of how to position these new products against competitive products was given little consideration—only $25 million was allocated to the advertising budget. The products were poorly introduced and, as a result, consumers were confused over exactly what the products were.

The steady stream of new products like TOPPELS®, Stuffers, and Kincaid's put a burden on the elite 9,400 salespersons who stock over 325,000 outlets. Frito-Lay prides itself on the notion that a customer should never bite into a stale chip or snack. The salespersons could not physically handle all the new products in the timely fashion that is a Frito-Lay custom.

Retailers were also left confused by the Frito-Lay onslaught of new products. Where would the products be shelved since only so much space is available? Would the new products take away margins earned from the powerhouse brands like FRITOS®, DORITOS®, and TOSTITOS®? When would the new product explosion stop?

Jordan listened to the signals he received from the environment—retailers, customers, competition—and stopped the frenzied activity in new product launches. Instead, he focused on the leading corn and potato chip brands that constituted 80 percent of Frito-Lay's sales. He also started to mend relations with retailers by instituting a trade promotion program that offered retailers rebates on increased sales volumes. Also, Frito-Lay dropped prices on leading brands by 10 cents or more per box.

Michael Jordan observed and listened to the environmental signals. Instead of letting Frito-Lay wait for consumers to come back, retailers to be satisfied with the firm's products, and competition to become less intense, Jordan took a proactive position. Frito-Lay didn't like what happened to them in their "marketing environment" and didn't want it to happen again.

SOURCE: Adapted from Rebecca Fannin, "Frito-Lay: The Binge Is Over", *Marketing & Media Decisions,* April 1987, pp. 54 and 60; and PepsiCo., Inc. Annual Report, 1986; personal communication with Frito-Lay, May 1989.

Questions

1. Would a company like Frito-Lay have to be concerned with damaging their product quality image by placing so many new products that were discontinued in the market? Explain.

2. Why is there a growing demand for healthier food products?

3. Why would a firm such as Frito-Lay want to satisfy such groups as retailers and their own salesforce?

4. What would a main competitor such as Eagle Foods (a part of the Anheuser-Busch Company) have to do to be effective against Frito-Lay brands?

PART
TWO

The Marketplace

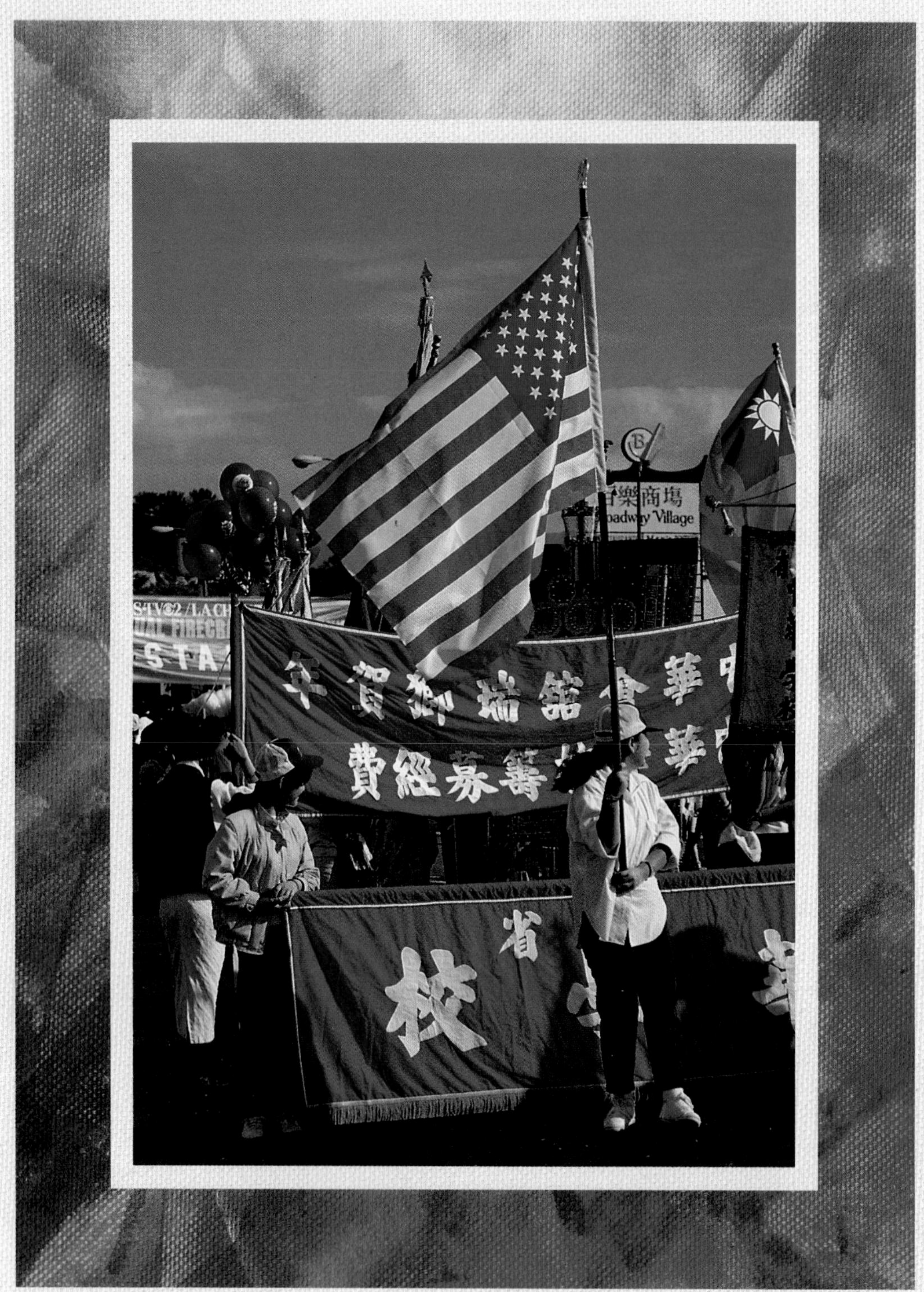

華會館瑞獅賀年
籌募經費
省
校
oadway Village

4

Market Analysis: Segmentation and Targeting

Learning Objectives

Upon completing this chapter, you will be able to do the following:

DEFINE
the terms *market* and *target market.*

DESCRIBE
the concept of market segmentation and the different ways to segment a market.

UNDERSTAND
the importance of income and other demographic variables to marketers.

IDENTIFY
the major categories of nondemographic segmentation variables.

DISCUSS
demographic changes and their importance to marketers.

EXPLAIN
what modifications need to be made in the marketing mix variables as a result of the changing demographic makeup of the United States.

MARKETING PROFILE

Campbell Soup Leads a Revolution

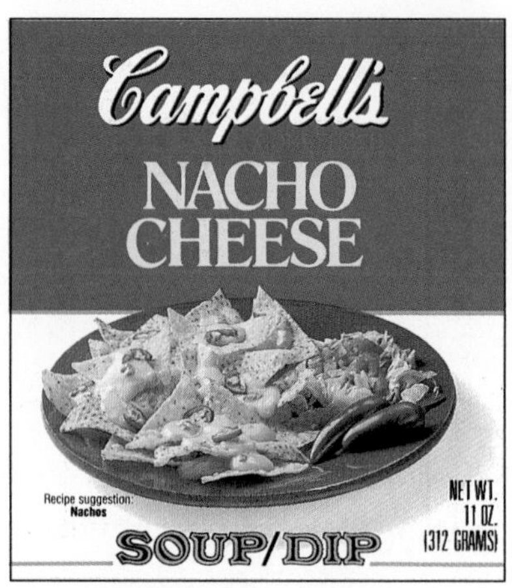

There is probably no more durable symbol of American mass marketing than the Campbell Soup can. The familiar red-and-white label is a machine-age icon of standardization, volume production, and national brand identity. For most of this century, it has stood for a line of products made the same way and sold the same way all across the country.

But what's this? In Texas and California, where they like their food with a little bit of a kick, Campbell Soup Co. now makes its nacho cheese soup spicier than in other parts of the country. The recipe calls for more jalapeña peppers—lots more. According to David Hackney, Campbell's manager of public relations, "We are convinced regional marketing is where the future lies."

Campbell's regional marketing program divides the country into 22 regions. The company promoted 88 employees, mainly from sales, to "Brand Sales Managers." They have had to retrain a sales force accustomed to one homogeneous national plan. Instead of one set of products and promotions, Campbell's is tailoring its products and marketing plans to each of the regions, taking into account the tastes of consumers, competition, and the retail grocery trade in the region.

Until January 1988, Campbell's program was "more public relations than substantial," according to Hackney. Recently, however, the company has been expanding the regional program, including "hitting harder on regional promotions." The company recently expanded its Mexican soup line in Southern California to appeal to the large Hispanic population there. They are conducting local radio promotions in a number of markets, such as one in New York highlighting the Giants football team for Swanson frozen dinners. In Nevada, Campbell's local marketers are giving samples of its soup of the day to skiers visiting ski resorts. These promotions are developed and implemented by the Brand Sales Managers, with each having control over the regional promotional budget.

Other companies are following Campbell's lead. American Airlines has been the first in its industry to develop distinctly separate campaigns in various areas of the country, typically pushing prices and destinations. Ads in California show beaches, sand, and seagulls stressing the number of nonstop flights to these destinations. On the East Coast, the spots stress north-to-south routes and frequency of flights. Meanwhile the national campaign promotes American's on-time performance. In other industries, Chrysler has developed a car just for the California market (better suspension and a high performance radio); Domino's Pizza offers different toppings in different regions (pineapples in Hawaii and anchovies in Texas); Lipton Tea sells its instant tea presweetened in New England and unsweetened in the Midwest.

There are risks, of course. Regionalization can drive up both manufacturing and marketing costs by reducing economies of scale. "Why did companies go to national marketing?" asks Alvin A. Achenbaum, chairman of Canter, Achenbaum Associates, a marketing consulting firm. "Because it's less expensive." And a barrage of conflicting local approaches may dilute a brand's overall image, the equity carefully built up by years of expensive national advertising.

For several reasons, however, the trend seems inexorable. The U.S. market for many products is slowly breaking up along regional and demographic lines—an ethnic market here, a suburban market there, a yuppie market here, an elderly market there. A recent study of 80 large consumer product companies found that 85 percent see definite competitive advantages in a regionalized approach to marketing such as that used by Campbell's. Tailored trade promotions are often the first step, with promotions targeted to regional chain stores. It is not surprising that many regional strategies start here, given that most companies already have regional sales forces. This is often followed by regional consumer promotions such as the Campbell's examples.

SOURCE: Christine Dugas, et. al., "Marketing's New Look," *Business Week* (January 26, 1987) pp. 64–69; Jennifer Lawrence, "American Air Books New Regionalized Ad Strategy," *Advertising Age*, September 12, 1988; Alix M. Freedman, "National Firms Find that Selling to Local Tastes Is Costly, Complex," *The Wall Street Journal*, February 9, 1987, p. 21; Scott Hume, "Execs Favor Regional Approach," *Advertising Age*, November 2, 1987, p. 36; and Judann Dagnoli, "General Foods Rethinks Regional Efforts," *Advertising Age*, November 21, 1988, pp. 1, 62.

The markets discussed in the Campbell's *Marketing Profile* can be described in many ways. One way is *size*, as in the $2.4 billion soup market. Another is the *people* who buy the product—such as the 22 million people living alone who make up much of the potential market for single serving food products. A market can be described by the *characteristics of the buyers*—"one quarter of the households with two unrelated adults of the opposite sex have children under the age of 15." Or it can be described by the differences in the *consumer behavior* of the buyers—in concern for sodium content among older consumers vs. younger ones, for example.

A market can also be distinguished by the *division among competitors* (our share of the market is 15 percent) or by the *products* comprising it (dry soups are 10 percent of the market, brand name condensed soups are 75 percent of the market, and private label store brand soups are 5 percent of the market). Finally, markets can be understood by looking at the *characteristics desired by consumers* ("we have the bulk of the traditional market, and they have most of the price-conscious market").

You can see how important it is for a marketer to be able to describe the market accurately. In this chapter, we will discuss how to analyze and segment markets; the importance of analyzing trends in demographics, and their impact on markets; how consumer expenditures are related to income and other demographic variables such as age, sex, occupation, and geography; and the importance of changes in attitudes and values in the analysis of markets.

What Is a Market?

Figure 4–1 shows the steps taken to define a market. Starting with the total population, the marketer must determine:

1. if there is a need for a product or service;
2. if those with a need are interested or potentially interested in buying the product or service;
3. if these consumers have enough money; and
4. if those with enough money are willing to spend it on the product or service.

Only those meeting all four criteria are included in the definition of the market for the product or service being studied. Consequently, in this book, a **market** is defined

Figure 4–1 Steps in Defining a Market

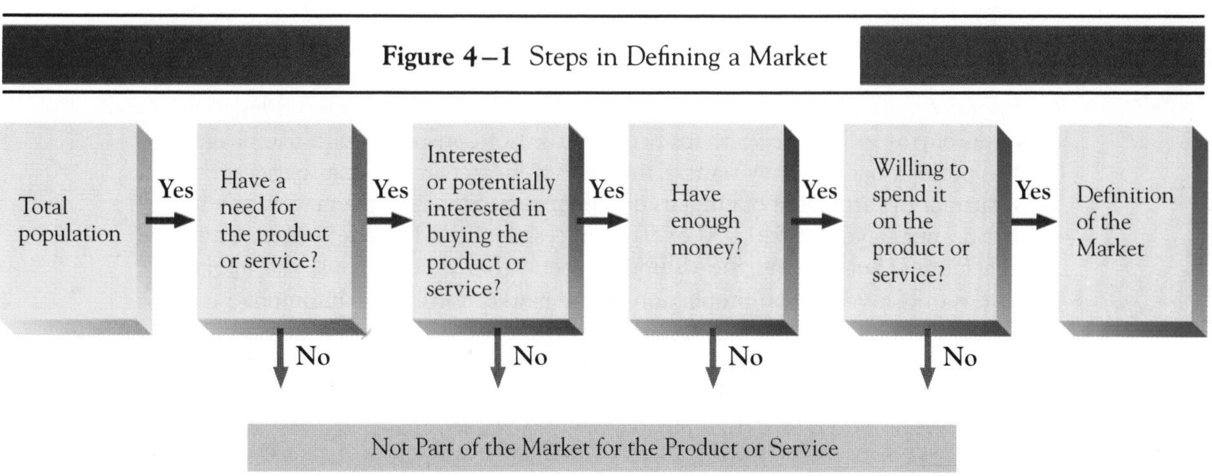

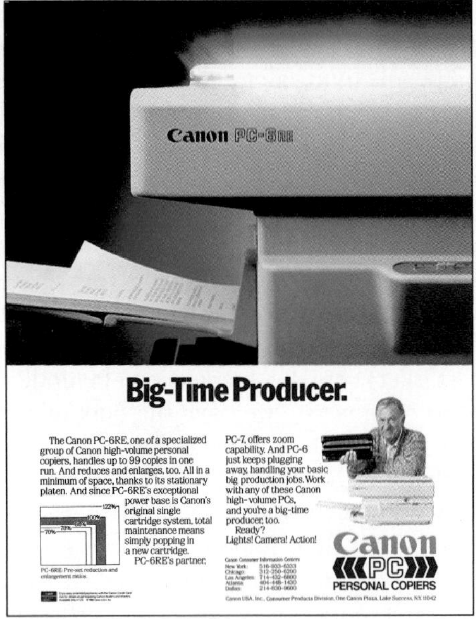

Canon copiers are sold in both the consumer and organizational markets.

as people or businesses with the potential interest, purchasing power, and willingness to spend the money to buy a product or service that satisfies a need.

Let's look at several examples to see how the definition can be applied. First, let's take a look at the maternity clothing market. To be part of the market, a person would have to have a need for the product and be interested or potentially interested in buying it. This would eliminate all women who were not pregnant and those who were pregnant but had no interest in buying maternity clothes (perhaps because they already have access to a complete maternity wardrobe). In addition, those with no money to spend on maternity clothes or who were unwilling to spend their money for this purpose would be eliminated. This process might result in a market of about 3 million women out of the approximately 95 million women sixteen years old and over.

Now let's examine another market to demonstrate the importance of specifically defining the market being analyzed. The definition of the market for Porsche is different from the one for luxury cars. Many individuals may have a need for a luxury car but may not feel any need to have a Porsche. They may have no interest whatsoever in buying a Porsche, perhaps because it is not consistent with the image they want to project, because they want to buy an American car, or because they are afraid it will attract the attention of burglars or kidnappers. Some people may want a luxury car but do not have the $40,000 or more necessary for a Porsche; others may have enough money, but may not be willing to spend that much. Thus, the market for Porsche is only a very small proportion of the market for luxury automobiles.

The definition of a market uses the words *people or businesses* to enable us to distinguish between consumer markets and industrial markets. A *consumer market* consists of buyers (or potential buyers) who intend to use or benefit from the product or service themselves rather than buying for the purpose of reselling the product. An *industrial market* consists of businesses, individuals, or organizations that purchase products or services for use in the production of other products or services, for use in their day-to-day operations, or for resale. In many instances, the same product is sold to both consumer and industrial markets. To be successful, though, a marketer must use different strategies to reach and meet the needs of different markets. For example, copying machines are now sold in both the consumer and the industrial markets, but the needs, wants, attitudes, and behaviors of the buyers are different. The consumer market wants low price, compactness, ease of use, and reliability; the industrial market is primarily interested in low cost per copy, quality of the copies, features such as reduction and collating capabilities, and reliability.

The quantity purchased, amount of personal selling needed, packaging, nature of pricing, and other marketing factors such as speed of delivery and credit are all very different for the industrial market and the consumer market. Each market must be analyzed separately, and different marketing strategies are required for each. The rest of this chapter examines consumer markets, while Chapter 6 looks closely at industrial markets.

Market Segmentation

Walk into any retail store, and you will undoubtedly be struck by the diversity of available products. For example, you will find soft-drink brands with and without sugar; with and without caffeine; in different flavors; in returnable bottles, cans, and nonreturnable bottles; in six packs and in individual containers; and in containers in a variety of different sizes. Some brands will be oriented toward dieters, some toward young people, and some toward cost-conscious consumers. This is the concept of **market segmentation,** the process of dividing large heterogeneous markets into smaller, homogeneous subsets of people or businesses with similar needs and/or responsiveness to marketing mix offerings.

Marketers have always had the option of treating a market as a single entity or as a group of separate submarkets or segments. Some marketers chose the former route, seeking to develop a product that appeals to the mass market. With this strategy, called **market aggregation** or **undifferentiated marketing,** a single product is handled using a single marketing mix strategy directed toward all consumers in a market.[1] It is sometimes called the total market approach. The strategy relies upon mass production, mass distribution, and mass communication to maximize economies of scale.

Most marketers today recognize that their markets are too varied to rely upon this kind of strategy. Instead of tying to satisfy the varied needs of the entire market, a marketer, using market segmentation, will divide the market into appropriate subsets, and then will identify one or more subsets on which to concentrate. This **target market** is a homogeneous segment of the market to which a marketer directs a specific marketing program. For example, the results of a recent study of the U.S. automobile market,[2] shown in Table 4–1, show that the markets for different types of cars vary substantially by age, sex, income, and education. Luxury cars tend to appeal to very high income, older males, whereas subcompacts are bought by younger, lower income males and females. Buyers of mini-vans are relatively high income, well-educated, middle-aged consumers. These types of cars are used for different purposes by different types of people. Of the marketing mix variables, only the distribution strategy is the same for the different cars; otherwise, the products, prices, and promotion strategies are very different for each target market.

Table 4–1 Who Buys New Cars? (Demographic Characteristics of New Car Buyers by Car Segment)

Percent of Market	all new-car buyers (100)	sub compact (24)	small specialty (12)	compact (13)	high-roof station wagon (2)	mid-size (2)	domestic mid-size specialty (5)	domestic standard (8)	import sport specialty (2)	luxury (4)	mini-van (5)
Men	57%	50%	53%	55%	56%	56%	60%	70%	70%	70%	68%
Women	43%	50%	47%	45%	44%	44%	40%	30%	30%	30%	32%
Median age	40	34	31	40	38	46	44	60	37	55	40
Median household income	$35,600	$27,600	$35,100	$35,300	35,700	$36,000	$35,600	$45,200	$65,200	$65,900	$45,400
College graduates	38%	37%	38%	41%	52%	39%	22%	29%	56%	47%	47%

SOURCE: Jim Schwartz and Jim Stone, "New Car Buyers," *American Demographics*, April 1987, pp. 33–36.

Benefits of Market Segmentation

Marketers engage in market segmentation in order to recognize the diversity that exists within markets.[3] Consumers are not alike, and the differences can have a major impact on market demand. The segmentation concept is also helpful in identifying unfulfilled consumer needs which translate into market opportunities. New products can then be developed to meet these unfulfilled needs, enabling the firm to grow and increase its profits. Specifically, market segmentation offers the following benefits:

1. It allows a more precise definition of the market in terms of consumer needs.
2. It strengthens marketers' abilities to meet changing market demands.
3. It allows a more efficient allocation of marketing resources. For example, product and advertising appeals can be coordinated better, enabling target consumers to recognize and distinguish products and promotion appeals directed at them.
4. It enables a marketing manager to better assess the strengths and weaknesses of the organization and competing firms. Segments where competition is thoroughly entrenched can be identified. This will save resources by avoiding a head-to-head battle with a competitor for a segment where there is little hope of market share gain.
5. It makes it possible to set marketing objectives more precisely. Targets can be defined operationally, and performance can be evaluated later against these standards.

Criteria for Effective Segmentation

For market segments to be useful, (1) the segment should be of sufficient size and potential to justify the expenditure of marketing dollars, (2) it must be possible to reach the segment, and (3) the segment should show clear variation in responsiveness to marketing programs in comparison with other segments.[4]

Size. A segment must be large enough to be profitable, although it is possible to treat each customer as an independent segment and still be profitable. This is commonly done with such large purchases as custom-designed houses, jumbo jet-airplanes and large computer systems. Typically, however, a marketer must determine if there are enough potential customers to justify treating the segment as a target market. For example, very short and very tall people might desire automobiles designed specifically for their needs, but the projected sales revenue would not justify the expenditures that would be necessary for a company to produce and market a product for those segments of the market.

Reachability. Often, large enough segments exist, but they cannot be reached feasibly through promotional or distribution efforts. For example, it is possible that people living in rural areas have different clothing needs from those living in urban or suburban areas. A clothing manufacturer might decide that it would not be profitable to sell to this segment, given the difficulty in reaching them through existing advertising media and channels of distribution.

Responsiveness to Marketing. Unless a segment responds differently from other segments to changes in marketing programs, there is no need to treat it separately. If all consumers had the same degree of price consciousness about a product, for example, there would be no need for premium-priced and low-priced alternative products. Marketers are most effective in selling to a segment when it differs from other segments on several marketing mix dimensions.

Segmentation in Consumer Markets

Managers are constantly seeking to find the best ways to segment their markets. In the following section of this chapter, we will describe the numerous alternatives for segmentation available to marketers, depending upon such factors as the personal characteristics, income level, and the consumer behavior of the potential buyers. Chapter 6 will discuss the possibilities for segmentation in *organizational* markets.

Geographic Segmentation

Geographic segmentation is an important basis of segmentation for most marketers. The total market can be divided into many different locations—regions, states, counties, cities, or even neighborhoods—depending upon the specific marketer's needs, objectives, and resources. For example, a snowmobile manufacturer might sell its products primarily in the Snowbelt, while a water-ski manufacturer might sell the bulk of its output in the Sunbelt. The population and growth rate vary in different locations, resulting in higher or lower market potentials for products. The Marketing Profile at the beginning of this chapter illustrates how one company, Campbell's Soup, uses geographical segmentation in the marketing of its products.

Although the population of the United States grew from the 226 million people counted in the 1980 Census to 246 million on January 1, 1989 (a 9 percent increase, or about 1 percent per year), all parts of the country did not grow equally. Table 4–2 presents information on the ten largest and ten fastest growing states. As shown in Figure 4–2, there are large population gains projected for the South and West between 1990 and the year 2000, while the Midwest and Northeast will experience modest gains or even losses in some states. Over half the population gain from 1990 to 2000 will come from three states—California, Florida, and Texas.

Tracking population shifts has traditionally been done using the U.S. Census Bureau *Standard Metropolitan Statistical Area* (SMSA), a geographically integrated,

Table 4–2 The Ten Largest and the Ten Fastest-Growing States

Ten Largest States, 1988

Texas moved ahead of Pennsylvania as the nation's third largest state, and Florida jumped from ninth place in 1970 to fourth in 1988. North Carolina moved into the top ten, displacing Massachusetts.

1988 Rank	State	1988 Population (in millions)	1970 Rank
1	California	28.3	1
2	New York	17.9	2
3	Texas	16.8	4
4	Florida	12.3	9
5	Pennsylvania	12.0	3
6	Illinois	11.6	5
7	Ohio	10.9	6
8	Michigan	9.2	7
9	New Jersey	7.7	8
10	North Carolina	6.5	12

Ten Biggest Gainers, 1980–1988

California, Texas, and Florida were the period's most powerful population magnets, together gaining nearly 9 million people—half of the nation's population growth for the period. However, impressive gains by small states mean the population is more dispersed than a decade ago.

State	Population Gain 1980–88 (in thousands)	State	Population Gain 1980–88 (in thousands)
1. California	4,646	6. Virginia	668
2. Texas	2,612	7. North Carolina	607
3. Florida	2,588	8. Washington	516
4. Georgia	879	9. Colorado	411
5. Arizona	771	10. Maryland	405

SOURCE: U.S. Department of Commerce News, December 30, 1988.

economic and social unit having a large population nucleus. In 1983, the Census Bureau changed the way it defined *metropolitan areas,* dropping the word *standard* and adding two new categories. A *Metropolitan Statistical Area* (MSA) is a free-standing metropolitan area surrounded by nonmetropolitan counties, with a large central city of 50,000 or more; or a Bureau of Census urbanized area of at least 50,000 and a total MSA population of 100,000. Each MSA has one or more central counties, containing the area's major population concentration, and may also include outlying counties which have close economic and social relationships with the central counties. The top fifty MSAs represented 109 million people, or 45 percent of the population, in 1988.

Areas with over one million population and two or more closely related metropolitan areas are designated *Consolidated Metropolitan Statistical Areas* (CMSAs). The

Figure 4–2 Projected Population Change in the United States 1990–2000

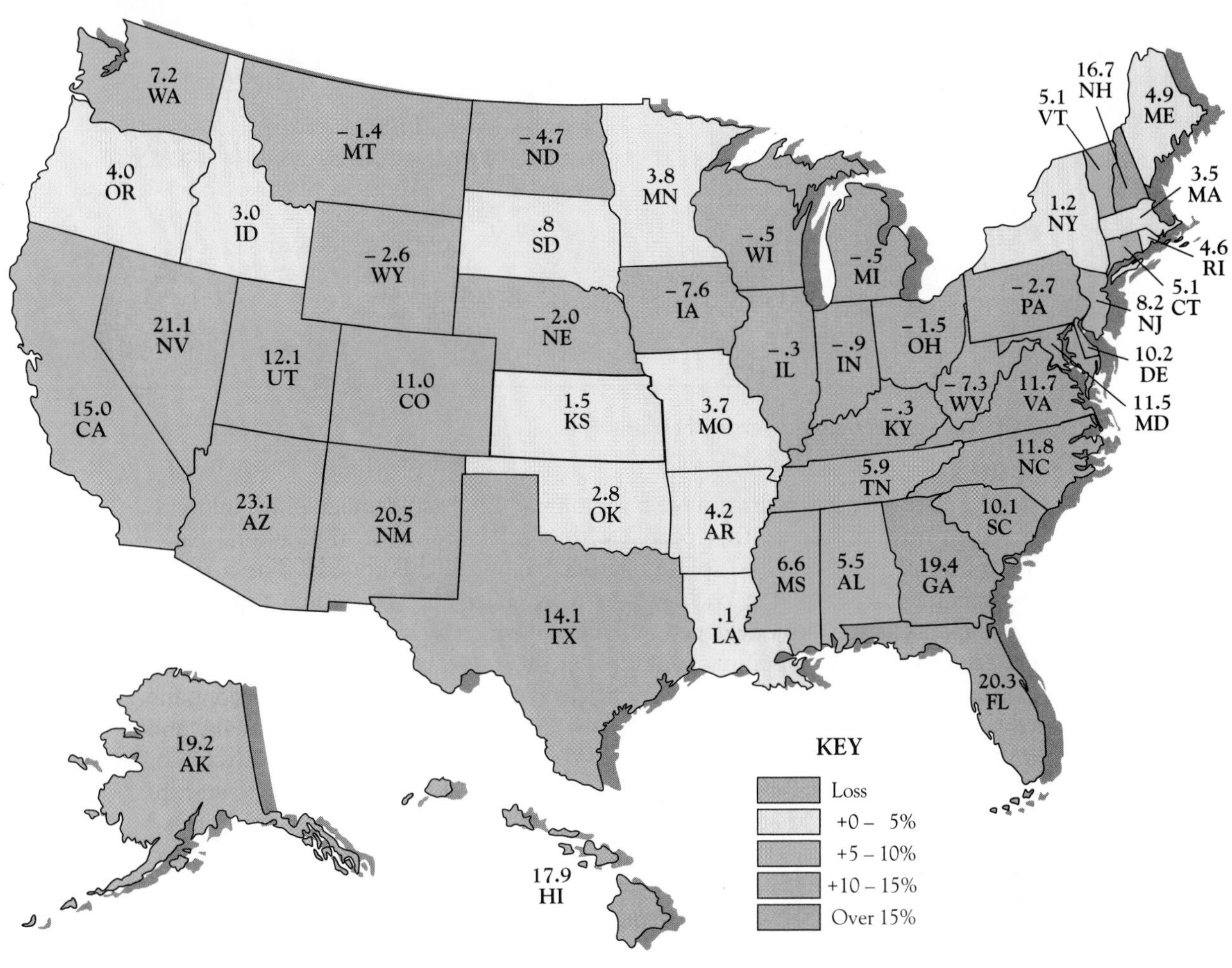

SOURCE: U.S. Census Bureau, *Commerce News*, April 1, 1988.

component metropolitan areas making up a CMSA are called *Primary Metropolitan Statistical Areas* (PMSAs), which are closely related metropolitan areas. Thus the Philadelphia-Wilmington-Trenton CMSA consists of the Philadelphia, Pennsylvania, Wilmington, Delaware, and Trenton, New Jersey PMSAs. Whereas the previous system lumped statistics from all metro areas together, whether the area had three million people or 70,000, the new system allows separate analysis of the individual metro areas.

One-third of the households in the United States (33 percent) live inside central cities, almost one quarter (23 percent) live in nonmetropolitan areas, and the largest number, 44 percent, live in the suburbs.[5] During the past few years, two-thirds of the population growth has been in the suburbs, with the remainder in nonmetropolitan areas. There are substantial differences in the distribution of the population by income, with 60 percent of the households earning $50,000 or more living in the suburbs vs. only 30 percent of the households earning $10,000 or less.[6]

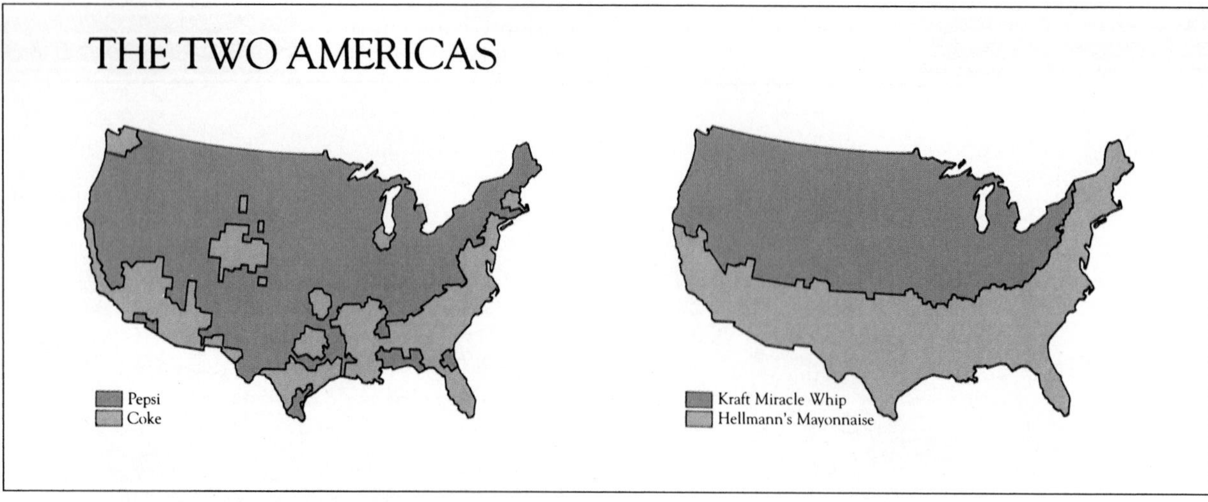

Marketers use geographic segmentation to target their products.

A number of research firms have begun marketing "geo-demographic" information, based on the premise that people with similar economic and cultural backgrounds and perspectives tend to cluster together in neighborhoods. The research firms combine data from the U.S. Census with geographical mapping techniques. For example, Claritas has developed a model called Prizm which has classified geographical areas into 40 different categories. Prizm calls Chappaqua, New York, and Winnetka, Illinois, *Blueblood Estates,* defined as "America's wealthiest socioeconomic neighborhoods, populated by super-upper established managers, professionals, and heirs to old money, accustomed to privilege." Weatherford, Texas, and Waverly, Ohio, are called *Shotguns and Pickups,* defined as "hundreds of small, outlying townships and crossroads villages that serve the nation's breadbasket and other rural areas." Banks, retailers, and marketers of many consumer products and services have used geo-demographics to define the characteristics of their customers.[7]

Other examples of the use of geographic segmentation include the following:[8]

- A savings and loan company determines its penetration of accounts and number of services used per account for each zip code in its markets.
- A leading insurance company measures actual sales vs. market potential by county and by zip code to determine exactly where new agents are needed the most.
- A major bank plots Census Data to determine the best locations for its automated teller machines.
- A major retailer analyzes sales and Census Data to select new outlets.
- A leading public utility compares energy usage by geographic area to help chart energy conservation campaigns and forecast future energy needs.

Because population shifts occur continuously, with about 20 percent of the population moving each year, it is important that marketers identify and follow mobile people, who usually have money to spend and need to make purchases of goods and services in their new locations. The astute marketing manager follows this migration so that he or she can alert the new people in the area to the firm's goods and services. This strategy is particularly important for retailers.

Demographic Segmentation

As mentioned earlier in this chapter, the starting point in defining a market is people. The study of people in the aggregate is called **demography.** A demographer is concerned about the size, birthrate, age, geographic migration patterns, and education levels of the population. Because the United States is now going through an era of significant demographic transition in many areas, demographic statistics can help marketing managers plan strategies for coping, including the identification and understanding of market segments.

Dividing the market into segments based on demographic variables—age, sex, family size, income, occupation, education, family life-cycle, religion, race, nationality, and social class—is called *demographic segmentation.* This is the most popular way marketers identify important market segments and target markets, primarily because consumer wants and needs are often closely associated with demographic variables which are relatively easy to measure. For example, sex is an important segmentation variable for cosmetics, age for "Top-40" records, and income for luxury automobiles.

Many changes are taking place in the demographic makeup of the United States, and it is important for marketers to monitor these changes over time. In this section, we discuss the major trends in American demographics—changes in age, family status, and sex roles—and their importance to marketers.

Aging of the American Population. The total population of the United States in the 1990s is projected to increase slowly, at a rate of less than 1 percent per year. Population growth depends on the rate of births, deaths, and migration. Death rates are very predictable. Net migration to the United States has averaged about 500,000 persons per year.[9] Thus, the most important factor in predicting increases in population is the birthrate. Changes in the birthrate and the fertility rate—the number of children born to the average woman in her lifetime—have had a dramatic impact on the population in the past twenty years and will continue to have a major impact into the twenty-first century.

Between 1947 and 1961, the fertility rate was 3.8, and almost 60 million Americans were born. This group (age 29 to 43 in 1990) now accounts for about 40 percent of the adult population. The 1970s brought on a baby bust, with the fertility rate down to 1.76 by 1975, dropping the number of births from 4 million per year to just over 3 million. The fertility rate has recently climbed back up to about 1.9, and because of the large number of women of childbearing age (those born during the post-World War II baby boom), the number of births was almost 3.9 million per year in the late 1980s.

The impact of these changes in fertility and birthrates is that the growth in the population has not been and will not be even across all age groups. Figure 4–3 shows the changes in population projected for the 1987–1993 time period, by age group segment. The largest percentage increases will come in the 35–44 and 45–54 age categories. The parents of these groups, especially those age 75 and up, and the children of these groups, age 5–14, make up the remainder of the growth categories. The number of people age 15–24 or 55–64 will actually decline during the 1987–1993 period.

The average age of the population was twenty-eight in 1970, increased to thirty in 1980, and is projected to increase to thirty-three in 1990. By the year 2000, the median age should reach thirty-seven. Some examples of the impact of the aging of the population on corporate changes in marketing strategy include the following:[10]

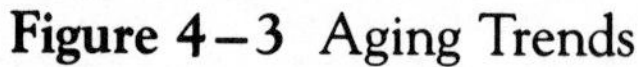

Figure 4–3 Aging Trends

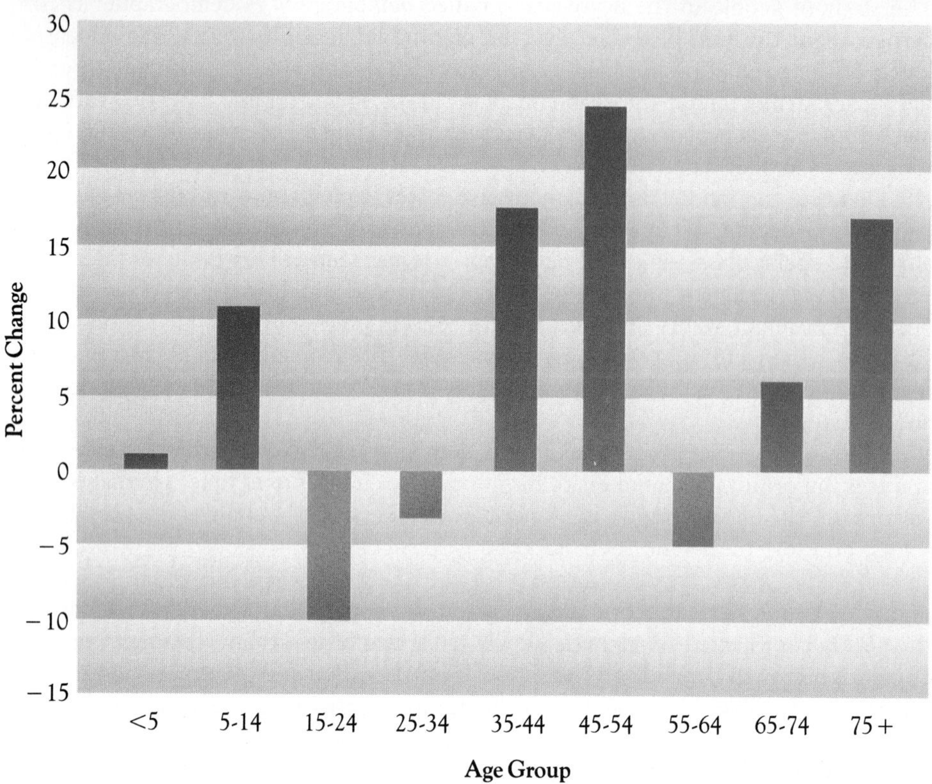

SOURCE: *American Demographics* magazine, cited in: "Changes in Age Groups; Changes in Markets," *The Wall Street Journal*, January 18, 1988, p. 21.

- Sears, Roebuck and Company formed *Mature Outlook*, a club offering discounts for people aged 55 and over.
- Blue Bell, Inc., emphasizes jeans that are "cut for the more mature figure."
- Selchow & Righter Co. developed a version of *Scrabble* with letters 50 percent larger than in the standard version of the game.
- Johnson & Johnson introduced Affinity, a new shampoo, especially formulated for people over age 40. The advertising says the product is for "brittle, hollowed-out" hair.
- Sharp Electronics is developing a VCR targeted at mature consumers that speaks the directions for ease of programming.
- AT&T offers older consumers emergency dialing attachments and amplifiers for the headset.
- Kellogg's has repositioned its 66 year old Bran Flakes as 40+ Bran Flakes.

Changing Status of Families and Households. The traditional definition of a typical American household was one that contained a husband, a nonworking wife, and two or more children. That type of household accounts for only about 9 percent of households today. Although the population grew by only 19 percent from 1970 to

Table 4–3 Growth in Households and Families 1970–1987

Household Type	Percent of Total: 1970	Percent of Total: 1987	Percent Increase: 1970–1987
Families	81	72	25
Married couples	70	57	15
Husband, no wife present	2	3	104
Wife, no husband present	9	12	90
Nonfamily Households	19	28	109
One person	17	24	95
Two or more persons*	2	4	252
Total	100	100	42
Total Number of Households (in millions)	63.4	89.5	—

*A significant portion of this group consists of unmarried couples who live together.
SOURCE: U.S. Census Bureau. Current Population Reports. Series P–20. No. 417.

1988, the number of households grew by 42 percent, to just over 90 million. As shown in Table 4–3, the number of families headed by married couples increased only by 15 percent; the majority of the growth in families came from those headed by a single parent. Nonfamily households (those without children) grew by 109 percent from 1970 to 1987, with households of one person and two or more people growing dramatically.

Married couples now make up only 55 percent of the households, and it is projected that this number will continue to decrease in the 1990s. Less that half (48 percent) of all married couples have children under age 18. There are now 21 million single-person households, 26 percent of the total. For many companies, such as General Electric and AT&T, the number of separate households is a much better predictor of their sales than raw population totals. This is certainly true for companies in the housing and appliance industries, because a household is likely to buy only one dwelling unit, washing machine, and dishwasher, no matter how many people live there.

The rapid changes in households are partly attributable to a significant increase in the number of divorces, but to a much greater extent, the changes come from the increasing tendency of young, single people to live apart from their parents, and for the elderly to live apart from their grown children. The average person living alone spends almost as much on restaurant meals as a married couple and just a bit less than a family of three. Campbell Soup has developed its Soup-for-1 product line and Stouffer's has introduced single-serving casseroles designed for the Single-Separated-Widowed-Divorced (SSWD) segment. Fifty percent of Ford's sales of specialty cars and Mustangs have been to singles, compared to 8 percent of Ford LTDs.

A number of trends have combined to create these changes in households. First, although the number of marriages is at an all-time high, only 10 of every 1000 people in the United States get married each year—over half (58 percent) of the women and three-quarters of the men between twenty and twenty-four are still single. A second trend is the higher divorce rate. The Census Bureau now predicts that about half of the first marriages of people between twenty-five and thirty-five years old may eventually end in divorce.[11] Finally, there is a widening gap between the life expectancy of males and females. Widows now make up one-third of one-person households. Life expectancy has been rising for both males and females, but women now outlive men by eight years, compared to only two years in 1900.

The impact of all these changes has been a declining average size of household. The average household size in 1960 was 3.33; it declined to 3.14 in 1970, and to a new low of 2.64 in 1988. Smaller households often have more income per person than larger households, and require smaller houses, smaller cars, and smaller package sizes for food products.

Changing Sex Roles. There are substantial demographic changes taking place in society that have resulted in a blurring of traditional sex roles. For example, women used to do most of the family's food shopping, and men typically purchased and arranged for the servicing of the family's automobile. These and other similar role stereotypes have begun to disappear. A major factor contributing to this change is the phenomenal increase in the percentage of women, especially married women and mothers, who are employed. Over half (52 percent) of all mothers with infants were working or looking for work in 1987, dispelling the myth that women wait until their children enter primary school before entering (or reentering) the work force. In 1982, only 43 percent of mothers with children aged one or younger were in the labor force. In 1977, only 32 percent were working.[12] Currently, 60 percent of mothers with children 2–5 and 72 percent of mothers with children 6–13 are working.

From 1948 to 1985, women's share of the labor force grew from 29 percent to 45 percent. Women are increasingly holding jobs that used to be held only by men such as lawyers (20 percent now vs. 5 percent in 1970), doctors (18 percent vs. 10 percent in 1970), computer scientists (28 percent vs. 14 percent in 1970), and college and university teachers (37 percent vs. 29 percent in 1970). Women started only 10 percent of the new businesses begun in 1960. By 1985, this figure had grown to one in three, and it is projected that by 1995 half of all new businesses will be started by women.[13] The Bureau of Labor Statistics projects that between 1986 and the year 2000, women will account for two-thirds of the growth in the labor force.[14]

The more education a woman has, the higher the probability she is working, and the increase in women's education is a major reason for the growth in the number of working women. In 1970, women were only 10 percent of the graduating class of the U.S. business schools, compared to 40 percent today. The same type of increase has been occurring in other professional schools as well.

Working women have become an increasingly important market segment during the last half of the 1980s. Producers of many products and services such as fast-food and take-out restaurants, labor saving appliances such as microwave ovens and food processors, convenience products, and services of all types have benefited substantially and should continue to do so in the coming years. Working women have numerous attributes important to marketers, including the following:[15]

- Their marketing behavior differs substantially from their nonworking counterparts. Time, their most important commodity, is a major factor. They shop at fewer supermarkets and make fewer trips to shopping malls.
- They are more cosmopolitan in their taste, more knowledgeable, and more demanding as customers, being less concerned with small differences in purchases than with service, convenience, and time.
- They and their families are better targets for goods and services because they have more money to spend. In addition to providing extras for their families, their jobs require separate goods and services for their own uses.

- They can justify expenditures for—and psychologically accept—expensive appliances and household goods such as microwave ovens and convenience foods, which help reduce the traditional wives' roles in important household tasks. Appliances that used to have an image of being for females, such as vacuum cleaners, have begun to take on a unisex image.
- They are more education-oriented and interested in travel, leisure, and self-improvement.
- They dislike the way they are depicted in advertisements, which often misrepresent both their desires and actual roles.
- They are typically unable to shop during regular retailing hours; therefore some shopping may be done by surrogates—daughters and sons. Shopping also is becoming more of a shared husband-and-wife activity, or even a family venture. Weekends and evenings are important shopping times. In addition, working women are heavy users of catalog shopping.

Family Life-Cycle. The demographic factors of sex, age, and family status often are not sufficient to explain variations in consumer buying behavior. Frequently, differences in consumption patterns among people of the same age and sex result from being in different stages of the family life cycle. **Family life-cycle** (FLC) is a segmentation variable consisting of a combination of age, marital status, and the presence or absence of children. The stages are as follows:[16]

1. Bachelor stage: young single people not living at home
2. Newly married couples: young, no children
3. Full nest I: young married couples with youngest child under six
4. Full nest II: younger married couples with youngest child age six or over
5. Full nest III: older married couples with dependent children
6. Empty nest I: older married couples with no children living at home, household head in labor force
7. Empty nest II: older married couples, no children living at home, head of household retired
8. Solitary survivor in labor force
9. Solitary survivor retired

The family life-cycle is a valuable variable to use for segmenting markets. Families' needs, income, resources, and expenditures are different at different life-cycle stages. See Table 4–4.

The life-cycle concept, as it has traditionally been used, ignores the substantial increase in terminated marriages and in married couples without children. To compensate for these deficiencies, a modernized family life-cycle has been developed;[17] it is presented in Figure 4–4.

The FLC can be an important segmentation aid to marketers. For example, the young divorced stage might be a promising segment for small appliances rather than large ones because the individual may be living in an apartment and may view this stage as temporary. Health spas, tennis clubs, and self-enhancement services would seem to be in demand by the more affluent of this group. Life insurance marketers may find the divorced woman interested in buying insurance for herself and, possibly, for her children. In the middle-age categories of the revised family life-cycle, those who remain without children may represent an excellent market for luxury goods such as expensive restaurants, extended vacation packages, and high-priced furniture. Middle-aged divorced parents, though, appear more interested in low-priced, functional products such as used cars, fast-food restaurants, and inexpensive furniture.[18]

Table 4–4 Characteristics of Family Life-Cycle Stages

Single Stage	Newly Married Couples	Full Nest I	Full Nest II
Few financial burdens Fashion opinion leaders Recreation oriented Buy: Basic kitchen equipment, basic furniture, cars, equipment for the mating game, vacations	Better off financially than they will be in the near future Highest purchase rate and highest average purchase of durables Buy: Cars, refrigerators, stoves, sensible and durable furniture, vacations	Home purchasing at peak Liquid assets low Dissatisfied with financial position and amount of money saved Interested in new products Like advertised products Buy: Washers, dryers, TV, baby food, chest rubs and cough medicine, vitamins, dolls, wagons, sleds, skates	Financial position better Some wives work Less influenced by advertising Buy larger sized packages, multiple-unit deals Buy: Many foods, cleaning materials, bicycles, music lessons, pianos

Full Nest III	Empty Nest I	Empty Nest II	Solitary Survivor: In Labor Force	Solitary Survivor: Retired
Financial position still better More wives work Some children get jobs Hard to influence with advertising High average purchase of durables Buy: New, more tasteful furniture, auto travel, non-necessary appliances, boats, dental services, magazines	Home ownership at peak Most satisfied with financial position and money saved Interested in travel, recreation, self-education Make gifts and contributions Not interested in new products Buy: Vacations, luxuries, home improvements	Drastic cut in income Keep home Buy: Medical appliances, medical care, products which aid health, sleep, and digestion	Income still good but likely to sell home	Same medical and product needs as other retired group: drastic cut in income Special need for attention, affection, and security

SOURCE: William D. Wells and George Gubar, "Life Cycle Concept in Marketing Research" *Journal of Marketing Research* (November 1966), p. 362.

REVIEW YOUR MARKETING KNOWLEDGE

• Assume you work for a company that makes tools for working around the house. Your boss asks you to evaluate whether or not the company should target the left-hand consumer market. Ten percent of Americans, 24 million people, are left-handed. How would you go about determining if this segment should be a target market for the company?

• Would using the family life-cycle be a better way to segment and target the tools market? Why? What about targeting working women?

Income and the New Economic Realities. At the beginning of this chapter, we indicated that one of the most important components in determining a market is the amount of money consumers have available to spend. Thus, income becomes an

Figure 4–4 Modernized Family Life-Cycle Flows

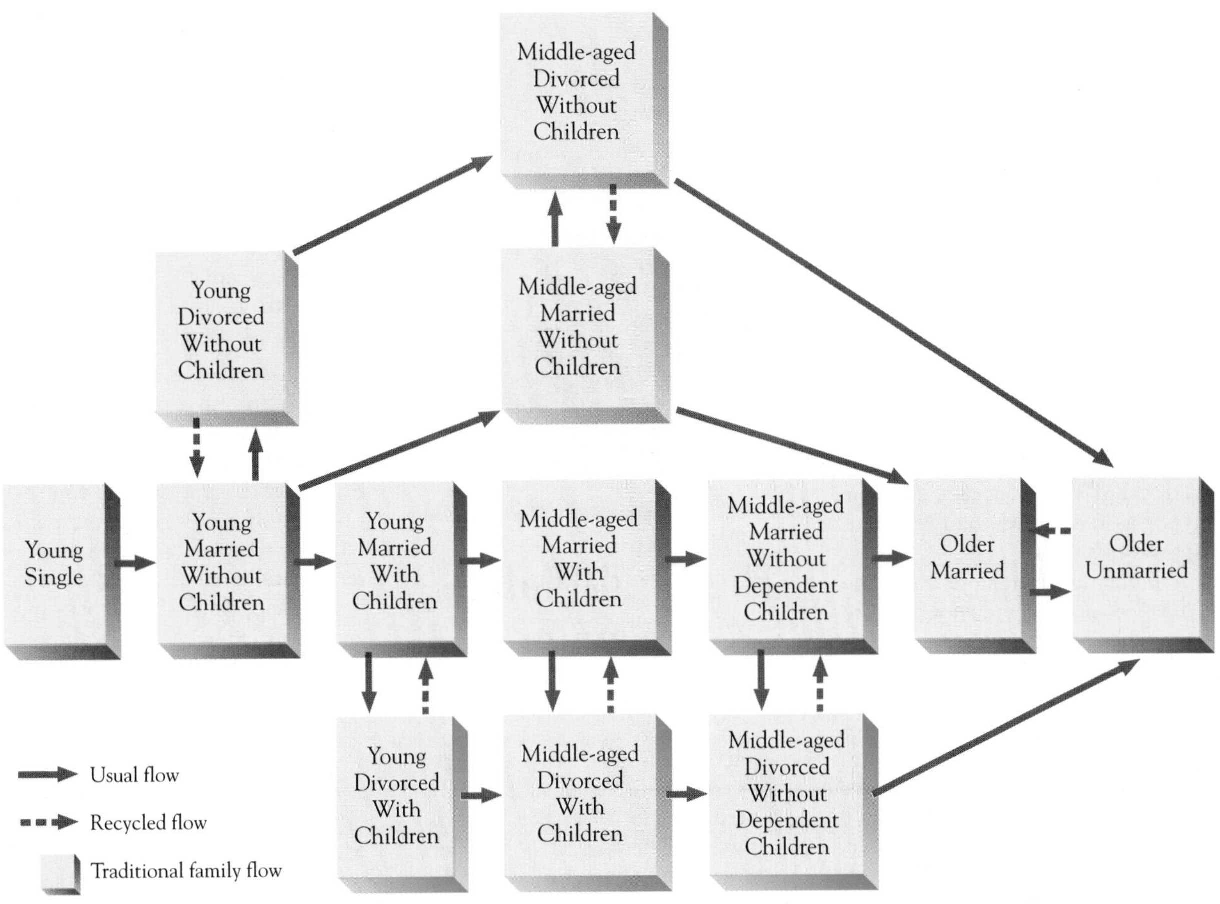

SOURCE: Patrick E. Murphy and William A. Staples, "A Modernized Family Life Cycle," *Journal of Consumer Research* (June 1979), pp. 16–17.

important segmentation variable. Median family income before taxes, and adjusted for inflation, increased about 1.9 percent per year from 1980 to 1990. In terms of the most commonly cited benchmark—pretax total money income—the average household income, adjusted for inflation, will rise from almost $27,500 in 1985 to over $35,000 in the year 2000 (in 1985 dollars).[19] Money income excludes such things as wages received in kind, the value of food and fuel produced and consumed on farms, and the net rental value of owner-occupied homes.

Figure 4–5 shows the distribution of total money income by category for 1985 and 2000. Several trends are evident. The $50,000-and-over group will increase dramatically. By 2000, this group will number more than 25 million. The $35,000 to $50,000 group will also increase. Much of the gain in high-income households will be attributable to the aging of the population and to the continued increase in the number of households with two incomes. The characteristics of wealthy people are described in the *Marketing in Action* feature, "The Gold-Plated Consumer."

MARKETING IN ACTION

The Gold-Plated Consumer

According to research conducted over the past 15 years by Dr. Thomas Stanley, Georgia State University, the affluent consumer may not be who you think. According to Stanley, there were about 1.2 million millionaires in 1987, up from 574,000 in 1980.

These people with a net worth of at least $1 million account for 11 percent of U.S. income. They are primarily entrepreneurs, business owners, and professionals whose goals are maximizing asset appreciation, often at the expense of short-term income. They are investing, not spending. For example, more millionaires drive Chevrolets than BMWs or Mercedes, and more have Sears' credit cards than American Express cards.

Millionaires read more than the average person, but trade journals are the number one thing they read, followed by *The Wall Street Journal*. Most are married (few have been divorced), and most didn't become millionaires until they reached the age of 50 or more. About 40 percent of the millionaires are over age 65. Almost 80 percent have college degrees. Six in ten own their own businesses.

Stanley's research indicates that all millionaires are not alike. He divides them into five categories:

"Parochial Wealth in Transition"—A high proportion of this group is in the transition stage between being an active business owner or manager and a retiree. This group only inherited $1 for every $22.70 of its net worth. They earned their money and are not inclined to take risks with it.

"Active Investors"—This group is in many ways the opposite of the parochial wealth in transition segment. This group, largely attorneys and professionals, enjoys the challenge of investing and likes to take risks. They often use credit for investment leverage.

"Loan-Prone Shoppers"—This group is the youngest segment, and has the highest concentration of entrepreneurs, business owners, and managers. Unlike the active investors, this group actually runs the businesses they invest in, seeking aggressive, long-term gains.

"Inheritor-Achievers"—The millionaires in this segment are the richest of all of the groups, and include the family names that are recognized by the general population as millionaires. The group contains the successful sons and daughters of millionaires. They are the most cosmopolitan of the groups and engage in publicized philanthropic activities. This group of millionaires generated $4.20 of net worth for every $1 inherited.

"Inheritor-Underachiever" — This segment typically includes the widow or ex-wife of an inheritor-achiever. More than one-half of their net worth came from inherited sources. The average income of this group is less than half the income of the inheritor-achiever, and is by far the lowest of all the segments.

SOURCE: Thomas J. Stanley, *Marketing to the Affluent*, Dow Jones-Irwin, 1988.

With this increasing level of affluence looming on the horizon, perceptive marketers have begun to get ready. They have improved customer service, added nontraditional hours of operation (especially for service), and focused on higher quality and dependability. By concentrating on time saving and higher quality, they should profitably expand in the following areas:[20]

- products that ease drudgery and household maintenance, automate chores, and demonstrate quality, reliability, durability, and luxury;
- products that support mobility and immediate gratification, such as instant photography, all-night restaurants, portable telephones and computers, emergency health centers, worldwide product services, 800-numbers, home entertainment centers, automated tellers, and instant credit;

Examples of ads targeted to working women and black families.

- products and services that will secure and protect individuals and property, such as sensing devices, home protection systems, security guards, insurance of various kinds, fire and burglar protection;
- products and services designed to enhance the physical self, particularly those perceived as maintaining and restoring youthfulness, such as cosmetics, skin-care products, health foods, vitamins, cosmetic surgery, spas, clothing consultants, exercise facilities;
- products and services that support the psychological self, such as counseling, education, stress management, and self-improvement books and courses; and
- entertainment and leisure activities, including services as varied as participatory and spectator sports, travel, gourmet foods, and the arts.

Other Demographic Bases for Segmentation. Depending on the product category, some marketers find it useful to segment their markets on the basis of occupation, education, and race or national origin. Each has a different impact on a market.

Occupation. According to the U.S. Census Bureau, about one-third of today's workforce are blue-collar workers, one-quarter are sales and clerical workers, one-quarter are managers or professionals, and the remainder are service workers or farmers. The biggest gains for the next decade are projected in sales, technical, and service workers.[21] The blue-collar market is projected to decrease during the 1990s but will still make up one-quarter of the work force in the year 2000. This market—craftsmen, first-line supervisors, machine operators, and laborers—is important because of the large increases in blue-collar income in recent years.

Education. For many products and services such as continuing education courses, books and magazines, travel, entertainment, and recreation, education is an impor-

JC Penney Markets to Hispanics

Today's U.S. population includes nearly 20 million Hispanics representing over $134 billion in purchasing power. Hispanics represent the fastest-growing ethnic segment of the U.S. population, sporting an annual growth rate of 6.1% vs. the Anglo population's 0.6%. U.S. marketers are finally starting to realize and act on this fact.

The J.C. Penney Co. was one of the earliest retailers to specifically target marketing programs toward Hispanics. Penney's targets a diverse Hispanic customer base. This base includes different social classes, as well as the subpopulations of Mexicans, Puerto Ricans, Cubans, and other Latin Americans. While cultural similarities exist between this entire group and its Anglo counterparts, the Hispanic segment as a whole and each of its various subsegments have cultural idiosyncrasies, both in buying patterns and media preferences. Penney's Hispanic ads are very different from its Anglo ads.

In 1978, JC Penney's catalog division produced a Spanish-language booklet explaining how to use an English-language JC Penney catalog to shop. Penney's was amazed at the overwhelming response. While the booklet had been targeted to select market areas, mainly in Florida, California, and Texas, requests poured in for the booklet in areas few considered important as Hispanic markets. Patricia V. Asip, Penney's manager of corporate Hispanic marketing, asserted, "This helped sensitize the company to the widespread existence of a customer out there who required a different kind of communication."

The assignment of the Argentina-born Patricia Asip in 1981 to a new position at the corporate level propelled JC Penney into the Hispanic market. Under her direction, the company has been actively advertising to Hispanics in a wide array of markets. An in-house Hispanic creative team produces all the ads, though the company also utilizes Hispanic freelance talent.

¡Descubra un nuevo mundo de conveniencia!
El Catálogo JCPenney

While radio spots and sales circulars are used occasionally, the largest share of the budget goes to television. Print is not as yet a popular medium in the Hispanic market. As Thomas Murname, senior vice president of Management Horizons, stated at the 1987 Retail West Midyear Conference, "Broadcast media is found to be more appealing than print when advertising to this population group. This is because second-generation Hispanics can converse in Spanish, but find it difficult to read or write in Spanish."

Ads are produced mostly for sale events. While they feature the same merchandise as the company's Anglo ads, they are produced entirely from scratch; they are not merely translations of the Anglo ads. Appealing to Hispanics often requires different approaches to the message as well as the media. One of the major differences is a much greater emphasis on children's apparel and on whole-family appeal. Advertising spots are generally shot in the context of the home. Children, mothers, and grandmothers are part of these Hispanic ads which have more of a story line than Penney's Anglo ads, making them "more 'real' and less cute." This message is effective with Hispanics, who tend to shop as a family unit. Appealing to this cultural preference is part of Penney's distinctly Hispanic orientation and reflects the high value placed on the total family in the Hispanic culture.

Asip also uses Hispanic directors and talent. Shots are often done on location in Miami and other relevant Hispanic-related sites. One fashion ad featured Laura Martinez-Herring, Miss USA of 1985. The key to success is "transcreation." Asip feels this is best accomplished by people familiar with and sensitive to all Hispanics. "There are big differences among people of Cuban, Mexican, and Puerto Rican heritage. We can't produce different ads for each segment, so we must carefully scrutinize our efforts to make sure ads don't contain language or references that will be interpreted differently by different Hispanics." While errors of grammatically correct translations can be disastrous, careful marketers can come up with Spanish translations that are appropriate for all Hispanic markets. By showing sensitivity to these and other uniquely Hispanic characteristics, JC Penney has established a strong foothold in the growing Hispanic market.

SOURCE: "The Hispanic Market," *Stores*, May 1988, p. 53–56.

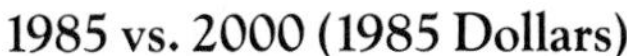

Figure 4–5 Household Income Distribution

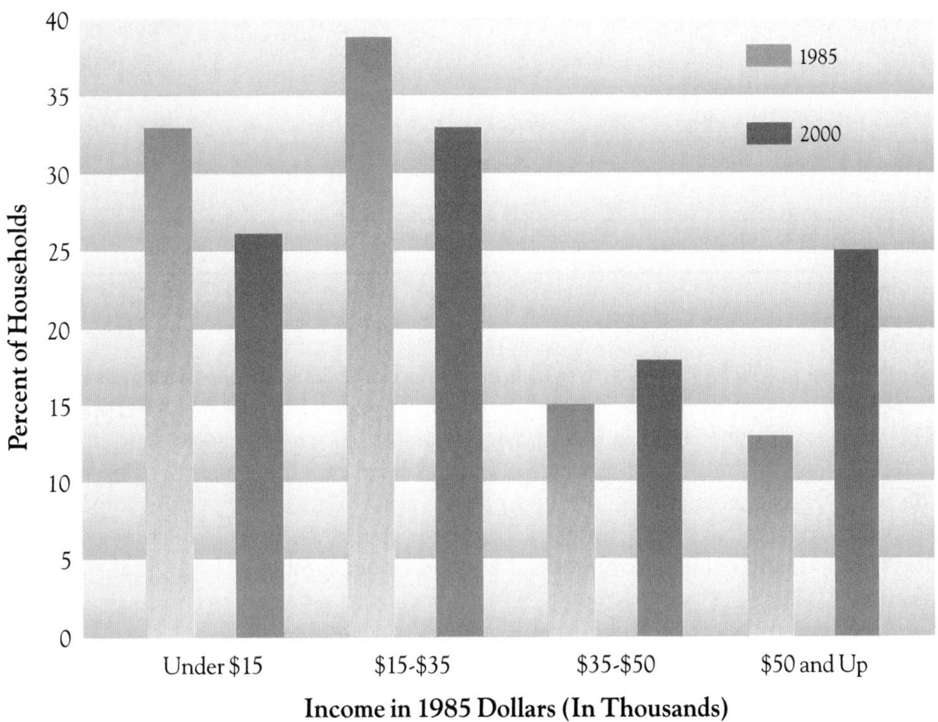

tant segmentation variable. One's level of education is closely related to his or her age—70 percent of those age sixty-five and over did not finish high school, compared to less than 15 percent for those age 25–44.

The total educational profile of the American population has been changing in recent years. By 1985, one person in five had a college degree, almost double the percentage in 1970. Thirty-six percent of adults had at least one year of college, and only 27 percent did not have a high school diploma. People age 70 and older account for one-fourth of those who have less than a high school education.[22] This trend toward increased education is important because higher levels of education produce consumers who are more sophisticated in evaluating alternative product offerings, more receptive to new products, and more demanding of quality and performance.

Race or National Origin. Although the population of the United States as a whole has been growing slowly, growth among various minority groups has been much greater. While the growth rate for the white population has been well under 1 percent per year, the black population has been growing two and a half times as fast. The Spanish-language market is growing about six times as fast as the white market (see Table 4–5). This trend is projected to continue throughout the 1990s.

An example of a successful attempt to market to minority consumers by a retailer is presented in the *Marketing in Action* feature "JC Penney Markets to Hispanics." Blacks and Hispanics are important for many consumer product categories. Blacks, with only 12 percent of the total population of the United States consume 39 percent

Table 4–5 Composition of the Population by Race

	Population (in millions)			Percent Increase	Percent Distribution	
	1980	1990	2000	1980–2000	1980	2000
White	195	210	221	13	86	83
Black	27	31	35	31	12	13
Hispanic	15	20	25	73	6	9
	227	249	267	18	104	105

Note: Figures do not add up exactly to totals because of the omission of minorities such as American Indian, Eskimo, and Asian, and because about half of Hispanics are also counted as white.

SOURCE: U.S. Census Bureau, Current Population Reports, Series P–25, 1988

of all the rice, drink 49 percent of the grape and orange soda produced, and spend 23 percent more per capita for shoes than the white population does.[23] After spending $12 million per year targeting blacks, McDonald's has seen its market share increase to 20 percent in the black consumer market, a level much higher than its share of the white consumer market.[24] Products that have a high index of consumption by Hispanics include baby food, movies, beverages (particularly fruit nectars and fruit drinks), canned groceries, cosmetics, hair conditioners and colorings, floor wax and cleaner.[25]

One reason the black and Hispanic markets offer so much potential is that they are very accessible. The vast majority of both groups live in metropolitan areas. More than half the Hispanics live in ten MSAs clustered in Texas, California, Miami, New York, and Chicago. Almost half the blacks live in fifteen major metropolitan areas. There are well-defined local and national media available to reach these two markets, and past experience has shown that these consumers will respond to marketing efforts. Of course, all blacks and all Hispanics are not alike, and there are often important segments within each of these markets.

REVIEW YOUR MARKETING KNOWLEDGE

- Many companies rely on geographic and demographic segmentation, using variables such as age, sex, and income. Very few companies have targeted minority markets. What might be some reasons why more companies don't target minority consumers?
- What advice do you have for a company segmenting by race for the first time?

Psychographic Segmentation

Up to this point we have discussed the segmentation of markets using geographic and demographic variables. We now turn our attention to ways to segment markets based on other important variables. The first of these is **psychographics,** a segmentation variable using consumers' activities, interests, and opinions.

The basic rationale for using psychographic variables as a way to segment a market is that they enrich the description of market segments beyond demographics. Psychographics tell us about attitudes and lifestyles, allowing the marketer to differentiate

Table 4–6 Life-style Dimensions

Activities	Interests	Opinions	Demographics
Work	Family	Themselves	Age
Hobbies	Home	Social issues	Education
Social events	Job	Politics	Income
Vacation	Community	Business	Occupation
Entertainment	Recreation	Economics	Family size
Club membership	Fashion	Education	Dwelling
Community	Food	Products	Geography
Shopping	Media	Future	City size
Sports	Achievements	Culture	Stage in life-cycle

SOURCE: Joseph Plummer, "The Concept and Application of Life-Style Segmentation," *Journal of Marketing*, January 1974, pp. 33–37.

between "swingers" and "homebodies," between liberals and conservatives, between those who admire sports figures and those who identify with movie stars.

The most common use of psychographics has been life-style segmentation through the measurement of activities, interests, and opinions (AIOs).[26] Psychographic, or life-style, segmentation concentrates on:

1. how people spend their time;
2. their interests, what they place importance on in their immediate surroundings;
3. their view of themselves and the world around them; and
4. some basic characteristics such as their stage in life cycle, income, education, and where they live.[27]

Table 4–6 lists some of the elements included in each of the major dimensions of life-style. The key premise of this type of segmentation is that the more you know and understand your customers, the more effective you can be in communicating and marketing to them. An example of how this might work in practice is shown in Table 4–7, which includes a sample of AIO statements taken from a larger inventory. The results illustrate differences between "heavy" moviegoers and nonmoviegoers. It is clear that frequent moviegoers have very different life-styles from those of nonmoviegoers. A marketer could use this type of information for targeting media; radio would appear to have great potential, for example. The data provide clues concerning copy appeals that might be successful; sacrilegious messages would appear to have a low probability of working, whereas messages oriented toward the individual's achievement, leadership, and willingness to take a chance might pay off. Movies containing sports cars, loud parties, or European environments would appear to be of interest to the "heavy" moviegoer population.

A study conducted by SRI International found the American population could be segmented psychographically into nine segments. The segments are derived by studying consumer values, and the technique is referred to in marketing circles as the use of "VALS." The VALS categories are as follows:[28]

- Survivors—poverty-level individuals who are just trying to stay alive. They make up 4 percent of the population, and don't have much enjoyment in their lives.

Table 4–7 A Psychographic Comparison of "Heavy" Moviegoers and Nonmoviegoers

AIO Statements	Percent in Agreement: Nonmoviegoers	"Heavy" Moviegoers
My greatest achievements are still ahead of me.	49	80
Five years from now, my family income will probably be a lot higher than it is now.	63	88
I'd like to spend a year in London or Paris.	19	42
I like to be considered a leader.	60	82
I don't like to take a chance.	71	51
I like parties where there is lots of music and talk.	37	65
I always have the car radio on when I drive.	49	82
Playboy is one of my favorite magazines.	13	48
I think I'm a bit of a swinger.	13	33
I like sports cars.	29	58
Liquor is a curse on American life.	59	36
A woman should not smoke in public.	62	36
If Americans were more religious, this would be a better country.	83	63

SOURCE: Glen Homan, Robert Cecil, and William Wells, "An Analysis of Moviegoers by Life-Style Segments," in Mary Jane Schlinger, ed., *Advances in Consumer Research,* Vol. 2 (Association for Consumer Research, 1975), p. 219.

- Sustainers—7 percent of the population that is just above the survivor income level but is striving to improve their position. They are combative and often feel left out of things.
- Belongers—the largest category, representing 35 percent of the population. They "follow the rules," own cats, like to garden, and watch daytime TV. The belongers conform, have lived at their present addresses for ten or more years, and like tradition.
- Emulators—constituting 10 percent of adults, these individuals blatantly emulate the rich and successful people they hope to become. They are young and ambitious and like to go to parties.
- Achievers—the second largest group, 23 percent of the adult population. Achievers are hard working, success-oriented people who like to acquire and enjoy the good things in life.
- I-am-me—making up 5 percent of adults, these people are young and individualistic. Many are students and others in a transitional stage.
- Experientials—representing 7 percent, these individuals are striving for intimate personal relationships and a "holistic" life.
- Societally conscious—the 9 percent that prefer to live a simplistic life, and are not very materialistic. Similar to the experientials, they prefer natural products and the outdoors.

The Man's Diamond. When a Woman Loves a Man.
"Our last anniversary,
I underwhelmed him
with a collapsible umbrella.
This time I could tell
I had overcompensated
beautifully."
A SAMPLE OF EXQUISITELY DESIGNED RINGS, WEDDING BANDS, CUFF LINKS, AND TIE GEAR TO DELIGHT AND BEGUILE. PRICED FROM $249 TO $1299. CALL 800 888-RING FOR THE GORDON'S JEWELERS NEAREST YOU. SELECTION WILL VARY BY LOCATION.
Gordon's JEWELERS
A diamond is forever.

Achievers like to acquire and enjoy the good things in life.

- Integrated—only 2 percent of the population, but the most likable. They lead a well-balanced life and have a true inner sense of who they are. They are people who can be trusted and have traits many people would like to have.

The VALS categories are often collapsed into three groups. The survivors and sustainers are called the *need-driven consumers.* Belongers, emulators, and achievers are classified as *outer-directed.* The final group is called the *inner-driven,* and consists of the I-am-me, experiential, societally conscious, and integrated groups. American Airlines has used VALS to identify its frequent-flyer customer group, the business traveler, as achievers and "societally conscious" people.[29] Other marketers, particularly in the food industry, have indicated that segmentation using VALS does not work for products with little or no emotional involvement in the buying process.[30]

Another type of psychographic segmentation is benefit segmentation, which is the identification of market segments by causal factors rather than descriptive factors.[31] The benefits people seek in a given product or service are the reasons for the existence of market segments. Proponents argue that the benefits sought by consumers actually determine their behavior, while demographic characteristics only serve as measurable substitutes for a position in life frequently associated with a type of behavior.

An example of benefit segmentation in the toothpaste market is shown in Table 4–8. The first segment is concerned about flavor and product appearance. The second segment is concerned about the brightness of their teeth, and the third segment is

Table 4–8 Benefit Segmentation of the Toothpaste Market

Segment Name	Principal Benefit Sought	Demographic Strengths	Special Behavioral Characteristics	Personality Characteristics	Life-style Characteristics
The Sensory Segment	Flavor, product appearance	Children	Users of spearmint flavored toothpaste	High self-involvement	Hedonistic
The Sociables	Brightness of teeth	Teens, young people	Smokers	High sociability	Active
The Worriers	Decay prevention	Large families	Heavy users	High hypochondriasis	Conservative
The Independent Segment	Price	Men	Heavy users	High autonomy	Value-oriented

SOURCE: Russell Haley, "Benefit Segmentation: A Decision-Oriented Tool," *Journal of Marketing* (July 1968), pp. 30–35.

oriented toward decay prevention. The final segment is interested in price. Although there are demographic differences, personality differences, and life-style differences among the four segments, benefit segmentation is the most important variable for a market segmentation analysis. The reason for this conclusion is that the other differences are caused by the benefit segmentation differences, rather than vice versa.

Behavioralistic Segmentation

Another major category of segmentation can be classified under the umbrella of behavioralistic variables. Consumers are segmented on the basis of their actual behavior rather than on their demographic characteristics or attitudes. Examples include usage rate, brand loyalty, and readiness stage.

Usage Rate. Segmentation by product usage rate is predicated by the importance of the "heavy user" to marketers. For many products and services, 20 percent of the users account for 70 to 80 percent of the sales (sometimes referred to as the "20/80 rule"). Under the usage-rate segmentation concept, the marketer first divides the market into heavy users, light users, and nonusers. Different marketing mix strategies are then directed toward each segment. A fast-food company like McDonald's would use advertising, special promotions, and contests to keep the heavy user coming back. Light users would be encouraged to come more often, using such techniques as premiums ("get a complete set of Muppet glasses") or the addition of new products to increase frequency of their visits. To attract nonusers, the company could add new products ("they don't like hamburgers, but maybe they will come in for chicken sandwiches") or even complete new meals (the addition of breakfast converted many nonusers into regular users at McDonald's).

Brand Loyalty. Different consumers will show different degrees of loyalty toward a brand. Some travelers will always stay at Holiday Inn, for example, while others will seek variety and change hotels often. It is important for marketers to identify those consumers that are most loyal to their brand and to design marketing strategies to meet the needs of this group. For example, many of the airlines have initiated Frequent Flier programs designed to encourage flying only, or mostly, on that airline's flights. The programs grant free prizes and trips for accumulating mileage on the airline's flights, encouraging brand loyalty.

Readiness Stage. At any given time, there are consumers in different stages of readiness to buy. Some consumers may be totally unaware of the product, others may be aware of it but not very knowledgeable about it, others may be knowledgeable but may have never tried it, some will intend to buy it, and others will have actually bought it and become loyal users.

Different strategies are required for each of these segments. Heavy advertising might be required to reach the unaware and unknowledgeable segments. Sampling would be effective in reaching the knowledgeable nonuser of the product, while personal selling might be required to convert those intending to buy into actual buyers. Advertising different from that used to create awareness could prove effective in converting current buyers into loyal users.

Personal Computer Exercise

Determining the market potential for the target market for a product involves the analysis of alternative market segments. Demographic data are often useful in determining the size of these alternative segments of the market, as demonstrated in this PC exercise.

KEY POINTS

• A market consists of people or businesses with the potential interest, purchasing power, and willingness to spend the money to buy a product or service to satisfy a need.

• A target market is a segment of the market to which a marketer directs a specific marketing program.

• Marketers typically divide markets into submarkets or segments, a process called market segmentation. Market segmentation allows a more efficient allocation of marketing resources, enables the marketer to understand better the needs of consumers in the market, and improves the organization's ability to satisfy the needs and wants of customers and potential customers.

• For market segments to be useful, they must be of sufficient size and potential, they must be reachable, and they should show clear variation in responsiveness to marketing programs in comparison with other segments.

• The major bases for segmentation are geographic, demographic, psychographic, and behavioralistic.

• The geographic distribution of the population in the United States is shifting to the South and West. Geodemographics and other regional marketing techniques are becoming increasingly important.

• Major demographic changes are occurring, changing the way managers view markets. The population is aging, and the number and proportion of single-person households is increasing. Many women have entered the labor force, creating affluent two-income households. Delays in getting married and an increase in the number of divorces have changed traditional views of the family life-cycle. The population is becoming more educated and is increasingly holding white-collar jobs. Minorities comprise a large part of the growth in population and are becoming more important to marketers.

• Psychographic segmentation—using consumers' activities, interests, and opinions—enriches the description of market segments beyond simple demographics.

• Behavioralistic variables enable managers to segment markets on the basis of consumers' actual behavior. Segmentation can be based on such variables as usage rate, brand loyalty, and readiness to buy.

ISSUES FOR DISCUSSION

1. The advertising manager for a major consumer electronics company was recently quoted as follows: "I'd say that psychographics is a crock. . . . With compact discs, we know we are going for the eighteen-to-twenty-four-year-olds; with TV and videocassette equipment, it's older and more income—$25,000-plus and ages twenty-five to fifty. We've found a definite correlation between income and education levels and the market for our product." Comment on the advertising manager's views about demographic vs. psychographic segmentation.

2. The director of marketing for Six Flags, a chain of theme parks, is concerned about the projected decline in the percentage of teenagers in the marketplace. How might the company respond to the changing demographics projected for the next decade?

3. What impact might the trend toward more working women have on banks? Airlines? Fast-food restaurants? Food companies? What impact will the changing age distribution of the population have on these industries?

4. The O.M. Scott Company, a large marketer of grass seed, is concerned about the best way to segment its market. It has found through research that the people spending the most on lawn care products care the most about their lawn, live in nicer neighborhoods, and make above average incomes. Should Scott segment the market using geographic, demographic, or psychographic segmentation? How should Scott define its target market?

5. Until recently, hotel marketers (such as Holiday Inns) used a market aggregation strategy to market their services. Now many hotel companies have several types of hotels, each targeted at a different segment. For example, Holiday Inn markets the following: a) Holiday Inn—"the world's leader in full-service, value-priced hotels;" b) Embassy suites—the leader in the all-suite hotel segment; c) The Residence Inn—accommodations with a residential flavor; d) Holiday Inn Crowne Plaza—"top-of-the-line hotels for the discriminating traveler;" and e) Hampton Inn—affordably priced hotels. What is the advantage to Holiday Inn to have so many different types of hotels? What are the disadvantages? On what basis is Holiday Inn segmenting the market? Does this seem like a wise strategy?

6. A major insurance company is considering targeting the segment of the market that owns Chevrolets and lower-priced cars. They would only go after this end of the market, refusing to insure Porsches, Mercedes, and other high-priced cars. What questions should they ask before implementing this strategy?

7. Most of the airlines have frequent flyer programs designed to appeal to heavy users of air travel and to generate increased brand loyalty. The rental car companies have begun to implement very similar programs. Should retailers of men's and women's apparel do the same thing, or are there other bases for segmenting and targeting, such as family life-cycle, that make more sense for these marketers?

8. Use the concept of market segmentation to explain why Coca-Cola sells so many different soft drink products, including Classic Coke, new Coke, Diet Coke, Tab, Cherry Coke, Sprite, Fresca, Fanta—in various versions, with and without caffeine, in so many different types and sizes of packages.

9. Can all markets be segmented? When might market segmentation not be used as a strategy?

10. What impact do geographic changes have on retailers? What demographic changes taking place will have the most impact on retailers during the 1990s? Give examples of what perceptive retailers can do to improve their abilities to satisfy consumer needs and demands given these demographic changes.

GLOSSARY

Behavioral segmentation: segmenting markets on the basis of actual behavior instead of on attitudes or demographics.

Benefit segmentation: the identification of market segments by causal factors rather than descriptive factors. Using this approach, marketers determine what benefits consumers are seeking from products or services.

Consolidated Metropolitan Statistical Area (CMSA): an area with over one million population and containing two or more closely related metropolitan areas.

Demography: the study of people in the aggregate, including population size, age, income, occupation, and sex.

Family life-cycle: a segmentation variable consisting of a combination of age, marital status, and presence or absence of children.

Fertility rate: the number of children born to the average woman in her lifetime.

Geodemographics: the neighborhood clustering of people with similar economic and cultural backgrounds and perspectives.

Gross National Product (GNP): the total national output of goods and services, valued at market prices, in a given year.

Market: people or businesses with the potential interest, purchasing power, and willingness to spend money for a product or service to satisfy a need.

Market aggregation: marketing a single product using a single marketing mix strategy directed toward all consumers in a market.

Market segmentation: the process of dividing large heterogeneous markets into smaller homogeneous segments of people or businesses with similar needs and/or responsiveness to marketing mix offerings.

Metropolitan Statistical Area (MSA): a freestanding metropolitan area surrounded by nonmetropolitan counties, including a large central city or urbanized area of 50,000 or more people.

Money income: income before the deduction of income taxes and Social Security taxes (excluding nonmoney items of income).

Personal income: the current income received by persons from all sources minus contributions for social insurance.

Primary Metropolitan Statistical Area (PMSA): a metropolitan area that is closely related to another metropolitan area and part of a Consolidated Metropolitan Statistical Area of one million or more population.

Psychographics: a segmentation variable based on consumers' activities, interests, and opinions.

Standard Metropolitan Statistical Area (SMSA): an integrated economic and social unit having a large population nucleus. Chicago is one example.

Target market: a homogeneous segment of the market to which a marketer directs a specific marketing program.

Undifferentiated marketing: see market aggregation.

NOTES

1. For a more thorough comparison of market segmentation with market aggregation or product differentiation, see the classic article by Wendell R. Smith, "Product Differentiation and Market Segmentation as Alternative Strategies," *Journal of Marketing,* July 1956, pp. 3–8.

2. Jim Schwartz and Jim Stone, "New Car Buyers," *American Demographics,* April 1987, pp. 33–36.

3. This section and the next one are based on James F. Engel, Henry F. Fiorilla and Murray A. Cayley, *Market Segmentation: Concepts and Applications* (Holt, Rinehart & Winston, 1972), pp. 2–3, 7–8.

4. *Engel et al.*, p. 7.

5. U.S. Bureau of the Census, *Current Population Reports,* Series P–60, No. 154, 1987.

6. U.S. Census Bureau, *Money Income and Poverty Status of Families and Persons in the United States: 1985,* 1987.

7. Thomas Moore, "Different Folks, Different Strokes," *Fortune,* September 16, 1985, pp. 65–68.

8. Thomas W. Osborn, "Analytic Techniques for Opportunity Marketing," *Marketing Communications,* September 1987, p. 54.

9. The net migration to the United States of 500,000 persons per year excludes illegal immigration. The number of illegal immigrants has been increasing rapidly, and estimates range as high as 1 million per year.

10. "U.S. Companies Go for the Gray," *Business Week,* April 3, 1989, pp. 64–67; Ronald Alsop, "Firms Try New Ways to Tap Growing Over-50 Population," *The Wall Street Journal,* August 23, 1984, p. 25; "Decade's Boom in Prime-Age Consumers Will Offer Vast Opportunities for Business," *The Wall Street Journal,* June 26, 1980, p. 29.

11. Paul Glick, "How American Families are Changing," *American Demographics,* January 1984, pp. 21–25.

12. Joe Schwartz, "A New High Water Mark," *American Demographics,* February 1988, p. 18.

13. Bureau of Labor Statistics data cited in David Bloom, "Women and Work," *American Demographics,* September 1986, pp. 25–30.

14. "New Mothers Return to Work Sooner," *The Wall Street Journal,* February 4, 1988, p. 27.

15. See Julie L. Erickson, "Marketing to Women: It's Tough to Keep Up With the Changes," *Advertising Age,* March 7, 1988, pp. S-1–S-10; Bickley Townsend, "Working Women," *American Demographics,* January 1985, pp. 4–7; Rena Bartos, *The Moving Target: What Every Marketer Should Know About Women,* New York: The Free Press, 1982.

16. William D. Wells and George Gubar, "The Life Cycle Concept," *Journal of Marketing Research,* November 1966, pp. 355–63.

17. Patrick E. Murphy and William A. Staples, "A Modernized Family Life-Cycle," *Journal of Consumer Research,* June 1979, pp. 12–22.

18. Murphy and Staples, pp. 12–22.

19. Fabian Linden, "Middle-Aged Muscle," *American Demographics,* October 1987, p. 4.

20. William Lazer, "How Rising Affluence Will Reshape Markets," *American Demographics,* February 1984, pp. 17–21.

21. Martha F. Riche, "America's New Workers," *American Demographics,* February 1988, pp. 34–41.

22. U.S. Bureau of the Census, "Educational Attainment in the United States: March 1982 to 1985," Series P–20, No. 415, 1987.

23. These data are taken from D. Parke Gibson, *$70 Billion in the Black,* (Macmillan, 1978), p. 4; and Richard

L. Green, "Black Buying Patterns Are Revealing," *Advertising Age,* April 16, 1979, p. S–34.

24. Marianne Paskowski, "Shades of Grey," *Marketing and Media Decisions,* March 1986, pp. 30–40.

25. Jack Feuer, "New Worlds Are Opening in Hispanic Marketing," *Adweek,* February 8, 1988, p. 30; Joe Schwartz, "Hispanic Opportunities," *American Demographics,* May 1987, pp. 56–59; Mark Watanabe, "A Profile Grows to New Heights," *Advertising Age,* April 6, 1981, p. S–23.

26. William Wells and Douglas Tigert, "Activities, Interest, and Opinions," *Journal of Advertising Research,* August 1971, pp. 27–35. For a review of other ways of defining and measuring psychographics, see William Wells, "Psychographics: A Critical Review," *Journal of Marketing Research,* May 1975, pp. 196–213.

27. Joseph Plummer, "The Concept and Application of Life Style Segmentation," *Journal of Marketing,* January 1974, pp. 33–37.

28. Arnold Mitchell, *The Nine American Life Styles* (Macmillan, 1983).

29. Tom Bayer, "American Accent," *Advertising Age,* July 28, 1986, p. 30.

30. Aimee Stern, "Marketers Question Value of Psychographics," *Adweek,* August 3, 1987, p. 41.

31. This section is based on Russell Haley, "Benefit Segmentation: A Decision-Oriented Tool," *Journal of Marketing,* July 1968, pp. 30–35.

CASE APPLICATION 4–1

Ramada's Marketing for Older Travelers

Ramada Hotels has launched a marketing and operations program that caters to older travelers. The program, called Best Years, includes a room discount and is backed by in-house training seminars for hotel employees.

According to Gail Brewer, director of specialty markets for Ramada and architect of the program, support materials are designed to help Ramada employees understand the needs of traveling seniors and to give employees specific suggestions for meeting the needs.

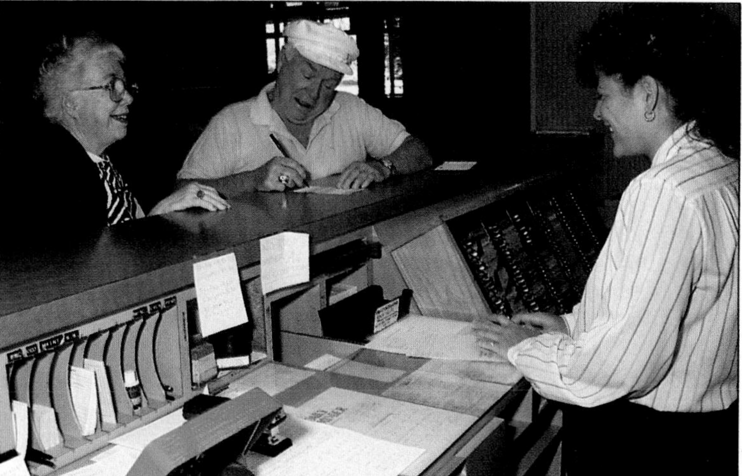

The overall effort is based on the same kind of market research and operations plan that Ramada started in 1982 with The Traveling Woman Program, which centered on the special needs and concerns of female travelers.

"By the end of the next decade, the mature traveler group will increase by more than 30 percent," said Brewer, "twice as fast as the overall population. Households headed by people 50 or older have twice the discretionary income of their younger counterparts."

All employees had completed the training by the end of 1984. The program includes front desk, housekeeping/maintenance, restaurant/lounge, and bell staffers.

Program recommendations for food and beverage people include the following:

• Because many seniors enjoy rising early and dining early, breakfast and twilight dinner specials are recommended for implementation.

• Dining room hosts can make meals extra comfortable by seating mature guests away from speakers, live music, serving stations, and air-conditioning vents. Hearing aids accent background noise so this is important to those who wear hearing-aid devices.

• Since 40 percent of seniors are often on special diets, chefs should make sure their menus include items such as decaffeinated coffee, fish, poultry, homemade soups, high-fiber baked goods, and cereals.

Management will also be involved in the new program. Recommendations include:

• Always be aware of the need for well-lighted guest rooms, hallways, lobbies, and especially front desk areas. A first-aid kit should always be handy at the front desk and all personnel should be instructed on how to react if emergencies occur.

Housekeeping efforts include:

• Keeping welcome amenities in the room. Amenities such as bath mats in tubs, an extra blanket in the closet, and night lights are important.

SOURCE: "Ramada Launches Marketing Program for Older Travelers," *Nation's Restaurant News*, November 23, 1983.

Questions

1. Looking at the steps to determine a market outlined in Figure 4–1 (page 101), does there appear to be a market for hotel services for the elderly?

2. Does age appear to be a good basis for segmenting the hotel market? How do the needs of elderly consumers differ from those of younger ones for services?

3. What criteria should other hotel chains use in deciding if they want to target the elderly consumer market?

4. What bases for segmentation other than age would make sense for Ramada?

Goya Crosses All the Borders

When Goya decided to develop a new pudding based on a traditional recipe, its marketing director checked around the Secaucus, New Jersey, office to see if anyone knew how to cook it. A Cuban clerk said she made it with corn flour, and a Puerto Rican secretary said she made it with rice flour. Both offered to make their own versions at home. When they brought the puddings in the next day, the staff—Dominicans, Colombians, and others—compared the puddings on taste, texture, and thickness. Goya eventually introduced two puddings, a Cuban version and a Puerto Rican version.

Informal test marketing like this isn't unusual at Goya Foods, Inc., the largest Hispanic-owned food manufacturer in the country. Celebrating its 50th anniversary this year, Goya not only serves countless Hispanics, but has begun serving Anglo consumers as well with the company's specialties. Goya isn't afraid of diversity—in its product line or consumer base.

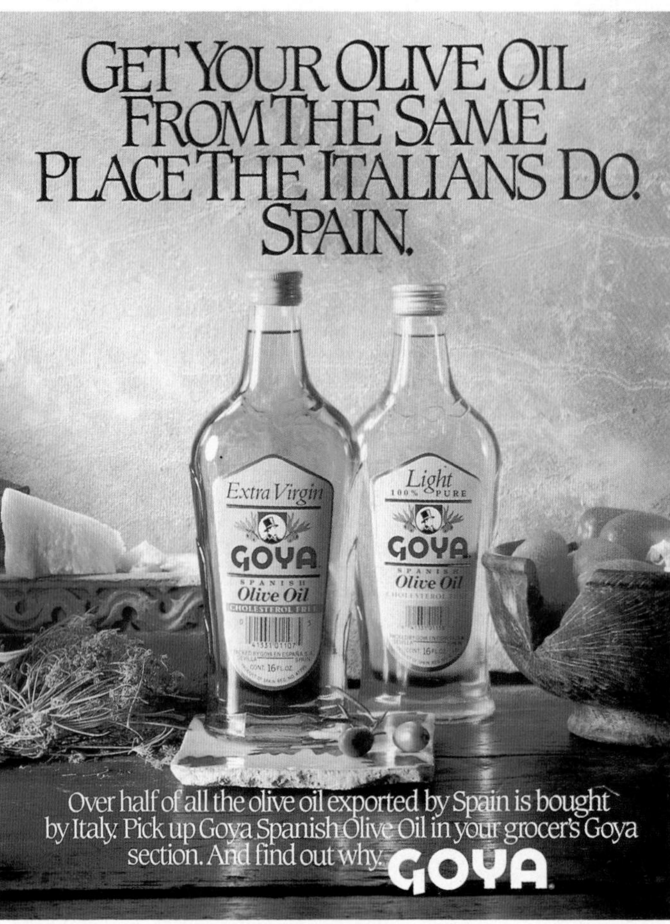

GET YOUR OLIVE OIL FROM THE SAME PLACE THE ITALIANS DO. SPAIN.
Extra Virgin
GOYA
SPANISH Olive Oil
Light
100% PURE
GOYA
SPANISH Olive Oil
Over half of all the olive oil exported by Spain is bought by Italy. Pick up Goya Spanish Olive Oil in your grocer's Goya section. And find out why.
GOYA

By Goya's estimates, Hispanics account for almost 90% of its $250 million in current annual sales, and the company holds its momentum by keeping a close eye on changes in this segment. Thirty years ago, most of its customers were Puerto Rican. Then came the Cubans in the 1960s, and the Dominicans in the 1970s. "Each time a new group comes in, it's a shot in the arm for Goya," says Joseph Unanue, Jr., Goya's director of marketing. "Now it's the Central and South Americans."

Goya's biggest sales are in the New York tri-state area, but distribution extends from Boston to Washington, D.C. In Florida, its primary market is the Miami metropolitan area, followed by Tampa, where it opened a warehouse facility last year. Other facilities are located in Chicago (serving Chicago to Milwaukee) and Houston. Since 1966, when annual sales were only $6 million, growth has been steady and impressive, with sales of over $250 million.

Keeping track of changing demographics on a day-to-day basis is part of the job of Goya's sales force, who are on their routes each day monitoring accounts from Spanish to suburban neighborhoods. "Before any statistics or census reports come in, our salespeople have identified what groups are moving in (or out), their relative affluence, and what they're buying," says Joseph Perez, purchasing director.

In Miami, for example, where the Hispanic population is mostly Cuban, Goya salesmen have carefully followed the arrivals of Colombians and, most recently, Nicaraguans. "They're arriving by the plane load, and, like the Cubans of the '60s, they're mostly middle class," says Perez. "Houston, which is primarily Mexican, is getting a large influx of Salvadorans."

When the salesmen spot a trend, they report it to headquarters, where the information is kicked around by the marketing staff. "Our strategy has been to identify a couple of products that each group consumes in high volume, and change our product line to meet the demand," says Unanue. For example, when Colombians began to arrive in large numbers over the past five years, Goya began producing Colombian soda crackers and block chocolate used in making hot beverages. If Goya feels the product has the potential to become one of its top sellers, it augments its research with more formal methods—mailings, surveys, sampling, and test marketing.

Recently, Goya's marketing group spent two weeks in Colombia doing surveys and visiting supermarkets. Based on research like this, recent additions to the product line include a precooked white corn flour (for Colombians) and a sausage (for Dominicans). Not all tailored products work out, however. One that backfired was a granular brown sugar aimed primarily at Colombians and Ecuadorans. "Traditionally, they get their brown sugar in a block the size of a large bar of soap, and scrape it to use in beverages," says Perez. "So we had the idea that we'd take the block and grind it up, but the idea never caught on. Apparently, part of the mystique was in scraping it off yourself."

Developing products for the Mexican-American market has been difficult, in part because Goya is more experienced with the needs and tastes of Caribbean consumers. After a false start with a product line that bombed in 1977, Goya has gone on to develop a new Mexican line that includes jalapeños, taco shells and sauce, refried beans, chili beans and nachos (which are lethally hot peppers, not chips). The Mexican line is available mostly in Houston, where it is selling well, and in Chicago, which has a large Mexican population. It remains targeted to Hispanics, but Goya expects that some Anglos will buy the products as well.

Goya sees great potential in non-Hispanic consumers—a market they've acquired by accident. In order to better serve second- and third-generation Hispanics, Goya fought its way into the major supermarkets in the late 1960s, where they were discovered by health-conscious baby boomers with a taste for ethnic foods. Goya management adjusted the company's strategies to fit the new retail environment. Popular crossover products include nectars (peach, pear, apricot, tamarind, mango, guava, papaya, and guanaban—a green fruit with white flesh), Coco Goya (a cream of coconut used in pina coladas), beans, olive oil, and seasonings. While Goya has no hard figures, it believes that non-Hispanics account for between 10% and 15% of its sales.

The diversity of Goya products might horrify the traditional American brand manager, but it makes eminent sense to Aldo Cunningham. "Most American companies are consumption oriented. We're service oriented," says Cunningham. "The item may move slowly, but when the buyer wants it, he won't have to turn to another brand." In all, Goya has more than 350 products; counting the different sizes, this comes to 738 items, sold through 9,300 *bodegas* (small local stores) and dozens of supermarkets.

Each sales representative—there are 120 in the New York area alone—wears a suit and tie at all times, and carries a pocket-sized computer that can feed orders over the phone into Goya's data processing system. With salespeople like these, Goya doesn't need brokers. Its fleet of trucks delivers its products directly to the bodegas (which still account for 50% of sales) and to the supermarkets, which get no volume discount. A Safeway buying 100 cases pays the same price per unit as a small grocery store buying only one. Seasonal discounts on best-selling items are given to all retailers as well.

Reaching out to its growing market is the job of Goya's ad staff. All of its Spanish language advertising—$4 million—is handled by Goya's four in-house agencies. Because Goya executives believe the most effective way to reach the highly fragmented Hispanic market is by decentralizing its media buying, each agency, in New York, Miami, Chicago, and Puerto Rico, makes its own media decisions. "TV is more effective than radio or print, because it's the cheapest way to reach a large Hispanic audience," says Unanue. Given the cultural differences in the Hispanic markets, Goya buys all Spanish TV on a spot basis, avoiding purchases at the network level. This way, Goya can target advertisements to different ethnic groups. If they're aiming a product at Cubans, for example, they won't show the ad in Chicago.

Radio is Goya's second media choice because of its wide reach and low cost. New York, with only four Spanish language stations, is considered a relatively easy buy. Miami, with 10 stations, is more complex; and Puerto Rico, with more than 100, takes the most work. So far, Goya does very little in Spanish language print. "It has little reach," explains Unanue.

Media decisions aren't the only things that are decentralized. So are the ads. Different versions are produced for different markets, such as Goya's bean ads. Puerto Ricans and Dominicans call beans *habichuelas*, and Cubans and Mexicans call them *frijoles*, so ads have to use different voice-overs, or even be filmed in two versions. "It's a little more expensive, but it's worth it," says Unanue.

SOURCE: Ellen Schultz, "Goya Crosses All The Borders," *Marketing & Media Decisions*, September 1986, pp. 78—84.

Questions:

1. How well has Goya responded to the demographic changes taking place in its environment?

2. Even though it closely tracks demographic changes in its markets, Goya has had several new products fail. Why? How can they minimize new product failures in the future?

3. Does their policy of offering no volume discounts for large orders from supermarkets make sense? Why or why not?

4. Should Goya be concerned that large food companies are now "discovering" the Hispanic market? What should they do to ensure their continued success with this segment?

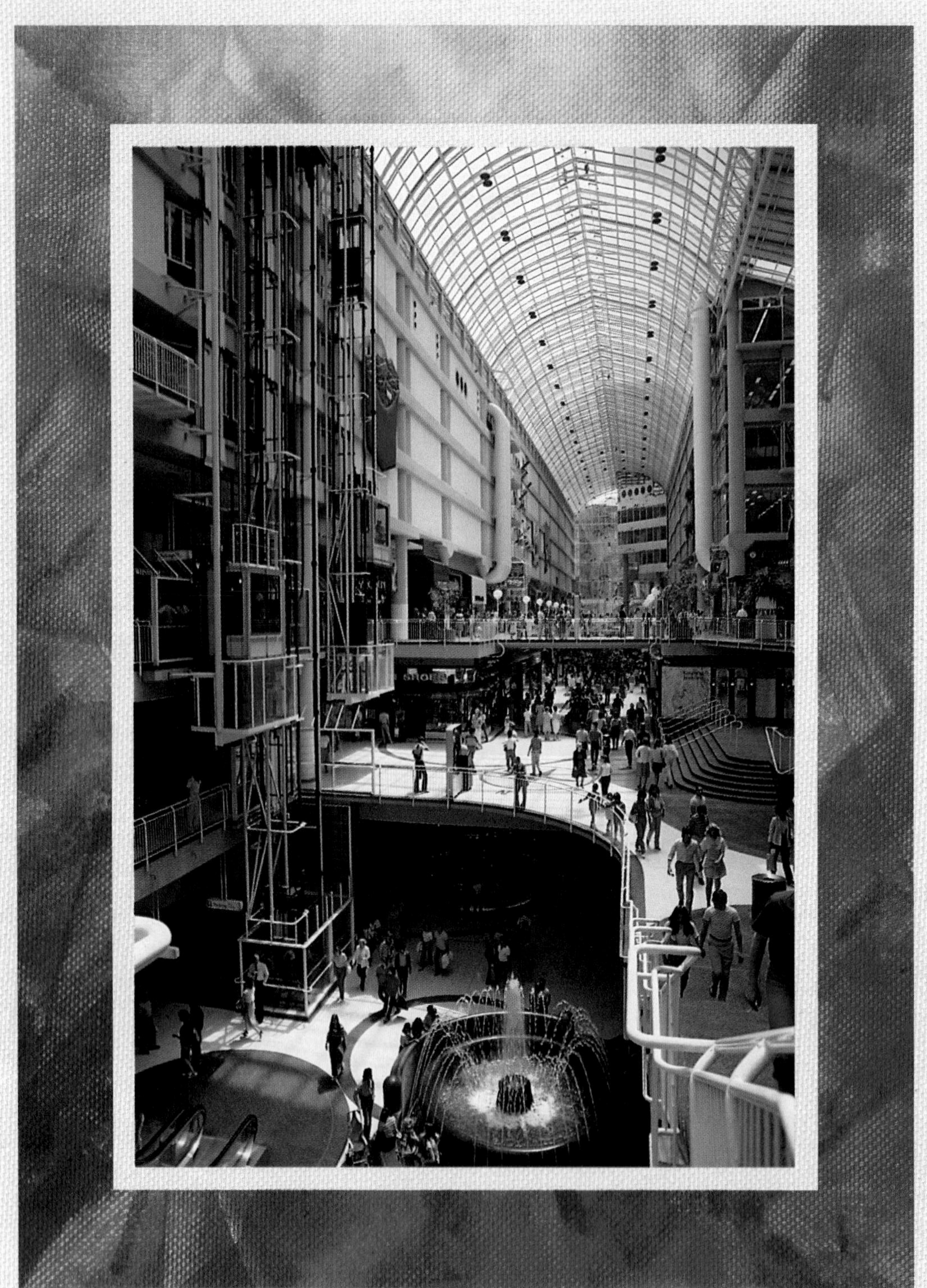

5

Consumer Buying Behavior

Learning Objectives

Upon completing this chapter, you will be able to do the following:

OUTLINE
the many aspects of consumer behavior and the steps in the purchase decision process.

UNDERSTAND
the consumer information-seeking process, including internal search and external search.

IDENTIFY
the types of problem-solving behavior used by consumers.

DESCRIBE
the major influences on consumer behavior, including psychological factors, culture, social class, reference groups, and the family.

DISCUSS
the impact on buyer behavior of such individual psychological influences as learning, perception, motivation, personality, and attitudes.

MARKETING PROFILE

Advertisers Put Consumers on the Couch

Researchers at the McCann-Erickson ad agency were baffled after interviewing some low-income Southern women about the insecticide brands they used. The women strongly believed a new brand of roach killer sold in little plastic trays was far more effective and less messy than traditional bug sprays. Yet they had never bought it, sticking stubbornly with their old sprays.

To try to understand this contradiction, the researchers asked the women to draw pictures of roaches and write stories about their sketches. What McCann-Erickson hoped to do was probe the women's subconscious feelings about roaches. Before advising a client on developing a new insecticide, the agency wanted to know how people really relate to roaches.

According to Paula Drillman, the agency's director of strategic planning, the roaches in the pictures were all male, symbolizing the men who the women said had abandoned them and left them feeling poor and powerless. "Killing the roaches with a bug spray and watching them squirm and die allowed the women to express their hostility toward men and have greater control over the roaches," Ms. Drillman says.

"We're using a whole battery of psychological techniques—some new and some old—to understand the emotional bond between consumers and brands," says Ms. Drillman. "You have to sell on emotion more than ever because it's a world of parity products out there. The days of having a competitive edge and a special product benefit are long gone."

The disastrous failure of new Coke in 1985 also has spurred advertisers to

pay more attention to consumers' emotional ties to products and rely less on standard focus group interviews and taste tests. "Brands are not just commercial products we buy and use; they're our companions in life as well," declares Rosalinde Rago, director of advertising research at the Ogilvy & Mather agency.

In addition to figure drawings, McCann-Erickson also is asking consumers to write newspaper obituaries for brands. The agency's researchers say they learn a lot about a product's image depending upon whether people describe the brand as young, virile, and the victim of a tragic accident or as a worn-out product succumbing to old age.

Other agency research executives insist that verbal techniques alone simply aren't sufficient. They maintain that people aren't able to express many of their feelings in words, either because they're not conscious of them or because they're uncomfortable sharing them with a stranger conducting the interview.

That's why the McCann-Erickson ad agency resorted to stick-figure sketches in research on its American Express Gold Card account. Focus group interviews hadn't made clear consumers' differing perceptions of gold-card and green-card holders. The drawings, however, were much more illuminating. In one set, for example, the gold-card user was portrayed as a broad-shouldered man standing in an active position, while the green card user was a "couch potato'" in front of a TV set. Based on such pictures and other research, the agency decided to market the gold card as a "symbol of responsibility for people who have control over their lives and their finances."

These examples illustrate the importance of both understanding consumers and figuring out what potential buyers want, how they perceive company and competitive offerings, and what their attitudes toward products and brands are. These issues and other aspects of consumer behavior are the focus of Chapter 5.

SOURCE: Ronald Alsop, "Advertisers Put Consumers on the Couch," *The Wall Street Journal*, May 13, 1988, p. 21.

As we indicated in Chapter 4, successful marketing strategies are based upon consumers' wants, needs, and behavior. The examples in the *Marketing Profile* illustrate how understanding consumer behavior is critical to developing products and promotions. It is also important in developing pricing and distribution strategies.

Many different factors influence consumer behavior. This chapter will help you identify these factors and understand how they affect the different kinds of decisions that consumers must make. A thorough understanding of consumer behavior is also important in understanding industrial buying behavior, which is discussed in Chapter 6.

The study of buyer behavior is really just the study of human behavior in the marketplace. Thus, we discuss the same principles of behavior that are discussed in sociology, psychology, and social psychology. Included in these principles are the decision processes consumers use to make purchases; the importance of individual or psychological factors (such as perception, motivation, attitudes, learning, and personality) and their impacts on consumer behavior; the influence of social factors (such as families and reference groups); and the role played by social-cultural factors (social class, culture, and subculture). In all of these areas, it is the *context* of the behavior that differentiates consumer behavior, not the nature of the behavior itself.

Understanding Consumer Behavior

Although many factors must be considered in designing marketing mix strategies, none is more important than consumer behavior. **Consumer behavior** can be defined as those acts of individuals that involve buying and using products and services, including the decision processes that precede and determine these acts.[1] This definition is very broad and covers both consumers and industrial buyers. The definition indicates that the study of consumer behavior includes not only the actions that the consumer takes in buying and using products, but also all the factors involved in the process that lead to those actions. Let us take a look at a specific transaction to illustrate this point:

> *The doorbell rings; it is answered by Mr. Johnson. A young girl is at the door selling Girl Scout cookies. She gives her sales pitch and, after excusing himself for a moment to go talk to his wife, Mr. Johnson returns and buys six boxes. Several days later the girl returns to deliver the boxes of cookies and to collect the money.*

In this example, several aspects of Mr. Johnson's consumer behavior are very clear, and some are not at all clear. We know that decisions were made to purchase the cookies and to buy a quantity of six boxes. We do not know, however, whether Mr. Johnson actually made the decisions or whether Mrs. Johnson made the decisions and Mr. Johnson merely performed the act of purchasing. We know nothing about the *why* behind the decisions. Do the Johnsons buy Girl Scout cookies every year? Do they buy because they like the cookies, or because they want to support the Girl Scouts? How important was price in deciding how many boxes to buy? If the price had been higher or lower, would they have bought fewer or more boxes? How will they use the cookies—will they eat them themselves, or will they serve them to friends to demonstrate their support of the Girl Scouts? These are examples of the many kinds of questions addressed by the study of consumer behavior.

Figure 5–1 Simplifed Model of Consumer Purchase Decision Process

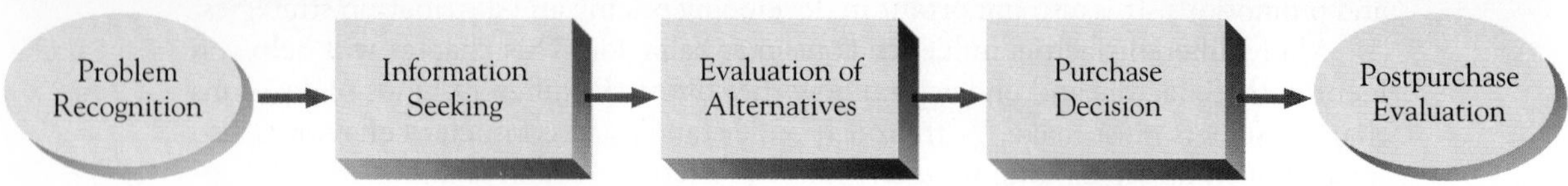

The Consumer Purchase Decision Process

The definition of consumer behavior presented earlier emphasized that consumer behavior is a process rather than a few discrete acts. A student interested in buying a new stereo will go through a complex decision-making procedure before choosing a system. He or she will seek out information from various sources to help evaluate the many alternative stereo systems available, agonize over a final choice, and will often have mixed feelings about the decision after it is all over. We refer to this as the **purchase decision process,** defined as the series of stages a consumer goes through in making decisions about which products to buy.

A simplified model of the consumer purchase decision process is shown in Figure 5–1. The model contains five stages, which are important for marketers to understand. They are the following:

1. problem recognition;
2. information-seeking;
3. evaluation of alternatives;
4. purchase decision; and
5. post-purchase evaluation.

Remember, though, that the buying process begins long before the decision is made and continues beyond the actual purchase.

Problem Recognition

Something triggers the consumer to begin the purchase decision process, and it is this first step that we call problem recognition. Put another way, problem recognition occurs when a person perceives a difference between an ideal state of affairs and the actual state at a given moment.[2] For example, the problem recognition stage for a student wanting to purchase a compact disk player may start after he or she gets a check from grandma, or it may start after a friend buys one. For a product like toothpaste, problem recognition may occur when a consumer sees a preferred brand on sale, or it may be triggered when he or she notices that the current tube is close to empty. Problem recognition often occurs gradually, but may also happen quickly, as in an impulse purchase.

Marketing efforts are also important in triggering the problem recognition stage of the purchase decision process. Many buying decisions are initiated by consumers after they notice advertisements for a product or notice that an item is on sale. Packaging can attract attention to a product. Personal selling can convince potential buyers that they have an unfulfilled need or want. A number of psychological factors, discussed later in this chapter, help explain what happens at the problem recognition stage.

Consumers go through several stages before deciding which item to buy.

Information-Seeking

After an individual recognizes a need, the next step is information-seeking. Often, the consumer does not even know what options are available, and much of the information search is concentrated on identifying products or services that are consistent with his or her needs. For example, the student buying a new stereo system might begin the search for information by visiting several stereo shops or talking with friends about different brands, necessary features, and technical specifications.

The amount and type of information gathered will vary, depending on the product and consumer. For some major purchases, such as stereo systems and automobiles, a great deal of information will be gathered from many different sources. For other frequently purchased, low-priced products like toothpaste and candy bars, only a minimal amount of information is typically gathered. In the purchase of toothpaste, for example, most consumers will only need information about the price and size (number of ounces) of one or two brands, and will obtain this information at the point of purchase. Many consumers are loyal to one brand or will always buy the same size. These buyers don't really need any information at all.

There are several different ways of classifying the types of information sought by consumers. The information-seeking process begins with a cognitive *internal search.*

This is the mental process of remembering information stored in memory that may be helpful in making a decision. After the internal search, the consumer may proceed through the other stages of the purchase decision process or may decide to undertake an *external search,* the search for information from sources other than memory.[3]

The major sources of external search are the following:

1. *Personal Sources.* Friends, relatives, and acquaintances are called personal sources of information and often provide the consumer with much information. In addition, personal sources are important because the consumer trusts them, even though the information is not always accurate.
2. *Marketer-Dominated Sources.* This type of information includes advertising, salespersons, packaging, displays, channels of distribution, and pricing. Much marketer-dominated information is typically available to consumers with virtually no search effort required.
3. *Public Sources.* These include magazine and newspaper articles, consumer rating organizations such as *Consumer Reports,* and government agencies. The information from public sources is often important to consumers because of its unbiased and factual nature.
4. *Experience Sources.* For a number of products, the most important information source comes from the consumer's own experience (not including past experience stored in the consumer's memory). Included in this category is handling the product, carefully examining the features, and actually using the product, as in a test drive of an automobile.

Table 5–1 presents the results of a recent study of appliance buyers, documenting the types of information used by the buyers and identifying the information sources that buyers found most helpful. The sources of information available to buyers of organizational products are somewhat different from the sources used by consumers. These will be discussed in the next chapter.

Evaluation of Alternatives

The information-seeking process helps clarify the various alternatives available to the consumer and helps evaluate those alternatives. Typically, the information search will yield an **evoked set,** or a group of brands that a consumer will consider when making a purchase decision. Even when a large number of brands are available in a product category, consumers will usually limit their evoked set to a relatively small number of brands.[4]

Several things are important in evaluating the alternatives in the evoked set. The first step is to identify the criteria that the consumer will use. For example, students buying stereo systems will use some combination of the following criteria:

- Price
- Brand name
- Quality of the sound
- Appearance of the system
- Amount of prestige associated with the system
- Warranty, number of amps, and other technical specifications
- Availability of features such as noise filters, Dolby adaptors, and audio muting switches

Table 5–1 Information Sources Used in the Purchase of Appliances

Information Source	Buyers Who Consulted	Buyers Who Found Source Useful	Buyer's "Most Useful" Source
1. Appliance Salesperson	59%	49%	41%
2. Newspaper Ad	39	28	13
3. Friend or Relative	38	31	13
4. Catalog	35	28	9
5. Brochures/Labels	28	25	9
6. Consumer Reports	20	18	9
7. Appliance Repairperson	14	10	5
8. Magazine Ad	12	7	1
9. TV Ad	10	5	1

*To be read: "59% of the buyers reported having consulted a salesperson as an information source. Almost all of these people (49% of the total sample) reported finding the salesperson to be a 'useful' source of information. When asked which source had been the 'most useful,' 41% of consumers reported that the salesperson had been."

SOURCE: William L. Wilkie and Peter R. Dickson, "Shopping for Appliances: Consumers' Strategies and Patterns of Information Search," Marketing Science Institute Report No. 85–108, November 1985, p. 13.

The second step is to determine the importance of each factor used. Although price may be used as a criterion by virtually all consumers, some people will give the price a very heavy weighting and others will consider it a relatively minor factor. Price is a minor factor if it is low relative to the buyer's income, or if the price differences among alternatives are not significant.

The third aspect of the evaluation process concerns consumer perceptions and values. Two consumers may use the same evaluation criterion and give it the same weighting, but they may still have very different consumer behaviors. For example, both consumers may determine that taste is very important in evaluating toothpaste alternatives, but one may rate Crest very high on this dimension, while the other may think that the taste of Crest is awful.

Advertising can be used to provide information to consumers which will influence the criteria used to evaluate alternatives. Note how the Crest ad on page 140 informs consumers about the merits of Crest toothpaste and stresses the endorsement of the American Dental Association.

Purchase Decision

Once the consumer has evaluated the alternatives, he or she will rank the brands in the evoked set and may arrive at a tentative decision to buy the top-ranked brand. The final decision may vary from this intended one, however, if, say, the preferred brand was not available. The consumer might purchase the second-ranked brand instead of waiting for the top-ranked brand. The actual purchase might also be delayed until the consumer had selected a retail outlet and completed any final price negotiations.

Crest. Because enamel
is more precious than gold.
A cavity can cost you one of your most valuable possessions.
A healthy tooth.
That's why you should help stop cavities before they have a chance to start, by brushing with Crest. The toothpaste that, over the years, has helped prevent more cavities than all others combined.
Because every time you prevent a cavity, you're saving something more precious than gold.
A healthy tooth.
The dentists' choice for fighting cavities.
Crest
Mint Flavor
ADA
"Crest has been shown to be an effective decay-preventive dentifrice that can be of significant value when used in a conscientiously applied program of oral hygiene and regular professional care." Council on Dental Therapeutics, American Dental Association. © P&G 1988

Some advertising provides consumers with important information to influence their purchase decision.

Postpurchase Evaluation

After the purchase has been completed, postpurchase evaluation takes place. Two outcomes are possible. First, the consumer may be satisfied if the product performance is consistent with the consumer's expectations. Information about the product will then be stored in memory, to be used the next time the consumer enters the problem recognition stage of the purchase decision process.

On the other hand, if the consumer is dissatisfied, he or she may behave differently. Consider a consumer in the market for a new car. If the consumer owned a Ford Mustang and loved it, he or she might find out only about the new models of the Mustang. The evoked set might only include Ford products, or even just Mustangs. If the consumer had been unhappy with the Ford Mustang, he or she probably would consider many more alternatives and would undoubtedly seek more information.

Types of Decision-Making Processes

As we have seen, consumer behavior for the purchase of a stereo system will be very different from behavior for the purchase of toothpaste. To distinguish among the various types of buying situations, Howard and Sheth have identified three different types of problem-solving buying behavior: extensive problem-solving, limited problem-solving, and routine response behavior.[5]

Extensive Problem-Solving. For products like stereo systems, automobiles, houses, and condominiums, consumers spend a great deal of time and effort at each stage of the purchase decision process. Consumers engaging in extensive problem-solving behavior tend to use a large number of criteria to evaluate alternative brands, have a relatively large evoked set of brands to evaluate, and spend a great deal of time seeking information and making their decisions. Marketers of products and services for which most consumers use extensive problem-solving must provide the target market with the information it needs to make decisions. Consumers usually haven't bought these products in a long time, if ever, and will thus need the information to help them make their decisions.

Limited Problem-Solving. In limited problem-solving situations, such as buying small appliances or clothing, consumers are typically familiar with the product class, but may not be familiar with all the alternatives available to them. As a result, much less information-seeking takes place, and much of the information search will occur at the point of purchase.

Take shirts as an example. Typically, several criteria, such as color, price, collar style, and brand name, are used to choose from among a number of alternatives and at least several alternatives would be included in the evoked set. A modest amount of thinking and a moderately long period for the purchase decision process are typical for limited problem-solving situations.

Routine Response Behavior. Our discussion of the purchase decision process for toothpaste is an example of routine response behavior, the least complex type of buyer behavior. For products in this category, consumers seek virtually no information and do not formally evaluate alternatives. Instead, the decision is automatic. For example, a hungry consumer passes a vending machine (problem recognition) and stops to purchase his or her favorite brand of candy bar. The purchase decision process is very quick; almost no thinking is involved in the process. Routine response behavior is normally associated with frequently purchased, low-priced consumer products.

Routine response behavior purchases are sometimes called *low involvement purchases,* indicating the product is not very important to the consumer, and the alternatives available are perceived as being similar. Examples include facial tissues, paper clips, and canned peas. *High involvement purchases* are those that are important to the consumer and are often closely tied to consumers' egos and self-images. Cosmetics, stereos, and automobiles are examples of high involvement products, which typically are associated with extensive problem-solving.[6]

So far in this chapter we have been discussing the stages of the purchase decision process. We now turn our attention to some of the many factors that influence that process. Figure 5–2 presents an expanded model of consumer behavior that includes the purchase decision process together with the direct and inferred influences on it. The direct influences include demographic factors (such as those discussed in Chapter 4), marketing mix factors, and situational factors. Among the inferred influences are psychological factors, social factors, and social-cultural factors.

Figure 5–2 Expanded Model of Consumer Behavior

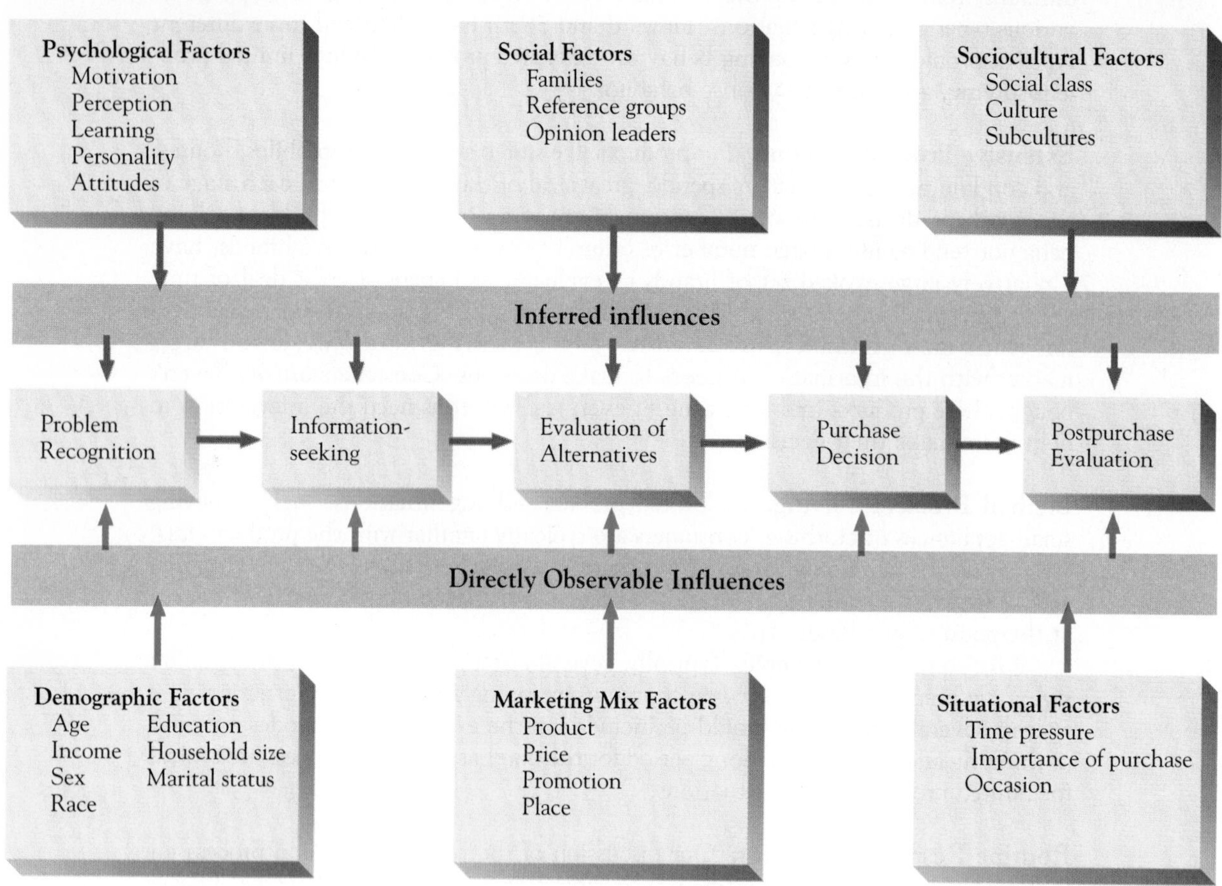

Directly Observed Influences on Consumer Behavior

Some influences on consumer behavior can be directly observed and measured, while others must be inferred. For example, the impact of a retailer placing a large "sale" sign in the window of his or her store can be an important influence in triggering the start of the purchase decision process for consumers walking by the store. Many of these consumers will notice the sign and quickly begin the problem recognition stage, stopping and entering the store to obtain information about the sale item. The sign is, thus, a very direct influence on consumer behavior.

Each year, close to 100,000 baby boomer consumers buy BMW automobiles, at prices ranging from about $25,000 to well over $50,000. If they are asked why they bought that kind of car when alternatives are available at less than half the cost, they may cite the quality, superior engineering, or resale value of the car. Many students of consumer behavior, however, would attribute the choice of this particular car to such social factors as a desire for prestige and acceptance by one's peers. It is extremely difficult to measure these influences, so their importance can only be inferred, but they are no less important to an understanding of consumer behavior.

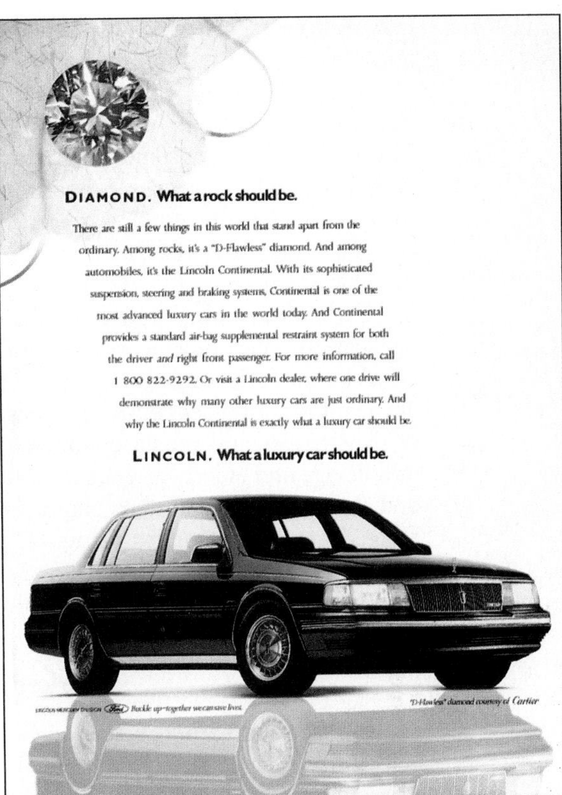

Prestige is an inferred influence on consumer buying behavior whether spending $40.00 or $40,000.

Marketers must thoroughly understand both inferred and direct influences on consumer behavior, which include demographic factors, marketing mix factors, and situational factors.

Demographic Factors

Chapter 4 dealt extensively with the demographic makeup and trends in the population of the United States. These demographic variables play an important role in the consumer purchase process. Depending on the product or service being considered, different demographic factors can have important impacts at different stages of the purchase decision process. Take another look at our stereo system example and look at the impact of income on the purchase decision process for this product.

A very wealthy consumer may enter the problem recognition stage each time a new breakthrough in technology occurs, purchasing a new stereo system every few years. An individual with far less income will enter this stage much less frequently and may be more likely to be buying a system for the first time rather than as a replacement. When his or her system does need replacement, this consumer may replace the system one piece at a time because of the prohibitive cost of replacing the whole system. At the information-seeking stage, the less wealthy consumer may be trying to find the lowest-priced system that meets his or her minimum quality level, whereas the wealthy consumer may only be trying to determine which system offers the highest quality available. The high-income consumer may seek out information from more expensive specialty stores, while a counterpart with less income may seek out discount outlets.

The two consumers would undoubtedly use different criteria to evaluate the alternatives and would also probably have different sets of alternatives to consider. The less wealthy consumer might have a much larger evoked set to evaluate and probably would take much longer to make a purchase decision. The factors used at the postpurchase evaluation stage could be very similar, but if the very wealthy consumer were dissatisfied, he or she might be triggered to enter the problem recognition stage again quickly.

Each of the other important demographic variables—age, sex, education, and occupation—can be important, and marketers must carefully examine the buyer behavior for each segment of their market. Age, for example, is often very important at the information-seeking stage, because younger people tend to have different kinds of experiences and media exposure. They use different media from those used by middle-age and elderly consumers. They listen to much more radio than other groups and choose different stations. They watch less television and they are much less likely to read newspapers or magazines. Companies like McDonald's, therefore, spend a portion of their media budget on radio to reach teenagers whom they might otherwise miss with their regular advertising program.

Marketing Mix Factors

As we discussed earlier, a thorough understanding of buyer behavior is necessary before marketers design their product, pricing, promotion, and distribution strategy. These marketing mix actions can also affect consumer behavior. A retailer putting up a "sale" sign in his or her store window can certainly trigger the problem recognition stage for many consumers. The communications initiated by marketers can certainly affect the information-seeking stage of consumers' purchase decision process and will have an impact on how information is processed.

The evaluation-of-alternatives stage of the purchase decision process can be influenced by the promotion strategy used by the marketer. Apple Computer initiated a program enabling potential computer buyers with acceptable credit to take home Macintosh computers for trial. The company used ads saying "Take Macintosh out for a test drive." A major purpose of the program was to encourage computer buyers to add Macintosh to their evoked sets and to influence the criteria that consumers used to evaluate the personal computers in their evoked set.

A company's marketing mix can also influence the postpurchase evaluation stage of the purchase decision process. The way a car manufacturer honors its warranty will have a direct impact on consumer satisfaction. The reliability and quality designed into the product itself will play a major role in consumers' postpurchase evaluation.

Situational Factors

The situations consumers find themselves in can also have direct influence on their purchase behavior. Consider, for example, the consumer behavior of a person who has a tire blow out one block away from a service station. The amount of information sought and the number of alternatives considered would vary substantially depending upon the status of the spare tire. Without a good spare, the consumer might purchase a new tire from the nearby gas station, particularly if it were the only seller of tires in the area. If, on the other hand, the spare were in good shape, the consumer might take considerable time in buying another tire, looking at which stores had tires on sale and perhaps calling or visiting several stores to identify and evaluate the alternatives.

The importance of the purchase can also have a direct influence upon the purchase decision process. A young woman buying a dress to wear to the junior prom might behave very differently from the way she would in purchasing a dress to wear to her afterschool job. A different set of information sources might be used, with personal sources, such as friends, playing a much more important role. She would probably have a different set of evaluative criteria. Price and versatility, for example, would probably be less important than style, color, and "social acceptability."

Review Your Marketing Knowledge

• Think of a major purchase you have made recently. What type of problem-solving behavior did this purchase represent? Why?

• Describe the purchase decision process you went through in this purchase. What information sources did you use, and what criteria did you use to evaluate the alternatives you considered?

Inferred Influences on Consumer Behavior

We now turn our attention to the many influences on consumer behavior that are less direct and observable; their impact on consumer behavior can only be inferred. The inferred influences discussed in this section are psychological factors, social factors, and social-cultural factors.

Psychological Factors

Much of what we know about how consumers behave is based on theories and research from the field of psychology, the study of individual behavior. In analyzing consumers' purchase decision processes, such psychological factors as motivation, perception, learning, personality, and attitudes are important to understand, since they can help explain the *why* behind consumer behavior. It is virtually impossible to directly determine the influence of these factors; thus, it must be inferred. It is impossible to observe directly what is going on in a buyer's mind. Often the consumers themselves do not know why they behave as they do. Other times they do know, but may not be willing to tell the researcher the true reasons for their behavior. So, marketers must study the psychological factors that are relevant to their products or services.

Motivation. Motivation is the basis of all consumer behavior. A basic question marketers must answer is, "What will motivate people to buy my product or service?" **Motivation** can be defined as activity directed toward a goal. This state is generated by tension, which is caused by an unfulfilled need. Consumers strive to reduce the tension by satisfying the need. The need is thus a critical component in the motivation process; when a need is aroused, it becomes a motive or drive stimulating behavior. For example, hunger is a basic need that, when aroused, becomes a motive for satisfying the need—by stopping at a McDonald's restaurant.

There is no agreement among psychologists or consumer behavior scholars on the best way to classify consumer needs. *Physiological needs* are biologically determined and include the need for food, clothing, and shelter. *Psychological needs* are generated by one's social environment; among these are the need for affiliation, belonging, distinctiveness, individualism, personal fulfillment, and status. Table 5–2 presents a

Table 5–2 Some Examples of Motives and the Promotional Appeals Used to Arouse Them

Motive	Areas of Use	Illustrative Appeals
Affection	Telephones, liquor, greeting cards, insurance, writing instruments, charitable organizations, and vacation resorts	Hallmark Cards—"When you care enough to send the very best" Kodak film—"For the times of your life"
Safety	Appliances, toys, air travel, batteries, toothpaste, burglar and fire alarms, and travelers' checks	Children's Tylenol tablets—"The one most pediatricians give their own children" Allstate insurance—"You're in good hands with Allstate" Michelin—"Because so much is riding on your tires"
Achievement	Books, sporting equipment, lawn care products, calculators, colleges, magazines, and liquor	Seagram's V.O. Whiskey—"This sign tells you that you've arrived" MasterCard Gold Card—"All it takes is success."

SOURCE: Adapted from David Loudon and Albert Della Bitta, *Consumer Behavior: Concepts and Applications* (McGraw-Hill, 1979), p. 306.

sample of three basic needs and the promotional appeals directed at arousing these needs in certain product categories.

After needs have been aroused, they can be classified as primary buying motives or selective buying motives. Primary buying motives are associated with categories of products or services. Selective buying motives refer to the selection of particular brands within the product categories. For example, a desire for warmth and beauty in one's home might be a primary motive in the decision to purchase carpeting over other floor coverings. Color, type of fiber, and price might be selective motives determining which specific brand of carpeting is purchased.

Another way to classify motives is to differentiate between product motives—those associated with the particular product or service—and patronage motives, which are associated with the place the product or service will be obtained. Examples of patronage motives include convenience of location, friendly personnel, assortment of products stocked, and services, such as credit and delivery.

Hierarchy of Needs. Abraham Maslow classified consumer needs into five hierarchical categories.

1. Physiological needs: satisfaction of hunger, thirst, and shelter
2. Safety needs: security, protection, order, and stability
3. Love needs: affection, belonging, friendship
4. Esteem needs: self-respect, prestige, success, and achievement
5. Self-actualization needs: desire for self-fulfillment[7]

According to Maslow, the lower-order needs, such as physiological and safety needs, must be satisfied before higher-order needs can emerge. Physiological needs are dominant until they become satisfied. In the United States today, these physiological needs have been satisfied for most consumers, and, thus, the higher-order needs have become the driving force behind much consumer behavior.

Perception. Consumer behavior is strongly affected by the way people perceive themselves and their environment. If two individuals perceive a product, its price, or its features in different ways, they are likely to behave differently with respect to the product. **Perception** can be defined as the process through which incoming stimuli are organized, interpreted, and given meaning.[8] More specifically, we can say that perception is a two-step process, as follows:

To perceive is to	see, hear, touch, taste, smell, *or* sense internally	⟶	some	thing, event, *or* relation	⟶ and to	organize interpret, *and* derive meaning from the experience.[9]

Several principles associated with the concept of perception are important for the marketer to understand. Perception is a process consisting of a series of interrelated activities. It is selective, and people perceive only a small proportion of all the stimuli with which they are bombarded. For example, although consumers may be exposed to a large number of advertisements on billboards, in the newspaper, and on television, they actually perceive only a small number of them. Their perceptions depend upon external stimuli and personal factors.[10]

The nature of the external stimulus itself is an important determinant of perception. Larger advertisements are more likely to be noticed that smaller ones, and color ads in magazines or newspapers are more likely to be noticed than black-and-white versions of the same ad. Frequency or repetition can also be important in getting one's message perceived by consumers.

Personal factors strongly affect consumer perceptions. A person's needs, values, attitudes, and experiences will affect the way he or she perceives various marketing stimuli. For example, a person who thinks of himself or herself as being "with it" is more likely to perceive and pay attention to an ad for a sports car than one for a station wagon. A person who has just completed several sets of tennis and is sitting in front of a television set to cool off is more likely to notice an ad for a soft drink than if he or she had seen the same ad at 7 A.M. while getting dressed. Past experiences also lead to product preferences; people are more likely to perceive ads for products they prefer.

Perception has a number of marketing implications. Consumers respond to a product offering in terms of its **brand image**—the meaning consumers give to a product based on the perceived benefits that the product provides. Thus, the *way* consumers perceive a product's benefits is much more important than the actual attributes are. For example, one brand of film might offer an extremely attractive value to the consumer; it might have comparable quality to another brand but sell at a much lower price. If the consumer, however, perceives that Kodak film is much better, the fact that a competitor's product actually is a better value will be irrelevant. Brand image and consumer's self-concept sometimes work together in the consumer purchase decision process. A famous study by Grubb and Hupp found that buyers of Volkswagens and Pontiac GTOs had different self-concepts, and, therefore, had different perceptions of the owners of each model car.[11] The buyers of Volkswagens, for example, thought that they had similar self-concepts to other Volkswagen owners, and they thought of themselves as different from owners of competing brands.

MARKETING IN ACTION

The Beef Industry Council Tries to Make Beef Appetizing Again

"What do you expect for 300 calories?" asks the narrator of a new set of commercials running on television screens across the country. With Beethoven's "Ode to Joy" providing background flavor, the surprising answer comes: beef, as depicted in a dozen concoctions from shish kebab to stew. The ads are part of a $10 million promotional campaign cooked up by the Beef Industry Council, the trade group that has taken on the formidable task of turning around a product gone lame. Says John Francis, director of marketing for the Beef Industry Council, "We've got to make our meat trendy."

Beef has been losing ground to chicken, leaving many ranchers in financial trouble. Because the red meat has come to be perceived as expensive, time-consuming to prepare, full of fat, and generally unhealthful, per capita consumption fell from a high of 94 pounds in 1976 to an estimated 75 pounds in 1985. Over the same period, per capita poultry consumption rose from 43 pounds a year to 70 pounds, nearly equaling beef consumption. Although 90 percent of the population still typically have red meat in the fridge, the percentage of respondents who characterize themselves as "meat lovers" in surveys conducted by the opinion research firm of Yankelovitch Skelly & White dropped from 22 percent in 1983 to 10 percent in 1985.

In fighting back, beef's proponents point out that their product is leaner, the result of 25 years of improved livestock. Indeed, the council is making much of new Department of Agriculture data that put beef in approximately the same nutritional ballpark as chicken—a well-trimmed, three-ounce sirloin steak has 185 calories and 75 milligrams of cholesterol; a three-ounce piece of boneless chicken breast has 140 calories and 72 milligrams of cholesterol. At many supermarket meat counters, display charts supplied by the industry will show a cut's calorie and cholesterol levels, together with other nutritional information, right alongside dietary standards recommended by the American Heart Association. In addition to the TV spots, which are running in the ten largest U.S. cities, ads in magazines such as *Bon Appetit*, *Glamour*, and *Parents* will blazon the industry's tag lines: "Beef. Good news for people who eat," and, "I've got a taste for some real food."

SOURCE: Edward Baig, "Trying to Make Beef Appetizing Again," *Fortune*, November 25, 1985, p. 64.

In another experiment on the impact of perception on buying behavior, Rolls Royce Motor Company ran an ad in *Architectural Digest* that let readers scratch a spot on the ad and smell the leathery Rolls interiors. Calls to the company increased by fourfold the month after the ad appeared.[12] An example of how the Beef Industry Council is trying to change consumers' perceptions of beef is presented in the *Marketing in Action* feature above.

Perception is also important in determining the price-quality relationship among brands.[13] For the many purchases where buyers have limited information available, price may serve as an indicator of product quality. Consumers appear to perceive a positive price-quality relationship: expensive products are perceived as being of better quality. Consumers may refrain from purchasing a product if they think a price is either too high or too low.

Perception is also important in evaluating the risk associated with a purchase. "Consumer behavior involves risk in the sense that any action of a consumer will produce consequences which he or she cannot anticipate with anything approximating certainty, and some of which, at least, are likely to be unpleasant."[14] This definition points out the two important dimensions of **perceived risk**—possible negative consequences and level of uncertainty (the probability the negative consequences will occur). Consumers generally strive to reduce risk in their purchase decision processes, either by reducing the negative consequences or by reducing the perceived probability that the negative consequences will occur.

There are several different types of perceived risk. *Financial perceived risk* is associated with the cost of the product, relative to the consumer's income. *Functional perceived risk* is concerned with product performance: Will the product function as it is supposed to? Another type, *psychosocial perceived risk,* is concerned with whether the product will enhance one's sense of self-concept or well-being: Will the product please others whose opinions the consumer values, and will the buyer feel good using the product? Functional risk may be more important to a consumer who is buying a carpet for a high traffic area and is concerned that it might wear out too fast. A consumer buying carpeting for a living room that is infrequently used might be much more concerned with psychosocial risk.

Perceived risk can be reduced either by reducing the negative consequences or by reducing the perceived probability of the negative consequences occurring. For example, General Electric sought to reduce consumers' perceived negative consequences by offering a "Satisfaction Guaranteed" 90 day refund or exchange option on all GE major appliances. Michelin seeks to reduce the perceived probability of negative consequences occurring for users of its tires by advertising "Michelin. Because So Much Is Riding on Your Tires" (and includes a picture of a baby next to a Michelin tire). If a product has high perceived psychosocial risk, consumers will tend to rely more on personal sources of information. If a product has high functional perceived risk, consumers will tend to seek out performance information, often from impersonal sources such as *Consumer Reports* magazine.

Learning. Consumer's perceptions and their motivation to buy or not buy products and services are primarily a function of learning. We define **learning** as changes in an individual's behavior resulting from previous experiences and information. Learning affects values, attitudes, personality, taste, and almost every other aspect of our behavior as consumers. To illustrate this, let's take another look at the purchase decision process. Consumers purchasing tennis balls for the first time will often do a considerable amount of information-seeking and may have some difficulty determining how to select from among the available alternatives. After they have purchased and used various brands of tennis balls a few times, however, they will have learned about the product category and the alternative brands available. This learning will enable them to conduct the information search by examining their memory instead of having to conduct an external search for information. After many purchases have been made, the consumer may engage in routine response behavior instead of limited or extensive problem-solving behavior.

Learning is a difficult concept to study because it is impossible to observe. Instead, we can only observe changes in behavior which, we can infer, come about because of learning. The stimulus-response model is the way most psychologists believe learning takes place.[15] The major components of the stimulus-response model are drive, cue, response, and reinforcement. We have defined drive previously as a state of tension caused by an unfulfilled need. The drive will stimulate action to reduce the tension. Hunger, fear, and a need for prestige are examples of drives. A **cue** is a stimulus in the environment that determines the type of response to a drive. Examples of cues include an advertisement for a fast-food restaurant, a coupon for fifty cents off one's next purchase, or an in-store display. **Response** represents an individual's reaction to cues or drives in the environment, such as the purchase of a hamburger

MICHELIN. BECAUSE SO MUCH IS RIDING ON YOUR TIRES.
Michelin is guided by a single overriding concept: tires are the most important pieces of equipment you can put on your car.
Therefore, making the best tires, regardless of cost, is an obsession with us.
That is why we make our own steel for our steel-belted radials. Why we take so long to develop and test each tire model.
That is also why Michelins perform as well as they perform. And last as long as they last. And why they cost more.
Though you may find, as many Michelin buyers do, they end up costing less to own in the long run.
MICHELIN

This ad reduces the perceived probability of negative consequences occurring.

at Wendy's. To the extent that a direct relationship exists between a stimulus and a response to that stimulus, learning has taken place. **Reinforcement** represents the reduction in a drive that results from a satisfying response. When reinforcement occurs, the probability that the same response will be duplicated in the future is increased—*habit formation* takes place. Thus, if the Wendy's hamburger is satisfactory, individuals may buy there again when they become hungry. If the response is not reinforced over time, *extinction* occurs, and the learned habit ceases.

Review Your Marketing Knowledge

- You are the head of marketing for a leading maker of tennis rackets. How much perceived risk do you think there is for buyers of this product? What type?
- What steps could you take to help consumers reduce the perceived risk?

Many of the products consumers buy are habitual responses resulting from previous satisfaction with products. The consumer demonstrates the close link between learning, habit, and brand loyalty. **Brand loyalty** exists when there is a favorable attitude toward, and consistent purchase of, a single brand over time.

The Coca-Cola Company found out the magnitude of consumers' brand loyalty to Coke when, in 1985, they changed the formula for the product. Millions of consumers protested by refusing to buy the new Coke product. Even though taste tests had shown that the new Coke was preferred in blind testing, it was obvious that consumers were loyal to the original Coke, and the company was forced to reintroduce the product, now named Coca-Cola Classic.

Personality. Some 200 studies have been reported in the marketing literature relating personality to consumer purchasing behavior, media choice, segmentation, and product choice, among others. A review of these studies has been characterized by the word *equivocal.*[16] One major review article concludes, "A few studies indicate a strong relationship between personality and aspects of consumer behavior, a few indicate no relationship, and a great majority indicate that if correlations do exist they are so weak as to be questionable or perhaps meaningless."[17]

Unfortunately, psychologists have not been able to agree on any definition of the term *personality*. Personality is a stronger concept than lifestyle, since personality reflects consistent, enduring behavioral responses to the stimuli one encounters in one's environment. Individuals tend to be consistently aggressive or submissive, extroverted or introverted, impulsive or orderly, or dominant or compliant. Marketers have long assumed that personality variables should be related to consumer behavior, even though there are very few examples from the research literature to support this conclusion.

Attitudes. Consumer attitudes are considered by many marketers to be accurate predictors of consumer behavior, making the study of attitude formation and change an important topic. **Attitudes** are learned tendencies to perceive and act in a consistent way toward a given object or idea, such as a product, service, brand, company, store, or spokesperson.[18] This definition emphasizes the impact on attitudes of several of the other concepts we have studied earlier in this chapter.

Attitudes, for example, are learned, and are derived from previous experiences and information. They are more strongly held and enduring than beliefs or perceptions and play a strong role in the formation of perceptions and brand images. Motivation is also involved in attitude formation. Attitudes are only *tendencies* to perceive and act; the behavior of consumers, however, may be more influenced by the particular situation. For example, a consumer may have a very favorable attitude toward a Nikon camera, but may purchase a Kodak, because he or she does not have enough money available to buy the Nikon. This example also demonstrates the importance of measuring the right attitude. One should measure the attitude toward *purchasing* the Nikon (which could be negative), not the attitude toward the camera itself (which may be positive).

According to traditional models, attitudes have three elements—a *cognitive* component (perceptions and beliefs), an *affective* component (evaluation, positive and negative feelings), and a *behavioral* component (intentions, preference, or purchase).[19] The three components of attitudes are typically congruent. For example, if consumers perceive that the product has the attributes they want, they are likely to have favorable feelings toward it and to be inclined to buy it. The three components reinforce each other. People's perceptions of the world influence their evaluations, which, in turn, affect their behavior.

A consumer may believe that Sony makes a high-quality television at a reasonable price, may rate Sony very highly, and may intend to buy one some day. However,

MARKETING IN ACTION

The Birth of USAir

In 1974, extensive marketing research by Allegheny Airlines showed that the nation's sixth largest airline was misperceived by a sizable percentage of the public as a small airline. Both quantitative and qualitative research produced findings that convinced the airline's management of a serious image problem: The public believed that small airlines were bad and big airlines were good. In actuality, since its 1972 merger with the former Mohawk Airlines, Allegheny had been the nation's sixth largest airline in terms of passenger boardings—ranking ahead of all but United, TWA, American, Eastern, and Delta.

The first and foremost chore of the marketing department was to change the public's perception, a task begun in early 1976 when J. Walter Thompson became the airline's agency and designed a "Big Airline . . ." campaign. The ads positioned Allegheny against the airlines already recognized as industry giants. "Big facts" point out that: Allegheny carried 4 million more passengers each year than Pan Am; Allegheny flew to "more American cities than American;" and Allegheny operated more daily flights than TWA. "It takes a Big Airline . . ." to do these things was the tag line reminder in all advertisements.

The 1974 research also made it clear that one of the reasons Allegheny could not shake the "smallness" image was the airline's name. "Allegheny" had regional connotations along with accompanying limitations. Management decided to change to a name that would more accurately represent the airline's new standing. But the time for such a change was not yet right. Officials wanted the new name to connote an airline of national scope and character, but Allegheny's service area was still confined primarily to the Northeast. It was decided that the airline had to grow geographically before changing its name. And the fuel crunch of 1973–74 was not helping the situation.

That time came in October 1978 with the advent of the Airline Deregulation Act. With deregulation came open and rapid entry into new markets during 1978 and 1979: Tampa, Orlando, and West Palm Beach, Florida; Birmingham, Alabama; New Orleans, Louisiana; Raleigh/Durham, North Carolina; Phoenix and Tucson, Arizona.

In March 1978, Chairman and President Edwin I. Colodny announced that Allegheny would become USAir on October 28. An internal working committee was formed by representatives of nearly every operating department within the company, and promotion and marketing plans were drawn up and budgeted. In partnership with J. Walter Thompson, the advertising and sales promotion department undertook the massive task of planning and executing an advertising and promotional campaign designed to quickly eliminate conscious recall of the Allegheny name while generating awareness of USAir as a new and growing major domestic carrier. By the late 1980s, they had acquired PSA Airlines and Piedmont Airlines, and had begun the process of putting these airlines' routes under the USAir brand name.

SOURCE: Harry T. Chandis, "The Birth of USAir," *Marketing Communications*, April 1980, pp. 30–32.

---

the actual behavior of buying a Sony TV may be influenced more by the consumer's financial status and the condition of the television already owned. A study of the relationship between buying intentions and purchases of automobiles indicated that 63 percent of those who planned to buy a new car within the next year actually did, and 29 percent of those who did not intend to actually purchased one.[20]

Once attitudes have been formed, they are not easy to change. Often, they change only after perceptions and beliefs have been changed. An example of the steps one company has taken to change consumer attitudes and some of the difficulties they encountered are presented in the *Marketing in Action* feature, "The Birth of USAir," above.

Social Factors

The inferred influences we have been studying to this point in the chapter have been the psychological factors of motivation, perception, learning, personality, and attitudes. These influences on consumer behavior all come from within the individual. But consumer behavior is also affected by social factors and other individuals. In this section, we will look at families, reference groups, and opinion leaders—three important social factors.

Families. Have you ever seen a family shopping together in a supermarket? If you have, you probably observed a number of discussions among family members concerning what to buy. Perhaps one of the children argued strenuously for a certain brand of cereal, and the father insisted upon a certain type of frozen pizza or dessert. This interaction among family members in making purchase decisions demonstrates the impact our families have on our purchasing behavior.

A recent study of husband-wife influence on buying decisions for 141 products, sponsored by 13 major consumer magazines, found that wives played the dominant role in the purchase of soft drinks, food products, most personal care products, home furnishings, stoves and refrigerators, and airline tickets for vacations. Husbands were dominant in the purchase of automobiles, beer and liquor, tires, 35 mm. cameras, personal computers, VCRs, stocks, and auto insurance. The decisions were jointly made for fast-food eating, film, microwave ovens, telephones, life insurance, and expensive jewelry.[21]

Children also play an important role in purchasing behavior for a number of different products. The extent of children's influence varies dramatically by product category. A major study by Ward and Wackman of the influence of children, ages five to twelve, found that 87 percent of mothers yielded to children's requests for specific breakfast cereals.[22] Children (particularly the older children) also had considerable influence on the purchase of products they consume, such as snacks, candy, soft drinks, games and toys, toothpaste, and clothing. Children had virtually no influence on the purchase of such products as gasoline, laundry soap, automobiles, cameras, and household items.

Consumer socialization is the process by which young people acquire skills, knowledge, and attitudes that help them function as consumers. A study by Moschis and Moore of adolescents' purchasing behavior demonstrated the importance of parents in the consumer socialization process.[23] They found that parents were preferred to friends as a source of information almost twice as often. For products where price, social acceptance, and performance is of great concern (such as watches, dress shoes, pocket calculators, and hair dryers), preference for parental advice was substantial. The use of peers as a source of information was important in buying decisions for items where peer acceptance was important, such as sunglasses and wallets.

Reference Groups. Did you ever wonder why so many people wear clothing with designer initials or symbols on them and why others put STP decals on their automobiles? These are all indications of the impact of reference group influence. A **reference group** is a group that the individual uses as a reference point in the formation of his or her beliefs, attitudes, values, and/or behavior. The individual also identifies with or aspires to membership in this group. Family groups, work groups, religious groups, fraternal organizations, civic or professional associations, and close friends are used by consumers as points of reference in determining their own beliefs, attitudes, values, and behavior.

Table 5-3 Reference Group Influence

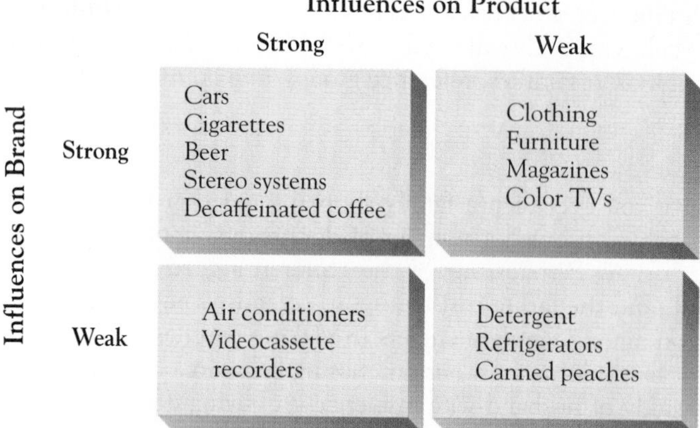

Influences on Brand	Influences on Product: Strong	Influences on Product: Weak
Strong	Cars Cigarettes Beer Stereo systems Decaffeinated coffee	Clothing Furniture Magazines Color TVs
Weak	Air conditioners Videocassette recorders	Detergent Refrigerators Canned peaches

SOURCE: Based on Francis S. Bourne, "Group Influence in Marketing and Public Relations," in Rensis Likert and Samuel P. Hayes, Jr., eds., *Some Applications of Behavioral Research* (UNESCO 1957).

The importance of reference groups in consumer behavior depends on the product category. In general, the more conspicuous a product is, the more important group influence will be. According to Bourne, reference groups (1) influence the purchase or product but not the individual brand selected, (2) influence the choice of a particular brand, but don't influence the decision to purchase the product, (3) influence both the product and brand decisions, and (4) don't influence the product or the brand.[24] Table 5–3 uses these categories to classify the reference group influence for a number of products.

Opinion Leaders. In introducing a revolutionary new type of golf ball, the Dunlop Corporation spent considerable resources trying to convince golf pros that the new product, the Maxfli DDH, was far superior to existing alternatives. They were successful in influencing a number of pros, who then encouraged other individuals to use the new product. This is an example of the concepts of opinion leadership and the two-step flow of communications. **Opinion leaders** are individuals who, because of their knowledge or expertise in certain product or service categories, are able to exert personal influence on other consumers of these products or services. Arnold Palmer and Chuck Yeager are two examples of opinion leaders. The **two-step flow of communication** is a process using the mass media to reach opinion leaders, who then can communicate the information to the followers.[25] Opinion leaders are important to marketers because they are likely to be the first consumers to purchase new products and are more likely to discuss products with other potential consumers.

It is difficult to identify opinion leaders, however. Often there are few demographic or psychographic differences between opinion leaders and followers.[26] But opinion leaders do display certain product-related characteristics, such as the following. They are:

- more knowledgeable about the product category;
- more interested in the product category;

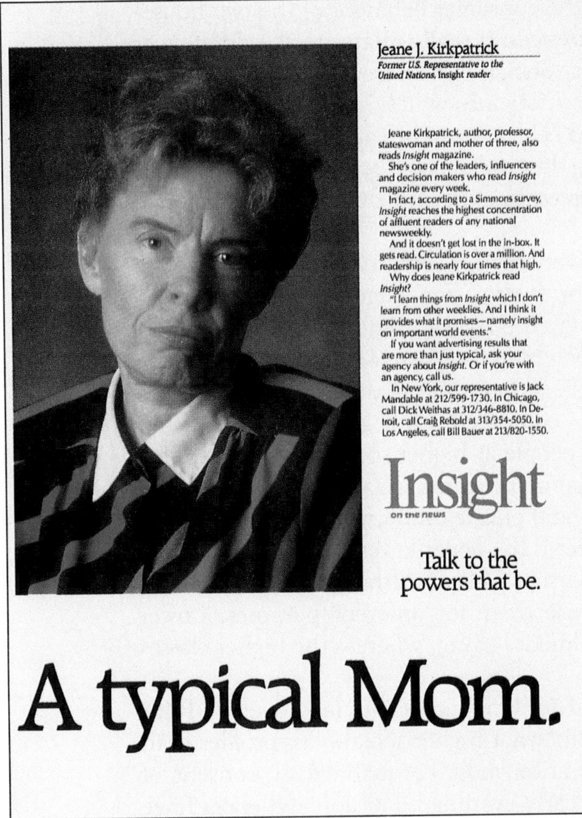

Opinion leaders are important influences on consumer buying behavior.

- more active in receiving communications about the product from personal sources; and
- more likely to read magazines and print media in their area of interest.[27]

Opinion leadership tends to be product-specific, and few generalizations can be made across product categories.

Social-Cultural Factors

In addition to psychological factors and social factors, there are other inferred influences on consumer behavior that we call social-cultural factors. These include the social class, culture, and subcultures to which individuals belong.

Social Class. Think of two households with the following characteristics: each, earning $30,000 per year, consists of a husband and wife in their early thirties with one child who live in a suburban area within a major metropolitan area. It would appear that each of these households, based on this demographic profile, would have similar attitudes, values, and consumer behavior. If another piece of information is added, however, this view might change. Suppose the first household consists of a first-line supervisor at the Ford assembly plant and his wife who works part-time, and the second household consists of an attorney working in the legal department at Ford and her nonworking husband. With this added information, one would assume that the two households did not have similar attitudes, values, and behavior.

The reason for the differences between the consumer behavior of the two households goes far beyond the occupational differences; it really relates to the differences in the social class of each of the households. **Social classes** are defined as relatively permanent and homogeneous divisions in a society into which individuals or families sharing similar values, life-styles, interests, and behavior can be categorized.[28] Although we tend to think of the United States as being the land of equal opportunity, numerous studies have shown that different social classes do exist and that they do influence consumer behavior.

Social class is useful as a segmentation variable for some types of products.[29] It can often be associated with a specific value system (for example, placing a high value on education), which leads to a specific life-style (attending college), which leads to specific consumption patterns (buying books). There are a number of value and life-style differences among the social classes that result in different consumption patterns. Manufacturers of china, silver, ski equipment, and golf equipment often define their markets as *upscale*, appealing to people at higher social-class levels. The markets for air travel, real estate, and financial investments are also typically upscale. Other products, such as bowling, bus travel, and plastic dinnerware, appeal to lower social-class markets. The largest market for beer is the upper-lower social class, whereas imported wines sell best to the upper-middle social class. Although most people in the United States have credit cards, they use them for different purposes. Lower classes tend to use bank credit cards for installment buying, whereas the higher classes use the credit cards for convenience.[30]

Different advertising media often appeal to different social-class levels.[31] Print media, especially magazines, tend to have somewhat higher social-class profiles than radio and television, although the generalization must be qualified by content of programming and time of day. For example, early evening television audiences have a heavier working-class composition, and the late evening audiences have more of a middle-class composition. Fashion, travel, and literary magazines are more often found in middle-class homes, and sports, outdoor, and romance magazines are more often found in working-class homes. Thus, marketers can reach different social classes by carefully selecting appropriate media.

Culture. Marketers must understand the importance of culture on consumer behavior. The impact of culture can be seen in Campbell Soup Company's loss of $1.2 million on its canned soup operations in Brazil.[32] Campbell's soups, mostly vegetable and beef combinations packaged in cans with a variation of their familiar red and white label, failed to catch on with Brazilian women. The Brazilian consumers apparently preferred the dehydrated products of such competitors as Knorr and Maggi, which they could use as a soup starter, adding their own ingredients. Those housewives who did buy Campbell's usually put it aside for an emergency, "like when she was late coming home from a tea party," according to the company's managing director.

What went wrong? Interviews that the company later conducted revealed that the Brazilian woman believed she was not fulfilling her role as a homemaker if she served her family a soup that she did not feel was her own. The company is now more thoroughly studying the local culture, and it may reintroduce a modified soup line more consistent with the Brazilian culture.

Culture is the set of values, attitudes, and ways of doing things that are transmitted from one generation to another within a given society. Culture is learned behavior and plays a large part in determining the customs, morals, and habits of members of a society. What we eat and how we eat it are just two examples of how culture affects our lives. Although cultural values tend to be relatively permanent, they also are dynamic, changing as societies change. For example, some of the cultural changes that have been taking place in the United States in recent years include (a) the changing role of women, (b) increased emphasis on materialism and self among the young, (c) more casual social values, (d) increased importance of children and family, (e) orientation toward individualism and competition over cooperation, and (f) concern for one's health.

As shown by the Campbell's Soup example, it is important for marketers to understand the culture of new markets they plan to enter. Other examples of blunders that have been made include: [33]

- An American firm sent a detailed business proposal to Saudi Arabia, bound in a pigskin cover. It was never read; Muslims are required to avoid hog products.
- A print ad for a men's cologne picturing a man and his dog was run in Northern Africa. The ad had performed well in the U.S., but failed in the new environment where dogs are signs of bad luck and symbols of uncleanliness.
- An American designer introduced a new perfume in Latin America emphasizing its fresh camillia scent. Unfortunately, sales were slow in this market where camillias are considered funeral flowers.

It is obviously very important for marketers to understand and anticipate cultural changes taking place in their markets, since these changes affect marketing strategies. Within any culture, there often exist subcultures, and these groups are also important to marketers.

Subcultures. In the past ten years, American marketers have become much more attuned to the special needs of a number of different subcultures. The most important of these subcultures have been based on race, nationality, religion, and geographic location. Chapter 4 discussed the importance of blacks and Hispanics in market segmentation strategies of marketers and presented a number of examples of companies successfully marketing to these groups. In general, subculture is most important for food products, clothing, furniture, and other items for the home.

Media habits are also substantially different among the various subcultures. Often very specific media, such as Spanish language radio stations, enable a marketer to target a specific subculture group. As subculture groups become increasingly important to marketers during the 1990s, more companies will design products, distribution channels, and promotion strategies to meet the needs of important subcultures.

Personal Computer Exercise

The evaluation of alternative brands involves both subjective and objective factors. This PC exercise enables you to see how subjective perceptions can be used together with objective measures of product attributes to evaluate alternative product offerings.

KEY POINTS

• The study of consumer behavior includes the actions consumers take in buying and using products, as well as the factors involved in the decision-making process leading to these actions.

• The purchase decision process is the series of stages consumers go through in deciding which products to buy. The five stages are problem recognition, information-seeking, evaluation of alternatives, purchase decision, and postpurchase evaluation.

• The amount and type of information gathered and used by the consumer varies according to the type of product and the characteristics of the consumer. The information-seeking process begins with an internal search, supplemented by an external search of personal, marketer-dominated, public, and experienced sources.

• Three types of problem-solving buying behavior are extensive problem-solving, limited problem-solving, and routine response behavior.

• The psychological factors of motivation, perception, learning, personality, and attitude play an important role in determining consumer behavior. These factors have an indirect impact, and the influence they exert must be inferred.

• Consumers respond to product offerings in terms of their brand images. The way consumers perceive the benefits of a product is much more important than the actual product attributes.

• Consumers generally strive to lower perceived risk in their purchase decision processes, either by reducing possible negative consequences or by reducing the perceived probability of the negative consequences occurring.

• Brand loyalty exists when consumers have a favorable attitude toward a single brand which they consistently purchase over time.

• Consumer behavior is also influenced by such social factors as family, reference groups, and opinion leaders.

• Social-cultural factors such as social class, culture, and subculture have a strong impact on consumer behavior.

ISSUES FOR DISCUSSION

1. Think back to your decision process about which college to attend and describe what took place at each stage of the purchase decision process.

2. Think of your most recent clothing purchase. How was your purchase influenced by your (a) perceptions, (b) motives, (c) attitudes, (d) learning, and (e) personality? What role was played by your family, reference groups, and opinion leaders?

3. Classify each of the following products as generally extensive problem-solving, limited problem-solving, or routine response behavior situations for most consumers.

a. automobile tires
b. fast food
c. swimming suits
d. compact disk player
e. soft drinks
f. life insurance policy

4. Describe how the concept of perceived risk applies to the marketing of small portable compact disk players. What marketing actions might a company like Sony take to reduce the perceived risk for consumers?

5. The people who buy central air conditioners are high-income consumers who spend a considerable amount of time and effort determining which unit to buy. Buyers of room air conditioners, on the other hand, often buy on impulse during a heat wave. How does this affect the marketing strategies for a company like Fedders, which markets both products?

6. Name some of the important cultural values in the United States today. What are the implications of these values for the marketing strategies of the following products:

a. BMW automobiles
b. McDonald's hamburgers
c. Reebok shoes
d. Haagen-Dazs ice cream
e. Merrill Lynch stock brokerage accounts
f. Disney World

7. Give two examples of products that satisfy the needs at each stage of Maslow's hierarchy of needs.

8. Discuss the importance of social class and reference groups in the marketing of home computers.

9. Sharp Electronics, a leading maker of copying machines and fax machines for small businesses, has recently targeted the "work at home" market, consisting of 24 million people who earn money by working part-time or full-time out of their homes. What information about buyer behavior would you want before developing a strategy targeted at this segment of the market?

10. What problems, if any, would a bank have in trying to use the two-step flow of communications to market checking accounts to students by enlisting the help of campus opinion leaders?

GLOSSARY

Attitudes: learned tendencies to perceive and act in a consistent way toward a given object or idea, such as a product, service, brand, company, store, or spokesperson.

Brand image: the meaning consumers give to a product based on the perceived benefits that the product provides.

Brand loyalty: a favorable attitude toward and exclusive purchase of a single brand over time.

Consumer behavior: those acts of individuals that involve buying and using products and services, including the decision processes that precede and determine those acts.

Consumer socialization: process by which young people acquire skills, knowledge, and attitudes that help them function as consumers.

Cue: a stimulus in the environment that determines the type of response to a drive.

Culture: the set of values, attitudes, and ways of doing things that are transmitted from one generation to another within a given society.

Drive: a state of tension caused by an unfulfilled need. The drive will stimulate action to reduce the tension.

Evoked set: the group of brands which a consumer will consider when making a purchase decision.

High involvement purchases: those purchases that are important to the consumer and are often closely tied to the consumer's ego and self-image.

Learning: changes in an individual's behavior resulting from previous experiences and information.

Low involvement purchases: those purchases which are not very important to the consumer, and whose available alternatives are perceived as being similar.

Motivation: activity directed toward a goal.

Opinion leaders: individuals who, because of their knowledge or expertise in certain product or service areas, are able to exert personal influence on other consumers of these products or services.

Perceived risk: the possible negative consequences of a purchase decision to the consumer and their probability of occurring (as perceived by the consumer).

Perception: the process of receiving and deriving meaning from stimuli present in our internal and external environment.

Purchase decision process: the series of stages consumers go through in making decisions concerning which products to buy.

Reference group: a group that the individual uses as a reference point in the formation of his or her beliefs, attitudes, values, and/or behavior. The individual also identifies with, or aspires to be a member of, this group.

Reinforcement: reduction in a drive that results from a satisfactory response to a stimulus.

Response: an individual's reaction to cues or drives in the environment.

Self-concept: the way an individual perceives himself or herself.

Social classes: relatively permanent and homogeneous divisions in a society into which individuals or families sharing similar values, life-styles, interests, and behavior can be categorized.

Two-step flow of communication: process of using the mass media to reach opinion leaders, who then communicate the information to the followers.

NOTES

1. James Engel, Roger Blackwell, and Paul Miniard, *Consumer Behavior,* 5th ed., (The Dryden Press, 1986), p. 5.

2. Engel, Blackwell, and Miniard, *Consumer Behavior,* p. 28.

3. For an excellent review of consumer external search, see Joseph W. Newman, "Consumer External Search: Amount and Determinants," in Arch Woodside, Jagdish Sheth, Peter Bennett, eds., *Consumer and Industrial Buying Behavior* (Elsevier North Holland, 1977), pp. 79–94.

4. For more detail on the concept of evoked set, see John Howard and Jagdish Sheth, *The Theory of Buyer Behavior* (Wiley, 1969).

5. Howard and Sheth, *Theory of Buying Behavior,* pp. 27–28.

6. Henry Assael, *Consumer Behavior and Marketing Action,* 3rd Ed., (Kent Publishing Company, 1987), pp. 12–14.

7. See Abraham H. Maslow, "A Theory of Human Motivation," *Psychological Review,* Vol. 50, 1943, pp. 370–96; and Abraham H. Maslow, *Motivation and Personality* (Harper & Row, 1954).

8. Kenneth Runyon and Daid Stewart, *Consumer Behavior and the Practice of Marketing,* 3rd ed., (Merrill Publishing Company, 1987), p. 423.

9. From Paul Thomas Young, *Motivation and Emotion: A Survey of the Determinants of Human and Animal Activity* (Wiley, 1961), pp. 298–99.

10. Thomas Robertson, Joan Zielinski, and Scott Ward, *Consumer Behavior,* (Scott, Foresman and Company, 1984), pp. 166–71.

11. Edward Grubb and Gregg Hupp, "Perception of Self, Generalized Stereotypes, and Brand Selection," *Journal of Marketing Research,* February 1968, pp. 58–63.

12. Nancy Gibbs, *Time,* June 27, 1988, p. 54.

13. Kent Monroe and Susan Petroshius, "Buyers' Perceptions of Price: An Update of the Evidence," in Harold Kassarjian and Thomas Robertson, *Perspectives in Consumer Behavior,* 3rd ed. (Scott, Foresman and Company, 1981) pp. 43–55.

14. Raymont A. Bauer, "Consumer Behavior as Risk Taking," in R. S. Hancock, ed., *Dynamic Marketing for a Changing World* (American Marketing Association, 1960); pp. 389–98. Also see Donald Cox, *Risk Taking and Information Handling in Consumer Behavior* (Division of Research, Graduate School of Business Administration, Harvard University, 1967).

15. This section is based on Thomas Robertson, et. al., *Consumer Behavior,* pp. 192–199.

16. Harold H. Kassarjian and Mary Jane Sheffet, "Personality and Consumer Behavior: An Update," in Harold H. Kassarjian and Thomas S. Robertson, eds., *Perspectives in Consumer Behavior,* 3rd ed. (Scott, Foresman and Company, 1981), p. 160.

17. Harold H. Kassarjian, "Personality and Consumer Behavior: A Review," *Journal of Marketing Research* (November 1971), pp. 409–19.

18. Martin Fishbein and Icek Ajzen, *Belief, Attitude, Intention and Behavior; An Introduction to Theory and Research* (Addison-Wesley, 1975), p. 6.

19. Milton J. Rosenberg et. al., *Attitude Organization and Change* (Yale University Press, 1960).

20. George Katona, *The Powerful Consumer* (McGraw-Hill, 1960), pp. 80–83.

21. "Purchase Influence 1985: A Major Study of Buying Influences Within the Contemporary American Household," Chilton Research Services, 1985.

22. Scott Ward and Daniel B. Wackman, "Children's Purchase Influence Attempts and Parental Yielding," *Journal of Marketing Research,* August 1972, pp. 316–19.

23. George P. Moschis and Roy L. Moore, "Decision-Making Among the Young; A Socialization Perspective," *Journal of Consumer Research,* September 1979, pp. 101–12.

24. Francis S. Bourne, "Group Influence in Marketing," in Louis E. Boone, ed., *Classics in Consumer Behavior* (PPC Books, 1977), pp. 211–25.

25. Elihu Katz, and Paul F. Lazarsfeld, *Personal Influence* (The Free Press, 1955).

26. James H. Myers and Thomas S. Robertson, "Dimensions of Opinion Leadership," *Journal of Marketing Research,* February 1972, pp. 41–46.

27. Assael, *Consumer Behavior and Marketing Action,* p. 433.

28. Engel, Blackwell, and Miniard, *Consumer Behavior,* p. 328.

29. Robertson, et. al., 1984, *Consumer Behavior,* pp. 518–521.

30. H. Lee Matthews, and John W. Slocum, Jr., "Social Class and Commercial Bank Credit Card Usage," *Journal of Marketing,* January 1969, pp. 71–78.

31. Robertson, et. al., 1984, *Consumer Behavior,* p. 521.

32. This example is from "Campbell Soup Fails to Make It to the Table," *Business Week,* October 12, 1981, pp. 66.

33. David A. Ricks, "International Business Blunders: An Update," *Business and Economic Review,* January-March, 1988, pp. 11–14.

CASE APPLICATION 5–1

Southwestern Bell Introduces the Silver Pages

Southwestern Bell Corp. learned a tough lesson about marketing to older people: If they look older and request an older-person's discount, they generally will get it—no questions asked.

That fact had completely eluded the regional telecommunications company's market researchers, and it ended up dooming the Silver Pages, a directory that lists retailers' discounts for older people. Earlier this month, Southwestern Bell announced it was ending publication of the Silver Pages and folding AD/VENT Information Services Inc., the unit that published the buyers' guide.

The problem: As the older population attracts more marketing attention, the directory's chief draw—discount promotions—is undercut by the growing availability of such offers. Increasingly, an older person can "get a discount merely by looking like a senior and asking for it," says R. M. Jennings, president of AD/VENT.

Silver Pages, a product planned before the Bell System breakup in 1984 and launched the following year in Southwestern Bell's hometown of St. Louis, had initially shown great promise. Distributed free to people 60 years of age or older, it carried alphabetical listings and advertisements from a wide range of merchants and purveyors of services—from clothing stores, theaters, and restaurants to barber shops and taxi operators. Eventually, it spread to 89 markets, with concentrations in states with large older populations, such as Florida.

Southwestern Bell began with a five-year business plan and in the first year exceeded projections. "We fell slightly short in the second year, and by the third year, it was clear revenue growth couldn't sustain publishing," says Mr. Jennings.

"The advertising community and seniors didn't embrace the product to the degree our research said they would," Mr. Jennings says. "All of our feedback said they were eager to get the product."

Mr. Jennings offers another possible reason for the failure of the Silver Pages: "My overall impression is that the habits (of older people) are slow to change."

The company won't say how much it had invested in the venture, but it expects that the costs of closing AD/VENT won't have any material effect. AD/VENT's other business, competing Yellow Page directories in markets outside Southwestern Bell's territory, will be transferred to another Southwestern Bell unit.

Southwestern Bell isn't the first to abandon the specialized-directory business. Since the seven regional telephone companies were created in the breakup of the Bell System in 1984, Pacific Telesis Group has launched and folded two such buying guides—one aimed at hotels and motels, the other at architects.

The older-people market, Mr. Jennings says, is "big, growing, and lucrative with special needs," and one that Southwestern Bell won't abandon. From the Silver Pages project, the company has generated an address list of about 14 million older people, and it still plans some form of targeted marketing to them.

"We've got to go back to the drawing board and reformulate what we do," Mr. Jennings says. But he acknowledges it is a difficult, diverse market.

"We may never find what is the right product," he says. "I don't know anybody who's got their arms around it in a big way" except the American Association of Retired Persons.

SOURCE: Mary L. Carnevale, "A Baby Bell Gets Some Gray Hairs As Older-People Buyers' Guide Flops," *The Wall Street Journal*, May 16, 1989, p. 26.

Questions

1. How could Southwestern Bell have done a better job of understanding the buyer behavior of the mature consumer market?

2. What types of influences are most important for this service and target market?

3. Why do *you* think the Silver Pages failed? Could the failure have been prevented?

CASE APPLICATION 5–2

Ford Motor Company

The Ford Motor Company gambled over $3 billion and is winning it back with the new Taurus and Sable passenger cars. The jelly-bean look of the aerodynamically designed cars has caught the public's fancy and helped Ford boost a lagging image for styling, attract a new set of young, wealthy buyers, and give its market share a swift upward kick. The high risks involved have also paid off in another way: For the first time in 60 years, Ford is expected to top industry leader General Motors in profits.

Ford Taurus SHO.
The car that will turn your idea of a four-door sedan inside out.

A pleased Ross Roberts, general marketing manager at Ford, can't help but pat himself on the back for this one. "We feel that the cars have done more to lift Ford's image than anything that had happened to us in a long, long time," he says. "We have hit a tremendous home run."

The achievements of the Taurus and Sable are far from a fluke. No car at Ford has ever had as much marketing research input—five years of both quantitative and qualitative studies. And no Ford car has ever had so much advertising support—a hefty $100 million was placed in television, magazines, and newspapers. The Taurus and Sable *had* to be successful, however, for Ford's long-term future. If they had failed, Ford would have been left with nothing to sell except small cars such as the Escort, or sportier, larger models like the Thunderbird. Their failure would also have cost Ford a serious morale blow. Ford had begun to pick up steam, managing record earnings three years in a row after the very bleak years of 1980 and 1981 when it lost $2 billion due to a series of stodgy cars that got stuck in the mud as the market shifted to smaller and more fuel-efficient, front-wheel drive autos.

The Ford look began to evolve in 1983 with the introduction of a rounded shape for the sporty Thunderbird and Cougar. This was followed a few months later with the compacts Tempo and Topaz. It wasn't until the Taurus and Sable, however, that Ford tried to revamp its bread-and-butter business—the mid-size models—which comprise one-quarter of its sales volume. "The previous cars laid the foundation for the aerodynamic look, but the Taurus and Sable punctuated it," notes Phillip Fricke, an analyst with Goldman Sachs.

As many as 340,000 Americans bought a Taurus or Sable last year, customers Ford believes might have turned instead to Japanese or European makes. Actually, Ford borrowed quite a few ideas from its overseas competitors. The company's engineers combed over 50 competitive models, including everything from the Audi 5000 to the Toyota Cressida and the Pontiac 6000, to determine the best features of each and to learn how to incorporate the ideas into Ford manufacturing plans. This exacting emphasis on placing drivers' needs first (above manufacturing assembly requirements, for instance) resulted in lots of nice extras, like color-coded service points under the hood and a net in the trunk to hold the groceries upright.

The Taurus and Sable helped Ford tag on an extra percentage point to its 20 percent share of the mid-size market. (Ford's total market share climbed only slightly from 18%.) By comparison, Chrysler managed to edge up only half a percentage point—to 13 percent—in this segment, while General Motors lost two percentage points to settle in at a 56 percent market share. "We're looking over our shoulder at them," admits Robert Jarboe, director of marketing at Oldsmobile.

With General Motors selling half the cars in the U.S., both Ford with an 18 percent share and Chrysler with a 12 percent stake are left to scramble to avoid going head-to-head with the leader. "Ford is saying eventually they have to differentiate themselves and this can be done via styling," comments Ted Sullivan, a consultant with Chase Econometrics. "This is probably a better move in the long run than what Chrysler is doing in trying to find holes in the marketplace with such products as the minivans. After a while, you run out of niches," Sullivan points out.

Ford also has scored a victory in attracting a new type of buyer to the company. The cars, which offer Japanese quality, European styling and ride for a modest price, are luring the young professional market that needs a sensible, yet stylish family sedan. But it was far from easy to make this leap. The first prototypes of the cars' design tested poorly at focus groups, and design teams were sent back to the drawing board. Two years later, in 1983, after they had been given the freedom to create a model they themselves found visually pleasing, they had a design that tested well with young professionals.

Statistics on who is buying the cars bear out the presumptions of market research. The average age of the Ford Taurus buyer, for example, is 47, compared to 59 for the replaced LTD. Likewise, the median income is $38,000 for the Taurus owner; $28,000 for the aged model. And a higher percentage (43%) have college degrees than the LTD buyer (29%). "We wanted to appeal to a group of people we call 'the influentials,' but even we were surprised by the results we were getting," says Ray Ablondi, director of market research, who oversaw a ten-stage research process on such seemingly minor details as the positioning of door handles. "We had never seen such huge jumps in demographic changes."

Another piece of good news has been that these new models attract more buyers who might have been inclined to buy imports. Prompted by favorable reviews from *Consumer Reports*, and such awards as *Motor Trend* Car of the Year, the Taurus and Sable have helped Ford make a dent in the rush to buy such makes as the similarly designed, but far more expensive Audi. According to Ablondi, previously only 5 percent of the trade-ins for a Marquis or LTD came from former import owners. That compares to 15 percent for the Taurus and Sable.

An essential part of the cars' success is due to the publicity bandwagon that preceded their launch in December 1985. With the goal of making half the nation aware of Ford's new vehicles, the company took a caravan of Taurus and Sable models cross-country. The team held press conferences in 110 key cities. Supplier plants were also visited so that workers could admire the results and management could perhaps drum up even more good will for the cars.

Meanwhile, the advertising strategy was being readied for its attack on the nation's psyche. Ford agency J. Walter Thompson and Lincoln/Mercury agency Young & Rubicam broke ads for the models months before the sale date. Their combined efforts resulted in 150,000 orders for the cars even before the launch.

SOURCE: Rebecca Fannin, "The Road Warriors," *Marketing & Media Decisions*, March 1987, pp. 60–66.

Questions

1. Evaluate the consumer behavior knowledge Ford has available in its marketing decision making.

2. How are attitudes about automobiles formed, and how important are these attitudes?

3. What consumer behavior concepts discussed in Chapter 5 are most relevant for a car manufacturer such as Ford?

4. What other consumer behavior information would you like to have if you were the vice president of marketing for Ford?

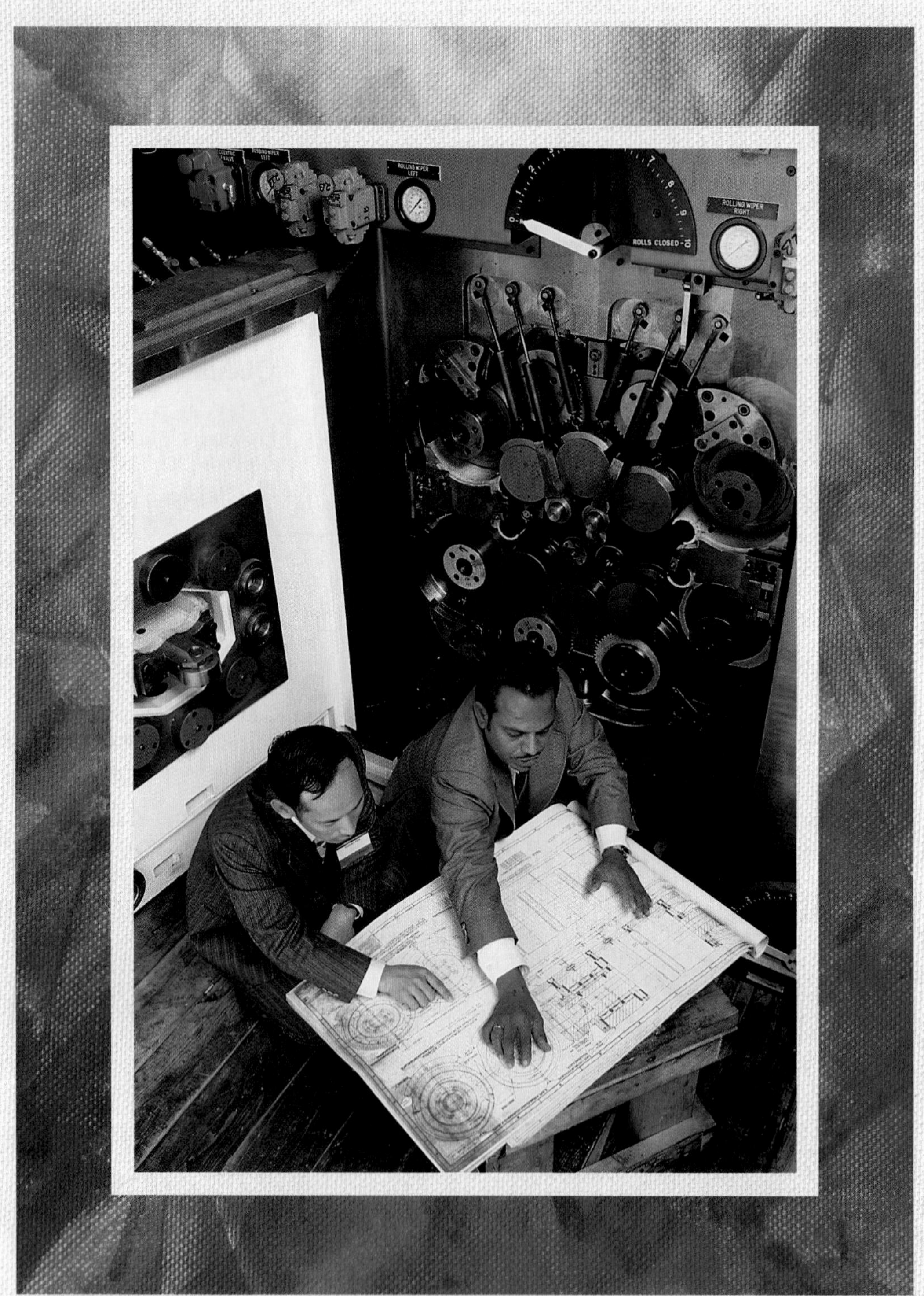
ROLLING WIPER LEFT
ROLLS CLOSED-10
ROLLING WIPER RIGHT

6

Organizational Markets and Buying Behavior

Learning Objectives

Upon completing this chapter, you will be able to do the following:

EXPLAIN
the ways to segment organizational markets, including the use of SIC codes.

DEFINE
the organization buying-center concept.

IDENTIFY
the various roles in organization purchasing behavior, including those of initiator, influencer, decider, user, and gatekeeper.

DESCRIBE
the stages of the organization purchase decision process.

DISCUSS
the advantages and disadvantages of selling to the government and how the government buying process is different.

UNDERSTAND
the types of buying decisions made by organization buyers.

LIST
the factors that are important in developing a strong supplier-buyer relationship.

COMPARE
organizational with consumer buying behavior.

MARKETING PROFILE

Zenith Personal Computers

When executives of Zenith Electronics Corporation met in 1982 to plot the marketing strategy for their line of personal computers, five of the six people present agreed that the firm should adopt a traditional "me-too" marketing strategy to sell their computers to businesses. Such a strategy would be centered on distributing Zenith PCs through computer retailers where business people typically bought their computers. Such a strategy would require a marketing plan and advertising campaign designed to enlist the computer retailers' support for the Zenith product line. Such a strategy would also be expensive, since these retailers expected heavy advertising to support their efforts.

The individual who disagreed with the group's plan was Jerry K. Pearlman, at the time Zenith's chief financial officer and the person credited with being the mastermind behind Zenith's decision to acquire Heath Co. in 1979. Zenith obtained the personal computer product line in that acquisition of Heath. Pearlman, who today is Zenith's chairman and CEO, argued that it was best not to compete head-to-head with other personal computer companies in the primary distribution channel. Instead, he argued that Zenith should seek to exploit and dominate smaller market niches such as the college and university market and the government market. A niche strategy, he argued, would be less costly in terms of advertising expenses, and niche markets were not receiving much attention from other PC makers.

Pearlman's strategy for marketing Zenith's personal computer was the one that was chosen and, looking back, it appears that it was a wise choice. The first break came in October 1983 when Zenith won its first government contract, a $30 million order from the Air Force. This got management's attention, since it was the biggest order the company had ever obtained. A year later they won their second Air Force contract, this time for $100 million for specially designed high security computers. More recently the company has been awarded contracts for 15,000 personal computers by the Internal Revenue Service, $104.5 million from the Department of Defense and $242 million by the Air Force, the largest PC order ever placed by the government.

Zenith began selling to the college market in 1982 when it received a large order from Clarkson College, one of the first schools to require all freshman to purchase a computer. The company now offers discounts of up to 40 percent to students, faculty, and alumni at campuses all across the country. They have staged "truckload sales," selling computers on campus from the back of a truck and in Fort Lauderdale, Florida, during spring break. Sales on college campuses represent an important part of the company's international strategy as well, accounting for 40 percent of its European computer revenues.

Numerous personal computer makers, including Columbia Data Products, Eagle Computer, and Victor Technologies, have gone bankrupt in recent years trying to compete head on with the IBM PC by fighting for scarce space on computer retailers' shelves. Zenith, however, is thriving, and is even having a hard time keeping up with demand from the government and university markets.

Zenith hopes its success in the government and educational markets will pay off in the business computer market. Nearly one half of all microcomputer sales (49%) are to businesses. Students that are used to using Zenith computer products in school are likely to request and specify Zenith after they graduate and go into the business world. Several defense contractors have followed the government's example and purchased Zenith. The computer retailer reseller market still does not sell Zenith in great volume, but this may change with the new models Zenith has recently introduced. The Zenith laptop is the first company product to be sold nationally by Computerland. In order to better serve the needs of the computer retailer chain stores and to increase their penetration of the business market, Zenith has begun to deal directly with the chains rather than through distributors.

This profile shows how the marketer of an industrial product has competed successfully by targeting specific market targets including governmental, institutional, and business. It also shows how a successful strategy in one market may be used as a springboard to exploit other markets. This example also indicates the concentration of buying power in the industrial market and how the marketing strategy used for industrial products will usually be different from the marketing strategy used for consumer products.

SOURCE: Lisa Kartus, "Zenith: Tail Wags Dog," *Financial World,* November 3, 1987, pp. 22–24 and Kenneth Dreyfack, "Zenith's Side Road to Success in Personal Computers," *Business Week,* December 8, 1986, pp. 100–103.

In Chapters 4 and 5 we examined the environment for the consumer marketplace and consumer buying behavior. In this chapter, we describe organizational markets and buying behavior. Some aspects of these topics are very similar to their consumer products counterparts, but a number are substantially different.

The starting point in understanding how to market an organizational product is the same as for a consumer product—defining the target market. For an organizational product, however, this is often more difficult. In the Zenith example, the company not only has to identify organizations likely to be prospects for their computers but also has to determine who within the buying organization will be the appropriate individual to target.

Even after someone in the organization has decided that they need to purchase a number of personal computers, his or her company may still have a somewhat complex process that must be followed before the product can be purchased. Specifications may need to be spelled out, alternative suppliers may have to be identified, and a set of buying procedures, including requests for proposals, bids, and purchase orders, may have to be completed before the product is approved for purchase. Other individuals, including plant engineers, production workers, and purchasing agents, may get involved.

In this chapter we will discuss the classification and segmentation of organizational markets, the types of decisions made by organizational buyers, the individuals involved in the organizational products buying process, and their various roles.

Organizational Markets

An *organizational* market has been defined in Chapter 4 as one which consists of businesses, individuals, or organizations that purchase products or services to use in the production of other products or services, in their day-to-day operations, or for resale. Although there is no perfect measure of the size of the American organizational market, *Sales and Marketing Management* annually estimates the "purchasing power" of the country's businesses. In 1988, it was estimated that 3.7 million business establishments represented $5.7 trillion in shipments.[1] This is a huge market.

In addition to the business part of the organizational market, there are two other markets of substantial size—the institutional market and the government market. The institutional market consists of organizations such as educational institutions, hospitals, prisons, and nonprofit organizations including museums, foundations, and libraries. The government market consists of the federal government, state governments, and the thousands of county and local governments throughout the country.

Classification of Organizational Products and Services

Although there are many different kinds of products sold to organizational buyers, they generally can be classified into one of seven categories: business services, heavy equipment, light equipment, consumable supplies, component parts, raw materials, or processed materials.[2]

Business Services. This category includes nontangible services purchased by a company, such as advertising and public relations services; legal, accounting, and consulting services; maintenance and janitorial services; and rental car, travel, and hotel services.

Organizational products are often bought in quantity, as demonstrated in this ad for dictating machines.

Heavy Equipment. These are capital goods which are typically purchased for a company's own use. The equipment can be purchased outright, or is sometimes leased by industrial user customers. Examples include machine tools (lathes, drilling machines, grinders), hydraulic presses, blast furnaces, forklifts, and electrical drive systems.

Light Equipment. This category includes goods which are not permanently affixed to the customer's physical plant, as in the case of heavy equipment. Light equipment can be purchased outright, or leased, and is considerably less expensive than heavy equipment. The buyers of these goods are normally the users. Examples of this category include power tools, copying machines, word processors, fax machines, and measuring instruments.

Consumable Supplies. These are goods that are used up or consumed by the purchasing organization in the normal operation of its business—cleaning compounds, cutting oils and fluids, drill bits, and business envelopes and forms.

Component Parts. These are goods that are purchased for inclusion into the final product of the buying organization. Examples are transistors, small electric motors, switches, screws, nuts, and bolts. These products are typically marketed to original equipment manufacturer (OEM) customers, who use the parts to produce their own products. Component parts are also often sold to both distributors who sell to OEMs and customers buying the parts for replacement purposes from various repair and service facilities.

Raw Materials. Raw materials are those products produced by extractive industries for use with little or no alteration in the production of other goods. Coal, crude oil, lumber, food crops, and copper are examples. These products are purchased by users—such as coal bought by a manufacturer for heating a furnace—and by OEMs.

Processed Materials. Processed materials differ from raw materials and component parts in that they are produced to the specifications of a customer. The buyers then use these processed materials in producing their goods. Typical examples include chemicals, sheet metal, plastics, and specialty steel.

Differences Between Organizational and Consumer Products

Table 6–1 presents ten major differences in the products sold to consumer and organizational markets. These differences come mostly from the nature of the technical specifications and the greater importance of presale and postsale service required in the organizational market. Many of the differences between consumer and organizational products are a function of the **derived demand** associated with most organizational products. Derived demand means that the amount purchased is determined by the demand for a related product. The number of tires purchased by the automobile companies is derived from the number of cars that they will sell to consumers. If gasoline prices rise substantially and consumers do less driving, the consumer demand for replacement tires may decrease substantially, and the tire companies will purchase less of the raw materials needed to produce tires. Thus, the derived demand for rubber and belting compounds will decrease.

The demand for organizational products fluctuates, due to the derived demand for them. If consumers cut back their purchases of tires slightly, retailers and wholesalers may find themselves with an excess of inventory. They, in turn, may cut off their purchases until their inventories have been reduced. This would have a major impact on the production of the tire factories and on their raw material purchases. Thus, a small change in consumer demand can have a major impact on the demand for these products.

Another characteristic of organizational products is the inelastic nature of the demand. By this we mean that price increases (or decreases) will not have much impact on the primary demand for the item. Thus, a large increase in the price of valves used in tires would not change the number of valves purchased by a tire manufacturer. This is particularly true when the item represents a small proportion of the costs of the end product, as is the case with the tire valves.

Table 6–1 How Organizational Products Differ from Consumer Products

1. The products in the organizational market are usually of a more technical nature.
2. Products in the organizational market are normally purchased on the basis of specifications.
3. There is multiuse of products in the organizational market, as different buying influences within a purchasing company may use the same product for a different use.
4. Organizational buyers purchase products for production inventories as opposed to immediate use.
5. There is a predominance of raw and semifinished goods found in the organizational market—these products are sold into the consumer market only on rare occasions.
6. There is tremendous emphasis on the importance of product service after the sale in the organizational market.
7. There is tremendous importance placed in the organizational market on presale servicing and technical assistance in setting up and operating products in the customer's plant.
8. Packaging is generally more protective rather than promotional in nature, although instances of the latter can be found, especially with distributor items.
9. There is tremendous emphasis placed in the organizational market on promptness and certainty of delivery of products, because of the effects of delays on production line operations, and other constraints.
10. Customers do not always have to purchase the products they require, but can sometimes produce them with their own production facilities. This is very rare in the consumer market.

SOURCE: R. Haas, *Industrial Marketing Management*, second edition, (Kent Publishing Company, 1982) p. 26.

Segmentation in Organizational Markets

As mentioned previously, organizational markets can be very different from consumer markets. The concept of market segmentation, however, is equally operative; many of the same bases for segmentation apply. Segmentation in organizational markets is often more complex.[3] For example, geographic segmentation is important in many organizational markets. The market for mobile-home components is concentrated in a handful of midwestern and southern states. Suppliers of automobile parts are concentrated in the Great Lakes region, and apparel manufacturers are located in the southeastern United States.

Most of the behavioralistic segmentation variables appropriate for the consumer sector are also useful in the organizational market sector. To illustrate, usage rate segmentation can be used by an organizational marketer to differentiate heavy users, light users, and nonusers. With most of the major oil companies concentrating on the heavy-user market, a smaller competitor like Superior Oil might find it profitable to concentrate on the light-user segment of the market.

Segmentation by benefit sought is also important in the organizational market. Benefit segmentation provides important information that is not obtained through traditional segmentation methods, such as demographic segmentation using SIC codes.[4] For example, some buyers of chemicals are interested in buying the lowest-priced product available, while others are interested in the finest quality available, often requiring specifications with extremely narrow tolerances. Still others, perhaps because

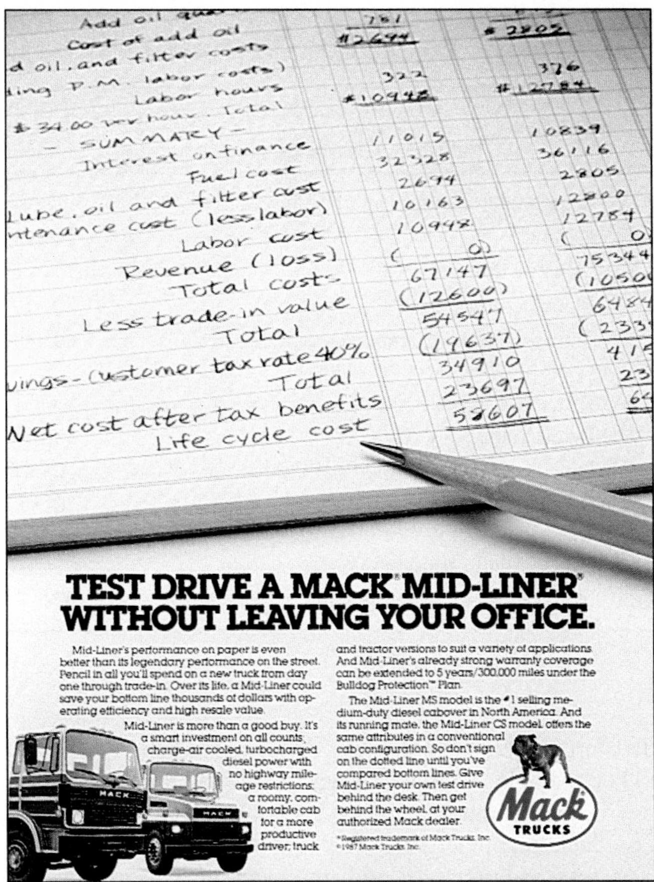

This ad illustrates some of the complexities of organizational product marketing.

of a lack of space for inventory or less working capital, might be mostly attracted by frequent, reliable deliveries of the chemicals.

Depending on the market, segmentation by brand loyalty or by readiness stage might be important. IBM, for example, has been particularly effective in developing and nurturing brand-loyal customers, trading them up to the faster, more expensive machines as their needs grow. IBM has also been successful in marketing to firms at various readiness stages through advertising, product demonstrations, strong personal selling, and user training.

Perhaps the most important segmentation tool in the organizational marketplace is the *Standard Industrial Classification System* (SIC). SIC is a detailed numbering system for classifying American establishments according to their economic activity.[5] Segmenting organizational markets by SIC codes is analogous to segmenting consumer markets by demographics.

Standard Industrial Classification System

The SIC system was developed by the United States government and divides the economy into eleven divisions; it assigns two-digit numbers to major industry groups

Table 6–2 The Standard Industrial Classification System

Division	Industries Classified	First Two-digit SIC Numbers Involved
A	Agriculture, Forestry, and Fishing	01, 02, 07, 08, 09
B	Mining	10–14
C	Construction	15–17
D	Manufacturing	20–39
E	Transportation, Communications, Electric, Gas, and Sanitary Services	40–49
F	Wholesale Trade	50–51
G	Retail Trade	52–59
H	Finance, Insurance, and Real Estate	60–67
I	Services	70, 72–73, 75–76, 78–86, 88–89
J	Public Administration	91–97
K	Nonclassifiable Establishments	99

within each division. (Table 6–2 lists the divisions and the two-digit codes within each division.) For example, Manufacturing, Division D, includes SIC codes 20, food manufacturers; 23, apparel manufacturers; 25, furniture manufacturers; and 34, fabricated metal products manufacturers. For each two-digit code, the Census Bureau publishes data on total industry sales and employment. This information is available for each SIC code for various geographical breakdowns, and is available for each county in the United States.

The industry groups are then divided into more specific three- and four-digit numbers, for industry subgroups and detailed industry classifications, respectively. For example, SIC 38 describes Measuring, Analyzing, and Controlling Instruments; Photographic, Medical and Optical Goods; Watches and Clocks. SIC 382 contains Measuring and Controlling Instruments, which is further subdivided into SIC 3822, Automatic Controls for Regulating Residential and Commercial Environments and Appliances. Going to the ultimate seven-digit code, 3822020, it is possible to identify the category for thermostats.

The importance of the SIC system is that companies in virtually every American industry have already been classified. Once a marketing manager identifies the SIC categories of interest, it is not difficult to combine SIC data with input/output analysis to develop market segments. Input/output analysis is based on the concept that the output (sales) from one industry is the input (purchases) of other industries. The U.S. Department of Commerce publishes national input/output models covering 83 primary industries.

It should be pointed out that all companies do not use the SIC system to segment and target their markets, and that a number of marketers are critical of it. Until recently, a number of marketers complained about the currency of the SIC codes, which had not been revised in over 10 years. In 1988, however, the Department of Commerce published a new SIC Revision. Some of the new SIC codes are shown in Table 6–3. Another criticism of the SIC system concerns the definition of industry

Table 6–3 New SIC Codes

SIC	Description	SIC	Description
3571	Electronic computers	7377	Computer rental & leasing
3572	Computer storage devices	7378	Computer maintenance & repair
3575	Computer terminals	7379	Computer related svcs., not elsewhere classified
3577	Computer peripheral equipment	7382	Security systems svcs.
3695	Recording media (blank disks)	7841	Video tape rental
7291	Tax return preparation svcs.	7991	Physical fitness facilities
7334	Photocopying & duplicating svcs.	8082	Home health care svcs.
7371	Computer programming svcs.	8741	Management svcs.
7372	Prepackaged software	8742	Management consulting svcs.
7373	Computer integrated systems design	8743	Public relations svcs.
7374	Computer processing & data preparation svcs.	8748	Business consulting svcs., not elsewhere classified
7375	Information retrieval svcs.		
7376	Computer facilities management svcs.		

SOURCE: "SICBP Debuts New SIC Sects," *Sales and Marketing Management*, May 1988, p. 32.

niches. For example, specific classifications are not available for recently created industries such as robotics, biotechnology, and home video recorders.

Only one SIC is assigned for the principal product per establishment, so if two or more products are produced at one location, the data for the secondary products are not captured by the SIC system. This creates over and under estimates for some industry categories. Finally, some people criticize the SIC system because the data are not collected frequently enough, often resulting in use of out-of-date information.[6]

In spite of the criticisms cited here, the SIC system is an important source of information about business markets. It is as important to business marketers as demographics are to consumer marketers. As an example, see the *Marketing in Action* on page 174, entitled "The 'Typical' U.S. Business."

REVIEW YOUR MARKETING KNOWLEDGE

- You have just been appointed head of marketing for the tax services division of a large public accounting firm. How might you use market segmentation to help you develop a marketing strategy?
- In what ways might the SIC system be helpful to you?

Understanding Organizational Buying Behavior

There are a number of major differences between consumer and organization buying behavior.[7] In comparison with consumer products, which are often purchased by millions of people, the base for organizational products is often very narrow. An active base of 4000 to 5000 customers is considered by some observers as very large

MARKETING IN ACTION

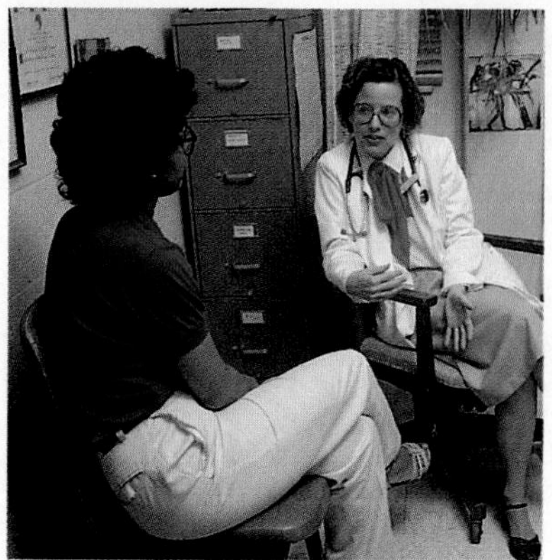

The "Typical" U.S. Business

What would the profile of the typical U.S. business look like? To arrive at the answer, Trinet—the company that prepares the business-to-business data contained in the *Survey of Industrial & Commercial Buying Power*—examined the median employment levels of all U.S. establishments, charted the most frequently occurring industries, and located the geographic center of business activity.

Trinet found that the typical U.S. business in 1987 was a medical office with six employees, located in the suburbs outside of St. Louis, MO. To some, it may come as a surprise that the typical U.S. business is a medical office rather than a manufacturing establishment, but with some 7 million employees, the health services industry has become the nation's biggest employer—providing twice as many jobs as the next largest industry. The aging of the U.S. population, coupled with increasing concerns for personal health, are also major contributing factors here, and expectations are that the growth of medical services will continue to outpace that of the rest of the nation's economy well into the next century.

As for employment, in a nation with gigantic corporations like IBM, General Motors, and AT&T, it might seem odd that the typical U.S. business has only six employees. But in spite of the presence of such huge conglomerates, we are still primarily a nation of small businesses. According to the numbers, there are nearly 5 million U.S. companies with fewer than ten employees, and millions of additional part-time, moonlighting, and work-at-home businesses—all of them quite small. It's this dynamic small business climate—with its high level of employment growth—that accounts for much of the vitality of the nation's economy.

In terms of location, the choice of St. Louis is directly tied to the fact that the population center of the U.S. has been moving steadily westward for the last 200 years. However, strong business performance in the Northeast, greater stability in the Midwest, and recent declines in energy-related businesses in the South and West have at least temporarily halted this westward movement.

SOURCE: "The Typical U.S. Business," *Sales & Marketing Management*, April 25, 1988, p. 9.

for an organizational product, and it is not unusual for 100 to 250 customers to account for a substantial portion of an industrial company's sales volume.[8] In some cases, such as with automobile component parts or jet engines, a handful of buyers comprise 100 percent of the market, a situation that would not be found in the consumer market. In these cases, each buyer is critical, for the marketer and the buyers exert a great deal of influence over the sellers.

Organizational buyers are professional buyers and are typically more technically qualified, making more rational, and less emotional, buying decisions. Organization buying behavior is seldom characterized by impulse purchasing motives, which are often found in consumer markets. Organizational buyers are normally well aware of their requirements and have detailed specifications available for potential suppliers to use in responding to their needs.

There are usually more buying influences and locations involved in organization buying behavior, leading to substantial complexity from the seller's viewpoint. Figure 6–1 illustrates the multiplicity of products, channels, and end-use markets, and the influencers involved in buying metal doors.[9] Even though consumer products can be sold through several different channels to different markets, it would be unusual for a consumer product to be sold through all channels to all markets, as are metal doors and many other industrial products. With each different channel, end-user, and influencer having different buyer behavior, the buying process can be extremely complex.

Figure 6–1 Multiplicity of Products, Channels, End-Use Markets, and Influencers for Metal Doors

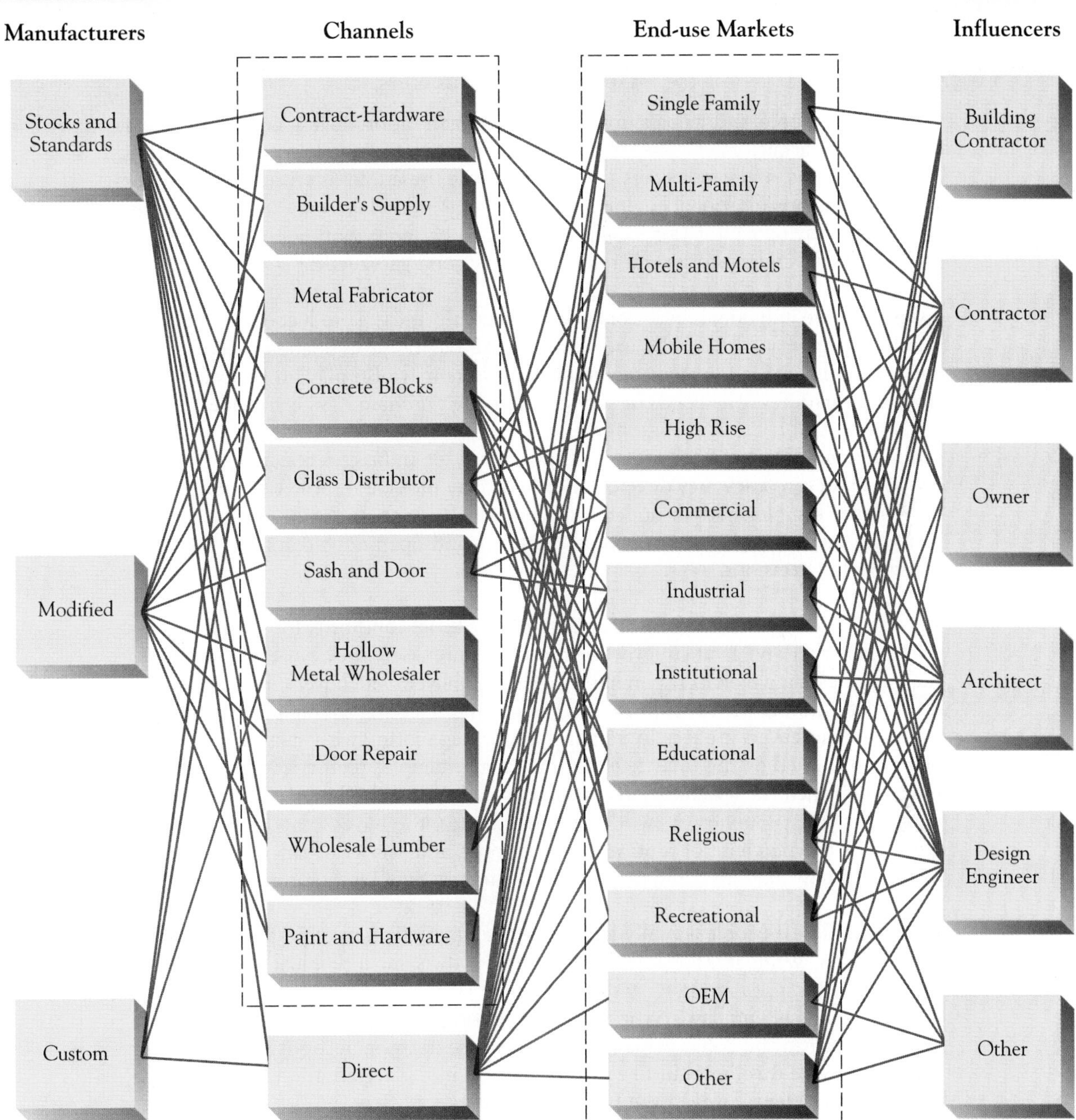

SOURCE: Thomas V. Bonoma and Robert Garda, *Industrial Marketing—What It Is and How It Works.* (Dartnell Corporation, 1982), p. 14.

There is typically more face-to-face contact between buyers and sellers of organizational products. For most consumer products, advertising and sales promotion are the major forms of communication between buyers and sellers, whereas for most organizational products, personal selling is the predominant form of marketing communication. Therefore, many aspects of the selling and buying functions are negotiated. This is true for a few consumer products such as automobiles, appliances, and houses, but, in general, prices are fixed in the consumer market.

A number of individuals are involved in most organizational purchases, whereas most consumer purchase decisions are made by one or two persons.

The Buying Center

The organization of individuals involved in the organization buying behavior process is called the *buying center*. The roles in the buying center include users, influencers, buyers, deciders, and gatekeepers.[10] Understanding these roles is critical to an appreciation of the organizational buying process. Several individuals may occupy the same role in the buying center (for example there may be more than one user), and one individual can undertake several roles (influencer and gatekeeper).

Users. These individuals in the organization actually use the product or service being purchased. In many cases, the users initiate the buying process and/or develop the specifications for the purchase requirements. Users may also play an important role in the evaluation of the goods or services after the purchase has been made.

Influencers. These members of the firm directly or indirectly affect the purchase decision process. They may develop criteria or may provide information that is used to evaluate the alternatives under consideration. In manufacturing operations, for example, technical personnel such as engineers and operations managers influence many buying decisions.

Buyers. These members of the organization have formal authority for actually selecting the supplier and arranging the terms of the purchase. They typically have titles such as purchasing manager, purchasing agent, or buyer. The buyer's most important role is determining the set of possible suppliers and selecting the supplier to be used. Although the buyers are usually responsible for negotiating with suppliers, they are often constrained by the influence of others. For example, technical personnel may have established the specifications in such a way so that the buyer is forced to deal with a particular supplier. As will be described later, the buyer's importance may be greater for the purchase of routine types of goods and services than it is for highly technical items that are being purchased for the first time by the organization.

Deciders. These people actually determine the final selection of products, services, and suppliers. While it is possible that the buyer is the same individual as the decider, often these two roles are split, with one individual making the buying decision and leaving the actual purchase to the buyer. Purchasing agents, for example, often have an upper limit in the dollar value for their purchase decision authority. Decisions for purchases above this limit must be made by others in the organization, such as a vice president, president, or even the board of directors.

Gatekeepers. These individuals have control over the flow of information into the buying center. Usually they are purchasing agents or buyers who are responsible for dealing directly with vendors and potential vendors. The flow of information from salespersons to users and influencers is often controlled by the purchasing department, whose influence is strongest at the stage of identifying buying alternatives.

The IBM advertisement in Figure 6–2 illustrates the various levels in the organization that might be included in a buying center and shows the roles that could be

Figure 6–2 The Concept of the Buying Center

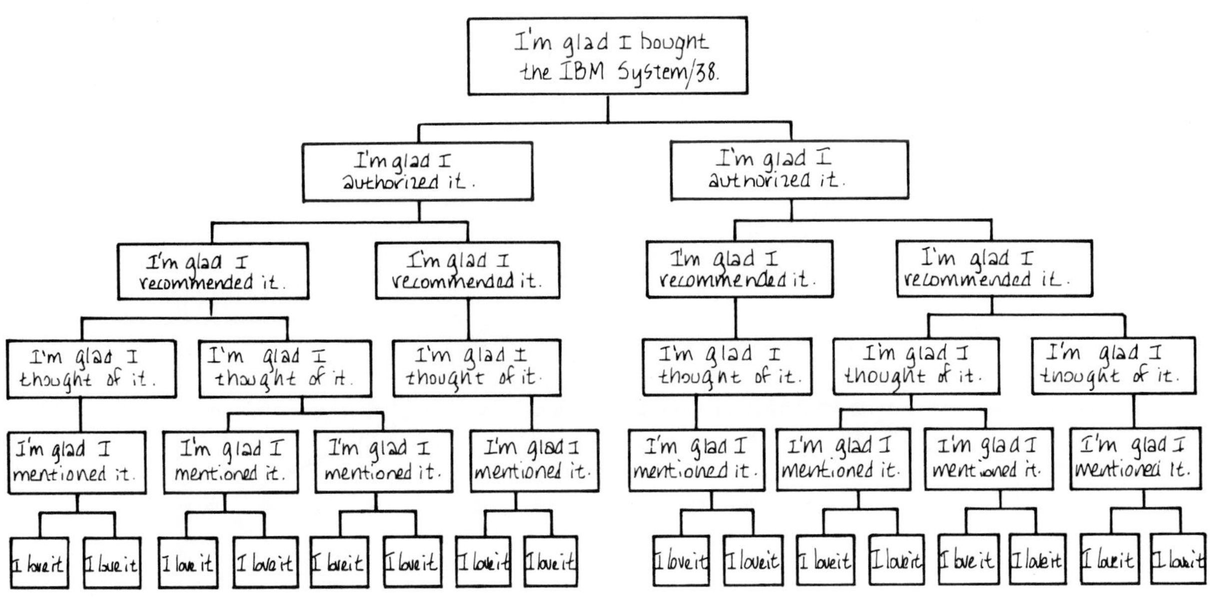

played by each member. With so many individuals involved, communication can be a complex process. Figure 6–3 outlines the communications picture among the various individuals involved in the buying process, including people from the vendor (seller) organization, the buying organization, and outside people such as consultants and purchasing agents from other companies. Note that communications take place across different levels of the organization vertically, as well as horizontally.

As might be expected, the number of people involved in a buying center increases as the importance of the purchase increases. This relationship was quantified by Johnston and Bonoma in a study of 62 capital-equipment and services purchases in 31 companies.[11] They found that, for the typical capital-equipment purchase, an average of four departments, always including purchasing and engineering, were represented. There were an average of seven people involved, serving in six different buying roles. The people came from three different levels of the organization. For services, five managers from four departments and two levels of management were typically involved. More complex buying decisions involved more people and more carefully considered decisions. There was little vendor searching or evaluation for packing supplies, but much in the purchase of a new boiler.

Some marketing scholars have been critical of the concept of the organization buying center.[12] Basically, these critics have questioned the usefulness of these concepts, indicating that practicing marketing managers cannot use the concepts to implement their marketing programs. They say, for example, that knowing that many different roles are involved in the buying center does not tell you who to call on or what to tell them. However, most organizational marketers find the concepts helpful to them even if they don't indicate exactly what should be done with each buyer. Just knowing that there are roles such as gatekeepers is important, even if it isn't crystal clear who the gatekeepers are.

Figure 6–3 A Communications Picture of a Buying Center

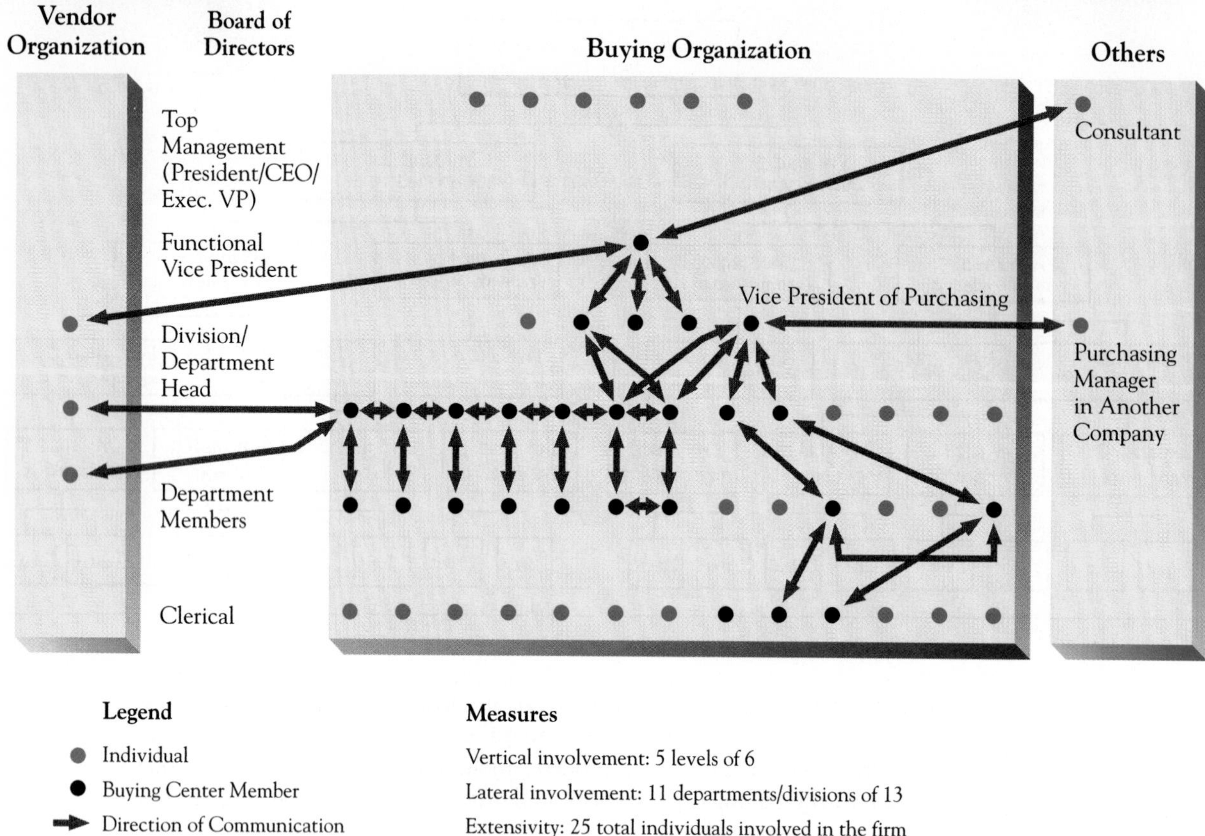

SOURCE: Wesley Johnston and Thomas Bonoma, "The Buying Center: Structure and Interaction Pattern," *Journal of Marketing*, Summer 1981, p. 147.

Types of Buying Decisions

The different types of buying decisions made by organizations have been called *buyclasses*, based on the newness of the problem to the company, the amount of information needed to make an informed decision, and the degree to which new alternatives are considered.[13] As shown in Table 6–4, the three types of buyclasses are new task situations, straight rebuy situations, and modified rebuy situations.[14]

New Task Situations. With new task situations, the buyer faces a requirement or problem that has not arisen before. He or she has little or no relevant previous buying experience, so a great deal of information is needed, and alternative suppliers are carefully considered. New task situations occur infrequently, but are very important to marketers because they set the pattern for the more routine purchases that will follow.

Table 6–4 Distinguishing Characteristics of Buying Situations

Buying Situation (Buyclass)	Newness of the Problem	Information Requirements	New Alternatives
New Task	High	Maximum	Important
Modified Rebuy	Medium	Moderate	Limited
Straight Rebuy	Low	Minimal	None

SOURCE: Patrick Robinson, Charles Faris, and Yoram Wind, *Industrial Buying and Creative Marketing* (Allyn & Bacon, 1967), p. 28.

Straight Rebuy Situations. These involve continuing or recurring requirements and are typically handled on a routine basis. Formally or informally, a list of acceptable suppliers exists, and no new suppliers are considered. Buyers, often in the purchasing department, have a great deal of relevant buying experience, and little, if any, new information is needed. The specific item purchased, the price, or delivery time may change somewhat from purchase to purchase, as long as these variations do not cause a new source of supply to be considered. Straight rebuy situations appear to be the most common in organizational buying.

Modified Rebuy Situations. These situations arise with continuing or recurring requirements where the buying alternatives are known but changed. A new evaluation of supplier offerings is done—prompted by the conviction that it is worthwhile to seek additional information and alternatives before a decision is made. Modified rebuy situations may arise internally because of new buying influences, or for potential cost reductions, quality improvements, or service benefits. They may arise because of external events such as an emergency or by the actions of a supplier. An example of a modified rebuy situation for hydraulic pumps, caused by the offer of a price reduction by a new supplier, is presented in Figure 6–4.

The Organizational Purchase Decision Process

We now turn our attention to how all the participants in the buying center are involved in the purchase decision process.[15] Figure 6–5 graphically represents how companies purchase goods and services. The process begins with someone in the organization anticipating a problem that can be solved with the purchase of some product(s) or service(s). Recognition of the problem may come from users, influencers, or even individuals not otherwise involved in the purchase decision process (for example, the president of the company telling the vice president of operations that raw materials costs should be lower).

The second step is the development of specifications for products or services to solve the problem. At this stage, *influencers* such as technical and engineering personnel may act as advisers. After the specifications are agreed upon, a requisition is sent to the purchasing department, and the search for alternative products, services, and sources of supply begins. Gatekeepers are particularly important at this stage of the process, since they control the flow of information to the influencers, deciders, and others involved in making the purchase decision.

Figure 6–4 Example of a Modified Rebuy: Hydraulic Pump

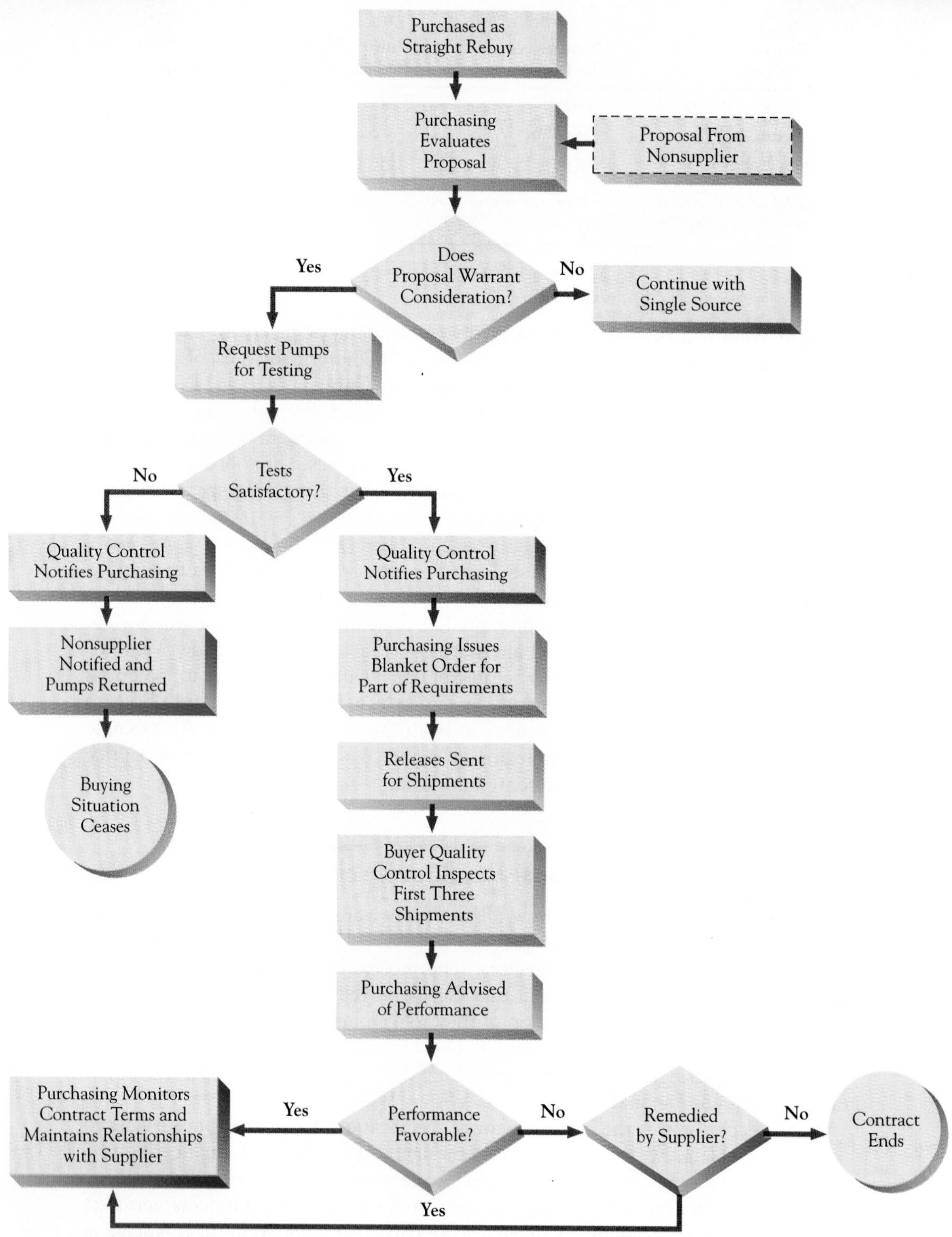

SOURCE: Patrick J. Robinson, Charles W. Faris, and Yoram Wind, *Industrial Buying and Creative Marketing*, p. 75. Copyright ©1967 by Allyn and Bacon, Inc., Boston. Reprinted by permission.

Figure 6–5 Organizational Purchase Decision Process

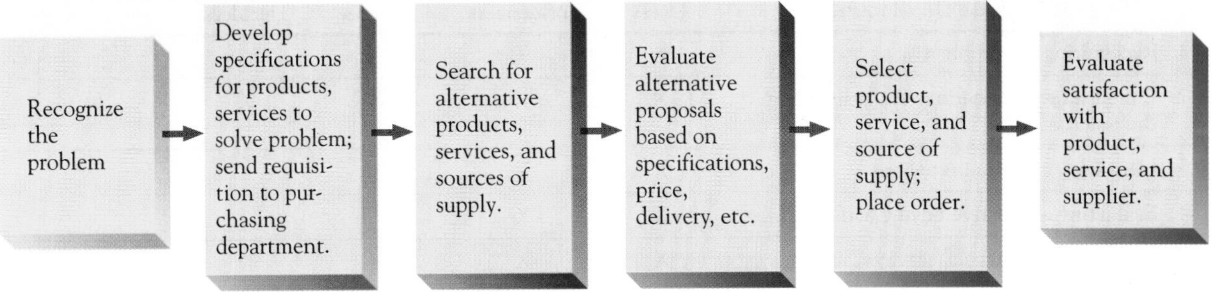

SOURCE: Based on R. Haas, *Industrial Marketing Management* (Petrocelli/Charter, 1976), pp. 56-60.

The third step in the process is to evaluate the alternative proposals obtained from the various possible sources of supply. The alternatives will be evaluated in terms of their ability to meet the specifications, particularly with respect to performance. Other factors that are typically used include price, delivery, seller reputation, and services provided. The price itself may not be as important as value analysis. *Value analysis* is the overall cost, including installation and servicing costs, reliability, and replacement costs. For example, a mechanical part that costs five times as much as an alternative may be a much better value if it results in substantially less down time for the piece of equipment in which it is used. After the alternatives have been evaluated, the decision is made and an order is placed. After the product or service has been received, it is evaluated, as is the supplier. This information will be compiled and used in the future when this product or service is again needed.

The various roles in the buying center have different degrees of importance during the industrial purchase decision process. Table 6–5 defines the influences the members of the buying center are most likely to have throughout each of the stages of the purchase decision process.

Power and Influence in the Purchase Decision Process

One of the most difficult aspects of organizational buying behavior is identifying the individuals with the most power and influence, the actual decision makers within the buying center. Those that have the most power are sometimes the individuals who are the least accessible to vendor salespersons; and the amount of power an individual has may vary substantially from purchase to purchase. For example, the power of technical personnel may be substantial for important, technically oriented new task situations. These same individuals may have very little say about what products should be procured in nontechnically oriented, straight rebuy situations.

An individual's influence may also vary within a specific buyclass, depending on the stage in the purchase decision process. Thus, a technical person may have substantial influence over the specifications for a new task purchase, but may have no say at all over the selection of the order routine or over the need for the product in the first place. A person with little power to decide which vendor should ultimately be selected may have the ability to eliminate one or more vendors during the selection process.

Table 6–5 The Organizational Purchase Decision Process and Buying Center Roles

Stage of Purchase Decision Process	Users	Influencers	Buyers	Deciders	Gatekeepers
1. Recognizing the problem	X	X			
2. Establishing specifications and scheduling the purchase	X	X	X	X	
3. Identifying buying alternatives	X	X	X		X
4. Evaluating alternative buying actions	X	X	X		
5. Selecting the products, services, and suppliers	X	X	X	X	
6. Evaluating the product, services, and suppliers	X	X	X		

SOURCE: Based on Frederick E. Webster, Jr., and Yoram Wind, *Organizational Buying Behavior* (Prentice-Hall, 1972), p. 80.

It is often extremely difficult to determine who has the power in a buying situation. Those who appear to be only gatekeepers or influencers may actually have the authority to make the final decision. Alternatively, other members of the buying center may have less power than they would lead one to believe.

Review Your Marketing Knowledge

- In many marketing situations involving organizational buyers, it is difficult to recognize the decision makers, gatekeepers, and key influencers. Why is it so hard to identify the various players in the buying center and their roles?
- Is it easier to identify the members of the buying center and their roles for straight rebuy situations or for new task situations? Why?

The Role of the Purchasing Agent

As we have seen, purchasing agents, while often not having the final authority, are heavily involved throughout the buying process. Often acting as gatekeepers, these individuals can help organizational marketers identify key personnel in their companies and can often play important roles in interpreting their companies' needs. They often establish the buying procedures and are responsible for "approving" suppliers. A profile of the purchasing professional in 1987 is presented in the *Marketing in Action* in this section of the chapter.

Two recent studies reveal the importance of the purchasing agent's role and influence on the buying process. The first, conducted among decision makers in the construction industry by Bellizzi and Walter, demonstrated that a purchasing agent's influence varied substantially at each stage of the buying process.[16] Influence was highest for the selection of an order routine (preparing the purchase order and expediting) or a search for information on alternative products and suppliers. Influence

MARKETING IN ACTION

Profile of the Purchasing Professional

Every few years, the editors of *Purchasing* magazine conduct a study of the backgrounds, job responsibilities, and duties of purchasing professionals. The results of the 1987 study (with appropriate comparisons to previous studies) of 2000 of these pros include the following findings:

- The average age is 43.7, down from 48 in 1977.
- Well over half have college degrees (73 percent of those with the title VP or Director of Purchasing); 22 percent have post-graduate degrees.
- Over half of the purchasing managers have had prior experience in production; more than a third in sales; and more than one-quarter in accounting.
- They spend their time as follows: 32 percent on paperwork, 21 percent negotiating, 18 percent on source selection, 15 percent on product research, and 13 percent on other things.
- The median amount of purchases is $11.5 million, up from $7 million in 1982.
- One-quarter of the items purchased, representing 39 percent of the dollars spent, are purchased under a contract, blanket order, or long-term agreement. The more money spent, the more likely that the long-term arrangement will be used.
- Over three-quarters indicate they are taking steps to consolidate their purchases with fewer suppliers.
- Overwhelmingly, they prefer to have more than one source for a given item purchased.
- Quality is their number one criterion in selecting suppliers, followed by delivery, technical service, and price.
- The average number of sales people seen per week is eleven.
- They average ten business trips per year, to investigate suppliers' facilities, to negotiate with suppliers, to attend trade shows and seminars, and to visit company facilities.
- Overwhelmingly they would again choose purchasing if given a chance to start their careers over.

SOURCE: Somberby Dowst, "Profile of the Purchasing Pro: 1987," *Purchasing*, October 22, 1987, pp. 63–73.

---

was lowest for performance feedback and evaluation, recognition of problem/need, and determination of specifications for needed items.

The second study examined the influence different levels of managers (purchasing, manufacturing, engineering, and senior management) had on decisions concerning which products to buy and which suppliers to use.[17] Five different categories of products were evaluated. The results, presented in Table 6–6, show that purchasing agents had far more influence on the selection of suppliers than on the products to buy. Engineers and manufacturing managers had substantially more influence on the products to be bought, and engineers were especially influential in the decisions for materials and component parts, probably because of their expertise.

Government Buying Behavior

The federal government is the largest consumer in the U.S., buying close to $200 billion worth of goods and services each year. In addition, there are over 75,000 local government units (cities, counties, and state agencies) that purchase goods and services. The buying process used by governmental units is somewhat different from that used by most businesses. First, the specification process is usually more formal-

Table 6–6 Relative Influence Allocations for Five Product Categories

	Management Level	Major Capital (%)	Minor Capital (%)	Materials (%)	Component Parts (%)	Supplies (%)
Product to Buy	Purchasing	30.33	34.44	23.63	27.21	32.69
	Manufacturing	20.11	20.27	20.48	15.82	19.04
	Engineering	35.44	28.06	40.77	45.98	22.59
	Management	11.33	8.47	6.65	6.72	5.13
	Other	2.78	8.75	8.46	4.26	20.56
Supplier to Select	Purchasing	50.22	60.69	70.06	64.61	63.48
	Manufacturing	13.78	11.64	7.02	5.43	11.17
	Engineering	26.22	18.61	17.42	24.02	12.69
	Management	7.78	6.69	3.38	3.98	4.24
	Other	2.00	2.36	2.12	1.97	8.43

SOURCE: Donald W. Jackson, Jr., Janet Keith, and Richard Burdick, "Purchasing Agents' Perceptions of Industrial Buying Center Influence: A Situational Approach," *Journal of Marketing* (Fall 1984), p. 79.

ized. For example, all federal purchases of $5000 or more must by law list the specifications required in the *Commerce Business Daily* and request proposals from potential suppliers. Businesses then may submit proposals in response to these requests for proposals (called "RFP's"). Evaluation committees then choose a supplier from the proposals submitted, and a formal contract is then negotiated for the order. There are many complexities in selling to the government, especially to agencies such as the Department of Defense. There is a substantial amount of paperwork involved, and, as a result, many companies have chosen not to target the government market.

Suss has created a list of positive and negative factors associated with selling to the government.[18] The positives include:

- Huge size of the market—for example, $203 million for furniture, $160 million for photographic equipment, $1.6 billion for instruments and lab equipment
- Diversity of products purchased—from paper clips to missiles
- Consistency—little variation from year to year
- Available information—easily obtainable information on past procurement patterns, including prices paid, detailed buying forecasts, specifications needed, etc.

The negative aspects of selling to the government include:

- Complexity—numerous channels of approval
- Risk—most of the risk is on the seller, for such things as quality control, assurance of compliance by subcontractors, delivery guarantees, and price (even though costs may escalate dramatically)
- Differences from commercial practices—paperwork requirements and fine print in government contracts can be burdensome, especially with the slim profit margins that are often associated with government contracts.

Many companies have chosen to sell to the government market. They avoid over-reliance on this market, however, by using it to supplement their regular business, not to replace their mainstream customers.

Developing an Effective Supplier-Buyer Relationship

It is virtually impossible for a supplier to be the *best* on every dimension, offering the highest quality product at the lowest price. Thus, suppliers regularly segment markets and target their efforts to those segments where they have the highest probability of profitably meeting the needs of buyers. The complications come when different individuals in the buying process evaluate suppliers differently, and it isn't clear where the decision-making power really lies.

Different people within the buying center will use different criteria in evaluating alternative product offerings and suppliers. For example, those individuals in production control will be more concerned with meeting production schedules and getting delivery quickly in an emergency. Those in quality control will be primarily concerned about meeting strict quality specifications on a consistent basis. And the financial people will be mostly concerned about competitive prices.

In many industries, the specifications are negotiated, as well as the other aspects of the product offering, such as delivery, payment terms, and price. However, sometimes this is done on a proposal and sealed-bid basis. How well a supplier and its products meet the needs of buyers will determine the strength and longevity of the relationship.[19] Some combination of the following seven factors determines the type of relationship that exists:

1. The unique or special capabilities performed by any one competitive product (performance)
2. Consistent quality equal to or better than the standards or specifications (quality)
3. The helpfulness of the relationship between a customer and the sales or technical people that serve the account (service)
4. The promised or expected delivery date (delivery)
5. The historical experience, favorable or unfavorable, the buying organization has had with the producer (past experience)
6. Delivered per-unit price (price)
7. The cost-benefit value of alternative products performing the same or similar functions (competitive value)[20]

Caterpillar Tractor has outlined the following sequence of events to select, evaluate, maintain, and terminate suppliers.[21]

Stage 1 Evaluate suppliers' quality capabilities. Quality control performs a detailed examination of potential suppliers' control over the materials received from their suppliers. Potential suppliers are expected to show the specification requirements of *their* suppliers; an approved supplier list; a method of inspection or their supplier field auditing; and the presence of appropriately trained personnel for raw material and finished goods quality control. Any deficiencies will be improved or corrected through mutual agreement with Caterpillar and the supplier. Caterpillar quality control periodically conducts follow-up quality audit visits.

Stage 2 Communicate quality requirements. After a supplier has been selected, the buyer communicates the technical specifications and requirements to the supplier.

Caterpillar maintains a series of manufacturing practices seminars and has a manual that assists suppliers to fulfill its requirements.

Stage 3 Preproduction sample approval. Suppliers provide samples according to the agreed upon sampling procedures for the item. Full-scale production begins when the samples are approved by the company. Preproduction sample approval does not relieve the supplier from sampling full production runs.

Stage 4 Production shipments. Any supplier's materials and components will be subject to dimensional, metallurgical, and functional inspection at the company. Inspection rates will be decreased as a good history is developed with suppliers and maintained or increased until a good history is developed. The company will also provide all suppliers with monthly or quarterly computerized delivery reports. These reports show the number of pieces or units shipped on time to each location, the percentage shipped early and late, and the rejection rate. When a supplier's sales representative or executive calls on the company, these reports, whether favorable or not, are always an item of discussion.

Stage 5 Measuring supplier performance. Caterpillar continually reviews each supplier's history relating to shipments in Stage 4, rejections, and any other nonconformance. Based on historical data, a status rating is assigned to each supplier. A less favorable status results in increased inspection and a decision to reduce the use of the source. Those suppliers who have continued excessive nonconformance are identified, and a program for improvement is established. Lack of response will result in reduced or terminated business. In this situation, Caterpillar will identify new potential suppliers and begin the process in Stage 1.

As we have seen throughout this chapter, organizational marketing involves complex buying and, therefore, complex selling. Until recently, marketers have focused on individual transactions. Recently, however, the emphasis has shifted to building relationships with customers that transcend individual transactions. In the words of marketing guru Theodore Levitt of the Harvard Business School, "A company's most precious asset is its relationship with its customers."[22] He indicates that, like all assets, these relationships can appreciate or depreciate depending on the marketer's actions.

What can marketers do to build strong relationships with customers? McKesson, a major distributor of drugs and health care items, found a way to develop closer ties with its customers.[23] It designed a system that provided pharmacies with hand-held terminals which were linked to McKesson's main computer. Instead of waiting for McKesson's sales people to call on them, the pharmacists could order by keying the items they wanted to buy into the terminals. This led to more productive salespeople, since they could spend more time selling new products and building personal relationships with new and existing accounts, instead of having to write up routine orders. The customers received faster service, when they wanted it, instead of having to wait for a salesperson to call. The computer also could be used to fill out insurance claims forms, saving the pharmacist time and speeding out the reimbursements from insurance companies. Pharmacists soon found it was easy to order from McKesson, effectively shutting out other suppliers.

The key to building stronger relationships with customers is to make it very unattractive for buyers to switch suppliers. This can be accomplished through the systems involved, as with McKesson, or it can be a result of totally understanding a customer's business and using that knowledge to meet the long-term needs of that

McKesson beat out its competition by supplying pharmacies with a computer hook-up from the pharmacy to McKesson's warehouse.

customer better than an alternative supplier could. If a strong relationship is built, both parties usually benefit greatly. The key is that the transaction is not ended with the purchase order or sale—the relationship is on-going, and what happens after the sale is as important as what happened before or during the sale.

Personal Computer Exercise

SIC codes are important in determining the size of organizational markets. This PC exercise allows you to use SIC data to examine the potential for each of several organizational markets. You will also be able to see how you can measure your firm's current market share for each of these markets.

KEY POINTS

- Organizational products can be classified into seven categories: business services, heavy equipment, light equipment, consumable supplies, component parts, raw materials, processed materials.
- There are many differences in the products sold to consumer markets versus those sold in organizational markets. Many of the differences are a function of derived demand, with the demand for the product arising from the demand for another product.
- The demand for organizational products fluctuates, caused by the derived demand for them. A small change in consumer demand can have a major change in the demand for organizational products.

• The demand for many organizational products is inelastic in nature, with price not having much impact on the level of primary demand (demand for the product category).

• Market segmentation is as important in organizational markets as it is in consumer markets. Bases for organizational market segmentation include geographic segmentation, behavioristic segmentation (including benefit segmentation, brand loyalty, and readiness states), and segmentation using the Standard Industrial Classification System (SIC).

• The number of potential buyers is often small in organizational markets. The buyers are typically more technically qualified than in consumer markets, and buying motives are usually, but not always, less emotional.

• A number of individuals are involved in most organizational purchases, and those included comprise the buying center. The roles in the buying center include users, influencers, buyers, deciders, and gatekeepers.

• There are three types of buying decisions, called buyclasses: new task situations, straight rebuy situations, and modified rebuy situations.

• The steps in the organizational purchase decision process are problem recognition; development of specifications; search for alternative products and sources of supply; evaluation of alternatives based on specifications, price, and delivery; selection of product/service, source of supply, and the placing of the order; and the evaluation of the product and supplier.

• The influence of purchasing agents varies at each stage of the purchase decision process. Agents have more influence in setting procedures and in selecting suppliers and less in selecting and evaluating products.

• The government market is huge, and, therefore, attractive to many marketers. Many different products are bought, and much information is available on the buying process. The process is complex, however, and is different from typical commercial buying, often resulting in considerable risk.

• The strength of supplier-buyer relationships is measured by such factors as performance, quality, service, delivery, past experience, price, and competitive value.

ISSUES FOR DISCUSSION

1. How might a marketer of facsimile machines like Xerox or Sharp segment the market?

2. Describe similarities and differences between consumer and organizational buying behavior. Discuss how the purchase of automobiles might be different for the two markets, using the college student market and the rental car company market as examples.

3. Describe the likely members of the buying center for each of the following products and services:

a. Federal Express Overnight Letter
b. annual contract with a major trucking firm
c. new personal computer for the marketing research department
d. new "super computer" system for the Research and Development laboratories of a major corporation
e. yellow pads and paper clips

4. What type of buying situation (new task, straight rebuy, or modified rebuy) would be represented by each of the purchases in Question 3?

5. How influential would you expect a purchasing agent to be in each of the purchases in Question 3?

6. Describe the buying process for the purchase of a $100,000 piece of medical equipment by a hospital. What information would be needed, and what criteria would be used to help make the purchase decision?

7. As a producer of jet engines (such as GE or Pratt & Whitney), what actions could you take to build and strengthen a relationship with Boeing (a major manufacturer of jet airplanes)?

8. How might the SIC system be helpful to a manufacturer of word-processing equipment? To a company selling poultry-processing equipment?

9. What is the impact of multiple buying roles on the marketing strategy of a postage machine manufacturer, a minicomputer marketer, and an office supplies distributor?

10. Give three examples of derived demand. How does derived demand affect the marketing strategies of these three products?

GLOSSARY

Buyclass: the classification of buying decisions based on the newness of the problem to the organization, the amount of information required, and the consideration of new alternatives.

Buying center: the organization of individuals involved in the organizational buying behavior process, including users, influencers, buyers, deciders, and gatekeepers.

Derived demand: demand for one product that arises from the demand for another product. The demand for many organizational goods is derived from the demand for consumer goods, such as the auto companies' demand for tires, which is a function of consumers' demand for cars.

Gatekeepers: individuals who have control over the flow of information into the buying center. Usually they are purchasing agents or buyers who are responsible for direct dealing with vendors and potential vendors.

Modified rebuy situation: a buying situation where a new evaluation is made of suppliers' offerings, prompted by the conviction that it is worthwhile to seek additional information and alternatives before a decision is made.

New task situation: a buying situation where the buyer has no previous experience, needs considerable information, and considers alternatives.

Organizational market: a market consisting of businesses, individuals, or organizations that purchase products or services to use in the production of other products and services, in their day-to-day operations, or for resale.

Standard Industrial Classification System (SIC): a detailed numbering system for classifying American industry according to its economic activity.

Straight rebuy situation: a buying situation involving a continuing or recurring purchase requiring little, if any, new information. No new alternatives are considered.

Value analysis: overall cost of a product, including installation and servicing costs, reliability, and replacement cost.

NOTES

1. "1988 Survey of Industrial and Commercial Buying Power," *Sales and Marketing Management*, April 25, 1988, p. 79.

2. This section is adapted from Robert Haas, *Industrial Marketing Management, Fourth Edition* (Kent Publishing Company, 1989) pp. 11–21.

3. Thomas Bonoma and Benson Shapiro, *Industrial Market Segmentation: A Nested Approach*, Marketing Science Institute, February 1983.

4. Rowland Moriarty and David Reibstein, "Benefit Segmentation in Industrial Markets," *Journal of Business Research*, December 1986, pp. 463–486.

5. Robert Haas, *Industrial Marketing Management, Fourth Edition* (Kent Publishing Company, 1989), pp. 35–62; "The New SIC Codes," *Sales and Marketing Management*, April 25, 1988; and Robert Haas, "Locating Industrial Customers," *Atlanta Economic Review*, September-October 1976, pp. 9–14.

6. John Couretas, "What's Wrong With the SIC Code . . . And Why," *Business Marketing*, December 1984, pp. 108–15.

7. These differences are described more fully in B. Charles Ames and James Hlavacek, *Managerial Marketing for Industrial Firms* (Random House, 1984), pp. 21–30, and Robert Haas, *Industrial Marketing Management* (Petrocelli/Charter, 1976), pp. 13–14.

8. B. Charles Ames and James Hlavacek, *Managerial Marketing for Industrial Firms*, p. 21.

9. This example is from Thomas Bonoma and Robert Garda, *Industrial Marketing—What It Is and How It Works* (Dartnell Corporation, 1982), pp. 13–14.

10. See Patrick Robinson, Charles Faris, and Yoram Wind, *Industrial Buying and Creative Marketing* (Allyn & Bacon, 1967) and Frederick Webster and Yoram Wind, *Organization Buying Behavior* (Prentice-Hall, 1972).

11. Wesley Johnston and Thomas Bonoma, "Purchase Process for Capital Equipment and Services," *Industrial Marketing Management* (Vol. 10, 1981), p. 253.

12. Wesley Johnston and Robert Spekman, "Special Section on Industrial Marketing and Purchasing Strategies: Introduction," *Journal of Business Research*, December 1986, pp. 461–462.

13. Robinson, Faris, and Wind, *Industrial Buying and Creative Marketing.*

14. Robinson et al., pp. 28–32.

15. This section is adapted from Robert Haas, *Industrial Marketing Management*, (Petrocelli/Charter, 1976), pp. 56–60.

16. Joseph Bellizzi and C. K. Walter, "Purchasing Agents' Influence in the Buying Process," *Industrial Marketing Management* (Vol. 9, 1980), pp. 137–41.

17. Donald Jackson, Janet Keith, and Richard Burdick, "Purchasing Agents' Perceptions of Industrial Buying Center Influence: A Situational Approach," *Journal of Marketing*, (Fall 1984) pp. 75–83.

18. Warren Suss, "How to Sell to Uncle Sam," *Harvard Business Review*, November-December, 1984, pp. 136–144.

19. B. Charles Ames and James Hlavacek, *Managerial Marketing for Industrial Firms*, (Random House, 1984), p. 60.

20. Ames and Hlavacek, 1984, p. 60.

21. Ames and Hlavacek, 1984, pp. 60–61.

22. Theodore Levitt, "After the Sale Is Over . . . ," *Harvard Business Review*, September-October 1983, pp. 87–93.

23. "McKesson Erects Computer Wall Against Competition," *Sales and Marketing Management*, March 11, 1985, pp. 123–124.

CASE APPLICATION 6–1

How to Sell Airplanes, Boeing-Style

November 7: United Airlines announces the purchase of 110 737s and six 747s. Price: $3.1 billion.

October 22: Northwest Airlines announces the purchase of ten 747s and ten 757s. Price: $2 billion.

October 9: International Lease Finance announces the purchase of two 737s. Price $50 million.

October 8: USAir announces the purchase of two 737s. Price: $50 million.

October 2: Western Airlines announces the purchase of twelve 737s. Price: $250 million.

October 1: Republic Airlines announces the purchase of six 757s. Price: $240 million.

Not a bad couple of weeks' work. And that's only the domestic sales—throw in international deals, and you'll have to add another $540 million. But you might expect that from a company with a 55 percent share of the market, a company whose average order this year is $34.9 million, and a company whose dedication to making a sale has been called obsessive.

The company is Boeing Commercial Airplane, a part of Boeing, the Seattle-based aerospace giant. So far this year, Boeing's customers have placed orders totalling $11.9 billion. But before you run out and decide to sell commercial aircraft (or even riskier, *make* commercial airplanes), remember that you will be working in an industry that, even in good years, only sells a few hundred units annually.

Also keep this in mind: there are only about 55 potential customers nationwide; your customers work in a business given to extreme cycles; it can take two to three years from the day you make your presentation to the day a sale is announced; and, in most cases, your company will not start to build the product until you have the order.

If all this sounds a little different, it is. Selling commercial aircraft is like no other business. In fact, Thomas Riedinger, director of marketing communications at Boeing, says, "It is the most expensive product in the world not sold by the bidding process."

It is expensive and time consuming. Salespeople for airline manufacturers could not make a quick sale (by normal standards) even if they wanted to. The selling process just takes too long. But despite its length—and the challenge involved in selling a complex, hi-tech item—the selling process does not differ greatly from the selling of any other industrial product. The salespeople determine needs, demonstrate how their product fulfills needs, and then make the case for their product.

Instead, it is how they do it that separates them from others. For example, in order to determine needs, salespeople become experts on the airline they are responsible for, much like a Wall Street analyst. They find out where the airline wants to grow, when it wants to replace planes, and its economic requirements. They analyze the airline's financial strengths and any alternatives the airline may have to buying from them.

Then there's fulfilling needs. The salespeople run their company's planes (and its competitors') through computer systems, simulating the carrier's routes, cost per seat, and so on to show how their planes are the most efficient. And, more than likely, they'll bring in financial, planning, and technical people to answer any questions.

Finally, there's the negotiations. Deals are cut, discounts made, training programs offered. Top officials—sometimes the CEO of both the airline and the manufacturer—are brought in to try to solidify the deal. The airline then tells the competing manufacturers of its choice, and a public announcement is made.

"It's not hard to sell these things, but it takes a lot of effort," says Riedinger. "It's just that it's much bigger than anything you're usually talking about."

Whether or not it is easy to sell airplanes, it is, in some ways, a "small" business. Despite the dollars involved, the limited number of potential customers and manufacturers (there are only three major ones: Boeing, Douglas, and Airbus) makes it an almost closed club.

Boeing gets more sales than its two major competitors combined. Jim MacKenzie, director of international marketing at Douglas Aircraft, Long Beach, CA, a division of McDonnel Douglas and Boeing's biggest competitor, says Boeing has a built-in advantage—size. "They have a broad product mix; something for everyone in the commercial business. And they are very aggressive."

Others agree that Boeing's success is not necessarily the result of a superior sales force. Says one industry observer: "It [the sales force] is probably the smallest part of the company's success. They benefit from having an excellent product to sell. Their salesmen start out with one foot in the door."

Once in the door, Boeing salespeople spend a lot of time keeping track of equipment needs. They call frequently, and the very nature of their jobs requires that they are in almost constant touch with their accounts. Salespeople are the day-to-day conduit who get the squawks and simultaneously observe the airline. It is through them that information is collected and contacts made so all other things can take place.

Boeing also has a reputation for paying great attention to detail. Explains John MacKenzie, an analyst with Foster Marshall in Seattle: "If you're a little start-up airline somewhere, Boeing is going to pay an awful lot of attention to you, so all of a sudden when you order five planes ten years from now, you'll remember them."

Size and reputation undoubtedly help Boeing. In a business where the customer is going to make a minimum purchase of several million dollars, it is easy to be swayed by the knowledge that the company is going to be around to service its product. Still, size isn't the only factor in Boeing's favor. While the competition is quick to point out that Boeing is a huge company without any competition in some areas (it is, for example, the only manufacturer of a plane the size of a 747), that is not the sole reason for its success.

Boeing's sales force, like those of its competitors, consists primarily of engineers and other technical people who have years of experience in the company before entering sales. There is no formal Boeing sales training (learning the products is an ongoing process because of constant refinements), and each salesperson is assigned to a handful of airlines that do not directly compete against each other.

They are, by all reports, smooth and knowledgeable salespeople who like to sell on facts and logic rather than promises and hyperbole. "They tend to be conservative," says Peter Rinearson, a business writer for *The Seattle Times* and author of *Making It Fly*, a book about the marketing of Boeing's 757. "For example, they'll always underestimate fuel efficiency. They'll say it's a five percent savings, and it'll be eight." Boeing's upstart competition, Airbus, the European consortium, is more likely to go the other way with its claims, say some industry observers.

Boeing, however, isn't being coy when it underestimates its planes' capabilities, says Rinearson. It is just the way that it does business. "An airline's whole business depends on those airplanes, so selling is on a whole different magnitude," says Boeing's Thomas Riedinger, "These are personal commitments as well as contractual, and they are perhaps more important than what's on paper."

SOURCE: Bill Kelley, "How to Sell Airplanes, Boeing-Style," *Sales and Marketing Management*, December 9, 1985, pp. 33–34.

Questions

1. Describe the buying center for the purchase of a jet airplane by a major airline. Who might be involved in this purchase decision? Who do you think has the most influence?

2. What type of buying situation is this for most buyers? What does this say about the marketing strategy required?

3. Evaluate Boeing's marketing strategy to date. Why has it apparently worked so well?

4. In what ways is the marketing of organizational products, such as jet airplanes, different from the marketing of consumer products?

Federal Express Faces Challenges to Its Grip on Overnight Delivery

Federal Express collects more than half the revenue in what is now more than a $10 billion industry. And at a time when deteriorating service is a national malady, this company claims to deliver more than 99 percent of its letters and packages on time.

But Federal Express faces some major obstacles in the months ahead. Its days of 40 percent annual growth are over. The market for shipping documents is saturated, forcing it to expand in areas like box hauling from warehouses. Its very mode of delivery is being challenged by new technology, most notably by the increasing use of facsimile machines.

And now, United Parcel Service, the package-delivery giant, is muscling into the overnight-express business, and it aims to grab a large piece of it. "It's the immovable object vs. the irresistible force," says Bernard La Londe, a transportation consultant.

To the people at Federal Express—employees as well as managers—this is no mere business challenge. They see it as a battle between good and evil, symbolized by such matchups as the lively orange and purple colors of Federal vs. the dull brown trucks and uniforms of UPS; the easy-going velvet-glove management of Federal vs. the stopwatch, highly engineered UPS style; Federal's up-the-ranks complaint system vs. UPS's union-grievance procedures; and publicly traded Federal vs. closely held UPS.

With an estimated $11 billion in revenue last year, UPS is about three times the size of Federal Express. That has given it the resources to build its overnight-delivery business from nearly zilch to an estimated $1.3 billion annually in five years. Already it has forced Federal to cut some prices, which may preserve customers but which then eats into historically lush profit margins.

Now UPS is spending millions of dollars to develop technology that will give it many of the same luxury services that Federal offers and enable it to truly go head to head—features like on-call pickup and continuous tracking of packages. UPS has also opened storefront counters and letter drop-boxes, and on January 1, 1988, it began offering air-express customers their money back if packages aren't delivered on time. It claims that it now delivers 99.5 percent of its packages by the noon deadline.

Fantastic Sams International Inc., for one, has switched its $5,000-a-month account to UPS. Federal's computerized tracking system is superior, says Victor Johnson, the traffic manager for the Memphis hair-care franchiser. But, he adds, "So what? UPS can get the package there by noon all the time. Federal is a good company, its trucks are cleaner, but I'm not that worried about how clean a truck is."

Federal Express Chairman Frederick Smith concedes that competition has made customers more prickly about price. Federal's basic overnight letter rate (by 10:30 AM) is $12, after all, and UPS's (by 3:00 PM) is $8.50. But Mr. Smith insists that extra service sets Federal apart and that in an era of intensifying competition, that is what's important. "The trick now is to keep differentiating," he says.

This wasn't the case before Mr. Smith hatched Federal Express, because there was no industry. As a Yale undergraduate in 1965, Mr. Smith wrote an economics paper criticizing the slow, unreliable cargo services available then and proposing an independent air-service system. His professor, believing the idea futile, gave the paper a C. But Mr. Smith started such a delivery business anyway, in April 1973, at the age of 28. At first, it still didn't seem like an "A " idea. Only after the airline industry was deregulated in November 1977 did Federal Express begin to take off. Once it was no longer restricted to 7,500 pounds of freight a plane, it made sense to buy larger airplanes and use its smaller Falcon aircraft to expand into small and medium-size markets. The company's operating profit rose from $19.5 million on revenue of $160.3 million in fiscal 1978 to $167 million on revenue of $3.88 billion in the year ended May 31, 1988.

As top strategist, however, Mr. Smith doesn't have a flawless track record. ZapMail, a document-transmission service, was started as a major diversification effort and proved a major embarrassment. Following a two-year effort, it was closed in September 1986 after a $190 million write-off. Mr. Smith says it proved to be "tremendously more complex" than expected.

But he doesn't apologize for the idea, because ZapMail was an effort to address a real and continuing problem. Facsimile machines, which transmit documents over telephone lines, are eating into Federal's overnight business. In just one year, the growth rate of Federal's letter shipments has been cut in half, to about 25 percent.

That's one big reason that Federal has begun to focus more on big-box delivery, or the "back-door" loading dock trade. But that move is risky, too. It targets a very different crowd from the white-collar clientele of Federal's "front-door" document-delivery business, and the company has had to fine-tune its marketing. A big new ad campaign shows transmission companies and fish producers sending big boxes, and the "absolutely, positively" tagline has been dropped.

The foray into boxes also moves Federal squarely into UPS's bailiwick. In the past, UPS's big brown trucks have crowded out most of the competition for the "back-door" market. Timing may be a problem, too. Federal is opening up this battle front just as UPS is launching its attack on Federal's overnight business.

So whom do the experts like in this high-stakes confrontation? Most are betting that Federal can prevail in the overnight market as long as it cuts its costs enough to keep its prices within hailing distance of UPS's. They argue that certain intangibles favor the reigning champ over the challenger. Says Kevin Murphy, a Morgan Stanley & Co. analyst. "There's a little bit of the Ayn Rand type of characters down there—freedom-fighting heroes, an intense pride."

Challenging Federal Express in Overnight Mail

The Company Still Dominates the Market...

1986 shares of the overnight air-express package-delivery market

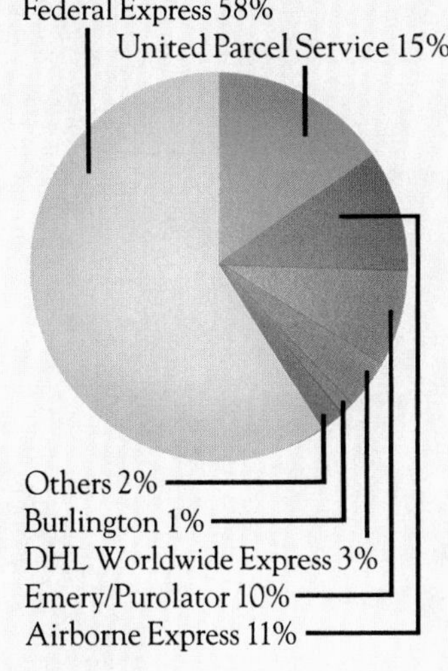

Source: Morgan Stanley & Co.

...But Competition Is Squeezing Profits

Federal Express net income per share; in dollars[1]

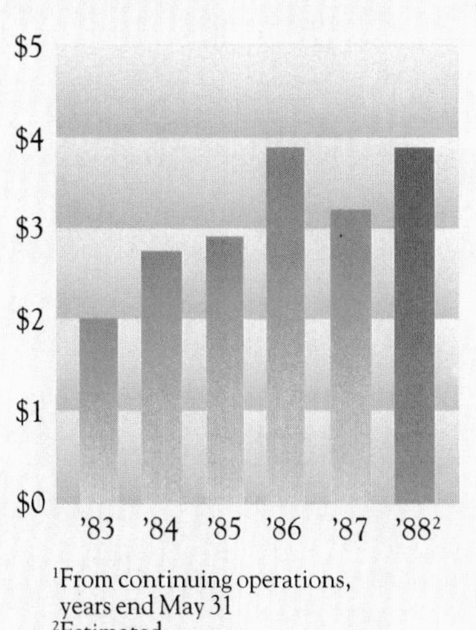

[1]From continuing operations, years end May 31
[2]Estimated

Source: Zacks Investments Research

SOURCE: Larry Reibstein, "Turbulence Ahead: Federal Express Faces Challenges to Its Grip on Overnight Delivery," *The Wall Street Journal*, January 8, 1988, p. 1, 10; personal communication with Federal Express, May 1989.

Questions

1. How would you segment the market for overnight delivery service?

2. How could a company like Federal Express or UPS use the SIC system to identify market opportunities and to evaluate their effectiveness to date?

3. What type of buying decision is represented here? What are the steps in the purchase decision process for this product?

4. What criteria do you think are important in the purchase of overnight delivery services? Are the criteria relevant for letters and reports sent by office personnel different from the criteria used by shipping and receiving personnel to decide how to send large boxes out of a warehouse? Given the criteria used, what can a company in this industry do to increase its marketing effectiveness?

5. Since 1973, Federal Express has had to adapt to changing external market conditions. List the external conditions and explain how Federal Express has altered its marketing mix to respond to the changing conditions.

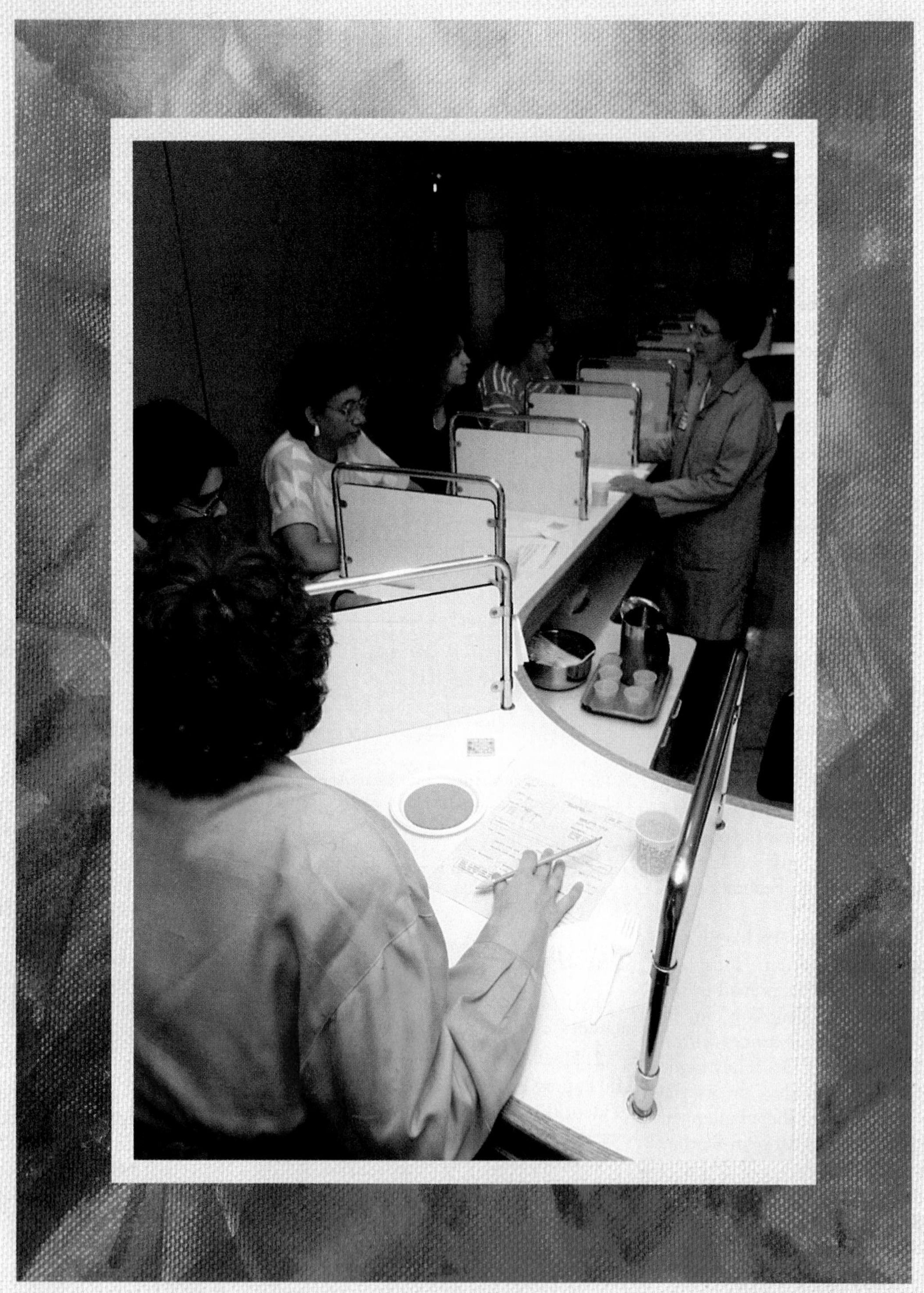

7

Marketing Research and Information

Learning Objectives

Upon completing this chapter, you will be able to do the following:

UNDERSTAND
the basic terminology of marketing research.

EXPLAIN
how marketing managers incorporate marketing research information into their decision making.

ILLUSTRATE
the potential uses of marketing research within an organization.

LIST
the steps in undertaking marketing research.

IDENTIFY
the cost and value of information to the decision maker.

DESCRIBE
the components of a marketing information system.

COMPARE
approaches to demand measurement and forecasting.

DISCUSS
procedures used to forecast market potentials and expected company sales.

MARKETING PROFILE

Colgate Palmolive's Irish Spring

Despite the company's previous tendencies to by-pass test markets, market research played an intrinsic part in Colgate Palmolive's introduction of its reformulated Irish Spring deodorant soap with skin conditioners. Consumer focus groups provided qualitative reactions to alternate product formulations and positionings. Consumer surveys gave a more precise measure of the market opportunities and current consumer soap usage. Test marketing was among the most significant marketing research techniques employed in the product's introduction process. The test markets allowed Colgate Palmolive to turn a narrowly positioned product with a low market share into a broader, more far-reaching success.

Colgate Palmolive's original Irish Spring soap had been positioned primarily toward men and held about a 5 percent share in the fairly flat bar soap market. Minute annual overall market growth meant that brands gain sales only at their competitors' expense. Thus, Irish Spring had to grow its market share to increase its sales. Colgate Palmolive saw that Dial and Zest, leaders in the deodorant soap market, were aimed at the entire family. Paul Brindak, group marketing manager for U.S. body cleaning products, noted that, "Marketing studies established the need for a deodorant soap that didn't dry out the skin. Our research showed business opportunities that were not being met."

Colgate Palmolive seized those opportunities. It saw great market potential for an all-family, skin-conditioning deodorant soap and repositioned itself accordingly. Market research on consumer attitudes and perceptions determined that the original product's formula, packaging, and ad campaign all contributed to its distinctly masculine appeal. These factors had to be changed. Yet the soap's fresh and outdoorsy image was highly compatible with the company's new strategy. Keeping the product's old name

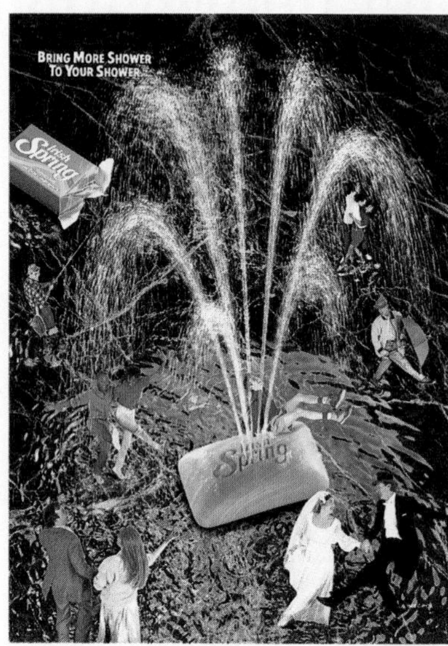

allowed the company to retain this positive association with "Irish Spring" and prevented alienation of the product's current users. This was one of the company's key objectives in structuring their test market.

Household panel data enabled Colgate to monitor its existing user base. Usage profiles tracked the brands that respondents had bought over the last two years. By defining new users, old users, loyal users, and dissatisfied users, Colgate Palmolive was better able to determine the causes of market shifts. The company then continued its successful approaches while identifying potential improvements.

The reformulated product was tested in three different "live" test markets from 1984–1987; it then underwent a detailed advertising and promotion testing by BehaviorScan in Marion, IN, and Visalia, CA. The extensive time spent in the testing stage was attributed to the numerous variables involved and the low success rate for new products in the bar soap market. Three different copy ads and a variety of promotion options were among the numerous variables tested. Based on its BehaviorScan test market, Colgate chose the "bumbling announcer" spots for its national advertising campaign. In this ad, the "bumbling announcer" stands amidst his listeners while water spouts from the bar of Irish Spring in his hand and "showers" all in its path. This ad scored well in consumer copy tests, and higher trial numbers indicate a strong impact in the final test market. Colgate also pin-pointed different consumer responses to its promotions.

Because bar soaps are sold in prepackaged groups of four, their purchase cycle is about eight weeks, and it takes about three months to collect good household data. The three-month mark indicated solid market penetration and the six-month mark produced the repeat sales indicative of a product's success. Although Colgate Palmolive won't reveal the exact figures, Irish Spring's numbers were strong and showed a significant improvement in market share (in a traditionally flat market). As Brindak said, "We wanted to fine-tune our promotion and maximize our position on the curve—that's why we went with a controlled market test." The numbers indicate that this was an effective decision.

This profile illustrates the effective use of both marketing research and management judgment in successfully reformulating and repositioning an old product. It shows how consumer panels, surveys, and test markets can forecast a product's success or failure and how an effective advertising program and packaging can support a product. These are but a few of the different methodologies used in marketing research.

SOURCE: Leslie Brennan, "Quick Study," *Sales and Marketing Management,* March 1988, p. 52–53.

This chapter is concerned with the effective use of information in marketing decision making. The quality of marketing managers' decisions depends on properly obtaining and using marketing information. Can you imagine yourself as a General Motors executive, deciding to introduce a new automobile without obtaining information on potential users' attitudes toward features and style preferences; or as the brand manager for RCA television, spending over $10 million on advertising without information on the possible effectiveness of various advertising messages; or even as the director of feature exhibits at the National Gallery of Art, making decisions on what admission fee to charge for the Egyptian exhibit without information on the impact of various fees? We trust that you would feel a great need for information in these types of decision situations. This chapter, then, is concerned with the mechanics of providing information for all types of marketing decisions.

Managers and Marketing Information

The *Marketing Profile* on the marketing of Irish Spring highlights the potential contribution that research can make to marketing decision making. However, it should be clear that Colgate's research could not answer all its questions with anything close to certainty. Other studies had to be conducted, and management judgment had to play a key role.

Sources of Information

Figure 7–1 illustrates, in a simplified way, the many sources of information available to a decision maker. The marketing decision maker has access to information from many sources, including marketing research studies, accounting reports, sales organization reports, and contacts with other managers. In reality, providing information to a decision maker is more organized than is implied in Figure 7–1. Organizing and supplying information often takes place within the context of a marketing information system (MKIS). The components and functioning of an MKIS will be discussed in detail later in the chapter. For now, note that an MKIS organizes diverse data into a form for a marketing manager to use in decision making.

The modern marketing manager often has a sophisticated marketing decision support system (MDSS) to allow manipulation and presentation of the information derived from the MKIS. MDSS will be discussed later.

Role of Experience

One other information source is directly available to the decision maker: experience. Information generated from a decision maker's experience is combined with other information inputs to yield a decision, but a manager must decide what weight to assign to each input source. It is possible that a manager is so sure of his or her judgment in a decision situation that new information inputs are ignored or not asked for in the first place. Consider the following examples:

- When Sony researched the consumer marketplace for a lightweight portable tape cassette player, consumers indicated that they would not purchase any tape player that would not record. The Sony chairman decided to introduce the Walkman, despite these results, and with great success.[1]
- General Electric undertook consumer research when the electric refrigerator was invented. The results were overwhelming: the consumer did not want this noisy, dangerous, expensive product. GE management decided

Figure 7–1 Sources of Information Available to a Marketing Decision Maker

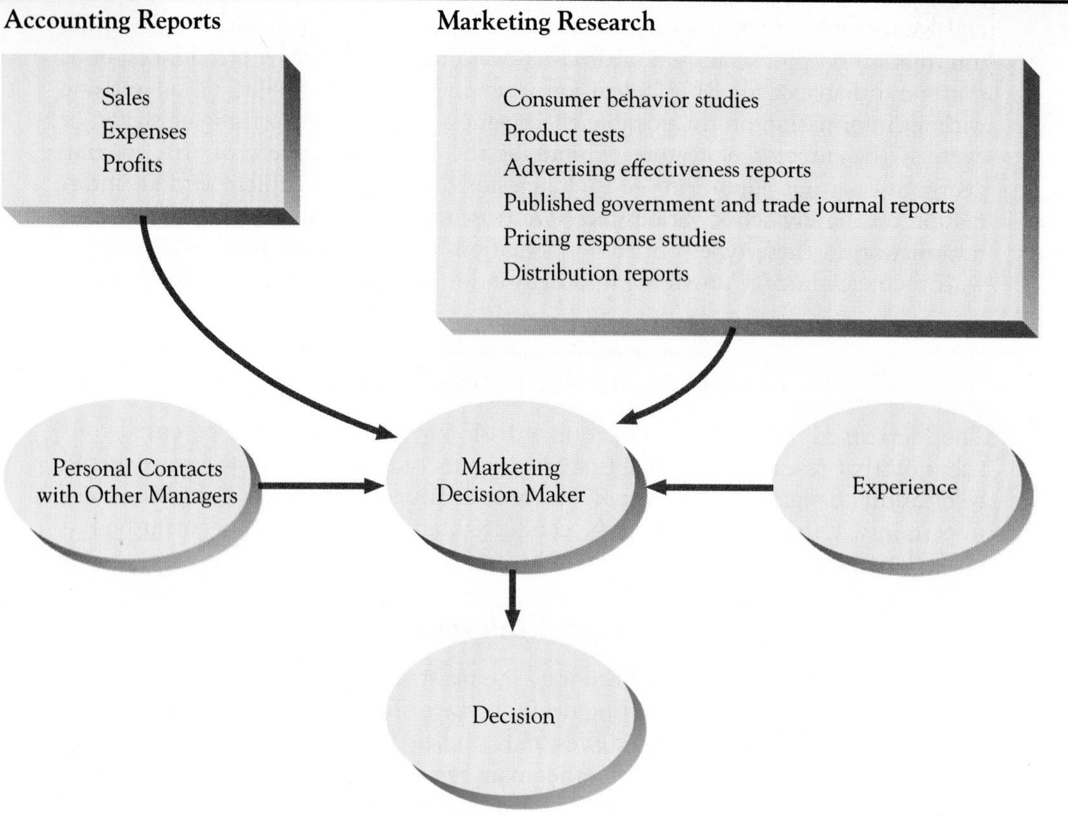

that the research did not properly indicate the long-run consumer reaction and went ahead and introduced the refrigerator anyway. (All ice cream eaters must applaud their judgment!)

Of course there are many examples where managers ignored marketing research results, and failure resulted. A classic example is in the marketing of the Susan B. Anthony dollar by the U.S. Bureau of the Mint. All marketing research evidence pointed to an unreceptive market among consumers and retailers, yet the Mint went ahead anyway, despite its earlier failure with the two-dollar bill. Yet we must recognize that it is part of the management function to make judgments. The management of marketing information is, thus, critical to effective decision making. We now turn our attention more formally to the concepts of marketing research, marketing information systems, and marketing decision support systems—that is, to the management of information.

Marketing Research and Decision Making

The function of marketing research is to provide information for decision making in an objective and systematic fashion.[2] Thus, we define **marketing research** as:

> . . . *the systematic and objective approach to the development and provision of information for the marketing management decision-making process.*[3]

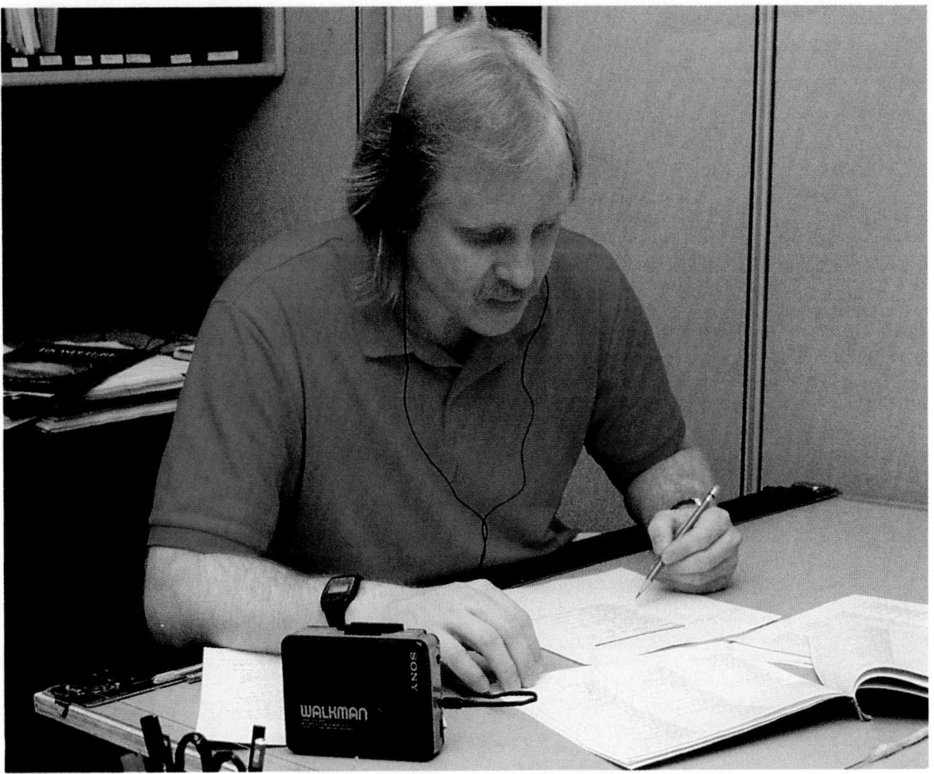

The Sony Walkman proved that sometimes managerial experience and judgment outweigh other marketing research information.

Systematic refers to the research being well planned in advance. It should be directly tied to the decision being made, and all aspects of the design will be developed in detail. *Objectivity* indicates that research should be undertaken in an unbiased and unemotional manner. It should be as free from political infighting as possible. It is thus *the application of the scientific method to marketing.* Finally, marketing research is tied directly to the *decision-making process.* Studies done without marketing decisions in mind are not marketing research; they are just data-collection exercises. Just what, then, is the decision-making process to which marketing research is so directly tied?

Figure 7–2 presents the steps a manager goes through in the decision-making process.

1. *Recognizing the Need to Make a Decision.* The brand managers for Maxwell House (MH) coffee may have been quite satisfied with their marketing program until sales reports indicated that sales had dropped. The need to make decisions became apparent when the sales results came in.
2. *Understanding a Decision Situation.* Having identified the need to make a decision, the manager now strives to better understand the situation by identifying the main issues and causal factors. MH might undertake research or creative thinking to determine if it is Folgers' competitive advertising activity for its coffee that appears to be causing consumers to switch from Maxwell House to Folgers.
3. *Identifying Alternative Courses of Action.* The decision maker explicitly identifies possible actions in such areas as product, price, place, or pro-

Figure 7–2 Steps in the Decision-Making Process

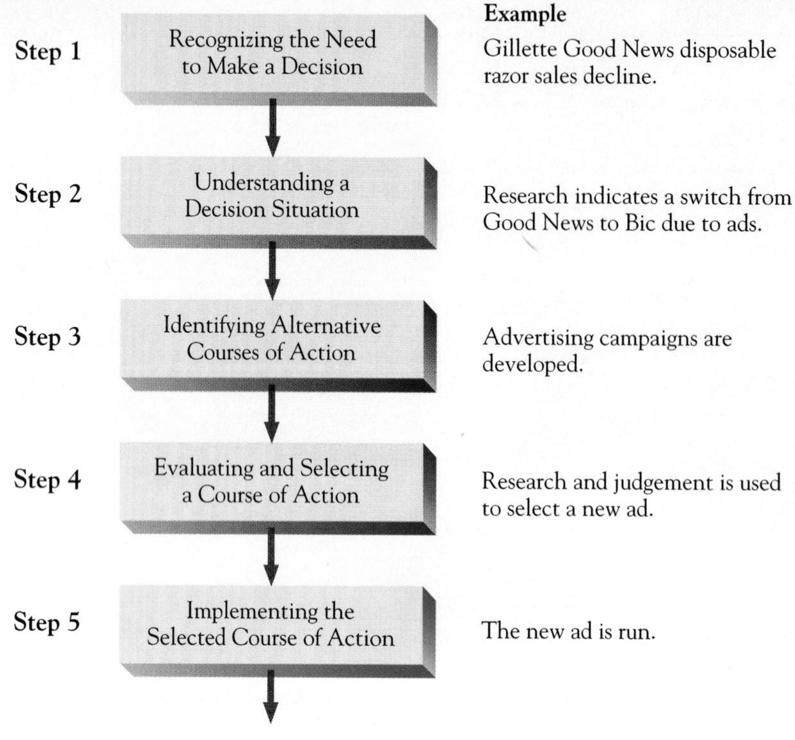
Example
Step 1
Recognizing the Need to Make a Decision
Gillette Good News disposable razor sales decline.
Step 2
Understanding a Decision Situation
Research indicates a switch from Good News to Bic due to ads.
Step 3
Identifying Alternative Courses of Action
Advertising campaigns are developed.
Step 4
Evaluating and Selecting a Course of Action
Research and judgement is used to select a new ad.
Step 5
Implementing the Selected Course of Action
The new ad is run.

motion, again by using research or creative thinking. The MH people may consider three new advertising campaigns as available alternatives.

4. *Evaluating and Selecting a Course of Action.* The MH people may select one of the three proposed advertising campaigns to run. They will do this by evaluating each campaign being considered. Again, research and judgment play a role.
5. *Implementing the Selected Course of Action.* The new MH advertising campaign will be developed and placed in the media. The results will be monitored.

Note that at each stage in the decision-making process the marketing manager can make use of both research and/or judgment. The type of research used at each stage will differ. We, thus, must classify different types of research and relate them to the steps in the decision-making process.

Types of Research

There are three types of marketing research, each playing a different role within the decision-making process, as shown in Figure 7–3. The three types are described as follows:

Figure 7–3 Types of Research in the Decision-Making Process

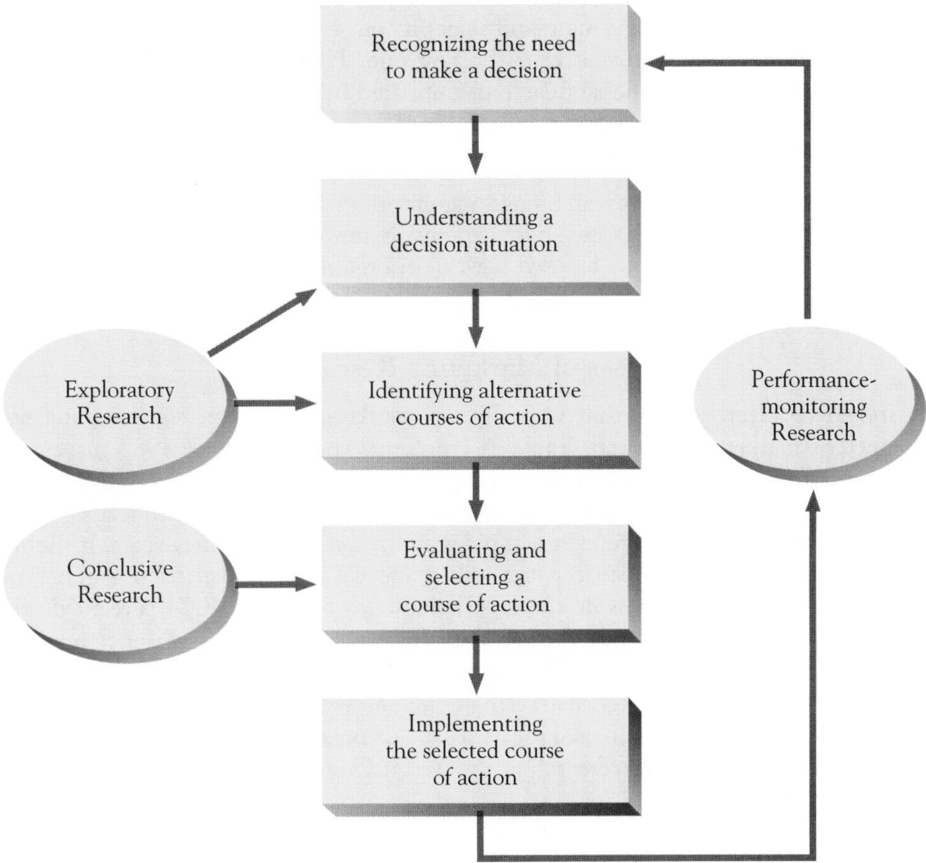

SOURCE: Based on Thomas C. Kinnear and James R. Taylor, *Marketing Research: An Applied Approach*, Third Edition (McGraw-Hill, 1987), p. 20.

1. *Performance-Monitoring Research.* This type of research provides feedback on an implemented marketing program. Basically, it answers the question: How well is the program working? In the MH coffee example, performance-monitoring research provided sales results, thus identifying the symptoms of problems or opportunities.
2. *Exploratory Research.* This information-gathering activity is used when the manager has not yet developed a good understanding of the decision situation or identified alternative courses of action. The fundamental objectives here are (a) to translate the symptoms identified by performance-monitoring research into statements of problems and opportunities, (b) to clarify vaguely identified problems and opportunities, (c) to understand better the factors affecting the situation, and (d) to identify possible courses of action. MH brand managers may have used this type

of research to decide their problem was the effectiveness of their advertising campaign and to reduce the number of possible new campaigns to three.

3. *Conclusive Research.* This type of research provides information that helps the decision maker evaluate and select a course of action. It answers the question: Which alternative is the best one? Here MH could undertake to test the effectiveness of each ad campaign by presenting the commercials in a theater to a group of consumers, or by doing actual television tests in different regions of the country.

Each of these types of research has an appropriate research design, and these will be discussed later in the chapter. First we must better understand the different ways that marketing research may be used within an organization and the organizational process necessary to initiate the studies.

Uses of Marketing Research

It should be clear by now that virtually any marketing decision can benefit from competent marketing research. Table 7–1 presents the results of a 1988 survey on the use of marketing research in 631 firms. All elements of the marketing mix and the marketing environment are represented. Marketing research is, indeed, greatly used in American industry, reflecting rapid growth over the last thirty years. It should also be clear that many decisions are still made without marketing research. For example, 39 percent of firms do no advertising-copy testing, and 24 percent do no new product acceptance or potential studies. Judgment based on experience remains the only input for decisions in many cases.

However, in sophisticated marketing companies the active integration of marketing research into decision making is a fact of organizational life. Consider the following uses of marketing research at Procter & Gamble (P&G):[4]

- The idea for Bounce dry fabric softener came when research on the use of liquid fabric softeners showed that consumers wanted something more convenient.
- P&G selected Coast deodorant soap's label based on research that gave the label a four-percentage-point advantage (33 percent vs. 29 percent) over a slightly different version.
- Luvs was selected as the name of P&G's new premium-priced disposable diapers when more consumers preferred it over the alternative, Harrah (80 to 64 percent).
- The bottle design for Dawn dishwashing liquid was selected because it was preferred 75 percent to 26 percent over competing brands.

Authorizing Marketing Research Studies

Before marketing research studies are undertaken, it is important to think through the major aspects of the problem at hand and the role of marketing research in this problem. In many organizations, this is formalized into a marketing research request form. Typical contents of these forms are the following:

- a statement of the background of the problem
- identification of alternative courses of action being considered
- a statement of the research objectives: what is expected to be accomplished by the research

Table 7–1 Types of Research Activity: 1988 Survey

	Sometimes Done	Frequently Done[1]	Done By Mkt. Res. Dept.	Done By Another Dept.	Done By Outside Firm[2]
A. Business/Economic and Corporate Research					
1. Industry/market characteristics and trends	37%	60%	66%	6%	14%
2. Acquisition/diversification studies	50	15	36	14	8
3. Market share analyses	30	62	64	6	11
4. Internal employee studies (morale, communication, etc.)	55	10	31	13	14
B. Pricing					
1. Cost analysis	36	35	31	24	3
2. Profit analysis	32	38	30	24	2
3. Price elasticity	40	15	31	12	5
4. Demand analysis:					
a. market potential	40	48	61	8	39
b. sales potential	38	45	53	12	4
c. sales forecasts	30	51	47	15	3
5. Competitive pricing analyses	41	36	46	16	4
C. Product					
1. Concept development and testing	48	34	50	6	17
2. Brand name generation and testing	37	9	30	5	14
3. Test market	40	13	34	8	10
4. Product testing of existing products	40	18	35	7	10
5. Packaging design studies	31	8	25	4	11
6. Competitive product studies	47	23	42	7	11
D. Distribution					
1. Plant/Warehouse location studies	24	6	14	9	5
2. Channel performance studies	28	8	20	7	5
3. Channel coverage studies	25	7	18	6	5
4. Export and international studies	19	6	16	5	5
E. Promotion					
1. Motivation research	36	11	29	3	14
2. Media research	43	25	30	9	22
3. Copy research	41	20	30	5	21
4. Advertising effectiveness	43	34	43	6	22
5. Competitive advertising studies	38	19	31	5	14
6. Public image studies	52	20	37	7	23
7. Sales force compensation studies	32	5	14	15	6
8. Sales force quota studies	25	7	14	14	3
9. Sales force territory structure	31	7	19	14	3
10. Studies of premiums, coupons, deals, etc.	34	9	28	5	7
F. Buying Behavior					
1. Brand preference	40	27	36	4	19
2. Brand attitudes	39	28	37	3	19
3. Product satisfaction	40	42	52	5	17
4. Purchase behavior	43	33	45	3	17
5. Purchase intentions	43	32	45	3	16
6. Brand awareness	41	32	41	3	20
7. Segmentation studies	47	28	45	3	18

[1]"Done" columns do not add to 100% since "not done" responses were omitted.

[2]"Done by" columns do not add to 100% since those responses indicating done by multiple sources were omitted.

SOURCE: Thomas C. Kinnear and Ann R. Root, 1988 Survey of Marketing Research, American Marketing Association, 1989, p. 43.

- the specification of what information is to be collected, including examples of the types of questions to be asked
- a statement of how the research results will be used in making the decision
- an estimate of the cost and value of the research.

This list clearly indicates that the requirements of the research be thought through completely before undertaking a study. This difficult task needs the active participation of both the decision maker and the researcher if the research is to address the real problems of marketing decision makers.

In the end, whether or not a study is sanctioned depends on the assessment of its potential cost and value. The costs of marketing research are quite straightforward and include the out-of-pocket expenses of the study, lost profits from delaying the marketing decision, and disclosing of plans and research results to competitors.

The value of marketing research is much more difficult to assess. Conceptually, research increases the probability of making better marketing decisions—that is, avoiding major errors and selecting the best alternative available. The problem from a measurement point of view is that there is a major subjective component: value is often in the mind of the manager. If he or she is sure about the results of a decision, then research has no value. As the manager's uncertainty about the decision increases, so does the value of research. For example, Charles Revson of Revlon made major decisions without doing marketing research. His knowledge and skill in the cosmetics business were such that he felt little uncertainty and, thus, assigned little value to research, even though the dollar consequences to Revlon of making a bad decision were very high. The dollar consequences of the decision being made are important in assigning value to research. Thus, in general:

Do research when
- the size of the market is large;
- the dollars earned per unit sale are large; or
- the manager is uncertain about the results of his or her actions.

Don't do research when
- the size of the market is small;
- the dollars earned per unit sale are small; or
- the manager is fairly certain about the results of his or her actions.

If the value of a study is greater than its cost, then the study should be done.

For example, the information that a test market would provide was not deemed worth the cost by the management for Fab 1 Shot in its competition with Procter & Gamble (P&G) for the single packet laundry product market.[5] Colgate's Fab 1 Shot is a single use packet that contains laundry detergent, fabric softener, an anti-static element, and a whitener. P&G has been in test market with its Tide Multi-Action Sheets in the Quad Cities area of Iowa and Illinois for some time. Fab 1 Shot management decided to take its product national without a market test. "Colgate figures they'd rather be first than careful," said Jay Freedman, an industry analyst. Subsequent product use problems with Fab 1 Shot occurred, requiring the product to be withdrawn from the market.

Review Your Marketing Knowledge

- You have just been appointed brand manager for a line of industrial chemicals that have been experiencing declining sales over the last six months. How would you approach the decision-making process for this situation?
- Under what conditions should you undertake marketing research in this situation? What type of marketing research is appropriate?

Steps in the Marketing Research Process

The marketing research process may be viewed as a series of steps. Both managers and marketing researchers are involved, to varying degrees, at each stage, as shown in Figure 7–4. The marketing researcher attempts to control the errors that can occur at every stage of the research process. It is common to distinguish between statistical sampling error and errors in other steps. Control of total error is the objective:

Total error = Sampling error + nonsampling errors.

Much of the rest of this chapter discusses how competent marketing research controls these potential errors.

Establish the Need for Information

Establishing the need for the information provided by marketing research is a critical step, and the manager who needs the information is highly involved at this stage. The researcher's function is to assist the manager in defining the problem at hand, usually by trying to determine its background, alternative courses of action, and how the research will be used. (See the questions listed in the section on sanctioning research studies.) The failure to do this properly is the main reason for unsuccessful marketing research studies. For example, a major package goods company undertook a study of its media mix (radio, television, and magazines) to determine how to better spend its advertising dollars and, thus, improve its declining market share. The study was well executed but was essentially useless, as the real problem turned out to be a shift in consumer tastes to lighter formulations of the product. Better thinking at the beginning would have identified this issue and led to a useful research study.

Specify Research Objectives and Information Needs

Research objectives describe the purpose of the study. Consider these objectives for three different studies:

- Measure the market potential for solar energy in the state of Maine.
- Determine which of three advertisements generates the highest consumer recall.
- Measure consumer preference for alternative formulations of a new, powdered soft drink.

Information needs represent a statement about the specific information necessary to satisfy the research objectives. It is, in essence, a listing of those issues that will comprise the research report. Thus, a report on the market potential for solar energy in Maine could include the following information needs:[6]

- The current energy use pattern of the residents of Maine (oil, gas, coal)
- The current market penetration level for solar energy
- The cost of current solar systems
- The factors considered by those having solar systems, and the evaluation of alternative energy systems using these factors; the same for nonsolar adopters
- The characteristics of segments of the energy market
- The likely size of the market in 1990, 1995, and 2000

Figure 7–4 Steps in the Marketing Research Process

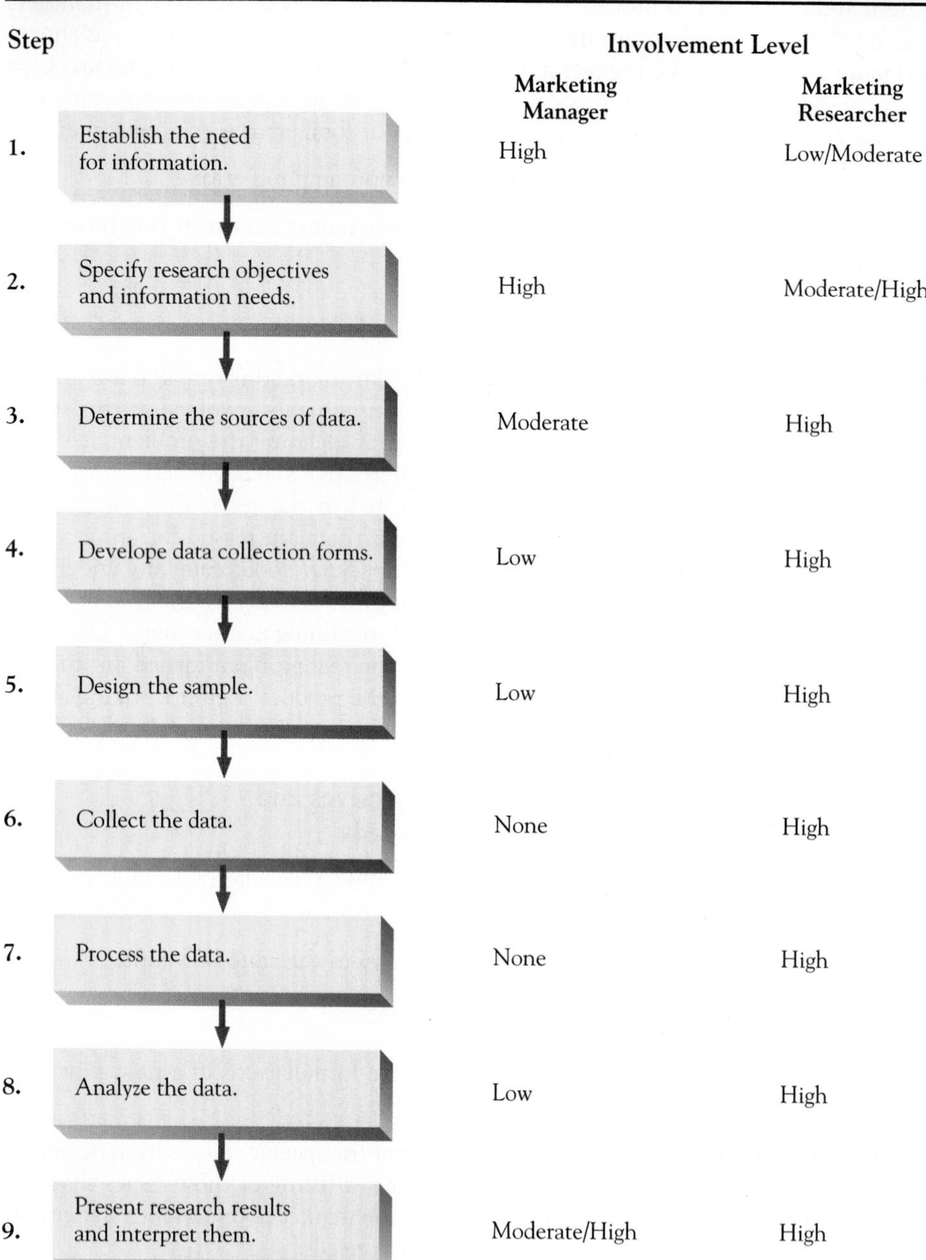

Step
Involvement Level
Marketing Manager
Marketing Researcher
1. Establish the need for information.
High
Low/Moderate
2. Specify research objectives and information needs.
High
Moderate/High
3. Determine the sources of data.
Moderate
High
4. Develope data collection forms.
Low
High
5. Design the sample.
Low
High
6. Collect the data.
None
High
7. Process the data.
None
High
8. Analyze the data.
Low
High
9. Present research results and interpret them.
Moderate/High
High

SOURCE: Based on Thomas C. Kinnear and James R. Taylor, *Marketing Research: An Applied Approach,* Third Edition (McGraw-Hill, 1987), p. 20.

For the remaining steps in the research process, the researcher is more involved than the manager because most of these steps involve major, technical research design issues. The next part of this chapter provides only an overview since this book focuses primarily on marketing principles and not on the details of marketing research design.

Determine Sources of Data

The researcher is confronted with three basic sources from which to obtain marketing data. These are respondents, experimentation, and secondary data.

Respondents. The most common source of marketing research data is from responses provided to specific questions. There are two types of research involving the questioning of respondents: *qualitative* and *quantitative.* Qualitative research usually consists of interviewing knowledgeable people, or groups of consumers, either individually or in groups of six to ten people, called *focus groups.* These interviews are usually somewhat unstructured and free-flowing. They are designed to provide insights into problems and help generate ideas for future research. For example, the product manager at one major company was heard to state after hearing a focus group interview, "Wow, I never thought that package design was a potential reason for our current situation." Clearly this type of data is most useful in an exploratory research study.

In contrast, quantitative research on respondents, which is often called *survey research,* is designed to put specific estimates on marketing phenomena. What percentage of consumers dislike the package design? How much does it affect their purchase behavior? These are examples of the types of questions addressed in quantitative research related to respondents. Quantitative research has its primary application in conclusive research. In the *Marketing Profile* at the beginning of this chapter, Colgate used both qualitative and quantitative marketing research. It is important that quantitative research have a sound conceptual basis, and qualitative research helps provide this.

In communicating with respondents, a number of data-collection methods are possible—*personal interviews, telephone interviews,* and *mail questionnaires.* Data may also be obtained by the *observation* of respondents. In observation, no communication goes on between the respondent and the recorder of the behavior. Both humans and mechanical devices may be used to record the relevant activities. For example, a human recorder may note the number of brands tested and the amount of time spent at a cosmetic counter by customers. Alternatively, mechanical devices are used to record the channel a television set is turned to, and automatic scanning devices in supermarkets are now used to record purchases by consumer panel members.

Experimentation. Experimentation is the second basic source of marketing data. Here the objective is to determine cause-and-effect relationships among marketing variables. For example, how much will sales change if we increase or decrease advertising dollars by ten percent? Is our new sales training program more effective than the old one? Which price level will be the most profitable? In experimentation, the researcher attempts to control all aspects of the situation so that he or she can be clear about one variable (for example, advertising) affecting another (sales). For experimentation to give effective conclusions, well-developed options must be tested. Thus, it is primarily appropriate for conclusive research.

The successful use of experimentation in marketing research is well documented. Examples include:

- the addition of a new stannous fluoride formulation to a toothpaste reduces user's cavities better than the previous formulation (Procter & Gamble's Crest)
- better allocation of advertising dollars among geographic regions to increase sales (Budweiser)
- more effective ads for V-8 Cocktail Vegetable Juice and Swanson Frozen Dinners (Campbell's)

This type of information is not easily obtained in a survey format. Survey respondents generally are either unable or unwilling to answer with reasonable accuracy. For example, a major home computer manufacturer asked a sample of target customers if they would buy the company's product if the price were reduced from $2400 to $1800. Fifteen percent of the respondents indicated that they would definitely buy at the lower price. When the price was lowered, only 3 percent of the target customers purchased the computer. The need to go beyond surveys to experiments for certain situations should be clear.

Secondary Data. There are two basic types of marketing data—primary and secondary. **Primary data** are collected specifically for the research needs at hand. **Secondary data** are already published pieces of information collected for purposes other than the specified one. Because secondary data were collected for other purposes, their fit with the specific problems of a manager may not be very exact. Thus, secondary data sources tend to be used for exploratory research purposes. The major sources of secondary marketing research data are internal company records, syndicated data, government data, and private data.[7]

Internal Company Records. The company itself often has available very useful data such as sales and cost information organized by territory, customer, and product. This type of data can help identify areas of strength and weakness in the marketing program, and major trends in these areas. Unfortunately, this data is often not detailed enough to provide useful analysis.

Syndicated Data. A number of private organizations collect and sell standardized data designed to serve the information needs of a number of organizations. This information is called syndicated data. For example, A. C. Nielsen's Retail Index provides market-share data on many package goods categories such as food items, cleaning products, paper goods, and drug products. Syndicated data are available on consumers, retail sales, wholesale sales, industrial products' sales and potential, advertising effectiveness, and media and audiences. Within a specific industry a trade association may have useful data available. Scanner data is also available on a syndicated basis as described in the *Marketing in Action* in this section.

Government Data. Governments at all levels collect and make available many kinds of data relevant to marketing. The federal government alone provides easy access to the following sets of data:

- *Census of Housing*—contains data on types of structures, year built, occupancy, appliances, value, rent, and ethnic category of occupant.
- *Census of Population*—includes information on age, sex, race, national origin, employment, income, and family composition.
- *Census of Manufacturers*—contains data on number, size, capital expenditures, output, inventories, and employment.
- *Census of Retail Trade*—provides information on number, size, sales level, merchandise, and employment for retail stores.
- *Census of Wholesale Trade*—presents the same type of data as the retail reports, but for wholesale operations.

Each census has data available at national, state, and local levels. The usefulness of this information to marketers cannot be overstated. Our list is a small part of the available data from the federal government, let alone from local and state agencies.

MARKETING IN ACTION

Scanners Revolutionize Marketing Research

The unobtrusive supermarket check-out scanner, which was first introduced by Kroger in the early 1970s, has revolutionized marketing research in the last few years. Originally, the device, which beeps as it reads the black bars of the Universal Product Code (UPC), was used to track inventory and improve shelf management, among other things. Due to the large amount of data the UPC generates, however, scanners have now become an indispensable tool for marketing researchers.

In their most simple application, UPC scanners provide data which can help both manufacturers and retailers determine price elasticities as well as the effects of coupons and other promotions. Scanners have been most revolutionary, however, when combined with other technologies. Information Resources, Inc. (IRI), a market research firm in Chicago, made a breakthrough in the early 1980s when it introduced BehaviorScan, a new tool in marketing research. BehaviorScan combines scanner technology with the use of split-cable technology to provide detailed information on the effectiveness of TV advertising on marketing programs. With split-cable technology, different TV advertisements for a given product may be targeted to different homes. The purchasing behavior of these homes is then individually tracked through the use of UPC scanners, after test families present a special ID at the grocery store. Researchers are then able to determine the effectiveness of different advertising programs within a given market.

In 1987, Information Resources introduced InfoScan—a faster, more comprehensive version of BehaviorScan. With InfoScan, Information Resources can provide its clients with weekly information on consumer purchasing, based on a sample of over 60,000 homes. InfoScan also provides complete data on the promotional conditions affecting these purchases. InfoScan gets information to its clients more quickly than competing data collection systems and allows marketers to closely track the effectiveness of their marketing programs.

SAMI/Burke, another leading market research firm, has taken scanner technology one step further. SAMI/Burke now offers a patented scanner wand which marketing research participants can use at home to scan their own purchases. By using this new technology, participants can help marketing research firms more accurately track consumer purchases of products from drug, convenience, and mass merchandising stores which generally do not use scanners. This new data collection technique gives marketers more complete data and greater flexibility.

SOURCES: Leonard M. Lodish and David J. Reibstein, "Keeping Informed," *Harvard Business Review,* January-February 1986, pp. 167–182. Ronnee Taylor, "Technology Offers Better, Quicker Test Market Results," *Marketing News,* June 19, 1987, p. 14. Thayer C. Taylor, "The Great Scanner Face-Off," *Sales and Marketing Management,* September 1986, pp. 43–46. "InfoScan—Breakthrough Tracking Service Delivered on Time," (Advertisement), *Advertising Age,* March 23, 1987.

At the federal level, the U.S. Department of Commerce is a clearinghouse for data from all censuses and from other federal agencies and departments. Customer service representatives gladly assist marketers in finding and using available data.

Private Data. Data are also published or made available for retrieval by many private organizations like magazine publishers, associations, advertising agencies, and research firms. Marketers can find useful data in *Advertising Age, Forbes, Fortune, Harvard Business Review,* and *Sales and Marketing Management* magazines, among others. The latter annually publishes a survey of population characteristics and expenditure data for all major markets in the United States. Other sources include the *Journal of Marketing, Journal of Marketing Research,* plus numerous industry-specific publications. The marketing research process requires access to an up-to-date and complete library of private data.

If secondary data are not available then primary data must be collected. The steps in the research process that follow relate to the collection of primary data. It should be noted, however, that the collection process for secondary data involved these same steps, when the data were originally obtained.

Develop Data Collection Forms

The fundamental data collection form used in marketing research is a survey questionnaire. Other forms include those used to record observations of behavior, and those used to record results of experiments. In structuring a questionnaire, some key rules must be kept in mind:[8]

- Avoid leading questions ("Doesn't this product work better than that one?").
- Avoid biasing questions ("Do you agree with the American Bar Association when it says. . . ?").
- Avoid double-barreled questions ("What do you think of this product's taste *and* texture?").
- Use simple words that the target respondent will understand ("white" instead of "Caucasian," as the U.S. Census Bureau does now).

There are many other issues in data collection form design that must be addressed. These are beyond the scope of this discussion, but they include the specific question content, the response format (*open*—what do you think—versus *closed*—check the appropriate response), question wording, and question sequence.

Design the Sample

In collecting primary data, decisions have to be made about who should provide the data. This is the issue of sample design. The option of selecting everyone (taking a census) is usually not a viable one in marketing; a census is too expensive and takes too long.

A **sample** is a group of elements (such as people, companies, or locations) selected from the population of elements that interests the researcher. For example, a population could be defined as business-school majors taking *Principles of Marketing* courses in the United States and Canada in 1991. Notice that both a time and a geographic reference are required to properly define the population.

The researcher has many ways to select a sample from the population. The fundamental distinction is between using a **probability sample** and a **nonprobability sample.** In nonprobability sampling, the selection of the sample is based, in some part, on the judgment of the researcher. In probability sampling, mechanical rules are used to select the sample, and each member of the population has a known chance of being selected.

Probability Sampling Procedures. There are three basic types of probability sampling: *simple random, stratified,* and *cluster.* The use of all of these requires having a list of all the elements of the population, called a *sampling frame.* For example, schools may provide us with a list of students in *Principles of Marketing* courses.

In *simple random sampling,* all elements in the population have an equal chance of being selected. Thus, in a class of 100 students, each student could be assigned an individual number between 1 and 100. The students comprising the sample would be those matching a set of randomly selected numbers. Simple random samples are

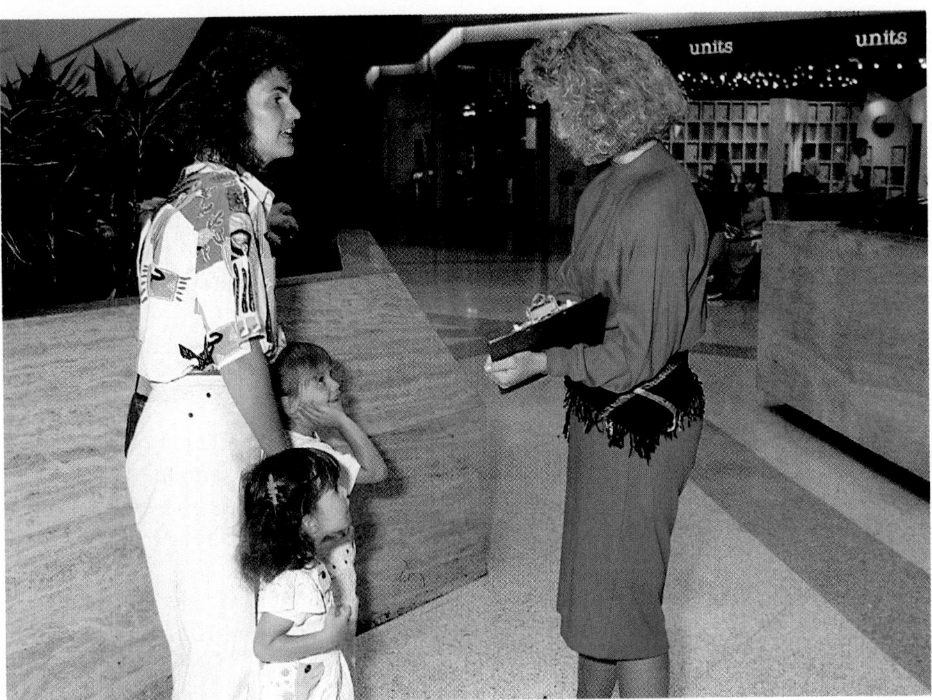

In-person interviews have many benefits, but they also have a high dollar cost.

expensive, especially for large populations, but they provide reasonably high statistical efficiency (small sampling error). They are not widely used because of their cost and the availability of more statistically efficient or cheaper procedures.

In *stratified sampling,* the researcher gains in statistical efficiency over simple random sampling. The cost is again high, but this procedure is moderately used. The benefits are gained by putting the population elements into groups, or strata, prior to sample selection. These groups are based on some criterion the researcher believes is related to the measures being taken. For example, the A. C. Nielsen Company measures sales levels of many products by sampling supermarkets. Since big stores generally sell more than small stores, the Nielsen researchers can meaningfully form groups of stores based upon their sizes. A simple random sample is then taken within the designated store groups. Because the stores within any group are more alike than all stores as a group, the sampling error is reduced. We say that the sample is more efficient. Common variables used to form groups or strata are size, days of the week, regions of the country, sex, age, race, and income.

Cluster sampling is used primarily to improve the cost dynamics of a sample. In doing so, some statistical efficiency is lost. There are two types of cluster sampling procedures: systematic sampling and area sampling.

Systematic sampling is a faster way to do simple random sampling. The results are virtually the same. The researcher selects every *k*th element (for example, every *10*th element) in a frame after a random start somewhere in the first *k* elements. You could select a sample of students in your class by simply selecting the students numbered 5, 15, 25, 35, 45, 55, 65, 75, 85, and 95.

Area sampling is very commonly used when geographic sections such as city blocks, counties, or regions of the country are being selected. The intent is usually to interview people living within the selected geographic area. For example, a *two-stage* area sample could proceed as follows: (1) form all blocks in the city into groups called clusters; (2) select a random sample of block clusters (first stage); (3) select households from within the selected block clusters (second stage).

Area samples have relatively large sampling errors, but for large national studies, they are much cheaper than other methods and, thus, are much used.

Nonprobability Sampling Procedures. The marketer also has the option of using one of three nonprobability sampling techniques: convenience, judgment, and quota sampling.

Convenient samples are selected on any basis that suits the researcher. Selecting those who volunteer to answer your questions or the first people to come past you are examples.

Judgment samples are selected on the basis of what the marketer or researcher thinks the selected elements will contribute to the study. For example, in test marketing, a judgment is made about which cities would constitute the best ones for testing a product's marketability. The usefulness of the sample is related to the skill of its selector.

Quota samples are special judgment samples. The sample is selected to match predetermined *control characteristics*. Common control characteristics for surveys of consumers are age, sex, race, region of the country, and income. A specific number of people who fit each control profile are selected. "We need 100 males age 25 to 34, who are white, live in the Midwest, and earn $25,000 to $45,000 per year." This directive would fill in one of the quota cells.

Nonprobability samples do not provide measures of statistical error. We simply do not know how good their estimates are. All nonprobability procedures are, however, inexpensive and easy to administer compared to probability procedures. As a result, they are highly used, with quota sampling being the most frequently used. Because nonprobability procedures provide no measure of sampling error, they are most appropriate in exploratory research. They can yield great insights and suggest possible courses of action. Once the sample has been selected, the researcher turns his or her attention to the actual collection of the data.

Collect the Data

Two major areas of concern arise in the data collection phase: (1) whether to conduct the interview in person, by telephone, or by mail, and (2) how to manage the field interviews.

Mode of Interview. The choice of how to collect the data involves a trade-off among a number of factors. Table 7–2 summarizes the characteristics of each mode against relevant criteria.

In-person interviews provide great versatility, can be done in a reasonable amount of time, give good control over who answers, and can potentially provide answers to a very long questionnaire. But these benefits come at a high dollar-cost per interview. In addition, the potential for interviewer cheating and biased responses to sensitive questions exists.

Telephone interviews are moderately versatile and inexpensive, provide reasonable sample control, are very fast, and allow for excellent supervision of interviewers. However, the amount of data one can collect is more limited.

Mail questionnaires are the weakest mode. However, a major benefit of mail is the amount of data that can be collected at a reasonable price. Unfortunately, this

Table 7–2 Three Modes of Data Collection

Criteria	In Person	Telephone	Mail
Versatility to adapt to special needs of respondent	High due to face-to-face contact	Moderate	None
Cost	High (average $30 per interview); travel time drives it up	Quite low (average $6 per interview); no travel time	Low (average $4 per completed interview), but can be much higher given poor return rate
Time	Moderately fast, depending on sample size	Very fast	Potentially quite slow, depending on interviewees' speed in returning questionnaire
Sample control (who answers the question)	High	High if there is a good list of numbers to select from	Poor
Quantity of data one can collect	Very large amounts	Moderate amount	Quite large amounts
Bias	Most biased response for sensitive questions Confusing questions can be clarified Interviewer cheating possible	Moderately effective on sensitive questions Clarification possible Close supervision of interviewers possible	Best on sensitive questions Clarification not possible

benefit must be weighed against the lack of versatility, slowness of returns, and poor sample control.

Field Operations. This phase involves the supervision of the actual data collection. In this regard, two major sources of potential biases have to be guarded against: nonresponse errors, and interviewing errors.

Nonresponse errors are of two types. The first occurs when a selected respondent is not at home. The field worker must call back to assure that the right sample elements are interviewed. The second is when the selected respondent refuses to take part in the study. The interviewer must do his or her best to interest the potential respondent in taking part. The potential bias in nonresponse is the concern that those who are left out of the sample may systematically answer differently from those who are interviewed.

Interviewing errors can also lead to biased responses. These include (1) leading the respondent to give a specific answer ("good answer"), (2) skipping questions on the questionnaire, (3) changing the question wording, (4) improper recording of the given response, and (5) cheating—the falsification of all or part of the response to a questionnaire.

Process and Analyze the Data

Once the data is collected in the field, it must be prepared for presentation to marketing management. The first step is to prepare the data into a computer-accessible data structure. This is called *data processing* and involves a number of steps:

1. Editing the data. This ensures its legibility, completeness, accuracy, and clarity.
2 Coding the data. Numbers are assigned to represent various responses. For example, for the variable *sex,* females are given the number 1, and males 2.
3. Putting the data into a computer-readable form. Typically, this involves keypunching it onto computer cards or directly placing it into a computer file from a computer terminal at the time of the interview.
4. Reading the data into a computer file and storing it on tape, or disk file.

Once the data is in a computer file, we are ready to do data analysis. *Data analysis* involves applying statistical techniques to summarize the collected data. It is vital that the techniques used be appropriate to the measurement scales. If the study is not properly designed and executed, no data analysis procedure will yield meaningful results. *One-way tabulations* answer questions like these: How many women were in the sample? What brand of toothpaste sold the most? *Two-way tabulations* answer questions about the interrelationships between two variables. For example, what is the association between age and brand choice? Or, is higher income associated with greater use of credit cards? More advanced statistical analysis procedures, or complex decision models, may also be applied to the data. No matter what techniques are used, the objective of the analysis should be to provide meaningful information addressed to the problem that was defined at the beginning of the research process. Many studies are not used, because the data analysis is not in tune with the study objectives.

Present the Results

The analyzed data should then be presented to marketing management both orally and in written form. The objective here is to be as clear as possible, leaving technical details to the appendices of the written report. A two-to-three page summary of the results is often all that interests the decision maker. This gives the most important findings of the research and their implications. Illustrations of some mistakes that can be made in marketing research are presented in the *Marketing in Action* feature "Some Questionable Research."

All Studies Follow the Marketing Research Process

It is quite common for a specific research problem to be addressed in stages, with different types of research being used. Thus, a problem may be noted by performance-monitoring research and refined in terms of definition and possible solutions by exploratory research. The solutions may be evaluated by conclusive research.

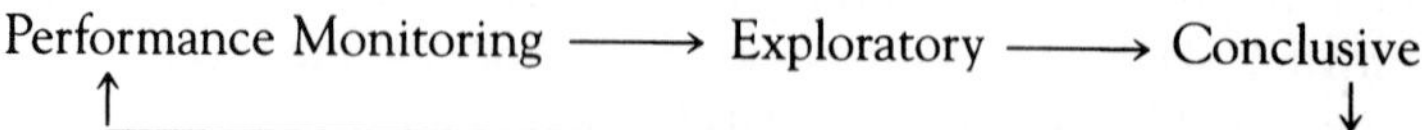

Note that performance-monitoring, exploratory, and conclusive research must complete each step in the research process. Each has issues of information needs, data sources, data collection forms, sampling, fieldwork, processing, analysis, and presentation. Thus the research process may be repeated many times in the solution of even one marketing problem.

MARKETING IN ACTION

Some Questionable Research

A. *A Political Survey*

A member of Congress mailed a questionnaire to his district households. The questions and results are listed below.

1. If the government will not stop inflating the money supply, do you think that it should amend the income tax law to provide protection for the purchasing power of people's savings?

Yes	No	Not sure
73%	4%	23%

2. Do you think that instead of increasing our taxes to increase welfare payments the government should repeal all monopolies and other privileges so that poor people—indeed, all people—would be able to buy what they need at fair, free-market prices instead of being gouged to enrich monopolists?

Yes	No	Not sure
84%	4%	12%

These responses were based upon 3248 respondents out of 24,732 questionnaires mailed. The member of Congress said about this: We received 3248 replies, and many included letters with further comments. The return rate was 13 percent (out of 24,732 sent out). Statisticians consider a response rate of about 6 percent to be normal, so again, it seems that the residents of this district have a greater-than-average interest in the politics of the federal government.

B. *A Magazine Readership Study*

Cosmopolitan magazine asked readers to respond to a questionnaire included in the magazine. It concerned the social habits and mores of readers. Some 106,000 women responded to the survey. *Cosmopolitan* compared this sample size to more academic studies that had "only 6000 women," and then claimed that "no survey as broad in scope as *Cosmopolitan's* had ever been done."

Commentary

A. Political Survey

- These were poorly phrased questions. How could anyone answer no to these questions?
- A response rate of 13 percent is extremely poor. No good marketing researcher (or statistician) would accept this, since seven out of every eight didn't respond, and these individuals may have very different views from those who responded.

B. Readership Survey

- Sample size is much less important than how the sample is selected.
- The *Cosmopolitan* sample is a self-selected sample. It is a convenience sample, which means that the reported results do not represent a broader segment of the population.

An Illustration. A good illustration of the effective use of all three types of marketing research is the turnaround of General Mills' Total Cereal.[9]

1. Performance-monitoring research, in the form of syndicated market-share data, indicated that Total was losing market share.
2. Exploratory research was then undertaken in an attempt to determine why. A series of focus groups were used. Out of this research came the hypothesis that Total was misperceived relative to so-called natural cereals. Specifically, Total was seen as being less nutritious than natural cereals, when, in truth, the opposite was true.
3. An advertising campaign was developed to convince cereal users that Total was more nutritious than natural cereals. Conclusive research, in the form of an experiment, then tested the effectiveness of the advertisements. They were judged to be extremely effective in changing consumer attitudes, and so were introduced nationally. The theme was that Total had 100 percent of the recommended daily allowance of vitamins, while natural cereals had much less.
4. Performance-monitoring research showed the effectiveness of the campaign, as market share increased dramatically and held at a higher level. This marketing strategy remains successful into the 1990s.

Review Your Marketing Knowledge

- Much marketing research that is technically well done fails to have significant impact on the marketing decision being made. Why might this happen? How might this be prevented?
- What skills should a marketing research analyst have to be effective?

Marketing Information and Marketing Decision Support Systems

Many firms are working toward integrating marketing research activity into the whole spectrum of information available to a manager. This is done through the development of a marketing information system (MKIS). A **marketing information system** is defined as:

> *a structured, interacting complex of persons, machines and procedures designed to generate an orderly flow of pertinent information collected from both intra- and extra-firm sources for use as the bases for decision making in specified responsibility areas for marketing management.*[10]

Simply put, an MKIS is designed to provide a marketing manager with the specific information needed to make decisions in his or her area of responsibility. For example, a sales manager needs sales information by product and by territory but does not need advertising recall data. An effective MKIS should provide information on a timely basis. You might ask: is this not the function of marketing research? Indeed, marketing research is a great part of an effective MKIS. However, MKIS goes beyond marketing research; it comprises data from all sources—both within and outside the company—including such areas as accounting, industry, and financial data. Also, marketing research usually deals with information about specific problems, whereas MKIS does not. It continually monitors and reports on the relevant information flow from all sources, including marketing research, as depicted in Figure 7–5.

The systematic provision of an orderly and relevant flow of information is not enough. Marketing decision makers must be able to use this information in an interactive fashion to answer *what is* and *what if* types of questions. The interactive computer interface between a marketing manager and the available information flow is called a **marketing decision support system** (MDSS). This system has certain characteristics: (1) the marketing manager is able to access the MDSS directly from his or her work without going through data processing professionals;[12] (2) the MDSS must provide answers quickly while the manager is interacting with the system; and (3) the software in the MDSS should allow analysis and presentation without requiring extensive computer expertise. The system must be "manager friendly." Figure 7–5 shows the pivotal place of MDSS in relation to the marketing manager and his or her information environment.

Modern marketing information and decision support systems are tied heavily to the computer. The systems are usually so large that the use of a mainframe or advanced minicomputer is required. The databases involved are too large for small computer systems. Two of the most successful MDSSs, the Express package of Management Decision Systems and the Evaluation Planning System of EPS, Inc. do need a main-

Figure 7–5 The Concept of a Marketing Decision Support System

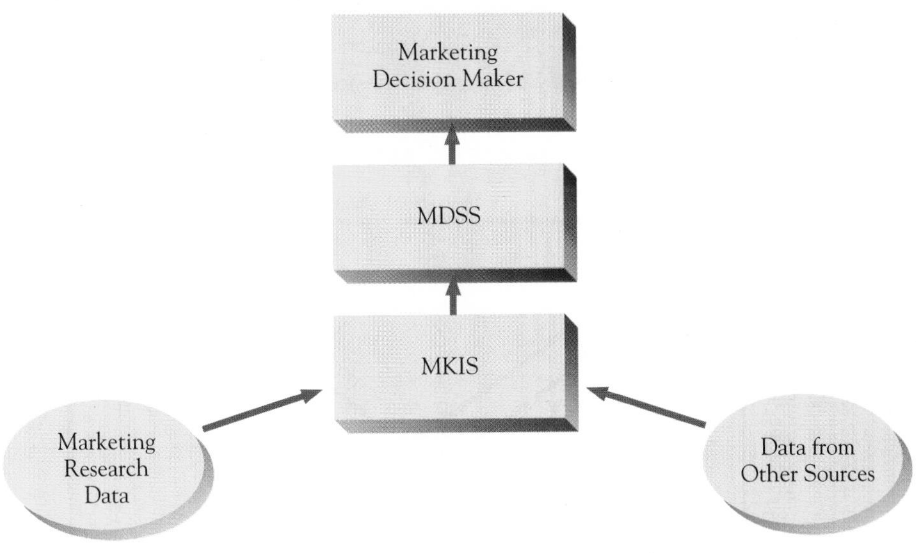

frame to take advantage of all their power. They are also integrated into a terminal or personal computer that resides at the manager's work place. In the future, as computer power for PCs increases, it is likely that these large systems will be self-contained in a PC or PC network. Some small MDSSs already are PC usable. The components of a modern MDSS are shown in Figure 7–6.

Components of MDSS

Figure 7–6 also shows how an MDSS is positioned between a manager and the information flows coming from all aspects of his or her environment, and represents each of the components of an MDSS operation: a data bank, a statistical bank, a model bank, and a display unit.

A *data bank* is the storage depot for the data flowing into the system. It is kept in an easily retrievable form. The *statistical bank* allows data analysis on stored data. This usually involves easy access to canned data analysis programs. Standard statistical procedures (tabs and crosstabs, and regression) are thus easily usable on stored data. The *model bank* contains operations research models that represent the real marketing world. For example, a marketer may have a model of his or her market in the bank. This model represents how consumers behave in the marketplace. The manager can then test so-called *what if* formations using the model. What if we decrease price 10 percent? What if advertising is increased 20 percent? The model provides quick and inexpensive answers to such questions. Of course, the model must mirror the real world enough to provide valid estimates of what will happen. The *display unit* is whatever form the system uses to give information to the manager. It could be a printed report or the display screen on a computer terminal.

Figure 7–6 Components of a Marketing Decision Support System

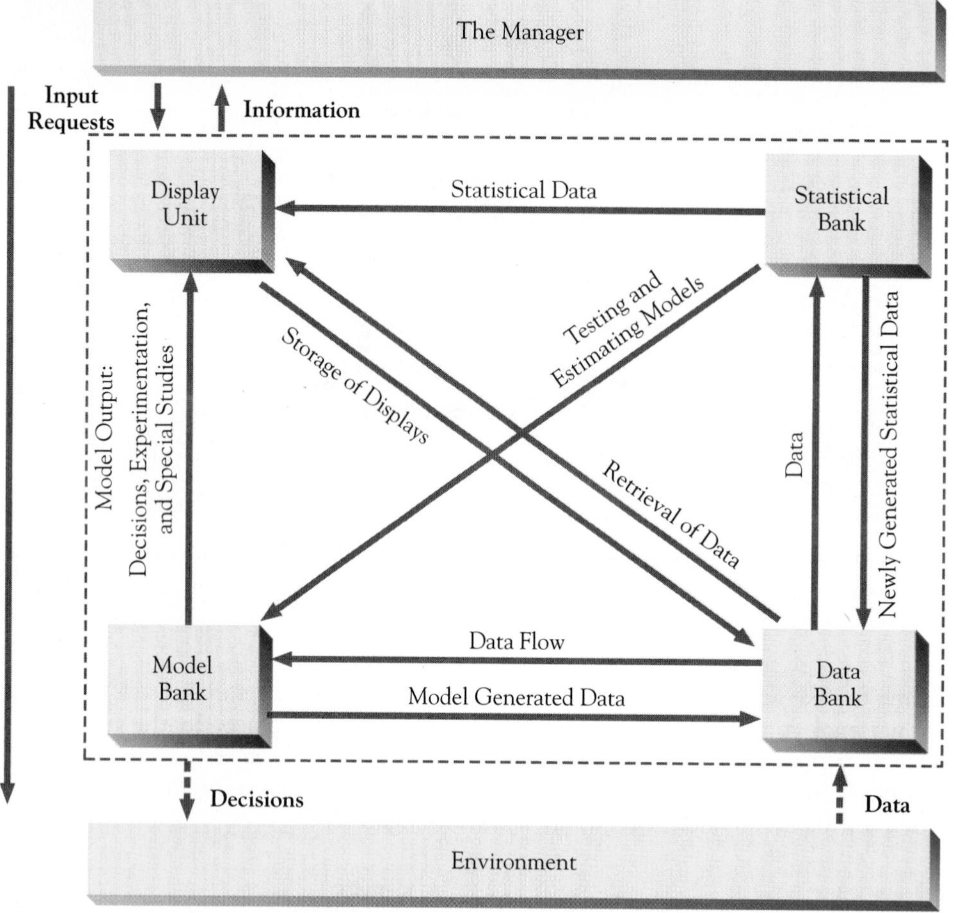

SOURCE: David B. Montgomery and Glen L. Urban, *Management Science in Marketing* (Prentice-Hall, 1969), p. 18, and John D. C. Little, "Decision Support Systems for Marketing Managers," *Journal of Marketing*, vol. 43 (Summer 1979), p. 10.

Status of MDSS

Despite the great potential for MDSS to assist the marketing manager in planning, control, and strategy research, MDSS, in its full potential, has not yet been widely used in organizations. The newness of the concept and the human problems of implementing such a system are major barriers. Technical MDSS people have often turned off marketing managers with their jargon and procedures, and the systems are not yet totally manager-friendly. MDSS remains for the most part an ideal to strive for. The effective implementation of an MDSS would seem to require the following:

1. Develop small systems first.
2. Develop systems relevant to current management practice and structure.
3. Don't overuse outside experts. Develop internal skills.

4. Involve the user in the design.
5. Build a flexible system to fit the many divergent information needs of managers.
6. Make the first use areas important ones to managers, and ones where success is quite likely.
7. Build the system in an evolutionary fashion. Add the complex models only after data storage and retrieval are successfully in place.

Demand Forecasting

Marketing research has many purposes within the organization, as noted in Table 7–1. Two key areas of marketing research activity are forecasting market potentials (with 88 percent of all firms undertaking such activity) and forecasting sales levels (with about 81 percent of all firms doing this). These are critical areas in the understanding of the marketplace. Both are complex topics sometimes involving statistical methodology. We present an overview here, leaving the technical complexities to courses in marketing research or forecasting. The difficulties and importance of demand forecasting are well illustrated in the *Marketing in Action* on the Delicare liability suit in this section.

There are a number of different levels at which measurement and forecasting can take place. **Market potential** for a product is the *maximum* total sales possible for all sellers of that product to an identified customer group within a specified time frame. It presumes a given marketing environment and combined marketing efforts of all suppliers. If the environment or marketing efforts change, the market potential will change. For example, the annual market potential for automobiles in the United States fell from about 12 million cars to about 10 million cars with increased gasoline prices from 1989 to 1990.

Sales potential is the *maximum* sales possible for one company's product as the company's marketing effort increases relative to competitors. Again, it is specified for a given environment, customer group, and time frame.

Sales forecast is the *expected* sales level of a company's product given a specified time frame, a designed marketing plan, and an assumed environment. The sales forecast serves as a basis for marketing and for financial and production planning within the organization. Note that the sales forecast presumes a given marketing plan and environment. It is illogical to develop a marketing plan on the basis of a sales forecast, since marketing effort causes sales, and not vice versa.

In forecasting market potential, sales potential, or expected sales levels, two general approaches may be used. These are the *top-down* (or *breakdown*) method, and the *buildup* method.

Top-Down Method

The **top-down method** first develops an aggregate measure of market potential. This typically is based upon an empirically derived relationship between the product of interest and some other measure. For example, the market potential for automobiles is highly related to the level and growth rate of the gross national product (GNP). Thus, a GNP estimate would be the starting point for the forecast. The forecaster then estimates total car sales and breaks down this total amount into units of interest to the organization. These units could be product lines, or customer groups, or geographic areas. The breakdown of the aggregate estimate of demand is usually based

MARKETING IN ACTION

Marketing Researchers Face Liability Suit

The marketing research industry was shaken in mid-1987 by a $24 million liability suit filed by Beecham, Inc. against Yankelovich Clancy Shulman (YCS). The suit asks that YCS be held liable for marketplace losses suffered by Beecham in its introduction of Delicare Cold Water Wash product. The product failed by a wide margin to meet the market share forecasts of Beecham's marketing research supplier, YCS.

Beecham attempted to obtain compensation for the $24 million in losses that it alleges occurred as a result of significant errors in a $75 thousand laboratory test market prediction model study done for Delicare Cold Water Wash. Delicâre was a product designed to compete with Woolite for the delicate fabric segment of the detergent market. The complaint stated that: "YCS forecast an extremely successful market performance for Delicare and urged Beecham to support the launch with massive advertising and promotional expenditures." The forecast was made that if Beecham did this, Delicare would take product category leadership from Woolite even if Woolite spent heavily to defend its dominant market position.

Beecham said it relied on the YCS marketing research in setting an $18 million introductory year advertising budget for Delicare. YCS had predicted that spending at this level would result in market share of between 45 to 52 percent. Delicare's share never reached 25 percent. Beecham charged that the inaccurate forecasts were the result of significant errors at YCS including "management malaise." More specifically, they charged YCS with negligence, negligent misrepresentation, professional malpractice, and breach of contract.

Many practicing marketing researchers reacted to this suit. "I will definitely be more cautious," said Norman Passman, president of Guideline Research Corp. "It won't stop me from making recommendations, but I will be more careful because you're always vulnerable." Another marketing researcher noted, "I have always maintained that marketing research is an art dancing around as a science and that we cannot profess to be 100 percent accurate. I feel a wise client will understand that."

The suit was settled out of court in 1989.

SOURCES: Jack Honomichl, "How Beecham Suit Affects Contracts," *Advertising Age*, August 17, 1987, pp. 23 and 38. Ellen Neuborne, "Researchers See 'Chill' From Suit," *Advertising Age*, July 20, 1987, pp. 3 and 50.

---

on some index that measures the potential sales in the subunits, relative to each other. For example, an estimate of total automobile potential may be broken down into geographic regions on the basis of the population within each geographic area. Once the market potential has been allocated to subunits, the market share for the company within each subunit can be estimated and the sales forecast developed.

Buildup Method

The **buildup method** starts at the lowest level of subunit aggregation, which again could be a product line, customer groups, or geographic areas. Estimates of market or sales potential and sales forecasts are made first at this level. The total estimates of market or sales potential and sales forecast, therefore, come from *adding up* all the subunits.

Both general approaches to forecasting require the use of certain techniques. In the following section, we discuss commonly used forecasting techniques; some are used mainly to estimate potential, while others are used more for sales forecasts.

Forecasting Techniques

We will present an overview of eight **forecasting techniques:** corollary product indexes, general buying power indexes, custom-made indexes, survey of buying intentions, test markets, sales force composition, causal relationships, and trend analysis.

Corollary Product Indexes. One method of forecasting sales potentials for a product involves using the sales of another product as an indicator. The two products in question must, of course, be related. For example, the number of residential building permits issued is a good indicator of the potential market for plumbing and electrical fixtures. The company would have to derive the exact relationship between the two empirically, using past data.

General Buying Power Indexes. It is possible to estimate the market potential in specific regions for many products by using indexes of relative buying power. The index may be either a *single-* or *multiple-factor* index. For example, a single-factor index might use summary Internal Revenue Service income data, by state, as a measure of market potential. If total American market potential for a product is estimated to be $100 million, and all potential buyers have incomes over $50,000, and California has 20 percent of all people with incomes above $50,000, then the estimated potential in California would be $20 million ($100 million × .2).

In industrial markets, a widely accepted single-factor index is the *Sales & Marketing Management Survey of Industrial Purchasing Power.* This annual index uses data on the value of shipments of industrial goods. The index is organized according to categories of the Standard Industrial Classification industry groups and uses geographic area as its measure of potential. For example, it would report the value of paper products shipped into the New England area.

It is usually more accurate to use *multiple factors* to construct an index. One very well-known consumer market index is the *Sales & Marketing Management Survey of Buying Power.* It is constructed by weighting population by two, effective buying income by five, and total retail sales by three. Data in this index are provided at the state, county, and city level. For example, if Texas is rated as having 10 percent of buying power, then 10 percent of the total American market potential would be allocated to Texas.

Custom-Made Indexes. Of course, general-purpose indexes may not provide accurate measures of potential for any specific product. In these circumstances, it may be possible to construct an index that is unique to a product. To do this, one must identify the most important factors that affect demand, obtain accurate data on these factors, and combine them into an index with weights assigned to each factor relative to its importance. The marketer, of course, must test the validity of the developed index as a predictor of potential. The index, once validated, would be applied in the same fashion as discussed.

Survey of Buying Intentions. One common way to forecast both market potential and sales is to undertake a survey of prospective buyers and ask them their intentions about purchasing either from the product category or a specific brand. This is often done by asking respondents to rate the probability (between 0 and 100 percent) that they will purchase a product in a given time frame. These measures usually overstate actual purchases, but if the marketers compare intended to actual sales over time, they can learn to apply the proper discount factor to intended sales to yield good forecasts. This method works best when there are relatively few buyers of large durable products.

Test Markets. A test market is a major step beyond a survey of intentions in forecasting, since it measures actual purchase behavior of consumers in the marketplace. Test marketing involves actually marketing the product in a few selected cities in the country, and then using the sales levels in the test market to predict national sales. Test markets are time-consuming (a year or more), expensive ($1 million plus), and can be monitored by competitors. Additionally, competitors may undertake unusual promotional activities within the test market, resulting in confusing conclusions. This has led many marketers to start using *simulated test markets.* These are controlled laboratory experiments where test consumers shop in a simulated store, and sales are forecast from these results. Research for Delicare was conducted in a simulated test market.

Sales-Force Composite. One buildup method of forecasting both potential and sales is to obtain from all salespersons and sales representatives an estimate of sales in their territories during a specified period. The total of all these estimates is the beginning point of an overall forecast. Again, there may be a tendency for these estimates to over- or understate actual sales. Thus, an empirically derived adjustment factor may be applied to the total estimate. If the sales force is competent and rewarded for accurate estimates, then this method can provide useful forecasts. It is best used when an organization has a small number of large customers.

Causal Relationships. This approach develops an empirically derived relationship among a set of marketing mix factors, environmental characteristics, and sales. For example, we may find sales of a paper product by using the following function:

$$\text{Sales} = .0001\ (\text{GNP} + .1\ (\text{Promotional Expenditures}).$$

These types of relationships are difficult to estimate and require constant updating. Usually, only large, sophisticated firms attempt this approach. Even in these firms, marketing managers often have difficulty understanding the method and results.

Trend Analysis. An alternative to trying to find causal relationships is to extend past sales trends into the future. It is a simpler and much less costly approach than surveys, test markets, or even the causal approach. The major assumption here is that whatever unspecified factors caused sales in the past will continue to affect sales. This method is thus very unreliable, except in very stable markets such as electric utilities. In preparing a forecast, a marketer may make use of a number of these procedures and compare the estimates generated.

Personal Computer Exercise

The use of marketing survey data can help determine the relative position that competing products hold in the minds of consumers. The PC exercise gives you the opportunity to analyze some data from a consumers' survey of product perceptions of competing brands. You should be able to identify the perception problems and opportunities facing each brand in your analysis of this data.

KEY POINTS

• Successful marketing decision making requires the skillful blending of new information with previous experience. This is not an easy task.

• Marketing research is designed to provide new information that is needed for decision making. The kind of information needed should be well planned out, objective, and relevant to the decision being made.

• Because of its importance in the quality of management decisions, marketing research is widely used in organizations. It will, however, never dominate all decisions, since judgment based on experience will always be needed.

• Marketing research can provide performance-monitoring information, produce insights by exploring new areas or ideas, and provide conclusive answers to well-defined alternative solutions.

• All marketing research involves the following: establish the need for information; specify the research objectives and information needs; determine the sources of data; develop data-collection forms; design the sample; collect data; process and analyze the data; and present the results.

• In sophisticated companies, marketing research information is being integrated with other information in a marketing information system (MKIS) and marketing decision support system (MDSS), and will increasingly be integrated in the future. These systems offer the hope of providing more relevant and timely information and hands-on interaction to the decision maker.

• In many decision-making situations, the success of the marketing program selected depends upon the quality of information the manager receives. The creative management of information is a required skill for marketers.

• One key research activity is in the forecasting of market potentials, sales potentials, and sales forecasts. Both top-down and buildup methods are commonly used in this forecasting.

• Major forecasting techniques include corollary product indexes, general and specific buying power indexes, surveys of intentions, test markets, sales-force composites, causal relationships, and trend analysis.

ISSUES FOR DISCUSSION

1. At a major global supplier of mining equipment, the results of a study of the rapidly changing marketplace were being presented. A short time into the presentation of the technically well done study, the general manager of the division stood up and noted in a loud voice that the study was nonsense and was not at all capturing the true market that he knew. He then walked out of the presentation. What was the value of research to this manager? What are the risks in his behavior?

2. At Procter & Gamble, a major marketer of packaged consumer goods (Crest, Tide, Head & Shoulders, Pampers, Crisco), the average age of a product manager is under thirty. If experience is so important in decision making, how can this be?

3. Some managers use exploratory research to select among alternative courses of action. Why is this risky? Why would they do this?

4. Your instructor is interested in knowing how many students will take a senior-level case course in marketing. What sources of data might be used to answer this question?

5. How might a sample of students in a principles of marketing course be selected to find out the number of students who will take the senior-level case course?

6. You have been asked to design a study on student perception of the student lounge at your school. Outline all the dimensions of a study design. How would you insure that the study would be used effectively by the managers of the lounge?

7. The technology of MDSS continues to lead the management capability to use such systems. How would you see that such systems were effectively implemented in a business that you managed?

8. One noted marketing executive was heard to say, "MDSS is doomed because it tries to reduce all marketing decisions to a set of mathematical equations." Evaluate this statement.

9. "A well-designed marketing information system and MDSS require an excellent marketing research department to work well. One should build the latter before undertaking the former." Evaluate this statement.

GLOSSARY

Buildup method: a procedure for developing an overall sales forecast by adding up estimates made at the lowest level of interest—usually product lines, customer groups, or geographic areas.

Coding: the process of assigning numbers to questions and other responses.

Conclusive research: research designed to help the decision maker evaluate alternative courses of action.

Data analysis: the application of statistical techniques to summarize the collected information in a survey.

Editing: the process of assuring maximum accuracy and unambiguity in a questionnaire.

Element: the unit selected in a sample.

Experiment: a research design that attempts to control all relevant variables in order to determine causality among them.

Exploratory research: research designed to formulate hypotheses about problems and give insights.

Forecasting techniques: procedures used to estimate potentials or sales. See chapter for specifics of various techniques.

Market potential: the maximum sales possible for all sellers of a product to an identified customer group within a specified time frame in a given environment.

Marketing decision support system (MDSS): the interactive computer interface between a marketing manager and the available information flow; composed of a database system, statistical analysis system, decision models, and a display system.

Marketing information system (MKIS): a system of machines, people, and procedures designed to provide a marketing manager with timely, organized, and relevant information from all sources.

Marketing research: the systematic and objective approach to the development and provision of information for marketing decision making.

Marketing research process: the steps required to properly complete a research study.

Nonprobability sampling: a procedure in which the selection of the sample is based, in part, on the convenience or judgment of the researcher.

Nonresponse errors: the differences on measures of interest in a study between those who respond and those who do not.

Performance-monitoring research: research that provides feedback on the operation of a marketing program.

Primary data: data collected expressly for the study at hand.

Probability sampling: a procedure in which each member of the population has a known chance of being selected.

Research design: the basic plan which guides the data collection and analysis phases of research.

Sales potential: the maximum sales possible for one company's product as the company's marketing effort increases relative to competitors.

Sales forecast: the expected sales level of a company's product within a specified time frame given a designated marketing plan and a specific environment.

Sample: a group selected from the population of elements that interests the researcher.

Secondary data: published data collected for reasons unrelated to the present study.

Top-down or breakdown method: an overall forecast allocated to product lines, customer groups, or geographic areas based upon some index of the potential in these subunits.

NOTES

1. This section follows the discussion in Thomas C. Kinnear and James R. Taylor, *Marketing Research: An Applied Approach,* Third Edition (McGraw-Hill, 1987), Chapters 1, 2, and 4.

2. Johnny K. Johansson and Ikujiro Nonaka, "Market Research the Japanese Way," *Harvard Business Review,* May-June 1987, p. 16.

3. Kinnear and Taylor, *Marketing Research,* p. 16. In 1989, the AMA adopted a new definition of marketing research that is consistent with our definition. The AMA definition is: *the function which links the consumer, customer, and public to the marketer through information—information used to identify and define marketing opportunities and problems; generate, refine, and evaluate marketing actions; monitor marketing performance; and improve understanding of marketing as a process.*

4. Richard L. Gordon, "Session with FTC a Turnabout for P&G," *Advertising Age,* October 15, 1979, p. 52.

5. Laurie Freeman, "Colgate Slam-Dunks P&G," *Advertising Age,* August 31, 1987, p. 1.

6. For details, see Duncan G. LaBay and Thomas C. Kinnear, "An Exploratory Study of the Adoption of Solar Energy Systems," *Journal of Consumer Research,* Fall 1981.

7. For a more complete cataloging of secondary data sources, see Kinnear and Taylor, *Marketing Research,* pp. 139–146 and 152–163.

8. Kinnear and Taylor, *Marketing Research,* pp. 403–23.

9. Taken from an oral presentation given by General Mills management at The University of Michigan.

10. Samuel V. Smith, Richard H. Brien, and James E. Stafford, "Marketing Information Systems: An Introductory Overview," in Samuel V. Smith, Richard H. Brien, and James E. Stafford, eds., *Readings in Marketing Information Systems* (Houghton Mifflin, 1968), p. 7.

11. For an excellent discussion of this topic see John D. C. Little, "Decision Support Systems for Marketing Managers," *Journal of Marketing,* Vol. 43, Summer 1979, pp. 9–26.

12. These criteria are from John D. C. Little, Lakshmi Mohan, and Antoine Hatoun, "Yanking Knowledge from the Numbers: How Marketing Decision Support Systems Can Work for You," *Industrial Marketing,* March 1982.

CASE APPLICATION 7–1

Japan, Inc.

Many Japanese companies practice a somewhat different style of marketing research than that generally undertaken in North America. Japanese marketers put much more emphasis on data they gather from wholesalers and retailers, and they do this on a much more frequent basis than most North American competitors. In addition, they use basically two types of data: "soft data" obtained from visits to wholesalers and retailers, and "hard data" about shipments, inventories, and retail sales. There is a belief that these data better reflect the behavior and intentions of end consumers than consumer surveys and other popular techniques used in the U.S. As the director of Matsushita's videocassette recorder business said: "Why do Americans do so much marketing research? You can find out what you need by traveling around and visiting the retailers who carry your products."

When Japanese companies do conduct consumer surveys, they want to interview consumers who have actually bought or used the product. They do not attempt to measure general attitudes and values as is popularly done in North America. For example, when Toyota sought to learn the preferences of Americans for features in small cars, they interviewed consumers who had driven the Volkswagen Beetle.

Both middle-level and senior managers get involved in soft data gathering. This impressionistic data is believed to give a manager a distinct feel for the marketplace. Most managers do not believe that surveys or quantitative research methods can supply this type of insight. Canon even used this type of approach in the U.S. to analyze the American market and the company's distribution structure for cameras. Through this process, Canon learned that dealers were not giving Canon much support because their sales forces were too small. The company also learned which cameras and promotional support would get dealers excited about Canon cameras. Although these methods may be less scientific than those practiced by American firms, they are by no means haphazard or careless. Japanese managers base their conclusions on very careful observation of the behavior pattern of consumers in stores and of the store employees.

Hard data on wholesale and retail shipments is done with such frequency that Japanese companies can often respond to a problem long before consumer panel or store audit data would even be available to a U.S. company that relied on this type of research. Warner Communications' Atari subsidiary in Japan would have never had the disastrous build-up of inventory at retail if it had not relied on a report on retail sales that had a six month lag.

The Japanese style of market research is perhaps most notable for the almost total absence of test marketing, which is used so much in the United States. Even when test marketing is done in Japan, it doesn't bear much resemblance to the American version. Japanese test marketing, when practiced, tends to be much shorter, and results may be skewed by sales force enthusiasm in the test market.

There are a number of reasons why the Japanese do not share the American interest in test marketing. Until about 1973 Japan was a rapidly expanding economy, with the GNP increasing at 10 percent or more per annum. Consumer demand slightly outpaced supply, and manufacturers did not worry about Japanese consumers being finicky. There was no real need for test marketing products in such an economic environment. Although Japanese economic growth has slowed since the 1970s and competition among manufacturers has consequently stiffened, the Japanese attitude toward test marketing has changed only slightly.

An important reason why the Japanese have resisted adopting American-style test marketing—despite the increase in market competitiveness—is the fear of tipping off competitors to the company's intentions. As a result, what test marketing occurs in Japan usually does not exceed six months—a period which American companies would think too short to get reliable results.

The experiences of two foreign consumer product giants seem to prove the dangers of lengthy test-marketing. According to J. Mitchell Reed, an executive for Japan's third largest ad agency, both Procter & Gamble (P&G) and Unilever suffered large market share losses after using 18-month test marketing for products in Japan. P&G went from an impressive 90 percent market share in Japan for its Pampers disposable diapers to 8 percent, in part due to the additional time test marketing gave its competitors. In addition, P&G failed to be as responsive to consumers' opinions about the product after it was on the national market and lost out to Japanese companies which were willing to make product modifications. Similarly, Unilever's lengthy test marketing of Jif sink cleaner also gave its competitors time to bring out rival products.

Product life cycles in Japan also tend to be shorter than in the U.S. Thus, there is less economic reason to conduct extensive test marketing on products which may quickly become obsolete.

From a cultural standpoint, the Japanese also see test marketing as being only marginally useful. Due to the high degree of Japanese cultural homogeneity, Japanese managers feel much more confident about understanding the tastes of their countrymen. As a result, they are much more willing to rely on hunches than American managers would.

Finally, there are simply fewer good test markets in Japan than in the U.S. Few cities in Japan meet the standards of media isolation which define a good U.S. test market. Therefore, Japan has only four cities—Hiroshima, Fukuoka, Shizuoka, and Sapporo—which are considered very desirable test markets, and they are used repeatedly. Such overuse of certain cities as test markets may in itself cause biased results.

In general, the Japanese proclivity for more qualitative and intuitive methods of market research, as well as the broad disinterest in test marketing, reflect certain basic characteristics of Japanese business. First, formal business education in Japan is still relatively uncommon. Instead of receiving academic business training, most managers develop their business skills through practical experience. As a result of this general pattern, Japanese managers seem to have less regard for those methods which apparently substitute a "quick fix" of highly quantitative methodology for knowledge developed through experience. Second, Japan's tradition of management by consensus allows less room for the development of a strong and separate marketing research unit than in a U.S. company. Major marketing decisions are made by high-level management and often reflect the experienced judgments of each individual, which are likely to outweigh the input of a marketing research department. Third, Japan's tradition of tight channel monitoring is closely related to the specialized nature of many Japanese firms. Due to limited diversification, Japanese management is better able to closely follow customer reaction toward a small number of product lines. By keeping close and constant tabs on its customers and distributors, the Japanese have less need to use American marketing research techniques.

Although Japan and the U.S. have distinct methods of conducting marketing research, there are indications that each country is experimenting more with the other's methodology. On the one hand, American managers are trying to get closer to their customers by listening more carefully to what distributors and the customers themselves have to say. In this way, American managers hope to keep their product lines in tune with customers' desires and their marketing practices more timely and competitive. On the other hand, some Japanese managers believe that using American-style marketing research may keep their firms competitive in global markets where their knowledge of consumer tastes is much less certain. Both the Japanese and U.S. styles of market research have their strong points, especially within their respective cultures. With the increasing globalization of business, however, it is likely that each will become more heterogeneous.

SOURCES: Jack Burton, "Testing Japanese-Style Mystifies Foreigners," *Advertising Age,* Feb. 20, 1984, pp. M–34–37. Johny K. Johansson and Ikujiro Nonaka, "Market Research the Japanese Way," *Harvard Business Review,* May-June 1987, pp. 16–22.

Questions

1. Why would the Japanese style be so successful in marketing cameras, automobiles, and consumer electronics?

2. Are there any potential problems with the Japanese style of marketing research? Be specific.

3. Under what circumstances would more broad-based consumer surveys and field experiments be appropriate than the Japanese style of research?

4. How might a MKIS and MDSS provide the benefits of both the Japanese style of research and those of the more quantitative approach?

CASE APPLICATION 7–2

New Coke: A "Classic" Marketing Research Blunder?

Spending millions of dollars and extensively measuring consumer opinion do not alone insure that a company has conducted reliable market research, as the experience of the Coca-Cola Company proves. In 1985, the Coca-Cola Company attempted to replace its longstanding Coke formula, after taste tests of 200,000 respondents indicated that consumers preferred a sweeter tasting Coke. Coca-Cola's market research failed to predict a high level of brand loyalty to the original formula, however. As a result, the company did not expect a consumer backlash against the new formula nor declining consumer interest in new Coke soon after its introduction on the market.

'Cheeseburger and a Coke . . . Is that the new Coke or the old Coke, or the new old Coke or the old new Coke, or the old, old . . .'

How did Coca-Cola misjudge the market so much after spending $4 million and more than two years to test a reformulation of Coke? According to some analysts, the company made serious methodological mistakes in constructing its taste tests. Also, Coca-Cola failed to take adequate account of psychological aspects of brand loyalty which are difficult to gauge using normal marketing research.

In taste testing a new Coke formula, Coca-Cola Company used three different formulations, which it tested against traditional Coke and Pepsi. Of the 200,000 consumers who took the test, however, only 30,000 or 40,000 actually tasted the new formula which was finally introduced. In addition, most consumers were not informed what they were tasting. In other words, most consumers simply made a "blind comparison" between unnamed products. They had no idea that their preferences were helping the Coca-Cola Company to decide whether it should introduce a new formula for Coke. If informed of the full ramifications of their preferences—in other words, a vote for new Coke also meant choosing to get rid of the old, standard Coca-Cola—perhaps many consumers, moved by an emotional attachment to the familiar soft drink, would have registered a preference for the old Coke. As the taste tests were constructed, however, a majority of consumers (about 53 percent versus 47 percent) who tasted both the old and new Coke liked the "new" Coke better than the original formula. This result was apparently instrumental in the company's decision to use this new formula to replace the old one.

Besides conducting taste tests, the company also surveyed a different set of consumers to see whether or not they favored the Coke change, in concept. As some researchers have pointed out, however, this survey consisted of simple yes/no questions and was not likely to reveal consumers' deep-seated feelings about Coke. Although consumers were asked to respond to "the idea of changing the formulation," they were not clearly advised that their responses might mean never being able to taste the old formula again. Under such hypothetical conditions, many consumers made a greater departure from tradition than they could in actuality.

Coca-Cola's marketing research also failed to consider consumer buying patterns. Therefore, in assessing consumer opinions, the company gave all the responses equal weight, despite the well-known phenomenon known as the "80/20 rule"—that a small minority of consumers usually accounts for the vast majority of purchases in a product category. According to a survey done by Pepsi soon after the introduction of new Coke, this segment of Coke loyalists overwhelmingly favored an unchanged Coke formula. If Coke had weighted their responses appropriately, it is unlikely that the company would have gone ahead with the reformulation.

Throughout its marketing research, the Coca-Cola Company focused more on Coke's physical properties than its symbolic character. The company failed to realize that many consumers identify themselves very closely with Coca-Cola. This phenomenon has been described as the "I use this, this is me" principle. According to a study by the Ogilvy & Mather advertising agency, such close identification with a product is usually most intense with products that are ingested or used close to the skin. Therefore, attempting to change the Coca-Cola formula apparently evoked deep psychological resistance from this type of consumer.

Coca-Cola also made a mistake by failing to note that many U.S. consumers strongly favor continuity and tradition over novelty. According to one well-known breakdown of the American population into consumer types, the largest single group consists of "belongers"—those who like stability more than change. For years, the Coca-Cola Company had successfully gone after this group by appealing to its members' traditional values. Reformulating Coke was like a slap in the face to those for whom Coke represented familiarity and tradition.

Knowing some of the errors the Coca-Cola Company made, what kind of marketing research would help reveal the psychological components of brand loyalty? First, a company can conduct careful, but unobtrusive observation of consumer interaction with different products in the same category. Is there any difference in the way the consumer handles the different brands? Subtle behavioral differences may be clues to different levels of emotional attachment to each product. Second, focus groups may be very useful in revealing consumers' attitudes toward different products. Focus groups also help reveal the hidden assumptions and fears behind consumer reactions which are often obscured by simple objective surveys. Third, researchers may use more exotic techniques such as simulated "psychodrama" to try to uncover consumer opinion. For example, consumers might be asked to imagine themselves as a beverage and then describe the beverage in detail. Through this technique, the researcher can often learn more about consumer preferences than through more direct methods.

Although New Coke has not attracted consumers as earlier marketing research had predicted, Coca-Cola's bold move to reformulate its flagship brand was not a debacle for the company. Soon after consumer interest in New Coke began to fizzle and fierce brand loyalty for the traditional formula became obvious, the Coca-Cola Company decided to reintroduce its old Coke as "Coca-Cola Classic." By remaining flexible and admitting its blunder, the Coca-Cola Company was able to correct a potentially grave marketing error. In terms of market share for New Coke and Coke Classic, the company remains about where it was with its traditional formula alone.

The New Coke/Coca-Cola Classic affair has not spelled either great success or great failure for the Coca-Cola Company. However, the company's dramatic marketing misstep offers some valuable lessons to the firm about the pitfalls of conducting market research. Fortunately, Coca-Cola's hard-won experience also provides valuable insight to all marketers. As we can see, good marketing research is more than dollars and numbers. Good marketing research—including both quantitative and qualitative techniques—gets to the root of how consumers really feel about a certain product. As Coca-Cola's experience proves, sometimes consumers' true feelings run even deeper than they realize themselves.

SOURCES: Anne B. Fisher, "Coke's Brand-Loyalty Lesson," *Fortune*, August 5, 1985, pp. 44–46. Betsy D. Gelb and Gabriel M. Gelb, "New Coke's Fizzle—Lessons for the Rest of Us," *Sloan Management Review*, Fall 1986, pp. 71–76. Robert C. Goizueta, "The Other Side," *Bank Marketing*, May 1987, p. 66.

Questions

1. What major mistakes did the Coca-Cola Company make in its marketing research before the introduction of "new" Coke?

2. How could Coca-Cola have changed its marketing research to get more accurate results?

3. In doing marketing research, should the opinions of each consumer be treated equally? Why or why not?

4. Give examples of other products which elicit a strong degree of psychological brand loyalty. What would you advise a company to do if it wanted to change one of these products?

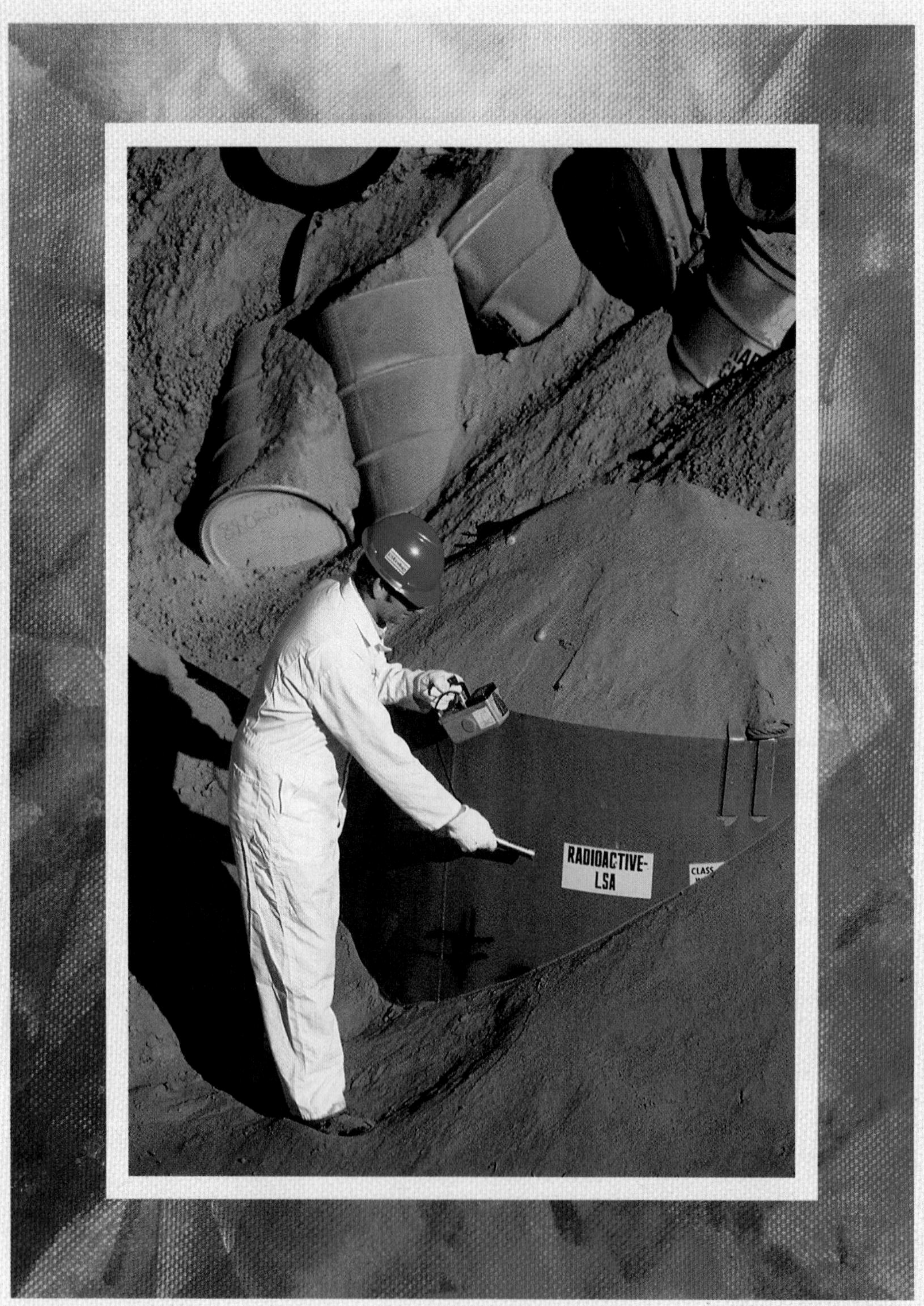
RADIOACTIVE-
LSA

8

Public Policy, Regulation, and Ethical Marketing Practices

Learning Objectives

Upon completing this chapter, you will be able to do the following:

LIST
the different types of public policy issues confronting marketers.

UNDERSTAND
the major pieces of legislation that affect marketing and know how the courts have interpreted these statutes.

DISCUSS
consumerism and the nature of consumer protection legislation.

COMPARE
the legal approach to regulation with attempts by marketers to regulate themselves.

IDENTIFY
criticisms of each element of the marketing mix and respond to these criticisms.

LIST
the components of the American Marketing Association Code of Ethics.

MARKETING PROFILE

The Impact of the FTC and the Courts

The actions of government regulatory agencies, such as the Federal Trade Commission (FTC) and the courts, greatly affect every part of the marketing mix. The following examples illustrate the breadth of this impact.

The FTC charged Montgomery Ward with making false and unsubstantiated claims in selling service contracts for products such as televisions, washing machines, dryers, and refrigerators. The complaint charged that Ward's sales staff falsely told consumers that these products needed routine maintenance and that *Consumer Reports* recommended service contracts to all appliance owners. In August 1988, Montgomery Ward and the FTC negotiated a consent agreement settling the charges. The agreement does not constitute admission of a law violation, but prohibits the company from misrepresenting service contract coverage and products' need for maintenance, adjustment, or servicing.

In another matter, the FTC ruled that the Massachusetts optometry board constrained competition by illegally restricting advertising and issued an order requiring the board to allow truthful advertising by optometrists in the state. The 1988 ruling stated that the board violated federal antitrust laws and prohibits restrictions on advertising or the offering of price discounts by optometrists.

Other FTC actions in 1988 included the filing of a number of suits against automobile dealers, funeral homes, and real estate companies for violations of various regulations requiring the disclosure of price and warranty information. They also amended food store advertising regulations, allowing grocery stores the option of offering rain checks or substitute products of comparable value when they run out of advertised items. Stores can now also comply with the regulations by disclosing in advertising that items are available only in limited quantities or only at some stores.

Under a 1988 Supreme Court ruling, manufacturers have the right to stop supplying merchandise to dealers who engage in heavy price cutting. In the *Business Electronics* vs. *Sharp Electronics* case, the Supreme Court, in a 6-to-2 decision, said that a manufacturer does not automatically violate the antitrust laws by terminating a relationship with a dealer, as long as they did not attempt to fix prices. In this case, a number of years earlier Sharp had terminated Business Electronics, a Houston business calculator dealer, after a rival dealer had complained about price cuts. The decision defines manufacturers' and dealers' rights, making it clear that manufacturers can require retailers to maintain certain types of support for their products, as long as they do not engage in price fixing.

In this *Marketing Profile,* we can see a number of the public policy issues that arise over and over again in marketing—concern of a government regulatory agency (FTC) for the false claims for products; concern for the restraint of competition in the marketplace; and concern for the consumer's right to receive full and accurate price, warranty, and availability information. Finally, we see the power of the Supreme Court to resolve issues in marketing.

Many other aspects of marketing interact with public policy. Product, distribution, promotion, and pricing decisions are all constrained by the workings of the regulatory agencies, courts, and the private legal actions of competitors and consumers. Imagine yourself making these decisions without understanding their legal and public consequences to your organization and to yourself.

SOURCES: "Montgomery Ward Charged with Making False Claims About Its Service Contracts," *FTC News Notes,* August 22, 1988, p. 3; "Massachusetts Optometry Board," *FTC News Notes,* June 27, 1988, p. 1–2; "FTC Votes to Amend Food Store Advertising Rule," *FTC News Notes,* May 2, 1988, p. 1; and Judith Graham, "Court Upholds No-Discount Tactic," *Advertising Age,* May 16, 1988, p. 74.

In this chapter, we explore the interaction between marketing and the public policy environment. These daily interfaces are important to the marketing practitioner (see Chapter 3). More specifically, we discuss the different types of public policy issues that affect marketing, including legal regulation, consumer protection, self-regulation, and social responsibility; the public policy interrelationship among marketers, their customers, their competitors, the government, and the community; the key pieces of major laws that affect marketing and the important judicial interpretation of these laws; consumerism and consumer protection laws; and marketers' self-regulation of their activities. Public policy in marketing is concerned with all these areas. In addition, we examine some of the criticisms of marketing and marketers' responses to these criticisms. The ethical dimension of marketing decisions is just as important as the legal dimension, so ethical issues are also explored in this chapter.

A Framework for Understanding Marketing and Public Policy

A look at a few recent newspapers and magazines indicates the extensiveness of public influence on marketing.[1] There is seemingly no end of public criticisms, legal actions by government and competitors, demands for change, and government regulation or deregulation of the marketplace. In this section, we present a simple model (see Figure 8–1) that we find useful for understanding important aspects of the public arena of marketing. We will discuss this model, part by part.

The model starts with a seller providing a product or service to a buyer at a price (arrow from Company to Customers). In practice, several companies usually compete for customer patronage, and we recognize this by distinguishing between an individual company's view of the marketing transactions and the industry's view (see arrows between Industry and Company).

Although companies compete, they sometimes recognize their interdependence and collude in their action in the market, perhaps tacitly agreeing to raise prices. To prevent such abuses, customers have used political pressures to insist that governments involve themselves in the marketplace because customers have not usually had the power to counteract the actions of big business. Generally speaking, governments have been expected to act as neutral referees in order to prevent unethical and fraudulent conduct and insure that business does not abuse its power. Most ethical businesspeople have accepted the need for some refereeing of marketers' conduct and for the establishment of "rules of conduct." In fact, many have urged government to become involved. The public has also urged politicians to develop programs for better economic and social conditions. One phrase often used to identify this set of demands is "quality of life." Thus government is at the center of the model (with arrows to Company and Industry), with the community's concern for the quality of life influencing the government (arrow from Community to Government via "Advocates").

Governments have intervened in the marketplace principally in two modes: *regulation of marketing conduct,* and *regulation of marketing institutions and industry structure.* Some industries are now very regulated by the policy of the government. For example, the fast-food restaurant's hamburger, with everything on it, is subject to about 41,000 different federal and state regulations,[2] and the American car has thousands of federal regulations that affect its whole physical makeup.

While most marketers have responded loudly to increasing government involvement in marketing, they have had to pay just as much attention to governmental developments in consumer purchasing behavior or competitive behavior. Marketers

Figure 8–1 The Full Marketing and Public Policy Arena

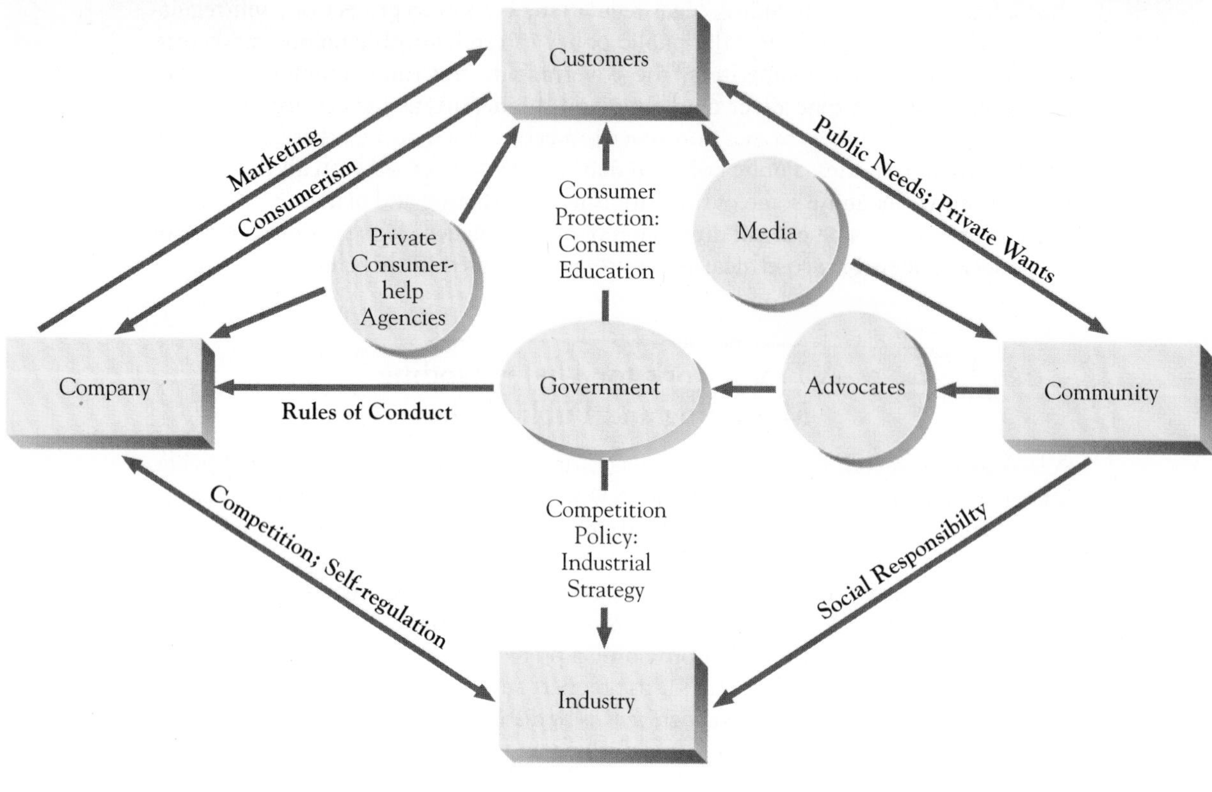

have been the objects of criticism from several societal groups as well as from governments. Community members, in their roles as citizens rather than customers, have become upset about issues such as package pollution, advertising to children, and the quality of breakfast cereals. Paradoxically, while citizens often seek marketing practices consistent with *public needs,* as consumers, with *private wants,* these same people act differently (see arrows between Community and Customers). For example, the soft-drink container controversy has clearly demonstrated that individuals *say* they want returnable bottles, but they *buy* nonreturnables. This kind of split-personality behavior leaves marketers in a dilemma: they're "damned if they do, damned if they don't." Nonetheless, there has clearly been an escalation in the expectations of community members.

The key concept is embodied in the term *social responsibility,* which refers to the duty of businesses to act in the public interest—a duty that goes beyond traditional economic performance (see arrow from Community to Industry). Unfortunately, the more goals we expect business organizations to achieve, the less likely they will be able to achieve any of them well.

Consumerism

Over the last twenty years, customers have increasingly begun to voice their dissatisfactions with marketing practices and institutions. The overall term given to this customer backlash is **consumerism;** it can be shown on our diagram as an arrow running from the Customers to the Company (see Figure 8–1). There are a number of ways to define *consumerism:* the expression of consumer dissatisfaction; the difference between what was promised and what was delivered; or "the shame of the marketing concept." It is ironic to note that, at a time when more and more marketers have had formal marketing education and have been exposed to the marketing concept, there has been increasing discontent with marketing practices (such as advertising) and marketing institutions (such as supermarkets). Probably the best definition of consumerism we've encountered was Stephen Greyser's "the revolt of the receiving-enders."

A host of reasons have been cited for consumerism, but most boil down to the increasing complexity and impersonality of the marketplace. In short, consumers often find shopping to be such a complicated phenomenon that many of them feel they have "been had" through no fault of their own.

Historically there have been three major waves of consumerism. The first occurred in the late 1800s and lasted until World War I. It arose to combat the abuses of the day: mail-order abuses, poor meat and food quality, fraud in the weights and measures of goods purchased, and drugs that didn't work. The second wave occurred from the late 1920s to the late 1930s. The abuses driving this movement were again food- and drug-related. Also, the Great Depression had made many people anti-big business; they wanted to protect the small businesses. The most recent wave of the consumer movement started in the late 1950s and continued through the 1960s and 1970s. With Ralph Nader as its champion, it addressed such issues as product safety, complete information disclosure, and high prices. During all of these waves, major pieces of legislation were passed that affect marketing. We will look at these later in this chapter.

Some feel that consumerism lost some of its influence in the 1980s; others believe that it is just maturing into a still active, but quieter, movement. As Bloom and Greyser noted, "It has become a diverse, differentiated movement, providing individual consumers with numerous ways to express dissatisfaction and pursue better shopping and consumption experiences."[3] Its legislative thrust is not as active now. However, it does remain an influential force at all levels, especially at the local one.

Marketers have responded to consumerism in three basic ways: by regarding it as a threat to be opposed vigorously; by ignoring it, hoping it will disappear; and by regarding it as a signal that something can and ought to be done to improve the buyer-seller relationship. Those who have adopted the last stance and regard consumer dissatisfaction as a marketing opportunity have fared far better than those marketers who have responded negatively or not at all. In many instances, companies have found it difficult to respond to consumer problems alone and have gone to industry associations and other groups, urging self-regulation on an industrywide basis. Sometimes these efforts have had noteworthy success; other times they have been short-lived failures. One of the success stories to date is the National Advertising Division of the Council of Better Business Bureaus, which has formulated and enforced standards of advertising accuracy.

Self-regulation is often difficult. The consumers and politicians are skeptical of marketers' motives from the outset. Often there are no effective sanctions to impose agreed-upon standards of conduct; and very often it is virtually impossible to get agreement on a set of standards.

The government has responded to consumerism in a variety of ways. The major responses are summarized in Table 8–1. The two most important government responses to consumerism are consumer protection and consumer education. **Consumer protection** refers to making buying less risky and buying mistakes less costly, usually

Table 8–1 Seven Major Government Responses To Consumerism

Government Activity	Purpose
Consumer Education	Making the buyer smarter and/or more realistic; focus is on prepurchase circumstances
Consumer Inquiry Handling	Providing prepurchase information to improve consumer choice-making in the marketplace
Consumer Complaint Handling	Mediating and/or arbitrating postpurchase disputes between individual consumers and individual marketers
Consumer Protection	Making buying less risky by requiring certain information disclosures Enforcing truth in information and standardized marketing methods (prepurchase) Making buying mistakes less costly by easing the rules of contract rescission and opening new avenues of redress (postpurchase)
Consumer Research	Conducting and funding studies (for use by all groups) that shed light on how consumers actually behave and on why and how they respond to variations in marketing approaches
Consumer Group Assistance	Providing funding and other forms of support to nongovernment groups and individuals who engage in consumer education, inquiry handling, complaint handling, investigation of marketing practices, and other forms of consumer advocacy
Competition Policy	Formulating and administering various incentives and disincentives to competition via antitrust and other legal methods; the purpose is to assist the consumer by making competition less imperfect

SOURCE: Michael R. Pearce, "The Public Arena of Marketing," in Cynthia J. Frey, Thomas C. Kinnear, and Bonnie B. Reece eds., *Public Policy Issues in Marketing* (Division of Research, Graduate School of Business Administration, University of Michigan, 1979), p. 8.

through legal action; **consumer education** refers to making the buyer wiser. All levels of government have become involved in consumer protection, especially in assisting consumers with postpurchase problems. An overview of consumer protection legislation is presented later in this chapter.

Consumer education appears to be a potentially useful long-run response to consumer problems, but it involves several operational difficulties. Where do we begin? How should it be done? How do we know if it is being done correctly? Who pays for it? Many attempts have been made by governments and private concerns. Most of us have encountered labeling changes, product fact sheets, *Consumer Reports,* and the like. Additionally, some companies, such as J.C. Penney, have been very active in consumer education by publishing materials and running educational workshops. Added to all of these, the media perform their role by reporting allegations of marketing wrong-doing and highlighting needed or attempted reforms. This is their function in a free society, but it makes them part of the public arena of marketing.

Figure 8–1 presents the full set of concerns and participants in the public policy aspects of marketing. This model serves several useful purposes. First, it shows the public policy environment in which marketers must operate. It clearly demonstrates that marketers must pay careful attention to the political and legal dimensions of their environment when formulating marketing strategies. (See Chapter 3 for a detailed discussion of environmental forces.)

Second, it helps put new developments in the environment into some perspective. For example, a new piece of legislation or a new attempt at business self-regulation can be positioned *vis-à-vis* other activities, developments, and interests in the environment.

Third, this model requires one to think about the interrelationships among the various interest groups that have a stake in any particular marketing issue. For example, the diagram can be used to better understand the positions taken and the course of events followed on such issues as product safety and advertising of alcoholic beverages. The diagram indicates that marketers now must operate in a public bargaining arena where marketing mix decisions are more political, and less economic, in nature.

Laws Affecting Competition

To understand the legal environment affecting the way marketers compete, it is necessary to examine (1) relevant *statutes,* (2) their related *interpretation* by the courts, (3) the nature of *enforcement* by the Justice Department and other agencies, and (4) the willingness of individual marketers to bring suit against one another.[4] This latter trend is illustrated in the *Marketing in Action* feature which describes how Avis, Wendy's, Stroh, and Kraft use the legal system. In this section, we will present an overview of the laws affecting marketing. Where required, we have left the discussion of the details of these laws for other chapters of the book. For example, pricing laws are discussed in detail in Chapter 17.

Table 8–2 summarizes the current major antitrust laws that affect marketing. Antitrust laws are designed to prevent or break up monopolies and deal with unfair methods of competition and deceptive practices.

In response to widespread monopolistic activity by corporations like Standard Oil, the **Sherman Act** was passed in 1890. Its key provisions deal with conspiracies among sellers to fix prices or divide markets (Section 1), and a firm's attainment of a monopoly position (Section 2). But the terms of the Sherman Act are very general. In order to allow legal action against more specific abuses, the Clayton Act and the Federal Trade Commission Act were passed in 1914. The key provisions of the **Clayton Act** made illegal:

1. the discrimination in price (to charge different prices) in sales among firms (Section 2), except where there were differences in grade, quality, or quantity of the commodity sold, or where the different prices reflected different costs of serving customers, or where the prices were good faith efforts to meet competitive prices;
2. the condition in buying a product that the buyer not deal in competitive products (Section 3); and
3. the acquisition of the stock of another company if the effect of this acquisition may be *substantially to lessen competition* or to *tend to create a monopoly* (Section 7).

The **Federal Trade Commission Act** created a quasi-judicial-administrative body called the Federal Trade Commission (FTC). The key section of the act is Section 5, which states that:

Unfair methods of competition in commerce are hereby declared unlawful.

It was left to the FTC and the courts to define *unfair.*

MARKETING IN ACTION

How Companies Use the Legal System

Action by government agencies and departments is only one side of the legal coin as it affects marketing; private suits by organizations are quite common. Listed below are descriptions of some recent suits.

• Ben and Jerry's Ice Cream Company sued Haagen-Dazs, a subsidiary of Pillsbury Company, over Haagen-Dazs' distribution policies, charging that the policies freeze competitors out of supermarket distribution. Haagen-Dazs countered, claiming that it is important that it be allowed to forbid its distributors to distribute competitive products.

• LeSportsac, Inc. sued Kmart after the retailer introduced a line of luggage, bags, and knapsacks which LeSportsac claimed was very similar in appearance to its bags. Kmart used the brand name "di Paris sac," with a logo, shape, and other features similar to the LeSportsac products, leading LeSportsac to claim that Kmart was causing confusion in the marketplace.

• Avis sued Hertz for $250,000, charging that Hertz violated truth-in-advertising laws. Hertz had alleged, in an ad, that it had more new cars than Avis had; Avis claimed that this was incorrect. Hertz stood by its claim and noted that $250,000 was more than they spent on the campaign containing the claim.

• Wendy's sued Big Bite, a regional chain in Ohio, for using a Wendy's lookalike in a negative fashion in its ads. Wendy's charged that this constituted a "trademark libel and disparagement of our mark and reputation by holding Wendy's up to public ridicule."

• Kraft Inc. sued Beatrice Foods to prevent it from employing former Kraft vice president of marketing for cream cheese and natural cheese brands, Norman Ross, as its vice president of marketing for cheeses. Kraft charged that Ross had resigned just days after attending a Kraft meeting where marketing strategy was discussed. Further, it charged that this was part of a campaign by Beatrice to employ Kraft executives with access to confidential data. Kraft sought to restrain Ross from working on Beatrice products that compete with Kraft's.

• Stroh Brewing Company is challenging the television networks' policy of giving an advertiser exclusivity in sporting events. Stroh charged that by giving its competitors exclusive rights to such events as NFL football and major league baseball, Stroh was prevented access to its prime target consumers. Stroh charged that this was a conspiracy in restraint of trade and asked for access to buy these times.

The Sherman Act dealt with existing monopolies, provided punishment for past actions, and laid down general principles. In contrast, the Clayton Act dealt with potential monopoly and its prevention. The Federal Trade Commission Act put public officials and financing behind the attack on unfair methods of competition. Previously, this had been left to individuals who filed lawsuits.

In 1936 the **Robinson-Patman Act** was passed to amend Section 2 (price discrimination) of the Clayton Act, which focused primarily on prevention of predatory pricing (by sellers). The Robinson-Patman Act was directed more at prevention of buyers' abuses of pricing (for example, preventing supermarkets from demanding discounts for high-volume business). It also removed quantity differences as a justification of price differences. The key provisions are points 1, 2, 3, and 5 listed under the Clayton Act in Table 8–2.

In 1938 the **Wheeler-Lea Act** was passed to amend Section 5 of the Federal Trade Commission Act. This law was passed because the courts had restricted the

Table 8–2 Summary of Major Antitrust Laws Affecting Marketing

Sherman Act (1890) prohibits:

1. contracts, combinations, or conspiracies in restraint of trade (Section 1).
2. monopolizing; attempting to monopolize, combinations or conspiracies to monopolize (Section 2).

Clayton Act (1914) prohibits:

1. price discrimination among purchasers that cannot be justified either by a difference in cost or as an attempt made, in good faith, to meet the price of a competitor (Section 2, as amended by Robinson-Patman Act of 1936, Section 2-a).
2. payment of a broker's commission if an independent broker is not employed (Robinson-Patman, Section 2-c).
3. providing supplementary services or allowances to a buyer unless such concessions are equally available to all buyers on a proportional basis (Robinson-Patman, Sections 2-d and 2-e).
4. geographical price discrimination, except under conditions in (1) above (Robinson-Patman, Section 3).
5. knowingly inducing or receiving an illegal discrimination in price (Robinson-Patman, Section 2-a).
6. tying and exclusive dealing contracts (Section 3).
7. mergers formed from acquisition of stocks or assets when the effect may be to lessen competition substantially, or to create a monopoly in any line of commerce in any section of the country (Section 7, as amended by Celler-Kefauver Act of 1950). Pre-notification of intent to merge is required under the Hart-Scott-Rodino Antitrust Improvement Act (1976).

Federal Trade Commission Act (1914) creates a commission whose orders are binding if not appealed to the courts by the defendant, and prohibits:

1. unfair methods of competition (Section 5).
2. unfair or deceptive practices in commerce (Section 5, as amended by the Wheeler-Lea Act of 1938).

FTC to involvement only when injury to competition was demonstrated; it had not been allowed to act when injury to consumers was the issue. Section 5 now reads:

> *Unfair methods of competition in commerce, and unfair or deceptive acts or practices in commerce are hereby declared unlawful.*

In 1950, the **Celler-Kefauver Act** was passed to toughen Section 7 of the Clayton Act (antimerger provision). The original Section 7 could not be used to prohibit acquisitions and mergers of physical assets as distinguished from capital stock. The coverage of amended Section 7 is listed in Table 8–3.

In 1976 the **Hart-Scott-Rodino Antitrust Improvement Act** was passed, requiring large companies, with intentions to merge, to notify the Federal Trade Commission beforehand. The intent was to allow the FTC to better prepare cases against these mergers.

Exemptions

The Congress of the United States has provided many exemptions to the antitrust laws. Historically, the most important of these to marketers was the concept of "fair

Table 8–3 Major Consumer Protection Legislation

Area of Concern	Year	Act	Main Features
Food, Drugs, and Cosmetics	1906	Food and Drug Act of 1906	Regulates interstate commerce in misbranded and adulterated foods, drinks, and drugs.
	1906	Meat Inspection Act	Provides for sanitary and standardized meat products.
	1938	Federal Food, Drug and Cosmetic Act of 1938	Strengthens the Food and Drug Act of 1906 by extending coverage to cosmetics; requires predistribution clearance of safety on new drugs; provides tolerance standards for unavoidable or required poisonous substances; and authorizes standards of identity, quality, and volume of container for foods.
	1958	Food Additives Amendments	Amend the Food and Drug Act by prohibiting use of new food additives until the promoter establishes safety and the Food and Drug Administration (FDA) issues regulations specifying the conditions of use.
	1960	Color Additives Amendment	Amends the Food and Drug Act, allowing the FDA to regulate the conditions of safe use for color additives in foods, drugs, and cosmetics.
	1962	Kefauver-Harris Drug Amendments	Require manufacturers to file all new drugs with the Food and Drug Administration; to label all drugs by generic name; and to pretest drugs for safety and efficacy.
	1966	Drug Abuse Amendment	Sets up regulations for the sale of amphetamines and barbiturates.
	1967	Wholesale Meat Act	Sets requirements making states' meat inspections meet Federal standards, and orders unsanitary meat plants to be cleaned up.
Fabric Identification	1939	Wool Products Labeling Act	Provides for proper labeling of the kind and percentage of each type of wool.
	1951	Fur Products Labeling Act	Provides that all furs show the true name of the animal from which they were produced.
	1959	Textile Fiber Products Identification Act	Covers the labeling of most products not covered by the Wool or Fur Products Labeling Acts.
Adequate and Accurate Consumer Information	1914	Federal Trade Commission Act	Establishes the Federal Trade Commission (FTC) to control, among other responsibilities, "unfair methods of competition," such as deceptive advertising.
	1958	Automobile Information Disclosure Act	Requires automobile manufacturers to post the suggested retail price on all new passenger vehicles.
	1968	Consumer Credit Protection Act (Truth-in-Lending Act)	Requires full disclosure of annual interest rates and other finance charges on consumer loans and credit buying, including revolving charge accounts.

Table 8–3 Continued

Area of Concern	Year	Act	Main Features
Adequate and Accurate Consumer Information (cont.)	1971	Fair Credit Reporting Act	Regulates the reporting and use of credit information.
	1975	Magnuson-Moss Warranty/ FTC Improvement Act	Requires warranty terms to be in easy-to-understand language, limits the ability of companies to restrict their warranty liability, and sets strict guidelines for what is a "full" warranty.
	1975	Fair Credit Billing Act	Sets up mechanisms for consumers to correct mistakes in their credit reports.
	1976	Energy Policy and Conservation Act	Requires the FTC to set rules requiring disclosure of energy efficiency ratings for appliances.
	1980	Fair Debt Collection Act	Makes it illegal to harass or abuse debtors; prohibits the use of falsehoods or other unfair methods to collect a debt.
Consumer Safety	1953	Flammable Fabrics Act	Prohibits shipment in interstate commerce of any clothing or material that could ignite easily.
	1966	National Traffic and Motor Vehicle Safety Act	Authorizes the Department of Transportation to establish compulsory safety standards for new and used tires and automobiles.
	1966	Child Safety Act	Strengthens the Federal Hazardous Substances Labeling Act of 1960 by preventing the marketing of potentially harmful products and permitting the Food and Drug Administration to remove inherently dangerous products from the market.
	1969	Child Protection and Toy Safety Act	Amends the Federal Hazardous Substances Labeling Act to protect children from toys and other articles intended for them that have electrical, mechanical, thermal, or other hazards.
	1970	Council on Environmental Quality Act	Authorizes the Secretary of the Interior to conduct investigations, surveys, and research relating to the nation's ecological systems, natural resources, and environmental quality and to establish a Council on Environmental Quality.
	1972	Consumer Product Safety Commission Act	Creates a permanent Consumer Product Safety Commission, which identifies unsafe products and warns consumers of their hazards.
	1976	Consumer Product Safety Commission Improvement Act	Expands the powers of the Commission and allows consumers to file suit against the Commission.

trade" or resale price maintenance, which allowed manufacturers to specify prices below which their products could not be sold by retailers. This is, in essence, vertical price-fixing. A number of states had laws to this effect, but these laws related only to goods sold in intrastate (within a state) commerce. In 1937, the **Miller-Tydings Resale Price Maintenance Act** was passed. It allowed contracts prescribing minimum prices for the resale of trademarked or branded commodities where state law allowed such agreements. This act amended Section 1 of the Sherman Act.

The intent of the act had been to bring all retailers of a product under pricing restriction. It effectively raised prices to end consumers by eliminating intrabrand retail price competition. However, the courts ruled that retailers who did not sign such an agreement were not bound. As a result, in 1952, the **McGuire-Keogh Act** amended Section 5 of the FTC Act to allow nonsigners provisions where sanctioned by state law; that is, if any single retailer of a commodity signed a resale price maintenance contract, all retailers dealing in that commodity were bound. In the 1975 **Consumer Goods Pricing Act,** Congress repealed these so-called "fair trade" laws and declared again that vertical price-fixing among producers and retailers was illegal.

Other exemptions to the antitrust laws have been allowed, including (1) agreements related to foreign trade; (2) tariff policy to exclude foreign competition; (3) labor policy—to protect workers; (4) organized baseball; and (5) soft drink bottlers.

Administration of the Antitrust Laws

The Antitrust Division of the Department of Justice has sole authority for enforcement of the Sherman Act and shares enforcement of the Clayton Act and Robinson-Patman Acts (focusing primarily on the criminal provisions) with the Federal Trade Commission. The Antitrust Division may bring criminal actions to punish violations or civil actions for restoring competition and providing relief to those injured. In a criminal action, the case must be proven beyond "a reasonable doubt," whereas in a civil action, guilt must be established by "a preponderance of evidence."

Federal Trade Commission (FTC)

The FTC is an independent administrative agency composed of five commissioners who are appointed by the President, with the advice and consent of the Senate, for terms of seven years. The President designates the chairperson. The FTC has a staff of about 800 people, consisting of lawyers, economists, and even some marketers.

In enforcing the FTC and Clayton Acts, the agency uses both voluntary and involuntary compliance methods. Voluntary compliance methods include:

1. Conferences—dialogue with affected businesspeople regarding the desirability of certain marketing practices.
2. Trade practice rules (since 1919)—written codes of suggested marketing practice formulated in conjunction with businesspeople.
3. Guides (since 1958)—administrative interpretations of its rulings prepared by the FTC.
4. Advisory opinions (by the staff for a long time and by the commissioners since 1961)—statements about the legality of *proposed* business activities. These statements contain no assurance that the FTC will not take action.

Involuntary compliance methods include:

1. Preliminary injunctions—temporary court orders requiring a firm to cease a marketing practice.
2. Cease and desist orders—permanent injunctions subsequent to administrative hearings.
3. Consent orders—specific agreements to resolve a dispute with no admission of guilt.
4. Miscellaneous remedies—corrective advertising or refunds of money to consumers.
5. Trade regulation rules.

Trade regulation rules (TRR) are statements prescribing a standard of conduct for a group of firms or an entire industry. Thus, instead of having to proceed on an individual case basis, the FTC could set rules for every company in an industry. This approach had little teeth in it until passage of the **Magnuson-Moss Warranty/FTC Improvement Act** of 1975, which gave explicit legal sanctions to TRRs. When Carter appointee Michael Pertschuk was chairperson of the FTC, the FTC attempted unsuccessfully to use this power to put TRRs in place to regulate a number of industries, including the funeral home, insurance, and used car industries. They also tried to prohibit advertising to children. The arrival of Reagan appointee James C. Miller as chairperson in 1981 changed this thrust dramatically. During the 1980s, Miller moved the FTC away from TRRs and back to proceeding more on a case-by-case basis. As in many other legal aspects affecting marketing, the law has not changed, but the enforcement emphasis has shifted to reflect the economic and political views of those charged with its enforcement.

The Important Court Decisions

Since the antitrust laws are very vaguely worded, the courts have had to put more detailed meaning into these statutes through judicial decisions in many cases.

Restraint of Trade

Section 1 of the Sherman Act proscribes "every contract, combination . . . or conspiracy in restraint of trade or commerce." An extended series of court decisions have interpreted this language as making illegal *per se* all agreements among competing firms to fix prices, to restrict or pool output, to share markets on a predetermined basis, or otherwise directly restrict the force of competition. Under a **per se** rule, the prosecution only needs to show that the alleged act was perpetrated. (The alternative to this is a **rule of reason,** where evidence would have to show that the act was also unreasonable or contrary to the public interest.) The rulings held that Congress had prohibited *all* agreements in restraint of trade—not just unreasonable ones.

The Control of Market Structures

Section 2 of the Sherman Act uses the word *monopolize,* but its definition is not clear. Would just dominating an industry be illegal? In early decisions, the courts developed a rule of reason. It worked as follows: the crime of monopolization involved two elements—the acquisition of a monopoly position and the intent to acquire that position and exclude rivals from the industry. If the actions of firms went beyond normal business practice, *intent* could be inferred. In the Alcoa case of 1945, a more *per se* position on monopolization was made the standing precedent. Alcoa, a manufacturer of aluminum products, had grown internally with the market by providing good service and good planning. This decision made legal actions possible against firms that dominate a market (such as IBM and AT&T). However, this type of action has been little used over the past two decades, and current government officials have indicated no desire to pursue this type of case.[5]

Mergers

Section 2 of the Sherman Act was supposed to prevent two firms merging together to form one firm and gaining an advantage over competitors. However, it did not prove to be a powerful statute in this regard. As a result, Section 7 of the Clayton Act was passed and later amended.

The courts have interpreted the revised Section 7 as a *per se* prohibition of horizontal mergers (those between direct competitors) of firms with substantial shares of the market. They have also interpreted it to prohibit vertical mergers (those between sellers and buyers in the channel) of firms likely to gain an appreciable share of some market. The emphasis has been on market structure. The exact share of market or definition of market area and composition has varied. The pre-1981 tendency was to take tight definitions of markets and fairly low combined market shares (for example, a 24 percent share in the Wisconsin beer market prevented a merger between Pabst and Blatz). Under the recent Republican administrations, the Justice Department and the FTC have taken a more open attitude toward mergers. The tendency is to give a green light to vertical mergers between suppliers and customers and conglomerate mergers between diverse companies operating in separate businesses. Horizontal mergers between competitors have also been made easier by raising the level of market concentration that the Justice Department considers to be a problem.

Price Discrimination

Section 2 of the Clayton Act outlawed charging different prices to different customers where the effect "may be to substantially lessen competition or tend to create a monopoly." This action is called **price discrimination.** However, discrimination because of differences in grade, quality, or quantity was exempted from the act, as was done for differences in cost or differences carried out in good faith to meet competitive pressures.

The quantity aspect proved to be a major loophole, making successful prosecutions difficult. As a result, the Robinson-Patman Act was passed to amend Section 2 of the Clayton Act. The effect of this amendment was to protect small independent enterprises against the price competition of large firms that discriminate in both their sales and purchasing functions. In essence, the law was designed to limit competition, not to enhance it. Enforcement of the Robinson-Patman Act has been vigorous. Chapter 17 discusses price discrimination in more detail.

Exclusion

Section 3 of the Clayton Act prohibits those contracts for sale or lease of commodities that impose a condition that the purchaser or lessee "shall not use or deal in the goods . . . supplies, or other commodities of a competitor," where the effect "may be to substantially lessen competition or tend to create a monopoly." It covers three main types of practices: *tying contracts, requirement contracts,* and *exclusive dealing* arrangements.

Tying contracts occur when the purchaser of some article agrees as a condition of purchase to buy the seller's supplies of some other commodity. If sellers require their full line to be carried, this is called *full-line forcing.* The courts have ruled that it is "unreasonable *per se* to foreclose competitors from any substantial market" by means of tying contracts. Violations will not be found unless there is monopoly power in the tying market, or unless a substantial volume of sales is foreclosed.

Under **requirement contracts,** the buyer agrees to purchase all its requirements for some commodity or group of commodities from a particular seller. The courts have taken a structural view of this area. Proof must be presented that "competition has been foreclosed in a substantial share of the line of commerce affected" for the contract to be voided.

Under an **exclusive dealing** arrangement, a buyer gets exclusive rights to resell a product by agreeing to sell only that product and no competitors' products. In order to be able to carry a brand of television, for example, a retailer may agree not to deal in other brands. Section 3 of the Clayton Act and Section 1 of the Sherman Act are relevant here. The court decisions have applied both a *per se* and a rule of reason approach. The latter seems to be the more dominant approach.

Another potential restraint of trade that arises in distribution occurs when a manufacturer attempts to control the actions of a wholesaler or retailer in terms of selling territory. In 1967, in the Arnold Schwinn & Co. case, the Supreme Court ruled this to be illegal *per se* under Section 1 of the Sherman Act, since intrabrand competition would be restricted. Schwinn was prevented from controlling the selling activities of its authorized dealers. However, in 1977, in the GTE Sylvania case, the Supreme Court overturned the *per se* rule. The rule of reason will now be applied to measure the interbrand and intrabrand effects of any restriction.

Unfair Methods of Competition and Deceptive Practices

Section 5 of the Federal Trade Commission Act (as amended by Wheeler-Lea) has been used to attack such things as price-fixing, boycotts of one firm's products by another firm, exclusive dealing and tying agreements, price discrimination, mergers, bribery, business espionage, disseminating derogatory information about rival products, harassing competitors, misrepresentation in advertising and promotion, misrepresentation of product ingredients, and false price representation (claimed bargain prices). The words *unfair* and *deceptive* have been given broad meanings by the courts.

Review Your Marketing Knowledge

- Review the laws and regulations discussed up to this point in the chapter. Are there any that you think should be repealed? Why?
- For those laws you think should be retained, why are they still needed? How rigorously do you think they should be enforced? What criteria should the government use in deciding which cases to prosecute?

Consumer Protection Laws

Another thrust of legislative activity has been in the area of consumer protection. It is important to note that, besides the laws presented in this section, the FTC Act is also concerned with protecting consumers.

Consumer protection legislation is growing annually. Table 8–3 outlines only some of the major proconsumer laws. Since the early 1960s, over thirty major consumer protection laws have been passed by Congress. Consumers and their spokespersons are continually pressing for and getting better treatment from business. Today, consumers have expectations that they will receive better product performance, more product safety, and better information to permit them to make better buying decisions.

Consumers have demanded what is called the *consumers' bill of rights,* legislation that protects them. The increase in consumer protection and the consumerism movement does not mean that *caveat emptor*—let the buyer beware—is replaced by *caveat venditor*—let the seller beware. Instead, it means that protecting the consumer is a role that the government has accepted and will enforce. John Kennedy outlined the rights of consumers as follows:

1. The right to expect the product they purchase to be *safe.*
2. The right to be *accurately and adequately informed* about products. This includes protection against fraud and deceit, plus misleading advertising and labeling. Also, the information needed to make an informed choice should be present.
3. *The right to choose* from a variety of offerings at a competitive price. This implies that there are a number of competitors in an industry.
4. *The right to be heard.* This means that the consumer point of view should receive a fair hearing by both business and government.

Two early laws of consumer protection were the **Pure Food and Drug Act** and the **Meat Inspection Act,** both passed in 1906. Upton Sinclair's vivid portrayal of conditions in the meat-packing industry in *The Jungle*[6] stimulated public support for passage of these acts. The Pure Food and Drug Act was revised in 1938 by the Food, Drug and Cosmetic Act, and more amendments were added, including the Pesticide Chemical Amendment in 1954, the Food Additive Amendment in 1958, and the Color Additive Amendment of 1960.

In order to oversee laws, the *Food and Drug Administration* (FDA) was established in 1927. Most of its activities are directed toward product purity, standards of potency, and truthful and informative labeling. False advertising of foods, drugs, and cosmetics is policed by the Federal Trade Commission.

The *Consumer Product Safety Commission* was established as a government agency in 1972 by the **Consumer Product Safety Act.** This independent consumer agency has the authority to set safety standards, to ban unsafe products, and even to jail marketing executives for noncompliance with requests. The Commission oversees the safety of toys, clothing, appliances, and the packaging of hazardous products. The Commission gathers information on the safety of products by using a call-in hot line to hear immediate consumer complaints. In addition, injury reports that reflect unsafe products are collected each day from hospital emergency rooms.

State Regulation

During the Reagan years, the federal government reduced its level of enforcement of both consumer protection and antitrust laws. This vacuum has been filled through increased regulatory activity by state and local governments.

When the safety of Saccharin was questioned, many companies switched to Nutrasweet.

The attorneys general in the individual states have coordinated their efforts, forming an organization called NAAG, the *National Association of Attorneys General.* By working together, they have found that they can share some of the costs of investigations and can wield more power. The threat to companies is much greater when they face possible prosecution from several states at once.[7]

NAAG has developed guidelines for advertising airline fares and rental car fees, and has been investigating for-profit vocational schools, the cable television industry, and airline reservation systems. New York's Attorney General reached a consent agreement with Panasonic, calling for the electronics company to pay $16 million in refunds to consumers to settle charges that the company threatened retailers with loss of supply unless Panasonic products were sold at prices dictated by the company. In other recent actions, state attorneys general have sued major insurance companies for alleged collusion to restrict certain policies, won a $16 million settlement from Chrysler for rolling back odometers, won a settlement of up to $4 million from Minolta on charges the company refused to let retailers discount their product, and challenged large corporate mergers ignored by federal regulators.[8]

Self-regulation

Self-regulation may be thought of as an alternative to government regulation. However, history clearly shows that it works best as a supplement to government. Self-regulation lacks the power of enforcement; it must rely on the good will of marketers. Unfortunately, an unethical person could ignore the proposals of self-regulators. This is why advertising associations actively encouraged the passage of the FTC Act and its Wheeler-Lea Amendments.

The most important self-regulation activities in marketing are (1) the local work of the Better Business Bureau; (2) the regulation of advertising by the National Advertising Division (NAD) of the Council of Better Business Bureaus (CBBB), in conjunction with advertising trade associations; and (3) the codes of the National Association of Broadcasters (NAB).

The Better Business Bureau is a nonprofit corporation that attempts to further business interests by actively promoting fair advertising and selling practices by industries. It works mostly at the local level to handle consumer complaints and attempts to work out solutions to disagreements between buyer and seller. Moral persuasion is its main technique.

MARKETING IN ACTION

The National Advertising Division Tackles Ad Disputes

In 1988 the Council of Better Business Bureau's National Advertising Division resolved 103 national advertising campaign disputes, up 5 percent from 1987. The largest number, 41, were brought to NAD's attention by competing advertisers. The NAD staff initiated 37 of the cases, with the remaining 25 disputes brought to NAD's attention by local Better Business Bureaus, consumers, industry associations, or other sources.

The largest product category was food ads, with 24 cases. This was followed by advertising directed at children, 23 cases, and automobiles, auto accessories, and car rentals with 10 cases. Among recent cases were the following:

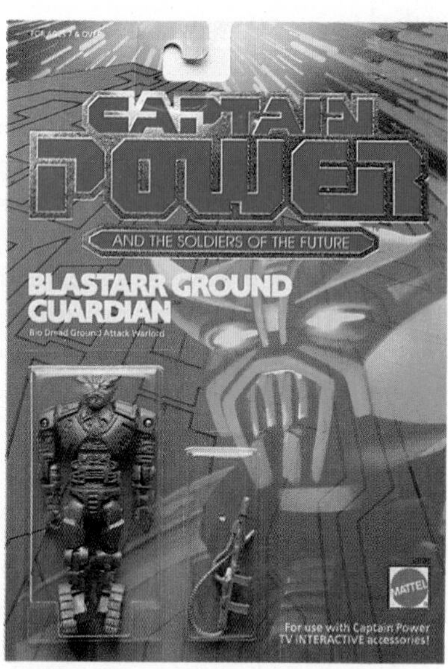

• Mattel's commercial for Captain Power and his Power Jet XT–7 (agency: Ogilvy and Mather, Los Angeles). Mattel was charged with confusing children by blending fantasy and programming with commercialism by advertising the product on the Captain Power & the Soldiers of the Future TV cartoon show in a manner that did not enable children to distinguish between program/editorial content and advertising. The company replied that the toy was shown clearly and realistically, and that it followed Children's Advertising Review Unit standards. NAD asked Mattel to change the ads and to ensure that in future ads children can distinguish between commercials and programs.

• Holly Farms Poultry Industries case. The company, a regional processor of branded fresh chicken, advertised that "Guarantees [of] the highest standards of quality and freshness in the world. And you can taste it." Other claims in the body copy of the advertising related to providing "the freshest chicken possible." The claims were challenged by NAD after a complaint by Perdue Farms, a competitor. NAD found that Holly Farms was able to substantiate the freshness claims, with plant records indicating its chicken was processed within 3 hours and delivery to most stores was made within 12 hours. The statistical reliability of the company's taste tests with "experts" were questioned by NAD, however, and the company agreed to expand the testing to include a representative panel of consumers to compare alternative products available in retail stores.

• Ashton-Tate case (agency: Chiat/Day, San Francisco). The company's ads for its dBase Plus computer software stated that, "So far, nobody has even come close to the versatility of the dBase programming language. Or found a way to let nonprogrammers create more sophisticated programs." A competitor, Microrim, complained that the copy disparaged its product, and submitted several articles from magazines that discussed the advantages and disadvantages of dBase. Ashton-Tate replied by submitting a number of review articles from computer magazines which supported its claims. NAD agreed that the ad claims were substantiated.

SOURCES: "NAD Tackles 103 Cases in '88," *Advertising Age*, January 16, 1989, p. 49; "NAD Clucks at Holly Farms," *Advertising Age*, May 16, 1988, p. 85; and "NAD Slams Spot from Mattel," *Advertising Age*, October 19, 1987, p. 6.

NAD actively solicits complaints about advertising from consumers and other advertisers and has some cases referred to it by the regulatory bodies (see the *Marketing in Action* on NAD). Complaints are either dismissed, or the adviser is asked to provide substantiation of claims. Once the evidence is examined, the complaint may be dismissed, or, if the substantiation is not acceptable, the NAD asks the advertiser to discontinue the advertisement. If the advertiser objects to the decision, the case is forwarded to the National Advertising Review Board (NARB). The NARB is composed of a chairperson and fifty members representing various segments of the industry and general public. When an appeal from NAD is received, the chairperson appoints a five-member panel to consider the case. If the NARB finds fault with the advertising, the advertiser is again asked to discontinue the message. If he or she refuses, the matter is referred to the government for action. NAD and NARB findings are made public. Most cases are settled by the NAD and, thus, never reach the NARB. Both NAD and NARB have outstanding records for gaining compliance for their decisions.

Review Your Marketing Knowledge

- Which is more effective in your opinion, government regulation or self-regulation? Why?
- Is government regulation more appropriate at the state level or the local level? Why?

Criticisms of Marketing

Criticism is healthy for any discipline because it leads to improvements and helps us better understand the issues involved. Individual consumers, consumer interest groups, government officials and legislators, and historians have all objected to aspects of marketing. In this section, we will summarize the opposition to each component of the marketing mix, together with marketers' responses to the criticisms. The criticisms tend to revolve around economic or social issues, and perhaps the most frequent complaint is that marketing costs too much.

Product: Criticisms and Responses

The critics raise a number of issues about products:

- Many products are of poor overall quality (for example, the Ford Pinto had defects in the gasoline tank, making the car susceptible to fire upon impact in even a minor accident).
- Service after the sale is sometimes nonexistent or is often done badly and without enthusiasm (delayed delivery of ordered furniture; warranty work on automobiles).
- Product advances are often very minor.
- Style changes cause consumers to purchase new products before the functional usefulness of the old ones is used up (style obsolescence in appliances and automobiles).
- Because materials and workmanship are of poor quality, products need to be replaced sooner than necessary (planned physical obsolescence).
- Product and brand proliferation confuse consumers in their purchasing (too many cereals).
- Some products are unsafe (like cap guns that give off sparks), while others provide no real benefit (candy).

Here are marketers' responses to these criticisms:

- Some of the criticisms are true for individual products or organizations, but not for marketing as a whole.

- The great majority of products (over 98 percent) work well, have good service, are safe, and provide benefit; the critics focus too much on the mistakes of a small percentage of organizations and on a small percentage of poor products.
- Consumers want style changes and new features; otherwise, life would be dull.
- It is not a marketer's role to be a moral judge of consumer needs.
- Individual product improvements may be small, but over a number of years they result in major improvements. Just compare a refrigerator now to one that is ten years old, or a new hand-held calculator or computer to an old one.
- Many different types of products and brands give consumers freedom of choice. Who in our society should be allowed to tell consumers how many products and how many brands should be available? Freedom of choice is one of the things that distinguishes a free society.
- Marketers will only market products and services if there is a demand.

Distribution: Criticisms and Responses

Critics of distribution focus on the following issues:

- There are too many levels of intermediaries in the channel.
- There are too many intermediaries at each level.
- Intermediaries are generally not necessary.
- Intermediaries earn excessive profits.

Marketers offer these responses:

- Critics have presumed that a shorter channel with few levels is more cost efficient in terms of the functions to be performed. This is generally incorrect since levels of channel intermediaries come into existence because there is a need to distribute goods more efficiently.
- The number of intermediaries at any level in the channel is dictated by competitive and economic forces, as it should be. If they provide a needed service at a competitive cost, they deserve to exist.
- Critics do not fully understand that someone must always perform the basic marketing functions.
- Intermediaries' profits are actually quite low (see Chapter 12).

Promotion: Criticisms and Responses

With so much money being spent in such a visible way on advertising and personal selling, questions about the economic and social effects are bound to arise. The following are the major criticisms:

- Once primary demand stimulation ceases, spending on advertising raises prices. Firms are just fighting over market share with no chance of overall economies resulting.
- Advertising is more concerned with persuasion than with information.
- Advertising can be misleading and deceptive.

- Advertising creates barriers to new-product entry by increasing the cost of entering a market. For example, a firm thinking about entering the frozen pizza market must at least match the $6 million advertising budgets of the established competitors. This added expense may dissuade entry.
- Much advertising is in bad taste and insults consumers' intelligence.
- Advertising is especially harmful to children, who do not understand its purpose.
- Advertising creates demand for products consumers would not otherwise want.
- Advertising increases the materialistic outlook of society.
- Salespeople use high-pressure tactics so that consumers are persuaded to pay too much for things they don't need. The door-to-door selling of magazines is a prime example.
- Personal selling is often manipulative. For example, appliance salespeople manipulate information about product offerings in order to sell the more expensive items in a line. The FTC charged Sears with this type of bait and switch in the late 1970s.
- Personal selling is deceptive. Statements like "This offer is a special one for today only, and is really only $100 above cost," are often outright deception.

In response, some benefits of advertising and personal selling should be noted:

- Advertising lowers the prices consumers would otherwise pay by making mass-production possible. Without advertising, demand would not be great enough to support large-scale production facilities. Advertising is increasing primary demand.
- Advertising provides information to consumers so that they can make competent choices about product, price, location, and competitive differences.
- Advertising makes new-product entry possible; without it, established brands could not be meaningfully challenged.
- Advertising supports the media; without it, the freedom of the press that we enjoy would be impossible, since no medium can be financially viable without advertising (except government and privately supported ones).
- Advertising itself is entertaining (for example, Federal Express, McDonald's, and Coke commercials).
- Advertising stimulates competitive activity, with resulting consumer benefits. Recent Federal Trade Commission action to stop lawyers, pharmacists, doctors, and other professionals from restricting advertising has resulted in lower prices to consumers. In all cases, prices have decreased when restrictions have been removed.
- Advertising provides jobs for people in advertising agencies, production companies, research firms, and the media.
- Advertising must be evaluated against realistic alternatives.
- The critics impose the unrealistic standard of perfect competition against which to evaluate the consequences of advertising.
- Personal selling can be too high-pressured, manipulative, and deceptive, but this occurs only in a small minority of all selling activity. Most selling today is very professional.

The debate on these issues is expected to continue into the future. In general, consumers apparently believe that the benefits of advertising and personal selling outweigh the potential negatives, but self-regulation and legal constraints are still needed to keep some potential abuses under close scrutiny.

Price: Criticisms and Responses

The complaints about price are heard almost daily:

- Prices are too high in general (lettuce at $1.24 a head, $500 a day for a hospital room, $13,000 for a basic midsized car).
- The poor and disadvantaged pay excessive prices. Stores in poor areas charge higher prices.
- Prices are too inflexible downward; when demand weakens, prices do not fall very much.
- Price competition is downplayed in the marketing mix.

Marketers offer the following responses:

- Price levels reflect the general level of inflation in the economy; they are not the cause of it.
- The poor *do* pay higher prices, but this is because they tend to be served by small, less efficient retailers. The returns earned by these retailers are typically not excessive relative to other retailers.
- Prices *are* inflexible downward because of rising costs to marketers.
- Other parts of the marketing mix are just as legitimate competitive variables as price is. This criticism is often based upon the model of the perfectly competitive world, which is unrealistic.

Many of the marketing criticisms reflect the critics' value judgments about the operation of society in consumption-related matters. They reject the premise that consumers should have freedom of choice; many wish to impose their judgments about what consumers should use. Sometimes the critics fail to identify or recognize the functions performed and the utility created by marketing.

Some of the criticisms we've listed certainly have merit. Indeed, marketing abuses by individual organizations are all too evident. However, the marketing system, as a whole, does pretty well. Winston Churchill described democracy as the worst system of government except for all others. In a sense, the marketing system is the same: it is imperfect, but is better than all alternatives at providing consumer welfare in a free society. As we noted previously, public and governmental efforts are constantly trying to make the marketing system better by removing abuses. Many of these efforts are supported by concerned marketing people. The National Advertising Division of the Council of Better Business Bureau's effort to regulate deceptive advertising is only one example.

Does Marketing Cost Too Much?

Another major criticism is that marketing costs too much. As we noted in Chapter 1, about 50 percent of the final price for products comes from marketing costs. Between 1840 and 1940, these total marketing costs increased as a percentage of sales from about 20 percent to 50 percent.[9] This increase, which has flattened out over the last five decades, does not indicate that marketing costs too much; it reflects a change in the nature of consumption in our society.

Table 8–4 American Marketing Association Code of Ethics

Members of the American Marketing Association (AMA) are committed to ethical professional conduct. They have joined together in subscribing to this Code of Ethics embracing the following topics:

Responsibilities of the Marketer

Marketers must accept responsibility for the consequence of their activities and make every effort to ensure that their decisions, recommendations, and actions function to identify, serve, and satisfy all relevant publics: customers, organizations and society.

Marketers' professional conduct must be guided by:

1. The basic rule of professional ethics: not knowingly to do harm;
2. The adherence to all applicable laws and regulations;
3. The accurate representation of their education, training and experience; and
4. The active support, practice and promotion of this Code of Ethics.

Honesty and Fairness

Marketers shall uphold and advance the integrity, honor, and dignity of the marketing profession by:

1. Being honest in serving consumers, clients, employees, suppliers, distributors and the public;
2. Not knowingly participating in conflict of interest without prior notice to all parties involved; and
3. Establishing equitable fee schedules including the payment or receipt of usual, customary and/or legal compensation for marketing exchanges.

Rights and Duties of Parties in the Marketing Exchange Process

Participants in the marketing exchange process should be able to expect that:

1. Products and services offered are safe and fit for their intended uses;
2. Communications about offered products and services are not deceptive;
3. All parties intend to discharge their obligations, financial and otherwise, in good faith; and
4. Appropriate internal methods exist for equitable adjustment and/or redress of grievances concerning purchases.

It is understood that the above would include, *but is not limited to,* the following responsibilities of the marketer:

In the area of product development and management,

- disclosure of all substantial risks associated with product or service usage;
- identification of any product component substitution that might materially change the product or impact on the buyer's purchase decision;
- identification of extra-cost added features.

In the area of promotions,

- avoidance of false and misleading advertising;
- rejection of high pressure manipulations, or misleading sales tactics;
- avoidance of sales promotions that use deception or manipulation.

In the area of distribution,

- not manipulating the availability of a product for purpose of exploitation;
- not using coercion in the marketing channel;
- not exerting undue influence over the reseller's choice to handle a product.

In the area of pricing,

- not engaging in price fixing;
- not practicing predatory pricing;
- disclosing the full price associated with any purchase.

In the area of marketing research,

- prohibiting selling or fund raising under the guise of conducting research;
- maintaining research integrity by avoiding misrepresentation and omission of pertinent research data;
- treating outside clients and suppliers fairly.

Organizational Relationships

Marketers should be aware of how their behavior may influence or impact on the behavior of others in organizational relationships. They should not demand, encourage or apply coercion to obtain unethical behavior in their relationships with others, such as employees, suppliers or customers.

1. Apply confidentiality and anonymity in professional relationships with regard to privileged information;
2. Meet their obligations and responsibilities in contracts and mutual agreements in a timely manner;
3. Avoid taking the work of others, in whole, or in part, and represent this work as their own or directly benefit from it without compensation or consent of the originator or owner;
4. Avoid manipulation to take advantage of situations to maximize personal welfare in a way that unfairly deprives or damages the organization or others.

Any AMA members found to be in violation of any provision of this Code of Ethics may have his or her Association membership suspended or revoked.

From 1840 to 1940 the number of retailers increased, providing better distribution and sales of goods, adding many services such as credit, delivery, and parking, and increasing dramatically the level of consumption-oriented activity. The cost increases were necessary to support the mass-production society that was developing. Also, the stability of marketing costs over the last four decades reflects the maturing of the consumption-oriented society in the United States.

The Ethical Issues of Alcohol Marketing and Underaged Drinking

Alarmingly high alcohol consumption rates have been reported among U.S. high school students. Half of the nation's fourth graders do not consider alcohol a drug. In a survey of 500,000 grade school students, 34 percent said they face considerable peer pressure to try alcohol by the time they reach fourth grade, and 26 percent believe other students are drinking. Marketing is blamed as a major cause of these growing problems.

Many people agree, including South Carolina Senator Strom Thurmond and Thomas V. Sessel, executive director of the National Council on Alcoholism, Inc. Senator Thurmond was especially incensed about the Spuds MacKenzie promotional campaign for Bud Light beer, which he cited as a prime example of the advertisements that "glamorize the use of alcohol" among young people.

Anheuser-Busch dismissed its critics' demands to halt the Spuds MacKenzie campaign, which centered on the notorious bull terrier. According to Stephen K. Lambright, vice president and group executive of Anheuser-Busch Cos., Inc., in St Louis, Spuds MacKenzie is "designed to sell beer only to those above the legal minimum age of consumption," and Anheuser-Busch takes pains to avoid "appearing to market to their children." Thurmond said that Spuds MacKenzie stuffed animals, children's toys, and T-shirts small enough to fit 12-year olds "indicate the real purpose of this campaign."

Wine coolers are a part of this issue as well. Thomas Sessel asserted that a lot of marketing efforts tend to obscure the fact that these products contain alcohol. He said that wine coolers are often packaged in boxes that look like soda pop containers, which he feels may confuse children.

Packaging is not the only alcohol marketing technique in question. Sessel feels that wine cooler makers should "stop using images that appeal to children." One ad that fit this bill featured a polar bear singing and dancing. In separate interviews, both he and Thurmond complained that these ads give the impression that wine coolers are actually soft drinks or fruit punch. In actuality, wine coolers contain as much as 6 percent alcohol, which is higher than the alcoholic content of most beers. While all of this activity is perfectly legal, it raises questions of ethics to many observers.

Both Sessel and Thurmond want mandatory health warning labels placed on alcoholic beverages. Thurmond says his repeated efforts to pass a bill to this effect have been thwarted because "the full power of the alcohol beverage industry is exerted against it." Sessel thinks these problems and misconceptions could be reversed if the alcoholic beverage industry would "live up to its own Code of Advertising Standards." Thurmond is not holding his breath. "I am not confident in the voluntary efforts of the industry to increase public awareness of the hazards of alcohol abuse. With 12-year-olds drinking wine coolers and wearing Spuds MacKenzie T-shirts, there is no basis for such confidence." "Just where are the ethical standards of these marketers?" asks another observer.

SOURCES: "Marketing Seen as a Factor in Kid Drinking," *Marketing News,* December 4, 1987, p. 24; "Senator Raps Spuds MacKenzie Promotion," *Marketing News,* December 4, 1987, p. 24.

Could the same marketing functions be accomplished at somewhat less cost today? There is really no data available to answer this question precisely, but to say that marketing costs are too high implies that one or more of the following conditions holds: (1) marketing intermediaries must earn abnormally high profits; (2) more services are being provided than consumers are demanding; (3) marketing functions must be performed in a grossly inefficient fashion; (4) consumption must be declining; and (5) total costs of production and marketing together must be increasing.[10]

The overwhelming weight of evidence is that none of these conditions holds, although it is possible that individual marketers may be overspending. But at an aggregate level, the marketing system does not cost too much for what it provides.

Marketing Ethics and Social Responsibility

Marketers have within their ranks a small number that operate outside the laws regulating the system. Unfortunately, these defrauders are all too present and visible to the general public. Even for those who operate within the law, questions come up about appropriate marketing behavior. Marketers continually make decisions that, although perfectly legal, may be considered unethical or socially irresponsible by some group. For example, advertising to children is considered unethical by one group, Parents Against Advertising to Children. Closing a Sears store in downtown Detroit brought the company into a conflict with a local community group in Detroit over social responsibility. Other ethical concerns are highlighted in the *Marketing in Action* on ethics.

Ethics are standards of behavior against which actions are judged. Proponents of social responsibility try to focus decision makers' attention on the broader social consequences of their decisions. Each of you reading this book will some day confront decisions that involve ethics and social responsibility, and each of you will, at that time, impose your own ethical standards and concern for social responsibility on those decisions. Each of you must reach your own decisions; however, you might find it instructive to see what some others think. Table 8–4 presents the Code of Ethics of the American Marketing Association (AMA). This code gives general guidelines to marketers but does not direct action in specific situations. Since compliance with the code is strictly voluntary, it has no enforcement power. Withdrawing someone's AMA membership has only symbolic impact. Professional groups such as doctors and lawyers can effectively take away one's ability to make a living by revoking membership in their organizations, but marketers are a long way from having this power. Also, people can take part in marketing without ever becoming AMA members.

Personal Computer Exercise

Marketing survey data is frequently used to determine if an advertisement is deceptive. This PC exercise allows you to play the role of a regulator, with the opportunity to determine whether or not you want to challenge the claims made in the ad. You will be asked to determine if the ad is unfair or deceptive, and if you rule it is, to determine what appropriate action should be taken.

KEY POINTS

• Marketing operates in a public arena composed of consumers, competitors, governments, advocates, the media, consumer help agencies, and the community.

• Government sets the rules of conduct for marketers. Some regulations that industries impose on themselves also form the rules of conduct. Marketers constantly deal with these antitrust and consumer protection regulations.

• The major statutes that affect marketing are the Sherman Act, the Clayton Act, and the FTC Act. The Sherman Act is used to attack conspiracies and agreements to fix prices and divide markets and to attack monopolization. The Clayton Act, as amended by Robinson-Patman, deals with price discrimination and tying and exclusive dealing contracts. As amended by the Celler-Kefauver Act, it can be used to attack anticompetitive mergers. The FTC Act set up a commission to deal with unfair methods of competition and unfair or deceptive practices.

• Consumerism represents attempts by consumers (customers) to gain rights and power in their dealings with marketers.

• Consumer protection laws have been passed to help give consumers more power in dealing with firms and to give them their rights to product safety, accurate information, a choice of products, and a hearing.

• Self-regulation is both an alternative and a supplement to government regulation, but works best in a supplementary role.

• Many criticisms have been raised about each area of the marketing mix. Some of these criticisms have merit. Abuses by individual organizations do take place all too often, but the marketing system works very well as a whole.

• A frequent criticism of marketing is that it costs too much, but the conditions necessary to demonstrate this truth do not hold.

• Ethics are standards of behavior against which actions are judged. In marketing we will all face decisions that have ethical aspects.

ISSUES FOR DISCUSSION

1. A major bank has determined that it loses money on personal and auto loans in inner-city areas and has decided to stop making these types of loans. It is also considering shutting down its branches in the inner city. What elements of the public arena of marketing would be involved? What advice would you give the president of the bank to help solve the problem?

2. Should beer advertising be removed from television? What would the consequences of this be to beer marketers, to beer consumers, to the media, and to alcohol abuse?

3. Is it an unfair practice for door-to-door salespeople of book companies to pretend to be conducting a marketing research study as a way of gaining entry to a prospect's residence? Why or why not? If you think so, what remedy would you suggest?

4. Increasingly, consumers are complaining about the intrusion of telemarketers, charging that they are called late at night or during dinner, creating an invasion of privacy. Many consumers especially resent calls from "talking computers." What regulations, if any, do you think the Federal Trade Commission should develop to regulate telemarketers?

5. How would you respond in the following circumstances, which are legal, but raise ethical issues?

a. Your company assigns you to work on a cigarette brand. You believe that cigarette smoking contributes to many diseases including cancer and heart disease.

b. You are in the final negotiations of a large contract with an international buyer when he or she asks you for "a personal payment to show good faith, as is the custom in my country."

c. An advertisement for your brand has been shown to be effective by marketing research. However, an organization representing a significant ethnic group has protested to you that the advertisement is offensive to the people of that group because of the way they are portrayed.

d. New technology has allowed you to reduce the size and weight of your product. It is now no longer economical to use a particular intermediary that your firm has been using with great success for twenty years.

6. Of all the criticisms of marketing listed in this chapter, which three do you think have the most legitimacy? Support your choice with good reasoning and examples. Suggest ways to remedy the criticisms.

7. Evaluate the American Marketing Association Code of Ethics. Is it specific enough? Is there anything that should be included that is left out? Do you think it will have any impact on the practice of marketing?

8. Examine such periodicals as *Business Week, Advertising Age, The Wall Street Journal,* and your local newspaper. Find a few examples of regulatory actions taken related to marketing. (We guarantee that it is easy to find lots of them.) Bring them to class for discussion.

GLOSSARY

Celler-Kefauver Act of 1950: a law passed to amend the Clayton Act (Section 7) by strengthening the antimerger aspects. It forbids acquiring stock or assets where the acquisition involves a substantial lessening of competition or tendency to create a monopoly in any section of the country.

Clayton Act of 1914: a law prohibiting price discrimination, with exceptions. It also bans tying, exclusive dealing, and requirement contracts, plus acquisitions by stock purchase that substantially lessen competition or tend to create a monopoly.

Consumer education: an approach to achieve better consumer decisions. It attempts to make consumers good marketplace decision makers by exposing them to materials that explain good consumerism.

Consumer Goods Pricing Act of 1975: a law repealing the retail price maintenance laws.

Consumer Product Safety Commission Act of 1972: a law that set up the Consumer Product Safety Commission as an independent government agency. The Commission sets standards for safety on products and bans unsafe products.

Consumer protection: legal action designed to give consumers more power in their marketplace dealings with businesses.

Consumerism: the consumers' movement for more rights relative to business.

Exclusive dealing: arrangement giving a buyer exclusive rights to sell a product if he or she agrees not to sell any competitors' products.

Federal Trade Commission Act of 1914: a law prohibiting unfair methods of competition. It also created the Federal Trade Commission (FTC), a regulatory body of five commissioners plus staff that enforces the FTC and Clayton Acts.

Hart-Scott-Rodino Antitrust Improvement Act of 1976: a law requiring large companies to prenotify the FTC of merger intentions.

Magnuson-Moss Warranty/FTC Improvement Act of 1975: a law expanding the FTC's Trade Regulation Rule powers and spelling out warranty requirements.

Marketing conduct: legal view of marketers' decisions on marketing mix variables and the process by which they make these decisions.

McGuire-Keogh Act of 1952: a law allowing all retailers of a given commodity to be bound to price maintenance if one retailer of that commodity in a state agrees to it.

Miller-Tydings Resale Price Maintenance Act of 1937: a law allowing retail prices to be fixed by manufacturers; an exemption to the Sherman Act.

National Advertising Division (NAD): an arm of the Council of Better Business Bureaus. It evaluates complaints about advertising.

National Advertising Review Board (NARB): a panel from industry and the general public that evaluates advertising cases appealed to it from the NAD.

Per se: a Latin phrase meaning literally *by itself* or *in itself*. It is used here to mean that an act is illegal based just upon the fact it happened; the act's reasonableness is not a relevant dimension.

Price discrimination: the practice of selling the same goods to different buyers at the same time for different prices.

Requirement contracts: an agreement in which the buyer purchases all its requirements of some commodity from a seller.

Robinson-Patman Act of 1936: a law amending Section 2 of the Clayton Act. It clarifies the legal meaning of price discrimination; is designed to protect small businesses from the buying power of large businesses; and also lays down rules for brokerage payments and promotional allowances by manufacturers.

Rules of reason: a principle for determining the legality of business practices. Illegality is determined on evidence concerning the effects of the action on the country, competitors, and consumers.

Self-regulation: standards of conduct developed and policed by members of an industry or groups of industries.

Sherman Act of 1890: a statute that outlaws contracts, combinations, or conspiracies in restraint of trade. It also forbids monopolization or combinations that monopolize.

Trade Regulation Rule (TRR): legal standards of conduct developed by the FTC for all companies in an industry or group of industries.

Tying agreement: a contract requiring the purchaser of some article to agree, as a condition of purchase, to buy some other article from the seller.

Wheeler-Lea Act of 1938: a statute amending the FTC Act, Section 5, to make unfair methods of competition and unfair and deceptive practices unlawful.

NOTES

1. This whole section is adapted from a paper by Micheal R. Pearce that was originally published in Kenneth G. Hardy, Michael R. Pearce, Thomas C. Kinnear, and Adrian B. Ryans, *Canadian Marketing: Cases and Concepts* (Allyn and Bacon Canada Ltd., 1978), pp. 458–65.

2. "Your Hamburger: 41,000 Regulations," *U.S. News & World Report*, February 11, 1980, p. 64.

3. Quoted from Paul N. Bloom and Stephen A. Greyser, "Exploring the Future of Consumerism," Marketing Science Institute, July 1981, p. 43. For a further discussion of this view see Paul N. Bloom and Stephen A. Greyser, "The Maturing of Consumerism," *Harvard Business Review*, November-December 1981, pp. 130–39.

4. The assistance of Michael R. Pearce in the preparation of this section is gratefully acknowledged.

5. Susan Samuelson and Thomas Balmer, "Antitrust Revisited—Implications for Competitive Policy," *Sloan Management Review*, Fall 1988, pp. 79–87.

6. Upton Sinclair, *The Jungle*, (Viking, 1905).

7. David Moskowitz, "Why the States Are Ganging Up on Some Giant Companies," *Business Week*, April 11, 1988, p. 62.

8. Paul Barrett, "Attorneys General Flex Their Muscles," *The Wall Street Journal*, July 13, 1988, p. 25.

9. Paul W. Stewart and J. Frederick Dewhurst, with Louis Field, *Does Distribution Cost Too Much?* (Twentieth Century Fund, 1939).

10. William J. Stanton, *Fundamentals of Marketing* (McGraw-Hill, 1981), p. 552.

CASE APPLICATION 8–1

Sears and New York City Go to Battle

Is one of the nation's most trusted retailers deceiving its customers? And why is it trying to torpedo New York City's consumer-protection law?

The questions arise in a bizarre legal battle between Sears, Roebuck & Co. and the New York City Department of Consumer Affairs. The city wants Sears to stop certain forms of advertising it considers misleading under New York law and is suing Sears in state court. One disputed practice involves promoting a discounted price, say "30% off," without explaining whether or not the markdown is based on the regular price of the merchandise.

Instead of changing its advertising and perhaps avoiding bad publicity, Sears is fighting back. Sears is suing New York City in federal district court, contending that it should be able to advertise as it sees fit. Besides, Sears says, its ads are accurate and are protected by the First Amendment. The company also asserts that New York is trying to interfere with its right to engage in interstate commerce.

Angelo J. Aponte, New York's consumer-affairs commissioner, says his office has negotiated advertising changes with more than a hundred retailers since the laws in question took effect 20 years ago. All the others have complied when contacted, he says, and Sears is the only retailer to offer serious resistance.

Sears is being accused, among other things, of advertising clothing discounts without explaining where prices started; promoting a tire sale without saying how much its more expensive tires sell for; and saying that a carpet cleaning bargain is about to end when, actually, the promotion is going to go on and on for months.

Stanley Lipnick, an outside attorney who Sears has assigned to the case, says that the company believes that its advertising hasn't misled any customers. "It's truthful," he says. W. Stan Knipe, a regional manager for Sears in New York, adds that the battle with New York regulators should do no harm to the company's image. "Our reputation for dealing with the American public is 100 years old. Our policies haven't changed: The phrase 'Satisfaction Guaranteed or Your Money Back' is still over the door at every store."

The dispute between Sears and New York actually began in 1987 when city officials spotted in Sears advertising what they now allege are violations of local law. For example, in its carpet-cleaning ads that ran in certain New York newspapers that September, Sears promised a $34.98 "Fall Savings Spectacular." It exhorted readers: "Hurry! Call by September 26." But the very next month it made the same offer, except for the date: "Hurry! Call by October 24." The same urgent pitch, with yet another expiration date, appeared on October 25. "This is the sort of thing you might expect from some small-time schlock operator," says Mr. Aponte, the consumer commissioner. "It's deceptive to imply this is some special offer when it goes on month after month."

Since health clubs, travel agencies, and car dealerships in New York do this sort of thing all the time and continue to do so, year after year, one has reason to wonder how common the abuse is and how consistent the law enforcement. The consumer-affairs department says it has ordered more than 100 merchants to stop such practices in the past ten years. But the department concedes that problems persist. The agency is going after Sears because the huge retailer affects substantial numbers of consumers. Sears' alleged violations, which it denied, have yet to be established in court; the company has never been found in violation of New York consumer laws.

Another Sears newspaper ad under fire in the city's lawsuit touted Sears Guardsman Radial Tires for "as low as $34.99." New York City law prohibits advertising offers of this sort that don't also cite the prices of similar but more expensive items. Such prices must be published in a type size "at least as tall and broad as the lowest price stated" according to the law.

Mr. Lipnick, the Sears attorney, says the tire ads aren't deceptive. "What about the car ads that say payments are from $95 a month without explaining how much higher they go?" he wonders.

Rather than contract the work out to its advertising agency, Ogilvy & Mather, Sears does all the work on its price-oriented advertising in-house. A company official says that even though the ads look fairly simple, more than 100 workers—copywriters, artists, layout experts, and marketing specialists—are involved in the preparation. There are also "people who do nothing but check over all the things that other people do to make sure we do nothing to offend a customer, violate our ad policies or Federal Trade Commission rules," says Thomas Morris, the vice president of the company's merchandise group.

Many of the ads are prepared a year in advance, when marketing officials pick items that will go on sale around the country. An artist's pencil draws up to five versions of the ad, with different print and photo sizes. Copywriters draft the words. That process sometimes takes weeks. Ultimately, attorneys check the ads, and Mr. Morris approves them. Most of these ads are "national," in that common ad styles are sent to newspapers and magazines across the country. Sometimes, Sears will send out a newspaper ad to different areas of the country, advertising perhaps a 30% discount on coats—even though its stores might not stock exactly the same styles.

This isn't the first time Sears has been in hot water over discounts. In 1983, California sued the company, alleging that it used misleading discount pricing in some of its promotions. Sears was charged in a civil lawsuit by the California attorney general's office with misrepresenting an artificially inflated price on certain items as the regular, or everyday, price. Sears agreed as part of a settlement to refrain from making untrue representations in ads; it also paid California $55,000.

New York City's civil suit in state court is seeking $500 for each alleged violation by the company. It also is asking the court to issue a permanent injunction against Sears to prohibit consumer-law violations of the sorts alleged. Sears, meanwhile, is asking the federal court to declare the city's consumer laws unconstitutional.

One securities analyst says he believes Sears' management is showing bad judgment in fighting consumer laws. "This is bureaucratic management rigidity, not good business sense," says Edward Weller of Montgomery Securities. "You'd think Sears would say, 'You're right. Let's get on the consumer side of this thing.' Instead, they seem to want to get dragged kicking and screaming into losing market share." But Sears, insisting that its ads are accurate, says altering them might drive up its retail prices.

SOURCE: Robert Johnson and John Koten, "Sears Has Everything, Including Messy Fight Over Ads in New York," *The Wall Street Journal*, June 28, 1988, pp. 1,17.

Questions

1. Do you agree with the New York Consumer Affairs Commissioner that Sears' ads are misleading and deceptive? Why or why not?

2. Evaluate Sears' arguments in defense of the allegations against it. What position would you take if you were in charge at Sears?

3. If Sears is found guilty, what would be an appropriate remedy?

4. Is it fair that a company complying with Federal laws can be sued for violations by individual states or cities where the laws are different?

A Test of Your Consumer Rights Knowledge

The Federal Trade Commission (FTC) receives many letters from consumers asking various questions about their rights under FTC-enforced laws and rules. Here are some of the most frequently asked questions. See how much *you* know about your consumer rights.

Questions

1. Your new washing machine spills water on the floor. The dealer's mechanics have repaired it several times under the warranty, but it still is not working right. Your warranty runs out, and two weeks later it spills water again. Do you have to pay for the repairs now?

2. You are shopping for a new TV. Can you compare warranties before deciding which model to buy?

3. The used car you bought less than one month ago developed transmission trouble. You consult your sales contract and discover you purchased the car "as is." What is "as is"?

4. You decided to buy a new house. The only thing stopping you from signing the contract is the leaky roof, which the builder promises to repair *after* you move in. How can you make sure the repairs are done as promised?

5. Your credit card is stolen. Before you can report it to the card company, the thief charges $1,000 worth of goods on your card. What is the most you will have to pay?

6. You lost your electronic fund transfer (EFT) card that lets you withdraw money using an automatic teller machine. You report the card lost a week after discovering it was missing. How much money can you lose?

7. A debt collection agency keeps calling you at home about a bill you owe. You want to pay the bill but you lost your job two months ago. Can you stop the collector from calling?

8. There is a mistake on your monthly credit card bill. To correct the error should you write or call the company?

9. You just had your eyes examined. What should you do if you want to shop around and buy your glasses somewhere else?

10. This morning a salesperson knocked on your door and sold you $200 worth of encyclopedias. Now you decide you do not want the books. Can you cancel the sales contract?

11. Last night you visited a health spa and signed a membership contract. Do you have three days to cancel the contract?

12. To help finance your new car, you need to take out a loan. What is the most important question to ask about financing?

13. You sent a mail-order company $20 for a new pair of shoes. Delivery was promised in two weeks. Six weeks later you have not heard from the company, and your shoes have not arrived. Are you entitled to get your money back?

14. You were recently divorced. Now you realize all your credit cards are in your ex-husband's name. How can you establish your own credit rating by using your past credit history?

15. You were told your loan application was denied because your sources of income—social security and retirement benefits—were not acceptable to the lender. Is this legal?

Answers

1. No. If you complained about the problem during the warranty period and it was not fixed properly, you are entitled to get it repaired. Your warranty rights do not run out for problems you complained about during the warranty period.

2. Yes. The Magnuson-Moss Act requires sellers to make copies of warranties available for products that cost more than $15. Although the law does not require manufacturers or sellers to provide warranties, if the product has a warranty, you must be allowed to read it before you buy. Different companies offer different warranties, so take advantage of this opportunity to compare before you buy.

3. "As is" means that the seller makes no promises to fix the item later. If you want warranty protection, make sure the seller puts repair promises in writing.

4. Make sure your warranty covers the leaky roof problem. If you do not have a warranty, have the roof repair written into the contract you will sign when you close on the house.

5. $50. If a credit card is lost or stolen and the card is used before you report it missing, the maximum you owe is $50. After you report the card missing, you are not liable for any purchases made by the unauthorized user.

6. $500. If your EFT card is lost or stolen, and you do not notify your bank within two business days after discovering it is missing, you may lose as much as $500. If you notify the bank within two business days, your liability is limited to $50.

7. Yes. If you write the debt collector a letter saying "stop bothering me," the collector must stop calling. However, this does not erase your debt; you still owe the money.

8. Write a letter and use the special billing error address provided by the company. While a phone call may resolve the problem quickly, sending a letter is the only way to trigger your rights under the Fair Credit Billing Act, a federal law which requires the card issuer to correct billing errors or justify the charges.

9. Ask the eye doctor for a copy of your prescription. An FTC rule requires eye doctors (ophthalmologists and optometrists) to give patients their eyeglasses prescription after an examination at no extra charge.

10. Yes. You have three days to cancel most door-to-door transactions of $25 or more. The seller is required to give you a cancellation form at the time of sale. Sign and mail it to the address given for cancellation any time before midnight of the third business day after the day of sale.

11. No. You usually do not get three days to cancel sales made at a merchant's regular place of business. However, a few state and local laws provide extra protection on some contracts like health spas. Check with your local consumer protection agency if you have questions.

12. Ask for the Annual Percentage Rate. The rates charged for loans may vary significantly. The Annual Percentage Rate is a unit price for credit which takes into account all the finance costs of the loan. Use the Annual Percentage Rate to compare loans and shop around for the best deal.

13. Yes. The FTC's Mail Order Rule allows you to cancel most orders and get a complete refund if you did not get delivery in the time period promised.

14. Apply for credit in your own name and list the accounts you shared with your former husband. If the creditor has trouble verifying these references because they were listed only in your husband's name, offer to provide additional information that would confirm your participation in payments of those bills. This might include cancelled checks where your name would show that you either paid the bills or that you shared the account with your former husband.

15. Under the Equal Credit Opportunity Act, creditors cannot discriminate because you receive public assistance income, such as social security. Creditors also must consider income from retirement benefits, as long as it is a consistent source of income.

SOURCE: "Consumer Quiz," Federal Trade Commission, March, 1984.

PART THREE

Product

9

Product: Basic Concepts

Learning Objectives

Upon completing this chapter, you will be able to do the following:

UNDERSTAND
the definition of a product.

RECOGNIZE
how to classify products.

EXPLAIN
the concepts of product line and product mix.

DISCUSS
the importance of the product life cycle and how it can be used by marketers.

DESCRIBE
the alternative types of branding strategies.

IDENTIFY
the functions of packaging.

MARKETING PROFILE

Rayovac Recharges Its Product Line

Rayovac Corp., the 81-year-old Madison, WI, battery and flashlight maker, resembled nothing so much as a flat D cell back in 1982. With declining sales of about $175 million, Rayovac was losing $20 million a year on an odd-lot mix of aging products sold in 1950s-vintage packaging. Longtime major accounts had dropped the line. Its battery market share, a lofty 35 percent in the 1950s, had drained to 6 percent or so, largely because Rayovac foolishly failed to charge into the market for alkaline batteries, which quickly became the industry standard. Things were so bad that the drugstore in the company's headquarters refused to stock Rayovac products.

Lights out? It should have been. But Rayovac proved to be rechargeable with a rich mix of new products, new packaging, and peppy marketing touches that smack of toothpaste, hair coloring, and cosmetics. No surprise: The new chairman and his vice-chairman wife, Thomas and Judith Pyle, came to Rayovac after selling toiletries, sewing patterns, makeup, wigs, and toilet paper for the likes of Procter & Gamble, Revlon, Clairol, and Esteé Lauder.

It must have been good training. Rayovac now generates "eight-digit" operating profits. It holds about 12 percent of the $2.5 billion U.S. retail battery market. Rayovac "Smart Pack" packages, holding six or eight batteries instead of the usual two, have helped boost sales 25 percent at stores that stock them. And new products like the Luma 2 flashlight—a sleek model combining a superbright krypton light with a lithium-powered, extremely long-lasting backup bulb—are again winning Rayovac shelf space at national and regional discounters such as Kmart and Caldor.

Rayovac's marketing resonates with two uncomplicated yet powerful themes. First, with limited distribution and advertising, Rayovac practices what Judy Pyle, 44, calls "nichemanship." Every product, especially the new ones, must incorporate features, designs, and prices focused tightly on a specific group of customers, not the entire market. Second, Rayovac's new products must be truly innovative, not "me-too" entries. In this largely commodity business, goes the thinking, only unusual new offerings will build a distinctive image for the company.

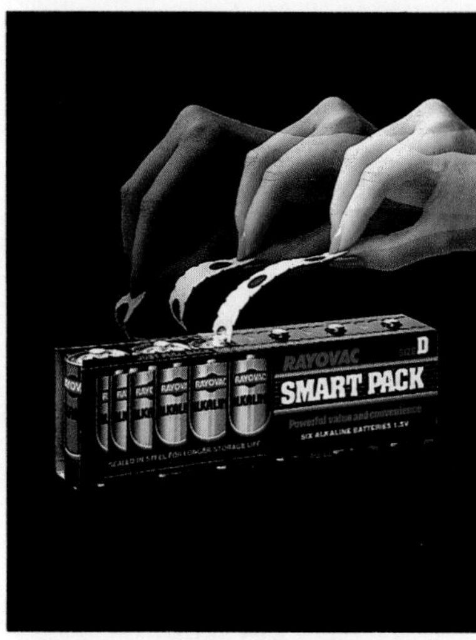

Another brainstorm: batteries sold in packages of six and eight instead of one or two on hanging cards. Although battery makers universally believe consumers buy cells on impulse, Rayovac's packaging caters to heavy users. Why? Studies showed that the average family uses 26 batteries a year, but many families use 100 or more. "And because of efficiencies in packaging and in our plant, we charge 15 percent less for batteries sold this way," says Tom Pyle, 46.

Rayovac's revival didn't come easy. The company was on the verge of liquidation when Pyle and two partners bought it in 1982. No new product had been introduced for nearly ten years.

One of the first changes was packaging. The company dropped its old color scheme of gaudy reds and blues and went into a modern look heavy on blacks, golds, and muted reds. The company's old packages had mummified flashlights behind plastic and cardboard. But Judy Pyle's cosmetics background taught her that customers like to get their hands on a product, so flashlights went into new cardboard packages that allow you to grip and heft them.

The first new product, introduced at the end of 1984, was the Workhorse flashlight with a space-age look of black-ribbed plastic and a high-intensity krypton bulb. Priced at $5 to $7, high for the time, it opened the premium "designer" market and gave Rayovac a stronger image plus a product with gross margins 50 percent higher than the rest of its line.

Judy Pyle figures that niche marketing will keep Rayovac's spark in the battery market and should boost its 21 percent share of the $415 million flashlight market. "We've made a statement in the market," she says.

Indeed they have. This little outfit is a dead cell no longer. Now it is a live wire.

This profile introduces a number of concepts, including the development of a product line, packaging, brand names, and product improvements and changes over time. These and other aspects of product strategy are discussed in this chapter.

SOURCE: Steve Weiner, "Electrifying," *Forbes*, November 30, 1987, pp. 196–98.

The Rayovac *Marketing Profile* illustrates many of the concepts that will be discussed in this chapter. You undoubtedly recognize the Rayovac brand name and may be familiar with the Workhorse brand of flashlights. Rayovac has a product line that includes some new products, some mature ones that have been marketed for many years, and some that are somewhere in between these two extremes. The company has recently developed some new forms for existing products, some new packaging innovations, and some new product categories. Some of the new products take on the brand names of existing products, and some have newly created brand names. The rest of this chapter will discuss all of these concepts and others associated with the product aspects of a firm's marketing program. Specifically, we will examine how to classify consumer products, the concepts of product line and product mix, the importance of managing a product over its life cycle, and strategies for branding and packaging.

What Is a Product?

A woman buys a gallon of Sealtest homogenized skim milk at a 7-Eleven convenience store, paying $2.39. A man buys a gallon of Sealtest homogenized skim milk at a Kroger supermarket, paying $2.29. Have these two consumers purchased the same product? The answer to this question depends upon one's definition of product. The narrowest definition of product would only consider the physical attributes of the purchase. On that dimension, both these consumers have purchased the same product. The problem with this narrow view of product is that it does not take into account the concept of exchange, which is the essence of marketing.

In the transaction described here, each of the two consumers has exchanged something, specifically $2.39 and $2.29, and, in return, received something. The man paid ten cents less than the woman did, but he also received less in return. Although they both received the same physical product, the woman received a number of other benefits, including being able to park at the front door, avoiding standing in line for several minutes, and completing the total transaction in two minutes or less. Also, she may have been able to complete the exchange late at night or very close to her home.

It should be clear that these two consumers did not purchase the same package of benefits, and, thus, we say that they did not purchase the same product. In this text we define product as every want-satisfying attribute a consumer receives in making an exchange, including psychological as well as physical benefits. This definition recognizes the importance of defining product from the point of view of the consumer and of expanding the definition of product to include much more than just its physical or tangible attributes.

Let's take another example. What is a person buying when he or she purchases a videocassette recorder? First, he or she is buying a metal box with electronic components in it (physical attributes). Much more important, however, the consumer is buying a means to greater entertainment. This is an example of a want-satisfying attribute. Other want-satisfying attributes that a consumer of a videocassette recorder might be seeking could include:

- special features, such as ability to program fourteen days in advance, stop action, and special effects;
- brand name for manufacturer and for retail outlet;
- guarantee and/or warranty;

Figure 9–1 Components of a Product

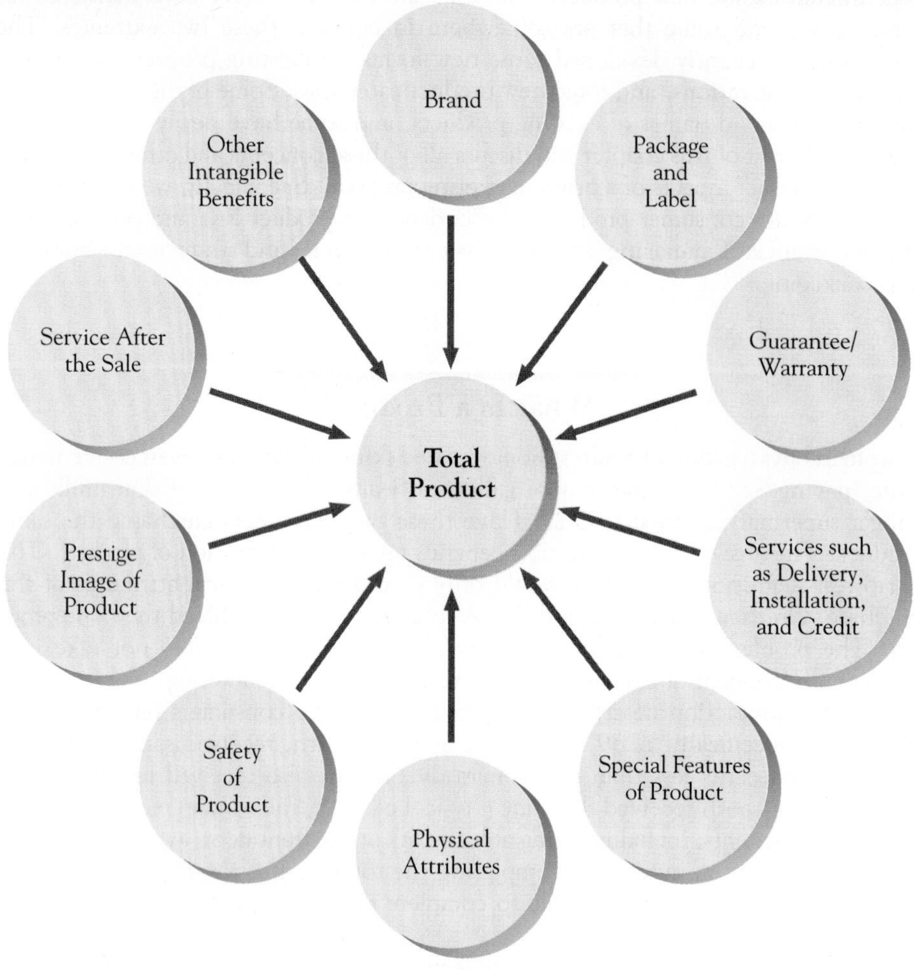

- services, such as help in making decisions concerning which model to buy, installation instructions, and credit;
- prestige and image of manufacturer, brand, and retailer; or
- availability of service after the sale.

Depending on the importance individual consumers place on each of these aspects, they will perceive different alternatives in the marketplace differently. This difference in perception (and, thus, difference in definition) includes the retail outlet. For example, consumers may perceive an RCA Model 650 videocassette recorder sold by a discount store as different from the same RCA Model 650 sold by a prestigious "full service" electronics retailer with highly knowledgeable sales and service personnel. In this case, the two retailers would be selling different products even though the physical attributes of the two products were the same. Figure 9–1 illustrates the many components that together define a product.

Our definition of product emphasizes the importance of concentrating on what consumers buy rather than on what marketers think they are selling. The two are not always the same; marketers sometimes overemphasize the technical aspects of the goods or services and underestimate the importance of the psychological, intangible benefits that people are seeking in purchasing the product.

Another important aspect of our definition is that products can be goods, services, or a combination of the two. There are often no physical attributes associated with services such as legal assistance, medical care, hair styling, or auto repair. The next section of this chapter presents ways of classifying products, and Chapter 21 discusses the differences between marketing of services and of goods.

Classification of Products

The most important aspects of classifying products are consumer attitudes and buying behavior, which form the bases for the various classification schemes used by marketers. In classifying products, it is important to use the same criteria that we use to classify markets. Products within a classification should be homogeneous, and the classification should be meaningful for product marketing.

The first way most products are classified is based on the ultimate user. Consumer products are products purchased for use by households or ultimate consumers. Industrial products are products sold for use in producing other goods or in rendering services.[1] Thus, Heinz Ketchup purchased by restaurants is classified differently from Heinz Ketchup purchased by the ultimate consumer. Even though the physical product may be the same in both cases, remember our definition of a product. Given the differences in what the buyers are purchasing, different marketing programs must be developed. The pricing, distribution, promotion, and packaging of the catsup will vary; these differences will be clear in the remaining chapters.

Classifying products as consumer products or industrial products is valuable, but the range of products within each of these categories is still too broad to be of much help to marketers. Therefore, each category has been refined further. (The classification of industrial goods was discussed in Chapter 6.)

Classification of Consumer Products

There are a number of problems in establishing a classification scheme for consumer products. The classification system should be based on consumer attitudes and buying behavior, but as we have already seen in Chapter 5, not all consumers think and act alike. For example, some consumers needing a battery will immediately go to Sears and buy a DieHard. Other consumers will engage in considerable shopping, visiting a number of stores, and will buy the one which they think offers the highest value for their needs. Still other consumers will not do any shopping for a battery, but will instead wait until their battery is completely dead, and then will buy a new one from the nearest service station. Thus, you must recognize that all products cannot be classified the same way for all consumers, and this explains why different products are marketed using different marketing programs to reach different segments of the market.

The traditional way to classify consumer goods is to define them as convenience goods, shopping goods, or specialty goods.[2] **Convenience goods** are those products bought with a minimum of time and effort. The battery purchased from the nearest service station by the consumer whose old one went dead is an example of a convenience good. Other examples are milk and food products, newspapers, Coca-Cola, candy, and gum. The small amount of money typically involved in the purchase does not justify extensive shopping. Also, the consumer has a high level of knowledge about the product prior to the purchase, so a substantial amount of shopping is not necessary. The consumer does not have strong loyalty to a single brand and is relatively indifferent to which one of several major brands he or she buys.

The key to the marketing of a convenience good is to have it readily available in a location convenient to the consumer. The product must be available when the consumer wants it and in a convenient location, or else the sale is lost. This implies intensive distribution. For example, Coca-Cola is available in supermarkets, convenience stores, restaurants, service stations, stadiums, and in vending machines everywhere. The burden of the promotion for a convenience product is on the manufacturer. The retailer typically carries several brands and is indifferent to which one the consumer buys.

Shopping goods are usually purchased only after the consumer has compared the price, quality, and style of a number of alternatives, often visiting several stores before making a purchase decision. Extensive information-seeking is necessary, because the consumer has incomplete knowledge at the early stages of the purchase decision process. Thus, the decision process follows the limited or extensive problem-solving behavior described in Chapter 5. Shopping goods are less frequently purchased and are generally priced higher than convenience goods. Brand loyalty is minimal, and the goods often have high social visibility. Examples of shopping goods are clothing, furniture and major appliances, automobiles, lawnmowers, and home repairs. A battery would be a shopping good for those consumers who "shop around" by visiting several retail outlets to find the lowest price for a certain quality-level battery.

The marketing strategy most appropriate for shopping goods is different from that used for convenience goods. Distribution does not have to be as intensive, because consumers will visit a number of retail outlets. Thus, the goods only need to be in enough outlets so that the consumer will encounter the product in at least one of the several stores visited. Promotion is often an important part of the marketing mix for shopping goods because of the need to inform consumers of the product and its price, but the retailer will often play the major role in this promotion. Price will also be an important marketing mix component, particularly for those products which are perceived as being similar to competitive alternatives. In this case, the consumer will usually identify several alternatives which are perceived as comparable in quality (such as painting contractors) and will then select the one with the lowest price.

Specialty goods are products for which no reasonable substitutes exist because of the unique characteristics and/or brand identification of the product. Consumers are thus willing to expend considerable effort to buy these goods. For the consumer who insisted upon a DieHard brand of battery, the product is a specialty good. Other examples of specialty goods are expensive stereo and photographic equipment, high fashion clothing items, restaurants, and certain brands of automobiles. In buying specialty goods, consumers are extremely brand-loyal and engage in routine response decision making. Consumers also are willing to pay a premium price.

Because consumers insist upon buying a particular brand, they will seek out the product from the retailer. Distribution is thus less important than it is for convenience and shopping goods, and relatively few outlets are needed. Advertising is used to let the consumer know where the product is, and the cost of this promotion is often shared by the retailer and manufacturer.

Product Line and Product Mix

The Rayovac *Marketing Profile* at the beginning of this chapter described changes the company is making in the marketing of some of its products. It is unusual today for a medium- or large-sized company to market a single product. In looking at the product offerings of an organization, we use the terms *product line* and *product mix*. A **product line** is a group of *closely related* products offered by an organization. Thus, Rayovac has two basic product lines: flashlights and batteries. An organization's **product mix** consists of *all the individual* products available through the organization. In Rayovac's case, there are many different products in their mix, counting all the different types of batteries and flashlights and all the alternative package sizes.

A firm's **breadth of product mix** is determined by the number of product lines it markets. Some firms such as Rayovac, Apple Computers, or Kellogg's have a very narrow product mix, offering a very limited number of product lines. Other companies, such as General Electric, have very broad product lines. General Electric sells light bulbs, major appliances, heavy equipment such as power plant generators, small electrical motors, medical equipment, aircraft engines, repair services, and electrical parts. An organization's **depth of product mix** is determined by the number of sizes, models, and colors available within each product line. Thus, Kellogg's product mix is deep, because it markets a number of different brands of cereal, each in several different size packages. Coors Beer has both a very narrow and a very shallow product mix, with only a limited number of lines, brands, sizes, and package types available for sale.

The specific product lines to be offered by an organization are determined by the overall strategic plan and objectives of the organization, including the segment and needs of the target market that the organization is trying to satisfy. Thus, Sony added a whole new product line when it decided to target young children. New product lines can be developed internally or can be acquired. The same two options are available for expanding an organization's product offering within each product line. The management of the product line is discussed in more detail in Chapter 10. The key idea is that the firm's product mix should be a function of its objectives, the target market, and the buyer behavior of that target market.

Product Life-Cycle

In 1971, 50,000 smoke detectors were sold in the United States; the market grew to a 10 million units per year business by 1978. The rapid growth attracted many competitors who flooded the market. The price of a smoke detector dropped from $50 in 1971 to under $15 in 1984. The market then started to decline and level off. It was only 8 million units in 1983, and only four of the twenty-five companies previously in the industry are still producing smoke detectors. By 1988, sales were still about 8 million units. What has happened in the smoke detector market is an example of product life-cycle. The **product life-cycle** is the series of stages that a product class goes through from its introduction until it is taken off the market. It is usually divided into four stages: introduction, growth, maturity, and decline.

Although some product classes have somewhat different patterns, the typical product life-cycle pattern is illustrated in Figure 9–2. Different marketing strategies are required for products at different stages of the life-cycle, so it is important for marketing managers to understand each of the stages.

Figure 9–2 Basic Product Life-Cycle Model

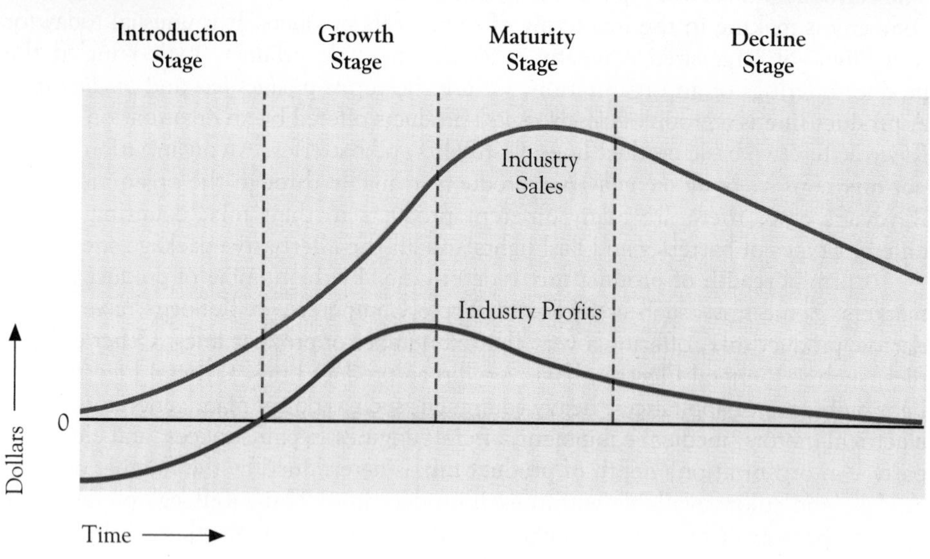

Introductory Stage

At this stage of the life-cycle, the product is launched into the marketplace, typically after a long period of development. Sales are zero at first and are still low even at the end of the introductory stage. Consumers are not aware of the product, its benefits, or potential uses. Thus, there should be an investment in advertising and promotion to educate potential customers and persuade innovators to try the new product. There are typically no important competitors, so this promotional effort is undertaken by only one firm. These high promotion costs and the cost of establishing initial distribution for the product usually mean that the profits will be negative during the introductory stage.

Growth Stage

During the growth stage as more and more consumers learn about and adopt the new product, sales volume increases rapidly. Profits also increase rapidly, but the growth in profits slows down before the end of this stage. This slowdown in profits occurs because competitors enter the market, which often results in a lowering of prices and creates the need to spend additional promotional dollars to tell consumers why the firm's product is better than the competition's. For example, the number of companies producing personal computers increased from a handful in 1977 to over 150 by the end of 1984. Prices also dropped considerably during this time period, fueling dramatic growth in the number of personal computers sold.[3]

Maturity Stage

In the early part of the maturity stage, sales continue to increase, but at a decreasing rate. By the end of the stage, sales have begun to decline. Major home appliances are an example of a product in the maturity stage of the life-cycle. As is happening

My First Sony.™
Because children are all ears and all thumbs.
There's a lot of sound thinking behind the My First Sony line of electronics for kids. It's all based on the idea that kids enjoy high-quality sound as much as adults. But since kids will be kids, they need electronics that can stand up to children hard at play.
That's why we've been hard at work, creating 5 new additions to the My First Sony family of products.
SONY
Announcing the world's first Compact Disc player for compact people. A wrist Walkie-Talkie that lets children walkie and talkie with their hands free. A Stereo Radio Cassette-Corder with sing-along microphone, so every kid can carry a tune. A Walkman™ personal stereo with an AM/FM radio for people who run more than walk. Plus a Cassette Tape Recorder with drum pads that won't miss a beat or a roar since they also make animal sounds.
If all this sounds too good to be true, wait till you hear what else they come with. The same Sony sound, child-sized controls and protective rubber accents that have My First Sony earmarked for success.
All told, our family keeps growing. Which means there will always be more My First Sony electronics designed to last at least a childhood.
my first Sony

Sony has added a new line of children's electronic products to its product mix.

in that industry, profits of both retailers and manufacturers begin to decline in the maturity stage, and many manufacturers cease their marketing efforts. Competition gets very tough, and some competitors cut prices to attract or hold on to business. At this stage, brands have quite similar physical attributes, and it is difficult for marketers to differentiate their products. Sales promotions of all types are used to encourage brand-switching by consumers and to encourage retailers to promote and give shelf space to the company's brands.

Decline Stage

Eventually, sales begin to decline, sometimes even rapidly. The causes of the decline may be market saturation (most households already have smoke detectors), new technology (color television sets replaced black and white models), or changes in social values (women now refuse to wear miniskirts). The decline in volume often results in higher costs. Therefore, it is important for marketers, at this stage, to eliminate those products that are no longer profitable or to find ways of cutting operational and marketing costs by eliminating marginal dealers and distributors, cutting advertising and sales promotion, and minimizing sales costs. These cuts could

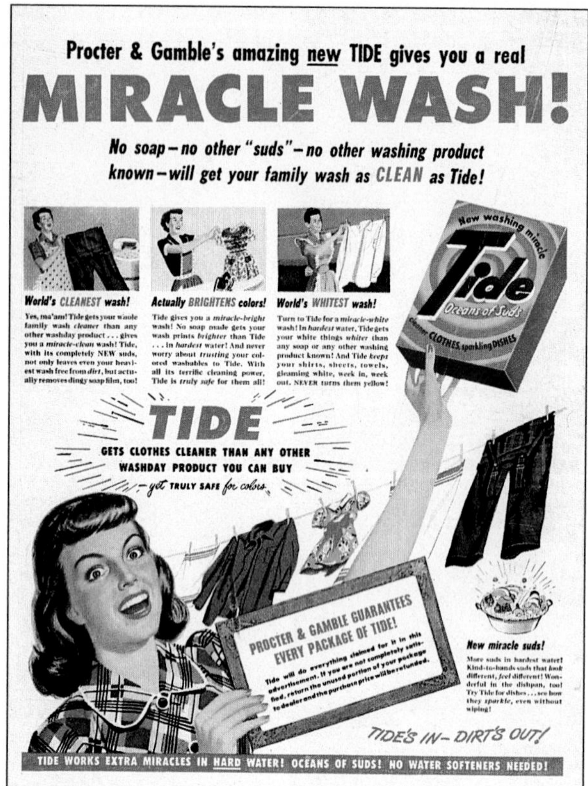

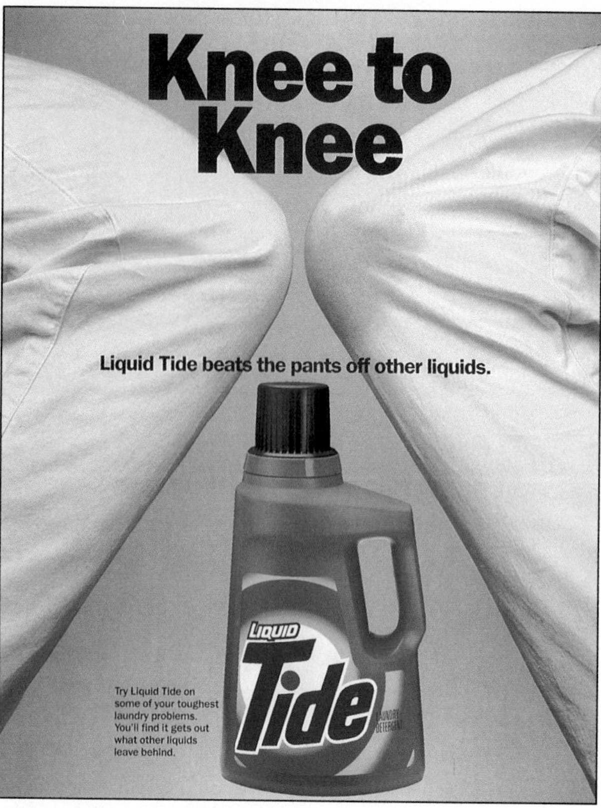

Tide detergent continues improving its product and increasing its sales, an example of a brand that has been well managed over the product life-cycle.

result in renewed profitability. In effect, the product is "milked"; that is, it is allowed to coast with decreased marketing support as long as it remains profitable. Those products which have developed brand loyalty among their customers will decline less rapidly than those products which have not been differentiated from their competitors.

Managing a Brand Over the Product Life-Cycle

Most marketers agree that it is possible to have some control over sales of their brand as the product category progresses through the stages of the product life-cycle. Consider the following examples:[4]

- Tide detergent was introduced more than forty years ago, and sales continue to increase year after year. The product has been improved some fifty-five times since its introduction, enabling the brand to forestall any decline in its market position.
- Alpo canned dog food has been the market leader for many years. In spite of an explosion of competitors and sales in the dry segment of the dog food market, Alpo has maintained its volume through effective advertising that emphasizes the important dog food benefits of meat, protein, and quality. The brand's marketing program has resulted in significant brand loyalty, which has preserved Alpo's volume and position.

- Arm & Hammer baking soda restored luster to its stagnant position by promoting the same product as an odor remover for the refrigerator, for litter boxes, and elsewhere. The innovative tactic greatly increased the product's sales.
- Johnson & Johnson Baby Shampoo was, for many years, used primarily by young children. The company's marketing people observed the trend toward increased frequencies of shampooing and promoted the Baby Shampoo for adult usage, stressing mildness and good grooming. Consumers responded, and volume increased substantially.

Some marketers argue that the product life-cycle concept should only be applied to product classes (for example, "tires") or product form (radial tires, bias belted tires) and not to individual brands.[5] Brands that are market leaders may enjoy profits throughout every stage of the product life-cycle, while weaker brands may never earn a profit. In the smoke detector product category, some brands never had any real product life-cycle, since their expected sales never materialized and they were withdrawn from the marketplace. Sales of other brands have continually increased even with the total market beginning to decline.

How can marketers control their brands through the product life-cycle? To answer this, we first must look at what determines its length and shape. Four factors are important:

1. *Consumer needs , wants, attitudes, and behavior.* How quickly will a new product or product modification be accepted by consumers? Consumers apparently want to be able to record television programs rather than just being able to buy programming; hence, the videocassette recorder had high sales and moved quickly into the growth stage while the videodisk player (which could not record programs off the television) never took off and eventually was taken off the market.

2. *Rate of technological change.* The faster the rate of technological change, the shorter the product life-cycle will be. There have been numerous technological breakthroughs in the personal computer market, resulting in a very short product life-cycle for most forms of the product.

3. *Competitive activity.* If patents, tariffs, or access to raw material supply slow down the introduction of competitive products, the product life-cycle will be much longer than it would be if there were ease of entry. The more vigorous the activity by competitors, the shorter the product life-cycle will probably be (at least for individual forms of the product).

4. *The organization's own marketing action.* As shown in the examples, an organization can take many actions to extend the product life-cycle. Table 9–1 shows how product life-cycle advocates view the implications of the cycle for marketing action.

Review Your Marketing Knowledge

- Cable television has moved from the growth stage to the mature stage of the product life-cycle. How will the marketing of this product have to change over the next few years?

- Suppose you are the new marketing manager for a cellular telephone (car phone) company. How can you use the concept of the product life-cycle to help you determine your marketing strategy to increase sales to the home (nonbusiness) market?

Table 9–1 Implications of the Product Life-Cycle (PLC) for Marketing Action

Effects and Responses	Stages of the PLC: Introduction	Growth	Maturity	Decline
Competition	None of importance	Some emulators	Many rivals competing for a small piece of the pie	Few in number with a rapid shakeout of weak members
Overall Strategy	Market establishment—persuade early adopters to try the product	Market penetration—persuade mass market to prefer the brand	Defense of brand position—check the inroads of competition	Preparations for removal—milk the brand dry of all possible benefits
Profits	Negligible because of high production and marketing costs	Peak levels as a result of high prices and growing demand	Increasing competition cuts into profit margins and ultimately into total profits	Declining volume pushes costs up to levels that eliminate profits entirely
Retail Prices	High, to recover some of the excessive costs of launching	High, to take advantage of heavy consumer demand	What the traffic will bear; need to avoid price wars	Low enough to permit quick liquidation of inventory
Distribution	Selective, as distribution is slowly built up	Intensive; employ small trade discounts since dealers are eager to store	Intensive; heavy trade allowances to retain shelf space	Selective; unprofitable outlets slowly phased out
Advertising Strategy	Aim at the needs of early adopters	Make the mass market aware of brand benefits	Use advertising as a vehicle for differentiation among otherwise similar brands	Emphasize low price to reduce stock
Advertising Emphasis	High, to generate awareness and interest among early adopters and persuade dealers to stock	Moderate, to let sales rise on the sheer momentum of word-of-mouth recommendations	Moderate, since most buyers are aware of brand characteristics	Minimum expenditures required to phase out the product
Consumer Sales and Promotion Expenditures	Heavy, to entice target groups with samples, coupons, and other inducements	Moderate, to create brand preference (advertising is better suited to do this job)	Heavy, to encourage brand switching, hoping to convert some buyers into loyal users	Minimal, to let the brand coast by itself

SOURCE: N. Dhalla and S. Yuspeh, "Forget the Product Life-Cycle Concept," *Harvard Business Review*, January-February, 1976, p. 104.

Branding

What products have you purchased recently? In thinking of your answer to this question, you undoubtedly remembered a number of brands. A **brand** is a name, term, symbol, design, or combination of these that identifies the seller's goods and services and distinguishes them from competitors' products.[6] A **brand name** is that part of a brand that can be vocalized, including letters, words, and numbers. A **brand mark**—a symbol, design, or a group of distinctive letters—is the part of the brand that is seen but not spoken. McDonald's, Coke, and NBC are all brand names. McDonald's golden arches, the distinctive lettering in Coca-Cola, and the multicolored NBC peacock are all examples of brand marks. If a brand or part of a brand is registered with the U.S. Patent and Trademark Office, giving it legal protection for the exclusive use of a seller, it becomes a trademark. There are currently about 1.5 million trademarks registered at the Patent Office. Trademarks are registered for twenty years and can be renewed for twenty years at a time if they have not been abandoned or surrendered through lack of use by the seller. A trademark may be a brand name or a brand mark or both. Brands and trademarks are comparable—*brand* is the commmonly used term, and *trademark* is a legal term meaning those brands that have been legally registered.

The Importance of Branding

Brands are everywhere. The government has estimated that the average American is exposed to approximately 1500 different brands every day.[7] Why is branding so prevalent? With increased technological capabilities enabling competitors to market extremely similar goods and services, a brand is often a product's most important distinguishing characteristic and may be the only part of the product a competitor cannot copy. Without the capability of using brand names, many organizations could not practice modern marketing.[8]

There are many advantages of branding for marketers. Retailers, wholesalers, manufacturers, and other marketers can develop loyal customers who identify what to buy through branding. Advertising a brand encourages consumers to buy and continue buying products. Branding allows marketers to more efficiently introduce new products. For example, Campbell's introduction of Chunky Soup required less advertising and achieved faster consumer acceptance than it would have if it had not used the Campbell's name. Bank Americard changed its brand name to VISA so it would be more effective in marketing the credit card throughout the world.

Branding is also important for retailers. Consumers often select a store on the basis of the brands it offers. Thus, consumers who desire Craftsman tools or Ann Page bakery goods must shop at Sears or A&P, because these brands are not available through any other retailer. The brands that a store stocks are an important part of its image for consumers. If retailers have exclusive rights to highly desired brands, they are less vulnerable to competition.

Branding offers consumers a way to distinguish between similar goods and services supplied by different producers. Consumers use brands to identify products they wish to purchase repeatedly, as well as those they wish to avoid. Brands simplify shopping, making the process much more efficient. Branding usually implies consistent quality, typically serving as a better indicator of quality than the price of a product. It also enables consumers to reduce the perceived risk in the purchase decision process. The power of some well-known brands is shown in the *Marketing in Action* on "America's Most Powerful Brands."

Selecting a Brand Name

Several years ago, Cadillac had to choose a brand name for its new scaled-down model. The firm considered several names, including Seville, St. Moritz, La Salle, and du Monde. The company's top executives were leaning toward the use of the La Salle name, a brand that Cadillac had marketed from 1927 through 1941 but had dropped because of poor sales during World War II. A study the company did, however, determined that 30 percent of Cadillac owners felt that La Salle gave the image of a cheaper and less genuine Cadillac; and many people were not sure how St. Moritz could be pronounced; virtually no one perceived that du Monde meant *one who was*

MARKETING IN ACTION

America's Most Powerful Brands

Quick, what is the most powerful brand name in America? If you said, "Coke is it," you're right, according to Landor Associates, a San Francisco design and image-consulting firm. Landor queried more than 1,000 U.S. consumers about their recognition and opinion of 672 brand names and tallied the results to produce its new "brand power" ranking.

Coca-Cola is so powerful it's practically off the charts. It is both the best known and most esteemed brand in America, and its overall score beat No. 2 Campbell's Soup by a greater margin than Campbell's beat No. 50, Dole. Other overall scores shed new light on old rivalries. Colgate (No. 35) nipped P&G's Crest (39); Mobil (82) outgassed Texaco (126) and Shell (150); Hershey's (12) beat Mars Inc.'s M&M's (42); NBC (13) outscored CBS (32) and ABC (47).

What accounts for brand power? Most of the top finishers have been around for decades. Some names—such as Levis, Kleenex, and Xerox, all in the top 30—are practically synonymous with their markets. Others are simply the product of superb salesmanship. For example, Philip Morris's Marlboro cigarette is 92 places ahead of RJR Nabisco's Winston.

Heavy advertising won't do the job by itself. Wendy's, Greyhound, and Volkswagen are among the 100 biggest advertisers on the list, but none makes the top 100 in brand power. Other brands are perhaps more infamous than famous. Playboy was 58th in recognition—but 670th in esteem.

Most Powerful Brands

Coca-Cola
Campbell's
Pepsi-Cola
AT&T
McDonald's
American Express
Kellogg's
IBM
Levi's
Sears

Least Powerful Brands

Export "A"
(Canadian cigarettes)
Klipsch
(loudspeakers)
Primerica
(diversified financial services)
Bang & Olufsen
(Danish consumer electronics)
Asahi
(Japanese beer)
Blue Mountain
(pet food)
Daewoo
(Korean industrial prod., electronics)
Gaggenau
(German cooking equipment)
Ricola
(Swiss cough drops)
Exide
(batteries)

SOURCE: Edward C. Baig, "Name That Brand," *Fortune*, July 4, 1988, pp. 10–12.

---

wise in the ways of the world. Seville, on the other hand, received no negative reaction and was remembered by many Cadillac owners as being a part of the Eldorado product line. This indicated to the executives that there might be savings in promotion costs for the new brand, and Seville was quickly adopted. The car soon became a profitable addition to the Cadillac line of cars.

This example gives you some insights into how companies select brand names. One study of the largest 200 consumer product manufacturers has identified a six-step process that companies go through in choosing brand names.[9] These steps are shown in Figure 9–3. The first step is to identify the objectives of the brand name and the criteria that will be used for the final selection. The study identified thirteen different criteria used by the companies. These are presented in Table 9–2 and discussed in the next section of this chapter (on the characteristics of a good brand name).

Figure 9–3 Steps in Selecting a Brand Name

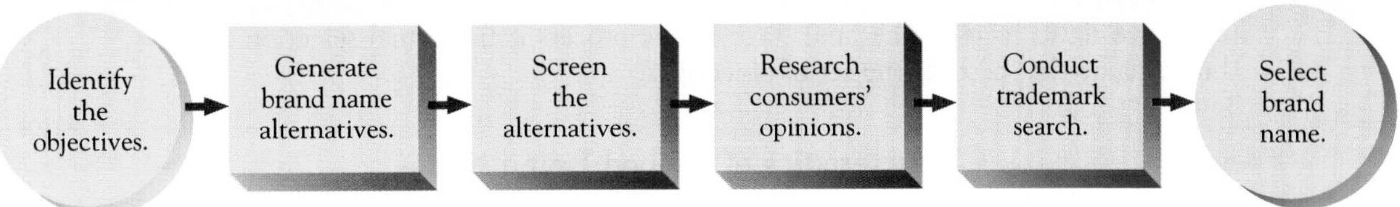

SOURCE: J. McNeal and L. Zeren, "Brand Name Selection for Consumer Products," *MSU Business Topics*, Spring 1981, pp. 35–39.

After the objectives have been agreed upon, the second step in the process is to generate alternative brand names. The most common way to do this is to have brainstorming sessions where a number of people generate as many brand-name possibilities as they can. In some cases, groups of consumers are shown the product and asked for their ideas. In a few cases, companies use a computer to generate alternative configurations of letters that could be used as brand names.

The third step is to screen all the alternatives to determine their appropriateness to the company's image and to identify the image they are trying to have the product project. In the Cadillac example, the screening stage yielded eight possibilities which served as inputs to the next stage, researching consumers' opinions. The research is done with consumers who are part of the target market for the product; the goal of research is to identify consumer opinions, understanding, perceptions, and preferences for each of the alternative brands.

Table 9–2 Criteria in Brand Name Selection

Criteria	Percentage of Firms Mentioning
Descriptive of product benefits	58.5
Memorable	46.3
Fits with company image and other products' image	46.3
Trademark availability	34.1
Promotable and advertisable	22.0
Uniqueness vs. competition	22.0
Length	15.9
Ease of pronunciation	14.6
Positive connotations to potential users	13.4
Suited to package	6.1
Modern or contemporary	3.7
Understandable	2.4
Persuasive	2.4

SOURCE: J. McNeal and L. Zeren, "Brand Name Selection for Consumer Products," *MSU Business Topics*, Spring 1981, p. 37.

Those brand-name alternatives surviving the consumer test are then subjected to a trademark search to determine their availability for the company's use. It is not unusual for this stage to have preceded the consumer research phase of the process, and often, the alternatives will include brand names that the company clearly has exclusive rights to use. The final stage in the process is the actual selection of the brand name that best fits the set of objectives.

Characteristics of a Good Brand Name

Think of the brand names Beautyrest, Weight Watchers, and DieHard.[10] What comes to mind? Probably you thought of mattresses, losing weight, and batteries, demonstrating the value of a good brand name. These three brand names are descriptive of the product benefits, are memorable, and fit with the images the companies are trying to project—the most frequently mentioned criteria presented in Table 9–2. There are four dimensions of a good brand name:[11]

1. It should identify the product and set it apart from the competition.
2. It should describe the product or the function it performs.
3. It should communicate an important quality inherent in the product.
4. It should be memorable and easy to pronounce.

Beautyrest, Weight Watchers, and DieHard clearly meet all of these criteria.

A brand name should fit the product. Thus, you wouldn't want to name a suntan lotion "Sizzle," nor would you want to have it packaged in boiled-lobster red. But the name Coppertone would seem to fit the product very well. As part of this category, the marketer should determine if the name is appealing and if it will work well visually and verbally. The automobile companies, for example, often try to present their cars as being exotic or romantic. Thus, we have brand names like Firebird, Fiesta, Cougar, Jaguar, Mustang, and Eldorado.

A brand name must also distinguish the product from its competitors. Sunlite by Hunt-Wesson beautifully describes the cooking oil as made from sunflower seeds and communicates that the product is naturally grown under sunlight and is light for frying. Turtle Wax clearly communicates that the product forms a hard protective shell that will shield the car from the elements.

Brand names like Home Box Office (HBO), Minute Rice, Shake 'n Bake, 3-in-1 Oil, and V-8 Juice describe the products or the functions performed. Liquid Plumbr, Head and Shoulders, Eveready, Cover Girl, Duracell, and Easy Off communicate their product's qualities and benefits.

Most marketers agree that the briefer the name the better, with one-word, one-syllable brand names the ideal. Consider, for example, Shout, Bold, Bounce, Brut, Jif, Zest, Pledge, Glade, Prell, and Raid. The shorter the name, the larger it can appear on a package. This leads to easy identification on supermarket shelves.

There are many examples of brands that violated these rules and were less successful than their competitors. Consider, for example Colgate 100, Good News, or Mennen E. Do they describe their products? Does Max Factor describe product benefits as clearly as Cover Girl does? Real Cigarettes used $40 million in advertising and its brand name to communicate that the product was all natural, something that consumers didn't expect, or want, in cigarettes.

There are many examples of products that violate these rules and still are very successful. For example, Haagen-Dazs, Riunite, Giacobazzi, and Michelob are neither short nor easy to pronounce. Thus, the criteria presented here should be considered as guidelines only, not as hard-and-fast rules.

A good brand name communicates an important quality inherent in the product.

Branding Policies

The first policy that a manufacturer must determine is whether to sell its products using a manufacturer's brand or a distributor's brand. A **manufacturer's brand** is owned by the manufacturer. These brands are sometimes called **national brands,** but in fact, they may be distributed on a regional or national basis. Examples of manufacturer's brands include Chevrolet, Pampers, Kodak, and Zenith. A **distributor's brand** is owned and controlled by a retailer, wholesaler, or other type of reseller. These brands are often called *private labels.* Examples of distributor's brands include Kenmore and Craftsman (Sears' brands), Radio Shack, Ann Page (A&P), and Kmart. Some distributors' brands are advertised heavily so that they resemble manufacturers' brands in the eyes of consumers. Two examples are Sears' DieHard and Radio Shack's Tandy personal computers.

The conditions that lead manufacturers to market products without using their own brands or in addition to their brands are the same ones that result in retailers and wholesalers seeking products to market under their own brands. These conditions include the following:[12]

1. The product class is past the midpoint in the growth stage of the life-cycle; some market segments may already be saturated.

2. Consumers are beginning to consider alternative offerings within the product class as undifferentiated substitutes for one another; that is, the product is approaching "commodity" status.
3. The reseller becomes more important than the manufacturer as a source of assurance of quality, style, or both to the customer and has greater economic power than the manufacturer.
4. Changes in the competitive environment stimulate manufacturers to provide distributors' brands, lest they lose distribution to competing manufacturers who will do so.
5. Economic slowdowns cause consumers to seek lower-priced products.
6. The distributors' volume becomes adequate to permit production of a custom product by the manufacturer and stocking and promoting by the distributor.

With distributors' brands, more of the marketing is shifted from the manufacturer to the distributor. Small manufacturers, in particular, may find this desirable, especially if marketing resources are limited. Manufacturers with excess capacity may also find that the additional business available from selling distributors' brands can improve profitability if additional sales can be obtained at a price above marginal cost of production. Distributors' brands offer the retailer and wholesaler a means of tying their consumers directly to them; if they are satisfied, consumers will return to them to buy the product in the future. Also, distributors' brands often enable retailers to earn greater margins while, at the same time, selling the product to consumers at a lower price than comparable alternatives.

Another major branding policy that marketers must determine is whether to sell products using individual brands or family brands. Companies having an individual branding policy use different brand names for each of their products. Thus, Procter & Gamble markets Pampers disposable diapers as well as Luvs and Attends disposable diapers. With **family brands,** a brand is applied to a line of products. GE, Scott Paper, Campbell's, Black & Decker, Xerox, IBM, Del Monte, Sears, and Kellogg's all use family brands. Some firms use a combination of individual and family brands. For example, automobile companies use names like Ford Taurus and Cadillac Seville. General Electric uses the GE family name on one line of appliances and uses a separate name, Hotpoint, on a different line of appliances.

Individual brands are most appropriate when the products are not similar in quality and/or price. The use of individual brands minimizes any confusion with other products in the company's product line. Firms can appeal to different segments of the market with different strategies. This explains why Procter & Gamble uses individual brand names like Tide, Bold, Cheer, and Oxydol for its line of detergents. Each of these brands stands on its own and has its own image targeted toward its own segment of the market. Use of an individual branding policy requires greater resources, however, because each brand must have its own promotional budget.

The use of family brands is most appropriate when the individual products are similar in quality. The family brand may offer greater economies in advertising and promotion as well as potentially higher impact. It is easier to obtain distribution, trial, and awareness of other new products that may be introduced later using the family brand. However, family brands also have potential disadvantages. If a new product introduced under a family brand fails, it may have an impact on the perception of the rest of the product line. A watch company like Rolex, for example, should be very careful about introducing a new low-priced watch under the Rolex brand. If consumers perceive the new product as a cheap watch, it could ruin Rolex's reputation for fine watches. Family brands work best when the quality, target market, channels, product classification, and usage are all very similar, as they are with GE refrigerators, GE ovens, and GE washers and dryers. Honda, on the other hand, used a different brand name and set up a completely different dealer structure when it introduced its higher-priced Acura line of cars.

Review Your Marketing Knowledge

- What benefits do brand names and marks offer to companies? To retailers? To consumers?
- Suppose you opened a new retail store specializing in discount compact disks. How would you go about choosing a name for your store?

Generic Brands

Recently a new type of brand has been established—the "no brand" or **generic brand.** These are sold with no identification other than the contents of the product. The products are labeled with names like *beer, corn flakes,* or *heavy-duty laundry detergent.* Generic brands were originated in 1976 in France by the Carrefour supermarket chain.[13] Carrefour called these *produits libres* (free products), which, it explained, were the same quality as the branded products it sold but free of the costly promotions and fancy packaging. The products were an immediate success, accounting for an average of 40 percent of sales in those categories where they competed with branded products.

The Jewel Foods supermarket chain was the first company in the United States to market generic brands, starting in 1977. The idea spread rapidly, and within a few years, generic brands became available in more than 320 product categories and in over three-quarters of all the supermarkets in the U.S.[14] On the average, generics cost about 40 percent less than nationally advertised brands, and 10–15 percent less than distributor private label brands. They also are generally of lower quality than manufacturers' and distributors' brands.

Studies conducted by Selling Areas-Marketing Inc., a marketing research company, have found that market shares for generic products have been dropping in recent years.[15] They peaked in 1982, during the height of an economic recession, with $2.8 billion in sales and a 2.4 percent share of all supermarket sales. By 1987, sales had slipped to $1.5 billion or about 1.2 percent of supermarket sales. Sales have been strongest in nonfood items such as paper goods, trash bags, disposable diapers, and coffee filters.

Sales of distributors' brands have been declining as well, falling from almost 15 percent of sales in 1982 to under 12 percent in 1987.[16] Apparently consumers perceive national brands to be of higher quality, and the tremendous increase in the use of coupons has brought the price of many advertised brands closer to the price charged by distributors' brands.

Packaging

Marketers have increasingly recognized the importance of packaging. Traditionally, a package was perceived as a container, and the emphasis was on the ability of the package to protect the product. Today marketers also recognize the importance of

A new package design can help increase a product's sales.

the promotional aspects of packaging and the ability of the package to contribute to substantially increased sales.[17]

A package has two important functions. First, it must have functional utility for the consumer and for the intermediaries in the channels of distribution. The package should protect the product, preventing breakage or spoilage and extending the product's life. In addition, it should be convenient for the consumer to use and convenient for the trade to ship, store, and stack on a shelf. Resellers prefer packages that help cut shipping costs and reduce shoplifting. The package should also be easily disposable.

Second, the package should facilitate promotional communication by allowing clear brand identification, promoting the product's features, and helping sell the product. A good label on the package, together with proper instructions on a product's use, for example, can reduce the amount of personal selling needed to convince the consumer to buy the product. Packaging—attractive Christmas boxes or distinctive shapes such as L'eggs hosiery or Janitor-in-a-Drum—can lead to a substantial increase in a product's sales. A properly designed package can communicate the quality level of a product, such as a slip-on box used for a high-quality book. Also, there is no question that attractive, innovative packaging can help a marketer obtain additional shelf space for the company's products. Some examples of successful packaging include the following:[18]

- Ralston Purina Company's Dog Chow® brand, the leading dog food, was losing market share. The company determined that the pictures of dog breeds on its package were old-fashioned and too rural. A new package, featuring a photo of a dog and a child, was designed, and sales have increased.

- When the price of fancy seafood rose rapidly, consumers of Wakefield frozen seafood noticed. The company developed a new, elegant box, featuring a photo of seafood in a silver serving dish. This helped position the product as a high-quality one worth the higher price.
- Kendall Oil learned that more motor oil sales were coming from supermarkets and hardware stores than from service stations. The company developed new packaging to make the product more appealing to do-it-yourselfers who buy through these channels of distribution.
- Planters Nuts and Weight Watchers have both undergone packaging changes to enable them to do a better job of selling several related products under a single brand name. The labels and colors of the packages were standardized to visually reinforce the concept of a related line of products.

Factors in Package Design

Several different factors must be considered in designing and developing a package. These include environmental and resource considerations, financial and cost factors, government regulations, and consumer behavior and product attributes.

Environmental and Resource Considerations. Marketers are under pressure to pay attention to the environmental impact of their packaging. Litter is always an important problem, and, additionally, the U.S. is running out of landfills and other places to put garbage. Environmental and resource considerations have increased the use of recycled paper and recycled beverage containers.

Financial and Cost Factors. Out of each dollar a consumer spends, close to 10 cents goes for packaging. For food, the amount is 13 cents, and for cosmetics it is nearly 30 cents.[19] A major change in packaging often requires new molds, dyes, and handling equipment, and thus can be very costly. The cylindrical cardboard package used for Pringles potato chips costs almost twice as much as the traditional potato chip package. A marketer must be confident that a more expensive package will contribute enough additional sales to justify the additional packaging cost. Consumers did not see much advantage in the Pringles package, and sales did not achieve expected levels.

Government Regulations. The Federal Fair Packaging and Labeling Act of 1966 contains a number of regulations about information that must be provided to consumers on packages. For example, the labels on food packages must contain a list of ingredients in order of the weight or volume of each. For certain types of products, so much information must be disclosed on the package that many packages are now filled with what designers call "mouse print." The Federal Hazardous Substances Act forbids the use of certain types of containers for products dangerous to ingest. The Consumer Products Safety Commission has a number of requirements for packages, the most famous of which is the childproof aspirin bottle. In addition, many states have outlawed certain types of packages such as nonbiodegradable packages and no-deposit, no-return beverage containers.

Consumer Behavior and Marketing Strategy Factors. A marketer is always interested in knowing how much a package will help sell the product. This, of course, depends upon consumer behavior. For example, Procter & Gamble put the cap for

MARKETING IN ACTION

General Mills Develops a New and Improved Betty Crocker

After spending millions of dollars on research, General Mills has found that American grocery shopping and cooking habits are changing: According to their surveys, 40 percent of grocery shoppers are now men as compared to less than 30 percent a decade ago; 34 percent of all men today over the age of 21 bake as compared to 22 percent a decade ago; 20 percent of all meals are prepared by teenagers as compared to 14 percent in 1975. People seem to be either cooking from scratch or are buying heat-'n-serve food products. What does this mean for a company like General Mills, whose Betty Crocker line of products typically involves some preparation prior to cooking, yet lacks the cachet of a totally "home-prepared" meal? Trouble. Time for a change.

To General Mills, the research confirmed what they were reading and seeing in the marketplace. Their objective was to make Betty Crocker, who was already an accepted institution, a relevant symbol for today's shopper—male or female, young or old, single or married.

The new Betty is younger looking, with a longer, more casual hairstyle. Her smile is friendly, approachable, yet confident. This makes her more appealing to men, working women, and teenagers, according to focus groups asked to compare the 1986 and 1980 portraits prior to the unveiling of the new Betty. The older Betty was seen as more formal and stiff.

General Mills' media relations plan was to reach two audiences. First, they had to communicate the change to their existing base of traditional homemakers in a nonoffensive way. Second, they had to reach men, working women, and teenagers who didn't have traditional baking habits.

Sales of Betty Crocker products are up since the introduction of the new portrait and sales of the revised Betty Crocker cookbook are breaking prior records. However, General Mills cautions against linking the increases to the new Betty alone because her makeover was part of a coordinated public relations, marketing, and advertising campaign.

SOURCE: Cathleen Toomey, "Betty Crocker: New and Improved," *Public Relations Journal*, December 1986, p. 15.

Wondra skin lotion on the bottom of the bottle to enable consumers to get every drop of lotion out of the bottle. The product's market share fell from 8 percent to 6 percent within a year. A study by a competitor later found that consumers did not feel comfortable changing their normal motion of grabbing the bottle, flipping open the cap, and turning the bottle upside-down. Thus, the Wondra bottle was inconsistent with normal consumer behavior, undoubtedly leading to its decline in market share.[20]

M&M/Mars did some consumer research to determine the appropriate size package for its candy bars. The company conducted a test in 150 stores, keeping the price of the candy the same, and varying the size bar from outlet to outlet. In stores where the dimensions were increased, sales went up from 20 to 30 percent, leading to changes in the company's whole product line.[21] Consumer response to packaging can differ by country. Thus, over 90 percent of the tennis balls sold in the U.S. come three to a can. Japanese prefer a two-pack and Europeans a four-pack. The *Marketing in Action* on Betty Crocker shows how General Mills has attempted to keep its packaging in line with consumer behavior.

Warranty and After-the-Sale Service

A warranty is a written statement of what the seller promises to do if the product is defective or does not perform as expected within a certain time period after the sale.[22] In addition to a written warranty, there are also implied warranties. The Uniform Commercial Code, a statute of the United States, together with many state laws, form the basis of implied warranties that guarantee to the consumers that the product purchased is fit for the purpose for which it was sold. The Magnuson-Moss Warranty Act of 1975 sets standards for the specifications of a warranty, should a company choose to offer one, and empowers the Federal Trade Commission to enforce the standards.

A written warranty must disclose to the consumer whether it is a *full warranty* or a *limited warranty*. If the warranty is limited, the major limitations (such as "includes parts only," or "does not include routine maintenance") must be clearly spelled out. The law also requires that the length of the warranty (for example, one year) be clearly communicated to the consumer.

Companies such as General Electric and Chrysler have made warranties and consumer satisfaction a major part of their product strategies. Whirlpool, GE, and many other companies have "800" toll-free telephone numbers that consumers can use to make complaints, ask questions, or find out the location of the nearest service center. Although these after-the-sale programs are costly, they can contribute additional sales and profits, because consumers value the companies' products more highly due to these services.[23]

Personal Computer Exercise

Product life-cycles are an important concept in determining marketing strategies. This PC exercise will help you evaluate product life cycles by examining the industry characteristics of different products. Are the market strategies you selected consistent with your description of the product's sales patterns?

KEY POINTS

- A product is the combination of want-satisfying attributes a consumer receives in making an exchange, including psychological as well as physical benefits.

- Consumer goods are products purchased for use by households, or ultimate consumers.

- Consumer goods can be further classified as convenience, shopping, or specialty goods. Different marketing strategies are required for each of these types of products.

- A product line is a group of closely related products offered by an organization. A product mix consists of all the individual products available through the organization. Breadth of product mix is determined by the number of product lines marketed by the organization. Depth of product mix is determined by the number of different sizes, models, and colors available within each product line.

- The product life-cycle consists of the stages—introduction, growth, maturity, and decline—that a product goes through from its introduction until it is taken off the market. The length and shape of the product life-cycle are determined by consumer needs, wants, attitudes, and behavior; the rate of technological change; competitive activity; and the organization's own marketing actions.

• A brand is a name, term, symbol, design, or combination of these that identifies goods and services and distinguishes them from competitors' products. There are many advantages of branding for marketers, resellers, and consumers.

• The steps involved in selecting a brand name include identifying objectives, generating brand name alternatives, screening the alternatives, researching consumers' opinions, conducting a trademark search, and making a final selection.

• A good brand name should identify the product and set it apart from the competition, describe the product or the function it performs, communicate the product's benefits, and should be memorable and easy to pronounce.

• Manufacturers may market their products under their own brands, or may choose to use distributors' brands or generic brands. The organization may use individual brand names or may apply a family brand to a line of products.

• Packages have a functional role and a promotional role. Environmental and resource factors, financial and cost considerations, government regulations, and consumer behavior and marketing strategy all influence package design.

• Warranties play an important role in the marketing strategy for some consumer products such as automobiles and major appliances.

ISSUES FOR DISCUSSION

1. General Electric announced it has developed a new type of light bulb that will last five times longer than ordinary light bulbs and will use only one-third the amount of electricity while generating the same amount of light. The bulb will cost $10 but will save $20 over its life in lower electric bills. Is this new light bulb the same product as the company's traditional light bulb? In what ways does it differ?

2. How would you classify each of the following products:

a. Vacation package to Hawaii
b. Paint for exterior of house
c. Leather wallet
d. Reebok shoes
e. Pepsi

3. Until recently, Kraft, Inc. marketed a number of food and dairy products such as Philadelphia Cream Cheese, Velveeta and other cheese products, Miracle Whip, Breyers Ice Cream, and Kraft Macaroni and Cheese, among others. In addition, Kraft sold Tupperware products, West Bend appliances, and Duracell batteries. Recently, they sold all the nonfood product lines. Why might a company like Kraft choose to *narrow* its product mix? Is breadth of product mix or width of product mix more important for a company like Kraft?

4. Using the list of characteristics of a good brand name in the chapter, evaluate the following brand names:

a. MCI (long distance telephone service)
b. *People Magazine*
c. Yoplait Yogurt
d. Canon Sure Shot Camera
e. Steak and Ale Restaurant

5. Holiday Inn markets hotel rooms under a number of brands, including Hampton Inns (budget motel), Embassy Suites (a suite for the price of a quality hotel room), Residence Inns (an apartment-like room for longer stays), and Crown Plaza (luxury hotel rooms). Why does the company use completely different names for these hotels, instead of using the Holiday Inn name to identify them?

6. The budget motel segment of the market has reached the end of the growth stage of the product life-cycle, and the suite segment is just beginning the growth stage. The longer stay type motel product is just being introduced into the hotel market. How might these three products (Hampton Inn, Embassy Suites, and Residence Inns) be marketed differently by Holiday Inn in the coming year?

7. Identify an example of a product for each stage of the product life-cycle. For each product, what should the marketing manager for the product expect to happen at the next stage?

8. What advantages might a company like Scott Paper see in selling distributor and/or generic brands? What are some disadvantages?

9. Considering the functions of a good package, how would you rate the packages for the following products:

a. L'eggs (hosiery)
b. Coca-Cola
c. McDonald's hamburgers
d. Kleenex facial tissues

10. Why do most major durable goods like automobiles and appliances have warranties, while many items such as food, clothing, and hardware don't?

GLOSSARY

Brand: a name, term, symbol, design, or combination that identifies a seller's goods and services and distinguishes them from competitors' products.

Brand mark: the part of a brand—in the form of a symbol, design, or distinctive letters—that is seen but not spoken.

Brand name: the part of a brand that can be vocalized, including letters, words, and numbers.

Breadth of product mix: number of different product lines marketed by an organization.

Consumer goods: products purchased for use by households, or ultimate consumers.

Convenience goods: those frequently purchased products which the consumer buys with a minimum of time and effort.

Depth of product mix: number of different sizes, models, and colors offered within each product line.

Family brand: a brand applied to one or more lines of products of one seller.

Generic brand: those products sold with no identification other than the contents of the package.

Industrial products: products sold for use in producing other products or in rendering services.

Product: every want- or need-satisfying attribute a consumer receives in making an exchange, including psychological as well as physical benefits.

Product life-cycle: the stages that a product class goes through during its time on the market, including introduction, growth, maturity, and decline.

Product line: a group of closely related products offered by an organization.

Product mix: all of the individual products available from an organization.

Shopping goods: products usually purchased only after the consumer has compared the price, quality, and style for a number of alternatives in several different stores.

Specialty goods: products for which no reasonable substitutes exist because of unique characteristics and/or brand identification. Consumers are thus willing to expend considerable effort to buy these goods.

Trademark: a brand or part of a brand that has been given legal protection for the seller's exclusive use.

Warranty: a written statement of what the seller promises to do for the buyer if the product is defective or does not perform as expected within a certain time period after the sale.

NOTES

1. Peter Bennett (ed.), *Dictionary of Marketing Terms* (American Marketing Association, 1988) p. 95.

2. Melvin Copeland, "Relation of Consumers' Buying Habits to Marketing Methods," *Harvard Business Review,* April 1923, pp. 282–89. For additional information on this classification structure, see Louis Bucklin, "Retail Strategy and the Classification of Consumer Goods," *Journal of Marketing,* January 1963, pp. 50–55; Richard Holten, "The Distinctions Between Convenience Goods, Shopping Goods, and Specialty Goods," *Journal of Marketing,* July 1958, pp. 53–56; and Patrick Murphy and Ben Enis, "Classifying Products Strategically," *Journal of Marketing,* July 1986, pp. 24–42.

3. J. Nicholls and S. Roslow, "The 'S-Curve': An Aid to Strategic Marketing," *The Journal of Consumer Marketing,* Spring 1986, p. 57.

4. Kenneth Derow, "Prolonging the Product Life Cycle," *Marketing Communications,* October 1981, p. 108.

5. Nariman Dhalla and Sonia Yuspeh, "Forget the Product Life-Cycle Concept!" *Harvard Business Review,* January-February 1976, pp. 102–12.

6. Peter Bennett (ed.), *Dictionary of Marketing Terms* (American Marketing Association, 1988) p. 18.

7. Sidney A. Diamond, "The Trademark: It Protects and Identifies," *Advertising Age,* January 7, 1980, p. 59.

8. James McNeal and Linda Zeren, "Brand Name Selection for Consumer Products," *MSU Business Topics,* Spring 1981, pp. 35–39.

9. J. McNeal and L. Zeren, pp. 35–39.

10. This section closely follows the discussion in Dennis J. Moran, "How a Name Can Label Your Product," *Advertising Age,* November 10, 1980, pp. 53, 56.

11. D. Moran, p. 53. Also see Daniel L. Doeden, "How to Select a Brand Name," *Marketing Communications,* November 1981, pp. 58, 61.

12. Richard Cardozo, *Product Policy: Cases and Concepts* (Addison-Wesley, 1979), pp. 44–45.

13. For information on the history and development of generic brands, see Brian F. Harris and Roger A. Strang, "Marketing Strategies in the Age of Generics," *Journal of Marketing,* Fall 1985, pp. 70–81.

14. B. Harris and R. Strang, pp. 70–71.

15. Julie Franz, "Ten Years May Be Generic Lifetime," *Advertising Age,* March 23, 1987, p. 76.

16. Ronald Alsop, "What's in a Name? Ask Supermarket Shoppers," *The Wall Street Journal,* May 9, 1988, p. 29; and "Private-Label, Generic Food Sales Drop," *Advertising Age,* May 13, 1985, p. 96.

17. See for example, Richard T. Hise and James U. McNeal, "Effective Packaging Management," *Business Horizons,* January-February, 1988, pp. 47–51 and Davis L. Masten, "Packaging's Proper Role Is to Sell the Product," *Marketing News,* January 18, 1988, p. 16.

18. Bill Abrams and David Garino, "Package Design Gains Stature as Visual Competition Grows," *The Wall Street Journal,* August 6, 1981, p. 25.

19. Walter McQuade, "Packagers Bear Up Under a Bundle of Regulations," *Fortune,* May 7, 1979, pp. 180–89.

20. Bill Abrams, "Packaging Often Irks Buyers, but Firms Are Slow to Change," *The Wall Street Journal,* January 28, 1982, p. 29.

21. John Keton, "Why Do Hot Dogs Come in Packs of 10 and Their Buns in 8s or 12s?" *The Wall Street Journal,* September 21, 1984, pp. 1, 18.

22. For an excellent review of the advantages of providing written warranties on products, see C. L. Kendall and Frederick Russ, "Warranty and Complaint Policies: An Opportunity for Marketing Management," *Journal of Marketing,* April 1975, pp. 36–43.

23. Karen Singer, "Marketing's New Watchword: 'Satisfaction Guaranteed,' " *Marketing Week,* November 2, 1988, pp. 59–61 and Sara Stern, "Guarantees at Fever Pitch," *Advertising Age,* October 26, 1987, pp. 3, 104.

CASE APPLICATION 9–1

A New Picture at Crayola

In 1903, Edwin Binney and C. Harold Smith were peddling sticks of dustless white chalk to schools in the Northeast when a group of teachers approached them with a problem. The chalk was all well and good, they said, but could the company make wax crayons for their students? So, the story goes, Binney and Smith returned home and developed a box of eight colors. Edwin's wife called them Crayola School Crayons—"cray" for the French word *craie,* or chalk, and "ola," for oleaginous or oily. Later that year, the pair sold their first set for a nickel.

Today, American consumers spend approximately $200 million each year on Crayola products, and they're not just buying crayons. In the four years since Hallmark Cards, Inc., acquired Binney & Smith, Inc., the Crayola brand name has appeared on a full line of arts-and-crafts products, including washable markers, fluorescent crayons and paints, glue, and scissors.

In 1988 the company introduced four products: Colorworks Color Sticks, an erasable drawing tool; a storage case for Crayola Markers; washable Crayola Water Colors paints; and, for young yuppies-in-training, Crayola's Special Collection crayons, which include metallic, fluorescent, and trendy pastel colors.

The move to expand is part of a strategy by Binney & Smith to make sure that the Crayola brand means as much to future generations as it does now to parents. "Up until recently, we were not aggressive with marketing or promotions or new products," says Steve Yanklowitz, vice president and general manager of Crayola products division. "We also concentrated only on schools. Now, we're focusing on the retail level as well."

While Crayola's educational roots have been deep, it sells five times the amount of products to stores as it does to schools. The turning point at the retail level came in 1986, when the company modified the packaging of its Crayola line to include tabs. With the tabs, the products could hang on pegs instead of laying flat on store shelves. "It allowed us to bring all of the Crayola products together in a display that can run up to eight feet wide," says Brad Drexler, a company spokesperson. "It's a highly visible anchor, and there's no way it can be missed."

The peg-board display organized all of the Crayola brands in one location at supermarkets, where space is often tight and where parents do much of their shopping for their children's art supplies. In the past, supermarkets would not carry more than a couple of boxes of Crayola, which it mixed in with other brands. But those stores quickly discovered that profits justified featuring all of Crayola's products in one location.

These days, the company rarely makes a move without first testing a product with a focus group. The successful introduction of washable markers in 1987, Yanklowitz says, is one example of this approach. "When we thought of markers, we found that mothers banned them because they stained," he says. "Then, after a year of development, the testing process began. We brought kids into the plant to play with them. We also gave the product to families and asked them to use them for a week. After that, we called them up for opinions. A lot of things happen in homes when products are used in a natural environment. Many of these problems can't be simulated in labs."

SOURCE: John Webb, "Crayola Comes of Age at the Retail Level," *Adweek's Marketing Week,* September 5, 1988, p. 19; personal communication with Binney and Smith, June 1989.

Questions

1. At what stage of the product life-cycle are crayons? What steps can the company take to expand sales in this stage of the product life-cycle?

2. What are the advantages to the company of using the family brand name?

3. How would you classify the company's products? How would you describe the company's product mix in terms of its depth and breadth?

4. What roles are played by the packaging for the company's products?

CASE APPLICATION 9–2

FireKing Tries to Satisfy Both Distributors and Consumers

It's the lament of small manufacturers everywhere. We make a wonderful product and consumers love it, but we don't sell to consumers. We sell to wholesalers or retailers, and they don't always have consumers' best interests at heart. Talk all you want about features and service, but these intermediaries focus most on margins and prices. What's more, we don't have the resources to try to reach consumers, so we have no choice but to fall into line and compete on price.

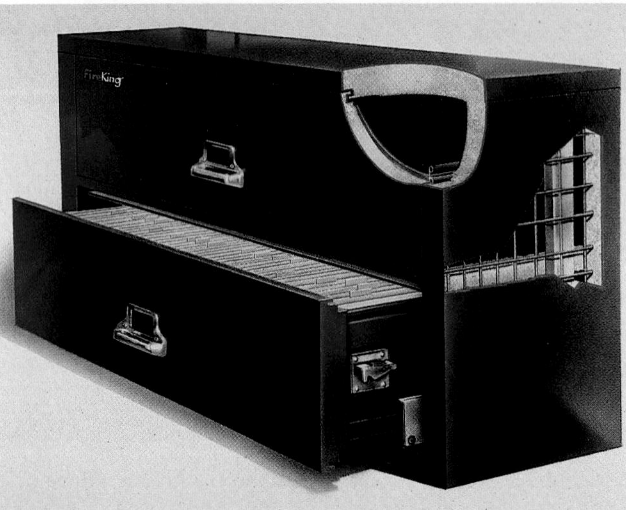

If Van Carlisle, the chief executive officer of FireKing International, Inc., in New Albany, IN, had accepted this argument thirteen years ago, when FireKing was the number six producer of fireproof filing cabinets in a field of six, he would still be there, instead of where he is today: number one, with annual sales of $16 million.

The story of FireKing is instructive for any company that has to sell through retailers, distributors, and other middlemen. It has become so expensive, and so inefficient, to maintain a direct-sales force that even the likes of Procter & Gamble Co. have turned to third-party sales organizations. But whereas the giants can run massive advertising campaigns to influence consumer choices, smaller companies seldom have that option.

In 1974, when Carlisle took over the company, the 50-employee business was losing money on its annual revenues of $750,000. Carlisle, grandson of the founder, decided to leave his job at a small regional elevator company and try his hand at running FireKing.

As he looked at the company, he saw a few strengths but many more weaknesses. Its primary strength was that consumers viewed FireKing's files "as the finest product around," Carlisle recalls. But even that strength created some problems. For one thing, the perception of quality was based largely on the files' weight. Fireproof files are insulated with a plasterlike substance that makes them heavy, and FireKing's, at 750 pounds on average, were the heaviest around. That made the company's freight costs the highest around as well. And even without the freight costs, FireKing's files were about the most expensive on the market.

What especially struck Carlisle, though, was the difference in how consumers and retailers looked at his product. Retailers' reaction was "They're better, so what?" His first task, he decided, was to identify and articulate what quality meant to retailers. And he quickly saw that the most effective way for FireKing to define quality was to compare its products with its competitors'.

From that perspective, Carlisle felt that FireKing's costly process of making separate insulating castings and curing them in drying ovens before placing them in the files was a special strength. Three of his competitors used a method that lowered costs, but created a problem if the files weren't sold quickly. Without the frequent opening and closing of drawers that occurs in offices, the insulation didn't dry completely, and the files rusted in the stores. In humid climates, they even rusted in offices. So FireKing began to define its quality to retailers in terms they could understand: "With us, they didn't have to worry about their inventory rusting." The tactic had mixed success, and FireKing began to establish itself in retailers' minds as a more aggressive competitor.

In 1977 and 1978, Carlisle addressed the nagging problem of weight. To consumers, weight meant quality. But to dealers, weight meant freight costs. FireKing's competitors, focusing on retailer concerns, constantly tried to lower freight costs by reducing their products' weight. But Carlisle didn't want to make his files lighter, since that would undermine their quality in consumers' minds and force him to lower prices. So he organized his own distribution system using contract trailers, getting lower freight costs and knowing in advance what they were. Then he began offering a prepaid freight program, which was an undeniable success. It emboldened Carlisle to further enhance FireKing's image of quality and to make life more difficult for the competition by distinguishing FireKing on the basis of its Underwriters Laboratories rating.

At the time, most fireproof files were referred to as either C or D; a C file was impact resistant and could withstand a 30-foot fall or a roof cave-in during a fire, while a D file wasn't impact resistant. Carlisle's competitors were turning out mostly D-rated files. Even the majority of FireKing's files were D-rated, but Carlisle felt they were such a high-quality D that they could inexpensively be upgraded to a C. So FireKing stopped making D-rated files altogether and priced its C files the same as its old Ds. The company could recover the price sacrifice by improving its volume, he reasoned. "That was one of the more successful things we did," Carlisle says. Retailers could improve their profitability and simplify their inventory. And competitors had to spend more than FireKing to bring their D-rated files up to a C. Perhaps most important, he says, "We forced a change in the industry. For the first time, we got competitors reacting to us."

It was now 1981, and FireKing's market share had increased from 3 percent in 1974 to more than 15 percent. At this point, Carlisle decided that he should use his heightened industry prominence to focus even more on issues associated with quality. In 1984, FireKing came up with a new scratch-resistant finish. And to counter the executive complaint that fireproof files are ugly, FireKing introduced attractive wooden files (at a price two and a half times the steel files). Whatever the tactics, the theme was consistent: "From the end-user standpoint, we're the best. From the dealer standpoint, we're the most profitable."

Even now, with a commanding 37 percent of the fireproof-file market, FireKing continues to look after both the retailer and consumer. Its market research in 1985 indicated that consumers wanted a smaller file cabinet. So FireKing added a new line of files that are 25 inches deep to go with the industry standard 31-1/2 inches. To ensure that dealers would go with the new cabinets, FireKing began offering them travel bonuses for reaching certain sales levels. That incentive—rather than price cuts or discounts—was chosen very deliberately. "The incentive travel program set us apart," says Carlisle. To encourage dealers to display and stock the FireKing files more extensively than they'd likely do on their own, Carlisle offers inventory financing by extending credit to dealers.

FireKing, with its 24 percent compound annual growth rate over the thirteen years Carlisle has headed it, may look as if it's leading a charmed life. But it's had its crises. Back in 1985, for example, one of Carlisle's suppliers produced 15,000 defective locks, each of which was on a FireKing file that had already been shipped. Without skipping a beat, Carlisle moved to placate both dealers and end-users. He offered to replace all unsold inventory, and he trained dealers to go out and replace defective locks on files already sold. He sent a new lock—together with installation instructions—to all the customers he could identify, offering to have a locksmith install it at FireKing's expense. Each customer received a $25 gift certificate for the trouble as well.

SOURCE: From "Which Customer Is Always Right?" by David E. Gumpert in *Inc.*, June 1987. Copyright © 1987 by Goldhirsh Group, Inc., 38 Commercial Wharf, Boston, MA 02110. Reprinted by permission.

Questions

1. Using the definition of product in this chapter, describe how FireKing's file cabinets differ from those of its competitors. How does the product distributors are buying differ from the product consumers are buying?

2. How would you describe FireKing's product mix? Would it make more sense for them to increase the width of their product line or the depth of their product line?

3. At what stage of the product lifecycle would you think fireproof file cabinets are? How does this affect FireKing's marketing strategy?

4. Evaluate the FireKing brand name.

5. How important is a warranty for a product like this one?

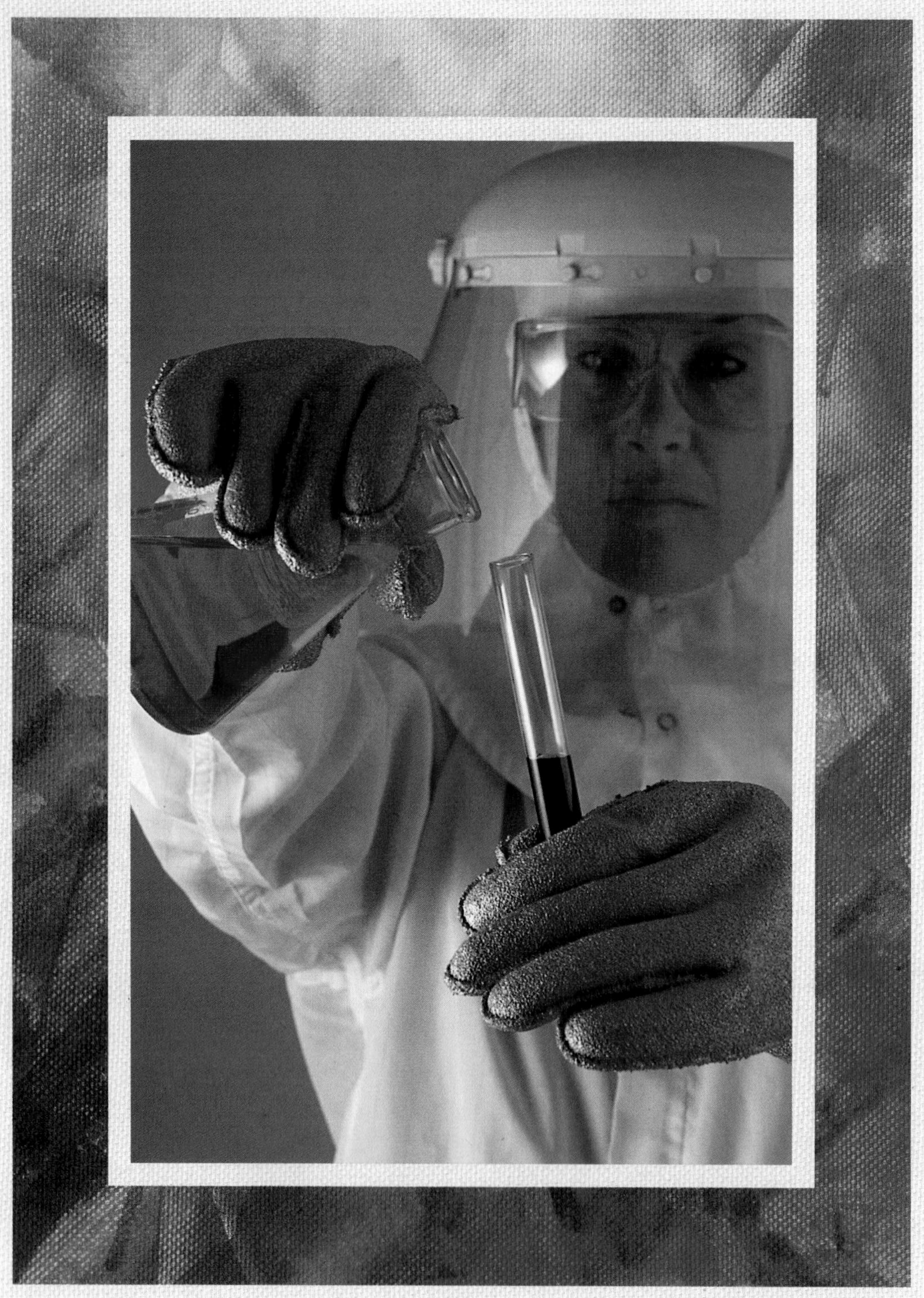

10

Product Development and Management

Learning Objectives

Upon completing this chapter, you will be able to do the following:

DEFINE
the concept of product positioning.

DISCUSS
the process of modifying existing lines.

KNOW
the importance of product innovation.

DESCRIBE
the development process for new products.

EXPLAIN
the reasons why many new products fail.

IDENTIFY
the factors that contribute to successful new products.

UNDERSTAND
the importance of quality and marketing's role in delivering it.

MARKETING PROFILE

Hasbro and the Development of Moondreamer Dolls

Crystal Starr, a 5 1/2-inch doll from Hasbro, Inc., was introduced to analysts and toy store executives in 1986. "Commercial toy companies might introduce a total of about 40 lines a year," said Henry Orenstein, the owner of Toy Builders, which develops toy ideas and advises toy makers. "Out of those, maybe three or four will be mega-hits, with retail sales of $100 million a year," he said. "At least 25 percent of the rest will be flops."

Crystal Starr was the central character in a line of dolls called "Moondreamers," which Hasbro spent two years developing. As a look at Moondreamers shows, creating a new toy isn't child's play. It has become a lengthy and expensive process as toy companies sift through countless ideas—Hasbro gets 4,000 a year—refine the best, shave pennies off production costs, and cater to the interests of retailers.

The idea for Moondreamers came from a Vermont illustrator in April 1984. The illustrator suggested a cast of characters called "Moon Beamers," who live in "Starry Up" and send dreams full of fun and adventure to children.

A line of mini-doll characters is hardly unique. Kenner Parker Toys' Strawberry Shortcake and similar lines sold by rival toy companies had been around for several years. But Hasbro believed that the falling sales of its competitors' mini-dolls offered an opportunity to fill a niche.

Still, the Moon Beamers idea needed a lot of fine tuning. Enraptured by the concept of dreams, the Vermont illustrator and Hasbro immediately agreed that the characters' names should be changed to Moondreamers. The toy maker also decided to aim the doll at little girls; thus, all but one of the original story's male characters were changed to females.

At the same time, the design team tried to develop what they considered the right look. Studies show that little girls love to play with long hair, so that

was a must. But designing the faces was trickier. Wanting to be a trend-setter, the designer finally found her inspiration in the face of a little girl on the EWOK Adventure TV show.

Going from sketches to models proved difficult. In some cases, sculptors made the eyes too big or the ears too pointy. Other sculptors left too much space between the eyes, nose, and mouth, making the faces look too mature. At the same time, problems arose with the dolls' body. The designer had sketched a fairly chunky body, but she didn't like the first prototypes. Crystal Starr "really looked fat when we put the clothes on," she says. As a result, the models were slimmed down to look more like "a little kid." The models took 4 months to complete.

For Crystal Starr's outfit, Hasbro wanted a shimmery, sheer, pink fabric with a high-tech look. The company sent samples to a Chinese manufacturer, but was told that the material would cost a steep $20 a yard. Instead, Hasbro settled for a cheaper imitation at $2.50 a yard. From start to finish, the costumes took eight months to complete in bulk.

Finally, confident it had a winner after nearly a year of development, Hasbro gave a sneak preview of the five-doll line to four top toy retailers. The retailers were unimpressed.

Before abandoning the project, Hasbro visited two shopping malls in New York and New Jersey and interviewed 100 little girls and their mothers to get their reactions. Among the results: 75 percent of the children rated mini-dolls as their favorite kind of doll; 96 percent said they would ask their mothers to buy Moondreamers; and 75 percent of the mothers said they would either definitely or probably buy Moondreamers.

Encouraged, Hasbro marketers and designers went back to the drawing board. They enlarged the line to nine dolls to give it more variety. But Moondreamers still needed something to make them stand out from other mini-dolls. The company decided to reexamine an idea that had been considered earlier, but seemed far-fetched at the time: hair that glows in the dark, a novelty in mini-doll land.

Seven months of work by Hasbro's resident chemist and others gave the company the hair it wanted. Hasbro gave another sneak preview of the improved Moondreamers to select retailers and received an enthusiastic reception. The glowing hair provided the "oooh and aaah they had missed in our other presentation," said Hasbro's marketing director.

However, despite all the hard work and research, sales on the Moondreamer Dolls did not meet expectations. Hasbro has pulled the dolls from the market, and toy stores are no longer stocking them.

SOURCE: Linda M. Watkins, "A Look at Hasbro's 'Moondreamers' Dolls Shows Creating a Toy Isn't Child's Play," *The Wall Street Journal*, December 29, 1986, p. 21; Personal communication with Hasbro, Inc., 1989.

Managing the product component of the marketing mix is the focus of this chapter on product development. We will discuss the management of existing products, as well as the development and management of new products. Chapter 9 presented the essential elements—such as product line, product life-cycle, branding, and packaging—of a successful product strategy. But product strategies are only successful when properly managed.

Product planning is often a complex process, as demonstrated by the Hasbro story. This chapter will describe the stages in the new product development process and the many decisions managers must make in determining the firm's products or line of products. We will look at the reasons why many products fail and the factors that contribute most to their success. Later, we will examine how marketing managers make changes in the product line, including the deletion of products.

Positioning Products

An important concept in the development of product strategy is **product positioning.** Product positioning refers to the place a product occupies in consumers' minds relative to competitors' offerings. The focus is, thus, on consumer perceptions of a product. Some well-known examples include Marlboro's positioning as a cigarette for macho consumers; Chivas Regal as a "super premium" Scotch whiskey; 7-UP as an un-Cola; Zale's, the diamond store; and Nyquil, the night time cold remedy.

A number of different bases can be used for positioning products:[1]

1. *Positioning by specific product features.* This is the most common approach to positioning, especially for industrial products. Price and specific product features are used as the basis for positioning. Budget Rent-A-Car's positioning as everything the major rental car companies give you, but at a lower price, is a classic example. Tyco has positioned its Super Blocks as "the Super Value Blocks," selling 600 pieces for the same price as Lego sells its 359 piece bucket (see ad on page 298).

2. *Positioning by benefits, problems, solutions, or needs.* This emphasis is on benefits, which is generally more effective than positioning on product features without referring to the benefits. Pharmaceutical companies position their products to doctors by stressing effectiveness and side effects. Other examples include Crest, which positions its toothpaste as a cavity fighter, and Federal Express, which uses its on-time performance record as a basis for its positioning.

3. *Positioning for specific usage occasions.* This approach is related to benefit positioning but uses the specific occasion as the major basis for the positioning. Johnson's Baby Shampoo is, thus, positioned as a product to use if you shampoo your hair every day, and Michelob Beer is for weekends and special occasions.

4. *Positioning for user category.* Examples here include "You've Come a Long Way, Baby" and "Breakfast of Champions." Age has been used as a basis for positioning by Geritol, by Colgate Junior toothpaste for children, and by Affinity shampoo for women over 40.

5. *Positioning against another product.* Although Avis never mentions Hertz explicitly in its advertising, its positioning as Number 2 in the rent-a-car market is an example of positioning against a leader. Savin Business Machine Corporation has positioned its plain paper copying machine directly against Xerox in its efforts to get industrial customers to perceive Savin as an alternative to Xerox.

6. *Product class disassociation.* This is a less common basis for positioning, but it can be effective when introducing a new product that is different from standard

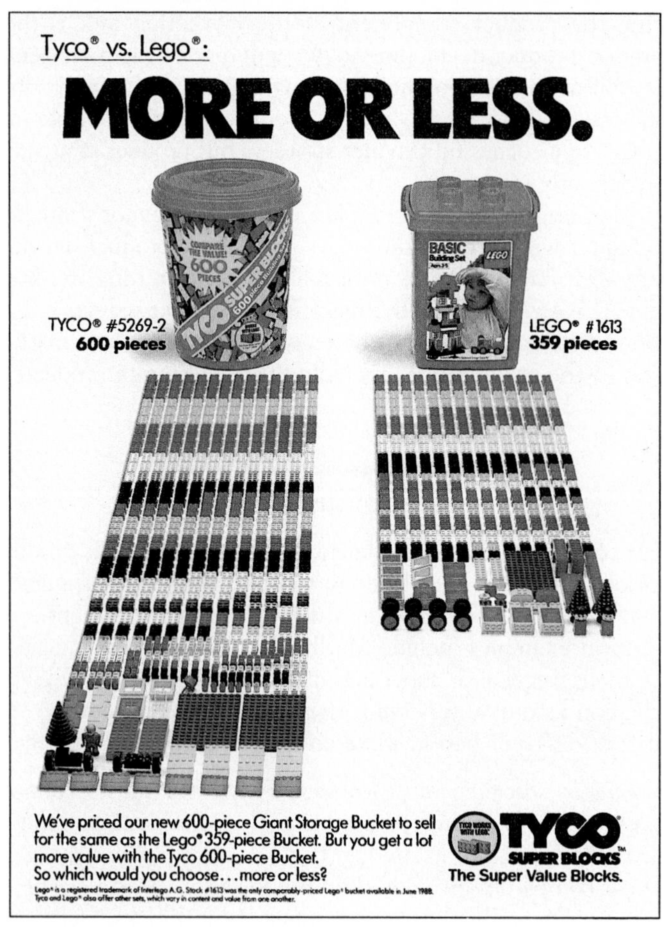

Price and specific product features can be used as a basis for positioning.

products in an established product category. Lead-free gasoline and decaffeinated coffee are examples of new product classes positioned against leaded gasoline and regular coffee. The 7-UP "no-caffeine" positioning is an example on the brand level.

7. *Hybrid basis.* Often, a positioning strategy will be based on several of these alternatives, incorporating elements from more than one positioning base. The Porsche positioning, for example, is based on the product benefits as well as on a certain type of user.

The basis actually used for product positioning will depend on the specific characteristics of the firm, the product, the target market, and the environment. Organizations will often refer to a *product positioning map* in determining positioning strategy. Figure 10–1 is a positioning map developed by Chrysler, based on a survey of car buyers.[2] The map positions the cars based on the product attributes of "touch of class" vs. practicality and appeal to young people vs. older people. On this map, Cadillac, Lincoln, and Mercedes are positioned as high class cars appealing to older people. Chrysler cars also appear to appeal to older people, but its image is not as high class as its competitors. Plymouth and Dodge are also positioned as being for older consumers, but are seen as much more affordable. Volkswagen is also perceived as prac-

Figure 10–1 Product Positioning Map for Sixteen Car Brands

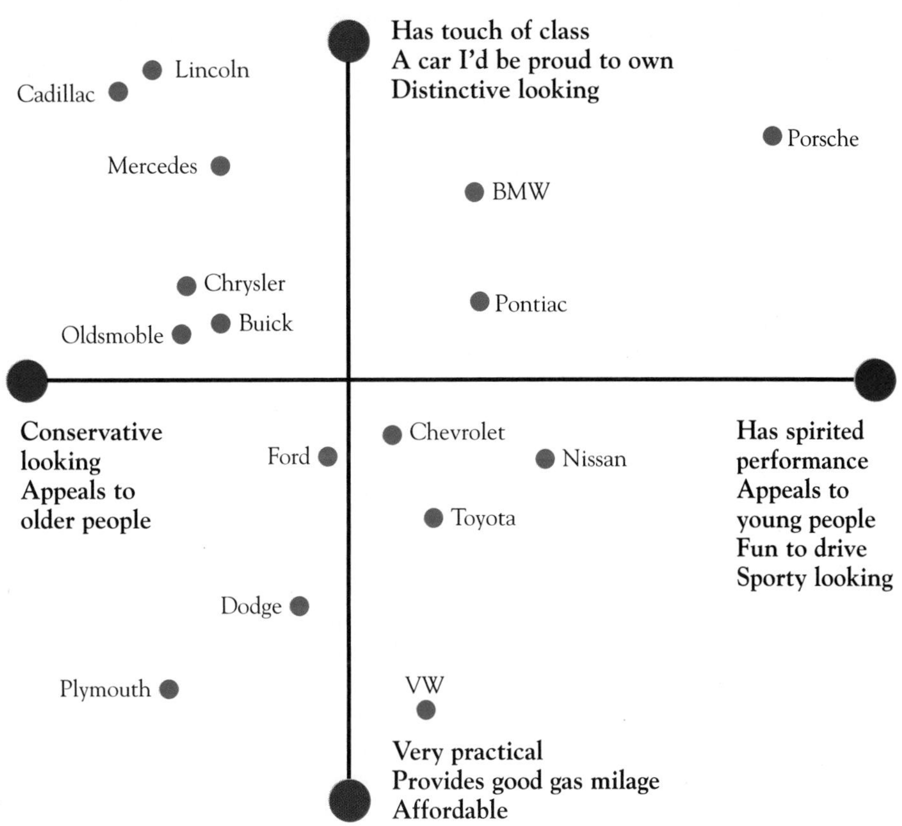

SOURCE: John Koten, "Car Makers Use 'Image' Map as Tool to Position Products," *The Wall Street Journal*, March 22, 1984, p. 33.

tical, but has a younger image. Chevrolet, Toyota, and Nissan have a younger image as well.

The closer the brands are positioned on the map, the more likely they are to be competitive. Thus consumers perceive the Chevrolet as being competitive with Ford, but not with Plymouth. Chrysler executives used this map to develop a strategy for its cars, determining that each of their car lines needed to improve their image to be more appealing to young people. The Dodge and Plymouth lines needed to improve their image on distinctiveness and luxury ("touch of class").

The portion of the map that appears to offer some potential is the lower right quadrant (the area representing practical, fun cars with good performance appealing to young people). This part of the map is *open,* and it might be possible for a new brand to be successful by occupying that position in the market. Suzuki has attempted to penetrate this segment with its low-priced, sporty, "Jeep-like" cars. Marketers must be careful, however, to carefully research such opportunities before developing new products. In the early 1980s, DeLorean developed a sports car for the high prestige, young, sporty segment of the market, and as it turned out, the company overestimated the demand for such a car.

Modifying Existing Product Lines

There are a number of reasons for modifying an individual product or a product line, including the desire to increase sales, profits, or market share; the support of the firm's overall marketing strategy; and a contribution to the objectives the organization has for its entire portfolio of products.[3] Marketing managers can modify an existing product line by changing any one, or combination, of the following attributes of a product line.[4]

1. Positioning
2. Physical characteristics
3. Package
4. Brand
5. Amount and nature of value added
6. Expansion or reduction of the product line
7. Composition of the product line

The first five of these attributes apply to individual products and/or product lines; the last two apply only to the set of products within a product line.

Positioning

One way to modify an existing product line is to change the positioning of one or more products within the line. Marlboro was repositioned from a cigarette targeted for women to one oriented toward men. Johnson's Baby Shampoo's positioning as a shampoo for babies was broadened to include adults who shampoo frequently. After originally achieving success in the male market, Right Guard deodorant was repositioned as a product that could be used by all members of the family, but, in the 1980s, has returned to the male positioning. Often, a product can be repositioned by changing the promotional strategy and/or distribution strategy. Sometimes it is necessary to change the actual product or its packaging.

Physical Characteristics

Marketers may change the physical characteristics of their products, by altering their qualities, performances, and appearances. For example, Sunkist removed the caffeine from its orange soda drinks, some cookie companies removed tropical oils from their cookies, and Florsheim shoes introduces new styles each spring.

The Package

Packages may be changed by altering the functional attributes or the communications attributes. Taylor California Cellars Wine is trying to increase sales by introducing the product in aluminum cans for use by airline companies. Campbell's Soup increased sales of several of its products by stamping "The Lite Ones" on the packages of individual soups that are low in calories.

Brand

Many marketers who sell under their own brand names have increased sales by marketing the same or similar products using a reseller's brand, and vice versa. The Whirlpool Corporation, for example, markets its products under its own brand name and under Sears' Kenmore brand.

Amount and Nature of Value Added

Value added refers to the change in the product characteristics from the time the ingredients enter the organization to the time the product is sold by the organization.[5] For example, Pillsbury changed its product line by altering the value added when it began marketing cake mixes in addition to its flour. Sold as a cake mix, the flour (together with other ingredients) had much more value to the consumer. Many companies have made their product more convenient to use, thus adding value for the consumer.

Expanding or Reducing the Product Line

In many product categories, consumers have a strong desire for variety, and to satisfy them, marketers frequently add new styles, models, or flavors. For example, Kellogg's frequently adds new cereals to its product line, McDonald's introduces new items on its menu, and Yves St. Laurent adds new styles to his line of clothing. For technical products, one segment will sometimes have more sophisticated requirements than other segments—in computers and communication equipment, for example. Marketers in these industries will often expand the product line to include new products with the latest technical specifications while maintaining the old products in the line to satisfy the needs of the less sophisticated users. Another reason for expanding a product line is to include *complementary products*—those for which demand is related to, but not competitive with, other products in the line. For example, the demand for brushes and clean-up supplies is complementary to the demand for paint, and a paint manufacturer may decide to satisfy the demand by introducing these complementary products.

Marketers also reduce the product line on occasion by eliminating products.[6] Usually, companies will only consider abandoning a product or product line after sales or profits have declined substantially. Managers often argue that they need a complete product line and that if they were to eliminate one product in the line, the sales of others might decline.

Composition of the Product Line

The composition of the product line may be changed by altering the individual products in the line. This can be accomplished by changing the product's style and characteristics, the options and accessories, or the pricing of the line. For example, a furniture manufacturer can change the composition of its product line by switching the emphasis from French provincial furniture to contemporary furniture. An appliance marketer can make certain features and accessories optional instead of standard, or vice versa. A men's pants producer might alter the composition of its product line by emphasizing the $49.95 and $59.95 pants, instead of the $29.95 and $39.95 pants.

Managing New Product Opportunities

Opportunities for developing new products can be classified according to product category and brand name. Whether the product is in a new or existing category and whether its brand name is new or existing is important.[7] Figure 10–2 presents the four possible opportunities available to an organization.

When a firm introduces a product that has a new brand name and is in a product category new to the organization, it is classified as a traditional **new product.** The

Figure 10–2 Alternative Product Opportunities

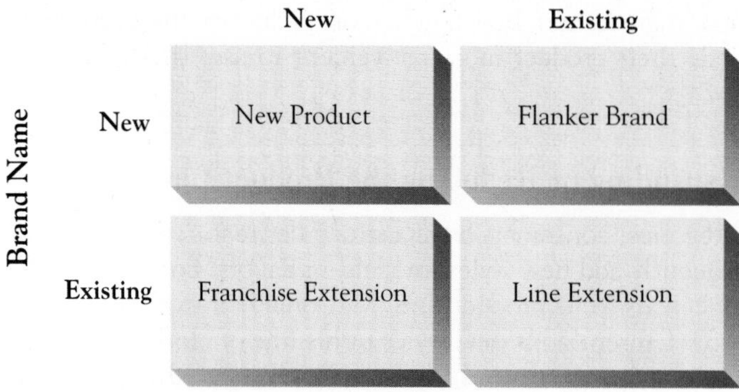

SOURCE: Edward Tauber, "Brand Franchise Extension: New Product Benefits from Existing Brand Names," *Business Horizons* (March/April, 1981), p. 37.

development of Pampers diapers by Procter & Gamble is a good example of a new product of this type. If the product that is developed uses a new brand name, but is introduced into a category where the organization already has products, the new item is called a **flanker brand.** Ralston Purina's Butchers' Blend Dry Dogfood is a flanker to its Dog Chow product line. Kraft has introduced Breyers and Light n' Lively ice cream as flanker brands to its Sealtest ice-cream line. If a firm produces new flavors, sizes, or models using an existing brand name in an existing category, they are called **line extensions.** Sunkist's Diet Sunkist Orange Soda and IBM's hard disk models of its floppy disk personal computer are examples of line extensions. The strategy of continually expanding the line by adding new models has enabled companies like Seiko (watches), Casio (calculators), and Campbell's (soup) to tie up a substantial amount of shelf space and "share of mind" in a product category.

The fourth opportunity is **franchise extension.** A firm introduces a product into a new category, using an existing brand name. Examples of franchise extensions include Honda lawnmowers, John Deere insurance, IBM copiers, and Woolite rug cleaner. This allows the organization to build on the consumer awareness, good will, and image of its established brand name and reduces the amount of money the firm needs to invest in the new product. It quickly conveys to the consumer many of the attributes of the old product, allowing the organization to enter the new category from a position of strength. Consumers' perceptions of the new item must be consistent with their perception of the brand name. Thus, Planters peanut-butter candy is a logical extension of the Planters franchise, but Planters ketchup would not be. There is some risk in franchise extension—the potential dilution of the brand franchise in the long run. For example, brands like General Electric, Quaker, and Gillette have been greatly extended and no longer have the strong consumer associations with specific products that they once had.[8] The Maytag *Marketing in Action* shows how one company has been successful in using flanker brands, line extensions, and new products.

How to fit six Hondas in a two-car garage.
That's easy. Just go to your nearest Honda Power Equipment Dealer and ask about the full line of Hondas you'll never see on the street:
Honda Lawn Tractors. The Hondas you ride on the grass. With our own automatic clutch for smooth shifting. 4-stroke engine standard. And 10HP, or 13HP models available.
Honda Generators. The portable powerplants. In a full line from 500 to 6500W maximum output. All featuring Honda's quiet, efficient engine. Great for running away from home with your favorite appliances. Or running almost anything in the house when the power's down.
Honda Lawn Mowers. The world's most advanced rotary mowers, with the world's most advanced mower engine: The Overhead Valve. Great for durability, fuel economy, size and lightness. Easy to start. Easy to maintain. Easy to operate. Some with Roto-Stop™ for stopping the blade but not the engine. Choose from 3.5HP to 5HP. Side or rear discharge.
Honda Tillers. With the ground-breaking power of Honda's durable 4-stroke engine. Also easy to start, easy to maneuver and easy to buy because there's one for everyone: 2.4HP to 7HP. Front or rear tine. For "city farmer" to professional.
Honda Outboards. For play you don't have to work at. With our popular 4-stroke engine, gas and oil never mix. Oil never burns. No smoky, water-polluting exhaust. Quiet, smooth-running. Greater fuel efficiency. And four models to choose from, from 2HP to 9.9HP.
Honda Snowblowers. As reliable as next winter's snowfall, thanks to Honda's famous Overhead Valve engine—smaller and lighter than any comparable 4-stroke you've known. Ask about "Tracks," a Honda feature for superb traction. From 3.5HP to 7HP. Wheels or tracks. Snowthrower or Snowblower.
HONDA

Equipment shown above are products of American Honda Motor Co., Inc. Advertising created by Dailey & Associates, Los Angeles, CA.

A well-known automotive company, Honda extended its franchise with lawnmowers and snowblowers.

Review Your Marketing Knowledge

- Assume you are appointed head of marketing for your college. Think of five different colleges in your geographical region, and draw a positioning map placing each of these colleges on the map. Which colleges are most similar and compete most directly for the same students?
- How might the college modify its product line?

The Importance of New-Product Development

Our previous discussion of the product life-cycle demonstrated the need for organizations to regularly develop new products to replace the decreasing sales and profits of existing products in the maturity and decline stages of the cycle. Just think of some of the important new products that have been introduced in the past few years, including Lotus 1-2-3 software, Chrysler minivans, Abbott Laboratories' AIDS antibody test, Apple's Macintosh, Kodak's lithium batteries, and Merck's cholesterol-lowering drug, Mevacor. Innovative companies such as 3M and Johnson and Johnson generate more than 25 percent of their sales from products new to the market within the past five years.[9] Johnson and Johnson introduced more than 200 new products in the past five years, but only two of them were "home runs" with sales of over $100 million.

Maytag Brands

Old reliable Maytag Co. was content for years to clean up with its expensive but durable washers and dryers. No more. The acquisition of Magic Chef Inc. has more than doubled Maytag's size and broadened its line dramatically to include virtually every segment of the home-appliance market. The company that characterizes its repairmen as the loneliest guys in town now plans to market some seven diverse brands without diluting the impact of its own well-respected name.

That won't be easy. The hardest part may be that the new Maytag has one tough act to follow: the old Maytag. By focusing on the high end of the washing-machine market and carefully controlling product quality, Maytag regularly got the best rating from Consumers Union for frequency of repair. It also regularly churned out an enviable operating profit margin—20% of sales in 1985. The industry average was about 10%, the same as Magic Chef's.

So why tinker with what didn't seem to be broken? Maytag Chairman Daniel J. Krumm, 60, started out with the company as a sales analyst at headquarters in Newton, Iowa, soon after graduating from the University of Iowa. And he finds it easy enough to see the meaning behind Whirlpool's acquisition of KitchenAid Inc., the dishwasher maker, and AB Electrolux's purchase of White Consolidated Industries. The $11 billion appliance industry is being consolidated, and Maytag has had to get into the act. "Because we were small, we were an easier target for our competition, as well as for unfriendly takeover attempts," Krumm says.

Counterattack. What's more, competitors are invading the premium-priced segment of the market, Maytag's home turf. Whirlpool Corp. has rolled out a full line of appliances under the name of KitchenAid, its new quality brand. General Electric Co. recently introduced its "Monogram" line of appliances for the carriage trade.

In addition to acquiring the necessary bulk to help fend off unwanted suitors, Maytag's acquisition enables it to counterattack in Magic Chef's medium-priced mass market. Magic Chef, the nation's best-selling brand of gas ranges, does a good business with homebuilders. Maytag's sales to builders, who represent 20 percent of the appliance market, have been minuscule.

More important, Magic Chef completes Maytag's line of major appliances. Appliance dealers, who are increasing their clout by banding together in giant buying groups, prefer to negotiate volume deals with manufacturers for a full line of products. Maytag has made dishwashers since 1966 and has also bought Hardwick Stove Co. and premium range maker Jenn-Air Corp. Now Magic Chef gives Maytag what it coveted most: refrigerators, sold under the Magic Chef, Admiral, Norge, and Warwick labels. These appliances accounted for an estimated one-third of major appliance sales last year, and Maytag wants even more of the market. On Jan. 16, the company introduced a refrigerator made by Admiral under the Jenn-Air brand. A refrigerator carrying the Maytag name is due out next year.

In case you lost count, that's six major brands of refrigerators from the same company. Carrying a large number of brand names is likely to test Maytag's marketing savvy. Convincing customers of significant differences in brands made in the same factory is essential. If consumers end up thinking all these items are of the same average quality, then Maytag's own respected brand could be tarnished.

Separate Niches. To protect it, and to maintain brand identities, Krumm has organized the company's appliance business into three highly autonomous divisions: Maytag, Magic Chef, and Admiral. The company will not roll out a Maytag refrigerator, he vows, until it can design a better appliance. "Our philosophy in the merge has been to keep our niches quite separate," he says. "You can't just take an Admiral and slap the Maytag name on it."

Meanwhile, Krumm is trying to get the usual merger turmoil behind him as fast as possible. Maytag has already absorbed all of the deal's one-time costs, which cut into earnings. Charles K. Ryan, an appliance analyst at Merrill Lynch, estimates that Maytag earned $115 million on revenues of about $2 billion in 1986. That's down from the $125 million the companies would have earned if they had been one in 1985. Little wonder that Wall Street's initial enthusiasm, which drove Maytag's stock to a record of nearly 55 after the merger won shareholder approval in May, has cooled. Maytag was trading recently at about 49. As consolidation progresses and Maytag realizes substantial tax savings, however, earnings could easily jump to $145 million this year, according to Ryan.

Less Lonely? Maytag has also moved to restructure its catch. On Jan. 13, Krumm announced the sale of Magic Chef's Toastmaster Inc. small-appliance unit to a group of Toastmaster executives. Krumm has also consolidated repair-parts and service operations. He says he will probably consolidate some manufacturing—component parts, for example—but he won't give specifics.

At least Krumm's customers seem inclined to give him the benefit of any doubts that the merger can succeed. "If any company can do this, Maytag can," says John Bevan, vice-president for appliances and electronics at Montgomery Ward & Co., the biggest retailer of Maytag products. If Krumm markets his new products effectively, his salesmen will escape his repairmen's lonely fate.

SOURCE: "Maytag's New Girth Will Test Its Marketing Muscle" by Kathleen Deveny, reprinted from February 16, 1987 issue of *Business Week* by special permission.

Figure 10–3 Stages in the New-Product Development Process

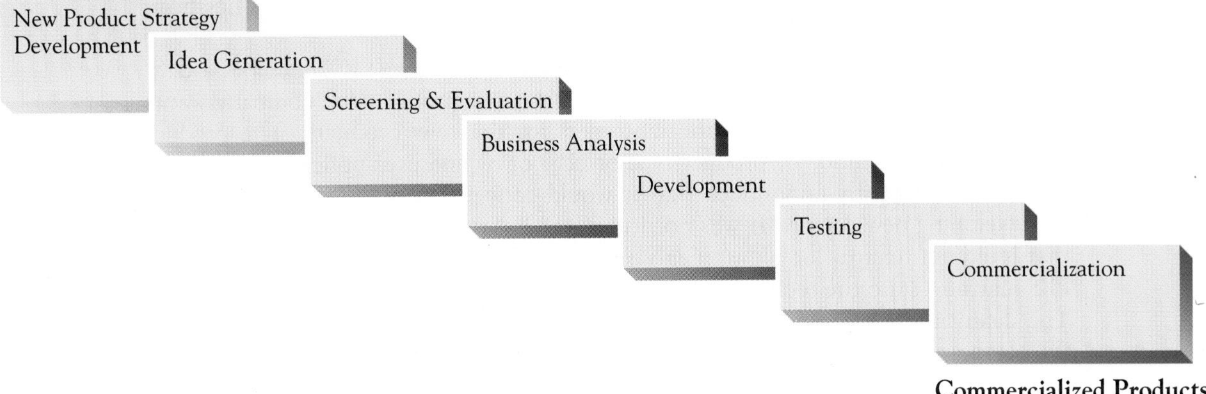

SOURCE: Booz, Allen & Hamilton, Inc.

Most innovative companies work on a portfolio of new products, generating a pipeline with different types of new products in different stages of development. At 3M, for example, about 10 to 15 percent of the new product development budget is spent on improving products in the company's four major product lines. Another 10 to 15 percent is spent on joint projects with manufacturing, pursuing ways to make their products cheaper or better. Slightly more than half the total budget is aimed at finding totally new products both related and unrelated to the company's current lines of business, and the remaining 15 percent is for longer term projects on the technological edge.[10]

New Product News tracks the new products introduced by major consumer products marketers. In the 23 years they have been monitoring this activity, they have reported on over 75,000 new items introduced into U.S. grocery and drug stores. There were 10,182 just in 1987.[11] The next section describes the process used by companies to develop new products.

The Product Development Process

The consulting firm of Booz, Allen & Hamilton has studied the product development process for more than thirty years, conducting numerous studies of the steps companies take to develop new products. The research has found that the most successful developers of new products first clearly define the company's mission, objectives, and overall corporate strategy. They also define the company's commitment to new products and determine the current situation for new products by analyzing the external environment and assessing the company's internal strengths and weaknesses with respect to new product development. Once all this analysis is done, the most common process in product development consists of seven stages: new product strategy development, idea generation, screening and evaluation, business analysis, development, testing, and commercialization (see Figure 10–3).[12]

New Product Strategy Development

The new product strategy is developed after the situation analysis is completed. The major parts of the strategy include the defining of parameters for the new products, the overall goals for the new product activity, and the programs to achieve the goals. The strategy statement containing these parameters, goals, and programs has been called the Product Innovation Charter.[13]

The parameters part of the **Product Innovation Charter** (PIC) includes a definition of the product category or categories for the new products the company wants to develop and a definition of the customers for the new products. The product category may be defined by product type or class or by end use application. Kellogg, for example, recently announced that it would concentrate its new product efforts on developing new cereals. It was not interested in fast food chains, toys, etc. Note that it did not refer to "breakfast meals" or to "products sold by supermarkets."[14] The PIC may also state the technology to be used for the new products to be developed. The definition of customers would typically include a statement outlining whether the company was seeking more business from current users vs. the business from new users. It might define the target customers in terms of demographics, psychographics, or other dimensions.

The goals of the new product activity would typically be stated in terms of growth (rapid vs. controlled), market share (aggressive seeking of an increase vs. protecting current share), and sales and profit targets. Other goals might be to diversify, to add to current product lines, to achieve a certain return on investment, etc.

The last part of the PIC is determining specific programs to achieve the goals. This might include a statement of whether the new product activity is to be primarily market driven (guided by customers or competitors) or technology driven (guided by the firm's technical capabilities). It might state the degree of innovation to be used, pioneering vs. imitative for example. A pioneering strategy usually has a higher payoff, but it is also much riskier than a strategy of imitating competitors. Many firms thus prefer to let their competitors innovate and then try to quickly copy and improve upon the innovation.

Here is an example of a PIC for a hypothetical chemical company:[15] The XYZ Company is committed to a program of innovation in specialty chemicals, as utilized in the automobile and other metal-finishing businesses, to the extent that we will become the market share leader in that market and will achieve at least 35 percent ROI from that program on a three-year payout basis. We seek recognition as the most technically competent company in metal finishing.

These goals will be achieved by building on our current R&D skills and by embellishing them as necessary so as to produce new items that are demonstrably superior technically, in-house, and have only emergency reliance on outside sources. The company is willing to invest funds, as necessary, to achieve these technical breakthroughs, even though 1991 and 1992 net income after tax may suffer.

Care will be taken to establish patent-protected positions in these new developments and to increase the safety of customer and company personnel.

Idea Generation

The idea generation stage consists of searching for new product ideas that are consistent with an organization's objectives. Some new products come from an organization's research and development personnel or from other company employees. Pampers, 3M's Post-it Notes, and Texas Instruments' talking calculators like Speak and Spell are examples of ideas that were generated by company employees.

Table 10–1 Sources of New-Product Ideas

Source	Industrial Products		Consumer Products		Total	
	Number	Percent	Number	Percent	Number	Percent
Research and Development	37	24.3	11	13.9	48	20.8
Internal—Other than Research and Development	55	36.2	25	31.6	80	34.6
Suggestions/Complaints from Users	24	15.8	10	12.7	34	14.7
Formal Research of User Needs	16	10.5	14	17.7	30	13.0
Analysis of Competitors' Products	41	27.0	30	38.0	71	30.7
Analysis of Published Information	12	7.9	9	11.4	21	9.1
Suggestions from Suppliers	19	12.5	3	3.8	22	9.5

NOTE: The percentages in this table are based on the number of products in each category (i.e., industrial products—152; consumer products—79; and total—231). Percentages in each column add to over 100 because more than one source was named for some products. Numbers also add up to more than 152 for industrial products and 79 for consumer products because more than one source was named for some products.

SOURCE: Leigh Lawton and A. Parasuraman, "So You Want Your New Product Planning to Be Productive?" *Business Horizons*, December 1980, p. 31.

Other ideas come directly from customers, either through unsolicited suggestions and complaints or more formal mechanisms. For example, Wang Laboratories added an automatic envelope feeder and addresser to its word-processing machine after suggestions by Wang's customers at the company's annual users' conference. The Pillsbury Bake-Off, started in 1949, has generated thousands of recipe entries by Pillsbury customers. Although the bake-off was intended primarily as a publicity tool, Pillsbury has brought several user-developed products to the marketplace. In some product categories, such as scientific instruments and other high technology industrial products, many products which are originally developed as prototypes by users are later introduced by companies that keep in very close contact with their customers.[16]

At both IBM and Digital Equipment Corporation, executives spend at least thirty days a year in contact with major customers. Both companies also use formal customer-satisfaction and other marketing research surveys to get ideas from customers. At Lanier Business Products, Inc., the twenty top executives in the company each spend at least one day per month making sales calls to keep in touch with consumer needs. Ideas for new products and product improvements are generated by these sales calls. Other sources include suppliers, consultants, distributors, wholesalers, and retailers. Finally, new product ideas are generated by careful analysis of competing products. Table 10–1 shows the sources of new product ideas identified in a study of 152 industrial products and 79 consumer products. Research and development and suggestions from suppliers were more common for the industrial products, whereas analysis of competitors' products and formal research of user needs were relied upon more heavily for consumer goods.[17] Although ideas can come from many sources, it is important for organizations to have a formal process for generating new products.

Screening and Evaluation

Screening and evaluation involve analyzing the ideas developed in the idea generation stage to determine which ones merit more detailed study. Since the later steps in the product development process—from business analysis through testing—can be very expensive, it is important to have this preliminary screening to identify the best ideas from among the many possibilities. During the screening stage, an organization attempts to avoid two types of errors—continuing to evaluate an idea that will not be successful, or discarding an idea that might lead to a successful new product. It is important, therefore, that the criteria used for the screening be neither too rigid nor too loose.

To avoid the two types of errors, many organizations use a screening process that involves several steps. At Texas Instruments, for example, ideas that are rejected during the preliminary screening process can be submitted to the company's IDEA program (for *I*dentify, *D*evelop, *E*xpose, *A*ction). When the inventor of the handheld calculator that could *talk* first proposed the idea in 1976, the idea was rejected as being "too wild."[18] Then one of the forty IDEA representatives within the company gave $25,000 from the IDEA funds to finance the long-shot project. Each of the IDEA representatives can allocate funds, without any other approval, as seed money for projects proposed by lower- and middle-level managers and engineers who don't have the influence to obtain money through the company's other research channels. Although more than half of all IDEA projects fail, sometimes whole new product lines, such as the Speak and Spell learning aid for children, are developed.

New product ideas are often filtered through several successive evaluative tests before they are turned over for business analysis and then for development. One firm's screening process is as follows:[19]

1. *Judgmental Screening.* The firm's new-product department makes the first rough judgment concerning the merits of each idea. Of the several hundred ideas submitted during a typical year, only twenty-five to thirty are selected for further screening.
2. *Preliminary Consumer Reaction Tests.* The ideas that survive the judgmental screening are then tested with small groups of consumers. Each idea is described in a few sentences, and prospective buyers' interest is measured.
3. *Preliminary Marketing Criteria Evaluation.* Each surviving idea is evaluated using criteria determined by management. These considerations include sales volume anticipated, product uniqueness, stage of the life-cycle, amount and type of competition, and inherent consumer appeal. The new ideas are rated on these attributes, and to go to the next stage, an idea must achieve a designated rating level.
4. *Preliminary Feasibility Evaluation.* New product ideas reaching this step are sent to the research and development department, where their feasibility in manufacturing is assessed. Rough estimates are also made of the time and capital expenditures required for development.

It is important for an organization to determine the criteria that will be used to evaluate new ideas. One of the major approaches is to develop checklists to judge specific new product ideas. A checklist used in the very early stage of the screening process would typically compare the new product idea with the objectives set for new products. For example, does the idea fit the type of products the company wants to introduce? Is the production process a required one that the company can perform? Can the item be handled by the existing distribution channels and sales force? Is the potential market for the product large enough, and is the growth rate acceptable? The better the organization has defined the criteria to be used for this preliminary judgment, the easier it will be to screen out unacceptable ideas. Some organizations have separated the screening criteria into two categories—those that must be met, and those that are desirable, but not absolutely required. Table 10–2 presents screening criteria used by Johnson Wax Company.

Table 10–2 Screening Criteria Used by Johnson Wax

Product Criteria	Marketing Criteria	Financial Criteria
• Is it safe • Effect on environment • Fit with existing technology, facilities, and skills • Is it high value added (vs. a commodity) • Is it a significant improvement for consumers • Compatibility with packaging capabilities • Proprietary position • Opportunity for logical extensions • Is labor content average or below • Extended product life-cycle (years vs. months)	• Does it utilize marketing capabilities • Does it utilize existing sales force • Does it have high advertising/promotion content • Opportunity to expand overseas • Use of existing distribution channels • Can establish a leadership role in the market • Not a major investment for consumers • Market growth potential	• Profit potential • Profit-risk ratio • Working capital requirements • Capital requirements average or below • Time required to achieve positive cash flow

SOURCE: Rodger L. DeRose, "New Products—Sifting Through the Haystack," *The Journal of Consumer Marketing*, Summer 1986, pp. 81–84.

The other major part of the screening process is the use of **concept tests.** These consist of reactions from individual consumers or small groups of consumers about new product ideas and concepts. Concept testing is especially relevant for new products that will require a change in consumer purchasing behavior. Concept testing may not be applicable, however, to true innovations—products totally new to the marketplace—since consumers may have difficulty in forming or even understanding the new concepts. Concept tests are helpful in determining the relevant market for a concept, identifying product attributes or benefits that are likely determinants of brand choice, defining how the concept is perceived relative to existing alternatives, describing consumer behavior with respect to the new concept, and predicting consumer preferences.[20]

Business Analysis

At the business analysis stage, the surviving ideas are evaluated according to the organization's requirements for initial estimates of sales, market share, profit, or return on investment. This analysis often requires studies of markets and competition as well as of costs and technical inputs. The purpose of this stage is to obtain a concrete business recommendation about the profitability of implementing the idea. It is important to determine estimates of sales, costs, and profitability before the product moves on to the development stage. If it is apparent that the product will not be able to meet the organization's objectives on these measures, then the considerable development costs can be saved and concentrated instead on products that are more likely to meet stated objectives. The key variables to determine are demand (sales), production and financial requirements, and compatibility with organizational objectives and policies.

Demand. The key to determining demand is the estimation of the total market for the product and its anticipated share. For new products designed for markets with which the company is already familiar, the estimation of the total market demand may be relatively easy. But determining these estimates for products designed for new markets, such as the first home computer, trash compactor, or new chemical process, may be extremely difficult. The manager must not only estimate the sales of the new product, but also must evaluate the probable impact on the organization's other products. In particular, it is important to avoid the cannibalization of the company's other products. **Cannibalization** occurs when sales of a new product come at the expense of sales of other products in the product line. Thus, if Coca-Cola were to introduce a new root beer product, it would want to make sure that the bulk of sales did not come at the expense of the company's Coca-Cola sales.

To estimate sales, some evaluation of the product life-cycle is necessary. Specifically, it is important to analyze four major elements: trial, first repeat, adoption, and frequency of purchase.[21] Early sales are primarily a function of the rate at which consumers try a new product and purchase it again. Over time, sales levels are determined by the proportion of consumers who adopt the product and the frequency with which they purchase it. In order to predict these sales, additional research may be necessary to determine consumer behavior. It is often easier for industrial products because information from a small number of potential customers may be all that is needed to predict these elements.

Production and Financial Requirements. In addition to sales, it is important to have a good estimate of costs to determine the likely profitability of a new product. The more similar the new product is to existing products, the easier it will be to estimate costs. In addition to production costs, it is necessary to estimate capital and marketing costs. If new equipment or production facilities are required, and if substantial marketing costs, such as the establishment of new channels of distribution or extensive promotion requirements will be incurred, accurate estimates of the capital required must be determined. It is important for marketing managers to understand what investment will be required *before* incurring substantial development costs. If it is unlikely the company would be willing to invest the required amount of money, then the new product should not be developed.

Organizational Objectives and Policies. Estimates of sales, costs, and investment then must be examined in light of the organization's objectives and policies. For example, some companies have a policy that all new products can lose money for the first two years, but must break even by the end of the third year and must recoup losses from the first two years by the end of the fifth year. Other organizations may have objectives that require any new product to have a given sales potential (for example, $1 million). Still other firms may have a policy that only allows development of products that are likely to have a return on investment greater than 20 percent (or some other target number). Some organizations only look at profitability, others use return on investment, and still others discount cash flows to determine the present value of alternative new product opportunities.

Development

After a product has made it through the business analysis stage, it then enters the development stage. Here the research and development personnel (R&D), often with the help of engineers, will fabricate the actual product, transforming it from merely an idea or concept into a prototype model. At the same time, a tentative marketing mix is developed, including the package and label, brand name, advertising message, and distribution strategy.

At the development stage, the product's technical feasibility is determined. The product should be able to be produced at a cost that will enable it to be marketed at an acceptable price to the consumer. The development stage often requires a large investment; it is not unusual to spend millions of dollars developing a new product, and many products take years to develop. For example, it took ten years for Crest toothpaste, eighteen years for Minute Rice, fifteen years for the Polaroid Colorpack camera, fifty-five years for television, and fifteen years for Xerox copying machines.[22] One reason the process takes so long is that a prototype must be built and tested with consumers, then a revised version may be developed and then tested again with consumers. This process may occur a number of times, until the firm develops a product which meets consumer needs, or until the project is abandoned.

The development process works best when the members of the research and development group are guided by marketing and financial considerations. They should be provided with a detailed description of the product concept and the customer so that they will have some idea of the target market. Members should receive a clear statement of the benefits desired by the consumers and the relative importance of each benefit. They also need to be told about pricing and cost targets and needed variations in style, size, or flavors. Finally, they should know about the probable channels of distribution and how the product will be shipped. The more information that marketing provides, the more likely it will be that the product developed will meet the needs of the target consumers, at an acceptable price.

An increasingly important aspect of development is product safety. The Consumer Product Safety Act of 1972 created the Consumer Product Safety Commission with broad powers to mandate safety standards for virtually all consumer products. Manufacturers are required to conduct a "reasonable testing program" to insure that their products conform to established safety standards. In addition, the law of product liability has been changing in recent years. The old rules held manufacturers and sellers liable only when they were negligent, or unreasonably careless, in what they made or how they made it. Today the courts are using a much tougher standard, called *strict liability*. Under this concept, if a defect in a product is legally established, the manufacturer is liable, regardless of the precautions taken.[23]

Manufacturers must anticipate the hazards and injuries that can occur when consumers use products inappropriately. For example, a teenager, trying to scent a candle, poured perfume made by Fabergé over a lighted wick. The perfume ignited and burned a friend's neck. The friend won a $27,000 judgment against Fabergé, because the company had failed to warn consumers of the perfume's flammability. Fabergé lost the appeal when the court rejected its argument that there was no way to foresee that someone would pour perfume onto an open flame.[24]

Testing

After the product and marketing programs have been developed, they are usually subjected to testing in the marketplace. A **test market** is the limited introduction of a product and marketing program, under controlled conditions, to determine its probable sales and profits. It is the first chance to see how the product will perform in the actual marketplace. A test market reduces the probability of bringing out a new product that will eventually fail under normal marketing conditions. In other words, it reduces the risk of introducing the new product on a national basis.

Another reason for test marketing is to learn how to market the new product most effectively. For example, Vaseline Intensive Care Lotion was tested in three

Table 10–3 List of 25 Most Frequently Used Test Markets

Albany, NY	Ft. Wayne, IN	Roanoke, VA
Albuquerque, NM	Fresno, CA	Rockford, IL
Binghamton, NY	Grand Rapids, MI	San Antonio, TX
Boise, ID	Green Bay, WI	South Bend, IN
Charleston, SC	Lexington, KY	Spokane, WA
Corpus Christi, TX	Omaha, NE	Syracuse, NY
Des Moines, IA	Peoria, IL	Tucson, AZ
Erie, PA	Portland, ME	Wichita, KS
Evansville, IN		

SOURCE: "A Telling Look at the 25 Most Frequently Used Test Markets," Erie, PA: *Times Publishing Company*, 1987.

markets. In two of the markets advertising was used, and in the third market, a combination of advertising and sampling was tried. The greater success in the third market led the company to introduce the product nationally using a combination of sampling and advertising.[25] At this stage of the new-product development process, the organization can test variations in the product or in the marketing mix, including alternative names, prices, and advertising budgets or messages. Depending upon the results of the test market, the product can be introduced nationally, withdrawn, or sent back to the product development stage for modifications in the product or marketing program.

Test marketing is very expensive and time-consuming. It is not at all unusual for market testing to cost well over $1 million. The length of time required creates a risk that the competition will find out about the new product, imitate it quickly, and enter the national market before the lengthy test market has even been completed. Therefore, in many situations, companies choose to skip this test market stage and directly enter a regional or national market. This is likely to happen if the company has considerable experience in the market for the new product, if the total investment is not large, if the production capacity is available, and if the brand name is already well known.[26] If the new product represents a "new business" to the company and is completely new or different enough to require a change in the buying behavior of consumers, test marketing is likely to be conducted. Sometimes a compromise, in the form of a simulated test market, constructed in a storelike laboratory, is used instead of a full test market.

In choosing where to test a new product, it is important to select "typical" markets. This means that the population in the cities selected should be representative of the national market—with respect to the product category—for such demographic characteristics as age, income, occupation, and buying habits. The competing products should be as similar as possible to those in the national marketplace, and the media available should also be representative. It is helpful if the test market city is relatively isolated, giving the firm better control of the distribution and media exposure, as well as making it more difficult for competitors to disrupt the test. In addition, it is important that the market have retailers who will cooperate. Finally, the market should have research services that can collect the necessary information to evaluate the success of the new product on such measures as new-product awareness, trial, repeat buying, attractiveness to different market segments, and whether

Table 10–4 Results of Simulated Test Markets

Action Taken After STM	Percent
Introduced it nationally	14
Test marketed, then went national	12
Test marketed, then discontinued	14
Recycled (changed, then another simulated test market)	16
Discontinued	44
	100

SOURCE: Jack Honomichl, "Buyouts Continue at Record Pace," *Advertising Age*, July 18, 1988, p. 24.

new-product sales are cutting into those of the company's other products or into those of the competition. Table 10–3 lists, in alphabetical order, the test market cities that are used most frequently.

As a reaction to the increased cost of traditional test markets, several additional means of market testing have been developed recently. The "controlled" test market, also called a "mini-market" or "forced distribution" test, consists of a testing program managed by a research company which guarantees distribution of the test product in stores in the test market cities. They warehouse the product, sell it to the trade, stock the shelves, and monitor sales on a regular basis. The results are obtained more quickly because the guaranteed distribution allows the start of the advertising and promotion two weeks after the start of the test. A traditional test market with regular distribution channels takes 60–90 days (and even then you are not sure that you will obtain the needed level of distribution). As a result, most controlled test markets can be completed within six months, at one-third to one-half the cost of a full blown test market. A disadvantage of the controlled test market, however, is the inferior information on the trade reaction, a result of the distribution being handled by the research firm (which pays the stores for the distribution) instead of by the company's own sales force.

A relatively new method for market testing new products is the simulated test market (STM). With STM, individuals are exposed to the new product's advertising, given samples of the product, and presented with an opportunity to buy (or rebuy) the product. Different research suppliers use different methodologies and procedures, but the purpose of the STM is to predict the awareness, trial, and repeat purchase levels for the product, thus simulating an actual test market. A typical STM takes 6–12 weeks, and costs about $50,000. It offers the added benefit of security, as it is hard for competitors to know that a new product is being tested. The disadvantages include inability to read the trade's reaction, and unreliability, since it is not conducted in actual stores. Thus STM's tend to be used where the risk is minor. If the risk is greater, controlled or full test markets are used after the STM (see Table 10–4).

Commercialization

Only about half the new products entering a test market show results justifying full **commercialization**—the introduction of the product into the marketplace. According to a study by Booz, Allen & Hamilton in 1968, it took fifty-eight ideas to yield one successful new product.[27] Some of the ideas are rejected at each stage of the product development process, as shown in Figure 10–4. In 1981, the company updated

Figure 10–4 Mortality of New-Product Ideas (By Stages of Evolution)

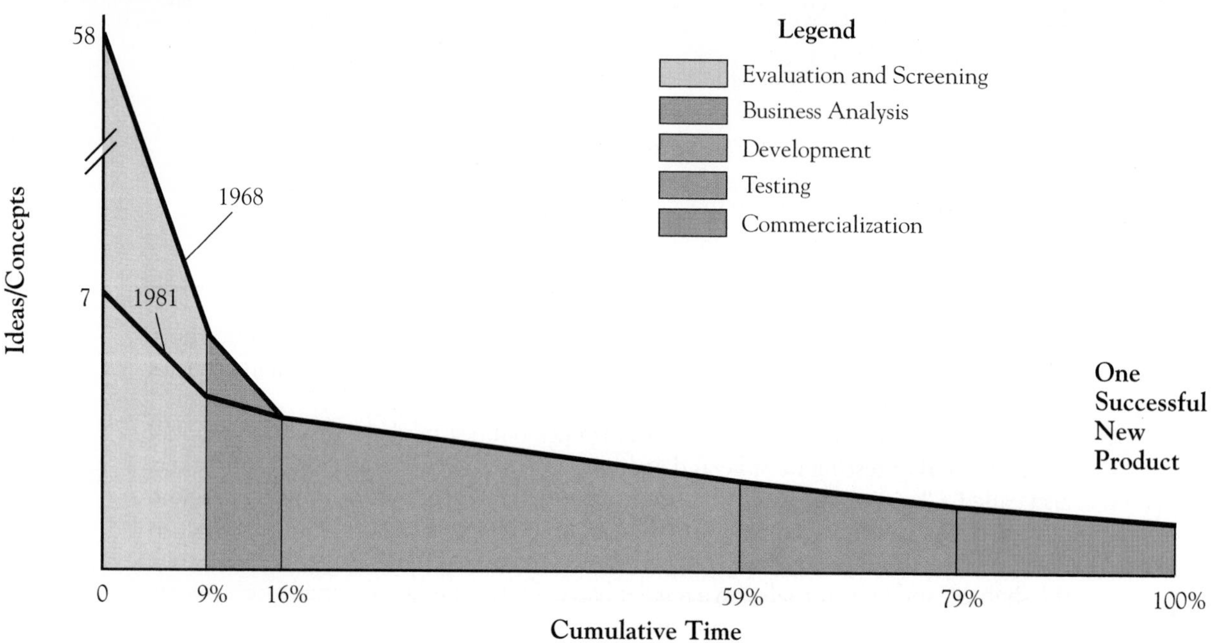

SOURCE: Booz, Allen & Hamilton, "More New Products Die Aborning than in 1968," *Marketing and Media Decisions*, May 1982, p. 48.

the study by contacting 700 companies and found that an average of only seven ideas were required for every successful new product.[28] Booz, Allen & Hamilton attributes this dramatic improvement to the increasingly sophisticated way that companies develop new products, doing a better job at the very early stages of identifying areas for new product development; thus they can concentrate all their efforts on those ideas that have the highest potential for success.

With better concept and product testing and evaluation at the earlier stages, there should be greater success at the commercialization stage, which can be an extremely expensive stage. New manufacturing facilities often must be opened, large amounts of inventory must be produced to supply the channels of distribution, and the introductory advertising and sales promotion costs often exceed $10 million during the first year. In addition, service facilities may have to be developed, spare parts produced, and expensive sales training undertaken before the new product can be introduced. A thorough plan must be developed, indicating who will do what, when, where, and how.

Because of the great expense, a new product will often be introduced using a regional "roll-out" strategy. A **roll out** is the introduction of the new product into one region at a time. Thus, it might take perhaps two years before the product is available nationally. With a regional roll out, a company's risks and capital requirements are reduced. Cash generated from sales in one region can be used to finance the introduction of the product into other regions.

After the introduction has taken place, the results must be carefully monitored. Consumer research may identify improvements that should be made in the product.

Table 10–5 Success Rates for Major New Products

Percent of Successful New Products	Percent of Companies Selling Primarily to	
	Industrial Markets	**Consumer Markets**
All succeeded	9	18
90 to 99%	7	4
80 to 89%	16	9
70 to 79%	11	11
60 to 69%	16	12
50 to 59%	15	15
40 to 49%	4	2
30 to 39%	9	9
1 to 29%	5	4
None succeeded	8	16
	100	100

NOTE: The success rate reported by each company represents the percentage of all *major* new products introduced to the market by the company during the previous five years which subsequently met management's expectations in all important respects.

SOURCE: David S. Hopkins, *New Product Winners and Losers* (The Conference Board, 1980), p. 6.

Also, opportunities may exist for the introduction of new sizes, flavors, or styles. It may be profitable to direct the product or a revised version of it to new market segments, perhaps with a different marketing program.

Review Your Marketing Knowledge

- You have been appointed to a new job, head of new product development, at your University. How might you go about generating ideas for new products and programs that the university might offer?
- How would you screen and evaluate these ideas? What kinds of information would you want to obtain for a business analysis of the potential new products or programs?

Why New Products Fail or Succeed

There is no standard definition for a new product's success or failure, but a new product can be called successful if it meets management's original expectations in all important respects. If it does not meet management's original expectations, it can be defined as a failure.[29] Using these definitions, one study of 148 major companies found that half of them achieved success with at least two-thirds of the new products they had introduced in the previous five years.[30] Table 10–5 contains the results of the study. Overall, the success rates for the industrial marketers were comparable to those of the consumer marketers.

Another major study, completed in 1981, reported that 35 percent of new products were unsuccessful, when success was determined by each company's own criteria.[31] When success was defined as a product still on the market, only 23 percent of the new products introduced in the previous five years were classified as failures. There are several other interesting findings:[32]

- One-third of all companies do not measure the performance of new products in a formal way. Those that do use sales volume, profits, and/or return on investment to measure success.
- Companies with successful new products do not spend any more as a percentage of sales on research and development and promotion of new products than companies who have unsuccessful products.
- Each time a company doubles its number of new products, the cost per new-product introduction drops 29 percent. Interestingly, there is no correlation between the number of new products and the percentage classified as successful.

Virtually no company expects a 100 percent success rate. In the words of the marketing vice president for an office supplies manufacturer, "To target a new-product development program to expect a 100 percent success rate would be counterproductive—extreme conservatism would rule with very few, if any, projects reaching fruition."[33] Firms may have to accept a certain percentage of new products failing as the cost of increasing the probability of successfully introducing innovative new products into the marketplace. Companies strive to minimize the cost of their failures and to maximize the amount they learn from these failures.

Failure Factors

Nine factors are most often mentioned as the major causes contributing to the failure of new products.[34] Examples of new product failures resulting from these causes are presented in the *Marketing in Action* feature on the Museum of New Products.

Lack of Product Uniqueness or Superiority. Virtually every study of new-product failures identifies the lack of meaningful product uniqueness as the major cause of failure. As shown in the study in Table 10–6, 74 percent of the successful new products offered the consumer better performance at the same or higher price, compared to only 20 percent of the failures. Eighty percent of the failures, on the other

Table 10–6 Performance Differences Between New Product Successes and Failures

Difference from Competitor	Percent of 50 Successes	Percent of 50 Failures
Significantly Better Performance, Higher Price	44	8
Marginally Better Performance, Higher Price	6	12
Better Performance, Same Price	24	0
Same Performance, Lower Price	8	0
Same Performance, Same Price	16	30
Same Performance, Higher Price	2	30
Worse Performance, Same or Higher Price	0	20
Total	100	100

SOURCE: J. Hugh Davidson, "Why Most New Consumer Brands Fail," *Harvard Business Review*, March-April 1976, p. 119.

MARKETING IN ACTION

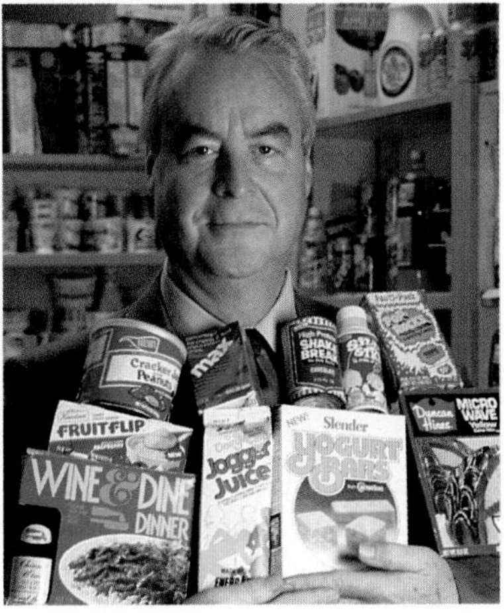

Museum Houses Shattered Dreams

The literature describes it rather grandly as a museum of shattered dreams, but anyone who chances on the converted granary here might think it is a sort of supermarket of the absurd. From soup to nuts, the shelves are packed with an immense range of products that eventually lost favor with consumers or, in a number of cases, never won it.

The Museum of New Products [its official title] is the property of Marketing Intelligence Service, a company that monitors products in test markets for some of the nation's leading packaged goods manufacturers. Although only 5000 products are on display at any one time, including successes as well as failures, there are some 75,000 different items in the museum's storerooms.

The museum's shelves provide an intriguing view of the lifestyles, diets, and fads of America during the last two decades that Robert McMath, the company's chairman, has been collecting new products. And the panoply of expensive flops—and, for that matter, of improbable successes—is testimony to the vagaries and unpredictability of the consumer.

Here is Singles, Gerber Products' food-in-a-jar that failed because consumers apparently associated it with baby food. "As I understand it, it was very tasty, but it was probably a marketing and packaging problem," said Steven Poole, a Gerber's spokesperson. Not only was the glass jar off-putting, he suggested, but so was the pitch that "it was for singles when they have to eat alone, which reminded them that they were alone."

There was a host of reasons for the failure of Scott Paper's Raggedy Ann and Raggedy Andy disposable diapers, color-coded and tailored for each sex; the girl's had thicker padding in the middle, the boy's had more padding up front. "It was a great idea," McMath said, but the stores refused to double the shelf space available to Scott. The company agrees that was a problem, but says that the diaper's main flaw was that it lacked a plastic backing and thus necessitated baby pants.

One of the costliest failures on the shelves here is New Cookery, a line by Nestle of some three dozen low-everything [salt, sugar, starch, fat] canned goods. New Cookery may have failed, McMath hypothesized, because the cream-colored packaging was simply too bland and its name suggested work; in contrast, the successful Lean Cuisine line connotes taste and trimness.

Another inspired idea whose time never came was Wine and Dine, a packaged dinner from Heublein that included a bottle of cooking wine [Chianti or Burgundy for the beef, Chablis for the chicken]. "A lot of people thought it was for drinking," said Richard Lawrence, Marketing Intelligence's president. "It wasn't clear until they read the fine print." Wine & Dine never got out of the test market.

SOURCE: Sandra Salmans, "Museum Houses Shattered Dreams," *Chicago Tribune,* March 10, 1985.

---

hand, had the same performance as brands already on the market, at the same or higher price, while less than one in five of the successes were characterized this way.[35]

A frequent reason for the introduction of products that are not unique or superior is insufficient or faulty marketing research. After a product has failed to meet its expectations, marketers often confess to "a serious misreading" of consumer needs, "too little field testing," or "overly optimistic forecasts of market need and acceptance."[36] Marketers and engineers, on occasion, simply decide what the marketplace wants without asking potential customers about their needs. This obviously can lead to disaster.

Poor Planning. The second most frequently mentioned reason for new product failure is poor planning.[37] Included here is poor positioning and segmentation, underbudgeting, poor overall themes, overpricing, and inadequate handling of all other facets of a plan. Again, the lack of adequate marketing research is often the reason why prices are set higher than consumers will pay and distribution or promotional efforts are inadequate or misdirected.

Improper Timing. In many cases of new-product failure, companies have been too slow or too fast in developing the new product, resulting in a poorly timed introduction. An example is the $25,000 DeLorean sports car that was introduced at the exact time that the economy was entering a downturn. Often, a new product will be hustled to the marketplace to meet or beat a competitive product. Sometimes the new product is not ready for introduction, having skipped some of the important steps of the development process.

Technical Problems. Sometimes the product has design problems, technical difficulties, or manufacturing deficiencies that contribute to its failure. Numerous products have had to be recalled from the marketplace because of unforeseen technical problems. Sometimes it is just impossible to produce the product in the huge quantities necessary to serve a large marketplace, and the quality produced is not the same as it was during the test market. Also, problems at the new production facility can doom a new product to failure.

Loss of Objectivity. Often the people involved in the new-product development process lose their objectivity. As a result, the firm may do inadequate marketing research on the size of the product's total market. Also, the managers may overestimate the product's benefits to consumers. People tend to fall in love with their new products, having invested so much time and effort in creating it. It is difficult to retain objectivity. Thus RCA marketers didn't recognize that consumers didn't value the high quality videodisc player as much as the videocassette player which could record TV programs off the air as well as play prerecorded movies. RCA lost $500 million on the videodisc player.

Unexpected High Product Cost. Sometimes production costs are greatly underestimated, making it impossible for the new product to generate a profit at the originally intended price. One alternative is to raise the price, but this may yield a market price above what customers are willing to pay. Consider what happened to a large machinery producer:

> *The problem developed while our new product was on exhibit. Many people liked what they saw—with the qualifications that just a few more functional capabilities would enhance its salability. Unfortunately, we listened to too many suggestions and proceeded to adapt additional features to the product. Its original $55,000 selling price became $80,000 as a result of these added features. We found the $80,000 product put us in a more unfavorable competitive position than if we had left it in its $55,000 configuration. The lesson learned was not to overengineer a product once it is developed for its specific market need.*[38]

Competition. Underestimating the effect of competitive actions can also contribute to new-product failure. Specifically, competitors may lower their prices, increase their promotional efforts, or take other defensive actions that may inhibit sales of the new product. An example is the Datril vs. Tylenol case where Datril failed to anticipate Tylenol's price reduction, which effectively eliminated Datril's main advantage.

Company Politics. On occasion, the politics within an organization may require it to introduce a new product—to meet company objectives for introducing new products, for example. In other cases, a new product may fail because no one within the organization had enough interest in the new product or enough clout to harness the resources necessary for a successful introduction.

Government. On occasion, government action may inhibit the sale of a new product, causing it to fail. Several tire companies have been forced by the National Highway Traffic Safety Administration to recall new tire products from the marketplace.

Success Factors

A recent investigation into the factors that separate successful and unsuccessful products tested a number of variables proposed by leading experts. The research, based on over 200 new product introductions, identified nine factors leading to successful new products. The three of the nine factors most strongly related to success were:[39]

1. *Product advantage.* The product offered unique features for the customer; was higher quality; reduced customers' costs; was innovative; was superior to competing products in the eyes of the customer; and solved a problem faced by the customer.
2. *Proficiency of predevelopment activities.* Undertaking proficiently a set of "up-front" activities, namely initial screening; preliminary market assessment; preliminary technical assessment; detailed market study or marketing research; and business/financial analysis.
3. *Protocol.* There was a clear definition, prior to the product development stage, of the target market; customers' needs, wants, and preferences; the product concept; and product specifications and requirements.

There were five other important success factors, including:

- having technical and production skills
- proficiency of market-related activities, including marketing research and marketing communications skills
- having a good fit between the project and the company's resources and R&D skills
- being in a large, high-need, growth market
- having a good fit with respect to marketing resources and skills, including distribution and sales force.

Top management support was also important, but this also seemed to be related to a number of the failures as well.

Product superiority, in terms of unique benefits for consumers, innovativeness, quality, and superiority in the eyes of customers, was found to be the number one factor in new product success. The proper management of the product development process, especially the early stages, was also vital to developing successful new products. These variables are within the control of marketing managers, and thus the success or failure of new products can be influenced by following the procedures.

Quality Issues in Marketing

In marketing, the word quality is used in many ways. However, a standard definition has been adopted world wide after many years of study and negotiation. *Quality* has now been defined as:

> *The totality of features and characteristics of a product or service that bears on its ability to satisfy stated or implied needs.*[40]

Quality and Productivity

In his book *Quality Is Free,* Phil Crosby states that building quality into a product does not cost the company more because of the savings in rework, scrap, and servicing the product after the sale, as well as the benefits of customer satisfaction and repeat sales. He states further that if features are added to improve fitness for use, fewer repairs are necessary, and the customer is pleased. Even though adding a feature may require a manufacturer to charge a premium price, the product cost over its lifetime may really be lowered.[41] IBM, Caterpillar, Michelin, Procter and Gamble, and Ford are some of the many companies that use this concept of quality in their overall strategy.

Marketing Responsibilities for Quality

A company's marketing department can perform a number of functions that will enhance quality as perceived by customers. Renowned quality consultants Feigenbaum, Crosby, Deming, and Juran all state that marketing departments have important functions in the achievement of product and service quality, as noted in the following actions.[42]

Product Development. Nothing will damage a customer's perception of quality more than receiving a finished product that does not satisfy its intended use. When a product is first ordered, a customer may not know all of the characteristics needed. This is especially true of complex equipment. Marketing people often have the most direct contact with customers. They can raise questions with customers to help ascertain all of the requirements and product characteristics wanted. These can then be brought to the design engineer's attention.

Marketing Personnel and Quality. When a product goes into production, the sales and marketing staff can take on certain responsibilities during the course of regular sales and marketing efforts. The careful salesperson can accurately determine a customer's requirements so that the correct product is purchased. If the intended use requires a modified design, the salesperson or product manager can make the engineer aware of these needs, sometimes arranging for the engineer to visit the customer personally. Any product limitations or potential problems can be brought to the attention of the user at that time. Potential problems should be recognized at this time, rather than after delivery. Firms such as IBM, Xerox, ITT, and Caterpillar attribute their success to providing quality products and services. The Japanese success has been attributed largely to the marketing of high-quality products that meet the customers' needs and desires.

Timely order processing and delivery fall into the category of quality and service as viewed by the customer. When products are delivered to the customer, sales personnel can ensure that instruction manuals are available, technical assistance is provided, and other needs are met. The marketing department can ensure that warnings accompany products to highlight any possible dangers when the product is used either as intended or in a forseeably unintended way.

After Delivery. Marketing personnel have important quality responsibilities after the customer has been using the product. Many companies use their service reputation as a prime selling point for their products. Rather than waiting for complaints, salespeople actively solicit feedback on product performance from their customers and report back to those responsible for product quality and improvement. Successful

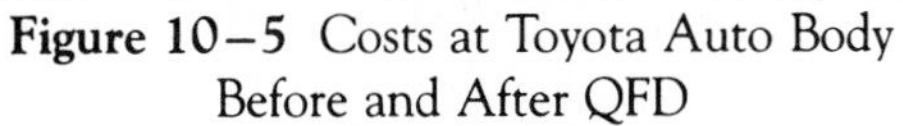

Figure 10–5 Costs at Toyota Auto Body Before and After QFD

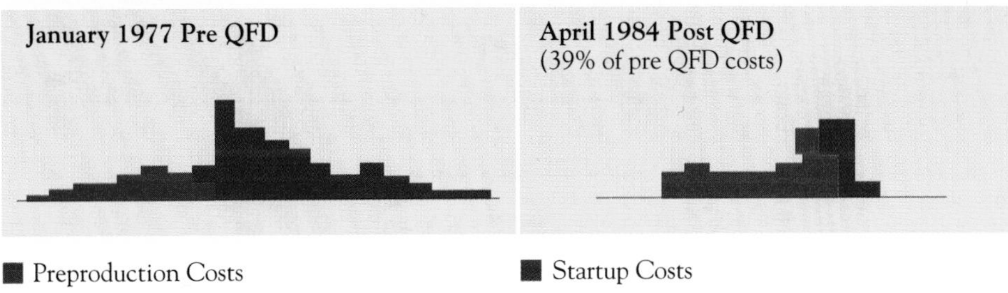

■ Preproduction Costs ■ Startup Costs

SOURCE: Lawrence P. Sullivan, "Quality Function Deployment," *Quality Progress*, June 1986, p. 39. © 1986 American Society for Quality Control. Reprinted by permission.

companies emphasize prompt action and response to customer complaints. Marketing people can actively participate in a corrective program to ensure that a customer is satisfied.

Quality Function Deployment: The "Quality House" Appproach

Quality Function Deployment, better known as QFD, is a Japanese-designed quality control system that implements these ideas. QFD is a set of planning and communication routines that focus and coordinate skills within an organization, first to design, then to manufacture and market goods that customers want to purchase and will continue to purchase. QFD's main design tool is "the house of quality." The house of quality is based on the belief that products should be designed to reflect customer desires and tastes—so marketing people, design engineers, and manufacturing staff must work together from the time a product is first conceived.[43]

By first examining customer needs and then designing across corporate functions, manufacturers can reduce prelaunch time and after-launch tinkering. Figure 10–5 compares startup and preproduction costs at Toyota Auto Body in 1977, before QFD, to those costs in 1984, when QFD was well under way. Early house of quality meetings reduced costs by more than 60 percent.[44]

Figure 10–6 shows a simplified version of the house of quality. This design tool is a conceptual map that provides a means for interfunctional planning and communications. A succession of steps must be undertaken to construct the "house."[45]

Determine what the customers want. The products and product characteristics that customers require are called customer attributes or CAs. CAs are usually reproduced in the customers' own words to minimize translation errors. They can be determined by both formal and informal consumer research and are often ranked into bundles of related attributes. In Figure 10–6, "water leaks," "wind noise," and "road noise" are all bundled under "Sealing." "Customers" are not limited to end-users. CAs can include the demands of regulators ("safe in a side collision"), the needs of retailers ("easy to display"), the requirements of vendors ("satisfy assembly and service organizations"), and so forth.[46] CAs are built into the left side of the house and listed along the array's vertical axis.

Figure 10–6 The "Quality House" Approach

Section of a quality function development table used to design a car door. The grid shows relationship between the requirements of a quality door and the features necessary to achieve the quality. For example, the blue symbol in the first line reflects a strong relationship between a door that does not leak and the seal material used. The "roof" shows where relationships between two quality features conflict or coincide.

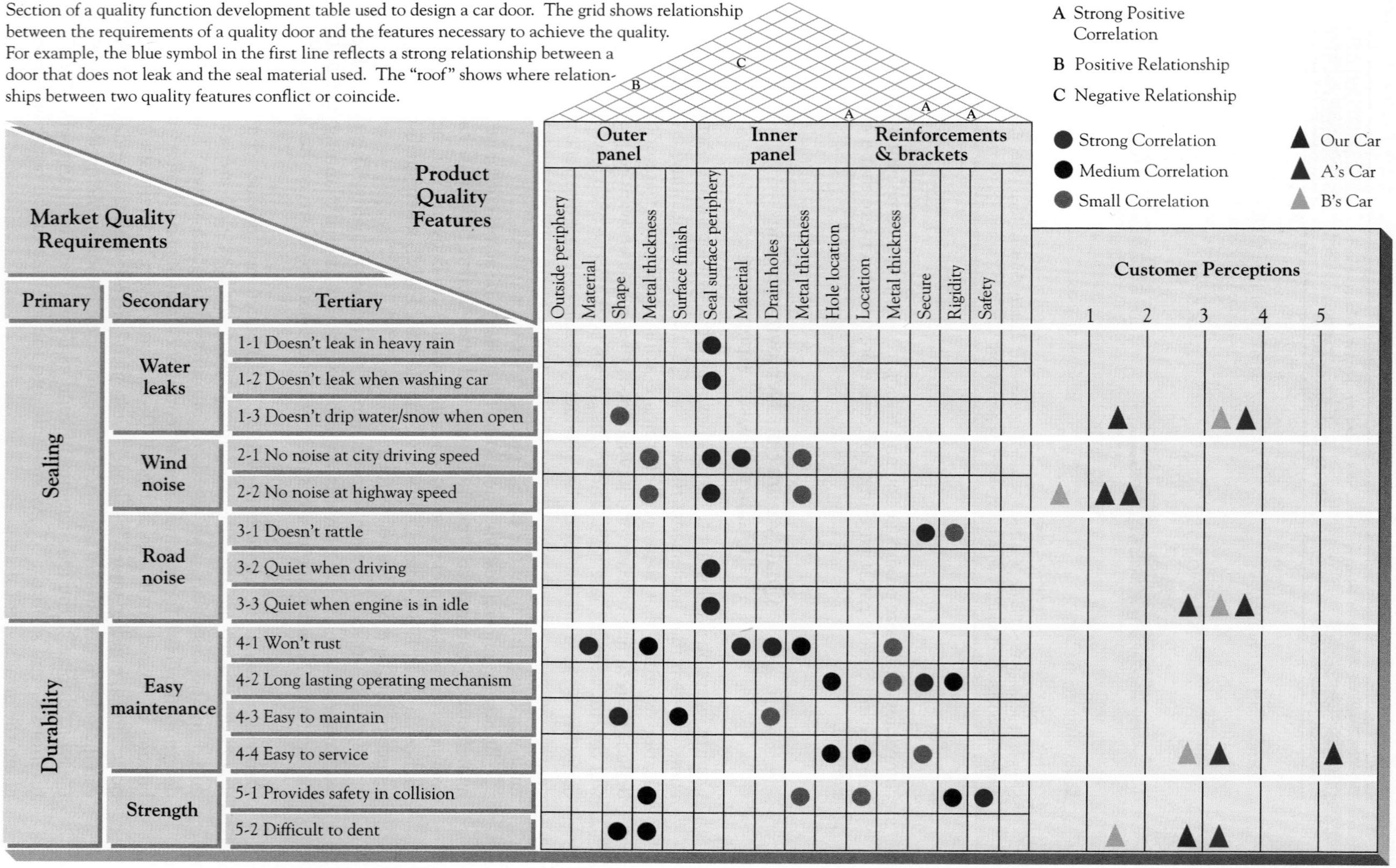

A Strong Positive Correlation
B Positive Relationship
C Negative Relationship

Strong Correlation
Medium Correlation
Small Correlation

Our Car
A's Car
B's Car

Market Quality Requirements

Product Quality Features

Outer panel: Outside periphery, Material, Shape, Metal thickness, Surface finish

Inner panel: Seal surface periphery, Material, Drain holes, Metal thickness, Hole location

Reinforcements & brackets: Location, Metal thickness, Secure, Rigidity, Safety

Customer Perceptions: 1, 2, 3, 4, 5

Primary	Secondary	Tertiary
Sealing	Water leaks	1-1 Doesn't leak in heavy rain
		1-2 Doesn't leak when washing car
		1-3 Doesn't drip water/snow when open
	Wind noise	2-1 No noise at city driving speed
		2-2 No noise at highway speed
	Road noise	3-1 Doesn't rattle
		3-2 Quiet when driving
		3-3 Quiet when engine is in idle
Durability	Easy maintenance	4-1 Won't rust
		4-2 Long lasting operating mechanism
		4-3 Easy to maintain
		4-4 Easy to service
	Strength	5-1 Provides safety in collision
		5-2 Difficult to dent

SOURCE: Adapted from *The New York Times*, January 5, 1989, p. B1.

Rank preferences. While creative solutions can sometimes be found that meet all needs, designers usually have to trade off one benefit against another. CAs are assigned weights according to the relative importance they hold for the customer. Weights are indicated by numbers or percentages or by the order in which the CAs are listed.

Determine if delivering perceived needs will yield a competitive advantage. Customer evaluations of competitors can be matched against a company's own ratings. "Conceptual maps," such as the one on the far right in Figure 10–6, which uses a 5-point rating scale, are one way to visually display these comparisons. Comparisons with competitive product offerings can identify opportunities for advantage in the marketplace. Figure 10–6 shows that our car is rated worst in leaking in heavy rain, indicating an area for improvement.

Determine how the product can be changed. While marketing tells us *what* to do with the product, the engineering domain tells us *how* to do it. Along the flat top of the house of quality, below the roof, the design team lists those engineering characteristics (ECs) that are likely to affect one or more of the customer attributes.[47] In Figure 10–6, these include various aspects of the outer panel, the inner panel, and the reinforcement and brackets.

Determine how much engineers influence customer-perceived qualities. The engineering team uses symbols or numbers to establish the strengths of these relationships. In Figure 10–6, the triangle symbol at the intersection of "material" and "won't rust" indicates that the chance that the door will rust strongly depends on the material with which the outer panel is made.

Determine how one engineering change will affect other characteristics. The "roof" shows where relationships between two quality features conflict or coincide. The letter "C" in figure 10–6 indicates a conflict between the door's shape and the location of the reinforcements and brackets. The roof is often the most critical information for engineers because it can be used to balance necessary trade-offs between CAs and ECs.

The Value of the House

The house of quality charts are prepared by a group that includes marketing and manufacturing specialists as well as engineers and designers. The house helps the team set targets. For engineers, it is a way to summarize basic data in usable form. For marketing executives, it represents the customer's voice. General managers use it to discover strategic opportunities. Perhaps most importantly, the house encourages all of these groups to work together to understand one another's priorities and goals, and to satisfy the customer.[48]

Personal Computer Exercise

Screening and evaluating new product ideas are important parts of the new product development process. This PC exercise provides you with an opportunity to make a variety of assessments concerning a new product and to see the implications of these assessments on the attractiveness of the new product concept. Depending on the weights you assign to each factor, you may change your decision on whether or not to pursue the idea.

KEY POINTS

• Product positioning—the place a product occupies in consumers' minds relative to those of competitors—is an important aspect of product strategy. Positioning can be based on specific product features, benefits, usage occasions, user categories, and competitive products, among other factors.

• Individual products can be modified by changing their position, physical characteristics, package, brand, or the amount and nature of value added. In addition, the set of products within a product line can be altered by expanding or reducing the product line or by changing its composition.

• In addition to developing new brands in product categories new to the organization, there are often opportunities for flanker brands, line extensions, and franchise extensions.

• New products are essential for organizations that want to grow. The rate of new product introductions has been increasing.

• The new product development process consists of seven stages: new product strategy development, idea generation, screening and evaluation, business analysis, development, testing, and commercialization.

• The Product Innovation Charter (PIC), defining the goals, product categories, and customers sought by the firm, is a key part of the new product strategy development stage of the process.

• New product ideas are generated from research and development personnel, other company employees, customers, suppliers, consultants, distributors, and retailers. A formal process for generating new product ideas is critical for new product success.

• New product ideas are screened to determine if the idea fits the type of products the organization wants to introduce. Other screening criteria include market size and growth, technical feasibility, fit with existing facilities and skills, and projected return on investment. Consumer concept tests are often used to help answer some of these questions.

• At the business analysis stage, trial, first-repeat purchase, adoption, and frequency of purchase are estimated to determine probable demand. The product's anticipated production and financial requirements and its compatibility with the firm's objectives and policies are evaluated.

• At the development stage, the product is transformed from merely an idea or concept into a prototype model. At the same time, a tentative marketing program is developed. The development stage often requires a large investment and may take a number of years to complete. An increasingly important aspect of product development is product safety and liability.

• Test markets help reduce the probability of introducing new products that fail. They are also used to learn how to market new products most effectively. But companies sometimes decide not to use them, particularly if there is a risk that competing firms will find out about the new product and imitate it quickly. Controlled test markets and simulated test markets are used when the risk is lower. They are quicker and less expensive than traditional test marketing.

• New products can be defined as successful if they meet management's objectives. Using this definition, about two-thirds of new products are successful.

• New products tend to fail if they are not unique or superior to competing products. Other factors contributing to new product failure are poor planning, improper timing, technical problems, lack of objectivity, high costs, competition, company politics, and government actions.

• Product advantage, proficiency of predevelopment activities, and a protocol describing the target market and product specifications are key factors leading to success with new products.

• The quality of a product's development and management is a major factor in that product's success or failure. Quality reflects the product's ability to satisfy customer needs. Marketing personnel can play a key role in achieving product and service quality.

• Quality Function Deployment is a Japanese-designed quality control system which coordinates diverse skills and perceptions within an organization. QFD integrates engineering, marketing, and manufacturing ideas into a product from the conceptual stage through post-production and service.

• The "House of Quality" is QFD's main design tool. It is a conceptual map that provides a visual means for interfunctional planning and communication. Visually resembling an actual house, the house of quality shows the relationships between customer requirements and engineering characteristics, pointing out conflicts and compatibilities and facilitating inevitable trade-offs.

ISSUES FOR DISCUSSION

1. What positioning strategy is used for the following products?

a. Disney World
b. Maytag washers and dryers
c. Wendy's restaurants
d. Apple computers
e. Federal Express overnight delivery service

2. Identify the following products as flanker brands, line extensions, franchise extensions, or new products.

a. McDonald's new ham and swiss cheese sandwich
b. Sears rental car service
c. Seiko computers
d. Acura cars (made by Honda)

3. Describe a number of ways that Pepsi-Cola Company could modify its product line.

4. Oranamics, Inc. has the American rights to distribute a new two-headed, Y-shaped, oversized toothbrush that cleans both sides of the teeth at the same time. What steps would you recommend before introducing the product?

5. How might a company like Xerox get ideas for new products? What techniques might they use to screen and evaluate the new ideas generated? What might be some of the more important screening criteria they could use?

6. Sentinel Technologies has developed floppy disks for personal computers that are available in a variety of bright colors. How important is it for the company to test market the new product? What could Sentinel learn from a market test of the new floppy disks?

7. Why is it important to develop the marketing program at the same time as the product?

8. Companies do a much better job of new product strategy development and "front end" thinking today in comparison to 1968, with the result that it only takes seven ideas to generate one successful new product vs. 58 previously. The research techniques available have been improved substantially during this time period. Yet the success rate for new products has not improved over the years. Explain how this can be.

9. Think of a new product which you wish were available for you to buy. Write a Product Innovation Charter for this new product.

10. Think of a new product you have seen recently. Reviewing the factors contributing to success and failure, do you predict the product will be a winner or a loser? Why?

GLOSSARY

Business analysis: the evaluation of new product ideas to determine estimated sales, market share, profit, and return on investment.

Cannibalization: sales of a new product that take away sales of another product in the product line.

Commercialization: the introduction of a new product into the marketplace.

Complementary products: products for which demand is related to, but not competitive with, other products in the line.

Concept tests: reactions from consumers to new product ideas and concepts.

Flanker brand: the introduction of a new brand into a product category where the organization already has existing products.

Franchise extensions: the introduction of a product into a new category, using an existing brand name.

House of Quality: a conceptual map that visually resembles an actual house and provides a means for interfunctional planning and communication by showing the relationship between a product's customer requirements and its engineering characteristics.

Line extensions: the introduction of new flavors, sizes, or models into an existing product category, using an existing brand name.

Product Innovation Charter (PIC): a new product strategy statement that includes parameters for new products, goals, and programs to achieve the goals.

Product positioning: the place a product occupies in consumers' minds relative to competitors.

Quality: the totality of features and characteristics of a product or service that bear on its ability to satisfy stated or implied needs.

Quality Deployment Function: a set of planning and communication routines that focuses and coordinates interfunctional skills within an organization, first to design, then to manufacture and market goods that customers want to purchase and will continue to purchase.

Roll out: the introduction of a new product into one region at a time.

Strict liability: a doctrine stating that if a defect in a product is legally established, the manufacturer is liable, regardless of any precautions taken.

Test market: the introduction of a new product and marketing program into a limited market as a way of determining probable sales and profits under actual market conditions.

Value added: the change in the product characteristics from the time the product ingredients enter the organization to the time the product is sold by the organization.

NOTES

1. Yoram Wind, *Product Policy: Concepts, Methods, and Strategy,* (Addison-Wesley, 1982), pp. 79–81.

2. John Koten, "Car Makers Use 'Image' Map as Tool to Position Products," *The Wall Street Journal,* March 22, 1984, p. 33.

3. This section closely follows the discussion in Richard Cardozo, *Product Policy: Cases and Concepts* (Addison-Wesley, 1979), pp. 31–60.

4. Cardozo, *Product Policy,* p. 31.

5. Cardozo, *Product Policy,* p. 47.

6. For more information on discontinuing products in the product lines, see Douglas Lambert and Jay Sterling, "Identifying and Eliminating Weak Products, *Business,* July-September, 1988, pp. 3–10; Richard Hise, A. Parasuraman, and R. Wiswanathan, "Product Elimination: The Neglected Management Responsibility," *Journal of Business Strategy,* Spring 1984, pp. 56–63; and George Avlonitis, "Industrial Product Elimination: Major Factors to Consider," *Industrial Marketing Management,* February 1984, pp. 77–85.

7. This section closely follows the discussion in Edward Tauber, "Brand Franchise Extension: New Product Benefits from Existing Brand Names," *Business Horizons,* (March -April 1981), pp. 36–41.

8. Tauber, "Brand Franchise Extension," pp. 38–39.

9. Kenneth Labich, "The Innovators," *Fortune,* June 6, 1988, pp. 50–64.

10. Labich, "The Innovators," p. 64.

11. Marty Friedman and Lynn Dornblaster, "New Food Products Hit a Belly-Busting Record in 1987," *Prepared Foods,* February 1988, pp. 117–119.

12. Booz, Allen & Hamilton, *New Products Management for the 1980s,* (Chicago: Booz, Allen & Hamilton, 1982).

13. C. Merle Crawford, *New Products Management Second Edition,* (Homewood, IL: Irwin, Inc., 1987), pp. 58–73.

14. Crawford, *New Products Management Second Edition,* p. 59.

15. Crawford, *New Products Management Second Edition,* p. 60.

16. Eric von Hippel, *The Sources of Innovation,* (New York: Oxford University Press, 1988).

17. Leigh Lawton and A. Parasuraman, "So You Want Your New Product Planning to Be Productive," *Business Horizons,* December 1980, pp. 29–34.

18. Lawrence Ingrassia, "Taking Chances: How Four Companies Spawn New Products by Encouraging Risks," *The Wall Street Journal,* September 18, 1980, pp. 1, 19.

19. E. Patrick Maguire, *Evaluating New Product Proposals* (The Conference Board, 1973), pp. 60–61.

20. C. Chaterji, Ronald Lonsdale, and Stanley Stasch, "New Product Development: Theory and Practice," in B. Enis and K. Roering, eds., *Review of Marketing 1981* (American Marketing Association, 1981), pp. 143–57.

21. Edward Tauber, "Forecasting Sales Prior to Test Market," *Journal of Marketing,* January 1977, pp. 80–84.

22. Lee Adler, "Time Lag in New Product Development," *Journal of Marketing,* January 1966, pp. 17–21.

23. See for example, "Terry Dworkin and Mary Jane Sheffet, "Product Liability in the '80s," *Journal of Public Policy and Marketing,* Volume 4, 1985, pp. 69–79; Michael Brody, "When Products Turn Into Liabilities," *Fortune,* March 3, 1986, pp. 20–24; and Carolyn Lochhead, "All Are Liable in Product Liability," *Insight,* February 15, 1988, pp. 46–47.

24. "The Devil in the Product Liability Laws," *Business Week,* February 12, 1979, pp. 72–78.

25. Jay Klompmaker, G. David Hughes, and Russell Haley, "Test Marketing in New Product Development," *Harvard Business Review,* May-June 1976, pp. 128–38.

26. Ronald Lonsdale and Stanley Stasch, "Do New Product Introductions Utilize Marketing Research the Way Textbooks Say They Do?" Paper presented at the Product Development and Management Association Conference, October 31-November 2, 1979.

27. Booz, Allen & Hamilton, *Management of New Products* (1968), p. 9.

28. Booz, Allen & Hamilton, *New Products Management for the 1980s,* 1982.

29. David Hopkins, *New Product Winners and Losers* (The Conference Board, 1980). For a review of the many different ways of defining product failures, see C. Merle Crawford, "New Product Failure Rates: Facts and Fallacies," *Research Management,* September 1979, pp. 9–13.

30. Hopkins, *New Product Winners and Losers.*

31. Bill Abrams, "Despite Mixed Record, Firms Still Pushing for New Products," *The Wall Street Journal,* November 12, 1981, p. 31.

32. Abrams, "Firms Still Pushing for New Products."

33. Hopkins, *New Product Winners and Losers,* pp. 10–11.

34. R. G. Cooper and E. J. Kleinschmidt, "New Products: What Separates Winners from Losers?," *Journal of Product Innovation and Management,* No. 4, 1987, pp. 169–84; F. Axel Johne and Patricia Snelson, "Success Factors in Product Innovation: A Selective Review of the Literature," *Journal of Product Innovation and Management,* No. 5, 1988, pp. 114–28; Calvin Hodock, "Rx for New Product Survival," *Marketing Communications,* February 1986, pp. 27–32, 61; C. Merle Crawford, "Marketing Research and the New Product Failure Rate," *Journal of Marketing,* April 1977, pp. 51–61; J. Hugh Davidson, "Why Most New Consumer Brands Fail," *Harvard Business Review,* March-April 1976, pp. 117–22; and David Hopkins, *New Product Winners and Losers,* The Conference Board, 1980.

35. Davidson, "Why Most New Consumer Brands Fail."

36. Hopkins, *New Product Winners and Losers.*

37. Crawford, "Marketing Research and the New Product Failure Rate."

38. Hopkins, *New Product Winners and Losers,* p. 17.

39. Cooper and Kleinschmidt, "New Products: What Separates Winners from Losers."

40. ANSI/ASQC. 1987. *Quality Systems Terminology, American Normal Standard.* A3, 1987.

41. Philip Crosby, *Quality is Free.* (McGraw-Hill, 1979).

42. Crosby, *Quality Is Free;* Edward W. Deming, *Out of the Crisis,* (Cambridge, MA: MIT Center for Advanced Engineering Study, 1986); J. M. Juran, *Juran on Planning for Quality.* (New York: Free Press, 1988).

43. John R. Hauser and Don Clausing, "The House of Quality," *Harvard Business Review,* May-June 1988, p. 63.

44. Hauser and Clausing, p. 65.

45. John Holusha, "Raising Quality: Consumers Star," *The New York Times,* January 5, 1989, p. B1.

46. Hauser and Clausing, p. 65–66.

47. Hauser and Clausing, p. 66.

48. Hauser and Clausing, p. 68.

CASE APPLICATION 10–1

The Development of the Taurus

The action is typically Japanese. Executives, plant managers, and production workers religiously gather to share ideas and map out strategy. But the scene is distinctly American: the new Ford Motor Company. Copying a page from the Japanese success manual, company chairman Donald Petersen has redesigned Ford; the boring cars and shoddy production methods have been junked, and he's silenced the internal squabbling. The reincarnated Ford now listens carefully to its customers; making cars right is the watchword, and its aerodynamic-designed cars are the auto world's hottest sellers. "Ford today is a very different sort of Ford," says Petersen. Louis Lataif, vice president of sales operations, agrees. "We have a whole new identity. Only the name is the same."

Ford has clearly transformed itself into the country's premiere master of automotive marketing. The company's metamorphosis began during the depths of the last recession when Ford was drowning in a sea of red ink—during one 18-month period alone the auto maker lost a record $3.2 billion. The very fact that Ford was floundering gave Petersen the chance to rapidly implement a risky rescue plan that called for total redesign of the company.

The first thing Petersen overhauled was Ford's archaic product development process. Until the early 1980s, Ford simply built the kind of cars it *thought* the public should have. Now, the company hardly makes a move without taking its cue from consumers. During the initial planning stages for the Taurus/Sable, for example, Ford asked consumers what they most looked for in a new car and, based on the answers from the largest marketing-research study in Ford's history, the company compiled a customer wish list of 1,400 "wants." Choosing 700 items from this list, Ford added such features as a net in the trunk to hold groceries upright and engines with oil dipsticks, batteries, and other parts labeled in yellow for easy identification.

The customers' contributions don't stop here. At ten set stages during the development process, Ford now turns to focus groups to see if its ideas are on track. At one session, consumers said they would prefer more chrome on the Taurus. The design was changed. The focus groups are considered so important, in fact, that Ford executives are present at all of them—something that never happened in the past.

Ford also took design cues from its competition. Using a little reverse engineering, Ford bought a Mercedes, Toyota, Audi, and other cars and stripped them down layer by layer to find out which had the best-in-class features. The Taurus' key insertion, door handles, gas pedal, tire jack, and dashboard were all copied from other cars. In all, Ford borrowed 400 features.

The company also tore apart the entire creative process and reassembled it so that everyone at Ford could have a say in designing new cars. Traditionally, the five-year new car development process consisted of sequential stages in which product planners, designers, engineers, and manufacturing all did their separate jobs without consulting each other. Petersen scrapped the old method in favor of a team concept. The first foray—Team Taurus—brought together design, engineering, manufacturing, and marketing people to plan the desired new car. As a result of this company-wide collaboration, over 300 ideas from employees were incorporated into Taurus' design and production.

Award-winning designs are a hollow victory if the cars aren't properly put together. Unfortunately, Ford and quality had not always been synonymous, so Ford launched a massive crusade for quality. Company president Red Poling was dispatched to crisscross the country to convert plant workers to Ford's new philosophy that stressed preventing problems during assembly, rather than attempting to detect them in the finished product. Petersen believes the plan is working well. Consumers obviously agree: complaints about car defects have been nearly cut in half.

Ford also demanded that its dealers upgrade their operations. Ford motivated dealers by making their jobs easier. The biggest innovation was the introduction of "option packages." Instead of offering buyers myriad options on every model, Ford decided to offer pre-set packages—a low- and a high-priced series for each model. The packages were a hit. For one thing, they lowered dealers' inventory costs since they now could keep fewer differently equipped cars on the lot. As an incentive, Ford also offered dealers $1,000 worth of options for $800. Customers liked the packages, too, because the confusing task of choosing options was done for them.

Ford also changed who it sells to, aggressively pursuing markets that GM had owned: younger, more upscale car owners. Because of the big-selling Taurus/Sable and aero-look cousins such as the Tempo and Thunderbird, the average Ford customer is now ten years younger and $10,000 richer. In addition, the company's share of the domestic market has risen thirteen points since 1980 to 29 percent.

The company's skyrocketing confidence is visible in its ads. Ford's pitch has a livelier and more optimistic tone. "Our ads are less apologetic," admits Louis Ross, executive vice president of North American operations, referring to the now little-used tagline, "Have You Driven a Ford Lately?" Ads for Ford cars and trucks now stress high quality, dependability, and superior design. Print ads for Ford took on the stylishly sleek look of the cars and, as a result, the ads jumped in Video Storyboard Tests' rankings from fifth place in 1985 to third in 1986.

Mercury's TV commercials are an even more startling deviation from the norm. Sable's emotion-packed pitches, for example, have a rich, sophisticated feel that's underscored by compelling rock music. "We developed a whole new ad strategy around style and lifestyle. We decided to use a lot more people in our ads so the consumer could easily put themselves behind the wheel," says Ross Roberts, general marketing manager.

"So far, we haven't been about to differentiate Mercury as a different car from Ford," says vice president of sales operations Louis Lataif. To that end, TV commercials will use a more futuristic look and music to stress that Mercury is the aero-wave of tomorrow.

SOURCE: from "Marketer of the Year: Ford's Don Petersen" by Kim Foltz in ADWEEK, August 1987. Reprinted by permission.

Questions

1. Evaluate the new product development process used by Ford to develop the Taurus.

2. Describe the product positioning for the Taurus and its sister car the Mercury Sable.

3. What do you think of the branding strategy and names for the two cars?

CASE APPLICATION 10–2

3M's Post-it Notes

3M Corporation is the world's most successful new product company with over 60,000 products ranging from Post-it Notes to heart-lung machines. The company's goal is to have 25 percent of sales coming from products which did not exist five years before. In 1988, these new products accounted for 32 percent of the company's $10.6 billion in sales. The 25 percent rule is an important yardstick at bonus time, and thus managers takes it seriously.

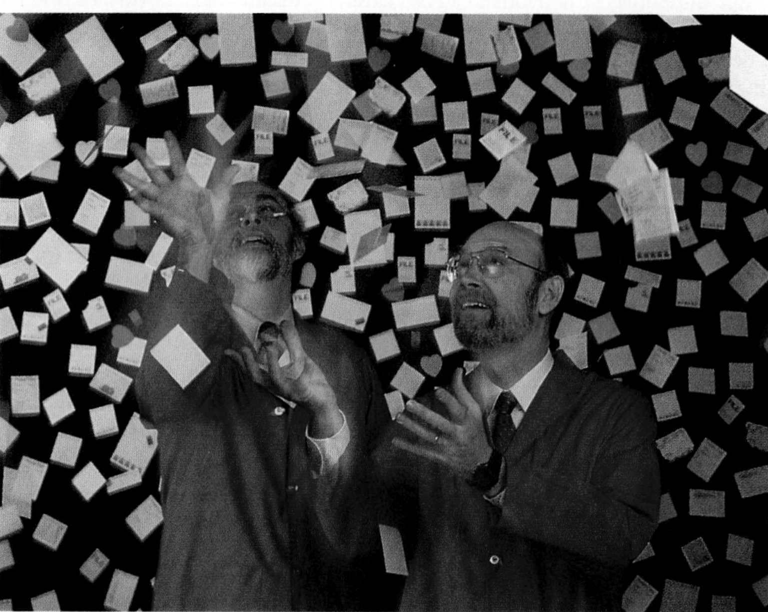

The company's success is largely attributable to the company's efforts to infuse an entrepreneurial spirit into a corporate setting. Each of 3M's 44 divisions has research and development autonomy, separate business planning, and its own profit and loss statement. The divisions are set up to market to narrowly defined markets, such as the electronics, automotive, or business office markets. This keeps employees focused on the needs of the consumer. The company has a "bootleg" rule which allows employees to spend up to 15 percent of their time on projects of their own choosing. There is a dual ladder career path, allowing scientists who don't want to manage to advance in the company by assuming additional responsibility for technologies instead of people or budgets. This means that researchers who are happiest working in the lab can stay there without losing pay raises or recognition.

Post-it Notes, introduced nationally in 1980, are a product which was developed by Arthur Fry using the bootleg rule. Fry sang in a church choir and marked sections in his hymn book with pieces of scrap paper. The bookmarks invariably fell out of the book or slipped between the pages. One day he remembered an adhesive that had been developed the year before, and he started working on marrying this adhesive to a piece of paper. He encountered serious technical problems right away. He had to develop coatings for the front and back of the paper so it could be bound in a pad, easily removed, and restuck to another surface over and over again.

Fry had permission to charge expenses to "Miscellaneous Accounts." He had been working on developing a shelf arranger tape for library shelves, so he had to bootleg the time to work on the Post-it Notes. Fortunately, his boss was very supportive and passed out samples of the product to secretaries of the senior executives. They quickly fell in love with the little yellow notes and before long their bosses began borrowing them. The lab started getting visits from senior executives now interested in the product. These executives became champions for the product.

"Once the laboratory perfected the process, we took Post-it Notes to the field for continued marketing research to determine how to get the concept across to the consumer," said Graydon Thompson, marketing manager—Post-it program. 3M tested the notepads in Richmond, Tampa, Denver, and Tulsa by selling them through the traditional mode of distribution—office supply stationers. Nothing happened in Richmond and Tampa, and the dealers there were less than enthusiastic about the product. But dealers in Denver and Tulsa ran promotions and put together a sampling brochure that they handed out to customers. "That was what clicked," he said.

"Getting notes into people's hands seemed to have some merit. However, the cost of sampling appeared to be prohibitive." Nevertheless, Thompson pushed for and won top management approval of the "Boise Blitz," an intense sampling and marketing campaign for Post-it Notes in Boise, Idaho, which proved to be the turning point for the product. They hand sampled and direct mailed to every office in Boise, in addition to advertising in the local newspapers. Marketing research showed an additional Post-it Note size, 3″ by 3″, needed to be added to the line before introducing it nationally.

"The formula: sampling, direct mail, and advertising. This has been the approach we've taken from the day we introduced Post-it Notes," Thompson said. The first brochure read, "We'd like you to sample the most exciting new office product since Scotch brand transparent tape. We ought to know; we invented both." Later 3M also introduced the Post-it Note Tray after marketing research showed the note pads were getting lost on customers' desks.

Developing standard printed Post-it Notes was the next step. 3M originally planned to have a full line of printed forms, but marketing research indicated the opportunity was limited to a route request form and a telephone message pad. In 1980 there were four Post-it products, and by 1984 there were 23 products in the line being sold through office stationers. By 1989 sales had risen to approximately $300 million. "All of this was possible," according to Thompson, "because of thorough marketing research, proven promotion techniques, a dedicated investment on the part of 3M management, and rapid line extension."

Even with 3M's emphasis on innovation, new ideas do sometimes fall through the cracks. Recently some employees complained that worthwhile projects were still going unnoticed despite the 15 percent bootleg rule. Guaranteed free time does not guarantee that there will be money to build a prototype, so the company created Genesis grants which give researchers up to $50,000 to carry their projects past the idea stage. A panel of technical experts and scientists awards as many as 90 grants each year.

SOURCE: Russell Mitchell, "Masters of Innovation," *Business Week*, April 13, 1989, pp. 58–63; Art Fry, "The Post-it Note: An Intrapreneurial Success," *SAM Advanced Management Journal*, Summer 1987, pp. 4–9; and "Post-it Notes Click Thanks to Entrepreneurial Spirit," *Marketing News*, August 31, 1984, pp. 21, 22.

Questions

1. How can companies better capture product opportunities identified by their employees? Why do you think 3M is so successful in coming up with new product ideas?

2. What are some criteria that a company like 3M should use to screen its ideas for new products?

3. How would you design a test market for a new product like Post-it Notes?

4. What, in your opinion, were the key components that led to the phenomenal success of Post-it Notes?

PART
FOUR

Distribution

J.CREW

11

Channels of Distribution

Learning Objectives

Upon completing this chapter, you will be able to do the following:

DEFINE
what is meant by the term *channels of distribution.*

DESCRIBE
the differences between conventional channels of distribution and vertically integrated marketing systems for distributing goods and services.

EXPLAIN
why intermediaries are needed in most marketing channels of distribution.

LIST
steps that can be taken when dual distribution problems exist.

ILLUSTRATE
the meaning of long and short channels of distribution for consumer goods and industrial goods.

MARKETING PROFILE

The IBM Clones

It looks, feels, and acts like the computer that revolutionized today's office, but where there used to be a label for International Business Machines (IBM), there is nothing. In fact, if you bought the parts separately and rented a video tape on how to assemble it, you could put your name on it. It is officially referred to as the "IBM compatible" or "IBM Clone". It runs all the software that the PC runs, and costs roughly one fifth of the price of the original (1981) IBM PC. In 1987, the IBM PS/2 rolled out on the market.* The first clones appeared about one year after the introduction of the original IBM PC, a few weeks after the IBM PC/AT, and the clones of the '386 machines actually appeared before the IBM machines were available. At first, only large manufacturing concerns like Compaq and AT&T were producing IBM "compatible" computers, but now it is not uncommon to find small retailers selling their own brand.

The key to the clones is compatibility. In order to be considered a clone, it must not only run PC software, but it also must have compatible disks, video, and expansion capabilities. This has resulted in many of the inexpensive clones being built to the exact specifications of the IBM equipment. The component parts of these clones have not only become similar, they have become interchangeable. This means that the small retailer/manufacturer can order cases (the IBM look-alike shells) directly from Pakistan, system boards from Taiwan, and power supplies from China with the security that they will fit and work together. Has this turned PC parts into commodities, and retailers into importers?

In the pre-clone era, if you wanted to sell personal computers, you had to be an official IBM dealer, work with a wholesaler and probably a distributor, and maintain some quota of individual and co-op advertising. Now, you can have a storefront operation, a salesperson, and a few contacts across the ocean in Taiwan. There is no need for intermediaries because manufacturing and retailing occur at the same location.

Although the clone industry looks like a perfect candidate for a direct channel system, intermediaries are needed in order to let the retailers concentrate on selling rather than importing. If the components are examined (instead of the finished product), it turns into a different industry. First, there is a great importing distance between the manufacturers of the components and the retailers. Second, the countries where the clone parts are coming from are not known for their consistent quality and timeliness. A large intermediary can use its buying power to gain concessions for defective merchandise. Third, manufacturers would rather deal with large wholesalers who can guarantee large orders. This allows the manufacturer to compete without an extensive sales network. Finally, the time lag between the orders and shipments would require retailers to hold large inventories in order to protect themselves against shortages. Intermediaries could hold inventory and break up large orders to supply several retailers.

This *Marketing Profile* emphasizes the fact that, although certain parts of the clone industry might appear to be without intermediaries, someone is performing the functions normally attributed to them. The utility of intermediaries in this case is not obvious to the consumer buying the computer, but without those intermediaries, the consumer might not be able to shop at a small retailer in the first place. In both consumer and industrial settings, then, intermediaries facilitate the movement of products from the manufacturer to the consumer. Chapter 11 highlights the various roles that intermediaries play in the marketplace.

* "Dvorak vs. Seymour," *PC Computing*, March 1989, pp. 29–30.

This chapter examines the following questions: (1) How do goods and services move through channels of distribution? (2) How are marketing channels of distribution organized? (3) What decisions are involved in managing a channel of distribution? (4) What major problems and issues must marketing managers consider in selecting channels of distribution? (5) How have vertically integrated marketing systems been designed to replace conventional channels of distribution? (6) How can the sales performance of channel members be evaluated?

We will show that the functions performed by intermediaries, while costly, are necessary for the convenience they provide consumers and industrial users. Intermediaries are like highways—they are expensive, but, without them, we could not easily get things from place to place. In the next two chapters, major channel intermediaries, retailers, and wholesalers will be discussed in detail.

The Realities of Waiting

The average consumer can visit a supermarket, department store, or hardware store and examine the hundreds of items each has available. The items in retail stores have typically been transported from distant locations. For example, the box of Wheaties on the supermarket shelf in Fort Wayne, Indiana, may have come from a General Mills plant in Lodi, California. The workbench in a hardware store in Arlington, Virginia, may have been shipped from a Black & Decker plant in Baltimore. The goods and services we consume are available because marketing managers have determined what they believe is the best method and route to bring products to us.

When Jennifer Wilson finally decided to purchase a food freezer, she did not expect to wait two months for delivery. Jennifer wanted a large, efficient, dependable freezer that was almond in color to match her other home appliances. The salesperson showed her many freezer styles, but all were white. Producers of food freezers simply do not mass produce almond freezers, choosing instead to concentrate on white, the most popular color. The store had decided not to carry them in inventory because of the risk and financial burdens involved. Thus, Jennifer's request had to be made as a special order to the producer.

The situation Jennifer faced occurs countless times every day in different marketing settings. The delivery of such goods and services as automobiles, furniture, mass transportation, police protection, airline tickets, legal advice, and health care is often delayed, resulting in lost sales today and lost or disgruntled consumers tomorrow. However, through effective marketing channels management, some inefficiencies associated with moving goods and services from producer to consumer or industrial user can be eliminated, and some delays can be significantly reduced.

Marketing Channels of Distribution: A Definition

The area of marketing that tries to find solutions to problems like Jennifer's is called **marketing channels of distribution.**

Most people have a general idea what the terms *marketing channels* and *distribution* mean. A marketing channel can be compared to a pipeline through which oil or gas flows. Distribution involves getting products to people. Thus, in a general sense, marketing channels of distribution make possible the flow of a product or service to a consumer or user.

Table 11–1 Major Types of Marketing Intermediaries

Middleman—an intermediary between manufacturer and end-user markets; synonymous with *reseller*.
Agent—an intermediary with legal authority to act for a manufacturer.
Manufacturer's Representative—an intermediary who sells a product but usually does not take legal title to or physical possession of it.
Wholesaler—an intermediary who sells to other intermediaries, generally retailers. This term usually applies to consumer markets.
Retailer—an intermediary who sells to consumers.
Broker— an intermediary who performs limited selling functions, usually writing orders to be turned over to the manufacturer for delivery and specializing in sales to a particular kind of customer, such as grocery stores.
Sales Agent—an intermediary who agrees to sell all the output of a manufacturer at a stated commission rate or for a stated fee, but who usually does not take physical possession of or legal title to the merchandise.
Distributor—an intermediary who performs a variety of distribution functions, including selling, maintaining inventories, extending credit, and so on. It is a more common term in industrial markets, but may also be used to refer to wholesalers.
Jobber—usually used in an industrial marketing context to refer to distributors, or in certain fields, such as paper and hardware, to refer to wholesalers characterized by broad lines and reasonably complete service offerings.

SOURCE: Adapted from Frederick E. Webster, Jr., *Marketing for Managers* (Harper & Row, 1974), p. 191.

In the marketing literature a more formal definition is offered. A marketing channel of distribution is defined as *any firms or individuals who participate in the flow of goods and services as they move from a producer to an ultimate consumer or industrial user.*[1] For example, a tube of Crest toothpaste may move from a plant in Raleigh to a wholesaler in Pittsburgh, a retailer in Denver, and finally a consumer in suburban Arvada.

The main concern of marketing channels management is making an offering available for consumption.[2] Specifically, managing marketing channels of distribution involves coordinating and directing performance so the consumer receives the good or service in a reasonable time.[3]

The channel always includes the producer and the ultimate user, as well as any intermediaries. The intermediaries include both merchants—people who take title and market (resell) on their own—and various agents—brokers and manufacturers' agents, who do not take title but who facilitate the flow from producer to user. The intermediaries in the Crest example include a wholesaler and a retailer.

The flow of some products involves numerous marketing intermediaries, many of whom are specialized by market, project, region, and even industry. Some of the more common marketing channel intermediaries are defined in Table 11–1.

An agent is a representative of buyers or sellers. A manufacturers' agent represents two or more manufacturers. They have a formal agreement covering price, territory, delivery schedules, warranties, and commission rates with each manufacturer they represent. Agents do not take title to goods. A purchasing agent makes purchases for buyers. They usually receive, warehouse, and ship goods to buyers.

Table 11–2 Intermediary Costs for a Compact Disc (1989)

Production of Disc	.74	
Packaging (Tuck Box, etc.)	1.72	
American Federation of Musicians Dues	.27	
Songwriters Royalties	.39	
Recording Artist's Royalties	1.01	
Freight to Wholesaler	.36	
Manufacturer's Advertising and Selling Expenses	1.74	
Manufacturer's Administrative Expenses	1.76	
Manufacturer's Cost	**$7.99**	
Manufacturer's Profit Margin	1.10	
Manufacturer's Price to Wholesaler	**$9.09**	←
Freight to Retailer	.38	
Wholesaler's Advertising, Selling, and Administrative Expense	.47	
Wholesaler's Cost	**$9.94**	
Wholesaler's Profit Margin	.80	
Wholesaler's Price to Retailer	**$10.74**	**$6.90**
Retailer's Advertising, Selling, and Administrative Expenses	1.76	
Retailer's Profit Margin	3.49	
Retailer's Price to Consumer	**15.99**	←

The difference between merchants and agents can be illustrated by following the distribution of coffee. Suppose a grower in Colombia owns beans and sells them to Nestlé Foods who produce Taster's Choice. The sales transaction between the grower and Nestlé is arranged by a broker, who never takes title to the coffee beans, but simply facilitates the transaction. The broker is an agent, the manufacturer is Nestlé, and the intermediaries are retailers who sell the coffee product to consumers in their stores. The broker is like a real estate agent who brings buyer and seller together.

Why Do We Need Intermediaries?

Occasionally one hears the cry "Get rid of the intermediaries; all they do is raise the price." However, the importance of channel intermediaries is clear in the coffee bean example. Growers cannot deal directly with ultimate consumers. They are not capable of producing, packaging, shelving, and selling cans or jars of coffee to shoppers in stores. A grower who engaged in these activities would have no time to plant, irrigate, and harvest a crop. Someone else is better able to perform the needed functions of marketing the coffee product. It seems the old marketing saying "You can eliminate the middlemen, but you can't eliminate what they do" still holds in marketing-oriented economies such as those in the United States, Canada, and Japan.

The costs of the intermediaries can seem high, but without intermediaries the costs of bringing buyers and sellers together would be even higher. Table 11–2 shows a breakdown of costs to produce and market a $15.99 compact disc.

About 43 percent of the price paid by the consumer ($6.90) goes directly to intermediaries. If intermediaries did not exist, Compact Disc producers like Sire,

Figure 11–1 How Intermediaries Simplify the Matching of Supply and Demand

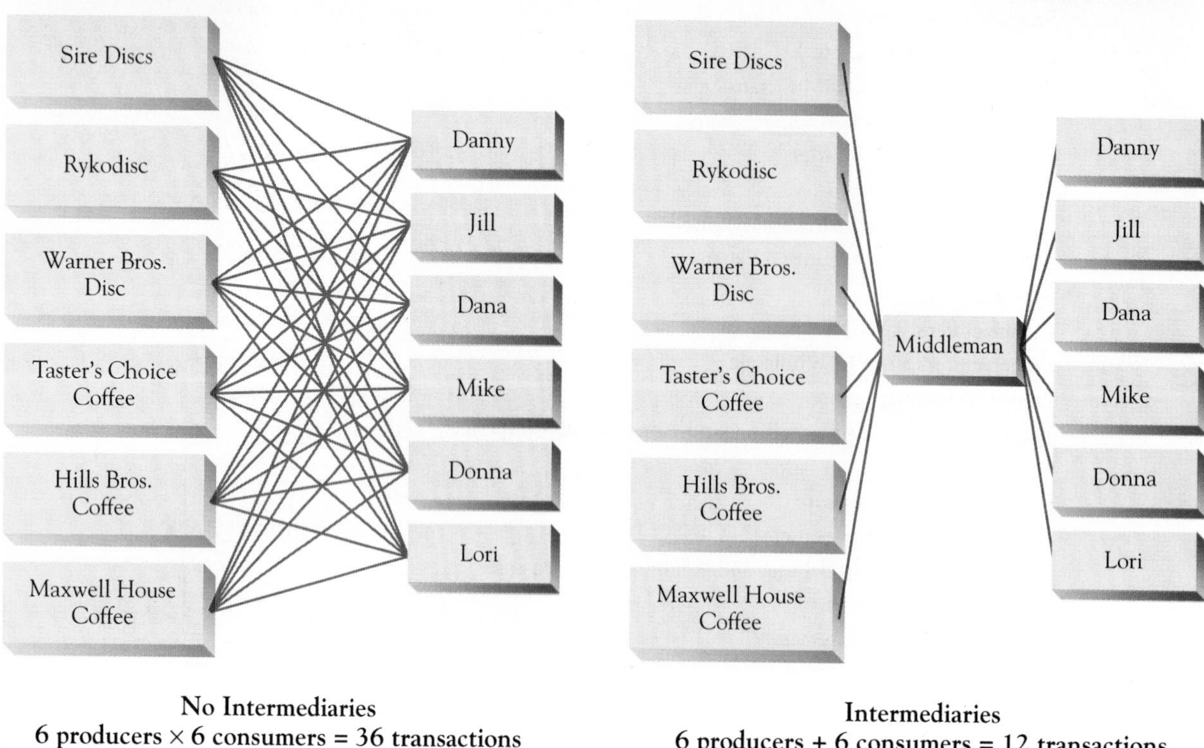

No Intermediaries
6 producers × 6 consumers = 36 transactions

Intermediaries
6 producers + 6 consumers = 12 transactions

Rykodisc, or Warner Brothers could sell directly to consumers, but there would be a number of inconveniences. For example, the consumer would have to travel to a Sire warehouse. Only Sire compact discs would be available, not those of other producers; producers would be scattered around the area, not clustered in stores in a shopping mall.

Despite what many consumers believe, intermediaries are necessary to bring buyers and sellers together. Can you imagine Americans going to Toyota plants in Japan to purchase cars, or Australian consumers flying to Houston to purchase Compaq computers? Also, remember the Colombian coffee bean growers. It would be impossible for them to sell beans directly to consumers in San Pedro, California, or Manchester, New Hampshire.

Sellers and buyers benefit from the existence of intermediaries, who help simplify contacts between producers and consumers. As Alderson has stated, "The goal of marketing is the matching of segments of supply and demand."[4] Figure 11–1 shows how this matching is simplified by intermediaries. Without an intermediary, each producer would have to market directly to each consumer. In the figure, this would mean thirty-six transactions or contacts. However, with a single intermediary who, in turn, contacts each customer, there would be only twelve transactions. Paperwork, personal inconvenience, time, and travel expenses are significantly cut by intermediaries.

Table 11–3 Marketing Functions That Can Be Performed in a Channel of Distribution

Transactional	Logistical	Facilitating
Selling—promoting a product to potential customers. **Buying**—purchasing a variety of products from various sellers, usually for resale. **Risk-taking**—absorbing business risks, especially risks of maintaining inventories and product obsolescence.	**Assorting**—providing an assortment of items (often interrelated) for potential customers. **Storing**—protecting a product and maintaining inventories to offer better customer service. **Sorting**—buying a quantity of items and breaking bulk items into amounts desired by customers. **Transporting**—physically removing the product between manufacturer and end user.	**Financing**—offering a credit to potential customers to facilitate a transaction; also providing funds to sellers to help them finance their activities. **Grading**—judging products and labeling them as to quality. **Obtaining Market Information**—obtaining information needed by manufacturers about market conditions, including expected sales volume, fashion trends, and pricing condition.

SOURCE: Based on Frederick E. Webster, Jr., *Marketing for Managers* (Harper & Row, 1974), p. 191.

The Utilities Created by Intermediaries

Intermediaries in channels of distribution have survived because they perform marketing functions more effectively and efficiently than anyone else. Certainly intermediaries add costs to products (see Table 11–2), but these costs are usually offset by the utilities they create. Also, these costs are lower than those associated with other modes of distribution.

The efforts of intermediaries create **form, time, place,** and **possession utilities** for ultimate users. Form utilities are those activities used to change the appearance or composition of a good or service to make it more attractive to potential or actual users. Time utilities make products available when consumers want them. Place utilities make the products or services available to consumers where they want them. Finally, possession utilities are those activities provided by middlemen who help consumers take possession of goods or services.

In creating these utilities, intermediaries perform the various marketing functions listed in Table 11–3. Each function has three things in common: it uses up scarce resources, it can best be performed by specialists, and it is shiftable.[5] If producers perform them, costs increase and so do prices; when intermediaries perform them, the producer's costs and prices are lower, but the intermediaries must receive something for their work. Therefore, they charge the producer a fee.

Whether one is discussing food freezers, coffee beans, compact discs, Wheaties, a workbench, or airline tickets, various marketing functions are necessary for effective distribution. These functions will be discussed in more detail in Chapter 12 (*Wholesalers*) and Chapter 13 (*Retailers*), and Chapter 14 (*Physical Distribution*). Intermediaries work to create form, time, place, possession, and information utilities. The following examples will show how this benefits the consumer.

Form Utility

The managers at a Memphis Winn-Dixie supermarket purchased over 200 pounds of flounder and prepared it in the fresh fish display case. Kelly Raymond drove to the store and selected three one-pound portions of the fish to prepare for dinner. Winn-Dixie was the intermediary that made available the fresh fish that Kelly selected. She closely inspected the fish and pointed out exactly what she wanted.

Time Utility

George Cannellos was vacationing in Sea Island, Georgia, and discovered that he forgot to bring a dress shirt. He had an important dinner engagement and needed a light blue dress shirt. He found a Davison-Faxon department store in a shopping mall and selected exactly the light blue shirt he needed.

Place Utility

Joy Henderson was traveling down a rural road late at night and noticed her gas gauge was nearing empty. She did not want to run out of gasoline in a desolate area. Fortunately, she found a Shell station that was open and was able to fill up.

Possession Utility

Jim Oganovich, a new arrival in New York, wanted to rent a reasonably priced apartment in Manhattan. Since Manhattan is so heavily populated, apartments are difficult to locate. Jim decided to use an agent who listed Manhattan apartments in his price range, facilitating his renting of a desirable apartment.

The marketing intermediaries in these examples performed valuable functions to create form, time, place, and possession utilities. Without these utilities, products would not get to consumers, or consumers would not buy them.

Review Your Marketing Knowledge

- If you were in the computer software business, why would you need marketing intermediaries?
- Describe the types of utilities created by intermediaries.

The Organization of a Marketing Channel

No one marketing channel is always superior; channels of distribution take the configurations that most efficiently meet the needs of the market and consumer.[6] In both consumer and industrial goods markets, manufacturers want control of distribution channels for better application and use of their marketing strategies.[7]

Consumer Products: Marketing Channels

Consumer products channels take many forms. Retailers are found only in consumer products channels, not in industrial channels. Figure 11–2 presents five patterns of distribution channels for consumer products. Channel I (the red arrow) is a *direct* channel from the producer to the consumer. Fuller Brush salespeople sell brushes directly to the consumer, and Mary Kay beauty consultants sell directly to customers. *Indirect* manufacturer-ultimate consumer linkages are spelled out in the Channels II–V (the grey arrows). For example, Channel III has two intermediaries, a retailer

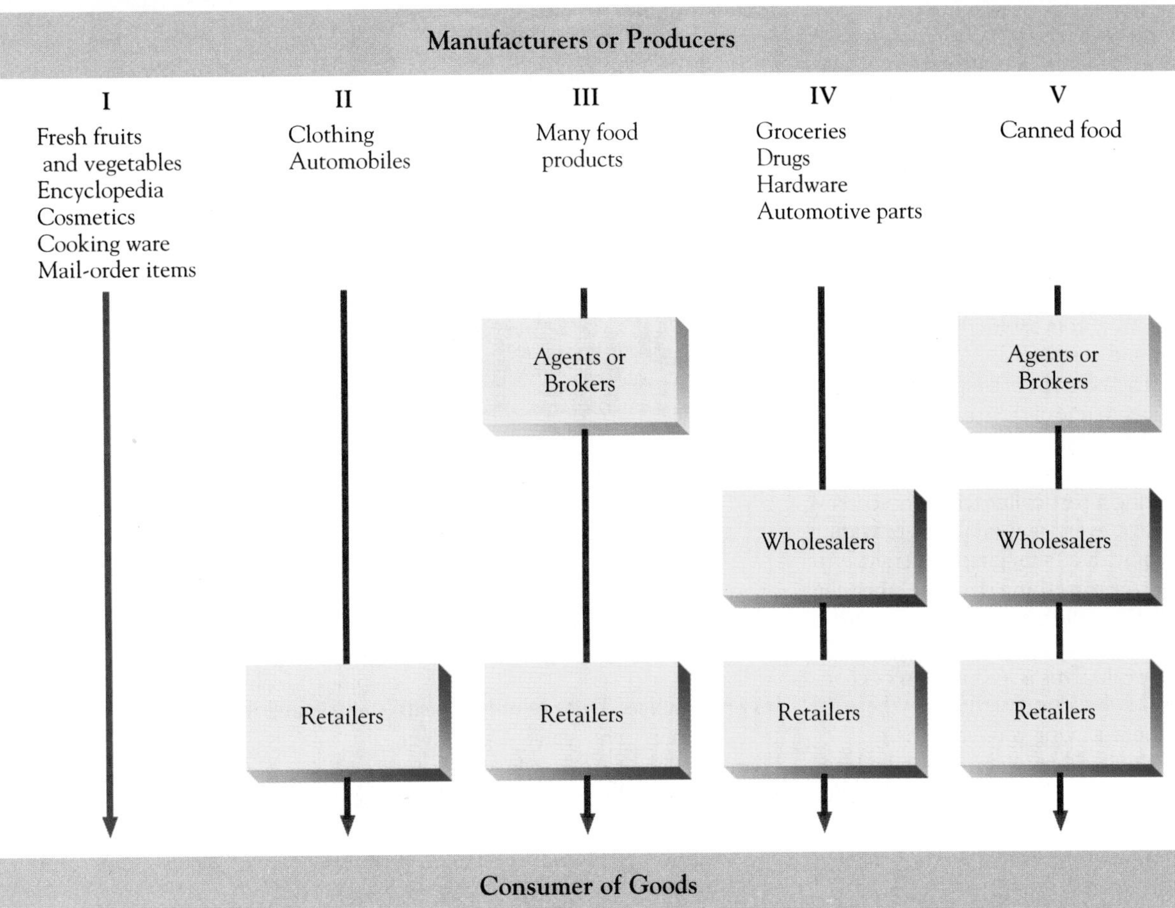

Figure 11–2 Marketing Channels of Distribution for Consumer Goods

and an agent or broker. Ocean Spray sells juices through brokers who then sell to retail stores. Channel V is the longest channel of distribution; it includes two retailers and wholesalers, as well as agents or brokers.

An example of an increasingly popular direct channel is home shopping. The *Marketing in Action* on direct channels points out the popularity of this channel arrangement.

Although there are many ways consumer goods pass through each channel, some patterns are more common than others. For example, fresh fruits and vegetables, cooking ware, and cosmetics often flow directly from the manufacturer to the consumer. The longer the channel, the more specialized are the functions performed by intermediaries. In most cases increased specialization means lower costs; each intermediary performs important functions in which he or she has become expert, and this efficiency results in prices relatively lower than if one person were performing all the functions.

A Short, Direct Channel of Distribution

If you have a TV, then you are probably used to seeing late night commercials pushing items by mail and flashing "800" numbers on the screen. If you have cable TV, you have probably seen the channels that are completely devoted to this type of shopping. This relatively new concept of home shopping has not only become very successful ($2.55 billion in 1987), but has received increased attention from cable companies, retailers, and customers.

The concept is simple. Consumers tune into one of the shopping channels (such as Home Shopping Network), and there is a "host" showing or demonstrating a particular item. These items change every few minutes, providing them with a "shopping" experience. If they see something they like, they can call the toll-free number and with a credit card have the item shipped within the week. This is a short, direct channel of distribution that can be used without leaving your easy chair.

Home shopping has several advantages over visiting a store or a mall. First, the consumer never has to leave his or her home. This not only appeals to consumers who can't leave their homes, but also to those who don't particularly enjoy driving to several locations, parking, and waiting in lines. Second, the consumer can see some items in ways that they could never see through retail and mail-order catalogs. Clothing can be modeled showing how it really looks, and records can be played (some complete with music videos) on the air to give the consumers a better idea of who the artist is and what they are buying.

Telaction Corp., a subsidiary of J. C. Penney Co., is planning to introduce a home shopping mall. So far, thirty-eight "video tenants" have signed on including J. C. Penney, Express Music Catalog, Marshall Field's, and Neiman Marcus. In this new concept, the consumers will be able to control where they shop and what items they see with their touch-tone phone. This concept of letting the consumer control more of the shopping process should increase the flexibility of home shopping. Technology has significantly eliminated the need for intermediaries.

SOURCE: Joanne Cleaver, "Consumers at Home With Shopping," *Advertising Age*, January 18, 1988, pp. 3 and 19.

Industrial Products: Marketing Channel

In contrast to consumer goods, industrial goods most often use a direct channel of distribution. The manufacturer sells directly to the industrial user through a sales force or other direct marketing technique (for example, mail order catalog). In comparison to the consumer market, the industrial market is made up of a smaller number of relatively large buyers.[8] In addition, buyers often are concentrated geographically. Thus, the advantages of using middlemen are sometimes not so clear for industrial goods manufacturers as for consumer goods manufacturers. Another reason for shorter channels for industrial goods is the complexity of many products, which require specialized knowledge or postsale service. Figure 11–3 presents three common channels of distribution for industrial goods.

Manufacturers' agents are used to market some industrial goods for the same reasons agent middlemen are used in consumer goods markets—the manufacturer is small, has a narrow product line, and sells in geographically dispersed markets. The industrial supply house in Channel III is a wholesaler. It is used primarily for supply and maintenance items and for low-cost, fairly standardized industrial equipment like lathe machines, shaft seals, electrical supplies, and grinding machines. Graybar Electric, for example, is a supply source for electric supplies. It advertises itself as a well-stocked, single source of electric supplies.

Figure 11–3 Marketing Channels of Distribution for Industrial Goods

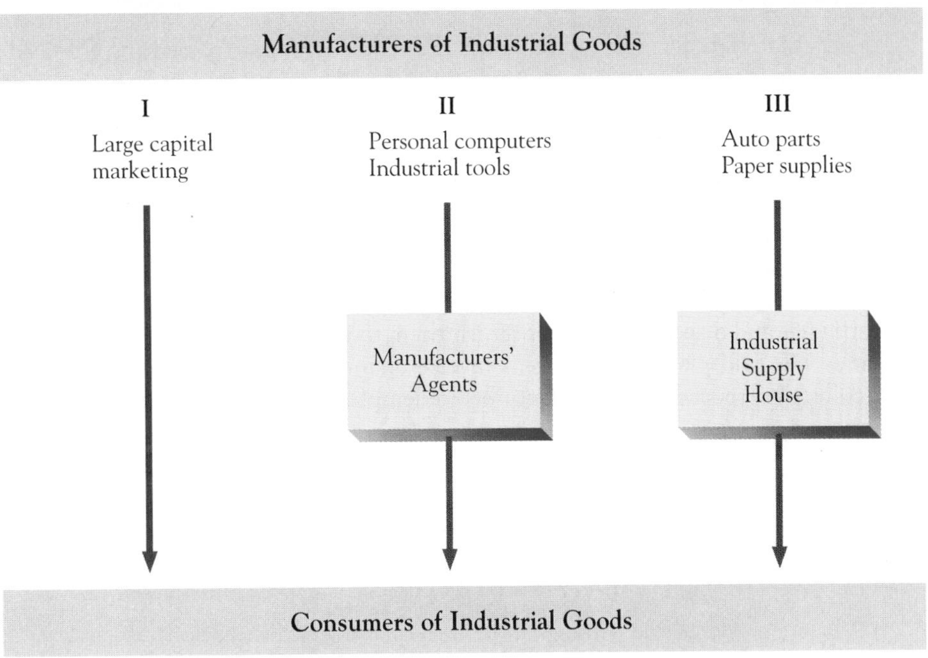

Multiple Channels

Organizations in some situations use more than one marketing channel for similar products. For example, multiple channels are used when the same product is marketed to consumers and industrial users. STP Corporation sells oil and gasoline additives to service stations and supermarkets. The STP products reach consumers who may have different purchasing patterns. Some people do not buy STP type products in supermarkets. However, there are some consumers who purchase what they need in any type of store because of the convenience.

In some situations the same product is marketed through a variety of retail outlets. Peanuts, for example, are sold in many grocery stores, but they are also sold in drugstores, restaurants, lounges, and service stations, as well as at baseball games. Goodyear automobile tires are marketed through Goodyear-owned retail stores, tire wholesalers (who sell them to service stations), and franchised Goodyear stores.

Reverse Channels

Marketing channels are traditionally thought to make possible the forward movement of products or services from producers to consumers or industrial users. However, there is increasing interest in reverse channels, in which goods flow back from consumers or industrial users to producers or other marketing intermediaries. The reverse channel is described in this discussion of the recycling process:

> *The recycling of solid wastes is a major ecological goal. Although recycling is technologically feasible, reversing the flow of materials in the channel of distribu-*

tion—marketing trash through a "backward" channel—presents a challenge. Existing backward channels are primitive, and financial incentives are inadequate. The consumer must be motivated to undergo a role change and become a producer—the initiating force in the reverse distribution process.[9]

As raw material shortages increase and litter-control laws are passed and enforced, the marketing of trash (bottles, cans, and cartons) will become an even more pressing problem, and consumers and producers will have to deal with it effectively. Reverse channels will be given more attention as such problems continue to demand efficient solutions.

Local government and private business have joined forces in creating a reverse channel that earns a profit in Camden, New Jersey. The *Marketing in Action* on recycling examines the reverse channel process used by Resource Recovery Systems.

The intermediaries in reverse channels are unique: they receive products from the consumer and dispose of them or return them to their manufacturer. Some intermediaries who will play major roles as reverse channels increase in importance are trash-collection specialists, manufacturers' redemption centers, and trash-recycling brokers.

Review Your Marketing Knowledge

- Describe a reverse channel of distribution that you have personally used.
- Why are groceries sold through an indirect channel of distribution?

Decisions About Marketing Channels: The Key Factors

Why are Electrolux vacuum cleaners sold door to door? Why can one find Saint Laurent fashions in only a few stores in large cities? Why does Goodyear use multiple marketing channels to sell automobiles tires? These questions must be answered if one is to see how a marketing manager chooses a channel arrangement.

There are some crucial issues marketing managers must consider if they want to avoid selecting inappropriate or inefficient marketing channel arrangements. Past successes and failures reveal which factors must be weighed in selecting appropriate channels of distribution strategy.

Strategic Thinking

In a common scenario, a manufacturer uses incentives and other short-term solutions to improve channel performance. For example, in Japan distribution is one of the most crucial and difficult challenges for foreigners.[10] Attempting to unravel the Japanese distribution networks without a long-term strategy is doomed to fail. For years foreign cars were sold in the same showrooms as domestic competitors. Deciding it wanted to be in Japan for years, BMW worked out a long-run plan to establish an independent dealer network.[11] Samsung, a South Korean consumer electronics firm, also worked out a long-term strategic distribution plan by entering into long-term agreements with large department store chains instead of wading through layers of Japanese wholesalers.[12]

MARKETING IN ACTION

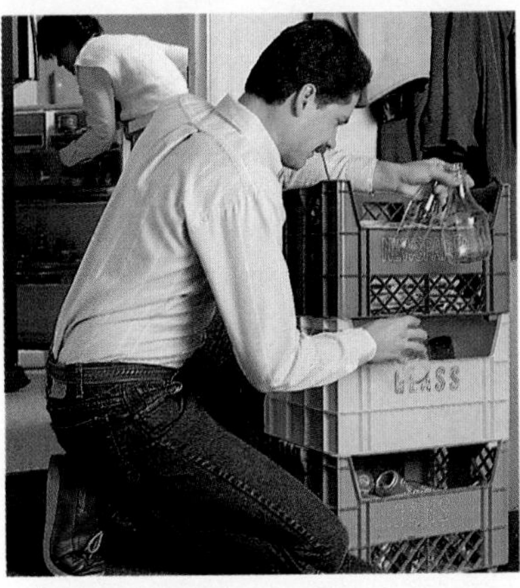

Recycling Success in New Jersey

In a time when a number of waste recovery operations are closing their doors, Resource Recovery Systems (RRS) is claiming success after success. RRS is providing solutions for a two-fold problem facing local governments: budget cuts and the increasing cost of waste management. Usually by working in concert with local municipalities, RRS is able to remove a large portion of a community's solid waste, which would otherwise be dumped in costly and scarce landfills. Once sorted and packaged, the revenues from the sale of the recyclable material is split by RRS and the municipality.

In Camden, NJ, the process starts with providing the neighborhood with a special container for all glass, aluminum, and tin/steel refuse. The recyclable material is collected on the same day as the other garbage and brought to the recovery site. There it is sorted by magnets, conveyor belts, and air blowers into specific sections of the site. Glass is separated by color and then shattered to produce marketable crushed glass cullet. Aluminum is flattened and blown into a truck trailer, ready to deliver to the Baltimore, MD, shredding plant of Reynolds Metals. Tin cans undergo a rubbing, turning, and beating process to remove paper labels and remaining food particles before they are shredded and sent to Vulcan Materials for further processing.

The capacity of the plant is 80 tons of material per day, which represents a savings of approximately $4,000 dollars a day for not dumping the material in a landfill, plus the profit associated with the sale of the material. The garbage-to-energy incineration plant cost is also indirectly helped when the bottles and cans are removed from the rest of the garbage. Overall, the efficiency of the RRS system with the flexibility of the residents has resulted in a more effective treatment of the municipality's waste.

This *Marketing in Action* describes a reverse distribution channel that earns a profit and also helps clean up the environment. The reverse channel means that materials are moved from the consumer to the manufacturer. The coordination of this effort is helped by the use of intermediaries as in a standard distribution arrangement.

SOURCE: "The Smell of Recycling Success," *Beverage World*, October 1987, pp. 224–25.

In order to develop a strategic perspective it is necessary to consider any distributor as a partner.[13] Any producer must first "market to distributors," convincing the distributor that it is important to be a partner. BMW and Samsung were able to do this in Japan. Next, the manufacturer must join with distributors to "market the product/service." Long-term thinking, partnership, and avoiding short-term incentives only to improve the partnership relationship are ingredients of a strategic approach to distribution. If American firms are going to fare well in Europe, Asia, South America, and elsewhere, the strategic approach to distribution will have to be included in marketing channels decision making.

Goals and Objectives

Every organization has a number of goals and objectives. Each would like to earn a satisfactory profit, be socially responsive, minimize complaints, satisfy consumer needs and wants, and take the lead in making improvements. In addition to these broad goals, each organization has specific objectives. For example, Turner Tool & Die Company of Columbus, South Carolina, wants to hire eight skilled millwrights and four computer specialists by June 1. Thus, an important issue in deciding on channels

BMW's long-term strategy in Japan includes marketing cars through an independent dealer network.

of distribution strategy is determining one's goals and objectives. These must be matched with the available resources (human, technical, financial) and constraints (legal, competitive, market mix).

Company Characteristics

Understanding the characteristics of a company is important in selecting appropriate channels of distribution. A strong financial position and a strong marketing work force allow an organization to engage in costly, but profitable, direct marketing. Conversely, a weak resource position may force a company to use powerful intermediaries, even when this requires giving up some power. The greater a firm's financial resources, the more control it exercises over its channels of distribution.

Customer Characteristics

The ultimate users and buyers must be considered in making choices about channels. The identity of ultimate users must be precise and up to date. Who are they? Where do they live? What are their needs and wants? What appeals to them?

The buying specifications of customers must be studied in detail. Typical buying specifications for the purchase of milk might be described as follows:

1. Purchased more than once a week.
2. Purchased usually on Friday or Saturday, plus early in the week.
3. Purchased in a supermarket along with other staples.
4. Purchased as needed to replenish supply.
5. Purchased according to an established brand preference, but brand preference may change if relative prices change.

In contrast, the typical buying specifications for the purchase of a high-quality personal computer system might be as follows:

1. Purchased only from a well-established, reputable local dealer.
2. Purchased only after considerable comparison shopping.
3. Purchased after extended, thorough review and consideration.
4. Purchased only from a dealer equipped to render prompt and reasonable product service.

If the manufacturer knows something about users' buying specifications, it can decide on the type of intermediaries to use. Matching consumer, or industrial user, buying specifications with a channel of distribution pattern is important.

Many firms have been very creative about the channels that serve the needs and wants of their customers. Here are a few examples.

- Tampa Compact Disc in Florida initiated the world's first drive-thru CD facility. An old instant print photo mart came equipped with a drive-up window, which the dealer turned into a marketing benefit: a convenient way for some to shop for their favorite CDs.[14]
- First Nationwide Bank is using a mixture of local savings and loan branches and outlets in grocery stores to sell its services. The bank is attempting to create an image of warmth and personal service.[15]
- There are now approximately 26,000 video rental/sales locations in the United States, some with over 12,000 tapes and titles. The video industry is now a $6.4 billion business. Consumers spend about $5.2 billion on rental tapes. Instead of going to the movie theater (retailer), the consumer rents the film from the video store (another retailer).[16]
- Brown & Jenkins Trading Co. is a fast growing mail-order coffee business in Burlington, Vermont. It fills orders and ships an average of 5,000 to 7,000 pounds of coffee each month. About 400 customers are members of its coffee-of-the-month club. The company appeals to customers who like such gourmet aromas and brands as Sumatra Mandheling, Brazilian Bourbon Santos, and Mexican Maragogipe.[17]

These examples illustrate that target markets can be aggressively addressed by creatively establishing new channels of distribution. Differences in the needs and wants of customers require diverse channels of distribution.

Product Characteristics

The characteristics of a product play a role in the selection of appropriate channels of distribution. As discussed in Chapter 4, consumer goods are categorized as convenience goods, shopping goods, and specialty goods. Bucklin has combined the traditional definitions of these three types of goods with definitions of stores based on patronage motives.[18] This interesting classification scheme can be useful in choosing an appropriate channel. Before discussing Bucklin's system, let us again illustrate the three types of goods:

convenience—small comparison gains to the customer (bread, milk, soft drinks, hair shampoos, and toothpaste).

shopping—large comparison gains to the customer (appliances, clothing, lawn equipment, and furniture).

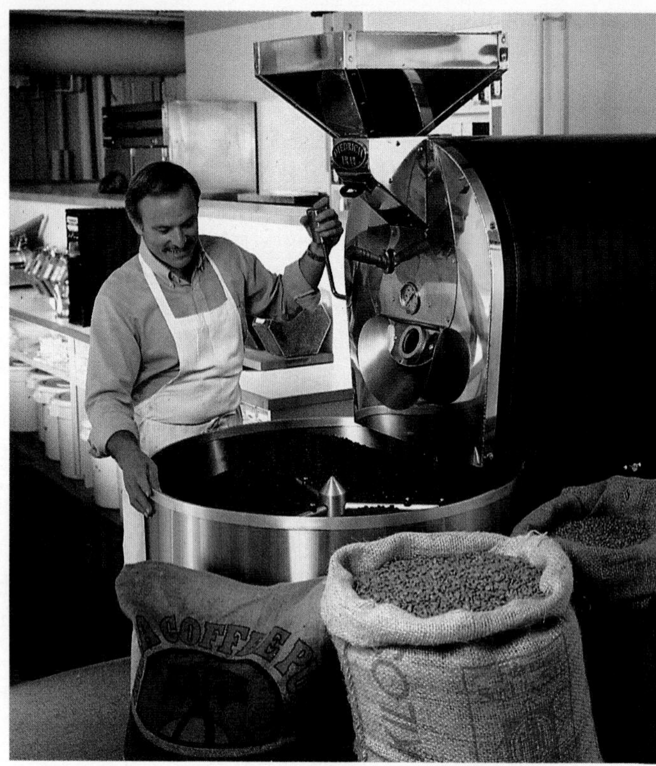

Brown & Jenkins Trading Co. targets an audience with gourmet tastes for their mail-order coffee business.

specialty—unique or special features for the customer (stereo systems, tennis rackets, and silverware).

Bucklin suggests that, on the basis of patronage motives, retail stores can be classified as convenience, shopping, and specialty stores. A Stop 'N Go Store is a convenience store, while the local deli is a specialty store. Marshall Field's, Macy's, Sears, and Dillard's are shopping stores, and Porsche dealerships, La-Z-Boy furniture stores, and Diet Centers are specialty establishments. The Bucklin ninefold system is outlined in Table 11–4. Marketing managers must study the market to determine where their consumers fall; the Bucklin system is a useful guide to understanding the importance of product and consumer characteristics.

Market Characteristics

The uses of a product, frequency of purchase, perishability, service required, value, bulk, and pricing margin are all important characteristics. Some experts believe the key determining characteristics of a good or service is its **replacement rate**—the rate at which it is purchased and consumed.[19] Milk has a high replacement rate, while a set of china has a low replacement rate; a man's shirt has a medium replacement rate.

A high replacement rate good usually has four characteristics: low unit gross margin, low adjustment factor (amount of change required to meet customers' needs), short consumption period (time needed to consume the product—a chocolate cake has a relatively short consumption period), and short search time (shopping time required to secure the good).[20] A low replacement item has the opposite character-

Table 11–4 Ninefold Classification Scheme of Shopper Types

Classification	Consumer Behavior	Most Likely Form of Market Coverage*
1. Convenience store/convenience good	The consumer prefers to buy the most readily available brand of product at the most accessible store.	Intensive
2. Convenience store/shopping good	The consumer selects the purchase from among the assortment carried by the most accessible store.	Intensive
3. Convenience store/specialty good	The consumer purchases a favorite brand from the most accessible store carrying the item in stock.	Selective/exclusive
4. Shopping store/convenience good	The consumer is indifferent to the brand of product but shops at different stores to secure better retail service and/or retail price.	Intensive
5. Shopping store/shopping good	The consumer makes comparisons among both retail-controlled factors and factors associated with the product (brand).	Intensive
6. Shopping store/specialty good	The consumer has a strong preference about product brand but shops at a number of stores to secure the best retail service and/or price for this brand.	Selective/exclusive
7. Specialty store/convenience good	The consumer prefers to trade at a specific store but is indifferent to the brand of product purchased.	Selective/exclusive
8. Specialty store/shopping good	The consumer prefers to trade at a certain store but is uncertain about which product to buy and examines the store's assortment for the best purchase.	Selective/exclusive
9. Specialty store/specialty good	The consumer has a preference both for a particular store and for a specific brand.	Selective/exclusive

*This form of market coverage (the number of intermediaries selling the good) will be discussed later in the chapter.
SOURCE: Louis P. Bucklin, "Retailer Strategy and the Classification of Consumer Goods," *Journal of Marketing*, January 1963.

istics: high gross margin, high adjustment factor, long consumption period, and long search time.

The importance of evaluating the replacement rate for goods is that a high replacement rate good requires more indirect routes of distribution. The reverse is true for low replacement rate goods like china or automobiles.

Some other guiding principles for using market characteristics to make channel decisions are these:

- Market size—in units and dollars, both current and potential
- Market structure—by geography, account size customization
- Market share—direct/indirect competition
- Market stability—volatility of user needs
- Market growth—in units and dollars

Pricing decisions are always extremely important. The margins earned pay the total channel and individual channel intermediaries' expenses and profits. The final price paid by a consumer includes the intermediary margins. As was shown in Table 11–2, 43 percent of the $15.99 price of a compact disc, or $6.90, goes to intermediaries. A larger gross margin can be used to motivate intermediaries to push a product harder than they usually do. Skil Corporation, a manufacturer of portable power tools, encourages its distributors to order in large volumes by offering discounts of up to 3 percent for carload orders.[21]

The **channel margin,** or difference between production costs (including the manufacturer's margin) and consumer price, has three components: distribution expenses, promotion expenses, intermediary expenses and profits.

Promotion expenses and intermediary profits are not as fixed as distribution expenses and are subject to bargaining. The amount of margin depends on expenses, profits, and the ability of the channel member to negotiate.

Environmental Characteristics

Chapter 3 covered environmental forces in detail. These forces are also important in reaching decisions about channels of distribution. Economic conditions and political, technological, social-cultural, ecological, and competitive environmental forces all affect the structure and efficiency of channels of distribution.

For example, channel competition can take four forms:

1. Competition between channel members, same level—retailer versus retailer, wholesaler versus wholesaler. One Walgreen Drug Store may compete with another two miles away.
2. Competition between channel members, different level—manufacturer versus wholesaler, retailer versus wholesaler.
3. Competition between channels—manufacturer-retailer channel versus manufacturer-wholesaler-retailer channel
4. Competition between channel members for the use of other channel members—manufacturer versus manufacturer for the use of a wholesaler or retailer, or wholesaler versus wholesaler for the use of a retailer.[22]

The competitive environment can result in decisions to change the pattern of distribution or the number of intermediaries. It can also result in conflict, which will be discussed later. Competition for the use of channel members can be as intense as price competition. For example, competition among manufacturers can give one an advantage over others. In the supermarket field, more and more retailers like Kroger, Dominick's, and Safeway are reluctant to increase the number of brand items they carry because they have only limited shelf space. Therefore, some brands make it to retailers' shelves and others do not.

In a study of the supplier-retailer level of distribution, Achrol and Stern examined the environmental factors affecting decision-making uncertainty in this channel relationship.[23] Four dimensions—diversity among consumers, dynamism, concentration, and capacity—are crucial in understanding decision-making uncertainty. *Diversity* refers to the degree of similarity-dissimilarity of such factors as needs, preference, and background of the customer; *dynamism* to the frequency of change in competition strategies and customer preferences; *concentration* to the economic power of competitors; and *capacity* to the number of opportunities and resources in the environment. These four environmental dimensions directly influence the degree of decision-making uncertainty expressed by channel members.

The legal system governing channels of distribution has evolved to encourage as much as possible full interchannel and intrachannel competition. The deregulation of some industries has created an array of channels for a variety of goods and services. For example, American Express is now a channel used by insurance companies.[24]

Federal, state, and local laws attempt to 1) prohibit uses of power that destroy competition in channels and 2) prevent use of practices and enticements that actually or potentially injure competition in the marketplace. Some critics, however, claim that, through inactivity in mergers and acquisitions, the government has encouraged less competition. For example, Whirlpool Corp. acquired Kitchenaid Inc., another appliance maker, and within five months dismissed all of Kitchenaid's former distributors. PepsiCo, Inc., which already owned Taco Bell and Pizza Hut restaurant chains, acquired Kentucky Fried Chicken. Wendy's, a competitor of Kentucky Fried Chicken, viewed this as a threat and banished PepsiCo products and substituted Coca-Cola in its hamburger outlets.[25]

There are many other ways environmental forces affect channels of distribution decision making. In developing design and strategy, one must carefully weigh environmental forces along with the other factors mentioned in this section. The task of weighing each characteristic may seem impossible, or extremely complex, but failure to thoroughly analyze these characteristics can result in the selection of improper, inefficient, or excessively costly channels of distribution. There is no one best channel of distribution, but some channels are better than others to meet a firm's general goals and objectives, as well as its marketing targets.

Market Coverage: How Many Channel Outlets?

Another important marketing channel decision involves choosing the number of channel outlets or intermediaries needed for the desired degree of market exposure—the number of resellers to include in the channel.[26] This decision requires determining the intensity of distribution to be used. How many retailers, wholesalers, and agents in a market should be included in the channel distribution network? There is no simple answer to this important question; possibilities are limitless, ranging from distribution through numerous outlets to having only one outlet in a market area.

Intensive Distribution

The maximum market coverage occurs through intensive distribution, where the manufacturer attempts to persuade as many retailers as possible in an area to carry the product. The advantages of intensive distribution are increased impulse purchasing, wider consumer recognition of the product, and greater consumer convenience. The disadvantages include lower margins, smaller orders, more inventory control and reorder problems, and less control.

Some items that are intensively distributed are Coca-Cola, Pepsi-Cola, Hershey candy, Frito-Lay chips, Kodak Film, Campbell's soups, General Mills Cheerios, and

Juicy Fruit gum. In the consumer market, almost all brand-name convenience items require intensive distribution because of consumers' tendencies to switch brands. For example, most consumers will switch breakfast cereals rather than travel to another store to get their favorites. In the industrial market, office supplies, small tools, and standard size fittings and seals are intensively distributed.

Intensive distribution can result in large sales volume. However, advertising and maintaining a large sales force are expensive. There is also the problem of motivating an intermediary to sell one's product more enthusiastically than another's. Gillette, Schick, and Wilkinson all want that extra push from intermediaries.

Exclusive Distribution

The use of a single retailer or wholesaler in a particular geographical area is referred to as exclusive distribution. For example, New York City, with a population of about 7.5 million, has only one Beltrami fashion store (that sells the famous polka dot shoes and handbag fashions). It has only a few Rolls Royce dealerships. And if you would like to purchase Caleche Perfume of Hermes in New York you must visit the exclusive Hermes store on East 57th Street.

Exclusiveness can mean significant marketing advantages for the manufacturer and intermediaries. Strong dealer loyalty and active sales support usually accompany exclusive distributorships. Exclusive intermediaries are motivated because they alone profit from their hard work and sales. Better forecasting and more efficient inventory control and retail control systems are possible when there is only one outlet. Exclusive distributors generally receive higher markups (the amount added to cost to cover expenses and allow for a reasonable profit—see Chapter 18) than other types of distributors. There is more consultation between producer and intermediary on decisions involving price, advertising, and inventory.

One disadvantage for a manufacturer in an exclusive distribution network is that sales can be lost because of the limited distribution. Furthermore, if a manufacturer has only one retail outlet, the firm is at the mercy of that outlet. The single retailer has the power of exclusivity.

Selective Distribution

Between the two extremes of exclusive and intensive distribution is a more moderate mode—selective distribution. This type of market coverage is used for products purchased by consumers who shop around. Such products are more expensive than convenience goods. For example, durable goods like typewriters, ceiling fans, stereos, and home appliances are selectively distributed.

With selective distribution, a manufacturer attempts to distribute only through outlets where sales volume, rate of inventory turnover, and order size result in a satisfactory profit. The decision to use a selective distribution system is often profitable for manufacturers of consumer shopping or specialty items and industrial accessory equipment, for which most users have strong brand preferences. Manufacturers like Florsheim (shoes), Baldwin (pianos), and Emerson (fans) find that selective distribution costs less than intensive distribution; because there are fewer intermediaries to call on, there is less intense competition and more cooperation between intermediaries.

Figure 11–4 presents three of the market coverage choices marketing managers face. Once again, careful analysis of goals, objectives, resources, and legal issues should precede any decision about how many outlets to use.

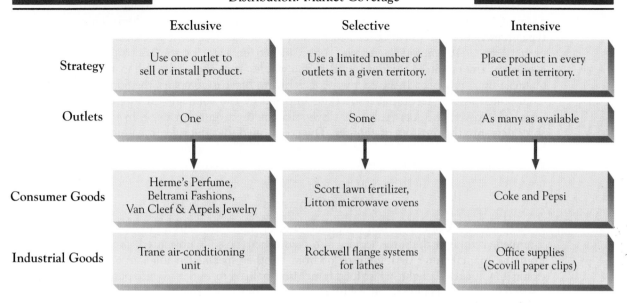

Figure 11–4 Intensive, Selective, and Exclusive Distribution: Market Coverage

	Exclusive	Selective	Intensive
Strategy	Use one outlet to sell or install product.	Use a limited number of outlets in a given territory.	Place product in every outlet in territory.
Outlets	One	Some	As many as available
Consumer Goods	Herme's Perfume, Beltrami Fashions, Van Cleef & Arpels Jewelry	Scott lawn fertilizer, Litton microwave ovens	Coke and Pepsi
Industrial Goods	Trane air-conditioning unit	Rockwell flange systems for lathes	Office supplies (Scovill paper clips)

Legal Issues in Marketing Channels

Manufacturers often attempt to influence the distribution of their product as it moves through the marketing channel by using control procedures. The following section will focus on three of these attempts and their legal implications.

Exclusive Dealing Contracts

With an *exclusive dealing contract,* the manufacturer prohibits an intermediary from carrying competing products. This type of contract is illegal in two situations. First, if the manufacturer's sales volume is a substantial part of the total volume in a market, competitors are closed out of the market. Second, when the contract is between a large manufacturer and a much smaller intermediary, the power imbalance can be a coercive threat and, possibly, a restraint of trade.

Exclusive dealing is not always illegal. If equivalent products are available to consumers, or if the manufacturer's competitors have access to equivalent intermediaries, an exclusive dealing contract may be acceptable. Such a contract is also acceptable when a manufacturer is just getting started in a market or when a manufacturer's share of the market is negligible.

Exclusive Sales Territory

An *exclusive sales territory* results when a manufacturer restricts the geographic territory of its intermediaries. The legal issue is whether restriction decreases competition and violates parts of the Sherman, Clayton, and Federal Trade Commission Acts. The courts seek to encourage competition among intermediaries handling the same brand, but exceptions are permitted when a manufacturer is new or its market share is negligible.

There are two types of sales territory restrictions—vertical and horizontal. With a *vertical restriction,* a manufacturer permits only one authorized intermediary. This type of restriction has usually been accepted by the courts because it promotes competing brands. A *horizontal restriction,* often judged unlawful by the courts, is an agreement among intermediaries (retailers and wholesalers) about who will market a manufacturer's products. In a case involving Schwinn Bicycle Company, the Supreme Court ruled against territorial restrictions imposed by the company on intermediaries.[27] However, the court ruled that Sylvania could prevent expansion by one of its dealers into the territory of another. The court ruled that the rule of reason must be used to decide if exclusivity harms competition.[28] Thus, granting exclusive territories depends on whether a firm can legally justify its actions to the courts.

Tying Contracts

A *tying contract* is one in which a manufacturer or franchisor sells a product to an intermediary only if the intermediary also buys other (possibly unwanted) products from the manufacturer or franchisor or from another specified manufacturer. For example, Chicken Delight, a fast-food franchisor, obliged its outlets to also purchase Chicken Delight's cooking and frying equipment, dips, and spices. The Supreme Court declared this tying contract system illegal and awarded the franchisees triple damages.

Tying contracts are often used when there are shortages of a desired product, and the manufacturer wants to push a less popular product. In franchise arrangements, franchisors often want each franchisee to purchase everything needed to run the business from them. In general, tying contracts of this type are illegal. On the other hand, tying contracts are often acceptable when a new firm is entering the market, the manufacturer (or franchisor) wants to maintain a quality product or service, or the exclusive intermediary is required to carry the manufacturer's full line of products but is not prohibited from carrying competing products.

Marketing Channels: Conflict and Cooperation

The need to properly manage channels of distribution is sometimes overshadowed by discussions of which pattern or how many intermediaries to use for optimal market coverage. Intermediaries, like manufacturers, are in business to accomplish goals and objectives. Certainly product, price, and promotion decisions are important, but properly managing the channels so these other marketing mix objectives can be achieved is also important.[29] Primary responsibilities of the key member (manufacturer, wholesaler, or retailer) in the channel are to plan, organize, control, and lead.

Types of Conflict

In our ealier discussion of environmental characteristics, a number of sources of interaction and conflict were pointed out. The existence of competition suggests that a channel is more than a structure or set of interdependent parts. It can also involve horizontal or vertical conflict.[30]

Horizontal conflict occurs between intermediaries at the same level—two or more retailers (for example, Kroger and Safeway) or two or more wholesalers. This type of

MARKETING IN ACTION

Conflict in the Channel

The discount merchandiser has been going through some structural changes of late, including fewer and fewer (but individually bigger) players in the industry. There has also been a philosophical metamorphosis that has resulted in "upscale discounting." Leaders in this change have been Target, Gold Circle, Richway, and Caldor. These firms fill their aisles with "woks and souffle dishes, duck decoys and designer jeans," and have influenced even the most traditional discounters such as Gemco, Murphy's Mart, and Ames to the point that they are moving to red interiors and racetrack designs.

What these changes point toward is a new interest in the quality image portrayed by discounters, and with it a responsibility to customers and the industry. A new proper mission statement has evolved because of the competition among discounters that reads, "large, clean, efficient, well-organized, single-stop, low-priced, always-in-stock, convenience store, with free parking, near home." This has resulted in some strain and conflict in the relationship among the discounters and between the discounters and their suppliers, a dramatic change from the past. On the positive side of this new intrachannel conflict situation is an emphasis on what the customers are now receiving:

- consistent specifications
- steady flow of replenishment
- quality control over color and fabric
- non-assorted piece-goods

Today's customer expects these niceties even if he or she has to pay modestly more for it. In order to insure these standards, discounters cannot spend all of their time finding one-time-only close-out purchases on which they cannot guarantee quality and availability. This type of purchasing, which is referred to as "dirty buying," should be a thing of the past in order to usher in the new quality image.

Thus, competition can result in horizontal conflict, which can result in some side benefits for the customer.

SOURCE: "The Word from Zayre to Apparel Vendors," *Discount Merchandiser*, Febraury 1988, pp. 30–32.

---

conflict also can be found between different types of retailers who handle similar products. Retail druggists (Eckerd's) compete with discount houses (Sav-On), department stores (J. C. Penney) quick-stop or convenience grocery stores (7-Eleven), and mail-order houses, all of which carry some of the same brands of products.

There is an ongoing battle between big retailers and big discounters involving the rights to market brand-name items, such as Lee and Levi jeans. The *Marketing in Action* on conflict points out how horizontal conflict can have some positive benefits for consumers.

Vertical conflict occurs between channel members at different levels—manufacturer with wholesalers, wholesalers with retailers, and so forth. It arises from such factors as differences in goals and objectives, misunderstandings, and poor communication.

Since marketing channels consist of individual organizations, there is always the possibility of horizontal or vertical conflict between channel members. *Role theory* explains why the potential for channel conflict exists. In role theory terms, each member in the channel is expected by other members to perform certain roles or functions. However, members' role expectations are not always in agreement. When a member acts in an unexpected or abnormal way, dissatisfaction, frustration, and inefficiency emerge.

Since channel members are separate organizations, they have their own pictures of channel member roles. For example, suppose a food producer like General Mills wanted intermediaries to promote Nature Valley granola bars in a particular manner. If a 7-Eleven store had a totally different picture of what was the best way to promote the product, channel member role conflict would exist.

Resolving Conflict

When continual breakdowns in communication, agreements, and trust occur, conflict is then dysfunctional. Reprisals, sabotage, anger, and frustration between manufacturers and intermediaries are not conducive to efficient marketing activities.

One way to resolve conflict is to follow the lead of a *channel captain.* A **channel captain** is often the member with the most power and authority, who directs, leads, and supports other channel members. IBM is a manufacturing channel leader; McKesson-Robbins is a dry wholesaler channel captain; and Wal-Mart and Sears, Roebuck are powerful retail channel captains.

Hardy and McGrath suggest a number of feasible conflict resolution strategies in specific manufacturer-intermediary conflict zones, as presented in Figure 11–5.[31]

1. *Conflict when manufacturers bypass intermediaries and sell directly to users.* This problem, called *dual distribution,* can be resolved by selling directly only to intermediaries. A manufacturer engaged in dual distribution sells to intermediaries while at the same time competing with them and selling directly to consumers. In more than 65 years of business, Steelcase, the over $1 billion office-furniture manufacturer, has never sold directly to users.[32] It has maintained that dual distribution activities are not good for business.

Another strategy to resolve or prevent this conflict is to adopt and use a policy of making direct sales only to a specific type or size of customer. And a third strategy is to compensate intermediaries for all manufacturer-to-user direct sales. The compensated rate is lower than the rate would be if intermediaries were in the channel.

2. *Conflict because the manufacturer is perceived to have permitted too many intermediaries in a geographic area.* One method used to solve this problem is the establishment of "master dealers." These dealers are given commissions on the sales of other intermediaries in the area. Another strategy is to assess the area carefully to decide on the appropriate number of intermediaries.

3. *Conflict over the margins members in the channel receive.* Intermediaries compare their margins with other channel members. The key to resolving this form of conflict is to establish margins on the basis of the effort and work performed. The manufacturer pays for work that is performed. If an intermediary doesn't stock an inventory, for example, it would not collect a portion of the margins for stocking.

4. *Conflict about sharing information on user identities.* Is user identity proprietary information?[33] Manufacturers may need user identity information to determine the type of customer using the product. Establishing trust with the intermediaries, increasing coupon redemption promotions, and jointly sponsoring intermediary-manufacturer marketing research are strategies for resolving this type of conflict.

Conflict will not spontaneously turn into neutral feelings or cooperation among channel members. Each channel member must work hard to create an efficient and cooperative channel of distribution. These four examples show only a few of the potential conflict zones that face channel members. Each channel member views the conflict, the relationship, and the tensions differently. However accurate each perception may be, it represents reality to that channel member.

Figure 11–5 Manufacturer/Intermediary (INT) Behavior in Five Zones of Conflict

Positive Relationship ↕ Negative Relationship

Zone	By Manufacturer	By Intermediary
1 NORMAL	Sells direct occasionally Sells direct to key accounts but discusses with distributor Uses multiple channels Does not overreact to distributor's muscle-flexing	Occasionally glances at private label but approaches key supplier first to offer the option Carries some competitive lines but de-emphasizes these in everday sale. May use only for bids.
2 ESCALATING CONFLICT	Removes formerly granted supports such as sales leads and spiffs Cuts margins Withdraws training of representatives for intermediary (INT) No more joint calls with middleman representatives Adds channels that manufacturer knows will heighten tension (squeeze play) Takes more and more business directly to end-customers	Selective cutbacks in inventory, line rationalization Adds competitive line of same quality and price positioning Gives competitive line more showroom space, catalog space, sales effort by representatives
3 COLD WAR	Does not talk to INT Does not return INT's phone calls Tries to renegotiate INT agreement unilaterally Bad-mouths INT customers Makes overt, stronger efforts to work with the INT's key competitor in the area	Demands private label Encourages customers to switch to competitive products Does not allow manufacturer representatives to work with middleman representatives Asks for customized literature and sales aids Demands excessive quantities of samples, literature, and displays
4 SHOOTING WAR	Removes or limits exclusives Conducts harrassment campaign delays INT's orders, hassles INT's regarding credit terms	Deliberately cuts prices to harm manufacturer and lower overall price levels in the market. Does so while substituting competing suppliers' lower-priced products
5 ALL-OUT SHOOTING WAR	Terminates relationship Sues INT	Denigrates manufacturer's brand performance Refuses to service or install items Instigates lawsuit, termination of arrangement

SOURCE: Kenneth G. Hardy and Allan J. McGrath, *Marketing Channel Management,* (Glenview, IL: Scott, Foresman, 1988), p. 104. Reprinted by permission.

The Vertically Integrated Market System

The analysis to this point of marketing channels of distribution may suggest that conflict, power, disorganization, individualism at the expense of team play, and occasional chaos are prevalent. The traditional view of marketing channels is that they are a loose confederation of actors (manufacturers, wholesalers, and retailers) who maneuver for position and bargain for a bigger margin. A more progressive approach to marketing channels of distribution design and strategy is found in vertical marketing systems. According to one author, *vertically integrated marketing systems* are "professionally managed and centrally programmed networks, pre-engineered to achieve operating economies and maximum market impact."[34] Three vertically integrated market systems are the *corporate, contractual,* and *administered.*

Corporate Vertically Integrated Marketing Systems (CVIMS)

The CVIMS involves the ownership of channel components. The integration is *forward* when a manufacturer operates its own distribution centers or retail stores. General Electric, Hart, Schaffner & Marx, Walgreens, and Singer are manufacturers with CVIMS. They own most of their channel components, excluding retail outlets. Sherwin Williams is a manufacturer with a CVIMS that also owns its retail outlets.

The integration in CVIMS is *backward* when a wholesaler or retailer owns a component upstream in the channel. Sears, J. C. Penney, Safeway, and Wards own substantial interests in a number of their suppliers. Sears has gained significant control of its distribution system, from the production of goods to the sale to users, by owning wholesaling and manufacturing companies. Many of Sears' products are derived from firms in which Sears owns a part of the business.[35]

Administered Vertically Integrated Marketing Systems (AVIMS)

Administered systems are slightly different from traditional marketing channels of distribution. In administered systems, distribution functions are coordinated by one or more channel leaders. Campbell, Gillette, and Kraft are channel leaders that can influence the policies of channel members. Because components can have disparate goals, the actions of individual members must be coordinated and controlled to develop a united team effort. Coordination is not achieved by ownership, as is the case in the CVIMS, but through the size and power of the channel leader(s).

Kraft uses an AVIMS. It says its marketing goal is "to participate in all meals, whenever consumed." Sales in 1988 were over $10.8 billion. The company can command unusual cooperation from its resellers in terms of shelf space, price policies, and promotional campaigns because its products account for over 60 percent of all dairy case volume, exluding milk, eggs, and butter. Kraft's well-known brand names include Velveeta (processed cheese), Parkay (margarine), Miracle Whip (salad dressing), Cracker Barrel (cheese), and Sealtest (ice cream). The success of Kraft's administered system depends on the popularity of its brands.

Contractual Vertically Integrated Marketing Systems (CONVIMS)

The most influential type of VIMS is the contractual. With this type of system, which accounts for about 40 percent of all retail sales, organizations draw up a contract to

Figure 11–6 Ten Largest Types of Franchised Businesses In 1988

Type of Franchised Business	Sales By Franchisees ($ Billion)	Example of Franchisor
Auto and Truck Dealers	$335.4	General Motors, Ford
Gasoline Service Station	91.9	Shell, Tenneco
Restaurants	63.2	Wendy's, Domino's
Retailers (Nonfood)	28.5	True Value, Ace Hardware
Soft Drink Bottlers	22.1	Pepsi-Cola, Coca-Cola
Hotels and Motels	19.7	Days Inn, Quality Inns
Business Aids and Services	16.8	H&R Block, Quick Copy
Automotive Products/Services	13.7	Firestone, Goodyear
Convenience Stores	13.6	Circle K, Stop N Go
Food Retailers	12.1	Independent Grocer's Association

SOURCE: Statistical Abstract of the United States, 1989, (Washington, D.C.: Government Printing Office, 1989, p. 760).

perform certain marketing functions in the channel. The three principal forms of contractual arrangement are wholesaler-sponsored voluntary groups, retailer-sponsored cooperative groups, and franchise systems.

A wholesaler, by organizing a number of independently owned retailers into a *wholesaler-sponsored voluntary group,* can provide goods and services far more economically than if it dealt with each retailer separately. Some better-known wholesaler-sponsored groups are Independent Grocers Alliance (IGA), Sentry Hardware, Western Auto, and Ben Franklin Stores. Sentry has over 4000 affiliated stores under contractual arrangement. It can exercise buying economies for products that will allow those stores to compete with large and powerful chains.

The *retailer-sponsored cooperative* came into existence because groups of retailers wanted to defend themselves against corporate chains. Retailers organize and operate their own wholesale companies, which then perform services for the member retailers. Each retailer is expected to purchase a minimum percentage of merchandise from the wholesaler. This cooperative is most commonly found in the food industry. Two of the largest cooperatives are Associated Grocers and Certified Grocers, both of which serve several thousand retail outlets.

Franchising is a form of marketing and distribution in which a parent company grants an individual (*franchisee*) or small company the right to do business in exchange for revenues from fees or royalties. The franchisee is given the right to use a seller's products, symbols, merchandise, and overall expertise in a defined territory. Franchising offers the manufacturer (*franchisor*) opportunities to obtain some control over the distribution outlets without owning them. The United States Department of Commerce forecasts that by the year 2000, franchising will account for 50 percent of all retail sales. There are currently approximately 480,000 franchised businesses in the United States and more than 30,000 American-owned franchised outlets outside the United States. Figure 11–6 lists the ten largest types of franchised businesses (each with sales exceeding $9 billion in 1988).

Many foreign countries are interested in opening U.S. franchises such as this Burger King in Caracas, Venezuela.

There is a growing interest among foreign countries in U.S. franchised businesses. Increased levels of disposable income, a growing demand for consumer goods and services, expanding urbanization, and higher consumer mobility are reasons behind the global attractiveness of franchising. Franchising, like the economy, is global. Entrepreneurs, consumers, and societies the world over are its beneficiaries. It has become not only a part of Europe, Japan, and Canada but also of Asia (over 1,400 franchises), South America (over 500 franchises), and Africa (over 600 franchises). McDonald's opened its first "Golden Arch" behind the Iron Curtain in Belgrade, Yugoslavia.[36] Another East European McDonald's, which claims to be the busiest in the world, is open in Budapest, Hungary.[37]

In most franchising arrangements, the franchisor offers initial and continuing services based upon performance accomplishments. Average start-up cost for a McDonald's franchise is $500,000, and average annual sales per unit is $1.4 million.[38]

As with any business, there are risks and pitfalls in franchising. Not every franchise is as well managed as McDonald's. Pizza Time Theater, Minnie Pearl Chicken, and Wild Bill's Family Restaurants were franchises that went bankrupt. Problems arise with contract interpretations. Franchisees may want to sell products other than those specified or may wish to buy nonfranchisor-supplied materials, items, or ingredients. Colonel Sanders of Kentucky Fried Chicken was known for checking on whether his "herbs and spices" recipe for chicken was being used properly. When it was not, the franchisee would hear about it immediately. In some cases franchisors do not deliver on promises concerning advertising, training, and pricing. Disputes and conflict result in non-cooperative behavior and legal actions in some cases.

The franchisor can occupy any position in the marketing channel. However, four types of franchise systems are especially popular:

1. The *manufacturer-retailer* franchise, as in automobile dealerships (Ford, General Motors, Chrysler) and service stations (Exxon, Shell, Gulf).

Figure 11–7 Comparison of Conventional and Vertically Integrated Marketing Distribution Systems

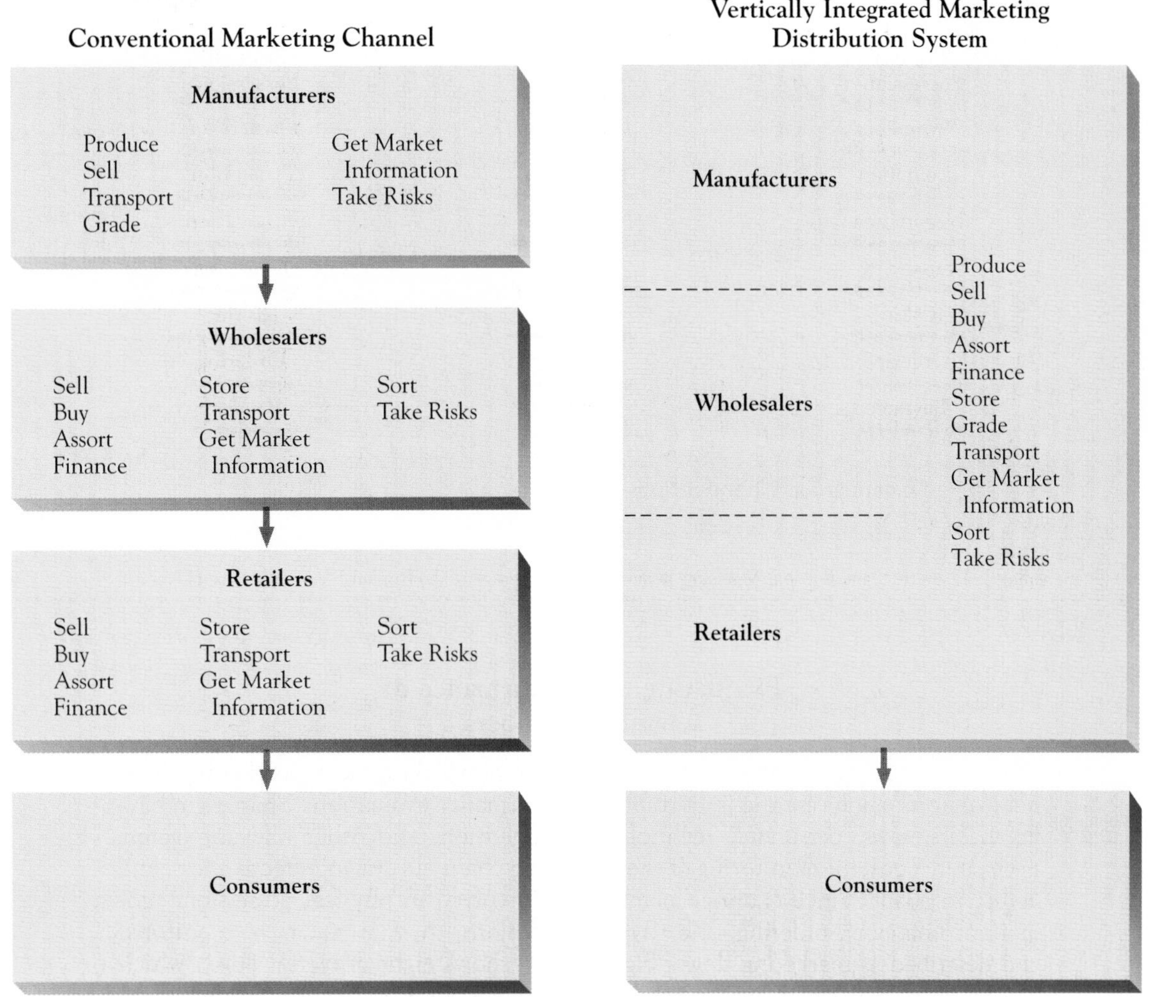

2. The *manufacturer-wholesaler* franchise, especially common in the soft drink area. Coca-Cola, Pepsi-Cola, and Seven-Up sell syrups to franchised wholesalers, who, in turn, bottle and distribute soft drinks to retailers.
3. The *wholesaler-retailer* franchise, as in Walgreen and Eckerd drug stores.
4. The *service-sponsored* franchise, such as Avis, Molly Maid, Jiffy Lube, Midas Mufflers, Holiday Camps, U.S.A., and H&R Block Co.

Vertically integrated marketing systems represent attempts to improve the effectiveness of marketing channels of distribution. They have been created in response to market condition changes, environmental forces, and the desire to survive and grow. They are also responses to the need to make conventional systems more dependent on team efforts. These two major forms of distribution are compared in Figure 11–7. Any benefits that accrue to members in marketing channels of distribution, conventional or vertically integrated, result from the quality of decision making. Decisions of such importance require information about the performance of channel members.

Figure 11–8 Marketing Flows in Channels

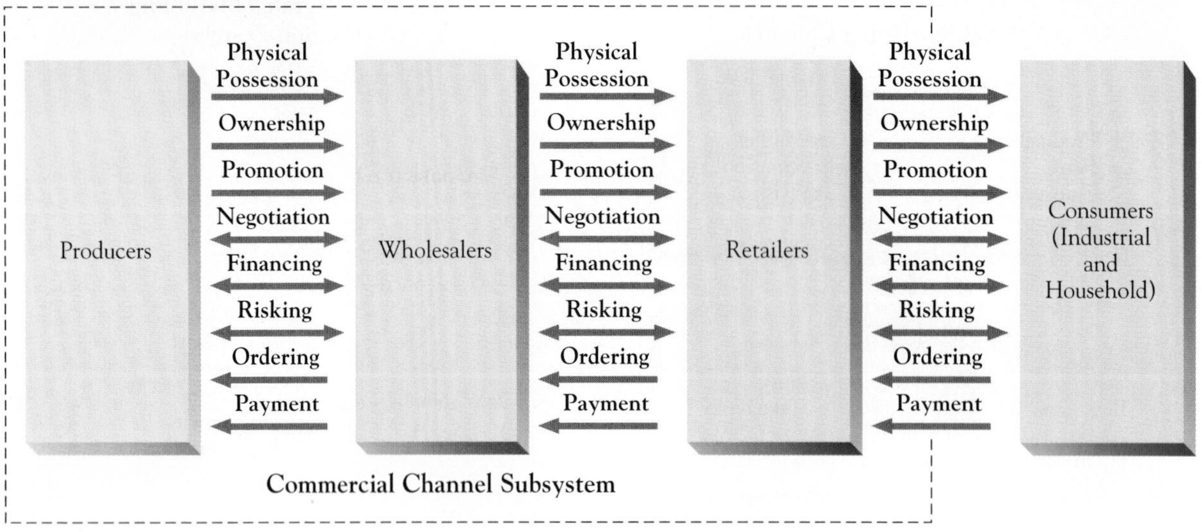

SOURCE: R. S. Valle, E. T. Grether, and R. Cox, *Marketing in the American Economy* (The Ronald Press, 1952), p. 113.

Evaluating the Performance of Channel Members

The issues, problems, changes, and continual decision making facing marketing channel managers emphasize the importance of performance evaluation. Changes in buying habits, laws, personnel, technology, competition, and other relevant factors necessitate constant monitoring of the marketing channel's design, effectiveness, and ability to adapt. Since channel members are involved in physical possession, promotion, financing, ordering, and payment functions, these areas can be monitored and described as marketing flows. Figure 11–8 shows eight universal flows, which can be measured. Exact measurement is difficult because no quantitative measures yield perfectly reliable and valid data on the efficiency of marketing flows, so marketing channels managers must develop their own performance-evaluation programs.

Determining the performance of intermediaries is extremely important for marketing managers who are supplying goods or services to middlemen. Sales performance is one indicator of the performance of marketing channel intermediaries. The manufacturer (or whoever is doing the evaluating) may decide to examine sales *to* an intermediary or sales *of* an intermediary to its customers. These two sets of data are rarely the same.

The supplier can examine sales trends by comparing current sales for a period with sales for a prior period, such as this summer versus last, one Labor Day versus another, or 1989 versus 1990. Daily, weekly, monthly, or annual comparisons permit the supplier to examine trends.

Another method of evaluating marketing channel performance is to compare the sales performance of each member in the channel with that of all members. The average sales for all members can first be calculated and then each member's performance compared to the average. This analysis can be used to examine total sales,

sales by product or region, and sales growth or decline. A second approach to channel-member comparisons is to calculate the average sales performance of the best-selling members. This aggregate average serves as a standard to which other members' sales performance can be compared.

Sales performance can also be evaluated on the basis of objectives achieved. Suppliers can set sales objectives alone or in consultation with channel members. Objectives can include the number of units sold in a period, total sales revenues, market shares, or total sales revenue/total sales cost ratios. Actual achievements of each channel member can then be compared by looking at the percentages of objectives accomplished.

Personal Computer Exercise

The costs and benefits of using intermediaries vary with intensive selective and exclusive distribution. In this PC exercise, you must determine the best distribution scheme for four different companies as well as rate the importance of various customer needs and company distribution goals.

KEY POINTS

• Marketing channels of distribution are pipelines through which goods and services flow from manufacturers to consumers and industrial users.

• The use of intermediaries increases the cost of goods, but less than other methods of distribution. Intermediaries also perform transactional, facilitative, and logistical functions in closing the gap between manufacturer and user. By performing these functions, middlemen create time, place, possession, and information utilities.

• A direct channel is one that finds a manufacturer selling directly to a consumer. An indirect channel has a number of intermediaries.

• Marketing managers, in deciding what channel is best for them at a particular time, consider such factors as goals and objectives, company strengths and weaknesses, customer characteristics, product characteristics, market mix characteristics, and environmental factors.

• The market coverage decision involves determining how many channel outlets to use. Intensive distribution or coverage involves using as many outlets as possible. Exclusive distribution involves the use of a single outlet in a geographic area. Selective distribution is an intermediate form of distribution.

• Manufacturers often attempt to influence intermediaries by exclusive dealing contracts, exclusive sales territories, and tying contracts. The legality of these contracts must be checked carefully before the contracts are implemented.

• Conflicts in marketing channels are inevitable but can be contained. Understanding vertical and horizontal conflict can help minimize conflict and improve cooperation.

• Channel captains can also improve cooperation. Channel captains emerge because of their expertise or power, by virtue of which they can influence others in the channel. Examples of manufacturer, retailer, and wholesaler channel captains can be easily found.

• Vertical marketing systems are professionally managed and centrally programmed networks engineered to achieve operating economies and maximize market impact. Corporate, contractual, and administered vertically integrated systems are used.

• Franchising is a form of marketing and distribution in which a parent company grants an individual (franchisee) or small company the right to do business in exchange for revenues from fees or royalties which the parent company collects.

• No matter what type of channel is used, manufacturers need to evaluate the performance of members. Evaluation permits the manufacturer to make necessary changes.

ISSUES FOR DISCUSSION

1. How does a firm like Campbell's provide form, time, place, and possession utilities for customers?

2. As more consumers conduct their banking transactions from their homes, what will be the impact on the traditional design (layout) and current staffing of banks?

3. Ping golf clubs can only be purchased by a select group of distributors. Why would some golfers prefer to use golf clubs sold selectively?

4. Why should a manufacturer evaluate the performance of channel members? Is such an evaluation useful in making decisions?

5. Why is a franchise such as McDonald's so expensive to start up?

6. What type of distribution system is being used in the video rental sales business? Why is their system so popular?

7. There are three main types of channel outlets—exclusive, intensive, and selective. Name a product that you or a friend has recently purchased that fits into each of these categories.

8. Why would an organization prefer to use a vertically integrated marketing system?

9. Why do consumers purchase products from channel leaders?

10. What criteria should be used to determine if the conflict that occurs between channel members has become dysfunctional?

GLOSSARY

Agent: Any intermediary with legal authority to act on behalf of a manufacturer. Agents do not take title to goods.

Broker: A wholesaler who does not take title to the goods and serves as a facilitator to bring buyers and sellers together.

Channel captain: The dominant member in a marketing channel, who helps coordinate, direct, and support other members.

Channel of distribution: Any firm or individual who participates in the flow of goods and services as they move from producer to ultimate user (consumer or industrial).

Exclusive distribution: A distribution approach in which one or a few outlets are selected to resell a product or service.

Form utilities: Activities used to change the appearance or composition of a good or service to make it more attractive to potential and actual users.

Franchising: A form of marketing and distribution in which a parent company grants a person or small company the right to do business in a prescribed manner over a specified period of time in a given location. The parent company is the franchisor and the person or small company the franchisee. The rights may include permission to sell the franchisor's products and to use a name, symbol, special ingredient, or store layout.

Horizontal conflict: Conflict between intermediaries who operate at the same level in a channel (for example, two or more retailers).

Intensive distribution: A distribution strategy in which as many outlets as possible are used to resell the product or service.

Merchant: An independently owned business that takes title to the products handled.

Middleman: An intermediary between the manufacturer and user.

Place utilities: Activities that make products or services available where purchasers want them.

Possession utilities: Activities provided by middlemen who help consumers take possession of a good or service.

Replacement rate: The rate at which a good or service is purchased and consumed. Milk is a high replacement-rate good, a set of china a low replacement-rate good.

Reverse channel: A channel in which goods flow from consumers or industrial users to producers or other marketing intermediaries.

Role theory: A behavioral science body of knowledge that attempts to clarify the importance of role expectations of channel members. Role theory can be used to examine the consequences of conflict among channel members.

Selective distribution: A distribution strategy in which only a limited number of outlets are allowed to resell a product or service.

Time utilities: Activities used to make a good or service available without the consumer wasting time.

Vertical conflict: Conflict between channel members at different levels.

Vertically integrated market systems: Professionally managed and centrally programmed channels of distribution designed to achieve operating economies and maximum market impact.

NOTES

1. Committee on Definitions, *Marketing Definitions: A Glossary of Marketing Terms* (American Marketing Association, 1960), p. 10.

2. Louis W. Stern and Adel I. El-Ansary, *Marketing Channels* (Prentice-Hall, 1989), p. 10.

3. Donald J. Bowersox, M. Bixby Cooper, Douglas M. Lambert, and Donald A. Taylor, *Management in Marketing Channels* (McGraw-Hill, 1980), p. 11.

4. Wroe Alderson, "The Analytical Framework for Marketing," in Delbert Duncan (ed.), *Proceedings: Conference of Marketing Teachers from Far Western States* (University of Calfornia, 1968), p. 15.

5. Philip J. Kotler and Gary Armstrong, *Principles of Marketing* (Prentice-Hall, 1983), p. 350.

6. Gul Butaney and Lawrence H. Wortzel, "Distribution Power Versus Manufacturer Power: The Customer Role," *Journal of Marketing*, January 1988, pp. 52–63.

7. Robert L. Heilbroner and Lester C. Thurow, *Economics Explained*, New York: Touchstone, 1987, pp. 59–60.

8. James D. Hlavacek and Tommy J. McCuistion, "Industrial Distributors: When, How, and Where?" *Harvard Business Review*, March-April 1983, p. 97.

9. William G. Zikmund and William J. Stanton, "Recycling Solid Wastes: A Channels of Distribution Problem," *Journal of Marketing*, July 1971, p. 34.

10. "Business Margins In Japan and The U.S.," *Journal of Japanese Trade and Industry*, January 1989, p. 55.

11. "Drive On Fritz," *The Economist*, October 22, 1988, pp. 75–76.

12. "Ways Into Fortress Japan," *The Economist*, October 22, 1988, pp. 18–19.

13. James A. Narus and James C. Anderson, "Strengthen Distributor Performance Through Channel Positioning," *Sloan Management Review*, Winter 1988, pp. 31–40.

14. "Drive-Thru Disc," *Digital Audio*, February 1988, p. 8.

15. Kate Fitzgerald, "Banking On Service," *Advertising Age*, March 7, 1988, p. 32.

16. Scott Hume, "Blockbuster's Plot," *Advertising Age*, March 7, 1988, p. 54.

17. Berkeley Rice, "Freshly Ground Success," *Profiles, Inc.*, March 1988, pp. 13–14.

18. Louis P. Bucklin, "Retail Strategy and the Classification of Consumer Goods," *Journal of Marketing* (January 1963), pp. 50–55.

19. Robert C. Weigand, "Fit Products and Channels to Your Channels," *Harvard Business Review*, January-February 1977, pp. 101–102.

20. Leo Aspinwall, *Four Marketing Theories* (University of Colorado, 1961).

21. "Skil Finally Breaks the Profits Barrier," *Business Week*, November 25, 1972, p. 50.

22. Kenneth G. Hardy and Allan J. McGrath, *Marketing Channel Management* (Glenview, IL: Scott, Foresman, 1988), p. 437.

23. Ravi S. Achol and Louis W. Stern, "Environmental Determinants of Decision-Making Uncertainty In Marketing Channels," *Journal of Marketing Research*, February 1988, pp. 36–50.

24. Mary Rowland, "Competition, Market Shifts Hit Staid Life Insurance Arena," *Dun's Business Month*, February 1985, pp. 77–80.

25. Allan J. McGrath and Kenneth G. Hardy, "When Mergers Rock Your Distribution Channels," *Business Marketing*, June 1987, pp. 68–75.

26. Martin L. Bell, *Marketing: Concepts and Strategy* (Houghton Mifflin, 1979), p. 282.

27. *U.S. v. Arnold Schwinn & Company* 388 U.S. 365 (1967).

28. Carol M. Larson, Robert E. Wegend, and John S. Wright, *Basic Retailing* (Prentice-Hall, 1976) p. 525.

29. "41st Annual Report On American Industry," *Forbes*, January 9, 1989, p. 148.

30. See John Gaski, "The Theory and Power of Conflict In Channels of Distribution," *Journal of Marketing*, Summer 1984, pp. 9–29 and also Stern and El-Ansary, Chapter 7.

31. This section draws information from Hardy and McGrath, pp. 101–111.

32. Phyllis Berman, "The Steel Behind Steelcase," *Forbes*, October 17, 1985, pp. 90–99.

33. Cynthia R. Milsap, "Conquering The Distributor Incentive Blues," *Business Marketing*, November 1985, pp. 122–125.

34. Stern and El-Ansary, *Marketing Channels*, p. 408.

35. Molly Wade McGrath, *Top Sellers U.S.A.*, New York: William Morrow & Co., 1983, pp. 66–67.

36. Richard T. Ashman, "Franchising Integral To Global Economy," *USA Today*, September 9, 1987, pp. 5B–10B.

37. "Yugoslavia Joins McDonaldland," *USA Today*, March 15, 1988, p. 2B.

38. Al Urbanski, "The Franchise Option," *Sales & Marketing Management*, February 1988, pp. 28–32.

CASE APPLICATION 11–1

Aslesens: The Oldest Distributor in the Twin Cities

Aslesens was one of the oldest food service distributors in the United States. They closed their doors in December 1987, after 108 years of business. The loss of Aslesens created an opportunity for other distributors in the Twin Cities market. Some of the major players in the market are Kraft/American, PYA/Monarch, CFS Continental, Sysco, and Sexton. There are also independents like Reinhart Institutional Foods and Upper Lakes Foods.

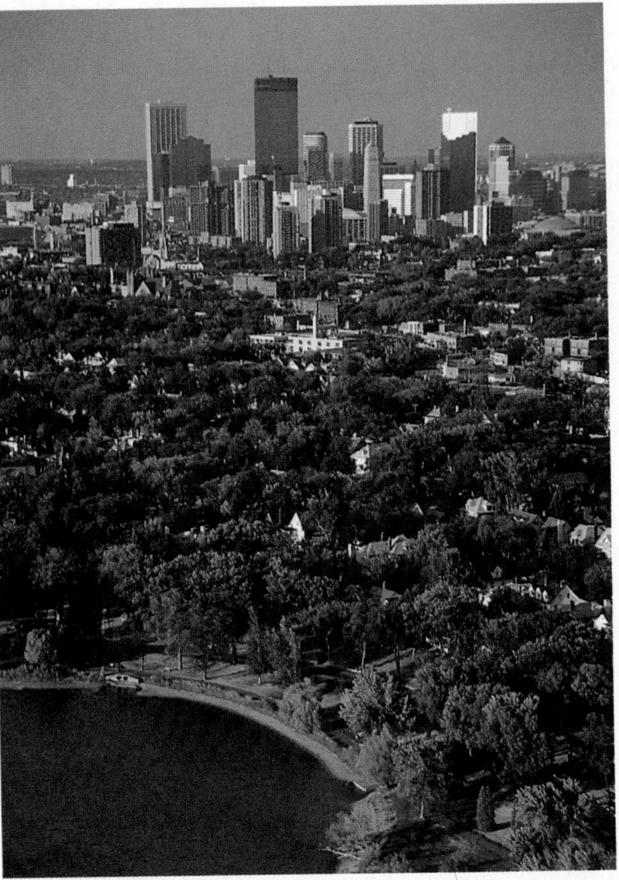

The Twin Cities market is the fifteenth largest metro food service market in the United States. Perhaps the major beneficiary of Aslesens' demise is Reinhart Institutional Foods, based in La Crosse, Wisconsin. They hired five of Aslesen's top salespeople as well as the director of sales. Reinhart also opened a sales office in the Minneapolis suburb of Hopkins. Moving closer to channel members is important in Reinhart's plan to capture a major portion of Aslesens' market share.

PYA/Monarch has also picked up ten sales reps from Aslesens. PYA/Monarch moved aggressively into the produce business and has continued to strengthen its healthcare and school food service distribution operations.

One might ask what brought about the demise of Aslesens, which was ranked high among local distributors in former years. Many see the roots of the problem going back long before the firm's acquisition in 1986 by American Food Service Supply Co., a New York-based holding company.

In fact, Aslesens' sales were virtually flat throughout most of the 1980s, and the distributor dropped out of the list of the nation's Top 50 distributors early on in this period. The company simply was behind the times in the competitive distribution arena, according to some. "Eleven years ago, nonfoods were more than half of Aslesens' volume," comments one area distributor executive. "They never really put it together with food, they never really focused on penetration, and they traveled long distances to make deliveries."

This observation was echoed by Wes Mainord, the last president of Aslesens. "This was primarily a supply company before its merger with American Food Service Supply," Mainord commented. "Sixty percent of its business was in nonfoods." According to Mainord, while Aslesens had been relatively flat for the previous five years, business was picking up and the distributor was anticipating dramatic growth for 1988. "We are running at the rate of $75 million for the calendar year," he said. This would have meant an increase of 35 percent, as compared with the modest gains of 5 to 6 percent during the prior five years.

This rate of growth, however, may have been more of a liability than an asset, for, according to some observers, an overambitious growth strategy in an attempt to turn the business around—compounded by outmoded accounting systems—may have been a major factor in the company's demise. This strategy reportedly included a new thrust on chain and other low-margin business.

At the same time, Aslesens acquired H. Brooks Co., Minneapolis, a local produce house. Aslesens was never able to integrate it efficiently with its other business.

SOURCE: Adapted from Stephanie Salken, "Shake-Up In Minneapolis," *Institutional Distribution*, February 1988, pp. 66, 68.

Questions

1. Why would being acquired by another firm be a reason why Aslesens started to have problems?

2. Why would customers become loyal, committed, and dependent on a firm such as Aslesens?

3. What lessons about integration are pointed out by this case?

CASE APPLICATION 11–2

Franchising Ideas, Experts, and Caution

The creativity that goes into franchising is endless. Every day approximately fifty new franchises enter the market. For example, if you're an arm wrestling enthusiast with a bad grip or a short arm, guess what? You're in luck. Jack Barringer has developed and franchised a World Class Arm Wrestling Machine. He has already sold over 35 franchises in the United States. Using the machine, which allows for singles or doubles competition, competitors grab onto rubber hands, eliminating unfair grip advantages. Elbow pads can be adjusted so that each competitor, no matter how short his or her arms are, has a fair chance. Franchisees pay a $25,000 fee that allows them the right to market the machine in a restricted geographic area.

If you're looking to invest in a franchise opportunity that serves a $4 billion market and gets a lot of its advertising for free, Sports Fantasy may be the one. Sports Fantasy offers officially licensed professional and college sports apparel, as well as sports-related gifts and novelties. Each outlet sells jerseys, jackets, hats, and other gear bearing the team logos and numbers of favorite sports personalities. Sports Fantasy has grown to seven franchises and thirteen company-owned stores. A $15,000 franchise fee and a 5 percent royalty on gross sales are needed to get started in business.

How would you like to wake up to an eight-foot birthday card in your front yard? Michael Hoefinger is the president of Yard Cards, Inc. For $35, anyone can have a personalized anniversary, get well, birthday, or congratulations card placed in someone's yard, home, or office for 24 hours. Franchisees are required to buy one of each of the ten copyrighted cards for $225 each.

Leslie and Douglas Alvey decided to sell cinnamon rolls in a shopping mall. Mom's Cinnamon Rolls Shop, Inc., became a very popular place. Now Mom's has 35 franchised stores, and people are waiting in line to get a franchise.

The Table on pp. 370–371 shows data on ten fast growing franchises.

A franchisor often makes promises. Buying a franchise, someone else's idea, or his or her expertise and support don't always lead to profits. One of the first steps a person must take is to carefully analyze the franchise. Here are 12 points to consider before becoming involved in a franchise of any kind:

1. *Franchisors who say you don't need to read the disclosure document.* According to a study by the Federal Trade Commission (FTC), approximately 40 percent of new franchisees sign an agreement without reading it.

2. *Franchisors who say you don't need to have a lawyer or an accountant look at the agreement.*

3. *A franchisor who doesn't give you a copy of the disclosure document at your first face-to-face meeting to discuss the franchise.* Federal fines of up to $10,000 are levied for each violation of this procedure. Report violations immediately to the Bureau of Consumer Protection at the FTC.

4. *Pressure to sign before the legally required ten-day waiting period.*

5. *Any franchisor you don't feel good about.* "An important rule in franchising is know your franchisor. It's like a marriage, and you wouldn't marry someone you met one afternoon," says Patrick J. Boroian, president of Francorp, Inc., Olympia Fields, Illinois.

6. *Thin management.* Make sure you're going to get the support you're paying for. Boroian suggests looking at how many supervisors the franchisor has. McDonald's has one supervisor for every twenty franchisees.

7. *A marginally successful prototype or no prototype at all.* "Most of those that fail are those that start franchising without a prototype," says Boroian.

8. *Franchisors who don't give you a list of all franchisees.* "Calling just one

Rank, Franchise, Location	Parent Company	Franchised Units	Company Owned Units	Founded	First Franchised Unit Opened
1. Master Works, Greenville, SC	Master Works International, Inc.	81	0	1986	9/86
2. Perkits Yogurt Shops, Atlanta	Perkits Yogurt, Inc.	52	4	1985	7/86
3. Blockbuster Videos, Dallas	Blockbuster Entertainment Corp.	51	59	1986	8/86
4. Park Inn International, Irving, TX	Park Inns Int'l Inc.	51	12	1986	3/86
5. Cindy's Cinnamon Rolls, Fallbrook, CA	Cindy's Cinnamon Rolls	43	0	1985	5/86
6. Laser Lube, Brooklawn, NJ	Lightning Lube, Inc.	40	0	1985	4/86
7. Ambus, Baton Rouge, LA	Ambus, Inc.	34	4	1986	2/87
8. Flying Colors, Houston	Int'l. Flying Colors Franchising Corp.	34	4	1985	8/86
9. Cinnamon Sam's Overland Park, KS	Cinnamon Sam's, Inc.	32	3	1985	3/87
10. The Elephant's Trunk, Midland Park, NJ	Tale of the Elephant's Trunk, Inc.	27	2	1983	9/86

or two franchisees is a mistake," says John E. Kinch, author of *Franchising: The Inside Story.* Be sure to ask about such things as start-up costs, income, and the quality of the franchisor's support.

9. *Franchisors who make projections about how much you can earn.* Any projections have to be based on what the franchisor itself is earning in its company-owned store. If projections are based on what franchisees have made, those figures must be disclosed in most states. "If they don't put it in writing and tell you orally, it's a violation of federal law," says Boroian.

10. *A franchisor who has no operations manual or a skimpy one.*

11. *A high franchisee turnover rate.* Terminations should be reported in the disclosure document.

12. *Litigation against the franchisor.* The fact that the franchisor has been sued doesn't necessarily mean you should decide against buying a franchise. However, you should look at the nature and the number of suits. Be aware that

Franchise Fee ($)	Other Start-Up Costs ($)	Royalty Fee	Notes
$13,500–14,995	$2,600–19,300	6%–10%	Industrial cleaning, including carpets and acoustical ceilings; name changed from Janimaster
20,000	70,000–98,800	6%	Founders Perk Evans and Kit Evans are still in their 20s
100,000	410,000–645,000	6%	Franchisor has an inventory of more than 150,000 tapes; stock trades on the OTC market
4,500–22,500	52,500–7,001,600	2.9%	Six out of every seven franchises were conversions; founder Robert L. Brock sold out of Brock Hotel
25,000	33,500–77,000	5%	This husband and wife team, Cindy and Thomas Harris, is rolling in the dough; typically located in malls
19,500	34,800–36,900	7%	Primarily conversions of old gas stations
25,000	39,600–40,200	10%	Brokerage services for buyers and sellers of small businesses
15,000	22,100–22,700	$1,000/ mo.	Touches-up auto paint jobs from specially equipped vans; most franchises sold in the Southwest
20,000	69,300–104,600	5%	Another cinnamon roll franchise on a roll; the chairman has majority interest in nine other companies
8,000	54,300–75,900	6%	If the Grimms had gone into retail instead of fairy tales, they might have dreamed up this children's gift store

only litigation that has to do with deceit, fraud, or cases where money or property were allegedly stolen have to be reported in the disclosure document.

SOURCES: "Man Wrestles Machine," *Entrepreneur,* February 1988, p. 119; "Attention Sports," *Entrepreneur,* March 1988, p. 108; Echo M. Garrett, "Franchises On A Role," *Venture,* March 1988, pp. 39–47; Jeannie Ralston, "Promises, Promises," *Venture,* March 1988, pp. 55–57.

Questions

1. Why is it fairly easy to present a franchise as an attractive business deal to a prospective franchisee?

2. Some claim that franchising is a complex distribution business. What do they mean?

3. Why would royalty fees and franchise fees differ across franchises?

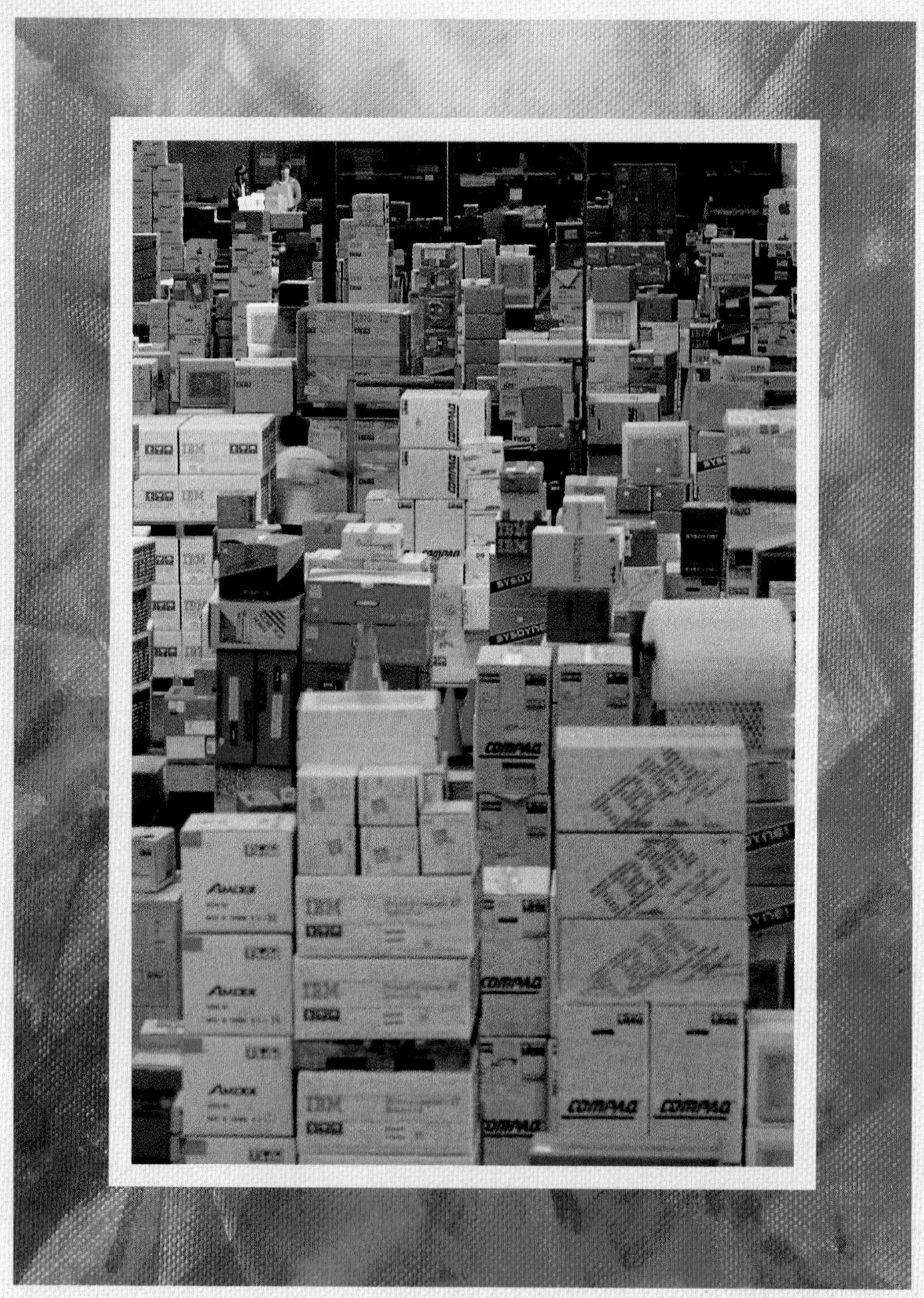
IBM
COMPAQ

12

Wholesalers

Learning Objectives

Upon completing this chapter, you will be able to do the following:

DEFINE
the functions performed by merchant wholesalers.

DESCRIBE
the types of wholesaling firms and their margin structure.

EXPLAIN
the importance of wholesaling in the economy.

LIST
the ways that wholesalers may be classified.

ILLUSTRATE
the institutions that perform marketing functions.

MARKETING PROFILE

The Wholesale Club Has Some Appeal

If you were to open a small restaurant business and needed sales receipts, ketchup, pens, salt shakers, and a cash register, where would you go? Traditionally, you could get the sales receipts and pens from an office supply wholesaler, the ketchup from a restaurant supplier, and the cash register from a business machine specialist. Generally, the items would be bought through a sales representative and would be delivered to your place of business complete with a new line of credit for further purchases. However, if you were willing to pick up the items yourself, pay by cash or check, and give up the personal attention of the sales assistant, you could buy the same merchandise at a wholesale club at substantial savings. This is exactly what many small businesses have turned to in order to get supplies they need in quantities that are manageable, with little or no waiting, and at low prices.

The concept began over twelve years ago in southern California, when Sol Price, of Price Club, decided to open a warehouse that catered to small businesses. This warehouse would act as a coop wholesale outlet for area businesses that didn't have the volume to attract wholesalers. Businesses were happy because they could save over conventional channels, and distributors were not upset because these smaller businesses represented more of a burden than a source of revenue. Thus the wholesale club concept was born. From then, it has grown into an $18 billion industry with over 350 whole-type clubs across the nation. These clubs span the nation from Price Company in San Diego, Pace Membership in Denver, The Wholesale Club in Indianapolis, and BJ's Wholesale Club in Natick,

MA. In this *Marketing Profile*, three leaders in the wholesale club industry talk about their philosophies concerning the role of the wholesale club, its future, and potential improvements.

Sam's Wholesale Club: Holding the lead in number of clubs (104), Jack Shewmaker, former vice-chairman Wal-Mart Stores, Inc., offers several reasons for the success of the wholesale club concept. First, some fast turnover items sell before vendors are paid. This "pretty neat trick in cash flow" is an incentive to keep high volume, fast turnover items in the club. Packaging has also saved costs for the club and, therefore, the consumer. Many times manufacturers shrink wrap five items and put Sam's tag on them, minimizing labor costs once the items are in the store. One financial success is the lower labor costs as a percentage of sales in the wholesale clubs, the result of fewer personnel providing service functions and more efficient check-out and check verification systems.

Price Savers: Thomas R. Grimm, president, feels that the new business can benefit the most from a wholesale club. Without having to develop relationships with suppliers, endure long-term agreements, or be penalized for small orders, the new business can gain all of the benefits of a wholesaler immediately with a wholesale club. One problem that he sees with the concept, though, is the "blinder effect": Many customers buy particular products, such as soft drinks, without looking to see if they can save on copier paper.

The Wholesale Club: The Wholesale Club has a responsibility to the customer, claims John Geisse, Chairman. Products need to be consistently in stock so businesses can rest assured they don't have to keep an otherwise large inventory. The prices need to be noticeably cheaper. If customers are not surprised by the low price, the club isn't doing its job. He feels wholesalers are successful because they are the next logical step in the national trend toward self-service.

The success and customer-orientation that is appealing suggests that wholesale clubs seem to be here to stay. This *Marketing Profile* illustrates the role that wholesalers can play as intermediaries. Wholesalers, like other intermediaries, serve the needs of customers who prefer price, service, and product mix.

SOURCE: "Wholesale Clubs," *Discount Merchandiser*, June 1988, pp. 54–68; Johnson, Jay L., "Five Wholesale Clubs Discuss Their Operations," *Discount Merchandiser*, November 1987, pp. 24–43; personal communication with The Wholesale Club, June 1989.

Each of us confronts many channel intermediaries every day. Even more important, each of us benefits greatly from the work performed, but we may not know about the role played by wholesalers.

Frank Jackson sets out early one Saturday morning in Dallas to pick up a few food items, get a new radio speaker for his car, get a prescription filled for some hand cream, and purchase some gardening items. Since many stores and pharmacies carry these items, his biggest decision is which one he should go to. He easily buys these items in about two hours time. (This includes a quick, reasonably inexpensive lunch at Denny's.) To accomplish these tasks in such a short period of time would be impossible in many countries.

The functioning of this system of intermediaries, which makes obtaining goods so easy for Frank Jackson and the rest of us, is all but invisible except when it does not work properly. (Think about the long lines at some supermarket checkout counters.) Of course, we see retailers, but have we ever thought about the functions they perform? Wholesalers are even more invisible. The dry skin prescription that Frank Jackson purchased was handled by McKesson Corporation, a wholesaler with over $2 billion in annual sales.

Wholesalers differ from retailers, such as Sears, in a number of ways. Most of the time, wholesalers sell to businesses. On the other hand, retailers sell in most cases directly to final customers. Wholesalers spend less time and money on promotion than retailers because of their customer base. The trade area of wholesalers is usually larger than the trade area of retailers.

In this chapter we explain how the wholesale structure works, why wholesalers are needed, and what functions wholesalers perform. In addition, we explore the organizational structure of wholesale institutions and describe their margin structure.

Functions of Intermediaries

In Chapter 1 we noted that exchange gaps exist between producers and consumers. These spatial, temporal, perceptual, ownership, and value exchange gaps are filled by marketing intermediaries like wholesalers and retailers who create place, time, possession, and form utility by performing certain functions.

The basic functions of marketing, discussed in Chapters 1 and 11, are divided into three types: (1) *transactional*, involving buying, selling, and risk-taking through taking title to goods; (2) *logistical*, involving transportation and storage, plus assembly and sorting goods; and (3) *facilitating*, including financing, providing information, grading, and postpurchase service.

It is important to note that none of these functions is attributed to any specific intermediary. The manufacturer, wholesaler, retailer, or even the end consumer could perform any or all of these functions. There are two critical points:

1. *These functions must be performed by someone in all cases.* One can eliminate specific channel members, but not the functions they perform.
2. *It is not necessarily cheaper to eliminate an intermediary.* A specific wholesaler or retailer may perform its functions more economically than producers.

Extension to Services

Thus far we have discussed the functions necessary in the flow of physical goods. Similar functions are also required for services and the activities of nonprofit orga-

MARKETING IN ACTION

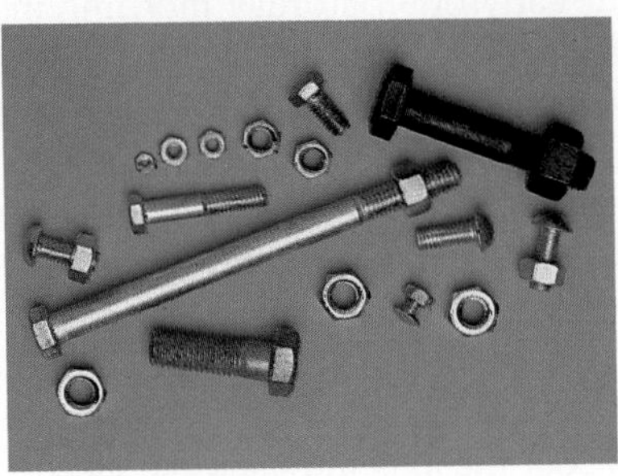

There Is a Place for the Service Wholesaler

Marley Cooling Tower Co., based in Mission, Kansas, was working on a Georgia Power & Light nuclear plant when employees discovered that they were short 15 bolts and 56 nuts in a hard-to-get 1 ¾-inch size. If the buyer had sent an order to Korea, the delay could have meant a week's stoppage. However, they called Special-T Metals in Lenexa, Kansas, instead, and the bolts were manufactured, shipped, and delivered to the site within three days. In this case, availability was more important than price, and Special-T Metals got the job done.

Special-T Metals' parent company, Sun Distributors based in Philadelphia, stresses that all of its companies sell service rather than products. The term that describes this type of approach is "value added," which means that the goods received by the wholesaler are somehow enhanced by alteration or expertise. There is an increasing void in the market as manufacturing concerns are offering less service and fewer products. "Value added" intermediaries can turn this into opportunity by filling in the gaps. One reason for the popularity of this approach is increasing costs in storage and delivery, and the availability of technology allowing the quick manufacturing of goods. This means that it is more cost effective for a "value added" wholesaler to manufacture items as needed or modify existing products to perform specialized tasks. Using this approach, engineers try to solve problems with standard equipment rather than manufacturing a new specialized machine.

Sun Distributors' Walter Norris unit sells the idea of retrofitting injection molding machines. Retrofitting is the remanufacturing of older machinery to meet existing needs. They have found that it is less expensive to remanufacture outmoded hydraulic machinery than to buy new, expensive, and possibly less durable machinery. Recently Walter Norris was hired to retrofit an injection molding machine at a Chrysler plant providing savings of $100,000 to the plant and $70,000 revenue to itself.

SOURCE: Ruth Simon "We Sell Service, Not Products," *Forbes*, March 7, 1988, pp. 98–103; personal communication with Sun Distributors, 1989.

---

nizations. They must deal with spatial, temporal, perceptual, and value gaps; the ownership gap is not usually involved. Thus, creating *place* and *time* utility is essential to these type of organizations. And the associated functions of location of facilities, hours of business, provision of information, and selling are all involved for services and nonprofit organizations. Consider the following examples:

- The Michigan Dental Society provides free *in-school* checkups.
- Hospitals run out-patient clinics at various neighborhood *locations* in Chicago.
- Banks *stay open* late on Friday nights and on Saturday morning in parts of the country and provide twenty-four hour automatic teller machines.

One example of a service wholesaler is Sun Distributors, discussed in the *Marketing in Action* above.

Participating Institutions

The performance of these functions in the marketing channel involves institutions other than the manufacturer, wholesaler, retailer, and end consumer. As Figure 12–1 shows, three are *facilitating and logistical agencies* such as marketing research firms, insurance companies, financial institutions, advertising agencies, storage firms, and transportation companies. These agencies are not involved in the *transactional func-*

Figure 12–1 Institutions Performing Marketing Functions

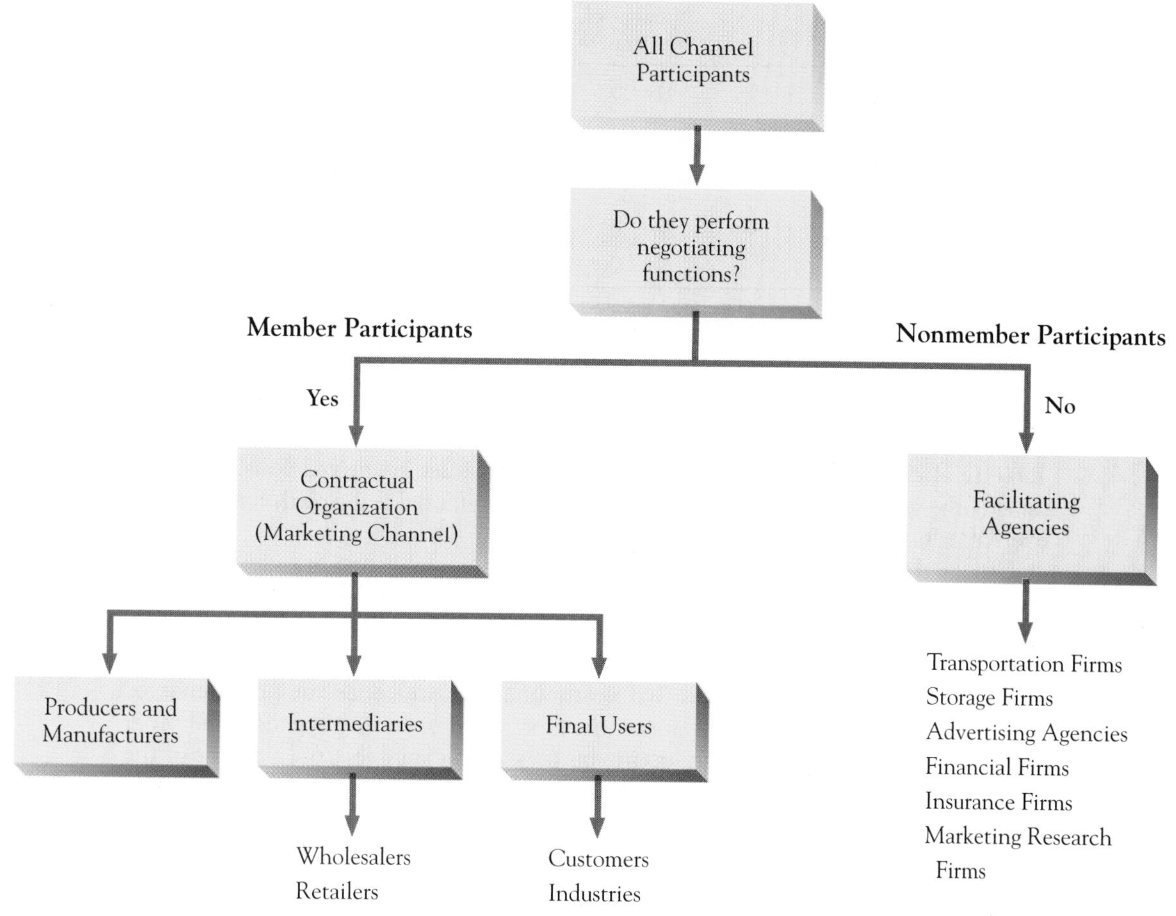

tion of buying and selling goods and services; they are specialty companies that perform their tasks based on agreements with the contractual organizations in the channel. They exist because they usually can perform their functions less expensively by specializing and spreading their costs among many clients. A channel member may take over any or all of these functions, and, of course, also pay the associated costs.[1]

Wholesaling

A **wholesaler** is a business unit that buys and resells merchandise to retailers and other merchants and/or to industrial, institutional, and commercial users; it does not sell in significant amounts to ultimate consumers.[2] The wholesalers' main customers are other businesses. Thus, sales by one manufacturer to another, or one retailer to another, are **wholesaling sales**. Our discussion here primarily concerns institutions where the majority of sales are in wholesaling—that is, where firms are primarily engaged in buying and reselling to other firms. Over six million people are employed in wholesaling.[3] The size of the wholesaling trade in the United States reached about

Table 12–1 Total American Wholesale Trade: Selected Years

Year	Number of Wholesalers	Wholesale Sales (in billions)
1986	416,000	$1998
1977	383,000	1258
1972	370,000	695
1967	311,000	460
1958	287,000	286
1948	216,000	181

SOURCE: *Statistical Abstract of the U.S.* (U.S. Government Printing Office, 1987), p. 764.

$2.5 trillion in 1988, up from $1,258 billion in 1977, and from $181 billion in 1948. Table 12–1 compares wholesaling dollar value to retail sales in selected years. Although some of the growth in dollar sales reflects inflation, substantial real growth has occurred, even after taking this into account.

Today there are approximately 415,000 wholesale establishments with total sales of over $2.2 trillion. It is estimated that about 60 percent of all manufacturers' products shipped in a year went through wholesalers.[4] Table 12–1 presents data on the size and growth of wholesaling in the United States.

Wholesalers perform services that cost money and influence the prices charged customers. Table 12–2 presents data on the gross profit operating expenses and other expenses wholesalers face in conducting business. For example, 26.2 percent of the price of Frank Jackson's prescription hand cream went to McKesson Corporation for assorting, sorting, transporting, and providing other services to the drug store. McKesson's before-taxes profit on the $4.19 jar of hand cream Frank purchased was about fifteen cents.

REVIEW YOUR MARKETING KNOWLEDGE

• Although wholesaling is such an important part of the economy, the public has little knowledge about wholesalers. Why?

• What kind of services does a wholesaler perform for a retailer? For an industrial producer?

Wholesaling Functions

Some wholesalers perform all of the marketing functions or services, while others specialize in performing one or some of them.[5] A full-service wholesaler might offer the following services for its *manufacturers* or *suppliers*.

1. *Provide a sales force* to sell the goods to retailers and other buyers.
2. *Communicate* manufacturers' advertising deals and plans.
3. *Maintain inventory*, thus reducing the level of the inventory suppliers have to carry.
4. Arrange or undertake *transportation*.

Table 12–2 Gross Profit, Operating Expenses, All Other Expenses (Net), and Profit Before Taxes for Wholesalers by Product Category[1]

Product Category of Wholesaler	Gross Profit (As Per Cent of Sales)[2]	Operating Expenses (As Per Cent of Sales)	All Other Expenses (As Per Cent of Sales)	Profit Before Taxes (As Per Cent of Sales)
Automobile equipment	30.1	26.5	0.6	2.9
Chemicals and allied products	25.4	22.7	0.5	2.3
Drugs and related items	26.2	21.9	0.8	3.4
Electronic parts and equipment	30.0	25.2	0.6	4.2
Flowers and florists' supplies	35.0	30.9	1.0	3.2
Coffee, tea, and spices	21.3	18.6	0.6	2.1
Fish and seafood	16.2	13.8	0.8	1.5
General groceries	16.9	15.4	0.4	1.2
Wine, liquor, and beer	22.8	20.2	0.6	2.0
General merchandise	34.8	30.0	1.2	3.5
Hardware and paints	29.7	26.3	0.8	2.6
Jewelry	29.3	24.4	1.2	3.7
Building materials	23.8	20.4	0.7	2.8
Fuel oil	12.4	10.5	0.1	1.7
Cotton	12.8	11.3	0.0	1.5

[1]In interpreting these data, RMA cautions that the Studies be regarded only as a general guideline and not as an absolute industry norm. This is due to limited samples within categories, the categorization of companies by their primary Standard Industrial Classification (SIC) number only, and different methods of operations by companies within the same industry. For these reasons, RMA recommends that the figures be used only as general guidelines in addition to other methods of financial analysis.

[2]Total costs of wholesaling, which include expenses and profit. There are some rounding differences.

SOURCE: Adapted from '85 *Annual Statement Studies* (Philadelphia: Robert Morris Associates, 1985). The data have been reproduced from the *all sizes column* on pp. 45–47. © 1985, Robert Morris Associates; reprinted by permission.

5. *Provide capital* by paying cash or quick payments for goods.
6. Provide suppliers with *market information* they cannot afford or are unable to obtain themselves.
7. Undertake *credit risk* by granting credit to customers and absorbing any bad debts, thus relieving the supplier of this burden.
8. *Assume the risk* for the product by taking title.

The wholesaler may perform the services listed below for *its customers:*

1. *Buy* goods the end market will desire and make them available to customers.
2. Maintain *inventory,* thus reducing customers' costs.
3. *Transport* goods to customers quickly.
4. Provide *market information* and business consulting services.
5. Provide *financing* through granting credit, critical to small retailers especially.
6. *Order* goods in the types and quantities customers desire.

The *Marketing in Action* on page 380 illustrates how Super Valu has fared in the retailing business. Super Valu is a wholesaler that supplies over 1500 small, independent food stores typically located in communities with fewer than 10,000 people. Its sales are about $2 billion.

MARKETING IN ACTION

Can Super Valu Do Everything?

In the past, Super Valu has done two things well: help people run supermarkets and operate grocery warehouses. In the last eight years it has grown into the largest grocery wholesaler in the country, supplying staples, produce, and dairy and bakery products to 3,006 stores in 32 states. Super Valu has built this empire by serving the needs of the retailers, providing them with advantages only the big chains are supposed to have: low prices, up-to-date stores, and good locations. Recently, however, it has expanded into other parts of the grocery business that could stall its performance.

In 1985, Super Valu bought Atlanta's financially troubled Food Giant supermarket chain figuring that it could use its industry expertise to make it profitable. Some also feel that it had little choice because it was Super Valu's biggest customer in the area. Since then, they have closed 16 and sold 33 of the original 57 stores, and they are still waiting for a profitable quarter. Despite the size and expertise of Super Valu, competitors have flooded into the Atlanta market, opening over one million square feet of supermarket space in 1987 alone.

A venture that has proven successful for Super Valu has been an innovative cross between a supermarket and a grocery warehouse called Cub Foods. The 42 stores in nine states blend wholesale and retail marketing into one store, a retail supermarket warehouse. Evidently the formula is working; Cub claims 43 percent of the market in Green Bay, Wisconsin, 16 percent in Columbus, Ohio, and 3 percent in Chicago. Some feel that this innovation, although profitable now, could pose problems in the future with Super Valu's foundation wholesale business. Claims of unfair price and distribution advantages by Super Valu's retail customers could surface if Cub Foods' sales begin to erode.

This *Marketing in Action* illustrates how a wholesaler can be an expert in an industry at the wholesale level, but flounder or produce conflict by stepping out of its traditional bounds.

SOURCE: Jan Parr, "Leader of the Pack," *Forbes*, February 8, 1988, pp. 35–36.

Classifying Wholesalers

The terms wholesaler, merchant, and agent are used when discussing the wholesaling business operation. Figure 12–2 is a classification system for intermediaries that conduct wholesaling activities. In most cases, wholesalers sell products and services to other businesses who either use what is purchased or resell it to the end user.

The merchant, company-owned sales branch, agents, and broker wholesalers activities can be described in terms of dimensions:

1. *Assumption of risk*—Merchant wholesalers take title to goods, while agents, brokers, and commission merchants do not.
2. *Type of ownership*—Merchant wholesalers and agent intermediaries tend to be independently owned, while manufacturers' sales branches and offices are owned by the manufacturer.
3. *Breadth of functions or services offered*—Full-service wholesalers are able to perform all wholesaling functions, while limited function wholesalers specialize in offering certain services. This difference in services performed is the main reason why operating expenses as a percentage of sales vary in Table 12–2. In general, the more services performed, the higher the operating expenses.

Figure 12–2 Classification of Wholesalers

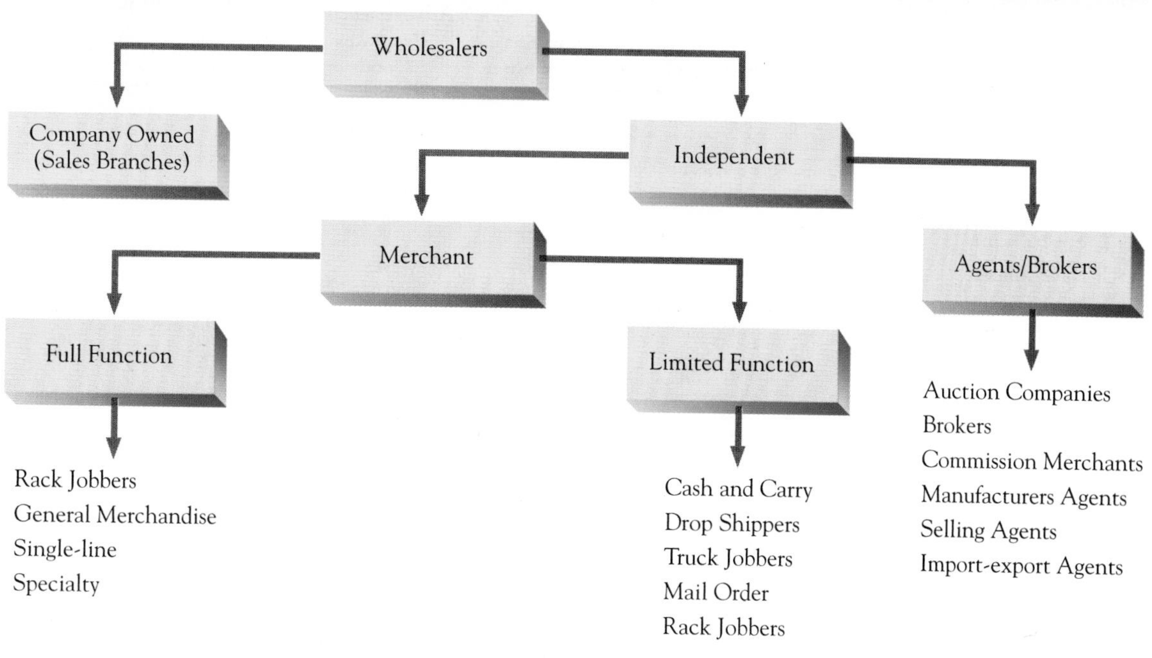

SOURCE: From Professor Kathleen A. Krentler, San Diego State University.

4. *Degree of specialization in product lines carried*—*General merchandise wholesalers* carry goods across product lines. For example, a hardware wholesaler may carry electrical, plumbing, and garden supplies, among other items. *Single-line wholesalers* carry a narrower line than general merchandise wholesalers. A single-line wholesaler may just sell plumbing supplies. *Specialty wholesalers* carry a very narrow product line. A wholesaler may specialize in ornamental fixtures for bathrooms and sell these to only hardware stores.

Table 12–3 summarizes the functions performed by all types of wholesalers.

Merchant Wholesalers. Merchant wholesalers are independent businesses that hold ownership to the goods they market and account for about 54 percent of wholesale trade. Super Valu Stores, Inc., is an example of a merchant wholesaler who considers itself more than a wholesaler.

Industrial distributors are merchant wholesalers who sell to producers rather than retailers. Electrical supplies, plastics, fasteners, machine tools, aluminum products, welding equipment, and bearings wholesalers are important in serving industrial markets.

Full-function Wholesalers. Sometimes called *full-service* or just *service* wholesalers, *full-function wholesalers* are active in each major function of marketing. They perform transactional, logistical, and facilitating functions. Full-function merchant wholesalers provide a range of services such as promotion assistance, a sales force, and storage and tend to earn a higher gross margin than other wholesalers. They may be

Table 12–3 Functions and Characteristics of Wholesalers

Wholesaler Type	Takes Title to Goods	Stores and Delivers Goods	Provides Sales Force	Advertises and Promotes Goods	Provides Credit	Percentage of Gross Margins Earned on Goods
I. Merchant Wholesaler Full-service						
1. General Line	yes	yes	yes	yes	yes	7–20
2. Special-Line	yes	yes	yes	yes	yes	12–25
3. Rack jobber	yes	yes	yes	yes	yes	10–15
4. Franchise	yes	yes	yes	yes	yes	6–15
II. Merchant Wholesaler Limited Service						
1. Cash and carry	yes	stores (yes) delivers (no)	no	no	no	5–10
2. Drop Shipper	yes	stores (yes) delivers (no)	yes	no	yes	5–8
3. Mail Order	yes	yes	yes	no	sometimes	6–10
III. Agents and Brokers						
1. Manufacturers	no	sometimes	yes	yes	no	5–6
2. Brokers	no	sometimes	yes	yes	sometimes	4–6
3. Commission Merchants	no	yes	yes	no	yes	5–6

general merchandise wholesalers, single-line wholesalers, or even specialty wholesalers, depending on the merchandise assortment they carry.

Certain **rack jobbers** who provide credit, sometimes called *service merchandisers*, constitute another type of full-function wholesaler. Rack jobbers typically sell nonfood, staple items to grocery and drug stores. These staple items include health and beauty aids, comic and other books, housewares, hardware products, and records. These items are usually displayed on racks as the name *rack jobber* implies. The rack jobber maintains the inventory and prices the product, thus relieving the retailer of all inventory ordering and control problems. Some rack jobbers bill the retailer when the items are sold; others insist upon cash payments when the rack is stocked. (This latter group is not providing financing services, so it is a limited-function wholesaler.) This is why the rack jobber is presented in Figure 12–2 as a full and a limited function wholesaler.

Rack jobbers came into existence to fill a need. As food stores' merchandise offerings included more nonfood items, they became a bother for retailers and traditional wholesalers to handle. The sales of any one of these items in a specific store were not large enough to justify the recordkeeping and ordering costs of the retailer; the traditional wholesalers were concerned about the reactions of their other customers. A drug wholesaler who sells to a supermarket runs the risk of losing the business of a nearby drug store. When serviced by a rack jobber, the retailer just provides floor space and collects money from customers at the check-out counter.

Because rack jobbers perform both the traditional wholesaling functions and many retail services, their operating costs are high—about 16 to 20 percent of sales—but gross margins are also high, running 12 to 16 percent.

Review Your Marketing Knowledge

- What risks are assumed by a merchant wholesaler?
- What kind of needs does a rack jobber satisfy for retailers that you do business with when you visit the supermarket?

Limited-Function Wholesalers. These intermediaries are merchant wholesalers who provide only a subset of the services of a full-function wholesaler. The major types of **limited-function wholesalers** are (1) cash-and-carry wholesalers, (2) drop shippers, (3) truck jobbers, (4) mail-order wholesalers, and (5) certain types of rack jobbers. Note, in Table 12–3, that these limited-function operators earn a smaller gross margin than full-function wholesalers.

Cash-and-carry wholesalers provide no credit, transportation, or selling effort. Their customers must come to them to buy and pick up purchased goods, for which they have paid cash. Small food-and-drug stores and garages, which are too small to be serviced by full-function wholesalers, have been able to stay in business because of cash-and-carry wholesalers.

Drop shippers, sometimes called *desk jobbers*, take title to the goods they sell but do not ever hold possession of these goods. They do not store, transport, or assemble these goods. Basically, they obtain orders for goods from retailers, industrial buyers, and other wholesalers; they then forward these orders to producers. Drop shippers operate almost exclusively with bulky products such as coal, lumber, fuel, chemicals, and building materials. These products are usually sold in carload lots and have high transportation and handling costs relative to their value. Thus, avoiding an extra handling of the goods in the channel saves money.

Truck jobbers, sometimes called *wagon jobbers or truck wholesalers*, specialize in the quick delivery of perishable or semiperishable items such as candy, bakery items, fresh fruits, potato chips, and tobacco products. They operate out of their own trucks and offer virtually all services except the provision of credit to their customers. They deal with smaller retailers that service wholesalers choose not to sell to. The combination of small orders from their customers and the great deal of service they provide makes them a high-cost operation.

Mail-order wholesalers make sales out of a catalog, distributed to small retailers and industrial buyers. They are most active in hardware, sporting goods, jewelry, and other general items. They sell mostly to smaller customers in outlying regions where the cost of undertaking a personal selling effort would not be supported by the sales that could be generated.

Rack jobbers were discussed in the previous section as a type of full-function wholesaler. If they choose to extend no credit to their customers, however, they are better classified as limited-function wholesalers.

Manufacturer's Sales Branches. The Census Bureau treats **manufacturer's sales branches** and offices as a separate wholesaling category. These branches are wholesale operations owned by manufacturers. There were over 40,000 such operations that sold about $600 billion in 1988,[6] representing the actions of manufacturers to take over the functions of merchant wholesalers by setting up semi-independent businesses. Major companies doing this include General Electric, IBM, Crane, and Hiram Walker in such major product categories as automobiles, chemicals, metals, commercial machines and equipment, farm machinery, paints, electrical equipment, tires, construction materials, and paper.[7]

Branches are usually justified when large retail or industrial customers are concentrated in large urban areas. These branches take the cream off the top of the market: although they represent only about 30 percent of wholesale businesses, they sell over 11 percent of wholesale dollar volume. Smaller and more geographically dispersed customers are left to other wholesalers. Branches perform functions in the transactional, logistical, and facilitating areas, have lower costs as a percentage of sales than merchant wholesalers, and earn higher gross margins (see Table 12–3).

Agents and Brokers. **Agents** and **brokers** are intermediaries that do not take title to goods. They also tend to perform far fewer services than limited-function merchant wholesalers.[8] Their main function is transactional—they facilitate buying and selling of goods and services. Agents and brokers provide knowledge of the market, usually have long-standing relationships with potential customers, and typically charge fees as low as 5 percent of their selling prices for their services. Their operating costs are low because of the limited services they provide. They account for about 10 percent of all wholesale trade or approximately $220 billion. There are over 35,000 separate agents and brokers, but this number is understated, since the Census excludes securities and insurance brokers and other service areas such as commercial real estate.

The most important groups in this category are (1) auction companies, (2) brokers, (3) commission merchants, (4) manufacturers' agents, (5) selling agents, and (6) import-export agents. Their functions are summarized in Table 12–3.

Auction companies bring buyers and sellers together. There are only 1,700 such companies in the country, but they are very important in such product classes as used cars, tobacco, livestock, fruit, and furs. For all these products, supply and demand change quickly, and inspection of the goods by prospective buyers is important. Demand and supply thus interact to set the price. Auction companies charge a fee or commission for their services and the use of their facilities, which are usually spartan, thus keeping overhead low. Sometimes, especially in agricultural sales, the auction company will set up at the seller's location.

Brokers, like auctioneers, also bring buyers and sellers together for a sale but rarely need physical facilities to do so. Their main function is to provide buyers and sellers with information about each others' needs, market conditions, alternative products, and price levels. They do not take possession of, or handle, the goods. They earn a commission once a sale is completed; the party represented by the broker pays the commission. Brokers, who can work for either buyer or seller, have no continuous relationship with either; they negotiate a deal with the buyer and then take this offer to the seller to accept or reject. The 4800 brokers in the United States have low operating costs—about 3 percent of sales—because of the small number of functions they perform and earn about 3 to 6 percent gross margin.

Brokers are especially active in product categories where sellers are not continuously trying to sell their products, like real estate, financial securities, certain complex capital machinery, and seasonal food items such as fruits, vegetables, and seafood. The seller has no solid relationship with prospective buyers and usually lacks market knowledge. The broker fills this gap. For example, a fruit cannery may operate only for a few months a year. The canner then hires a broker to sell the product to food wholesalers and chain stores. Once the year's production is sold, the broker's services are dropped until the next year.

Auction companies are useful wholesalers for products such as livestock where supply and demand change quickly.

Commission merchants operate mostly in agricultural markets. Typically, they take possession of a commodity sent to them at a central market area by a small farmer. They handle the logistics of the goods, find a buyer, negotiate a price, and complete the sale. The monies earned are returned to the farmer minus the commission earned. There are about 7,500 commission merchants in the United States. Their costs are relatively low—about 4.8 percent of sales—and they earn about 5 percent gross margin.

Manufacturers' agents, or *manufacturers' representatives*, as they are often called, are agents designated by a manufacturer to sell all or some part of their product offering in a specified geographic area. They, in essence, become the manufacturer's sales force in that territory. There are about 20,000 manufacturers' agents, earning 5 to 7 percent gross margin, with costs running 6.6 percent of sales. Commissions average about 6 to 7 percent of sales, but may run as high as 20 percent for slow-moving items, or as low as 2 percent for large-volume products. Japanese camera companies first entered the American market by using these types of representatives.[9]

Manufacturers' representatives operate year-round. They usually carry many related product lines from several noncompeting manufacturers. Thus, they can spread the cost of a sales call among a number of different products. They do not set the sales price for items they sell and often do not carry inventories. They generally do not give technical advice or handle repairs or installations. They are most active in industrial products, especially machinery and equipment, but also sell automotive products, clothing, cameras, and food products.[10]

Manufacturers' agents who specialize in marketing processed foods are called *food brokers*. (The term *broker* is inappropriate since they now act on a permanent basis as manufacturers' representatives, calling on wholesalers and large retailers.) These food brokers earn about 5 percent commission and are typically specialized geographically. A company like General Mills gains national distribution using about 70 to 100 food brokers.

In general, manufacturers' agents are used when:

1. a manufacturer wants to develop a new sales territory and the cost of one's own sales force would be prohibitive, given early sales levels;
2. a firm wishes to add a new and unrelated product line to its product offering, and this product does not fit the experience or end customers of its current sales force (the company's sales force and its agents will operate in the same geographic territory);
3. a small firm has no sales force of its own. Alternatively, a large firm may operate in a particular territory that is too small to support a sales force.

Manufacturers' agents can sell across national boundaries. For example, M.J. Daniel Co., a manufacturer's agency in Dallas, ships Apple Computers to U.S. military PXs in West Germany for resale to military personnel there.[11] Paul E. Moss & Co. concentrates on selling industrial goods and auto equipment in the Middle East. Quinto, Dawson & Associates of Orlando, Florida, specializes in the Caribbean market. There is a growing number of manufacturers' agents like these who are finding lucrative new opportunities ahead for United States marketers.[12]

Selling agents are independent intermediaries who perform the manufacturers' entire marketing task. They set prices, determine promotional activities, distribution policies, and advise on product offerings. They are most active with financially weak producers who cannot afford their own marketing effort.[13] They are important intermediaries in coal and textiles and are found in the clothing, metal products, lumber, and food industries. There are about 1,700 selling agents doing about $6.5 billion in wholesale trade. Operating expenses are about 3.2 percent of sales, and gross margins are about 5 percent.

Import-export agents, numbering about 1,000, are intermediaries who specialize in international trade. Some operate as brokers, while others are more like manufacturers' representatives or selling agents. Their understanding of foreign markets and their ability to provide financing make these intermediaries crucial in international trade.

Prospects for Wholesalers

In the nineteenth century, wholesalers dominated the marketing scene. The small producers and retailers of the day found their services to be essential. However, the growth of large producers and retailers in the first half of the twentieth century led to many manufacturers setting up their own sales forces and to large chain stores taking over the wholesaling function. Many claimed that the wholesaler was wasteful and unnecessary. Wholesale trade declined from 1929 to 1939.

Many who tried to bypass the wholesaler found distributing by themselves more expensive. This, combined with the growth in the economy since the 1940s, has led to great growth in wholesaling, especially among merchant wholesalers, the very group some predicted would disappear. At the present time, wholesalers appear to be a strong and durable set of intermediaries. As long as they provide needed services in a cost-justified fashion, they will survive. Those that do not will disappear, and new wholesalers will develop to provide new services.

Are wholesalers wasteful? You be the judge. A survey of wholesalers dealing in thirty-two product lines revealed the following:[14] (1) median net profit exceeded 3 percent of sales in only ten product lines; and (2) the highest profit wholesale products were commercial machinery and equipment (4.2 percent), chemicals (3.4 percent), and industrial machinery and equipment (3.3 percent). In contrast, meat, poultry, tobacco, and grocery wholesalers earn less than 1.3 percent on sales after taxes. Even a giant wholesaler like Super Valu Stores earned only about $135 million in 1988 on total sales on $10 billion.[15] In trying to bypass the wholesaler, many manufacturers have found that their costs of performing the wholesaling functions exceeded the wholesaler's costs and profit margins combined.

The emphasis on the quality of wholesaling activities is becoming a major concern. An example of the quality push is the case of Sysco Corporation, the nation's largest food distributor supplying restaurants, hospitals, and other institutions. Sysco in 1987 had only about a 3 percent share of the $80 billion food-distribution business. However, it had a reputation of being quality conscious. Tuna sold under the Sysco label must be caught on lines so that there are no struggle marks from the nets.[16] Sysco has also turned down truckloads of ham that contained too much water. Samples from every product lot are tested at Sysco for quality. If wholesalers are going to earn a reasonable profit margin, then the Sysco enthusiasm for quality appears to be something that must be addressed.

For most wholesalers, future productivity gains and maintaining a reasonable profit margin seem to lie in the improved use of computers. Inventory turnaround is critical, and wholesalers are concerned about picking up not just weeks or days, but hours. To that end, most of the large wholesalers such as Sysco, Farm House Foods, Phibro-Solomon, Alco Standard, Amfac, and McKesson have installed complex control computer networks.[17] When the store manager at your local supermarket decides to order Wheaties, he or she doesn't have to talk directly to anyone. The manager waves an electric wand over the product label on the Wheaties box and then uses the telephone lines to relay that order to the wholesaler. This instant ordering helps the store manager satisfy customer needs more efficiently.

Staley Continental, Inc., needed more computer capability to help run their $40 million "super" distribution center in Los Angeles and a smaller, $16 million outlet outside of Washington, D.C. The effective use of computers permits Staley to respond quickly to the needs and requests of its fast-food chain clients. Staley distributes supplies to Ponderosa, Chi-Chi's, Burger King, and McDonald's. When McDonald's requests, Staley must respond quickly and correctly. McDonald's Corp. alone accounted for 16 percent—or $550 million—of Staley's total 1987 sales.[18]

Personal Computer Exercise

This PC exercise will allow you to choose an appropriate wholesaler for three companies and determine the price to the channel and to the end customer. How did using an intermediary affect profit, demand, and expenses for each company and its wholesaler? Would you choose to use a wholesaler in this situation? Why or why not?

KEY POINTS

- The transactional, logistical, and facilitating functions of marketing must be performed to fill the exchange gaps that lie between producers and consumers. Wholesalers and retailers actively perform these functions. Wholesalers sell most of the time to other businesses who then either use the product or resell it to final users.

- If channel intermediaries are eliminated in a flow of goods, the functions they perform must still be undertaken by some agency.

- It is not necessarily cheaper to eliminate the wholesaler from the channel of distribution.

- Any sale made to anyone except the ultimate consumer is a wholesale sale.

- Wholesale sales reached $2.2 trillion in 1988.

- Merchant wholesalers, who take title to goods, account for about 55 percent of the $2.2 trillion wholesale market. Manufacturer sales branch wholesalers constitute about 30 percent of the wholesale market. The branches are wholesale operations owned by manufacturers.

- In the future, computers are likely to play an increased role in the activities and functions performed by wholesalers.

ISSUES FOR DISCUSSION

1. Are brokers and commission merchants performing the same functions? Explain.
2. How do the nature of the following products and their end consumers affect the type and extent of the wholesaler used?
    a. Industrial chemicals
    b. Fresh fruit
    c. Cold remedies
    d. Home appliances
    e. Used cars
    f. Machine tools
3. Why would a firm use an agent instead of a merchant wholesaler?
4. Why is the computer becoming a necessary resource for large wholesalers?
5. What would be some of the reasons why a producer would bypass using the services of a wholesaler?
6. Why are wholesalers not as well known as retailers?
7. What are the differences in the services provided by a manufacturer's agent and a selling agent?
8. What type of power does a large wholesaler such as McKesson Corp. have as an intermediary in the channel of distribution?
9. How can the performance of a wholesaler be evaluated?
10. Why would a company like General Mills use over 70 food brokers instead of utilizing a much smaller number (e.g., 10 brokers)?

GLOSSARY

Auction company: an agent wholesaler who brings buyers and sellers together to buy and sell goods, usually at the auction company's facilities.

Brokers: agents who bring buyers and sellers into agreement for a sale, usually without buyers and sellers meeting at the broker's physical facilities.

Cash-and-carry wholesalers: intermediaries who provide a wholesale store where small retailers make cash purchases and carry the merchandise away themselves.

Commission merchants: wholesalers who take possession of and sell agricultural commodities in central markets.

Drop shippers: wholesalers who arrange the sale of goods, passing these orders to their customers without ever taking possession of the goods.

Full-function wholesalers: merchant wholesalers who are active in each major marketing function (facilitating, logistical, transactional). See *merchant wholesalers*.

Limited-function wholesalers: merchant wholesalers who provide only a subset of the services of full-function wholesalers. See *merchant wholesalers*.

Mail-order wholesalers: intermediaries who make sales to retailers from catalogs.

Manufacturers' agents: representatives designated by a manufacturer to sell all or some part of their product line in a specified geographic area.

Manufacturers' sales branches: wholesale operations owned by manufacturers.

Merchant wholesalers: independent businesses that hold ownership to the goods they market to retailers, other merchants, or industrial customers.

Rack jobber: a full-service wholesaler who sells nonfood, staple items to grocery and drug retailers. These items are displayed on racks in the store that are maintained by the rack jobber.

Retailing: all activities related to sales and service to the ultimate consumer.

Selling agent: an independent intermediary who performs the manufacturer's entire marketing task.

Truck jobbers: wholesalers who operate from trucks and specialize in the quick delivery of perishable items.

Wholesaler: a business unit that buys and resells merchandise to retailers, other merchants, and/or to industrial, institutional, and commercial customers.

Wholesale sale: any sale made to anyone except the ultimate consumer.

NOTES

1. James A. Narus and James C. Anderson, "Industrial Distributors Into Partners," *Harvard Business Review*, March-April 1986, pp. 66–71.
2. Committee on Definitions, *Marketing Definitions: A Glossary of Marketing Terms* (American Marketing Association 1960), p. 23.
3. *The 1989 Information Please Alliance*, New York: Houghton Mifflin, 1988, p. 67.
4. *Census of Wholesale Trade*, May, 1985, p. 207.
5. Louis W. Stern and Adel L. El Ansary, *Marketing Channels*, (Englewood Cliffs, NJ: Prentice-Hall, 1989).
6. *Census of Wholesale Trade*, May, 1985, p. 207.
7. Kenneth G. Hardy and Allan J. McGrath, *Marketing Channel Management* (Glenview, IL: Scott, Foresman, 1988) p. 325.
8. Jim Gibbons, "Selling Abroad With Manufacturers' Agents," *Sales & Marketing Management*, September 9, 1985, pp. 67–69.
9. Donald A. Ball and Wendell H. McCullock, Jr., *International Business* (Plano, TX: Business Publications, Inc. 1988), p. 55.
10. Harold J. Novick, "Yes, There Is a Perfect Rep," *Business Marketing*, February 1989, pp. 73–76.
11. Richard W. Noel, "From Peddlers To Professionals," *Electrical Wholesaling*, April 1986, pp. 42–46.
12. "The Ratios," *Dun's Review*, October 1979, pp. 144, 146.
13. "The Business Week Top 1000," *Business Week*, April 1988, p. 252.
14. "The Ratios," Dun's Review, October 1989, pp. 144, 146.
15. Super Valu, *Annual Report*, 1988.
16. Jo Ellen Davis, "Food Distributor: The Leaders Are Getting Hungry For More," *Business Week*, March 24, 1986, pp. 106–107.
17. Michael Granturco, "The Supernets Are Coming!" *Forbes*, February 27, 1989, pp. 112–114.
18. Brian Bremmer, "Staley Dishing Up Growth In Food Distribution Units," *Crain's Chicago Business*, February 29, 1988, p. 21.

CASE APPLICATION 12–1

Lingard Publishing Products Division

Tom Nielsen, the project manager of Binding Systems for Lingard Publishing Products Division, hung up the phone and sighed. He had just finished speaking with Eric Moss, the company lawyer, about an upcoming meeting between the two of them and Lee Wells, a sales agent appointed by Lingard to handle the selling of Binding Systems to the magazine- and book-publishing industry.

Wells had requested a meeting with the Lingard executives to determine whether to launch suit against them for withholding $27,000 in sales commissions that he believed was owed to him for the sales of three master binding systems. Wells' lawyer, Ted Traynor, would also be attending their meeting.

Lee Wells, 57, was a retired former vice president of Manufacturing for one of America's largest publishers of trade magazines. He had been appointed as an agent to sell Lingard's new high-speed binding systems because of his influential contacts with the top twenty publishers of trade journals, text books, paperbacks, and popular magazines in the eastern United States.

An agent for four years, Lee had been successful in assisting Tom Nielsen to place thirty-seven units at $100,000 per unit. Over this time period Lee was also an agent for a German manufacturer of printing presses that sold for more than $1 million per press. It was known that Lee had assisted in placing three such presses in accounts over the last nineteen months.

Based upon an assessment of the accounts that had sufficient volume to provide a satisfactory payback on the initial capital outlay, the total market for Tom Nielsen's products was estimated at sixty-two units.

As project manager, Tom was the sole salesperson, marketing representative, and technical advisor to the book-publishing industry for the eastern United States. With worldwide sales of over a billion dollars, Lingard was the world's largest supplier of various metal-embossing equipment. Their largest market was in metal embossing for labels used on appliances, motor vehicles, and machine tools.

A typical master binding system sale normally involved five steps.

1. Tom would make head-office presentations to major American publishers to sell their manufacturing management on the concept of high-speed binding and potential savings. Many of these calls were based on leads obtained from trade shows or word-of-mouth referrals from satisfied Lingard customers.
2. Tom would make follow-up written proposals to interested accounts, based upon their own individual machine needs and volumes processed.
3. Tom would enter detailed negotiations with accounts over price, machine installation schedules, and so on. These negotiations usually involved the publishers' top financial personnel and production people.
4. Tom would arrange the delivery and installation of the equipment by Lingard.
5. Tom would remain in the account for three weeks to insure the machinery was functioning properly. He would make adjustments as required and he would train machine operators to use and maintain the equipment properly.

Lee Wells, the sales agent, initially had been involved in introducing Tom to influential contacts in key accounts. The first nine machine placements stemmed directly from Lee promoting the Lingard concept to many of his former colleagues. Lee also had written feature articles in trade journals or given seminars at trade shows as Lingard's "ambassador-at-large." Lee had earned a 9 percent commission on each of these nine placements.

Lee had been relatively inactive for the last year and a half. Six months earlier, he had telephoned Tom and briefly tipped him that an account that had purchased a German press through Lee might be interested in a binding system. After receiving the phone call, Tom had done all the follow-up work to sell the account, from the written proposal stage through installation and start-up of the three units. This work had taken six months of concentrated effort.

Thus, when Lee had contacted Tom about his commission check, Tom had been very surprised. Tom had argued that Lee's phone tip had certainly assisted him somewhat in the timing of the sale. But Tom pointed out that he had called on that account several times in the past, and indeed, had even written proposals to them and entered detailed pricing negotiations. Tom believed the deciding factors in the account's decision to purchase were the availability of capital to spend and an impending 9 percent price increase announced by Lingard.

Tom pointed out that Lee had no correspondence at all to support his claim that his contact with the publisher had created the sale of the three units. Lee countered that a dinner meeting he had set up with the publisher's president had given rise to the sale, as well as placement of the German printing press. Lee also contended that the placement of three Lingard binding systems at one time was evidence of his influence with the publisher, because all other sales of Lingard systems to date had been single placements normally followed a year later by an additional placement.

Lee brought the Letter of Understanding (Exhibit 1) that Lingard had used to commission his services, to the meeting with Tom and Eric Moss. Tom asked himself again if Lee was owed a $27,000 commission. Should he have used an agent in the first place? And what about now?

SOURCE: Written by Kenneth G. Hardy and Allan J. McGrath, *Marketing Channel Management* (Glenview, IL: Scott, Foresman) 1988, pp. 335–337.

Questions

1. What kind of services did Lee Wells perform that he was paid for as a sales agent?

2. Does Lingard owe Lee Wells the $27,000 commission? Why or why not?

3. How could this type of disagreement and conflict between an agent and the publisher have been avoided?

Exhibit 1 INTERNAL CORRESPONDENCE

To: L. G. WELLS

From: R. T. NIELSEN—LINGARD INC.

Subject: SALES AGENCY ARRANGEMENT FOR THE SALE OF MASTER BINDING SYSTEMS TO THE BOOK PUBLISHING INDUSTRY

This Letter of Understanding shall serve as a working agreement between yourself and Lingard, Inc. In your case you will provide Lingard with the benefit of your influence to sell key publishers the Master binding systems. Such influence should include making sales calls on such accounts, distributing literature about Lingard's line to important customer buying influencers; writing and speaking to influential contacts about Lingard systems in the trade press or at key trade shows; providing to potential customers the names of current satisfied Lingard system users.

In return for such services you will be provided with: a 9 percent commission on the installed sale price of a Master binding system by Lingard; business cards signifying that you are an agent of Lingard; and any and all literature required for your discussions with prospective customers. This could include spec sheets, technical bulletins, photographs, data on placements in various states, and written testimonials from Lingard users.

You will be paid your commission after completed installation when Lingard has been paid by its customer.

Claims for commissions on placements for which Lingard's own sales representative has been instrumental in gaining the account will be disallowed.

Account-development activities completed by Lingard considered "instrumental" in final sale include submission of a written proposal tailored to the accounts' needs and a written exchange of pricing quotes and prospective installation dates. Such activities are deemed "instrumental" because they provide conclusive proof of an on-site audit having been completed of the publishers' production line, and quotes reflecting a customized interface of the accounts' process to the preferred binding system configuration.

Where the sales agent, however, is instrumental in closing a sale by *overcoming* unspecified obstacles to purchase, regardless of sales development activities by Lingard's own rep, a commission will be paid to the agent in full.

This agreement is automatically renewable unless notice of cancellation is sent, in writing, to arrive thirty days prior to the annual anniversary date.

Deductions for income tax from commission checks will not be withheld by Lingard.

This agency agreement shall also preclude you from representing any other vendor with directly competing binding systems sold to the Publishing Industry.

Signed, Cosigned and Acknowledged,

R. T. Nielsen
Project Manager

L. G. Wells

CASE APPLICATION 12–2

Industrial Wholesale Distribution: Bergen Brunswig Corporation

Based in Orange, CA, Bergen Brunswig Corporation is made up of two subsidiaries: Bergen Brunswig Drug Company, a drug wholesaling unit and Commtron, a consumer electronics and pre-recorded video cassette distributor. Accounting for nearly 90 percent of Bergen Brunswig's annual revenues, the drug wholesaling unit is the heart of the company. This unit distributes its drugs primarily to hospitals, regional drug chains, and independent drug stores.

In 1975, Bergen Brunswig pioneered both the primary-supplier concept of drug wholesaling and the use of computers as a sales and marketing tool. The company introduced its pharmacy and other retail customers to a series of computer-based order-entry programs designed to speed ordering and delivery. Several of these programs gained immediate popularity.

"Space Management℠," a merchandising program based on product sales data gathered by Bergen Brunswig, "makes sure the retailer has the right products in the right place at the right time," according to Leo Granucci, Bergen Brunswig Drug Company's vice president of sales. For a monthly fee, one of Bergen Brunswig's merchandisers advises customers on product and shelf arrangements and updates this personalized system every month. "CompuPhase™" provides retailers with a pharmacy computer system for processing prescriptions, storing patient information, and updating prices. "The Good Neighbor Pharmacy℠" advertising program offers retailers the opportunity to participate in the advertising and other benefits enjoyed by chains, but without sacrificing their local identity. Monthly circulars, electronic media, and newspaper ads are offered, along with other benefit programs.

Following Bergen Brunswig's lead, all drug wholesalers have computerized their businesses and these computerized wholesalers now dominate drug distribution. Wholesalers control 70 percent of the $20 billion pharmaceutical industry. The advent of more sophisticated computer programs and telecommunication links between distributors and drug manufacturers is expected to increase this market share to 85 percent over the next few years. This increasingly competitive wholesale industry forces distributors to distinguish themselves if they want to succeed. Bergen Brunswig's extensive service programs provide this vital mark of distinction.

Service is continually stressed at Bergen Brunswig Drug Company. Merchandisers and salespeople are called "consultants" to emphasize the service aspect of their jobs. All top management personnel are expected to make 100 sales calls a year, while consultants make monthly calls on their customers. Covering 44 states from 35 distribution centers, Bergen Brunswig's 235 salespeople and 70 merchandisers service over 9,500 independent, chain, and hospital pharmacies.

Bergen Brunswig did not stop with order entry, shelf management, and inventory control systems. The company expanded its service offerings to include financial and asset management programs. They generate good will in pharmacies with free services such as one-stop coupon redemption. Granucci feels Bergen Brunswig distinguishes itself from the competition through the company's ability to effectively execute the plans it designs. A comprehensive training program ensures that Bergen Brunswig Drug Company salespeople can implement any service program that Bergen Brunswig offers. This training program lasts several months and incorporates an extensive training manual with hands-on learning experience in all departments of the company, as well as in actual pharmacies.

Retailers have become more cautious about choosing distributors. As information systems become indispensable links in drug distribution systems, customers become locked into their distributor's computer system. Since this makes switching wholesalers and computer systems an expensive proposition, pharmacists' initial wholesaler choice is an increasingly complex decision. Bear Stearns analyst John McCrae asserted that this choice "boils down to the quality of service offered, and Bergen Brunswig excels in this area."

Customers seem to agree. Bergen Brunswig Drug Company was rated No. 1 in reputation among customers in *Sales & Marketing Management*'s 1987 Best Sales Force Survey. Richard Shapiro, owner of the independent Mel-Rich pharmacy, has been a Bergen Brunswig customer for 11 years. "I stay with them because they're always there when I need them. They have the marketing information I need to be successful, and their salespeople and merchandisers are in my stores at least once a month to update me on sales promotions and management programs. It's a very close relationship. I count on them."

Bergen Brunswig's service programs were designed to help customers run their businesses more efficiently and profitably. They did this and more. Bergen Brunswig's service programs generated two-way benefits, exceeding their original objectives for their customers, broadening the company's drug sales territory from 9 states to 44 states, and significantly increasing company revenues.

SOURCES: "Bergen Brunswig Locks in Sales with Service," *Sales & Marketing Management*, June 1987, p. 48; "Bergen Brunswig Writes a Winning Prescription," *Sales & Marketing Management*, January 17, 1983, pp. 38–39; "How to Select a Business Partner," *Industrial Distribution*, May 1989, p. 103; personal communication with Bergen Brunswig, July 1989.

Questions

1. What wholesaling functions were performed by Bergen Brunswig Corporation?

2. What type of wholesaling firm is Bergen Brunswig?

3. What competitive advantages, if any, did Bergen Brunswig provide for its customers?

4. How does Bergen Brunswig and the functions it performs affect both the manufacturers and the retailers? How would the relationship between the manufacturers and the pharmacies differ if Bergen Brunswig did not exist?

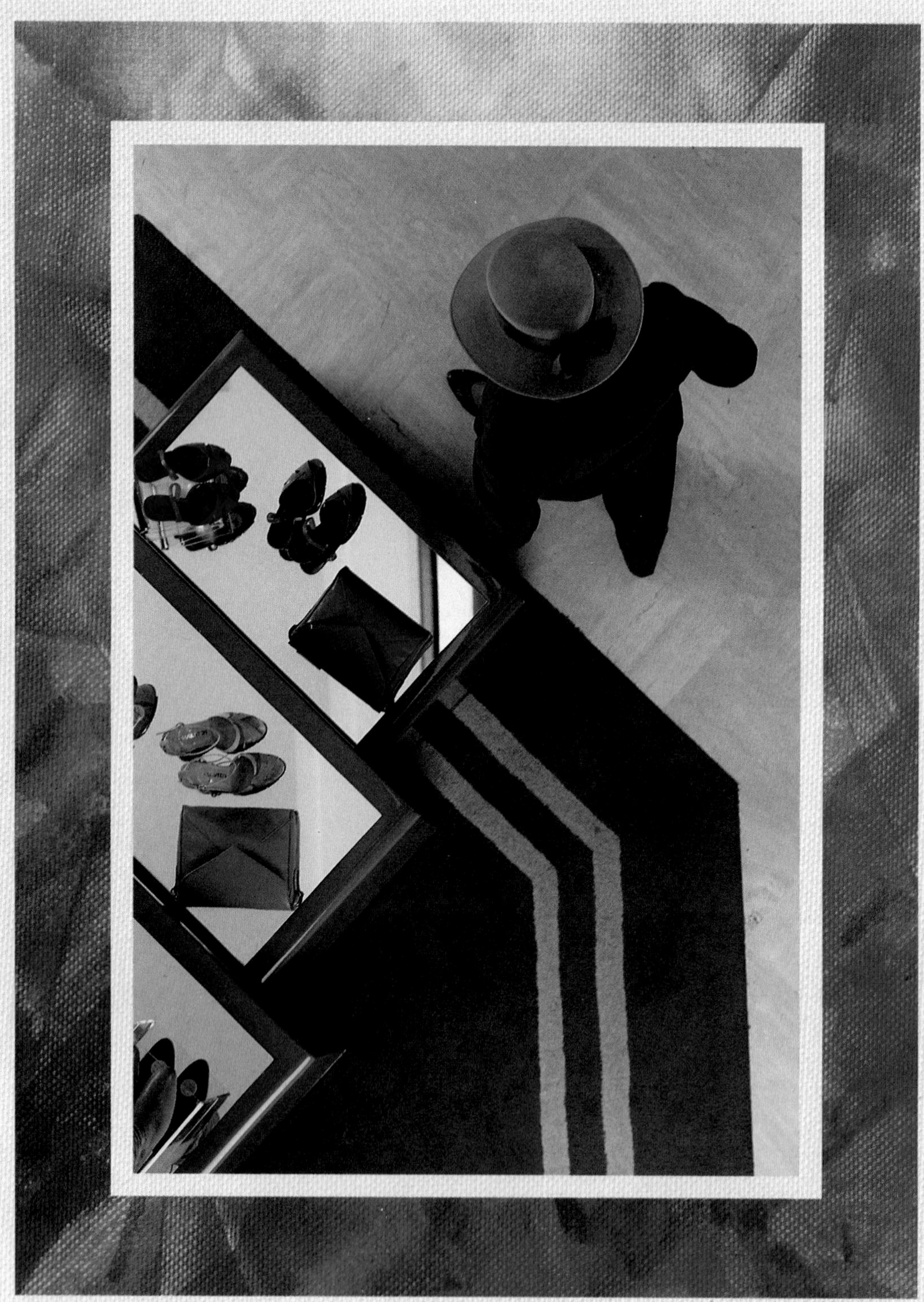

13

Retailers

Learning Objectives

Upon completing this chapter, you will be able to do the following:

DEFINE
the terms retailing, the wheel of retailing, and hypermarket.

EXPLAIN
why the creation of a retail store's image and ambience is more art than science.

DISCUSS
why the target market of Kmart is different from the target market of Nieman-Marcus.

ILLUSTRATE
the differences of service found in a limited service variety store and a full service department store.

LIST
the type of information that can be provided to a retail manager by an effective retail decision support system.

MARKETING PROFILE

What's Behind Iron Curtain Number One?

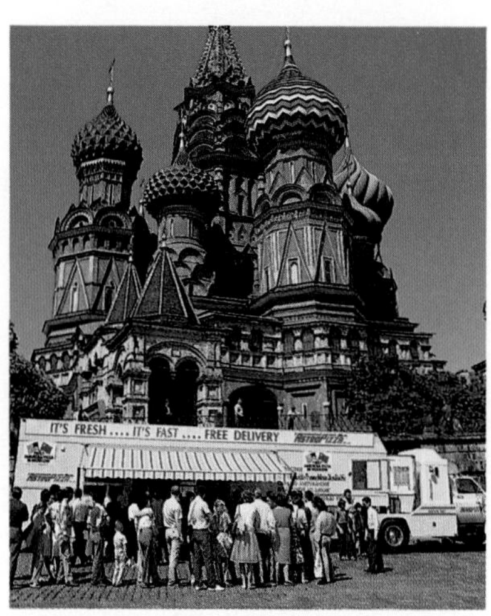

U.S. firms are lining up to sell their wares to the virtually untapped market of the U.S.S.R. Representing 280 million consumers, the Soviet Union is attracting investment from fast food to personal hygiene companies. In recent years, the political ice has started to thaw, resulting in increased interest in U.S.S.R. investment and a number of joint ventures.

Mikhail Gorbachev has promised a restructuring of the Soviet Union's economic system. He calls the restructuring *perestroika*. Could this mean more retail shops, stocked with goods, and a move away from rationing soap, laundry powder, butter, eggs, and meat? Currently, the Soviet Union is a long way away from having a modern marketing system with retailers, wholesalers, and an efficient physical distribution system. The start of major changes to move the Soviet Union from a production-oriented to a marketing-oriented society has been initiated by Gorbachev's new reforms. For the first time, Soviet citizens are becoming aware of the gap between their system's failures with material goods and the successes in the West.

Under Soviet joint venture laws, the Soviet partner must have controlling interest (51 percent) and thus appoints the board. Generally, the Western partner's responsibility is to supply most of the capital and expertise in the business. The Soviet's contribution is generally in supplying the labor. Profits are restricted, usually limited to local reinvestment or the purchase of Soviet-made goods to export. Many times joint ventures open identical restaurants side by side, one that accepts hard Western currency and one that accepts rubles. Despite these limitations, several companies are making strides toward opening new businesses or introducing new products in the U.S.S.R.

When you think about selling "American," you can't forget McDonald's and Coca-Cola. Both firms intend to expand their operations in Russia, but they are not the leaders. Pepsi has been sold in the Soviet Union since 1974 and is the most widely available U.S. consumer product. Zieger Enterprises and Roma Foods have introduced their mobile Astro Pizza truck in Moscow. It is in direct competition with at least 18 state pizzerias already in existence and is making a splash. PepsiCo is not far behind with its plans to open Pizza Huts soon.

Soviet interest in high quality health care products has produced a heated battle for exclusive rights. Because of the probability that only one firm per product will be allowed to manufacture behind the Iron Curtain, several companies have jumped into the race. The most intense competition is for the exclusive right to make tampons. They are not available in the Soviet Union, and sanitary napkins are in short supply. Currently, Johnson and Johnson and Tambrands are the contenders for this market. In a Western health care products exhibition, Soviet women stood five deep at Tambrands and Johnson and Johnson displays, demanding samples and information.

Visa International has come to an agreement with Vao Intourist, which oversees tourism, to be the first issuing agency in the Soviet Union. The card will be offered to Soviet citizens who travel extensively, as well as to foreigners living in the Soviet Union. This represents the first credit card marketer to enter into a venture with a Russian agency.

The Soviet Union has a long way to go in marketing. The big GUM department store in Leningrad has a scruffy look. Food stores have limited goods to choose from, and people wait in long lines to see if they will get their allotments of four cartons of soap powder each week. However, a few years ago no one would have imagined Gorbachev's reform, his push to increase retailing types of businesses, and his overtures to retailers to consider the Soviet Union as a promising market. One of Gorbachev's major goals is to allow Soviet managers to respond to market forces. Soviet citizens are responding by demanding more choices when they shop.

This *Marketing Profile* outlines new directions that are being taken by retailers to satisfy a need in the market.

ADAPTED FROM: Richard I. Kirkland, Jr., "Why Russia Is Still in the Red," *Fortune*, January 30, 1989, pp. 173–176, and Peter Brimelow, "Empire of the Will," *Forbes*, January 9, 1989, pp. 53–56, and Nancy Giges, "Capitalists Eye Russian Front," *Advertising Age*, March 21, 1989, pp. 28–29.

Retailing, a dynamic marketing activity that attempts to satisfy the needs of consumers, is a major influence in the economy. Other institutions such as wholesalers and manufacturers do some retailing business. However, businesses whose sales come primarily form selling goods and services directly to consumers to satisfy their needs are called retailers. Sears, F. W. Woolworth, Jostens Jewelers, Nordstrom, and Dillard's Department Stores are retailers. The Fuller Brush salesperson, the orthodontist, and the CPA are also retailers.

Retailers in our society do not produce a physical product. This important job is left to manufacturers. Instead, *retailers* purchase goods for purposes of resale at a profit. The merchant retailer also makes important decisions about which products to place in over two million stores for consumers to consider for purchase. The retailer selects what to carry because he or she believes a customer will try the product. These products are placed and found in the following retail establishments:

Supermarkets—A Kroger store carries about 10,000 to 12,000 different items.

Discount stores—A Wal-Mart carries about 50,000 different items.

Department stores—A Macy's carries over 100,000 different items.

Drug stores—An Eckerd's carries about 8,000 different items.

Many consumers appreciate a wide selection of brands, sizes, colors, prices, and designs.[1] It is the retail merchant who provides the assortment of products that we prefer to consider.

A retailer sells directly to the consumer for personal, nonbusiness use.[2] This selling includes all forms—in stores, at home, and by mail order. Retailing involves all activities related to sales and service to consumers. This chapter provides a systematic look at the topics of retailing and retailers. We will examine the various types of retail establishments, the decisions retailers must make, and trends in retailing.

Evolution of Retail Institutions

A number of changes in the retail institutional structure have occurred over the past century. Table 13–1 presents some of the more provincial changes and the stages of maturity. The *retail life cycle* is a series of stages through which a retailing institution moves from its inception until its decline and disappearance from the marketplace.[3] The retail life cycle stages are *innovation*, *accelerated development*, *maturity*, and *decline*.

At the innovation stage there are few competitors, rapid growth of sales, and some profitability. During the accelerated development stage many new competitors enter the market, profitability is good, and management attempts to develop stronger market distribution. At the maturity stage, price competition is intense, the rate of sales growth is slow, and attention is focused on achieving efficiency of operations to reduce the costs of doing business. During the decline stage competitors drop out of the market, profitability is low, and the rate of sales growth is either slow or negative.

Table 13–1 illustrates the fastest period of growth for the various institutional types and the stage of the life cycle each type is now experiencing. The institutions are what this chapter will discuss.

Theories of Retail Institutional Change

It appears that cycles or stages of growth/decline characterize retail institutions. New retail institutions come along and then vanish or become less important. There is an

Table 13–1 Life Cycle of Retail Institutions

Institutional Type	Fastest Growth	Inception to Maturity (Years)	Stage of Cycle	Example of Business
General store	1800–1840	100	Decline	A local store
Specialty store	1820–1840	100	Mature	Hickory Farms
Variety store	1870–1930	50	Decline	Morgan-Lindsay
Department store	1860–1940	80	Mature	Dillard's
Mail-order house	1915–1950	50	Mature	Spiegel
Corporate chain	1920–1930	50	Mature	Sears
Discount store	1955–1975	20	Mature	Highland
Supermarket	1935–1965	35	Mature	Kroger's
Shopping center	1950–1965	40	Mature	Dallas-Galleria
Gasoline station	1930–1950	45	Mature	Shell
Convenience store	1965–1975	20	Mature	Circle K
Fast-food store	1960–1975	15	Mature	Burger King
Computer store	1980–	?	Growth	Computerland
Hypermarket	1973–	?	Early Growth	Hypermarket USA
Warehouse retailer	1970–1980	10	Late Growth	Sam's Warehouse
Catalog Showroom	1970–1980	10	Late Growth	Best Products

ever-changing pattern of growth, development, and rebirth. A number of theoretical explanations call attention to retail institutional changes.

Wheel of Retailing

The *wheel of retailing* explanation was originated by Malcolm McNair, a Harvard professor.[4] His theory states that new types of retailers enter a market as low-margin, low-priced, low-status merchants. This is called the *entry phase*. Gradually, they add to their operating costs by providing new services and improving displays and facilities, a phase referred to as *trading up*. As time passes, they become high-cost merchants and are challenged by new competitors, a phase called *vulnerable*. These concepts are shown in the wheel of retailing, portrayed in Figure 13–1. As indicated, higher margins become necessary to support new services and upgrading.

The four main hypotheses stated by McNair are:

1. A new innovator or operator develops a low-cost institution (supermarket or discount store). The low cost is possible because of a new procedure for lowering or eliminating operating expenses (no credit or self-service.)
2. The innovator increases market share because of low prices and attracts numerous competitors who copy this approach.
3. In order to differentiate their firm from the others and to hold on to customers, these innovators "trade up" their goods and service offerings. The competitive activity increases operating costs. Prices increase to cover increased cost. (For example, the original discount stores were in out-of-

Figure 13–1 The Wheel of Retailing

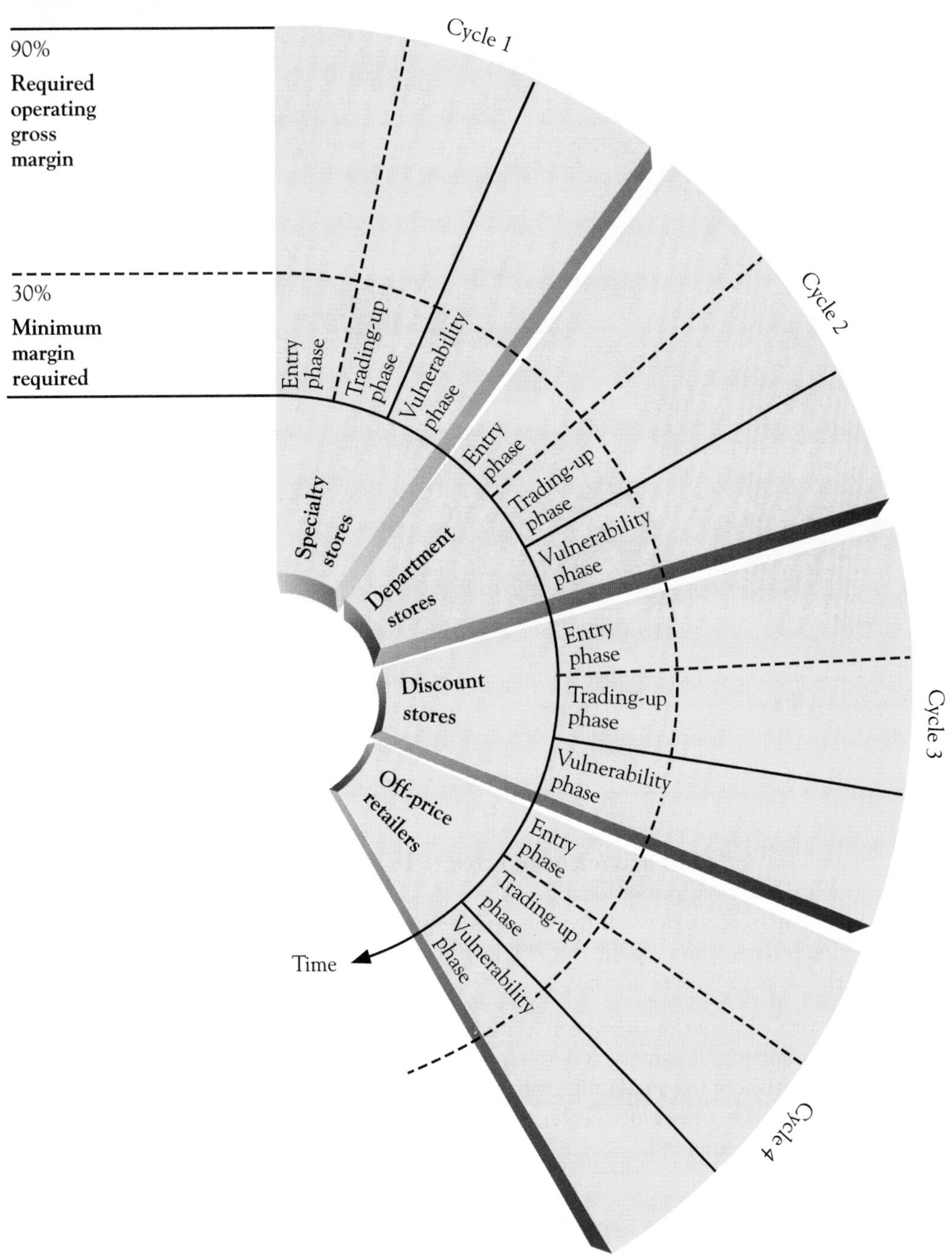

SOURCE: Adapted from Dale M. Lewison and M. Wayne DeLozier, *Retailing Principles and Applications* (Columbus, Ohio, Charles E. Merrill Publishing, 1982), p. 36, and published in Jack G. Kalkati, "Don't Discount the Off-Price Retailers," *Harvard Business Review*, May-June 1985, p. 87.

The Galleria in Dallas is a shopping center in the mature stage of the retail institution life cycle.

the-way locations and offered no credit. Today stores such as Kmart and Wal-Mart hold prime locations.)

4. At this point a new innovator emerges under the umbrella of high costs and prices created by the trading up of the now traditional operators. Thus the wheel revolves again.[5]

McNair's explanation has been criticized as being too narrow because not all institutions begin as low-margin outlets. For example, department stores and expensive suburban shopping malls did not follow the wheel of retailing cycles. On the other hand, catalog discount outlets and convenience stores did follow the entry, trading up, and vulnerability cycle.

The Retail Accordion

The *retail accordion* argues that changes in the merchandising mix are a better way to explain changes in retail institutions than the prices and margins of the wheel of retailing.[6] It proposes that retail institutions evolve over time from broad-based outlets with a wide assortment of products to institutions offering specialized narrow lines. Then in another cycle the outlets start to offer a wide assortment of products. This is the opening-closing-opening concept of an accordion.

According to this theory, the general store was the starting point for modern retailing. It had a wide assortment of foods, clothing, feed, and other merchandise. The next era brought in the more specialized, larger department store. This specialization became more pronounced with the single-line (bookstore and specialty store, for example). But then the specialty store began to add more merchandise. Today, some supermarkets sell cosmetics, drugs, automobile parts, banking services, videos, liquor, and a variety of other goods.

The Dialectic Process

A third explanation, called the *dialectic process*, uses the thesis, antithesis, synthesis view that change begets change and adaptation:

> *In terms of retail institutions, the dialectic model implies that retailers mutually adapt in the face of competition from "opposites." Thus, when challenged by a competitor with a differential advantage, an established institution will adopt strategies and tactics in the direction of that advantage, thereby negating some of the innovator's attraction. The innovator, meanwhile, does not remain unchanged. Rather . . . the innovator over time tends to upgrade or otherwise modify products and institutions. As a result of these mutual adaptations, the two retailers gradually move together. . . .*[7]

The theme of the dialectic process is "if you can't beat them, join them" (see Figure 13–2). For example, the department store was developed to offer a wide variety of goods and services (the thesis). The response to the department store was the discount store (the antithesis), which offered similar goods in a less attractive facility at lower costs. The promotion department store (the synthesis) emerged as an integration of the department and discount store (Mervyn's and Kohl's are examples). They have found a niche within the retail institutional structure.

Each of these three theories views the evolution of the retail institutional structure slightly differently. By combining the thoughts, hypotheses, and assumptions of all three, a more comprehensive view of changes in retailing emerges.

The use of theories to understand retailing must be supplemented with the knowledge that retailing is a constantly changing field. For instance, customers today are older. In the 1980s, the number of 35 to 44 year olds in the U.S. increased by 36 percent, while the 14 to 25 year old age group declined nearly 14 percent. This change has dramatic implications for retailers.[8] Retailers must come to grips with different spending patterns of the various age groups. Older customers want sales and bargains. As Kurt Barnard, publisher of *Barnard's Retail Marketing Report*, an industry newsletter, has put it, "Retailers had done so well for the past twenty years almost without paying attention to market changes. Now they have to."

Review Your Marketing Knowledge

- What is retailing?
- In straightforward terms explain what is called the dialectic process.
- How would a retail manager use knowledge about the present stage in the life cycle of his or her business?

Figure 13–2 The Dialectic Pattern of Retail Evolution

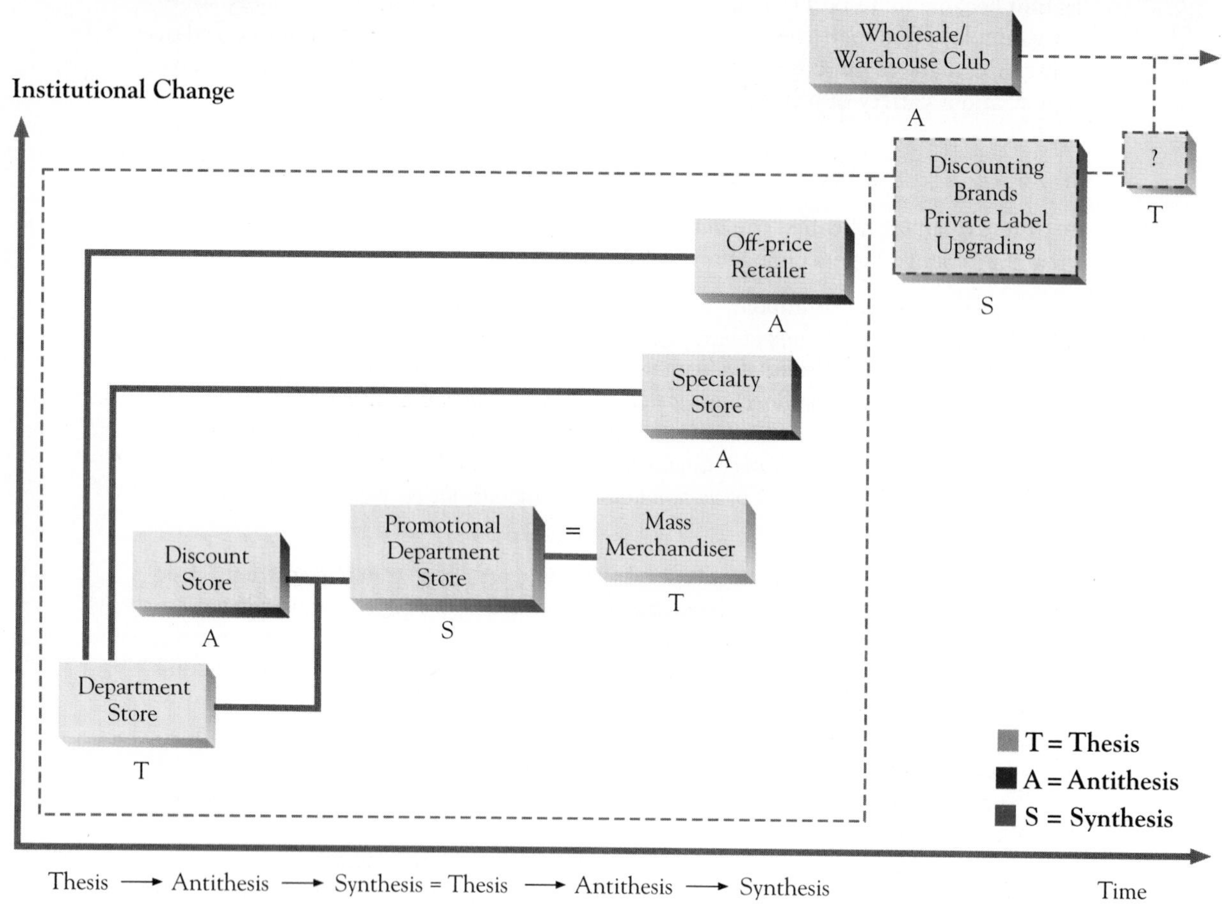

SOURCE: Sylvia Kaufman, "Coping with Rapid Retail Evolutions," *Journal of Consumer Marketing* 2, no. 1, Winter 1985, p. 170.

Retailing: Functions, Market, and Costs

Retailers provide place, time, possession, and sometimes form utility for their suppliers and their customers by actively performing transactional, logistical, and facilitating functions. Like wholesalers, not all retailers are active in each of these three functional areas; some choose to specialize.

For suppliers the retailer anticipates ultimate customer needs, provides inventory storage and transportation, finances inventories, breaks bulk, provides market information, assumes product risk, and provides personal selling and advertising effort. *For ultimate consumers*, the retailer anticipates their product and service needs, provides product storage and delivery, breaks product bulk into acceptable size, provides credit, provides product and service information, and assumes risk by giving guarantees and aftersale service.

Figure 13–3 Illustrations of Marketing Management Decisions

	For Marketing-Oriented Manufacturer	For Marketing-Oriented Retailer
Product	Product-design characteristics Brand-name selection Packaging Creation of product line Labeling—level of information Other	Product design (for private label) Brand-name selection (private label) Selection of brands to carry Creation of assortments by departments Signing-level of information Other
Place	Which markets to distribute in Which intermediaries to distribute through Desirable shelf space or display location Other	Trade-area analysis Site location Number of branches Store layout Variations of assortment plan by store location Other
Promotion	Creation of national campaign—extended time period Promotional appeals for national market Should a sales force be used? Use of point-of-purchase (POP) materials and their nature Contests, coupons, stamps, and other sales promotions Shall co-op advertising be offered? Other	Typically, creation of local advertising—immediate time period Promotional appeals for local market Should sales clerks be available? Will manufacturer's POP materials be permitted in store? In-store promotions and mall-promotion participation Use of co-op advertising Other
Price	Price strategy over product life cycle Trade and functional discount structure Periodic promotional pricing Shall suggested retail price be established? Prepricing? Other	Full- or discount-price orientation Reduction plans for store employees and markdowns Periodic promotional pricing—off-retail strategies Shall suggested retail price be honored or promoted against? Other
Service	Nature of return policy Nature of warranty Delivery policies (to store) Credit policies Product-information availability Other	Nature of return policy Nature of warranties beyond manufacturer Delivery policies (to home) Credit policies Consumer-information availability Other

SOURCE: Ronald W. Stampfl, "Marketing vs. Merchandising Mentalities in Retailing Management, *Proceedings of the American Marketing Association*, Joseph Gultenien and Dale Achabal, eds., American Marketing Association, 1986.

To be successful, retailers must develop an efficient marketing mix. Price, product, place, and promotion decisions must be made to fit the firm's retail situation. The marketing mix of retailing firms is called the *retailing mix*. In this mix, price, product, place, promotion, and service decisions must be made. Like the manufacturer, the retailer must meet customer needs while at the same time meeting the firm's goals. In Figure 13–3, Stampfl captures the marketing mix decisions of the manufacturer and the retailer.[9] Similarities and differences in the kinds of decisions that must be made to be successful stand out clearly.

Table 13–2 Margins and Profits for Selected Retailers

Type of Retailer	Gross Margin (Percent of Sales)	Net Profit After Tax (Percent of Sales)
Motor vehicle dealer	13–15	1.1–1.5
Gasoline service station	23–25	2.4–3.0
Liquor stores	18–23	2.5–2.8
Food stores	18–21	1.0–1.8
Department stores	35–37	1.9–2.0
Variety stores	36–37	2.0–3.7
Jewelry stores	45–48	4.5–7.7
Drug stores	30–35	1.7–1.9
Hardware stores	28–32	2.1–4.5
Building materials dealers	24–27	2.4–3.5
Furniture stores	40	2.1–4.4
Appliance stores	28–35	1.5–3.6
Apparel and accessories stores	35–37	
Children's and infant's wear		2.0–4.8
Women's ready-to-wear		2.2–5.0
Men's and boy's clothing		2.8–4.0
Shoe stores		3.0–5.2
Restaurants	50	N.A.*

*N.A. = not available

SOURCE: Dun and Bradstreet; Internal Revenue Statistics, Robert Morris Associates

The Retail Market

In the United States, there are about 2.0 million retail stores, up from about 1.8 million in 1967. Another 33,000 retailers are doing business directly with consumers without the use of store facilities.[10] Total retail sales are estimated to be $1.63 trillion in 1988, up from $723 billion in 1977, $310 billion in 1967, and $200 billion in 1958. Even after allowing for inflation, retail sales volume has grown substantially over this period, as has per capital retail sales volume. About 80 percent of all retail sales occur in the nation's 300 largest metropolitan areas—the Metropolitan Statistical Areas (MSA) of the Census Bureau. These MSAs account for about 75 percent of the population.[11]

Retail Costs and Margins

Average retail expenses, other than the cost of the retail goods themselves, run about 25 to 30 percent of retail sales—two to three times the average cost of a wholesaling operation. This difference reflects the nature of doing business with end consumers. Relative to a wholesaler, a retailer has higher costs for physical facilities (rent or purchase), has more personnel per dollar of sales, buys in smaller volume, and sells in smaller average volume per sale.

The gross margins and profit levels of retail operations are different for various types of retailers, as you can see from Table 13–2. Retailers in the same business can

Figure 13–4 Classification of Retailers

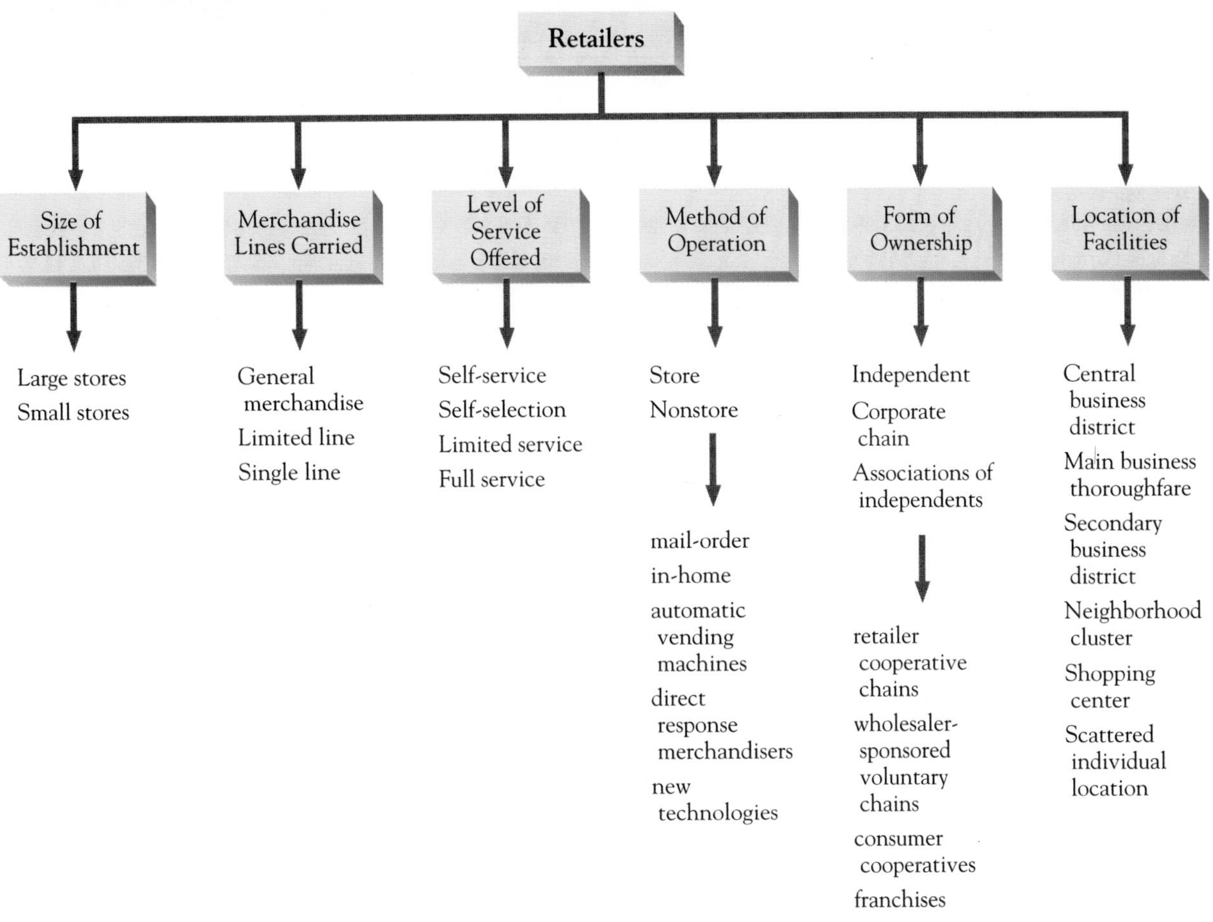

choose to operate in different ways. For example, one hardware store may take only 28 percent gross margin and have a 2.1 percent profit on sales. This "discount" dealer may earn more profit, however, than a competitor who takes 32 percent margin and earns 4.5 percent on sales, because the discounter may do a much bigger volume than its competitor.

Classifying Retailers

The seemingly endless variety of retailers that we confront daily may be classified based upon six dimensions, as depicted in Figure 13–4. These dimensions are size of establishment, merchandise lines carried, level of service offered, method of operation, form of ownership, and location of facilities. In this section we will briefly describe each of the dimensions.

Size of Establishment. The total retail sales volume is, of course, not evenly spread across all retailing firms. The largest 6 percent of retail firms do 57 percent of retail sales volume, and the largest 52 percent account for 92 percent of sales. Thus, the

Table 13–3 The Ten Largest Retailers: 1988

Company	Sales	Profits		Employees		Profits as percent of sales		Stockholders Equity	
	$ Millions	$ Millions	Rank	Number	Rank	%	Rank	%	Rank
Sears Roebuck (Chicago)	50,251.0	1,453.7	1	304,700	1	4.7	85	14.6	79
Kmart (Troy, MI)	27,301.0	803.0	4	24,600	23	0.6	68	10.3	53
Wal-Mart Stores (Bentonville, AR)	20,649.0	837.2	2	35,595	20	1.2	58	16.5	26
Kroger (Cincinnati)	19,053.0	34.5	40	16,700	34	1.3	56	13.5	39
American Stores (Irvine, CA)	18,478.4	98.3	26	52,000	8	1.5	54	24.4	10
J.C. Penney (Dallas)	14,833.0	807.0	3	37,661	16	7.8	12	26.9	5
Safeway Stores (Oakland, CA)	13,612.4	31.2	41	17,778	30	6.7	16	25.5	7
Dayton-Hudson (Minneapolis)	12,204.0	287.0	10	17,876	29	1.1	59	9.4	58
May Department Stores (St. Louis)	11,921.0	534.0	6	45,144	11	3.9	31	12.4	44
Great Atlantic & Pacific Tea (Montvale, NJ)	9,531.8	103.4	24	61,400	7	1.9	52	0.6	71

SOURCE: *Fortune*, June 6, 1989, pp. 358–359.

smallest 48 percent of retailers do only 8 percent of retail business, each doing less than $100,000 in business per year. The ten largest retailers, doing over $183 billion in sales per year, are listed in Table 13–3.[12]

One of the reasons so many small retailers exist is the ease with which one may enter the retailing business on a small scale. By renting a location and having product suppliers grant credit, the capital requirements can be held to a minimum. Virtually anyone can open a retail store. One side effect of this is a high failure rate among small retailers, many of whom lack the competence and experience of the larger retailer, who also fails on occasion for the same reasons. The bankruptcy of W.T. Grant and Korvette have been attributed to management incompetence.

The large retailer has advantages over the small retailer in the division of labor and management skills, buying power, efficient use of the media, financial resources, possible integration into wholesaling and manufacturing, and use of private brands. Small retailers have the advantages of greater flexibility in store layout, merchandise carried, and services offered. They have lower cost operations with smaller overheads.

Merchandise Lines Carried. Retailers may also be classified according to the product lines they carry. Sales patterns can be thought of as flowing through three different types of stores: (1) general merchandise stores, (2) limited line stores, and (3) single line stores.

General merchandise stores carry many different product lines, but with varying degrees of depth depending on the specific type of stores. Department stores, variety stores, and discount stores are the modern-day descendants of the old general stores that still operate in some rural areas.

The **department store** is a large retail institution that carries a wide variety of merchandise grouped into well-defined departments, usually with substantial depth for each product line. Six of the ten largest retail institutions presented in Table 13–3 are department stores. Items carried include household linens and towels, family wearing apparel, furniture, home furnishings, appliances, and radios and televisions. Department stores usually offer many services such as credit, delivery, money-back guarantees, and personal selling assistance. There are well-known, national stores, such as Sears, J.C. Penney, Montgomery Ward, as well as such regional ones as Filene's (Boston), Rich's (Atlanta), and Marshall Field's (Chicago).

Variety stores tend to carry a large number of small and inexpensive product items such as writing paper, housewares, toys, jewelry, buttons, and apparel. They have less depth than department stores and give none of the service. Perry's and F. W. Woolworth are variety stores. Today variety stores are considered obsolete.

One variety store that has not failed and is still competitive is Kmart Corporation. Today Kmart is attempting to upgrade some outlets, experimenting with such activities as providing banking services and selling Wendy's fast foods.

Discount stores price merchandise at a relatively low markup and offer limited customer services. They handle many different types of merchandise, but tend to concentrate on specialty goods and avoid convenience goods. Appliances, cameras, sporting goods, jewelry, silverware, as well as some apparel and fabric are all featured products in discount stores. Target, Toys "R" Us, and Wal-Mart are examples of discount stores.

One theory is that the best way to bring customers into a retail store is to heavily promote price cuts. Toys "R" Us and Wal-Mart have done well keeping prices low all the time. Sears, Montgomery Ward, and Dillards have attempted to do the same.[13] Sears intends to keep its prices low year round, acting more like a discounter because of lost market share. Today most shoppers do not like to wait for sales. Keeping prices low all the time is the weapon Sears, Wards, and Dillards are using to combat the major discounters like Wal-Mart and Target.[14]

Level of Service. Another way to classify the retail structure is to examine the level of service performed for customers. Table 13–4 shows the possible range of services. Since services cost money, the more services retailers offer, the higher their costs—and their prices. Full-service outlets tend to focus on fashion and specialty items. Self-service and self-selection retailers tend to offer lower prices and deal in staple convenience goods that require little customer service. Retailers have a great deal of choice in the service level they offer, even within a category that, by tradition, provides a certain service level. They can satisfy different customer needs by targeting to different segments.

Method of Operation: Store vs. Nonstore Retailing. Certain other types of stores are important as a group. These include supermarkets, box stores, superstores, convenience stores, and catalog showrooms.

Supermarkets, such as Kroger's, Lucky Stores, and Albertson's, are large self-service food stores that often carry some nonfood items. They developed during the Depression as low-cost, low-price alternatives to small, personal-service food stores; today they dominate food sales. Today, the supermarket connotes self-service, large-scale and low-cost physical facilities, and a wide assortment of merchandise. There are non-food supermarkets, such as Toys "R" Us. Supermarkets at the low-price and no-service end of the scale are called *discount supermarkets*.

Table 13–4 Classification of Retailers by Service Level

	Decreasing Services ← Self-Service	Self-Selection	Limited Service	→ Increasing Services Full Service
Characteristics	Very few services Price appeal Staple goods Convenience goods	Restricted services Price appeal Staple goods Convenience goods	Very limited variety of services Much less price appeal Shopping and convenience goods	Wide variety of services Fashion merchandise Specialty merchandise
Examples	Warehouse retailing Supermarkets Mail-order Automatic vending	Discount retailing Variety stores Mail-order retailing	Door-to-door Telephone sales Variety stores	Specialty stores Department stores

SOURCE: Larry D. Redinbaugh, *Retail Management: A Planning Approach* (McGraw-Hill, 1976), p. 12.

One special type of discount supermarket is the **box store**. These stores are smaller, carrying fewer staple product lines and no perishables. The goods are displayed in their shipping boxes (hence the name), and few national brands are carried. The success of these stores has led some traditional supermarkets to have special "box" sections in their stores or to feature generic brands.

Limited-line stores carry great depth in their merchandise but only in a few associated product lines. They tend to be named for the product lines they carry. Thus, we have furniture stores, hardware stores, food stores, and jewelry stores. The advent of **scrambled merchandising** has complicated this classification scheme, especially for food, drug, and hardware stores. Scrambled merchandising occurs when retailers carry product lines that are unrelated to their primary business. Drug stores are selling camera and photo supplies, hardware stores are handling sporting goods and luggage, and supermarkets are selling electric appliances. In each instance, this merchandise represents a small proportion of overall store sales. Scrambled merchandising developed as retailers sought to find products with higher profit margins and as they tried to satisfy consumer's desires for one-stop shopping.

Single-line stores, sometimes called *specialty stores*, specialize in one product line. Florists, card shops, bakeries, furriers, computer stores, camera stores, and automobile dealerships are examples.

Designs of Chestnut Hill, Massachusetts, has used a *single-brand store* concept. The *Marketing in Action* in this section explains this retailing idea.

Another related development is the advent of the **superstore**, sometimes called a **hypermarket**. Imported from France in the 1970s, this concept involves combining a general merchandise discount offering with a supermarket. A hypermarket is about twice the size of a supermarket and carries four times as many items. The French originators of the hypermarket opened their first U.S. store, Carrefour, in February 1988 in Philadelphia.[15] The early results have been sluggish. What was successful in Europe and Latin America hasn't translated into profits yet for the French.

MARKETING IN ACTION

Single Brand Retailer: A New Classification?

Stores often concentrate on a particular line of merchandise, such as kites or t-shirts. But in Chestnut Hill, MA, Designs is claiming a new single-line store concept. In a Designs store you can buy shirts, shoes, jeans, and jackets, but all of a single brand. This is because Designs (full name Designs, exclusively Levi Strauss & Co.) buys only from Levi Strauss & Co., one of the nation's largest suppliers of jeans and related sportswear items. Calvin Margolis, chairman, claims that Designs is the only major chain of its kind (only Levi Strauss) and that the name association is a terrific benefit since Levi's™ is considered to be the second most recognized name in the world—second only to Coca-Cola.

Several benefits are associated with such a close relationship between a supplier and a retailer. First, Designs is connected to an inventory control system called LeviLink™ which monitors stores' sales and automatically replenishes basic stock when needed. Second, because the buyers know the Levi's™ line so well, they are able to take advantage of off-price goods (discounted by Levi Strauss & Co.) and benefit from the increased margin. Finally, Designs stores are actively recruited by malls because of their name, fine reputation, and past sales record, and they are often able to secure prime mall locations at advantageous rents. The major downside to the dependence on one supplier is the risk that the Levi's™ brand of clothing could fall out of fashion. With downsized buying staff and inventory control so closely linked to a sole supplier, large costs would be associated with adding other lines. But as the single-brand store becomes widespread, the list of retail classifications could become a little longer.

ADAPTED FROM: "Designs Expands Single Vendor Concept," *Chain Store Age Executive*, January, 1988, pp. 78–80.

Wal-Mart Stores, Inc., and Cullum Cos., Inc., opened a 220,000 square-foot Hypermarket USA store in Garland, Texas, in December 1987.[16] The store has thirty-five general merchandise departments in addition to a full-line supermarket. The size of the Hypermarket USA store is reflected by these data: twenty truck loads of merchandise are received daily; there are 500–600 full- and part-time employees, 48 permanent scanning cash registers and 12 additional registers, and 50,000 to 70,000 customers shopping in the store each week.

The success to date of Hypermarket U.S.A. and the sluggish returns for Carrefour are an interesting contrast. Hypermarket U.S.A. promoted the store, and the store is well known and crowded. Carrefour elected to open their stores quietly, which is customary in France. This was a major blunder. One-stop shopping with super low prices is something that apparently needs to be announced and promoted to be successful in the U.S.

Still another development is the **convenience store**. Examples include 7-Eleven, Stop-N-Go, Jiffy, U-Tote'M, and Circle K. These stores carry a limited assortment of products, are usually quite small, and have higher prices than those in traditional supermarkets. Their emphasis is on proximity to the customer, long store hours, easy parking, and fast checkout.[17] Using the retail accordian view of retail evolution, the convenience store reflects elements of the single-line grocery store of the early 1900s.

What about a convenience store for video rentals? The Video 1st example in the *Marketing in Action* on the next page presents a new retailing concept.

Catalog showrooms are discount retail stores that sell general merchandise, using as their main promotional pieces large catalogs mailed to prospective customers. The

MARKETING IN ACTION

Drive-in Movies

Imagine a Fotomat-type kiosk that has two drive through windows renting new release and hit videos for $2.95 a night. That's exactly what Todd W. LeRoy and Michael L. Adkinson, co-founders of Video's 1st, think will become the "hottest franchise in the country." Despite skepticism by professionals in the video industry, the entrepreneurs feel that consumers will pay a premium price (average rental price is under $2) for the convenience of a drive through with the guarantee that they will be able to rent the movie that they want to see (or at least a hit). By keeping several copies of popular and new release movies in a low overhead store, they feel that they can better serve the needs of movie renters.

Traditional movie rental operations come in three formats: the storefront, the rack jobber, and the superstore. Video's 1st feels that these approaches are already tapped and cite the following shortcomings:

• The storefront operation is the most seen, usually in a strip shopping center, about 2,089 square feet, 3,478 tapes, with 2,417 titles. This means that there are few copies per title and a greater chance that the movie that you want to see is checked out.

• The rack jobber supplies convenience stores and gas stations with a small list of titles and relies on the employees to perform the rental activities. The high turnover nature of such employees precludes training to do a good job.

• The superstore, with costly start-up and several thousand titles, has already been built in most of the areas big enough to support its large volume.

Overall, the only approach left untapped is the fast-to-serve, cheap-to-build, and well-stocked "top forty" type kiosk.

FROM: "Drive-In Movies" by Tom Richman in *Inc.*, February 1988.

---

customer identifies the item he or she wishes to purchase, either from the catalog or an in-store display, and the order is filled from a warehouse attached to the showroom. Although they carry general merchandise lines, catalog showrooms tend to feature items on which they can offer large discounts—jewelry, luggage, small appliances, toys, and sporting goods.

These outlets have grown dramatically during the 1970s and early 1980s. Annual business was about $7 billion in 1980. Some major catalog retailers are Spiegel ($1.2 billion), Service Merchandise ($527 million), Zales, and Gordon Jewelry Corporation ($390 million).[18]

Although discussed earlier in the chapter, *discount stores* warrant a further look. These stores originally featured brand-name hard goods (appliances, televisions, cameras, watches) at low prices relative to traditional retailers. Their margins were about half the 30- to 40-percent margins of traditional retailers. Their costs—about 20 percent of sales, compared to 30 to 40 percent for traditional retailers—were lower, because they offered fewer services and cheaper locations.

Over time, discount stores added other products. Traditional retailers responded by opening discount subsidiaries (see Table 13–5). Today we find the range from general merchandise discounters (Kmart) all the way to specialty discount stores (T.J. Maxx), as well as drug, food, and appliance stores. Two of the largest discounters are Kmart ($26.9 billion) and F.W. Woolworth ($7.1 billion).[19]

There are about 33,000 nonstore retailers in the United States; their sales are about 10 percent of all retail sales. The most important ones are (1) mail-order

Table 13–5 Discount Operations of Traditional Retailers

Store Type	Example	Discount Operation
Variety Stores	F.W. Woolworth	Kmart
	Neisner Brothers	Big N
Department Stores	May's	Venture
	L.S. Ayres	Ayr-Way
	Rich's	Richway
	Federated Department Stores	Gold Circle, Gold Triangle
	Dayton-Hudson	Target
Supermarkets	Grand Union	Grand Way
	Food Fair	Pantry Pride
	Kroger	Thriftown
	Jewel	Turn-Style
	Stop & Shop	Bradlees

SOURCE: David J. Rachman and Elaine Romano, *Modern Marketing* (Dryden, 1980), p. 389.

retailers, (2) in-home retailers, (3) automatic vending machines, and (4) direct response merchandisers. In addition, technological advances have allowed the development of new types of nonstore retailers, including *videocassette* and *videodisc catalogs* and *interactive cable television.*[20]

Videocassette and videodisc catalogs display the printed pages of a catalog on a home television set. (Of course, the consumer needs the right in-home equipment to do this.) An interactive cable television system allows viewers to buy products displayed on their television sets by pushing cable system buttons that record and charge the purchase to a credit card or bank account. Many other similar systems are being established, or have been proposed, by such companies as AT&T, Cox Cable, Dow-Jones, and Time, Inc. This type of retailing is referred to as *teleshopping* since consumers are able to buy what they view on their television sets.

An example of teleshopping is Silverman's, Inc., a clothier in Grand Forks, North Dakota. The company used Viewtron, a shop-at-home system operated out of southeast Florida. Steven Silverman, the vice president of Silverman's, Inc., believes that the use of Viewtron changed his firm from a one location, one market operation to a multiple-market one. There are only 45,000 people in Grand Forks, and 650,000 in all of North Dakota, but Silverman's clothing was seen via Viewtron by some 1.6 million people in the metropolitan Miami area alone.[21] Viewtron subscribers called up a display of Silverman's clothing wares on their television sets and punched in their orders directly. Orders were taken all day long, seven days a week.

Some retail outlets are offering toll-free 800 service. Harrod's Department Store in London, England, was the first store in Europe to offer AT&T international 800 service. U.S. customers can order by dialing direct—even before the store opens for business in London.[22]

Telemarketing is a growing form of direct marketing. In 1988, consumers spent an estimated $100.00 billion in ordering goods and services by telephone. There are some complaints about this type of marketing, especially about when calls are made. Calling at dinner time is popular, a timing that has annoyed many customers and legislators. U.S. Senator Albert Gore, Jr., is sponsoring a bill to lay out standards dealing with customer refunds, merchandise deliveries, when calls may be made, and use of a three-day cooling-off period.[23] Passage of legislation may slow the growth of telemarketing.

There are about 11,000 *mail-order retailers*, who account for about $50 billion in sales annually.[24] Over 6.7 billion catalogs are distributed each year, offering everything from personal computers to battery-operated timers for garden hoses.[25] The top mail-order industries are insurance (Colonial Penn, Geico), general merchandise (Sears and Penney's), magazine subscriptions, books (Time-Life, Doubleday), ready-to-wear clothing (New Process, Lane Bryant), collectibles (Franklin Mint, Bradford Exchange), sporting goods (L. L. Bean, Eddie Bauer), crafts, foods (Swiss Colony, Harry and David), and records and tapes (Columbia Record Club, RCA Music Service).

Mail-order customers receive promotion about products in the mail, but they may order the merchandise by mail, phone, or even at a store's catalog order desk. The goods are then shipped directly to the customer or to the store for customer pick-up.

In-home or *direct retailing* involves presenting goods to customers in a face-to-face meeting at the customer's home or by contacting the customer by telephone. This solicitation can be done without advance selection of consumers or follow-ups based upon prior contact at stores, or by phone or mail. The well-known Tupperware party fits in this category. Here a person has a social gathering where everyone know a sales presentation will be made. Besides Tupperware, some of the largest companies operating in this type of retailing are Avon (cosmetics), Electrolux (vacuum cleaners), Amway (household products), and World Book (encyclopedia and books). Despite the great cost savings of having no store and no inventory, labor costs make this form of retailing expensive. Expenses are estimated to average about 50 percent of sales, compared to about 26 percent for all retailing. Sales in 1987 of in-home or direct retailing merchandise were $8.8 billion.[26]

Automatic vending machine retailers do over $20 billion in business.[27] There are more than 13,000 operators, with six million machines, accounting for 25 percent of all soft drink sales, 16 percent of cigarette sales, and 20 percent of candy bar sales in the United States.[28] Coffee and soft drinks account for about half of their total dollar sales.[29] Total sales are about two percent of all retail sales.

Direct-response merchandisers solicit customers through the use of mass media promotion. These goods are "not available in any store." The customer orders the goods either by a toll-free phone call or mail. Broadcast media are sometimes paid a commission on sales or inquiries instead of being paid for the advertising time used. Records, small housewares, books, and magazines are popular direct-response items.

Form of Ownership. Another dimension we can use to classify retailers is their form of ownership. We distinguish among independents, corporate chains, and associations of independents.

An **independent retailer** owns a single store that is not affiliated in any way with other retailers. About 90 percent of all retail stores fall into this category.

A **corporate chain** is a group of *two or more* stores that is *centrally owned and managed*, and that deals in the same line of merchandise. This technical definition by the Census Bureau is probably too broad. Many merchants operate a few units and probably do not consider themselves chains. About 31 percent of all retail store sales are made by chains, which account for about 90 percent of all department store sales, and 45 percent of shoe store sales. The great majority of these sales are made by chains with more than ten stores. Since chains gain economies in purchasing goods and in promotion, they can often underprice independents.

In response to this cost and promotion disadvantage, independent retailers have combined to gain the advantages of a large-scale operation. The resulting retailer *cooperative chains, voluntary chains, and franchise* systems that have been formed were discussed in Chapter 11.

Other small independents ("mom and pop retailers") have survived because they have a special location advantage, give better or more personal services, and carry unique products.

Location of Facilities. The last dimension we will use to classify retailers is the *location of their facilities*. We distinguish five types of locations:

1. *The central business district* or *downtown shopping area* contains the larger chain and department stores in a city or town.
2. *Main business thoroughfares* or *string streets* are heavily traveled streets leading to the central business district or other important commercial areas.
3. *Secondary shopping districts* are usually located in outlying and suburban areas, closer to consumers' homes.
4. *Neighborhood clusters* are small groups of stores located in or near residential areas.
5. *Scattered individual locations* are held by some stores apart from other retailers, usually in residential areas (for example, a convenience store).

Additionally, we need to distinguish whether a store is located in a **planned shopping center**. This is an integrated unit, planned in advance, that is composed of different types of stores to satisfy customer needs. Free, off-street parking is usually provided. Larger centers are often enclosed and attractively designed. A single owner, frequently a developer or large major department store, owns and manages the center.

Centers vary greatly in size. The smallest is the *neighborhood shopping center*, consisting of ten to fifteen stores, selling mostly convenience goods such as food, drugs, and hardware items. A supermarket is often the anchor store. These centers serve from 2500 to 20,000 people and average 54,000 square feet of selling space. Next largest is the *community shopping center*, which contains both specialty and convenience stores and has a small department or discount store as the anchor unit. These centers serve from 50,000 to 100,000 people and average 162,000 square feet of selling space.[30] The largest are the *regional shopping centers* or *malls* that are anchored by two or more department stores and have 100 or more stores. These centers serve as alternatives to downtown shopping and average 481,000 square feet of selling space. The largest ones can be one million square feet.[31] There is a trend toward larger centers. These centers feature shopping and specialty goods, but they have some convenience goods also and may serve from 100,000 to 200,000 people coming from distances as far as fifty miles away. There are almost 19,000 shopping centers in the United States, with sales of over $245 billion.[32]

A new generation of shopping center is called a "power center."[33] It resembles an oversized strip or community shopping center (200,000 to 500,000 square feet) but is smaller than a regional shopping center. The power center contains as many as seven promotional anchors, such as discounters, destination-oriented retailers, or superstores. Typical anchor tenants in power centers are presented in Table 13–6.

Table 13–6 Typical Anchor Tenants For Power Center

Retail Type	Gross Square Feet	Specific Merchants
Discount department store	80,000–100,000	Kmart Target Wal-Mart
Promotional softlines department store	70,000–80,000	MainStreet Mervyn's
Off-price apparel	20,000–30,000	Marshall's Ross Dress For Less T.J. Maxx
Toys/children's	25,000–40,000	Children's Palace Kids "R" Us Toys "R" Us
Consumer electronics	20,000–25,000	Circuit City Fretter Highland Superstores
Catalogue showroom	20,000–50,000	Best Products Luria's Service Merchandise
Deep-discount drugstore	25,000–45,000	Drug Emporium F&M Phar-Mor
Supermarket	50,000 +	—
Consumer-oriented home center	70,000–100,000	Builders Square HomeClub Home Depot
Cinema	8+-plex	—

SOURCE: Howard L. Green & Associates, Inc. from Jane E. Primo, "Picking Power Center Tenant Mix," *Marketing News*, December 5, 1988, p. 10.

One of the developers of power centers is Edward De Bartolo & Co. of Youngstown, Ohio. The firm has a 1.6 million square foot power center in Orlando, Florida. It is De Bartolo's opinion that power centers can be opened adjacent to or opposite regional malls. Economies of scale by marketing to the malls and the center are what De Bartolo plans to achieve.[34]

Summary of Retail Classifications. The six dimensions we have discussed can be used to classify virtually any retailer. Table 13–7 compares a J. C. Penney store and a local hardware store according to these classifications.

Review Your Marketing Knowledge

- How are retailing institutions classified?
- What is a nonstore retailer?
- What would be some limitations or reasons why some consumers would not like teleshopping?

Table 13–7 Retail Classifications: Two Examples

Classification Dimension	J.C. Penney	Lincoln Ace Hardware Store
Size of store	Large	Small
Merchandise lines	General merchandise	Limited line
Level of service	Self-selection	Limited to full service
Method of operation	Store and mail order	Store
Form of ownership	Corporate chain	Voluntary chain (Ace)
Location of store	Secondary shopping district—in a regional shopping center	Main business thoroughfare—in a neighborhood shopping center

Retail Management: Strategy and Decisions

The retailer today doesn't simply find the best products, display them, and make it easy for customers to see and buy the goods. Retailing in the 1990s requires strategic planning of important decisions in such areas as promotion, pricing, and selection of a proper location. The successful retailer addresses such questions as: What business are we in? How are we different from competitors? Who is our target customer?

Developing a strategy means that a firm carefully plans how it will compete so that worthwhile objectives are accomplished. Figure 13–5 illustrates how four strategic levels of planning are blended at J.C. Penney.[35] At the corporate level, an overall corporate plan is specified. At the business level, each division develops a strategy that is integrated with each of the other strategic plans (e.g., corporate, functional, operating). Functional strategy involves making decisions about financial plans, marketing plans, physical facility plans, and human resource plans. The daily operations at J.C. Penney are carried out at each store using an operating level strategy.

In retail management at J.C. Penney, Wal-Mart, or Avon Cosmetics, the decision process begins only after the mission of the firm is clearly stated. A *mission* is what the firm plans to accomplish in the markets it enters. The *mission statement* clarifies what the firm wants to accomplish to employees, owners, competitors, and consumers. J.C. Penney has stated its mission as, "to sell merchandise and services to customers at a profit, primarily but not exclusively in the United States, in a manner that is consistent with our corporate ethics and responsibilities."[36]

A number of retail management decisions must be made once the business mission is clearly portrayed. The decision areas are illustrated in Figure 13–6.

Target Market Selection

Target markets are the segments of the population that management decides to serve. *Market positioning* is how the retail management team plans to compete in target markets.[37] The objective is to satisfy the needs of customers within the target market. McDonald's hamburger chain can be used to highlight the target-type decisions.

Type Business—Hamburgers, fast food

Market Segments—Age, income level

Figure 13–5 Levels of Strategy in the J.C. Penney Company

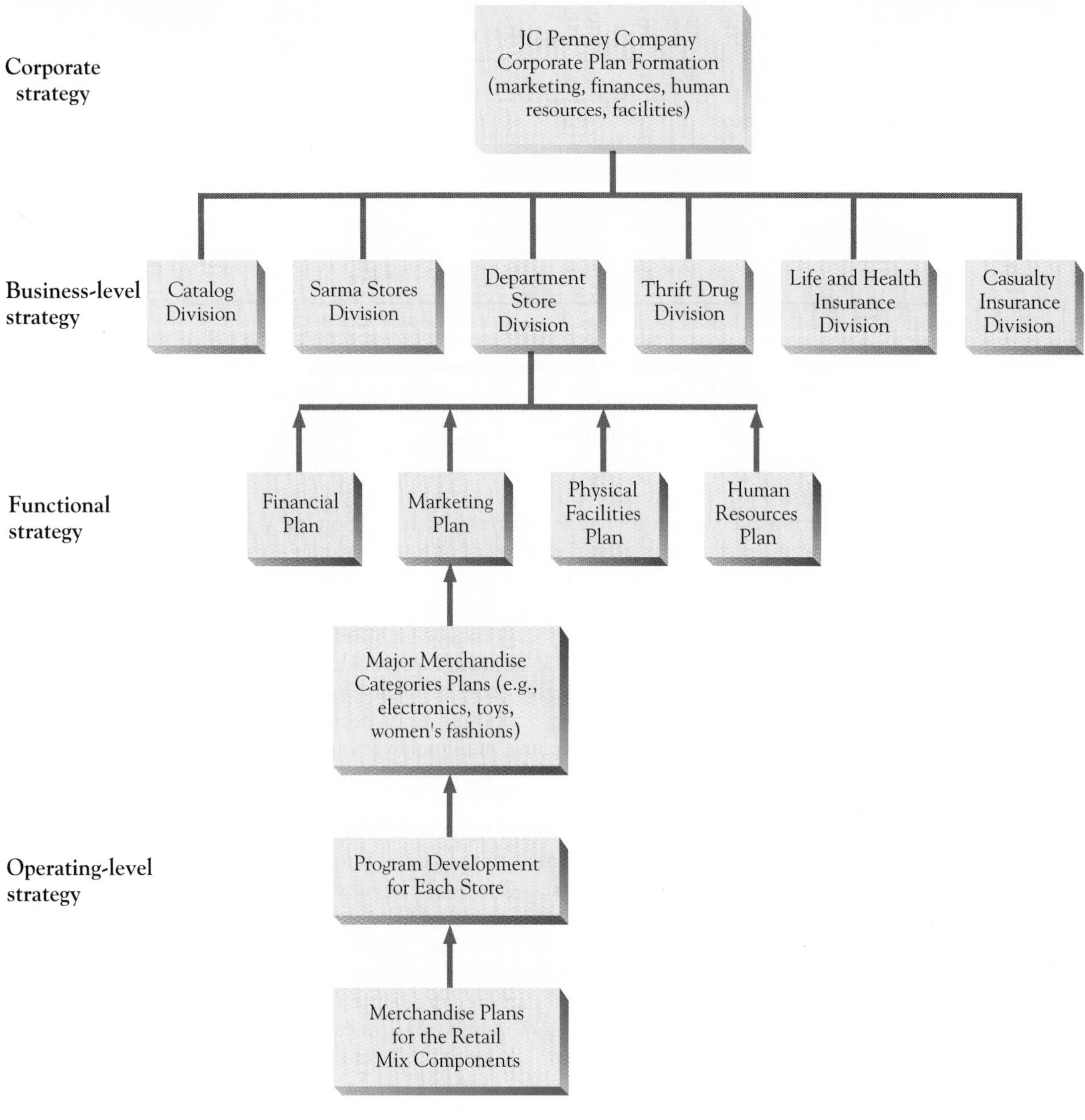

Target Market selected—Teenagers—Early adults 15–19, average income, average education

Positioning Strategy—Provide a high quality meal at an average price in attractive and clean outlets.

Figure 13–6 Retail Management Decisions: Some Issues to Consider

Target Markets	What business should we be in? Who are competitors (local, national, international)? How can we gain competitive advantage? How much of the target market are we satisfied with? How can we gain our target market share? How much will we spend to achieve our goals?
Decision Support Systems	What information do we have about our markets, competitors, and resources? What research information is available? How can information be formulated to achieve optimal value? When is information needed?
Merchandise Mix	What products should be carried? What style, how many? What type of inventory system is needed? How should merchandise be displayed?
Pricing	What are competitors charging? What will our customers pay? What price is needed to attract more customers? If we use a pricing strategy, how will competitors respond?
Store Image and Convenience	What do our customers like in terms of ambience? What furniture, colors, and layout are most appropriate? Where will parking be? How many parking lots?

McDonald's has generated a large share of their business with individuals under 19 years old. Although McDonald's competes with Wendy's, the target markets and positioning strategies of the two firms are different.[38] There is no specific formula for selecting target markets, but it is usually important to consider age, income, education, and occupation. Once such factors are differentiated, retail managers can determine how their products and services fit the target markets.

The Retail Decision Support System

The firm needs timely, accurate information about the environment, consumer needs, tastes, perceptions, and competitors' merchandise offerings. D'Lites of America (a chain of nutritious fast food restaurants) uses trade-area serving information to develop demographic profiles of their customers. The firm also uses telephone surveys to test advertising and product awareness. D'Lites uses primary and secondary information to forecast best future sites for new restaurant locations.[39]

Retail management needs a steady flow of quality information to supplement its experience when making decisions about strategy, positioning, price, promotion, product offerings, and location. A retail decision support system is the people, equipment, and procedures used to gather, analyze, and use the information needed for more efficient decision making. The *Marketing in Action* on Mrs. Fields' Cookies illustrates how, on a daily basis, information is used to make important retail decisions.

An example of an information system for a hotel is presented in Figure 13–7. The multiple sources of information used by the hotel provide information about

MARKETING IN ACTION

Artificial Intelligence at Mrs. Fields Cookies

Every morning, managers at each of the 700 Mrs. Fields cookie stores begin their day by striking up a conversation with their computer. The computer asks questions like: What day of the week is it? Is it a holiday? Is it a special sale day? After comparing the answers to dates in memory, it responds with how much cookie dough should be made, when it should be baked, and what sales should be like at different time intervals during the day. During the day, the store manager enters actual sales data and the computer revises estimates, providing up-to-date expectations along with sales and promotion ideas aimed at boosting sales. Sounds a little spooky? "Actually, it's a little peculiar," admits Randy Fields, owner.

The computer's artificial intelligence attempts to emulate the decision processes found in humans. In this case, Debbi Fields' (owner) extensive experience of different days, sales, and sales techniques can be taught to the computer. The result is a computer in every store that thinks as she would, eliminating much of the corporate communication while standardizing across stores.

For each of the stores, the computer takes care of labor scheduling, acts as a time clock, does production planning, keeps track of inventory, reorders when necessary, and keeps track of maintenance for the various machines in the store. Because many of the functions of a retail manager are taken care of automatically, the Fields feel that the system allows managers and personnel to ignore traditional functions and concentrate on selling cookies.

Just selling cookies may have been the cause for Mrs. Fields' missteps and losses. Despite the use of computers, the single-product line and the difficulty of sustaining growth has resulted in some changes. Mrs. Fields is opening combination stores. LaPetite Boulangerie, a chain of baking stores, will merge with Mrs. Fields. Even with sophisticated computers, Mrs. Fields expanded rapidly and into international markets on its own. The strategy wasn't sound, and now with mergers, joint ventures, and more carefully planned growth, Mrs. Fields is attempting to become profitable again.

ADAPTED FROM: Buck Brown, "Mrs. Fields Sees Cookie Empire Crumble," *The Wall Street Journal*, January 27, 1989, p. 5; Anonymous, "Mrs. Fields Automates the Way the Cookie Sells," *Chain Store Age Executive*, April, 1988; personal communication with Mrs. Fields, Inc., 1989.

---

individual guests, group guests, occupancy needs, guest satisfaction and preferences, and advertising effectiveness. This array of information helps the hotel evaluate its reservation system, services, and relationships with travel agents, tour operators, and associations. A thorough evaluation can result in better future decision making in each of these areas.

Merchandise Mix Decisions

Managing the merchandise mix involves making decisions about what products to carry; what styles, models, colors, sizes, and price ranges; and how many units of each product to have in inventory. A customer does not typically think of a supermarket or a department store as a good place to buy a product. He or she usually shops at one store because of the variety or assortment of goods available. The merchandise mix provides a store with a certain character or atmosphere, an ambiance.

The size and content decisions of any store are determined largely by the space available. Having adequate space to display an assortment of products is important for customer comfort. Thus, an important decision involves the range of products that are essential to satisfy customer needs. There is likely to be a small number of

Figure 13–7 Marketing Information System in a Hotel

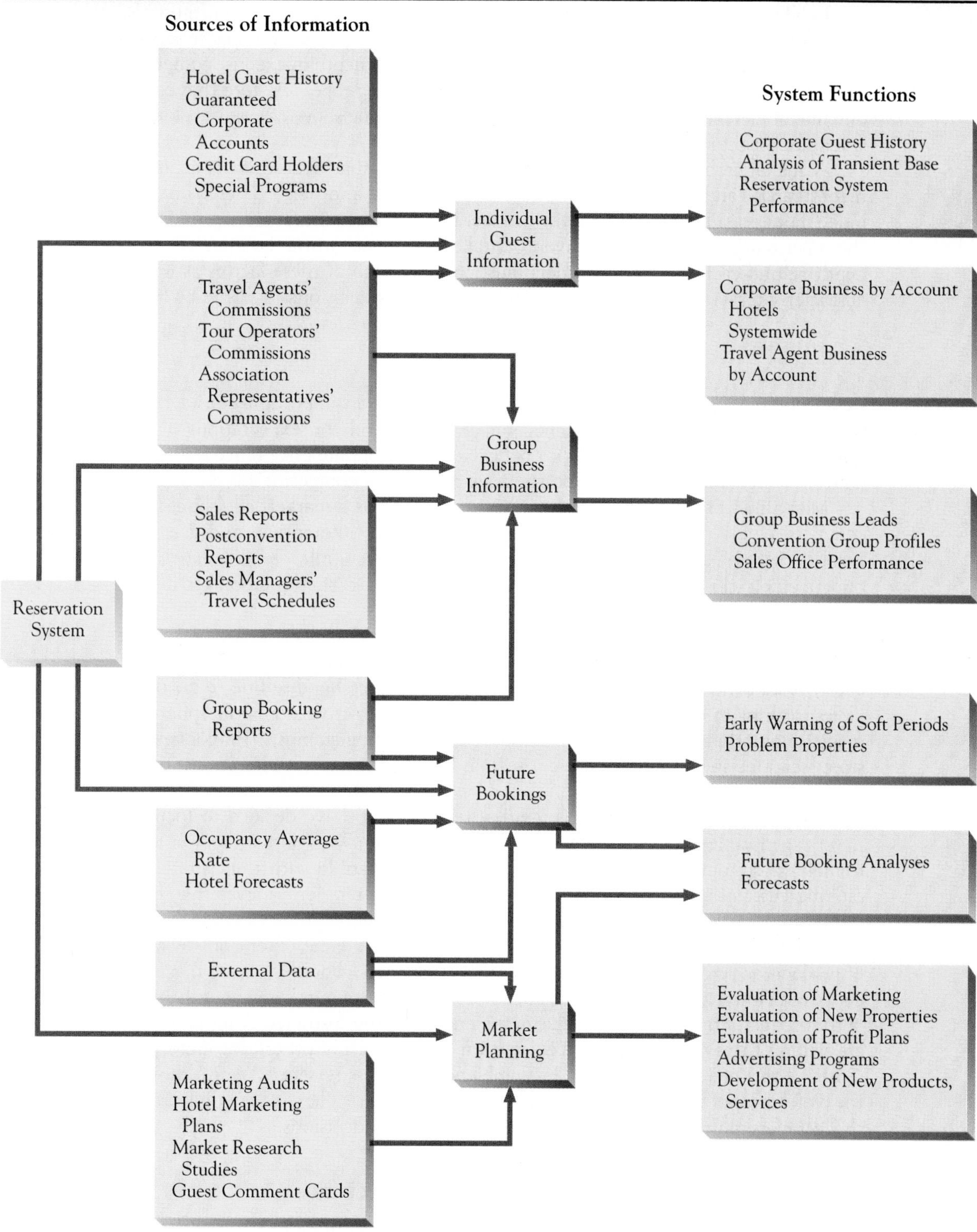

SOURCE: A. Neal Geller, "How to Improve Your Information System," *Cornell H.R.A. Quarterly*, August 1985, p. 25.

products that account for large sales volume. These products deserve special attention and need to be stocked. Being out of preferred and highly demanded goods creates a negative customer impression of the retailer.

In addition to having a wide assortment of products on hand, retailers must also have stock depth—that is, sufficient quantity on hand behind each product to support sales. Oshman's sporting goods stores carries considerable depth in exercise equipment from rowing machines to universal gym sets to stretching ropes. A store that carries one line of merchandise, such as a ski shop, a scuba diving shop, or a sports clothing store, also has stock depth.

A major problem of merchandise management is that decisions about assortments, range, and depth are often in conflict with one another.[40] There is only so much money available to expand the product line and to maintain an inventory. On the other hand, building up an inventory takes money away from building adequate depth behind each product. Retailers must consider each of these factors as well as customer satisfaction when making merchandising mix decisions.

Pricing Decisions

Retail pricing is a difficult but necessary task. Price is an important consideration when matching the retailer's assumed target market and the expectations of customers. Customers develop what they believe is an appropriate price range for various kinds of merchandise. There is also the issue of prices of competing stores.

Many lines of merchandise have what is accepted as a market level price. It is common to find prices for candy, groceries, hardware, automotive, and drugstore items to be based on a standard markup percentage that is similar for all competitors. Supermarkets closely adhere to almost identical prices so that competitors do not have a price advantage.

In some cases a store may have something to offer that permits it to set prices higher than competitors'. Some of the factors that permit pricing above the market are 1) more personal service, 2) exclusiveness of the merchandise line (e.g., petite ladies clothing or tall and big men's clothing), 3) an attractive store atmosphere, 4) special promotions, such as triple coupon days or trading stamps, 5) a convenient store location, and 6) special service, such as home delivery, free alterations, or 90-day free credit.

Pricing below market levels is used by retailers who have decided to focus on lower expenses, less service, and less store ambience. The Wal-Mart strategy of being friendly to customers, in a rather bland store, is compatible with their strategy of offering customers lower prices. The no-frills discount retailer believes that lower prices will be sustained by volume selling and some cutbacks in service.

The pricing decisions made by a retailer depend to a great extent on the value of products as perceived by the target market. Customers, whether paying market or above or below market prices, make decisions at the time of purchase about the value of the product. Price reflects the value of the product to the customer. Some customers are willing to pay more for services and atmosphere, while others are more price sensitive and prefer lower prices, less ambience, and less service. Again, knowing the preferences of the target market and its thoughts about value is an ongoing process that retailers must deal with daily when making pricing decisions.

Store Image and Ambience Decisions

Customers offer more than money when purchasing something of value; they offer time and effort. In most cases, the merchandise and customer exchange occurs in a physical store. A store's ambience, reflecting its mood, character, tone, and atmosphere, is something that a customer can feel.[41] The retailer can artfully create ambience. A jewelry store on Rodeo Drive in Los Angeles, for example, has ambience because of its location.

Other factors that contribute to ambience are the merchandise carried, how merchandise is displayed, what is to be emphasized in a display, the interior design and decoration of a store, and the customer services offered. A comparison of the Nieman-Marcus, Dillard's, and Kmart stores can show how these factors create a different feel or tone. Together they create a store image in the minds of customers and potential customers—that is, a composite attitude they have about the retail store (company).

Stew Leonard's is not a typical supermarket; the owner has worked hard on ambience and image. Located in Norwalk, Connecticut, Leonard's has annual sales of $80 million.[42] Customers travel long distances for ambience; excitement; fresher, better-quality products; and often lower prices than can be found at other supermarkets.

Stew Leonard stores carry only 700 products, while the average supermarket stocks over 10,000. He talks personally to customers, listens to their suggestions, and is a stickler for clean floors, tasty food, and being friendly. He states, "When I see a frown on a customer's face, I see $50,000 about to walk out the door." His good customers buy $100 worth of groceries a week; over ten years, Stew claims, that is about $50,000. The way merchandise is displayed, the friendly atmosphere, the cleanliness are all part of Stew Leonard's special emphasis on image and ambience.

Trends in Retailing

The United States retailing establishment has been labeled a "Baskin-Robbins" society, implying the market is so diversified that every product and service is available in 31 different shapes, sizes, and forms.[43] The marketplace of the 1960s offered consumers few alternatives. There were three major television networks, a limited number of automobiles to choose from, and three or four major department stores in large cities. Today there are choices and more choices.

Some marketplace fragmentation has occurred, creating benefits and problems. There has been some shaking out in retailing, and stores like Gimbels and Hudsons have had to close their doors and lay off employees. Other retailers have had to manage more effectively to survive the influx of new retailers, new forms of retailing, and changes in the lifestyles of consumers. There is now more than ever a strong consumer orientation in retailing. Simply minding the store and offering a limited assortment is not going to do the job. Retailers have to search continually for new ways to meet changing consumer needs.

Through improved merchandising practices, cost reductions, and strategic planning retailers are seeking to improve their productivity and profit margins. Forecasters have agreed that only moderate growth in retail sales is expected in the 1990s.[44] This will place more emphasis on sustaining market share performance at acceptable levels. The implications of moderate sales growth include:

- Increased competition for consumers' patronage and spending.
- More attention to improving productivity for improved profitability.
- More awareness of consumer changes such as the aging of the population, better informed and discriminating consumers, working couples, and single-parent households.

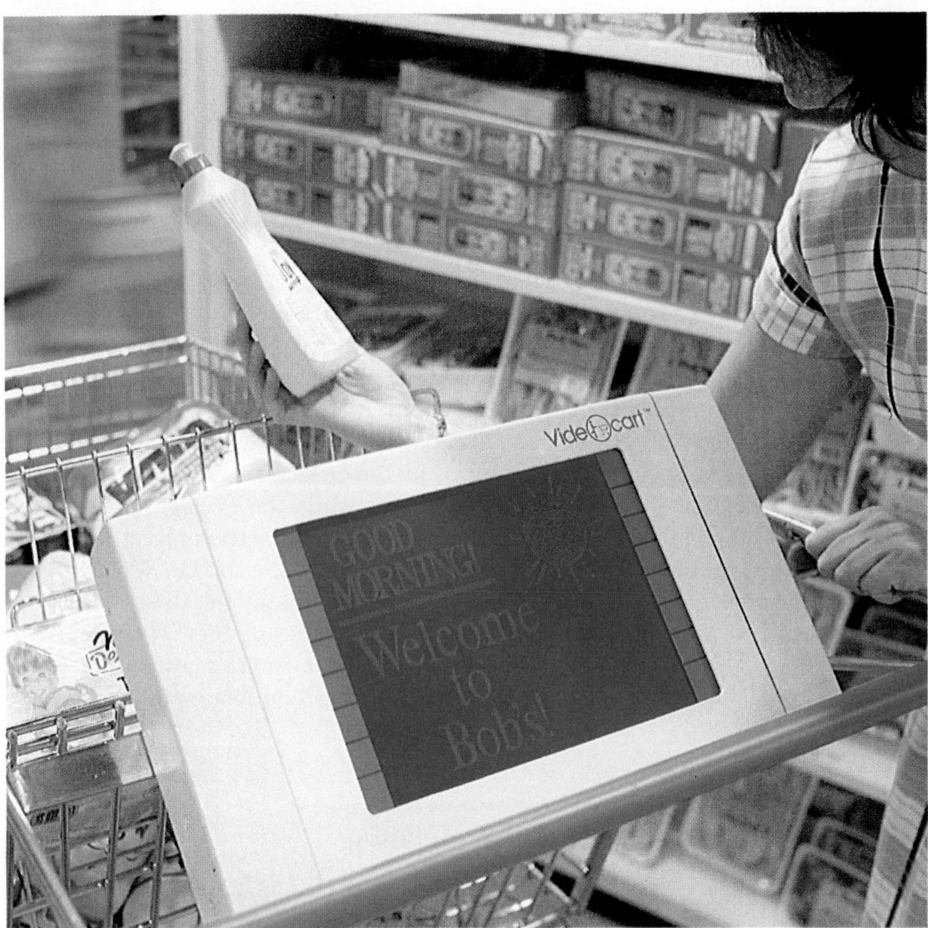

The VideOcart advertises to customers as they push their shopping carts down the aisle.

The astute retailer will cash in on these retailing opportunities. For example, although there is increased competition, everyone seems to be going about competing in the same manner as in the past. There is what some describe as "very little creative competitive marketing being executed in most retail lines of trade." Innovation, creative styles, and decisions can be the key to securing and holding on to a distinct market share in the 1990s. An example of innovation is the television home shopping business.[45] Originally, it was assumed that by showing certain segments of the audience low-priced items in a brief time period, a sale would be made. Today, the idea is to give customers more information, choices, and time to make decisions. TV home shopping sales are projected to grow from an estimated $1.75 billion in 1987 to about $3.3 billion in 1991. This will happen by injecting a stronger entertainment flavor to the presentations. Games, prizes, and selling enthusiasm are increasingly used as innovative ways to improve TV shopping sales.

The retail life cycles will likely be shortened. Store concepts reach maturity quickly and innovation is almost mandatory. Some refer to retail stores as "locaters." If this analogy is correct, changing the "scenery" to attract and keep customers is going to become more important. Banana Republic has changed from safari outfitters to broader-based, travel-oriented stores. Merchandise and promotional themes are changed. Montgomery Ward stores have sublet space, adding to the idea of changing scenery. Changing the decor, the goods, and the overall scenery is likely to become more important as retailers face increased competition.

Technological changes are likely to occur in retailing. Electronic funds transfer systems will become more widely used in retail stores. The use of scanners and wand devices will grow. Hand-held electronic inventory equipment and other electronic devices, such as VideOcart, an electronic point-of-purchase ad medium, will be found in more stores. As a customer pushes a VideOcart down a supermarket aisle, the manufacturers' ads for brands on the shelves being passed at the moment will be triggered. The manufacturer of VideOcarts expects to have 10,000 U.S. supermarkets outfitted with the computer-equipped shopping carts by 1991.[46]

Retailers have been using lick-and-stick trading stamps since 1986.[47] However, a new generation is receiving electronic cards resembling credit cards. The card has a magnetic strip that records all transactions at the cash register.

The successful retailers of the 1990s will have to be immersed in strategic planning, paying careful attention to consumer needs and environmental changes. They will need to develop creative ways to satisfy consumer needs and improve productivity by using technological advances correctly. The 1990s will neither repeat nor even resemble the 1960s. Thus, paying attention to detail, listening and observing carefully, and finding the best market niche must become a part of the retailer's daily routine.

Personal Computer Exercise

The use of productivity, price, and cost data can help you understand the small net profit after tax margins enjoyed by retailers. This exercise will provide specific information on both the importance of improving productivity and why retailers must find strategic options to bring about such improvements.

KEY POINTS

- The retail merchant provides an assortment of products that consumers can observe, purchase, and use.
- The retail life cycle is a series of stages through which a retailing institution moves from its inception until its ultimate decline and disappearance from the marketplace.
- A number of theories exist that explain how retail institutions have evolved. The wheel of retailing, the retail accordian, and the dialectic process are three explanations.
- Retail establishments can be classified on the basis of size of the establishment, merchandise lines carried, level of service offered, method of operation, form of ownership, and location of facilities.
- Retailers are becoming more involved in thinking in terms of strategic planning: What business are we in? How are we different from competitors? Who is our target customer?
- Increased competition, marketplace fractionation, and changing tastes among customers are now the rule. These changes and situations require an aggressive and innovative stance by retailers. In order to survive, the theme of "business as usual" has to be discarded by retailers. Finding innovations that appeal to customers is the main alternative available to retailers.

ISSUES FOR DISCUSSION

1. There are national service chains in real estate, dentistry, and optometry. Why did these kinds of retail establishments emerge in society?

2. What change in retailing have you noticed the most in the past five years?

3. What is meant by the notion that retail management must emphasize a marketing orientation to survive in the future?

4. Is there one accepted model for explaining the evaluation of retail institutional changes?

5. Why has strategic planning become an important process for retailers in the past decade?

6. What factors suggest that competition is intense in the retailing industry?

7. How do changes in the family unit (structure, income, size) influence retailing?

8. How has the computer affected retail management practices and decision making?

9. What would cause a retail establishment to fail or not survive?

10. What factors result in what is called "moving the wheel of retailing"?

GLOSSARY

Box store: a small food store that displays its low-priced goods in shipping boxes. It carries no perishables and fewer staple product lines than a supermarket.

Catalog showrooms: discount retail stores that sell general merchandise lines displayed in a catalog and, to a lesser extent, displayed at the showroom.

Convenience store: a small food and staples store with a limited assortment of products, locations near the consumer, long store hours, and fast checkout.

Department store: a large retail institution that carries a wide variety of merchandise grouped into well-defined departments, usually with substantial depth for each product line.

Dialectic process: A theory of change in retail institution structure based on the premise that retailers mutually adapt in the face of competition from opposites. When a retailer is challenged by a competitor with an advantage, the retailer will adopt strategies that proved to be successful when used by the competitor.

Discount store: a retail institution that offers few services and features low prices.

General merchandise store: a store that carries many different product lines with varying degrees of depth.

Hypermarket: an extra-large supermarket and a general merchandise store under one roof.

Independent retailer: one who owns a single store that is not affiliated with other retailers.

Limited-line stores: retail stores that carry great depth of merchandise but only a few associated product lines.

Planned shopping center: a group of stores that is planned in advance as an integrated unit.

Retail accordian: a theory that retail institutions evolve over time from broad-based to specialized and then back again to broad-based outlets.

Retail life cycle: a series of stages through which a retailing institution moves from its inception until its ultimate decline and disappearance from the marketplace.

Retailer: a merchant whose main business is selling directly to the ultimate consumer for personal, nonbusiness use.

Retailing: all activities related to sales and service to the ultimate consumer.

Scrambled merchandising: the carrying of product lines that are unrelated to a retailer's primary business.

Single-line store: a retail outlet that carries only one line of goods.

Supermarket: large, self-service food stores that often carry some nonfood items, too.

Variety store: a retail store that carries a large number of small and inexpensive products.

Wheel of retailing: the theory that new retail institutions start as low-cost/low price operators and "trade up" services (costs) and the price over time.

NOTES

1. William R. Davidson, Daniel J. Sweeney, and Ronald W. Stampe, *Retail Management* (New York: John Wiley & Sons, 1988), p. 5.

2. Committee on Definitions, *Marketing Definitions: A Glossary of Marketing Terms*. American Marketing Association, p. 19.

3. William R. Davidson and J. L. Sheppard, "Retailing Challenges For The 80's," *Business Forum*, Fall 1982, pp. 21–24.

4. Malcolm McNair, "Significant Trends and Development In The Post-War Period," In A. B. Smith (ed.) *Competitive Distribution in a Free, High-Level Econ-*

omy and Its Implication for a University. (Pittsburgh: University of Pittsburgh Press, 1958), pp. 1–25 and Malcolm P. McNair and Eleanor May, "The Next Revolution of the Retailing Wheel," *Harvard Business Review*, September-October, 1978, pp. 81–91.

5. This interpretation of McNair is from Ron J. Marken and Calvin P. Duncan, "The Transformation of Retailing Institutions: Beyond the Wheel of Retailing and Life Cycle Theories," *Journal of Macromarketing*, Spring 1981, pp. 58–59.

6. J. Barry Mason and Morris L. Mayer, *Modern Retailing* (Plano, TX: Business Publications, Inc., 1987), pp. 43–44.

7. Thomas J. Maronick and Bruce J. Walker, "The Dialectic Evolution of Retailing." In Barnett Greenberg (ed.) *Proceedings: Southern Marketing Association* (Atlanta: Georgia State University, 1974), p. 147.

8. Susan Caminiti, "What Ails Retailing," *Fortune*, January 30, 1989, pp. 61–64.

9. Ronald W. Stampf, "Marketing vs. Merchandising Mentalities in Retailing Management." Proceedings of The American Marketing Association, Joseph Guiltinan and Dale Achabal (eds.), American Marketing Association, 1986.

10. Statistical Abstract of the United States 1989, Washington, D.C. The U.S. Department of Commerce, Bureau of The Census, 1989, pp. 751–57.

11. Statistical Abstract of the United States 1987.

12. "The 50 Largest Retailers," *Fortune*, June 5, 1989, pp. 378–79.

13. Steve Weiner, "Price Is the Object," *Forbes*, February 20, 1989, pp. 123–24.

14. Francine Schwadel, "The Sale Is a Failing Retailing Tactic," *The Wall Street Journal*, March 1, 1989, pp. B1 and B6.

15. Diana Fong, "Cherchez la Store," *Forbes*, January 9, 1989, pp. 311–314.

16. "Hypermarket USA," *Dallas Morning News*, December 27, 1987, K1–K10.

17. Martin I. Horn, "Old Ways Expected to Die as the New Century Dawns," *Marketing News*, March 28, 1988, p. 11.

18. "Business Week Top 1000," *Business Week*, April 15, 1988.

19. "Retailing," *Forbes*, January 9, 1989, pp. 188–190.

20. J. Barry Mason, Morris L. Mayer, and Hazel F. Ezell, *Retailing*, (Plano, TX: Business Publications, Inc., 1988), pp. 24–25.

21. "Only 10% of Consumers Interested in Shopping at Home Via 2-Way TV," *Marketing News*, May 29, 1981, pp. 1 and 3.

22. "London's Harrod's Department Store," *Sales & Marketing*, January 13, 1986, p. 83.

23. Stephen Barbas, "U.S. Gets Ready to Restrict Telemarketing," *Marketing News*, September 12, 1988, pp. 1 and 3.

24. Erika Kotite, "It's in the Mail," *Entrepreneur*, February 1988, pp. 68–71.

25. John Stevenson, "The State of the Industry," *Direct Marketing*, May 1989, pp. 58-60.

26. "Direct Markets Adapt to New Lifestyles," *Marketing News*, June 19, 1989, p. 7.

27. "Direct Marketing: An Aspect of Total Marketing," *Direct Marketing*, June 1989, p. 14.

28. "Total Vended Dollar Volume," *Vending Times*, September 1988, pp. 14, 16, 19, 27.

29. "Total Vended Dollar Volume," pp. 16, 19, 20, 21.

30. John Branston, "Malls: Urban Fad of 1970s Raises Questions for '80s," *The Commercial Appeal*. Memphis, TN: September 4, 1986, pp. A1, A8.

31. Faneuil Hall Marketplace, Inc. "Fact Sheet," Boston, MA: 1988.

32. Lou Ziegler, "Canadian Mall: Wonder Under a Roof," *USA Today*, January 3, 1986, p. 1.

33. Brent H. Felgner, "Power Centers Pack Punch in Mature Market," *Marketing News*, December 5, 1988, pp. 1 and 10–11.

34. Joan E. Primo, "Picking Power-Center Tenant Mix," *Marketing News*, December 5, 1988, pp. 10 and 11.

35. Mason and Mayer, 1988, pp. 80–81.

36. See J.C. Penney Annual Report, 1987.

37. Al Ries and Jack Trout, *Bottom-Up Marketing*, New York: McGraw-Hill, 1989.

38. Jason Zweig, "Bunnyburgers," *Forbes*, March 20, 1989, pp. 42–43.

39. "Restaurant Chain Credits Marketing for Growth," *Marketing News*, February 1, 1985, p. 21.

40. Heikki Rinne and William R. Swingard, "Retailing Strategy: Developing a Desired Fidelity," *Exchange*, Fall 1988, pp. 8–11.

41. Patricia Sellers, "Getting Customers to Love You," *Fortune*, March 13, 1989, pp. 38–49.

42. Tom Peters, *Thriving on Chaos*. New York: Alfred Knopf, 1987, pp. 98–99, 104, 233, and 316.

43. Sallie Hook, "Retailers Turn to Narrowcasting to Survive," *Marketing News*, February 15, 1988, p. 9.

44. Frederick W. Langrehr, "10 Trends in Retailing," *Exchange*, Fall 1988, pp. 12–13.

45. Diane Schneidmann, "Better Goods, Entertainment," *Marketing News*, February 1, 1988, pp. 1–2.

46. VideOcart Shopping Cart with Computer Screen," *Marketing News*, May 9, 1988, pp. 1–2.

47. "Electronic Cards Replacing Green Stamps at Grocery Stores," *Marketing News*, January 30, 1989, p. 16.

CASE APPLICATION 13–1

The Hispanic Market: Fiesta's Approach

The Ed Sullivan Show in the 1950s and 1960s was a Sunday night ritual for middle America. Today in the Hispanic communities of Houston, Los Angeles, Chicago, and Miami, the family television ritual is Sabado Gigante. The variety show is a marketer's dream. Brands such as Coca-Cola, Kinney shoes, Tide detergent, and Coors are advertised, again and again. The weekly audience is estimated to be between four and eight million.

The U.S. Census Bureau counts 18.9 million Hispanics, now 7.5 percent of the population. Is this a market that should be served by retailers? This is a question that has not been answered clearly. The Hispanic population is expanding at four times the national rate. The opportunities seem to be obvious. As Hispanics begin to enjoy affluence, they are gaining more clout to get the products and service they want.

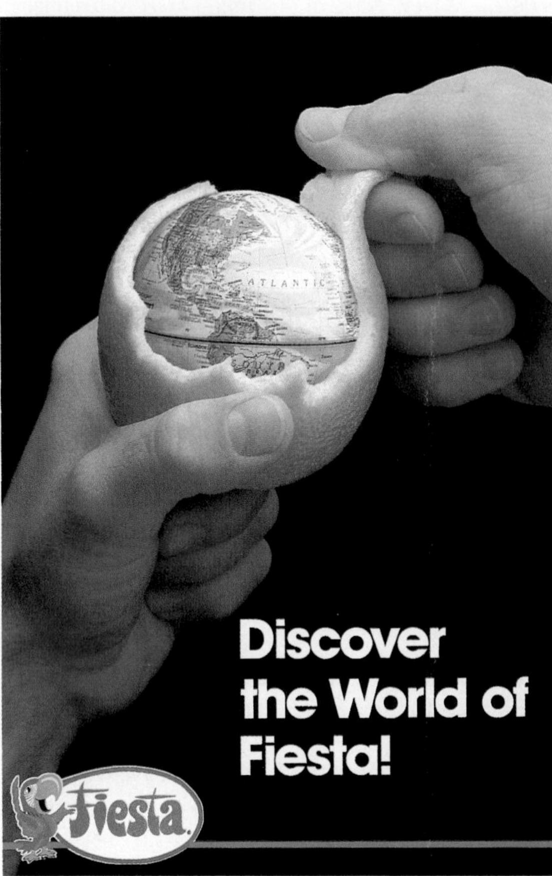
Discover the World of Fiesta!
Fiesta

Fiesta Mart, Inc., a Houston grocery chain started in 1972 by Donald Bonham, caters to Hispanics in the inner city. In 1989 the firm had a total of sixteen Houston area stores. The 110,000 square foot store at Bellaire and Hillcroft has money exchange machines that handle currency from Mexico, El Salvador, and Guatemala. Plans are to have 22 stores operating by 1990, including a 200,000 square foot gigantic store in Clear Lake, close to the Johnson Space Center (NASA). In Houston, the major retailers like Kroger and Safeway are nervously watching Fiesta grow larger and larger and gaining increased market share.

Fiesta attempts to provide foods and merchandise that customers are used to in their home countries. Korean, Cuban, Vietnamese, African, French, Greek, and Colombian products are among the different types of foodstuffs available in the specialty foods departments. Some of the stores also include a dental clinic, pharmacy, beauty salon, optician office, and travel agency.

The Fiesta stores have developed a sensitivity to the eating habits of the Hispanic market. They have segmented the market on the basis of different countries and what kind of foods are preferred. In addition, the stores carry more fresh produce and fresh seafood to accommodate the trend toward lighter, healthier food. Crayfish, catfish, fish filets, octopus, and squid are in high demand. They also sell tulapea fish, which is used by Fiesta's Middle Eastern customers.

Fiesta's buyers pride themselves on searching out products for the distinctive tastes of customers. Asking customers, listening to their preferences, and then finding the food is how Fiesta believes in applying the marketing concept.

The Fiesta chain has been able to keep its prices down by buying direct from producers. Surveys indicate that Fiesta prices are about 15 percent lower on produce. The company also buys up close-out items to stock its apparel department; prices there are about 50 percent lower than those in department stores. And by taking a lower margin on retail prices and dealing in a higher volume, the company stays about 3 to 5 percent lower on price on normal grocery items.

The sixteen operating stores have annual sales of $350 million. Fiesta ranks fourth in market share among grocery chains in Houston. They plan to become the number three chain in the next five years. The strategy is to expand Fiesta's appeal to other groups—Afro-Americans, Orientals, and Caucasians.

The Hispanics of Houston and other cities pose a special challenge to marketers because they aren't disappearing into the melting pot as fast as earlier immigrant groups. Because of their numbers, local concentration, and frequent contact with their homelands, they are clinging to their language and culture. Many Hispanics are not fluent in English. Fiesta realizes this and advertises in Spanish, posts signs in Spanish, and hires many store personnel who can speak fluent Spanish. Like Ronaldo McDonald, who sells *hamburguesas*, Fiesta stores sell *El Rey de Cervezas* (Budweiser) to their number one customers.

SOURCES: David D. Medina, "The Fiesta Maker," *Houston Post*, March 26, 1989, pp. F1, F7, and F10, Diane Freeman, "Fiesta Mart Adding Stores, Wares," *The Houston Post*, March 20, 1988, and "Fast Times on Avenida Madison," *Business Week*, June 6, 1988, pp. 62–67.

Questions

1. Why would a retailer such as Fiesta be so concerned with and interested in the Hispanic market in Houston?

2. What is Fiesta's strategic plan in terms of ethnic markets?

3. What would happen to Fiesta's approach if Hispanics become more integrated into the American melting pot?

4. Is it possible that a local retailer like Donald Bonham can beat the national giants like Kroger? How could this occur?

CASE APPLICATION 13–2

Retailers Better Pay Attention to Customers: True or False?

The United States is getting beat in semiconductors, construction, autos, steel, appliances, and financial services by Koreans, Japanese, West Germans, French, and other international markets. Some suggest that protectionism, closed markets, aggressive marketing by dumping, and differences in labor costs are the reasons. Others think that customers have the answer. Quality of goods and services has decreased and until it improves, American products will be battered again and again.

Keeping a customer depends on customer satisfaction with quality value. Retailers in a competitive market must find ways to add value to the customer relationship. For example, the Southland Corporation, which operates 7-11 stores, invites employees who have performed superior feats of customer service to join in on a company sweepstakes, with the winner receiving a cool $1 million.

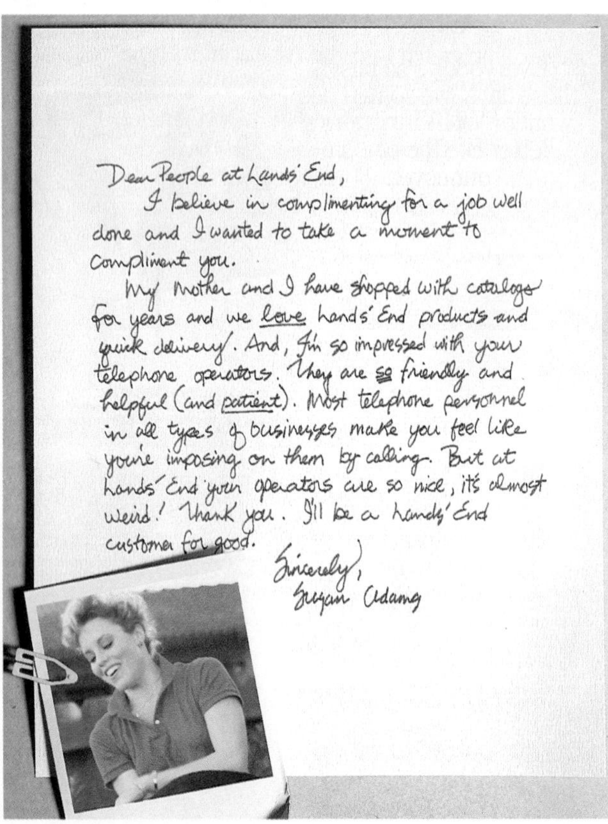
Dear People at Lands' End,

I believe in complimenting for a job well done and I wanted to take a moment to compliment you.

My mother and I have shopped with catalogs for years and we love Lands' End products and quick delivery. And, I'm so impressed with your telephone operators. They are so friendly and helpful (and patient). Most telephone personnel in all types of businesses make you feel like you're imposing on them by calling. But at Lands' End your operators are so nice, it's almost weird! Thank you. I'll be a Lands' End customer for good.

Sincerely,
Susan Adams

© Lands' End, Inc.

Some retailers have overlooked the fact that customers want dealing with the firm to be easy. Making it easy for a customer to complain or order goods is still a crucial practice. In the 1960s, one retailer that led the way in expediting customer complaints was J.C. Penney. The procedure for returning unwanted merchandise or poor goods or simply complaining was spelled out on every packing slip accompanying the mail order goods. Some managers felt that this procedure would significantly increase merchandise returns. It did not. Customers want an outlet, a procedure, an easy way to order. Penneys, Sears, and Wards have made it easy for customers to measure body dimensions. They concluded correctly decades ago that customers do not know or recall their sizes—neck, waist, inseam, arm length, chest, etc. Habard Company, a retail clothier, includes a paper tape measure, folded in with their direct mail offerings.

Customers must always be first. The retailers' credo for the 1990s might look like this:

- Think of yourself as the customer.
- Listen actively to your customers.
- Have every employee understand the importance of the "customer is first."
- Make it convenient for customers to do business with you.
- Closely observe and monitor service—how are customers being treated?

There are many examples of this credo in use. For example, Four Seasons Hotels is a Toronto-based chain that beats the industry averages in occupancy rates. Keeping in contact with customers is a rule. Each of seven regional vice presidents must serve as general manager for one of the hotels that they oversee. Customer preferences (e.g., Does he like a rare kind of tea? Is she allergic to smoke?) are recorded in a customer-profile data bank. When a customer visits any Four Seasons Hotel, management knows a little about his or her preferences.

Tom Monaghan, president of Domino's Pizza, is a customer-first practitioner. He gets his "Dominoids," as he refers to employees, to pay close attention to customers by linking pay to customer satisfaction. Domino's pays 10,000 "mystery customers" $60 each to buy twelve pizzas throughout the year at its 5,000 units and evaluate quality and service. Was the pizza good? Was it served on time? Was the pizza hot? Monaghan bases managers' compensation partly on what the 10,000 "mystery customers" have to say.

Lands' End is a mail-order catalogue company founded by Gary Comer. He started the firm as a catalogue supplier of hardware and other equipment for sailboats. He added a small clothing section which eventually drove out the hardware. Lands' End now concentrates on apparel and mails out 76 million 150-page catalogues several times a year. The underlying theme of the catalogue is that quality is the most important feature of a Lands' End product. Polite, knowledgeable operators take calls at the toll-free number in Dodgeville, Wisconsin. The first contact with the operator is a pleasant experience. Customers often make comments or suggestions to operators or directly to the firm. Each month a three-inch thick computer printout of customer comments lands on managers' desks. What happens to the comments? Many are acted on. When many callers wanted a turtleneck in a gray sweatshirt fabric, the company decided to do it.

Tom Peters, the author of the best seller *In Search of Excellence*, holds back nothing when he warns retailers that, "You have no choice." He means that customer service is a must-do to survive. Ask what have you done for the customer today or you will have no customers left to ask about.

SOURCES: Adapted from Patricia Sellers, "Getting Customers to Love You," *Fortune*, March 13, 1989, pp. 38–49; Susan Caminiti, "A Mail-Order Romance: Lands' End Counts Unseen Customers," *Fortune*, March 13, 1989, pp. 44–45; M. John Storey, *Inside America's Fastest Growing Companies*, New York: John Wiley, 1989 and Tom Peters, *Thriving on Chaos*, New York: Knopf, 1987.

Questions

1. Are Tom Peters' warnings too severe for retailers to pay attention to, or is he correct? Explain.

2. Why is customer service not always the top priority of retailers?

3. What do you like and dislike about tying Domino's compensation for managers partly to "mystery customer" opinions?

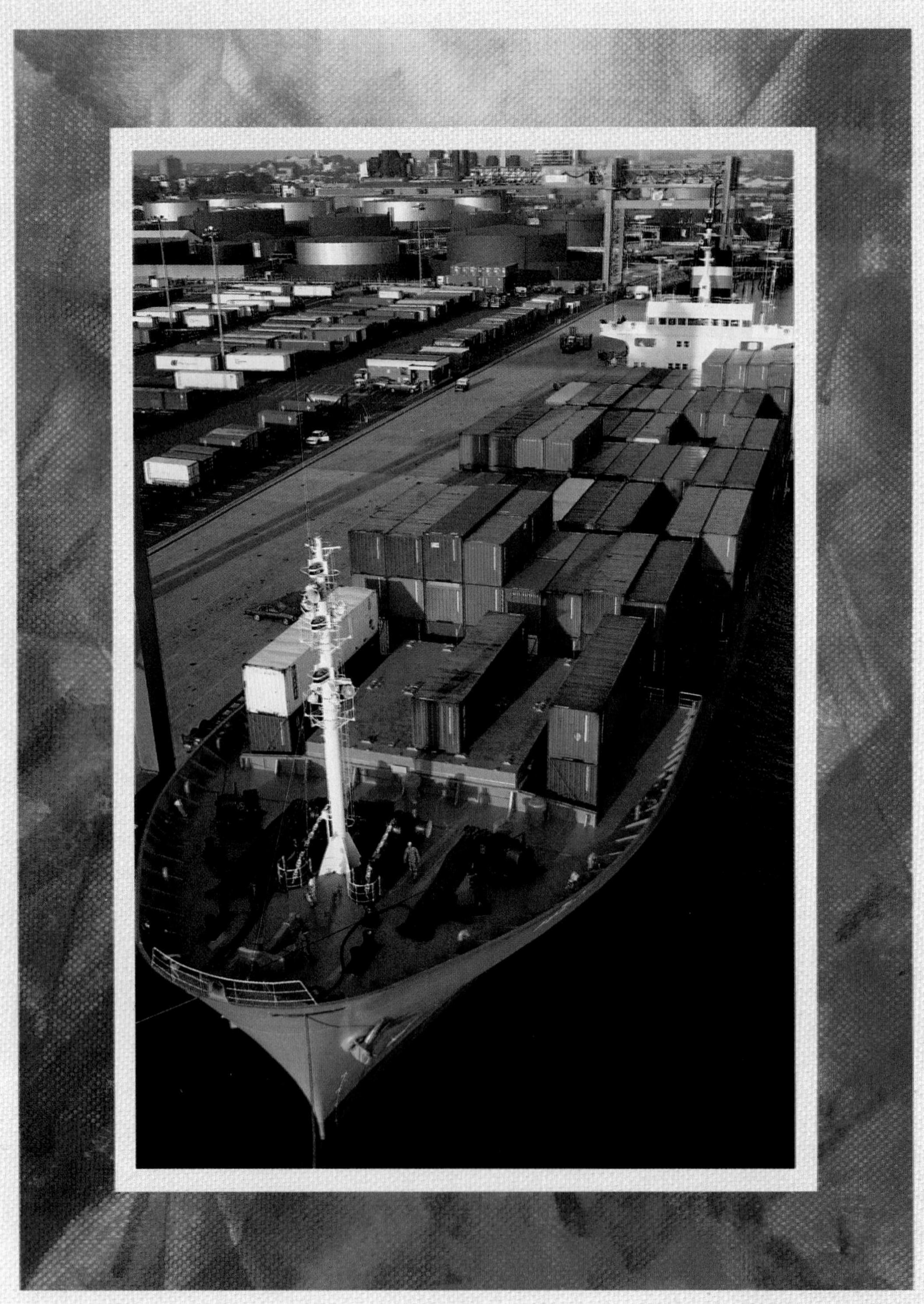

14

Physical Distribution

Learning Objectives

Upon completing this chapter, you will be able to do the following:

DESCRIBE
the importance of physical distribution in successfully implementing a marketing program.

IDENTIFY
the major objectives of physical distribution.

LIST
the main means of moving and transferring goods.

ILLUSTRATE
what is meant by cost trade-offs and minimizing total costs.

DEFINE
the functions of a physical distribution system.

MARKETING PROFILE

Intermodal Transportation: New Developments in Distribution

The intermodal concept is simple. Items are loaded into containers that can be put on ships, trucks, trains, or planes depending on which is most effective. Currently, rail is the mode of choice for long-haul domestic shipping, especially heavy freight. Trucks are more versatile in short line shipping, and water transport constitutes the remainder of the business. What this means for shippers is that instead of unloading the items from one mode and loading onto another (e.g., train to truck), they simply move the containers. In addition, these containers can be stacked at the shipping terminals, a space saving feature that was not available with boxcars or semi-trailers.

American President Domestic Co. (APD) did not foresee their large role in the intermodal market when they decided to introduce domestically a stack train system developed for their American Presidents Lines Ltd. for transporting Asian imports. The stack train design uses special boxcars that allow two or more intermodal containers to be stacked on them. Now they have 140 of these stack trains running from city to city each week, and they expect to transport 400,000 containers annually across the United States. The recent acquisition of American President Trucking is paving the way to intermodal expansion into the trucking industry. APD's goal is to "provide 50-hour transit, for example, between Chicago and Los Angeles, that allows cargo to be grounded and delivered by, say, eight o'clock in the morning." This dedication to providing speed and flexibility is certainly one of the reasons that APD has succeeded in the field.

Although intermodal containers have been used to transport dry goods, chemical producers can now enjoy the benefits of intermodal transport as well. Before, bulk liquid shippers were limited to drums (55 gallons), parcel tankers (7,000 gallons), or rail tankers (30,000 gallons). Now they can move the load intermodally, in 5,000 gallon tanks. The other advantage is that they can avoid transferring the sometimes toxic or flammable liquid to and from modes.

The standard intermodal tank container is the iso-tank, which meets all the specifications of liquid transport. Eythl Corp. started using these iso-tanks in 1974 and currently has about 525 units in their fleet.

The increased use of intermodal transportation has helped shippers focus on what the customers want: flexibility, timing, and capacity. This has spurred other developments addressing the same issues. Some of these are rail-truck transloading and the use of short line railroads.

Rail-truck transloading is a service provided for customers that usually involves some long-haul railroad and warehousing. In the automobile industry, Rail-Truck transloading has become an important part of many of the auto manufacturers' Just-In-Time inventory systems. Because inventory shortages could mean assembly line stoppage and millions of dollars in lost revenue, transloading helps guarantee shipment. Conrail has addressed this with its AutoNET system, which uses rail to bring in supplies, stores them in their warehouses, and ships the equipment as needed via short-run trucking. In this way, the shippers provide manufacturers with short line convenience and bear the costs of storage in return for the volume business. The main benefit of transloading is that standard rail equipment is used, avoiding the costs of intermodal containers.

Short rail lines are used in busy and expensive metropolitan terminals. A short line can store, move, and transfer both intermodal and standard shipments with terminals just outside major metropolitan hubs. Massachusetts Central Railroad operates such a terminal near the junction of Canadian National's Vermont Railway and Conrail connections, which are also near the Massachusetts Turnpike. With a customs station on the site, customers can save both time and money in all types of processes.

This *Marketing Profile* outlines some of the recent trends in transportation that attempt to better serve the needs of the customers. This chapter discusses the distribution functions that occur before, during, and after the physical transportation.

ADAPTED FROM: Robert J. Kursar, "American President Domestic: A Matter of Organization," *Traffic World*, April 18, 1988, pp. 8–9 and Kurt Hoffman, "Short Line Railroad Industry Making Intermodal Connections," *Traffic World*, April 18, 1988, pp. 10–12 and James Abbott, "Rail-Truck Transloading Services Grow as Intermodal Alternative," *Traffic World*, April 18, 1988, pp. 14–17 and Allen R. Wastler, "Intermodal Tank Containers Winning Shipper Converts," *Traffic World*, April 18, 1988, pp. 17–18.

Up to this point we have studied various marketing channels of distribution. In this chapter, we will specifically address the issue of physically transporting goods in an efficient, effective flow between key distributive institutions. The growing importance of this phase of marketing is highlighted by the fact that physical distribution activities account for about one-half of all marketing costs.[1]

We will examine the objectives, management, and organization of physical distribution systems and discuss their main functions. We will look at marketing management's role in decisions involving various tasks. Finally, we will describe two companies currently practicing physical distribution to illustrate the efforts necessary to plan and control distribution activities and cost expenditures.

Marketing and Physical Distribution

In 1988 U.S. industry spent an estimated $500 billion on physical distribution functions like transportation, warehousing, inventory carrying costs, and general management.[2] This figure is not expected to decrease. In fact, to continue creating place and time utilities in an environment of change and increasing complexity, managers will have to devote even more money and attention to physical distribution. By providing customers with place and time utilities, physical distribution implements the marketing concept. As Robert Woodruff, former president of Coca-Cola, put it, Coke's organization policy was to "put Coke within an arm's length of desire."

From a marketing viewpoint, physical distribution can be seen in two ways. It can be viewed as a support for a firm's marketing objectives. With this perspective, physical distribution is usually dispersed throughout a firm as a backup function. Figure 14–1 shows the organization of a company where physical distribution activities are conducted in three departments. This dispersion often results in conflicting objectives—marketing wants more inventory to meet customer needs, while finance and accounting want to hold inventory down to reduce carrying costs.

However, physical distribution can, if used efficiently, give a firm a competitive edge in the marketplace. To achieve this competitive edge, some believe that physical distribution functions should be unified in a full-fledged organizational unit. Physical distribution, through consolidation, can provide service to other units. Figure 14–2 represents such a unit as a freestanding member of a firm's team.

There are some stumbling blocks to the creation of freestanding physical distribution departments. In many firms, marketing or production is dominant. If the structure were changed from that of Figure 14–1 to the one presented in Figure 14–2, it might be perceived as a threat to the power of the dominant unit. The responsibilities and goals of each of the three departments are in conflict. For example, marketing wants to maintain a large inventory to meet customer demand. However, finance and accounting prefer to keep the size of inventory down and to aggregate ordering if at all possible. They feel that fewer orders mean less ordering and administrative expense.

The important thing is that those involved in physical distribution must understand it as a marketing function and, instead of competing with the marketing manager, they must work together. The debate over the fit between physical distribution and other areas like marketing, production, and finance will undoubtedly continue.[3] However, as managers continue to face increasing physical distribution costs, more intense competition, and increasing customer service demands, their resistance to new methods will weaken. Experts in physical distribution believe that the structure shown in Figure 14-2 is what the modern, up-to-date company needs to compete effectively. They believe the hard facts of rising physical distribution costs, growing

Figure 14–1 Distribution Task Responsibilities and Potentially Conflicting Departmental Goals

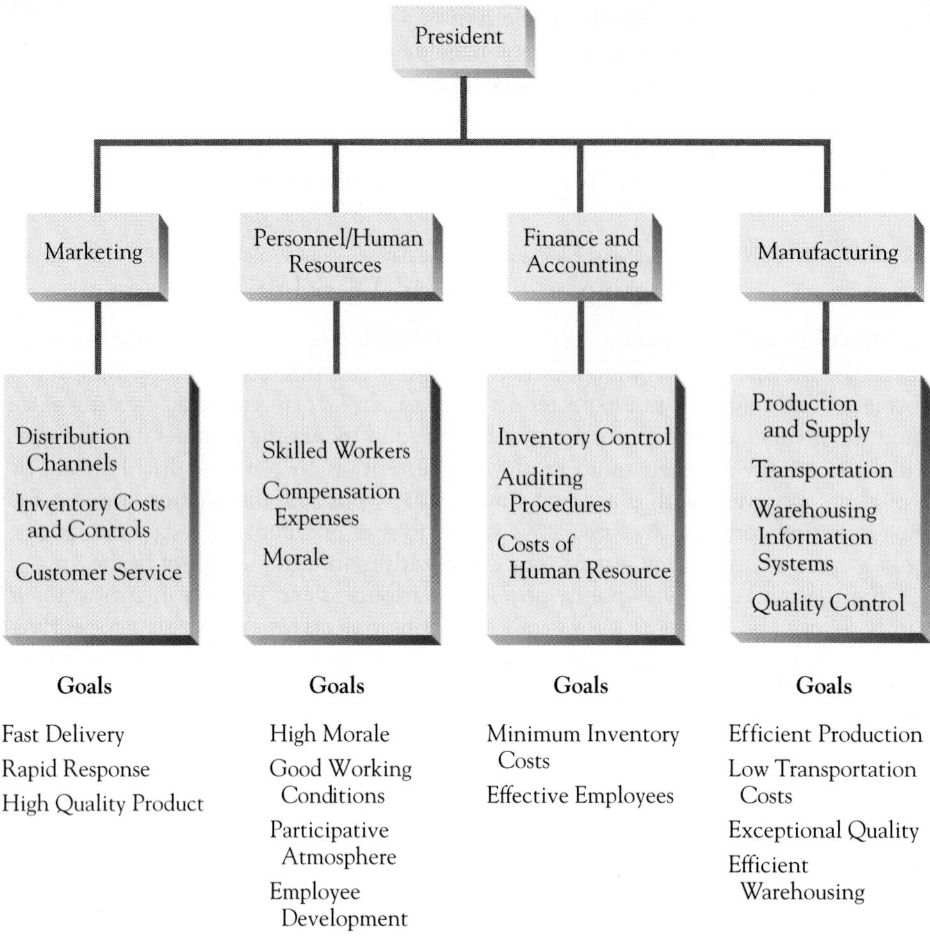

customer service demands, increased competition, and shrinking profits will push physical distribution into a freestanding system, equal with other business functions such as marketing.

The Nature of Physical Distribution

The terms *physical distribution* and *logistics* are sometimes used interchangeably to refer to activities associated with the physical transfer of goods. The National Council of Physical Distribution Management (NCPDM) has defined physical distribution as:

> *. . . the movement of an item from the place where it was made or grown to the place where it is consumed. . . . All the activities involved in moving goods to the right place at the right time (as opposed to manufacturing them) can be described under the broad term "distribution." The components of the physical distribution system include: customer service, demand forecasting, inventory control, materials*

Figure 14–2 The Physical Distribution Organization as a Consolidated Unit

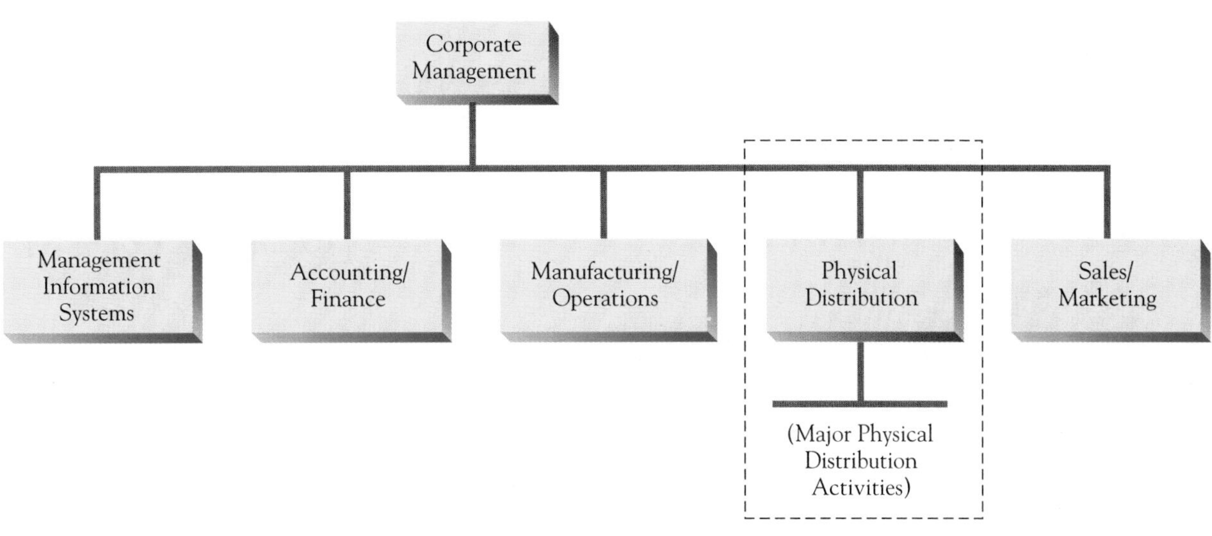

handling, order processing, packaging, traffic and transportation, warehousing, and distribution communications.[4]

The term *logistics* is borrowed from the military and has a broader definition, including "'the procurement, distribution, maintenance, and replacement of material and personnel."[5] *Physical distribution* is the preferred term in the marketing context and is concerned with the physical movement and transfer of finished and semifinished goods within and across marketing channels.

Figure 14–3 presents one view of distribution. Generally, movement and transfer have two major markets. One consists of consumers or other companies who use the product. The second consists of intermediaries, wholesalers, and retailers who do not consume the product but offer it for resale, usually to other intermediaries or to consumers.

An important difference among markets is the volume in which they buy. Single consumers usually purchase small amounts of a product, while intermediaries and other companies often buy in large quantities. The physical distribution system needs to be flexible enough to meet the different levels of purchase requested by customers.

Physical distribution flow includes inventories sent directly to consumers, direct resale shipments from intermediaries, and shipments from field warehouses. If large quantities are needed, shipments are made from inventories, the production line, or vendors. Since transportation rates are lower when full vehicle loads are transferred, this method of movement is the least expensive.[6] If quantities requested will not fully load a vehicle, it may be more cost efficient to distribute through warehouses. By strategically locating warehouses as close to customers as possible, manufacturers can improve service and lower distribution costs.

The physical transferring of goods is not necessarily finished upon customer receipt. Sometimes goods are returned, necessitating a return-of-goods procedure as part of the physical distribution system. Reasons for returning products include damage, receipt of the wrong product, a customer's changing need, or failure of the customer

Figure 14–3 The Flow of Goods in the Physical Distribution System

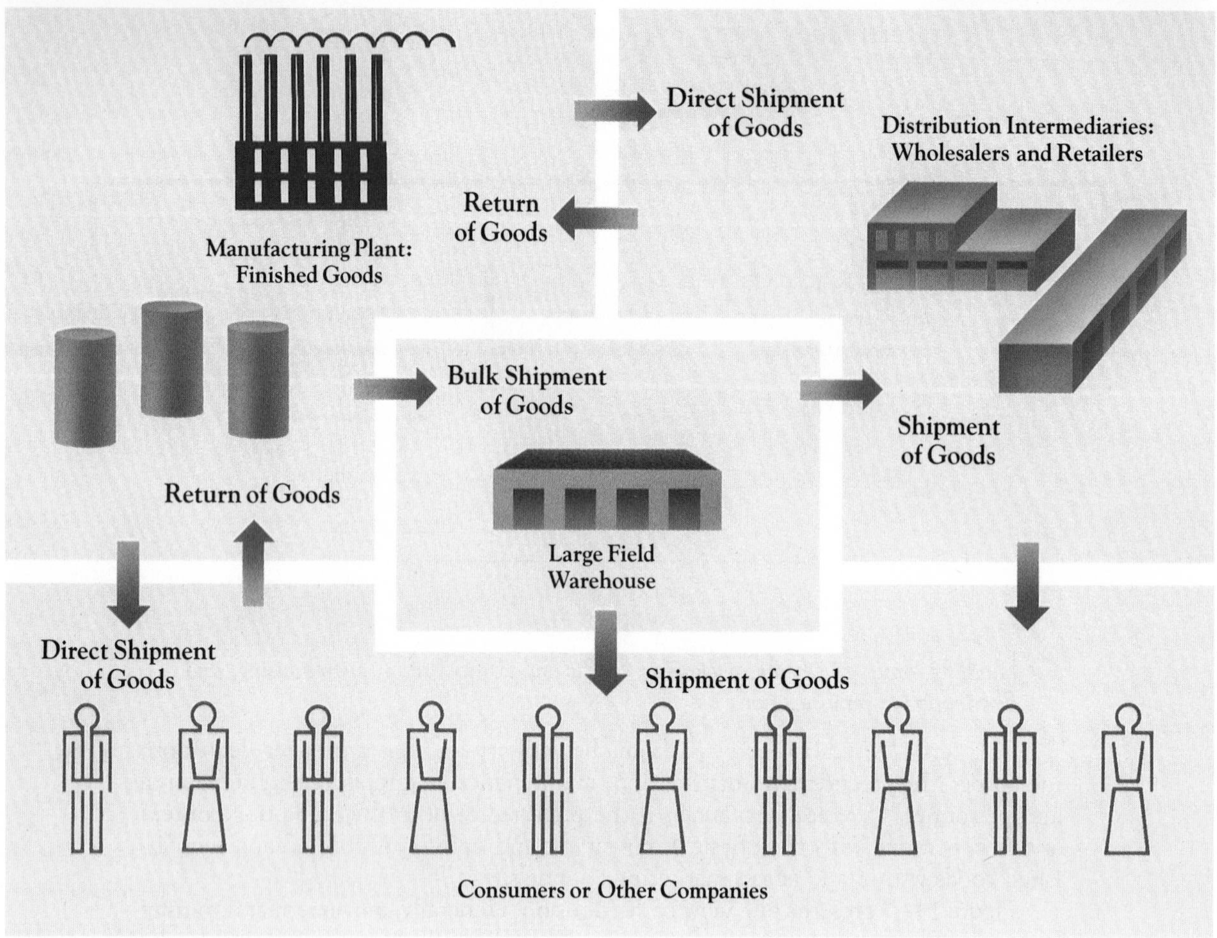

to pay. A number of cases involve returning goods because of safety problems. Cyanide found on three Chilean grapes resulted in destroying over $80 million of produce to protect consumers. Matsushita Electric recalled over 300,000 color television sets because of radiation transmission. Ford Motor Company recalled more than 375,000 automobiles because of steering column problems. The necessary corrections were made by supermarkets, Matsushita, and Ford at no expense to customers.

Figure 14–4 provides only a skeleton view of the flow of goods in the physical distribution system. To effectively distribute goods like home computers, automobiles, detergents, central air-conditioning units, and lamps involves a number of physical distribution elements not displayed in the figure. The typical functions of physical distribution systems for firms like Merck, Rubbermaid, Digital Equipment, and Lever Brothers are shown in Figure 14–4. As with product, price, and promotion decisions, the starting point in physical distribution decisions is the customer.

Eastman Kodak, in the past, failed to efficiently serve its customers. The aggressive promotion of its new instant camera resulted in rising customer interest. Customers liked features of the Kodak product and wanted to buy it. However the

Figure 14–4 Functions in the Physical Distribution System

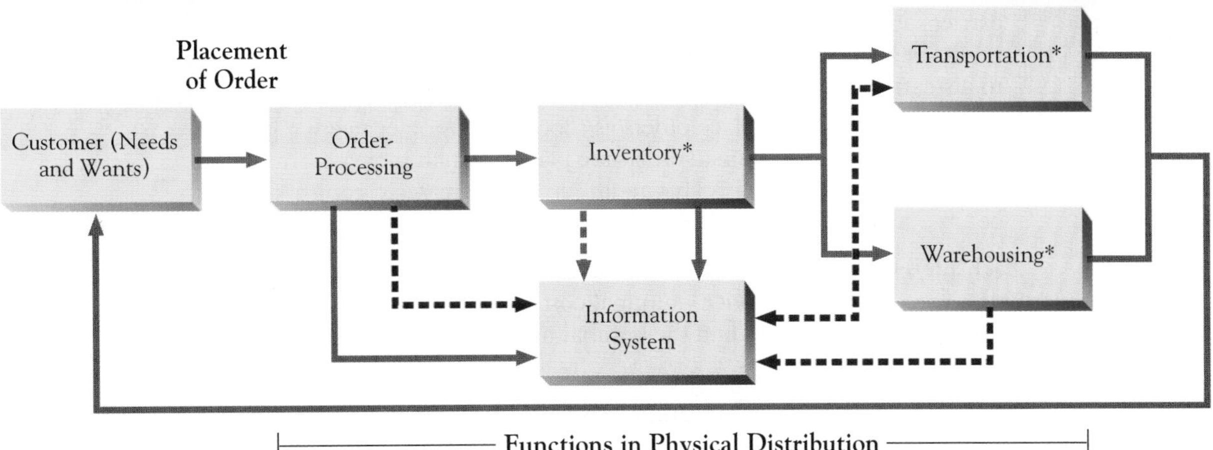

*Materials handling function occurs in these three areas.

NOTE: Dotted lines indicate information flows. For example, orders flow into the system. Transportation data also flow into the system, but there is a reciprocal flow back to the transportation point.

company did not provide sufficient quantities of the camera to retailers, so Polaroid stepped in and made the sales. This example illustrates the importance of distributing a product so that customers can get it when their interest is at a peak.

Hitachi Sales Corporation distributes the firm's consumer goods in the United States.[7] Its management decided to install the CO-OP order entry system, so that it could monitor transportation and warehousing information. Prior to this installation, one employee could spend an entire day determining inventory levels. Now this job would be done instantly when an order was placed. A computer terminal screen permitted an operator to see and double-check inventory amounts. With CO-OP, Hitachi could reduce order errors, consolidate shipments of goods, and conduct credit checks.

Shipments of goods from Tokyo, Japan, to Compton, California, to Boston, Massachusetts, at minimal cost and increased customer satisfaction are made possible by Hitachi's physical distribution program and system. Cost savings and customer satisfaction are enhanced because physical distribution is being managed, timely decisions are being made, errors are being minimized, and efficient physical transfers of goods are being made. Hitachi is one example of how distribution should be handled, and it illustrates some of the activities that are becoming more necessary in the competitive marketing environment.

Objectives of Physical Distribution

Balancing customer service, costs, and a firm's profits is a Herculean feat. The expenses in each phase of physical distribution are usually inversely related.[8] For example:

- A decision is made to ship goods by motor carriers to reduce transportation expenses. Motor transport is only moderately fast but is dependable, frequent, and available. However, because most customers want goods promptly and because motor carriers are slower than air carriers, customer satisfaction is often reduced.

- A firm decides to use air carriers to transport goods. However, the air carriers are far away from the source of the goods. Again, customer ill will results because goods must first be shipped from the plant by motor carrier to air-carrier facilities resulting in more distribution time.
- A decision is made to place orders as soon as a customer needs a product. The result is that many small orders are placed, which increases the administrative cost of ordering. This results in an increase in returned goods, because many customers receive the wrong orders.

Each physical distribution activity must be studied in conjunction with other activities. Good customer service, minimal costs, and high profits are certainly worthy objectives, but it's hard to find the optimal mix of physical distribution activities.

The Customer Service Objective

The main physical distribution objective is providing *customer service.* If no customers existed, concerns about cost and profits would be meaningless. Customers are interested in receiving goods when needed, receiving appropriate order sizes, receiving usable goods, being able to return goods when necessary, purchasing goods at fair and competitive prices, and placing orders easily.

Each of these desires is important. One way companies can emphasize their importance is to state them in terms of performance objectives. Victoreen, an electronics manufacturer in Chicago, does just that. Its customer service objectives are the following:

> The number of orders shipped within 24 hours of demand should represent 90 percent of all orders placed.
>
> No customer will wait more than 96 hours to receive an order. Customers waiting more than this time will receive at least a 10 percent reduction in the total full cost of the order.
>
> At least 96 percent of all goods delivered will be in perfect working condition.

Victoreen management has been setting specific, quantifiable, customer service objectives every year for two decades. It believes this is one reason it has been successful in the highly competitive electronics parts industry.

To some firms, customer service is the ultimate objective that must be fulfilled; consequently, customer preferences must be determined.[9] Studies have shown that customer service preferences can be determined by informal questioning and formal surveying.[10] The intent of such probing is to establish physical distribution objectives that are meaningful, timely, concise, and, if at all possible, quantifiable.

The Total Cost Objective

Total cost includes all costs incurred in accomplishing the customer service objectives of the physical distribution system. Physical distribution experts believe it is less important to minimize the cost of any one component (for example, transportation or ordering) than to minimize the total cost.[11] Since the various physical distribution functions are interrelated parts of the system, a change in one part can have an effect on other parts. If management wants to increase the number of warehouses, it should study the effects on inventory, processing, and transportation.

Figure 14–5 Total Cost Analysis for Providing Customer Service

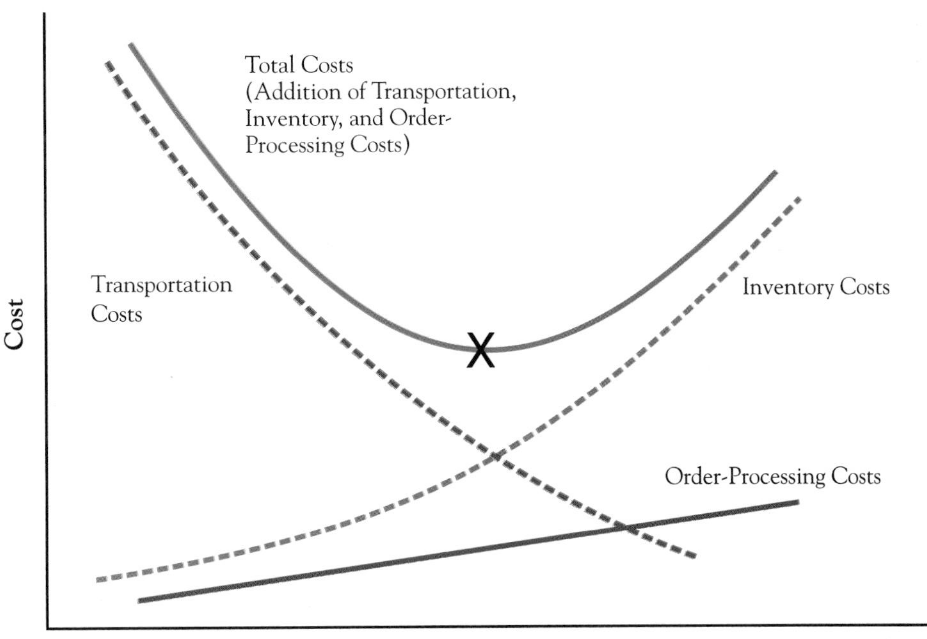

In Figure 14–5 the minimum total cost is noted by an X. This point is different from the lowest points of the three components, because it is the determination of the lowest total cost for the *system,* a combination of transportation, inventory, and order processing. A lower cost in one area may be offset by a higher cost in another.

In analyzing total cost, managers often must make transportation mode decisions. They must decide how their companies should ship goods—by air, truck, rail, or some other mode. Suppose a large machine manufacturer in San Francisco was interested in shipping goods to a market in Boston. Three major modes of transportation could be considered—air freight could deliver the machines in an average of three days, while truck or rail would take about nine. Although order-processing costs do not vary with the mode of transportation, inventory costs typically do. In most cases, the faster the movement of goods, the lower the inventory carrying expense. As shown in Table 14–1, the rail transportation cost is lowest, but air is least expensive in total cost, because there is less inventory expense. Thus, examining total cost would help the manufacturer choose air as the transportation mode. Using a total cost approach means viewing physical distribution as a system of functions.

Distribution Cost Trade-offs

Physical distribution managers must often weigh **distribution cost trade-offs,** which occur when cost increases in one area lead to cost decreases in other areas. As Figure 14–5 illustrated, costs are often in conflict with one another. A manager typically faces three types of costs—inventory, transportation, and order-processing.

Table 14–1 Annual Costs of Moving Machines from San Francisco to Boston

Cost Factor	Mode of Transportation		
	Air	**Truck**	**Rail**
Transportation	$600,000	$520,000	$500,000
Inventory carrying	265,000	390,000	410,000
Damage	20,000	35,000	25,000
Order-processing	NR	NR	NR
Total Cost	$885,000	$945,000	$935,000

NR = Not Relevant

If a decision is made to increase the number of warehouses, transportation costs decline. However, at the same time, inventory and order-processing costs may increase. The cost of inventory increases with the number of warehouses because more stock is stored, and order-processing costs increase if orders are placed from each warehouse because more personnel are needed.

Review Your Marketing Knowledge

- What is the difference between physical distribution and logistics?
- Why is it important to *balance* customer service, costs, and profits?
- When discussing physical distribution, some believe that a freestanding department can be effective, while others view it as a supportive activity. What are the strengths and weaknesses of these views of physical distribution?

Functions of the Physical Distribution System

A physical distribution system consists of a set of interrelated functions with specific boundaries. Figure 14–4 showed how these functions were interrelated. The physical distribution manager must address how orders should be placed (order-processing), where goods should be located geographically (warehousing), what amount of goods should be on hand (inventory management and control), what mode of transportation should be used to move goods (transportation), how goods should be moved within company boundaries (materials-handling), and what type of information system is needed to link producers, intermediaries, and customers.[12]

Order-processing

The old proverb that "time is money" points up the importance of order-processing. The distribution of goods does not begin until customer orders have been received, processed, and filled. Carrying out these activities as quickly and efficiently as possible results in profits, customer satisfaction, and repeat business. **Order-processing** refers to all those activities involved in collecting, checking, and transmitting sales-order information. It is the handling of all paperwork associated with the sale of an organization's goods and services.

Filling out an order form by a salesperson or customer and transmitting it to the warehouse constitute order entry. Preparing the bill of lading, checking credit, and carrying out the order make up order-processing. Order filling from warehouse inventory stocks and delivery of the goods complete the order cycle.[13]

Order-processing can be handled in many ways. In general, firms want to fill orders with speed and accuracy. However, these objectives need to be achieved within cost limits. Two types of systems, manual and automated, are used to achieve speed and accuracy objectives.

An example of a manual system is that used by the Samson-Packard Company, manufacturer of custom hoses, valves, and hosing for industrial customers.[14] The firm processes about fifty orders a day. A full order cycle includes order-processing, manufacture of the quantities requested, and delivery of the orders.

The application of electronic technology to order-processing has progressed rapidly. Sears, Roebuck & Company has an automated order-processing system designed to supply an instant flow of sales and merchandising information to all levels of Sears at widely dispersed retail locations.[15] Sears is the world's largest retailer, accounting for 1 percent of the gross national product. Its distribution system includes 20,000 retail merchandising departments.

The first step in the Sears system is the receipt of the product from the warehouse or supplier. If the product is a lamp, for example, an automatic ticketmaker produces a ticket that lists the lamp's color, price, and stock number and the clerk's department number. When a customer takes the lamp to the checkout counter, the clerk keys the numbers into the register or uses the reading wand. If the customer wants to pay with a credit card, the wand picks up a magnetic code and, in less than one second, clears the card through the store's minicomputer.

Lamp sales are stored in the minicomputer until the end of the day, when they are automatically transferred to one of the company's twenty-two regional data centers. The information is processed, the customer's credit account is charged, sales and tax figures are entered into the accounting department's records, and the clerk's commission is recorded by the payroll department.

Sales data also enter the lamp department's inventory control system. If the day's lamp sales drop the inventory below a predetermined reorder point, the computer automatically prints a purchase order, which is sent by messenger to the department manager. If the manager decides to buy more lamps, the reorder is sent to the supplier. At the same time, lamp sales data are sent from the regional data center to a central data processing center in Sears' Chicago-area headquarters, where national unit-sale information is compiled.

The Sears system clearly indicates how order-processing, inventory control, manufacturing, and transportation activities can be tied together. Each function plays a part in the Sears physical distribution system. Failure in one function of the system results in problems and the possible loss of customers. Sears customers can just as easily purchase children's clothes, automobile tires, paint, and fishing tackle at J.C. Penney, Ward's, or discount stores like Wal-Mart or Kmart.

Inventory Management and Control

Eventually, any business must manage inventories of goods.[16] The manager must procure stocks of goods to meet demand. One dilemma involves minimizing total inventory costs within demand, cost, and customer service constraints. The major objective of inventory management and control is to inform managers how much of a good to reorder, when to reorder the good, how frequently orders should be placed, and what the appropriate safety stock is for minimizing stockouts. Thus, the overall goal of inventory is to have what is needed, when it is needed, and to minimize the number of times one is out of stock.

One way to examine the inventory dilemma is to consider the demand for goods. There are continuous, seasonal, and erratic demand patterns.[17] **Continuous demand** products have a long history of sales with demand basically unchanged throughout the year. Products such as Wrigley's chewing gum, Tide detergent, and Crest toothpaste are continuously demanded and require continual stock replenishment. Inventory decisions involve forecasting the continuous demand level, judging when replenishment should occur, and determining the size of the replenishment order. When these decisions are effectively made, customer service and profit objectives are met.

A **seasonal demand** product experiences high demand at regular points in time. Christmas tree ornaments, stuffed Easter bunnies, and ballots to select major league baseball all-star players are some examples. These products require accurate forecasting of the level of seasonal demand. If the forecast is off, inventory levels will be incorrect.

Erratic demand is a generally unpredictable pattern of demand. The demand for compressors, cement mixers, automobiles, and trailers makes inventory management and control difficult. The response time to fill orders, the size of the inventory, and the delivery approach are difficult to plan and implement.

Three important costs of inventory are carrying costs, procurement costs, and out-of-stock costs.[18] **Carrying costs** are all costs associated with holding a quantity of goods for some time. For example, there is the cost of capital that is tied up and could be used for other purposes. There are also the costs of taxes and insurance for carrying inventory. With the exception of a few states, a property tax is levied on all or some inventories in warehouses. Fire and theft protection insurance is needed to protect the inventory from losses. There are also storage space costs. Finally, a risk cost must be considered because damage, obsolescence, and deterioration of inventory occur. Carrying costs can average as much as 25 percent of inventory value. Thus, good reasons, such as fulfilling customer service objectives, increasing profit, or improving public image by having goods in stock, must exist before large inventories are carried.

Procurement costs occur when stock must be replenished. Costs for processing orders, transmittal expenses, materials handling costs, and the price of goods make up procurement costs.

If there is a demand for goods that are out of stock, a firm incurs an **out-of-stock cost** because of lost sales and backorder expenses. Customers prefer to receive goods as soon as possible. The customer who cancels an order because the firm is out of stock usually goes elsewhere. The lost sales cost is the profit lost at the time of the outage, as well as the ill will suffered by not having the goods available. Backorder costs result if clerical and ordering expenses must be incurred to fill the order as soon as possible.

Balancing carrying, procurement, and out-of-stock costs is an important objective of inventory management. The larger the inventory in a warehouse, the higher the inventory levels. Fewer, but larger, replenishment orders are needed to keep goods in inventory. The conflicting costs of inventory are illustrated in Figure 14–6. The total cost curve is derived by vertically summing the other three curves. The optimal order quantity is represented as R_Q on the replenishment axis.

Just-in-time (JIT) is a Japanese addition to efficient inventory management. There is still some confusion about what this buzz-word means, but, no matter how you define it, the bottom line is that it can control costly inventories. JIT is a control technique that has, as its principal goal, the elimination of waste in the inventory process. At General Motors, where parts are needed on the assembly line at specific

Figure 14–6 Conflicting Costs Involved in Inventory Management and Control

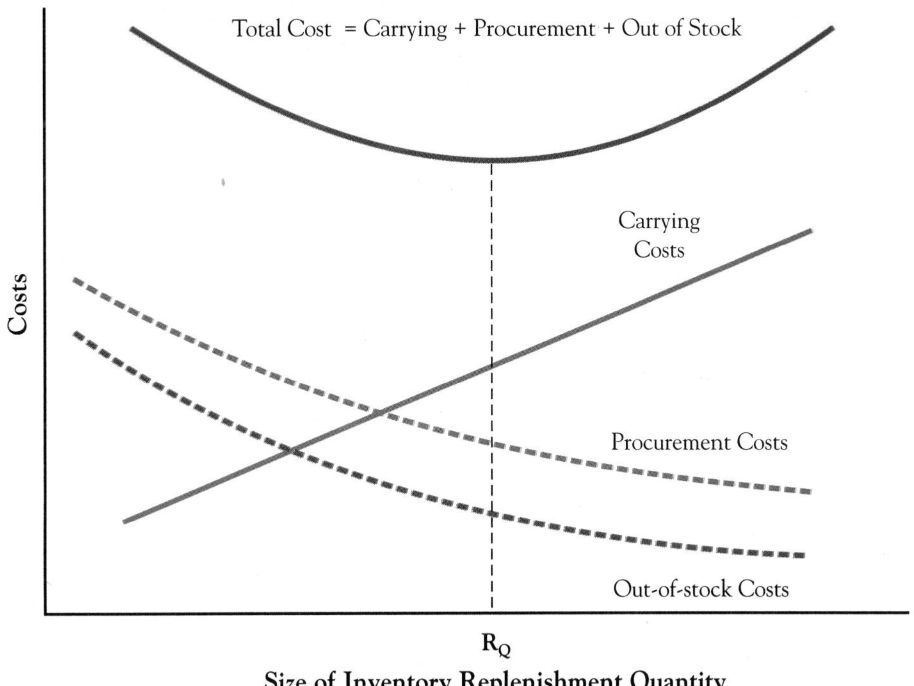

times of the day and in the right sequence, this means receiving the exact number of required parts every four hours. For a tool manufacturer in central Maine, it means getting a shipment of metal within a day of its expected delivery. For Hewlett-Packard, General Electric, Black & Decker, Westinghouse, and Ford Motor Co., all enthusiastic supporters of JIT, it means having inventory where it's needed, when it's needed.

General Motors is spending almost $2 billion to make its Osharon, Ontario, plant one of the most efficient JIT facilities anywhere. Before installing JIT, GM attained 24 turns of inventory at its Oshawa plant.[19] The use of JIT will result in 50 turns of inventory. Each inventory turn is worth $1 million in savings. GM's goal is to have only one day's worth of material at its assembly plants. Maintaining such a lean inventory, however, presents risks—being out of stock, delays, and shut downs of assembly lines. GM has decided that being lean in terms of inventory is worth the risks.

Warehousing

Organizations cannot manufacture goods in every possible market location. Thus, warehouses maintained by middlemen or the manufacturers themselves must be strategically located in or near centers of demand. There are two types of warehouse facilities, private and public. **Private warehouses** are either owned or leased and are used when a large volume of goods must be regularly stored to meet customer demands. Although owning warehouse space may be expensive, private warehouses are popular when a firm needs flexibility in the design of facilities, wishes to maintain control

Table 14–2 A Comparison of Private and Public Warehouses

	Type of Warehouse	
	Private	**Public**
Fixed investment	Very high	No fixed investment
Unit Cost	High, if volume is low Very low, if volume is very high	Low; charges are made only for space needed
Control	High	Low managerial control
Adequacy for product line	Highly adequate	May not be convenient
Flexibility	Low; fixed costs have already been committed	High; easy to end arrangement

SOURCE: Louis W. Stern and Adel El-Ansary, *Marketing Channels* (Prentice-Hall, 1977), p. 150.

over its warehouse operations, has special handling and storage requirements, and has a high volume of goods flowing through its facilities.[20] In contrast, public warehouses, which are rented, are desirable for firms that do not want to be burdened with operating a warehouse. Public warehousing is also popular if a firm needs flexibility in placing its inventory because of uncertain or seasonal demand for goods. The customer using a public warehouse pays only for the amount of space used. Table 14–2 shows some major considerations in choosing what type of warehouse to use.

At Disney World, warehousing is not as up to date as some critics claim it should be. The *Marketing in Action* in this section points out some issues of concern in terms of warehousing efficiency.

Distribution Centers

A major development in private warehousing is the **distribution center.** Distribution centers differ from conventional private warehousing operations because they are centralized warehouse operations that serve regional markets, process and regroup products into customized orders, maintain a full line of products, consolidate large shipments from different distribution points, frequently use computers, and are highly automated.[21]

Although each function can be performed by some public warehouses, most distribution centers are owned or leased for private use. Many organizations, including Levi Strauss, IBM, Pillsbury, Atlantic Energy, and Anchor Hocking, operate distribution centers. These firms use the centers as a primary means of moving goods, rather than as a storage facility.

Walgreen Company, an industry leader in revenues and profits, uses a network of six strategically located warehouses (distribution centers) to service its over 1,100 stores. The distribution costs of the firm have been reduced by 35 percent because of more optimal, rapid decisions being made with regard to physical distribution functions.

MARKETING IN ACTION

Disney's Magic Is Not in Warehousing

If you have ever visited Disneyland, you might have wondered how all of the shops and restaurants kept their shelves and kitchens stocked. Each night, between 1:00 and 7:00 AM, up to 2500 items are delivered to as many as 110 locations within the park. In keeping with the park's fantasy image, this is a fantastic feat and great selling point, but from a physical distribution angle, it can be a nightmare.

The message that is preached from the boardroom to the lunchroom is that the entire operation of the park is a giant "show." This show surrounds guests during their stay and nothing should bring them back to reality. This means that on an operational level, all cleaning, repairing, and replenishing functions must occur after the park is closed. This "graveyard shift" is totally responsible for getting the park ready for the next day.

The warehousing system at Disneyland uses outdated inventory systems and thus large amounts of labor to perform distribution needs. The purchasing is performed off-site, with little input from the warehouse concerning the timing of shipments. This results in a swell in the number of workers from 70 to 140 during peaks. A recent shift to overseas suppliers (intended to cut costs) has further increased this variability (larger and fewer orders).

The items are received from the docks, where they are entered into the system and sent for pricing. Each item must be hand priced *before* it is sent into the park. Price adjustments are also handled centrally, adding to the bottleneck. Once items have been priced, they are loaded onto carts that are wrapped with cellophane when full and connected into trains. These trains have to wait until the park closes before the merchandise can be delivered. This puts the final responsibility of distribution on the graveyard shift. The process is further constrained by small stock rooms in most of the stores, which means that much of the inventory must be kept at the warehouse.

It seems in this case that Disney is more concerned with the "show" than the physical distribution of the "show." With investments in technology and a concentration on communication, they could turn an inefficient, labor-intensive black hole into a well-controlled cost center. At Disneyland, a strong commitment to physical distribution and its contribution to overall organizational efficiency should be a major theme.

ADAPTED FROM: E. J. Muller, "Behind the Magic Kingdom," *Distribution*, January 1988.

Because the distribution center serves as a temporary station for goods prior to their rapid movement to customers, the costs of storage are decreased. Transportation costs may also be lowered. Instead of shipping to ninety key market locations, General Mills transports its products to only fifteen. The loads are larger, and bulk loads usually are cheaper to transport than small loads.

More and more distribution centers, such as those of Montgomery Ward, Pillsbury, and Hallmark, are using computerized information systems. At Ward's, a computer is involved in processing orders, guiding conveyor systems, and guiding stacker cranes to move goods from place to place. Distribution centers are costly to build, but management believes the improved customer service is well worth the investment. In addition, management believes that greater order accuracy, better control, and improved efficiency will aid its drive to significantly expand its business.[22] In other words, one must spend money to make money—and this is one of the things the money must be spent on.

Transportation

The United States has the most sophisticated transportation network in the world. Despite deregulation bills enacted between 1978 and 1986, the transportation network is still closely monitored by government agencies. The Interstate Commerce Commission (ICC) helps regulate railroads, pipelines, motor carriers, and inland water carriers. It also regulates the Federal Marine Board (FMB). The Civil Aeronautics Board (CAB), which was phased out in 1985, regulated air carriers. Some specific deregulation laws include the following:

- *Airline Deregulation Act of 1978*—Carriers can choose new routes or phase them out, and can cut fares by half or raise them by 5 percent on routes where they control less than 70 percent of the traffic.
- *Motor Carrier Act of 1980*—Carriers can raise or lower rates by 10 percent without ICC approval. Any fit, willing, and able carrier who provides a public service can enter the regulated trucking industry.
- *Household Goods Transportation Act of 1980*—Moving companies can give customers guaranteed pick-up and delivery dates at an extra charge. They must pay the customer a specific amount if they miss these dates.
- *Staggers Rail Act of 1980*—ICC jurisdiction over rates is limited to cases in which railroads exercise market dominance. Carriers were permitted to raise rates up to 6 percent a year through October 1984 and can now raise rates 4 percent annually.
- *Surface Freight Forwarder Act of 1986*—This act substantially deregulated the nonhousehold goods segment of the surface freight forwarder industry. This legislation retains Federal regulation over all surface freight forwarders in the areas of cargo liability and claims settlement procedures. Freight forwarders are responsible for any loss or damage to the cargo they handle.

The deregulation trend in the United States affects all classes of carriers. *Common carriers* are transporters that maintain regular schedules and accept goods from any shipper. *Contract carriers* are for-hire transporters who transport goods for anyone for an agreed-on sum. They are generally subject to less governmental regulation than common carriers. *Private carriers* are company-owned transporters that carry goods only for the company. Since they are company-owned, they are subject to little government regulation. *Exempt carriers* are shippers that are exempt from state and federal regulation. They usually move unprocessed agricultural products by truck.

Rate Regulation. Even with the general trend toward deregulating the transportation industry, there is still some rate control by the ICC. *Transportation rates* are the prices for-hire carriers charge for their services. *Class rates* are rates charged for goods that are shipped in small amounts. Only about 7 percent of the total revenue for railroads comes from class rates. *Commodity rates* are special low rates for the shipment of large quantities or regular use. About 90 percent of the total tonnage of railroads and a large percentage of the tonnage of inland water carriers is shipped under commodity rates.[23]

Most rates are based originally on supply factors or the costs of providing services—loading, special handling, product liability, and so on. The rates actually charged, however, are determined largely by competition among carriers and alternative modes of transportation. The physical distribution manager searches out, bargains for, and selects the best rate. By receiving the best rates, routes, and service, firms can best accomplish their physical distribution customer service, cost, and profit objectives.

Modes of Transportation. There are numerous ways of physically moving goods, but most goods are moved by rail, motor, water, pipe, and air.[24] A number of transportation agencies facilitate the movement of goods. Figure 14-7 shows how the transportation network works to achieve customer service goals.

Figure 14–7 Transportation Modes and Agencies Used to Physically Move Goods

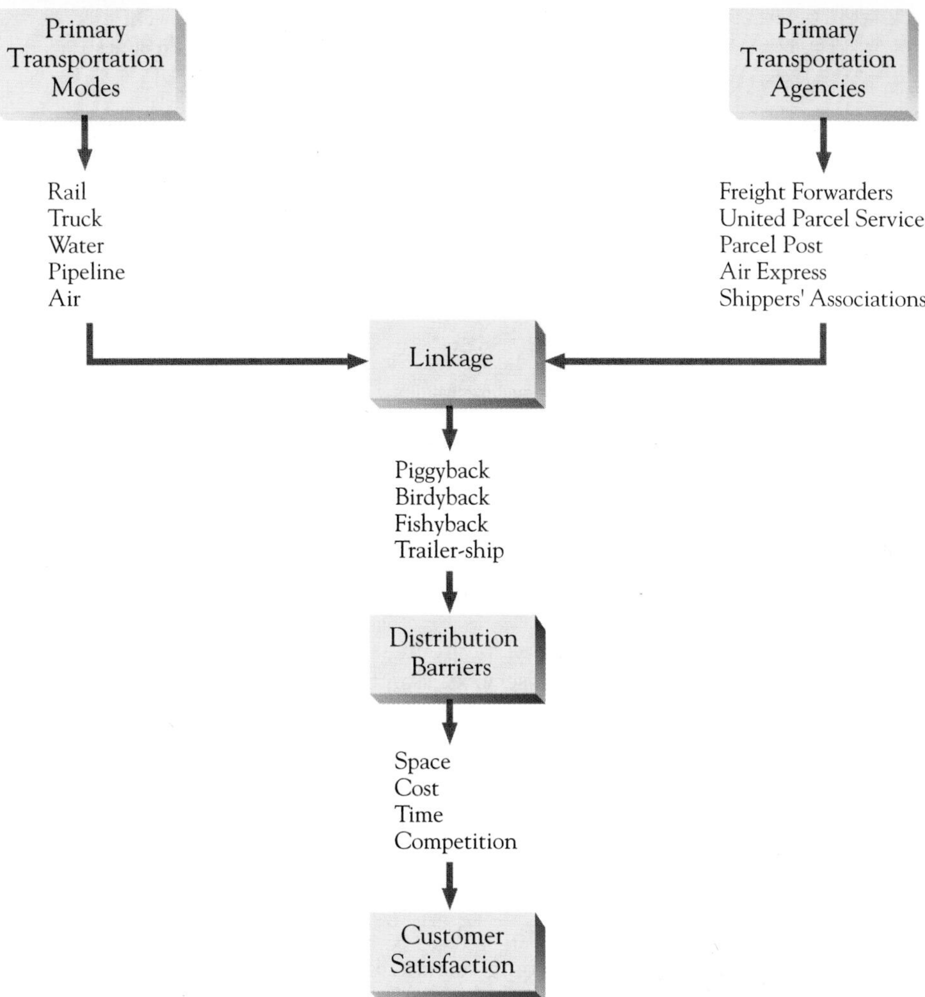

SOURCE: William Lazar, "The Distribution Mix—A Systems Approach," in Eugene J. Kelly and William Lazar, eds., *Managerial Marketing: Perspectives and Viewpoints*, 3rd ed. (Richard D. Irwin, 1967), p. 529.

The relative importance of the five transportation modes is shown in Table 14–3. The latest data indicate that railroads haul about 36 percent of total ton-miles. (A ton-mile is one ton of freight moved one mile.) Motor vehicle and oil pipeline ton-miles have increased slightly in the past few years, to about 24 percent each. Air freight has shown the most dramatic growth. The increase from 1950 to 1981 was over 1500 percent. Despite this growth, air freight still represents less than 1 percent of ton-miles shipped. Air freight accounted for about 8.7 billion ton-miles in 1987 compared to 976 billion railroad ton-miles in 1987.[25]

The importance of a particular mode of moving goods depends largely on the type of freight being hauled. For example, *pipelines* are efficient means for moving liquids such as oil and gas products over long distances (from Alaska to California).

Table 14–3 Trends in Freight Traffic in the United States; 1970–1987 (billions of ton-miles)

Year	Total	Railroads		Motor Vehicles		Inland Waterways		Oil Pipelines		Airways	
		No.	%	No.	%	No.	%	No.	%	No.	%
1970	1936	771	39.83	412	21.28	319	16.46	431	22.26	3.3	.17
1975	2066	759	36.74	454	21.97	342	16.55	507	24.54	3.7	.19
1977	2307	834	36.15	555	24.06	360	15.95	546	23.67	4.2	.18
1981	2438	924	37.90	535	21.94	423	16.82	564	23.13	5.0	.21
1983	2333	838	35.93	551	23.62	359	15.26	582	24.95	5.5	.24
1985	2414	898	37.20	600	24.86	382	14.42	562	23.28	6.4	.26
1987	2671	976	36.50	666	24.90	435	16.30	587	22.00	7.1	.30
% Increase 1970–1987	37.9		26.60		61.60		36.30		36.20		151.10

SOURCES: *The 1989 Information Please Almanac*. New York: Houghton Mifflin, 1989, p. 73 and *1989 Statistical Abstract of The United States* (Washington, D.C.), p. 605 and 607.

Today over 200,000 miles of pipelines (not including the Alaskan pipeline, which stretches about 900 miles from Prudhoe Bay, Alaska, to Valdez, Alaska) weave through the United States.[26]

In contrast, *air freight* is best suited for products that can trade off higher transport costs per ton-mile against improved service. Common goods shipped by air are computing and accounting machines, special dies and tools, medical supplies, live lobsters, and electronic parts. These products generally have high value compared to their weight and must get to customers quickly.

Air freight in moving mail has become a big business. Federal Express is a $4.6 billion firm that is buying up firms like Flying Tigers Line.[27] Federal is currently the nation's largest overnight carrier, responsible for more than 45 percent of the U.S. market and now delivers to over 109 countries. United Postal Service (UPS), a major competitor of Federal, has drivers throughout the world, including 6,000 German employees. Air freight service is going to remain popular because of the speed of delivery, even though facsimile machines might slow some of the unprecedented growth.

Water transportation is a major means of hauling products in bulk. Coal, oil, grain, and sand in bulk amounts are shipped over waterways. These products are of low value relative to their weight and are not perishable. The movement of these goods is slow, but time is not a crucial consideration.

Motor vehicle transportation is a flexible mode of shipping a variety of products, including food, metal castings, rubber belts, and apparel. Motor vehicles can move goods short or long distances, and offer customers relatively fast, consistent service at a reasonable cost. In 1984, there were 30,481 motor carriers in the United States.[28] Regulated motor carriers (those that answer to the ICC) earned $1.1 billion in 1983 on $46.5 billion in revenues—a 2.4 percent profit margin.[29]

Railroads are the most widely used method of transportation, although this dominance has been weakened by the development of other modes of transportation. In 1988, for example, railroads carried about 37 percent of all intercity freight, a drop from 57 percent in 1950 and 44 percent in 1960. There are today over 200,000 miles of railroad lines in the United States. Along these lines move such goods as pulp, paper, coal, sand, and lumber. Rail is a relatively low-cost form of transportation,

MARKETING IN ACTION

Futures Contracts in Transportation

For many years, contracts for commodities such as gold, wheat, and pork bellies have been sold on the futures market. A futures contract is an agreement to acquire a commodity at a set price at a future date. This set-up insures the delivery of raw materials for producers so that production can continue. An example of a futures contract would be Nabisco's buying a future contract for wheat (for their cookies) to be delivered in six months. When that date arrives, Nabisco is assured that their wheat was not sold to another buyer. For Nabisco, this guarantees a supply, and for the farmer, this guarantees a buyer.

Burlington Northern Railroad has launched a new program in which it sells futures contracts for the availability of their covered grain hopper. The contract is a promise that a 54 car unit train to carry grain will be delivered at a specified date in the future. The reasoning behind this introduction is that during harvest season, they are unable to supply enough grain hopper trains, which could mean that some customers would be willing to pay a premium for the guarantee.

Initial reactions of other shippers to the system have been negative, but train contracts have been selling for $116,500, which represents a premium of 15 percent over the regular rate. Plans are in store to increase the percentage over the regular rate to the maximum of 40 percent of their operations.

ADAPTED FROM: David M. Cawthorne, "Traffic World," *Traffic World*, January 18, 1988, pp. 8–9 and James Abbott, "BN Grain Car Futures Program Is Challenged by Shipper Group," *Traffic World*, March 14, 1988, pp. 7–8.

especially for heavy cargoes such as coal, chemicals, and farm products.[30] An interesting notion in the rail industry is the use of futures contracts. The *Marketing in Action* above discusses such an arrangement.

Deciding How to Transport Goods. Transportation modes can be used in combination, as well as exclusively. At some point a decision must be made about how to transport goods. To aid in making the best decision, six criteria are important: *speed of delivery, dependability, frequency of shipments, availability in different locations, flexibility in handling products,* and *cost*. For example, the cost of transportation varies greatly. Air is the most expensive, but it is also fast. On the other hand, water is the least expensive, but it is slow. Of course, any comparisons must consider the type of commodity shipped and the other criteria listed in Table 14–4. One can't ship Maine lobsters to Muncie, Indiana, by rail because no one will buy a dead lobster. Although air is expensive, it is the only way fresh lobster can arrive in Muncie. In other words, the price of a lobster dinner includes a few ounces of jet fuel.

Coordinated Services. Recently there has been increased interest in combining the services of various modes of transportation. This is often referred to as *intermodal coordination of transport services.* A major feature of the use of coordination is the free exchange of equipment between modes.[31] For example, a truck can be carried aboard an airplane, or a rail car can be shipped fully loaded on a water carrier.

Piggyback is the most widely used form of coordinating modes, now available between 1,400 cities in the United States and Canada. Also known as trailer-on-flatcars (TOFC), piggyback involves transporting truck trailers on railroad flatcars, usually over long distances. Piggybacking combines the flexibility of trucking with

Table 14–4 Operating Characteristics of Five Major Transportation Modes

Operating Characteristics	Railroads	Motor Trucks	Waterways	Pipelines	Airways
Speed[1]	3	2	4	5	1
Availability[2]	2	1	4	5	3
Dependability[3]	3	2	4	1	5
Capability[4]	2	3	1	5	4
Frequency[5]	2	5	1	3	4
Cost per ton-mile[6]	3	4	2	1	5

[1]Door-to-door delivery time. [2]Number of geographic points served. [3]Ability to meet schedules on time. [4]Ability to handle various products. [5]Scheduled shipments per day. [6]Illustrative costs per ton-mile are pipeline, $.27; waterways, $.30; railroad, $1.43; motor truck, $7.70 and airways, $21.88.

SOURCE: Donald J. Bowersox, *Logistical Management*, 2nd ed. (Macmillan, 1978), p. 120.

the long-distance rate economy of railroads. The overall cost per ton-mile is less than for trucking alone, and the combination permits trucking to extend its range of service.

With another form of intermodal coordination, called *birdyback,* motor carriers, picking up and delivering shipments of goods, are transported on air carriers. There is also *fishyback,* in which motor carriers are loaded on water carriers.

Yet another intermodal service is *containerized freight.* This involves the placing of goods in containers, which are then placed on a trailer's chassis. With a truck-rail combination it is possible to haul only the containers, thus eliminating the cost of the dead weight of the motor vehicle. This particular combination is called *container-on-flatcar* (COFC).

On March 23, 1981, the ICC deregulated all truck and rail services provided by the railroads in connection with TOFC and COFC movements to give the railroads more marketing flexibility. This deregulation allowed the railroads to counteract the efficiency advantages gained by motor carriers with their 1980 deregulation.

Review Your Marketing Knowledge

- What transportation legislation has a direct impact on the physical distribution activities of a manufacturing firm?
- Is Just-in-time an inventory management procedure that can be used in the United States, Brazil, and Portugal? Explain.
- What types of products would be moved primarily by railroads, motor vehicles, and airways?

Materials-Handling

Materials-handling, or the physical handling of goods, is an important activity in inventory, warehousing, and transportation. The characteristics of a product determine, to a large extent, how it will be handled. For example, radioactive wastes, bulk chemicals, and gases require special handling and storage.

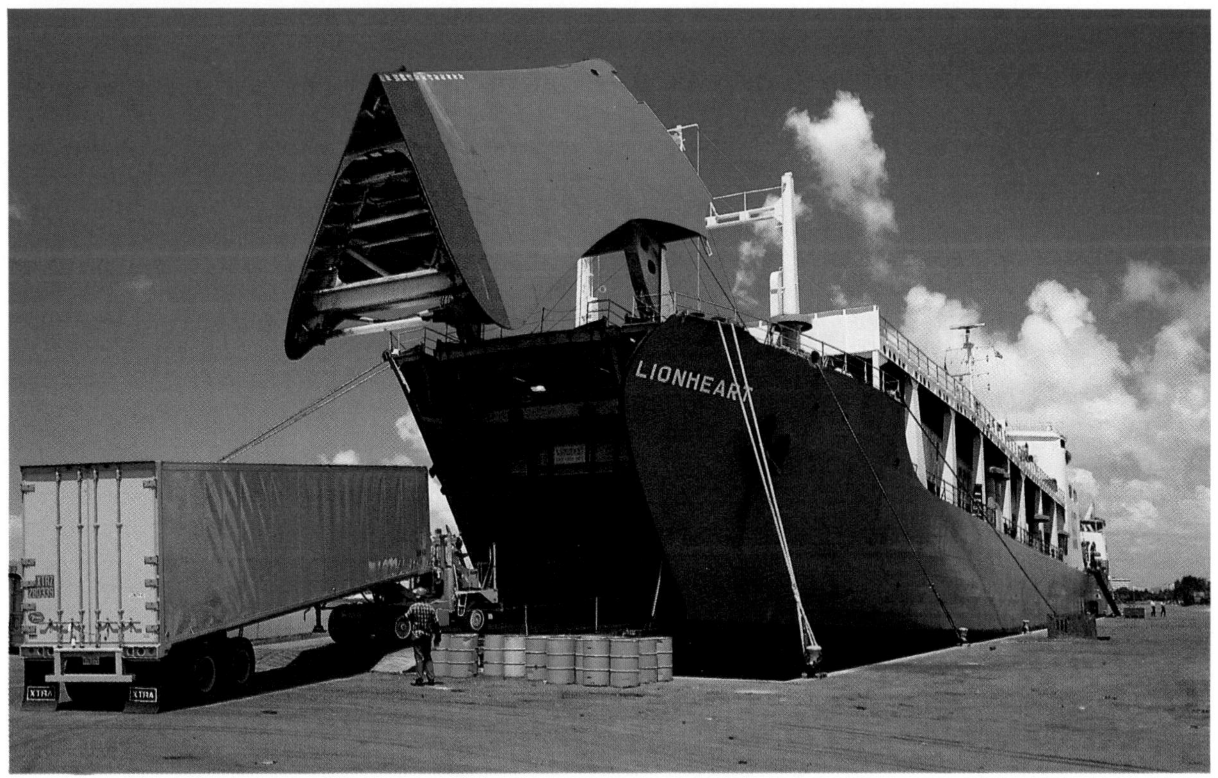

Intermodal coordination allows for more efficient transportation of goods.

A variety of equipment is used to handle a wide range of product sizes, shapes, volumes, and weights. The most popular materials-handling equipment includes trucks, conveyors, and cranes, which can minimize losses from breakage and spoilage. General Mills carefully monitors the handling done by forklift operators in its warehouses. Rough and careless handling can break boxes that are being stacked. Damaged boxes are put in off-storage, the area reserved for boxes that must be destroyed. Of course, General Mills loses money on products that must be destroyed. To minimize such losses, the company has its forklift operators attend materials-handing classes and tests them periodically.

Information Systems

The use of computerized information systems for physical distribution has become very popular. Computers, memory systems, display equipment, and other forms of information-processing technology are being used to link producers, intermediaries, and customers. Del Monte, Campbell's, American Motors, Southland, Winn-Dixie, Tandy, R. J. Reynolds, and Standard Brands are among the firms that have introduced major computer information systems.

Defying inflation, computer costs continue to decline, while speed and reliability of equipment used in order-processing, inventory control, warehousing, and transportation scheduling improve annually. Today minicomputers and microcomputers are replacing older computers in many physical distribution areas.

MARKETING IN ACTION

Lotus 1-2-3 Can Be a Powerful Distribution Tool

James Nurss, manager of distribution for the consumer products division of NutraSweet, had the following problem. "We have a plant in Phoenix, Arizona, and are shipping to Texas, Oklahoma, and part of Louisiana. I want to determine if it would be effective to ship in volume to Dallas and use a pool distributor."

Lotus 1-2-3 uses commands called macro statements that can perform several calculations in a row. These can be used to make custom programs. Users have only to enter the name of the macro to repeat the complex mathematics. Using such macros, Nurss was able to develop a system that would check prices to determine the lowest cost method of shipping. It automatically checks the different ways of shipping and provides an instant comparison.

The program also allowed the user to experiment with different shipment sizes within the program, allowing the user to ask "what if?" types of questions in the optimization of costs. Overall, the program which took just over a week to develop, allows the user to perform what used to be weeks' worth of calculations in a matter of minutes.

Steve Arkin, Rayovac's general traffic manager, has developed several programs with Lotus that allow the distribution department to better manage their requirements. From freight claims management to the tracking of pallets, Rayovac has used 1-2-3 in concert with word processing programs to automate several functions of the department. The claims program is in two parts. One tracks open claims and the other handles historic claims records. Printing of claims is handled by the word processor and has reduced the time spent on the tedious task. However, since the information has been organized on the computer, the number of claims filed dropped from 2,500 in all of 1987 to just 384 in the first five months of 1988.

The chart on the following page shows how many distribution functions can be solved using spreadsheet and word processing programs on personal computers.

ADAPTED FROM: Walter Weart, "Lotus 1-2-3: This Basic Software Isn't Just for Number Crunching Anymore," *Distribution*, February 1988, pp. 38–44.

One thing that leading-edge firms have in common is their use of information systems. Over 380 firms participating in a survey conducted by Donald J. Bowersox of Michigan State University indicated how their firms applied computers. The results of the Bowersox research is presented in *Traffic Management* and is shown in Figure 14–8. A few examples can illustrate how computers have taken over.

- P-I-E Nationwide, Inc. and Matson Navigation are using direct computer link-up in the Hawaiian Islands. The motor carrier's Honolulu link-up with Matson enables it and its delivering agent, Hawaii Transfer Co., instant access to status reports on all P-I-E containers arriving in Honolulu. This is important for providing up-to-date and timely information on every delivery.[32]
- Sea Cloud Concepts, Inc. of Woodland Hills, California, has released an updated version of its Shipmate traffic analysis and reporting system. Shipmate is designed to replace manually generated daily shipping logs, inbound shipment records, or receiving logs. Operating on IBM or compatible per-

Rayovac's Lotus Applications Directory

Program Name	Use	Program Name	Use	Program Name	Use
Allowance	Accesses rates to ascertain freight allowances for customer pickups.	LTL Rates	Accesses inbound LTL bureau and carrier Zip rates for selected carriers. Allows for instant comparison of carrier rates and is excellent for negotiating.	DC/Customer	Program allows user to download shipment history from distribution center to customer from the mainframe. The LOTUS program computes by DC the size and weight ranges. It provides data used to determine the effect of consolidations.
Open Claims/ Closed Claims	Loss and damage claim data which is stored, sorted and printed to provide management reports.	Volume Rates	Accesses inbound volume rates for selected carriers. Program sorts to arrive at the most economical carrier. Useful in establishing preferred carrier routes.	Private Truck Operation Reports	Program presently requires the use of the IBM mainframe using ADRS software to record the shipment data, and the PC to combine the ADRS data with PC-generated equipment and driver invoices to provide management reports.
Export/Import	Monitors import and export shipments which are stored, sorted and printed to provide management reports.	Savings	Provides management reports for traffic department cost improvement obtained through vendor charge backs, vendor returns, and negotiated pricing programs.		
Pallets	Allows management reports of pallet usage and location.				
Fuel Analysis	Analyzes fuel consumption of private fleet. Prints reports for cost per gallon and miles per gallon by tractor.				

sonal computers, it accumulates and reuses daily inbound and outbound shipmate data to provide instant access to shipment information from on-screen inquiries.[33]

- NutraSweet Consumer Products, Inc., in Skokie, Illinois, and Rayovac Corp., in Madison, Wisconsin, address cost-effective shipment problems, production scheduling-shipping problems, claims requests, and distribution center work flows by using LOTUS 1-2-3 and dBase III software packages.[34] The *Marketing in Action* in this section provides more detail on NutraSweet's and Rayovac's application of LOTUS 1-2-3.
- Proposed international standards for electronic data interchange (EDI) are about to become reality. EDIFACT are standards that would allow companies around the world to communicate with each other. All importers, exporters, forwarding agents, customs brokers, and carriers would use EDIFACT for trade-data interchange. The United States, the European Economic Community, and Japan would use EDIFACT data to make phys-

Figure 14–8 Physical Distribution Applications of Computer Programs

Application	Present Company Installations: Leading Edge*	Norm	Emerging	All Companies	Planned (3–5 Years): All Companies
Order Entry	95.3%	87.8%	69.4%	62.9%	3.7%
Order Processing	93.8%	87.0%	75.8%	62.9%	3.1%
Finished-Goods Inventory Control	93.8%	85.0%	58.1%	56.0%	5.3%
Supporting Financial Programs	89.1%	71.3%	59.7%	49.2%	7.9%
Performance Measurement	87.5%	53.5%	17.7%	18.7%	19.7%
Freight Audit/Payment	84.4%	63.8%	37.1%	70.6%	16.3%
Warehousing	82.8%	63.4%	45.2%	82.1%	10.8%
Raw-Material Inventory Control	78.1%	72.8%	53.2%	63.7%	9.0%
Sales Forecasting	76.6%	61.0%	30.6%	89.5%	11.6%
Outbound Freight Consolidation	71.9%	35.8%	14.5%	85.5%	19.2%
Purchasing	71.9%	64.2%	48.4%	25.8%	13.2%
Materials-Requirements Planning	65.6%	49.2%	32.3%	16.6%	11.0%
Distribution Modeling	56.3%	24.0%	6.5%	38.4%	25.5%
Vehicle Routing/Scheduling	40.6%	24.4%	16.1%	72.4%	22.6%
Inbound Freight Consolidation	39.1%	12.6%	9.7%	53.4%	22.9%
Distribution-Requirements Planning	34.4%	17.7%	6.5%	26.6%	19.0%

*Organizations defined as the most progressive

SOURCE: Jack W. Farrell, "How Top Companies View the Role of Computers", *Traffic Management*, May 1988, p. 47.

ical distribution decisions. The EDIFACT data would not have to be translated, which is an important reason for the appeal among physical distribution decision makers.[35]

Despite the accelerating rate of computer use, there are some problems. Staffing information-system units and retaining qualified specialists are becoming more difficult. At present, there is a shortage of qualified personnel. In addition, there are problems with obtaining the information needed to make inventory, warehousing, and transportation decisions.[36] By holding back or slowing down the flow of information, employees sometimes display their resistance to the increased use of computers in physical distribution.

The major functions of a physical distribution system have been presented in this chapter. However, it is important to be able to trace the actual operations of systems in practice. Consequently, an example of a physical distribution system is presented to show how an organization has attempted to accomplish its distribution objectives—good customer service, cost containment, and high profits.

MCA Distributing Corporation

The recording business is often highly unpredictable.[37] Artist, compact disc, or album acceptance is based largely on current tastes in music, which change rapidly, especially in the young adult and teenage markets. To further complicate the distribution process, most song hits enjoy only a brief life span. The industry places great emphasis on point-of-purchase displays to generate sales dollars. Thus, distribution managers must ship CDs, cassettes, and records on time at reasonable costs and have related promotional materials at the retail outlet when albums arrive.

MCA Distributing Corporation, headquartered in Los Angeles, uses tight control systems and cost-effective carrier services to accomplish its goals. Performers on the MCA label span the popular music spectrum, from rock groups like Night Ranger and Boston to singers like Patti LaBelle, Tiffany, and Elton John. MCA customers include music stores, department stores and mass merchandisers, and independent record distributors.

One MCA distribution responsibility is the timely shipment of point-of-purchase material. These items, designed to stimulate consumer demand, include posters, books, T-shirts, buttons, and belt buckles.

For some time MCA's distribution management faced a problem. The point-of-purchase and other promotional materials from the Los Angeles vendors were not ready in time for East Coast and Midwest truck deliveries. Even parcel post was too slow. Thus, the company had to use regular air freight transportation systems to meet its in-store deadlines, even though air freight was very expensive.

In an effort to correct the problem, the company began using a program called Freight Miser, offered by Northern Air Freight, Inc. At rates below those for regular air freight, Freight Miser delivered MCA's promotional items to East Coast and Midwest customers in three to five days, and MCA was charged for the amount of space used rather than for the weight.

Personal Computer Exercise

This PC exercise will examine the trade-off among various forms of physical distribution. You will have the opportunity to rate the importance of different shipping objectives and discover how distribution affects the ultimate cost of the product.

KEY POINTS

- Physical distribution involves the physical movement and transfer of finished and semifinished goods within and through marketing channels.

- Physical distribution activities represent a major portion of marketing costs. In 1988, American industries spent more than $500 billion on transportation, warehousing, inventory control, and general distribution management.

- There are two ways physical distribution can be interrelated with marketing activities. As a backup to marketing programs, physical distribution is dispersed throughout a firm. As a freestanding unit, it is equal in status with other functional units. Experts believe that most future physical distribution systems will be freestanding.

- The interrelated functions of the distribution system are order-processing, warehousing, inventory management and control, transportation, materials-handling, and information systems. Each function plays a major role in accomplishing the primary objective of providing optimal customer service.

ISSUES FOR DISCUSSION

1. Why should a marketing manager understand the total cost approach to physical distribution?

2. Would a company like Toyota use air transportation to ship automobiles from Japan to the United States? Why or why not?

3. What type of physical distribution system would you suggest using for the following products:

a. A special medication for a seriously ill patient
b. A delicate electronics part for a nuclear waste disposal unit
c. A child's toy
d. Natural gas from Texas to be sold in South Dakota

4. What role would physical distribution play in a firm like Walt Disney, Inc.?

5. What has government deregulation meant to the physical distribution manager?

6. How can a physical distribution system's effectiveness influence the sales of a firm, such as Amway, that sells household products?

7. Is the objective of a physical distribution system to operate at the lowest costs? Why or why not?

8. In what kind of firms would the Just-In-Time (JIT) inventory control technique be very effective?

9. Why have computers become so important in the physical distribution industry?

10. What is likely to happen if order processing and inventory management and control are treated as separate tasks instead of being treated as interrelated functions of a distribution system?

GLOSSARY

Carrying costs: All costs associated with holding a quantity of goods for some period of time.

Continuous demand: Demand for products that have a long, relatively stable history of sales.

Distribution center: A large, centralized warehouse that serves regional markets and processes and regroups products into customized orders that can be shipped in large quantities to various distribution points.

Distribution cost trade-offs: Trade-offs that occur when cost increases in one area lead to decreases in other areas.

Erratic demand: An unpredictable pattern of demand for a good, such as the demand for large automobiles.

Freight-forwarder: A transportation intermediary who works with different freight carriers, aggregating small shipments and shipping the total by an efficient mode available to customers for a fee.

Logistics: A concept borrowed from the military to refer to the procurement, distribution, maintenance, and replacement of material and personnel.

Order-processing: All those activities involved in collecting, checking, and transmitting sales.

Out-of-stock costs: Costs of lost sales and back-orders resulting from not having goods available.

Physical distribution: The physical movement and transfer of finished and semifinished goods within and through marketing channels.

Private warehouse: A storage facility owned or leased by a firm.

Procurement costs: Costs that occur in replenishing stock.

Public warehouse: A storage facility that is rented by a company.

Seasonal demand: Product demand that is high only at certain regular points in time.

NOTES

1. Stephen B. Oresman and Charles D. Scudder, "A Remedy for Maldistribution," *Business Horizons*, June 1974, p. 61.

2. John J. Coyle, Edward J. Bardi, C. John Langley, Jr., *The Management of Business Logistics* (St. Paul: West Publishing, 1988) p. 20.

3. "The Not-So-Nifty '90s," *Distribution*, January 1989, pp. 30–35.

4. National Council of Physical Distribution Management, *Careers in Distribution* (Oak Brook, IL, 1983), p. 3.

5. William Morris, (ed.), *The American Heritage* (1982).

6. Ronald H. Ballou, *Basic Business Logistics* (Prentice-Hall, 1978), p. 27.

7. The discussion of Hitachi is based on Francis J. Quinn, "Effective Distribution Helps Hitachi Compete in U.S. Market," *Traffic World,* October 1979, pp. 50–52, 55–56.

8. Philip Kotler, *Principles of Marketing* (Prentice-Hall, 1989), p. 369.

9. Graham Sharman, "The Rediscovery of Logistics," *Harvard Business Review,* September-October 1984, pp. 71–79.

10. Tom Eisenhart, Advanced Research Funds a New Market," *Business Marketing,* March 1989, pp. 51–61.

11. Robert J. Bowman, "Going the Extra Mile," *World Trade,* Winter 1988–1989, pp. 34–43.

12. Donald F. Wood and James C. Johnson, *Contemporary Transportation* (New York: McMillan, 1989), p. 81.

13. Tom Eisenhart, "Automating the Last Frontier," *Business Marketing,* May 1989, pp. 41–46.

14. Ballou, 1978, p. 310.

15. Francine Schwadel, "What Looks Like a Sale, But Isn't a Sale?" *The Wall Street Journal,* April 27, 1989, p. B1; and Steven Weiner, "Price Is the Object," *Forbes,* February 20, 1989, pp. 123–124.

16. "Automated Inventory on the PC," *Distribution,* February 1989, pp. 61–64.

17. "Casebook: Hewlett-Packard," *Distribution,* March 1989, p. 66.

18. Hal F. Mather, "The Case for Skimpy Inventories," *Harvard Business Review,* January-February 1984, pp. 40–42, 46.

19. Andrew Tausz, "How GM-Canada Makes JIT Go," *Distribution,* March 1988, pp. 38–40.

20. Walter Weart and Robert Steiler, "Warehousing: A Review for Management," *Distribution,* June 1988, p. 72.

21. "Wake Up to Computers," *Distribution,* May 1989, pp. 25–28.

22. Francis J. Quinn, "Montgomery Ward Distribution Center Stresses Materials Handling, Efficient Traffic Controls," *Traffic Management,* May 1980, pp. 51–57.

23. Samuel P. Delise, "Interstate Commerce Commission Regulation, 1887–1987: The Carrier Viewpoint," *Transportation Practitioners Journal,* Spring 1987, pp. 262–291.

24. Robert J. Bowman, "A Survey of International Carriers," *World Trade,* Spring 1989, pp. 56–62.

25. *The 1989 Information Please Almanac.* New York: Houghton-Mifflin, 1989, p. 73.

26. See Charles A. Taff, *Management of Physical Distribution and Transportation* (Richard D. Irwin, 1986).

27. "Mr. Smith Goes Global," *Business Week,* February 13, 1989, pp. 66–72.

28. Daniel L. Anderson and William J. Rennicke, "The Contestable Market Defense: Measuring Competition in Freight Transportation," *Transportation Practitioners Journal,* Winter 1987, pp. 199–220.

29. Ruth Hamel, "Trucking Industry: Game's Changed," *USA Today,* August 8, 1984, p. 1B.

30. "Freight Train Cargo," *USA Today,* March 27, 1989, p. 1.

31. Francis J. Quinn, "Intermodalism Finally on the Right Track?" *Traffic Management,* April 1988, pp. 46–53.

32. "P-I-E Links up with Matson," *Traffic World,* April 4, 1988, p. 54.

33. "Sea Cloud Concepts Updates Reporting System," *Traffic World,* April 25, 1988, pp. 48–50.

34. Walter Weart, "LOTUS 1-2-3," *Distribution,* February 1988, pp. 38–44.

35. "Global EDI Language May Have Finally Arrived," *Traffic Management,* April 1988, pp. 17–18.

36. Colin Barrett, "Off-the-Shelf Computer-Ware Can Be Better Than Customized," *Traffic World,* April 25, 1988, p. 51.

37. This discussion is based on Francis J. Quinn, "Record Distribution: Keeping Pace in a Volatile Market," *Traffic Management,* June 1979, pp. 44–46.

CASE APPLICATION 14–1

The Largest Distributor of Foodservice Products: SYSCO

Americans will spend over $220 billion on meals away from home this year, about 40 percent of their food budgets. Sysco Corporation's business is to supply the food and related products to the restaurants, hotels, hospitals, schools, and other institutions that provide those meals. Since its founding in 1969, Sysco has grown from an idea to a $7 billion food marketing distribution organization. Today the company serves more than 225,000 food service customers, in the forty-eight contiguous states and Canada, with approximately 150,000 different food and related products. Sysco also markets and distributes frozen foods to 2000 supermarkets, primarily in the New York and San Francisco metropolitan areas. The demand for thousands of ethnic and specialty foods has provided Sysco with the unique opportunity to service these demands. Sysco can provide food, at the right place and time, prepared for patrons who want varied menus. For example, Sysco carries beef stroganoff, Italian tortellini, and Indian chicken curry.

Sysco management also pays especially close attention to customer service. It stresses that full customer service is its primary goal. Full service at Sysco means:

- immediate access to a broad line of quality products;
- dependable delivery of specified quantities at specified times;
- evaluation of the quality and economy of alternative products and brands to determine which can best meet customer needs;
- menu testing and planning with the aid of Sysco's dieticians and nutritionists; and
- service of multiunit locations on a systemwide basis to ensure consistent product quality over a diverse geographic area.

Sysco emphasizes that it merchandises not only products and service but also a nationwide distribution capability. Customers receive total food-distribution service. The entire package is backed by talented sales, marketing, and distribution experts. As a function of the marketing and distribution of products, Sysco's distribution system works to optimize productivity. The distribution department conducts studies of the mechanics of materials-handling, energy conservation, and a vehicle and equipment performance, as well as safety and warehouse design to improve practice and overall productivity. Improvements in transportation techniques, including environmentally controlled compartments in trucks, has enabled Sysco to provide fresh California strawberries to East Coast markets. Now the strawberries, after a five-day trip, can still look and taste as fresh as the day they were picked.

When you enter a restaurant, think about Sysco's tough job. You have to make choices like "Do I want boeuf bourguignon or the fish of the day?" The chef has to translate your wants into "Do we have enough mushrooms (from Taiwan), olives (from Spain), orange sections (from Florida), and lettuce (from California)?" The restaurant owners and chefs depend on Sysco to get these foods into the kitchen.

SOURCE: *Sysco*, 1988 Annual Report; personal communication with Sysco Corporation, June 1989.

Questions

1. Are Sysco's full-service statements specific enough, or can they be converted into more quantitative objectives?

2. What does Sysco mean when it says its distribution system works to optimize productivity?

3. Does Sysco really have a difficult job servicing restaurants that require foods from around the world? Why or why not?

CASE APPLICATION 14–2

Tradeport: Atlanta's International Distribution Center

In the early 1800s, it was known as Terminus. It was a city built on transportation systems, and as far back as 1837, it was the junction point for the Western & Atlantic Railroad. Today Atlanta is a major distribution center. In its Southside section, a 260 acre Tradeport project is underway. Tradeport is a joint venture of Wilma Southeast, the United States arm of the Danish developer, Wilma, Inc., and two Japanese firms, Mitsui, USA and Shimizu Land Corporation. The objective of this joint venture is to make Atlanta a fully integrated, multi-modal international trade center.

The $300 million Tradeport joint venture will link Europe, the Far East, and the deep South by offering a dynamic globally oriented distribution center. Wilma and Mitsui will market the services of Tradeport in Europe and the Far East. Ideally, companies can locate an entire operation within the complex: warehouses, materials-handling, offices, and even light manufacturing operations (the Tradeport has Foreign Trade Zone status).

Tradeport's proximity to Atlanta's Hartsfield Airport, as well as the Port of Savannah and railroad lines, indicates many advantages for using it as an international distribution center. It is a quick five minute truck drive from the airport, and containers shipped from Savannah will arrive at Tradeport the same day they leave the docks. The traffic flow, ease of access, and room for expansion are important factors in the plan to promote Tradeport.

The Tradeport project has three phases of development. Phase I, the air freight service center, is completed. It offers over 124,000 square feet of office space and warehouse space. Air freight companies, forwarders, customs brokers, and hi-tech businesses are customers for this operation.

Phase II will involve constructing a modern, expansive distribution facility, which will be used to link national and international businesses. Parts, goods, and equipment will flow into and out of the large distribution facility.

Phase III will be an International Trade Center, complete with office buildings, hotels, banks, international business services, and retail shops. This facility will permit trade negotiations, the distribution of goods and services, and the ideas of individuals from various nations to take place under one roof or within close proximity. The Tradeport model of distribution is so attractive that similar developments will likely be found in other major U.S. cities as well as in England, Japan, West Germany, and Taiwan.

A key to the success of Tradeport or any other similar distribution center is having a facility that is at the crossroads of air, water, rail, and land transportation systems. Hartsfield has in a short time period become a major airport. Nonstop international flights are added regularly, and 80 percent of the U.S. market can be reached within two hours flying time. New York, Los Angeles, Houston, and Chicago are also centers or crossroads of transportation systems. These cities are likely candidates for Tradeport type centers because of their airports, waterway access, rail systems, and highway systems. It is the airport system that serves as a major draw for the businesses that become involved in a distribution center.

The Tradeport project is likely to add to the economic development of Atlanta. New jobs to conduct the work of a distribution center are being created. In addition, other businesses such as hotels, restaurants, car rental, and recreational are likely to emerge in the Tradeport area.

SOURCE: E. J. Muller, "Atlanta Goes International," *Distribution*, May 1988, pp. 84–85.

Questions

1. Why would an investor be interested in a project like Tradeport?

2. What economies of scale can be realized by having a massive international distribution center such as Tradeport?

3. What type of marketing will have to be conducted to promote the advantages of doing business at Tradeport?

4. Why is location such a critical factor in making Tradeport a successful international physical distribution center?

PART
FIVE

Promotion

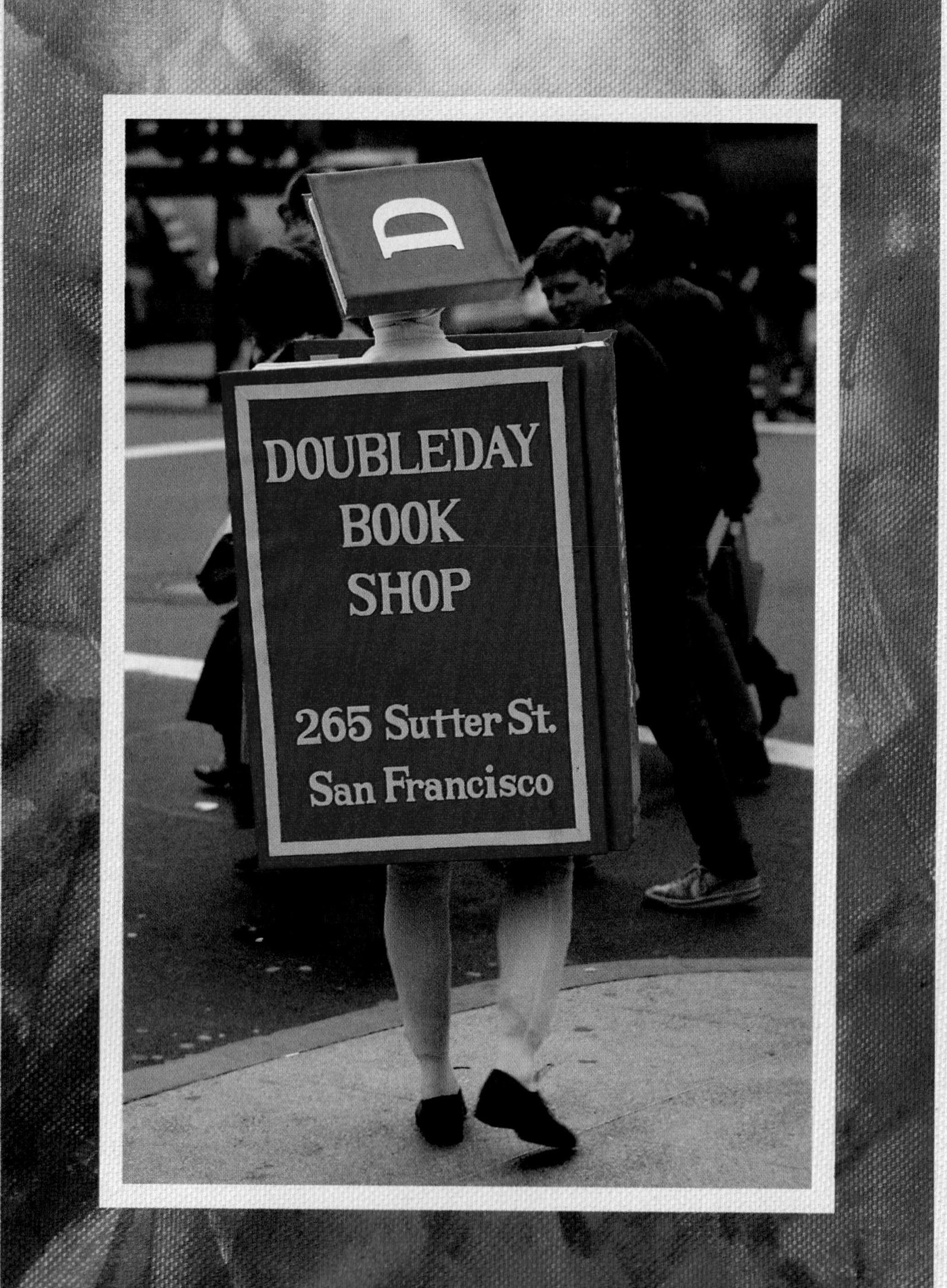
D
DOUBLEDAY
BOOK
SHOP
265 Sutter St.
San Francisco

15

Promotion: Basic Concepts

Learning Objectives

Upon completing this chapter, you will be able to do the following:

IDENTIFY
the components of a promotional mix.

DEFINE
advertising, sales promotion, publicity, and personal selling.

EXPLAIN
how communication takes place and how it influences promotion.

DESCRIBE
the components of properly stated promotional objectives.

LIST
the factors that determine an organization's overall cost of promotion.

EXPLAIN
the various budgeting procedures for determining promotional expenses.

DISCUSS
the factors that influence an organization's choice of a promotional mix.

MARKETING PROFILE

Black & Decker Selects a Promotional Mix

During the past three years, Black & Decker, a manufacturer of household appliances and power tools, has accomplished two important tasks. First, with the acquisition of GE's small appliance division, B&D successfully incorporated over 150 former General Electric products under the B&D logo. Second, it revitalized and restructured its core business in power tools. Financially, the company has solidified its performance with sales up 8 percent in 1987 to $1.93 billion. B&D has been able to maintain sales growth through the use of several promotional tools—sales promotion, advertising, and personal sales.

The B&D/GE brand transition has been smooth and profitable. Advertising was used to inform consumers of changes in the product line. Kenneth E. Homa, vice president of marketing for B&D's household products, said "there's the feeling that you have to talk with consumers a lot. The ad budget is sacred."

B&D spends $30 million annually on advertising for small appliances with 50 percent of the budget in TV, 45 percent print and 5 percent radio. It also uses direct mail to increase consumer awareness of its household products. Five mailings will be done this year, targeting women 25–54. And although sales promotions have been reduced, the division's profitability has not suffered. Rebates, used extensively by competitors, have been discontinued, without a loss in market share.

Personal sales efforts are important to B&D's success. Steps have been taken to improve relationships with both retailers and customers. A team of 30 retail-merchandising agents have full-time responsibility of monitoring stores and assisting in-store merchandising. A spokesperson for Best Products said

that B&D "is a terrific marketing group that helps create demand for the retailer." Other trade members still see room for improvement in terms of providing inventory when needed.

Black & Decker has also instituted new marketing plans in its power tool division. New products include more step-up products, such as a Master Series of power tools aimed at professional users, and a larger accessories line with the highly successful Bullet Pilot Point drill bits. Improved personal sales efforts serve customers better. The salesforce has increased from 175 to 275. Marketing programs can now be tailored to the needs of B&D's diverse distributors.

The advertising budget has doubled since 1986 to $10 million domestically. The worldwide ad budget is $30 million for power tools. TV is used for image spots and individual products, and magazines such as *People, Popular Science,* and *Esquire* have gift guide inserts geared toward special occasions such as Father's Day.

B&D's 1988 promotional budget for power tools is between $30 and $50 million, up 10–15 percent from 1987. The company's choice of promotional mix has competitors taking notice. Makita U.S.A., Inc.'s market research manager Roy Thompson said, "We respect Black & Decker in many ways. Their pricing and programs are competitive, and they have some strong and much improved leadership."

This profile shows a company making use of advertising (radio, magazines, direct mail, and telephone), sales promotion, and personal selling to reach its sales objectives. How a company uses the available promotional tools indicates its success or failure in the marketplace. Communicating an effective message so that the response of the consumer is to buy the product or use the service is a difficult problem to solve. By developing a promotional mix that works, the company maximizes its possibility to communicate. The profile shows that Black & Decker has identified the issues for its company and has developed activities to stimulate consumer interest. It also illustrates the synergy among these different promotional activities. Chapter 15 explores the role of these and other promotional tools in marketing.

SOURCE: Paula Schnorbus, "B&D Turns On the Power," *Marketing and Media Decisions,* May 1988, pp. 57–64.

In this chapter we examine the different promotional tools available to a marketer. Although some people consider advertising synonymous with marketing, it is but one of the many promotional tools a marketer can use. And promotion is just *one* of the major decision areas within marketing.

Promotion is the *communication* mechanism of marketing, the exchanges of information between buyers and sellers. Its task is to *inform, remind,* and *persuade* consumers to *respond* to the product or service being offered. The desired response may take many forms, from awareness of the product or service to actual purchase. This response issue will be discussed in more detail later in the chapter.

Making promotional decisions in marketing is both exciting and difficult. Can you imagine yourself working for Upjohn, trying to develop an advertising program directed at doctors for a new cancer drug, or as the national sales manager for special alloy steels at U.S. Steel, trying to determine programs of compensation, training, and evaluation for your sales force? These are but two illustrations of the dynamic and complex nature of promotional activity. Chapter 16 focuses in more detail on advertising and sales promotion, while Chapter 17 explores personal selling.

In this chapter we will cover the different types of activities constituting promotion; the dynamics of the communications process; setting promotional objectives; determining promotional expenditures; and selecting a promotional mix.

Components of Promotion

The marketing manager has four broad types of promotional devices available:[1]

- **Advertising:** any paid form of nonpersonal presentation and promotion of ideas, goods, or services by an identified sponsor in such media as magazines, newspapers, outdoor posters, direct mail novelties, radio, television, bus posters, catalogues, directories, programs, and circulars.
- **Personal Selling:** an oral presentation in a conversation with one or more prospective purchasers for the purpose of making sales.
- **Sales Promotion:** those marketing activities—other than personal selling, advertising, and publicity—that stimulate consumer purchasing and dealer effectiveness, such as displays, shows and exhibitions, demonstrations, coupons, contests, and other nonroutine selling efforts. These are usually short-term activities.
- **Publicity:** nonpersonal stimulation of demand for a product, service, or business unit by generating commercially significant news in published media or by obtaining a favorable presentation on radio, television, or stage. Unlike advertising, the media costs of this form of promotion are not paid for by the sponsor.

The combination of these four promotional tools forms the **promotional mix** of an organization. The goal is to *communicate* a message to some person or persons in order to get a *response* (attitude change or purchase). It is necessary to understand this marketing communication process to develop effective promotional plans.

Marketing Communications

Figure 15–1 depicts the communications process. All communications require a source and a receiver.[2] The **source** is the originator of the communication and could

Figure 15–1 The Communication Process

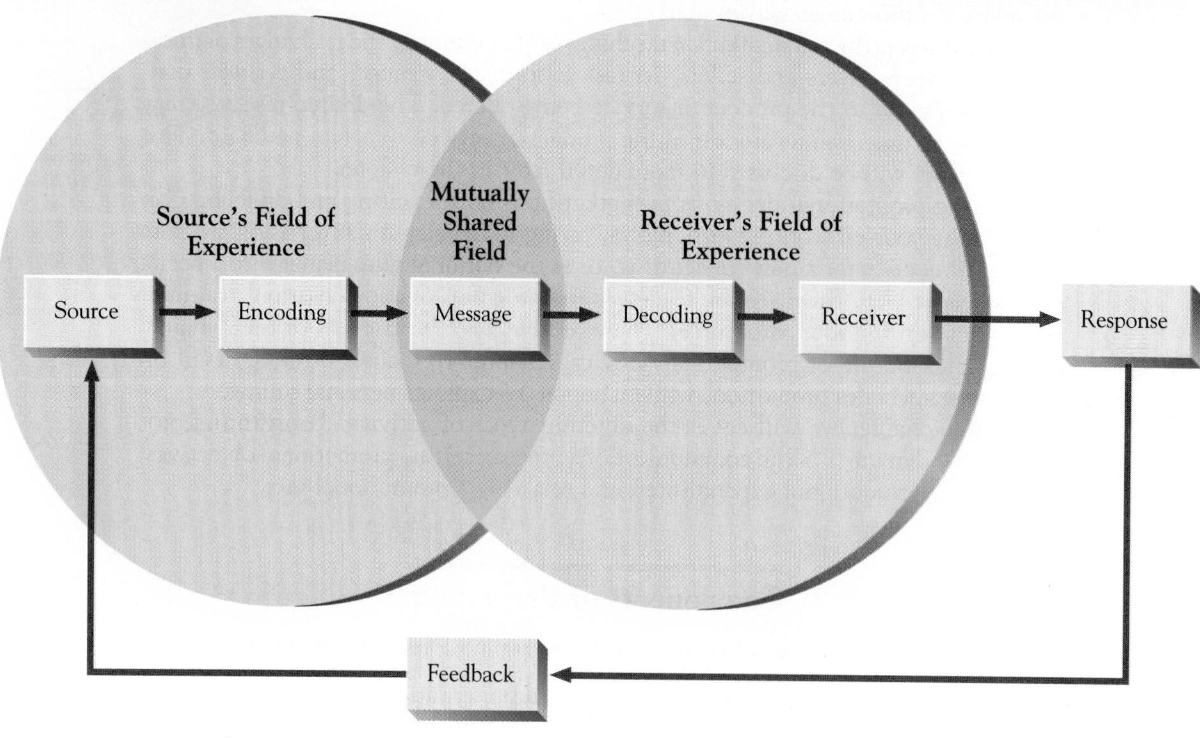

be a salesperson, advertisement, or coupon; the **receiver** is the target of the communication. Although communication does not depend upon the proper understanding of the message nor the intent of the source to send one, it does require that the targeted receiver attend to the sender's signals. Marketers thus have two major problems: first, to communicate only when and in the ways they intend to; and second, to communicate the specific message intended—and no others.

In order to communicate effectively, the sender must arrange ideas into symbolic forms such as words and pictures. This process is called **encoding.** The encoded *message,* the exact set of symbols used by the sender, is then transmitted through a **channel.** The channel can be many things, including the spoken word (personal selling) or the mass media (advertising). If the channel delivers the message to the receiver, the receiver may attempt to assign meaning to the symbols in the message. This process is called **decoding.** The successful communication of the source's intended message thus requires proper encoding and decoding plus a clear channel for transmitting the message. All these requirements are difficult to meet, even in the best of times. Advertisers may use words that people misinterpret, or a salesperson's presentation to a potential buyer may be interrupted.

Communication is facilitated when the source and receiver share common backgrounds, experiences, social influences, and needs. When this occurs, they are said to overlap in *psychological fields.* The higher the overlap, the greater the chance for accurate communication. Marketers must be able to put themselves inside the head of the intended receiver in order to speak their "language." Table 15–1 on failed communications illustrates communication attempts that did not work.

Table 15–1 Failed Communications

Below are some real-world examples of unsuccessful communication. They all failed because of the breakdown of some part of the communications process. These examples come from marketers' attempts to directly take an English language ad campaign and put it into French.

Original English	French Version	Meaning to a French Person
Open with care, use other end (referring to a package)	Ouvrez soigneusement avec l'autre main	Open carefully with other hand
Three times per annum (referring to the application of a floor care product)	Trois fois par voie rectale	Three times in the rectum
Big Mac	Gross Mac	Sex maniac

Once the message has been received (not necessarily accurately), the receiver will make some *response* to the message. The response could be a purchase, an attitude shift, or even just a physical gesture. The part of the overall response that is measured by the sender is called *feedback.*

Interpersonal vs. Mass Communication

Both interpersonal and mass communication are important in marketing. Personal selling requires interpersonal communication, while advertising, sales promotion, and publicity use mass communication techniques. Table 15–2 presents a summary of the advantages and disadvantages of the two communication modes.

A mass communication, such as an advertisement in a magazine, can more accurately deliver the same message to a larger audience than can an interpersonal communication, such as a salesperson's presentation to a customer. The latter changes with each attempt to communicate. The cost of reaching an individual through the mass media is substantially lower as well. However, mass communication is one-way; it has less likelihood of gaining the potential audience's selective attention, and it suffers from slow, and many times, inaccurate feedback.

Interpersonal communication has the benefits of being fast and allowing two-way feedback. A buyer can respond instantly to a salesperson's presentation, and the salesperson can ask for clarification of the response. This greater flexibility in feedback allows the communicator to counter objections from the buyer and thus attain a greater change in attitude and behavior than is possible with mass communication. Interpersonal communication is much more efficient than mass communication. Unfortunately, interpersonal communication used for a large audience is slow and very expensive. One must thus compare the efficiency of using a particular type of communication with the cost involved. This comparison of communication efficiency with cost leads to what has been referred to as the *communication-promotion paradox.* One set of authors noted:

> *It is obvious that the mass media present some significant communication problems. Advertising and publicity through the mass media will always represent inefficient communication, even with precise definition of market targets, motivation research,*

Table 15–2 Comparison of Interpersonal and Mass Communication

Factor	Interpersonal Communication	Mass Communication
Reaching a Large Audience		
Speed	Slow	Fast
Cost per individual reached	High	Low
Influence on the Individual		
Ability to attract attention	High	Low
Accuracy of message communicated	Low	High
Probability of selective screening	Relatively low	High
Clarity of content	High	Moderate to low
Feedback		
Direction of message flow	Two-way	One-way
Speed of feedback	High	Low
Accuracy of feedback	High	Low

SOURCE: James F. Engel, Martin R. Warshaw, and Thomas C. Kinnear. *Promotional Strategy*, 6th ed. (Irwin, 1987), p. 49.

and feedback of results through various media. This is because of the very nature of the communication process. Nevertheless, a mass market generally can be reached economically only with mass media. This leads to the seeming paradox that advertising provides efficient promotion through inefficient communication.[3]

Thus, promotion activity is evaluated in terms of its communication power relative to its cost. Table 15–3 gives an example of the communication process for the four promotional elements.

Communication Flows in Marketing

Every sale of a product or service in marketing involves many communication flows. Table 15–4 illustrates how the nature of the product involved and its distribution structure influence the choice of communication mode. The more direct the purchase transaction between buyer and seller, the fewer mass communication devices will be used. For example, a house sale is a very direct transaction and is thus dominated by interpersonal communication. At the other extreme is a packaged good; here the seller uses advertising and marketing research to communicate with prospective buyers. Without these devices, the seller would have no direct influence on the sale of the product.

Push vs. Pull Strategies

The marketing manager may direct promotional activity at any or all end consumers, distributors, and retailers. Two broad classes of promotional strategies have been identified. Figure 15–2 on page 472 illustrates these. The first is called a **pull** strategy. Promotional activity (usually advertising and sales promotion) is directed primarily *at the end consumer,* with the objective of developing demand for the product. The

Table 15–3 The Communications Process in Promotion

	Source	Encoding	Media	Receiver	Decoding	Feedback
Personal Selling	DuPont sales engineer	Words, gestures, appearances	Sales visit	Purchasing agent at Burlington Mills	Mannerisms of salesperson distract buyer from fully understanding message	Buyer asks questions to clarify information
Advertising	General Foods' ad for Jello	Words, pictures, color, social setting	Television commercial	Viewer in Chicago	Consumer gets positive feeling about new Jello recipe	Consumer purchases Jello; sales increase
Sales Promotion	Armour's coupon for Dial Soap	Size and shape of coupon, words, money-back offer	Local newspaper in top 50 markets	Reader of the LA Times	Consumer clips coupon from paper	Consumer redeems coupon, sales increase
Publicity	Interview of Chrysler Chairman Lee Iacocca	Words, gestures, appearance, office image	Television news show	Viewer in Portland	Viewer dislikes "big business" image of Iacocca	Consumer does not buy products. No research done so Chrysler unaware of reaction

hope is that the consumer will require retailers to carry the product, and that retailers will, therefore, demand it from wholesalers. Thus, the promotion to end users has *pulled* the product through the channel. Many consumer package goods use this emphasis to obtain a space on crowded supermarket shelves.

The alternative to this strategy is to **push** the product through the channel. With a push strategy, the promotional activity (usually personal selling, trade deals, and advertising) is directed *at channel members.* A producer only promotes the product to the closest level; that channel member then promotes the product to the next level. This process continues until the ultimate consumer is reached. Many clothing products and industrial products are promoted in this way.

Of course, push and pull strategies are extremes; virtually all products make use of both schemes. Thus, a major chemical producer may advertise to end users, even though a personal selling push is the key ingredient in the promotional plan. DuPont advertises its fibers this way so that consumers will accept them when clothing manufacturers use them in their clothing lines. Further, even the most advertised package good has push effort put behind it. Procter & Gamble prides itself on its sales force, which promotes its products to retailers who then promote them to the consumers, who are the ultimate users.

Uncontrolled Communication

Marketers control the design and execution of advertising, sales promotion, and personal selling; therefore, they bear the costs. Publicity is only partially within marketers' control and is not paid for by them. For example, well-placed news releases

Table 15–4 Role of Personal and Impersonal Communication in Consumer Transactions

	House Sale	Automobile Sale	Appliance Sale	Soap Sale
Role of Intermediaries	Important	Exclusive retailers only	Distributor and nonexclusive retailers	Chain retailers and wholesalers
Personal Selling to Consumer	Very important	Very important by retailer	Important by retailer	None at retail
Need for National Advertising	None, except for intercity relocation to give agency name recognition (for example, Century 21)	Important, but not relative to cost	Somewhat important relative to cost	Very important
Need for Local Advertising	Very important	Somewhat important	Very important	Not important
Need for Research Feedback	None	Important relative to cost	Somewhat important relative to cost	Very important

generated a substantial number of positive newspaper and magazine articles, plus much television coverage, for Chrysler's minivans; but the results of medical studies in the mid-1980s, showing a relationship between the use of children's aspirin for treatment of flu and chicken pox and the potentially fatal disease Reyes Syndrome, generated substantial negative publicity for Saint Joseph's Aspirin for Children. This latter communication falls into the category of hard news and was beyond the marketer's control.

Another type of communication that is always beyond marketer's control is *word of mouth* communication—consumers talking to other consumers about products. This type of communication is well documented and is potentially influential. For example, word-of-mouth is the most effective type of communication in the adoption of a new food product; it was twice as influential as television advertising and about four times as influential as store displays. The power of word-of-mouth to help or hurt product success should not be underestimated. Haven't you told friends about records, movies, cars, or stereos that you've liked or disliked? The *Marketing in Action* about the need for Procter & Gamble, McDonald's, and Stroh to fight rumors clearly shows the power of word-of-mouth.

Setting Promotional Objectives

Promotional objectives are directly related to the *response* desired from communication. The ultimate response would be a purchase, of course. However, purchases occur because of the complex interaction of all marketing activity, not just promotion. Further, purchases are affected by uncontrollable environmental factors such as competition. Thus, marketers must look at a hierarchy of possible responses to promotion. The two most used response hierarchies are the *AIDA* and *hierarchy-of-effects* models.

MARKETING IN ACTION

The Power of Uncontrolled Communication

Procter & Gamble has, on many occasions over the last few years, taken action to fight a rumor that its man-in-the-moon logo was a Satanic symbol, and that P&G was in league with the devil. In one year P&G received over 12,000 phone calls per month on its toll-free line about this issue. Later the company was still receiving about 3000 calls per month, with most of the callers threatening to boycott P&G products. Finally, P&G gave in and dropped its long-standing logo.

Over the years McDonald's has been the target of a number of widespread rumors. One was that its hamburger meat contained worms. More recently trading in McDonald's stock was stopped for a short time on the New York Stock Exchange because of a flood of sell orders resulting from a rumor that someone had died after eating a McDonald's hamburger. Although totally false, both rumors were widely believed and talked about. They forced McDonald's to take action to forcefully deny the rumors.

In 1983, Stroh, the nation's third largest brewer, took out ads in local newspapers in Illinois and Indiana to call attention to the fact that Stroh did not make any financial contributions to various presidential candidates. This eye-catching ad had a headline stating, "STROH OFFERS $25,000 TO STOP RUMORS!" and offered the reward for the identification of those responsible for circulating the allegations. Although the reward was never granted, the unique ad was successful in stopping further rumors about Stroh.

Response Models: AIDA and the Hierarchy of Effects

AIDA is an acronym for the stages a consumer is expected to go through before purchasing a product. These stages are the following:

1. To get the consumer's Attention (sometimes called awareness)
2. To create and hold Interest
3. To arouse Desire
4. To motivate Action

A promotion may have as its objective any part or parts of AIDA. For example, marketers may want to motivate action (a purchase) with a cents-off coupon, and they may want to create interest in a product with a television advertisement.

The **hierarchy of effects** is a more elaborate version of AIDA. It proposes more steps in the sequence: *awareness, knowledge, liking, preference, conviction,* and *purchase.* Again, promotion objectives may be expressed at any level on the hierarchy. Figure 15–3 presents an advertisement for the Mystery Guild; its fundamental objective is the completion of a purchase. The advertisement, which is essentially the only chance the Guild has to complete a sale, is called a *direct action* advertisement. In contrast, the advertisement presented in Figure 15–4 is intended to have an effect on consumers at a lower level in the hierarchy. The intent here is probably to generate awareness and knowledge of this relatively new product.

The AIDA and hierarchy of effects models are related. This can be more readily seen if we divide the stages into more generic psychological terms: *cognitive, affective,*

Figure 15–2 Push vs. Pull Strategies

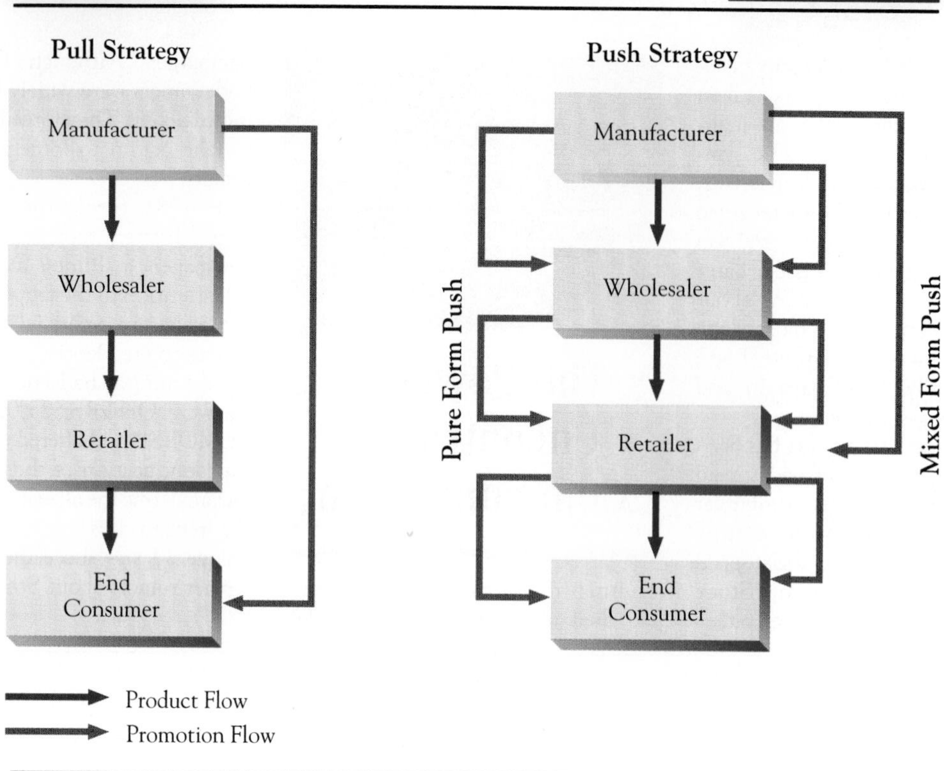

and *behavioral,* as Table 15–5 shows. Cognitive response refers to awareness and knowledge, or attention; affective response refers to liking and preference, or interest and desire; and behavioral response refers to conviction (intention-to-buy) and purchase, or action. We have also added an additional level to the hierarchy. This is the *outcome* of the purchase: to what degree is the consumer satisfied? This is a critically important question that marketers interested in long-term success must answer.

The more detailed specification of steps in the hierarchy-of-effects model makes it more useful than AIDA for collecting feedback on promotion activities. However, the AIDA formulation (or, as we now could call it, AIDAS, to explicitly consider the satisfaction level) does serve to remind us, in a simple way, of the tasks promotion must accomplish along the road to purchase. AIDAS is also useful in understanding personal selling (discussed in Chapter 17).

Diagnostic Power of the Hierarchy. Marketers can collect feedback about their promotional activities by measuring the effectiveness of promotion on each level of the hierarchy of effects. Consider the following possible response profiles in the total market for two products (total = 100 percent). The percentages given are cumulative; that is, for Product 2, the 10-percent satisfied represents 10 percent of the target consumers, but 25 percent (10%/40%) of those target consumers who were aware of the product.

Figure 15–3 An Example of a Direct Action Ad

Product 1	*Product 2*
Awareness 90%	Awareness 40%
Knowledge 60%	Knowledge 30%
Liking 20%	Liking 25%
Preference 10%	Preference 20%
Conviction 8%	Conviction 15%
Purchase 4%	Purchase 12%
Satisfied 3%	Satisfied 10%

Product 1's profile suggests that the consumers understand the communication about the product very well (60 percent knowledge) but did not particularly care for these attributes (only 20 percent liking). A major reworking of the message, or a new product with more liked attributes may be needed. Product 2's profile suggests a real winner that needs to be better known (40 percent awareness) in the marketplace.

Figure 15–4 An Ad Designed to Stimulate Awareness

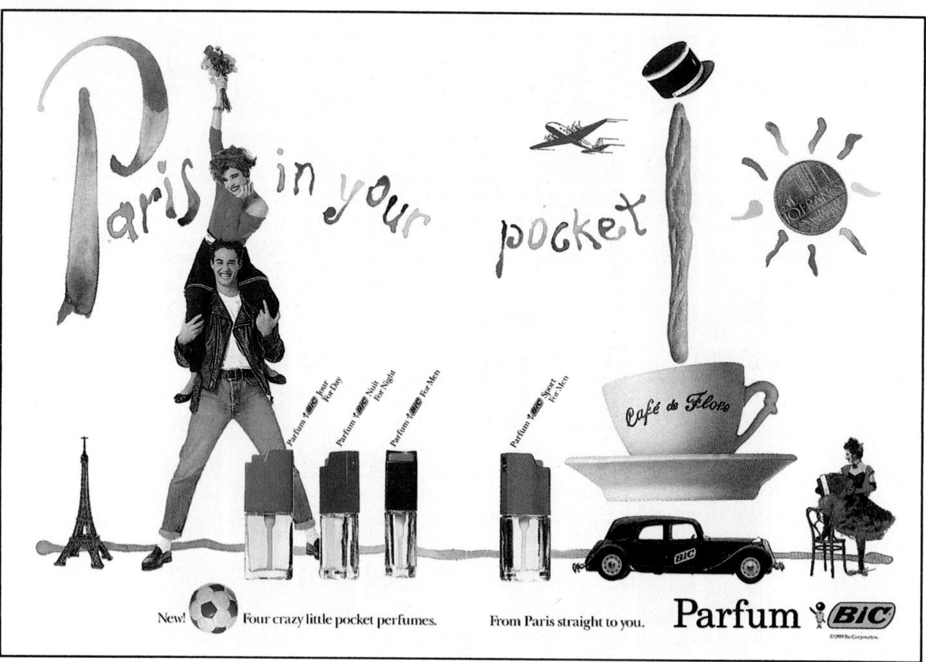

These diagnostic tests are very useful in setting promotional objectives. For example, building awareness would be the prime objective for Product 2. The power of the hierarchy to guide promotional planning is thus clear.

Alternative Ordering in the Hierarchy. It would be very misleading to presume that every consumer automatically passes through the hierarchy of effects in order. Researchers have found that this **learning hierarchy** does not hold in certain circumstances. The alternatively ordered hierarchies are the **low-involvement hierarchy** and **dissonance** (or action-first) **hierarchy.**

The basic learning hierarchy holds when the consumer is highly involved with the product or purchase process, when highly differentiated products exist, or when mass media advertising is important, such as with new, highly technical consumer products like video tape recorders and home computers. In the low-involvement hierarchy, the consumer has little involvement with the product or purchase process, perceiving products as similar to each other. The ordering in this hierarchy is awareness, knowledge (minimal), purchase, liking, preference, conviction. Usually the product is in the later phase of maturity in the product life-cycle and so broadcast media are important. It is very hard for consumers to get involved, for example, with tonic water or detergents. Thus, switching from Canada Dry to Seagram's is likely to follow the low-involvement pattern. A Canada Dry user is aware of Seagram's and has some minimal knowledge about it. The specific attitude change will occur after the switch: "I'm glad I tried Seagram's tonic water; I prefer it to Canada Dry."

The dissonance (or "action-first") hierarchy is ordered: awareness, purchase, knowledge, liking, preference, conviction. It is called the dissonance hierarchy because the buyer is presumed to have some second thoughts about the purchase since so

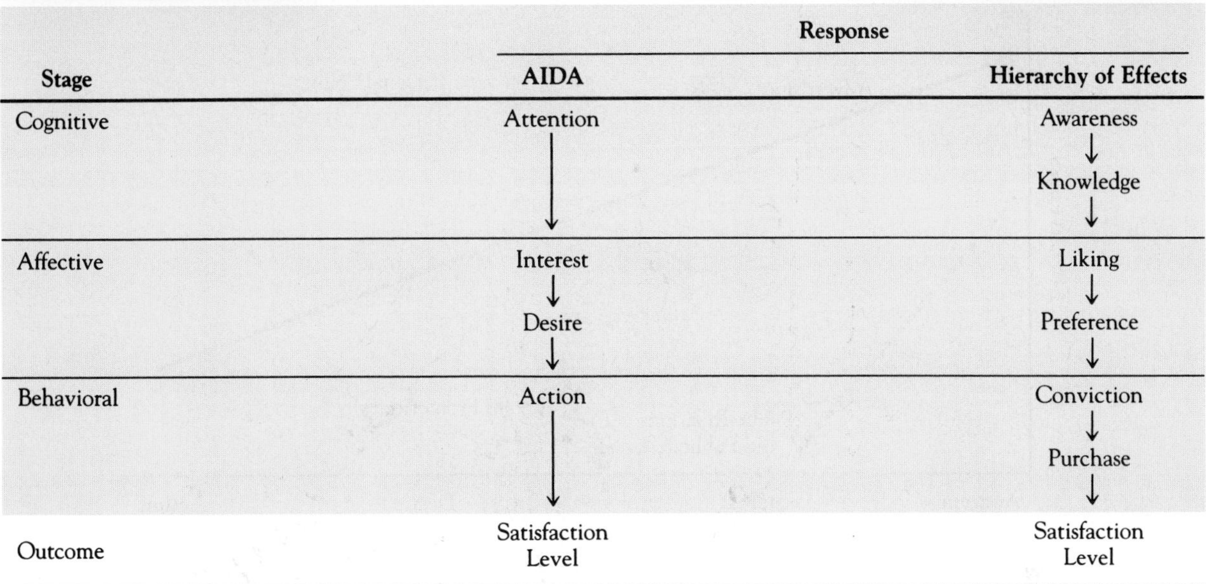

Table 15–5 Relationship of Response Models

Stage	Response: AIDA	Response: Hierarchy of Effects
Cognitive	Attention ↓	Awareness ↓ Knowledge ↓
Affective	Interest ↓ Desire ↓	Liking ↓ Preference ↓
Behavioral	Action ↓	Conviction ↓ Purchase ↓
Outcome	Satisfaction Level	Satisfaction Level

many similar products exist. These second thoughts are dissonance. What follows in the hierarchy after the purchase is that consumers make their attitudes consistent with the purchase, thereby reducing the dissonance. This, of course, presumes that the purchase was not an obvious mistake.

The dissonance hierarchy holds when the buyer is highly involved with the product or the purchase process and when little product differentiation exists. Personal selling, or nonmarketing sources of information, are usually high, and the product is often in the early phases of maturity. A businessperson in charge of buying one of hundreds of essentially similar word-processing machines may make a quick decision because the task of assembling and processing information on all machines is just too overwhelming. The businessperson, in this situation, makes the decision and then gathers information to make the attitude consistent with the actual purchase. This may involve just noting ads or reading the accompanying brochure.

Promotional Tools and Consumer Response

The different promotional tools generally have different impacts on the various levels of the hierarchy. Figure 15–5 shows the relationship between the four AIDA stages and various promotional tools. Note that while advertising has its greatest impact on creating attention or awareness and developing interest, it is generally much less effective at inducing action. Personal selling shows just the opposite pattern. Sales promotion is best at stimulating action. Finally, publicity is limited to creating awareness and generating a low level of interest.

Elements of Good Promotional Objectives

Just what constitutes a good promotional objective? Certain characteristics are a must:[4] a designated target market, a statement of exactly what is to be accomplished, a goal stated in quantitative terms, and a designated time period. Consider the

Figure 15–5 The Impact of Promotional Tools on Consumer Response

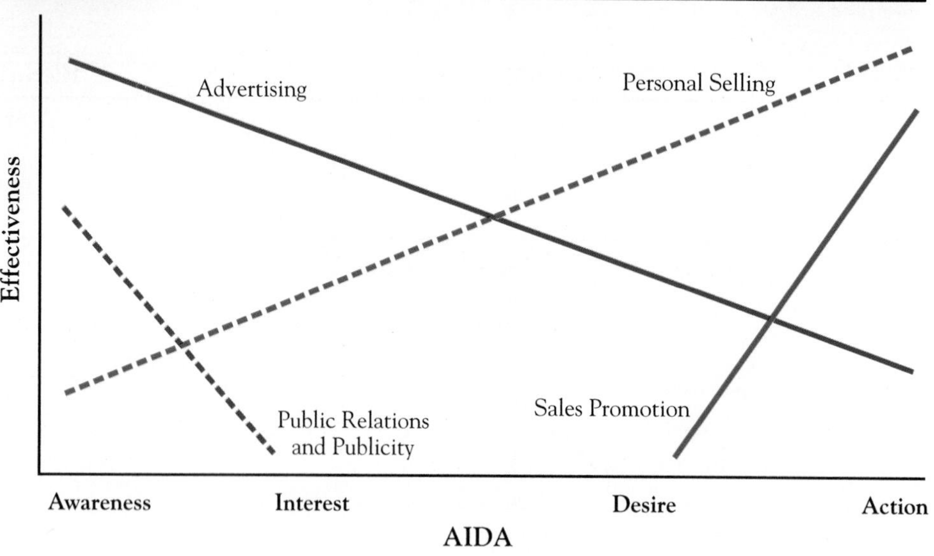

following hypothetical examples of good and bad objective statements. The bad ones are deficient in one or more of the above criteria.

Good	*Bad*
1. To increase sales of Apple Macintosh II computers by 25 percent to males 40 to 50 years old within the next year.	1. To increase sales of Apple Macintosh II computers.
2. To reach 90-percent awareness levels for Kodak 35mm cameras among women 18 to 35 in the next six months.	2. To create high levels of brand awareness for Kodak 35mm cameras.

The bad objective statements are unmeasurable. One can never be sure whether the objectives have been reached or not. Consider the second objectives statement, for example. What is high awareness? Who do I ask about their level of awareness? When do I interview them? Objectives must be clearly stated so that promotional activity can be evaluated. It is also important that objectives be attainable—that is, realistic.

Unfortunately, the criteria used to judge campaign success are often different in practice from the original objectives. For example, the objective for a Welch's grape juice campaign was "to convince parents that the product was the best drink for children because of its nutritious value and good taste." Although increased knowledge and conviction were the objectives, success was measured in terms of sales; there were no measurements of knowledge and conviction. If sales were the true objective, then the objective should have been so stated; otherwise, the sales criterion is an invalid measure of the worth of the campaign. Unfortunately, many business campaigns are evaluated in terms unrelated to campaign objectives.

Objectives designed for each promotional element should be complementary. Marketers expect them to combine with other marketing mix activities to reach overall marketing objectives. It is important that the role of each promotional tool be well thought out and that each be assigned a well-stated objective. Once objectives are in place, marketers can turn their attention to determining how much money needs to be spent to attain them—the costs of promotion.

Review Your Marketing Knowledge

• For each component of promotion used by Black & Decker as described in the marketing profile in this chapter, describe the source, the encoding, media, receiver, decoding, and feedback.

• In the promotional activity for your job search, describe your objective related to each level of the hierarchy of effects.

• Write out a good objective for the advertising for a play being performed at the theater guild at your school.

Understanding Promotion Costs

Figure 15–6 shows an estimate of promotion expenses as a percent of sales in several industries. These figures, which come from an examination of government studies, are just averages, but it is clear that there is great variation in promotional spending across industries. It is equally true that variation in expenditure levels among firms within an industry also exists. Why is it, then, that such differences exist? Why do the pharmaceutical, breakfast cereal, and office equipment industries spend, on average, over 20 percent of sales on promotion, while producers of canned food, paper, textiles, and primary metals spend less than 10 percent? The following factors contribute to these differences:

1. channel involvement in promotion;
2. overall strategy;
3. number and accessibility of customers;
4. complexity of decision-making units;
5. standardization of products and customer needs;
6. customer recognition of product benefits;
7. frequency and timing of purchases; and
8. product line turnover.

Channel Involvement in Promotion

Promotion costs at a given level of the distribution channel depend somewhat on the promotional activities undertaken at other levels of the channel. The more a manufacturer can get intermediaries to carry the promotional load, the lower that manufacturer's promotional costs will be. For example, the paper industry has historically had greater promotional support from the channel than the industrial machinery or office equipment industries have had. This helps explain some of the expenditure differences we see in Figure 15–6.

Figure 15–6 Average Promotional Expenditures for Selected Industries

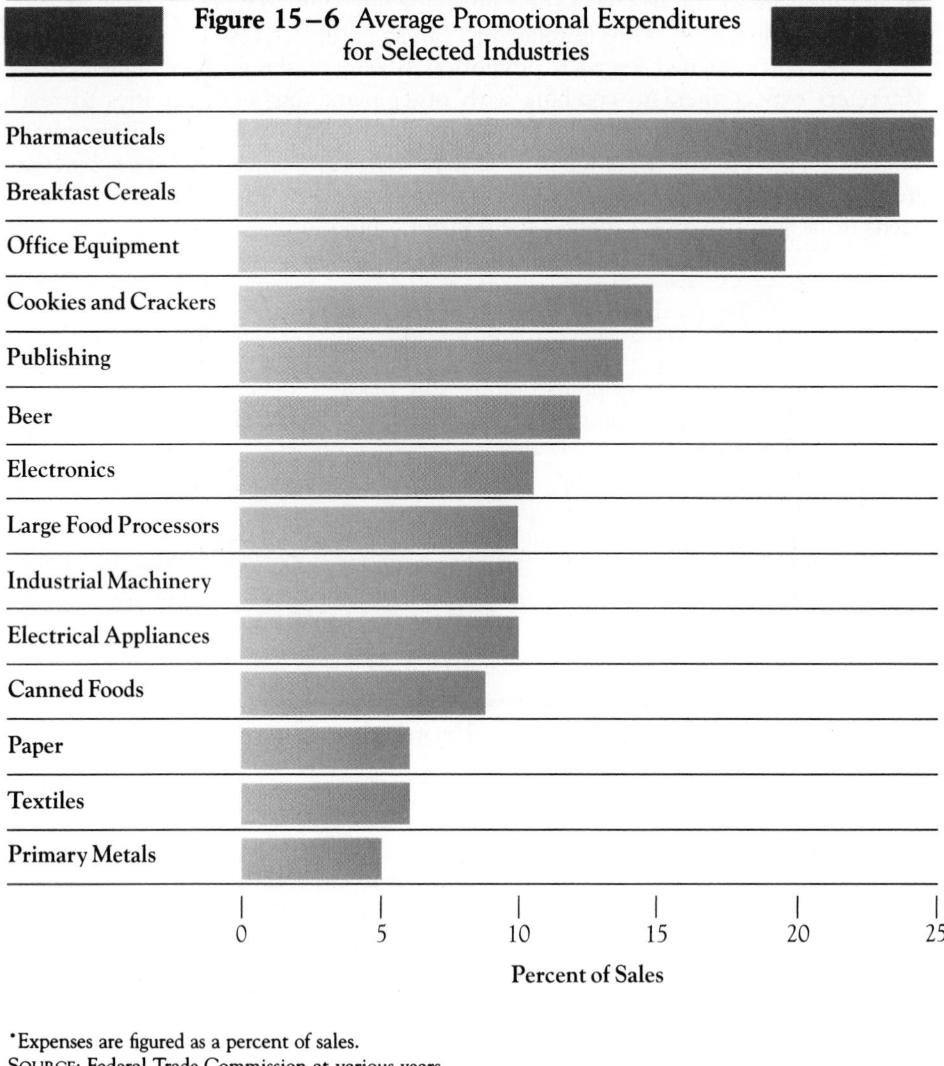

*Expenses are figured as a percent of sales.
SOURCE: Federal Trade Commission at various years.

Overall Strategy

Other elements of a firm's marketing strategy can affect promotional activity. Some product and pricing decisions require more promotional support than others. For example, firms or industries with great emphasis on product innovation (pharmaceuticals and office equipment) need more promotional support than those less active in innovation (textiles and primary metals). Similarly, a pricing strategy that leads to constantly changing prices requires more promotional effort than a stable pricing strategy.

Number and Accessibility of Customers

The fewer the number of potential customers and the easier the access to them, the less promotional costs will be. Primary metals and textiles are two examples of industries with a small number of very accessible customers. On the other hand, breakfast cereal customers are measured in the millions and are difficult to reach.

SAND
On the beach. In the hourglass. One of the most abundant materials on the face of the earth. Yet in its simplicity, an almost unlimited potential that stretches from fine art to state-of-the-art technology.
SILICONE
Sand, transformed. And its potential, realized. Silicones, in various forms, demonstrate unique abilities. To lubricate. To seal. To protect. To do much more.
BEAUTY
In the pursuit of beauty, silicones – and in turn, Dow Corning – play a vital role. From cosmetics that adorn the face to treatments that soften fabrics.
Recently, Dow Corning worked with a leading manufacturer of hair care products to develop a unique hair conditioner that changes its conditioning performance in accordance with the needs of the hair.
In such partnerships, silicones have a multitude of beautiful possibilities. As many as there are grains of . . . sand.
DOW CORNING
Dow Corning Corporation
Dept. A-8016
Midland, MI 48686-0994
Original sand painting by John Kleber

High promotional activity and effective advertising can help consumers understand a chemical company's product line.

Complexity of Decision-Making Units

If a decision-making unit involved in a purchase decision is complex, the more complex and costly its promotion will be. For example, office equipment decisions are made by a combination of purchasing agents, office managers, office personnel, and even senior-level executives. In contrast, primary metals and paper would probably be purchased solely by a purchasing agent. The task of promoting office equipment is, thus, much more complex than it is for primary metals, and we would expect the promotional expenditures to be higher.

Standardization of Products and Customer Needs

The more a product is standardized within an industry, and the more customers and their needs are similar, the less promotional activity there will be. Commodity products such as primary metals, textiles, and paper are examples. Highly differentiated products with multiple uses, such as pharmaceuticals and office equipment, need much higher promotional support than commodity items.

Customer Recognition of Product Benefits

When a product is well known and understood by customers, the need to promote it diminishes. Since users of steel and aluminum (automobile and airplane industries, for example) are well aware of their benefits, little promotion is required. On the other hand, the pharmaceutical industry's product line is not well understood by customers because of its rapidly changing nature. Consequently, there is a greater need for high promotional activity in pharmaceuticals.

Table 15–6 Factors Affecting Promotional Expenses

Factor	Increased Spending	Decreased Spending
Channel involvement in promotion	Low channel support	High channel support
Overall strategy change	Other marketing mix activities change	Other marketing mix activities change little
Number and accessibility of customers	Many, hard-to-reach customers	Few, easy-to-reach customers
Complexity of decision-making units	More complex	Less complex
Standardization of products and customer needs	Differentiated product and nonhomogeneous customer needs	Highly standardized product and very homogeneous customer needs
Customer recognition of product benefits	Not well known or recognized	Well known and recognized
Frequency and timing of purchase	Purchased often and in small quantities	Purchased infrequently and in large quantities
Product line turnover	High level of turnover	Low level of turnover

Frequency and Timing of Purchases

When products are purchased frequently and in relatively small quantities, the product must be promoted almost continuously. The chance for competitors to take customers away is always there. This is one of the main reasons that promotional activities are higher in the consumer package-goods business (breakfast cereal) than in industrial or institutional markets (industrial machinery).

Product Line Turnover

The more a product line changes, the greater the need for promotional activity. Annual model changes in the automobile and appliance industries are prime examples. These changes require promotion just to inform customers of their existence. Other examples of industries with high product line turnover include pharmaceutical, office equipment, publishing, apparel, and movies.

Thus we can see that setting a level of promotional spending is complex, involving trade-offs among many factors (summarized in Table 15–6). These trade-offs and specific budgeting techniques are discussed in the next section.

Establishing the Promotional Budget

The factors discussed in the previous section help explain the different levels of promotional spending across industries. However, we still need to deal with the question of setting a specific dollar budget for a company, or even a brand within the company. How much money should we spend on all promotional activity this year?

The Theoretical Budget

The answer to the budget question is very easy in theory but very difficult in practice. The theory approach, using *marginal analysis,* does help us understand what it is we are attempting to do when we set a budget.

Figure 15–7 Short-Run Determination of Promotional Budget by Marginal Analysis

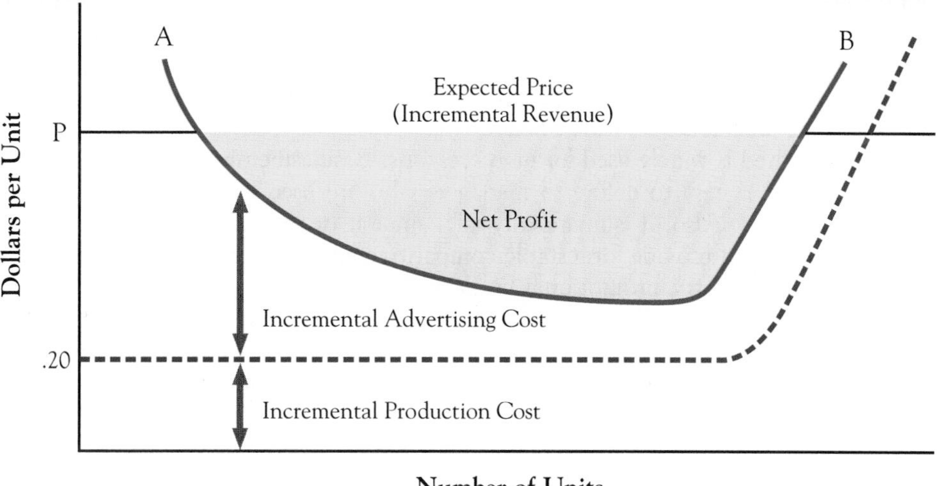

Figure 15–7 illustrates the theoretical approach. The horizontal axis is the number of units produced, while the vertical axis represents the dollars allocated to promotion. Price is presumed to remain constant over the possible range of production; this is realistic, since price seldom changes during a short-run planning period. Also, per-unit production costs are assumed to be constant at $.20 over the relevant range of production but rise rapidly when certain capacity limits are reached. The line *AB* represents the promotional costs per unit. Promotional expenditures are usually substantial, no matter what sales volume is. Thus, at a very low sales volume we find the cost of promotion exceeding price (*AB* is above *P*). However, as sales prospects are won over, the promotion per unit drops rapidly. At some later point, the response to promotion diminishes as few additional prospective buyers are being motivated to buy, and cost per incremental sale rises. At what point, then, should we stop spending on promotion? Notice that net profit is represented in Figure 15–7 by the shaded area. Profits result when promotion costs per unit are below the price per unit. Thus profit continues to be earned until the promotional-cost line *AB* exceeds the price per unit. In general, *a firm should spend on promotion until the cost of acquiring new business (the marginal sale) equals the sales revenue per unit (the marginal revenue).*

The main problem with this theoretical approach is that it is extremely difficult in practice to determine the promotion response per unit sold. Just what does line *AB* look like for Tide detergent, American Express Travelers Checks, or DuPont Silverstone? Anyone reading this book who can do this with any accuracy will get rich quickly as a consultant. The theoretical approach does focus our attention on profitability as the key criterion for budget setting, and it does serve as a standard against which to judge other procedures that are used to determine promotional budgets. These procedures are percentage-of-sales, competitive parity, "all you can afford," return on investment, and objective and task. As we discuss them, we will judge them against their capacities to approximate marginal analysis.

Percentage-of-Sales Approach

One of the most common promotional budgeting approaches is to use percentage of sales. The budget is determined by applying a fixed percentage to either past or forecasted sales. A common variation is to allocate a fixed dollar amount per unit for promotion and then multiply this by the sales forecast to obtain the budget. The proportion of sales allocated to promotion may be based upon past results or on management judgments about the future.

This method is widely used for many reasons. Besides being simple to calculate, it is exact and is easy to define to managers who are used to thinking of costs in percentage terms. Also, it is financially safe, since it ties expenditures to sales revenue. Finally, it can provide for a stable competitive environment. If it is widely used throughout an industry, promotional levels will be proportionate to market shares.

The major problem with the percentage-of-sales approach is its inherent fallacy to *view promotion as a result rather than a cause of sales.* This even holds when one uses forecast sales: How can one forecast sales without knowing the level of promotional spending? In addition, spending by competing firms may change or other environmental influences may shift, making old percentage-of-sales levels irrelevant to current realities. But this method can legitimately be used as a starting point for budgeting and can offer good direction in a very stable competitive environment.

Competitive Parity Approach

In the competitive parity approach to promotional budgeting, firms may adopt the average ratio of promotion costs to sales for their industry (Figure 15–6 gives examples of average promotion-to-sales ratios for selected industries); adopt the average ratio of promotion costs to sales for an important individual direct competitor; or spend the same absolute dollar amount as the competitor.

This approach adds the consideration of spending levels of competing firms to the budget-setting process and has many major shortcomings. It assumes that competitors know how to expend promotional dollars properly and that they are in the same position this firm is, have the same objectives, and compete with the same promotional game plan. Avon, competing heavily with personal selling, and Revlon, competing heavily with advertising, clearly would gain little by setting budgets in this way. Neither would a cosmetics competitor who used an industry average calculated from such diverse spending levels. Further, the only competitive promotional data are past data. They may not reflect the future promotional behavior of competitors very well. What many firms do is anticipate competitors' future promotional expenditures and match them.

"All You Can Afford" Approach

Some firms do set promotional budgets on the basis of available funds. Here the company spends as much as it can afford without impairing financial liquidity, or it limits budgets because it wants a satisfactory profit in a given year. Thus, the budget adopted and the monies needed to accomplish the required marketing task may be totally unrelated. On the one hand, the firm could miss opportunities because of underspending, while on the other hand, it could easily spend too much.

Return On Investment Approach

Some people believe that promotion expenditures should be treated like any other long-term investment decision for a business. Using this approach, firms view promotional expenditures in terms of their ability to generate profits over many years. Promotional budgets compete for scarce resources with other possible investments. It thus encourages data-gathering to measure the impact of promotion and assures more objective decision making. The major defect of this approach is that management can usually do little more than guess at the likely future returns for promotional dollars. Also, managers are conditioned to think of promotional spending as an expense for a given year. Overcoming this mental set would be difficult; therefore, this method has received little, if any, managerial use.

Objective and Task Approach

None of the methods discussed so far is without major fault, and none closely approximates the theoretical standard. We believe the objective and task approach—or the *build-up* approach, as it is often called—has the most merit. This method requires that promotional objectives be stated well and that the expenditure necessary to reach these objectives be determined. Implementing such a method is somewhat more complex. Table 15–7 outlines the required steps and applies the method to the advertising component of promotion for Gallo Chablis Blanc wine. The complete promotional budget would include other items whose cost would be determined in a similar manner.

This method avoids arbitrary thinking and emphasizes research and sound management judgment. It also requires managers to explicitly define what they believe to be the relationship between the desired objective (sales, awareness) and expenditures. The major weakness of this method is the difficulty managers have in defining how much it will cost to attain the objective. Even with the best research, this remains a difficult task.

Having set the total promotional budget, we now need to know how this money should be divided among the available promotional methods. That way, we can determine the direction of our promotional activity.

Determining the Promotional Mix

Thus far, we have discussed promotional activity without deciding the relative emphasis that should be put on advertising, sales promotion, or personal selling—an important aspect of a firm's promotional strategy. The exact combination of promotional elements is called the *promotional mix* or *promotional blend.*

There is no one correct promotional mix for a company because all the promotional elements are, in a sense, substitutes for each other. For example, both Desenex foot powder and Sinutab sinus tablets attained dominant brand status in their product categories with heavy emphasis on personal selling over advertising (a push strategy). Managers for both these brands subsequently changed the emphasis to a pull strategy, with advertising dominating personal selling. Both brands improved their positions with this change. In all likelihood, they would have continued with great success under the old strategy. This does not mean that promotional mix decisions do not matter. In these circumstances, it happened that advertising and personal selling were good substitutes for each other.

Figure 15–8 shows the distribution of promotional dollars between personal selling and advertising/sales promotion in selected industries. The differences noted among these industries will be used to illustrate the factors—discussed in the following section—that guide the promotional mix decision.

Table 15–7 Steps in the Objective and Task Method

Step	Description	Example: A Budget for Gallo Chablis Blanc
1. Determine and set objective.	Completely analyze the situation and state specific objectives.	*Establish the market share goal.* Gallo wants 8 percent of the market—4 million of the 50 million wine drinkers.
2. Measure benchmark levels on variables in objective statement.	Determine, through research, the firm's current position with respect to the objective. This analysis is sometimes part of Step 1.	*Determine the percent of the market that should be reached by advertising.* Gallo intends to reach 40 million wine drinkers (80 percent) with its advertising.
3. Determine the relationship between expenditures and the stated objective.	This requires an extensive program of marketing research and good judgment.	*Determine the percent of aware wine drinkers that should be persuaded to try Chablis Blanc.* Gallo wants 25 percent of all wine drinkers to try Chablis Blanc. This is because it is estimated that 40 percent of the *triers,* or 4 million people, will become loyal users. 4 million people is the market goal.
4. Set a specific program to reach the objective; determine the cost.	Using the results from Step 3, set up the program. The budget, then, is the cost of the required program.	*Determine the number of advertising impressions per 1 percent trial rate.* Gallo estimates that 40 advertising exposures for every percent of the population will bring a 25 percent trial rate. *Determine the number of gross rating points that have to be purchased.* A gross rating point is one exposure to 1 percent of the target population. Since Gallo wants to achieve 40 exposures to 80 percent of the target population defined as wine drinkers, it will buy 3200 gross rating points (40 × 80 percent = 3200). *Determine the necessary advertising budget on the basis of the average cost of buying a gross rating point.* To expose 1 percent of the target population to one exposure costs about \$3277. 3200 gross rating points will cost \$3277 × 3200 = \$10,486,400. This is the budget for Year One.
5. Execute program.	Implement the program devised in Step 4.	
6. Evaluate the program.	Undertake research to determine if the objective was met.	

Theoretical Optimum Mix

There is a theoretically optimal way to divide promotional dollars among the available elements. Simply put, one should spend any given dollar on the promotional element that has the highest *marginal* impact on the objective being sought. Every available dollar should thus be evaluated in terms of the marginal return available from each promotional element. The mix would be optimal when the budget is totally used up in such a way that the *last dollar spent on each promotional element generates the same return.*

For example, consider the breakfast cereal industry in Figure 15–8. For the first dollar of the promotional budget in this industry, the returns to advertising/sales promotion are much higher than personal selling. However, as more and more money is spent on advertising/sales promotion, the *marginal results* eventually diminish—

Figure 15–8 A Distribution of the Promotional Budget for Selected Industries

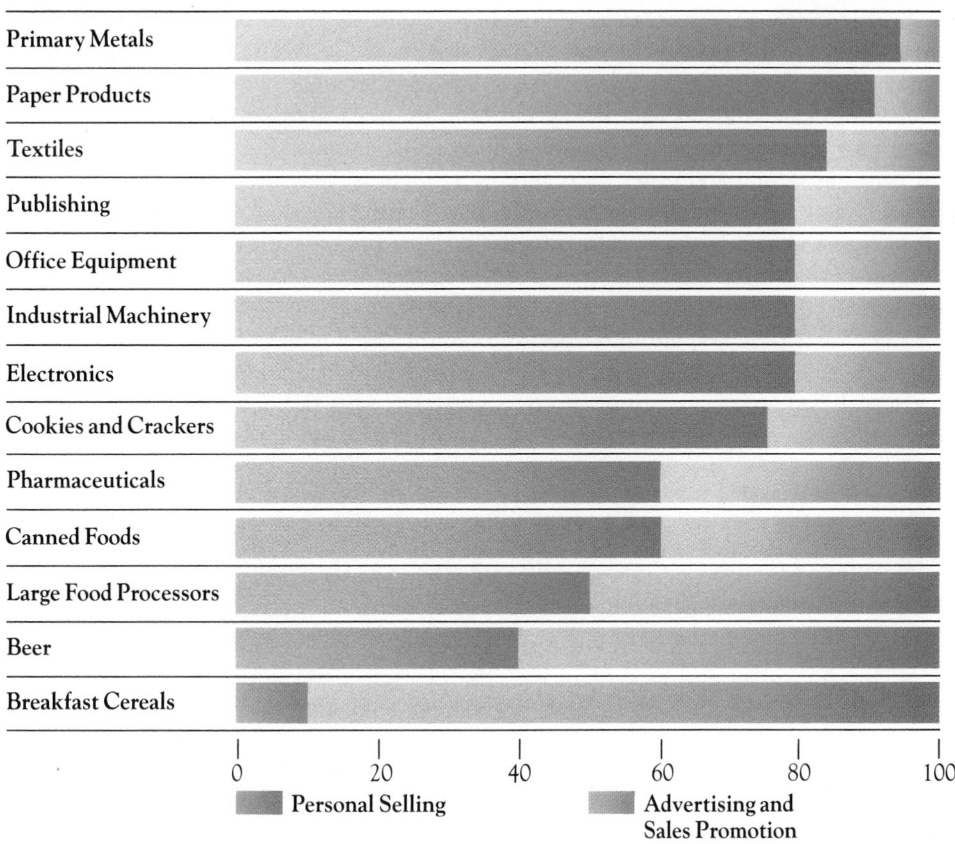

SOURCE: Federal Trade Commission at various years.

new prospects become harder to motivate. At some point, they diminish so far that they fall below the marginal returns to personal selling, justifying spending money on personal selling. The returns associated with spending money on personal selling diminish much faster in the breakfast cereal industry than those for advertising/sales promotion. Thus, the marginal impact of personal selling falls below that of advertising/sales promotion at a much lower dollar level. This process continues until the budget is used up. The marginal return patterns in the primary metals industry are, of course, just the opposite of the breakfast cereal industry (see Figure 15–8). Here the marginal impact of personal selling diminishes much more slowly.

These response functions required by the theoretical approach are, of course, difficult to measure in marketing practice. However, a number of factors can guide the marketer in the direction of the optimal mix, including:

1. the resources available,
2. characteristics of the product,
3. characteristics of the target audience,
4. stage of the product life-cycle, and
5. company policy.

Resources Available

The amount of money available to an organization has a direct impact on promotional mix decisions. Small companies with small budgets, or even small brands in large companies with small budgets, are unable to afford the $150,000-plus that it costs for a thirty-second placement on "The Cosby Show" or "Dallas," or the $750,000-plus it costs for the Super Bowl. The dollar requirements of running an effective advertising campaign in almost any medium are not for those with small budgets, except for local spot ads or direct mail. The emphasis in such circumstances is usually on personal selling and other push activities, such as trade level deals. A company could hire and support three salespeople for a year for the cost of one thirty-second ad in prime-time television. The advertising may be a more efficient way to reach customers, but these marketers must turn to less efficient personal selling for lack of funds.

The next time you are in a drugstore, count the number of brands in the store that you have never seen advertised. The unadvertised brands are often "pushed" because these companies cannot afford to advertise. This also demonstrates the power of push, because all these brands sell enough to hold their shelf space.

Product Characteristics

The nature of the product itself contributes greatly to the promotional mix decision. Personal selling tends to dominate when the product:

- *has a high unit value.* In these circumstances, the consumer often needs intense persuasion to explain why the product justifies such a high price. Also, with such a high revenue per product sold, the cost of personal sales efforts can be carried. Business computers and capital equipment are typical examples; indeed, the IBM sales force is legendary as a key to IBM's sales success.
- *is technical in nature.* A highly technical product requires skilled sales personnel to explain it to customers. It is quite common for salespeople to have to explain the need for a new technical industrial good to purchasing agents, engineers, and senior executives.
- *requires demonstration.* When a product's feature "must be seen to be believed" and understood, the power of personal communication is needed. An office word-processing system or a home personal computer requires extensive personal selling efforts.
- *must be tailored to the specific needs of customer groups.* Here the marketer must make personal contact with the potential customer in order to understand his or her particular needs and explain how the product has been altered to satisfy these needs. Capital equipment systems such as computer controlled machines and investment analyst services are two areas where this factor is critical.
- *is purchased infrequently.* Here the product just cannot support a heavy advertising program relative to personal selling. Home appliances and major business purchases are examples.
- *involves the consideration of a trade-in for purchase.* The existence of a trade-in requires negotiation on the value of the old item.

The above characteristics match those of industrial products very well, but some of them do apply to certain consumer goods such as cars and appliances. This is not

Figure 15–9 The Enhancement by Advertising of Personal Selling Efforts

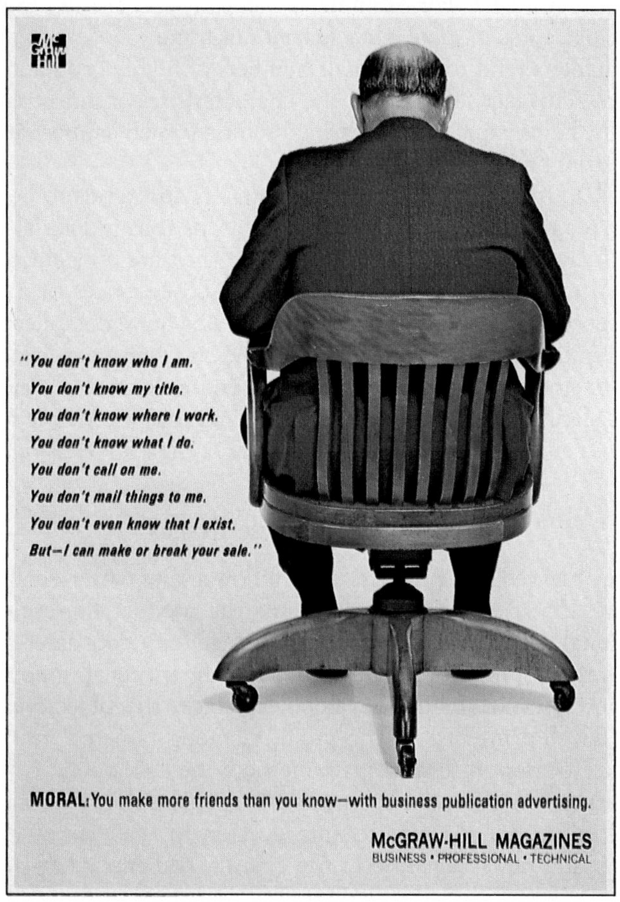

"You don't know who I am.
You don't know my title.
You don't know where I work.
You don't know what I do.
You don't call on me.
You don't mail things to me.
You don't even know that I exist.
But—I can make or break your sale."
MORAL: You make more friends than you know—with business publication advertising.
McGRAW-HILL MAGAZINES
BUSINESS • PROFESSIONAL • TECHNICAL

to say that for industrial products one need not advertise. Indeed, there is an important role for advertising in industrial marketing. Personal selling performance increases an average of 25 percent when supported by advertising. The advertising serves to open the door for the salesperson. Figure 15–9 presents an ad for McGraw-Hill Business Publications that reinforces this point.

Target Audience Characteristics

The *size* and *geographical dispersion* of the target audience has a direct impact on the promotional mix. If the target audience is large and widely distributed, then advertising is, by far, the most economical procedure to reach the audience. The cost of personal selling would be prohibitive. Most consumer products have large, widely distributed markets. This is why advertising is so dominant for companies like Procter & Gamble, General Foods, General Mills, McDonald's, and Coca-Cola, and even for some agencies of the government.

At the other extreme, markets with small numbers of highly geographically concentrated customers readily justify the cost of personal selling. Mass media methods here would lack the necessary target precision. Far too many people outside the target audience would be reached by mass appeals. This is not to say that advertising cannot be useful in these circumstances. The advertising would be very specifically targeted, using special interest media. For example, a company specializing in plant-cleaning equipment may place ads in *Plant Management* magazine.

Industrial markets tend to have small numbers of highly geographically concentrated customers. This fact, along with the characteristics of industrial products discussed previously, helps explain why personal selling is such a dominant promotional device for industrial products.

Promotional activity to wholesalers and retailers also tends to be dominated by personal selling for the same market-oriented reasons that industrial situations are. There are relatively few of these institutions and they are concentrated enough to warrant personal attention. Also, the economic consequences of a successful sale help justify the cost, and often the specific sale may be quite complicated. For example, a sale to a retailer may involve coupons to the end consumer, cents-off packages for the retailer to stock, and the use of a special end-aisle display. Personal selling is clearly needed. Managers at Procter & Gamble claim that the selling their sales force does to retailers is as important in their success as is their advertising.

Product Life-Cycle Stages

In Chapter 9 we observed that products often follow a sales pattern called the product life-cycle. Figure 15–10 graphically represents the product life-cycle, noting how typical promotional activity varies by life-cycle stage for a consumer good.

Note that both the promotional objectives and the specific promotional activities change over the life-cycle. In the development stage, the objectives are to create awareness and develop interest in the product among targeted innovators—those who are expected to adopt first. The main methods used are publicity and some well-directed advertising. Consider the compact laser digital disk player, a major advance in the playback of sound. Prior to its introduction to the market, virtually every major newspaper and news magazine in the country had carried an article about it. Also, long before it was nationally distributed, Pioneer was running ads in magazines that have high socio-economic groups as readers.

At the introductory stage, the main objective is to increase awareness of the product in general and, to a lesser extent, to publicize the specific brands. The emphasis is on stimulating primary demand. Ads are often informative. Other objectives include generating product trials among consumers and gaining distribution penetration. Advertising and publicity are used to stimulate primary demand. Sales promotion is used to generate product trial (coupons, free samples, and rebates); and trade deals and personal selling to dealers are used to gain access to distribution channels.

As the product matures, the main objective of promotion changes to developing brand preference. Here ads become more persuasive and less informative. Selective demand becomes key. Holding and continuing to gain distribution are also important objectives. Advertising to a greater mass market than before becomes more important. Sales promotion and personal selling are still needed, but they are less important.

At the maturity stage of the life-cycle, holding brand preference and distribution, plus the possible communication of new uses for the product, become dominant objectives. Advertising and dealer support programs are key promotional activities. Advertising reinforces brand choice (Hallmark's "when you care enough to send the very best"), and presents new uses (Grandparents' Day cards). Programs, such as special discounts, rebates, and displays, are designed to hold dealer support.

Figure 15–10 The Generalized Product Life-Cycle and Promotional Activities

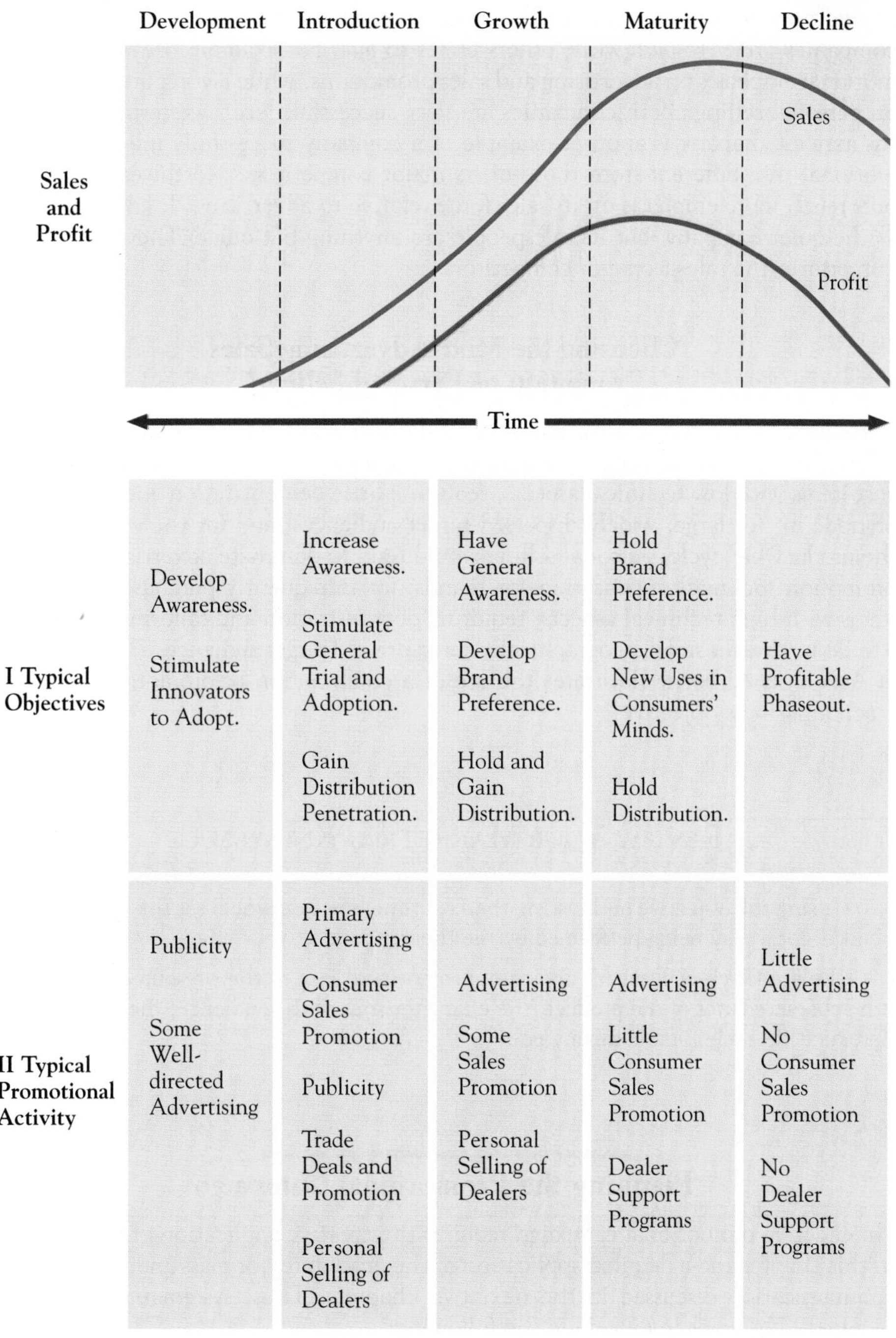

Development
Introduction
Growth
Maturity
Decline
Sales
Profit
Sales and Profit
Time
I Typical Objectives
Develop Awareness.
Stimulate Innovators to Adopt.
Increase Awareness.
Stimulate General Trial and Adoption.
Gain Distribution Penetration.
Have General Awareness.
Develop Brand Preference.
Hold and Gain Distribution.
Hold Brand Preference.
Develop New Uses in Consumers' Minds.
Hold Distribution.
Have Profitable Phaseout.
II Typical Promotional Activity
Publicity
Some Well-directed Advertising
Primary Advertising
Consumer Sales Promotion
Publicity
Trade Deals and Promotion
Personal Selling of Dealers
Advertising
Some Sales Promotion
Personal Selling of Dealers
Advertising
Little Consumer Sales Promotion
Dealer Support Programs
Little Advertising
No Consumer Sales Promotion
No Dealer Support Programs

In the decline stage, the objective is to phase out the product profitably. Thus, all promotional costs are reduced dramatically. Some advertising is targeted to still interested consumers to remind them that the product is still available.

Company Policy

Along with the previously discussed factors, management choice helps to explain differences in promotional mixes. In these circumstances, long-standing preferences or traditions for one promotional approach over another can come into play. Some companies prefer to *push* while others prefer to *pull.* For example, Revlon puts promotional emphasis on advertising and sales promotions, while Avon puts its emphasis on personal selling. Both companies are very successful. Northwestern Mutual Life Insurance Company is another example of a company successfully following a promotional mix different from those of its major competitors. Northwestern Mutual puts much more emphasis on its sales force relative to advertising. It advertises itself as the quiet company, but its salespeople are anything but quiet. They consistently outperform the salespeople of competitors.

Choosing the Mix: Advertising/Sales Promotion or Personal Selling?

In summary then, advertising and sales promotion would tend to dominate personal selling for organizations or brands with large resources; for frequently purchased, low-cost items with low technical aspects, requiring little demonstration and no tailoring or trade-in; for large, widely dispersed target audiences; and for the early stages of the product life-cycle. Personal selling would tend to dominate advertising and sales promotion for small organizations or brands; for infrequently purchased, high-cost items with high technical aspects, requiring demonstration and tailoring and having a trade-in; and for small, geographically concentrated target audiences. The *Marketing in Action* on Airborne illustrates the use of a combination of promotional tools to reach a business objective.

Review Your Marketing Knowledge

- Using the objective and task method, outline how you would set the promotional budget for a play being performed by the theater guild at your school.
- Relate Black & Decker's choice of promotional mix to their resources available, the characteristics of the product, the characteristics of the audience, the stage of the product life-cycle, and company policy.

Planning the Promotional Campaign

An effective promotional campaign requires the creative application of the concepts in this chapter and a detailed application of the procedures for mass and interpersonal communication discussed in the next two chapters. Thus, systematic planning is required. The steps involved are the following:

1. analyze the situation facing the organization or brand;
2. establish objectives;
3. determine the budget;

MARKETING IN ACTION

Airborne Uses a Combination of Promotional Techniques

With an aggressive advertising campaign, Federal Express grabbed a large share of the overnight air express service industry. Network buys were used to focus attention on the importance of overnight deliveries to corporations. Airborne Express has slowly been capturing market share from Federal Express with a marketing strategy that employs a different promotional mix of direct mail and personal sales.

Kent Freudenberger, executive vice president of sales and marketing for Airborne, said, "We are faced with the problem of having little or no awareness in the small package marketplace. By deploying a very aggressive direct sales force, we were able to capitalize on that network exposure among corporate accounts. However, we didn't appreciably penetrate the large market of infrequent users. We decided that putting that money behind our direct sales organizations was the best way to go."

To maintain larger corporate accounts, Airborne relies on personal sales. However, they turned to other forms of direct marketing to build clientele among small to medium-sized businesses. Through a network of direct salespeople, drivers, and other sources, Airborne has built a database of these smaller businesses.

Direct mail and telemarketing contacts follow the initial call. Businesses that do not send a package with Airborne within 45 days receive resolicitation packets encouraging them to try the company's service. "We have several channels of direct mail. If the customer uses us, we have an automatic program thanking the customer and offering one or two sales messages that our marketing specialists feel are pertinent to that type of customer," said Freudenberger. "The results of these efforts are demonstrated in the substantial growth of this area of our business."

The shift away from mass marketing to a more direct, business-to-business campaign has been a successful move for Airborne Express. They have used this strategy to capture an increasingly larger share of the corporate overnight air express market. This approach has led them to be the fastest growing company in the industry in each of the past five years.

SOURCE: Personal communication with Airborne Express, May 1989; Kurt Hoffman, "Shift Gets Airborne Out of Holding Pattern," *Advertising Age*, Direct Marketing Special Report, May 18, 1987, pp. S29–30.

4. manage the specific programs for selling or advertising;
5. measure effectiveness, evaluation, and follow-up.

The whole process is iterative and requires considerable skill from promotional managers and their staffs. The next two chapters discuss these issues in detail.

Personal Computer Exercise

Setting a promotional budget requires determining clear objectives. This PC exercise gives you an opportunity to experiment with different approaches to setting a promotional budget given an objective and your own assumptions.

KEY POINTS

• Effective marketing requires skillful communication among buyers and sellers. This communication is a key function of marketing activity. The marketing techniques used to communicate with potential customers are called promotion techniques.

• Advertising, sales promotion, publicity, and personal selling all play important roles in promoting products and services.

• The quality of the promotion decisions made by a firm strongly influence its success or failure.

• Two major theoretical models used to explain consumer response to promotional activity are AIDA and the hierarchy of effects.

• Good promotional objectives must include a designated target market; a statement of exactly what is to be accomplished; a goal stated in quantitative terms; and a designated time period.

• Promotional costs vary from industry to industry. The factors affecting costs are channel involvement in promotion; overall promotional strategy; number and accessibility of customers; complexity of decision-making units; standardization of products and customer needs; customer recognition of product benefits; frequency and timing of purchases; and product line turnover.

• Of the many approaches used to determine the promotional budget, the objective and task approach (sometimes called the build-up approach) is the most logical.

• The promotional mix is the exact combination of advertising, sales promotion, personal selling, and publicity used in a promotional strategy.

• The factors that guide marketing managers in establishing the optimal promotional mix include available resources (the firm's budget), product characteristics, target audience characteristics, the product's stage in the life-cycle, and company policy.

ISSUES FOR DISCUSSION

1. Why does so much miscommunication occur in advertising? In personal selling?

2. In what ways could a customer give feedback to a retail salesperson during the purchase decision process for a major appliance?

3. In what ways could a purchasing agent give feedback to a salesperson?

4. For a major purchase that you have recently made (stereo, television, renting an apartment, selection of a college), identify all the communications that you received which were related to the purchase. What role in the AIDA model did each communication play? How could a marketer possibly have better communicated with you?

5. Is sales an appropriate measure for promotional objectives?

6. Identify three products or services that you think would fit each of the three response hierarchies. Why do you think so?

7. Why do bar-soap marketers spend more of a sales dollar on promotion than do appliance marketers such as Westinghouse?

8. Using recent newspapers or magazines, identify an example of publicity for a product that was probably initiated by the marketer and one that was probably beyond the marketer's control.

9. Why is a specific budget for promotion so difficult to set in practice?

10. "To get effective push, one must also pull." Evaluate this statement.

11. What general mix of advertising/sales promotion and personal selling would you use for each of the following products? Assume you have a large budget. In each case, give reasons for your answer.

a. prescription drugs
b. minicomputers for business
c. candy bars
d. automobiles
e. universities

GLOSSARY

Advertising: any paid form of nonpersonal presentation and promotion of ideas, goods, or services by an identified sponsor.

AIDA: an acronym for a consumer response model to promotion: Attention, Interest, Desire, Action.

AIDAS: adds satisfaction outcome to AIDA.

Channels: the media used to transmit a communication.

Decoding: assigning meaning to a communication by the receiver.

Dissonance hierarchy: a response model in which purchase occurs only after awareness, and attitude change occurs after purchase.

Encoding: the symbolic representation of the ideas in a communication.

Hierarchy of effects: a consumer response model to promotion: awareness, knowledge, liking, preference, conviction, purchase.

Learning hierarchy: the standard hierarchy-of-effects response model.

Low-involvement hierarchy: a response hierarchy in which purchase occurs before liking, preference, and conviction.

Personal selling: oral presentation in a conversation with one or more prospective purchasers for the purpose of making sales.

Promotion: the communication mechanism of marketing designed to inform and to persuade consumers to respond.

Promotional mix: the combination of promotional techniques used in a campaign.

Promotional objectives: the marketer's promotional goals.

Publicity: nonpersonal stimulation of demand for a product, service, or business unit by generating commercially significant news about it in a print medium or obtaining favorable presentation of it in radio, television, or on stage. This form of promotion is not paid for by the sponsor.

Pull: promotional strategy that is primarily directed at the end consumer, such as advertising.

Push: promotional strategy, such as personal selling and trade deals, that is primarily directed at channel members.

Receiver: the person or persons who attend to a communication.

Sales promotion: those marketing activities—other than personal selling, advertising, and publicity—that stimulate consumer purchasing and dealer effectiveness such as displays, trade shows and exhibitions, demonstrations, coupons, contests, and other nonroutine selling efforts.

Source: the originator of a communication.

NOTES

1. Adapted from *Dictionary of Marketing Terms,* (American Marketing Association), 1988.

2. This section follows a more detailed discussion presented in James F. Engel, Martin R. Warshaw, and Thomas C. Kinnear, *Promotional Strategy: Managing the Marketing Communications Process,* 6th ed. (Irwin, 1987), pp. 42–45.

3. Engel, Warshaw, Kinnear, *Promotional Strategy,* p. 52.

4. This section follows Engel, Warshaw, and Kinnear, pp. 193–209.

AT&T, MCI, and Sprint

American Telephone and Telegraph, MCI Telecommunications Corp., and US Sprint Communications Co., the nation's three largest carriers for long distance telephone service, are turning their attention away from residential users to the highly profitable business segment. With the completion of the equal access period in most major cities, targeted promotions and ad campaigns are being used to attract new corporate clients.

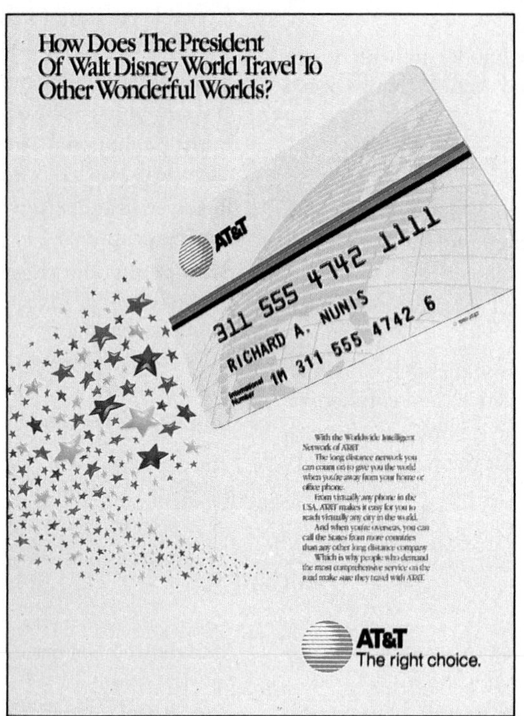

Most of the carriers' promotions are geared toward telecommunications procurement executives. Blair Pleasant, a consultant with the Yankee Group, which tracks the telecommunications industry, said "quality" is the only real attribute the carriers can promote now. "They've got to keep talking faster and better, and of course, cheaper," said Ms. Pleasant. "The average business customer doesn't really care what the technology behind it is. They want to see that their transfer of data is moving quicker and that the sound quality is better."

US Sprint gained 2 million customers with its "Charter Customer" 10 percent discount promotion, for residential and business customers, which ran for over three months. Edward Carter, senior vice president of sales and marketing for Sprint, said, "The influx of business customers we got through that promotion has brought us into many places we would never have gotten into before. Sales keep going up because of referrals and exposure and the confident attitude of our sales force."

Sprint and MCI are involved in a "me-too" contest, with each firm trying to top the other in volume discounts, free installations, and sporting events sponsorships that increase their visibility in the corporate community. AT&T sponsors events such as the annual golf tournament at Pebble Beach, California. Charles Mitchell, business advertising and promotion director for AT&T's Business Marketing Group, said these types of sponsorships are "big with business" and make business "interested in what we have to say when we advertise during the events." Roy Gamse, MCI vice president of marketing said, "You have a great deal of high-level executives who are avid watchers of these things."

Sprint uses direct mail to target managers. "We know who lives behind the door," said Mr. Carter, "and often these are the ones who can say to their firm's telecommunications managers, 'Hey, I've got Sprint. Ever thought about them before?'"

AT&T's "Partners" program incorporates a monthly newsletter sent to businesses with direct response reply devices that allow companies to receive free information on new and upcoming telecommunications features and provide their opinions. Mr. Mitchell said, "The 'Partners' plan is more than just advertising. It is a resource center for any business problem that can be helped through technology."

With the increased competition among the three major carriers, promotions will help gain new customers. MCI's Mr. Gamse noted, "We will try many attractive incentives, and we will change them often. Promotions will help close the deal."

SOURCE: Richard Laermer, "Carriers Vie for Corporate Segment's Numbers," *Advertising Age*, Special Report—Sales Promotion, March 23, 1987, pp. S11–13.

Questions

1. What role do advertising, sales promotion, and personal selling play in the promotional strategies of AT&T, MCI, and Sprint?

2. What objectives would be reasonable for each of these promotional techniques?

3. If these competitors were targeting residential customers, how would the promotional mix change? What role would each type of promotional technique play in these circumstances?

4. Some have argued that these competitors are over-using sales promotions with potential negative impact on consumer loyalty and profits. Comment.

CASE APPLICATION 15–2

Barksdale Controls is a Los Angeles-based division of Imo Industries, Inc. Its product line consists of many types of pressure transducers/transmitters, electromechanical pressure and temperature switches, solid-state pressure and temperature switches, as well as directional control valves. It markets its products primarily to original equipment manufacturers (OEMs), for use in these companies' products. The USER community is serviced largely through independent distributors. Within this market, Barksdale offers products for eighty-one major OEMs and sixty-six major users' market segments. The range of customers is from manufacturers of medical equipment to manufacturers of trash compactors. Barksdale shares a sales force with Imo Industries, Inc. It makes sense to do so as the products from several Divisions of the parent firm complement each other and are sold to the same customers. However, Barksdale then must strive to maintain a separate image and reputation for its products. To do this Barksdale utilizes a broad range of promotional activities.

Barksdale Controls

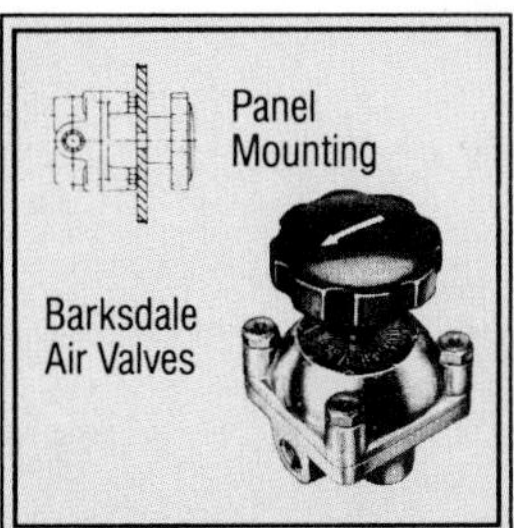

Avoid accidental actuation while saving panel space with Barksdale's easy-grip knob. A pointer indicates flow position, while spring detents hold the valve in center, or 45° right/left positions. Available in 4-way and manipulator flow patterns, ¼," ⅜" and ½" npt port sizes, and 0 to 350 psi air or oil service. Four threaded holes are provided in the valve body for secure panel mounting. Metal-to-metal seals lap themselves with each valve operation, assuring years of leak-proof, maintenance-free actuation. The seals need no lubrication. Prices are low because of our high production tooling. For more information, contact Imo Delaval Inc., Barksdale Controls Division, 3211 Fruitland Ave., Los Angeles, CA 90058, (213) 589-6181.

Barksdale

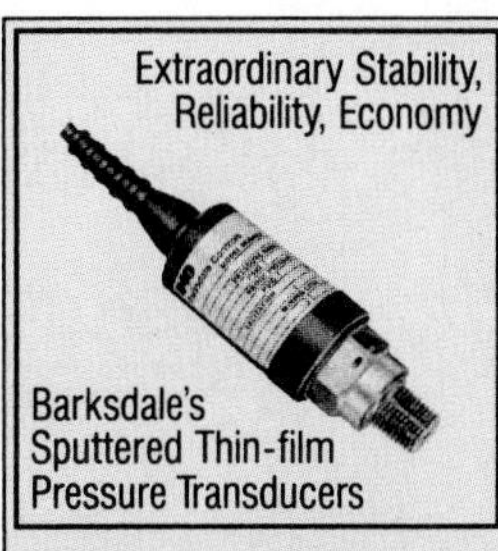

Extraordinary Stability,
Reliability, Economy
Barksdale's
Sputtered Thin-film
Pressure Transducers

We wrote the book on stability with this new line of transducers, experiencing less than 0.1% zero drift after 18 months. Stress isolated sensors and all stainless steel wetted parts allow our sputtered thin-film transducers to operate over a range from 15 to 6,000 psi at temperature extremes of −65°F to +250°F with a static error band of 0.2% to 0.25%. Designed and manufactured to the most exacting standards, they are ideally suited to a broad range of industrial applications: hydraulic systems, machine tools, process monitoring and control, test stands, depth and level measurement. Submersible and 4-20 mA models are also available. For more information on these products, built on 25 years experience in high performance transducers, contact Imo Industries Inc., Barksdale Controls Division, 3211 Fruitland Avenue, Los Angeles, CA 90058, (213) 589-6181.

Barksdale

Advertising efforts are mostly educational, designed to inform the target customers that Barksdale's key feature is quality. The target of these advertisements is the product design engineer. The objective is to have Barksdale be the name most often thought of for the application being designed. The total advertising budget is in the area of $500,000. About $300,000 of this is for media space, with the balance for direct-mail and trade shows and collateral material.

The media schedule consists of fifteen publications serving the OEM and USER market, in general, and design engineers, in particular magazines such as *Machine Design, Design News,* and *Instruments and Control Systems.* While Barksdale's products are used as components in many end markets, there is no advertising aimed at creating preferences for Barksdale components in the products these consumers buy. The target is strictly the design engineer in the OEM company and not the buyer in the user company. All advertising is designed to invite inquiries after the designer has been educated. A so-called "bingo card" is always present in the magazine so that a reader can ask for more information from the advertiser by mailing the card to the designated address. The card is screened to identify the specific market segment from which it emanates. Then the field sales application engineer follows up to better determine the needs of the respondent.

Direct mail is a second advertising procedure used. It is used as a highly targeted supplement to the broad-based space advertising program.

Piece design covers both specific products and catalog offers, and offers services for technical and applications "freebees" on a scheduled basis. The yield from the direct mail program, as well as selected SIC responses from the space ad program, feeds the Division's telemarketing effort. Telemarketing objectives are to pre-qualify responses prior to delivery to the Field Sales organization for follow up.

Trade show participation by Barksdale is limited to a few key events and is directed largely at introduction of new products. Support is provided for Distributors of Barksdale products at some local exhibits such as those run by the Sensors Expo., Design Show, Fluid Power Shows, and Instrument Society of America.

SOURCE: George deLucenay Leon, *Marketing and Media Decisions,* Business-to-Business Special 1984, pp. 80–82. Personal communication with Barksdale Controls, July 1989.

Questions

1. What objectives should Barksdale set for each of the components of its promotional mix?

2. It has been recommended that Barksdale make more extensive use of magazines targeted to the end users of the OEM's products. Evaluate this proposal.

3. What role does each component of Barksdale's promotional mix play in relation to moving a prospective new customer through the hierarchy of effects?

4. How do the factors that decide what percentage of sales that a company should spend on promotion affect Barksdale?

16

Advertising, Sales Promotion, and Publicity

Learning Objectives

Upon completing this chapter, you will be able to do the following:

UNDERSTAND
the role of advertising for the individual organization and for the economy.

IDENTIFY
the major American advertisers and advertising agencies.

DESCRIBE
how creative and media choices are made.

DISCUSS
how advertising effectiveness is measured.

ILLUSTRATE
each of the different types of sales promotion techniques and define their role in promotion.

EXPLAIN
the nature and role of publicity in the promotional mix.

MARKETING PROFILE

Hanes vs. Fruit of the Loom

With Jockey International's men's underwear campaign featuring Jim Palmer and Calvin Klein's controversial advertising campaign generating lots of consumer attention, manufacturers of men's underwear began to recognize that they were not dealing with a commodity product. Although designer brands have not achieved a large portion of market share even among status seekers, manufacturers have realized that a more fashionable product means increased sales. The two largest firms in the industry, Fruit of the Loom and Hanes, are fiercely competing to increase sales with more fashionable products. Strong advertising campaigns are key to each firm's success in this $1.4 billion industry.

Hanes, the second largest firm in the industry with a 23 percent market share, began the fight in July of 1987 with an advertising campaign featuring its spokeswoman, Inspector 12, and copy proclaiming Hanes' better fit and lower shrinkage rate. Fruit of the Loom responded quickly in order to defend its 35 percent market share, going as far as suing Hanes to stop the ads as well as introducing its own product superiority campaign. An out of court settlement resulted in the cancellation of both firms' TV spots.

Fruit of the Loom is trying to diversify into other types of apparel while maintaining a strong base in underwear. A $25 million campaign is being run with the theme "We Fit America," demonstrating Fruit of the Loom's plans for expansion. Banking on its strong name recognition, the company plans to be a force in socks, activewear, women's panties, and men's fashion briefs.

These diversification plans have been put on the back burner because of Hanes' attempt to gain market share. Hanes has changed its distribution system, loosening ties with department stores and developing business with discount chains such as Wal-Mart. Aggressive price promotions have also been employed. A new advertising approach was developed stressing quality and backed by a $15 million budget. "There is a huge opportunity in this market. We know we have a superior product, and we have the marketing savvy, too," said John Ceneviva, director of marketing at Hanes. The media plan included more sports buys, such as the Super Bowl, to target male purchasers. The print schedule was broadened to include *Sports Illustrated, People,* and *Life.* With this new campaign, Hanes' market share increased from 18 percent in 1986 to 23 percent in 1988.

Hanes and Fruit of the Loom both copy the products of the trendsetters in the industry and then use their huge distribution networks to keep challengers such as Jockey or Calvin Klein from gaining share points. Jockey has increased its advertising budget by 10 percent to over $5 million in order to stay in the fight. Store brands such as Sears and J.C. Penney have been hard hit by the battle between the big two. Kmart even got out of the business. Trade and consumer deals are also extensively used by all brands.

Fruit of the Loom's premium BVD brand has increased its advertising budget by 22 percent to $4.5 million to increase its share of the upper end of the market. A new advertising campaign has been developed and is planned to run on cable networks such as ESPN. Sean Driscoll, group senior vice president at Warwick Advertising, BVD's agency, said, "Our strategy is to communicate quality and steal business from other premium brands."

Both Hanes and Fruit of the Loom are in the battle for market share for the duration. "We have gotten more aggressive because we want to shake up the market and be the leader," said Hanes' Ceneviva. Fruit of the Loom has responded to Hanes' challenge quickly and aggressively. Men's underwear certainly can't be classified as a commodity product any longer.

The conclusion that can be drawn from the marketing profile is that great care must be taken with advertising and sales promotion decisions because of the financial commitment and complexity of this area. Imagine yourself being responsible for a $25 million advertising and sales promotion budget—quite an exciting and challenging prospect! This chapter will explore these exciting aspects.

SOURCE: Rebecca Fanin, "Underwear—Inspector 12 Takes on the Fruits", *Marketing and Media Decisions,* April 1988, pp. 55–60.

This chapter focuses on those promotional activities directed at a mass audience: advertising, sales promotion, and publicity. It will explore ways that marketers make decisions about the size of the budget and about the creative content of ads by looking at: the role of advertising in the organization and in the economy; some of the significant advertisers and advertising agencies; the creative presentation in ads; media selection; the ways of measuring advertising effectiveness; and sales promotion and publicity.

Advertising

Advertising is the most visible marketing activity and is often thought of as synonymous with marketing. To readers of this book, it should now be clear that it is but one of marketing's many facets, although it plays a significant role in many organizations and in the economy as a whole. Advertising is *any paid form of nonpersonal presentation and promotion of ideas, goods, or services by an identified sponsor.*

Expenditure Levels

In 1987 the total volume of American advertising was $109.65 billion; it was $118.8 billion in 1988 and $127.7 billion in 1989.[1] Table 16–1 gives the dollar amounts that were spent in the available mass media. Newspapers have the highest percentage

Table 16–1 Advertising Expenditures: 1988

Medium	Dollars (in millions)	Medium	Dollars (in millions)
Newspapers		Direct Mail	21,115
Total	$ 31,197	Business Publications	2,610
National	3,586	Outdoor	
Local	27,611	Total	1,064
Magazines		National	628
Total	6,072	Local	436
Weeklies	2,646	Yellow Pages	
Women's	1,504	Total	7,781
Monthlies	1,922	National	944
Farm Publications	196	Local	6,837
Television		Miscellaneous	
Total	25,686	Total	14,531
Network	9,172	National	10,461
Spot (national)	7,147	Local	4,070
Syndicated Barter (national)	901	Total	
Cable (national)	942	National	65,610
Spot (local)	7,207	Local	52,440
Cable (local)	254	Grand Total	$118,050
Radio			
Total	7,798		
Network	425		
Spot (national)	1,418		
Spot (local)	5,955		

SOURCE: *Advertising Age*, May 15, 1989, p. 24.

Table 16–2 Top Ten National Advertisers 1987

Company	Total (in millions)	Distribution of Total: News-papers	Business Publi-cations	General Magazines	Farm Publi-cations	Newspaper Supplement	Spot TV	Net-work TV	Cable TV Networks	Spot Radio	Net-work Radio	Outdoor
Phillip Morris Cos.	$1,557,846	$ 49,740	$2,893	$243,331	$ 0	$ 9,060	$111,888	$330,778	$20,522	$29,489	$ 8,937	$50,207
Procter & Gamble Co.	1,388,710	5,576	3,579	79,611	0	2,217	238,049	377,552	23,713	7,906	23,665	842
General Motors Corp.	1,024,852	174,889	9,658	153,985	3,355	7,789	103,522	272,953	7,968	34,829	18,906	1,996
Sears, Roebuck & Co.	886,529	NA	761	21,608	0	6,411	25,765	89,973	2,327	21,211	52,701	772
RJR Nabisco	839,589	20,242	4,338	105,674	0	12,518	31,272	209,777	14,688	8,788	2,226	63,065
PepsiCo Inc.	703,973	8,178	187	936	0	32	271,069	140,342	3,742	19,766	5,203	4,518
Eastman Kodak Co.	658,221	2,866	6,045	32,884	247	1,232	15,000	145,961	7,989	960	3,941	1,096
McDonald's Corp.	649,493	NA	14	7,192	0	1,236	129,010	216,067	1,820	4,548	0	6,607
Ford Motor Co.	639,510	100,690	5,448	125,491	4,267	615	50,292	161,177	6,118	14,861	19,766	1,787
Anheuser-Busch Cos.	635,067	11,409	1,099	11,893	0	421	83,767	186,948	22,943	43,550	23,456	9,580

SOURCE: *Advertising Age*, September 26, 1988, pp. 10–12.

of total advertising revenues, with 26.4 percent; television has 21.8 percent; radio, 6.6 percent; magazines, 5.1 percent; direct mail, 17.4 percent; and outdoor, 1 percent. Other media, including the Yellow Pages and farm and business publications, have about 21 percent of total expenditures. American advertising expenditures as a percentage of gross national product (GNP) have remained fairly stable at about 2 percent over the years.

In other countries this percentage is lower. For example, in the Netherlands the figure is 1.6 percent; in Australia, 1.6 percent; in Switzerland, 1.5 percent; in the United Kingdom, 1.4 percent; and in Japan, 1.0 percent. The 1985 advertising expenditures for Japan, were $12.81 billion; for the United Kingdom, $6.44 billion; for Australia, $2.32 billion; for the Netherlands, $2.03 billion; and for Switzerland, $1.49 billion.[2]

Outside the United States total advertising expenditures in 1980 were estimated to be $56.4 billion. By 1990, this total was $133 billion, and by the year 2000, it will be about $450 billion. In the year 2000, American advertising expenditures are predicted to be $350 billion. These projections would make total worldwide advertising expenditures about 1000 times greater at the start of the twenty-first centuy than they were at the beginning of the twentieth century. Clearly, advertising is a growth area.

The Big Spenders

Many firms spend large amounts of money on advertising. In 1987, the 100 leading national advertisers spent $28.4 billion on advertising in major media, about 26 percent of all advertising that year. Table 16–2 presents the top ten national advertisers and the media in which they spent their money. The big names in consumer goods marketing lead the list: Procter & Gamble, General Foods, Sears, Roebuck & Co., General Motors, Philip Morris. Table 16–3 notes the advertising-to-sales ratios for some leading national advertisers.

Table 16–3 Advertising-to-Sales Ratios for Selected Advertisers: 1987

Product Category	Advertiser	Advertising Dollars (in millions)	Advertising as Percent of Sales	Advertising Rank
Airlines	United	$ 138	1.7	64
	Delta	109	1.6	80
Automobiles	General Motors	1,025	1.2	3
	Ford	640	1.2	9
Chemicals	DuPont	149	0.7	59
Drugs	Bristol-Myers	359	9.1	26
Electronics	Kodak	658	8.1	7
	IBM	241	1.0	39
Food	General Mills	572	11.0	13
	McDonald's	650	6.1	8
Gum and Candy	Hershey Foods	123	5.0	69
Retail Chains	Sears	887	1.8	4
Soaps	Procter & Gamble	1,387	11.1	2
	Unilever NV	581	10.0	12
Telephone Service	AT&T	531	1.6	16
Tobacco	American Brands	152	6.0	57
Petroleum	Mobile	166	0.7	50

SOURCE: *Advertising Age*, September 28, 1988, p. 152.

At the brand level, we get an even better feeling for the specific responsibility one has in spending advertising appropriations. Listed in Table 16–4 are some specific brands and their 1988 total media budgets. Try to imagine yourself as a brand manager with marketing training, in your late twenties or early thirties, in charge of these specific brands.[3] With a good idea of the stakes involved in advertising decisions, we now turn our attention to issues in the management of advertising.

Advertising Decisions

Marketing managers must make a number of advertising decisions, including:

1. setting advertising objectives;
2. establishing the advertising budget;
3. selecting the media to be used;
4. scheduling the ads over time;
5. choosing a creative approach;
6. measuring advertising effectiveness by pre-testing the ads and post-testing the ads; and
7. selecting and working with an advertising agency.

The next sections of this chapter present an overview of each of these decision areas in advertising.

Table 16–4 Advertising Budgets of Selected Brands: 1988

Brand*	Budget (millions of dollars)
Pepsi-Cola	69.5
IBM PS/2 Line	38.2
Miller Lite Beer	78.3
Marlboro Filter Cigarettes	29.0
McDonald's Restaurant	405.0
Hallmark Cards	38.3
Chevrolet Corsica	22.9
Midas Muffler	49.2
Pizza Hut	83.3
American Dairy Association	32.9
Safeway Food Stores	46.6
Kellogg's Raisin Bran	23.4
Northwest Airlines	40.3

*Brands are selected to illustrate expenditure levels and do not represent the top thirteen advertised brands.

SOURCE: *Marketing and Media Decisions*, July 1989.

Setting Advertising Objectives

In Chapter 15 we discussed the importance of setting proper objectives for promotional activity. The same principles can be directly applied to setting objectives for advertising. Undertaking any task without knowing, in measurable terms, what is to be accomplished does not make much sense. Objective-setting requires taking very careful and accurate measurement both before and after the campaign. Advertisers who fail to do this will only have an intuitive feeling about the effectiveness of their campaigns. This concept seems so obvious that it is hard to believe that many organizations do not follow it.

Advertising objectives should specify:

1. *what* is to be accomplished, including *how much* (for example, 75 percent awareness of brand name);
2. the *target market* or segment (college students); and
3. the *time period* for accomplishing the objectives (by June 1993).

The Association of National Advertisers has supported the use of communications objectives in advertising. This view has become known as the **DAGMAR** (Defining Advertising Goals, Measuring Advertising Results) philosophy. This view of advertising objectives has not gone unchallenged. As was pointed out in Chapter 15, some marketers think that the sequence of stages in the response hierarchies can be reversed, with behavior (usually sales) preceding attitude change. Also, they point out that there are considerable difficulties in properly assessing the effects of advertising, even if communications objectives are used.

Setting reasonable advertising objectives is part of the art of marketing. The first time a manager sets objectives, it will probably be an educated guess, despite the logical analysis that may have gone into the choice. In time, however, experience in setting objectives and observing the actual results of particular advertising programs

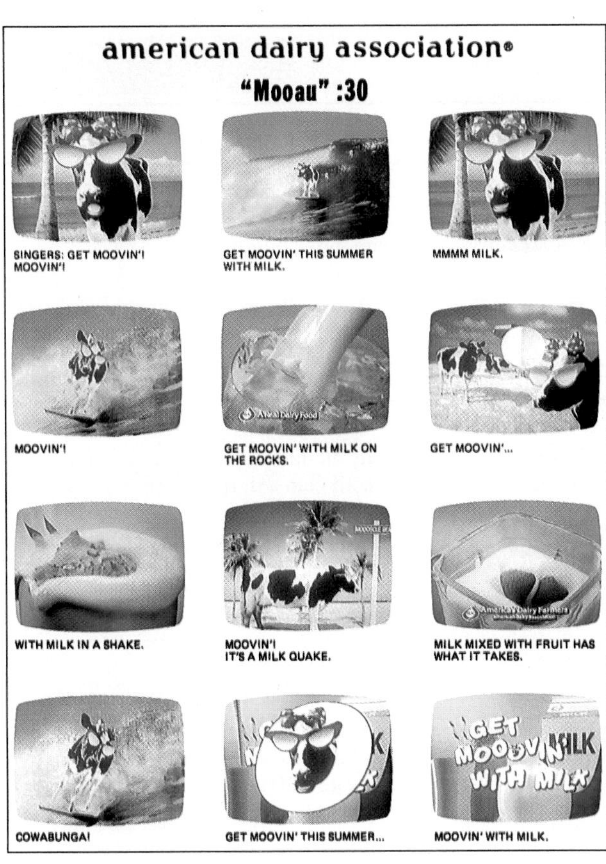

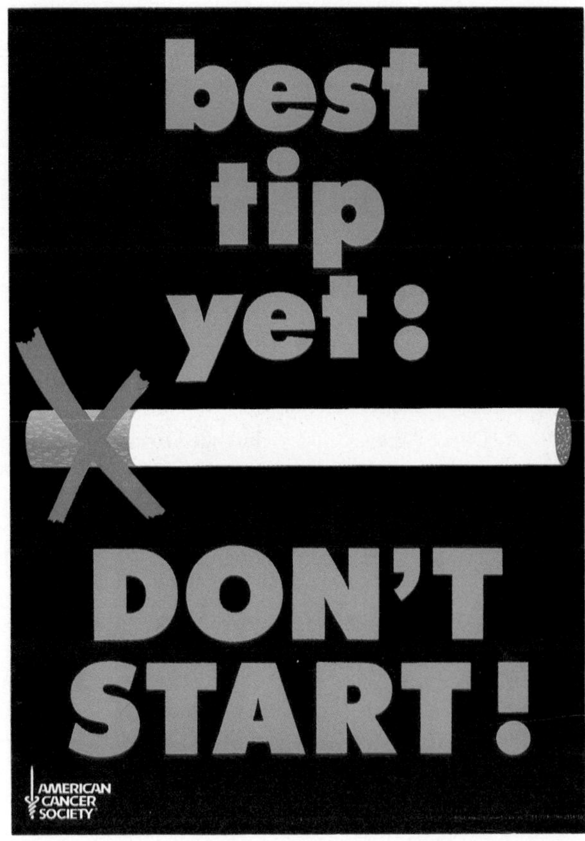

Examples of advertising campaigns directed at primary demand and public service.

will allow the manger to set much more realistic objectives as standards or norms of performance are developed.

Stating the advertising objectives leads directly to determining the types of ads that will be presented. They can be oriented toward:

1. primary or selective demand;
2. direct or indirect action;
3. consumer, industrial, or trade;
4. product or institutional;
5. vertical cooperative or horizontal cooperative; or
6. commercial or public service.

Table 16–5 defines these types and gives examples of campaigns for each.

Establishing Advertising Budgets

Advertising expenditures constitute a significant outlay of money, as Tables 16–1 and 16–3 clearly show. Even for much smaller firms or brands, setting an advertising budget constitutes a significant decision. What variables affect the size of the advertising budget?

In Chapter 15 we examined a number of procedures that can be used to determine the budget for all marketing promotion. These same procedures can be used to design an advertising budget. The objective-and-task method again is the best compromise

Table 16–5 Possible Types of Advertising

Type	Definition	Example
I. Primary vs. Selective Demand		
A. Primary-Demand Oriented	Intended to affect the demand for a whole product category and not simply a specific brand	American Dairy Association attempts to increase milk consumption.
B. Selective-Demand Oriented	Intended to affect the demand for a specific brand	Folgers coffee, "It's mountain grown," designed to indicate Folgers superiority over Maxwell House.
II. Direct vs. Indirect Action		
A. Direct Action	Intended to cause the prospective consumer to purchase the product upon seeing the ad	Virtually all direct mail campaigns; book and record club ads; special offers on TV, not available in stores.
B. Indirect Action	Intended to attract attention, build awareness, or create favorable attitudes for possible effect on a future sale	Car and appliance advertising by manufacturers; Pepsi-Cola, McDonald's.
III. Consumer, Industrial, or Trade		
A. Consumer	Directed at end users in households.	DuPont advertises its Rain Dance car wax to readers of *Car and Driver* magazine.
B. Industrial	Directed at industrial buyers and influences	DuPont advertises its Rain Dance car wax to corporate car fleet managers in *Fleet Management* magazine.
C. Trade	Directed at wholesalers and retailers in the channel of distribution	DuPont advertises its Rain Dance car wax to retailers in the *Discount Merchandiser* magazine, emphasizing advertising support, coupon availability, and a special trade price.

between an ideal and a pragmatic procedure. Unfortunately, marketers often use the percentage-of-sales, competitive parity, and "all-one-can-afford" methods, because of the difficulty and expense of estimating the required response of sales or some communications measure of advertising.

Various factors affect the profitability of advertising (see Table 16–6). Advertising should be used only if the product or service warrants it. This method of marketing is not always appropriate, even for consumer products.

Choosing the Media

Advertising media decisions involve specifying the following:

1. the **media types** to be used (That is, will the product be advertised on television, radio, in magazines, newspapers, or by direct mail?)
2. the **media vehicles** to be used (That is, what television station and program, what radio station and program, what specific magazines and issues will be involved?)
3. the number of *inserts* (specific ads) in each media vehicle.

These specifications constitute a **media plan.**

Table 16–5 Possible Types of Advertising
continued

Type	Definition	Example
IV. Product vs. Institutional		
A. Product	Intended to promote a specific product or service, either by manufacturers or channel members	Mobil 1 motor oil is advertised as reducing oil consumption.
B. Institutional (Corporate)	Intended to build an overall favorable image about the organization and its product offering; not intended to sell specific products	Mobile advertisers in favor of free enterprise and explains how it is working to get energy supplies.
V. Cooperative: Vertical vs. Horizontal		
A. Vertical*	Advertising by a wholesaler or retailer that is partially paid for by a manufacturer; support is usually based on sales levels.	Newspaper appliance-store ads featuring Hotpoint appliances.
B. Horizontal	Members of a group, at the same level in a channel, pool resources to sponsor ads	Wisconsin Dairy Association pushes "real" dairy products and says, "Don't forget the cheese"; IGA ads for their stores.
VI. Commercial vs. Public Service		
A. Commercial	Ads intended to result in an exchange that has production and media paid for by the sponsors; the organization may not be a business, but the ad is still paid for to facilitate exchange	Tide detergent; political parties; hospitals—some activities.
B. Public Service	Ads intended to result in an exchange that have production and media costs given by the Advertising Council and other organizations	United Way: March of Dimes; anti-smoking campaign.

*Vertical cooperative advertising is also considered by manufacturers to be a type of sales promotion activity, as discussed later in this chapter.

Four characteristics are at the heart of good media decisions: the characteristics of the product to be advertised; the characteristics of the target market; the characteristics of media types; and the characteristics of media vehicles.

The media decision maker must consider these four sets of characteristics when making choices. However, the size of the advertising budget, the specification of audience reach and frequency objectives, and creative strategy all constrain the final media vehicle choices.

1. *The Size of the Advertising Budget.* The vehicles selected and the number of insertions in each vehicle are limited by the amount of money available. This is true even for advertising budgeting using the objective-and-task method (see Chapter 15).

2. *The Specification of the Audience Reach and Frequency Objectives.* The total number of persons in the target market exposed one or more times to a particular ad from any media is called **reach. Frequency** is the average number of times that those who are reached in the target market are exposed to an ad. Given a fixed budget, both reach and frequency objectives cannot be increased, for as frequency increases, the reach possible must decrease, and vice versa.

The combination of reach times frequency defines what is known as **gross rating points** for a campaign. Particular reach and frequency objectives can significantly

Table 16–6 Factors Affecting the Profitability of Advertising

Advertise a product or service more:
1. if it possesses unique, salient attributes.
2. if it possesses "hidden qualities" important to prospects.
3. if it is bought largely on the basis of powerful, emotional motives.
4. if the primary demand trend for it is favorable.
5. if the market potential for it is large enough.
6. if competitors do not possess too much brand loyalty.
7. if general economic conditions are favorable for this type of product or service.
8. if the organization is financially able and willing to spend the amount of money required.
9. if the organization possesses sufficient marketing expertise to successfully market the product or service.

constrain media choices. For example, if reach is deemed to be primary, advertisers are then most interested in *unduplicated* audiences (those persons not previously exposed to their ads). Therefore, they will use more diverse media vehicles than those advertisers whose primary objective is frequency and who try to reach the same audience over and over again.

3. *Creative Strategy.* The vehicles selected must fit the particular creative strategy being used. For example, it would not make much sense to place an ad for Old Milwaukee beer in *The New Yorker.*

Characteristics of Media Types. Media types may be evaluated according to a number of characteristics. Table 16–7 rates the major media types on the basis of the following characteristics:

1. *Intrusiveness:* the extent that the consumer cannot avoid being confronted with ads in that media.
2. *Product Demonstration:* the extent that the use of the product being advertised can be shown.
3. *Package Identification:* the extent that the package, as it is available in the store, can be indicated to the audience.
4. *Short-term Action:* the ability of ads in media types to generate a fairly immediate consumer response.
5. *Cost:* the expense of an insertion relative to audience size.
6. *Economy of Production Costs:* the cost of preparing an advertisement for use in a media type.
7. *Coupon Vehicle:* the ability to distribute consumer coupons in the media.
8. *Major Market Penetration:* the ability of the media to reach the largest urban areas.
9. *Flexibility:* the ability to use media types for regional markets, test markets, seasonal brands, and major markets only.

Rating media types using these above characteristics can help the advertiser select the types of vehicles that should be used. For example, assume you must develop a media plan for a product that (1) needs to be demonstrated to be effectively sold; (2) needs a strong package identification because it will be purchased in a self-serve fashion, and (3) will be marketed only in major markets. Which medium seems to be most appropriate for this product? The data presented in Table 16–7 suggest that television is the best choice.

Table 16–7 Comparative Ratings for Media Selection

Characteristics	Broadcast: Television	Broadcast: Radio	Print/Indoor/Outdoor: Magazine	Print/Indoor/Outdoor: Newspaper	Print/Indoor/Outdoor: Outdoor
Intrusiveness	Very High	High	Low	Low	Very Low
Product Demonstration	Excellent	Poor	Fair	Fair	Poor
Package Identification	Good	Poor	Excellent	Good	Good
Short-Term Action	Good	Excellent	Fair	Excellent	Fair
Cost per Audience Exposure	Good	Excellent	Fair	Good	Fair
Production Cost, Economy	Poor	Excellent	Fair	Fair	Poor
Coupon Vehicle	—	—	Good/Exc.	Good	—
Major Market Penetration	Excellent	Excellent	Fair	Excellent	Good
Flexibility					
i. Regional Buys	Good	Good	Fair	Excellent	Good
ii. Major Markets	Excellent	Excellent	Poor	Excellent	Good
iii. Use of Test Cities	Excellent	Excellent	Poor	Excellent	Good

Characteristics of Media Vehicles. Specific media vehicles may also be evaluated according to the size of the vehicle audience and target audience and the cost.

The first action that should be taken when examining a media vehicle is to determine the size of its audience. This information is usually available from the medium itself or from syndicated research services. Figure 16–1 shows the relationships among the various concepts of audience size. First to consider is a vehicle's basic *distribution level.* For a newspaper, this would be the size of its circulation; for radio or television, it would be the number of sets existing in households. However, more than one person may see the same newspaper, or listen to or watch the same program from the same radio or television. This fact leads to the *vehicle exposure* concept of audience size. Not all the people exposed to an advertising vehicle are exposed to the ad of interest. Therefore, *advertising exposure* is then less than the vehicle exposure and could conceivably be less than the vehicle distribution. Of those exposed to an ad, only a proportion will *consciously perceive* it; of these, only a proportion will maintain any *effects* of the communication (obtain knowledge, formulate liking, preference, or conviction).

Marketers are interested in knowing who takes *action* after exposure to an ad in a vehicle. Ideally, we would like to compare these responses to an ad in various media vehicles. If that is not possible (as is likely), we would prefer measures of the other concepts of audience size in order, moving from communications to perception to advertising exposure to vehicle exposure to distribution. Most firms are unwilling or unable to do research on advertising exposure, perception, communication, or behavior because it is very time-consuming and costly. Additionally, so many factors affect behavior that accurately separating out the part attributable to advertising is very difficult and sometimes impossible. These measures are specific to the individual ads of individual firms. On the other hand, vehicle exposure and distribution are common to all advertisers and are usually readily available. As a result, these latter two concepts of audience size are most often used in media planning.

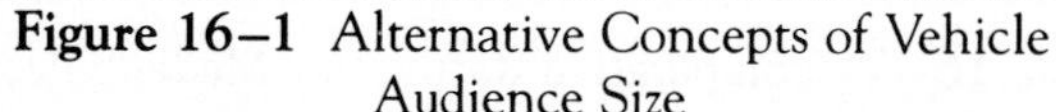
Figure 16–1 Alternative Concepts of Vehicle Audience Size

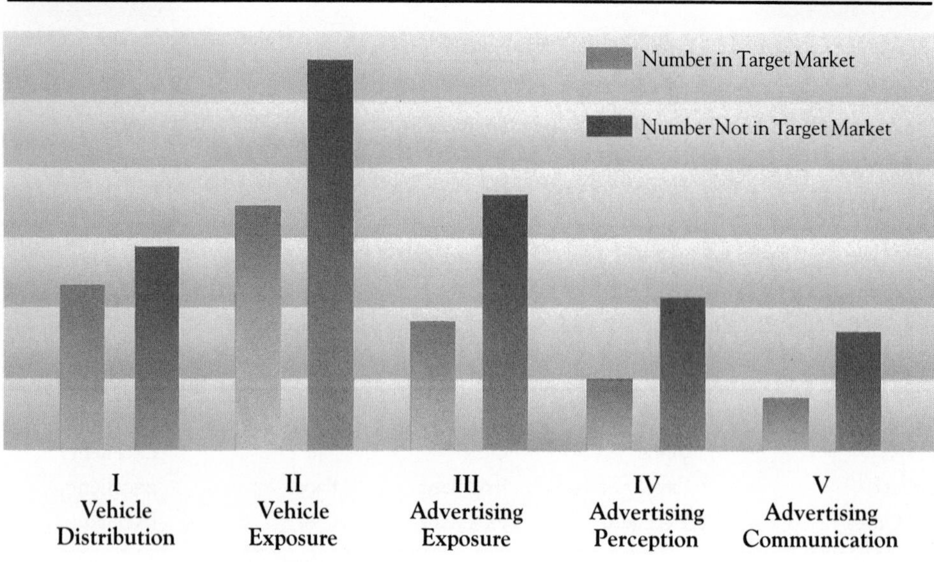

When considering audience sizes, marketers also need to distinguish between those in the target market and those not in the target market. This is represented in Figure 16–1 by two different groups of bar lines. We are really interested in the target audience; therefore, in assessing the audience for vehicles, we must reduce the total audience (for whatever size concept used) to include only those in the target segment.

Knowing the vehicle's target market audience is not good enough. We must also know the cost of reaching these audiences. Some costs for well-known vehicles are shown in Table 16–8. The **cost per thousand** (CPM) rate, the cost to reach a thousand users of the media vehicle, is typically used to summarize the cost effectiveness of various vehicles. The CPM for what base, we must ask. Some media planners use CPM per total media vehicle audience, but this could be a misleading measure: we may have a low CPM but not be reaching our target market. Therefore, CPM *per target audience* is a more meaningful measure. Vehicles are compared to their CPM from this base, and ads are placed in the vehicles with the lowest cost per thousand, up to the limits of the budget available.

You are probably saying to yourself that media selection is a complex process. Well, you are correct. This complexity has given rise to many computer models that attempt to help marketers make media decisions. These models vary greatly, but, in general, follow the type of process we have outlined here. Advertisers constantly monitor the cost/benefit of alternative media types and media vehicles within media types. The following example on Maybelline illustrates this appraisal.

An Example of Media Choice: Maybelline Cosmetics

The rapidly rising costs of network television have forced many advertisers to reevaluate their advertising campaigns. Maybelline USA cut network TV spending by as much as 30 percent and reallocated at least $15 million to cable TV, print, and radio.

Table 16–8 Costs of Selected Media Vehicles

		Four-color	Black and White
Magazine (per page):	Newsweek	$86,500	$54,095
	Fortune	45,040	29,440
	Motor Trend	32,695	20,435
	Ebony	29,990	22,199
	Golf Digest	44,100	29,400
Network Television (per 30-second vehicle in prime time):	Super Bowl	$750,000	
	60 Minutes	160,300	
	The Cosby Show	369,500	
Spot Television (per 30-second vehicle in prime time):	New York: WABC	$3,000	
	Chicago: WFLD	2,400	
	San Francisco: KHBK	1,800	
	Knoxville: WRJZ	480	
Radio (per 60-second vehicle): 30-seconds = 80 percent of the 1-minute rate	New York: WNBC	$408	Mon.–Sat. 5–10 A.M. Sat. 10 A.M.–3 P.M.
	Chicago: WFYR	348	Mon.–Fri. 5:30–10 A.M. Sat. 10 A.M.–3 P.M.
	San Francisco: KSFO	366	Mon.–Fri. 5:30–10 A.M. Sat. 7–10 A.M.
	Knoxville: WRJZ	114	Mon.–Sat. 5:30–10 A.M. Sat. 10 A.M.–3 P.M.
Newspaper (per page):		**Daily**	**Sunday**
	New York Times	$37,280	$44,832
	Detroit Free Press	29,754	32,234
	San Jose News	8,938	10,219

SOURCES: Newspaper SRDS, July 12, 1989; Consumer Magazine SRDS, June 27, 1989; *Advertising Age,* January 4, 1988; Julia Flynn Siler, "Soaring Super Bowl Costs Face Advertiser Challenge," *The New York Times,* February 4, 1988, p. 25.

Executive vice president Gary Mulloy said, "At some point you have to say, 'Sorry, that's enough. We'll go somewhere else like print, where we can still reach numbers through massive quantities of appearances. Or cable, where everything is very negotiable and there are a number of side benefits, like billboards.'"[4]

With new agency DDB Needham, Maybelline planned to spend between $50 and $60 million in 1988. DDB Needham was chosen by Maybelline because of its creative work as well as the strength of its media planning services. Mr. Mulloy said, "They had a fresh approach and we saw potential there."

Print ads featured the theme "Smart, Beautiful, Maybelline" and displayed the product apart from the model in the layout. Exclusive cosmetics rights have been bought on Point of Purchase Radio, an in-store broadcasting network. Maybelline will also use a 36 page "magazine within a magazine" advertorial advertising section to run in *Seventeen* and programs with Whittle Communications, such as poster advertising, in high schools. Television is used selectively for new product introductions and existing products according to vice president of advertising David Blanton.

Scheduling the Ads

Marketers must be concerned with the sequencing of advertisements. First, how should the total advertising budget be spaced over the year? Second, what should the detailed spacing and pattern of advertisements be during those times of the year when it is appropriate to advertise?

There are basically six different types of timing media schedules, often called the **flighting pattern.**

1. *Steady.* Monies are expended evenly throughout the year. If 26 insertions in *Sports Illustrated* are purchased, they would appear every other week.
2. *Seasonal Pulse.* For products with sales patterns that vary during the year, the advertising dollars are increased during peak sales times. For example, most toy sales and advertising occur in the Christmas selling season.
3. *Periodic Pulse.* Advertising activity is exerted at regular intervals during the year. Budweiser did this very successfully to gain more impact in its advertising.
4. *Erratic Pulse.* Advertising dollars are spent at irregular intervals. A company may spend for a few weeks, then stop for some time, and then resume spending at a different rate for some other length of time.
5. *Start-Up Pulse.* Advertising dollars are more heavily spent at the start of a new campaign or selling season or even for a new product introduction.
6. *Promotional Pulse.* Advertising dollars are often spent to support sales promotion activity. Figure 16.2 presents a media schedule and an advertising plan for a fast-food company.

If a product has no seasonal fluctuations in sales, we would generally advertise it evenly throughout the year. It is when a product has a seasonal sales pattern that scheduling becomes complex. Consider this example. The U.S. Office of Tourism knows that its peak tourism period will be in July and August, and that a tourist's decision about a vacation is made approximately two months ahead of the actual vacation, on average. Given this situation, the tourism office might spend most of its advertising budget between March 1 and May 15 in order to heavily advertise during the period in which most tourists select their vacation spots.

Selecting a Creative Approach

What *message* and what type of *presentation* should an advertisement have? The answers to these questions are determined by the creative approach the ad takes. The decisions are very important, since the effectiveness of a whole campaign can depend on an ad's specific message and presentation. Advertising results per dollar can vary from 5 to 1 depending on the message and presentation. For example, Oldsmobile's creative campaign theme, "This is not your father's Oldsmobile," has been credited with changing the stodgy image of Olds, and with substantially reducing the average age of buyers.

The message in an advertisement is often called the *copy.* Copy results from a combination of analytical thinking based upon a clear understanding of the brand situation and a liberal use of creativity and imagination. The copy must fit both company and advertising objectives; it must also be consistent with the target audience and the product itself and take account of competitive activity. In addition, the copy must fit the editorial position of the media vehicles being used. Royal Dalton china would fit better in *The New Yorker* magazine than in *Modern Romances.*

This is not your father's Oldsmobile.

Cutlass Supreme

We think your Dad would readily agree. We also think he might be right behind you when you go to the showroom. Because this new Cutlass Supreme is the most researched, refined and remarkable car in our history.

Who wouldn't love it? The power comes from a 2.8-liter V6 with multiport fuel-injection.

As for handling, it's remarkably precise. Each wheel boasts a separate suspension system, with MacPherson struts up front and coil springs in the rear.

And remember, behind it all is GM's new 3-year/50,000 mile Bumper-to-Bumper Plus warranty. See your dealer for terms of this limited warranty.

On this car, everything looks good for a highly technical reason. A whole new generation of Cutlass watchers will be snapping heads when this beauty whizzes by.

Want in on the fun? Visit your Oldsmobile® dealer for a test drive. Or for more information, call toll-free 1-800-242-OLDS, Mon.-Fri., 9 a.m. to 7 p.m. EST.

The New Generation of OLDSMOBILE.

A creative campaign theme can change a product's image.

Figure 16–2 Fast Food Promotional Plan

Some details of a fast-food company's promotional plan, including the advertising themes, sales promotion activity, and public relations actions, appear below and on the next page. The promotional plan specifies timing during the year, identifies specific creative themes, and details the media plan that will be used.

Fast-Food National Media Plan

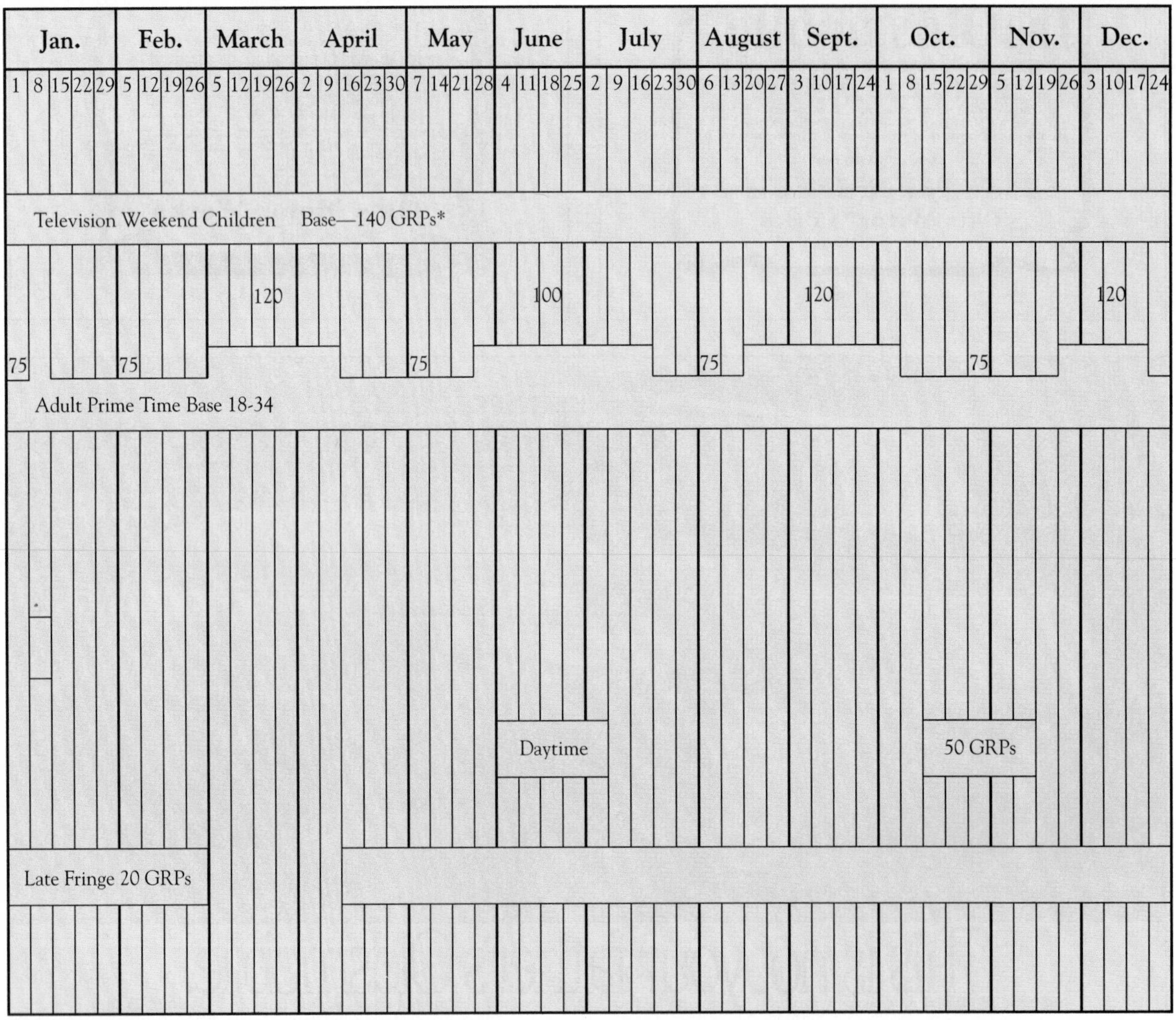

Jan.	Feb.	March	April	May	June	July	August	Sept.	Oct.	Nov.	Dec.
1 8 15 22 29	5 12 19 26	5 12 19 26	2 9 16 23 30	7 14 21 28	4 11 18 25	2 9 16 23 30	6 13 20 27	3 10 17 24	1 8 15 22 29	5 12 19 26	3 10 17 24

Television Weekend Children Base—140 GRPs*

120 100 120 120

75 75 75 75 75

Adult Prime Time Base 18-34

Daytime 50 GRPs

Late Fringe 20 GRPs

*GRPs = Gross Rating Points = Reach Times Frequency

Figure 16–2 Fast Food Promotional Plan
continued

Fast-Food Marketing Plan

		D	Jan.	Feb.	March	April	May	June	July	Aug.	Sept.	Oct.	Nov.	Dec.
National Advertising	Adult	Hamburger Theme*	Breakfast	Kid's Day	Fries	4-9 Family Dinner	Food Service	Hot Dog	4-9 Use Occasion	Christmas				
National Advertising	Children	Hamburger/Cheeseburger	Breakfast	Fries	Dinner	Sundaes	Hamburger/Cheeseburger	Dinner	Christmas					

Promotion Recommendations	Items (left to right)
	Continuity Subjects
Vertical Continuity	Breakfast Day; Happy Meal; Hot Dog Continuity; Christmas Gift Ornament
Supportive	Coloring Calendar; Valen-tines; Milkshake; Fries (Kids); Sundaes; Self-liquidator
Crew Motivation	Crew Motivation; Crew Motivation; Crew Motivation; Crew Motivation
National Community Calendar Opportunities	Hamburger Theme/ Washington's Birthday/ Valentine's Day/Black History; Milkshake/ Breakfast/Easter/ Kid's Day/Fish; Fries/Mother's Day/Spanish/ Seniors; Family Dinner/ Grads/Memorial Day/Father's Day; 4th of July/ Sundaes; Labor Day/ Back to School; Dinner/ Halloween/ Thanksgiving; Christmas

Public Relations	Items (left to right)
	Hamburger Theme; Kid's Day; M-D; Christmas Gift
	Children's Classics; Children's Classics
	All American Basketball; All American Basketball
	Olympics; M-D; All Amer. Band
	Charity Drive
	Films/Educational Programs; Films-educational Programs
	Black History

Figure 16–3 The "Argument" Approach

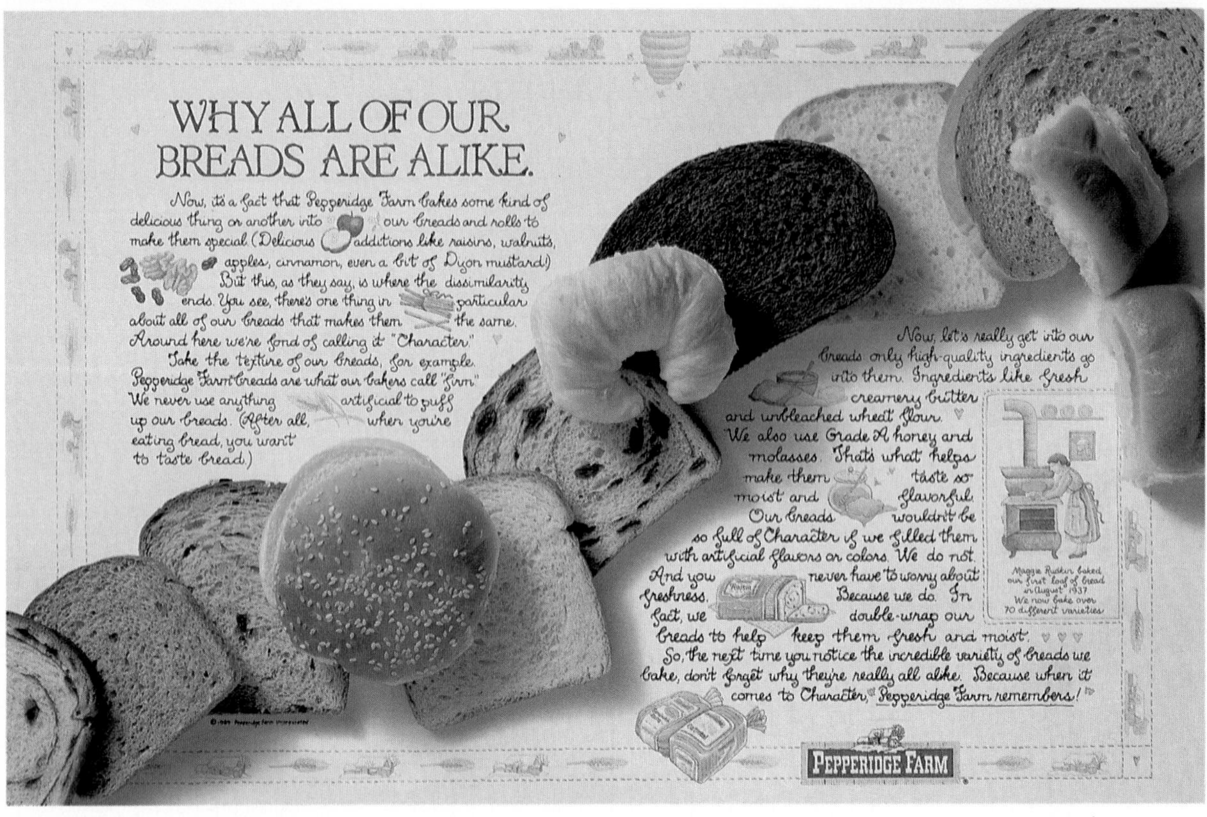

Types of Presentations. Once ad copy has been generated, there are many types of presentations that can be used.[5]

- *Information.* This presentation sticks right to the facts, without any argumentation or explanation of the relevance of the facts.
- *Argument or Reason-Why.* The ad is set up in the form of a logical argument. Facts or expected consumer benefits form the basis of the argument. Many industrial ads use this format. Figure 16–3 shows this form of presentation.
- *Motivation with Psychological Appeals.* This type of ad, seen in Figure 16–4, makes use of emotional appeals. The ad creates a mood. Cosmetics and beer tend to use this form of advertising.
- *Repeat Assertion.* This is a hard-sell technique. Statements are made and repeated in ads, but the reasons why the statement holds are not explained. Nonprescription drugs and taste-related products often use this style. For example, Sanka is presented as "tasting like real coffee because it is real coffee."
- *Command.* This presentation is in the form of an order. "Uncle Sam wants you," and "Give the United Way" are two well-known illustrations.

Figure 16–4 The "Emotional Appeal" Approach

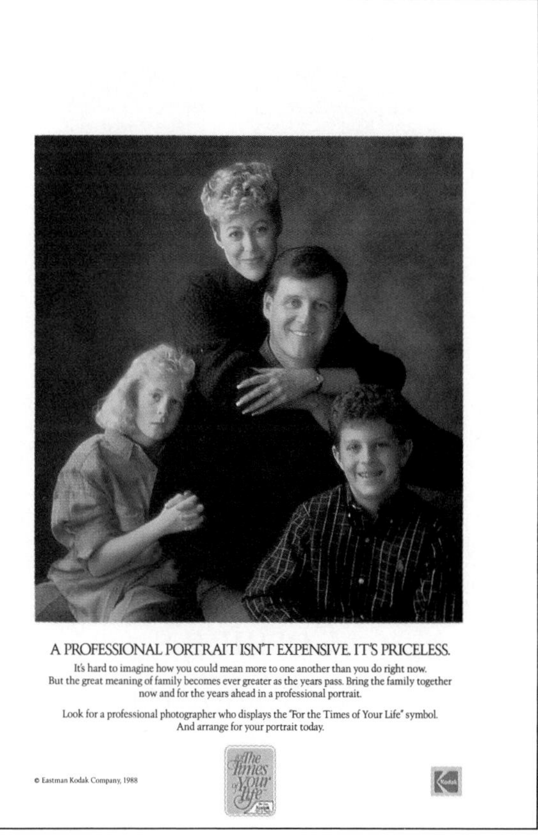

A PROFESSIONAL PORTRAIT ISN'T EXPENSIVE. IT'S PRICELESS.
It's hard to imagine how you could mean more to one another than you do right now.
But the great meaning of family becomes ever greater as the years pass. Bring the family together now and for the years ahead in a professional portrait.
Look for a professional photographer who displays the "For the Times of Your Life" symbol.
And arrange for your portrait today.
© Eastman Kodak Company, 1988
The Times of Your Life

Reprinted courtesy of Eastman Kodak Company.

- *Symbolic Association.* Here the product is linked to a person, or music, or situation that is viewed positively by target customers. The product and the symbol become highly connected (see Figure 16–5). The Green Giant, the Qantas Koala, and the Rock of Prudential are the prototypes.
- *Imitation.* The ad, as seen in Figure 16–6, offers situations or presents people for the prospective consumer to imitate. Famous people in testimonials and status appeal are two common forms of this type of ad.

The power of advertising to enhance marketing performance is illustrated in the Corning *Marketing in Action* on the next page.

Execution. Any given copy combined with any given presentation type can be executed in a number of ways. For example, an ad may use a straight *spokesperson* execution, a *slice-of-life* (showing the product used in a real-life context), a *testimonial, hyperbole* (overstatement), *comparison* (direct evaluation of the product against competitors), or even *humor.* Additionally, the use of colors, particular actors, headlines, copy layout, and even graphics all contribute to the execution of the copy and presentation type. Clearly, there are an infinite number of copy, presentation types, and execution combinations available. Choosing a specific combination is truly a

MARKETING IN ACTION

Effective Advertising Enhances Corning's Performance

Corning Glass Works used an attention grabbing television commercial to build competitiveness and regain profitability. The company lost $26 million in 1985 and was facing strong competition from foreign manufacturers of kitchen items. "Corning finally realized the need to market its products," said Ed Schollmeyer, an analyst at Paine Webber. "There's been a great transformation at the company over the past few years, largely due to the introduction of products like Visions and the revitalization of the entire line of dinnerware and cookware." An expensive restructuring effort costing Corning around $40 million has paid off with a return to profitability.

Corning had positioned its products by emphasizing their durability. With increased foreign competition, consumers were able to purchase less expensive products with greater variety in style. Durability was no longer a major factor in the purchase decision. To counter these developments, Corning introduced a new product line, Visions, in 1985. Visions is the first see-through cookware available for the microwave as well as stove top cooking. Corning estimates that Visions has 34 percent of the top of the range cookware market, a substantial lead over its competitors.

In order to rejuvenate the image of Corning's cookware and dinnerware among younger consumers, the advertising budget was almost tripled to $20 million per year beginning in 1984. Much of the credit for Visions' success has been attributed to the television commercial showing an aluminum saucepan melting inside of a Visions dish on the top of a stove. A voice delivers the advertising slogan, "Turning ordinary saucepans into sauce."

"The Visions television commercial, for example the melting pot ad, has been remarkably effective," said Edward Fogerty, head of the consumer products division. Fogerty said that the ad was the "driving force behind the growth of this major new brand."

In 1986, Corning returned to profitability with earnings of $25.9 million. In 1987, earnings increased significantly to $55.2 million. In addition to the successful TV campaign, Corning attributes its turnaround to the revamping of several existing product lines including Corelle Living Ware, Pyrex Bakeware, and Corning Ware. A line designed for microwave use was added. Analysts such as Chuck Ryan at Merrill Lynch feel Corning has done a good job. "Corning is very well established, and despite a probable slowdown in the consumer market, Corning has positioned itself well.

SOURCE: "A Hot TV Ad Pays Off for Corning", *The New York Times*, April 2, 1988, pp. 17, 19.

creative process. The amount of money in an ad's production and the media time used require that this creative process be subject to evaluation by research. A four-color magazine ad can cost up to $15,000 to produce and over $90,000 for each insertion in a major national publication like *Time.* A thirty-second television commercial costs about $65,000 to produce on average. One Levi's ad, using a combination of real people, animation, and special effects, cost $250,000—just to produce. With an average prime time TV network thirty-second buy costing $115,000 and a special like the Super Bowl costing over $750,000 per thirty-second buy, the need to do research on advertising should be clear.

Measuring Advertising Effectiveness

Good advertisers put considerable effort into testing an ad's effectiveness. Ads may be tested at any one of a number of stages—as a concept, as a set of rough drawings,

Figure 16–5 The "Symbolic Association" Approach

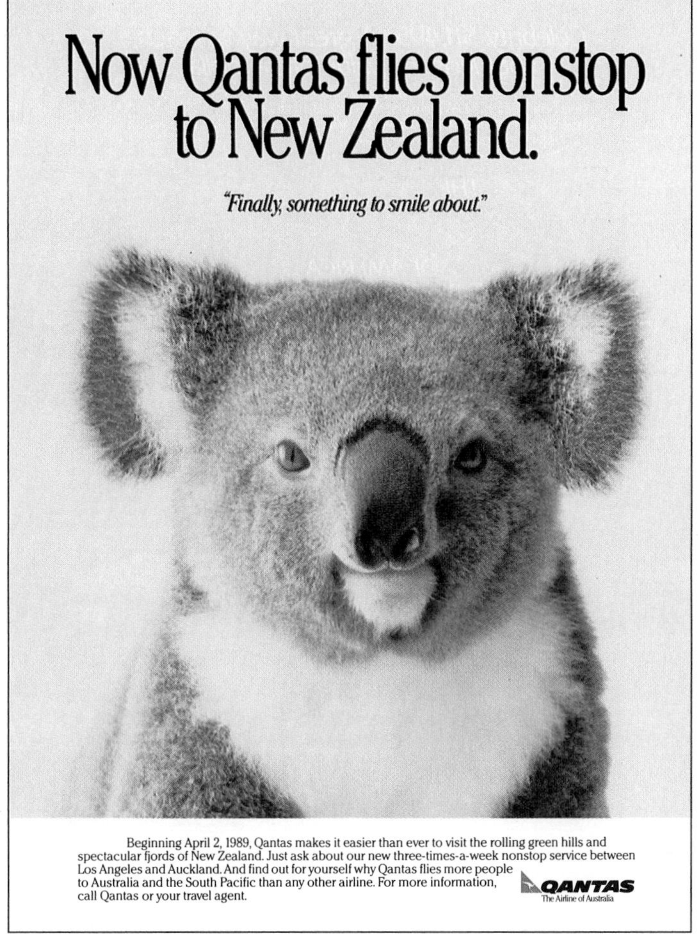

Now Qantas flies nonstop to New Zealand.
"Finally, something to smile about."
Beginning April 2, 1989, Qantas makes it easier than ever to visit the rolling green hills and spectacular fjords of New Zealand. Just ask about our new three-times-a-week nonstop service between Los Angeles and Auckland. And find out for yourself why Qantas flies more people to Australia and the South Pacific than any other airline. For more information, call Qantas or your travel agent.
QANTAS
The Airline of Australia

or as a finished ad, both before and after media exposure. An ad is *pre-tested* if the test occurs before media dollars are committed; tests after commitment of funds are designated as *post-tests.* The question at hand is: What constitutes a good test of advertising effectiveness?

Criteria for Judging Advertising Tests. The scheme presented as a series of questions is a useful starting point in determining criteria for judging advertising. The "ideal" responses to these questions indicate which criteria to use.

- *What measure should be taken?* What level or levels in the consumer response models, discussed in Chapter 15, should we aim for? Ideally, we would like to know the sales and profit implications of our advertising.
- *What form should the ad be in?* Should we test a rough sketch of the ad, cheap film or videotape version, or the final version? Ideally, we would like to test the final version, since this is the one people will be reacting to. However, cost and time may require the use of a less finished version.

Figure 16–6 The "Imitation" Approach

- *Should we measure the effect of one ad or of a whole campaign?* Ideally, we would like to know the effect of our entire campaign.
- *How should the measurement be made?* Should the ad be exposed in a normal advertising vehicle or in a less normal fashion? How many times should it be exposed? Should the sampling and measurement techniques be technically correct? Clearly we would prefer repeated exposures in a normal fashion with a truly representative sample.

Of course, time and money force all advertising measurement procedures to compromise on these points. However, the procedures provide a good benchmark to work from. Deviation from that benchmark should be backed up with reasoning.

Pre-testing. There are a number of commonly used testing procedures.

1. *Focus-Group Interviews.* In this procedure, about six to ten target audience consumers are brought together with a group leader. They are then exposed to an ad or a part of an ad. The leader encourages group members to interact with each other and asks probing questions about the ad. What do they understand from the ad? Does it interest them? Do they believe it? Would they try the product? This technique is most commonly used during an ad's development.

2. *Folio Tests.* In this procedure, an interviewer takes a looseleaf binder containing the test ad and others to the consumer's home and asks the consumer to look through the ads, noting what he or she remembers or finds interesting. This technique is designed exclusively for testing print ads, usually in a finished or nearly finished form. It measures an ad's attention-getting abilities. In addition, it provides insights into motivational and comprehension aspects and measures potential attitude changes.

3. *In-Home Projector Tests.* A rough or finished version of a television commercial is shown, in a consumer's home, as a short sequence from a television program or film. This procedure does not measure attention-getting aspects, but does give a measure of comprehension, motivation, credibility, and possible consumer attitude change if attitude measures are taken both before and after the ads are shown.

4. *Trailer Tests.* Trailer tests are less expensive ways to evaluate television commercials. A trailer is parked in a shopping center parking lot, and people are asked to take part in a marketing research study. They are put in a waiting room with magazines and a television set. This set shows a closed circuit version of a prerecorded program in which the test ad is aired. The subject is then interviewed to determine the attention-getting impact of the ad, plus comprehension, credibility, and motivation. Alternatively, respondents may be shown an ad directly and asked for their reactions. This latter procedure negates getting information about the attention-getting aspect of the ad.

5. *Theater Tests.* An audience is recruited to view a number of test television programs. On arrival they fill out questionnaires about their opinions and preferences for the product categories and brands of interest. Then they see television shows with the relevant commercials inserted. Another questionnaire is done, giving measures of attention-getting power, credibility, motivation, and preference.

6. *In-Magazine Recall Tests.* Syndicated services regularly interview people who read magazines to determine which ads they remember seeing, how much of the ads they read, what associations they draw, and the interest level attained for the products advertised. They are asked questions about the ads they remember, then shown each ad and asked whether they remember it and to what extent they read it.

Pre-testing print ads is also done in a similar fashion. The test ad is inserted into a dummy magazine containing editorial sections, other real ads, and some benchmark ads. The benchmark ads give reference points for meaningful comparisons with the test ad. This dummy magazine is placed in respondents' homes, and a few days later, an interview similar to the one for in-magazine recall takes place.

7. *Live Telecast Tests.* An ad is shown, usually on a television program. The next day television interviews are conducted with respondents who viewed the show in question. They are asked what ads they remember seeing on the show (*unaided recall*). If the ad of interest is not mentioned, the brand in question is identified, and respondents are asked if they remember seeing an ad for this brand (*aided recall*). Those remembering the ad are asked to describe it, yielding measures of video impact, music, and other characteristics. This test is quite often the final pre-test before full commitment of media dollars occurs. Burke Marketing Services made this type of research well known under the name day-after-recall (DAR) test.

8. *Test Market.* A number of advertising approaches may be tested in the marketplace. Here, the intent is to measure the impact of the ads on sales. Communications measures are also usually taken in test areas at the same time. This approach requires a heavier commitment of funds to research than the other methods.

Post-testing. In post-testing, those exposed to ads in such media as print, television, and radio are questioned about their unaided recall, aided recall, recognition, comprehension, believability, brand awareness and preferences, product trial, satisfaction, and usage.

For example, the Starch Advertisement Readership Service gives post measures of print ad effectiveness in a number of ways: (1) *noted*—a person who remembered having previously seen the advertisement in the issue being studied; (2) *seen-associated*—a person who not only noted the advertisement but also read some part of it that clearly indicates the brand or advertiser; and (3) *read most*—a person who read half or more of the written material in the ad. The service gives a number of measures, including the percentage of a magazine's readers in each of these three categories, and the number of "readers" an ad obtains per dollar spent. Many other syndicated organizations are available to provide information on any of the measures we've discussed, or the impact of the campaign on sales. Of course, a company may do its own testing. Post-testing allows the advertiser to determine how well the objectives have been achieved.

Review Your Marketing Knowledge

• What are the advertising decisions that a marketing manager must make? Relate each of these to the Hanes versus Fruit of the Loom profile that began this chapter.

• Evaluate the creative approach used by Corning using the "types of presentations" outline presented in the chapter. Also apply this outline to three other print advertisements of your choice.

Choosing Advertising Agencies

Many large firms perform all the functions necessary to effectively advertise themselves. If they do this, they have an *in-house agency*. However, most firms make use of some of the following types of outside advertising agencies to do some or all of their advertising work.

- *Media-Buying Services.* These agencies execute the media strategy developed by a firm by doing the actual purchasing of media vehicles.
- *Creative Boutiques.* These firms specialize in the development and production of the advertisements themselves.
- *Full-Service Agencies.* Full-service advertising agencies are capable of performing any or all activities related to a firm's advertising, including development of overall marketing strategy. These agencies are the most common form of advertising firm. Table 16–9 lists the ten largest advertising agencies and some of their clients.

Advertising agencies have traditionally been paid a straight 15 percent commission on the value of the media that they purchase for clients. However, because of cost pressures and a great diversity in the functions of agencies, many compensation systems are being used. For example, Gillette and Lorillard pay a smaller percentage as their advertising expenditures increase; American Home Products and Lipton use only limited agency services and pay 7.5 to 10 percent. Others, such as Best Foods, pay on a fee-for-service basis. DuPont pays more than 15 percent on small industrial brands.

For advertising to be effective, client and agency must work well together in an atmosphere of respect and trust. When this atmosphere does not exist, agencies often

Table 16–9 The Top Ten Advertising Agencies in World Billings and Income: 1988

Rank	Agency	Billings (in millions)	Gross Income (in millions)	Some Major Clients
1	Young & Rubicam	$5,390.3	$757.6	AT&T, Chevron, DuPont, General Foods, Kodak, U.S. Army
2	Saatchi & Saatchi Advertising	$5,053.9	$740.5	General Mills, Johnson & Johnson, Paine Webber Inc., Procter & Gamble, Sara Lee Corp., Tyson Foods
3	Backer Spielvogel Bates Worldwide	$4,677.9	$689.8	British Airways, Dole, Fischer-Price, Mars Inc., The Prudential, Wendy's
4	McCann-Erickson Worldwide	$4,381.0	$656.8	Coca-Cola, General Motors, L'Oreal, Nestle, Texas Instruments
5	FCB-Publicis	$4,357.6	$653.3	Brown Foreman Beverages, RJR Nabisco, Mattel, Marriott Hotels
6	Ogilvy & Mather Worldwide	$4,110.1	$653.2	American Express, AT&T, Campbell Soup, General Foods, Owens Corning, Seagram's
7	BBDO Worldwide	$4,051.2	$585.9	Apple Computer, Delta Airlines, PepsiCo Inc., Pizza Hut, U.S. Navy, Visa
8	J. Walter Thompson Company	$3,857.5	$559.3	Bell Atlantic, Lever Bros., Miller Brewing Co., Nestle, Warner-Lambert
9	Lintas: Worldwide	$3,585.6	$537.6	Carnation, Chevrolet, Johnson & Johnson, MasterCard, Noxell Corp.
10	Grey Advertising	$21,868.5	$432.8	Pan Am Shuttle, Corning's Revereware, Mitsubishi's Eclipse, Canon Cameras

SOURCE: *Advertising Age,* March 29, 1989, p. 8.

are fired or resign accounts. Firms like General Motors, Levi Strauss, and Procter & Gamble rarely change agencies.

Sales Promotion

Sales promotion activities supplement both advertising and personal selling. Recall, from Chapter 15, that sales promotion involves *those marketing activities other than personal selling, advertising, and publicity that stimulate consumer purchasing and dealer effectiveness.* Sales promotion holds a middle ground between advertising and personal selling. It is usually not directed at as large an audience as advertising, but instead is directed at much larger groups than a typical personal selling effort. Included are such activities as trade shows, exhibits, couponing, sampling, premiums, trade allowances, cents-off packs, point-of-purchase displays, demonstrations, and dealer incentives. Note that sales promotion is intended to aid both consumer *pull* and dealer *push.* Figure 16–7 categorizes common sales promotion techniques in terms of their consumer or dealer focus.[6]

It is very difficult to accurately measure the amount of money spent on sales promotion. The authors' best estimate is that it is currently between $100 billion and

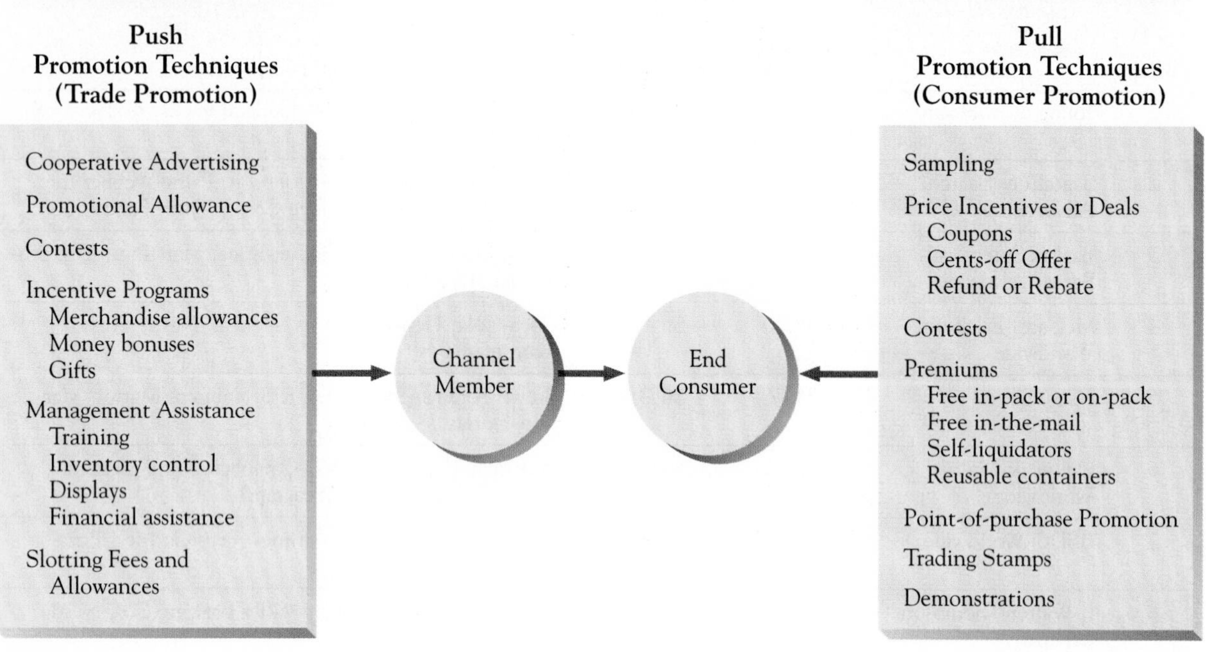

Figure 16–7 Sales Promotion: Push and Pull Techniques

$120 billion per year. Given their diversity, sales promotion activities are designed to reach many target audiences and to achieve a wide set of objectives, such as:

- identifying sales leads (trade shows);
- inducing consumers to try a new product (free samples);
- increasing the share of an established brand (multipacks giving three for the price of two);
- gaining more retail shelf facings (promotional allowances to retailers for setting up special displays).

These objectives are usually all near the action end of the response hierarchy (AIDA).

Sales promotion has a number of distinct advantages. First, it involves primarily the consumer or channel member. For example, consumers must return coupons to get the values, or they must use free samples or throw them away. These are sometimes called *forcing techniques,* since they "force" the consumer to act. Additionally, sales promotions give true value to the user; actual savings of money usually occur. Finally, they can be directed to narrowly defined market segments. For example, free samples can be mailed to prospective users in high-income areas in Los Angeles.

Consumer-Directed Sales Promotions

These sales promotion activities are the ones that we are most familiar with as consumers.[7] They are pull-oriented activities (on the right side of Figure 16–7).

Sales promotion, such as this computer vendor trade show in New Orleans, holds a middle ground between advertising and personal selling.

Sampling. Sampling a product means giving away free quantities of it, usually in a smaller size than the regular package. Few people throw away such free items. Marketers hope that the sample usage will lead to future purchase. Sampling is expensive and presents a very complex distribution problem. Mail, home delivery by private services, distribution in stores, and advertising it on the package of another product are but some of the ways it can be done. A variety of service firms are available to distribute samples. Reuben H. Donnelley Corporation is one such firm that can handle samples with mass mailings, handouts, or door drops.

Free samples seldom help mature products, since their problems usually run much deeper than just consumer failure to try them. It is not appropriate for perishable items, very personal-care products, or items with slow in-store turnover.

Price Incentives or Deals. Lowering prices in the short run to encourage new product trial or more consumption of an established brand is called a **price incentive** or **consumer deal.** These deals are often presented to the consumer by means of *cents-off coupons* ads in packages, on labels, or may even be mailed to the consumer. About 40 billion coupons are distributed each year. The coupon may be returned to the store to get money off on the purchase or directly to the manufacturer for redemption.

Deals work best when (1) the price incentive is used only infrequently, at widely spaced intervals; (2) when a brand is relatively new; (3) when the manufacturer avoids dealing as a strategy to force the retailer to stock in the hope of offsetting acceptance of a price offer by a competing brand; and (4) when deals are not used as a substitute for advertising. Fraudulent redemption of coupons is a major problem, as is misredemption (on the wrong size or item).

Consumer deals may be presented on the package itself as a *cents-off offer* at the store or *cash refund* from the manufacturer (*a rebate*), thus avoiding the coupon. This method is easier to control but may cheapen a brand's image if overused, and may require special handling by the retailer.

Contests and Sweepstakes. Promotional activities that involve consumers in games of *skill* are called **contests,** while those involving consumers in games of *chance* are called **sweepstakes.** Their advantages include high consumer involvement, added retailer support, and added excitement about or interest in products or advertising themes. Responses to these activities never involve more than 20 percent of the target audience and are prohibited in certain states.

Premiums. A premium is the offer of some article of merchandise, either free or at a lower price than usual, as an inducement to purchase another product or visit the location where the latter product is sold. The intent is to induce consumers to purchase the product to which the premium is tied. The goal may be to increase trial of a new product or encourage more consumption of an established product. About $12–$15 billion is expended annually on premiums. Common types of premiums include the following:

- *Free Premiums.* These are items that the consumer receives or may obtain as a result of buying the product. Small toys in cereal boxes, the Cracker Jacks "prize," and a towel attached to a Duz detergent box are all examples of *in-pack* or *on-pack* free premiums. Alternatively, the premium may be offered *free-in-the-mail.* The offer of the premium is presented in a coupon or advertisement. The consumer mails the request to the manufacturer or a designated redemption center.
- *Self-Liquidating Items.* Here the customer is offered the chance to buy merchandise at a special price, usually just enough to cover the cost of the premium. These offers can reinforce the brand's image and its advertising. Marlboro overtook Winston as the number-one-selling cigarette, in part because of a very effective "store" of self-liquidating cowboy-related items (hats, belts, shirts).
- *Reusable Containers.* The product package itself can be an effective premium. Maxwell House coffee has had great success with special carafes, as has Dunkin' Donuts with storage cannisters.

Point-of-Purchase. Point-of-Purchase promotions (POP) are those special displays, racks, signs, banners, and exhibits that are placed in the retail store to support the sale of a brand. With the increasing importance of self-service, POP has become more important. These promotions serve to remind customers that a product is available at a given location (a GE or Sony sign in the window or Budweiser sign over the bar); as one final attempt to influence the customer to select a specific brand (the Gillette display right at the cash register); and to encourage impulse buying. Sometimes it is necessary to pay the retailer in order to obtain a prime POP location, such as right at the cash register. The payment may be in cash discounts or even free goods. With a proven, successful display, the retailer may pay to get the POP materials. The yearly expenditures on POP are about $8 billion. Studies indicate that these dollars are well spent when effectively coordinated with advertising and other promotional activity. Retailers often do not use a firm's POP materials because:

1. too much material is supplied by too many firms;
2. displays do not fit the retailer's needs in terms of size or durability;
3. the quality of display material is inferior;

4. the salesperson merchandises the display material badly to the retailer, or it is not seasonally appropriate, or it is difficult to assemble;
5. the profit available on the product is insufficient to warrant the space.[8]

The POP must fit the retailer's and end consumer's needs. It has been said that if retailers put up every display offered to them, there would be very little room in the store for anything else. The next time you are in a food or drug store, be alert to the POP displays that are present.

Other Techniques. Two other sales promotion techniques are worth noting briefly: *trading stamps* and *demonstrations.* Trading stamps are special coupons distributed with a purchase that are redeemable for merchandise or cash. Some consider them to be a type of premium. It is usually the retailer who distributes the stamps on the basis of total purchase in the store. Trading stamps are owned by a stamp company, such as S&H, and sold to the retailer for about 2 to 3 percent of face value of store merchandise cost. They were very popular in the 1950s and 1960s, but have fallen out of favor because they drove up retailers' costs, and consumers perceived that they helped increase prices.

Demonstrations are sometimes used by manufacturers to gain attention at the retail level. They involve a personal presentation of how a product works or tastes. Cosmetic firms often have their own people in stores to show how to properly use their products. Microwave oven companies effectively used this technique in recent years. The labor-intensive nature of demonstrations makes this a very expensive technique, and, thus, it has limited application.

Channel-Directed Sales Promotions

Sales promotion activity is also directed at wholesalers and retailers.[9] These promotional activities, often called **trade promotions,** are designed to increase sales by motivating channel members to more actively sell products to their customers, to place larger orders, to feature these products in local advertising, and to allocate more shelf space or allow special displays for the product. They are a critical part of overall marketing success. The most important ones are discussed below (and shown on the left side of Figure 16–6).

Cooperative Advertising. This is an agreement in which a manufacturer pays a portion of a retailer's local advertising costs. These costs are shared on a fifty-fifty basis up to a specified limit, usually related to the amount the retailer purchases from the manufacturer.

Promotional Allowances. In circumstances where effective in-store display is critical to the success of the product, an allowance may be made for a retailer who puts a display in a specific location. It may be a payment or a discount from the usual cost of merchandise. Expenditures in this area have grown rapidly over the last ten to fifteen years from about $1 billion to over $15 billion. It is estimated that 60 percent of all manufacturers' sales to food and drug retail outlets are accompanied by a trade deal averaging 12 percent.

Contests and Incentive Programs. Manufacturers often sponsor *contests* with prizes like free merchandise, trips, and plaques to dealers who reach certain specified sales levels. Additionally, they may get free *merchandise allowances* or even *money bonuses* for reaching sales performance goals. Once in a while, there is a sweepstakes, where "lucky" dealers can win substantial prizes. For example, Fisher-Price Toys had great success with a sweepstakes that gave cooperating dealers a chance to win a trip to Puerto Rico. These types of programs may also be directed at in-store sales personnel for their individual sales performances. A direct payment by a manufacturer to a channel member salesperson is called a *spiff.* This is very common at the consumer level for consumer durables and cosmetics, and at the wholesale level for beer and records. Another version of a spiff is when retailers pay their salespeople to push certain items. Clearly, this practice makes it possible for consumers to be deceived by a salesperson attempting to earn *push money.* As a result, these types of payments are controversial.

Management Assistance. Manufacturers may also provide channel members with management assistance in running their businesses. Among these services are personnel training, inventory control, store displays, and financial management.

Slotting Fees or Allowances. Recently, power in the channel has shifted more toward retailers, and many have been able to extract an additional type of fee or allowance from manufacturers. These so called *slotting fees* or *allowances* are cash payments made by the manufacturer to the retailer for access to shelf space in the store or warehouse, or for special shelf locations or displays. A common fee structure would be: $1,000 per store to get shelf space for a new product, $10,000 to get into the warehouse, and $250 per store for an end-aisle display.[11] Slotting allowances are very unpopular with manufacturers and very controversial in the consumer package goods business. Some consider these payments as a close cousin to extortion. The long-run viability and structure of slotting fees is very much an open question at this time. Some retailers are even asking for discontinuance allowances to be paid when a product is dropped from retail distribution. This fight will continue.

Review Your Marketing Knowledge

- Look through four or five magazines and observe at a supermarket to identify different types of consumer-directed sales promotions. Classify each one you identify.
- With more power in the channel shifting to distributors and retailers, the importance of channel-directed sales promotions has increased. Why would this happen?
- Ask a retailer what type of trade deals would be required for a new product to get shelf space. What do you think he or she would say?

Publicity

Publicity is another means that marketers can use to promote their products to mass audiences. It involves free promotion about the product or organization in the media. For example, as the result of an effective publicity campaign, a majority of prospective moviegoers were aware of "Batman" before the film was introduced and before any advertising dollars had been spent on it. The campaign included news releases and feature stories in news and movie magazines.

Publicity can play a strong role in product marketing, but often it is also the cornerstone of a company's *public relations* campaign. A firm's publicity experts are often located in the public relations department. **Public relations** *evaluates public attitudes, identifies the policies and procedures of an individual or an organization with the public interest,* and *executes a program of action to earn public understanding and accep-*

tance.[12] The public involved may be consumers, employees, suppliers, stockholders, the investment community, government administrators, or the community at large. The public relations role in organizations involves the use of many communications approaches, including institutional advertising, personal selling by senior corporate executives, and publicity. The latter strongly supports public relations but has a role that extends far beyond this.

Topics Available

Organizations have many topics available to them that have potential for publicity. Among them are new products, special events, changes in the marketing mix, charity activities, athletic sponsorships, sales and profit positions, and speeches by executives. For a topic to generate effective publicity, it must be truly newsworthy. Unfortunately, not all publicity is within the control of the organization. Negative stories may appear in the media whether well-founded or not. For example:

- The Exxon *Valdez* spilled millions of gallons of oil into Alaskan waters, resulting in harsh public reaction against Exxon.
- A study was published in the *New England Journal of Medicine* that linked coffee consumption with cancer. This, on the other hand, was later debunked, due to the limitations of the study.

Both these incidents generated substantial national press coverage. So it seems that firms must not only be concerned with generating positive publicity, but also with responding to negative publicity.

Publicity Techniques

The main techniques for gaining publicity are news releases, feature articles, press conferences, personal appearances, records, and films. *News releases* are short statements about a product or organization typically containing about 250 to 300 words. *Feature articles* contain up to 3000 words and are usually prepared for a specific publication. *Press conferences* involve inviting newspeople to hear a specific announcement and ask questions. *Records* and *films* can also be produced to serve as filler on radio and television stations, be shown in schools, or to social or civic groups. For example, Phillips Petroleum makes a number of films on science available to television and to the schools.

Managing Publicity

Publicity needs to be managed carefully. Objectives need to be set, budgets determined, media targeted, and performance evaluated. This should be done with the same care and with the same procedures used in advertising. Publicity is a powerful promotional device if managed properly.

Personal Computer Exercise

Preparing an advertising and sales promotion plan involves the careful analysis of the cost and likely sales impact. The PC exercise provides you with data on these issues for a product and allows you to prepare alternative advertising and sales promotion plans. What are the advantages and disadvantages of these plans?

KEY POINTS

• The skillful blend of advertising, sales promotion, and publicity is an important building block in successful marketing programs.

• Total advertising expenditures are growing rapidly in the United States but are fairly stable as a percentage of gross national product.

• Marketing managers must set advertising objectives and budget levels, choose creative approaches, make media choices, determine the timing and placement of advertisements, test advertising effectiveness, and select and use an advertising agency.

• There are many different types of advertising, including primary or selective demand; direct or indirect action; consumer, industrial, or trade; product or institutional; vertical or horizontal cooperative; and commercial or public service.

• Sales promotion techniques aid in both consumer pull and dealer push. Costs of sales promotion activities about equal those for advertising.

• Pull approaches include free samples, price incentives or deals, contests, premiums, point-of-purchase displays, trading stamps, and demonstrations.

• Push approaches include cooperative advertising, promotional allowances, contests, incentive programs, and management assistance.

• Publicity can also be useful to marketers in the promotion of their products or organization.

• Among the techniques used to generate publicity are news releases, feature articles, press conferences, and records and films.

ISSUES FOR DISCUSSION

1. A firm that markets a major package good was about to undertake a study of the relationship between its advertising dollars and its sales. One member of the management team argued that this could be misleading, because other advertising factors beyond the amount of money spent also affected sales. These include the media used and the creative execution. Discuss.

2. How does advertising affect the prices consumers pay for products?

3. The cost per thousand readers of *The New Yorker* magazine is many times greater than that for *Time* magazine. Why, then, would one advertise in *The New Yorker?*

4. Pick two consumer products ads and two industrial products ads from magazines.
   a. List the objectives of each ad.
   b. Evaluate each ad's fit with the editorial environment of the magazine.
   c. Explain how you would test the effectiveness of the ads.

5. The brand manager for a new entry into the shampoo market is planning the consumer and trade promotions for the first year of the product entry. What might be the composition of this program?

6. How might a sales promotion program for the Macintosh II personal computer be structured?

7. What different activities might an advertising agency perform for its client? Why would a company drop an agency that had produced award-winning commercials (McDonald's move from Needham, Harper, and Steers to Leo Burnett for example)?

8. Identify some publicity about a product or organization that is positive. Explain how the organization might have generated this publicity.

9. Nutrasweet has been extremely well received in the marketplace as a sugar substitute. Recently, in the press, some scientists have questioned its safety, saying that it can cause brain disorders in some people. How should the management of Nutrasweet respond to this publicity?

10. From recent magazines, select two ads. For each (a) describe the target market; (b) identify the type of presentation used; and (c) rate the ad for effectiveness.

GLOSSARY

Contest: a game requiring some skill on the part of the participant.

Cooperative advertising: an agreement in which a manufacturer pays a portion of a retailer's local advertising costs.

Cost per thousand (cpm): a measure used to summarize the cost effectiveness of media vehicles; it gives the cost per thousand persons in the vehicle's audience.

DAGMAR: (Defining Advertising Goals, Measuring Advertising Results): a philosophy requiring advertising goals to be stated and evaluated using communications objectives.

Flighting: the timing pattern of media expenditures throughout the year.

Frequency: the average number of times a person is exposed to an ad.

Gross rating point (GRP): the combination of reach times frequency.

In-house agency: a department in an organization set up to do the work usually performed by an advertising agency.

Media plan: the media types, vehicles, and inserts used to advertise a product or service.

Media type: the distinction between broad classes of media—newspapers, magazines, television, radio, and so forth.

Media vehicles: the specific units for purchase within media types (the CBS Evening News or the December issue of *Life*.)

Point-of-purchase promotion (POP): special displays, racks, signs, banners, and exhibits that are placed in the retail store to support the sales of a brand.

Premiums: offer of some article of merchandise either free or at a lower price than usual to encourage consumers to buy another product or service.

Price incentives or deals: short-run price decreases.

Public relations: activities that evaluate public attitudes, identify the policies and procedures of an individual or an organization with the public interest, and execute a program of action to earn public understanding and acceptance for the firm.

Reach: total number of persons exposed to a particular ad.

Sampling: giving away quantities of a product.

Slotting fees or allowances: cash payments made by a manufacturer to the retailer for access to shelf space in the store or warehouse, or for special shelf locations or displays.

Sweepstakes: a game of chance.

Trade promotions: sales promotion activity directed at wholesalers and retailers.

NOTES

1. Joanne Lipman, "Estimate for '88 U.S. Ad Spending Is Sliced by Prominent Forecaster," *The Wall Street Journal,* June 16, 1988, p. 24.

2. *Marketing and Media Decisions,* May 1988, p. 109. Provided by McCann-Erickson.

3. For a complete list of the top 200 advertised brands with their media expenditures, see *Marketing and Media Decisions,* July 1988.

4. Pat Sloan, "Maybelline Cuts TV Ad Spending," *Advertising Age,* March 7, 1988, pp. 3, 79.

5. For a more developed presentation of this scheme, see Julian L. Simon, *The Management of Advertising* (Prentice-Hall, 1971), pp. 174–206.

6. For a more detailed presentation of this area see Katherine E. Jocz, "Research on Sales Promotion: Collected Papers," Marketing Science Institute, July 1984, and Al Urbanski, "Sales Promotion's New Aura," *Sales & Marketing Management,* November 14, 1983.

7. For a more detailed discussion, see James F. Engel, Martin R. Warshaw, and Thomas C. Kinnear, *Promotional Strategy: Managing the Marketing Communications Process* (Irwin, 1987), pp. 438–460.

8. For detailed evaluation see "Display Effectiveness: An Evaluation," *The Nielsen Researcher,* Number 2, 1983, pp. 2–8, and "Display Effectiveness: An Evaluation Part II," *The Nielsen Researcher,* Number 3, 1983, pp. 2–10.

9. For a more detailed discussion, see Engel, Warshaw, and Kinnear, *Promotional Strategy,* pp. 513–44.

10. Monci Jo Williams, "The No-Win Game of Price Promotion," *Fortune,* July 11, 1983, pp. 92–102.

11. Judann Dagnoli and Laurie Freeman, "Marketers Seek Slotting-Fee Truce," *Advertising Age,* February 22, 1988, pp. 12 and 68; and Rebecca Fannin, Planograms: "Friend or Foe?" *Marketing and Media Decisions,* May 1988, pp. 48–54.

12. Bertrand R. Cansfield and Frazier Moore, *Public Relations: Principles, Cases, and Problems,* 6th ed. (Irwin, 1973), p. 4.

CASE APPLICATION 16–1

The Frozen Entrees Industry

Frozen food entrees gobbled up almost $2.7 billion in supermarket sales alone last year, says *Progressive Grocer* magazine. Stouffer's Food Corp., which has been at the top of the heap with its higher-priced "red-box" prototype and Lean Cuisine entree lines, found its volume down between 7 percent and 10 percent last year, according to John McMillin, food industry analyst for Prudential-Bache Securities. Meanwhile, the more wallet-conscious Weight Watchers, Banquet, and Budget Gourmet's volumes were on the rise.

The All American Gourmet Co., which makes Budget Gourmet, opened up its offerings three years ago with its Slim Select entrees. Now the company is test marketing the new Eating Right selection, a 14-entree line of low-calorie, frozen entrees that will be priced competitively with both Lean Cuisine and Weight Watchers entrees.

It is no secret that manufacturers spend millions on advertising their products to reach female homemakers, who do most of the grocery buying. Sources say that the introduction of All American Gourmet's Eating Right entrees alone will be close to $15 million, the same amount spent for all Budget Gourmet lines, which include side dishes, dinners, and entrees.

Basically, the usual advertising vehicles, such as TV, magazines, and couponing, are in the marketing and media plans. Manufacturers are also working with the trade more to get their products better play. One frozen-food buyer in the Midwest says that Stouffer's has come out with billback features they never had before. "They're finally doing what their competitors are doing," he says. "Stouffer's used to bring out new items, and it was almost, 'Take it or leave it, you will be forced to buy it because it's so good,'" he says facetiously. But with Budget Gourmet, says Jack DeMoulas, vice president, frozen food and dairy of the Market Basket Inc., which has 42 stores in Massachusetts and New Hampshire, "I can buy everything on deal with them all year long."

Following are the six biggest frozen-entree brands based on 1987 overall retail sales, according to Business Trend Analysts Inc. They are Lean Cuisine, with 19%; Banquet, 17%; Stouffer's and Weight Watcher's, both 16%; Budget Gourmet, 11%; and Swanson, 10%. Keep in mind that the least expensive are Banquet, Budget Gourmet, and Swanson. Their media budgets are as follows:

Lean Cuisine

Although the Lean Cuisine name and the notation on the package—"less than 300 calories"—may suggest that only dieters consume the entrees, a look at an ad suggests a bigger target. One magazine ad in particular shows an expensive leather briefcase, purse and gloves, car keys, and the upper-right-hand corner of a newspaper, subtly but obviously *The Wall Street Journal.* A box of Lean Cuisine's veal lasagna lies on top of the leather goods, and the words at the top of the page read, "Don't forget your lunch box."

Says Marguerite Tremelin, marketing services coordinator, "These are more upscale products and appeal to those with a fast-paced lifestyle, but they don't want to sacrifice quality for convenience."

Tremelin says that from the beginning, "Lean Cuisine was designed to appeal to a much broader audience than just dieters—people interested in lighter eating and maintaining their weight. It's a lifestyle rather than a diet mode."

Lean Cuisine was rolled out nationally in 1982 after 10 items went into test market a year earlier. There are now 28 entrees, including unusual offerings such as stuffed cabbage and

Frozen Entrees' 1987 Media Expenditures (000)

	Total	Network* Television	Spot* Television	Cable TV* Networks	Syndicated* TV	Spot** Radio	Magazines	Sunday Magazines	News-papers***
Lean Cuisine	11,523.9	6,646.7	391.0	85.4	1,410.9	—	2,335.7	654.2	—
Budget Gourmet	7,352.0	—	5,268.7	—	—	—	2,072.6	—	10.7
Stouffer's	6,156.2	387.6	2,201.8	8.1	—	284.4	2,810.5	—	463.8
Swanson	5,435.6	4,226.3	139.5	187.7	629.5	—	99.8	98.0	54.8
Weight Watchers	3,130.7	—	—	—	1,716.8	—	660.2	471.4	282.3
Banquet	119.7	—	—	—	—	—	—	—	119.7

SOURCES: Leading National Advertisers; *Broadcast Advertisers Reports as reported to LNA; **Radio Expenditure Reports; ***Media Records. No network-radio or outdoor expenditures were reported. From *Media and Marketing Decisions*, September 1988, p. 101.

herbed lamb. Lean Cuisine may average four to five new entrees a year.

A cross promotion was called "The Lite Show," and touted to be "a great-tasting combination under 391 calories." It "starred" Diet Coke, Lite Lite Tofutti and Lean Cuisine. Thirty-cents-off coupons were available for each of the products.

According to Leading National Advertisers and Broadcast Advertisers Reports, for the first quarter of this year, Lean Cuisine advertised on network, spot, cable, and syndicated TV and also magazines and Sunday magazines. About $5 million was reported in media expenditures, with TV getting the bulk and magazines coming in second. The 30- and sometimes 60-second spots, says BAR, have appeared on *ABC News This Morning, All My Children, Mr. Belvedere, Donahue, Hour Magazine, Jeopardy,* and *Entertainment Tonight.* On cable, the entrees have appeared on TBS' movie presentations and *National Geographic.*

LNA reports, for the first half of the year, Lean Cuisine ads were in magazines such as *American Health, Cosmopolitan, Bon Appetit,* the *Los Angeles Times* and the *New York Times* magazines, *Southern Living, Sunset,* and *Working Mother.*

Banquet

Conagra's Banquet features a variety of entree presentations, such as Family Entrees that can feed mom, dad, and a couple of kids; Cookin' Bags, which were the answer to not heating the oven; and Banquet Supreme, which is Banquet's answer to good food at a good value.

Tom Studer, vice president of marketing, Conagra Consumer Frozen Food Co., which markets Banquet, says that although Banquet Supreme is being sold at cut-rate prices—as low as $1.29—it can't really be compared to the Budget Gourmet. Conagra's Sensible Chef is positioned more closely to the Budget Gourmet, both of which have more of a "linguini with clam sauce" upscale appeal, while Banquet Supreme, which has eight entree offerings, has a "lasagna" or family appeal. Banquet entrees always target the family, or a more "blue-collar-oriented," broad target of those 25 to 49 with a $25,000 and under annual household income.

The family entrees, which average about $1.99 each at retail, have 16 different items. Banquet entrees have always been pushed through consumer promotions such as free-standing inserts (FSIs), direct mail, ROP, and localized programs through the trade.

Stouffer's

We have Stouffer's to thank for frozen entrees, born 34 years ago. The marketing message remains the same: quality, convenience, and variety. These have been promoted since day one, says Marguerite Tremelin, marketing services coordinator.

There are now 56 entrees for the regular line, or "red box" as some call it, ranging in price from 99 cents to $2.99. Stouffer's, like Lean Cuisine, also has been price promoting against its competitors, for example through increased couponing, and also playing up the quality aspect of Stouffer's name. One magazine ad reads, "If you can have 32 different entrees priced about $2 each, and they all have the name Stouffer's, why would you buy anything else?"

The target audience is pretty much the same as Lean Cuisine, and that is upscale but with a fairly broad reach. Tremelin describes it as one- and two-member households where one or both people are working.

For the first quarter of 1988, LNA reports that Stouffer's spent $3.4 million in ad expenditures. Commercials appeared on spot TV in 35 markets on shows such as *Family Ties, The Today Show, Wheel of Fortune,* and *Entertain-*

ment Tonight, according to BAR. According to LNA, in the first half of this year, Stouffer's frozen entrees were advertised in *Bon Appetit*, *Better Homes and Gardens*, *Cosmopolitan*, *Ladies' Home Journal*, *Life*, *Metropolitan Home*, *New Woman*, *People*, *Reader's Digest*, *Redbook*, *Smithsonian*, *Southern Living*, and *Sunset*.

Weight Watchers

"This Is Living" may be the long-running tagline of Weight Watchers, but it also may be the tagline of the company itself, which has been gaining ground through the years.

Weight Watchers' 35 entrees, priced at $1.89 to $2.89, are targeted to primarily female, weight-conscious frozen-meal users who are 25 to 54 years old and make more than $25,000 a year. "We think working women are probably our most important subsegment," says Douglas Haines, Marketing General Manager. "I think the employment status is more important than age or income. To the working woman, time is money."

TV is the primary advertising medium for the entrees. "We generally have a good presence in prime time, fringe, and prime access. Network, spot, cable, and syndicated TV are used, and BAR lists *ABC Monday Night Movie*, *Dallas*, *MacGyver*, *48 Hours*, *Divorce Court*, and *Wheel of Fortune* as some of the more recent TV Shows used. On cable, the entrees have appeared on Cable News Network, USA, CBN, and TBS, according to BAR. Spots are 15- and 30-seconds.

Haines says the entrees participate in a "fairly substantial magazine plan. Anything from the Seven Sisters to *Vogue* or fitness books like *Shape* and, of course, *Weight Watchers* magazine. Newspaper ROP ads haven't been used because the ads "look much better in color," says Haines. Newspapers have been used in selected markets.

Promotionally, Weight Watchers is always on the lookout for companies to be tie-in partners. Last year, the company ran a joint promotion with Diet Coke and Kellogg's Special K cereal. Free-standing inserts and coupons on the cartons were used. Weight Watchers also sponsors a women's cycling team.

Haines says last year's LNA estimate of $3.1 million in expenditures is "awfully low." He puts last year's media expenditures as more to the tune of $10 million. LNA also reports that for the first quarter of 1988, about $6 million was spent on the entrees.

Budget Gourmet

Here's a product that has made the other frozen entrees shudder in their cases. Budget Gourmet's entrees, born five years ago, cost only $1.89 for the regular entrees and $1.99 for the three-year-old Slim Selects. But last year Budget Gourmet commanded an 11 percent market share based on retail sales.

A spokesman for the All American Gourmet Co., now a unit of Kraft/General Foods, Inc., says All American has almost tripled in size from three years ago. He adds that the marketing is very regional, and the fundamental message hasn't changed: "Great tasting food at great prices."

"We try and coordinate our marketing efforts with trade customers as much as possible," explains the spokesman. "We try to be flexible in terms of the local broker and what his needs are in terms of timing." He adds, "We want them to push our product hard, so we give them the tools to do it," such as price promotions and coupon drops. "We'll buy space in their TV programs, too."

Women are the primary target for Budget Gourmet products, especially for the Slim Selects. More specifically, the target is middle-class women who may or may not be short on time. "Men play an important role, but women do most of the grocery shopping," reasons the spokesman, who says single men are part of the audience, but they have discretionary income and tend to eat out more than women with responsibilities at home.

For 1988 LNA reports that Budget Gourmet spent more than $8 million in media. BAR says that Budget Gourmet advertised, for example, on *Dynasty*, *thirtysomething*, and *Cosby*. For the first half of 1988, Budget Gourmet advertised in *Good Housekeeping*, *McCall's*, *Ladies' Home Journal*, and *People* magazines.

Swanson

As the Swanson aluminum frozen dinner tray finds its place in the Smithsonian Institution, so goes Swanson off in search of new demographic groups to conquer with is microwaveable, plastic-tray-encased Swanson Homestyle Recipe Entrees, introduced in June 1987.

The Homestyle entrees, which are below $2, had been even less expensive, but the new plastic trays are pricey, so a $1.29 entree went up to $1.49. When the Homestyle entrees came out last year, there were three price points. Chicken cacciatore and seafood creole with rice boil-in-bag entrees were more than $2 each, the highest price point, and were designed for image enhancement to "stretch beyond what people think Swanson is," explains Swanson's Marketing VP. However, he also noted that boil-in-the-bag entrees are less convenient, so those products have been dropped, though a bag of spaghetti and meatballs remains.

Swanson's 15- and 30-second TV commercials air on network and cable. For the introduction of the entrees last year, a wide mix of media was used, including prime, daytime, sports, and news. No radio or magazines are used currently. Local marketing is managed by 21 regional offices that do newspaper advertising, primarily ROP. FSIs are used also.

LNA reports that $1.8 million was spent on ad expenditures for the first quarter of 1988. According to BAR, Swanson Homestyle Recipe entrees were advertised on the Barry Manilow special, ABC *World News*, *Our House*, *227*, and *Star Trek—The Next Generation*. On cable, *Celebrity Chefs* and the *Young People's Special* are a sampling of programs.

SOURCE: Paula Schnorbus, "Freezer Burn: Brand Report No. 155, Frozen Entrees," *Marketing and Media Decisions*, September 1988, pp. 101–16.

Questions

1. What role does advertising play in the marketing of this type of food product? Relate this role specifically to the Weight Watchers brand.

2. What role do consumer and trade deals play in this industry? Relate this specifically to the Weight Watchers brand.

3. Discuss the appropriateness of the media choices for each brand discussed in the case. Why is the Weight Watchers brand media schedule so different from the other major brands?

4. How should the advertising budget for the Weight Watchers brand be set? Is the current budget appropriate?

CASE APPLICATION 16–2

Merrill Lynch Financial Services

The stock market crash on October 19, 1987, sent financial brokerage services plummeting to the bottom of the popularity polls. Consumers lost confidence in the industry. Mergers, staff and budget cuts, and profit decline followed. Brokerage firms found themselves immersed in an atmosphere of client distrust. This situation demanded a new approach to marketing financial services and products.

Merrill Lynch, industry leader in media expenditures, immediately took action with new creative presentations in its ads. TV spots and a new print campaign started within days of the crash. Gone was the "Your world knows no boundaries" campaign. Merrill Lynch discovered the hard way that this is not the case. In the midst of financial chaos, clients wanted reassurance. Risk and adventure were out, security was in.

Several competing financial services companies chose to dramatize the market's severe downturn, while others chose to ignore it. Merrill Lynch met the situation head-on with a straightforward, informative approach, deciding that educating consumers by addressing their questions and needs was preferable to entertaining them or provoking their thoughts. In a ground-breaking move, "straight-talk" television commercials featuring William A. Schreyer, Merrill's chairman and CEO, were created in hopes of calming unhinged investors. Their message was to assure investors that "the nation and the economy were going to be OK despite the market's nasty jolt." Debbie L. Mandelker, vice president and manager of marketing services, said that Merrill Lynch wanted to take a "very public position and be quickly out there to calm investors with information on the market situation and how it was going." One of the company's main promotional objectives was to establish and increase dialogue between clients and their brokers.

The tainted title of "stockbroker" was replaced by the more informative and less offensive term "financial consultant." Thirty second TV spots featured these financial consultants examining different areas of investment and answering actual questions the company perceived its clients may have had at the time. This straight-talk series was done in groups of four commercials. Each was made without a script to better convey the sense of answering real people's questions. Old commercials were continuously replaced with more timely messages. Another group of four commercials were historical vignettes demonstrating Merrill Lynch's commitment to its clients. This group of ads, designed to imply a return to "the good old days," was accompanied by the tagline, "A Tradition of Trust." The bull, Merrill Lynch's symbol, reappeared, but it had also been noticeably changed by the crash. This new bull adopted a more controllable, electronic form and it now ran across tickertape instead of rambling through china shops and across open landscapes.

Merrill Lynch's main target segment was the group of adults, primarily in their mid 40's, "slightly more affluent" with annual incomes of $50,000 or more. Young emerging investors and small to medium-sized businesses were secondary targets. Merrill's strategy, given the market situation at the time, was to focus on the relationship between clients and financial consultants and the diversification of Merrill's products. Again, reassurance was a key factor.

In addition to its straight-talk campaign, Merrill Lynch's promotional mix included 60 second local and network radio spots, as well as print ads in local newspapers and *The Wall Street Journal.* The print ads provided an 800 number, facilitating customer service. Mandelker said Merrill felt its message was "better and more openly received in an environment where people take you seriously." As a result, business magazines such as *Forbes* and serious lifestyle books such as *Smithsonian* and *Harper's* were employed.

The firm felt that it was more effective to own a few events than to sponsor bits and pieces of many. TV show sponsorship was not even considered, but sports and cultural events were high on the company's list of promotional targets. These events often provide publicity as well. Merrill Lynch employed this "event media" approach in promoting itself during the 1988 Winter Olympics and presidential election-oriented events.

Marketing was also done on the local level, where customization and personal selling were more important and feasible. Branches reported their individual needs and the national office provided them with material on specific products and services. Local seminars grew in importance, and print advertising was the standard local medium. An in-house agency took care of local advertising, while the New York agency of Bozell, Jacobs, Kenyon & Eckhardt managed national promotion.

Merrill Lynch was on to something. By September of 1988, the nation's top brokerage firm found its innovative promotional approach being used by second-ranked Shearson Lehman Hutton, as well as AT&T, the struggling long distance service leader. The reasons were evident. Research determined that the format was extremely effective, and management felt the feedback from Merrill's clients and brokers was "terrific." In a struggling industry, Merrill Lynch's 1988 profits reached $463.2 million, an increase of 38 percent over the previous year.

SOURCES: "The Confidence Game," *Marketing and Media Decisions*, May 1988, pp. 133–147; "Shearson, Merrill Ads Butt Heads," *Advertising Age*, September 26, 1988, p. 84.

Questions

1. What role does advertising play in the Merrill Lynch promotional mix?

2. What external and internal constraints on Merrill Lynch caused the development of a new advertising campaign?

3. Evaluate the media vehicle choices made by Merrill Lynch.

4. Evaluate the creative approach used. Is this creative approach appropriate in the 1990s?

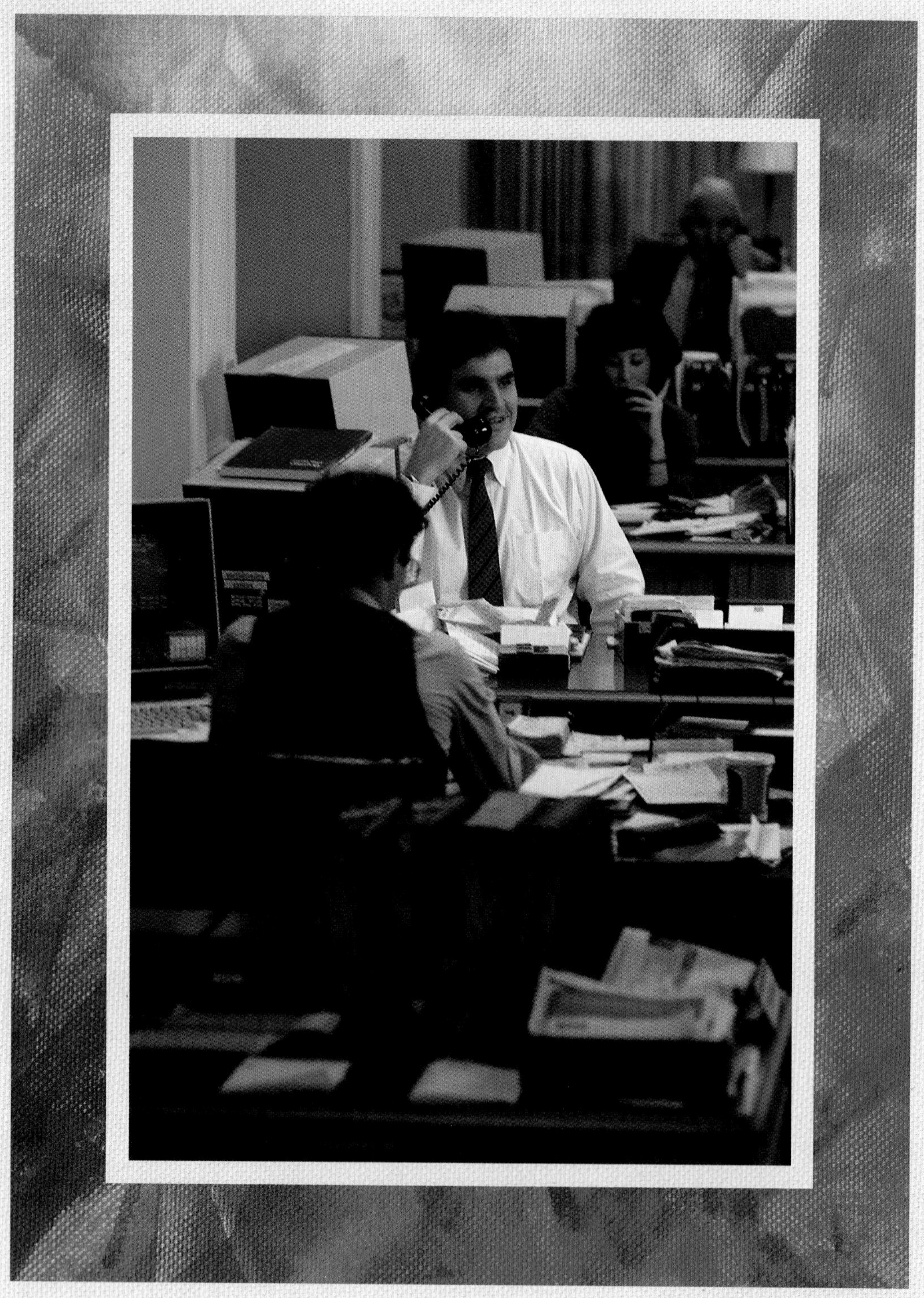

17

Personal Selling

Learning Objectives

Upon completing this chapter, you will be able to do the following:

DEFINE
the need satisfaction approach to selling.

DESCRIBE
the nature and importance of personal selling.

IDENTIFY
the different types of sales jobs.

LIST
the basic steps in the selling process.

ILLUSTRATE
why closing is such an important phase in the selling process.

EXPLAIN
the activities sales force managers are involved in.

MARKETING PROFILE

The Laptop May Be the Salesperson's Best Friend

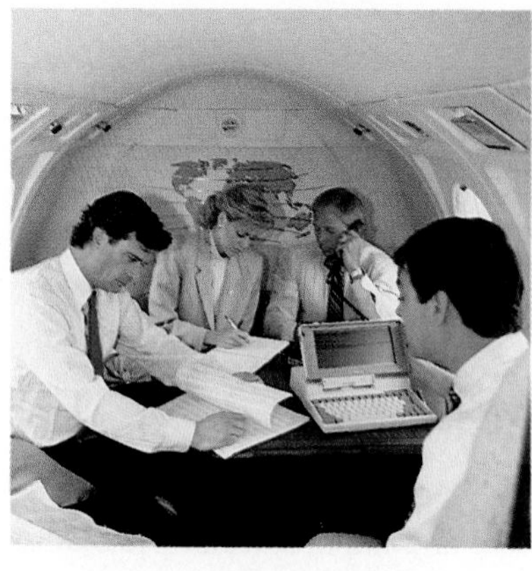

Imagine a salesperson who can effectively keep track of price and availability information for all of the products he or she is selling. This person has the ability to determine the status of a customer's order at any time and at any location. Also, this person could produce letter-quality correspondence at a moment's notice. Does this sound too good to be true? Many companies are envisioning this type of flexibility for their salespeople as a result of laptop computers.

Laptop computers are portable battery powered personal computers that can do virtually everything that their desktop counterparts can do in the office. Most of them use a "clamshell" design where the flat LCD (Liquid Crystal Display) screen can be folded down covering the keyboard when moved. The result is a fully functional PC that can be carried in a briefcase and operated at any location.

The first wave of laptop sales were being sold to middle management presumably to make plane trips more productive and help maintain communication when out of the office. However, due to falling prices, most of the laptops sold recently have been going into the hands of lower level personnel such as field engineers and sales personnel. These recipients are using the machines for word processing, data processing and spreadsheets, retrieving and reviewing data from a central computer via phone lines, and collecting data from customers for use on the central computer. In this way, they bring functions that historically were confined to the office to the customer.

For the salespeople, laptop PCs mean that they no longer have an information tether connecting them to an office. Salespeople can use laptops to shorten the time needed to get important information. Millions of bytes of information can be stored to help determine how much an order will cost the customer and when the products will be delivered. At Northwestern Mutual, Milwaukee, Wisconsin, punching a few buttons can show how different options can change the cost of a policy, according to vice president of sales, Dennis Tamscin. Before laptops and remote access to their main computer, this was done through the mail. At DuPont's chemical pigments department in Wilmington, Delaware, laptops equipped with special programs determine whether customers have to redesign their equipment to accommodate DuPont products. Overall, the portable computer is used to shortcut the information loop generally encountered in sales.

Results have been favorable by many companies. IBM's Michael Sinneck, director of area systems and applications for their marketing services group, claims that "reps that use laptops save, on average, 4.4 hours per week on tasks that were formerly required, such as travelling to branch offices to get answers to customer queries." Inland Steel's Stephen Korbecki estimates a 20–25 percent reduction of clerical errors for the laptop users. Kodak's Ted McGrath thinks salespeople with laptops "have gained two to three hours a week in selling and servicing time." Other organizations such as Black and Decker and Xerox have seen improvements in the form of increased log-on time with the main computer and increased use of district budgets for computer hardware. This shows that the laptops are not only helping productivity, but their ease of use could be winning over some noncomputer users.

However, there are some executives who feel this transfer could have a negative impact on profitability. James Huguet, president of marketing consultant Northeastern Organization, Trumbull, Connecticut, claims, "If I'm paying a salesperson $40,000 or $50,000, plus $10,000 to $20,000 in expenses, I'd be seriously concerned if he used the laptop mostly for writing letters. That makes him a very expensive typist." This doesn't seem to be a majority view, since more and more companies are introducing laptops.

Many of the functions of the salespeople that can be helped by laptops in this *Marketing Profile* are vital to their doing a good job. This chapter helps define these and other functions and processes involved in personal selling.

ADAPTED FROM: Geoff Lewis, "Is The Computer Business Maturing?", *Business Week*, March 6, 1989, pp. 68–78 and Thayer C. Taylor, "How the Best Sales Forces Use PC's and Laptops," *Sales and Marketing Management*, April 1988, pp. 64–74 and Thayer C. Taylor, "Make Way for the Salesman's Best Friend," *Sales and Marketing Management*, February, 1988, pp. 53–56.

Promotion involves communication with potential customers, and personal interaction is often the best way to persuade someone to purchase a good or service. Each of us engages in acts of persuasion by convincing a friend to drive carefully, telling an employer of our abilities and skills, or selling used furniture to browsers at a garage sale. Since we all *must* do it, we might as well learn to do it *well.* In simple terms, personal selling uses human relations skills.

In this chapter we will examine personal selling as an extremely important and necessary part of the promotion mix. The job is done by salespeople, who attempt to establish two-way communication with potential buyers.[1] The old maxim "Nothing happens until a sale is made" is worth keeping in mind when analyzing the importance of personal selling.

We will review each step in the personal selling process in this chapter. In addition, we will discuss the job of managing the personal selling force, including deciding how many salespeople to hire, what kind of salespeople are needed, how to motivate the sales team, and how to evaluate their performances.

The Importance of Personal Selling

Personal selling involves interactions between people. Consequently, compared with other parts of the promotion mix, personal selling is more human, flexible, and dynamic.[2] The salesperson can tailor the communication to fit the prospective customer's needs, expressions, and overall behavior.

This up-close type of communication is needed in our economy. United States Census Bureau statistics suggest that about 8 percent of the labor force, or approximately 7 million people, work in sales. Many of those simply collect money at check-out counters, but others find customers, sell creatively, close sales, and service customers afterwards. Even those at the cash register help "sell" the store to the customers, though they are not always aware of their impact.

Historically many types of products have needed the creativity of personal selling to gain acceptance in the marketplace.[3] Most consumers are hesitant to change from old, familiar products or ways of doing things. Someone must communicate the advantages of and demonstrate the new products before they are accepted. This type of communication and demonstration has occurred with many products most people take for granted today, such as televisions, microwave ovens, vacuum cleaners, videocassette recorders, exercise equipment, vacations to Hawaii and soft contact lenses. Through the creative efforts of salespeople, these products have become integral parts of modern life.

Some salespeople serve as communication links with the public. These "boundary spanners" continually receive, process, and transmit information from the public to the organization and vice versa. They can sense the needs and desires of the marketplace, and provide their firms with data that can be eventually converted into goods and services.

The salesperson is the *image agent* of the company. He or she is the contact person, the representative of the company who affects and controls the customer's perceptions and evaluations of the company and its products and services. The salesperson is also the communication link from the customer back to the company. As *liaison agent* the salesperson should be trained to report customer dissatisfactions with the company, its programs, products, and services. This feedback helps reduce unnecessarily lost sales and bad word-of-mouth. The salesperson is in a good position to act as *intelligence agent* and report to the company changes in the marketplace, such as changes in customer choice criteria, competition, and the environment (technological, legal/political, and so forth).

The work of salespeople is also related to the work of many other people in society. This is because a chain reaction follows each sale, starting with the first reorder through the wholesaler to the larger replacement orders for factory production with basic items that come from farms and mines.

Although their function is extremely important to economic growth, a high standard of living, and full employment, salespeople still have negative images. This may be due to a misunderstanding about their roles by salespeople in the past.[4]

The Sales Stereotype

Three thousand college students were asked to jot down the first five words that came to mind when they heard the word *salesperson*.[5] The ten most common replies were *travel, money, personality, sales, fast-talker, commission, appearance, products, high-pressure,* and *aggressive*. This list reveals some of the negative stereotypes surrounding salespeople. Since salespeople are the most visible of all performers in business, they will probably continue to be at the center of stories and movies. Arthur Miller's play *Death of a Salesman* helped perpetrate the old salesman stereotype. Willy Loman attempted to create an illusion of success, but everyone saw right through it, including Willy. The questionable stereotype is brought out in the *Marketing in Action* on the need for salespeople.

In contrast to the jaded stereotype are the many professional salespeople who are experts in particular areas and are trained to render valuable services to customers. For example, sales personnel in many firms determine the needs of customers, deliver and service goods, and receive and process customer responses about the products. They perform many roles in a professional and ethical manner. Like all occupations, the job of selling is always developing, but today it is usually more a mix of art and science than an exercise in high pressure, glib talking, and conning.

The emphasis on the art side of selling is displayed by Nicholas Barsan, one of the top salespersons among the 75,000 Century 21 real estate brokers.[6] He sells a house every four days in the Jackson Heights area of Queens, New York. He is persistent, excited about selling, and loves to talk with customers. A third of Mr. Barsan's $1.1 million in commissions last year came from repeat customers. He literally knocks on the doors of old customers and asks if they are ready to sell.

The professionalizing of the sales job has come about gradually, with standards being established by various accreditation groups. The American College of Life Underwriters offers a Chartered Life Underwriters certificate to salespeople who complete a rigorous course of training and study. Colleges and universities educate the public by offering courses in marketing and personal selling.[7] Today, the salesperson's responsibilities require more education and technical training than the old "traveling salesman" had and the role, at present, is that of communicator, advisor, coordinator, information-processor, problem-solver, and supportive individual.

Review Your Marketing Knowledge

- What has caused the negative image of sales jobs that many people have?
- Explain the meaning of, "Nothing happens until a sale is made."
- Why are communication skills so important for anyone in a sales job?

MARKETING IN ACTION

A Need for Sales and Salespeople

James Koch, Chief Executive Officer of the Boston Beer Company, Boston, Massachusetts, is an advocate of selling. He feels that in recent years "manufacturers perceive marketing as a magic solution that takes away their responsibility for making a good product." Instead of making a better product and selling it, companies make a product that is just as good as the competition and expect that good marketing will make the product successful. Koch feels that consumers know what quality is and buy quality rather than slick advertising campaigns. He cites the example of Japanese cars in the early 1970s. The Japanese manufacturers were not recognized in America and used awkward marketing campaigns. The American consumers, however, saw that they could buy a reliable, efficient car for less money.

Part of the reason for the decreased emphasis in selling, says Koch, is that the salesman's job has become "devalued." "If you go to a cocktail party and you're asked what you do for a living, and you reply, 'I'm a salesman,' people look at you like you've got crumbs on your shirt. Tell them you're a marketing director, however, and they say, 'How interesting.' It is this type of attitude, one that salesmen are hucksters trying to make a buck, that places an 'inferior' tag on the profession."

When he was starting his Boston Beer Company, Koch had a revealing conversation with his uncle who happened to be one of his financial backers:

"So," his uncle asked, "what did you do today?" He told him that he had spent his day shopping for a computer system. When his uncle asked why, he explained that he need it to keep track of sales, payables, etc. "Oh yeah," the uncle replied, "sales. By the way, have you got any?" When Koch admitted that he hadn't, his uncle demanded, "So what . . . are you doing buying a computer?" and continued, "You know Jim, I've seen a lot more businesses go broke because they didn't have enough sales than I've seen go under from lack of computers. Why don't you work on first things first?"

From this he realized that he had started from the wrong end. He didn't need a computer, he needed a customer. From that day on, he put a few cold beers in his briefcase, and started cold-calling on bars. Even though the business has grown to $7 million in sales, he still pounds the pavement and feels the job of salesman can make or break a company.

Types of Sales Jobs

Personal selling jobs differ on such dimensions as necessary training, personal freedom, many rewards, location and type of customers, and creativity. Generally, as the number of potential customers decreases, the complexity of the product increases or the economic value of the product grows, and the role of personal selling becomes more important.[8] Based on the functions they perform, salespeople can be classified into three groups: order-getters, order-takers, and support personnel.[9]

Order-Getters

Order-getters are salespeople who are concerned with selling and generating more sales. The order-getting job is to find new buyers and to increase sales to old customers by creative selling. As this chapter's opening Profile indicates, a few years ago receiving orders for the laptop computer was almost impossible. However, thanks to screens that are as legible as monitors on office terminals, microprocessors as powerful as those in the best desktop machines, and vastly improved memory capacity, buyers are lining up.[10] Eastman Kodak, Ciba-Geigy, and Touche Ross are sold on the laptop. Ciba-Geigy is providing up to 1,000 pharmaceutical salespeople and sales managers with nine-pound laptop computers from *G R I D* Systems Corp. in Fremont, California. The GRID sales team was able to creatively show how their machine was as capable and as powerful as office desktops.

Manufacturers of all types of goods, but especially industrial goods, need order-getters to find new prospects, present the products, and facilitate the exchange of goods. Order-getters often tell customers how a product can be used, reordered, and modified. The persuasive skill of the order-getter becomes especially important when many competitors exist. In these situations, order-getters must clearly show how their products can do the job better and save money. Creativity is especially important. An order-getter for GRID 1530 must be able to show why the laptop meets the needs of the customer better than a Compaq III or a Toshiba T 1500.

In wholesaling, order-getters must work closely with customers and often serve as counselors to retailers, advising them how to sell the goods. They provide services such as checking inventory, performing product demonstrations, advertising, and conducting special promotions.

At the retail level, order-getters are needed to increase the sales of unsought and shopping goods. Convincing a customer that he or she needs a set of pots and pans, encyclopedias, or Xerox copiers can be difficult. Order-getters must persuade customers that the goods, which may cost $200 to $2500, will satisfy important needs. For example, an encyclopedia is sold as a good that can provide information and enjoyment for many years. Reluctant customers must be persuaded that these needs are worth their cost.

Order-getters are also needed to sell shopping goods. Buyers of cameras, furniture, automobiles, and clothing are often looking for the best price and quality. Order-getters who are helpful, informed, and interesting can be invaluable. Two Fuller Brush order-getters are discussed in the *Marketing in Action* in this section. Charles F. Terrasi and Toshie Legg are order getters who have been very successful.

Order-Takers

Order-takers complete sales made to regular or repeat customers. They do fairly routine work, but it should not be underestimated. Without order-takers, the regular or repeat customer might well purchase goods elsewhere.

Order-takers at the manufacturing level often have a regular sales route. As part of the job and in the process of making calls, they often serve as information sources and trainers. They inform customers about prices, terms, and new developments and train them in the proper use of the products. The wholesale order-taker exists to serve the customer, regularly calling on industrial customers or retailers and then making sure the order is filled on time and accurately.

Order-taking at the retail level—at a Toys "R" Us checkout counter or supermarket bakery counter—is routine. The goods are brought to the counter and sales are rung up. The order-taker completes the sale by wrapping or bagging and making change. At the retail level the order-taking job is not as challenging or well-paying as other forms of order-taking. However, good order-takers often act as order-getters; by their attention to customers they enhance sales. A wine steward at a restaurant can often sell more, better, and more expensive wine through the personal attention given to customers.

MARKETING IN ACTION

Soft Sell Technique Works for Fuller Brush Veterans

Charles F. Terrasi, 73, uses humor and a soft sell approach to bring in sales for the Fuller Brush Company. He has been known to use funny quotes or sayings to generate attention, such as the following song lyrics he had reprinted as a newspaper advertisement:

> Roaming in the gloaming,
> With my suitcase in my hand,
> Making calls each evening,
> Making sales to beat the band,
> When all the folks are home to rest,
> Fuller Brushes sell the best.

"The whole idea of these songs was to create a sense of humor, a soft sell, and have the people talk to you," said Terrasi. "It's a low-pressure business. Many women have someone pushing their door bells all the time, and they can't get rid of the salesman." He knows the advantages of a low-key pitch. One of his longstanding customers, Phyllis A. Crumbaker, said of Terrasi, "I am very slow about trying new products, but I trust Mr. Terrasi's recommendations. He knows what I like and what I don't."

Terrasi feels that you should never sell over the telephone to new customers. He starts by phoning new clients and asking if he can tell them about Fuller Brush Co. On his first visit he leaves a catalog and drops by later for an order. If they are not interested, he will usually leave a free gift. The relationship between the salespeople and the customer is one that must be carefully cultivated and could initially involve multiple calls to the same house, long days, and small orders. He says that this is necessary to gain people's trust, arguing that "too many salespeople are greedy and want sales for no work."

Fuller Brush lady Toshie Legg, 45, agrees with Terrasi that the relationship between the salesperson and the customer is one that must be carefully cultivated. "It's necessary to build the relationship over a period of time to gain peoples' trust," says Legg.

Women like Legg, in fact, represent the new wave of Fuller Brush's direct sales team. Eighty percent of Fuller Brush's 13,000 representatives are women. Toshie Legg earns more than $1000 a month selling Fuller Brush products and recruiting new sales representatives.

Both Legg and Terrasi build relationships with customers in a soft-sell manner and visit them regularly. "That way, the sales don't take a big hunk out of their paychecks and you're building a regular customer base," says Terrasi. Other strategies he uses are stockpiling popular items on sale and passing the savings on to the consumers, and giving gifts for baby and wedding showers and engagements. "Gifts cement your relationship with the families," said Terrasi. "Besides, when they have been purchasing for so many years, I think you owe them something."

For this service and care, Terrasi has built up a large and supportive clientele that will be buying from him as long as he comes around.

ADAPTED FROM: Associated Press, Framingham, Massachusetts. "Fuller Brush Man Uses Soft Sell, Humor to Boost Sales," January 18, 1988, p. 3; *Shrewsbury Register*, Shrewsbury, NJ, "Woman Has 'Brush' with Big Success," October 3, 1988, p. 1.

Support Personnel

Support personnel are involved in the selling process but typically do not get orders themselves. They are primarily used to market industrial products. In general, support personnel locate prospects, educate customers, foster good will, and provide postsale service. Support personnel include missionary salespeople, trade salespeople, and technical specialists.

Missionary Salespeople. The missionary salesperson (also called the *detail person*) works for manufacturers and calls on their intermediaries and customers.[11] He or she

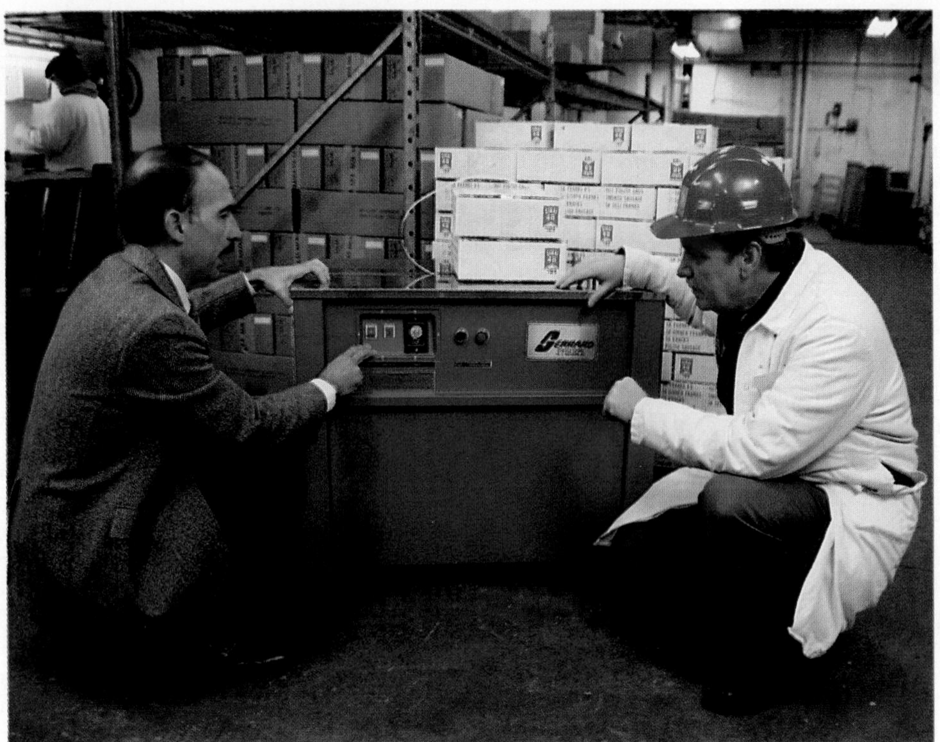

A technical specialist, such as this product sales representative, can explain the functions of new machinery to the manager of the firm's shipping department.

visits professional people such as doctors and dentists, giving them literature and leaving samples of the company's products. Missionary salespeople describe the products, answer questions, and pave the way for later sales. They attempt to stimulate demand, build good will, and train their intermediaries' salespeople. Merck, Hospital Supply, Eli Lilly, and Smith Kline Beckman are manufacturers that use missionary salespeople to promote their products to retail druggists, physicians, and hospital pharmacists.

Trade Salespeople. The trade salesperson is not only a support person, but often an order-taker. However, the main part of the job is to help customers promote products. Nabisco, Kellogg's, and Sunshine Bakery use trade salespeople to arrange shelf space, set up displays, distribute samples, and provide in-store demonstrations.

Technical Specialists. Technical specialists act as consultants and often help design products or systems to meet a client's needs. A background in engineering or the physical sciences is often needed to be a technical specialist. Brown & Root Engineering and Construction Co. has technical specialists who work with customers to design highways, distribution facilities, and electrical utility plants.

The three types of sales jobs—order-getters, order-takers, and support—are used only as a general classification system. Many sales jobs do not fit neatly into one type. A salesperson, working in a store or showroom or calling on a customer, may do all of these jobs. The job may be routine in many respects but still require creativity.

Figure 17–1 Position Description: Sales Representative—FMC Corporation

Position Description

Position DISTRICT SALES REPRESENTATIVE
Reports to REGIONAL SALES MANAGER
Division(s), Plant(s), Branch(es) FOOD PROCESSING MACHINERY

Purpose of Position:

To sell and/or lease all manufactured and agency equipment and parts in the assigned territory and/or to assigned customers, and assist on national account promotions and sales.

Position Responsibilities:

1. Manage territory as an Industry Representative from FPMD to create and maintain an environment for a customer or potential customer to buy, use, and recommend products from FMC and agency suppliers.
2. Call regularly on major, unpenetrated accounts to build future business.
3. Complete studies and quotations, make technical and sales presentations, close sales and leases, draw sales contracts and other sales documents on machinery, obtain parts orders.
4. Maintain representation between customers and all departments of FPMD, other FMC divisions, and agency suppliers to gain and maintain a high level of acceptance in customers' organizations.
5. Work with the Service and other departments to insure prompt and adequate service to customers to include using sound business judgment in handling pricing problems, pressures for concessions, and difficult negotiations.
6. Monitor competitive market posture to advise on necessary redesign of equipment, modification of pricing policy, or similar changes as may be indicated.
7. Assist the Credit Department in establishing customer's financial condition.
8. Maintain expenses at a prudent level and evaluate entertainment and conference expenditures to ascertain their potential to generate sales.
9. Implement aggressively divisional product line promotional programs.
10. Manage time and utilize available resources to provide adequate coverage to customers.
11. Assist management in preparing accurate sales forecasts, quotas, and financial reports.

Position Requirements:

A. Knowledge and Experience
   1. B.S. degree (Engineering, Technical, or Business).
   2. One to three years experience in the food industry plus two to five years experience in field sales of capital equipment to food processors.
   3. Willing to relocate.

B. Supervision—Not Applicable

The type of person needed to do the sales job and the compensation involved depend primarily on the mix of sales tasks performed.

The mix of tasks necessary for a specific sales job can be found in its **job description,** a general statement about the tasks and behaviors required to perform the job. A job description for a sales representative of FMC Corporation, which manufactures food-processing machinery, agricultural machinery, and chemicals, is presented in Figure 17–1. This description suggests that the district sales representative would be an order-getter and order-taker and provide support to customers.

The Personal Selling Process

There is a notion that successful salespeople are born. For example, Colonel Sanders was a natural at selling fried chicken, Lee Iacocca has a flair for selling a company image, and Walt Disney was great at selling laughter and feeling young. However, most successful salespeople are not born with the required attributes, style, intelli-

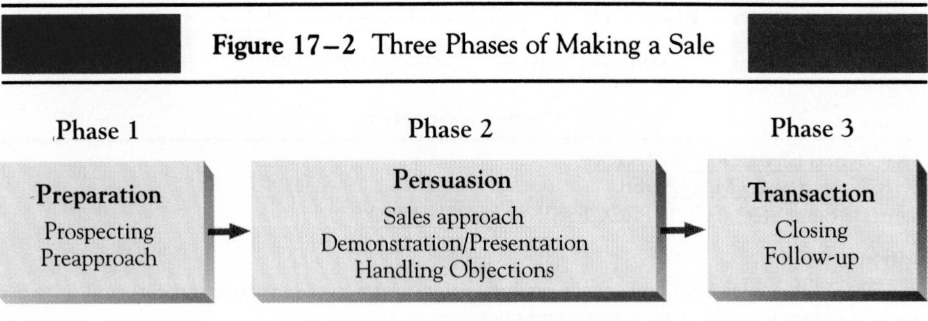

Figure 17–2 Three Phases of Making a Sale

gence, and personality but develop them through hard work, dedication, positive attitudes, and proper training. The personal selling process includes a number of steps people can be trained to perform effectively.

A sale of a product or service has three major phases.[12] The activities in each phase differ for each type of sales job. The phases described here generally fit the order-getting type. First is the *preparation* phase, which includes everything that takes place before the customer is approached. Next is the *persuasion* phase, in which the potential customer is shown what need he or she has and how the salesperson can help fill it. Finally there is the *transaction* phase, in which the sale is finalized. Figure 17–2 presents the three phases and their respective activities.

Although these steps seem logical, they are not always followed. Some salespeople use shortcuts or disregard various steps; others have never been adequately informed. Hints about making a sale and following a sequence of steps have been offered by theorists, researchers, and practitioners. The following guidelines are offered to those interested in learning more about the personal selling process.

1. The more closely matched the physical, social, and personal characteristics of customer and salesperson are, the more likely there will be a sale.
2. The more believable and trustworthy the customer perceives a salesperson to be, the more likely there will be a sale. To be believable, a salesperson has to believe in the product or service.
3. The more persuadable a customer is, the more likely there will be a sale.
4. Be gentle and remove objections from a customer cautiously. Remove objections without the customer noticing.
5. The more a salesperson can make prospective buyers view themselves favorably, the more likely there will be a sale.

Prospecting

Before face-to-face, buyer-seller communication begins, the necessary groundwork must be done. This involves finding prospective customers, or **prospecting.** Prospects may come from many different sources: current customers, previous customers, friends and relatives, advertising leads, other sales personnel selling noncompeting lines, and newspapers. The prospects' list identifies possibilities, but does not suggest which are most likely.

Another phase of prospecting is deciding how much time to spend. Judgments must be made on the basis of potential sales, likelihood of repeat sales, and the financial situation of the prospect. Some type of ranking from "live, good prospect" to "cold, unlikely prospect" should be developed, since each prospect cannot be covered in the same way. Some may require continuous attention and cultivation, while others may be checked with a telephone call.[13]

If a salesperson's product has widespread demand, he or she may resort to the *cold canvass* method of prospecting, in which calls are made to every person or company in a group. Since no advance information on the needs or financial status of each prospect is available, the salesperson relies on the law of averages to generate sales. H. J. Heinz Company was launched by cold canvassing.[14] Henry J. Heinz made his first big sale after a cold call on the largest supply house in London. Today Heinz is a $4.6 billion business.[15]

The increasing cost of making calls has increased the popularity of telemarketing. A single sales call can now cost as much as $200–300, and it may take five or six personal visits to complete a sale.[16] Telemarketing, the use of the telephone to make sales calls, is being used in a variety of ways. These include communicating company and product information to prospects and customers, conducting marketing surveys, creating sales strategies, prospecting for new sales, screening sales leads, responding to toll-free 800 numbers for orders, and direct sales solicitations. The daily average a telemarketer can contact is 21–42 prospects, while a sales rep will only be able to make three to six in-person calls.[17]

Preapproach

Before the contact, the salesperson should learn as much as possible about the prospect in order to anticipate questions and indicate to the prospect the salesperson's seriousness.[18] The salesperson might want to know something about the products or brands the prospect is using, personal likes and dislikes, and preferences for service. When calling on a company, a salesperson can consult annual reports, Dun and Bradstreet reports, the Census of Manufacturers, newspapers, and salespeople of noncompetitive goods or services for information.

Sales Approach and Presentation

The approach is the communication phase of making the sale. Therefore, its timing—morning, afternoon, or evening—is important. Some prospects are impossible to reach at certain times. The salesperson needs a plan to apply the marketing concept—bringing together the buyer, his or her needs and preferences, and the product or service. A number of theories offer guidelines for the sales approach. Each theory is based on the psychology of consumer behavior. Four insightful theories are AIDAS, black-box, formulated, and need-satisfaction.[19] We covered the AIDAS (Attention, Interest, Desire, Action) model in Chapter 15.

The Black Box Approach. The **black box approach** is also referred to as the *canned, packaged,* or *prepared* presentation. This notion is built on stimulus-response theory, which was developed in Pavlov's experiments. It can be summarized as follows:

Drive ⟶ Cue ⟶ Response ⟶ Reward

A *drive* is a stimulus strong enough to impel a prospect into activity, while a *cue* is a stimulus that guides the response of the prospect. Cue may be visual or auditory, or may rely on tasting, smelling, or feeling.

The logic behind the canned approach is that a prospect will give the desired yes response to a persuasive sales approach and presentation. In this theory, the

Table 17–1 The Special Features of Sales Approaches and Presentations

Approach	Communication Skills	Listening Skills	Knowledge of Prospect's Thoughts	Stimulus Value	Application
AIDAS	Important	Somewhat important	Not very important	Important	Sales of automobiles, food products, equipment, preventive health methods (diet modification or exercise)
Black-box	Important	Not very important	Not important	Extremely important	Door-to-door sales and telephone canvassing
Formulated	Important	Important	Important	Extremely important	Sales of office and house furniture, interior decorating, and paintings
Need-satisfaction	Important	Extremely important	Extremely important	Important	Sales of business or home computers

prospect is passive and simply responds to the right stimulus. The encyclopedia salesperson (an order-getter), describing learning as a lifetime experience that begins at birth and ends only at death, or the salesclerk who says, "The hat was made for you, it is simply beautiful," is using a canned approach. What goes on in the prospect's mind (the black box) is not important; only finding the right stimulus to make the sale counts.

Need-Satisfaction Approach. In contrast to the "me-oriented" black-box and formulated approaches, the **need-satisfaction approach** is marketing concept oriented. Need-satisfaction emphasizes the internal motivation of the prospect, pinpointing specific wants, instead of throwing out cues in the hope that one or more will be on target.[20] The need-satisfaction approach is often used to sell insurance, individual retirement accounts, stocks and bonds, and farm machinery.

Understanding what a prospect really needs or wants calls for skills such as excellent listening, problem-solving, careful observance of nonverbal communications, and an attempt to take the place of the other person. The salesperson needs to be a student of internal motivation and to understand the behavioral sciences to fully develop the need-satisfaction approach.

Sometimes a salesperson using the need-satisfaction approach may not recommend a product or service to a customer if it will not satisfy that customer's needs. This decision is made to avoid creating ill will after the sale. The astute salesperson, however, will report back to the company, providing information needed to create better products in the future.

These theories, used separately or in various combinations, emphasize the importance of persuasion. Each approach relies on communication skills. A comparison of the special emphases of these approaches is presented in Table 17–1.

Whatever the sales approach or presentation, it is usually supported with visual and audiovisual aids, such as movies, brochures, manuals, slides, product samples, and maps. Anything within reason is used so the prospect can see, touch, or handle the product. A prospect who can handle a product will become better acquainted with it and remember its features and uses.

Handling Objections

Objections are excuses for not buying that slow down the momentum needed to make a sale. Usually they are polite ways of informing the salesperson, "I am not interested." Even if there is a match between the product or service being offered and the needs of the prospect, psychological resistance to closing a sale may build up. Resistance to spending too much time with the salesperson, a preference for maintaining established routine or habits, a lack of desire for what the salesperson is offering, reluctance to spend money on the good or service, bad feeling about salespeople in general, resistance to being dominated by salespeople, a preconceived idea about the good or service, and dislike for having to make a final decision are just some of the causes. Other objections may be very logical, focusing on price, product characteristics, delivery schedule, or type of company selling the product.

Tactics for handling any type of objection, psychological or logical, require communication and negotiating skills. There are six techniques:

1. *Ignore* the prospect's remark.
2. Meet the prospect's statement *head on* and deny it.
3. First *agree* with the prospect, then go on to *refute* the objection.
4. *Convert* the objection into a logical reason for buying.
5. Ask the prospect *why* and attempt to stimulate further discussion.
6. Ask the prospect to *work through* the situation.[21]

These techniques stress calmness, minimal interruption of the prospect, no downgrading of competitors' products, and anticipation of objections before they are raised. In essence, the salesperson is asked to be not only an astute communicator but a proficient negotiator. These human relations skills are important in each step of the personal selling process.

Closing

Every step taken to this point moves toward one goal—making the sale. If the salesperson fails to close properly, everything is lost. If the prospect's objections are handled, the closing begins. The salesperson may attempt a *trial close,* which is designed to test the customer's willingness to buy by asking, "When would you like this delivered?" or, "Do you want the car with the stick or the automatic shift?" Answers to these questions indicate how close the prospect is to making a decision. The trial close can also bring out the most important objections, which can then be addressed.

Another closing approach is the *assumption technique.* The salesperson assumes that the prospect is going to buy and says, "Did you decide on the blue or the green model?" or, "What day of the week should we deliver your videocassette recorder?"

In today's economy salespeople are using the *urgency* close approach more and more. Consumers are informed, "Prices are going up 15 percent next week," or, "Because of shortages, this is the last group we will have available for four months."

The best closers appear to be salespeople who are always in what can be called a state of closing.[22] They know that closing begins the minute the salesperson and the prospect meet. The *Marketing in Action* in this section emphasizes how important closing is in the selling process.

MARKETING IN ACTION

Salespeople Should Know Their ABC's (*A*lways *B*e *C*losing)

There are many aspects of the selling process, but if a salesperson cannot close the sale, the others are meaningless. Surveys have shown that 60 percent of the time salespeople never even ask for an order. If the customer does not take the initiative, the sale is lost. A company that trains their salespeople in closing or recruits those that excel in closing could have a large competitive advantage.

Closing can be thought of as actually asking whether the customer wants to buy the product. However, in asking, the salesperson must assess the needs of the customer and match the benefits of the product with these needs. Timing, therefore, can be of utmost importance so that closing begins just when the customer is convinced that the product is needed. Tip-offs that the customer might be ready to make a sale could be agreement with the salesperson or increased attention. Questions can also be tip-offs, especially if they are about guarantees, product service, terms of payment, or delivery.

Sometimes the obvious tip-offs are not present and salespeople have to use their best judgment to interpret behaviors as tip-offs to close. The following could be such behaviors:

- The buyer appears restless when being shown more merchandise.
- The buyer sets one item aside from a group of products.
- The buyer re-examines one item.
- The buyer demonstrates the product.
- The buyer picks up the article.
- The buyer nods in approval.
- The buyer smiles when a particular benefit is brought up.

These are not guarantees that the buyer will make an order, but they provide the salesperson with more information to determine whether closing should be the next step.

Even if salespeople recognize that a presentation is over, there is a chance that they will fail to close. These are some of the common reasons:

- Fear of rejection.
- Lack of conviction about the product or its price.
- Failure to build agreement throughout the sale.
- Ineptitude in asking for the order.
- A perception that buyer hesitation/frustration at the moment of decision may indicate probable rejection.
- Difficulty in handling objections positively.
- The misconception that closing is a separate step, rather than an integrated and continuous process.

This *Marketing in Action* outlines when a sale should be closed and some behaviors that could help a salesperson determine when a buyer is ready to close the sale.

ADAPTED FROM: Joseph P. Vaccaro, "Best Salespeople Know Their ABC's (Always Be Closing)," *Marketing News,* v. 22, March 28, 1988, p. 10.

Follow-Up

A salesperson's tasks do not stop once the sale is made and the order placed. The relationship between seller and buyer has been expressed as being much like that between husband and wife.[23] The salesperson must make sure promises of delivery, service, and performance are met. Most businesses depend on repeat sales, which depend on following up promises.

The follow-up work is designed to reduce the buyer's *cognitive dissonance,*[24] or postdecision anxiety. According to cognitive-dissonance theory, once a decision is made, anxiety often occurs because the buyer seeks reassurance that the best purchase was made. The salesperson can reduce dissonance by emphasizing the positive features of the product or service, complying with all prepurchase promises, and relating what other satisfied customers have said about their purchase.

Table 17–2 Sales Costs: Metro (A) and Non-metro (B) Areas

Industry	Total Direct Sales Costs	Calls per Territory per year		Cost per Call per Territory	
		A	B	A	B
Consumer					
Range	$25,000–$120,000	561–1,122	374–748	$22.28–$213.90	$33.42–$320.86
Median	$72,500	841.5	561	$118.09	$177.17
Industrial					
Range	$20,000–$155,000	561–935	374–748	$21.39–$276.29	$26.73–$414.44
Median	$87,500	748	561	$148.84	$220.58
Service					
Range	$21,000–145,000	748–1,496	374–935	$14.04–$193.85	$22.46–$387.70
Median	$83,000	1,122	654.5	$103.95	$205.08

SOURCE: "A User's Guide to the Survey of Selling Costs," *Sales & Marketing Management*, February 20, 1989, p. 5.

REVIEW YOUR MARKETING KNOWLEDGE

- What type of customer response does a salesperson need to hear to suggest that the buyer is ready to make a purchase?
- Provide some examples of order-getters and order-takers that you do business with on a regular basis.
- Do you believe that successful salespeople are born?

Sales Force Management

The selling process requires a great deal of managerial guidance and coordination, and is, therefore, costly. Table 17–2 lists the costs of a sales call for consumer, industrial, and service salespeople as surveyed annually by *Sales & Marketing Management*. Compensation is presented as the total direct sales costs. A cost-per-call is calculated for A and B territories. An A territory is defined as a metropolitan area where customers and prospects are heavily concentrated. A B territory reflects an area where customers are widely dispersed. Because of rising costs, efficient management of the sales force is becoming a major concern and an important responsibility.

One of the biggest personnel promotion mistakes made by firms is to assume that the most successful salesperson can manage the sales force. In fact, the job of managing a sales force involves much more than learning and following the steps in the selling process. The core of the management job is to plan, organize, control, and direct the individual efforts of salespeople and to build these salespeople into a team that achieves objectives compatible with the marketing objectives of promotion. It is extremely important for the sales manager to clarify what the sales task and objectives are.[25] The specific activities engaged in by sales force managers are listed in Figure 17–3.

Figure 17–3 Activities of Sales Force Managers

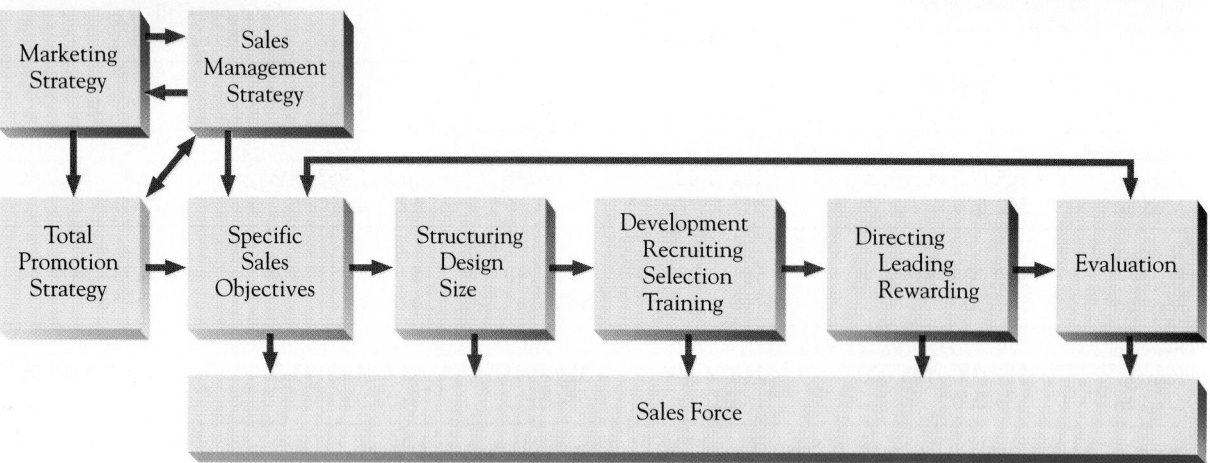

SOURCE: Maurica I. Mandell and Larry J. Rosenberg, *Marketing* (Prentice-Hall, 1981), Figure 20-3, p. 500.

Specific Sales Objectives: The Manager and the Salesperson

The policies and *objectives* established for the total sales force are linked to the overall marketing strategy of the organization. In addition, the objectives are linked to the overall promotion strategy. Table 17–3 presents a few major target areas for which sales managers' objectives can be determined. A sales manager's *objectives* are specific, measurable, and time-based goals.

Sales managers also expect salespeople to establish objectives for each step in the selling process. For example, a set of *prospecting objectives* could be the following:

- To find at least six new prospects a week in the western territory for the July 1–December 31 period.
- To close at least one sale from among these six prospects each week for the July 1–December 31 period.
- To have at least one repeat sale every two months from the new group for the next year.

Guiding the sales force's objective-setting is a responsibility of the manager that requires understanding each salesperson's ability, motivation, and goals. It also requires evaluating meaningful, clearly stated, challenging, and timely objectives.

Structuring the Sales Force

Establishing the structure of the sales force is another responsibility of sales managers. In Chapter 20 *(Marketing Organizations)* a number of different forms of organizational design for the total marketing department will be presented. These forms of structure can and are applied to the sales organization.

The complexities of managing a sales force have been addressed by increased use of computer-based decision support systems. It is expected that such systems will continue to increase in use. The introduction of business-to-business software has

Table 17–3 Target Areas* for Establishing Sales Force Manager Objectives

Sample Target Areas				
Total Sales	**Recruiting**	**Training**	**Motivation**	**Evaluation**
Increase volume.	Improve job offer-acceptance ratio.	Improve sales presentation.	Reduce turnover.	Develop equitable system.
Increase repeat sales.	Develop clear job descriptions.	Develop subordinates.	Improve sales performance.	Provide personal development feedback to salespeople.
Improve customer mix.	Improve hiring of minorities.	Train for new product.	Develop sales contest.	Improve counseling skills.

**Target areas* are short forms of more elaborate objectives that include a quantitative measure, time frame, and cost of accomplishment estimate. For example, the second recruiting objective could be written: Objective—To develop a complete set of job descriptions for sales representatives in eastern region by June 15, 1993, at a cost not to exceed $16,000.

resulted in better sales management and follow-up of leads.[26] It is now possible to gain data on the status, quantities, classes, and potential and actual revenue generation of leads gained from an advertisement, trade-show, or customer referral list. The software permits the maintenance of a central marketing data base of suspects, prospects, and customers. The salesperson's performance in following leads and selling effectively can be monitored. Figure 17–4 presents a view of the Marketing and Sales Management (MSM) system that is available to sales managers.

Structuring by Territories. The simplest sales structure is one in which each salesperson sells the firm's full product line in a specific territory and is responsible for successes and failures in that territory. Because of this direct responsibility, the salesperson is encouraged to work hard at selling and cultivating business ties.

The territory sales-management hierarchy often includes a district sales manager, a regional sales manager responsible for several districts, and a national sales manager. This hierarchy can serve as an incentive for those interested in being promoted from personal selling into administrative positions. The sample corporation hierarchy in Figure 17–5 shows possible career paths available, from technical sales representative to managerial positions. It is typical for a technical representative to stay in the job for about six years and then to move to corporate headquarters as an instructor. After about two years as an instructor, a person would be moved to a staff position; after three years as a staff employee, the person would be promoted to a managerial position.

Structuring by Products. In product structuring, the sales task is split up among different sales managers, each of whom directs operations for part of the product line. The decision to use the product line organizational structure depends on the benefits of product specialization outweighing the additional expenses. Since multiple sales forces are needed, this could result in higher administrative and travel expenses.[27]

Structuring by Customers. Companies sometimes arrange their sales forces along customer lines. This method is suitable when similar products are marketed to several types of customers. With the customer arrangement, special attention can be paid to the needs of each type of buyer. For example, the computer needs of colleges, man-

Figure 17–4 Market and Sales Management System

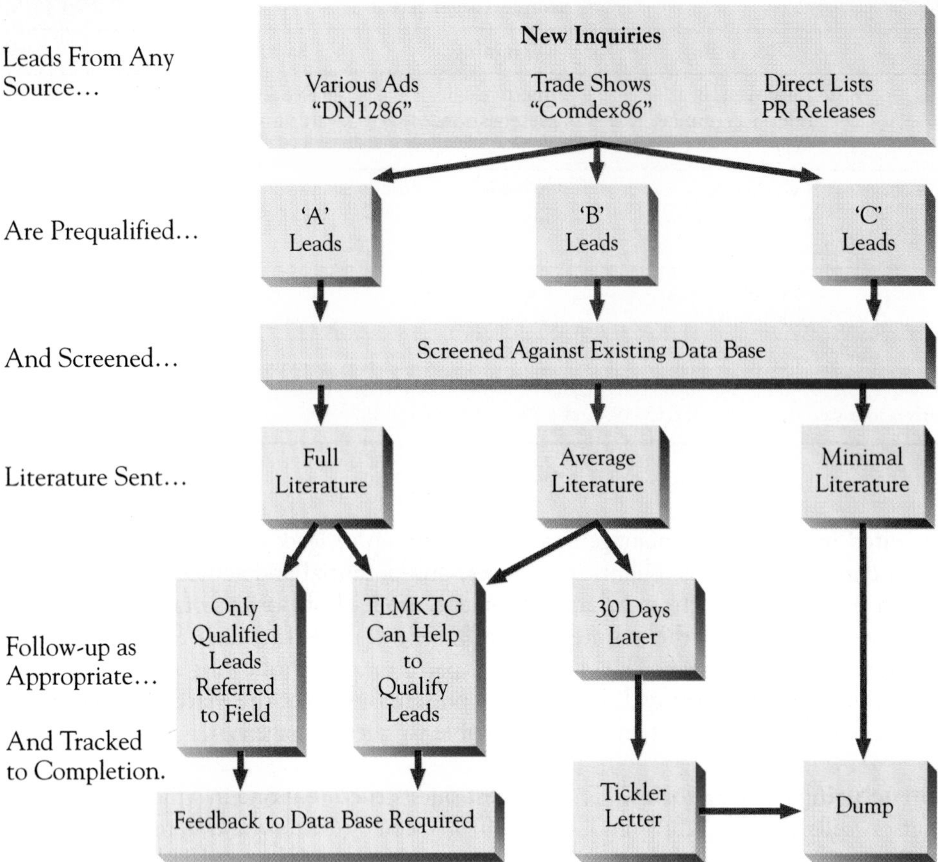

SOURCE: Used by permission from Christopher Stockwell, "Be Concerned With Quality, Not Quantity, of Sales Leads," *Marketing News*, March 14, 1988, p. 11.

ufacturing firms, retail stores, and banks are quite different. National Cash Register Corporation recognizes these differences and assigns its sales force on the basis of industry categories—retailing, financial, and educational.

Multiple Bases for Structuring. Few companies use a single method of structuring the sales force. Most use a combination, dividing the selling task into multiple arrangements. Nearly every sales department uses a territory arrangement combined with the product or customer design.

Deciding How Many Salespeople to Use. Once the strategy, objectives, and structure are in place, the issue of sales force size must be addressed. Sometimes the sales force is very large, which means larger market coverage, as well as more expense. For example, Nabisco has more than 3,000 salespeople.

A common approach to determining the size of the sales force is **workload analysis.** A firm like IBM, General Electric, or Polaroid might determine the number of salespeople needed by estimating the extent of the selling task and dividing this by

Figure 17–5 The Sales Hierarchy at Eastman Kodak

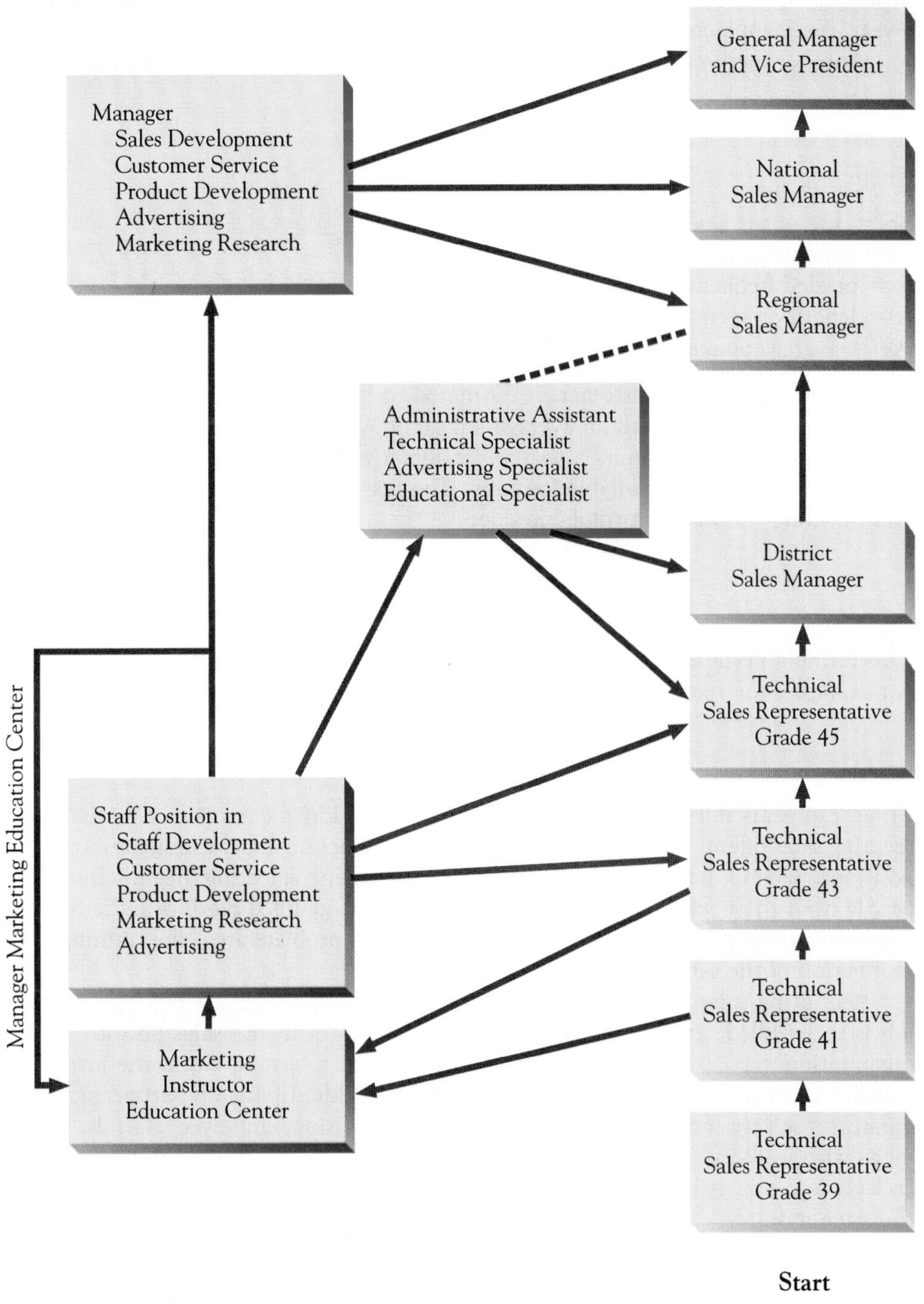

the amount a single salesperson could effectively handle. IBM has redeployed 11,800 manufacturing employees into what are called "marketing rep" jobs.[28]

Suppose, for example, an appliance manufacturer sells toasters to two types of customers: discount stores and retailers. Suppose further that in a selected market there are approximately 600 retailers and 10 discount stores. The sales force management team might, after careful analysis, decide to calculate how many salespeople are needed to make five calls on each retailer and five calls on each discount store in a year. A simple calculation would reveal that the sales force would have to make 5(600) + 5(10), or 3050 calls a year. If the average salesperson could make 750 calls a year, the manufacturer would need about four full-time salespeople (3050 ÷ 750).

Another method of determining the size of the sales force is by the formula

$$SS = \frac{C \times F \times L,}{A_T}$$

where:

SS = size of the sales force,
C = number of customers,
F = needed frequency of making calls on customers,
L = length of average customer call, and
A_T = average amount of time each salesperson has available.

Suppose the number of customers is estimated to be about 5000 and about six calls a year should be made, with an average length of 30 minutes (.5 hour). The average salesperson works 2000 hours a year (40 hours a week × 50 weeks), but has only about 30 hours a week available for calls. The rest of the time is spent in meetings and traveling. Using the formula produces

$$SS = \frac{5000 \times 6 \times .5}{1500} = 10.$$

This formula permits the sales manager to change variables and data as necessary. For example, the number of customers or the time for calls may change.

Development of the Sales Force

Three problems must be overcome for an organization to compete effectively in securing sales talent. First, the organization must attract qualified candidates for sales positions. Second, it must identify potential selling talent, selecting the most qualified people from those who apply for sales jobs. Without qualified recruits and effective selection, the organization will never reach the third problem area, the training and motivation of the sales force.[29]

Recruiting is largely influenced by answers to two questions: What type of sales job is to be filled, and what requirements are there to fill the sales position? The organization may attempt to locate candidates for the job from within the firm, but if this is not possible, an outside search must begin. Identifying and attracting candidates for selection screening are done through advertising, employee referrals, interviews with walk-ins, and referrals from public and private employment agencies and colleges and universities. Salespersons may also be located in other organizations in the same industry.

In some cases organizations attempt to recruit and then select a person with what are considered ideal traits for the job. The dilemma is identifying those traits. Presenting a list of traits that will ensure success in sales is like identifying the stock purchases that will make you wealthy tomorrow. Studies have been conducted, and one list after another has been offered for consideration. Some of the more popularly cited attributes for sales success are high level of energy, ambition, tolerance, self-confidence, reflectiveness, intelligence, and friendliness. There still is no isolated and accurate model that can predict what makes a successful salesperson.[30]

Selection

Selection refers to the steps employed by the firm to identify and assess individuals and place them in sales positions. Such selection steps as tests, interviews, background checks, and physical examinations represent hurdles. If the candidate overcomes them, he or she is presumed able to do the job.

Psychological testing is a gauge used by many firms to measure, in a consistent manner, characteristics related to effective sales performance and the degree to which a candidate possesses these characteristics. These guidelines are required by federal law.[31] Such tests are only used as a supplement to other selection criteria, which include application forms, interviews, background or reference checks, and physical examinations. The decision to hire comes after every selection step has been passed. Applicants are rejected for many reasons (lack of ability, poor work record, criminal record).

Training

Once a person is hired, the sales manager must continue developing the sales force by offering training, usually in one of three forms. First, new salespeople must often be taught what their job entails, how to do it, what their competition will be, and what is expected of them. This training involves some orientation, knowledge acquisition, and work on specific selling skills. Training needs are usually identified by analyzing the tasks of the sales job. An important principle to remember is that training should be done at the trainee's level.[32]

Sales training increases product knowledge and improves selling skills; it also builds self-confidence among members of the sales force. When people know what is expected of them, they are better prepared for the challenges and disappointments of a sales career. Effective sales training can point out and reinforce positive behaviors that can contribute to a very successful sales career.

Finally, there is a need for long-term development, aimed at increasing the firm's long-run effectiveness. The organization's objectives, strategy, and environment are all considered when planning the sales force development program. Development may involve providing salespeople more responsible jobs, more autonomy, and more decision-making power. These are assumed to help salespeople prepare for future assignments. The ultimate long-term objective is to increase the sales of the firm. The direct relationship between sales and training is elusive, because so many things can influence sales (such as the economy, shortages, and size of sales territories). Nevertheless, sales training is considered a significant activity.

Directing

The job of directing individual salespeople and integrating their needs and goals with the objectives of the firm is continuous. The exact style and procedures to direct the sales force depend largely on the leadership provided and the reward system used.

Leadership. The ability to influence others to accomplish desired goals is called *leadership*. The responsibility of a sales manager to lead is derived from the formal position he or she has in the hierarchy and the respect and cooperation he or she inspires because of personal traits and expertise.

The extensive literature on leadership suggests there is no one best way to lead subordinates.[33] For years attempts were made to isolate and identify a "best" leadership

Figure 17–6 Leadership Styles and Situational Considerations

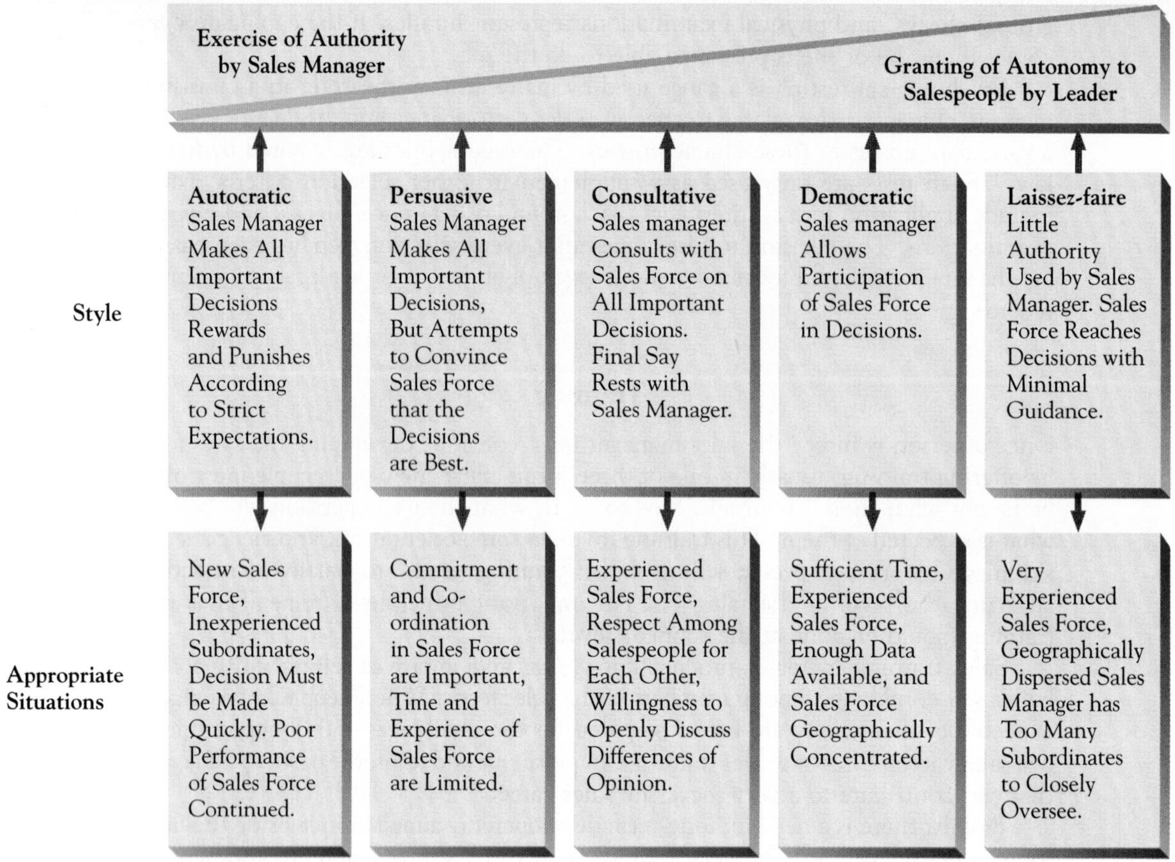
Exercise of Authority by Sales Manager
Granting of Autonomy to Salespeople by Leader
Style
Appropriate Situations
Autocratic
Sales Manager Makes All Important Decisions Rewards and Punishes According to Strict Expectations.
Persuasive
Sales Manager Makes All Important Decisions, But Attempts to Convince Sales Force that the Decisions are Best.
Consultative
Sales manager Consults with Sales Force on All Important Decisions. Final Say Rests with Sales Manager.
Democratic
Sales manager Allows Participation of Sales Force in Decisions.
Laissez-faire
Little Authority Used by Sales Manager. Sales Force Reaches Decisions with Minimal Guidance.
New Sales Force, Inexperienced Subordinates, Decision Must be Made Quickly. Poor Performance of Sales Force Continued.
Commitment and Co-ordination in Sales Force are Important, Time and Experience of Sales Force are Limited.
Experienced Sales Force, Respect Among Salespeople for Each Other, Willingness to Openly Discuss Differences of Opinion.
Sufficient Time, Experienced Sales Force, Enough Data Available, and Sales Force Geographically Concentrated.
Very Experienced Sales Force, Geographically Dispersed Sales Manager has Too Many Subordinates to Closely Oversee.

Adapted and reprinted by permission of *Harvard Business Review.* An Exhibit from "How to Choose a Leadership Pattern," by Robert Tannenbaum and Warren H. Schmidt, May/June 1973.

style. It now appears that what is good leadership in one situation, or at one time, is often disastrous in another situation, or at a different time. Research evidence suggests that situational and personal variables must be seriously considered before a style is adopted.[34]

An important aspect of applying a leadership style is determining how authority is used. Figure 17–6 indicates five styles of leadership and ways trade-offs between authority and autonomy can be made. The *autocratic* style emphasizes top-down decision making, while the *consultative* places a premium on receiving input from subordinates before making a decision. Different situations lend themselves to different styles.

Note that there is no one ideal style of leading salespeople. The style that works best depends on the sales manager, situation, and sales force. Whichever style is selected, the leader will eventually have to implement a reward system to motivate the sales force.

Rewarding. One directing activity a sales manager engages in is the administration of rewards. Rewarding salespeople is tied closely to evaluation. The objectives of a reward system are to attract people to join the firm, to keep them coming to work, and to motivate them to perform at high levels. Salespeople exchange their time, ability, skills, and effort for valued rewards that sales managers then distribute as they see fit.

Extrinsic rewards are those that are external to the job. Included in this category are financial rewards, such as pay, fringe benefits, and sales bonuses, as well as promotions and good working conditions. **Intrinsic rewards** are associated directly with the job itself. Being challenged and having freedom to make decisions are intrinsic rewards.

A reward must be important to the salesperson if it is to influence his or her behavior. In all occupations, an important reward is the compensation received for working. Sales compensation is an extrinsic reward distributed by a sales manager. The best mix and type of compensation programs depend on such factors as the compensation plans of competitors, costs of sales force turnover and poor morale, compensation plans for nonsales personnel in the organization, and amount of nonsalary selling expenses.

Many sales compensation programs reimburse salespeople for their selling expenses and provide some fringe benefits and compensation. Three popular methods of compensation are straight salary, straight commission, and a combination of salary and commission. In a **straight salary plan,** the amount received by salespeople is based on the time worked. A **straight commission plan** bases compensation on the sales generated in a period of time. The commission may be based on a straight percentage of sales or a sliding scale in which the percentage earned increases as sales increase. In a **combination plan,** salespeople are paid a fixed salary and a commission based on sales volume. Some combination plans require the salesperson to generate a certain level of sales before a commission is paid.

Some advantages and disadvantages of these three types of compensation plans are presented in Table 17–4. The combination method is the most popular, but each has strengths and weaknesses that should be considered when rewards are analyzed.

Another extrinsic reward used in some organizations is the sales contest. Its purpose is to increase the volume of sales. Prizes in such a contest have included merchandise, vacation trips, titles such as "Salesperson of the Month," trophies, pins, and certificates. Of course, the success or failure of a sales contest is often influenced by the attractiveness of the award.

The use of **intrinsic rewards** has received too little attention in the personal selling literature. Sales managers need to foster the job conditions necessary for salespeople to experience intrinsic rewards. In essence, an intrinsic reward permits salespeople to reward themselves. Allowing the salesperson to make decisions without being closely monitored, encouraging the sales force to set challenging and realistic goals, and providing good feedback on performance are intrinsic rewards that can be built into the motivation package by creative sales managers.

Table 17–5 presents data on the Dartwell Profile of Sales personnel. The profile is based on surveys of 122,000 salespeople at more than 300 companies in 36 industrial classifications.[35] The data suggest that experienced sales reps—those who have been selling for three years or more—are earning an average of $40,000 per year. It now costs about $14,435 to train a salesperson and field expenses now cost about $14,666, compared with $16,781 two years ago. Women comprise 18 percent of all salespeople. Sales reps are willing to work in a job for about 4.7 years.

Table 17–4 Comparison of Compensation Methods

Compensation Method	Usage by Firms	Situations in Which Useful	Advantages	Disadvantages
Straight Salary	17.4%	When compensating new salespersons; when firm moves into new sales territories that require developmental work; when salespeople must perform many nonselling activities	Provides salesperson with maximum security; gives sales manager great control over salespeople; is easy to administer; yields more predictable selling expenses	Provides no incentive; necessitates closer supervision of salesperson's activities; during sales declines, keeps selling expenses at same level
Straight Commission	6.5%	When highly aggressive selling is required; when nonselling tasks are minimized; when company cannot closely control salesforce activities	Provides maximum amount of incentive; by increasing commission rate, allows sales managers to encourage salespeople to sell certain items; selling expenses relate directly to sales resources	Gives salespeople little financial security; gives sales manager minimum control over sales force; may cause salespeople to provide inadequate service to smaller accounts; makes selling costs less predictable
Combination	76.1%	When sales territories have relatively similar sales potentials; when firm wishes to provide incentive but still control activities	Provides some financial security; provides some incentive; allows selling expenses to fluctuate with sales revenue	May make selling expenses less predictable; may be difficult to administer

SOURCE: The percentages are computed from "Alternative Sales Compensation and Incentive Plans," *Sales and Marketing Management*, February 17, 1986, p. 57. Characteristics are based on John P. Steinbrink, "How to Pay Your Sales Force," *Harvard Business Review*, July-August 1978, p. 119.

Behavioralists and practicing managers agree that both extrinsic and intrinsic rewards must be used to encourage sales performance.[36] It is also clear that the following conditions must exist for rewards to motivate sales performance:

1. Rewards must be *important* to the sales force.
2. Both *extrinsic* (money incentives) and *intrinsic* (allowing more autonomy in making decisions) rewards must be used by the sales manager.
3. Information must be made *public* (for example, through a company newsletter) about how rewards are distributed to the sales force.
4. Sales managers must be able to *explain* the firm's reward system to salespeople so that they can easily understand it.
5. Sales performance should be *measured* with the most objective system available, using specific numbers when possible. Keep in mind that perfectly objective systems are probably not feasible.
6. Rewards can be varied, depending on the conclusions reached with the *performance evaluation* system.

Table 17–5 Dartnell Profile: The American Sales Professional

National Averages

- 36 years old
- 82% male
- 18% female
- 81% some college or degree
- Most likely to leave after 4.7 years
- Average length of service—7.3 years
- Incentive Payment Frequency:
  Annual—15%
  Semi-Annual—5%
  Quarterly—26%
  Monthly—54%
- Automobiles:
  Company—29%
  Leased—21%
  Personal—54%

- Trainee makes $23,000
  Semi-experienced makes $31,000
  Experienced makes $40,000
- Costs $14,435 to train

- Length of training—6 months
- Sales call costs $56.68
- Sales calls per day—5.5
- Number of calls to close—5
- Field expenses cost $14,666
- Value of benefits—$8,218
- Average sales volume—$1,579,707
- Spends 45 hours per week in selling activities
- Spends 15 hours per week in nonselling activities

If these conditions do not exist, the sales manager is likely to have major problems directing the sales force. In practicing effective sales force management and in having an efficient reward system, it is necessary to evaluate sales performance.

Review Your Marketing Knowledge

- Explain how a workload analysis can be used in planning for salesforce size, additions, or subtractions.
- What does the sales hierarchy at Eastman Kodak (Figure 17–5) state about job opportunities for recent college graduates? Where would they start in the firm?

Evaluation

An important and difficult task sales managers face is the evaluation of each person in the sales force. The job is *judgmental,* because verdicts must be made about whether each person has met sales objectives, and is also *developmental,* because the future growth of salespeople depends on performance evaluation and feedback.

The sales manager and each salesperson must know how well objectives are being met. To acquire this information, a formal evaluation program is usually developed and implemented. The search for the "perfect performance evaluation" has been going on and producing controversy for years.[37] The ideal evaluation continues to center on minimizing or eliminating traditional complaints from raters (sales managers) and ratees (salespersons). Specific complaints center on inequities in ratings, poorly trained evaluators, ambiguous performance standards, the subjective nature of evaluations, and excessive emphasis on weaknesses.

In spite of this controversy, there are a number of reasons why performance evaluations are necessary and should be done:

- They can provide feedback to salespeople on their job results, enabling them to match expectations to reality.
- They can provide information for training, compensation, and motivation programs.
- They serve as a basis of control. Projected efforts and results can be compared to actual efforts and results.
- They point out strengths to maintain, as well as weaknesses to correct.
- They provide information for the sales manager to use in working out a plan for career progress and development.

Formal evaluation programs used by firms like IBM, General Mills, Sears, J.C. Penney, First City National Bank, and Procter & Gamble usually follow five steps:

1. The sales job is analyzed and objectives are set.
2. A job description (a factual description of duties, responsibilities, and requirements of the sales job) is prepared.
3. Sales performance measures (quantitative and qualitative standards) are developed.
4. The evaluator observes when possible, measures, and evaluates sales performance.
5. The evaluation is fed back to the salesperson and some form of reward or sanction is distributed.

The sales manager's role is crucial in an evaluation of sales force performance. Basically, the manager is asked to observe, evaluate, counsel, and coach the sales force as well as to administer rewards and sanctions. To accomplish these duties, the sales manager must use some standards.

Based on the situation, job analysis, and job description, a number of quantitative and qualitative criteria can be developed for measuring and evaluating sales job performance. Of course, the criteria used will also depend on the objectives of the firm. *Quantitative* measures indicate specific levels of performance in objective terms—dollar sales volume, number of new accounts, sales volume as a percentage of sales quota. The emphasis is on output or objective results. *Qualitative* measures involve more personal judgments about the contribution of the salesperson (see Table 17–6).

The sales manager making the evaluation needs to appraise sales performance

Table 17–6 Quantitative and Qualitative Criteria Evaluations of Three Salespeople

Evaluation Criteria	Joan Wester	Rob Davis	Nick O'Dell
Dollar Sales Volume			
1. Projected objective	$220,000	$250,000	$200,000
2. Actual accomplishment	260,000	230,000	180,000
3. Effectiveness rate (2 ÷ 1)	1.18	.92	.90
4. Weight	3.00	3.00	3.00
5. Weighted performance (3 × 4)	3.54	2.76	2.70
Gross Profits			
1. Projected objective	$42,000	$46,000	$38,000
2. Actual accomplishment	40,000	46,000	44,000
3. Effectiveness rate (2 ÷ 1)	.95	1.00	1.16
4. Weight	4.00	4.00	4.00
5. Weighted performance (3 × 4)	3.80	4.00	4.64
Average Number of Sales Calls a Month			
1. Objective	90.00	100.00	80.00
2. Actual accomplishment	100.00	130.00	100.00
3. Effectiveness rate (2 ÷ 1)	1.10	1.30	1.35
4. Weight	1.00	1.00	1.00
5. Weighted performance (3 × 4)	1.10	1.30	1.35
Skills in Problem Solving			
1. Manager's rating (0 poor to 1.0 excellent)	.6	.7	.7
2. Weight	1.0	1.0	1.0
3. Weighted performance (1 × 2)	.6	.7	.7
Dependability			
1. Manager's rating (0 poor to 1.0 excellent)	.6	.5	.5
2. Weight	1.0	1.0	1.0
3. Weighted performance (1 × 2)	.6	.5	.5
Overall Sales Evaluation on Basis of Five Weighted Criteria	3.54	2.76	2.70
	3.80	4.00	4.64
	1.10	1.30	1.25
	.60	.70	.70
	.60	.50	.50
	9.64	9.26	9.79
Overall Effectiveness—Sums of Total Evaluation Divided by Weights	**96.4%**	**92.6%**	**97.9%**

on a multiple range of measures. For example, the number of new accounts may tell the manager nothing about the average size of orders. Furthermore, the effort of salespeople must be considered along with the results. A salesperson's productive effectiveness is based on quantitative results, as measured by dollar sales volume and gross margin, and qualitative efforts, as indicated by enthusiasm, ability to overcome objections, and appearance.

The sales performance evaluation in Table 17–6 presents five criteria—three quantitative (dollar sales, gross profits, and average number of sales calls) and two qualitative (skills in problem solving and dependability). The example illustrates how quantitative and qualitative factors can be used by the sales manager. Which quantitative and qualitative measures to use, what weights should be applied, and the objectives themselves are decided on by the sales manager.

Personal Computer Exercise

The overall sales effectiveness of five salespersons will be examined, analyzed, and interpreted. Which of the salespersons should receive a promotion to sales manager? If there is to be a reduction in the sales force of one person, which of the five should be let go? Suppose that the salesforce wanted an explanation of the weighting (how are weights determined) system? What would you be able to say?

KEY POINTS

- Personal selling involves the interactions that occur between people.
- The old-fashioned view of a salesperson is that of a glib talker who travels a lot and is inclined to use any tactic to make a sale.
- Today the professional salesperson is trained to provide valuable assistance to customers.
- Three main types of sales jobs are order-getter, order-taker, and support. The order-getter, who seeks out business, is the most creative. Order-takers are primarily involved in completing sales. Support salespeople perform missionary, trade, and technical sales tasks.
- The selling process involves three major steps—preparation, persuasion, and transaction. The preparation phase involves everything that takes place before the customer is approached by the salesperson. The persuasion phase occurs when the potential customer is shown that he or she has a need the salesperson can help fill. In the transaction phase, the sale is finalized.
- The manager of a sales force is involved in setting objectives, structuring the sales force, developing salespeople, rewarding, and evaluating performance. Each activity is important in achieving sales services.

ISSUES FOR DISCUSSION

1. What role can the computer play in helping sales force managers accomplish their various selling objectives?

2. Why is it important for performance criteria to be clearly understood by salespersons?

3. Why does a sales manager need to monitor the way a salesperson is calling on customers and closing sales?

4. How are personal selling, economic growth, and the national standard of living related?

5. Why is creativity generally a more important attribute for order-getters than for order-takers?

6. What personal characteristics would be important for individuals who serve a support personnel in the selling process?

7. Suppose that you are a salesperson and you have the kind of day none of us likes—people are complaining about your product. Answer the following objections:

a. "Your competitor can deliver the product a week before you can."

b. "Do you have a two year warranty? Why not?"

c. "Your product doesn't come in the color I need to go with my wallpaper."

8. What aspects of the service salesperson's job make the job of selling difficult?

9. On what basis should a salesperson's rewards (compensation, promotion opportunities) be based?

10. There are some who believe that the job of a salesperson is not compensated well. How would you reply to this claim?

GLOSSARY

Black-box approach: The use of a "canned" or prepared sales presentation. This builds on the stimulus-response model developed by Pavlov's experiments.

Cognitive dissonance: The tension one experiences after making a decision.

Combination plan: A system in which a salesperson is paid a fixed salary and a commission based on sales volume.

Extrinsic rewards: Rewards, such as salary, that are external to the job.

Formulated approach: An approach that is tailored to a prospect's wants and needs.

Intrinsic rewards: Rewards associated with doing the job, like having autonomy to make important decisions.

Job description: A general statement about the tasks and behaviors to perform a job.

Leadership: The ability to influence others to accomplish desired goals. Some important factors to consider when examining leadership style include leader-follower relations, position power, job structure, and personalities of the leader and followers.

Need-satisfaction approach: A sales presentation relying on the notion that customers have needs that must be satisfied. The good or service must be able to satisfy these needs if this approach is used.

Order-getter: A salesperson who is concerned with getting or seeking out business.

Order-taker: A salesperson who routinely closes a sales transaction.

Personal selling: Selling that relies on personal interactions between buyer and seller.

Prospecting: The step before any buyer-seller communication begins, during which likely customers are found for the good or service.

Straight commission plan: A system in which a salesperson's pay is based on the amount of sales generated for a period of time.

Straight salary plan: A system in which a salesperson is paid on the basis of time worked.

Support personnel: Salespeople who are in the selling process but do not get orders themselves.

Workload analysis: A mathematical approach to determining sales needed for a salesforce.

NOTES

1. Frank V. Cespedes, Stephen X. Doyle, and Robert J. Freedman, "Teamwork for Today's Selling," *Harvard Business Review,* March-April 1989, pp. 44–54, 58.

2. E. Jerome McCarthy and William D. Perreault, Jr., *Basic Marketing* (Richard D. Irwin, 1987), p. 399.

3. C. Robert Petty, *Managing Salespeople* (Reston Publishing, 1979), p. 3.

4. Joseph W. Thompson, *Selling* (McGraw-Hill, 1973), p. 15.

5. Donald L. Thompson, "Stereotype of the Salesman," *Harvard Business Review,* January-February 1972, pp. 20–22, 24–25, 28–29, 159–61.

6. "What Makes a Great Salesman," *The Wall Street Journal,* June 20, 1988, p. 10.

7. Douglas J. Dalrymple, *Sales Management: Concepts and Cases* (John Wiley & Sons, 1982).

8. McCarthy and Perreault, *Basic Marketing,* pp. 401–403.

9. McCarthy and Perreault, *Basic Marketing,* pp. 402–405.

10. Frederic Paul, "Laptops on Desktops," *P/C Computing,* March 1989, pp. 88–93.

11. Michael Waldholz, "How a Detail Man Promotes New Drugs to Tennessee Doctors," *The Wall Street Journal,* November 8, 1982, pp. 1 and 18.

12. Ronald D. Balsley and E. Patricia Birsner, *Selling: Marketing Personified* (Chicago: Dryden Press, 1987), p. 47.

13. Thomas V. Bonoma, "Major Sales: Who Really Does the Buying?" *Harvard Business Review,* May-June 1982, pp. 111–19.

14. "The Fortune 500," *Fortune,* April 30, 1984, p. 182.

15. "The Fortune 500," *Fortune,* April 25, 1988, p. 11.

16. "Industries Add Telemarketing to Fight the High Cost of Sales," *Marketing News,* August 15, 1988, p. 8.

17. "Telemarketing Is 'Smarter' When Used with Other Tools," *Marketing News,* August 15, 1988, p. 8.

18. Ralph E. Anderson and Joseph F. Hair, Jr., *Sales Management* (Random House, 1983), pp. 582–86.

19. For an excellent discussion of this, see Philip G. Zimbardo, *Psychology and Life* (Scott, Foresman and Company, 1985), pp. 190–194.

20. A. H. Maslow, *Motivation and Personality* (Harper & Row, 1954).

21. Daniel K. Weadock, "Your Troops Can Keep Control—and Close the Sale—By Anticipating Objections," *Sales & Marketing Management* (March 17, 1980), pp. 102–106.

22. Joseph P. Vaccaro, "Best Salespeople Know Their ABC's (Always Be Closing)," *Marketing News,* March 28, 1988, p. 10.

23. Theodore Levitt, "After the Sale Is Over . . . ," *Harvard Business Review,* September-October 1983, pp. 87–93.

24. Original thoughts about cognitive dissonance can be found in Leon Festinger, *A Theory of Cognitive Dissonance* (Stanford University Press, 1957).

25. Benson D. Shapiro and Stephen X. Doyle, "Make Sales Task Clear," *Harvard Business Review,* November-December 1983, pp. 72–76.

26. Christopher Stockwell, "Be Concerned with Quality, Not Quantity, of Sales Leads," *Marketing News,* March 14, 1988, p. 11.

27. Scott Matulis, "Building a Sales Force," *Entrepreneur,* September 1988, pp. 43–48.

28. Patricia Sellers, "How IBM Teaches Technies to Sell," *Fortune,* June 6, 1988, pp. 141–146.

29. John M. Ivancevich, *Foundations of Personnel/Human Resource Management* (Business Publications, Inc., 1989).

30. Patricia Sellers, "How IBM Teaches Technies To Sell," *Fortune,* June 6, 1988, pp. 141–146.

31. Chapter XIV, Equal Employment Opportunity Commission Part 160–67, Guidelines on Employee Selection Procedures. Also see Floyd L. Ruch, "The Impact on Employment Procedures of the Supreme Court Decision in the Duke Power Case," *Personnel Journal,* October 1971, pp. 777–83.

32. Maynard M. Garfield, "Make a Salesperson and You Make a Sale," *Marketing News,* February 27, 1989, p. 16.

33. Victor H. Vroom and Arthur G. Jago, *The New Leadership* (Prentice-Hall, 1988).

34. In the leadership literature this is called a "contingency approach."

35. "Sales Reps Are Earning More Than Ever Before," *Marketing News,* June 6, 1988, p. 16.

36. Edward E. Lawler, III, "Reward Systems," in J. Richard Hackman and L. Lloyd Suttle (eds.) *Improving Life at Work* (Scott, Foresman, 1977), pp. 163–226.

37. Martin Levy, "Almost-Perfect Performance Appraisals," *Personnel Journal,* April 1989, pp. 76–83.

CASE APPLICATION 17–1

Sales Incentives: Can They Motivate?

In some organizations, incentive systems are looked at as another tool to manipulate employees. This is a viewpoint that sales managers have to overcome. One way to improve the image of an incentive system is to design a program that satisfies the needs of the salespersons. A number of programs that are used indicate that designing a well-received program is not easy. Creativity, equity, clarity, and communication are all features that need to be incorporated.

Lincoln Liberty Life Insurance Company took its top sales personnel and their spouses on a vacation to Hong Kong and China. The winners of this vacation were sales representatives who had earned between $40,000 and $150,000 in commissions from new accounts. Each month two newsletters were sent to the sales rep advertising "Hong Kong—A World of Mystery and Adventure." The reps were encouraged to compete for the reward to visit Hong Kong. The trip was promoted and there was a high degree of interest in winning among the sales reps.

Travel agents are also becoming involved in incentive reward programs. National Car Rental Systems has offered a $125,000 prize to the top travel agent. RPM Rent-A-Car provides a Sony Walkman to travel agents who book fifty rentals of three days or more.

The Hyatt Corporation is giving travel agents with the best sales rewards of $4 million worth of free rooms at its Waikoloa resort in Hawaii. Continental Airline offers top selling agents flights anywhere in the U.S. for $50.

Union Foods of Costa Mesa, California, spent $100,000 to send eight sales volume winners and their spouses to the 1988 Summer Olympics. At Wordperfect Corporation in Orem, Utah, salespersons who doubled their annual sales were sent for an all-expense paid week in Hawaii. They were also given $300 of spending money.

Travel, jewelry, spending money, and other incentives are being used to increase sales and to reinforce productive selling techniques. Do incentive systems work? An apocryphal story highlights the positive and negative sides of incentive systems.

An experienced insurance agent quite unexpectedly finds himself at the Pearly Gates talking to St. Peter.

Agent: I can't be dead. I'm only 37 years old.
St. Peter: I'm sorry, our records indicate that you are 61.
Agent: Please, St. Peter, check again. I know I'm only 37. (St. Peter leaves and after 30 minutes returns with a huge work report book.)
St. Peter: I'm sorry. My assistants and I checked and rechecked our records. I assure you that our books are completely accurate.
Agent: I don't understand. Your records are off by 24 years. Here look! I've got a birth certificate in my wallet. Look, this proves I'm 37.
St. Peter: Sorry sir. Our records are perfectly accurate. You are 61 years old.
Agent: How can your records be more accurate than an official birth certificate?
St. Peter: Let me show you why our system is accurate. (St. Peter uses a calculator and adds up some totals.) According to our work ledger, you completed 9,500 insurance applications. Put on over 1,000,000 miles on your cars, and traveled to fifteen foreign countries. You made over 12,000 telephone calls and attended 100 professional meetings. According to the blue book used to estimate the times allocated for insurance agent tasks, you must be 61!

An incentive system may have motivated the insurance agent to extraordinary work. If incentive systems are to be motivational, they must recognize and satisfy a salesperson's needs.

SOURCE: Adapted from Leslie A. Westoff, "As Incentive, Anything Goes," *The New York Times Magazine*, April 2, 1989, pp. 60, 80–81 and Robert L. Rose, "Travel Agents' Games Raise Ethics Issue," *The Wall Street Journal*, November 23, 1988, p. B1.

Questions

1. Would travel vacations be an extrinsic or an intrinsic reward in the type of incentive systems discussed in the case? Explain.

2. What kinds of ethics issues are associated with travel agents selling customers on an airline offering an incentive package?

3. How would a sales manager determine a salesperson's needs so that an effective incentive program could be designed?

CASE APPLICATION 17–2

Appealing to Customer Needs in Selling

Attitudes, needs, emotions, preferences, and the future are what salespeople need to tune into to be successful. The competition in all fields of selling has become so intense that educated, trained, and dedicated personnel are important just to be successful and survive in the marketplace. Is there anything new about the need for a professional approach to selling? Not really. Today some obvious and important "how to sell" pointers can go a long way. This is no different than what worked in the past, but today the intense competition makes simple pointers seem more important.

In the 1950s and 1960s, most home builders paid little attention to furnishing their model homes. A rug, a couch, some chairs, some nice-looking paintings, and the house was established as a showpiece home. The salesperson would take customers in and sometimes a sale would be made. Today, builders and salespersons are paying more attention to decorating their model homes. The average U.S. home buyer sees about a dozen models before making a selection. The model that does not stand out, appeal to the buyer, affect attitudes, and provide a message of being somewhat distinct is passed over.

Colors are chosen to appeal to the interests and preferences of target audiences. Homes for first time buyers are decorated with bold, primary hues, while units for older people use pastels. Furniture ranges from antiques for the older couple without children to sturdy items for younger couples with children.

Selling has not only changed in home buying, but also in selling art. Again, customer needs and obvious follow-up techniques seem to be successful. Hanson Galleries is a $25 million a year business with stores in Sausalito, New Orleans, and San Francisco. The philosophy used at Hanson is that sales efforts should be directed to repeat customers. It is the Hanson philosophy that selling to people that have already bought art from you is easier than selling to new customers. All the groundwork has been laid. Creating a desire and the need to make the second, third, and other purchases is what Hanson sales personnel are trained to accomplish.

Hanson Galleries sells limited-edition graphics of such artists as Marc Chagall, Peter Max, Thomas McKnight, and Erte to mostly middle-class collectors who buy multiple works and keep buying. The sales invoices indicate that the middle-class buyer will spend about $4,000–$5,000 on art that they want and like. To convert customers into repeat buyers, Hanson Galleries concentrates on attitude and follow-up. The salespeople work on creating a collector, not a single purchase, attitude. Then they follow-up to reinforce the "I am a collector" attitude.

The Hanson salespersons ask questions, find out about customer preferences, home style, colors, and interests. They find out what artists customers like and provide background details about the preferred artist. The salesperson works to create a personal relationship—a feeling that buying and collecting art is not frivolous, and that the customer is an intelligent and knowledgeable buyer.

Education is crucial to repeat sales. Videotapes, catalogs, private viewing rooms, and personal communication are part of the Hanson selling approach. This type of personal attention permits the salesperson to learn about preferences, needs, and the total customer. A detailed customer information card is prepared so that the salesperson can call and mail information on a regular basis. Making art collection exciting and a rewarding personal experience is what Hanson sales personnel work on constantly.

The new home and art businesses are different, but methods of selling to appeal to the emotions, needs, and preferences of customers are similar. A trained salesperson in either industry must work to educate and satisfy buyers. The glib, aggressive, and uninformed salesperson is not likely to succeed in selling homes or working for Hanson Galleries. Although the lessons offered in the new home sales industry and at Hanson Galleries are straightforward, too many salespeople ignore or refuse to learn them.

SOURCE: Adapted from Tom Richman, "Come Again," *Inc.*, April 1989, pp. 177–78 and Ruth Simon, "Hit the Prospect at Every Emotional Level," *Forbes*, January 9, 1989, pp. 310 and 317.

Questions

1. Why would one conclude that the home buying and art collecting examples in this case could be explained by using the need satisfaction approach?

2. What makes following up on customers a difficult task that many salespeople ignore?

3. What aspects of the Hanson approach to selling suggest that more than order-taking is necessary to get customers back for repeat sales?

PART SIX

Pricing

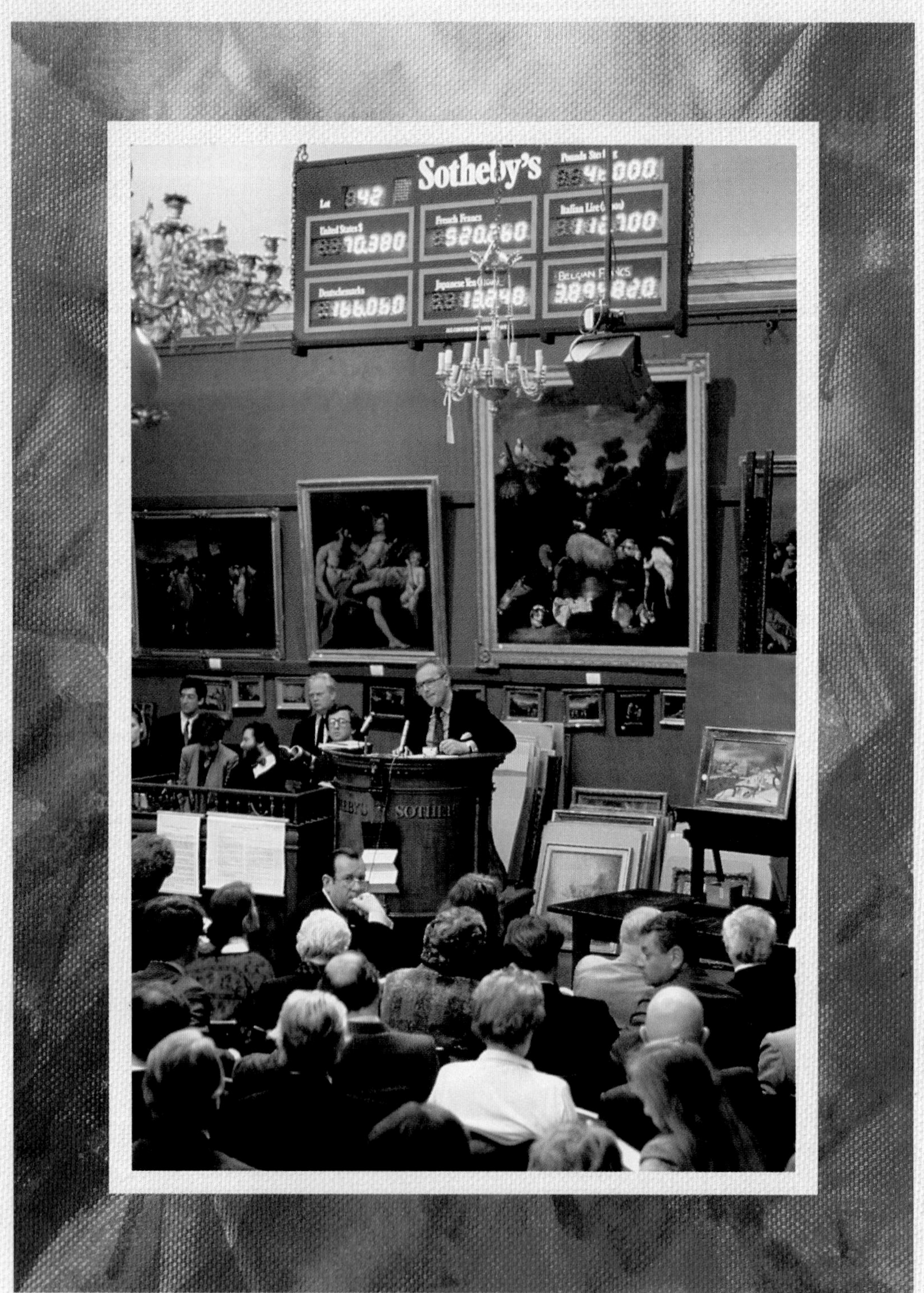
Sotheby's

18

Pricing: Basic Concepts

Learning Objectives

Upon completing this chapter, you will be able to do the following:

DISCUSS
the meaning of price to consumers and marketers.

UNDERSTAND
the role and importance of pricing in marketing.

IDENTIFY
alternative pricing objectives.

COMPARE
various pricing policies and methods of quoting prices.

EXPLAIN
different types of discounts and allowances that determine the price buyers actually pay.

DESCRIBE
different types of geographical pricing schemes that take delivery charges into account.

ILLUSTRATE
the effect of government regulation on pricing.

MARKETING PROFILE

Price Wars for Airline Passengers

Over the last ten years, airlines in the United States have been involved in a continuing series of price wars. American Airlines pitched its latest set of fares as "ultimate super savers" and found itself matched in fares by the other major airlines and some of the smaller ones. This is but a continuation of an ongoing struggle for the air travelers' business.

United and American Airlines engaged in a battle with Continental for the New York area to Chicago traveler. It started when Continental set its Newark International to O'Hare one-way fare at $59 for off-peak times and $79 for peak times, compared to the then current fare of $258 for an unrestricted seat on United and American. United's response was quick. It cut fares, but, for the most part, it did not match Continental's rates. United's management thought that the consumer would pay for the additional services United offered that Continental did not have. United set its fares on the Newark-Chicago run at $89 off-peak and $109 peak. It would match the Continental fares with advanced-purchase and minimum-stay provisions. United also lowered its fares from New York's Kennedy and LaGuardia airports to $20 above its Newark rates. American's response was to match United's fares.

The battle for the California market and the market that it feeds was no less hard fought on the price dimension. United Airlines set out to make San Francisco its western hub, much as O'Hare is its midwestern hub. On one day it added twenty-seven daily flights at San Francisco. Other carriers responded by adding capacity and by slashing air fares. PSA was the dominant airline in the lucrative San Francisco-Los Angeles route and its president, Paul Barkley, stated strongly that, "PSA has no intention of allowing any carrier to replace it as the dominant carrier in the corridor." Both carriers cut fares to $35 one-way from the discounted fare of $55 and regular fare of $75, as did other carriers such as AirCal. All this price activity put pressure on the airlines' profitability. AirCal lost almost $35 million dollars that year.

Many other airlines also had substantial profitability pressures because of price competition in many regions of the country. Braniff Airlines, in its attempt to rise from bankruptcy, continued to have great financial problems by trying to compete. Braniff had adopted a reduced-fare strategy when its full service, full fare pricing strategy failed to attract enough customers. Continental Airlines, in its fight to recover from financial reorganization, featured ads that showed passengers from other airlines wishing that they had flown Continental so that they could have saved money.

This continuing price war mentality, which is pervasive in the airline industry, appeared to doom a number of airlines. Some critics petitioned the federal government to intervene to protect the smaller airlines from what they saw as predatory pricing practices of the larger carriers. Recently, Continental and others have been attempting to drop some discount fares. In 1989, a long strike at Eastern Airlines allowed Delta, its main competitor in the Atlanta hub, to substantially cut back on discount fares.

This profile identifies many of the dynamics having an impact on the marketing manager when he or she makes pricing decisions. Consumers' reactions to prices, competitive behavior, cost dynamics, and services offered relative to competitors are just some of the factors that must be addressed in making these important decisions. Imagine yourself charged with setting prices for American when the success or failure of the whole airline could depend on your decision. This chapter and the next one discuss the complex and interesting area of pricing.

SOURCES: Scott Hume and Robert Raissman, "American Joins United to Blunt People Fare Cut," *Advertising Age*, August 13, 1984, pp. 1 and 66; Tom Bayer, "Air-war Ads Draw Battle Lines," *Advertising Age*, September 10, 1984, pp. 2 and 102; "War in The Crowded Skies," *Business Week*, September 26, 1983, pp. 72–74; Leonard Sloane, "Why an $873 Flight Can Also Cost $124," *The New York Times*, April 2, 1988, pp. B1, B39.

The airline industry pricing activity described in the *Marketing Profile* points out the great dynamics of pricing in marketing and illustrates many of the factors one must consider when making pricing decisions. Major concerns that have an impact on pricing are consumer demand, cost pressures, competitive activity, and even government regulatory action. Balancing these factors while making pricing decisions is a difficult but exciting task.

In this chapter, we describe basic concepts that underlie pricing decisions. (The description of actual procedures for setting prices, explained in Chapter 19, requires a good understanding of the concepts presented in this chapter.) The first step is to define *price* and discuss its importance in marketing. Then we examine the different types of pricing objectives and the role they play in pricing. Later, alternative pricing policies and methods for quoting prices—including discounts, allowances, and the handling of freight charges—are introduced. The chapter ends with a discussion of the impact of government regulation and legislation on pricing.

The Meaning of Price

Price is not a simple concept. It can be defined in many ways and can take many forms. Table 18–1 lists a number of these forms, indicating what is usually received in return. It is the fact that something is received in return that defines the pricing relationship. *Price is the value that one puts on the utility that one receives for goods and services.*

The utility received can be any of the types we discussed in Chapter 1: form, time, place, and possession. One pays a price for some or all of these utilities.

In our high-level economic society, it is common to think of price in money terms. However, at a broader level, price can be anything of value that is exchanged for something else.

The price, or value, of a good does not have to be expressed in monetary terms. For instance, barter—the exchange of goods or services for each other, in lieu of cash—was the basis for history's earliest pricing system. Although monetary price systems have supplanted barter as the basis of all modern economies, bartering has made a resurgence in recent years as a small but increasingly important segment of the U.S. economy. Bartering is now being used by companies, both large and small, to solve problems in operations, finance, and marketing.[1]

Bartering has become particularly popular for companies with rapidly changing technology, such as in the computer industry, where suddenly outmoded inventory can be a problem. Bartering allows such companies to unload still-valuable products that are no longer marketable through retail outlets in exchange for needed goods or services. Bartering is also used by firms that have accumulated more current inventory than their distribution channels are able or willing to handle. Cash flow problems may also be circumvented by bartering. A company strapped for cash to buy needed raw materials may barter finished products to pay for what it needs.

Barter has also helped many firms broaden distribution for their products—often inadvertently. For example, the unexpected payoff for a lighting manufacturer of a recent barter sale was entry into a market segment it had not penetrated before. After completing a barter deal for $2 million worth of lighting fixtures, the fixtures ultimately found their way into a number of hotels that had never used the firm's products before.

The development of a small barter economy has been facilitated by several barter companies that act as clearinghouses for corporate exchange. In addition to serving

Table 18–1 The Meaning of Price

Alternative Terms	What Is Given in Return
Price	Physical merchandise
Tuition	College courses; education
Rent	A place to live or the use of equipment for a specific time period
Interest	Use of money
Fee	Professional services: for lawyers, doctors, consultants
Fare	Transportation: air, taxi, bus
Toll	Use of road or bridge, or long-distance phone rate
Salary	Work of managers
Wage	Work of hourly workers
Bribe	Illegal actions
Commission	Sales effort

as middlemen for bilateral exchanges, barter companies may also bundle goods and services from several companies, thus facilitating multi-party exchanges.

Even if companies find little reason to use bartering as a tool of domestic trade, they may find it a *quid pro quo* for engaging in trade with developing countries strapped for hard currency. This kind of barter is known as "countertrade." Many governments require foreign companies they buy from to accept full or partial payment in locally manufactured goods or raw materials in order to bolster their own economies.

Bartering offers many companies advantages over making cash deals. Although money may not change hands in barter arrangements, barter prices are still genuine prices. As such, management must use care in developing barter prices so that they reflect the company's objectives just as monetary prices do.

This *bartering* of goods is still common in other societies. Even today in our society, the price of one good is sometimes defined in terms of other goods. Other examples of bartering in our society include:

- consultants exchanging their time and knowledge for products from the companies they help, and medical people exchanging treatment;
- advertising media accepting the products of their advertisers in return for advertising time;
- athletes being exchanged by teams, with no cash involved.

Many transactions involve a price consisting of both money and goods. This practice occurs in the purchase of durable goods, such as cars and appliances, where a trade-in is part of the price paid.

Price has a *subjective* and *temporal* meaning. Consider the following examples:

- Bob and Carol both purchase a General Electric color twenty-seven-inch television set. Bob pays $650, while Carol pays $525. Clearly, Carol has made a better deal, right? Well, not necessarily so. Bob purchased his TV from a store that gives home delivery, in-home tuning, extended service at the store, carries many brands, and is located close to his home. Carol, on the other hand, bought her TV from a discount store that is twenty miles from her house, offers no service, carries few brands, and required Carol

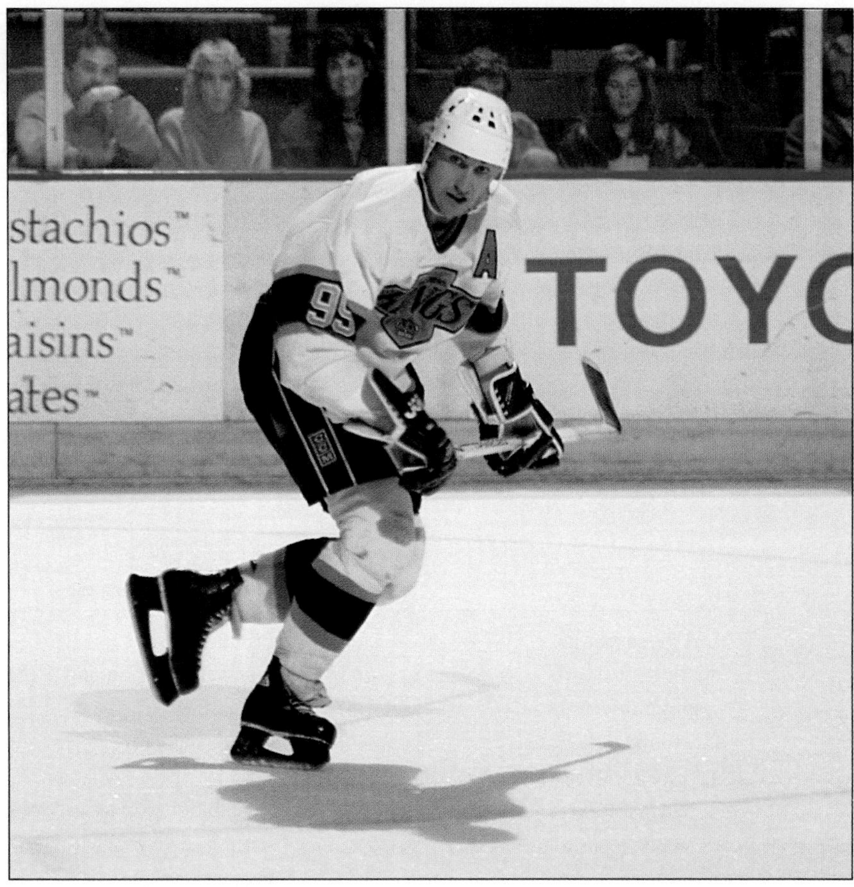

Wayne Gretzky cost the L.A. Kings one player, three draft choices, and $15 million in cash.

to take the set with her. The bundles of utility received by Bob and Carol are different, and the value they subjectively attach to them are different. This example helps explain why one can buy fruits and vegetables from a farmer at the produce stand on the highway much more cheaply than in the supermarket; different things are being exchanged.

- In 1988 the Edmonton Oilers of the National Hockey League exchanged hockey's greatest player, Wayne Gretzky, to the Los Angeles Kings for second year standout player Jimmy Carlson, $15 million in cash, three future first round draft choices, and some other considerations. Gretzky had led the Oilers to four championships in five years. Directly after the exchange, the Oilers fell to third place in their division, while the Kings attained previously unheard of levels of success. The Kings subsequently eliminated the Oilers in the playoffs and were then defeated by Calgary. The long-run value received by each party in the exchange is as yet unknown. However, *at the time of the exchange,* both parties perceived the price to be equal.

In our society, price is typically a monetary amount and can be thought of as part of an equation of exchange. Table 18–2 presents this equation from both the consumer's and the retailer's points of view. The table clearly shows *price as the value assigned to a bundle of form, time, place, and possession utility.*

Table 18–2 The Equation of Exchange

	Price Paid	Bundle of Utility Received
Consumer	**List Price Minus** store discounts coupons rebates trade-ins	**Product:** features style quality packaging **Place:** location delivery service **Promotion:** image confidence of quality information about use
Retailer	**List Price Minus** quantity discounts seasonal discounts functional discounts advertising allowances display allowances return of goods allowances transportation allowances	**Product:** brand recognition and preference warranties service support **Place:** availability of inventory of models, sizes, etc. speed of delivery **Promotion:** advertising support to end consumers sales promotion activity to end consumers sales training

The Importance of Price to the Economy

The price variable plays an important role both for the individual organization and the economy as a whole. For the economy, price brings the supply and demand for productive inputs (land, labor, capital, and entrepreneurship) and outputs into balance. It helps direct and allocate resources to their most productive uses.

The effects of pricing on supply and demand and on resource allocation can be seen in the pricing decisions of a monopoly firm or of the government. For more than twenty-five years, the federal government held the price of natural gas at levels well below what a free market would have set for it. As a result, more people adopted natural gas heating systems than they otherwise would have. The end result was a shortage of natural gas, caused by excessive demand, and a limiting of supply. Both the excessive demand and the limiting of supply are the result of consumers and businesses using price to make decisions in their own best interests. Rent controls have the same impact on the availability of apartments in New York City.

Alternatively, for years the price of many agricultural commodities has been held above market prices by government policy. As farmers have increased supply and

MARKETING IN ACTION

Price Reform Plays a Key Role in China's Economic Reforms

Price reform is a key element of the massive economic reforms that the Chinese government has been undertaking for more than a decade. In China, as in every country, prices give signals to all actors in the economy—producers, consumers, investors, or government bureaucracies—and so prices must be rational in order for the economy to function smoothly. In the case of the People's Republic of China, however, the country's communist leaders had strictly controlled most prices until 1978 in order to maintain political and social stability. As a result, by 1978 the price system did not accurately reflect the absolute or relative value of many commodities.

For instance, extremely low prices for coal and other energy sources discouraged energy production on the one hand, while encouraging industrial wastefulness on the other. As a result, China now faces a severe energy shortage, especially in its highly industrialized Southeast. Its current situation is largely attributable to irrational energy pricing, since China does not lack natural resources, although they are unevenly distributed. Similarly, from the 1950s until 1978, government procurement prices for grain remained relatively unchanged. At those prices, however, peasants had little incentive to increase grain production. In 1979, the government recognized the gap between the price and value of agricultural commodities and increased procurement prices. The result was a dramatic increase in agricultural productivity.

Price reform is a necessary complement to many of China's other economic reforms. For example, as more and more of China's enterprises become responsible for their own profits and losses, prices will have to be adjusted in order to give each firm a fair chance to be profitable. Under China's unreformed price system, certain industries, such as those which manufactured watches, bikes, and other consumer goods, had a natural advantage due to high prices and high profit margins. At the same time, other firms were at a disadvantage due to low prices.

Price reform, especially of food commodities, is proving to be both an economic and political challenge for the Chinese government. While they may recognize the theoretical need for price reform, the Chinese populace is not happy to see inflation return after decades of stable prices. The urban population has been especially hard hit. After years of subsidizing the high grain procurement prices paid to farmers, the Chinese government is now shifting the burden of higher grain prices to the urban consumers.

Due to the political delicacy of implementing price reforms, the Chinese government is moving forward cautiously in this area. The Chinese leadership does not want to provoke too much intense popular dissatisfaction which might further destabilize the government and upset the economic reforms. Still, China's top leaders seem to understand the importance of rational pricing and intend to move China toward that goal. However, the ruthless crushing of the "Democracy Movement" by the hardline communist leaders may cause much of the economic reform to be put on hold.

---

consumers have cut back on demand (compared to what it would have been at lower prices), a surplus of these products has been created. Of course, there are public-policy reasons for these types of government actions.

In both of these cases, the government, or some other organization, must take steps to correct the problems created by having artificial prices. If the price is kept too low, the resulting shortage must be handled either by forcing an increase in supply or by rationing. The government has set up lottery systems to identify who is eligible for particular units in government-built apartment buildings in rent-controlled areas. When the price of farm produce is too high, the government often steps in and buys the surplus. The *Marketing in Action* on China's economic reform illustrates the importance of price to the economy.

Foreign automobiles compete with American products on a price basis.

The Importance of Price to the Organization

The rapidly changing nature of the marketing environment in recent years has caused pricing decisions to grow in importance. Studies done twenty years ago found that managers ranked price third in importance behind product and promotion;[2] today, however, many people feel that it is the most important marketing decision area.

The importance of price in the decision making of the individual organization increases in the following circumstances:

- The pace of *technological advance increases,* pushing a product through its life-cycle more quickly and making it more difficult to remedy pricing errors. The pricing of home video games and computer chips are two examples of the importance of proper pricing in gaining early market position.
- *Foreign competition* increases, putting substantial pressure on prices; many foreign goods, such as shoes, clothes, toys, electronics, and automobiles compete with American goods on a price basis to a great degree.

- *Shortages* of raw materials and energy occur, putting great upward pressure on prices. For example, the price of the paper used to print newspapers has risen from $125 per ton in 1973 to over $700 per ton today. These price increases were generated fundamentally by the increased costs of the energy, the raw wood, and chemicals required to make newsprint paper. In this environment, one is constantly dealing with pricing decisions.
- The firm is preparing to introduce a *new product.* The need to set a proper price is difficult but necessary.
- A *competitor attempts to gain market share* using price decreases. For example, Sanyo's low prices in microwave ovens forced competitors to reassess their pricing structures.
- A *substitute product* is introduced into the market, making the pricing of the original product very important. The advent of margarine, synthetic fibers, and long-distance telephone services after the breakup of AT&T are examples of the importance of the pricing response of established products in determining the market penetration of the new products. For example, the price of butter was held artificially high, and margarine gained high market penetration.
- In a *highly inflationary economy,* consumer demand patterns may change greatly, requiring the firm to carefully consider the amount each product's price should be increased. A general price increase across the product line may not give the best solution.

The importance of price to the individual firm can be clearly seen from the profit equation:

$$\text{Profit} = \text{total revenue} - \text{total cost}$$

or

$$\text{Profit} = (\text{prices} \times \text{quantity sold}) - \text{total cost}.$$

What makes this even more important is that the price affects the quantity sold. Thus, the task is to set a price that generates enough total revenue to yield an acceptable profit.

Finally, we must recognize that the price set for goods and services has a direct impact on consumers, who use it to determine their *cost of living.* They will get angry at some prices (gasoline, utility costs), show elation at others (appliances, home video equipment), and dramatically change their behavior (conversion to foreign cars, shopping at discount stores) in response to others. The consumers' perceptions of how well they are doing from year to year are determined by measuring the prices they get for their labor (wage or salary) against the prices they pay for goods and services (as reflected in the inflation rate).

Price, then, plays a major role in the economy as a whole, is increasingly important to the individual firm, and has a direct impact on consumers. The importance of price can clearly be seen in the *Marketing in Action* feature about Suave shampoo, Breck, Downy, and Purina's Alley Cat.

Key Factors in Price Determination

Determining a specific price for a product or service involves a dynamic trade-off among certain key factors (see Figure 18–1):

1. pricing objectives
2. corporate and marketing objectives and policies

MARKETING IN ACTION

Using the Price Variable

Helene Curtis' Suave shampoo developed one of the largest market shares in the shampoo business by advertising that "we do what theirs does for less than half the price." Competitors were either named or their labels were clearly shown. This strategy transformed Suave from an also-ran to a market leader. Its success did not go unnoticed by Shulton whose market position for Breck shampoo was faltering. Its response was to reduce the price of Breck 24 percent. Shulton's intention here was to reposition Breck as a price-value competitor.

Market leaders also may use price to respond to a challenge. Procter & Gamble's Downy fabric softener was the long-standing market leader. To attack this position, Lever Bros. developed Snuggle and positioned it as a less expensive alternative, offering the same benefits as Downy. In response, P & G reduced the price of Downy to slightly above Snuggle's price. Proctor & Gamble was making it clear to the industry that it would fight to keep its market share.

Price may also be used to define the positioning of brands in a product line. Purina's Alley Cat brand was given a moderate price relative to other Purina cat food brands so that Purina would have a brand positioned in every price category in the market. Before this, Purina already held the largest share of this market, with about a 62 percent share. This price move was designed to solidify Purina's position as the market leader before some other company could exploit this moderate price point.

3. demand behavior
4. cost dynamics
5. the competitive situation and behavior of competitors
6. legal and ethical constraints

In the remainder of this chapter, we discuss the basics of pricing objectives, policies, and legal constraints, while in Chapter 19 we examine the factors that help set prices in practice: demand behavior, cost dynamics, and the competitive situation in a given market.

Pricing Objectives

The objectives set for any marketing activity greatly influence specific decisions that are made. This is as true for pricing as it is for promotion and product policy. Regrettably, not many firms develop explicit, written pricing objectives. Instead, these objectives tend to be held as implicit understandings by the firm's management. Objectives, whether explicit or implicit, fall into three broad classes: profit objectives, sales objectives, and competitive position objectives.

Profit Objectives

Profit maximization and target return are two major types of profit objectives. With a *profit maximization* objective, the firm attempts to earn the largest profit possible. To do this, the firm sets the price at the point where the additional revenue generated by a sale of one more unit just equals the additional cost of producing and marketing

Figure 18–1 Key Factors in Price Determination

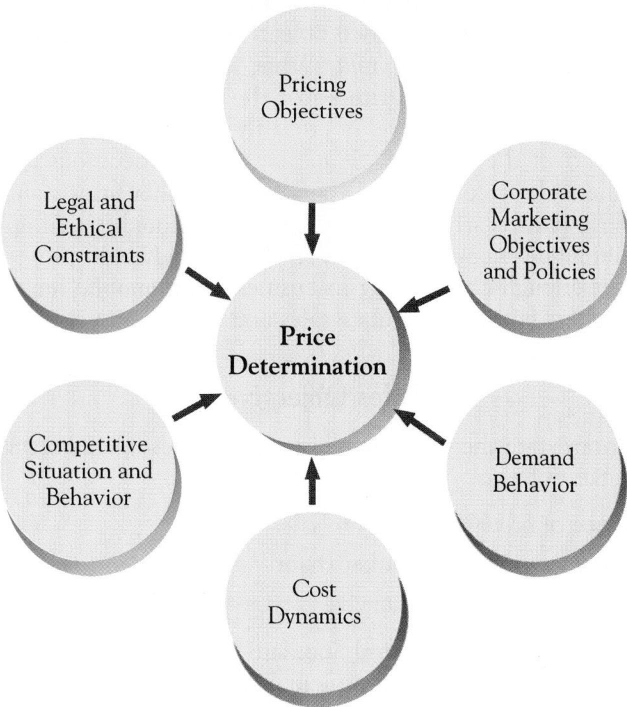

this additional sale. In practice, this objective is difficult to attain because it requires detailed knowledge of demand and costs. This objective is even more difficult to implement in multiproduct companies. The firm may accept little or no profit on one product to gain large profits on another. For example, Polaroid sells cameras at a low price and profit to gain high profitability on film; Gillette sells razors at a lower price in order to sell razor blades. Managers strive for a certain profit level for the firm, not just for an individual product item.

One point should be made clear. Even if a firm did use a profit maximization objective, it would not necessarily mean a high price for the product in question. Profit maximization does not mean price gouging, excessive profits, and consumer rip-offs. Depending on demand and cost behavior, the profit-maximizing price may be quite low, since the firm might be most profitable selling a large volume at a small profit on each sale. Selling at a higher price could decrease demand and increase unit costs; profits might be far below what the lower price option would generate. Supermarkets and discount stores operate on this principle.

With the many operational difficulties of the profit-maximization approach, many firms have turned to using a *target return on investment* (ROI) objective. ROI is the ratio of profits to capital investment, such as plant, equipment, and accounts receivable. Companies like Alcoa (20 percent target ROI before tax), General Electric (25 percent ROI after tax), General Motors (20 percent ROI after tax), International Harvester (10 percent ROI after tax), DuPont, Exxon, Johns-Manville, Union Carbide, and U.S. Steel all reportedly use this type of pricing objective.

A twist on this objective is to set a *target return on net sales,* where the targeted profit is a specific percentage of a sales dollar. Retailers and wholesalers often use this type of objective. The typical supermarket earns 1 to 2 cents profit on a dollar sale; the typical department store, about 4 cents; and wholesalers, about 2 cents. Firms may also set other types of profit-related objectives. Some less aggressive companies may set *price to earn a satisfactory profit.* What is considered satisfactory varies by company and is affected by the attitudes of the managers, stockholders, and the financial community. Often the level of profit that managers believe the public will consider *fair* is part of the decision. Sometimes pricing decisions reflect managers' desires to avoid attacking competition too severely. Other firms want to generate a positive cash flow, particularly when they have their liquidity tied up in inventory. Some condominium developers have sold off their already built properties at distress prices just to get enough cash to stay in business. Automobile rebate programs do not generate a profit, but they stimulate sales and decrease inventories.

Sales Objectives

Many organizations state their pricing objectives in sales-related terms. These goals can take a number of forms.

- Maintenance or growth in absolute sales
- Maintenance or growth in market share
- Minimum sales necessary to survive

American Can, Swift, Kroger, and Standard Oil of Indiana are all firms with the maintenance of market share as their principal pricing goal. Growth in market share appears to be the objective of A&P, Sears, and Bic.

The major risk in a sales orientation to pricing is that the profitability of such an approach is uncertain. However, recent research from a large cross-section of firms concludes that market share and profitability are highly related. The *Profit Impact of Marketing Strategies* (PIMS) project found that pretax ROI was about 8 percent for firms with under 10 percent market share, over 14 percent for those with 10 to 20 percent market share, 22 percent for those with 20 to 30 percent share, 24 percent for those with 30 to 40 percent, and 29 percent for those with over 40 percent market share. Thus a market-share objective has a possible long-term side benefit of yielding good profits, although this is not expected when trying to gain market share. Even Sanyo's aggressive acquisition of market share in microwave ovens had minimum gross margin expectations involved. It should be noted, however, that sales objectives for pricing are often made with a minimum acceptable profit level in mind.

Competitive Position Objectives

Some firms set pricing objectives in relationship to the actions of their competitors. Their goals may be the following:

- *To meet or prevent competition.* Many firms, such as Goodyear, Gulf Oil, and National Steel, attempt to match the pricing of competitors. This pattern is very common in industries where one firm dominates and serves as the *price leader*—the firm that usually is first to change prices in the industry. U.S. Steel (USX) serves this role in the steel industry and R.J. Reynolds in the cigarette industry.

- *To stabilize prices.* Here the objective is to have similar prices throughout the industry, so that competition will not be based on price. This is often the objective of price leaders. Their power in the industry allows them to "police" the prices they set. The smaller firms fear a price reprisal from a large firm if they deviate from the normal price in the industry. Steel, paper, chemicals, and aluminum appear to follow such a pattern. Kennecott's (a metals and mining company) stated objective is to stabilize prices.

REVIEW YOUR MARKETING KNOWLEDGE

- For most consumer goods, the same brand can be found at different retail stores at different prices. What is the nature of the exchange between store and customer that leads to these different prices? Give an example for consumer durables (televisions, etc.) and for package goods (cereal, etc.).

- Tuition at some state supported universities has been held down below "market tuition" by actions of state legislatures and governors. What are the likely long-run consequences of such actions to the university administrations and students involved?

Pricing Policy and Structure

Within the guidelines set by pricing objectives, a firm must develop *pricing policies,* which define approaches to setting prices for the long run. For example, Cadillac will never offer discount prices, since this is against its policy of selling high-priced cars. This was true even when it entered the small-car market with the Cimarron. In addition, a firm must develop a policy for quoting prices in terms of discounts, allowances, and freight cost absorption. These latter areas of pricing policy are often referred to as *pricing structure.* Without an overall pricing policy and a detailed pricing structure, managers would have to recycle their thinking completely every time a price had to be set. There are two general pricing policies that are important: *quoted price levels relative to general market price* and the *degree of price flexibility.*

Setting Price Levels

The firm has three options for determining price levels: (1) pricing above the market price, (2) pricing at market price, or (3) pricing below the market price. The choice must be consistent with the overall marketing program of the product in question. Firms with products that offer extra qualities—such as BMW, Chivas Regal, and IBM computers—are able to price above the market. For other firms, pricing below the market makes the most sense. Kmart became the second largest chain store in the country using such an approach. Helene Curtis (see the Suave example in the *Marketing in Action* feature in this chapter), European newsprint companies, and independent gasoline retailers also use this approach.

For certain commodity goods, pricing at the market is the most common pattern. These goods include basic chemicals and steel, which are sold in large markets with only a few competing firms (undifferentiated oligopoly). Since pricing above the market in these circumstances usually results in a substantial loss in sales, the higher-priced competitor will lower the price back to the market level. Pricing below the market usually results in a substantial increase in sales relative to higher-priced competitors, and the higher-priced competitors tend to match these lower prices quickly. Thus, all prices are eventually about the same. It is in each firm's best interest to price at the market level. However, when all competitors have reduced prices to match the lowest price, the total revenue earned in the industry will decrease. The firms moving to match each other's prices in their own best interests are said to be operating in a *conscious parallel* fashion. As long as there is no conspiracy to fix the price, the fact that they all have the same price is perfectly legal.

Price Flexibility Policies

The marketer can determine the *degree of price flexibility* by setting a *one-price policy* or a *flexible-* or *variable-price policy*. With a one-price policy, the product is sold for the same price and terms of sale to all customers at the same level in the channel. *Terms of sales* means the timing and method of payment and the discounts and allowance that apply. Most goods in the United States are sold under a one-price policy. This saves a great deal of time, since bargaining over price is not part of the transaction. Can you imagine how long it would take you to shop if you bargained over price for every item in a supermarket, record store, or department store? One-price policies are less common in less-developed countries, where bargaining over price in open markets is the custom.

With a flexible-price policy, the product is sold at different prices and terms to different customers at the same level in the channel. Purchasing a car by bargaining over price with the dealer is a common example. Appliances and houses are other goods where this tradition has remained. The existence of a trade-in is a means to set flexible prices. Flexibility in prices has been increasing lately in American industry, as illustrated by the following examples:

- To fight Japanese imports, Ford and General Motors are charging less for subcompacts on the West Coast than elsewhere in the country.
- In the chemical industry, a rush of "temporary" allowances or prices have been given to certain key customers.

Agreement about price often depends upon the power of the bargainers. The nature of the competition in the market also greatly affects the final price and terms. Flexible pricing allows the marketer to respond to specific market conditions quickly. In industrial selling, it allows the salesperson to get orders that might have been lost. The risks are that profit will be bargained away and that those paying the higher price will become upset and take their business elsewhere. There is also a risk in flexible-price sales that illegal price discrimination will occur.

Discount Pricing Structure

In sales made between firms, it is common practice to quote a *list* or *base price* for a product and then quote discounts, or lower prices, that are available. These discounts occur in three circumstances:

1. sales made in different quantities, or at different times
2. sales made to different intermediaries performing different functions
3. sales made with different credit and collection terms

Quantity and Timing Discounts

As an incentive for their customers to purchase larger quantities of an item, marketers at all levels in the channel often offer quantity discounts. For example, one firm offered the following discount schedule to its customers on automatic temperature controls:

Annual Volume	*Net Price*
50–349	$17.35
350–999	16.45
1000 and up	15.90

At the retail level, supermarkets often offer discounts of three cans of vegetables for $1.00 or a single can for $.37. Those buying appliances can easily bargain for a discount if more than one item is being purchased.

Quantity discounts may be either *cumulative* or *noncumulative. Cumulative quantity discounts* are based upon the total amount of a product purchased within a specified time—usually a year. The discount schedule for the temperature controls was cumulative. This type of discount is an incentive to the buyer to stick with one supplier, since the reduced price applies to the quantity purchased in the entire period. When a buyer's volume level qualifies him or her for a lower price, the seller makes an adjustment to account for items purchased earlier at a higher price.

Noncumulative quantity discounts relate to the size of an *individual* purchase. They encourage large purchase orders, but unlike cumulative quantity discounts, they do not tie the buyer as tightly to the seller over the long run. Quantity discounts sometimes give "free" amounts of the product being purchased instead of reducing the cash price. Thus, a retailer might get one free carton of Tang for every twenty-four cartons purchased.

The purpose of quantity discounts is to gain economies for the seller in production, marketing, and order handling. Since fixed costs of getting and filling an order are the same whether the order is large or small, spreading them over a large number of units reduces costs. Also, fewer orders are obtained and processed during the period, giving additional cost savings. For noncumulative discounts, the buyer, of course, must compare the discount savings against the additional costs to carry more inventory associated with the larger orders.

The marketer may also give discounts based on the *timing* of a purchase order. Automobile rebates always have a specified time frame, as do most special retail sales (for example, Midnight Madness Sale—from midnight to 6:00 A.M.). *Seasonal discounts* are tied to the purchase of a product during a certain time of the year. Their intent is to get buyers to stock up on an item ahead of its selling season. Snow blowers, air conditioners, lawn mowers, coal, fuel oil, and toys are all sold in this fashion. This aids manufacturers in production planning and decreases their inventory carrying costs.

Functional Discounts

Functional or trade discounts are reductions of the list price given to resellers on the basis of the *level* they hold in the channel and the marketing activities or *functions* they are expected to perform. It is quite common to quote price in the following form:

List price: $300 less 30/10/5.

Table 18–3 The Chain of Functional Discounts

Terms:	List price $300 less 30/10/15	
	Manufacturers' suggested retail price (MSRP)	$300.00
Less:	Retail margin, 30 percent of MSRP	90.00
Yields:	Retail cost price or wholesaler's selling price (WSP)	$210.00
Less:	Wholesale margin, 10 percent of WSP	21.00
Yields:	Wholesale cost price or jobber seller price (JSP)	$189.00
Less:	Jobber margin, 5 percent of JSP	9.45
Yields:	Jobber cost price or manufacturer's selling price	$179.55

The $300 is the manufacturer's suggested retail price. The 30 is the percentage of the suggested retail price available to the retailer to cover costs and provide a profit ($300 × .3 = $90). The first number given always refers to the retail end of the channel. The next number refers to the wholesalers closest to the retailer in the channel. These wholesalers get 10 percent of their selling price ($300 − $90 = $210). Thus, they get $21 per unit sold ($210 × .1). The next group of wholesalers (probably a jobber) in the channel who are closest to the manufacturer get 5 percent of their selling price of $189 ($210 − $21) or $9.45 ($189 × .05). Trade discounts are just subtracted one at a time starting with the manufacturers' suggested retail price, making sure that a relevant discount is applied to that level of the channel's selling price. The end result of this is that we can determine the manufacturer's selling prices to the wholesaler closest to them in the channel. In our example, this price is $179.55 ($189 − $9.45). Table 18–3 presents the example in more detail.

This chain of discounts is what the manufacturer proposes the margin should be at the various levels in the channel. The channel members may vary from this schedule if they wish. Retailers or wholesalers may increase the discount from the producer's list price, while others may decrease it. Quite often trade discounts are determined by the custom for a given product. Thus, these types of discounts tend to be very similar across brands.

Credit and Collection Discounts

An additional deduction from list price may be given if a buyer pays a bill for goods and services within a specified time frame. For example, a bill may be quoted as $800, 2/10, net 30. This means that the bill for the product is $800, but that the buyer can take a 2 percent discount and pay $784 if payment is within ten days. Otherwise, the total $800 is due within thirty days. It is usually in the buyer's best interest to take this *cash discount.* If a buyer does not take advantage of it, he or she is paying a very high interest rate for the use of money. For example, 2/10, net 30 means that the buyer would pay 2 percent interest to gain twenty days use of this money. In a 360-day year, this translates to an effective annual interest rate of 36 percent (2 percent × 360/20 = 36 percent). Because the effective rate is so high, it is normally in the firm's best interest to borrow money at bank rates to take advantage of cash discounts. Cash discounts relate to both the financial management and marketing areas of a company, and these two divisions make joint decisions about them.

Table 18–4 An Example of Multiple Discounts

The Hardware Distributing Company Order	10 ladders @ $30	$ 300
	6 ladders @ $50	300
	10 ladders @ $90	900
	5 ladders @ $120	600
	4 ladders @ $150	600
	Total	$2700
Applying the Quantity Discounts	Total order amount	$2700
	Discounts, $2700 × 0.05	135
	Net order amount	$2565
Applying the Trade Discounts	Net order amount	$2565.00
	Less 40% discount	1026.00
		$1539.00
	Less 10% discount	153.90
		$1385.10
	Less 5% discount	69.26
	Amount due manufacturer	$1315.84
Applying the Cash Discount	Amount due manufacturer	$1315.84
	Less 3% discount	39.48
	Net remittance	$1276.36

SOURCE: Kent B. Monroe, *Pricing: Making Profitable Decisions* (McGraw-Hill, 1979), p 171.

Multiple Discounts: An Example

To see how all these different types of discounts are related, let us consider the following situation:

The Stepup Ladder Company sells five different types of ladders priced at $30, $50, $90, $120, and $150.[3] The channel for those ladders is through a jobber to a merchant wholesaler to department and hardware stores. *Functional* or trade discounts are 40/10/5. Additionally, Stepup gives a *cash* discount of 3/10, net 30 and gives a *quantity* discount of 5 percent for orders of $1000 or more at list price. An order is placed by the Hardware Distributing Company. Table 18–4 shows how the discounts apply. Note that the quantity discount comes off first, as is customary, then the trade discounts and finally the cash discount. If all the discounts are taken, an order that lists at $2700 retail yields $1276.36 to the manufacturer.

Allowances

In addition to all the discounts already noted, the buyer may be able to obtain certain allowances from the seller. We are all familiar with *trade-in allowances.* It is quite common in car, appliance, and even textbook purchasing. A seller can change a true price substantially without changing list price by changing the value given on the trade-in. It is also possible for a buyer to qualify for *promotional allowances.* These types of allowances are given as a discount in selling price, as "free" goods, or as a cash payment. In return, the wholesaler or retailer undertakes certain promotional activities for the seller. (These were discussed in Chapter 16.)

Geographic Pricing Structure

One other major decision area affects the way prices are quoted: the *cost of transportation* of goods from seller to buyer. Recall from Chapter 14 that this cost runs into billions of dollars annually. There are two general procedures for quoting prices related to transportation costs: *F.O.B. origin pricing* and *delivered pricing* methods.

F.O.B. Origin Pricing

F.O.B. means *free on board.* Prices are quoted F.O.B. to some specific point. For example, *F.O.B. Omaha* means that the buyer becomes responsible for the transportation costs, plus picking the specific mode of transportation, designating a carrier, and handling all damage claims, once the seller delivers the goods to Omaha. Typically, the seller quotes a location at or near his or her factory. The major advantage of such a system is that the seller obtains the same net amount from each sale of like quantity for a given channel level, since the buyer pays the freight from the F.O.B. location.

The big disadvantage is that this system effectively raises the price of goods the farther away the buyer is from the seller. Sales can suffer, especially when demand is responsive to price differences and little product differentiation exists among competitors. If all sellers in a product class used an F.O.B. plant system, then each would have a price advantage in their local area. The net result would be regional monopolies. Many firms have multiple plant locations and, therefore, use delivered pricing methods.

Delivered Pricing Methods

In a *delivered pricing* structure, the price quoted by the seller includes transportation costs. The price is quoted as *F.O.B. buyer's location,* and the seller maintains responsibility over all aspects of transportation of the goods. Under this general framework, a number of different delivered pricing methods are possible: (1) single-zone pricing, (2) multiple-zone pricing, (3) F.O.B. with freight allowed, and (4) basing-point pricing.

Single-Zone Pricing. Under a single-zone pricing method, each buyer pays the same delivered price for goods regardless of proximity to the seller. This system is also called *uniform delivered pricing or "postage stamp pricing,"* because this is in essence how American postage rates are established. A first-class letter from Detroit to Houston costs the same to mail as it would from Detroit to Chicago. Under such a system, those customers at greater than average distance from the shipper have their transportation costs subsidized by those who are closer than average to the seller. All buyers effectively pay the average transportation cost. The net return to the seller, then, varies depending on where the goods are begin shipped. Pizza stores offering "free" delivery are really requiring all customers to pay an average delivery charge for their pizzas.

Multiple-Zone Pricing. Under a multiple-zone pricing method (sometimes called *zone delivered pricing*), sellers divide their selling territory into two or more geographic areas called zones. Within any one zone, the delivered price to buyers is uniform, but prices across zones are different. For example, a long-distance call from San Francisco to Seattle costs less than one from San Francisco to Memphis. Similarly, metropolitan transportation systems often divide cities into zones, charging a specific amount for each zone traveled through. Or, a manufacturer may quote different prices for New England, the Midwest, or other regions. The price quote for a zone reflects the average transportation costs within a zone and the competition and level of demand within the zone. A zone system makes it easier to sell in markets that are farther from the shipper.

F.O.B. with Freight Allowed. Under this system, called *freight absorption pricing*, prices are quoted as F. O. B. *plant-freight allowed.* The seller *absorbs* the transportation costs; the buyer is allowed to deduct freight expenses from the list price of the goods. This system is used by sellers trying to expand their geographical market coverage. A twist on this is to allow freight absorption equal to the freight costs of the competitive seller closest to the prospective buyer. This approach can severely cut into profit margins if freight costs are large relative to product selling price.

Basing-Point Pricing. Another delivery pricing scheme designed to expand a seller's geographic market area by giving distant buyers prices similar to nearby buyers is the *basing-point pricing system.* The seller may select either a *single* basing point or use *multiple* basing points.

With a *single basing-point pricing* system, the price set by the seller is the list price for the product plus the freight charges from the selected basing-point to the purchaser. The place where the goods are actually produced is not usually the basing point. Thus, the amount the seller charges the customer for freight is often quite different from the actual freight costs. Consider the example of a company with three mills (see Figure 18–2). The basing point used by the company is the location of Plant A. Thus, the price to the customer from all three mills is $500 base price plus the $50 of actual freight from Plant A to Customer X ($550). Under this scheme, Plant B must absorb $30 of freight charges, while Plant C can collect $30 for freight that never existed. This nonexistent freight is called *phantom freight.*

The most famous basing-point pricing system was the "Pittsburgh-plus" pricing system used in the steel industry for a long time. Although steel producers did have many mills around the country, prices were quoted containing freight charges from Pittsburgh. Thus, a steel buyer in St. Louis would pay freight charges from Pittsburgh even though the steel involved may have been produced and shipped from a mill in Gary, Indiana. After a time, buyers' objections to paying phantom freight led to the use of multiple basing-point systems.

Under a *multiple basing-point* system, more than one geographic location is designated as a basing point. The price quoted to a customer is the base price plus the freight charges from the closest basing point to this customer. If the seller ships the goods from a plant that is farther away from the buyer than the closest basing point, then the seller absorbs the differential in actual freight charges. For example, assume that both Pittsburgh and Gary are pricing points for steel. The buyer in St. Louis would pay the freight cost from Gary. If the seller shipped to St. Louis from Pittsburgh, the seller would pay the freight costs over and above the charges from Gary to St. Louis.

Figure 18–2 An Illustration of Single Base-Point Pricing

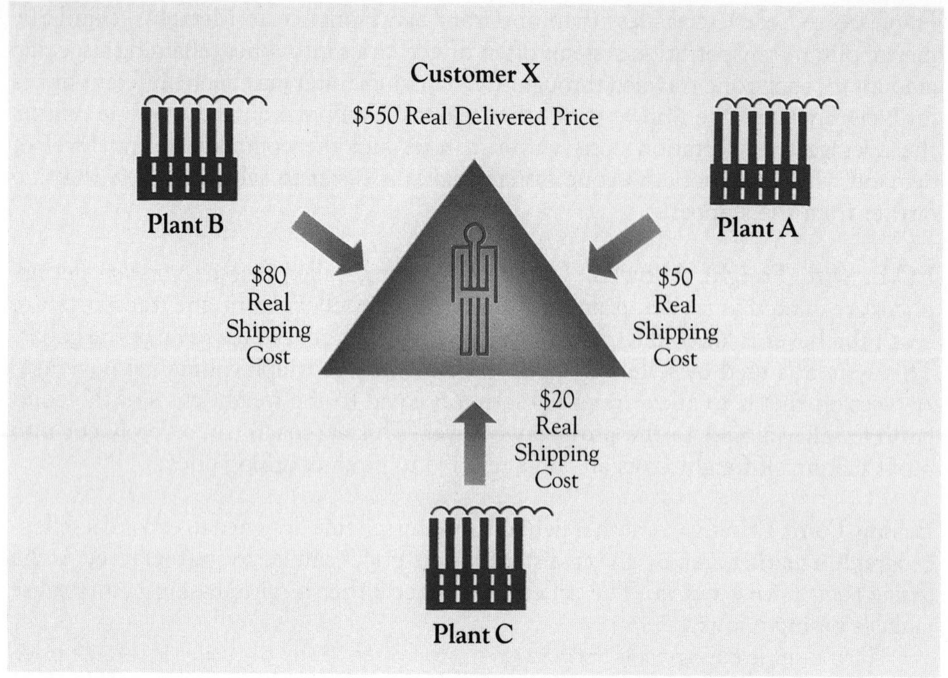

Review Your Marketing Knowledge

- Airfares are sometimes thought of as the ultimate example of flexible pricing. What drives airlines to allow such diverse prices?
- A product is listed by a manufacturer as list price: $950 less 35/12/20. What is the manufacturer's selling price to the channel?

Legal and Regulatory Constraints

Virtually all aspects of pricing may be influenced by legislation and other government regulation. These occur in six major areas:

1. price fixing
2. price discrimination
3. geographic pricing
4. price controls and guidelines
5. deceptive pricing
6. predatory pricing

Price Fixing

Section 1 of the Sherman Act states that every contract, combination, or conspiracy in restraint of trade or commerce is illegal. Price fixing may be thought of as a sinister conspiracy, for it eliminates one major aspect of free competition among firms. The conspirators are those competitors who work together to attempt to fix prices.

The standing legal precedent related to price fixing is the Sacony-Vacuum case.[4] The courts ruled in this case that price fixing, or even the attempt to fix prices, was illegal *per se* (See Chapter 8). That is, the reasonableness or economic impact of the fixed prices is not a defense; the conspiracy itself is illegal. This *per se* illegality has been applied to many forms of cooperative price setting by competitors,[5] including efforts to lower prices; indirectly raising prices by taking excess supply of merchandise from an alternate channel; splitting markets by rotating who has the lowest bid for contracts; maintaining prices by distributing price lists to competitors; agreeing on mark-ups or discounts; and for members of professions (for example, lawyers), publishing and circulating minimum fee schedules within the profession. All are illegal *per se* and have resulted in fines and sometimes prison terms for errant marketers. This is one area where the law is quite clear and the Justice Department's enforcement is vigorous. Recently the Federal Trade Commission has sought to extend these illegal circumstances to contexts where no direct collusion occurs, but where market signaling is used to communicate a company's intentions about prices. In the DuPont and Ethyl Corp. case the FTC ruled that the following were illegal: (1) giving customers more than 30 days notice of price changes to allow competitors knowledge of one's intention, (2) granting "most favored customer status" to a company that guarantees a price at least as low as any other, thus discouraging spot discounts, and (3) using a uniform delivered pricing system that gives one price throughout the country so that competitors can easily determine what one's price is. This decision is currently in appeal in the federal courts.

We most commonly think of price fixing among competitors at the same level in the channel. That is, manufacturers or retailers conspire to fix prices. This is *horizontal* price fixing, since the conspirators are at the *same* level in the channel.

It is also a conspiracy under Section 1 of the Sherman Act for organizations located at *different* levels of the channel to fix prices. However, for a period of almost thirty years, this *vertical* price-fixing was expressly exempted from coverage of the Sherman Act. The Miller-Tydings Act of 1937 and the McGuire-Keogh Fair Trade Enabling Act of 1952 allowed vertical price fixing to occur in states that passed laws allowing it. The practice was called either *resale price maintenance* or *fair trade*. It allowed a manufacturer, in effect, to set retail prices across an entire state. All retailers would be bound to this price, even if only one dealer in the state had agreed to this price with the manufacturer. Thus, no intrabrand competition could occur on prices in the state. In 1975, the Consumer Goods Pricing Act was passed, repealing the Miller-Tydings and McGuire Acts and making vertical price fixing illegal *per se*.

The major intent of the fair trade legislation was to protect small retailers from the price cutting practices of large chains and discount stores. Also, it was intended to protect a manufacturer's brand name from being used as a discount item for attracting customers to stores. The image of the brand would thus be protected. But "fair trade" put constraints on free competition of prices and kept prices to consumers higher than they might have been. The mid-1980s found some confusion on this issue. The Federal Trade Commission, under its Reagan-appointed chairman, moved toward application of a *rule of reason* to resale price maintenance agreements; that is, the FTC wanted the economic consequences of these agreements to be the tests of their legality. This policy change of the FTC brought protests from retail discounters

Table 18–5 Types of Legal Price Discrimination

Class	Bases of Discrimination	Examples
Personal	Buyer's income or earning power	Doctors' fees, royalties paid for use of patented machines, professional association dues
Group	Age, sex, military status, or student status of buyer	Children's haircuts, ladies' days, airline tickets, magazine subscription rates, theater admission charges, senior-citizen rates
	Location of buyers	Zone prices ("prices slightly higher west of the Rockies"), in-state vs. out-of-state tuition
	Status of buyers	New magazine subscriptions, quantity discounts to large-volume buyers
	Use of product	Railroad rates, public utility rates
Product	Qualities of products	Deluxe vs. regular models
	Labels of products	National, private, or unbranded
	Product size	Family, economy, giant size
	Peak—off peak services	Off-season resort rates, airline excursion rates, evening and holiday telephone rates

who discount brand-name merchandise. They actively lobbied Congress to stop the FTC from changing the meaning of the law. Kmart even handed out protest cards that customers could send to their members of Congress. It continues to be an ongoing struggle.

Price Discrimination

Section 2 of the Clayton Act of 1914 and the amendments to Section 2 contained in the Robinson-Patman Act of 1936 prohibit price discrimination. This does not mean that all price differences granted to buyers in a market are illegal. On the contrary, most are legal. First, these statutes exclude sales to ultimate consumers. Second, in sales between businesses, certain bases for price differentials are explicitly allowed. Table 18–5 illustrates a number of bases for legal price discrimination among ultimate consumers. Figure 18–3 illustrates the many different fares that an airline can legally charge on the same flight.

Section 2 of the Clayton Act (1914) attempted to make price discrimination between firms illegal. Its purpose was to prevent sellers from cutting prices in areas with strong competition while maintaining higher prices in less competitive areas. It was found to have so many loopholes that the Robinson-Patman Act (1936) was passed to amend it.

Section 2(a) of Robinson-Patman defines the conditions that constitute price discrimination. It must be shown that (1) the same seller, (2) charged different prices, (3) to two or more different purchasers, (4) for use, consumption, or resale within the United States or any territory, and that (5) there were two or more sales, (6) reasonably close in time, (7) involving commodities, (8) of like grade, and quality, (9) and that at least one sale was in interstate commerce.

Figure 18–3 Typical Price Differentials in Airfares

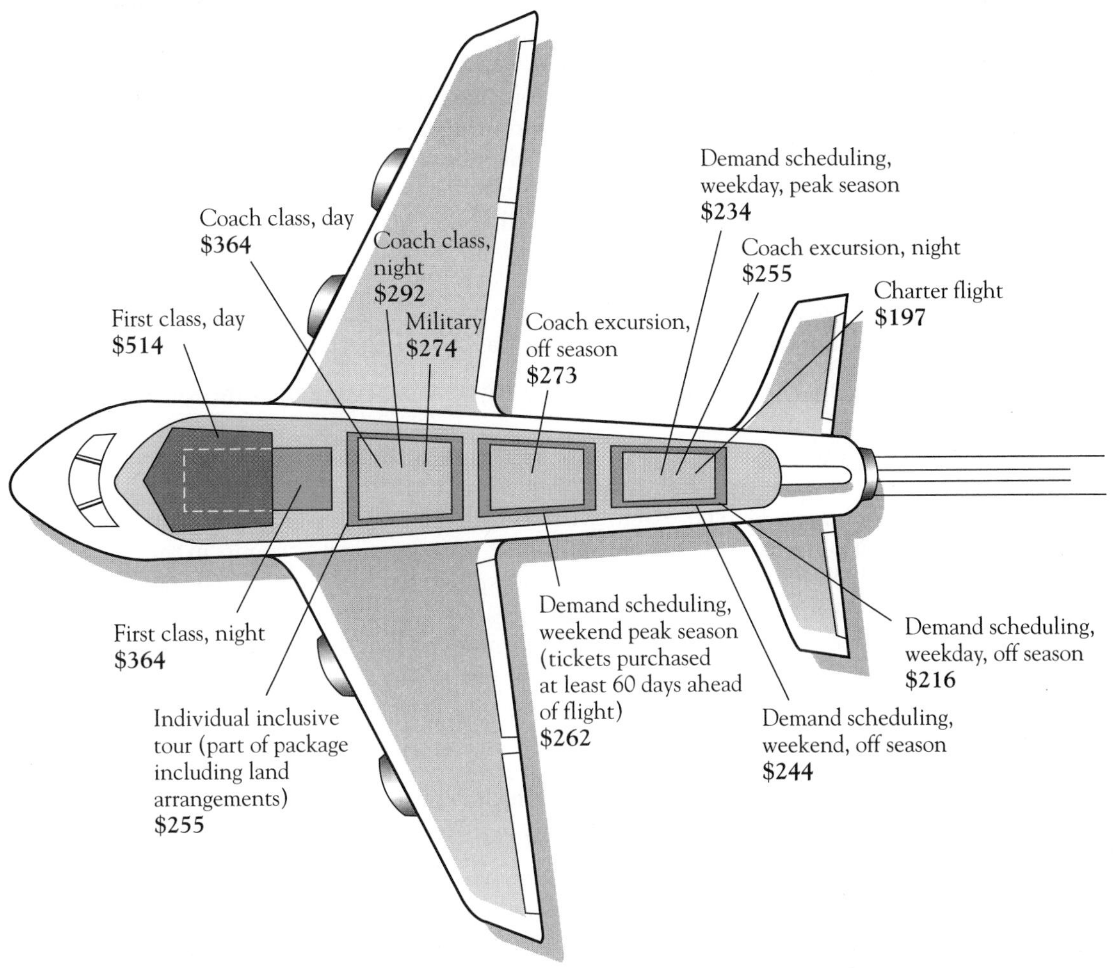

The Federal Trade Commission is empowered to act to stop the price discrimination if it believes these nine conditions hold. Even in these instances, though, the action is not illegal *per se.* The marketer may present a number of defenses. If any one of these defenses holds, then no illegal price discrimination exists. Also, Section 2(f) makes it illegal for a buyer to knowingly induce or receive a discrimination in price. The intent here is to keep large buyers from coercing suppliers.

Defenses to Price Discrimination

The seller may use eight defenses against a price discrimination charge. The first three attempt to refute some of the nine conditions in Section 2(a) of the Robinson-Patman Act.

1. *The item in question is not a commodity* (physical product).
2. *The sale is not in interstate commerce.*
3. *The items being sold are not of like grade and quality.*

Products that are not physically identical may still be considered of like grade and quality. The relevant issue is that they are functionally or commercially equivalent.[6] Perceived product differences do not justify this defense. This was demonstrated in the Borden case, when the courts ruled that privately labeled milk manufactured by Borden was legally the same as Borden branded milk, even though consumers perceive the former to be inferior.

Other defenses against price discrimination charges arise out of the general wording and some specific provisions of the Robinson-Patman Act. At a general level, the effect of the price discrimination under Section 2(a) must "be substantially to lessen competition or tend to create a monopoly, or to injure, destroy, or prevent competition," for the differences in price to be illegal. This leads directly to two more defenses.

4. *The buyers of the goods are not in competition with each other.* Competition cannot be injured if the buyers do not compete. This has three important dimensions:

a. *geographic location* of the markets. The buyers must compete in the same geographic area.
b. *timing* of the sales. The courts have held that both price quotes and the delivery of goods must be reasonably close in time.
c. *level of distribution.* The extent that retailers and wholesalers are not in competition constitutes the only justification of *functional* discounts in the channel. Robinson-Patman makes no explicit place for functional discounts; they must be justified on other bases. Thus, a functional discount given to one channel member who performs extra functions and not given to another at the same level who does not is illegal unless some other defense can be found; the argument that they perform different functions carries no weight.[7]

5. *No injury to competition has occurred.* The defendent may show that no significant injury to competition has occurred at any of three different levels of distribution.

a. The first, the *primary level* injury, occurs when a direct competitor at the same level in the channel as the price discriminator is hurt by discriminatory pricing.
b. The wholesalers who buy from the price discriminator may sell farther down the channel at different prices because of Manufacturer A's different prices to them. Those getting a lower price may undercut those paying a higher price and thus gain a competitive advantage. This advantage of one buyer over another buyer is called *secondary level* injury.
c. Finally, *tertiary level* injury involves injury to the customer of a customer. This occurs when the seller has two separate channels of distribution. One channel uses wholesalers, while the other involves direct sales to retailers. If the retailer receiving direct sales pays either a higher or lower price than the retailers buying from the wholesaler are paying, then one group has a potential advantage over the other. The classic case here involves Standard Oil, which sold its gasoline to jobbers at 1.5 cents below its price to retail service stations in the same area.[8] These jobbers then resold the gasoline to other retail outlets at a price below Standard Oil's price to directly competing stations, with resulting injury at the tertiary level.

In addition to the two general provisions about competitive effects, three specific defenses are allowed under Robinson-Patman.

6. *The differences in prices are based upon cost differences in serving the customers.* Section 2(a) allows price differences "made only due to allowance for differences in the cost of manufacturer, sale or delivery resulting from different methods or quantities." Thus, we see that *quantity discounts* have no legal standing in themselves. They must be justified by cost differences in serving buyers purchasing different amounts.

7. *The seller is meeting the equally low price of a competitor.* Section 2(b) allows one to meet, but not beat, a competitive price.

8. *The price differential is caused by changing conditions.* Section 2(a) states that prices may be changed to reflect "changing conditions affecting the market for or marketability of the goods." Included here would be such conditions as: (1) actual or imminent deterioration of perishable goods, (2) obsolescence of seasonal goods, (3) distress sales under court process, and (4) sales in good faith in discontinuance of business in the goods concerned.

As if all the complexities of price fixing and discrimination were not enough, marketers must also be concerned with the legality of their delivery pricing structure.

Pricing Based on Geographic Location

F.O.B. origin pricing is legal, since there is no price differential based upon the geographic location of buyers. In single-zone pricing schemes, there is inherent price discrimination since some buyers pay more and others pay less than the cost of transportation. However, since there are no price differences at the point of destination, the Federal Trade Commission (FTC) and the courts have traditionally viewed this system as not being illegal. Recently, in the DuPont and Ethyl Corp. case, the FTC has tried to make this type of pricing system illegal when it is believed to be part of a system where competitors are making it easier to know each other's prices. The Supreme Court's view of this change remains to be known. Multiple-zone systems have run into legal problems only when evidence of collusion exists in setting up the zones. The existence of zones with identical boundaries and identical price differences across zones is, in itself, evidence of illegal collusion to the FTC. F.O.B. freight-allowed systems are also perfectly legal as long as no collusion on the price schedules is present.

Basing-point pricing systems are illegal if firms collude in developing them, choosing the cities, or administering them. Another major issue involves the existence of phantom freight. When two buyers compete with each other, and only one pays phantom freight because of the basing-point system, the one who pays this freight may be injured competitively. This would appear to be illegal price discrimination. Unfortunately, all cases that have reached the Supreme Court have involved some collusion, and, thus, the legality of the basing-point system is not completely clear. In the current regulatory environment, it is not likely that the FTC will attack any form of delivery pricing structure in the absence of collusion between firms.

Price Controls and Guidelines

Most marketers in recent history have made pricing decisions under some form of federal price controls or guidelines. Presidents Kennedy, Johnson, Nixon, Ford, and Carter all set price guidelines that industry was "jawboned" not to exceed. Additionally, President Nixon imposed price controls for a time during his Presidency. The problem with all such attempts is that the primary forces that drive prices, such as demand and supply, are ignored (see Figure 18–1). A brief history of price controls is presented in the *Marketing in Action.*

MARKETING IN ACTION

Price Controls: A History of Failure

In times of rapid price increases, many ancient rulers, and even modern American presidents, have attempted to impose some form of price controls on products and services. The list includes the Athenian ruler Pericles, the Roman Emperor Diocletian, and Presidents Richard Nixon and Jimmy Carter. The overwhelming lesson from all of these attempts is straightforward: price controls do not work.

In ancient Athens the death penalty was prescribed for those selling their grain above the price established by an administrative body. Despite the harsh penalty, the price of grain fluctuated according to the supply available and the demand in the market. The whole price setting administration eventually collapsed. The same result was evident in Rome when the Emperor, Diocletian, in response to inflation caused by war expenditures, imposed wage and price controls. The death penalty again was used, with the result that the farmers stopped bringing grain to market. The grain shortage resulted in the law being abolished.

The American Continental army nearly starved at Valley Forge as a result of price controls imposed by the Continental Congress. Under the pleading of John Adams that "if not repealed, [the act] will ruin the state and introduce a civil war," the Continental Congress revoked the act.

The price controls imposed by Richard Nixon in the 1970s held prices down for a while. However, as soon as the controls were lifted, the Consumer Price Index increased by the largest amount in twenty-two years. The controls did not deal with the causes of the inflation. President Carter tried a voluntary set of price controls that were tied to tax incentives. This, like all other Presidential jawboning on prices, ended in failure. President Bush indicates that the he is totally opposed to price controls. History suggests that this is a wise position. However, it would be interesting to see what he would do if rapid inflation returned to the United States. History also suggests that the temptation to impose controls is great.

Deceptive Pricing

Marketers often use special low prices as a means of promoting their products. To the end consumer, we are familiar with all types of retail "sales." Sale prices are potentially illegal under Section 5 of the Federal Trade Commission Act, which prohibits "unfair and deceptive practices." The FTC is likely to act if it believes that the marketer has deceived the buyer about the true nature of his or her prices. These pricing practices, like price discrimination, are subject to the rule of reason. There are five different price promotions that have the potential for legal action.

1. *Bait and Switch.* This activity is "an alluring but insincere offer to sell a product or service which the advertiser does not intend or want to sell." The marketer offers a very low price on a product (the bait) in order to get the customer into the place of business. Once in the store, the prospective buyer is persuaded to purchase a higher priced item (the switch). The switch is made by such tricks as criticizing the quality of the promoted item, failing to have the item in stock, refusing to take orders for the item, or failing to deliver the item in a reasonable time. Sears recently signed an agreement with the FTC agreeing to take great care not to practice bait and switch in its sewing machine, washer and dryer, and major home appliance lines.

2. *Former Price Comparisons.* In one of the most used forms of a bargain price, marketers offer a reduction from their own former price for an item. If the former price is the actual price at which the item was regularly offered to the public for a reasonably substantial period of time, it provides a legal basis for a price comparison. But if the former price is fictitious, then the discount being offered is deceptive.

3. *Comparable Value Comparisons.* Another commonly utilized form of bargain price is to offer items at prices lower than those charged by others for the same merchandise in the same trading area. The person making the claim should be reasonably certain that the higher price, used as the reference price for the sale, does not appreciably exceed the price at which most of the item's sales are being made in the area. This also holds when comparisons are made to other brands of like grade and quality. For example, Retailer A promotes Brand X pen as having "comparable value of $15.00." Unless a reasonable number of the principal outlets in the area are offering Brand Y, an essentially similar pen, for $15.00, the price offer would be deceptive.

4. *Advertising Manufacturer and Retailer Suggested Retail Prices.* The FTC holds that "many members of the purchasing public believe that a manufacturer's list price, or suggested retail price, is the price at which an article is generally sold." If these list prices do not correspond to prices at which a substantial number of sales of the item are made, the bargain price is deceptive.

5. *Bargain Offers Based upon the Purchase of Other Merchandise.* Often marketers offer additional merchandise, to be given or sold at a special price to customers, on the condition that they purchase a particular item at a price usually offered by the marketer. Such offers as "Buy One—Get One Free," "2 for 1 Sale," "Half-price Sale," "1¢ Sale," and "50 Percent Off" all are relevant here. When the seller, in making these types of offers, increases the regular price of the item the customer must buy to qualify for the bargain, or decreases the quantity or quality of that item, or otherwise attaches conditions beyond the specified purchase, then the consumer may be deceived, according to the FTC. The Mary Carter Paint Company was found guilty of deceptive pricing of this type. Its claim was that for every can of paint purchased, the buyer would get a "free" can of equal size and quality. The FTC charged that Mary Carter had never sold single cans of paint and that the quoted one-can price was really a two-can price, thus deceiving consumers. The Supreme Court agreed.

In addition, retailers' use of such terms as *wholesale* and *factory* in referring to prices can also be considered deceptive. Unfortunately, all of us confront these pricing practices by some retailers. This fact reflects the enforcement difficulty of these provisions. The FTC's budget and priorities do not allow it to police deceptive pricing well. Enforcement is often left to state and municipal governments.

Predatory Pricing

Predatory pricing occurs when a firm charges a very low price for a product, with the intent to drive competitors our of business. Having driven out the competition, the firm raises prices. This practice is potentially illegal under Section 2 of the Sherman Act as an "attempt to monopolize," or under Section 5 of the Federal Trade Commission Act as an "unfair practice." It is likely to be judged illegal if the firm is selling at prices below its cost. Certain states have statutes that require minimum mark-ups of about 2 percent at wholesale and 6 percent retail. Thus, the marketer must take care not to appear too aggressive in price-setting, or predatory intent may be inferred.

A Look Ahead

This chapter has laid the foundation for our discussion of pricing decisions in Chapter 19. Marketers make these decisions within the context of issues discussed here: corporate and marketing pricing objectives and policies, the goals set for the price variable within the marketing mix, and the legal framework for pricing regulation. In the next chapter, we discuss the role that consumer demand, cost structure, and competitive environment play in determining price.

PERSONAL COMPUTER EXERCISE

In marketing management, the ability to examine the revenue and profit dynamic of alternative price discounts and geographic pricing schemes in conjunction with the financial area of business is important. The PC exercise gives you the opportunity to set alternative list prices, price discounts, and geographic pricing methods. The revenue and profit implication of these alternatives can then be examined with the PC.

KEY POINTS

• Pricing is an essential component of the marketing mix. In times of high inflation or high unemployment, or both, the price decision takes on even greater importance.

• The price set for goods and services serves as the basis of exchange in our society and is an index of value for goods. Price is the value assigned to a bundle of form, time, place, possession utility.

• The price of goods and services goes by many names (other than price) including tuition, rent, interest, fee, fare, toll, and salary. In all cases, it is the index of value for the item.

• Price plays an important role for the economy as a whole by bringing demand and supply into balance. When price is not allowed to move with supply and demand, imbalances occur. These may be shortages that result from prices that are too low, or surpluses that arise when prices are too high.

• Price increases in importance to the organization with increasing technological advances, increased foreign competition, shortages of raw materials and energy, the advent of substitute products, and inflation.

• Key factors in price determination are pricing objectives, corporate and marketing objectives and policies, demand behavior, cost dynamics, competitive situation and behavior, and legal and ethical constraints.

• Pricing objectives should be explicit but may be implicit. They are typically based on profits, sales, or competitive position.

• Pricing policy refers to the quoted price levels relative to the general market price and to the degree of price flexibility the marketer has in setting prices. Both aspects guide the specific price that is set.

• Price quotes between firms include a base price, discount structures, and geographical freight payment methods.

• Firms use quantity, timing, functional, and cash discounts in their pricing.

• Geographical pricing may involve either F.O.B. origin pricing or delivered pricing. The latter includes single-zone and multiple-zone pricing, F.O.B. with freight allowed, and basing-point pricing.

• Major areas of price regulation include price fixing, price discrimination, geographical pricing, price controls and guidelines, deceptive pricing, and predatory pricing.

ISSUES FOR DISCUSSION

1. What is the price paid for each of the following: (a) the principles of marketing course you are now taking, (b) a standby flight to Hawaii, (c) police protection, (d) a free hot lunch program, and (e) a direct one-for-one player trade in baseball.

2. In each of the situations in Problem 1, what is being exchanged for the price paid?

3. How has price contributed to a shortage of rental apartments in New York City and a surplus of cheese in the United States?

4. What factors have led to price becoming more important in the marketing mix? Do you see this changing?

5. Some economists view profit maximation as the only appropriate price objective, whereas marketing managers use many different price objectives. What difference in perspectives causes this? Who is right?

6. "Salespersons should be given a great deal of flexibility in setting prices to their customers." Evaluate this statement from a managerial and legal point of view.

7. The Teckac Computer Company offers two different versions of a computer printer, with retail base prices of $400 and $300, respectively. The trade discounts are 40/15, and Teckac gives sales terms of 2/10 net 30. A 10 percent quantity discount is available on purchases of over $2000. The Computer Mart, a large Chicago retailer, ordered ten printers at $400 and 20 at $300. They paid within thirty days. What are the net proceeds to Teckac?

8. The Teckac Computer plant is located in Madison, Wisconsin. As a result, it operates at a significant freight cost disadvantage relative to sales made in both the East and the West. What methods of quoting prices could Teckac use to make itself more competitive in these markets?

9. "All forms of geographic pricing schemes are unfair to some buyers." Comment.

10. A manager from the tenth-largest company in the paperboard industry happened to meet a manager from the fifteenth-largest company in this industry. In conversation, they discussed future prices of products within their industry and companies, and concluded that they were powerless to affect the industry price, which was set by the largest competitors. Have they violated the law? Why or why not?

11. A manufacturer of computer chips has been accused of price discrimination. On what basis can it defend against such a suit?

12. Instead of imposing price controls, how should government approach the problem of rapid increases in prices?

GLOSSARY

Allowances: reduction in the actual price paid resulting from a trade-in or an agreement to participate in promotional activity.

Barter: a price set in nonmoney terms.

Basing-point pricing: prices quoted as list price plus freight from a specific location.

Cash discounts: reduction from the list price given to the buyer for paying for the goods or services within a specified time period.

Deceptive pricing: specially promoted price deals that mislead consumers.

F.O.B.: "free on board," meaning that the seller pays freight charges to a designated location and the buyer pays the remaining freight expenses.

F.O.B. with freight allowed: an agreement allowing the buyer to deduct freight expenses from the list price.

Functional discounts: reductions from list price given to a firm because of the position it holds in the channel or because of the activities it is expected to perform. Also called trade discounts.

Multiple-zone pricing: A system in which prices vary depending on the buyer's geographical area.

Predatory pricing: The practice of setting low prices, with the intent of driving competitors out of business.

Price: the value that one puts on the utility one receives for goods and services.

Price controls: legal limits on price levels.

Price discrimination: the practice of charging different prices to different buyers for goods of like grade and quality.

Price fixing: a conspiracy among competitors to set prices for a product either at the same level in the channel (horizontally) or at different levels in the channel (vertically).

Price guidelines: government-sanctioned targets for price levels.

Price policy: an overall approach to setting prices.

Price structure: the use of discounts, allowances, and freight cost absorption in stating price.

Quantity discounts: reduction from list price based upon the amount of purchases a buyer makes. They may be based upon a specific purchase (noncumulative) or on total purchases over a period (cumulative).

Seasonal discounts: reduction from list price based upon the time of year a purchase is made.

Single-zone pricing: a scheme in which all buyers pay the same price no matter what their location.

NOTES

1. Arthur Bragg, "Bartering Comes of Age," *Sales & Marketing Management,* January 1988, pp. 61–63.

2. John G. Udell, "How Important Is Pricing in Competitive Strategy?" *Journal of Marketing,* January 1964, pp. 44–48.

3. This example is from Kent B. Monroe, *Pricing: Making Profitable Decisions,* (McGraw-Hill, 1979), p. 171.

4. *U.S.* v. *Sacony-Vaccuum Oil Co.*, 310 U.S. 150 (1940).

5. Joe L. Welch, *Marketing Law* (PCC Books, 1980), p. 55.

6. Welch, *Marketing Law,* p. 73.

7. Welch, *Marketing Law,* p. 74.

8. *Standard Oil Co.* v. *FTC,* 340 U.S. 231 (1951).

CASE APPLICATION 18–1

Upjohn Company

For years the Upjohn Company dominated the arthritis prescription drug market in the United States with its product Motrin. Motrin was made under a license from Boots Pharmaceutical of Britain. It represented more than 30 percent of all of Upjohn's earnings. Its one significant brand competitor was the brand Rufen that was made by Boots Pharmaceutical. Upjohn had not expected Boots to be a significant American competitor when it entered into the licensing agreement. However, Boots had aggressively entered the American market by buying an American drug company and pricing Rufen competitively. Boots had a cost advantage over Upjohn in this product since Upjohn had to pay a licensing fee to Boots. Rufen sold for about 30 percent less than Motrin and captured 25 percent of the market volume of prescriptions. This share was up from about 10 percent the year before.

For the aging arthritic...
Efficacy that's easy to live with
Effective yet well-tolerated treatment of arthritis in the aging.
Motrin®
ibuprofen
400, 600, & 800 Tablets mg
Please see adjacent page for a brief summary of prescribing information.
Upjohn
The Upjohn Company
Kalamazoo, MI 49001, USA
© 1989
The Upjohn Company

Additionally, by mid-1984, over-the-counter variants of the product began to bring even more significant competition. Boots had licensed American Home Products to produce one of these over-the-counter brands, while Upjohn itself licensed Bristol-Myers. Because these products were lower-dose versions of the prescription products, Upjohn was concerned that some arthritis patients would switch to these cheaper products and just take more of them.

Upjohn was dropping market share to both the over-the-counter products and to Rufen. Additionally, the patent on Motrin's active ingredient, ibuprofen, was due to run out in late 1984 and, as a result, significant price competition from generic versions of Motrin was expected.

Upjohn had considered a number of responses to this competitive activity. It had developed an extended line of Motrin products that were expected to be introduced within a year or so. This included a liquid form, a form with codeine, and a time-release capsule.

However, Upjohn management decided to take action on price prior to the availability of these line extensions. In mid-June, 1984, Upjohn cut the list price of Motrin 30 percent to 35 percent, intending this price cut to preserve its market share and, thus, give its line extension a solid base on which to start. Said Upjohn executive vice president Lawrence Hoff, "We had to protect the franchise for Motrin."

The reaction from Boots was swift and effective. It cut the price of Rufen by 30 percent, effectively eliminating Upjohn's advantage. Upjohn continued to drop market share to the again lower-priced Rufen and the over-the-counter products. Upjohn was left with a market share that was continuing to shrink and with much smaller margins than it had before. The stock market reacted to these pricing moves quite negatively. The price of Upjohn stock fell, in a month, from over \$61 a share to about \$48 a share.

Questions

1. What do you believe was Upjohn's pricing objective for Motrin in the short run? Could their long-run objective have been different? How?

2. What do you believe was Boots' pricing objective for Rufen?

3. Why did Boots respond so aggressively to the price reduction on Motrin?

CASE APPLICATION 18–2

General Motors

Price is an important component of the marketing mix for a product. At the same time, a company's pricing strategy should be carefully coordinated with its overall marketing strategy. Prices should help the firm achieve its objectives in profit, sales, or competitive position. Sometimes, however, a firm's pricing system lacks focus either because it is not well coordinated with the goals of the company or because those goals are unclear.

In 1986, pricing by General Motors for its cars and trucks did not exhibit much strategic character. The lack of focus in pricing stemmed primarily from GM's lack of commitment to a well defined corporate objective. GM, which had watched its U.S. market share sink from about 48 percent to 38 percent from 1978 to 1986, wanted to regain lost market share. At the same time, it wanted to achieve certain ROI goals. As a result, GM's prices fluctuated wildly as the company tried to attain these two distinct and often competing goals.

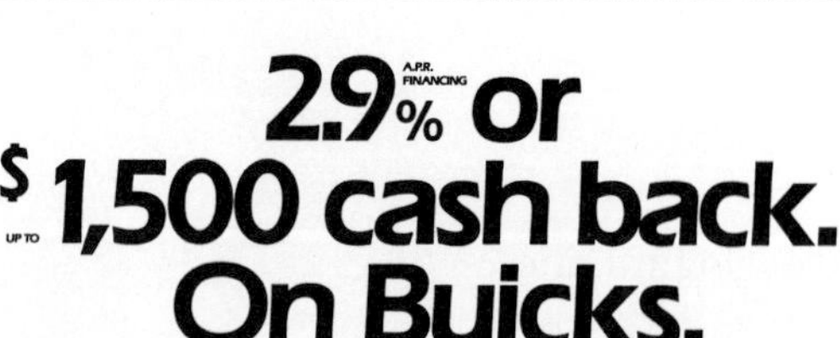

With the expectation of winning back lost market share, GM maintained high levels of production in 1986. Sales were weak, however, during the first few months of the year. In response to high levels of inventory, GM introduced 9.9 percent financing incentives, which effectively lowered the price of its vehicles. The 9.9 percent finance rate GM offered was only slightly lower than the rate offered by most banks. As a result, GM's financing incentive failed to attract a large number of car buyers. In fact, sales in March 1986 were 6 percent lower than in the previous year. After failing in its attempt to increase sales through a reduction in the effective price of its cars, GM made an about face and began to concentrate on profitability. In April 1986, the company cancelled financing incentives and raised the sticker price of GM vehicles by 2.9 percent. GM argued that the elasticity of demand for cars is so low that a 2.9 percent price hike—worth about $350 per car—would be insignificant to most buyers.

Although GM solved some of its short-term profitability problems by raising prices in April, the problem of mounting inventories and mediocre sales was not solved. Faced with excessive inventories as the 1987 model year approached, GM made the dramatic decision in late August to offer 2.9 percent financing—a figure previously unheard of from any of the automakers. In addition, GM also offered rebates of up to $1,500 on some of its cars. Even though GM's low financing rate was matched by Ford and beaten by Chrysler (at 2.4 percent) and American Motors (which offered free financing), GM's price incentives were enormously successful as a sales mechanism. GM's sales jumped from an annual rate of 8.1 million units for the first 8 months of 1986 to a record 18 million unit rate during the first part of September. Inventories quickly dropped from a 79-day supply of vehicles to a 28-day supply. The price paid for such sales success, however, was a large loss of potential profits. At the height of the September incentives, GM had reduced its profit per car by about half.

Although GM's pricing machinations had solved the company's immediate problem of excess inventory, the pricing system itself remained unfocused. In 1987, GM continued to use financing incentives—albeit less enticing than the low rates offered in 1986—as well as rebates to boost sales when inventories began to pile up. Since consumers had become somewhat inured to rebates and special finance offers, though, such incentives became less effective at sparking sales. Some analysts at the time even suggested that car buyers would become so used to special incentives that they would not buy cars if such special deals were removed. While this has not proved to be true—it seems GM's assessment of demand inelasticity for cars is fairly accurate—the potential for price incentives to increase sales and control inventories has diminished.

After using pricing to pursue, less and less effectively, its market share and profit objectives, GM has finally realized the limitations of its strategy. In April 1988, the company announced plans to close some of its auto assembly plants. This move is intended to bring production capacity more in line with GM's market share position, which stood at 36.4 percent in 1987. With production geared more appropriately to demand, GM should not be forced to use pricing to control inventory levels to the extent it did before.

Although GM's move clearly suggests that the company has abandoned its former dual focus in favor of emphasizing profitability, GM has not entirely resigned itself to its current market share. Despite closing some of its assembly plants, the company still hopes to improve its current market share by running its facilities at capacity. In order to run at capacity, however, GM will have to increase demand for its products. Fortunately for the company, General Motors has apparently realized that the key to capturing market share lies in manufacturing cars that people want to buy rather than simply manipulating prices. As evidence of its new market awareness, GM is now working hard to differentiate its car lines in order to dispel the criticism that many GM cars look and perform alike.

At this stage, it is impossible to determine the practical components of GM's future pricing strategy as the company downsizes and implements its new marketing plan. Whatever the case, it seems that GM's price system will be part of a comprehensive marketing strategy for the company, rather than a substitute for having no clear strategy at all.

SOURCES: Paul L. Edwards, "Auto Boomerang? Promotion Pros Decry Finance Ploys," *Advertising Age*, September 8, 1986; William J. Hampton, "GM's Price Hikes: Foresight or Folly?" *Business Week*, April 14, 1986, p. 36; William J. Hampton and Russell Mitchell, "Detroit's Feast-or-Famine Cycle Is Getting Worse," *Business Week*, September 29, 1986, p. 41; James B. Treece, with Robert Ingersoll, "GM Faces Reality," *Business Week*, May 9, 1988, pp. 114–122.

Questions

1. Why do you think GM used rebates and financing incentives to lower the effective price of its cars, rather than simply lowering sticker prices?

2. What is the relationship between pricing strategy and marketing strategy?

3. What were GM's apparent short-run pricing objectives? Long-run objectives?

4. In the future, what strategy should GM adopt for setting prices? Why?

Mobil
Self Serve-Cash
Reg. Unl.
1.14 9
1.26 9
1.34 9
Mobil Mart

19

Pricing Procedures

Learning Objectives

Upon completing this chapter, you will be able to do the following:

EXPLAIN
the role of demand analysis in pricing and the major concepts of demand as they relate to pricing.

DESCRIBE
the major concepts of cost and their relationship to pricing.

ILLUSTRATE
the role that competing firms and other environmental influences play in pricing.

IDENTIFY
major approaches to setting prices in practice.

COMPARE
alternative pricing strategies for new products.

UNDERSTAND
the dynamics of price leadership.

DISCUSS
pricing approaches for the complete product line.

MARKETING PROFILE

Competition in the Gasoline Market

The 1980s found the California gasoline market in the midst of an intense struggle between Atlantic Richfield (ARCO) and Union Oil (Union 76). The objective of both companies was to increase their share of the California market, and in the early and mid 1980s, the availability of a relatively plentiful supply of oil and falling world oil prices set the stage for this competition.

In eliminating its credit card operations and moving significantly to being a self-serve operator, ARCO dramatically lowered its cost. This allowed ARCO to drop the price of gasoline to its distributors by about three cents a gallon while maintaining its margins. Costs at the dealer level were cut significantly by the move to self-service, thus reducing labor costs in pumping gas. Additionally, many of these outlets dropped their mechanic service and eliminated those costs. The differential in price at the pump between ARCO and Union 76 was about nine cents a gallon on regular gas and seventeen cents on super-unleaded.

Union 76 retained its full-service orientation and image, based upon studies identifying five basic consumer segments in the market. The first two groups, "self-serve saves money," and "the car is just transportation," buy self-serve. The third group, "full-serve is worth the money if you can afford it," buys self-serve most of the time. The last two groups, "full-service is best," and "the car is personally important," buy full-serve and use credit cards. Union 76 scored highest with the last two groups in attitude studies.

The aggressive marketing activity by both ARCO and Union 76 increased their gasoline sales market shares. In its 1900 service stations, Union 76's share rose about one percent to almost thirteen percent, an increase that would normally be considered an excellent performance in the tough California market. ARCO's results were even more spectacular, with an increase of five share points to reach near the 18 percent share level in its 500 service stations.

Until 1989, prices in the industry in California generally moved downward. This was partially the result of a fall in the world price of oil and partially the result of a decrease in the demand for gasoline among California consumers who had responded to high gasoline prices by driving less. Finally, the overall price level was driven down by ARCO's aggressive pricing posture in the market. Competitors responded to this pricing strategy in order to protect their market shares. The prime benefactors of this competition were the gasoline consumers of California who at that time had more choices and paid lower prices.

The situation in 1989–1990 found substantial increases in gasoline prices due to the limiting of supply by OPEC and a jump in demand by consumers. This higher price caused both ARCO and Union Oil to begin rethinking their strategy.

We see in the pricing of gasoline in the California market many of the factors that affect price determination and the success of pricing decisions—consumer demand in relation to price and the services offered, competitive activity in the price area, the costs inherent in doing business in a particular way, and the impact of the broader environment in the supply and price of world oil. How to balance these types of issues in price-setting forms the structure of this chapter. It is this balancing of price with demand and the costs of doing business that determines the profitability of the enterprise. Once again, imagine yourself having to balance all these factors to make price decisions—certainly a challenging assignment.

SOURCE: Liz Murphy, "Pumping Up for the Great California Gasoline War," *Sales and Marketing Management,* April 2, 1984, pp. 51–54; ARCO and Union Oil Annual Reports, 1988; 1989 oil price news reports.

In this chapter we examine how prices are determined in the real world. Price-setting occurs within the constraints imposed by corporate and marketing objectives, the objectives set for the price variable in the marketing mix, and the legal environment. (All these aspects were discussed in Chapter 18.) In addition, price-setting should be based on a careful analysis of (1) consumer *demand* behavior with respect to price, (2) the *cost* structure of the product in question, (3) the *competitive* environment in which the product is marketed, and (4) the potential impact of other *environmental forces* such as economic conditions, political climate, or even weather. We first discuss each of these cornerstones of the pricing decision, assuming that whatever price we set is consistent with the various corporate, marketing, and price objectives, and that it is legal. Later in the chapter, we discuss the major approaches to pricing, including demand-based pricing, cost-based pricing, return-on-investment pricing, and competitive bidding. Finally, we investigate how prices are set for new products and a complete product line.

Demand Analysis

At the heart of price-setting is a good understanding of how demand reacts to various prices. These estimates of demand then allow one to forecast the revenue that will be generated for the firm at various prices. One basic tenet of economics and marketing is that as the price of an item increases, the demand for that item will decrease. This is a very intuitive concept and is one that real-world experience supports. We present this general result by means of a downward-sloping **demand curve** showing the quantity of a product that is expected to be sold at various prices. Figure 19–1 presents hypothetical demand curves for several different products. Clearly, the responsiveness of these products to price varies greatly. What we need is a measure of the degree to which consumers respond to changes in prices. This measure is called the *price elasticity of demand.*

Price Elasticity of Demand

The **price elasticity of demand** is defined as the *percentage change in quantity demanded relative to the percentage change made in price.* This is expressed as:

$$\text{Elasticity} = \frac{(\text{original quantity} - \text{new quantity})/\text{original quantity}}{(\text{original price} - \text{new price})/\text{original price}}$$

or

$$E = \frac{(Q_1 - Q_2)/Q_1}{(P_1 - P_2)/P_1} = \frac{\Delta Q/Q_1}{\Delta P/P_1}$$

where P_1 = original price; P_2 = new price; Q_1 = original quantity demanded; Q_2 = new quantity demanded; E = elasticity; $\Delta P = P_1 - P_2$ the change in price; $\Delta Q = Q_1 - Q_2$ the change in quantity.

Let us illustrate this concept with two different situations. First, assume that the price of a small computer in January 1989 was $800 and 20,000 units were sold over the year. In January 1990, the price dropped to $700 and 22,000 units were sold during the year.

Figure 19–1 Selected Demand Curves

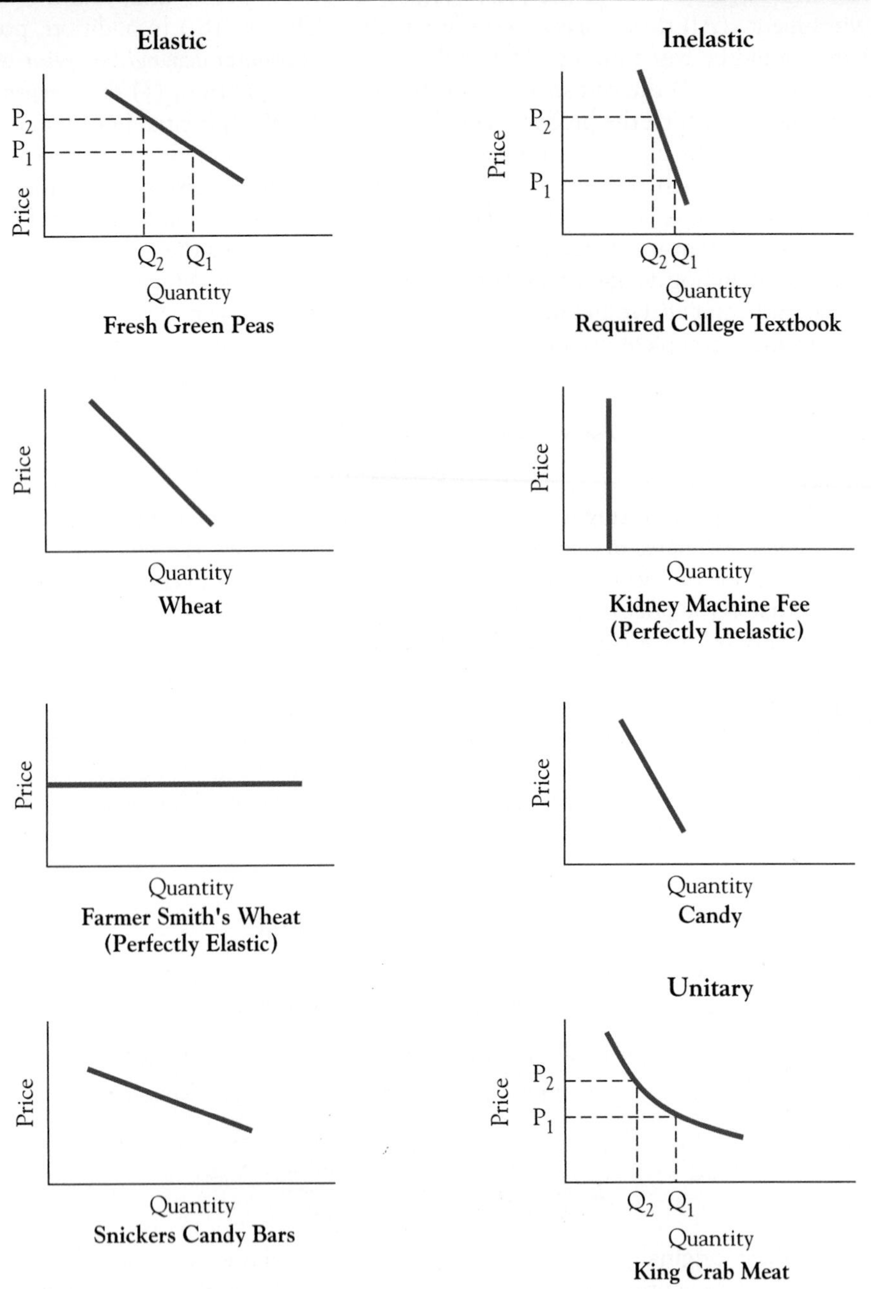

$$E = \frac{(20{,}000 - 22{,}000)/20{,}000}{(\$800 - \$700)/\$800} = \frac{-2{,}000/20{,}000}{\$100/\$800}$$

$$= \left(-\frac{2{,}000}{\$100}\right)\left(\frac{\$800}{20{,}000}\right) = -.8$$

The minus sign reflects the fact that demand increases as price decreases, and vice versa. Since it is not customary to express the minus sign, we will suppress it in the remainder of this chapter. Note here that the total revenue generated at the 1989 price is greater than that generated at the 1990 price.

Old situation: $\$800 \times 20{,}000 = \$16$ million (total revenue)

New situation: $\$700 \times 22{,}000 = \$15.4$ million (total revenue)

In situations where the total revenue generated after a price decrease is smaller than the original total revenue, the product is said to be *price inelastic.* This is reflected in a calculated elasticity of demand of *less than one,* and is typically portrayed by a demand curve that is close to vertical. In Figure 19–1, the demand for a required textbook and candy bars are price inelastic. The demand for the use of kidney machines is the extreme case of inelasticity: it is *perfectly inelastic,* which means that the same number of units will be sold regardless of price. A perfectly inelastic demand curve suggests that no matter how high the price rises, consumers will not cut back on demand.

Now assume that, in January 1991, the price of the computer is reduced further, to \$550. The quantity sold in 1991 is 40,000 units.

$$E = \frac{(22{,}000 - 40{,}000)/22{,}000}{(\$700 - \$550)/\$700} = \frac{-18{,}000/22{,}000}{\$150/\$700}$$

$$= \left(-\frac{18{,}000}{\$150}\right)\left(\frac{\$700}{22{,}000}\right) = 3.8 \qquad \text{(minus sign suppressed)}$$

Note that the total revenue after the price decrease is *greater.*

Old situation: $\$700 \times 22{,}000 = \$15.4$ million

New situation: $\$550 \times 40{,}000 = \$22$ million

In situations where the total revenue generated after a price decrease is larger than the original total revenue, the product is said to be *price elastic.* This is reflected in a calculated elasticity of demand of *greater than one,* and is typically portrayed by a nearly horizontal demand curve. In Figure 19–1, note that the demand for fresh green peas, wheat, and Snickers candy bars is price elastic, and that the demand for Farmer Smith's wheat is the extreme case of elasticity. It is *perfectly elastic,* which means that Smith's wheat brings the same price regardless of how much he produces. Also the demand for gasoline, as illustrated in the *Marketing Profile* at the beginning of this chapter, appears to be an example of inelastic price demand.

It is also possible for the total revenue generated both before and after a price decrease to be identical. This is called *unitary price elasticity* and occurs when the elasticity of demand *equals one.* King crab meat illustrates this situation in Figure 19–1. The small computer example points out a very important aspect of price elasticity of demand: in general, it is *not the same value over all possible prices for a product.*

The price elasticity of demand is determined by a number of factors. The first is the degree to which substitute products are available. If a product has close substitutes, it tends to be elastic; if a product does not have close substitutes, it tends to be inelastic. For example, apples have many possible substitutes in a meal and, therefore, are very elastic, while gasoline has almost no substitutes and is very inelastic. Second, goods that are necessities, such as medical services and required textbooks, tend to be inelastic, while luxuries like vacations and fine dining tend to be elastic. Third, goods that constitute a large proportion of one's budget tend to be elastic while those that use little of the budget tend to be inelastic. Cars, housing, and television sets are elastic, while napkins, stationery, and matches are inelastic.

Primary vs. Selective Demand

It is important to draw a distinction between the price elasticity for *primary* and *selective* demand. As we pointed out in Chapter 4, primary demand is the size of the market for a product class as a whole. (It is also called *generic demand.*) In Figure 19–1, the demand curves for fresh green peas, a required textbook, wheat, candy, king crab meat, and kidney machine services all represent primary demand. Alternatively, the demand curves for Farmer Smith's wheat and Snickers candy bars represent the impact of price on *selective* or *brand demand.* This is demand for one specific brand offering within a product class.

The wheat and candy examples in Figure 19–1 illustrate the distinction between primary and selective demand elasticity. They also point out that it is possible for *primary demand to be inelastic while selective demand is elastic.* That is, the total market may not be very responsive to price changes, but the choice of a specific brand may be very much affected by price differences among brands. This situation often occurs when primary demand is a *derived demand*—that is, when the demand for a product is affected by the demand for some other product. Industrial products fit this pattern very much. For example, the demand for steel is partially derived from the demand for new cars, and the demand for building products such as bricks and lumber is derived from the demand for new structures. The following generalization is important:

> *For industrial products, the primary price elasticity of demand is often inelastic, while the selective price elasticity of demand is often elastic.*

This same pattern can occur in consumer products when the market is mature and when brands are considered to be reasonable substitutes for each other. For example, candy and gasoline as categories are price inelastic while specific brands are price elastic. Also, although a required textbook is price inelastic, stores may sell the same book at different prices, creating a very elastic situation. In marketing it is important to know both the primary and selective price elasticity of demand.

Demand and Revenue

Demand level leads directly to the amount of revenue generated for the firm, and this, in turn, is related to the price elasticity of demand.[1] We recognize three different concepts of revenue:

1. *Total revenue (TR).* This is simply the total amount of money received from all buyers of a product, or

   $$TR = P \cdot Q \qquad (19\text{–}1)$$

   where P = price of the product
   Q = quantity sold.

   We noted earlier the effect that price elasticity had on the total revenue generated.
2. *Average revenue (AR).* This is simply the average amount of money received per unit sold, which we know is the price of the units sold. It is the total revenue divided by the quantity sold. As a simple manipulation of Equation 19–1 we get:

   $$P = TR/Q = AR$$

Table 19–1 Impact of Downward-Sloping Demand Curve on Revenue

Price (P)	Quantity Sold (Q)	Total Revenue (TR = PQ)	Marginal Revenue (ΔTR/ΔQ)	Average Revenue (TR/Q) = P
$10	1	$10	$10	$10
9	2	18	8	9
8	3	24	6	8
7	4	28	4	7
6	5	30	2	6
5	6	30	0	5
4	7	28	−2	4
3	8	24	−4	3
2	9	18	−6	2
1	10	10	−8	1

SOURCE: Adapted from Richard E. Leftwich, *The Price System and Resource Allocation* (Holt, Rinehart and Winston, 1986), p. 191.

Because average revenue equals price at any given quantity, the plot of the average revenue curve will be identical to the plot of the demand curve.

3. *Marginal revenue* (MR). Marginal revenue refers to the amount of change in total revenue resulting from one additional unit of sales. In formula:

$$MR = \Delta TR/\Delta Q.$$

With the standard downward-sloping demand curve, marginal revenue will be less than average revenue, because, in order to gain additional sales, the price has to be lowered on the entire quantity that would have been sold at the higher price. Table 19–1 illustrates the impact of a downward-sloping demand curve on total revenue, average revenue, and marginal revenue.

Note that with the exception of the first unit, marginal revenue is always less than the price or average revenue at each sales level. This becomes clear if we look at the revenue effects of moving from a $9 price to an $8 price. On the incremental unit sold, the firm earns $8. However, to get this sale it gives up $1 on the two units that would sell at $9. Thus, the marginal revenue of the incremental unit sold is $8 − $2 = $6. Graphically, then, the marginal revenue curve will always lie below the demand curve (see Figure 19–2).

Note also, from Table 19–1, that marginal revenue becomes negative when the amount of money given up on sales that could be made at higher prices exceeds the price of the incremental unit. By moving from a price of $5 to a price of $4, we gain $4 for the incremental unit but give up $1 each on six units that would sell at $5. Thus marginal revenue equals $4 − $6 = −$2. When marginal revenue is negative, total revenue is decreased.

Figure 19–2 The Relationship of Demand and Marginal Revenue Curves

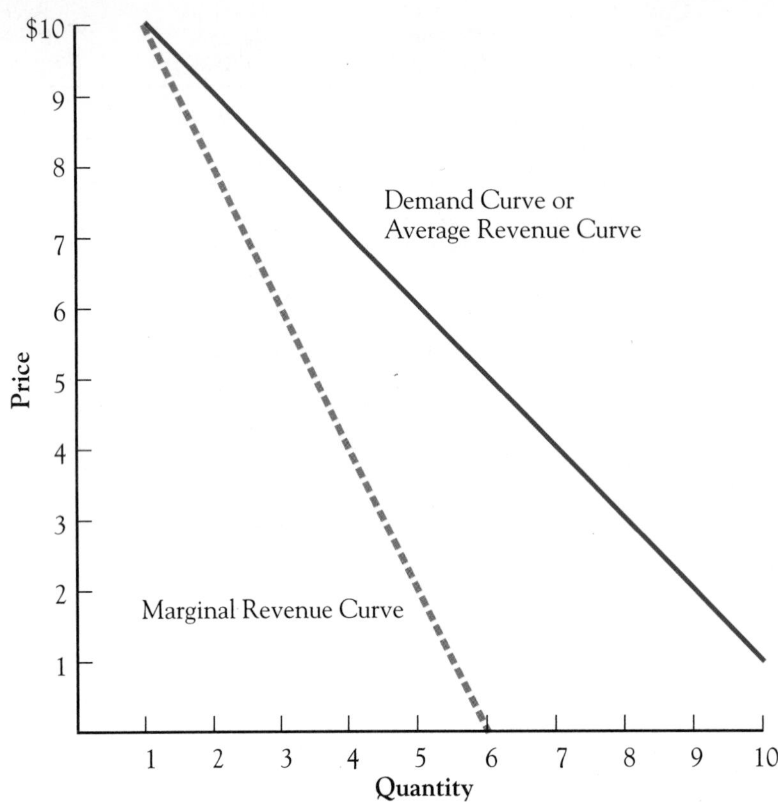

Marginal Revenue and Elasticity

Marginal revenue and elasticity are related as follows:

$$MR = P - P/E.$$

This leads to important generalizations about the impact on marginal revenue for price increases and decreases at various elasticities. These revenue effects of various elasticities are summarized in Table 19–2. This summary makes clear that for total revenue to increase, marginal revenue must be positive and vice versa. Note that (1) if P and TR move in the *same* direction, demand is inelastic, and (2) if P and TR move in *opposite* directions, demand is elastic.

These concepts help explain why the automobile companies in the 1980s undertook price rebate programs. With an elastic demand for cars (in the short run), they increased their total revenues by decreasing the price. Buy why, then, do so many analysts believe the automobile companies actually *lost* money in their rebate programs? The answer probably lies in the cost dynamics of the industry, which will be discussed later in the chapter.

Table 19–2 How Elasticities Affect Revenue

	Effect on Total Revenue		Effect on Marginal Revenue	
Elasticity	**Price Increase**	**Price Decrease**	**Price Increase**	**Price Decrease**
Inelastic $E<1$	Increase	Decrease	Positive	Negative
Unitary $E=1$	Zero	Zero	Zero	Zero
Elastic $E>1$	Decrease	Increase	Negative	Positive

Nonprice Competition and Demand

The other elements of the marketing mix, besides price, are intended to affect demand in two ways. First, the marketer hopes to sell more of a product at any given price than would be possible without the "nonprice" activity in channel availability, promotion, or product offering. This makes it possible, in effect, to shift the demand curve to the right, as illustrated in Figure 19–3, Panel A. RCA has been able to increase the *demand* for $600 video tape systems from 100,000 to 120,000 units by effective promotion and distribution penetration and support. Effectively, they have shifted the demand curve D to D'. In contrast, by using price competition alone, RCA could only change the *quantity demanded* by moving up or down their demand curve (D).

A second major objective of nonprice competition is to make the firm's demand curve more inelastic (see Figure 19–3, Panel B). Here RCA, due to effective promotion, has been able to change from demand curve D to curve D'. On curve D', it can increase price from $600 to $650, with demand only falling from 100,000 units to 95,000. Total revenue has increased from $60 million to $61.75 million. If RCA had remained on the original demand curve D, demand at $650 would have been 85,000 units. Total revenue would have fallen from $60 million to $55.25 million. The benefits of insulating oneself from price competition through other marketing activities thus becomes clear. Many firms aggressively attempt this, and it remains a very controversial area in marketing.

Any demand curve assumes a given and fixed environment with respect to all other elements of the marketing mix and consumer tastes. We talk about a demand curve being accurate if "all other conditions are held constant." Since, in the real world, these other conditions change, we must also expect demand curves to change. Fortunately, these changes usually occur slowly enough to allow the marketer to deal with a reasonably stable demand curve in the short run.

Estimating Demand

The importance of demand estimation should be very clear by now. The question then naturally arises: How does one go about estimating the effects of price on demand? We addressed this issue to some degree when we discussed marketing research and demand forecasting in Chapter 7. Basically, the same techniques are available to help identify demand curves. These techniques include surveys of buyers' intentions, laboratory and field experiments measuring buyers' purchase behavior related to price, and the statistical analysis of past price and sales data.

Figure 19–3 Demand for RCA Videotape Systems

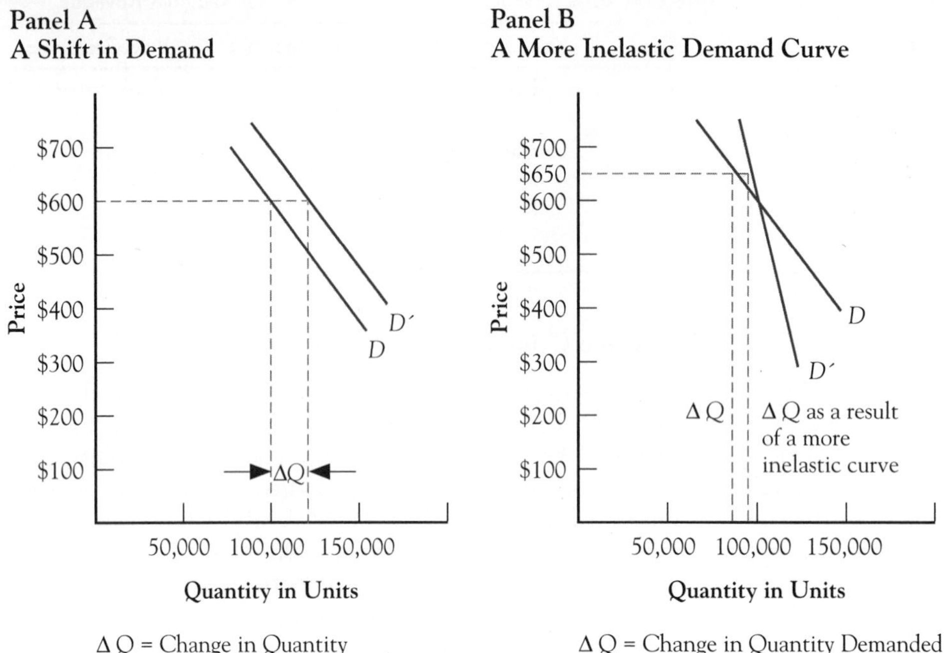

Cost Analysis

The nature of the demand for a product determines the revenues that will be generated. However, whether these revenues will yield a profit depends on the *costs* associated with generating that revenue. In fact, some approaches to price-setting only examine costs, as we shall see later in the chapter.

Types of Costs

We must develop an understanding of six different costs if we are to be good price setters.

- **Total fixed cost (TFC)** is the sum of the financial obligations of the firm that remains at the same level no matter how many units of a product are produced and marketed. Amortization charges for capital equipment and plant, plus such charges as rent, executive salaries, property taxes, and insurance are examples.
- **Average fixed cost (AFC),** or fixed cost per unit, is the amount of fixed cost allocated to each unit. It is simply the TFC divided by the number of units.
- **Variable cost (VC)** is directly tied to production. It includes direct labor and raw materials charges.

RCA increased the demand for video tape systems through effective promotion and distribution penetration and support.

- **Average variable cost (AVC),** or per unit variable cost, is the variable cost per unit produced. It is simply the sum of all variable cost (TVC) at a given production volume divided by this volume. AVC usually starts out high and then decreases as production and purchasing efficiencies are obtained with increased volume. Beyond a certain point, the costs of trying to overwork labor or overcrowd a plant drive AVC up again.
- **Total cost (TC)** is the sum of TFC plus TVC at a given output.
- **Marginal cost (MC)** is the change in total cost of producing and marketing one additional unit. Usually MC will fall sharply at low volume levels but will then level off and then rise sharply as volume increases. It could equally well be defined with identical results as the change in total variable cost associated with one additional unit of volume. This is true because this one unit increase raises total cost and total variable cost by the same amount. Note in Table 19–3 that the increase from 1 to 2 units changes total variable cost from $40 (1 unit × $40) to $70 (2 units × $35). The difference is the MC of $30.

Table 19–3 Types of Costs and Their Behavior

(1) Quantity Produced and Marketed	(2) Total Fixed Cost	(3) Average Fixed Cost (2) ÷ (1)	(4) Average Variable Cost	(5) Average Total Cost (3) + (4)	(6) Total Cost (5) · (1)	(7) Marginal Cost
1	$100	$100.00	$40.00	$140.00	$140.00	
2	100	50.00	35.00	85.00	170.00	$30
3	100	33.33	28.33	61.66	185.00	15
4	100	25.00	24.00	49.00	196.00	11
5	100	20.00	20.80	40.80	204.00	8
6	100	16.67	18.33	35.00	210.00	6
7	100	14.29	16.43	30.72	215.00	5
8	100	12.50	15.00	27.50	220.00	5
9	100	11.11	14.00	25.11	226.00	6
10	100	10.00	13.40	23.40	234.00	8
11	100	9.09	13.18	22.27	245.00	11
12	100	8.33	13.33	21.66	260.00	15
13	100	7.69	13.85	21.54	280.00	20
14	100	7.14	14.72	22.86	306.00	26
15	100	6.67	15.93	22.60	339.00	33
16	100	6.25	17.50	23.75	380.00	41
17	100	5.88	19.41	25.29	430.00	50
18	100	5.55	21.67	27.22	490.00	60
19	100	5.26	24.27	29.53	561.00	71
20	100	5.00	27.20	32.20	644.00	83

SOURCE: Adapted from Richard E. Leftwich, *The Price System and Resource Allocation* (Holt, Rinehart and Winston, 1986), p. 139.

Table 19–3 presents the costs associated with the production and marketing of a specific product. For these per unit costs, graphed in Figure 19–4, note the following generalizations:

- *Average fixed cost (AFC)* declines across the whole output level.
- *Average variable cost (AVC)* forms a U shape. Early economies in production and purchasing eventually give way to inefficiencies of overworked labor and overcrowded production facilities. A major calculator company lost control of variable cost in this way and eventually went bankrupt.
- *Average total cost (ATC)* is the sum of AFC and AVC. As a result, it, too, is usually U-shaped. Because AFC continues to fall after AVC starts to increase, the lowest point *of ATC is at a higher level of output than* AVC. For ATC, the lowest point is at 13 units at an ATC of $21.54. For AVC, the lowest point is at 11 units at a cost of $13.18.
- *Marginal cost (MC)* always equals ATC at the latter's *lowest level.* In Table 19–3, note that MC equals ATC at between 12 and 13 units of output. ATC decreases as long as MC is less than ATC and increases once MC is above ATC.

Figure 19–4 Behavior of Average Cost Curves

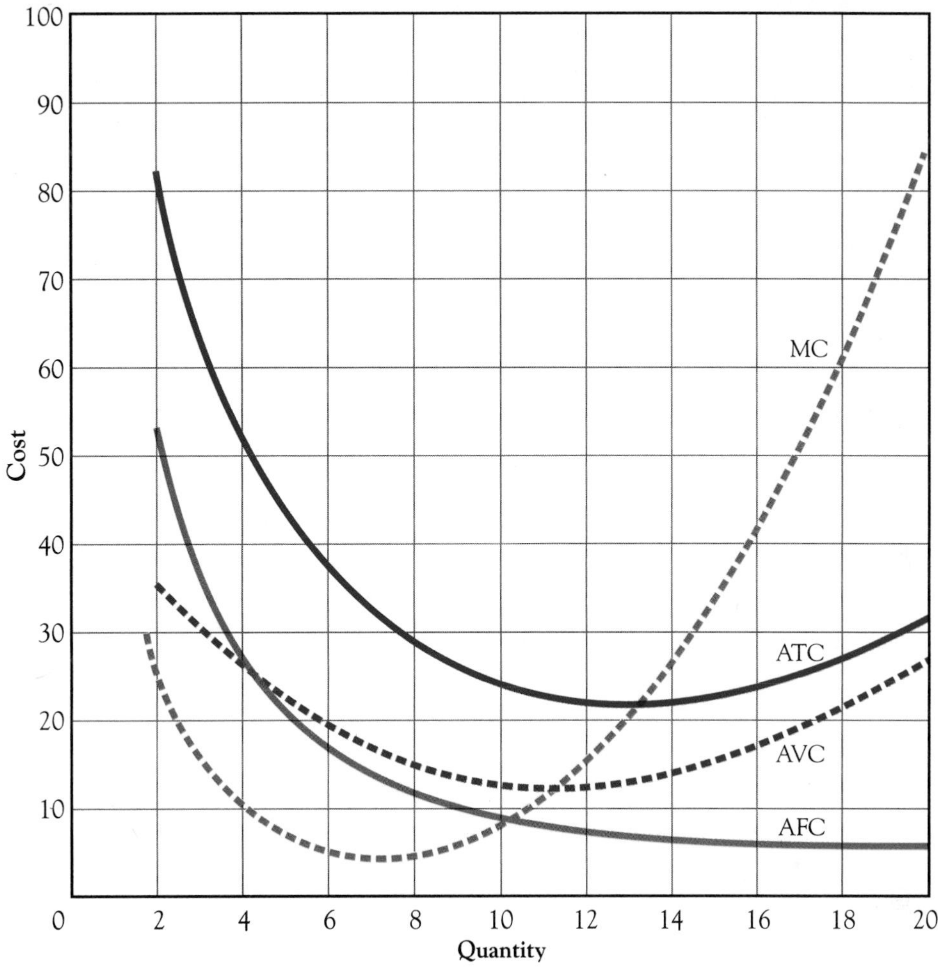

SOURCE: Richard H. Leftwich, *The Price System and Resource Allocation* (Holt, Rinehart and Winston, 1986), p. 140.

We can use these concepts of cost and the demand concepts we developed earlier to determine a profit-maximizing price. This approach is called *marginal analysis* because it uses the concepts of marginal revenue and marginal cost to reach the optimal pricing level.

Maximizing Profit Through Marginal Analysis

Table 19–4 combines relevant data on cost from Table 19–3 and adds information on demand: price, quantity sold, total revenue, and marginal revenue. In addition, it shows maximum profits possible for various combinations of price and cost. It also demonstrates the overriding principle of profit maximization:

Profit is maximized when MC = MR.

Table 19–4 Using Marginal Analysis to Get Maximum Profit-Producing Price

	(1) Price	(2) Quantity Sold	(3) Total Revenue (1) · (2)	(4) Marginal Revenue	(5) Marginal Cost (See Table 19–3)	(6) Total Cost (See Table 19–3)	(7) Profit (3) – (6)	
	75.00	1	75	75	—	$140	–$65	
	70.00	2	140	65	$30	170	– 30	
	66.00	3	198	58	15	185	13	
	62.50	4	250	52	11	196	54	
	59.00	5	295	45	8	204	91	
	55.00	6	330	40	6	210	120	
	51.50	7	361	31	5	215	146	
	47.50	8	380	19	5	220	160	
	43.50	9	392	12	6	226	166	
(Optimal Price)	40.00	10	400	8	8	234	166	(Maximum Profit)
	37.00	11	407	7	11	245	162	
	34.50	12	414	7	15	260	154	
	31.00	13	403	–11	20	280	123	
	27.50	14	385	–18	26	306	79	
	24.00	15	360	–25	33	339	21	
	20.00	16	320	–40	41	380	– 60	
	16.00	17	272	–48	50	430	–158	
	12.00	18	216	–56	60	490	–274	
	8.00	19	152	–64	71	561	–409	
	4.00	20	80	–72	83	644	–564	

Up to this point, when MC = *MR*, the incremental total revenue generated from an extra unit of sale exceeds the total incremental cost of it. Thus, profitability increases. Beyond this point, however, the incremental cost exceeds the incremental revenue and profits decrease (see Figure 19–5). In our example, MC = *MR* at 10 units. The optimal price is then $40.00, and profit is $166.

Note that if we would have set a price based upon the *minimum average total cost,* we would have made less profit—at 13 units ($21.54 *ATC,* from Table 19–3) and a price of $31.00, for example, profit is down to $123. Also, a price based upon *minimum average variable cost* is also not optimal. At 11 units ($13.18 *AVC,* from Table 19–3) and a price of $37.00, profit is $162. The dangers of pricing based upon some markup over some average cost should be clear. Unfortunately, it is quite common for firms to set prices based upon average cost.

A more detailed look at cost analysis is presented in Appendix B, *Financial Concepts for Marketing Analysis.* It also discusses breakeven analysis, operating statement analysis, analytical ratios, and computing markups and markdowns.

The marginal approach to price-setting does have some practical problems.

1. *Demand curves are difficult to estimate accurately.*
2. *Costs often are not in the form needed for marginal analysis.* Costs are much more accurate than demand estimates. However, there are many ways to

Figure 19–5 Pricing for Maximum Profit

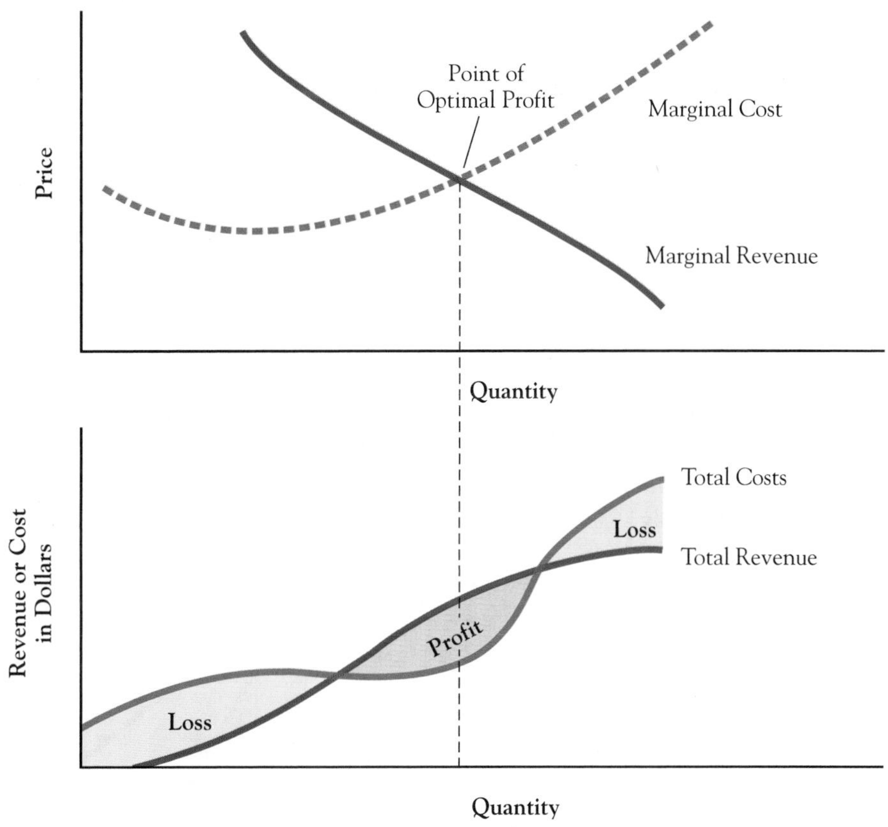

account for costs, and costs assigned to products often include nonrelevant overhead.

3. *Firms often have goals other than profit maximization,* as we noted in Chapter 18. For example, a firm, using the data in Table 19–4, might set its price at $20 with the explicit understanding that it would take a loss in order to gain market share.

Most operating managers do not know exactly what their marginal revenue and marginal cost curves look like. They must approximate them using research and good judgment. However, some firms—including major airlines, catalog retailers, and gas and electrical utilities—explicitly use marginal analysis to make pricing decisions. In all these instances, they do have a good understanding of their demand and cost structures. Other organizations may attempt to make optimal pricing decisions in other ways. We will examine these procedures later in this chapter.

Of course, all price-setting, whether marginal analysis is used or not, takes place in a competitive environment. In the next section, we examine the role of competitive analysis in price-setting.

Figure 19–6 Demand and Marginal Revenue Curves for Competitive Structures

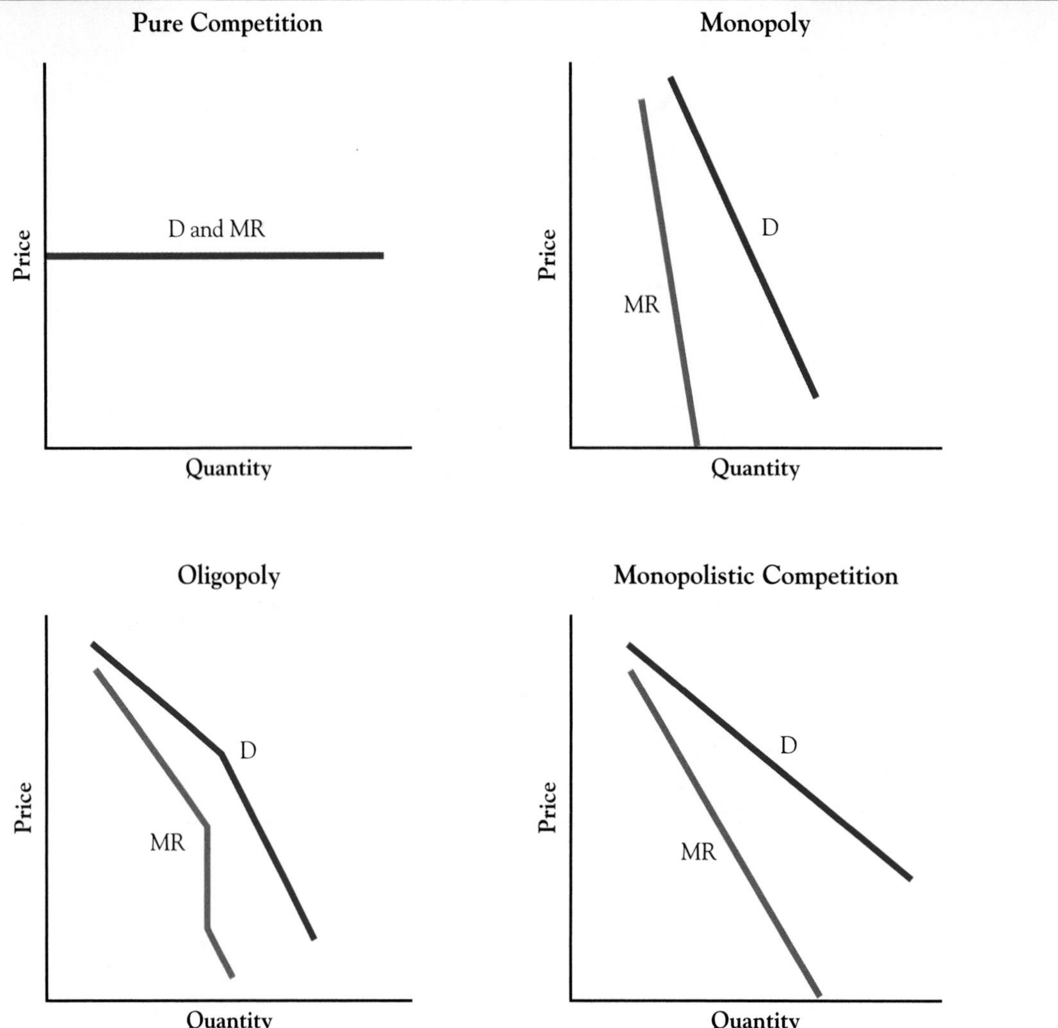

Competitive Analysis

The assessment of demand and cost must take place within the context of a specific competitive environment. That environment directly affects the demand curve faced by an *individual firm.* Two aspects of competitive analysis are important: the *competitive structure* of the firm and the *pricing behavior* of competitors.

Competitive Structure

Recall that there are four general classes of competitive structure: (1) pure competition, (2) monopoly, (3) oligopoly, and (4) monopolistic competition. (The characteristics of each were discussed in Chapter 3 as part of the marketing environment.) The demand and associated marginal revenue curves for these structures are shown in Figure 19–6.

Figure 19–7 Pure Competition

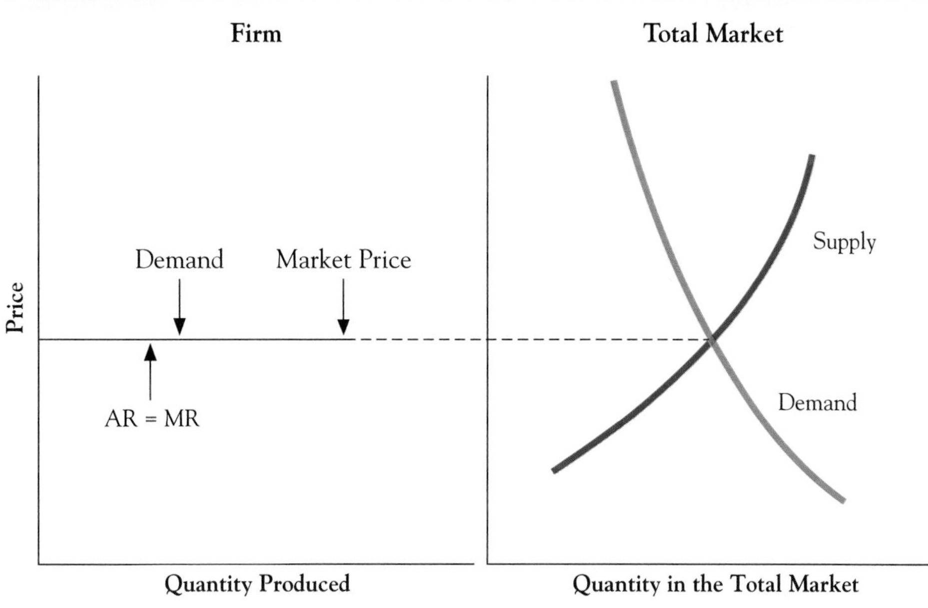

The monopolist's demand curve in Figure 19–6 is the least elastic, since this is where the fewest product substitutes are available. Because our society considers monopoly to be a societal negative, the pricing policies of monopolies are usually regulated. This is certainly true of our public utilities. Also note the "kink" in the oligopolist's demand curve. With oligopolies, there is usually a uniform or market price at which most competitors sell a product. If one firm lowers its price below the market price, the competitors will match this price quickly so that they won't lose sales. Thus, the sales gain from lowering price will be small or nonexistent, and total revenue will be less due to the price decrease. Below market price, then, the demand curve for the firm in an oligopoly is very inelastic. However, if one competitor raises prices above the market price, the competitors may not match this price. The result is that the competitor raising the price loses sales as customers switch to competitive products. Thus, above the market price, the oligopolist's demand curve is very elastic.

The demand curve for an individual firm in pure competition is perfectly elastic, because the firm has no impact on price. Price is determined completely by the interaction of supply and demand in the total market (see Figure 19–7), and the market price, then, represents the demand curve for the firm. A marketer, as far as price is concerned, is completely at the mercy of the demand and supply conditions in the market. The agricultural sector of our economy, which comes closer to pure competition than any other, has even taken steps to mitigate the power of the overall market to set prices by forming cooperatives to try to differentiate products (for example, Sunkist oranges) or to agree on the amount of product that will be supplied to the market.

If we added the marginal cost curve of the individual firm to each of the competitive demand and marginal revenue curves shown in Figure 19–6, we could find the profit-maximizing price. This is, of course, the point where marginal cost equals marginal revenue ($MC = MR$). It is illustrated in Figure 19–8 on the next page.

Figure 19–8 Pricing for Maximum Profit in Different Competitive Structures

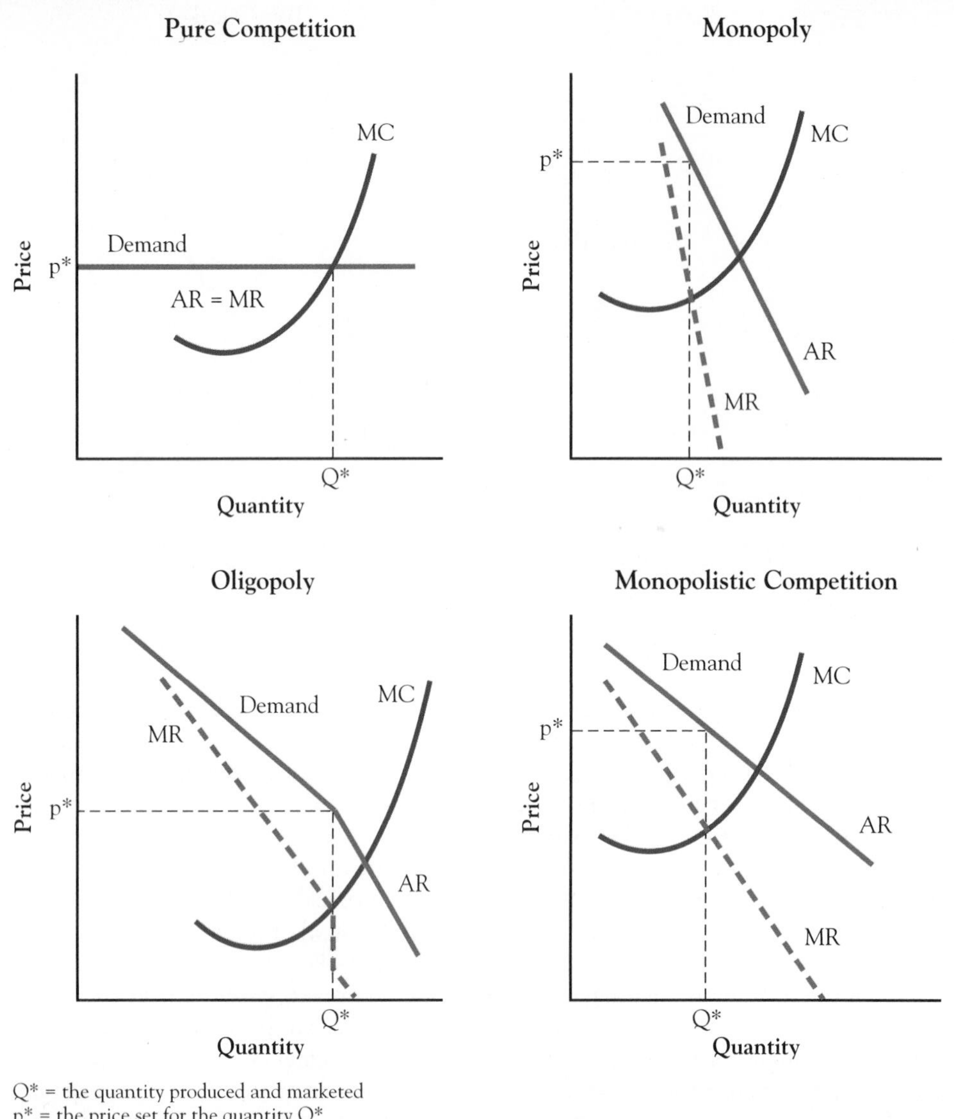

Q* = the quantity produced and marketed
p* = the price set for the quantity Q*

The exact profit could then be calculated by taking the total revenue generated at this price and subtracting the total cost.

This approach to price-setting suffers from the previously noted limitations of marginal analysis. However, it does serve as a conceptual standard because it considers *demand, cost,* and *competitive environment.*

Competitors' Pricing Behavior

Within the monopolistic competition and oligopolistic market structures that represent most of our economy, price choices are available to the firm and its competitors. In setting price, a firm must consider the *pricing behavior* of its competitors.

Table 19–5 The Effect on Price of Environmental Factors

	Factor	Impact
Demand	Government price supports for butter	Decrease in demand for butter
	Promotional program and tax incentives for home insulation	Increase in demand for home insulation
	Government drops support for air bags in cars	Decrease in demand for air bags; increase in demand for seat belts
Cost/Supply	OPEC increases oil prices	Increase in cost of all products using oil in any form
	Freeze in Brazil's coffee fields	Increase in cost of coffee marketing
	Pollution standards lowered for the steel industry	Decrease in cost of doing business for the steel industry
Competition	Government subsidizes Texas Savings and Loans	A competitor kept in the market for financial services
	Government sells its own aluminum plants to Kaiser and Reynolds	New competitors for Alcoa enter market
	U.S. and Japan agree on limit on imports of Japanese cars	Aggressive competitors actions on price are limited

- How many competitors are there?
- What market share does each have?
- What are their total financial resources in and how much money has been committed to the competitive product?
- What is their cost position relative to ours?
- What pricing behavior have they exhibited in the past?
- How is demand affecting them?

From the answers to these questions, the manager attempts to forecast competitors' prices. It is not an easy task, as the makers of a new product called Datril (an aspirin substitute) found out. They decided to price their product below the price of the established aspirin substitute Tylenol. They reasoned that Tylenol would not match their price. The day Datril was introduced, with a large advertising campaign claiming that it had a lower price, Tylenol's price was cut to match Datril's, and Tylenol sued Datril for deceptive advertising. Upjohn did not expect Boots Pharmaceutical to aggressively respond to its price decrease (see Case Application 18–1). Thus, forecasting competitors' pricing behavior is a difficult but necessary job.

Other Environmental Influences on Price

Other factors in the environment—such as government price supports, foreign conspiracies to fix raw materials prices (OPEC), weather, and tariff policy—all have an indirect impact on price-setting. They affect demand, cost/supply, or competition. Table 19–5 presents examples of some potential influences on price and indicates how they affect demand, cost/supply, or competition.

MARKETING IN ACTION

Price and Frost in Florida

The 1985 orange crop in Florida was devastated by one of the worst winter freezes ever. Almost immediately the retail price of fresh oranges and frozen orange juice in the supermarkets of the United States and Canada jumped about 20 percent. Wholesale prices went up even further. This was true even though the impact on supply at the supermarket level was actually many months away.

For the most part it was impossible for stores to replace the lost Florida oranges. "Florida oranges are critical to us," noted a spokesperson for one of the Midwest's largest supermarkets. President Reagan did move to lower tariffs on South American oranges. However, there weren't enough available to the United States to make up for the losses in Florida. The California orange crop could not replace the destroyed crop, and the price of these oranges increased, along with the price for what was left in Florida.

Most supermarkets that had been using oranges as a promotional item stopped. A number of supermarkets ran ads recommending that consumers switch to other fruits. However, the price of potential substitute fruits rose also as the demand for them from consumers increased.

On the demand side, in the early 1980s, the federal government undertook a promotional program for the installation of insulation in homes by giving tax incentives. This program has increased the demand for insulation. On the cost/supply side, a freeze in the orange groves of Florida substantially increased the cost associated with the marketing of oranges. The *Marketing in Action* on orange prices traces the impact of such a freeze on the consumer and on the wholesale and retail trade. As a final illustration, the American government's decision to agree with Japan to restrict the number of Japanese cars imported into the United States affected the competitive structure of the industry and made the Japanese automobile companies less likely to compete on price. The Japanese car companies then moved to compete more in the luxury markets with the Acura (Honda), Lexus (Toyota), and Infiniti (Nissan).

With this grounding in the basic foundations of pricing, we turn our attention to how prices are actually set in the real world. Many of these approaches suffer because all three factors of demand, cost, and competition are not considered simultaneously. But one approach—integrative pricing—does take into account all three.

Review Your Marketing Knowledge

- For the gasoline pricing profile that began this chapter, describe the demand curve for the California market as a whole, and the demand curve for ARCO.
- What type of cost analysis should ARCO be performing to prepare its pricing strategy?
- A supermarket has many thousands of items for sale. What role should demand, cost, and competition play in setting a price for a specific item?

Table 19–6 Classification of Pricing Methods

Demand-based	Cost-based	Competition-based	Integrative
Value pricing	Cost-plus pricing	Price leadership	Marginal-approach pricing
Prestige pricing	Return-on-investment pricing	Customary pricing	Multistage-approach pricing
Odd-even pricing	Experience-curve pricing	Market-share pricing	Competitive-bidding pricing
Price lining			
Leader pricing			

Setting Prices in the Real World

When setting prices in the real world, marketers commonly use their understanding of only demand, cost, or competition, and exclude the other factors. Thus, we end up with *demand-based* pricing methods, *cost-based* pricing methods, and *competition-based* pricing methods. Fortunately, some marketers do attempt to consider more than one of these factors in setting prices. Thus we have *integrative* pricing methods. Table 19–6 summarizes the specific pricing methods within these classifications, and the next sections of the chapter discuss these methods in more detail.

Demand-Based Pricing

Value Pricing

Value pricing, or *value-in-use pricing* as it is also called, works to assign a price to a product based upon its value to the consumer in the use of the product. For example, 3M Corporation's Post-it Notes (paper with a special light glue on it that allows it to be attached to other paper and then easily removed without damaging the host paper) is priced high relative to its cost. However, this price is consistent with the value that the end-user places on the product. Companies like 3M and Hewlett-Packard have used this pricing method to gain a competitive edge in the marketplace.

Figure 19–9 illustrates the concept of value pricing in an industrial context.[2] The vertical bar on the left side of Figure 19–9 shows the full cost to the end customer over the life-cycle of a computer networking product. The life-cycle cost is made up of the product's price, start-up costs, and service and maintenance costs, for a total of $1000. Our product, represented by the next vertical bar, offers major advantages over the first product. It has lower start-up and service costs and offers extra product features (it is faster at feeding information in the network, for example). We put an estimated value of $100 on this feature. Since the customer is willing to pay $300 for the competitive product, he or she should, in theory, be willing to pay up to $600 for our product—the base of $300, plus the $200 saving on start-up and service, plus the $100 for the extra feature.

Figure 19–9 An Illustration of Value Pricing

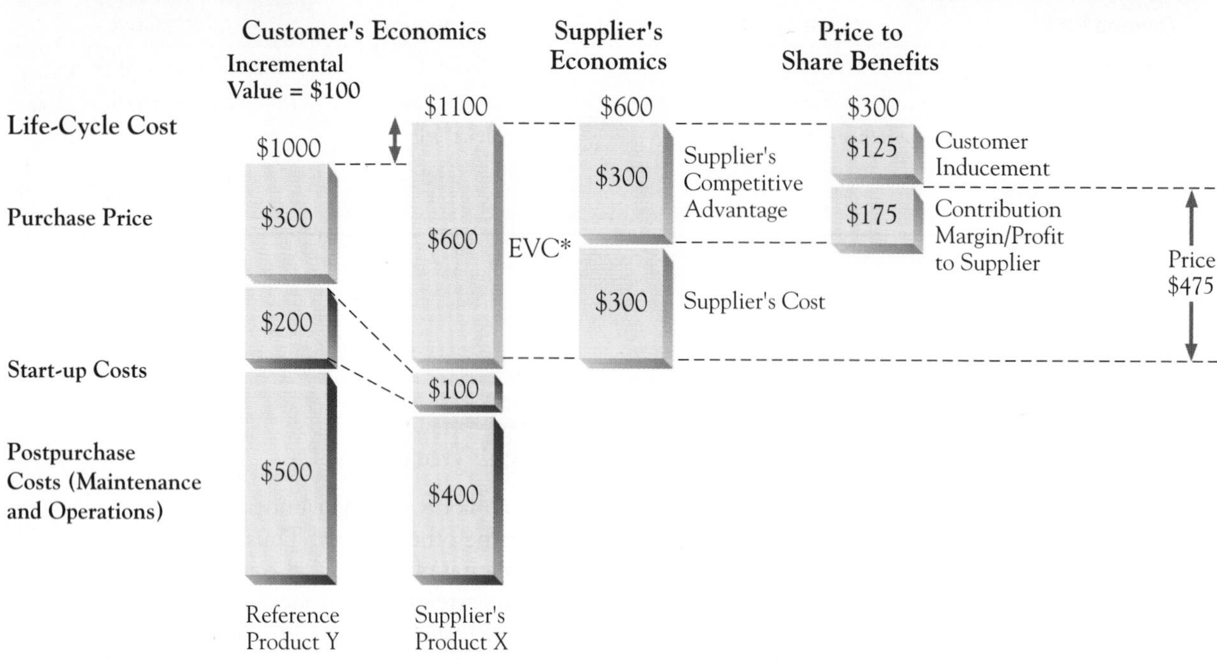

*Economic value to customer

Source: John L. Forbis and Nitin T. Mehta, "Value-Based Strategies for Industrial Products," *Business Horizons,* May 1981 p. 33

These calculations only look at the customer's point of view. From the supplier's side, it costs us $300 to make the product (the third vertical bar). Any price over $300 will then return us a profit. Any price under $600 will give the consumer a better deal than he or she has with the current product in use. The $300 difference between our cost and the value limit is our competitive advantage. The last bar (on the right side) gives one possible price. Setting the price at $475 would give us $175 in profit, while offering the consumer an economic advantage of $125 over the currently used product. This $125 is the consumer inducement to buy our product. The final price set then reflects the value of the product to any given end-user and the amount of inducement (from the competitive advantage) the supplier wishes to give the customer.

Special Demand Curves

The traditional demand curve that we have discussed may not always hold. The reason for this is simply that people respond to prices in personal, and, not necessarily, in rational ways. This behavior has resulted in some very nontraditional, and even strange-looking, demand curves. These curves form the basis of three demand-based pricing methods: *prestige pricing, odd-even pricing,* and *price lining.* In addition to these three, we will look at *leader pricing,* which is based upon demand relationships among different products.

Figure 19–10 Nontraditional Demand Curves

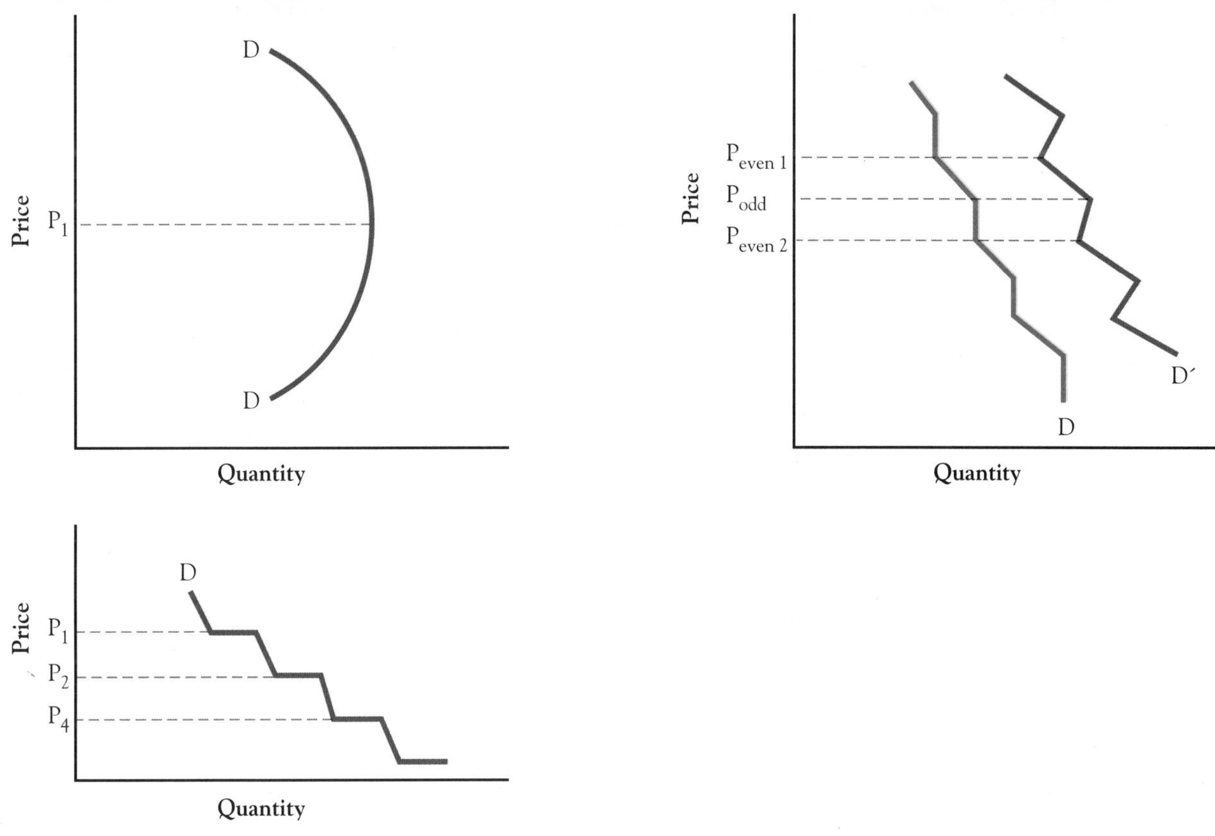

Part 1 Prestige Pricing *(upper left)* Part 2 Odd-Even Pricing *(upper right)* Part 3 Price Lining *(lower left)*

Prestige Pricing Figure 19–10, Part 1, illustrates the demand curve for products like diamonds, furs, European sports cars, certain retailers, perfume, and whiskey, when consumers use price as a measure of prestige or quality. These products may not sell as well if the price gets too low. At point P_1, the curve turns back to the left. Up to that point, consumers have perceived the products as being at bargain prices and have purchased more. But as price becomes even lower, consumers become suspicious of the quality or image of the merchandise (a diamond ring for $50?), and actually demand less. Toni home permanents had this problem when first introduced in the 1950s. Consumers had trouble believing that a product that cost so little could do the job properly. A price rise helped overcome this problem, causing demand to increase.

Odd-Even Pricing This strategy is common at the retail level and is based upon the belief that consumers will respond more positively to prices ending in certain numbers. Thus, we see prices of $6.95 instead of $7.00, $2.99 instead of $3.00, and $499.99 instead of $500.00. For retail goods under $50, prices ending in 9 are the most common, followed by prices ending in 5 and 3. With products selling for over

$50, the most common prices are $1 or $2 below the even dollar amount. The presumption is that consumers will buy the same amount, or even less, of a product as prices are lowered below an odd-price point. Then, as the price approaches a new odd-price point, demand will increase dramatically. There is some evidence that consumers perceive these slightly reduced odd prices to be more below the even price above them than they really are.[3]

The resulting demand curve has a jagged look to it (see Figure 19–10, Part 2). On curve *D*, between the even price, $P_{even\ 1}$, and the odd price below it, P_{odd}, the demand is much more elastic than between this odd price and the even price below it, $P_{even\ 2}$. Thus, the benefit of increased total revenue is derived from lowering the price over the elastic part of the curve. However, no further benefit would be obtained from dropping the price over the inelastic part of the curve. In fact, total revenue would decrease, as we noted earlier in the chapter, since demand here is inelastic. Curve *D* shows demand being the same below the odd-price point as it is at this price point. If demand decreased at prices below the odd-price point, the curve would slant back to the left between P_{odd} and $P_{even\ 2}$, as illustrated by the curve identified as *D′*.

Price-Lining This term describes the practice of offering a product line with items placed in the line at specific pricing points. For example, a clothing retailer may offer men's shirts at $12, $17, and $25, and at no points in between. Figure 19–10, Part 3, illustrates the type of demand curve that is being presumed by a retailer using this pricing scheme. The demand at all three pricing points—P_1, P_2, and P_3—is assumed to be very elastic. However, between the pricing points, the demand is assumed to be very inelastic. In our shirt example, the presumption is that the retailer would sell about the same number of shirts at prices just below $25 to just above $17, but that as soon as the price hit $17, demand would increase. Again, from just below $17 to just above $12, the demand would be about equal. But as the price reached $12, the demand would expand greatly.

In retail outlets that offer many different product classes—with many brands within a product class, and many different package sizes within a brand—consumers may become confused about which item is the best price offer. Consider the following prices for two sizes of Sugar Frosted Flakes, and with a third option of a special deal: (a) 10 oz. $1.09, (b) 13 oz. $1.56, and (c) two 18 oz. boxes for $3.98. Which offer is the best deal? With *unit pricing* one can tell, because both the price of the item and the ounce, pound, or other unit of measurement is marked on the shelf in the store. In our example, the unit prices are (a) 10.9¢ per ounce, (b) 12¢ per ounce, and (c) 11.1¢ per ounce. In this case, larger packages and special offers are really less of a bargain than the standard price on the smallest package. Unit pricing, which grew out of the consumer movement, is used by some large supermarkets. Although unit pricing does add to costs, retailers hope that the social benefit of consumers making better purchase decisions will offset this cost.

Leader Pricing With this strategy, the marketer sets very low prices for one product, intending to stimulate its sales and those of other complementary products. Marketers assume that there is a *highly positive* price *cross elasticity* of demand between the "leader" product and the other products involved. That is, by stimulating demand for the "leader" product, they will increase the demand for complementary products. Retailers often have "door crasher specials" or feature sale items to generate store traffic and, thus, stimulate sales of all items. Ames Company puts low prices on its medical diagnostic machines in order to sell the test materials required by the machines; Gillette sets low prices on its razors in order to sell razor blades. If the price is so low on the leader item that it is below cost, it is referred to as a *loss leader*. Of course, if the intent of a leader price is really to bait and switch, the price would be illegal. The marketer must be willing to sell the leader item at its promoted price, even to *cherry pickers* (people who only buy the leader item).

Cost-Based Pricing

To price without concern for cost is very dangerous. To be fair, we must note that those who use demand-based pricing methods probably have one eye on the cost of the products involved. Because costs are so important in determining profitability, and because they are much easier to estimate than demand, many marketers set prices utilizing cost-based procedures. The most common are (1) cost-plus pricing, (2) return-on-investment pricing, and (3) experience curve pricing.

Cost-Plus Pricing

This is the most commonly used form of price-setting. One simply adds a specified amount to the cost of an item. The added amount is a percentage of the cost. Usually the cost is based on average total cost for a planned number of sales. However, average variable cost is sometimes used. In formula:

$$\text{Using Average Total Cost} \quad \text{Price} = ATC + m\,(ATC)$$

$$\text{Using Average Variable Cost} \quad \text{Price} = AVC + m\,(AVC)$$

where m is the percentage added on to cost. Thus, if the target markup on ATC was 25 percent and ATC was \$100, then

$$\text{Price} = \$100 + .25\,(\$100) = \$125.$$

The simplicity of this approach to setting prices is its biggest strength. All one needs is a cost schedule and a set of decisions about the appropriate markup. It is also useful because marketers often do not know demand schedules very well and so cannot estimate total revenue. In addition, it is easy to justify a price that covers total cost; this is especially important in government contract work.

This approach to pricing is most appropriate in product categories where demand and competitive structure are quite stable over time. This would include food (milk, bread) and other household staples. But it has a number of weaknesses, too. First, it assumes an accurate assessment of cost. In inflationary times and in high technology industries, assessing cost is not an easy task. The inability to accurately estimate costs is a constant problem for military contractors, for example. Further, when using ATC, the product has some of the firm's general overhead allocated to it; but just how much of the president's salary or the employee recreation area should be allocated to each product? There are many ways to allocate these costs, each way resulting in a different ATC. Price then becomes the slave of an arbitrary accounting system. The cost allocation system is also set up to fully absorb these overhead costs at some specified planning volume. If the sales exceed this amount, then too many overhead costs are absorbed. Alternatively, if actual volume is below the planned volume, then not all overhead costs are covered.

Intermediary Pricing

Cost-plus pricing is the dominant mode in the wholesaling and retailing areas, where it is called *markup pricing.* We must have some sympathy for these marketers, since they often carry thousands of items. They have neither the time nor money to develop demand schedules for each item. (The way their margins are quoted and calculated was presented in an overview in Chapter 19.) In fairness, we should note that their prices are not totally unrelated to demand. They do assign different percentage markups to different items based upon their sales experiences and will quickly lower prices if an item is not selling. Also, the intermediary's price is based upon a markup on manufacturer's selling price, or discount from manufacturer's suggested retail price (see Appendix B for details of these calculations). The manufacturer may have done a more complete demand and competitive analysis in setting the price and discount schedules.

Return-on-Investment (ROI) Pricing

With this method, marketers attempt to set a price that will enable the firm to reach a specified return. Sometimes called *target ROI pricing,* this method requires the firm to forecast a *planning volume* in order to determine both cost and profitability levels. This planning volume is the quantity the firm expects to sell over the next year, or is some average of sales expectations over a number of years. Target ROI price is set using the following formula:

$$\text{Price} = AVC + \frac{TFC}{PV} + \frac{r(INV)}{PV}$$

where

AVC	=	average variable cost
TFC	=	total fixed cost
PV	=	planning volume
INV	=	investment
r	=	target ROI

Let us illustrate how this formula can be used. Assume that AVC is \$1.50 per unit for a 35mm film product, the TFC is \$2 million, total investment is \$10 million, target ROI is 25 percent, and planning volume is 20 million units. Then the price should be:

$$\text{Price} = \$1.50 + \frac{\$2{,}000{,}000}{20{,}000{,}000} + \frac{.25\,(\$10{,}000{,}000)}{20{,}000{,}000} = \$1.73.$$

Basically, this formula says that the set price must cover the average variable cost, the average fixed cost per unit, plus the average return on the investment per unit.

Note that if the targeted planning volume (PV) is not attained, then AFC/PV and $r(INV)/PV$ will be larger than before. Thus, to reach the target ROI, the price must be raised. Therefore, one would raise prices when confronted with falling demand, a seemingly counterproductive action. Yet this is precisely what the automobile companies have done to attempt to meet their target ROIs. Of course, this price increase could further depress demand, inventories could build up, and ROI could actually become negative. Like cost-plus pricing, this method is based on total costs being allocated to products, and distortions are possible.

Experience-Curve Pricing

Average total cost (in constant dollars) of a product declines as the firm produces and markets more of it. This occurs because labor becomes more skilled, automated equipment can be used, and purchasing and marketing costs can be lowered on average because the firm is able to obtain discounts at higher volume. An *experience curve* is a representation of the relationship between average total cost and cumulative experience in producing and marketing a product.

Firms that maintain a cumulative volume advantage over competitors may thus have lower costs. If they then price at a small markup over these costs or what they expect their costs to be given experience projections, they may make other firms unprofitable. This was Texas Instrument's pricing strategy with digital watches and calculators, and it is the pricing strategy of Japanese producers of 256K computer chips. In some industries the low-cost producer provides a *price umbrella* for the industry. This happens when this producer sets its markup above cost at a high enough level that the other companies are profitable. This has historically been General Motors' approach to pricing.

Experience-curve pricing is a variation of cost-plus pricing. Here the cost used is the projected cost, adjusted for inflation, given a certain volume level and experience curve effects.

Competition-Based Pricing

Neither demand- nor cost-based pricing methods explicitly take competition into account. A number of price-setting procedures assign the dominant role to competition. These include (1) price leadership, (2) customary pricing, and (3) market-share pricing.

Price Leadership

In some oligopolistic industries—with their kinked demand curves for firms—the job of assessing competitors' prices has been made easier because of **price leadership** in the industry. A price leader takes the first step at raising and lowering prices in an industry. Others then generally follow. U.S. Steel plays this role in the steel industry, as does General Motors in the automobile industry. The price leader is usually the largest competitor in the industry, although it is not uncommon for the second or third largest firm to play some role in price leadership. Sometimes the leader is not the first firm to make a price change, but the leader's response to another price change will set the market price. For example, Chrysler often announces price increases first, but then adjusts its prices based upon what General Motors does in response.

It is quite common for competitors to *signal* one another by announcing price changes effective at some specified time in the future. The fact that the competitors have the same price and change price together is not illegal. Under the Supreme Court doctrine of *conscious parallelism,* the FTC or Justice Department must also prove the existence of a conspiracy to make equal prices and/or price moves illegal. This whole area of enforcement has been brought into question by the recent Federal Trade Commission ruling in the DuPont and Ethyl Corp. case (see Chapter 18). It appears that the FTC will be proactively seeking out nonexplicit conspiracies.

In setting prices, the price leader must consider the demand and cost situation of all competitors, not just itself. For example, a price that does not allow some competitors to make a profit may cause these competitors to secretly cut prices to gain needed volume. A price war might follow. In addition, the temptation to conspire to fix prices or divide the market increases in these circumstances. This would, of course, be illegal under Section 1 of the Sherman Act.

Customary Pricing

With **customary pricing,** certain traditional pricing points are used by all competitors. For example, retail prices for virtually all candy bars are 40 cents. Firms do not sell candy bars for 41 cents or 46 cents. In times of changing cost, the product itself is changed, not the price. Thus, the size of an M&M's package changes with the cost of chocolate, but the retail price of an M&M's package remains the same. In periods of extreme cost changes though, the customary pricing point can shift, as it has for candy bars in recent years from 10 cents to 35 cents to 40 cents.

Vending machines used at the retail level give further impetus for customary pricing. One finds prices in these machines that are divisible by 5 cents. For example, local phone calls are 25 cents, not 17 cents, and even on long distance calls where one is actually putting coins in the phone, the charge always ends in a multiple of 5. Beverage, food, and other vending machine product prices also conform to this pattern.

Although customary pricing occurs mostly at the retail level, it is still common at the wholesale and manufacturer level. This is most true when all manufacturers of the same product type quote the same retail and wholesale margins. Tradition dictates what this margin should be, and one takes a big risk in deviating from it.

Market-Share Pricing

The objective of **market-share pricing** is designed to take market share from competitors. Sometimes called **penetration pricing,** it is most commonly used after a brand is introduced. The hope is to make the price so low that consumers will give up their usual brands and switch to the new entry. It is often said that the new entry is "buying market share." The cost of purchasing market share is usually the short-run profits for the brand. The firm hopes that once an acceptable level of market share is attained, prices can be raised and profits earned. If competitors attempt to prevent the new entry from getting share, a price war may occur, and all competitors may become unprofitable. The eventual winner will be the firm with the lowest costs or the most resources to commit to its brand. The prices of all brands of smoke detectors fell when Sears entered the market with a penetration price of $19.95 against the market price of $25.00. In this case, the competitors were able to fight back. In the case of Japanese 256K chip manufacturers, using a penetration price based on an experience curve, some competitors were not in a strong enough cost position to fight.

If the firm takes market-share pricing so far that it starts to gain a monopoly position, it runs the risk of being charged with *predatory pricing* (as we discussed in Chapter 18).

Integrative Pricing

Pricing decisions should take demand, cost, and competition into account. The approaches to pricing, discussed so far, that focus on only one of these factors are logically incorrect and can cause big mistakes in price-setting. Fortunately, a number of pricing procedures are available that simultaneously consider all three factors. These are (1) marginal-approach pricing, (2) multistage pricing, and (3) competitive bidding pricing.

Marginal-Approach Pricing

Setting prices by determining the price at which $MC = MR$ was discussed in the first part of this chapter. We should recognize this method as an *integrative approach* to pricing because it does simultaneously consider demand, cost, and competitive aspects. The difficulties of implementing it, as we noted earlier, have limited its use. However, some organizations, such as public utilities and airlines, do attempt to implement this type of approach. What we really need is an approach that is capable of simultaneously considering demand, cost, and competition, and is more usable in practice: multistage pricing.

Multistage Pricing

The multistage approach to pricing is designed to get marketers to think through all the aspects of setting a price. It is a *checklist* of things to do in setting prices. The term *multistage* in reference to pricing was first used by Oxenfeldt,[4] who proposed the following stages:

1. Selection of target markets
2. Specification of the brand image that fits the selected targets
3. Decision on the marketing mix and pricing role in it
4. Setting a pricing policy to assure consistency in pricing decisions
5. Selection of a pricing strategy to fit the current environment
6. Designation of a specific price

His approach emphasized the importance of setting prices within the framework of other marketing decisions. This checklist remains a good one but does not go far enough with respect to setting a specific price. Kent Monroe developed a more complete checklist that put the emphasis on all the parts of the pricing decision we have discussed in the two pricing chapters: setting objectives; identifying alternative prices; acquiring relevant information on demand, cost, and competition; developing the mechanics of the decision itself; and maintaining feedback and control about the price actually set.[5] These guidelines are reproduced in Table 19–7.

These approaches do not lead to the setting of one price for a given product class, as the *Marketing in Action* on personal computer software pricing illustrates. Each competitor follows the approach to its own conclusion.

Competitive Bidding

Another special circumstance in pricing that requires an integrative approach is when sales are awarded on the basis of *competitive bids*. The competitive bidding process may be either seller- or buyer-initiated. For products such as livestock, art, government land, and used cars, the seller initiates the competitive bidding by holding an *auction*. Prospective buyers offer prices for products in face-to-face exchange so that all competitive buyers know what others are offering, and buyers can bid more than one time in the process as the price is bid up. For seller-initiated bidding, the highest bid gets the product.

In industrial marketing and government contract work, the buyer often initiates the process by announcing the specifications of products and asking for bids. Often the bids are *sealed* or *closed* so that a bidder does not know what other bidders have bid. Usually, a bidder may only submit one bid, and the contract is awarded on the

MARKETING IN ACTION

Personal Computer Software Pricing

The personal computer software business is characterized by dramatic polarization in the pricing of similar products. At the top end of the scale are such standards as Lotus 1-2-3 and WordPerfect, which may list for more than $500. At the bottom end are a range of programs that often claim to offer what the top-of-the-line programs do, but at a bargain price—often less than $100. The wide variation in software prices suggests that a broad range of factors—including a company's reputation and its corporate objectives—affects the pricing decision. The actual cost of developing a program may play a minor role in determining its price.

Low-priced software producers began to appear around 1985. These firms apparently wanted to gain market share and also increase the size of the software market by setting prices far below current industry standards. The author of *Intuit,* a program manufactured by Noumenon Corporation, suggested that high prices for software were "choking off" the high volume of software sales that should be expected with a flourishing personal computer industry. Based on this calculation, Noumenon conducted an unusual pricing experiment with *Intuit,* which had found few buyers when priced at $395. With no special advertising, Noumenon dropped the price of *Intuit* to $50 and then raised its price by $20 each week until sales began to falter. Noumenon discovered that dollar sales peaked at a price of $130 and unit demand had been highest at $90. As a result, Noumenon decided to price *Intuit* at $89.95.

The move by Noumenon and some other low-priced manufacturers to deviate from the software industry's high pricing standards did not cause the revolution in industry pricing that was predicted by some analysts. According to an executive with a large software distributor, only a small percentage of computer owners make software decisions based on price. Business customers, in particular, are often worried about losing ground to competitors by failing to use the most reputable, and often priciest, software. As a result, the market for high-priced software remains strong, although a price-sensitive market has also been opened up. Until price-conscious individuals become a higher percentage of the PC market or until business buyers exhibit less of a "follow-the-leader" mentality about hardware and software purchases, the software market will continue to permit large and seemingly arbitrary price differences.

SOURCES: Kelly Walker, "Software Economics 101," *Forbes,* January 28, 1985, p. 88. Erik Sandberg-Diment, "Lowering the High Cost of Software," *The New York Times,* Nov. 24, 1985, p. 16–F.

---

basis of this one bid. It is common practice for the lowest bidder to get the contract, but this is not always true. Sometimes the special skills or reputation of one bidder allows the contract to be awarded to a firm that does not offer the lowest bid. In addition, in government work, the price actually bid may not end up being the final price. Cost overruns on such projects as the stealth plane and $500 toilet seats are legendary. The government usually pays for these extra costs or cuts back the number of units ordered. Often the alternatives are either not getting the product at all or bankrupting the supplier.

In preparing competitive bids, the marketer must consider demand, cost, and competition. Fortunately, the demand aspect is taken care of, since the buyer specifies the exact number of units that will be purchased. The marketer must carefully develop cost estimates, usually making experience-curve projections in doing so. Finally, the marketer must forecast what competitors will bid based on his or her assessment of

Table 19–7 Pricing Guidelines

Set consistent objectives.	1. Make sure that objectives are clearly stated, operational, and mutually consistent. 2. When there are several objectives, develop priorities, or otherwise clarify the relationships between the objectives. 3. Make sure that everyone concerned with a pricing decision, at any level in the firm, understands the relevant objectives.
Identify alternatives.	1. Identify enough alternatives to permit a sensible choice between courses of action. 2. Avoid traditional thinking, encourage creativity.
Acquire relevant information.	1. Be sure that information about buyers and competitors is current and reflects their current and future situations. 2. Make sure information is for the future, not just a report of the past. 3. Involve market research people in the pricing problem. 4. Make sure cost information identifies which costs will be affected by a particular pricing alternative. 5. Communicate with and involve accounting people with the cost aspects of a pricing decision. 6. Analyze the effect a particular alternative will have on scarce resources, inventories, production, cash flows, market share, volume, and profits.
Make the pricing decision.	1. Make full use of the information available. 2. Correctly relate all the relevant variables in the problem. 3. Use sensitivity analysis to determine which elements in the decision are most important. 4. Consider all human and organizational problems which could occur with a given pricing decision. 5. Consider the long-run effects of the pricing decision. 6. Base the pricing decision on the life-cycle of each product. 7. Consider the effect of experience in reducing costs as the cumulative production volume increases.
Maintain feedback and control.	1. Develop procedures to ensure that pricing decisions fit into the firm's overall marketing strategy. 2. Provide for a feedback mechanism to ensure that all who should know the results of individual price decisions are fully informed.

To summarize, pricing decisions should be logically made and should involve rigorous thinking, with minimum difficulty from human and organizational factors. Further, it should be recognized that judgment and prediction are needed about the future, not the past. Finally, pricing decisions should be made within a dynamic, long-run marketing strategy.

SOURCE: Kent B. Monroe, *Pricing: Making Profitable Decisions* (McGraw-Hill, 1979), pp. 277–78.

their costs and competitive strategies. Getting accurate information on competitors' costs and probable strategies is a major problem in developing bids.

Bidding often reflects a cost-plus approach. The risk in doing this is that a competitor may have lower costs than your firm or may be "buying into" the market by sacrificing profits in the short run. Actually, below-cost bidding is quite common for government contracts. A cost-plus approach is clearly inappropriate. A bidder must ask what the probability of getting the contract is at various bid levels, and trade this off against the profits or losses that will occur at these bids.

With an understanding of different pricing approaches in hand, we now look at two special topics: new-product pricing and pricing the complete product line.

Review Your Marketing Knowledge

• The General Electric magnetic resonance scanner (used to do brain, chest, etc., scans in hospitals) sells for over $2 million and is the most expensive such device in the market. It is also the sales leader in units sold in this market. How could this situation be explained by value pricing analysis?

• What role does cost play in setting PC software prices (see the *Marketing in Action*)? What role does competitive positioning play in the setting of these prices?

• How do competitors signal each other as to their intended pricing behavior? Should such practices be illegal?

New-Product Pricing

There are different types of new-product entries, each having to do with how "new" the product is. First, the product may be entering an already well-established market where its price will be largely determined by the prices of established competitors. The pricing of Aim toothpaste to compete with Crest and Colgate was such a circumstance.[6] Second, the form of the product may be new, but it will compete against established products on a functional basis. The prices of the competitive products strongly influence the new product's price. The introductory price of Maxim freeze-dried coffee was greatly influenced by the prices of established regular and instant coffees. Third, a product may be completely new and unique. This is the type of new product that interests us here. The product, in essence, has a monopoly position to start with. Examples include the original RCA color television, the Polaroid camera, Sony Betamax recorder, digital watches, trashmasher, liquid soap, and DuPont Silverstone. These products may still compete indirectly with others, but a great deal of latitude exists for price. Two broad alternative pricing strategies are possible in this context: *skimming* and *penetration.*[7]

Skimming involves setting a high initial price for a new product and aiming for the market segment that is willing to pay it. The price-setter is "skimming the cream" off the top of the market. Polaroid cameras, Sony Betamax, hard-cover books, and Magnavox videodisc systems are but a few examples of products that have used this entry strategy. Over time, the price is lowered so that the product may "*slide down the demand curve*" to pick up other price segments. The soft-cover version of a hard-cover edition of a book is an example. Another example is DuPont's marketing of nylon, rayon, cellophane, and Silverstone.

Penetration involves setting a low price for the new product in order to attract the mass market. Some new books come out in paperback immediately. Texas Instruments' calculators and digital watches, Casio watches, and new Xerox photocopiers used penetration pricing. At its extreme, this method may be labeled *pre-emptive pricing,* since its intent is to foreclose competitive entry by making the profit potential unattractive for prospective competitors.

The choice between skimming and penetrating involves trading off a number of factors. Table 19–8 lists these factors and indicates when one would tend to use one strategy over the other. Of course, these are just suggestions; for any product, the factors may point in different directions. For example, for United Techtronics, a manufacturer of a new large-screen projection television system, demand and competitive aspects pointed to penetrating, while cost and company resources pointed to skimming.[8] It is up to the marketer to decide which of the factors are the most important and make the decision.

Table 19–8 Factors Affecting the Choice of Skimming or Penetration

Factor	Use Skimming If:	Use Penetration If:
Price elasticity of primary demand	Inelastic	Elastic
Price elasticity of selective demand	Inelastic	Elastic
Cost of production and marketing relative to potential competitors	Higher	Lower
Economies of scale	No	Yes
Ease with which competitors will enter the market	Difficult for them to enter	Easy entry
How new the product concept is relative to ones the consumer knows	New concept	Known concept
(Rate at which the consumer will accept the concept)	(slow)	(fast)
Market segments based on price	Exist and can be taken one segment at a time	Only a mass market exists
The firm's resources to produce and market the product	Small or restricted	Large

Pricing the Product Line

So far we have concentrated mostly on pricing individual products or services, but many firms market a complete product line or a number of interrelated product lines. For example, Kodak not only markets many different still cameras, but also film, projectors, movie cameras, screens, and other related items. These products are likely to have both demand and cost interrelationships. We saw some of the effects of this interrelationship in our earlier discussion of *price lining*.

In pricing the product line, the marketer must (1) determine the lowest-priced product and its price, (2) determine the highest-priced product and its price, and (3) determine the price differentials for all other products in the line.

The role of each item in the product line must be understood. For example, the lowest-priced item may serve as a price leader to get prospective purchasers to trade up to other items in the line. At the other end, the highest-priced item may serve to add prestige to the line. In both instances, the price of the item may bear little relationship to its cost. When pricing, the marketer seeks to cover the total cost of the full line, not necessarily on each specific item. The automobile companies have historically used prices that gave them much higher margins on larger cars, particularly on the most expensive models of the larger cars.

For the leader items in a product line, average variable cost is likely to be the floor below which prices will not be set. At prices above this level, the item makes a positive contribution to the fixed costs of the whole product line.

Both the lowest- and highest-priced item in a product line are critical for establishing the buyers' perception of the total line. With too low a price at the bottom, the whole line may be considered cheap; with too high a price at the top, buyers may perceive the line as above the mass market. Would one really take seriously a Porsche priced at $5000? This price would cheapen the whole line's image. Additionally, price differentials between items in a line should be associated with perceptual differences in the value of the products offered. The price differences must make sense to customers. There is some behavioral evidence to suggest that the price differentials should get larger as one moves up the product line.[9]

In price lining, the marketer places items in a product line at specific pricing points to cover the whole range. One twist in this approach occurs when marketers identify a pricing point that consumers will respond to, but no items exist at that position. Research and production people are then asked to develop and produce an item that will sell at that retail price. Essentially, marketers subtract all relevant channel margins for the target retail price to determine the price they must charge. Then they subtract their expected profit per item to establish the cost at which the product must be produced. This type of pricing is sometimes called *market-minus pricing* or *demand-backwards pricing.* It is common for many retail products, especially when customary pricing or price lining is used. In addition, the gift market is one where customers seem to have upper limits on spending. So products are developed for the $10 gift or the $25 gift.

PERSONAL COMPUTER EXERCISE

Setting a specific price for a product or service involves the analysis of demand, cost, and competitive dynamic. The PC exercise gives you the opportunity to explore alternative prices for an item, given data on demand, cost, and competition.

KEY POINTS

- Setting an appropriate price for a product has always been a difficult and complex task. In times of inflation and recession, this decision has become even more complex and important.

- A proper approach to setting prices involves a detailed analysis of demand, cost, and competition. The legal environment must also be clearly understood, as we discussed in Chapter 18.

- Price elasticity of demand measures the responsiveness of demand to price. It is the percentage change in quantity demanded relative to the percentage change in price. Marketers must be concerned with both primary and selective price elasticity of demand.

- The responsiveness of demand to price determines the total revenue and marginal revenue earned at various prices.

- Nonprice competition affects both the position and elasticity of a product's demand curve. In general, marketers hope to shift it to the right so that more is demanded at any price, and to make it more inelastic so that price increases will increase total revenue.

- Cost analysis is important in price-setting. Marketers need to understand fixed cost, variable cost, total cost, average fixed cost, average total cost, and marginal cost.

- Profit is maximized by setting prices at the point where marginal cost equals marginal revenue. The nature of marginal revenue and marginal cost is different for different competitive environments, and marketers must understand the competitive environment in which they set prices.

- There are different real-world approaches to setting prices. These include demand-based approaches, cost-based approaches, competition-based approaches, and integrative approaches. Demand-based methods include prestige, odd-even, price lining, and leader pricing. Cost-plus, return-on-investment, and experience-curve pricing comprise the cost-based methods. Competition-based approaches include price leadership, customary, and market-share pricing. Finally, marginal, multistage, and competitive bidding pricing are all integrative approaches.

- The unique pricing problems of new products and product lines also require special attention. In new-product pricing, skimming and penetrating are two broad alternatives.

ISSUES FOR DISCUSSION

1. In 1979, in many parts of the United States, there were long lines of cars waiting to buy gasoline. At that time, the retail price of regular gasoline was about $.75 per gallon. One analyst commented that "if the price of gasoline were allowed to reach slightly over $1.00 per gallon, there would be no shortage." Comment on the truth of this statement.

2. Distinguish between primary and selective price elasticity of demand.

3. For each of the following, indicate whether the primary and selective price elasticity of demand would likely be elastic or inelastic:

a. automobiles
b. fertilizer
c. steel ingots
d. fast-food burgers
e. a college degree

4. How is demand related to total revenues, average revenue, and marginal revenue?

5. "Price competition is ethically superior to non-price competition." Comment.

6. The retail selling price of a small appliance item was quoted as $24.00, with trade margins of 25 and 15 percent. The variable cost of the product was $6.00, while the relevant fixed costs of production and marketing were $6 million.

a. What is the breakeven point in units and dollars?
b. How many would have to be sold to earn a profit of $1 million?
c. What additional information would one need to determine the point of maximum profit?

Hint: Be sure to review Appendix B in order to answer parts (a) and (b).

7. "If you take the average total cost of a product and add a markup, this may not give you the optimal profit, but it will assure you of earning a profit on this product." Evaluate this statement.

8. Within your local retail community, identify examples of prestige pricing, odd-even pricing, price lining, and leader pricing.

9. Should cost-plus pricing be required in regulated markets such as natural gas, telephones, etc.?

GLOSSARY

Cost concepts: see the *cost analysis* section for definitions of *TFC, AFC, VC, AVC, TC,* and *MC.*

Cost-plus pricing: a price-setting method that adds a markup to average total cost or variable cost.

Customary pricing: a practice in which all competitors use certain traditional pricing points.

Demand curve: a graph of the quantity of products expected to be sold at various prices, given that other factors are held constant.

Experience-curve pricing: a price-setting method using a markup on the average total cost as forecast by the cost trends as sales volume accumulates.

Leader pricing: the practice of setting very low prices on one product with the intent of stimulating sales of it and complementary products.

Marginal revenue: the change in total revenue resulting from one additional unit of sales.

Market-share pricing: a price-setting method aimed at gaining market share.

Odd-even pricing: the practice of setting prices to end in certain odd numbers.

Penetration pricing: setting a low initial price for a new product.

Prestige pricing: a strategy based on the assumption that consumers use price as an index of prestige or quality for certain products. The result is that greater quantities are sold at higher prices.

Price elasticity of demand: the percentage change in quantity demanded relative to the percentage change made in price.

Price leadership: the tendency in some industries for one firm to take the first step at raising and lowering prices.

Price lining: the practice of placing items in a product line at specific pricing points.

Return-on-investment (ROI) pricing: a price-setting strategy aimed at reaching a target ROI.

Skimming pricing: the practice of setting a high initial price for a new product.

Value pricing: the method of setting price based upon the relative value the product gives a specific consumer or group of consumers.

NOTES

1. This section follows an excellent discussion in Kent B. Monroe, *Pricing: Making Profitable Decisions* (McGraw-Hill, 1979), pp. 29–31.

2. This section is based on John L. Forbis and Nitin T. Mehta, "Value-Based Strategies for Industrial Products," *Business Horizons,* May 1981, pp. 32–42.

3. "Strategic Mix of Odd-Even Pricing Can Lead to Increased Retail Profits," *Marketing News,* March 7, 1980, p. 24.

4. Alfred R. Oxenfeldt, "Multistage Approach to Pricing," *Harvard Business Review,* July-August 1960, pp. 125–33.

5. Monroe, *Pricing,* pp. 277–78.

6. This scheme is suggested in Monroe, *Pricing,* pp. 128–29.

7. See Joel Deal, "Pricing Policies for New Products," *Harvard Business Review,* November-December 1976, pp. 141–53.

8. See Kenneth L. Bernhardt and Thomas C. Kinnear, *Cases in Marketing Management* (Business Publications, Inc., 1988), pp. 475–77.

9. Monroe, *Pricing,* p. 156.

CASE APPLICATION 19–1

Standard Machine Corporation

Standard Machine Corporation manufactures and sells machine tool equipment. Its state-of-the-art milling, grinding, and boring machines are reputed to be among the best in the world. Standard Machine prides itself on quality, reliability, and innovation. Development and customer service are mainstays of Standard's competitive advantage. On-time delivery, installation, operator training, machine integration, and emergency services, (such as rush orders on parts), are "standard" extensions of the company's products. To assure continuance of these value-added services and the company's success, Standard Machine has long maintained a fixed-price policy for its products.

Occidental Aerospace has been one of Standard's major customers for over 20 years. During that time, Occidental purchased and installed Standard equipment in its plants on an almost exclusive basis. Standard's state-of-the-art automation played a major role in maintaining Occidental's manufacturing edge. Occidental was sold on Standard's products and services.

Other factors have recently come into play. Occidental's purchasing department is now under pressure to cut costs. Last month they adopted a more aggressive competitive bidding policy which meant that Standard would no longer be the only supplier Occidental considers. Occidental's search for cost-competitive suppliers came amidst increasing global competition. Especially of concern to Standard was "the Asian invasion," a term referring to the increased competition from Asian manufacturers, (whose lower production prices often allow lower product prices), and the dwindling market shares of U.S. manufacturers.

Occidental needed a computerized milling machine for its new training center. This machine was to be acquired under the company's new competitive bidding policy. Long-time supplier Standard Machine submitted a bid of $429,000. Two competitors submitted lower bids: Kakuchi bid $390,000 and Akita Limited bid a little over $400,000. Joanne Bracker, Occidental's purchasing agent, felt that Standard's bid was $22,000 too high. (Standard sales representatives had recently attended a trade show in Munich where other salespeople had complained of losing large accounts because of price competition. Akita was named as one of the major causes.)

Bracker was more than satisfied with Standard's past performance, knowing that the company's products and services had always served Occidental very well. She also realized that accepting a new supplier meant risking the quality Occidental had come to count on from Standard. Rumors suggested that Akita's and Kakuchi's training and service were far from superior, and none of their present customers' plants were as big as Occidentals'. Yet other U.S. accounts stood behind these two competitors, their new software looked promising, and Akita's service had been steadily improving since building field centers in the U.S. Quality and service aside, Bracker still had the new cost constraints to consider.

Standard is adamant about sticking to its traditional fixed-price policy. The company feels it is necessary in order to maintain its high standards. Yet Occidental is serious about its new cost-competitive policy. Occidental is also planning to build two new plants over the next four years, and those plants hold a lot of potential business. Bracker sees Standard's current pricing decision as an indicator of the company's attitude toward the future, not just the price of one machine. Bracker tells Standard that she cannot accept a bid over $407,000, and gives the company two weeks to submit its final bid.

SOURCE: "The Case of the Pricing Predicament," *Harvard Business Review,*" March-April 1988, p. 10–12.

Questions

1. What roles do demand, cost, and competition play in the price of the machine tools?

2. How is Standard Machine's behavior affecting the price of the milling machine?

3. What pricing action should Standard Machine Corporation take at this time?

4. What are the probable long-run consequences of Standard's decision? Why?

CASE APPLICATION 19–2

Computer Chip Pricing

The history of price changes for computer memory chips offers clear evidence that product pricing is often influenced by a wide variety of factors besides manufacturing costs. These factors include the level of competitiveness in an industry, the market share goals of each company, and governmental trade restrictions, among other things. Of course, pricing in each industry is affected by factors peculiar to that industry. Nevertheless, an analysis of the semiconductor industry permits some generalizations about pricing in high-tech commodity industries and highlights the complexity of pricing.

The computer-chip industry has some notable characteristics that strongly influence pricing. First, the learning curve phenomenon is well pronounced. For instance, with every doubling of chip production, manufacturing costs drop by about 30 percent, resulting in a steady decline in prices in the expanding chip industry. Second, demand has been very cyclical, reflecting cyclical trends in the personal computer industry, a key purchaser of computer chips. Third, competition is extremely intense because of the original attractiveness of high chip margins. Among the competitors are several Japanese electronics giants.

Beginning at a price of $30 in 1980, 64K DRAM chips had dropped to about $.75 in 1985. Learning curve-induced efficiencies caused much of this decrease. However, the "suicidal" decrease from a price of $3.50 in 1984 to $.75 a year later was largely the result of a price war among chip makers. Coming out of a chip boom in 1983, the semiconductor industry fell into a price war for several reasons. First, demand for chips was off due to a downturn in the personal computer industry and a corresponding inventory glut. Second, new capacity for the semiconductor industry, which had been contracted during the 1983 boom, was beginning to come on line. In addition, Japanese suppliers continued to flood the market with chips despite the glut, according to American semiconductor manufacturers.

Faced with low demand and fierce competition, Micron Technology Inc., a small memory chip maker in Boise, Idaho, began the price war in September 1984 by lowering prices for 64K DRAM chips from $3.40 to $1.95. Micron reasoned that it was necessary to sacrifice some profits in the short run in order to gain vital market share. By price cutting, Micron logged a flood of orders, including some from new, larger customers. Nevertheless, Micron's move was quickly met by industry competitors, and Micron's advantage was soon lost.

Although drastic price cutting damaged all competitors in the industry, no company was able to resist the downward price spiral without risking extinction. Even large firms, such as Texas Instruments, which had a relatively strong position in the market, were driven to continue the price cutting trend in order to liquidate inventories. Although restricting chip production would have propped up prices by restricting supply, no firm was willing to do so. The players in the semiconductor industry wanted to run their production lines as close to capacity as possible so that they could retain skilled workers and could continue to amortize their investment in new production equipment. As a result, all firms maintained high levels of production and drove prices of both 64K and 256K DRAM chips to new lows.

By 1984, the large Japanese producers of memory chips—Hitachi, NEC, and Fujitsu—already had a substantial advantage over U.S. competitors in manufacturing costs. In fact, as early as 1979 these Japanese firms had scared three U.S. firms—Mostek, Intel, and Advanced Micro Devices—out of the memory-chip market by achieving lower cost structures. Therefore, by the time of the 1984–85 price war, the Japanese were well prepared to follow the American lead and eventually beat American prices. Although U.S. firms had been instrumental in driving prices downward, they were quick to call "foul" when the Japanese met and exceeded their cost cuts. In desperation, several

U.S. semiconductor firms finally filed complaints with the Department of Commerce and the International Trade Commission in late 1985, charging Japanese firms with dumping memory chips in the U.S. market. As a result, Japan and the U.S. came to a trade agreement on July 30, 1986, regarding chip prices. The agreement did not set a uniform export price for Japanese semiconductor firms, however. Thus, low cost producers, such as NEC, were still allowed to maintain a cost advantage over high cost manufacturers such as Fujitsu. Nevertheless, under the terms of the agreement, prices for memory chips shot up 100–200 percent over what they had been before the agreement was reached.

Although the trade agreement was designed to improve conditions for American semiconductor manufacturers, U.S. computer makers were hard hit by the new, higher chip prices. Some computer manufacturers were even forced to discontinue some of their low-margin lines. At the same time, computer makers were also suffering from slackening demand for their products. As a result, chip purchases declined. Thus, despite the trade agreement, U.S. producers still could not make a profit on memory chips.

In 1987, U.S. semiconductor manufacturers, still in desperation, appealed to Congress to take further measures to stem the flow of Japanese memory chips into the U.S. market. The result was an embargo on Japanese chips, especially the popular 256K DRAM type. Because of the limited supply of chips, coupled with a strengthening demand for computers in late 1987, the price of 256K DRAM chips increased from about $5 in 1987 to about $14 by mid-1988. But Japanese firms were the main beneficiaries of the new, higher prices since many computer manufacturers chose to remain with Japanese suppliers because of their strong reputation for quality.

As higher prices offered U.S. memory-chip manufacturers an opportunity to recover from the devastating price decline of 1984–85, the few remaining U.S. contenders seemed to be following the lead of Intel and Advanced Micro Devices, which very early moved out of commodity chips into specialty chips. The remaining U.S. memory chip manufacturers are all diversifying into specialty chips, perhaps in advance of getting out of memory chips altogether. These firms may fear that current price increases will help the Japanese broaden their lead in memory chips by permitting higher R&D expenditures.

The critical situation that the U.S. semiconductor industry reached in the late 1980s, particularly in the area of memory chips, cannot be entirely blamed on price considerations. Quality and technology issues are also important. Nevertheless, recent developments in the industry prove that pricing has been an important factor in the fortunes of U.S. memory-chip producers, and has produced wide-ranging ramifications for the industry. For example, because of the commodity nature of the industry, price decreases were only marginally successful in increasing market share for individual firms, yet seriously impaired the profitability of the entire industry. Similarly, price increases, as dictated by government intervention, have served to benefit foreign competition as well as domestic marketers. In summary, pricing decisions, especially in highly competitive commodity industries, must be made with careful consideration of the strengths and resources of the individual company as well as the possible reactions of competitors.

SOURCES: Subrata N. Chakravarty, "We've Heard All That Before," *Forbes*, December 31, 1984, pp. 34–36; J. S. Taub, "Chipmakers Hang on as Battle Rages," *Business Marketing*, December 1985, pp. 19, 28. Bro Uttal; "The Coming Glut of Semiconductors," *Fortune*, March 19, 1984, pp. 125–40; John W. Wilson, "The Bloodbath in Chips: There's No Relief in Sight," *Business Week*, May 20, 1985, p. 63; John W. Wilson, with Michael Berger and Peter Hann, "The Chip Market Goes Haywire," *Business Week*, September 1, 1986, pp. 24–25.

Questions

1. What roles did demand, cost, and competition play in the price of memory chips?

2. What should memory chip producers do to deal with the cyclical nature of demand for their product?

3. Was Micron Technology smart to drop the price of its chips from $3.40 to $1.95?

4. What do you think of the policy of maintaining full production and unloading inventories at any price?

5. What are the possible long-run consequences of a trade embargo on memory chips?

PART
SEVEN

Marketing Applications: Situations, Trends, and Issues

20

Marketing Organization

Learning Objectives

Upon completing this chapter, you will be able to do the following:

DESCRIBE
what is meant by the terms *organizational structure, authority,* and *responsibility.*

EXPLAIN
why downsizing a marketing unit or department may have a point of diminishing positive returns.

IDENTIFY
the four distinct stages of the development of an organization.

LIST
five dimensions on which marketing organizational structures differ.

ILLUSTRATE
in graphic form the functional, territorial, product, and customer structures traditionally used in marketing units.

DESCRIBE
the advantages and disadvantages of a matrix organizational structure applied to a marketing unit.

MARKETING PROFILE

They Know How to "Roast A Pig"

In 1882 Charles Lamb wrote an essay entitled *A Dissertation on Roast Pig,* a satirical account of how the art of roasting was discovered in a Chinese village that did not cook its food. It seems that a mischievous child accidentally set fire to a house that had a pig inside, and the villagers, poking around in the embers, discovered a new delicacy. This discovery led to a series of fires and many homeless Chinese. The moral of the roast pig story is: You have to burn a whole house down every time you want a roast pork dinner if you don't understand how the pig gets cooked.

An organization that wants to cook a pig does not necessarily have to burn its house down. Although it has been assumed for years that large firms, with their many layers of managers, red tape, and bureaucratic minutiae, *suppressed* innovation and creativity, it appears possible that one can be big, structured, layered with managers, and still be considered an innovative and creative heavyweight. All it takes is the establishment of a "protected unit" that is structured so that the creative and innovative ideas of its employees provide the spark for product development.

American Airlines, Apple Computer, Campbell Soup, General Electric, Intel, Merck, Minnesota Mining and Manufacturing, and Philip Morris are recognized as structural giants that foster creativity. These eight heavyweights all are convinced that the need to innovate is essential for survival. Furthermore, they believe that markets can speak, and that listening to customers takes precedence over any bureaucratic factor. Two companies, Apple and Intel, have survived by staying on the leading edge of technology. Their structures permit ideas to be taken from inception to conclusion. Apple used the Macintosh technology to set a new course in the microcomputer area instead of following IBM's example.

In each of these eight firms, people in marketing, production, research and development, and finance are not permitted to become isolates. Business units that combine people from different disciplines encourage and require interaction. Meetings, committees, and discussion groups bring people from different parts of the structure to discuss problems and processes.

Another organization that highlights change, tinkering with the structure, and taking risks is Frito-Lay. The company is famous for its store-door delivery system. The 2,000 salespeople who call on and deliver to major outlets are called merchandisers. They use the larger trucks and trailers to transport snacks. The other 8,000 salespeople continue to be called salespeople and sell to smaller outlets and convenience stores, using the fleet of Frito-Lay vans. The separation structurally is contingent upon the need to fit service with the different needs of the outlet. Frito-Lay also arranges jobs of some marketing personnel from headquarters to work side by side with salespeople. Frito-Lay makes structural changes and shifts personnel to fit the situation.

The toughest job of all in the innovative, large company is to maintain the enthusiasm of employees to experiment and take risks. The impersonal bureaucracy has a tendency to intimidate and shut off enthusiasm.

If innovation and creative units are permitted in the structure and are rewarded, then new ideas and new products are likely to emerge. Searching for a way to permit these units to flourish is a worthy objective of any manager dealing with the question of how a firm should be structured. Learning the best way to "roast a pig" will create an organization that is both productive and profitable.

This chapter presents various organizational structures. In examining each one, ask yourself: could innovation and creativity flourish within this arrangement? Why? Understanding how to capitalize on innovation and creativity is important if a company wants to avoid facing the "roast pig" problem.

SOURCES: Craig R. Hickman & Michael A. Silva, *The Future 500.* (New York: NAL Books) 1987, pp. 209–210; "3M's Aggressive New Consumer Drives," *Business Week,* July 16, 1984, pp. 114–22; and Rosabeth M. Kanter, "Change Masters and the Intricate Architecture of Corporate Cultural Change," *Management Review,* October 1983, pp. 18–28.

In this chapter we will explain how creating an organizational structure for the marketing department affects people, their jobs, and the groups they work in. In order to structure an organization effectively, a manager must know the goals of the organization, the skills, needs, and goals of subordinates, the available resources, and the time and environmental constraints that exist; the manager must bring together human, technical, and financial resources.

Human resources are brought together in units, teams, or projects so that special skills and training can be best used. The marketing unit or department interacts with the personnel of other major functional areas. All units must act together to accomplish the overall mission and goals of the total organization. Thus, the marketing organization must be structured effectively so that it can work together with production, finance, personnel/human resources, and research and development units. The responsibilities, tasks, and goals of each functional area are different, and no one department can or should take precedence over any other.

The organization chart, a blueprint or representation of how a firm is structured, was developed by Daniel McCallum in 1854. The chart McCallum presented resembled a "tree".[1] Its roots represented a president and board of directors. The charts he developed for the New York and Erie Railroad were used to show authority and reporting relationships, and as a basis for analyzing operations. Today, organizational charts are used for similar purposes by marketing managers to examine how jobs, groups, and departments should be arranged. However, today the organizational "tree" is upside down—president and board of directors are at the top.

One constant refrain in this chapter is that no one marketing structure fits every organization. Human emotions, perceptions, and needs hinder the creation of structurally perfect arrangements of people, jobs, and groups. Instead, the focus is on the ways the human elements (for example, salespeople, product managers, and marketing researchers) fit and work together. It is also more realistic to think about alternative structures available to marketing managers. Thus, we will highlight structures that have been, are, and will be used in marketing organizations. We will show why some form of marketing organization is needed to accomplish objectives and how managers can best serve their organizations by using a *contingency perspective* to address structural decisions.

Some Important Terms

Organizational structure, the particular arrangements of people and units that give a firm its form, is obvious to anyone who has contact with organizations. Structure describes how organizations like Magnetek, GAF, Tyson Foods, and Conagua are divided into units and how these units interact. For the newly hired employee, structure is imposed when he or she is told, "You will report to Mr. Danly, the marketing department manager."

The organizational structure of a marketing unit provides a means of delegating authority and responsibility. In organizations people are expected to perform distinct roles. **Authority** gives the Heinz ketchup product manager the right to take action and use resources. Any occupant of an organizational position has the authority that goes with that position. The use of decentralized authority is highlighted in the *Marketing in Action* on KYTV, a television station.

Responsibility, or the obligation to carry out a job, is also specified by structure. Managers with authority often delegate responsibility to subordinates. Ultimate

MARKETING IN ACTION

At KYTV, Decentralized Authority Is the Key to Success

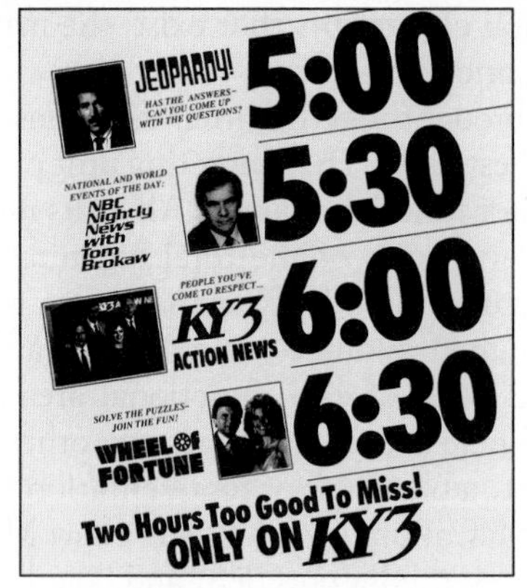

KYTV is the number one television station in Springfield, Missouri, and it looks like it's going to stay in that position for a while. Many believe that its strength is a result of its marketing structure, which promotes decentralized decision making and cooperation.

Schurz Communications, Inc., the parent company of KYTV, is different from many station owners because they let the station manager make most, if not all, of the local decisions. When problems arise, they make suggestions but leave the final word to the local station manager. They feel that this "responsible autonomy" gives the managers a feeling of ownership and pride. The system exemplifies feelings expressed by Schurz over and over again that local managers know their market better than anyone else. Someone constantly looking over their shoulder would only make them nervous.

KYTV's station manager, Stan Pederson, likes decentralization and has tried to use the same philosophy in running his station. The local marketing structure is headed by a decision-making team rather than just Pederson. The committee consists of eight key managers from business, sales, engineering, programming, promotion, news, public affairs, and production departments. Pederson claims, "I'm not smart enough to do it all," so he relies on department managers to provide information and help make decisions that are in their areas of expertise.

This round table approach has not only made decisions more effective, but has expanded the organizational awareness of the department managers. When they make decisions, they know how they will affect other areas of the business. This helps to reduce the possibility of stepping on another department's toes. The end result is a team spirit among the managers rather than competitive or adversarial attitudes.

This *Marketing in Action* demonstrates how the marketing structure and level of centralization can affect how a company performs.

SOURCE: adapted from D. Keith Denton, "Behind the Cameras and Lights," *Management World*, May/June 1988, pp. 27–28; personal communication with KYTV, June 1989.

responsibility, however, cannot be delegated and is based largely on the hierarchy of authority. The vice president of marketing at Coca-Cola can delegate authority to the advertising manager, but he or she is responsible for the ultimate success or failure of Coca-Cola's marketing program. Once the structure is in place the marketing strategy of a firm can then emerge and be implemented.[2]

An example of a marketing strategy that has emerged from a structure is found in Matsushita, a Japanese firm with sales of over $30 billion annually and over 130,000 employees.[3] Americans are familiar with its brand names Panasonic, Technics, and Quasar. The founder of the company, Konosuke Matsushita, focused on structuring the firm properly. In the 1930s, he devised a divisional structure similar to the one created by General Motors. His divisional managers (marketing, production) were given a great deal of autonomy. Matsushita made sure they all learned about each other's jobs. Every year, 5 percent of the employees were rotated to different divisions. The structure at Matsushita is always present, and the human resources are always rotated so that different views of authority and responsibility can be acquired through personal contact. Marketing personnel learn to understand how manufacturing personnel view the job by transferring into the manufacturing unit.

Three Improper Structure Decisions

There is ample evidence that as an organization grows, its competitive power can increase geometrically. Specialization of functions such as marketing, finance, and production can also increase. There is even more evidence, however, that improper structure decisions can burden a firm. Consider these three situations.

- *Situation One:* A packaged food products manufacturer eliminated the position of vice president of marketing and reassigned the various tasks to the vice president of sales, the controller, and the director of planning. Although various reasons for the organization changes were offered, the changes were made primarily to make more acceptable the company-enforced early retirement of the vice president of marketing.
- *Situation Two:* A company overreacted to an announcement of a significant new product by its principal competitor. It set up a separate marketing department to promote and sell its own product to special-industry markets. In fact, the actual threat wasn't as serious as first thought because the competitor had overestimated certain performance features of its new product.
- *Situation Three:* A small, multiproduct manufacturer decided to decentralize by setting up product divisions in its existing structure and acquiring a number of small divisions. It then found that the market and engineering requirements for the product lines were not mutually exclusive. This meant there was a great deal of expensive duplication and not enough engineering talent to solve problems. Also, there was a shortage of marketing managers to operate the numerous divisions.

Situation One illustrates one approach to solving a personnel or people problem. By reorganizing, the company disrupted an already efficient unit. Because one person is not performing a job is no reason to eliminate a function. Situation Two demonstrates the tendency, common in dynamic and growing companies, toward ill-planned, premature reorganization. Familiar patterns of authority and responsibility are disrupted, and communication systems go haywire. Situation Three shows the failure of considering the linkage between marketing and other functional areas, like engineering. The issue of human resources and the availability of managerial talent were also overlooked.

Usually these types of organization changes are caused by misunderstanding, overreaction, and guessing. Too often impulses dominate marketing organization decision making. There are no hard-and-fast rules about the structuring of a marketing group, but a marketing manager can avoid organizational pitfalls by choosing carefully from a variety of forms.

Symptoms of Inappropriate Organizational Structures

An important issue to consider in marketing structure decisions is the cost to an organization if it uses the wrong structure, given its products or services, human resources, goals, and the environment in which it operates. To be effective, an organization should adapt to its environment, be structured to allow employees to do their work to the best of their abilities, and maximize customer service to maximize the company's success.

There are certain clues about the ability of an organization to adapt and use the skills of its employees.[4]

- Those with authority and responsibility may not be able to anticipate problems. Reaction times may be too slow because information is not available. Toymaker A. C. Gilbert (American Flyer trains and Erector sets) failed to recognize market changes at first. When it did, it frantically responded and made successive product, planning, and pricing mistakes.
- Poor forecasting of costs and trends is common because of insufficient coordination across units. In 1963 DuPont developed a new material called Corfam that was supposed to replace leather in shoes.[5] DuPont analysts had estimated that, by 1982, there would be a 30 percent shortage of real leather, and Corfam would fill the gap in shoe manufacturing. However, after seven years of heavy losses, ranging from $80 million to $100 million, Corfam was dropped. Production expenses significantly above predictions were one reason for Corfam's failure. Marketing expenses were twice the forecast figure. Furthermore, the material did not breathe like leather, resulting in a hot, uncomfortable shoe. Customers did not like Corfam and were unwilling to pay a high price for it. By trying to go after the high-price market with an uncomfortable shoe, DuPont missed the mass shoe market.
- Information for making decisions may not be directed to the right point. For example, division managers may have information that quality and liability standards on their products are unrealistically high. However, because of decentralization and lack of coordination, this information may never get to the staff groups that set policy in this area. William Batten, assistant to the president of J.C. Penney, wrote a memo to the board of directors criticizing the conservatism of the company.[6] He stated bluntly that Penney's would not survive with outdated policies and programs. The memo seemed to spur the board to make changes and become more growth oriented. Interestingly, a few years later Batten was made president of J.C. Penney.
- If decision makers are overloaded with requests and information to process, their responses to their environments may slow down. PepsiCo moved quickly against the sluggish, slow reaction of Coca-Cola Co. by entering the supermarket business. Coca-Cola had about 36.5 percent to Pepsi's 28 percent of the $25 billion soft-drink business.[7] A strong advertising and price-cutting campaign caught Coca-Cola by surprise. The result was an initial loss of market share by Coca-Cola and a fierce counter-attack. In April 1985, Coca-Cola changed the taste of its soft drink—a major risk. Coca-Cola dared to tamper with a 99-year-old formula to bring out a "new" Coke. This so outraged some consumers that they demanded "old" Coke be brought back. In July 1985, a red-faced Coca-Cola Company did an about-face and reintroduced, as Coca-Cola Classic, the old formula. Today, Coke controls 56 percent of the soft drink market. Coke is now preparing for the end of common market barriers in 1992 by consolidating bottling operations throughout Europe. Coca-Cola is now an example of a company that anticipates and adapts to its environment—competitive, customer tastes, and changing economic conditions.[8]
- Management teams or ideas change too quickly. The management team of Airbus Industries involves British, West German, French, and Spanish

managers and owners. These owners share ideas, make suggestions, and attempt to compete against Boeing Co. and others. Airbus has been subsidized by four governments and is incorporated in France as a hybrid joint venture.[10] Decision making, problem analysis, and management and marketing programs are dispersed, occasionally disorganized, and involve owners and four governments. Attempts to establish the best structure to compete have often met with squabbling. Deciding how to set up the best structure is an ongoing debate with ideas flowing and changing all the time. Only one major company benefits from the internal bickering and changes—the main competitor, Boeing.

These and other symptoms can be indicators of poor marketing organization. Monitoring the impact of structure so symptoms can be picked up and problems corrected is a responsibility of the chief marketing executive. The monitoring, done over a period of time so comparisons can be made, can be accomplished by means of an interview between a superior and his or her subordinate, as part of the performance evaluation system, or during a career planning session. The manager should examine the subordinate's access to information, workload, role expectations, and relationships with colleagues and other departments. In addition to, or in place of, interviews, some organizations, such as Cooper Industries, Control Data, Teledyne, Brunswick, and Cummins Engine use attitude surveys to monitor employee attitudes. These surveys reveal information that is useful in restructuring departments, transferring personnel, developing training programs, and acquiring a general picture of what employees are thinking. Although attitude surveys cost money and require time, the potential benefits include identifying symptoms of inappropriate marketing structure.

An example of using information flow effectively in structuring an organization is found at Ballard Medical Products, Inc. The *Marketing in Action* in this section illustrates how Ballard uses its information flow to accomplish its mission.

Review Your Marketing Knowledge

- How can authority in an organization be decentralized?
- Why is forecasting of marketing trends so difficult to do accurately?
- What does *organizational structure* mean?

Downsizing Organizations: A Structural Strategy

In recent years, economic recessions, increased foreign competition, and large fluctuations in energy prices have forced many companies to reevaluate their current organizational structures and change the way they do business. One result is that many firms are trying to get "lean and mean" in their marketing efforts; at the organizational level, this downsizing has eliminated excess or "fat" positions, departments, and even divisions.[10]

To remain competitive, companies are trying to increase the amount of work per person and run the business using minimum resources. This can have a positive effect unless the cutting of jobs and opportunities is taken too far.[11] After a point, the cost-

MARKETING IN ACTION

Ballard Medical's Structure Is Not Just Boxes and Lines

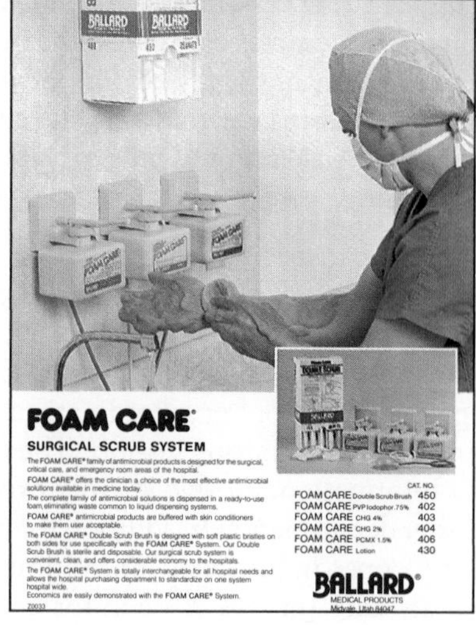

In a typical organizational chart, boxes represent functions and lines represent channels of information and/or chain of command. New products develop in R&D, R&D tells Marketing, and Marketing tells Sales. Dale Ballard, founder of Ballard Medical Products, Inc., has a different view of his company's chart. He feels that communication and product development are not functions connected by lines, but by a continuous loop. The loop includes product design, marketing, sales, service, and refinement. The direction and order that information travels in the loop is not mandated, but changes for each situation. Virtually any person in any department can enter a new product idea into the loop, and this innovative spirit helps maintain a constant flow of new products.

Although the system is very informal and loosely defined, there are three straightforward criteria for new products:

• The medical product has to be unique—what salesman Sam Maravich Jr. calls a "concept sale." Ballard Medical won't produce a clone or a commodity product to sell on its price alone.

• It has to appeal to one of the two niche markets the company sells in: the hospital intensive care unit and the operating room.

• The product should eventually be good for at least $1 million in annual sales.

In defining the boundaries of the innovation, Ballard gives employees an idea of what the organization wants to sell and what types of products would complement its current line.

Information-flow philosophies and sales techniques are as nonstandard as the product development. Customers are seen as the primary source of information which drives a relationship intensive sales program. Sales are made only to hospitals that agree to use the product for a month and agree to allow Ballard personnel to train the nurses in using the product. This approach has two purposes. First, it helps educate the nurses from old to new techniques. Secondly, it establishes an information outpost where Ballard has personal relationships with actual users of the products. This helps improve existing products and determine problems that could be solved with new products.

By including everyone in the organization as well as the customer in the information and developmental loop, Ballard is able to use an informal organizational structure with open communication to remain innovative in the medical supply industry.

ADAPTED FROM: Tom Richman, "Seducing the Customer," *Inc.*, April 1988, pp. 96–104.

---

cutting measures could weaken the organization, especially if it loses the ability to grow back in the case of an economic upturn.

In order to determine whether the cutback program is having a destructive effect on a marketing unit's productivity, morale, and/or flexibility, a manager needs to be aware of a number of indicators. Three of the indicators are external, having to do with how the company is interacting with its customers:

1. Some usually loyal customers complain that they rarely see your representatives, and they therefore have begun to try your competitor's products.

Much like a waitress with too many tables, salespeople can have too much territory to cover effectively. They are forced to either give less attention to all clients or to concentrate on the larger accounts. Usually the latter is chosen, leaving opportunities for the competition.

2. Communication and follow-through on marketing programs to end users or resellers fall off.

If salespeople are short on time, many types of services they are expected to provide after orders are placed are at risk. These services can be handling of customer complaints, marketing intelligence gathering, and communication of marketing program details. Over time their absence could force customers to look elsewhere.

3. Distribution channels show markedly less enthusiasm for the manufacturer's product lines, except the proven best sellers, and resellers are less willing to list, promote, or aggressively endorse any new product.

Intermediaries are losing confidence in the vitality and growth of the product line. They want to know that the manufacturer will provide enough "pull" marketing to sustain sales.

Three other indicators of excessive cutting back are internal, pointing to a breakdown of systems within the organization:

1. Sales agents' and marketers' morale falls as the company continues to downsize.

This falling morale is similar to fatigue following intense combat. Earlier layoffs could have produced a rallying attitude among the salespeople, but as cutbacks increase, time and resources become scarce and productivity reaches a plateau. This can lead to questioning of company policy, regret, and bitterness.

2. Market opportunity-seeking behavior by sales agents and marketers lessens considerably.

Because of the many hours that new ventures or creative marketing campaigns can take, sales and marketing personnel tend to experiment less and avoid uncharted markets. This can hurt the organization in the long run by cutting off possible avenues of expansion.

3. Individual learning curves on new products, markets, and applications become extended.

Managers have less time to train sales and marketing personnel as territories increase. One-on-one coaching is too time consuming, and feedback is less frequent. With less direction for the sales personnel, mistakes and misquotes increase.

These indicators tell marketing management that if the current situation continues, more serious problems will develop.[12] Most vulnerable are new programs, growth areas, and entrepreneurial opportunities. Thus, the company that cuts too far could have trouble sustaining current levels as markets mature or change. The key to downsizing is to cut only what is truly unnecessary, leaving enough resources to not alienate remaining forces.

One way of doing this is through concentrating on markets where premium prices are possible by upgrading or customizing current lines. For example, American Express has expanded its services for its gold card customers. In this area, they have strong market share and customer loyalty. Many oil companies have reinstated premium gasolines, stressing their detergent and performance qualities. A commodity product like gas is transformed into a premium product that can be differentiated from the others.

Another way to effectively downsize is through restructuring costs to get more marketing for the same expenditures. Sharing costs with other firms and utilizing marketing methods such as telemarketing or direct mail are ways of using funds more efficiently. Sears is testing an interactive video program in Atlanta, Chicago, and Los Angeles that allows customers to pick curtains, blinds, and shutters through video monitors. The customer chooses the product, places the order, and the goods are received usually the next day from a central warehouse, saving the company space, storage, and sales personnel expenses.

Stages of Organizational Development

Since no one best structure exists, a more realistic approach to organizations is to become aware of a firm's stage of development. For example, the structure that fits a small sandwich shop relying on business traffic in the financial district in San Francisco is not likely to fit a large, multiproduct firm like Tenneco. Stages of development can overlay the organizational continuum. The designs on one end fit smaller firms with limited market coverage, limited product lines, and a particular management philosophy, while those on the other end complement large, complicated firms that do business in widely diverse areas. Both types of firms must consider size, market coverage, product lines, managerial goals, and philosophy, but on different scales. Four stages of organizational growth have been identified.[13]

Stage I

A Stage I firm is a one-owner firm and is an extension of that person. For the most part, it focuses on a single product (sandwiches), market (a neighborhood in Philadelphia), and distribution channel (seller to buyer). The owner is an entrepreneur who has daily contact with employees and customers. He or she makes all decisions about marketing, personnel, and financial matters. As a result, the firm's strengths and weaknesses depend on the owner's style, efforts, and resources.

Stage II

Stage II organizations are larger than those in Stage I and create a need for managerial specialization. Instead of an owner who also manages everything, there is group management. Many Stage II organizations divide managerial responsibilities along classic lines: marketing, production, personnel, and so on. Within these units there may be subunits. For example, the marketing department of University Computing Systems of Oklahoma City has subunits to handle sales, dealer relations, advertising, product development, market research, and product management.

Stage III

Stage III includes organizations whose operations, though concentrated in a single field or product line, are large and scattered over a wide geographical area. All the units report to corporate headquarters and conform to corporate policies, but they still have the freedom to develop and select their own channels of distribution and to buy and sell on their own behalf on the open market.

Typical of firms in this category are breweries, steel mills, and foundries with production facilities and sales organizations in several geographically distinct markets. A unique Stage III organization is Hard Rock Cafe, an unusual multinational restaurant chain.[14] Fast food outlets such as Kentucky Fried Chicken, McDonald's, and Wendy's have exported their formulae to many areas of the world, but it's unusual for a traditional, full-service restaurant to be successful overseas. Hard Rock Cafes are found in such diverse places as Bombay, Bangkok, Amsterdam, Houston, Manila, Chicago, Stockholm, and San Francisco. Two Americans, Isaac Tigrett and Peter

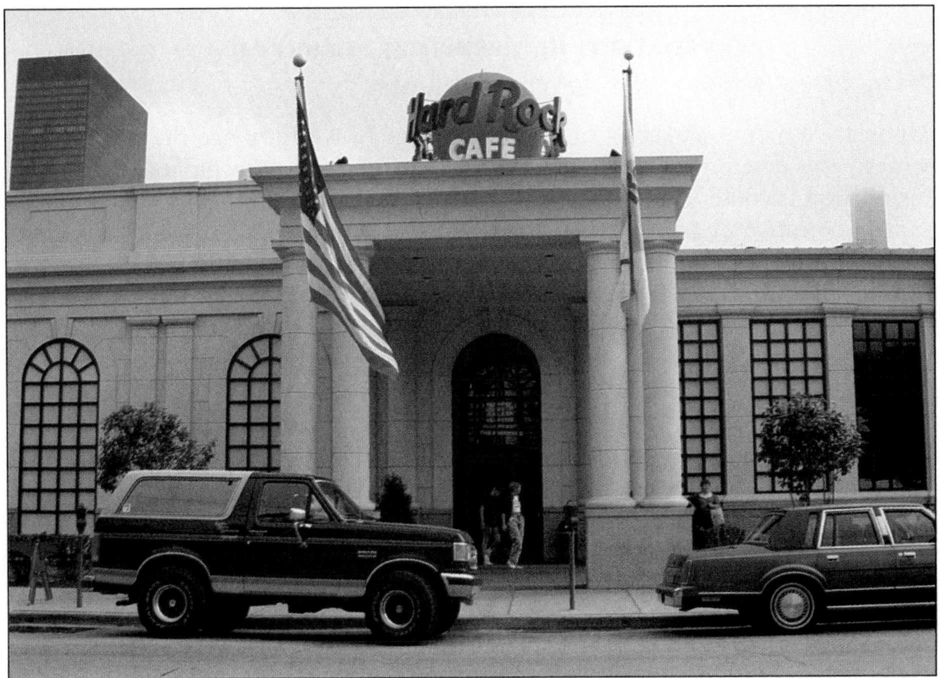

The Hard Rock Cafe, a multinational restaurant chain, serves American food with lots of noise and atmosphere on the side.

Morton, started the business in London in 1970. Each Hard Rock Cafe has a decidedly American menu and is loud and noisy, with a lot of turnover. Today, after a falling out, ex-partners Tigrett and Morton have divided the United States and the world in half. There are now two Hard Rock Cafe owners who have given local managers some autonomy to run the restaurants, but the theme and noise remain the same.

Stage IV

Large, multiproduct, multimarket, multiunit organizations decentralized along product lines comprise Stage IV. As with Stage III companies, the semiautonomous operating units report to a corporate headquarters and comply with company policies. However, each operating unit pursues its own line of business and marketing strategy. Typically, each unit is headed by a general manager who has profit-and-loss responsibility. Decisions for the units are made at the unit rather than corporate level. Some Stage IV companies are General Electric, Exxon, ITT, and DuPont.

The discussion of these four stages of development illustrates how the strategy follows the structure of the company. Organization structure changes, in most cases, when product-market-technology relationships change. A firm need not move from Stage I toward Stage IV. In fact, some firms retreat to earlier stages. For example, DuPont's textile fibers were originally grouped into five business units—rayon, acetate, nylon, orlon, and dacron.[15] As a result, five salespeople, promoting different synthetic fibers, called on customers, who understandably became annoyed at being solicited by so many people. So DuPont consolidated the units into a textile fibers department with one multifiber sales force. DuPont also set up market programs for four broad market segments—menswear, womenswear, home furnishings, and industrial products, each of which had a potential use for the five fibers.

Variations in Marketing Structural Arrangements

A primary use of a marketing organization structure is to manage the relationship between the enterprise and the market so that the long-term profitability of the organization is conserved.[16] This view needs some explanation. First, even when a primary objective of a firm is not profit, such as with a state university or public hospital, a marketing unit may be required. Nonprofit organizations must manage their relationships with users of their output (see Chapter 22). Second, managing the relationship between the firm and the market requires matching the expertise and competence of the firm with the needs of the market. If no match occurs, the primary goals of the organization cannot be achieved. An example of a mismatch occurred with an advertising campaign for Rheingold beer. The makers of Rheingold, once the top-selling beer in New York, decided to go after the working-class beer drinker. They felt there was a market for a tasty beer with good flavor and consistency that appealed to the blue-collar worker, so they produced television commercials featuring Italians, blacks, and Irish drinking Rheingold. The results were disastrous. Some ethnic groups seemed to be alienated because other groups were drinking the beer. Considerations of ethnic pride were not properly weighed in the Rheingold strategy to sell more beer.

Whether the primary task involves profit, service, good will, public responsibility, or some combination of these factors, there are major differences in the organizational structures available. Philip Sadler has identified five differences:

1. the extent to which marketing functions are clearly differentiated from other functions (marketing versus production versus finance);
2. the extent to which tasks within the marketing function are specialized (sales, advertising, marketing research);
3. the manner in which the marketing activities are grouped into organizational units;
4. the shape of the organization, as indicated by the number of subordinates reporting to a manager and the number of levels of managers (manager, assistant manager, management trainee); and
5. the organizational arrangements for managing which interface with the market.[17]

Marketing Unit Differentiation

In small firms, marketing is often only one part of the manager's or chief executive's responsibilities. The marketing function is not even represented on the organizational charts of many small firms. Larger firms have separate marketing functions defined as divisions or units on organizational charts. In most single-product companies, a marketing director or manager is the chief executive in the unit.

When a company markets more than one product, as with Colgate-Palmolive and Georgia-Pacific, it may be organized into product divisions, with each division having its own manufacturing and marketing activities. Normally, in such cases, the head of the product division has overall responsibility for marketing, but, in reality, this is usually delegated to a marketing manager who has equal status with the financial, personnel, and production managers. In very large companies, separate marketing companies may be subsidiaries of manufacturing parents.

Figure 20–1 Merck Sharp & Dohme Division

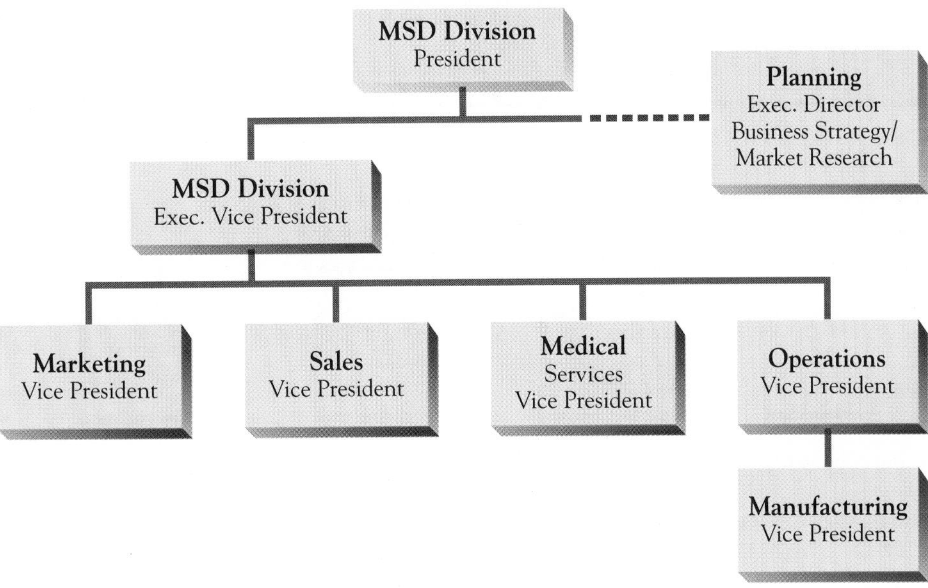

SOURCE: Courtesy of Merck Sharp & Dohme, West Point, Pennsylvania.

Marketing Unit Specialization

To manage the organization's market relationship, various task decisions must be made. In a straightforward single-product case, a marketing department will conduct a whole range of decisions and activities for a market. In a more complex multiple-product case, there may be multiple marketing units, each performing a unique set of decisions and activities. In between the simple and complex are marketing units with varying degrees of specialization. A common form of specialization is for sales activities to be separated from other marketing activities, as is presented in the Merck Sharp and Dohme organization chart in Figure 20–1. The form of specialization within the marketing unit varies from one marketing situation to another.

The Market Interface

Organizations can use a direct or indirect marketing interface, or both. Some firms sell directly to customers by means of their sales force (Avon), direct mail-order selling (Spiegel), or their own retail outlets (McDonald's). Other organizations use a third party, such as wholesalers, retailers, or agents, to bridge the gap between the marketing organization and the customer or client (Procter & Gamble). The structures used to manage the market interface vary from direct line control to advisory staff arrangements.

Figure 20–2 Marketing Division at Coca-Cola (Partial Chart)

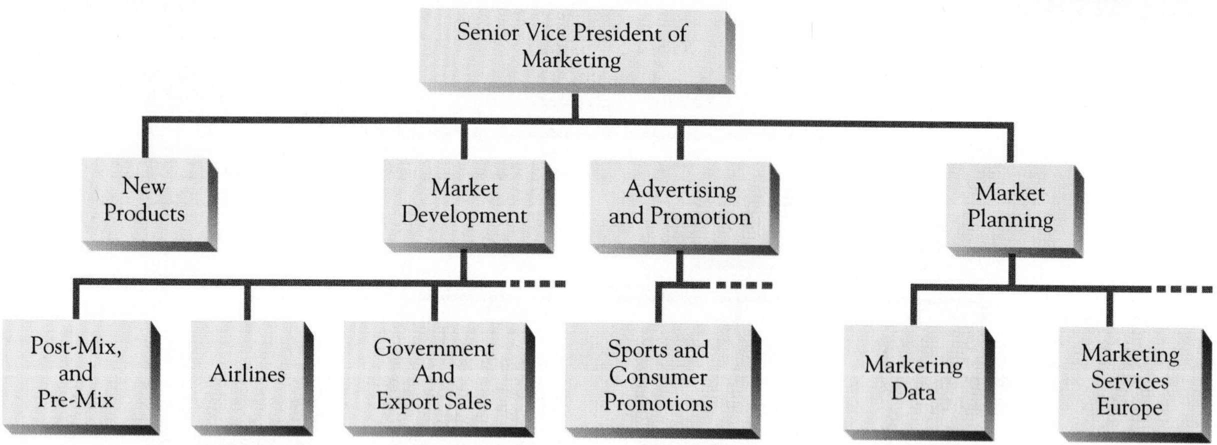

■■■■ indicates other units are part of the organization but are not shown here.

SOURCE: Courtesy of the Coca-Cola Company.

Alternative Marketing Organizational Structures

An examination of the organization charts of Borden, Levi Strauss, NCR, Greyhound, Brunswick, and Federated Stores reveals numerous types of organizational structures. Remember, no one best structure exists. The forms are usually spin-offs of traditional functional, territorial, product, and customer designs.

Functional Marketing Structure

One of the most common structural arrangements is the *functional marketing structure.* In this arrangement, managers report to a marketing manager. Figure 20–2 shows Coca-Cola's four marketing managers, for new products, market development, advertising and promotion, and market planning, each of whom reports to the senior vice president of marketing. The senior vice president reports directly to the president, as do the vice presidents of production, finance, personnel, and other functions. The simple, direct flow of communication between the senior vice president and the four managers is a major advantage of this type of structure. A shortcoming of the functional structure is that it cannot cope with increases in market size and product line. No one person is responsible for a product or market, and determining responsibility is difficult with any functional arrangement.

Today, General Foods still uses a functional structure, but it also has incorporated a territorial reporting system for its three product sectors: General Foods U.S.A., General Foods Coffee and International, and Oscar Mayer Foods.[18] These three units report directly to Philip Morris Companies.

Figure 20–3 Organization Chart of a Major U.S. Food Corporation

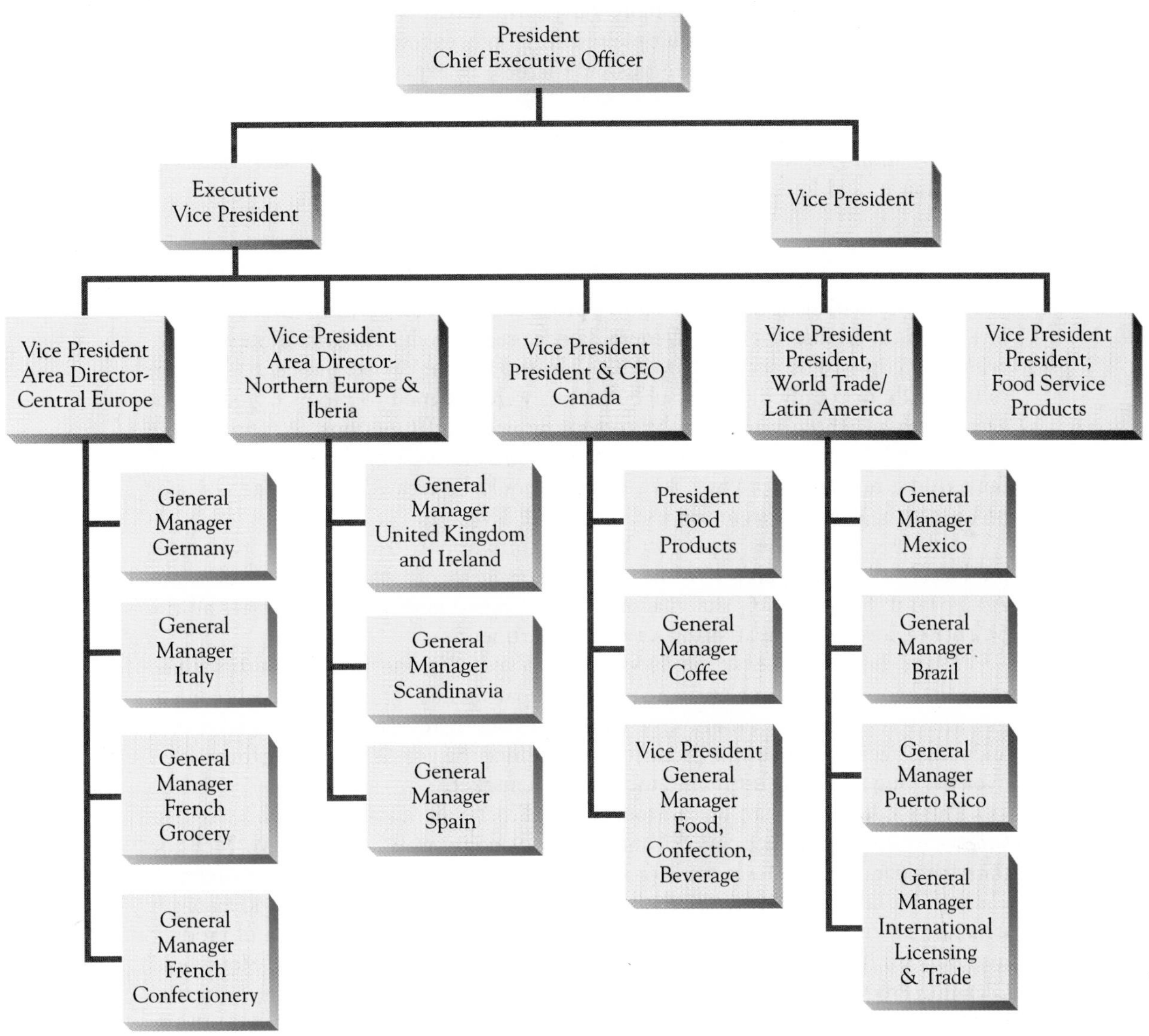

Territorial Marketing Structure

As an organization begins to serve customers who are spread over a growing geographical area, a **territorial marketing structure** becomes a viable design. With this system, the market is divided into geographical units according to certain criteria (customers, sales potential, and distance). Figure 20–3 shows an organizational chart illustrating how a firm can be divided into geographical units.

Territorial structural arrangements have several advantages. First, local markets can be cultivated by personnel familiar with the history of customers in the area. Second, the company and its sales force can respond quickly to changes in the competitive environment. Third, closer contact between managers familiar with a territory and their subordinates is possible. Finally, because management is familiar with local conditions, it can make quicker decisions.

As the product line becomes more varied, the territory structure becomes more cumbersome. The creation of multiple territorial offices results in the duplication of services and administrators, and, thus, an increase in expenses. Furthermore, competent managers must supervise territories. Sometimes duplication results in the appointment of less qualified individuals to supervisory positions. The long-run effects of having unprepared or weak managers in territories may be lost sales, damaged public image, and lower morale among employees.

Product Marketing Structure

Traditionally marketing divisions follow a **product market structure**—that is, a structure based on product families. General Foods used a product organization structure prior to changes that occurred in 1987.[19] In the General Foods product structure, substantially or totally different subbusinesses were assigned to product group managers, each of whom was given key operating and staff functions. As long as the products, markets, and customers were diverse and mutually exclusive, there was no limit to the number of product divisions that could be created. The General Foods product management system was used in its five divisions.

Anheuser-Busch uses a product-based organizational structure. It considers its product structure an appropriate and efficient arrangement for its marketing division. As shown in Figure 20–4, the vice president of brand management oversees all the product teams and the marketing services department.

When different types of products are involved, divisions are likely to include research and development and engineering departments. This allows each general manager to operate like an entrepreneur. He or she is responsible for both current and future decisions about the product market, since the goal is increasing the market over the long run, not just maintaining today's market.

The product structure was introduced by Procter & Gamble in 1927. At that time, a new soap product called Camay was not doing well, and Neil M. McElroy (later president of P&G) was made product manager with the responsibility to improve Camay's market.[20] The structure that evolved is now referred to as the brand manager structure at Procter & Gamble. The P&G brands are organized by type of product into nine similar divisions: Packaged Soap and Detergents, Bar Soap and Household Cleaning Products, Toilet Goods, Paper Products, Food Products, Coffee, Industrial Foods, Industrial Cleaning Products, and Special Products.

Product or Brand Manager's Job

The product or brand manager follows the product from its conception to the time when it is made available to consumers. He or she coordinates information relating to the product, and, for this purpose, uses all the departments in the company. Figure 20–5 illustrates how the product or brand manager is linked to various company operations. Some specific tasks of a brand manager at Procter and Gamble are the following:

1. Gather and centralize all information relating to the product.
2. Prepare product strategy alternatives.
3. Prepare forecasts.
4. Define the means of achieving the planned objectives.

Figure 20–4 Product Structure at Anheuser-Busch Co.

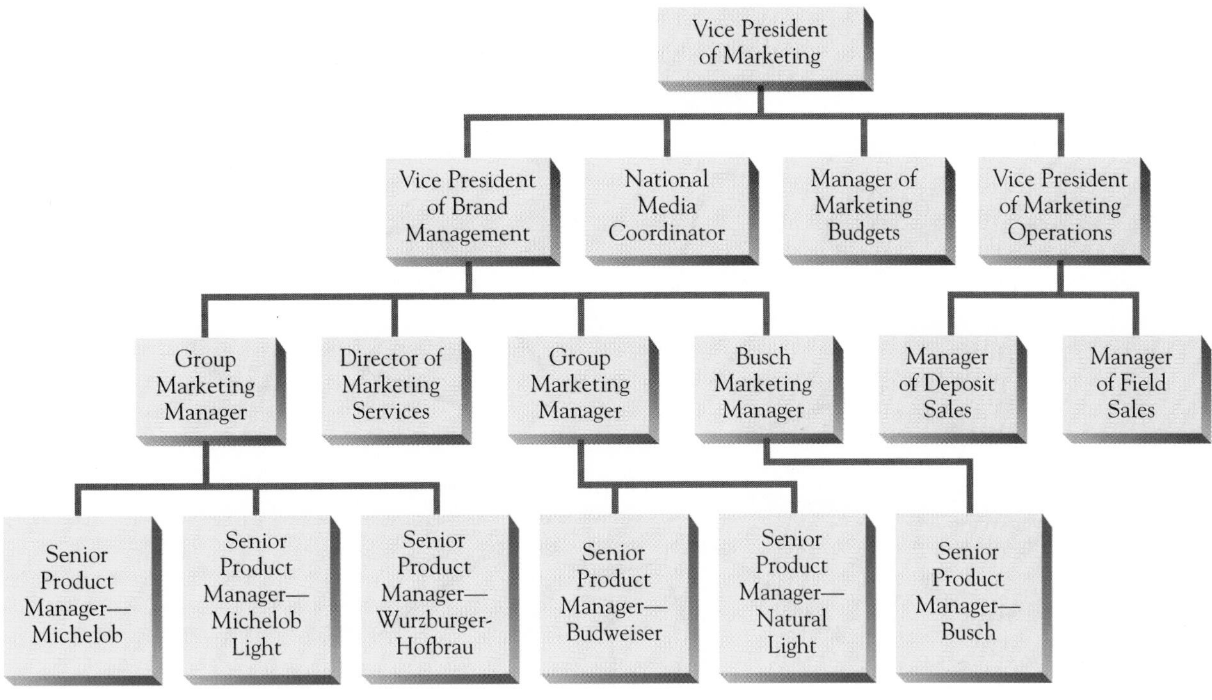

SOURCE: Courtesy of Anheuser-Busch Co.

5. Ensure the profitability of the product and monitor its life-cycle.
6. Monitor the accomplishment of programs previously drawn up.
7. Suggest ways to improve or create products.

These seven basic functions are common to both P&G consumer and industrial brand managers. However, some noticeable differences exist.[21] Consumer brand managers usually manage fewer products than industrial product managers. They also spend more time working with other specialists from market research, advertising, sales promotion, and general sales. The industrial brand manager is more technically oriented and spends large amounts of time with technicians, engineers, and research and development personnel.

One of the biggest problems with the product-manager system is that, although these managers have major responsibilities, they often have little authority. For example, product managers are responsible for sales plans, but have no authority to direct and monitor the sales force. They also have profit responsibilities, but, in some companies, they do not set prices, determine advertising expenditures, or control product expenses. They have to coax other specialists to provide the support needed to achieve desired results. This is very time consuming and detracts from other functions that must be performed. Furthermore, the ability to influence others is a major interpersonal skill that is not learned overnight. It requires a thorough understanding of oneself and of human behavior in general.

Figure 20–5 The Product Manager's Links in the Organization

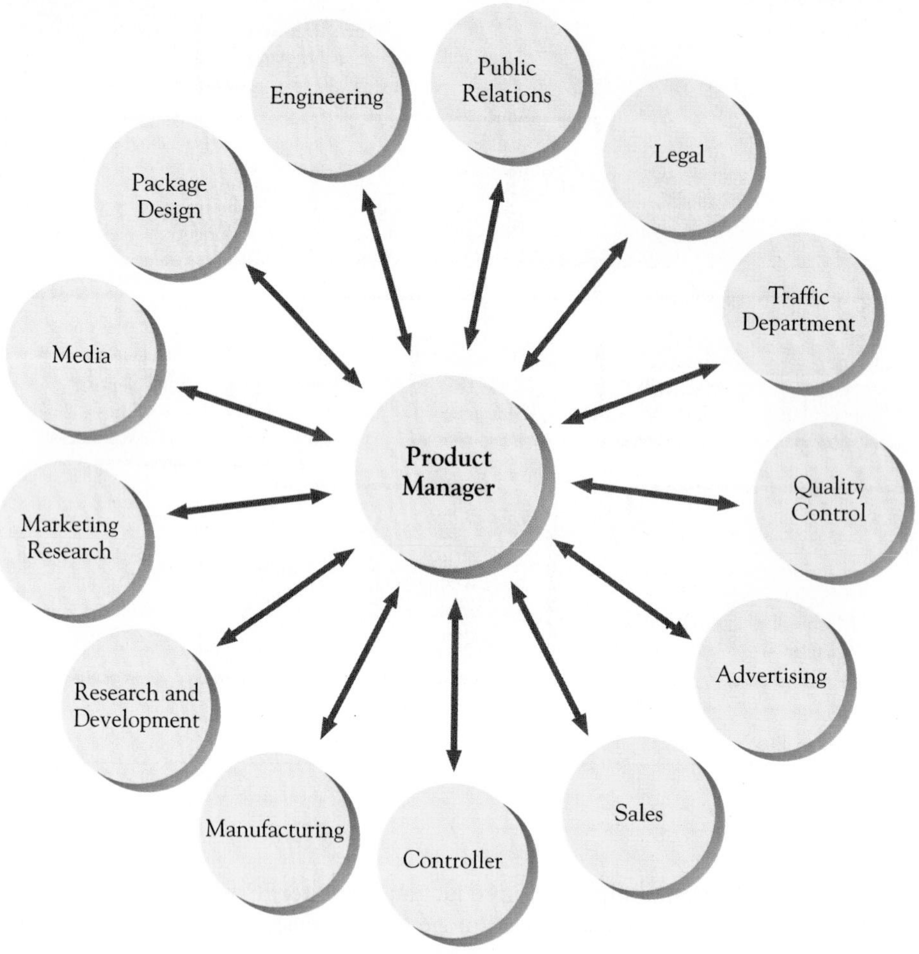

Philip Kotler identifies four courses of action an organization can take to improve or replace the product management structure.[22] First, training programs in forecasting, interpersonal skills, planning, motivation, and control can improve the ability of product managers to do the job. A second course is to switch from a product manager to a product team approach in which the product manager works with assistants to perform those activities necessary to market the product effectively. Another alternative is to eliminate product managers of minor brands and divide those brands up among the remaining product managers. This is feasible when the product line appeals to similar consumer or industrial user needs. A fourth alternative is to establish divisions around the major company products and use functional structural arrangements within divisions.

Despite the problems involved in the product or brand structure, it can be very successful. A key to its success is that the managers receive top management support and are allowed to operate within reasonable cost, planning, and resource boundaries.

Without top management support, product or brand managers have a difficult time gaining the cooperation needed in such crucial areas as advertising, marketing research, and sales.

A product line structure is used in many well-known firms, such as Lever Brothers, Max Factor, Genesco, Uniroyal, Pillsbury, and Colgate-Palmolive. For example, at General Mills the theme is that managers are in charge of, and have responsibility for, their own businesses. This management control and responsibility approach was needed because of the vast array of secondary products added to the original General Mills product line. The addition of product lines became the impetus for putting managers in charge so that control could be exercised at the managerial level.[23] It initiated the shift to a product type structure. Other firms have abandoned the product structure. In the early 1980s, it became very difficult for the chief marketing officer at PepsiCo, Inc., to coordinate all the firm's marketing efforts, since PepsiCo, Inc., was a one-product firm; its other products were related in some way to Pepsi-Cola.

One motivational advantage of using product or brand managers is that, since the manager has many tasks, he or she is faced with stimulating and challenging job activities. Boredom is not usually a problem faced by product managers, who are probably the closest thing to entrepreneurs within organizations. Unfortunately, product managers are often not given the authority that should accompany their challenging and complex tasks.

Customer Marketing Structure

Sometimes companies find their products are being used for other purposes or are being purchased by different customer groups. This may require creation of a **customer marketing structure,** in which separate sales forces are used to deal with the unexpected usage or diverse customers. For example, distribution to consumer and industrial markets usually requires different sales techniques, pricing procedures, and territorial organizations. The salesperson dealing with consumer groups in the customer-oriented structure would become familiar with their needs, attitudes, and preferences. Again, specialization is possible under a structure that permits firsthand understanding of and contact with the ultimate consumer.

Figure 20–6 presents General Electric's customer-oriented organization structure for the consumer and industrial products groups. The vice president of marketing delegates authority to two subordinate marketing managers. In terms of the marketing concept, the GE customer structure is consumer oriented, as it meets the needs of each class of customer.

The data-processing division of IBM is another unit that uses a customer-oriented structure. One group of sales personnel sells to the financial industry (brokerage houses), another to the aircraft and missile industry (firms like Lockheed and General Dynamics), still another to universities, and another to the textile industry (for example, Cannon Mills and West Point Pepperell).

Market-Centered Structure

Mark Hanan urges companies to structure their business to fit their markets.[24] He uses the term **market-centered** to describe the wide range of structural forms that center on a group of customer needs, rather than a region, product line, or function. *Market-centered* also describes an organization that is decentralized by market. In effect, a market center is a profit center.

Figure 20–6 General Electric: Partial Organization Chart

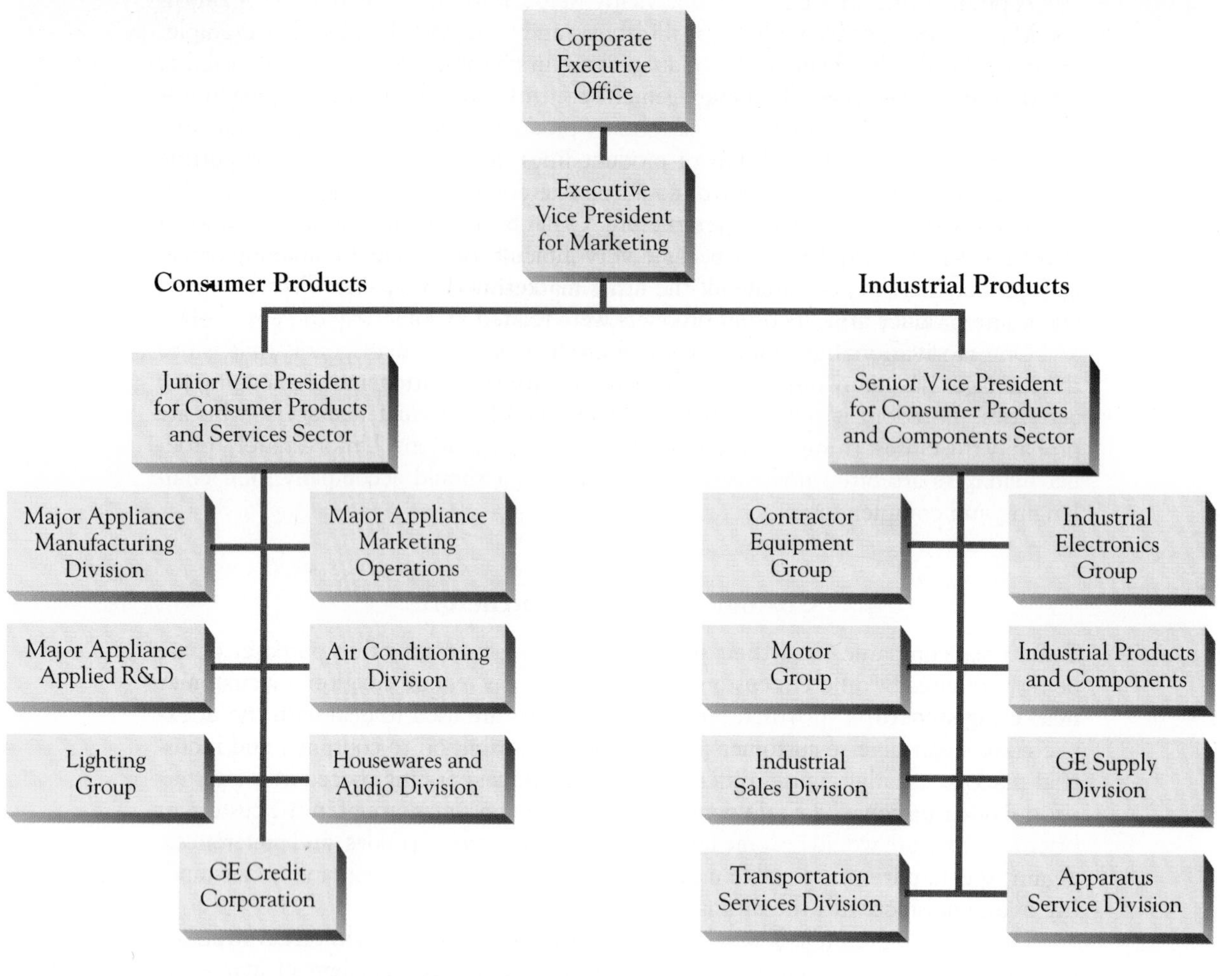

SOURCE: Courtesy of *General Electric 1983 Annual Report.*

Organizations in the following situations are suited for the market-centered structure:

1. *Market leadership is threatened by a competitor.* Market-centering can restore a competitive advantage by improving knowledge of customer, distributor, and retailer needs.
2. *New-product famine has hit the firm.* Market-centering can stimulate new ideas because the firm's technical specialists receive more information about market needs.
3. *A product manufacturer wants to diversify into high profit margin services or to market systems of related products or services.* Again, market intelligence is valuable in making this transition.

4. *A manufacturer who has been selling product performance benefits shifts marketing strategy to feature the financial benefits of customer profit improvement.* Market-centering makes it easier to gather information on how customers make their profits.
5. *A marketer wants to attract a more entrepreneurial manager.* Market-centering offers an individual manager wide responsibility and a variety of supervisory duties.[25]

Market-centering has been adopted by Xerox, Mead, PPG Industries, Borg-Warner, Monsanto, Revlon, General Electric, and NCR.

McKinsey Corporation, a consulting group, provided General Electric with a plan to restructure its operations.[26] The plan was to superimpose a **strategic business unit** (SBU) structure on the existing line hierarchy structure. For ongoing operations, managers would report according to the group-division-department structure. Only those units designated as SBUs would prepare strategic plans. The general characteristics of an SBU were defined as: a unique set of competitors in external markets, a unique business mission and strategic plan, and autonomy to make decisions crucial to the success of the business.

Of the original 43 SBUs at General Electric, four were groups, 21 were divisions, and 18 were departments. This resulted in the number of strategic business plans being reduced from 190 (under the traditional structure) to 43 (under the SBU structure).

Review Your Marketing Knowledge

- Why are structural experts so convinced that no one best structure exists?
- What are some weaknesses of organizing along functional market lines?
- What kind of job tasks does a product manager perform?

Divisionalization

Some successful companies grow beyond the size at which organizational structuring by market, territory, product, or some combination of these is adequate. One solution to this situation is to break the business up into divisions representing separate business units. Each unit is responsible for profits, and in many cases large divisions have their own marketing departments.

Division marketing may also be structured by product, market, customer, or some combination. Often a new division starts with a functional organization, but changes to one structured by product, customer, or market as business increases.

The divisional structure raises the issue of whether any marketing functions should be performed at the corporate staff level. Some companies maintain a minimum marketing service structure at the corporate level. For example, market research, advertising, and media planning services are provided to each territorial division in Los Angeles, New York, Houston, and Pittsburgh from a corporate staff group in Chicago. The decision whether to maintain some corporate-level marketing staff services depends primarily on the size of the division. If a division is large enough to afford its own marketing structure, it will usually have one.

Matrix Structure

The functional structure is efficient for establishing specialist resources but weak for integrating functions. On the other hand, divisionalization introduces effective integration at the expense of resource specialization. The **matrix organization** seeks the best of both. Firms such as Unilever, Shell, Dow Chemical, Texas Instruments, and TRW use various forms of matrix organizational structure.

The matrix approach began in the United States aerospace industry. A *matrix* is any organization that employs a multiple "boss" arrangement. For example, a person could have a *functional* boss and a *product* boss. Matrix structures have been used in manufacturing, service, professional, and nonprofit organizations. A marketing specialist is a member of two units, one of which is, more or less, a permanent home (the base function, such as marketing) and the second is a temporary home (the product group). Thus, the matrix structure combines the idea of specialized departments with the idea of self-sufficient, somewhat autonomous units.

In an organization that uses a matrix structure, one must cut across departmental boundaries to get a job done. A team working on a job is comprised of a group of specialists, so the ability to work together is very important. Figure 20–7 illustrates how teamwork among production, marketing, and finance specialists (functional) is required to complete projects. The key feature is that the functional and product lines of authority are overlaid. Managerial authority over people in each cell (indicated by the circles) is shared by the product and functional managers.

The matrix structure has had some application in large-scale retailing organizations. In a typical retailing matrix structure, the sales unit manager reports to two bosses, the relevant merchandiser and the relevant operations manager. The responsibilities and directions of each boss are spelled out.

Once a matrix structure is in place and people accept the processes and procedures, greater harmony between specialists is likely. In a matrix, it is difficult for one group to gain more power than the other, so specialists learn to accommodate each other. A recurring complaint, however, is that people are confused about who they report to and for what. Since there is shared authority, it is hard to reach decisions. The matrix is certainly not one of the simplest arrangements used to structure an organization.[27] Therefore, most applications at the matrix structure are limited to a particular part of the organization rather than used in the entire firm. Many multinational firms have moved away from the matrix structure because it is considered too rigid for responding quickly to far-flung markets. The matrix is considered by many multinationals to be too bureaucratic.[28]

The Contingency Theme

Many other marketing organizational structures could be discussed, but it is more important to tie together the main points already raised. Managers today appear to need what experts call a **contingency perspective** to organize marketing units and departments. This perspective holds that an organization's structure should be consistent with its needs. Lawrence and Lorsch put it this way:

> *During the past few years there has been a new trend in the study of organizational phenomena. Underlying this new approach is the idea that the internal functioning of organizations must be consistent with the demands of the organization task, technology, or external environment, and the needs of its members if the organi-*

Figure 20–7 Matrix Organizational Structure

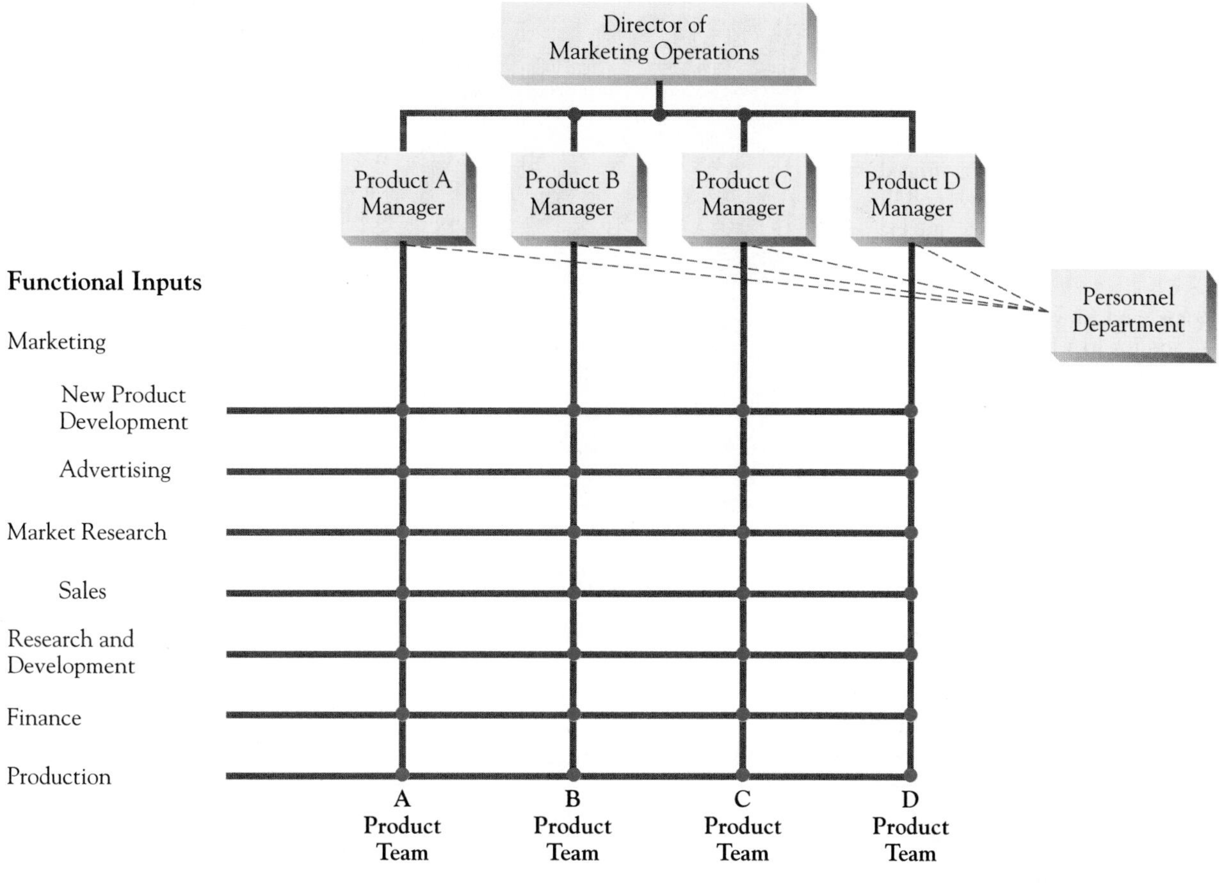

zation is to be effective. Rather than searching for the panacea of the one best way to organize under all conditions, investigators have more and more tended to examine the functioning of organizations in relation to the needs of their particular members and the external pressures facing them. Basically, this approach seems to be leading to the development of a "contingency" theory of organization with the appropriate internal states and processes of the organization contingent upon external requirements and member needs.[29]

The contingency perspective assumes a functional relationship between environmental factors (markets, competition, political and legal requirements), employees' needs, and the appropriate structure to optimize goals. Direct causality between environmental and human factors and a specific structural arrangement is not implied by the contingency perspective. In other words, environmental or human needs do not cause the structure to develop. There is merely a relationship between these variables.

An example of a contingency based perspective involves the development of full- and part-time employees in marketing and other units working out of their homes.

MARKETING IN ACTION

A Growing Number of Professionals Are Moving Into Their Homes

Until recently, working out of your home meant that all the company records, client lists, and other resources were out of reach. But today, with telecommunication capabilities via computers and modems, low-priced fax machines for hard copy and image transmissions, and an abundance of overnight delivery services, the gap has been bridged. Professionals can now stay home and stay productive as well. According to a 1985 study by the U.S. Labor Department, as many as 2.24 million people (excluding homemakers) work entirely in their homes. The professions include computer salespeople and middlemen, programmers, systems analysts, professors, research scientists, physicians, management consultants, and stock brokers. The largest groups were technological (593,000), managerial (553,000), and service (504,000).

Although many of the professionals-at-home were self-employed, large corporations can also benefit by offering home employment as an option. The following represent some of the benefits:

Flexible Work Hours: A salesperson or distribution agent can choose his or her schedule from a 24-hour day and 7-day week. If, for instance, a salesperson from a regional sales division feels most productive from 10:30 AM to 4:00 PM, he or she can work then. This type of schedule allows the salesperson to work during his or her peak productivity.

Freedom: Many marketing personnel who work at home enjoy the freedom they gain and their ability to control their lives. Autonomy is important to some individuals, and not being restricted by a formal routine and reporting relationship is satisfying.

Productivity: Some employers that use home workers claim that the home workers are almost 60 percent more efficient than office workers. Office politics also seem to be reduced when all the correspondence is limited to the telephone and writing.

Other benefits are limited to certain groups such as single parents, elderly, and disabled persons. For single parents or women on maternity leave, marketing work can be done at home, saving the cost of child care and using time that would be otherwise lost. Employees that must restrict their movement, such as elderly, handicapped, or injured employees, can also be employed at home, where they can juggle daily needs with work.

These benefits are not without their costs, and the following represent reasons why home workers might not jump at the chance not to come into work every day.

Costs: There are several hidden costs involved with working out of your home, including telephone and utility bills, higher taxes, office furniture, and mail and delivery services. Sometimes these can offset the savings in gas, parking, and travel time associated with an office job.

Career Progression: Staying at home can have an effect on how others perceive you. In some circumstances, the day-to-day contact helps to remind your employer of your abilities and thus qualifications for advancement. For the self-employed, working out of the home could mean that you lose some credibility and possibly not be taken seriously as a business.

Social Isolation: Sometimes the social aspects of the office or factory can be a benefit, especially for young singles. Sometimes this interaction with friends and associates can be important to the job itself, such as a group of engineers solving complex problems.

Self-Perception: For some people, working at home gives them a feeling that they are not really working. For them, the commute to the office helps them separate their home roles and their work roles. In a work-at-home situation, the distinction could be difficult to make and therefore decrease productivity. The work-at-home arrangement can be an effective way to organize some jobs. If this type of structure and working arrangement is productive, then it can be used as another alternative to matrix, functional, product, or other designs. Since the work-at-home structure is not suited for everyone or every job, it can be referred to as a contingency based organizational practice.

ADAPTED FROM: Anonymous, "Working Out of Your Home," *Hispanic Business,* July 1988, pp. 16–24.

Yes, they are part of the organization, but they are not expected to be at work in an office or on the factory floor. The *Marketing in Action* in this section emphasizes the contingency features of working at home to help satisfy needs of employees.

A classic study by Alfred D. Chandler highlights the value of using a contingency perspective to analyze and implement marketing organization structures. Chandler set out to test the hypothesis that organization structure follows managerial strategy. He studied the development of four American firms: DuPont, General Motors, Standard Oil of New Jersey, and Sears, Roebuck, gathering data from company records, interviews, reports, and correspondence.[30] Each company eventually became less centralized in response to environmental changes, employee needs, and advances in organizational structure practices. DuPont went from a centralized to a decentralized structure in order to accommodate a management strategy of product diversification. General Motors was originally run by one man with iron control, William C. Durant. In 1920 it switched to Alfred P. Sloan's organization plan, which called for centralized control over decentralized operations. Standard Oil of New Jersey moved toward decentralization on a piecemeal basis. Sears, Roebuck started off with a decentralized structure, but this proved unsuccessful because of unclear channels of authority and communication and poor planning. Next Sears tried a highly centralized structure, but this also proved ineffective. Gradually the company returned to a decentralized structure.

Although Chandler's research was concerned with the relationship between managerial strategy choices and structure, he made clear that some structures are more effective than others.

> *As long as enterprise belonged in an industry whose markets, sources of raw materials, and production process remained relatively unchanged, few entrepreneurial decisions had to be reached. In that situation such a weakness was not critical, but where technology, markets, and sources of supply were changing rapidly, the defects of such a structure became more obvious.*[31]

Besides the importance of external environmental factors, Chandler recognized that internal environmental variables such as territorial expansion, product diversification plans, and growth rate affected the strategy and structure adopted by the companies studied.

No matter what the future holds, the flexibility of the contingency perspective makes it a more feasible structural decision-making approach than searching for an elusive "one best" marketing organization. Today's slow-growth economies require that various factors, previously given minimal thought, be given more attention now. Lower productivity, high inflation, energy conservation, and diminishing resources are shaping marketing organizational structures.

Peter Drucker summed up the importance of structure extremely well:

> *The simplest organization structure that will do the job is the best one. What makes an organization structure "good" are the problems it does not create. The simpler the structure, the less that can go wrong. . . . Above all, the architect of an organization needs to keep in mind the purpose of the structure he is designing.*[32]

It is Drucker who also predicts that the organizations of the 1990s will resemble a symphony orchestra.[33] In an orchestra, each of the musicians is a "high-grade specialist" taking direction straight from the conductor, or CEO. There are no intermediaries or conductors in the middle. This is the simple, flat organization that permits rapid response because fewer layers have to be involved in decision making.

Personal Computer Exercise

The allocation of marketing resources among product managers or strategic business units is an important issue in organizational structure. This PC exercise will allow you to allocate a yearly budget across a company's business groups. What system did you use to decide which groups should receive increases in funds?

KEY POINTS

• Despite some claims to the contrary, there is no one best way to structure an organization.

• In making structural decisions, managers consider environment, strategy of the organization, and resources of superiors and subordinates.

• Some organizations move through four stages of development, from small, one-owner operations to large multimarket, multiproduct, multiunit companies.

• A variety of structural arrangements are used in organizations. Some of the more publicized include the functional, territorial, product, customer, and matrix. Each structure has its own advantages and disadvantages.

• The contingency approach, in which structural decisions are based on careful diagnosis of internal and external environmental forces on organizations, has become popular within organizations. Chandler's work illustrates the contingency approach. There is also a contingency perspective found in permitting employees to work from their homes.

ISSUES FOR DISCUSSION

1. Is a product manager in the matrix structure the same, in terms of power, authority, and responsibility, as a product manager in a product arrangement structure?

2. How could structure get in the way of innovation and creativity being displayed by a firm's employees?

3. Does a contingency theme of structure mean that there is no one best way to design a marketing department?

4. Why do some people believe that an organization's structure is the best control mechanism that a firm has in its arsenal?

5. What are some of the costs of downsizing a marketing department?

6. You probably frequent some fast-food restaurant—McDonald's, Wendy's, Kentucky Fried Chicken. Observe the activities in that restaurant and then draw an organization chart. Ask to speak with the manager and compare your chart with what he or she describes as the structure. How accurate were you?

7. What are some of the problems associated with having an improper structure?

8. What would be some of the differences in managerial activities found in a centralized versus a decentralized organizational structure?

9. Does an organization chart such as that presented in Figure 20–7 show how much autonomy each of the four product managers has? Explain.

10. Suppose you were starting a business. How would you arrange its structure? What factors would you consider in developing the structure?

GLOSSARY

Authority: The right to take action and to use available resources.

Centralization: The holding or maintaining of the authority and responsibility to make decisions at a central point or with one person or group.

Contingency perspective: A view that the structure of any organization must be consistent with the demands of the organization's tasks, technology, environment, and members' needs. It argues against the adoption of a one best way design.

Customer marketing structure: A structure that uses a specialized sales force to deal with diverse customer groups.

Decentralization: Pushing downward and delegating decision-making responsibility in the organizational hierarchy.

Downsizing: The elimination of levels, units, groups, or individuals in an organization.

Functional marketing structure: A structure in which specialists report directly to a marketing manager.

Market-centered: A term to describe structural forms in which customer needs are the center of the business. Such forms use decentralization by markets and make each market center a profit center.

Matrix organization: An organization that uses a multiple command system. Individuals work in a permanent unit (for example, marketing) and a temporary unit (for example, organized by product).

Organizational structure: The arrangements of people and units that give a firm shape and form.

Product manager: A person with the authority and responsibility to follow a product from its conception to its availability to consumers.

Product marketing structure: A structure established on the basis of products or product families.

Responsibility: The obligation that a person has to carry out a job.

Strategic business unit (SBU): A unit whose manager has complete responsibility for integrating all functions in a plan being used to meet competition. General Electric uses this type of unit.

Territorial marketing structure: A structure that is based on dividing the market into geographical units.

NOTES

1. Alfred D. Chandler, Jr., "Origins of the Organization Chart," *Harvard Business Review,* March-April 1988, pp. 156–157.

2. Thomas J. Peters, "Strategy Follows Structure: Developing Distinctive Skills," *California Management Review,* Spring 1984, pp. 111–25.

3. Milton Moskowitz, "*The Global Marketplace*" (New York: Macmillan, 1987) pp. 348–349.

4. Some of these symptoms are discussed by Robert Duncan, "What Is the Right Organization Structure?" *Organizational Dynamics,* Winter 1979, pp. 59–80.

5. Robert F. Hartley, *Marketing Mistakes* (Grid, 1976), pp. 59–80.

6. Hartley, *Marketing Mistakes,* pp. 71–80.

7. Al Ries and Jack Trout, *Bottom-Up Marketing* (New York: McGraw-Hill, 1989) pp. 111–113.

8. Gary Hector, "Yes, You Can Manage Long Term," *Fortune,* November 21, 1988, pp. 65–76.

9. John Rossant, "A Reorganization at Airbus May Never Get Off the Ground," *Business Week,* May 16, 1988, p. 56.

10. A. J. Magrath, "Are You Overdoing Lean and Mean?" *Sales and Marketing Management,* January 1988, pp. 46–50.

11. Anne B. Fisher, "The Downside of Downsizing," *Fortune,* May 23, 1988, pp. 42–52.

12. "America's Leanest and Meanest," *Business Week,* October 5, 1987, pp. 78–84.

13. For a more detailed discussion of the four stages, see Arthur A. Thompson, Jr., and A. J. Strickland III, *Strategy Formulation and Developmentation* (Business Publications, 1984) pp. 202–207.

14. Milton Moskowitz, *The Global Marketplace* (New York: Macmillan, 1987) pp. 248–50 and Robert Heller, *The Naked Market: Marketing Methods For The 80's* (London: Sedgewick & Jackson, 1985).

15. E. Raymond Corey and Steven H. Star, *Organization Strategy: A Marketing Approach* (Division of Research, Harvard University Graduate School of Business Administration, 1971) pp. 23–24.

16. Philip Sadler, "Task and Organization Structure in Marketing," in Eric J. Miller, ed., *Task and Organization* (John Wiley & Sons, 1976) pp. 173–92.

17. Sadler, "Task and Organization," p. 177. Each of these points is discussed in this source.

18. Calvin Sims, "General Foods to Split Itself," *The New York Times,* August 19, 1987, p. 21.

19. Sims, 1987, p. 21.

20. Philip Kotler, *Marketing Management: Analysis, Planning, and Control* (Prentice-Hall, 1988), p. 81.

21. Kotler, *Marketing Management,* p. 87.

22. Kotler, *Marketing Management,* p. 89.

23. Ann M. Morrison, "The General Mills Brand Manager," *Fortune,* January 12, 1981, pp. 99–107.

24. Mark Hanan, "Reorganize Your Company Around Its Markets," *Harvard Business Review,* November-December 1974, pp. 63–74.

25. Hanan, "Reorganize Your Company," pp. 63–74.

26. Francis Joseph Aguilar, *General Manager in Action* (New York: Oxford University Press, 1988) pp. 262–266.

27. Thomas J. Peters and Robert H. Waterman, *In Search of Excellence* (Harper & Row, 1982).

28. Fred V. Guterl, "Goodbye, Old Matrix," *Business Month,* February 1989, pp. 32–38.

29. Jay W. Lorsch and Paul R. Lawrence, *Studies in Organization Design* (Irwin, 1970) p. 1.

30. Alfred D. Chandler, Jr., *Strategy and Structure: Chapters in the History of the American Industrial Enterprise* (MIT Press, 1962).

31. Chandler, *Strategy and Structure,* p. 41.

32. Peter Drucker, *Management: Tasks, Responsibilities, Practices* (Harper & Row, 1974), pp. 601–602.

33. Neal E. Boudette, "Networks to Dismantle Old Structures," *Industry Week,* January 16, 1989, pp. 27–31.

Structural Changes at Beatrice

Millions of Americans who watched the 1984 Olympics were introduced to a $9 billion company that went public—Beatrice. Until then, Beatrice had been a faceless conglomerate of vaguely related businesses: Swiss Miss Cocoa mix, Samsonite luggage, La Choy Chinese food, Playtex intimate apparel, and Tropicana Orange Juice were household names, but the identity of their parent company was not. Consumer awareness levels of the Beatrice name were a paltry 4 percent, compared to an impressive 98 percent for General Foods.

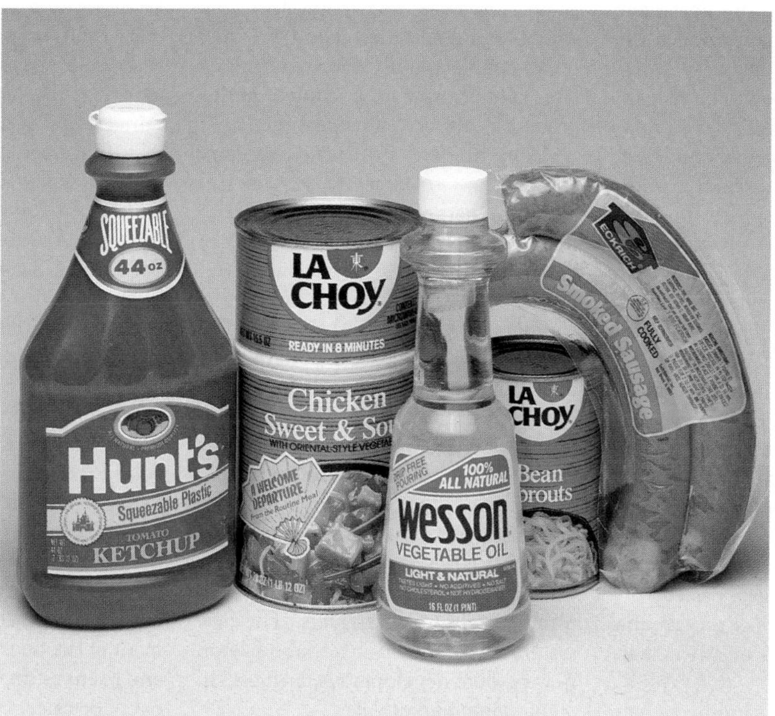

In an effort to become the world's "premier marketer," Beatrice employed a "cluster" advertising campaign. Using the tagline, "Beatrice—you've known us all along," Beatrice ads featured a kaleidoscope of its best-known brands. The name "Beatrice" was repeated as each product was displayed. The corporate logo, a red stripe, was displayed on many of the company's products. Corporate recognition did increase as thousands of consumers were amazed by the vast number of products Beatrice owned. Where did this huge conglomerate come from, and where was it going?

In 1894, George Hoskill and William Bosworth formed a partnership in Beatrice, Nebraska, to buy butter, eggs, and poultry from farmers. By 1899, Beatrice was churning out 940,000 pounds of butter a year. In 1943, Beatrice bought its first nondairy business: La Choy Food Products; by 1972, they were big enough to buy Swift-Eckrich meats; and, in 1978, they acquired Tropicana Foods.

Beatrice employed this acquisition strategy with increasing intensity throughout most of the 1960s and 1970s. Diversification was a key concept of the era, and Beatrice took it to heart. By the time Jim Dutt took over as CEO in 1979, Beatrice was a collection of 430 disparate businesses. Its small, financially minded corporate staff bought money-making businesses, consolidated the balance sheets, and earned attractive profits. Only those firms headed by independent-minded entrepreneurs were brought into the fold. Commodity-oriented businesses were excluded because of unpredictable price swings. Companies in head-on competition with such powerhouses as Kellogg's and Campbell Soup were avoided.

Beatrice appeared to be a success story. The company's extensive buying spree had led to 26 years of consecutive increases in sales and earnings, indicating that Beatrice's diversification strategy was a great success, at least on a short-term production - oriented basis. These impressive figures also hid one of Beatrice's most serious underlying problems: the absence of a cohesive marketing program. The recession of the early 1980s took its toll, and by 1983 Beatrice saw its earnings drop 89 percent to $43 million. It was obvious that changes were imperative.

The company examined the current marketplace as well as its operations. Their findings were alarming. Many of their units were not in categories with bright growth prospects, were not low-cost producers, and often were not market leaders. The giant conglomerate's overall success had masked these significant divisional problems.

Strategic changes took hold. Beatrice focused its product mix into six operating groups: Refrigerated Food/Distribution Services; Beverage; Grocery; Consumer/Commercial; Specialty Chemicals; and International

Food. The days of "buying earnings" were gone. The new acquisition criteria at Beatrice became, "Are they (potential acquisitions) viable from a long-term perspective in the marketplace?" Over 50 companies were slated for divestiture. Old acquisitions that were not on the marketing fast-track or did not fit into the new product mix were sold. Adopting a popular 1980s' strategy, Beatrice wanted to be "a lean, mean fighting machine."

Decentralized management had been like a religion at Beatrice for years. Management decided to turn the company's 450 autonomous profit centers into a centralized marketing giant with 25 strategic business units. The maze of 450 profit centers, reporting to 81 groups, reporting to 22 divisions, reporting to corporate headquarters in Chicago, was simplified. Formerly independent companies were consolidated into the six major operating groups. Outsiders were hired to form a corporate level (top) marketing department. The company's financially oriented middle managers passed control on to this new team of professional marketers. This was a massive structural rearrangement.

Beatrice felt its streamlined chain of command would help business units react more quickly to changes in the marketplace. This had been a major problem in the old company. But success depended on coordination among the six units themselves, as well as coordination with the new corporate marketing department. The new lines of authority were still unclear, and this uncertainty bred insecurity. The new structure required as very different attitude from divisions that had previously operated autonomously. The corporate office was packaged as a "resource" in an attempt to decrease divisional resentment over lost independence.

The new structure increased efficiencies. Beatrice reduced its number of advertising agencies from 140 to seven. Each agency was responsible for one particular medium. For example, Bozell & Jacobs bought all radio time for any Beatrice brand. This allowed Beatrice to concentrate its media buying to get price discounts. Similar products, which had formerly competed against each other in the market, could now be joined to produce one strong consumer line. Food brokers, trade contacts, and distribution systems could be shared. Lucrative, multiproduct deals were now possible.

Doug Stanard, corporate secretary and assistant to James Dutt, and Hal Handley, marketing chief, pointed out that decentralized management was not dead. Profit responsibility now fell on business units instead of individual companies. Each unit set its own ad and promotion budgets, but the corporate group now had the power to review the budgets or "advise" them on changes. This change did alleviate one major problem that had plagued the old corporation. The company's previous emphasis on consistently producing profits each quarter had kept managers from spending sufficient marketing funds to underwrite new products. The new system incorporated internal focus on new product development, a "must" in a changing marketplace.

The restructured Beatrice Co. continued to develop and prosper until 1986, when the company was sold to Kohlberg Kravis Roberts & Co. for $8.2 billion in one of history's largest leveraged buy-outs (LBO). Beatrice's self-contained operating units, each with its own corporate headquarters, had made it a prime target for corporate raiders. One or more units could easily be broken off and sold without disturbing the respective unit's operation or the rest of the company.

Feeling that the parts were more valuable than the whole, KKR placed Donald P. Kelly in the CEO's seat and Kelly proceeded to dismantle the Beatrice empire. In 1986, Playtex International was sold to its management for $1.25 billion; Los Angeles Bottler was sold to Coca-Cola for $1 billion; Americold was sold to its management for $480 million; Meadow Gold was sold to Borden for $315 million; Avis was sold to Wesray Capital for $263 million (Wesray then resold the company to Avis employees for $750 million). In 1987, International Foods was sold to the TLC Group (The Lewis Co.) for $985 million; E–II Holdings which included the company's Samsonite, Stiffel and Culligan units, was sold to its management for $1.1 billion; Bottled Water was sold to Perrier for $450 million. In 1988, Tropicana Products, Inc., was sold to Joseph E. Seagram & Sons for $1.2 billion. Several of these former Beatrice subsidiaries have since been resold. All that remains of the old Beatrice company are four original businesses from the domestic foods operations: Hunt-Wesson, Swift-Eckrich, Beatrice Cheese, and La Choy Food Products.

How did the structure created by the Beatrice leveraged buy-out affect the success of the company and its subsidiaries? The quick sale of at least a few units was necessary to begin repayment of the huge debt incurred by KKR and its investors in their leveraged buy-out of Beatrice. In an assessment of Food Company Takeovers, *The Wall Street Journal* felt that little benefit had resulted in terms of greater efficiency or improved management: "Following the Beatrice LBO, Beatrice was saddled with a big debt lead, which depressed profits and made the company more vulnerable to an economic downturn. Management upheaval hurt morale and slowed marketing momentum. Productivity suffered. Massive restructuring and divestitures at Beatrice eliminated more than 20,000 jobs. Profits plunged despite sales gains, and improved results for ethnic foods proved elusive. Managers were distracted by what one called 'the feeling we have to pay off debt and pay it off fast. We have to slam these two companies together.' "

Frederick B. Rentschler, former head of BCI's domestic food operations and CEO since Don Kelly's retirement in October of 1988, agreed that reducing debt and selling assets had distracted management's attention from marketing and product development. Asserting that former unit sales had been necessary to give BCI the focus it had lacked for so long, and declaring 1987 "an investment year," plans for capital spending and broadening current brands were touted as effective solutions to these plaguing problems. Further asset sales developed; positive results did not. In 1985, before the leveraged buy-out, Beatrice's net income was a gain of $392 million. After the 1986 LBO, net income was a loss of $12 million in 1986, a loss of $118 million in 1987, and a loss of $105 million in 1988.

How did the former Beatrice subsidiaries fare? While some are still struggling to pay the debts they received with their independence, most have achieved higher sales, improved profits, and/or expanded markets. Most people running former Beatrice subsidiaries feel that Beatrice was too big; it was involved in too many different businesses without being sensitive to their differences. The former subsidiaries enjoy being a core business instead of just "one of the crowd," and feel their "single-minded dedication to reducing overhead and increasing profits makes a difference." Meadow Gold's acquisition by Borden is a prime example of matching like businesses to provide advantageous economies of scale in purchasing, marketing, and distribution. These efficiencies have increased Meadow Gold's profit margin from 4 percent to 5 percent, and Borden hopes that it will soon reach 6 percent.

Another major advantage of independence is being able to do what is best for a particular business rather than merely hitting headquarters' corporate goals. According to Robert Katz of Webcraft Technologies, Inc., boosting quarterly income at Beatrice was so important that "if managers added too many net assets, it hurt their bonuses. Now we're not only looking for short-term profits but long-term investments." This allows higher spending on marketing, new equipment, and product development.

The former subsidiaries have their problems. Many are plagued by high levels of debt. An economic downturn could prove their undoing. Yet new owners insist their narrower focus and other changes have better equipped them to handle whatever comes along. Only time will tell if their present, independent structures are better than their former conglomeration for succeeding in today's world.

SOURCES: "Beatrice Says Goodbye to the Bean Counters," *Sales & Marketing Management*, February 6, 1984, p. 30–33; "Beatrice Make-Over," *Marketing & Media Decisions*, May 1984, p. 74–77; "Beatrice's Sell-Off Strategy," *Fortune*, June 23, 1986, p. 44–49; "Getting Top Dollars for Beatrice's Leftovers," *Business Week*, July 6, 1987, p. 50–51; "Donald Kelly Is Flipping Companies Like Flapjacks," *Business Week*, February 15, 1988, p. 30; "How Sweet It Is to Be Out from Beatrice's Thumb," *Business Week*, May 9, 1988, p. 98–99; "A Big Raider Gets the Last Laugh," *Fortune*, July 4, 1988, p. 62–69; "Food Company Takeovers: Mixed Results," *The Wall Street Journal*, October 21, 1988, p. A3;1; "Tarnished Trophy: Beatrice, Once Hailed Deal of the Century, Proves Disappointing," *The Wall Street Journal*, November 21, 1988, p. A1;6–A10;1.

Questions

1. What are some of the human resource (people) problems that Beatrice may have incurred from its various structural changes?

2. The absence of a cohesive marketing program was a major problem in the original Beatrice Co. What changes were made to correct this problem? Were they effective?

3. What advantages and disadvantages were created by the various structures of the Beatrice Co.?

CASE APPLICATION 20–2

The Campbell Sales Company

While companies selling in foreign countries have recently been interested in global marketing, the domestic divisions of some important consumer goods companies have begun to take a more regional focus in their U.S. marketing efforts. As part of this shift in focus, some companies, such as Campbell's Soup, have made major changes in the structure of their marketing organizations.

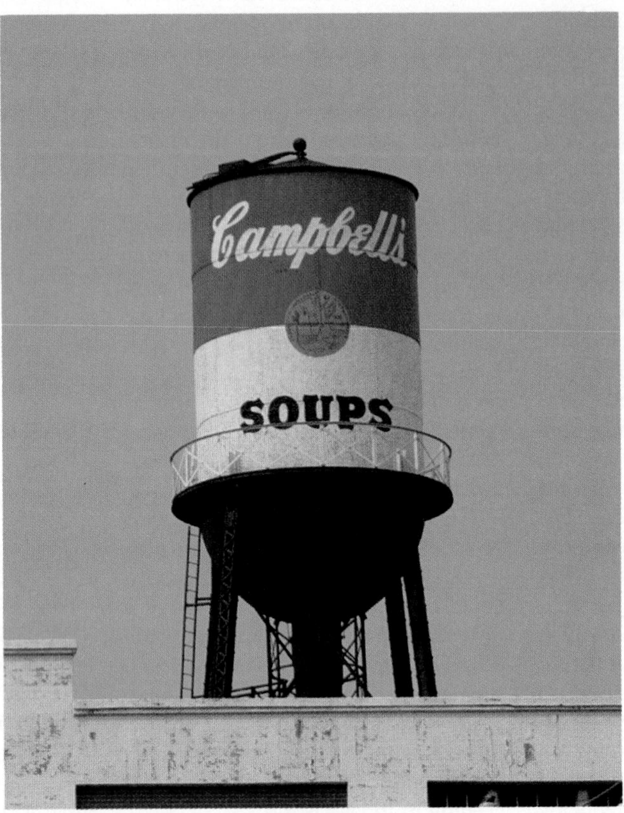

Formerly, the Campbell Sales Company—the sales arm of Campbell Soup—was organized by product line into four separate sales and marketing units. The separate units comprised canned foods, frozen foods, special products, and fresh food. Each unit was further subdivided along geographical lines into divisions and districts. As a result of this organizational structure, individual retailers had as many as four or five Campbell people, representing different product lines, calling on them. Such a system was potentially confusing to retailers and also became less suitable with changes in the food industry.

Three major changes made Campbell rethink the structure of its sales organization. First, after R. Gordon McGovern took over as Campbell's CEO in 1980, the company rapidly expanded its number and type of products. Spurred on by an entrepreneurial spirit throughout the company, Campbell ventured into new areas, resulting in a larger number of Campbell products. Second, with the widespread use of scanners, marketing power has shifted more and more to the supermarket retailer, who now has data on which products are selling and what kind of promotions are most effective. As a result, retailers are demanding that manufacturers develop more individualized marketing programs. Third, due in part to the increasing popularity of VCR's, national TV advertising now reaches a smaller percentage of consumers than it did before. This tendency, coupled with the retailers' desire for more individualized marketing, is making nationwide promotions less popular.

In response to the change in its marketing environment, Campbell Sales redesigned its structure along geographical lines. It now is divided into four large units—West, Central, South, and East—that are headed by general managers. These large geographical areas are further subdivided into regions. Due to this geographical focus, salespeople now represent a much broader line of Campbell products than they did before.

Although Campbell Sales' new structure emphasizes geographical distinctions, certain positions within the organization still retain a product emphasis. For example, on the regional level there are now four "brand sales managers," each responsible for one of four product areas: soups, frozen foods, beverage and grocery items, and fresh and refrigerated food. Even though these brand sales managers are product-oriented, however, the new geographical structure of the organization encourages them to be more targeted than brand managers in general. According to Julian Handler, publisher of the *Food Industry Newsletter*, the new structure has moved brand managers closer to "where the action is." In other words, brand managers are involved in developing more regionalized and more effective marketing strategies for their brands.

Although brand managers are active in developing marketing programs for brands in their regions, field salespeople have also been given a great deal of new authority and accountability, especially for developing local promotions. Campbell Sales' president describes how this new system works: "Rather than having the business units construct a trade promotion plan and a local marketing plan in Camden (Campbell's New Jersey headquarters) and negotiate it, the better way is to train the local sales force to develop a local promotion. You give them the budget, they develop a promotion, you approve it, they execute it, and you hold them accountable for the results." CEO McGovern anticipates that the sales force will control about 10–20 percent of the marketing budget under this system. Even when the sales force is not directly responsible for developing a promotion, however, opinions of the sales force will be sought before developing the marketing program. According to Michael Newton, vice president, administration and sales promotion, "[Under the old system] sales input was generally sought after the strategic plan and marketing plan were developed. Now we anticipate total involvement on the part of the Sales Company."

Of course, giving the sales force new marketing responsibilities also requires giving them more advanced training. As a result, brand sales managers have each received 250 hours of specialized training in marketing skills. At the same time, emphasis has been placed on developing the computer skills of the sales force. Although Campbell previously made limited use of personal computers out in the field (for placing orders), computers now will be used by salespeople to access research and marketing data from Campbell's mainframe and to help create marketing programs. In addition, Campbell is also offering incentives, such as contests, to encourage greater creativity and better results in sales promotions.

Campbell believes that the restructuring of its sales organization marks the beginning rather than the completion of a process. Campbell even foresees a day when its ad copy may be modified to suit regional tastes. In any case, Campbell believes that its geographical emphasis will help the company to be a more agile and effective marketer, and thus the company is strongly committed to its process of regionalization. Since Campbell has increased responsiveness to local needs, it seems they may be on the leading edge of a trend toward regionalization within the consumer products industry.

ADAPTED FROM: Rebecca Fannin, "Hit the Road, Jack," *Marketing and Media Decisions*, July 1987, pp. 118–24. Rayna Skolnik, "Campbell Stirs Up Its Sales Force," *Sales and Marketing Management*, April 1986, pp. 56–58.

Questions

1. What are the positive and negative points of organizing a sales/marketing unit along product lines? Geographical lines?

2. Campbell Sales' new form of organization has been described as "labor intensive." Can you suggest any other form of organization that might allow Campbell to enjoy the benefits of regionalization while keeping its personnel costs down?

3. Which industries (e.g., consumer goods, transportation, etc.) are well-suited for organization along product lines? Geographical lines? Why?

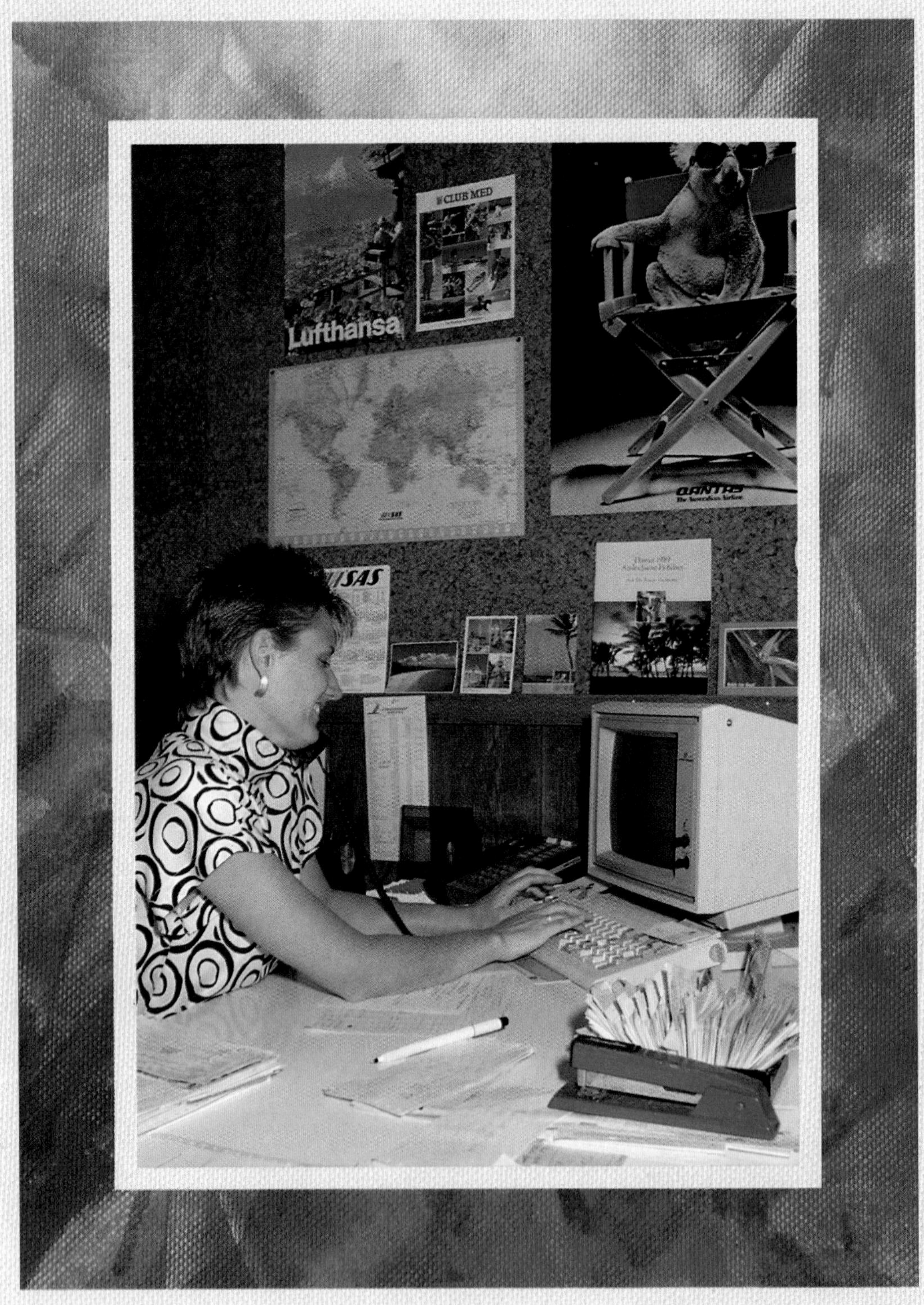
CLUB MED
Lufthansa
QANTAS
SAS

21

Marketing of Services

Learning Objectives

Upon completing this chapter, you will be able to do the following:

DEFINE
what is meant by the term *service*.

DESCRIBE
the five main features of services.

IDENTIFY
three insightful ways of classifying services.

LIST
some steps that can be taken to increase the quality of services.

ILLUSTRATE
how firms can use marketing analysis, promotion, and pricing techniques to market the services they perform.

MARKETING PROFILE

Chick-fil-A Serves Its Customers

Chick-fil-A, an Atlanta-based $250 million sales fast food chain, is the originator of the breast of chicken sandwich. The founder of Chick-fil-A, Truett Cathy, developed the sandwich in response to a problem he had in his original restaurant, the Dwarf House. He could cook hamburgers and steaks much faster than he could cook chicken, causing problems with serving everyone in a party at the same time. After years of experimenting with skinning and deboning a chicken breast and pressure frying it with various seasonings, he came upon a combination that allowed him to prepare the chicken sandwich in four minutes.

He later continued to innovate, being the first to introduce chicken nuggets. Many of the menu items, including fresh-squeezed lemonade, lemon meringue pie, carrot and raisin salad, cole slaw, and potato salad, are made fresh in each of the 400 restaurants in 31 states. Product quality is a key part of the company's success, and in a 1988 *Restaurants and Institutions* magazine poll of fast food customers, it was voted the best chicken restaurant in the U.S.

An important part of Chick-fil-A's strategy is its unique distribution setup. About 380 restaurants are in large, regional shopping malls. This guarantees constant traffic in front of the Chick-fil-A restaurants, reducing the need for the heavy advertising its fast food rivals must use to generate customers. Each restaurant is run by an operator, who makes an investment of $5000, a fraction of the investment required by the major competitors. The operator actually subleases the restaurant from Chick-fil-A, and the profits are split fifty-fifty. This results in highly motivated people running the restaurants, which is important in a business where close attention to details and customer service are critical to success.

Sales promotion is heavily used, especially product sampling. The chain strongly believes that if potential customers taste the product, they "will love it for good." Striving for the highest possible "QSC" (quality, service, and cleanliness) dominates the operations of the organization. The goal is to provide customers with their orders within one minute ("60 second service"), and to make sure they get a perfect product every time. The chain invests heavily in training its store crews, and grants close to $1 million per year in scholarships to motivate and keep its crews. Mystery shoppers visit each restaurant monthly to ensure that the restaurant is clean, the staff courteous, and the food fresh, warm, and consistently good.

Chick-fil-A's marketing challenges are considerably different from those encountered by producers of tangible consumer and industrial goods. This chapter will illustrate how marketing is used in service organizations. The use of marketing by health care organizations, financial service companies, law firms, and other professional service organizations, telecommunications companies, and other service firms has been the fastest growing area within the field of marketing. Whereas many service firms ignored marketing in the past, they are now embracing it, recognizing its ability to help these firms succeed in meeting their goals.

The Chick-fil-A case demonstrates another aspect of services marketing—the relationship between tangible attributes and intangible ones. Most services contain some attributes that are tangible, such as the chicken sandwiches in Chick-fil-A's case, and others that are pure services, such as speedy service, courteous employees, and convenience. Many products that are primarily physical goods have important service attributes such as after-the-sale service or delivery. The attention paid to the service aspects of the product is what differentiates the marketing of services from the marketing of tangible goods, as we will show in this chapter.

Since the end of World War II, the fastest growing part of the American economy has been the service sector, accounting for over 60 percent of all private-sector jobs. Out of every dollar spent today by consumers, about 50 cents goes for services. Forecasts indicate that services will continue to grow in importance in the next decade, with 90 percent of new jobs expected to come from the services sector.[1] According to Dun & Bradstreet, every one of the ten fastest growing categories of new businesses are service-based businesses, including health clubs, beauty shops, medical services, investment management services, real estate businesses, travel agencies, and hotels.[2] Unfortunately, the marketing of services has received much less attention than the marketing of goods. Thus, services marketing has remained somewhat underdeveloped, misunderstood, and unimaginative, although this has been rapidly changing in recent years.

A major reason for this lack of attention is the belief that product marketing techniques apply equally to services. Certainly, there are many similarities; at the same time, the ingredients of the marketing mix for services and products possess some significant differences.[3] In this chapter, we will clarify some of the issues, problems, and characteristics of marketing services, and we will examine some of the implications. We will discuss marketing professional services and how to measure quality in the service area.

What Is a Service?

The United States has changed in the past one hundred years from an agricultural economy to an industrial economy and has become the world's first service economy. What does the term *service* mean? There is no widely accepted definition in marketing. In fact, there is no clear distinction between those firms that are part of a marketing channel for products and those firms that market services. Fast food restaurants are often classified as food distributors because they compete with supermarkets, but these restaurants also provide services to customers.

The American Marketing Association (AMA) years ago defined **services** as *activities, benefits, or satisfactions which are offered for sale, or are provided in connection with the sales of goods.*[4] This definition is rather sketchy and uninformative. More recently, a comprehensive and very detailed definition of *services* was offered.

> *Services are products, such as a bank loan or home security, that are intangible, or at least substantially so. If totally intangible, they are exchanged directly from producer to user, cannot be transported or stored, and are almost instantly perishable. Service products are often difficult to identify, since they come into existence at the same time they are bought and consumed. They are composed of intangible elements that are inseparable, they usually involve customer participation in some important way, cannot be sold in the sense of ownership transfer, and have no title.*[5]

We will define **service** as an *identifiable* and *essentially intangible* activity that provides the user with some degree of *performance satisfaction* but does not involve *ownership*. In most cases, it cannot be *stored* or *transported*. Note that our definition indicates that a service is essentially intangible. If it can be made more tangible, it can provide customers with a feeling of being able to touch something. The bank credit card is an example of creating a more tangible representation of a service. Customers receive the service when a plastic encoded card is used to make purchases. VISA and others have been able to overcome the drawbacks of intangibility; they have allowed customers to make credit purchases without having to visit the bank.[6]

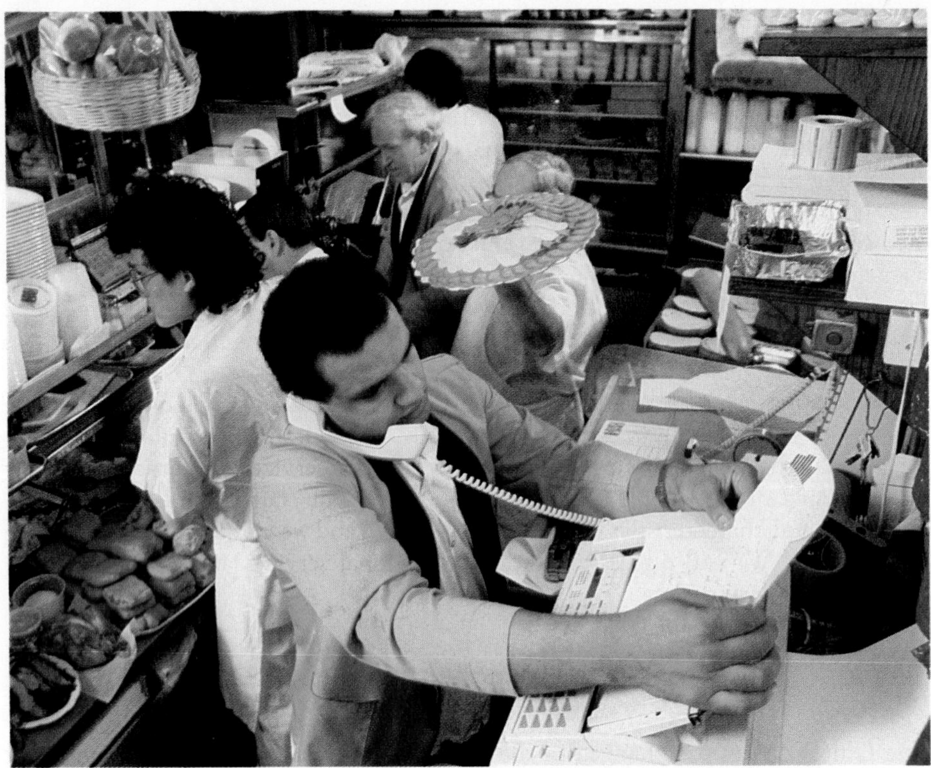

This deli offers several services, among them fast specialized food and a fax machine for orders.

The services provided by an insurance company or an airline are *performed.* Thus, the intangible activity provides performance satisfaction. Furthermore, the performance of the services does not involve *ownership* of an actual product. As you can see, marketing's place in the exchange process is different when products and services are considered. Goods like Wheaties, Crest toothpaste, or French's mustard are produced, sold, and then consumed. Services are first sold and then performed and consumed simultaneously. You purchase an airline ticket to Atlanta, and the airline transports you (performs the service) at the same time you consume the service.

Our definition suggests that services:

- include activities such as accounting, banking, medical care, lodging, transportation, communication, advertising, consulting, and personal care (for example, laundry and beauty care);
- exclude activities in which the principal aim is the production of tangible products that buyers will keep permanently, such as cars, food, and appliances;
- are performed by profit-making organizations; and
- can be sold to both consumer and industrial market groups.

Products can be classified on a goods-services continuum on the basis of tangibility-intangibility. For example, a microwave oven is a tangible product, while teaching is considered an intangible activity. Figure 21–1 uses the goods-services continuum as a system for comparing products on the basis of tangibility.

Figure 21–1 A Goods-Services Continuum

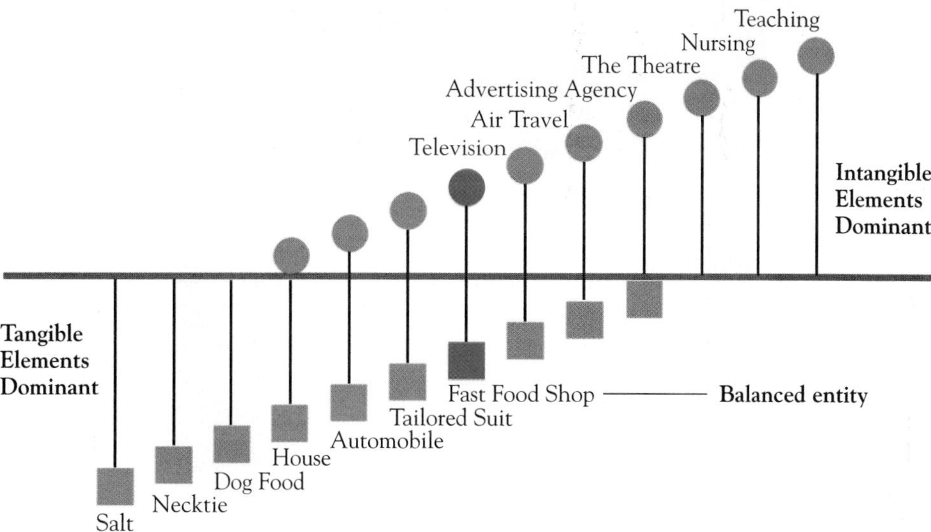

SOURCE: G. Lynn Shostack, "How to Design a Service", *European Journal of Marketing*, Vol. 16, No. 1, 1982, p. 52.

Features of Services

Although consumer and industrial services are themselves quite varied (ranging from barber shop to legal counsel), there are some features that are applicable to all.

Intangibility

A microwave oven, a bottle of Pepsi, and a videocassette recorder are products that can be seen, tasted, or heard before they are purchased; a new haircut, a visit to the doctor for a sore throat, and the cleaning of a soiled garment are services performed by the seller for the buyer. When a service is purchased, there is generally no object to show for it; it has the quality of **intangibility.** Money is exchanged, but there is no new automobile in the driveway or blender in the kitchen.

Since there is nothing to touch, service providers often attempt to improve the buyer's feeling of receiving something of value. Insurance companies promote the benefits of having money available for a child's college education or having necessary dollars for retirement. Insurance policies are designed to look impressive so that customers feel they have bought something of value. Another way to enhance buyers' feelings about services is to use celebrities to promote the service. Hertz Rental Cars uses sports stars O. J. Simpson and Arnold Palmer, American Express uses a number of entertainment and sports figures, and assorted health clubs use singer-movie star Cher, to create confidence among consumers for their services by making the service tangible through the link to the celebrity.

Another way service companies make the service more tangible is through the dramatization of their "product," showing consumers the benefits of using it. For example, Carnival Cruise Lines uses television advertising showing vacationers din-

Why The Portman hotel leaves broom bristles scattered about.
It's a trick.
To help us serve you better. Because at The Portman, San Francisco's ultimate luxury hotel, the last thing we want to do is disturb you in any way.
So to be sure your room is always perfect in every way—and to avoid knocking on your door—our personal room valets place a broom bristle against it instead. Then, when you leave, the bristle falls (invisible to everyone but the watchful valet). A sign that you've left your room. And he can have it cleaned.
Through the day, your room will also be "tidied up" as necessary. Ashtrays emptied. Bed straightened. Mini-refrigerator restocked. Towels replaced.
The Portman.
From the moment you arrive to the moment you leave, you'll be swept away by the service.
THE PORTMAN
SAN FRANCISCO
A PENINSULA GROUP HOTEL AFFILIATE
500 Post Street • One block from Union Square
(415) 771-8600 • For reservations call (800) 533-6465 • A member of The Grande Collection of Hotels

Continual cleaning is a service offered by the Portman Hotel.

ing, dancing, and enjoying the pleasures of exotic places, putting viewers "on the ship." Federal Express's advertising cleverly dramatizes the unpleasant experiences of those who don't use their service.[7] The Portman Hotel, a San Francisco "ultra luxury" hotel, makes its high service level more tangible by leaving broom bristles outside the room as evidence that it will be serviced each time the guests leave the room. (See the ad for the Portman Hotel above.)

Simultaneous Production and Consumption

Services are typically produced and consumed at the same time. The physician listens to the patient, analyzes the problem, and suggests a solution—all at once. In the case of services, the provider is usually physically present when consumption occurs, while with tangible goods, this is not the case. A car manufactured in Michigan may be driven by someone in New Mexico.

It is important to recognize *how* the provider distributes the service.[8] In marketing, time and place utility are extremely important. Having the good at the right place at the right time to satisfy the customer is a vital marketing management concern. With services, special emphasis is also placed on distributing the service in the "right way." How physicians, bank tellers, lawyers, auto repair specialists, or consultants conduct themselves in the presence of the customer can influence future purchasing decisions. A microwave oven is not rude, abrasive, or careless, but people providing services can be, and occasionally are. When they are, customers may look for a different and more courteous service provider. The result is not only a lost sale, but a lost customer.

Less Standardization

Consumers expect products to be standardized. A tube of Crest toothpaste is the same every time it is bought; Kellogg's Raisin Bran is Kellogg's Raisin Bran. However, the consumer's expectation about medical service, tax help, or car repairs is less certain. The skills of one doctor are different from the skills of another doctor; the skills of one accountant are different from those of another. Each situation that requires a service is different, and each provider conducts himself or herself differently. Also, since each situation that requires the service is different, standardization is not wholly appropriate.

This general lack of standardization requires firms to check on the quality of service they are performing. One method to determine quality is to monitor customer satisfaction. Banks often conduct attitude surveys, restaurants use opinion surveys, and airlines ask passengers to rate their service. Some service organizations pay close attention to the recruitment, selection, placement, and training of personnel, so that the best available people are hired and retained to provide services promptly, courteously, and continuously. These human resource management and development efforts are attempts to provide as much standardization as possible, minimize uncertainty, and improve customer confidence.

Perishability

A microwave oven can be stored in a warehouse until it is sold, but an idle H & R Block tax accountant represents business that is lost. Physicians, lawyers, and dentists have charged patients for missed appointments because the service value only existed at the time the patient or client was not present. A missed doctor's appointment or an empty seat on yesterday's flight is lost; it is perishable.

The perishability of services is not a major problem if demand is continuous and steady. However, when demand fluctuates considerably, providers of services have difficult resource decisions to make. For example, how many city buses should be running during non-peak time? How many tellers should be in the bank's drive-in section?

Making resource decisions requires an analysis of the supply of and demand for a service.[9] For example, managing demand for services can be conducted through the following:

- *Differential Pricing.* Movie theaters attempt to shift some demand from peak to off-peak times by offering early matinee rates; telephone companies like AT&T and MCI offer lower rates at night and on weekends.
- *Developing Non-Peak Demand.* Resort areas have developed special vacation packages for off-season customers.
- *Complementary Services.* Banks have added automatic teller machines to service customers.
- *Reservation Systems.* Preselling services is a way to determine demand in advance. This is used by airlines, railroads, buses, sports teams, hotels, and motels.

Banks extend their services by providing 24-hour automatic teller machines.

Managing supply can be practiced by the following:

- *Using Part-Time Employees.* When there is peak demand in a restaurant, hire part-time help.
- *Peak-Time Efficiency Practices.* During peak hours only, practice the most necessary procedures. Paramedics have been invaluable in aiding physicians when there is peak demand.
- *Increasing Consumer Participation.* Have patients fill out their own medical records or customers bag their own groceries.
- *Sharing Services.* Have several service firms share resources, such as hospitals using the same laboratory or other special medical equipment.

Client Relationship

In many service transactions, the buyer is a client rather than a customer; the client, when buying a service is, in a sense, "in the hands" of the seller. Consider the physician and the patient or the airline and the passenger. The buyers are not free to simply use the service when they wish, as would be true if a product were purchased. The buyers must abide by the conditions established by the seller. Airplanes with passengers do not simply take off when passengers tell them to; they follow a departure and arrival schedule. They also have rules, procedures, and policies for passengers to follow. Passengers abide by these programs so that services, such as in-flight meals, can be performed on time and efficiently. The rules, procedures, and policies are usually in the best interest of the customer.

Figure 21–2 Types of Service Businesses

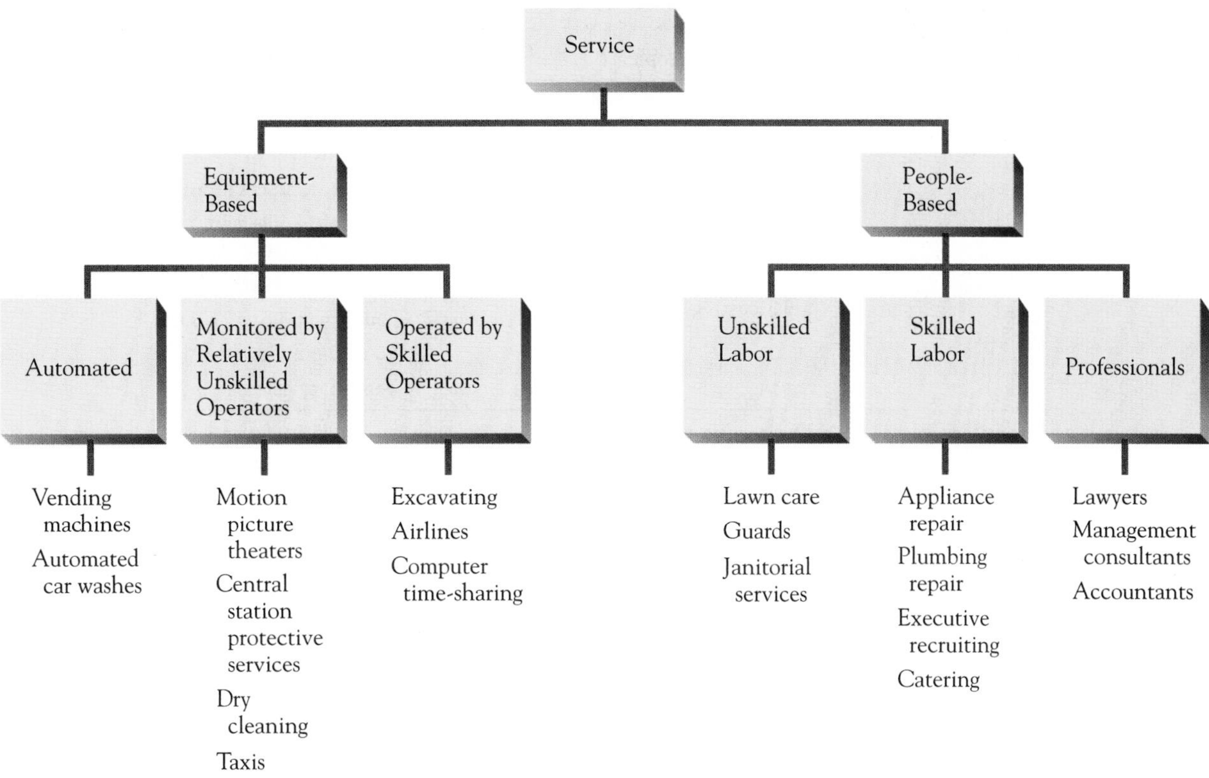

SOURCE: Reprinted by permission of *Harvard Business Review*. An exhibit from "Strategy is Different in Service Businesses" by Dan R. E. Thomas, July/August 1978.

Classification of Services

Establishing a classification system can help us understand services more clearly and also can provide insight into how marketing principles can be applied to the service sector of society. There is no one generally accepted classification system. Thus, we have elected to discuss service classifications in terms of (1) equipment versus people, (2) the recipient of service, and (3) the method of service delivery.[10] These three provide an excellent background and insight into the nature of services in society.

Numerous services are performed for consumers and industrial users. In some cases, they are provided by special machinery with little personal assistance (such as vending machines dispensing sandwiches). In other instances, the services are provided by skilled professionals (teachers) who do not use much special equipment. Figure 21–2 classifies services as either equipment-based or people-based.

Equipment-Based Services

These services involve automated equipment (the automatic car wash), equipment monitored by relatively unskilled operators (the dry cleaners), and equipment operated by skilled operators (excavating vehicles).

Table 21–1 Recipients of Service

What Is the Nature of the Service Act?	Who or What Is the Recipient of the Service? People	Things
Tangible Actions	*Services directed at people's bodies* Health care Passenger transportation Beauty salons Exercise clinics Restaurants Haircutting	*Services directed at goods and other physical possessions* Freight transportation Industrial equipment repair and maintenance Janitorial services Laundry and dry cleaning Landscaping/lawncare Veterinary care
Intangible Actions	*Services directed at people's minds* Education Broadcasting Information services Theaters Museums	*Services directed at intangible assets* Banking Legal services Accounting Securities Insurance

SOURCE: Christopher H. Lovelock, *Services Marketing* (Englewood Cliffs, NJ: Prentice-Hall, 1984), p. 51.

People-Based Services

People-based services are provided by professionals like lawyers; skilled labor, like plumbers; and unskilled labor, like janitors and plant guards. Classifying services as either people- or equipment-based allows us to place them in particular groups for further analysis, but exact placement is difficult for two reasons: (1) as service businesses evolve, they often move along the spectrum from people-based to equipment-based or vice versa, and (2) many companies are in a number of service businesses. For example, when transferring and storing funds, banks use equipment to perform services, but when financing a car loan, the bank's loan officers talk and work with customers.[11]

Services can be directed at people and things, as shown in Table 21–1. For example, a surgeon can remove a patient's appendix. Or a janitorial service, hired by Kroger, can clean and wax floors in a large supermarket. The surgeon and the janitorial services are directing tangible actions toward people or things. On the other hand, an educational television station provides an intangible action (a program) to viewers. Intangible actions are also provided to make a transaction in a bank customer's account. Of course, providing a service may fit more than one category. An airline, by transporting a passenger from Chicago to New York in less than two hours, permits the person to make an important meeting. The passenger feels psychologically good about this, but he also has physically moved from Chicago to New York.

The recipient classification system identifies what the service provider actually provides. The benefits of each service can be highlighted. This classification system

Table 21–2 Methods of Service Delivery

Nature of Interaction	Availability of Service Outlets	
	Single Site	**Multiple Sites**
Customer goes to service organization.	Beauty salon Local deli	Bus service Fast-food chain
Service organization comes to customer.	Lawncare service Taxi	Mail delivery AAA emergency repairs
Customer and service organization transact at arm's length (mail or electronic communications).	Credit card company Airline reservations	Broadcast network Telephone company

SOURCE: Christopher H. Lovelock, *Services Marketing* (Englewood Cliffs, NJ: Prentice-Hall, 1984), p. 60.

also helps answer the question of whether the person must be physically present to receive the benefits offered or provided by a service.

A better understanding of service distribution can be provided by classifying services on the basis of delivery. Table 21–2 presents three forms of customer-service organization interactions. Customers, in some cases, must travel to receive service. For example, a person may have a favorite beauty salon or fast-food restaurant. In other cases the service organization travels to the customer to provide the service, as is the case with a taxi cab or Federal Express. There is also the possibility that the person and service provider transact business without either engaging in travel. This is called an arm's length interaction. For example, an airline will provide flight information, reservations, and tickets by telephone instead of requiring customers to come to an office.

Developing a Program for Marketing Services

Developing a sound marketing program for services is extremely challenging because of their characteristics. Intangibility, simultaneous production and consumption, less standardization (than products), perishability, and client relationships require somewhat different marketing-mix decisions than those for marketing products.

The Marketplace Analysis

Analyzing the marketplace for products and services is very similar. In marketing a service, the characteristics of the consumer or industrial market must be determined; the demographics of the market must be carefully reviewed. The service provider also needs to examine customer needs, wants, income levels, and preferences. Pacific Select Corporation conducted a marketplace analysis for the Houston Astros who play baseball in the Astrodome. The audience profile of baseball fans attending games in domed stadiums (Houston, Minnesota) is different from that of fans in the non-domed stadiums (Chicago's Wrigley Field, Boston's Fenway Park). Pacific Select determined that the Astros had not been targeting their marketing promotions to the proper markets—couples forty-five and older without children. This information was used to redirect the Astros' promotional efforts.[12]

Review Your Marketing Knowledge

• Using the classification schemes presented in the chapter, classify day care centers, a local electric utility, a major league baseball team, and an overnight package delivery service.

• In what ways, if any, are the classification schemes helpful in determining the marketing strategy for these services?

Product

Product planning and development has its counterpart in the marketing of services. Here the "product" is the service. Unlike tangible products (a cassette recorder), however, most services (legal advice) cannot be held, seen, or evaluated before they are purchased. The service buyer must make decisions based on past experience, word of mouth, reputation or brand names, and promotional campaigns.

Observers have claimed that information is the product that causes people to buy from a service organization, but what they receive are service benefits. For example, people might be motivated to go to a Bruce Springsteen or Alabama concert because of the publicity for the events, but what the customers receive is the pleasure of listening to music. The more they appreciate good music, the more the entertainment might mean to them.

Some service firms provide a standard product—one that is the same for all customers. Cleaning and laundry rates, savings account interest at banks, full-service automotive care, and the cost of delivering a package through air freight are the same for all customers. Other service organizations vary the product for each customer. Lawyers, physicians, and consultants usually vary the service product; they offer more of an individualized service than one directed to the masses. However, some lawyers offer a standard fee for preparing a will or reviewing a contract.

Brand names in service industries are extremely important for product differentiation. The names of Holiday Inn, Ramada, Hilton, H & R Block, United Airlines, Pan Am, Merrill Lynch, Federal Express, and F. Lee Bailey are important in establishing a competitive advantage for marketing services. The customer associates quality with the names of these well-known service providers.

The packaging of the service "product" is another marketing activity not usually considered; however, the impact of a package is important. Goods manufacturers constantly work on providing a cost-efficient and physically attractive package to customers. Morton Salt Company, for example, has designed an attractive package that performs the "service" of keeping its salt dry and in usable form in all weather.

A preventive medicine center in Houston that caters to business executives had searched for months for a way to present medical examination results to patients. After a thorough, five-to-six hour physical exam, the center had used a personal letter and a visit with the physician to inform patients about their health and well-being. Patients complained about the impersonality and lack of clarity of this method. The center's director concluded that business executives were used to reviewing charts and figures; thus, he established a bar chart medical report form. This director had packaged the preventive medicine diagnostic report to provide patients with a convenient, clear, and familiar format that enabled them to follow and observe their physical well-being. In other words, results were presented in the customer's terms, rather than the center's, to facilitate communication.

Figure 21–3 Channel Alternatives for Services

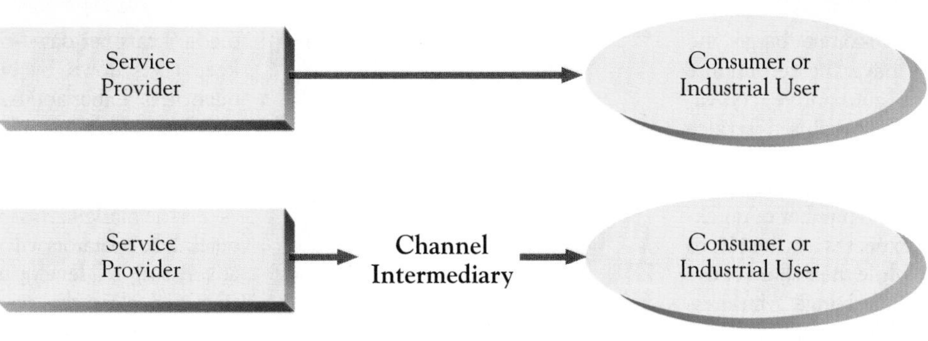

Distribution

Some people assume that because services are intangible, heterogeneous, and perishable, distribution becomes much less important. It is true that most services are sold directly from the provider to the consumer or industrial user. (Recall the various methods of service delivery shown earlier in Table 21–2.) No intermediaries are used when a lawyer or accountant evaluates a client's needs and prescribes some action, and follows up. However, some service providers use agents, brokers, or other channel members as intermediaries. The channel alternatives for services are presented in Figure 21–3. For example, companies selling entertainment, insurance, or securities typically use independent brokers or agents to sell their services. In other instances, such as with employment agencies, day care centers, or dance studios, individuals are trained to perform a service and are franchised to sell it. (See the *Marketing in Action* on Quick-Lube Centers.) Intermediaries for services are less concerned with warehousing, transportation, inventory control, and materials handling than are marketers of goods.

An important issue in the distribution of services to customers is site location. Banks, motels, hotels, physicians, dentists, and physical fitness facilities all seek convenient locations. Banks have attempted to locate branch offices in well-traveled areas in or near shopping malls. Physical fitness centers attempt to locate facilities in areas that are easily accessible to customers, especially before and after work hours.

Service industry distribution systems are becoming more involved in a number of industries. For example, when retailers extend a bank's credit to their customers, the bank becomes an intermediary. In the marketing of credit card plans such as VISA or MasterCard, banks rely heavily on the retail merchant to encourage customers to apply for and use the cards.[13] In fact, many banks compensate merchants through incentive programs. Thus, when banks become engaged in credit card programs, they become active intermediaries in the channel of distribution.

In health care, the health maintenance organization (HMO) is altering views about the distribution of medical care, and changing the nature of competition in the medical field. An HMO is a group of physicians, nurses, technicians, and pharmacists who work as a team to increase the availability of health services for members. It acts as an intermediary between providers and patients and includes generalists and specialists. Since fees are prepaid, there is a greater tendency to visit the health-care providers more frequently, practicing a more preventive approach to medicine.

MARKETING IN ACTION

Quick-Lube Centers Striking Oil

People have the five-minute burger and fries. Now cars have the ten-minute quick-lube. The automotive equivalent of fast food, franchised service centers specializing in cheap, fast oil changes are following a similarly rapid growth pattern. The number of quick-lube outlets is expected to double to 5,000 by 1990, while their share of the $7.7 billion oil-change business increases from 4.5 percent to 11.5 percent.

Jiffy Lube, Minit Lube and Grease Monkey, the three major franchisors, are hoping that rate of growth will transform them into the industry's McDonald's or Burger King.

"It's a great idea, just as a good hamburger in five minutes is a great idea," says David MacDonald, vice president of marketing for Grease Monkey. "Whenever you can think of a good idea at a good price, it's going to grow." Like fast-food restaurants, quick-lube centers provide service in ten to twenty minutes and are usually located at heavily trafficked areas. Oil changes usually cost $20 or less.

There's plenty of room to grow, too. With roughly 14.5 percent of the market, full-service gas stations still do about three times as many oil changes as franchise outlets, but the full-service gas station is rapidly going the way of the doctor's house call. "There are fewer gas stations, and people have less time to spend and less patience," says automotive analyst Maryann Keller of Furman Selz Mager Dietz & Birney.

Charles Glovsky of Alex Brown & Sons says the growth of quick-lube centers will come at the expense of gas stations and car dealers, whose numbers have eroded in the last 10 years. Full-service gas stations are down to 110,000 from 192,000 in 1973, while car and truck dealerships have declined to 25,000 from 36,000 in 1975. Moreover, owners are depending less on dealerships for service as the numbers of cars on the road that outlive their warranty periods increase: The average age of cars has grown from 6.6 years in 1980 to 7.5 years in 1985.

[Quick-lube centers] generally provide services that gasoline stations and car dealers can't make money on," says Glovsky. By handling a high volume of customers—last year Jiffy Lube centers in operation for two years or more handled 60 cars per day—the centers can keep costs down by buying in large quantities. Labor and training costs are also lower. "It's not a high-tech operation," says Keller. "This is pretty basic stuff."

As the market grows, Glovsky adds, quick-lube operators will use more media advertising to develop name recognition and alert the two-thirds of car owners who change their own oil. Until then, quick-lube franchises depend on consumer impulse. "The choice is being made in a parity situation," says Grease Monkey's MacDonald, who believes none of the companies has managed to win brand loyalty. "It's based on a person's experience after they've done it once."

Ann Thompson, vice president of communications at Precision Tune, agrees that "in the past our messages haven't been that dissimilar." Precision, which offers engine tune-ups as well as oil changes at its 340 centers in 32 states, is going for a "more high-tech image," she adds, since most new cars now have computerized equipment that consumers believe only their dealers can service.

But the race for dominance could depend on which firm gets the most centers up fastest. Jiffy Lube is the current leader with 422 outlets; Minit Lube is a distant second with 133. But all are growing. MacDonald says Grease Monkey, which currently has 78 centers in 36 states, is opening two to three centers a month and has 275 in some stage of development.

SOURCE: from "Quick-Lube Centers Striking Oil" by Stephen Battaglio in ADWEEK'S MARKETING WEEK, December 8, 1986. Reprinted by permission.

Promotion

It is generally easier to promote something tangible. A product can be seen and demonstrated and lends itself to customer evaluation. It is difficult to evaluate something that cannot be touched. Thus, marketers of services must make the service seem more tangible.

Table 21–3 Price Terminology in Some Service Industries

Nature of Services	Typical Price Terminology
Communications	Rate
Consulting and Business Facilitating	Fee, commission, retainer
Education	Tuition
Finance	Interest
Health	Fee, charge
Household Operations	Rate, charge
Housing	Rent
Insurance	Premium*
Legal	Fee, retainer
Personal	Charge
Recreation	Admission
Transportation	Tariff

*In the case of life insurance, premiums must be adjusted for dividends and cash surrender value (savings) to arrive at the true price.

SOURCE: John M. Rathmell, *Marketing in the Service Sector* (Winthrop Publishers, Inc., 1974), p. 72.

Promotions build interest in service benefits and help distinguish one service from another. Other forms of service like professional sports, travel agencies, and tax preparation benefit from coverage on radio, television, billboards, and newspapers. These media build interest in watching a sports event like the World Series, or traveling to the Grand Canyon, or completing your tax returns properly.

An indirect form of promotion is the volunteer work and community activities done by physicians, accountants, and lawyers to make themselves more publicly known. Eventual customers come in contact with the volunteers, who acquire reputations for helping the community.

Some service firms attempt to promote the real benefits provided to users. For example, by using promotion, the insurance industry has made it easier for consumers to perceive what is being sold.[14] Think about these well-known efforts to promote insurance protection (an intangible) with a specific tangible object:

- Allstate—You're in good hands with Allstate
- Prudential—The rock of Prudential
- Travelers—Protected by the Travelers' umbrella
- Nationwide—The Nationwide blanket of protection

Hands, rocks, umbrellas, and blankets are promoted to give customers a picture of a tangible object they can associate with an insurance firm.

Pricing

Interestingly, the term *price* is rarely used in marketing services. Service firms often use the terms *fee, charge, rent, interest, admission,* or *retainer* to describe the cost of the buyer-seller exchange. The terms in Table 21–3 are actually the prices being charged for the services being provided. The pricing strategies used vary across industries.

Some service industries, such as utilities (electricity and telephone), have their prices regulated by the government; other service firms charge users according to the season or time of day (resorts, motels, and movie theaters). Some service prices are based on age, with lower charges for children and senior citizens (restaurants and movies), while others (doctors, lawyers, accountants) set rates on the basis of a customer's ability to pay.

In general, service pricing tends to be flexible but is similar to that used in setting product prices. An important consideration is the cost of providing quality service. Most services, especially if they are people-based, are labor intensive (involving people's time, expertise, efforts), and prices must cover these labor costs, plus capital costs and an allowance for a satisfactory profit. Supply and demand also influence the price of services. The supply of outstanding diamond cutters is limited, and demand for their services has skyrocketed in the last decade. Thus, the supply-demand imbalance has resulted in high prices for this type of service.

The method of paying for a product and a service often differs. Since a service that is not paid for cannot be repossessed like an automobile or a dining room set, some service firms require payment before the service is performed or at the time it is provided. A house painter requires at least a down payment before he or she starts to work. Sports teams and entertainers require payment before performing. Auto repair businesses require payment at the time the service is provided. These advance or time-of-delivery payments are designed to prevent losses, and they keep the service provider in business so that the service can continue to be rendered.

Professional Services: a Reluctance to Practice Marketing

A **professional service** is defined as being advisory and problem-solving in orientation, although there may be some amount of routine work performed for a client.[15] The *professional services*—health care, law, accounting, engineering, and architecture—have been especially slow to accept and practice marketing. Some of this reluctance has been based on the following:

- *A disdain for commercialism.* Professionals view their areas of expertise as more scientific than business. Furthermore, many of them do not like to publicly discuss fees or rates for services, considering it crass or unprofessional.
- *Association code of ethics.* Many professional associations have established rules against advertising, direct solicitation, and referral commissions.
- *The notion that marketing is selling.* Many professionals have equated marketing with selling. As we have discussed throughout the book, marketing encompasses more than just selling.[16]

These barriers have slowed the development of marketing professional services. However, the U.S. Supreme Court has held that self-imposed ethical restrictions against advertising prices or services, intended to inhibit the free flow of commercial information and to keep the public ignorant, are illegal.

Recent Changes in Professional Services Marketing

Since the Supreme Court ruling in 1977, the professional services have increased their use of promotion. For example, according to the Television Bureau of Advertising, lawyers spent $45 million on television commercials in 1986, four times the amount spent in 1982.[17] It rose another 26 percent in 1987 to $59 million.[18] The other professions have also experienced dramatic increases.

Most professionals, however, still don't use the services of experts like marketing researchers. In fact, numerous professional service firms attempt to execute marketing plans, ignoring marketing specialists who have the necessary skills and know-how. Many of the plans have been poorly conceived and have actually diminished the image and business of the professional practitioners.

The first attempt to franchise the delivery of professional legal services began recently. Jacoby & Meyers, a franchisor, established thirty-four clinics in southern California. They now have over 300 lawyers in 150 branch offices in six states. To promote this growth, they have heavily invested in television advertising, spending $6.5 million in 1988 to foster the idea that legal services are within the budgets of most people.[19]

A recent study conducted by the Association of Legal Administrators found that more than 5000 law firms have hired outside public relations or advertising agencies. This is only a small percentage of the 45,000 law firms with five or more attorneys, however, and only a few law firms are spending as much as 0.5 percent of total revenues on "practice development" activities.[20] The *Marketing in Action* on how law firms have adopted marketing techniques suggests some ways lawyers are using advertising, public relations, and sales promotion to attract new clients, thereby increasing revenues for their firms.

Unfortunately, many professionals still like to think that they do not need to use marketing techniques and plans. To generate business, some professionals prefer to rely on their reputations and word of mouth, which are actually forms of marketing. However, court rulings, increased competition, and clients' demands for better service are changing the professional service marketplace.

Those professionals who are becoming more involved with marketing have accepted the following ideas:

- *Marketing is not only selling.* Marketing professional services involves pricing, promotion, and place decisions.
- *Business marketing procedures are not only commercial.* Successful business leaders use scientific methods to analyze markets, provide people with what they want, and, after delivery of a good, handle complaints. They are as ethical, moral, and motivated as professionals.
- *Aggressive market analysis and planning is an essential part of a successful marketing program.* If marketing is to be done effectively, marketing analysis and planning must be done. As professional services competition increases, these marketing activities will have to be done in accordance with each profession's canons of ethics.

The real issue in professional services is not whether marketing is needed, but how it can be done effectively. Those professionals who accept the marketplace challenges will be better able to meet competition head on, cope with spiraling service costs, and improve the quality and delivery of the services performed. In general, the successful marketers of services in the future will be the people who can capitalize on what customers, clients, and patients want and need—which is what the systematic application of the marketing concept is all about.

MARKETING IN ACTION

Law Firms Adopt Marketing

Law firms are being prodded toward marketing by an increasingly competitive market. The megafirms—the half-dozen or so with more than 500 lawyers—are opening branches in major cities and aggressively wooing business from local rivals. Meanwhile, corporations are paring legal budgets and forcing outside law firms to bid competitively for their business.

Law firms walk a fine line in devising marketing that brings in new business without offending conservative partners or old-line clients who value discretion. Also, there's still a confusing array of laws and bar-association rules governing lawyers' marketing in many states. So it's not surprising that initial forays into marketing have been timid and clumsy at times.

Glossy brochures are a hot item, as are newsletters on legal developments that give firms the opportunity to catch a client's eye periodically. Yet these efforts often seem to be testaments to the profession's discomfort with self-promotion.

Some firms, for instance, try to appear worldly. Instead, they come off as crass. ("Facing Robins Zelle in court is a little like encountering Genghis Khan on the steppes," says the Minneapolis law firm in its promotional brochure.) Others err on the side of caution and wind up sounding fusty or arrogant.

Unintended irony distinguished one vanity-press offering: "Conversations with McGuire, Woods & Battle," a hardcover book containing four chapters of "actual conversations" with partners of the Richmond, Va., firm. The final chapter of the gold-embossed tome emphasizes the necessity of "staying lean." (The firm recently merged with another firm; its new name is McGuire, Woods, Battle & Boothe.)

Some efforts are becoming sophisticated, if also slick. One law firm in Cleveland now distributes its newsletters on videocassettes. Another Ohio firm recently surveyed its 1,500 newsletter readers and produced a computer analysis of their keenest legal concerns. The firms' lawyers use the results to tailor pitches for more business from those clients.

Advertising to the public in newspapers and on television is still seen by most firms as ineffective and unprofessional. But legal clinics and small personal-injury firms are increasingly aggressive retail advertisers, especially on television.

Restrictions against other kinds of legal advertising are loosening in many states. Last fall, for example, a federal appeals court overturned an Illinois rule barring direct-mail advertising. Outright sell "is the next marketing frontier," says Stephen Gillers, a law professor at New York University Law School. "Soon, a lawyer who sees a 'For Sale' sign on a house will be able to go up and ring the bell without violating any ethical rules," he says.

Many states effectively continue to restrict marketing with a profusion of rules governing matters as detailed as the wording of brochures. Some states, for example, ban the words "specialty" when used to advertise legal expertise. Yet even some large, conservative firms are flouting some rules and daring the state to discipline them. "The attitude is 'Let them come after us,'" Mr. Burke says. "Firms want to look progressive."

Image is important to the firms. Cutting a high public profile is a top priority at many. To that end, some are hiring publicists to court the media and to groom their lawyers for interviews and speeches. Paul, Hastings, Janofsky and Walker, a 270-lawyer firm in Los Angeles, recently hired a staff public-relations specialist. Earlier this month, when a judge handed down a favorable ruling on one of its cases, the PR person, Byron G. Sabol, alerted about a dozen major newspapers and magazines. The goal, he says, "is to raise the firm's visibility."

SOURCE: Patricia B. Gray, "More Lawyers Reluctantly Adopt Strange New Practice—Marketing," *The Wall Street Journal*, January 30, 1987, p. 25.

REVIEW YOUR MARKETING KNOWLEDGE

- How does the marketing of professional services differ from the marketing of other services?
- What suggestions can you make to the head of a local architectural firm concerning the marketing strategy the firm should use?

Service Quality

Everyone has experienced situations in which he or she was disappointed in the quality of a service, whether it was at a restaurant, in a hotel with lots of noise down the hall, from an auto repair shop, or at a doctor's office where a long wait was encountered. In a recent Gallup poll, real estate firms, public transportation companies, auto repair firms, and airlines were rated particularly low by consumers in the delivery of quality service. Banks, restaurants, and hospitals received relatively high ratings, with over half the consumers rating these industries an 8 out of 10 or better (1 represented low quality and 10 signified very high quality).[21]

What determines whether consumers perceive a service as high quality or not? In a series of studies on service quality, five dimensions of service that differentiate between good and bad have been identified:[22]

- Tangibles: the physical facilities, equipment, appearance of the personnel;
- Reliability: the ability to perform the desired service dependably, accurately, and consistently;
- Responsiveness: the willingness to provide prompt service and help customers;
- Assurance: employees' knowledge, courtesy, and ability to convey trust and confidence; and
- Empathy: the provision of caring, individualized attention to customers.

Reliability was found to be the single most important factor, with about half or more of credit card, repair-and-maintenance, long distance telephone, and bank customers saying this dimension was the single most important factor in determining the quality of service received.

What causes consumers to be disappointed with the quality of the service they receive? Consumers have certain expectations concerning the five dimensions of service just described, leading to an overall expectation of service quality. The expectations are also affected by consumers' past experience, personal needs, and any word of mouth they might have heard about the service (see Figure 21–4). If there is a gap between what they expect and what they perceive they actually receive, consumers are disappointed in the quality of the service.[23] Quality lower than expected can also be caused by top management not understanding what consumers expect, by standards being set by management lower than what consumers expect, by employees not delivering what management has set as the standard, and by advertising, selling, and other communications exaggerating the level of service quality, creating unrealistic expectations.[24]

Many companies work hard to ensure that a high level of service quality is delivered to consumers. A recent survey revealed the following companies as the best in their industries: American Airlines, American Express, J. P. Morgan (commercial banks), Fidelity (discount stock brokerage), Embassy Suites (subsidiary of Holiday Inns), and L.L. Bean (mail order merchants).[25] What do these companies do to deliver superior service quality? Among the tools they use are the following:[26]

- American Express has over 100 programs to recognize and reward employees who take unusual care of customers, including cash bonuses of up to $1000. The company also spends hundreds of millions of dollars on the latest technology to maximize its service delivery levels.
- Embassy Suites motivates its employees by posting a daily report on occupancy rate, average room rate, and estimated profits, along with comments

Figure 21–4 Determinants of Perceived Service Quality

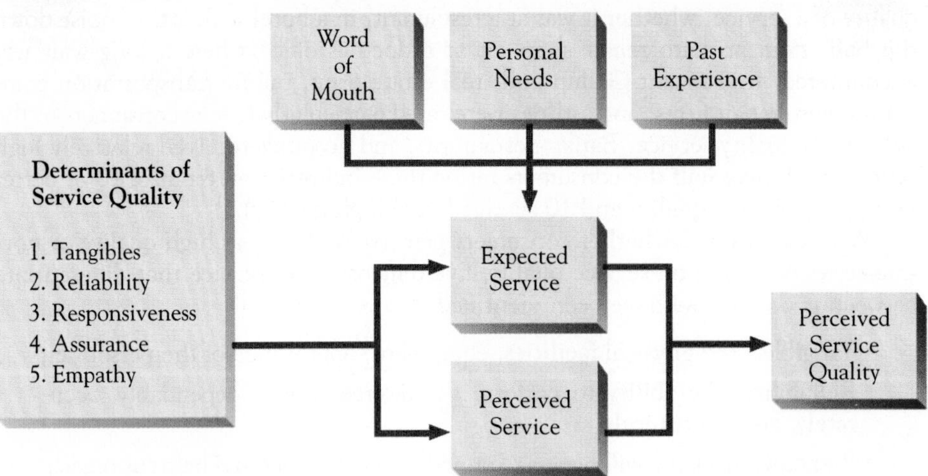

SOURCE: Adapted from A. Parasuraman, V. Zeithaml, and L. Berry, "A Conceptual Model of Service Quality and Its Implications for Future Research," *Journal of Marketing*, Fall 1985, p. 48.

from five customers interviewed at random the day before. Monthly bonuses of at least $100 are paid, even to the lowest level employees, if the hotel achieves its goals. Raises are based on skills and are given for taking optional extra training.

- Fidelity puts on extra staff at peak periods, ensuring its customers can get through to customer service agents to execute their trades.
- L.L. Bean employees are given 40 hours of training before they talk with their first customer. Much of the training deals with how to be helpful and courteous to the customer. Computers are used extensively to achieve a 99.8 percent accuracy rate in order fulfillment.

All of these companies continually do research with customers to measure how they are doing and to identify ways to improve their service. They do all this because they know it pays off, enabling them to increase sales, and to sell at a higher gross margin than their competitors because consumers will pay for higher quality service.

Personal Computer Exercise

As demonstrated in this chapter, the level of service quality a firm provides can determine its success or failure. Service firms thus often conduct surveys to measure their level of service quality in comparison to their competitors. This PC exercise will enable you to measure a firm's service quality on the five dimensions discussed in the chapter to determine what changes might be needed to improve the firm's quality.

KEY POINTS

• The marketing of services is similar in many ways to the marketing of products. However, there are some distinct differences in promotion, pricing, and distribution that should be recognized.

• The service sector is expected to continue to grow. It already accounts for $.50 of every dollar spent by consumers and 60 percent of all private sector jobs.

• Service businesses can be classified as equipment-based (automated car washes) or people-based (legal counsel from a lawyer), the recipient of a service, or the method of service delivery.

• The distinct characteristics of services include intangibility, simultaneous production and consumption, less standardization than products, perishability, and client relationships.

• Marketing concepts, tools, and programs have been slow to catch on in services firms. However, more service firms are beginning to incorporate their own form of the marketing mix today.

• The marketing of professional services presents some significant challenges. Even today, many professionals are reluctant to engage in marketing activities. However, increased competition and customers' demands are placing pressure on professionals to market their services.

• Service quality has become increasingly important. Tangibles, reliability, responsiveness, assurance, and empathy are the critical dimensions of service quality. It is important for companies to deliver a level of quality consistent with consumer expectations.

ISSUES FOR DISCUSSION

1. List reasons why service-oriented firms generally are not as up-to-date and sophisticated in performing marketing activities as goods-marketing firms are.

2. Which of the different ways of classifying services do you like best? Why? Can you think of any other ways to classify services?

3. Discuss the characteristics of services using the following examples:

a. KinderCare day care centers
b. MCI long distance service
c. A major accounting firm
d. H & R Block income tax service

4. How might each of the services in Question 3 be made more tangible?

5. There are now about 670,000 lawyers in the United States, with estimates that there will be over one million by the mid-1990s. What kind of changes in advertising and public relations do you foresee for lawyers in the 1990s?

6. What actions might a company like Chick-fil-A (see the *Marketing Profile* at the beginning of the chapter) take to increase its service quality?

7. Why do some professionals believe that marketing means selling? Why don't they want to be associated with this practice?

8. When someone comments that maintaining an inventory of services is not feasible, what do they mean?

9. Think of the advertising for a fast food company, a bank, and one other service company of your choice. Why might the service advertise this way? How effective do you think it is? Why?

10. Would being a marketing manager in a service firm involve different decisions and managing style than being one in a product firm?

GLOSSARY

Intangibility: A feature of most services. It means that the service of a physician or other performer cannot be touched or handled. On the other hand, a product like an automobile is tangible—it can be touched and handled.

Professional services: Activities performed by practitioners such as physicians, accountants, engineers, lawyers, or architects.

Service: An identifiable, and essentially intangible, activity that provides the user with some degree of performance satisfaction, but does not involve ownership.

NOTES

1. Joan Berger, "The False Paradise of a Service Economy," *Business Week*, March 3, 1986, pp. 78–81. For statistics on service industries see "1986 Service Annual Survey," U.S. Department of Commerce Bureau of the Census, September 1987.

2. "Entrepreneurs Find Success in the Service Sector," *Business Week*, September 28, 1987, p. 68.

3. See Leonard Berry, "Services Marketing Is Different," *Business*, May-June 1980, pp. 24–28; Christopher Lovelock, "Distinctive Aspects of Services Marketing," in Christopher Lovelock, *Services Marketing* (Prentice-Hall, 1984) pp. 1–9; and G. Lynn Shostack, "Breaking Free from Product Marketing," *Journal of Marketing*, April 1977, pp. 73–80.

4. Committee on Definitions, *Marketing Definitions: A Glossary of Marketing Terms* (American Marketing Association, 1960), p. 21.

5. Peter Bennett (ed.), *Dictionary of Marketing Terms*, (American Marketing Association, 1988), p. 184.

6. James H. Donnelly, Jr., "Service Delivery Strategies in the 1980s—Academic Perspective," in Leonard L. Berry and James H. Donnelly, Jr. (eds.), *Financial Institution Marketing: Strategies in the 1980s* (Consumers Bankers Association, 1980) pp. 143–50.

7. Leonard Berry and Terry Clark, "Four Ways to Make Services More Tangible," *Business*, October-December 1986, pp. 53–54.

8. Berry, "Services Marketing Is Different," p. 25.

9. See Leonard Berry, A. Parasuraman, and Valerie Zeithaml, "Synchronizing Demand and Supply in Service Businesses," *Business*, October-December 1984, pp. 35–37; and W. Earl Sasser, "Match Supply and Demand in Service Industries," *Harvard Business Review*, November-December 1976, pp. 133–40.

10. An excellent discussion of service classifications is provided by Christopher H. Lovelock, *Services Marketing* (Prentice-Hall, 1984), pp. 50–62.

11. Dan R. E. Thomas, "Strategy Is Different in Service Businesses," *Harvard Business Review*, July-August 1978, pp. 158–65.

12. Frederick A. Russ and Charles A. Kirkpatrick, *Marketing* (Little, Brown, 1982), p. 489.

13. Paul J. Peter, Lawrence X. Tarpey, and James H. Donnelly, Jr., *A Preface to Marketing Management* (Business Publications, Inc., 1982), pp. 189–90.

14. Berry, "Services Marketing Is Different," p. 27.

15. Evert Gummesson, "The Marketing of Professional Services—25 Propositions," in James H. Donnelly and William R. George (eds.), *Marketing Services* (American Marketing Association, 1981), p. 27.

16. Philip Kotler and Richard A. Connor, Jr., "Marketing Professional Services," *Journal of Marketing*, January 1977, pp. 71–76.

17. Patricia B. Gray, "More Lawyers Reluctantly Adopt Strange New Practice—Marketing," *The Wall Street Journal*, January 30, 1987, p. 25.

18. Lenore Skenazy, "Jury Is Still Out," *Advertising Age*, April 11, 1988, p. 76.

19. Skenazy, 1988, p. 76.

20. W. Randolph Baker, "Counsel to Counsel," *Public Relations Journal*, February 1988, pp. 24–27, 43.

21. "Americans Voice Opinions on the Services Industry," *Marketing News*, November 20, 1987, p. 18.

22. L. Berry, A. Parasuraman, and V. Zeithaml, "The Service-Quality Puzzle," *Business Horizons*, September-October 1988, pp. 35–43.

23. A. Parasuraman, V. Zeithaml, and L. Berry, "A Conceptual Model of Service Quality and Its Implications for Future Research," *Journal of Marketing*, Fall 1985, pp. 41–50.

24. Parasuraman et al, 1985, pp. 41–50.

25. Bro Uttal, "Companies That Serve You Best," *Fortune*, December 7, 1987, pp. 98–116.

26. Uttal, 1987, pp. 98–116.

CASE APPLICATION 21-1

The Airlines Survey the Passengers

Air Marketing Research is an organization that conducts passenger surveys for airline firms like American, Eastern, TWA, United, and USAir. Listed below are some of the questions that were asked in a survey of airlines.

Questions

1. How would the airlines use the data collected from Part 1, Section B in the Air Marketing Research survey?

2. Why would the airlines be interested in the passenger responses to Part II?

3. Is the type of marketing research information collected by a service business like an airline that much different from the type a manufacturing firm like Campbell's Soup would be interested in? Explain.

4. What type of personal information (would marital status be important?) should Air Research collect for the airlines? Why?

I. Please tell us about your impressions of various airlines.

A. Based on all the things you've heard or know about airlines, please indicate the *one* airline you most associate with each of the phrases listed below.

	Northwest	**United**	**TWA**	**American**	**USAir**	**All the same**
Has the best overall reputation	64-1 □	-2 □	-3 □	-4 □	-5 □	-6 □
Is the first to offer new services	65-1 □	-2 □	-3 □	-4 □	-5 □	-6 □
Satisfies business travelers best	66-1 □	-2 □	-3 □	-4 □	-5 □	-6 □
Provides an inconsistent level of service	67-1 □	-2 □	-3 □	-4 □	-5 □	-6 □
Offers the most value for the money	68-1 □	-2 □	-3 □	-4 □	-5 □	-6 □
Satisfies vacation travelers best	69-1 □	-2 □	-3 □	-4 □	-5 □	-6 □
Is the most warm and friendly	70-1 □	-2 □	-3 □	-4 □	-5 □	-6 □
Makes flying easiest for the public	71-1 □	-2 □	-3 □	-4 □	-5 □	-6 □
Goes to the most destinations	72-1 □	-2 □	-3 □	-4 □	-5 □	-6 □
Provides the most efficient, hassle-free experience	73-1 □	-2 □	-3 □	-4 □	-5 □	-6 □
Frequently provides poor service	74-1 □	-2 □	-3 □	-4 □	-5 □	-6 □
Has the most widebody planes	75-1 □	-2 □	-3 □	-4 □	-5 □	-6 □
Offers the lowest fares	76-1 □	-2 □	-3 □	-4 □	-5 □	-6 □
Provides the best all-around service	77-1 □	-2 □	-3 □	-4 □	-5 □	-6 □
Flies the aircraft people prefer	78-1 □	-2 □	-3 □	-4 □	-5 □	-6 □

B. Usually airlines use a particular theme or tag line. For each of the phrases listed below, please indicate the *one* airline you most associate with each theme.

	Northwest	**United**	**TWA**	**Pan Am**	**American**
We fly the world the way the world wants to fly	79-1 □	-2 □	-4 □	-5 □	-6 □
Fly the friendly skies	80-1 □	-2 □	-4 □	-5 □	-6 □
We better be better	81-1 □	-2 □	-4 □	-5 □	-6 □
Airport Express	82-1 □	-2 □	-4 □	-5 □	-6 □
Doing what we do best	83-1 □	-2 □	-4 □	-5 □	-6 □
We have to earn our wings everyday	84-1 □	-2 □	-4 □	-5 □	-6 □
You're going to like us	85-1 □	-2 □	-4 □	-5 □	-6 □

II. Please tell us a bit about your current trip. On this trip, which of the following have you done/are you likely to do? (Check all that apply.)

98-1 □ Rent a car
99-1 □ Stay in the downtown section of a city
100-1 □ Visit more than one city
101-1 □ Visit the home of a business associate
102-1 □ Attend a meeting/conference
103-1 □ Visit the home of a friend or relative
104-1 □ Go shopping
105-1 □ Visit a national park, monument, or historic site
106-1 □ Entertain business associates at your hotel/local restaurant
107-1 □ Be entertained by business associate(s)
108-1 □ Use public transportation
109-1 □ Visit a nightclub/theater/cinema
110-1 □ Spend a quiet evening alone
111-1 □ Read local newspapers
112-1 □ Watch a professional/collegiate sports event
113-1 □ Participate in recreational sports
114-1 □ Visit a museum
115-1 □ Eat dinner alone in local restaurants
116-1 □ Other ______________________ (Please specify)

Days Inns of America

Cecil B. Day, Sr., had only a few rules when he opened his Days Inns motels in 1970. He insisted on building inexpensive hotels, primarily along highways in the Southeast; owning most of them rather than franchising; and, consistent with his religious belief in abstinence, never serving alcohol.

But since the chain was sold in 1984, six years after Mr. Day's death, the old rules have changed. Atlanta-based Days Inns has expanded to all 50 states, opened several hotels with rooms that cost a lot more than $100 per night, sold all of its company-owned properties to franchisees, and allowed cocktail lounges serving alcohol to open in its hotels.

The transformation is all part of Days Inns of America, Inc.'s grand plan to be a major hotel chain. And the new owners say the strategy is succeeding despite the fact that the chain's founder might not recognize the company today.

"Cecil's was very much of a family owned and operated lodging chain. The new ownership is big business," said Hank B. Staley, director of the leisure-time industry group at the Atlanta office of Laventhol & Horwath. "They are just very, very different. They are interested in expansion at a very rapid pace. That was not necessarily the goal of the Day family."

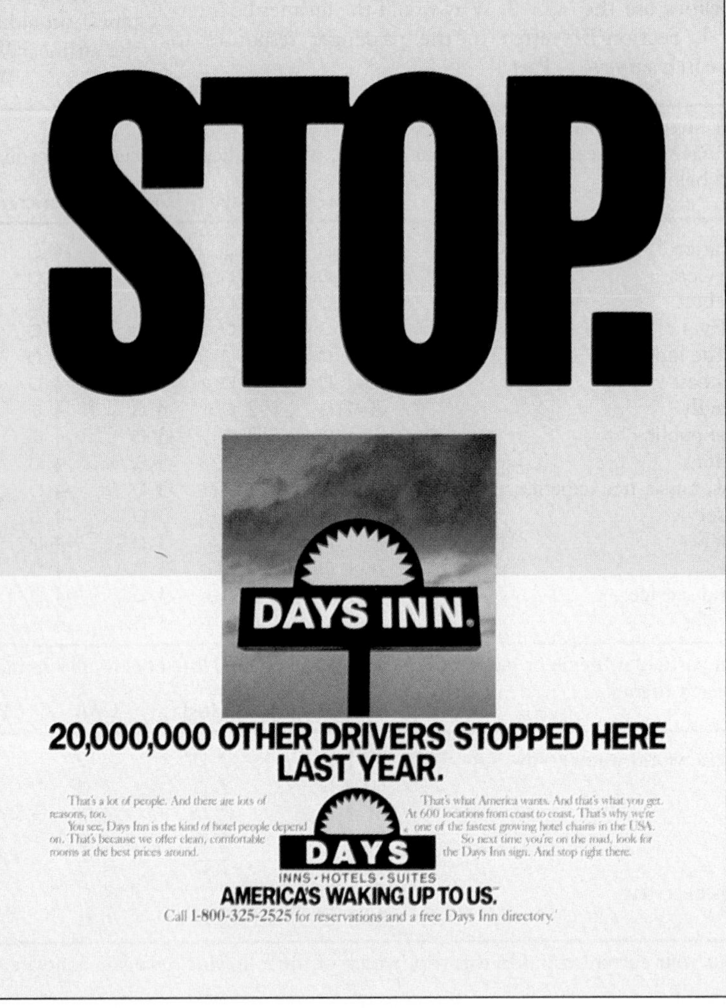

The company has been doing well at expanding its hotel business, largely by broadening its appeal. Since 1984, the chain has grown from 285 properties to 900 hotels worldwide. Franchise and management fees in 1987 were $40 million. That number increased to $52 million in 1988 and is projected to be $87 million by 1990, largely as a result of the fact that the company sold off many of the properties it owned in order to concentrate on franchising.

Rather than remaining almost exclusively an economy chain by the side of the road for Southern travelers, Days Inns has concentrated on opening franchises in major cities, near airports, and near suburban office parks; locations that are particularly attractive to business customers. There are now Days properties at all of the nation's 50 busiest airports.

The company says its numbers clearly show that business travelers are turning to Days Inns when they travel. According to Michael A. Leven, the company's president and chief operating officer, business travelers comprised 35 percent of the company's guests in 1988, up from 20 percent a year earlier. "A major thrust of the advertising recently has been aimed at the business person because we always went over well with other markets," said Joel M. Babbit, the president of Babbit & Reiman Advertising, the firm that created the chain's current "America's Waking Up To Us" advertising campaign.

Although executives traveling on big expense accounts are more apt to choose

Days Inns of America: The Chain at a Glance

	Company-owned properties	Company-managed properties	Franchised properties	Total	Number of rooms
1984	115	0	170	285	45,030
1985	88	3	199	290	46,594
1986	22	32	389	443	66,392
1987	25	50	515	590	84,832
1988	0	46	702	748	100,839

SOURCE: Days Inns of America Corp.

the Ritz-Carlton or other luxury hotel than a Days Inn, there is a large group of business travelers for whom Days properties are attractive. "I think Days Inns is basically targeting the Chevrolet, Pontiac part of the market," said H. Mark Daley, who owned a Holiday Inn franchise for 14 years before buying three Days properties in North Carolina.

The company has also expanded the Days name to include not just inns but also Days Suites, Days Hotels and, most recently, Daystops. Room rates at Days Inns range from $25 to $125 per night, depending upon location. System average rate is about $40 per night. Days Suites, of which there are four, were created in 1988 to compete with similar chains that offer fewer amenities but more room space. These properties rent for an average of $44 per night.

The fifteen Days Hotels, the high-end properties the company introduced last year, are priced at $58 per night on average. Daystops, which are designed to compete directly with budget-price chains such as Motel 6 and Econo Lodge, cost about $25 per night on average.

SOURCE: L. Eric Elie, "A New Day That Dawned for Days Inns," *The Atlanta Constitution*, February 7, 1989, pp. 1D, 10D; personal communication with Days Inns, Inc., June 1989.

Questions

1. In what ways is the marketing of Days Inns similar to the marketing of consumer goods? How is it different?

2. How might Days Inns measure the quality of its service?

3. How do the five features of services discussed early in Chapter 21 apply to Days Inns? What are the implications for Days Inns' marketing strategy?

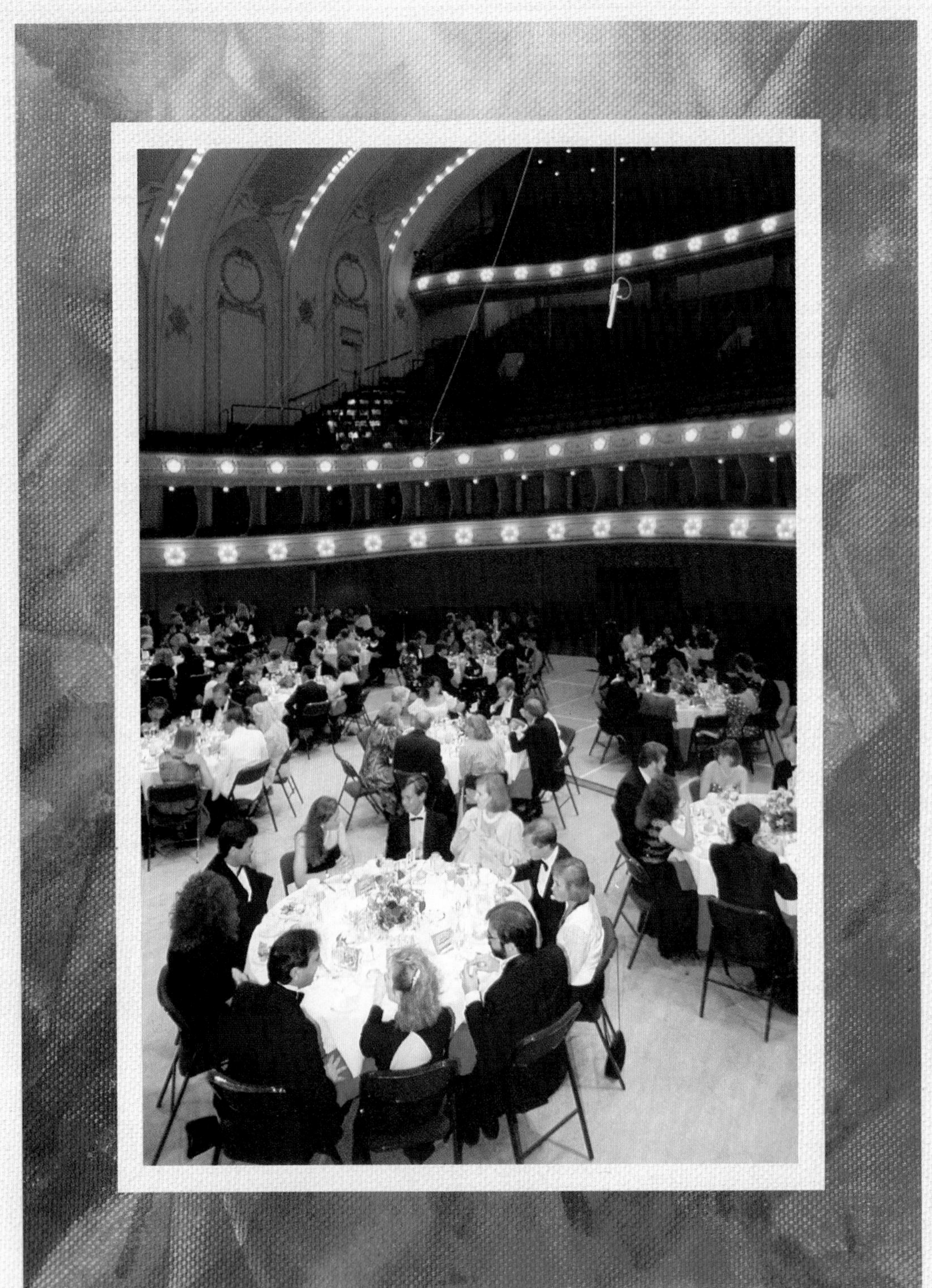

22

Marketing in Nonprofit Organizations

Learning Objectives

Upon completing this chapter, you will be able to do the following:

IDENTIFY
the many types of nonprofit organizations.

DESCRIBE
the characteristics of nonprofit organizations and how they differ from business firms.

EXPLAIN
the importance of marketing for nonprofit organizations.

ILLUSTRATE
how product, price, promotion, and distribution concepts can be effectively applied in nonprofit situations.

DISCUSS
strategies for introducing marketing into nonprofit organizations.

MARKETING PROFILE

Colleges Learn to Use Advertising

In the kind of close-up testimonial that's a staple of consumer advertising, four students speak simply and convincingly about all the good reasons to become a student at Boston's Northeastern University.

The ads focus on the school's innovative Cooperative Education program, which allows students to alternate classroom time with jobs in business and industry. School officials felt that if more students knew about Northeastern's program, a greater number would be interested in learning more about it. The strategy paid off with a record 7,000 inquiries.

Northeastern's aggressive, nontraditional approach to college recruitment is an example of a nationwide trend. Colleges and universities are bracing for a demographic disaster as the baby boom gives way to the birth dearth. And just as any marketer must scramble to wrest potential customers from competitors' clutches, so colleges are using ever more creative strategies to woo high school graduates.

According to the Center for Education statistics, a 15-year decline in the number of high school graduates began in 1977. Peaking that year at 3.2 million, the number will taper off to 2.7 million by 1992.

But so far, the vast majority of the nation's 3,389 institutions of higher learning are in better shape today than they were ten years ago. And all have started to ease the impact of the baby bust with revamped recruitment efforts, image overhauls, and state-of-the-art advertising.

Northeastern University first turned to television seven years ago. "We tried radio," says Philip McCabe, dean of admissions, "but it didn't work. When kids are listening to their rock stations, they're not interested in hearing about cooperative education." After some experimentation, it became clear that TV gave the best results. Today,

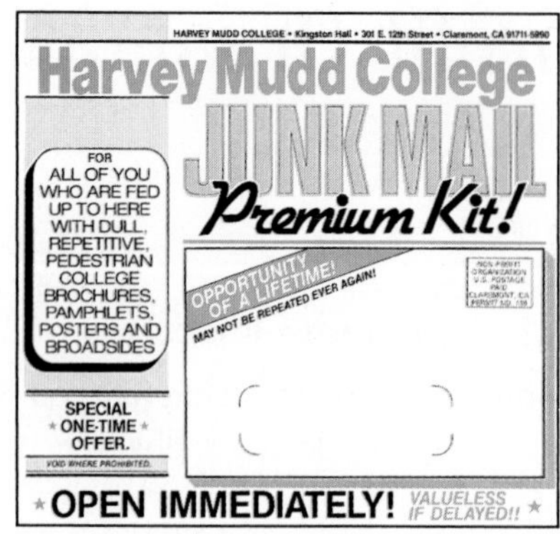

Northeastern's commercials are seen across the country, reaching potential students well beyond the school's traditional New England market.

Other colleges face problems different from those of large, urban schools such as Northeastern. Jim Jarvells of Campus Crossroads, an academic news service in Keene, NJ, explains: "As demographics change in the '90s, schools affected the most are small, independent liberal arts colleges, predominantly rural in nature." Cornell College is one example. A small liberal arts school in Mt. Vernon, Iowa, Cornell could be facing trouble as the next decade approaches—but it probably won't. "We've had a 40 percent increase in enrollment since 1982," says Peter Bryant, Cornell's dean of admissions.

Cornell advertises its competitive edge through general direct mail in 40 states. It also uses market research to determine which strengths to stress. Earlier recruitment literature, for example, played down the school's small-town setting until research revealed that for many students it was a big plus.

Duncan Murdoch has been working magic as director of admissions for Harvey Mudd College, a small engineering school in Claremont, California. In the early 1980s, when he was asked to bring a fresh approach to their recruiting process, Murdoch came up with the Harvey Mudd College Junk Mail Premium Kit, a blatantly tacky brochure specially designed for students ". . . who are fed up to here with dull, repetitive, pedestrian college brochures, pamphlets, posters and broadsides." The layout looks more amateur than a badly done high school yearbook; the photos are tinted a downright ugly orange and gray; the copy is most irreverent, packed with information, and hard to put down once you start reading.

Murdoch says the Junk Mail brochure wasn't immediately well received by the rest of the college. "I kind of snuck it in," he says. "I got a lot of direct flak from the faculty, but I stood my ground because I had the support of the president and senior staff." The support paid off. Harvey Mudd gets a 22 percent response rate from the Junk Mail piece, double the national average for college direct mail efforts.

Harvey Mudd College, Northeastern University, and Cornell College are bright exceptions in the college information dissemination game. But not for long. Schools still relying heavily on traditional recruitment techniques are being forced to re-examine the efficacy of their programs. The recruitment process is multifaceted, and no single change can work miracles. But college recruitment seems destined to rely more heavily on advertising—whether through the mass media, direct mail, or the strategic use of alumni.

SOURCE: from "Colleges Take a Crash Course in Creative Advertising" by Robin Nagle in ADWEEK, May 23, 1988. Reprinted by permission.

The *Marketing Profile* on Northeastern, Cornell College, and Harvey Mudd illustrates some of the topics covered in this chapter on marketing in nonprofit organizations. Nonprofit organizations are those organizations created for a purpose other than making a profit. Colleges need to go through the same steps that a profit-oriented organization would go through in developing and implementing a marketing program. Cornell College, for example, used marketing research to help identify and describe the attitudes and behavior of its target market. It then used the same marketing mix tools available to corporate marketers to increase the number of applications from potential students.

The same techniques can be used by government agencies, hospitals and other health-care organizations, charitable organizations, museums, and the arts to achieve their objectives. In this chapter, we will study the characteristics of nonprofit groups and how they differ from profit-making firms, focusing on how these differences affect marketing strategies. Nonprofit marketing is a relatively new application in marketing, still in its infancy, even though numerous organizations have begun to recognize the contribution that marketing can make to an organization's effectiveness. Thus, one additional purpose of the chapter is to present ways in which nonprofit groups can introduce marketing into their operations.

Nature and Scope of Nonprofit Marketing

Some marketers prefer the term *nonbusiness marketing* to *nonprofit marketing;* in this book we will use them interchangeably. Nonprofit, or nonbusiness, marketing applies to intangible goods or services, such as education, health care, entertainment, and religion, or to ideas or viewpoints, such as the prevention of forest fires, the use of seat belts, the prevention of cruelty to animals, and the advantages of donating blood. The marketing of ideas or social causes is sometimes called **social marketing.** Nonprofit organizations also market goods, such as Girl Scout cookies, but this is not as common as marketing services or ideas.

The concept of exchange is the basis of marketing by nonprofit organizations, just as it is in marketing goods and services. A marketing manager for a consumer product is typically only concerned with the exchange relationship between the company and its target market consumers, but a hospital marketer must be concerned with the exchange flows among a number of different client groups—patients and their families, physicians, medical staff, donors, and suppliers (see Figure 22–1).[1] The hospital provides medical services to patients and receives dollars in return. It provides the use of the medical facility to physicians in return for business from patients. The hospital gives donors gratitude, recognition, and a feeling of "doing good," and receives contributions of money or time in return. Patients, physicians, and donors are thus all treated as consumers. As we will see in later sections, different marketing strategies are required to effectively meet the needs of each of these groups. The tools of market analysis, product, promotion, distribution, and price are the same as those used in marketing consumer or industrial products. *How* the tools are used, however, is different.

The Differences in Nonprofit Marketing

Lovelock & Weinberg have identified four key differences between nonprofit and profit-oriented organizations.[2] Nonprofit organizations are characterized by the following:

1. *Multiple Publics.* Most nonprofit organizations direct marketing activities to at least two different publics—those involved with resource attraction and those involved

Figure 22–1 Exchange Flows Between a Hospital and Its Client Groups

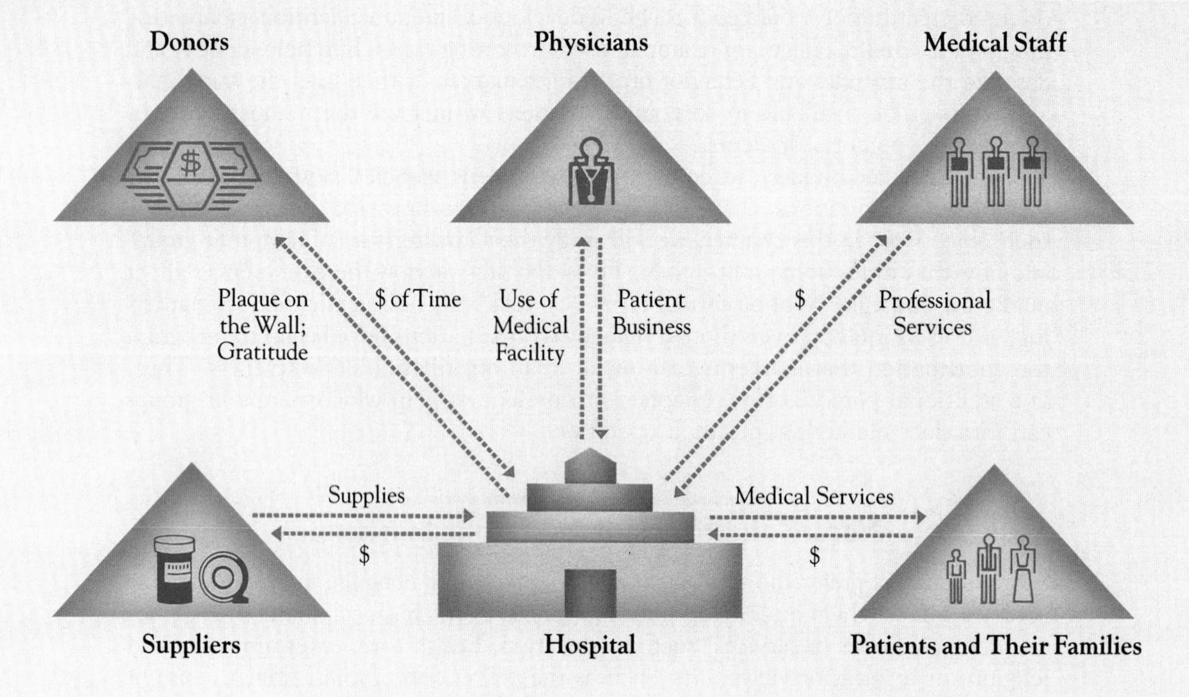

SOURCE: Reprinted by permission of publisher from *Management Principles for Nonprofit Agencies and Organizations*, by Gerald Zaltman.

with resource allocation. In Figure 22–1, donors represent resource attraction, and patients represent resource allocation (even though they also give the hospital resources to pay for the services they receive). The American Cancer Society engages in fund-raising to attract resources and then provides many services in allocating its resources. It can be argued that businesses also have multiple publics, but marketers are only involved in exchange relationships with consumers. Although business firms must attract resources from the sale of stocks or bonds or the negotiation of loans from financial institutions, marketers are rarely involved in these exchange relationships.

2. *Nonprofit Objective.* All marketing decisions should be evaluated in terms of ability to contribute to their objectives. In the case of a for-profit organization, strategies and tactics that contribute the most to the profit of the firm can be selected. With nonprofit organizations, there are multiple objectives that do not involve profit. With multiple and often unmeasurable objectives, it becomes difficult to evaluate alternative marketing programs or activities. For example, let's assume a zoo was trying to decide whether to enlarge the reptile section or to add a room where children could pet certain animals. The decision would depend on whether the zoo was trying to increase the total attendance (and revenues), maximize the satisfaction of those coming, or increase the educational value of a visit.

3. *Services Rather Than Physical Goods.* Nonprofit organizations are more involved in marketing services than they are in marketing physical goods. (Chapter 21 outlined

the differences between the marketing of services and the marketing of physical products.) Marketers in nonprofit organizations must not only adapt the marketing tools used by consumer goods firms to account for these differences but also must make adjustments for the kind of products to be marketed.

4. *Public Scrutiny and Nonmarket Pressures.* Many nonprofit agencies, at least the public ones, are subject to close scrutiny because of their roles in providing public services. For example, the review of proposed price increases for mail delivery by the U.S. Postal Rate Commission illustrates how public hearings and testimonies from trade associations, special interest groups, and heavy users of mail services must all be involved in the price-setting process. In addition, nonprofit organizations often are expected, or even required, to provide services or serve market segments that a profit-making organization would find uneconomical. The U.S. Postal Service is required to maintain rural post offices, and many mass transit companies are forced to maintain service on unprofitable routes.

Developing Marketing Strategies for Nonprofit Organizations

Marketing tools are just as applicable to nonprofit organizations as they are to organizations dedicated to making a profit. The sections that follow demonstrate how market analysis and segmentation, product, distribution, promotion, and pricing strategies can be effectively implemented in nonprofit organizations.

When nonprofit groups do think of marketing, it is often only the functions of advertising and personal selling that are used. Not many managers (or volunteers) in nonprofit organizations think in terms of total marketing programs or in marketing language. For example, colleges tend to think in terms of educational programs, not products; tuition, not price; catalogues and brochures, not advertising or sales promotions; college recruiting, not personal selling; and branch campuses and correspondence courses, not distribution. We will now take a closer look at each of the major areas of marketing to see how marketing tools can be (and have been) successfully applied to nonprofit marketing situations.

Market Analysis and Segmentation

Most decision makers in nonprofit organizations overlook the needs or wants, attitudes, and consumer behavior of their target market consumers. They either assume they know the needs of their "customers" or think of the market in total, not perceiving the various segments that exist. For example, many colleges treat all alumni equally in their fund-raising efforts. Stanford University, however, uses market analysis and segmentation strategies with separate marketing programs for each group.[3] Stanford first categorizes alumni by school and year of graduation. These groups are divided into subgroups according to their estimated potential for donations—$1000 or more, $100–$999, and less than $100. Personal contact is then used to solicit donations from the first two groups; mail solicitation is used to solicit funds from those likely to give less than $100. The last group is further divided into seven segments based on when the alumnus last donated money to Stanford, whether it was the first time he or she gave, and whether the amount was over or under $25. Five letters are sent to those who gave more than $25 the year before for the first time, and only two letters are sent to those who have never given. The letters sent to each of the groups contain different messages and appeals.

An organization must obtain information about the needs, attitudes, and behavior of different segments of the market before developing its marketing programs. For example, charities like the Multiple Sclerosis Society or the March of Dimes may find that people give money to them for the following reasons:[4]

1. *Need for self-esteem.* These people attempt to build their self-esteem and self-image by playing "God," or feeling good from giving. The opposite of this would be shame or guilt.

2. *Need for recognition from others.* These people attempt to build their social status or enhance their prestige in the eyes of others. They have a strong need to belong.

3. *Fear of contracting the problem.* This need centers on people's fear that they or members of their families will contract a particular disease or fall into poverty or neglect in their old age. They hope in some sense to buy "protection."

4. *The habit giver.* These people give out of habit for no real reason other than a desire not to be embarrassed by not contributing to the cause. They are indifferent to contributions, but feel that they must give to someone because everyone else does. A benefit may be not having to agonize over choosing charities (for example, *not* giving to a needy cause).

5. *Nuisance giver.* These people only give to get rid of the caller. They feel that contributing to a cause is of no real significance, but would rather donate a few dollars than be troubled by others.

6. *Required to give.* These people are required to give at work; they feel they are under pressure from superiors to donate part of their checks to a fund. They therefore demand efficiency and credibility from the organization that they contribute to.

7. *Captive givers.* These people feel real sorrow for someone they know who has a particular problem. They are other-centered in that they earnestly would like to aid the victim in some way. Givers in this category may contribute at the death of a friend rather than sending flowers, etc.

8. *People-to-people givers.* These people have a real feeling of the "commonness of man," a solidarity with other people. This group of people has internalized the idea of helping others because they want to.

9. *Concern for humanity.* This segment of givers is concerned about others for religious reasons and because they are "God's children." They feel a moral obligation to contribute to a charity. They have accepted the love-for-humanity idea because it is a requirement of their faith.

Once an organization has used market analysis to identify the different segments and the potential contributions from each segment, it can design marketing programs to maximize the contributions obtained from each segment. Table 22–1 gives some examples of fund-raising methods that might be used to obtain contributions from four different segments of the market.

There are some problems with respect to market analysis and segmentation encountered in the marketing of nonprofit organizations and social causes.[5] There are often no good secondary data available about consumers and consumer behavior, few research studies are available, and most nonprofit organizations do not have funding for their own marketing research studies. Also, it is often much more difficult to conduct research. It may be more difficult for consumers to explain why they gave money to a charity, what they expect from their church, or what they expect from their hospital than it is for them to tell you what they want in an automobile or camera.

Table 22–1 Fundraising Methods for Different Market Segments

Segment	Methods	
Mass Anonymous Small Gifts	Charity cans in stores Direct mail Door-to-door solicitation Street and sidewalk solicitation TV and radio marathons Thrift shops Plate passing	Raffles Rummage sales Sporting events Tours Walkathons, readathons, bikeathons, danceathons, jogathons, swimathons Yearbooks
Members and Their Friends	Anniversary celebrations Art shows Auctions Benefits (theater, movies, sports events) Bingo games Book sales Cake sales	Dances Dinners, suppers, lunches, breakfasts Fairs Fashion shows Parties in unusual places Telethons
Affluent Citizens	Convocations Dinners (invitational and/or testimonial) Letters from high-status individuals	Parlor meetings Telephone calls from high-status individuals
Wealthy Donors	Bequests Celebrity grooming Committee visit to person's home, office Memorials	Testimonial dinner for wealthy individuals Wealthy person invited to another's home or club

SOURCE: From *Strategic Marketing for Nonprofit Organizations*, 3rd ed., by Philip Kotler and Alan R. Andreasen. Copyright © 1987 by Prentice-Hall, Inc. Reprinted by permission of Prentice-Hall, Inc., Englewood Cliffs, N.J.

Review Your Marketing Knowledge

- You have just been named director of fundraising for your school's alumni association. Review the reasons people give money. How could this list be helpful in developing programs to raise money for the school?
- What methods would be most appropriate for raising funds from alumni?

Product

Nonprofit organizations and governments are more likely to market services and ideas rather than physical goods. It is no less important, however, for the nonprofit organization to define its product broadly, including such things as brand, packaging, and warranty. How the product is positioned will play a critical part in how it should be

MARKETING IN ACTION

Positioning the Jacksonville Symphony Orchestra

Founded in 1950 and with an operating budget of $2.5 million, the Jacksonville Symphony lost about 1,200 annual subscribers when it changed auditoriums and altered its program from classical music to more upbeat popular offerings. Because Jacksonville is a growing city, symphony subscriptions didn't decline, but grew at a lower-than-expected rate.

"We had moderate growth instead of tremendous growth. And, we had a lot of discontent," says Dean Corey, executive director of the symphony. "We had to get those 1,200 people back, and we wanted to know what the people wanted from their symphony."

According to Corey, they polled major orchestras across the country, and found little quantitative research on what the general public wants. An exception is the San Francisco Orchestra, which uses J. Walter Thompson for its marketing advice. "In the past, we, and other cities, have relied on institution and experience. We decided we needed to view us as a product," Corey says.

Jacksonville used focus groups to determine key issues surrounding the symphony. Location, programming, guest artists, and packaging were all gauged, then the perceptions were quantified through phone interviews with 500 persons by Message Factors, a marketing research firm.

"We learned exactly what types of things people wanted from their symphony. We learned about their lifestyles and what it would take for someone to subscribe, or for someone to renew their subscription," says Russell Boyd, managing director of Message Factors. "We finally knew what were the key issues and concerns of the people the symphony needed to reach."

Both Boyd and Corey say there were some startling findings. "We learned that our audiences aren't as shallow as we thought they were," says Corey. "People say that compact discs and video tapes have replaced the experience of going to the theater or a concert. That's not true; the CDs reinforce the experience. But we thought our audience only wanted the experience to see and be seen and mingle in the lobby. It's deeper than that. They want to meet people to confirm their opinions about the performance. They want to talk about how they're connecting with the music." The Jacksonville Symphony now "gives its audience an experience. That's the key. People want to live the music. We now sell it as an event," Corey says.

Boyd says the research showed two distinct audiences—classical and pop-oriented—and recommended not trying to mix the two. "They didn't want to alienate the current subscribers, who are more classical, but they needed to increase the base by changing the programming and location to attract the others. We saw them taking a two-prong approach to their season."

Which is exactly what the Jacksonville Symphony did. For one thing, the orchestra plays two distinct musical series in two halls. It reformulated its concert mix, its schedule, and its ticket-buying procedures. Since much of the potential audience is single and didn't want to commit to specific performance times, a flexible system was started wherein a subscriber buys six tickets and turns them in for any performance. "The person can use one ticket for six performances or use six tickets for one performance. They get flexibility, but they lose a guaranteed seat," Corey says.

"A lot of orchestras aren't making it and it's because they don't know who their market is," Corey says. "We now know who we need to reach. Before, we'd send out a glitzy brochure and maybe it worked—but we never knew why." Last year the symphony "squeaked by" with 6,800 subscribers, but it expects 8,000 to sign up this year. "It's beyond what we expected," Corey says.

SOURCE: Mary Welch, "Message Factors Finds Its Niche in the Music," *Atlanta Business Chronicle*, February 29, 1988, p. 6–A.

---

promoted, distributed, and priced. The concepts of product line, product mix, and product life-cycle are just as important for nonprofit organizations as they are for businesses.

The *Marketing in Action* feature on the Jacksonville Symphony Orchestra illustrates some of these concepts. The symphony was in the mature stage of the product

After determining what its customers wanted, the U. S. Postal Service developed guaranteed Express Mail overnight delivery.

life-cycle before it repositioned itself as an exciting experience tailored to the needs of its two major market segments. The symphony reformulated its concert mix, its schedule, and its packaging of tickets to meet the needs of its audience.

A critical ingredient in product strategy is, of course, a definition of what the customer wants to buy. The U.S. Postal Service has conducted a substantial amount of research to determine what its customers wanted to buy and, based on that research, developed a series of new products. Recognizing that consumers really were buying the ability to transmit communications (rather than mail service), the postal service has developed and introduced Express Mail overnight delivery service (with money-back guarantee if not delivered the next day) and Zip + 4 Presort Mail for large mailers willing to sort their outgoing mail by nine-digit zip code in return for a postage discount. These new products have been branded and are heavily promoted to businesses. Other products developed by the U.S. Postal Service include stamp albums, first day covers, and commemorative stamps for collectors.

Many nonprofit organizations have paid increased attention recently to their product mix. Universities have offered new product lines to meet the demand for degree programs in such new areas as information systems and health technology. Noncredit adult education courses of all types have been added and product lines such as MBA programs have been deepened through the addition of evening programs and Executive MBA programs taught on weekends. Zoos have altered product mixes by adding categories of animals and more animals within each category.

Distribution

Most channels of distribution for nonprofit marketers are very short, as they are with services. The channel typically goes directly from producer to consumer without intermediaries. Thus, Planned Parenthood markets its information and services directly to consumers, colleges work directly with students and potential students, and museums and performing arts organizations deal directly with their patrons. Occasionally intermediaries are involved. For example, some performing arts organizations have independent firms market their tickets, and certain charities hire professional fund-raisers to implement programs for soliciting contributions.

Physical distribution strategies may also be important for nonprofit organizations. The easier it is to donate money, the more money will be donated. Thus, the Salvation Army is extremely successful in its fund-raising efforts during the Christmas season by accepting donations on what seems like every single street corner in town. Universities have added branches in suburban areas, at corporate headquarters, and even on commuter trains. Symphony orchestras have tours that take concerts to people in rural areas and make recordings to distribute their music. Libraries have established branches in shopping malls and use large vans to create mobile branches throughout many cities. The U.S. Postal Service has opened self-service branches, in the parking lots of many shopping centers, open twenty-four hours a day, with no employees.

While it is important to distribute a product in locations attractive to consumers, this is not always possible with nonprofit organizations. Many hospitals and performing arts organizations are saddled with physical structures in downtown locations that are unattractive to the suburban part of their market. Since the cost of creating new facilities in the suburbs would be prohibitive, the other parts of the marketing program must be designed to overcome the disadvantage created by the distribution of the product.

Promotion

Promotion is the one marketing mix factor that most nonprofit organizations have learned to use. In fact, many equate marketing with promotion, not recognizing the importance of the other three marketing mix areas. Although many nonprofit groups have used advertising, personal selling, public relations, and/or sales promotion, very few have developed strong communications programs integrating all aspects of the promotion mix. Here are some examples of how colleges have attempted to increase applications through the use of aggressive promotion without making any real improvements in their competitive product positioning, services, or quality.[6]

- Bowdoin College in Maine recently advertised in *Black Enterprise's* annual "Careers & Opportunities" issue, using the headline, "In 1826, Bowdoin College graduated its first Afro-American: John Brown Russman. How many colleges can point to such a long-standing commitment to black Americans?"
- The University of Colorado at Denver featured its president, with his customary bow tie and suspenders, growling at the camera in a TV ad, "Gordon Gee wants *you*!" Other TV ads and billboards featured faculty and minority students. Its applications are holding their own for the first time in years.

- Carleton College in Minnesota has tried regional marketing in its direct mail efforts, based on research it conducted, emphasizing outdoor activities and the school's informal atmosphere to Westerners. Easterners were provided with statistics concerning the scholarly standing of the Carleton students and faculty.
- New York University has set up an in-house advertising agency to promote its continuing education and graduate programs.
- The admissions staff of one college distributed promotional frisbees to high school students vacationing during Easter break at Ft. Lauderdale, Florida.

Although a number of nonprofit groups such as symphonies, theater groups, the United Way, and the Armed Forces have advertised for many years, others such as colleges, hospitals, and social welfare groups have only recently effectively utilized this tool. The promotional strategy of nutrition and health groups in the Third World is presented in the *Marketing in Action* feature in this section. Churches have long advertised in weekend newspapers, and the American government has advertised mass transit, energy conservation, the use of seat belts, military recruitment, and the prevention of forest fires. In 1989, the federal government will spend $300 million on its paid and public service advertising campaigns. It was number 29 on the list of the top 100 advertisers in 1987.[7]

Most nonprofit organizations use public service announcements (PSAs), advertisements run by the media as a public service, at no cost to the advertiser. Unfortunately, many PSA campaigns are not effective, for a number of reasons.[8] Few public service advertisers pretest their ads. The ads are often created by committees, with no clear objectives in mind and no clear media strategy. With PSAs, the advertiser has no say about when or where the ads are run—on TV, they could be in the daytime or in the middle of the night, and, in magazines or newspapers, they go wherever there is space available. Often there is not enough money available to produce high-quality ads, and the ads are typically not run with enough frequency to have much impact. For the most part, nonprofit groups of this type are too short of funds to support effective promotion campaigns.

Personal selling is often an important promotional tool. Many charitable organizations find that a small proportion of their donors contribute a large portion of the total amount of funds raised, and they use personal selling to reach the large contributor. College alumni directors personally "sell" large contributors on their school, and the same holds true for fundraisers in organizations such as the American Cancer Society, the United Negro College Fund, the Humane Society, and museums and performing arts organizations. The army uses personal selling to recruit new soldiers. Certain religious groups use missionaries to sell their religion. College admissions personnel engage in personal selling when they visit high schools to recruit students.

Sales promotion can also be important for nonprofit organizations. Brown University created a gift catalogue offering an endowed faculty chair at a cost of $1 million. For a $10 million gift, with a 10-percent discount for cash, a contributor could have the building housing the geology and chemistry departments named after him or her.[9] Brochures, films, special events, contests, and catalogues can all be effective sales promotion tools.

Finally, public relations is also often used by nonprofit organizations. Many nonprofit marketers have become adept at getting publicity for their organizations by staging "events" and nurturing the press.

MARKETING IN ACTION

When the Product Is Life Itself

Promotional techniques have had a significant impact on the education of Third-World families in the proper prenatal and postnatal care of babies. Fifteen years ago most nutrition and health educators disdained the mass media and, especially, advertising. They believed that the latter was so closely attached to commercial marketing that it could not possibly work for the advancement of health and nutrition. Today advertising is a major instrument in Indonesia's Nutrition Education Improvement Program and in Central and South American infant feeding programs. The power of marketing, particularly advertising, has been demonstrated.

The approach for nutritional and health advertisers requires meaningful content and rational presentation. In Indonesia, the Nutrition Education Improvement Project uses radio to inform rural mothers about dietary practices for pregnant and lactating women and their infants, for treating diarrhea, and for monthly weighing of infants.

Consumer research, using focus groups and questionnaires, was done to determine the concerns and practices of the identified target audience. Based upon this research, specific advertising copy themes were identified, and the appropriate media-matching to the target was done. In Indonesia, the different advertising messages were rotated over commercially paid-for radio so that each one had a reasonable frequency with its particular audience. In addition, the messages were displayed in separate posters that were distributed among village mothers. The copy of one Central American ad follows:

Lita: Mama, what are you putting in my baby's lugaw (a rice and water weaning food)?

Grandmother: A drop of oil, some chopped green vegetables, and fish.

Lita: Where did you get the strange idea?

Grandmother: From the doctor on the radio. Listen!

Doctor: After six months a baby needs lugaw as well as breast milk, but lugaw must be mixed with fish that gives some protein for muscles and brain, green vegetables for vitamins, oil for weight on the baby's body.

Lita: But mama, a six-month-old baby can't digest such foods.

Grandmother: Shh. Listen to the doctor on the radio.

Doctor: A six-month-old can digest these foods. Just wash the salt from the dried fish, chop the vegetables and cook them well, add a little oil, and mash with the lugaw.

The ad continues with the grandmother directing Lita to put aside old, outdated ways and learn from the doctor on the radio.

SOURCE: Richard K. Manoff, "When the 'Client' Is Human Life Itself," *Advertising Age*, August 22, 1983, pp. M–4 and M–5.

Pricing

Pricing in nonprofit organizations is often determined differently from that in profit-oriented businesses. The differences between the two groups relate to their objectives. Often, with nonprofit groups, the objective in setting a price is recovery of costs, and there are times when prices are set knowing that even this will not be accomplished. It is not unusual for tuition at public colleges and universities to cover less than one-third of the cost of educating a student. Operas, symphonies, and ballets rarely cover their costs through ticket sales; they must rely upon grants and contributions from foundations, businesses, and individuals. If prices for buses and subways were set to cover operating costs, many individuals would not be able to afford to ride them.

It is also important to recognize that prices charged by nonprofit organizations involve more than money. Nonmonetary costs can include time, effort, inconvenience, and pride. Alcoholics Anonymous, for example, charges a very high price—a public commitment to stop drinking and an admission of a drinking problem in front of one's peers.[10]

Review Your Marketing Knowledge

- Why do many nonprofit organizations concentrate most of their marketing efforts in the promotion area?
- How could a hospital utilize distribution and pricing concepts more effectively? How might a public hospital go about adding products to its product mix?

Different market segments may be charged different prices. Performing arts groups charge different prices for different seat locations. Season ticket holders are given quantity discounts; the prices they are charged are lower on a per-ticket basis than prices charged individual ticket buyers. Sometimes different types of consumers, such as students and senior citizens, are charged lower fees. Members of an organization may receive discounts. Contributors to nonprofit organizations also pay different prices by contributing different amounts. Often levels such as donors, patrons, sustaining members, family members, and individual members are offered.

Some organizations have tried to get a better idea of their costs and have begun to base their pricing on these costs. A few colleges have adjusted tuition charges, for example, to reflect the fact that juniors and seniors often cost more to educate than freshmen and sophomores. Since 1977, the University of Minnesota has priced its tuition using a formula that includes the cost of faculty salaries, support services, utilities, and equipment. This has resulted in a 13 percent higher tuition for students in the College of Forestry than the tuition for students in the College of Liberal Arts. And students in the College of Biological Sciences pay 19 percent more than the liberal arts students.[11]

Introducing Marketing into Nonprofit Organizations

There are a number of ways of integrating marketing into nonprofit organizations, but it is first important to understand the role that marketing is to play within the organization. Figure 22–2 presents an organizational chart for the marketing function within a transit authority.[12] Note that there are many different aspects of marketing included on the organizational chart and that a number of different people would be needed to execute all these functions. Although this organizational structure is recommended by the U.S. Department of Transportation, it is doubtful that many mass transit organizations are structured this way. Even though it makes sense to marketing people, pricing and service changes are probably not under the authority of the marketing manager in most transit system operations.

Figure 22–2 Recommended Marketing Organization and Functions for a Transit Authority

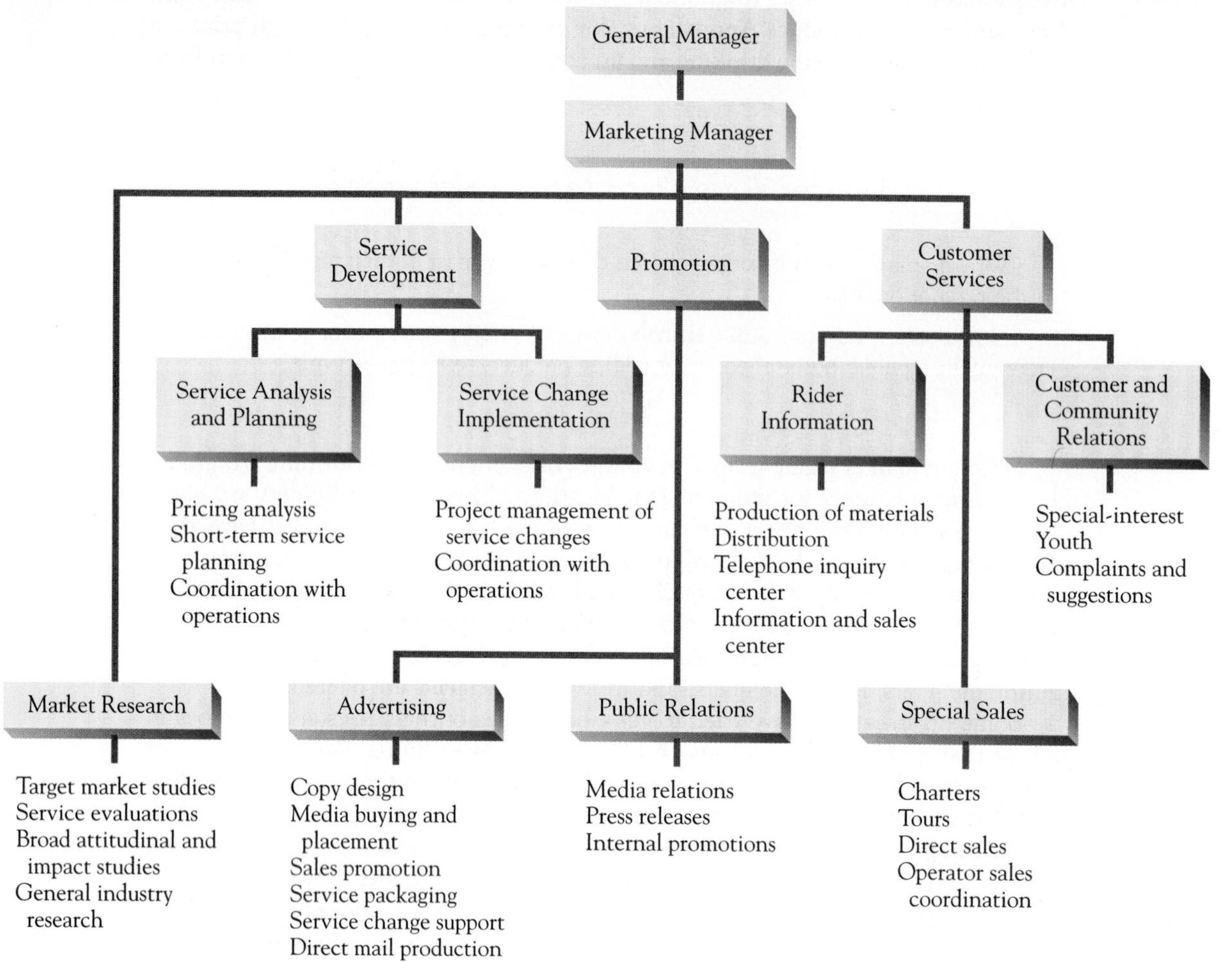

SOURCE: Office of Transit Management, Urban Mass Transportation Administration, U.S. Department of Transportation, *Transit Marketing Management Handbook: Marketing Organization,* as excerpted in C. Lovelock and C. Weinberg, eds., *Readings in Public and Nonprofit Marketing* (The Scientific Press, 1978), p. 85.

Kotler recommends the following ways of introducing marketing into a nonprofit institution.[13]

1. *Marketing Committee.* The function of a marketing committee is to examine the institution's problems and the potential for the marketing function. The committee objectives are to (1) identify the marketing problems and opportunities facing the institution; (2) identify the major needs for marketing services; and (3) explore the possible need for a full-time director of marketing.

2. *Task Forces.* The chief administrator should appoint task forces to conduct an institutional audit to discover how the institution is seen by its key publics, what its constituencies want the institution to be, which programs are strong and which are weak, and so on.

Figure 22–3 Job Description: A University Director of Marketing

Position title: Director of Marketing

Reports to: Vice-President, University Relations

Scope: University-wide

Position concept: The Director of Marketing is responsible for providing marketing guidance and services to university officers, school deans, department chairpersons, and other agents of the university.

Functions: The Director of Marketing will:

1. contribute a marketing perspective to the deliberations of the top administration in its planning of the university's future
2. prepare data that might be needed by an officer of the university on a particular market's size, segments, trends, and behavioral dynamics
3. conduct studies of the needs, perceptions, preferences, and satisfactions of particular markets
4. assist in the planning, promotion, and launching of new programs
5. assist in the development of communication and promotion campaigns and materials
6. analyze and advise on pricing questions
7. appraise the workability of new academic proposals from a marketing point of view
8. advise on new student recruitment
9. advise on current student satisfaction
10. advise on university fundraising

Responsibilities: The Director of Marketing will:

1. contact individual officers and small groups at the university to explain services and to solicit problems
2. prioritize the various requests for services according to their long-run impact, cost-saving potential, time requirements, ease of accomplishment, cost, and urgency
3. select projects of high priority and set accomplishment goals for the year
4. prepare a budget request to support the anticipated work
5. prepare an annual report on the main accomplishments of the office

Major liaisons: The Director of Marketing will:

1. relate most closely with the President's Office, Admissions Office, Development Office, Planning Office, and Public Relations Department
2. relate secondarily with the deans of various schools and chairpersons of various departments

SOURCE: From *Strategic Marketing for Nonprofit Organizations*, 3rd ed., by Philip Kotler and Alan R. Andreasen. Copyright © 1987 by Prentice-Hall, Inc. Reprinted by permission of Prentice-Hall, Inc., Englewood Cliffs, N.J.

3. *Marketing Specialist Firms.* Specialist firms such as advertising agencies, direct mail consultants, and marketing research firms should be used on special projects to help the institution identify its mission, objectives, strategies, and opportunities.

4. *Marketing Consultant.* An independent marketing consultant may be hired to conduct a comprehensive marketing audit of the organization and present a set of findings and recommendations concerning the institution's marketing efforts.

5. *Marketing Director.* Eventually the organization may become ready for a director of marketing. This requires the development of a job description containing the functions, responsibilities, and major liaisons of the position. Figure 22–3 presents a job description for a director of marketing for a university.

6. *Marketing Vice President.* According to Kotler, the ultimate solution is the establishment of a vice president of marketing, an upper level management position with more scope, authority, and influence for marketing.[14]

Personal Computer Exercise

This PC exercise will illustrate the tradeoffs that have to be made in not-for-profit organizations with multiple objectives. The exercise presents you with a set of program alternatives that have different impacts on the organization, and you will have to decide which of the programs should be undertaken. Some will generate net revenues over the costs, and others will deliver greater benefits to the recipients of the organization's services. You will see the difficult choices that managers of these organizations face every day.

KEY POINTS

- The concept of exchange provides the basis of marketing by nonprofit organizations. Marketing managers in businesses are typically concerned only with the exchange relationship between the company and its target market consumers; nonprofit marketers typically are concerned with exchange flows involving a number of different publics.
- In addition to being concerned with multiple publics, nonprofit marketing differs from marketing in profit-oriented organizations in several other ways: it has a nonprofit objective, it focuses on services rather than physical goods, and it must deal with public scrutiny and nonmarket pressures.
- The tools used in marketing nonprofit organizations are the same as those used by businesses. How the tools are used differs, however, because of the differences in the products and organizations.
- It is important for nonprofit organizations to conduct market analyses and segment their markets, but marketing research is often difficult, and there is usually not much secondary information available.
- Nonprofit organizations should develop strategies regarding product positioning, branding, packaging, and product mix.
- Channels of distribution for nonprofit organizations are very short, going directly from producer to consumer without using intermediaries.
- Nonprofit organizations often use promotional tools, including public service advertisements.
- Pricing strategies for nonprofit organizations are often different from those used by profit-oriented businesses because the objectives are not the same.
- Marketing can be integrated into a nonprofit institution through a marketing committee, task forces, marketing specialist firms, marketing consultants, a marketing director, or a marketing vice president.

ISSUES FOR DISCUSSION

1. In what ways might the marketing manager's job in a public, not-for-profit hospital differ from his or her counterpart in a private, profit-oriented hospital?
2. Identify some relevant market segments for each of the following organizations:
   a. the American Red Cross
   b. a church
   c. the United Way of America
   d. Amtrak
   e. the American Cancer Society
3. What tactics could be used by the Partnership for a Drug Free America for product, price, promotion, and distribution to get people to stop using drugs?
4. Think of some relevant publics for your college or university. For each, describe the exchange relationship that exists.
5. Think of a nonprofit organization with which you are familiar. How marketing-oriented is this organization? What steps might it take to become a better marketer?

6. Can marketing be used to (a) get people to wear seat belts, (b) get people not to litter, (c) get people to be organ donors, or (d) prevent forest fires? What are the limits of such marketing?

7. Why do people give money to organizations like the Society for the Prevention of Cruelty to Animals? What methods would you recommend to this organization to help them increase the amount of funds they raise?

8. Why, in your opinion, haven't nonprofit organizations made better use of marketing?

9. Describe how marketing could be used by the following organizations:

a. a local theater company
b. the YMCA or YWCA
c. Mothers Against Drunk Driving (MADD)
d. a local museum

10. In many nonprofit organizations, *marketing* is a dirty word, associated with the rough world of commerce and with real or imaginary abuses. What would you say to a person who directs a nonprofit organization who holds these attitudes?

GLOSSARY

Nonbusiness marketing: Marketing conducted by nonprofit organizations.

Nonprofit organizations: Those organizations created for a purpose other than making a profit. Colleges and symphony orchestras are two kinds of nonprofit organizations.

Public service announcements (PSAs): Advertising run by the media as a public service—at no cost to the advertiser.

Social marketing: The marketing of ideas or social causes.

NOTES

1. This example is drawn from Melanie Wallendorf, "Understanding the Client as a Consumer," in G. Zaltman, (ed.), *Management Principles for Nonprofit Agencies and Organizations* (AMACOM Division of American Management Associations, 1979), pp. 256–60.

2. Christopher Lovelock and Charles Weinberg, "Public and Nonprofit Marketing Comes of Age," in G. Zaltman and T. Bonoma, eds., *Review of Marketing 1978* (American Marketing Association, 1978), pp. 413–52.

3. "Stanford University: The Annual Fund," in C. Lovelock and C. Weinberg, eds., *Cases in Public and Nonprofit Marketing* (Scientific Press, 1977), pp. 73–88.

4. From *Strategic Marketing for Nonprofit Organizations,* 3rd ed., by Philip Kotler and Alan R. Andreasen. Copyright © 1987 by Prentice-Hall, Inc. Reprinted by permission of Prentice-Hall, Inc., Englewood Cliffs, N.J.

5. Paul Bloom and William Novelli, "Problems and Challenges in Social Marketing," *Journal of Marketing,* Spring 1981, pp. 79–88.

6. See, for example, Robin Nagle, "Colleges Take a Crash Course in Creative Advertising," *Adweek,* May 23, 1988, pp. 28–29; Lawrence Ingrassia, "Colleges Learn to Use Fine Art of Marketing," *The Wall Street Journal,* February 23, 1981, p. 25; J. Gilbert, "The Stepped-Up Search for Student Bodies," *Madison Avenue,* February 1986, pp. 71–75; Philip Kotler, "Strategies for Introducing Marketing Into Nonprofit Organizations," *Journal of Marketing,* January 1979, pp. 37–44; and Brad Edmundson, "Colleges Conquer the Baby Bust," *American Demographics,* September 1987, pp. 26–31.

7. Janet Myers, "Learning to Deploy a Strategic Weapon,"*Advertising Age,* November 9, 1988, p. 94.

8. Joe Adams, "Why Public Service Advertising Doesn't Work," *Ad Week,* November 17, 1980, p.72.

9. "Keeping Brown in the Black," *Time,* May 24, 1982, p. 84.

10. Benson Shapiro, "Marketing for Nonprofit Organizations," *Harvard Business Review,* September-October 1973, pp. 123–32.

11. David Garino, "Some Colleges Try New Ways to Raise Fees," *The Wall Street Journal,* May 19, 1982, p. 31.

12. Office of Transit Management, Urban Mass Transportation Administration, U.S. Department of Transportation, "Organizing the Marketing Function for Transit Authorities," in C. Lovelock and C. Weinberg, eds., *Readings in Public and Nonprofit Marketing* (The Scientific Press, 1978), pp. 81–86.

13. Kotler, "Strategies for Introducing Marketing into Nonprofit Organizations," pp. 37–44.

14. Kotler, "Strategies for Introducing Marketing into Nonprofit Organizations," p. 43.

CASE APPLICATION 22–1

Media-Advertising Partnership for a Drug-Free America

The ad shows a young mother clutching her nursing infant to her breast. The image is touching, warm, life-giving. Then the copy begins: "Little Tammy's a lucky girl. Her mom used cocaine all through her pregnancy and Tammy came out healthy . . . but Tammy's luck may be running out. You see, her mom is still using cocaine. And because she breast-feeds her baby, Tammy is still getting quite a dose of that drug . . ."

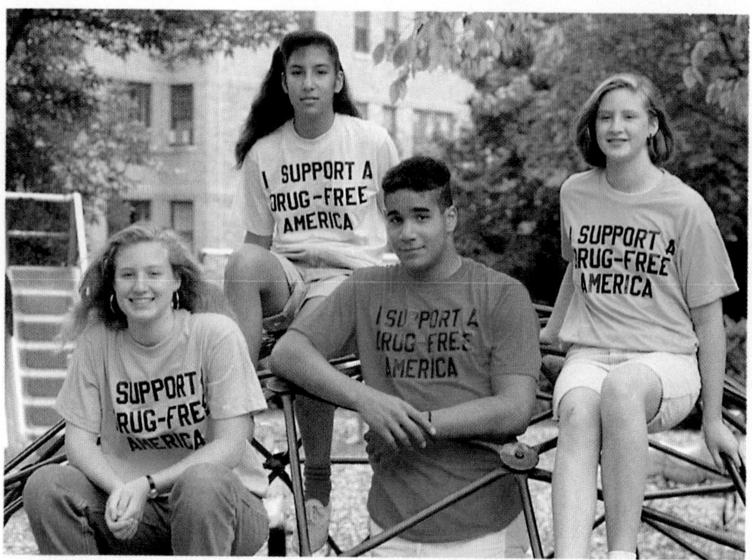

This modern-day Madonna and Child, photographed delicately and lovingly, is a portrait of a life doomed before it ever had a chance. It is an image that will linger in the mind, especially if you happen to be a young mother yourself—a young mother who might be doing drugs.

"Tammy"—prepared by Backer Spielvogel Bates—is among the many TV commercials, print ads, radio spots, and outdoor boards addressing the problem of drug abuse in the U.S. The work is being done by agencies participating in the Media-Advertising Partnership for a Drug-Free America. Organized through the American Association of Advertising Agencies, it has been called "the largest single *pro bono* advertising effort in U.S. history."

"Drug abuse is this country's leading socioeconomic problem," says Tom Hedrick, executive director of the Partnership. "We are trying to unsell the idea of using cocaine, crack, and marijuana. Our mission has been to try to change social attitudes about drug use, to combat the *normalization* of its use. We're trying to turn around the consumer demand for the substances from all segments of society. It's no longer just a problem of the urban poor."

"We've pulled together top people in advertising, healthcare, and marketing research to help formulate a strategy: We are approaching the problem posed by the $110 billion illegal drug industry from a marketing point of view," he says. "What we're doing is competing with drug pushers for market share of *nonusers*." It's competition for share of mind.

"Everything we've been doing goes back to the belief in advertising's power to communicate messages strong enough to change attitudes and affect behavior over time. That was the foundation for the Partnership," Mr. Hedrick says.

In February 1987, Gordon S. Black Corp., Rochester, NY, a marketing research company, conducted the first of two major surveys completed thus far on behalf of the Partnership. This first "base wave research" consisted of 7,325 mall-intercept interviews conducted nationwide—the largest mall-intercept study done to date. Respondents were asked to fill out a questionnaire concerning their attitudes toward illegal drugs and their use of those drugs. All respondents remained completely anonymous.

"We had several objectives. The first was to gather quantitative information regarding the attitudinal basis of drug use," Mr. Black says. "We wanted to get a handle on the advertising's targets and develop models to reach them." The four groups identified were 9–12 year olds, 13–17 year olds, college students, and adults.

"The study was designed to reveal the matrix of attitudes that form the basis of drug abuse—rather than focus on the phenomenon of drug abuse itself—and to track attitudinal change over time." This, of course, would support the Partnership's position that the advertising was contributing to that change. "Our findings also helped to focus the creative efforts," Mr. Black says.

The base-wave study identified several important factors:

- The age of first drug use.
- The importance of friendship networks and how they affect or inhibit drug use.
- The influence siblings exert on the behavior of their younger brothers and sisters.

The research formed the basis of several campaigns, according to Mr. Black. "We found that in the 9–12 group, contact with older siblings was the greatest reference for drug behavior—and older siblings feared they would influence their younger brothers and sisters. We recommended an ad that implied, 'Regardless of whether you think you're doing it, you're influencing them.' We thought this could be a powerful message to deliver to teenagers and young parents. We also found that one of the most powerful predictors of teen drug use was whether your friends were using it. Teens often want to do something about their friends' drug involvement, but they're afraid." A memorable TV spot by Leo Burnett USA, "Catching Up to Her," was based on that finding. In the spot, a teenage girl is forced to make a life-or-death decision regarding her drug-abusing girlfriend.

With the base-wave study completed, a "Wave I" study was done a year later with about the same number of respondents and with the same methodology. Had exposure to the partnership's advertising messages made a difference in attitudes? Some of the major findings included:

- Many attitudes and orientations have become more antagonistic toward drug use, with the most pronounced change overall in the college sample.
- In areas of high media exposure, the changes were greater on most variables than in the balance of the U.S. The ads themselves were generally very positively received.
- Among college students, there were statistically significant declines reported in cocaine consumption, notably among the "occasional users."

SOURCE: Cecilia Reed, "Partners for Life," *Advertising Age*, November 9, 1988, pp. 122–26.

Questions

1. How is the use of marketing different in this case in comparison to its use to increase sales of products?

2. What publics are involved in this marketing campaign?

3. What other marketing activities could be used to reduce drug abuse?

CASE APPLICATION 22–2

The U.S. Department of Defense

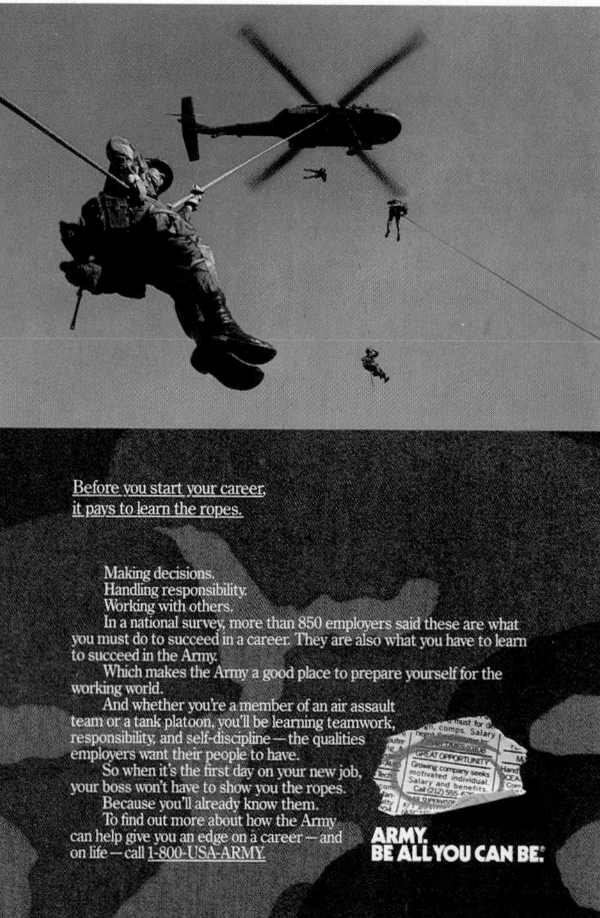

Before you start your career, it pays to learn the ropes.
Making decisions.
Handling responsibility.
Working with others.
In a national survey, more than 850 employers said these are what you must do to succeed in a career. They are also what you have to learn to succeed in the Army.
Which makes the Army a good place to prepare yourself for the working world.
And whether you're a member of an air assault team or a tank platoon, you'll be learning teamwork, responsibility, and self-discipline — the qualities employers want their people to have.
So when it's the first day on your new job, your boss won't have to show you the ropes.
Because you'll already know them.
To find out more about how the Army can help give you an edge on a career — and on life — call 1-800-USA-ARMY.
GREAT OPPORTUNITY
Growing company seeks motivated individual. Salary and benefits.
ARMY.
BE ALL YOU CAN BE.

The government's biggest success story of the 1980s is the U.S. Army's "Be All You Can Be" campaign, created by N W Ayer, New York. No other campaign can claim so much credit for turning around the declining fortunes of the all-volunteer force. "Be All You Can Be" changed the image of the Army. No longer the ditching ground for losers, the Army—through this campaign—became a place in which young men and women could earn money for college while they were learning high-tech skills.

The campaign was born out of desperation. In 1980, the seven-year-old, all-volunteer force had hit rock bottom. During the three previous years, Army recruiters had not achieved their goal of enrolling about 100,000 men and women a year. Not only were fewer recruits signing on, those who did were the least desirable: 46 percent were high school drop-outs, and 75 percent tested below average on intelligence tests.

The army's advertising in the 1970s was unfocused; the messages frequently changed, often at the whim of the Army and congressional leaders. Congress would look for advertising with "blood and guts," arguing that the Army wasn't for sissies. They didn't want advertising to glamorize it. The ad slogans of those years were "Today's Army wants to join you," "Join the people who've joined the Army," and "This is the Army." One ad showed soldiers slogging through a swamp. Suddenly, one man was sucked under the slime. "One recruiter said that every time he showed it, five people would walk out," recalls retired Col. William S. Graf, who was the U.S. Army Recruiting Command's director of advertising and sales promotion from 1980 to 1984.

Then, in late 1979, Maj. General Maxwell R. Thurman, commanding officer of USAREC, hired a New York marketing consultant, Canter, Achenbaum, which recommended the Army improve its product before launching a new campaign. Thurman persuaded Congress to provide for an Army College Fund, which would give recruits with two-year hitches $15,200 toward their college educations. With the incentive in place, USAREC set about to revitalize the Army's stagnant image.

The Army's longtime agency, N W Ayer, tackled the problem. Some of its early choices were "The 21st Century Army" and "We'll Show You How." But everyone involved agreed that "Be All You Can Be" best expressed the potential of Army service for young people. "When I was thinking of a line, I wanted one that could be used in the Army, not just in the ads," says Earl Carter, the former Ayer copywriter who is credited with writing the line. "I thought it was the kind of line a sergeant could yell at someone. He couldn't yell, 'This is the Army' when a guy was rappeling down a cliff."

According to a history of the marketing effort that Col. Graf wrote in 1986 while at the Army War College, both client and agency decided a high-tech focus to the campaign would be the way to dispel the Army's battered image. A patriotic theme was considered but dropped because "everyone considers himself patriotic," Col. Graf wrote in his study. "Patriotism doesn't have to be expressed by joining the Army." Nor could career development serve as a campaign theme because that would appeal most to those with no other options.

The advertising that resulted—all with superb production values—was fast-paced and showed healthy young men and women using high-technology equipment and benefiting from the Army's challenges. One spot said, "We do more before 9 A.M. than most people do all day."

The campaigns worked. The number of recruits testing in "category IV," or lowest intelligence, fell from 56 percent in 1980 to 30 percent in 1981 to 19 percent in 1982. In 1981, the percentage of high school graduates zoomed to 80 percent from 54 percent in 1980, and to 86 percent in 1982. By 1984, the percentage of high school graduates was 91 percent, where it remains today, and 63 percent of the new recruits scored above average on intelligence tests.

Today, the Army has retained "Be All You Can Be," even though it has changed ad agencies. Young & Rubicam, successor to Ayer on the $100 million account, has added the line, "Get an edge on life." With this twist, it is attempting to attract the brightest recruits by showing them how their Army experiences will benefit them later as civilians.

But the Army, as well as the other branches of the armed forces, faces a tough battle ahead. Now wise in the ways of advertising and how it affects the quality and quantity of the nation's military, Department of Defense ad strategists are studying ways to set up smaller media budgets, which have been cut from 10–50 percent in the last two years, depending on the service.

One cost-effective deployment of ad funds is to pursue smart prospective recruits. The reasoning is, the smarter the recruit, the cheaper he or she is to train. Military recruiters now favor ads attracting those bright candidates. Thus, the Navy, when it dropped long-time agency Backer Spielvogel Bates in August 1987 in favor of BBDO, also ended its 12-year-old "Live the Adventure" campaign. The adventure theme was considered too frivolous. Instead, the Navy, copying the Army's success, focused on high-tech machines and career enrichment. Its new campaign uses the theme, "You are tomorrow. You are the Navy."

The Defense Department also is grappling with the problem of how best to divide ad dollars among the services, says Lt. Col. Darrell Supak, assistant director of advertising, the department's ascension policy office. Should more money go into the "joint" military services—or corporate umbrella—campaign? Or will too broad a corporate campaign result in lower quality recruits for some of the individual services?

Lt. Col. Supak believes the military can attract better quality recruits with fewer ad dollars, "because we're more sophisticated in our advertising. We're applying the lessons we've learned over the last few years."

SOURCE: Janet Myers, "Learning to Deploy a Strategic Weapon," *Advertising Age*, November 9, 1988, pp. 94–96.

Questions

1. Describe the target market the Pentagon is trying to reach.

2. What is the product the military is marketing to the target market?

3. Some critics say the American government should not pay for advertising and that marketing the military is inappropriate. Do you agree? Why or why not?

4. Do you think the Pentagon will achieve its recruiting goals? How else could marketing be used to help?

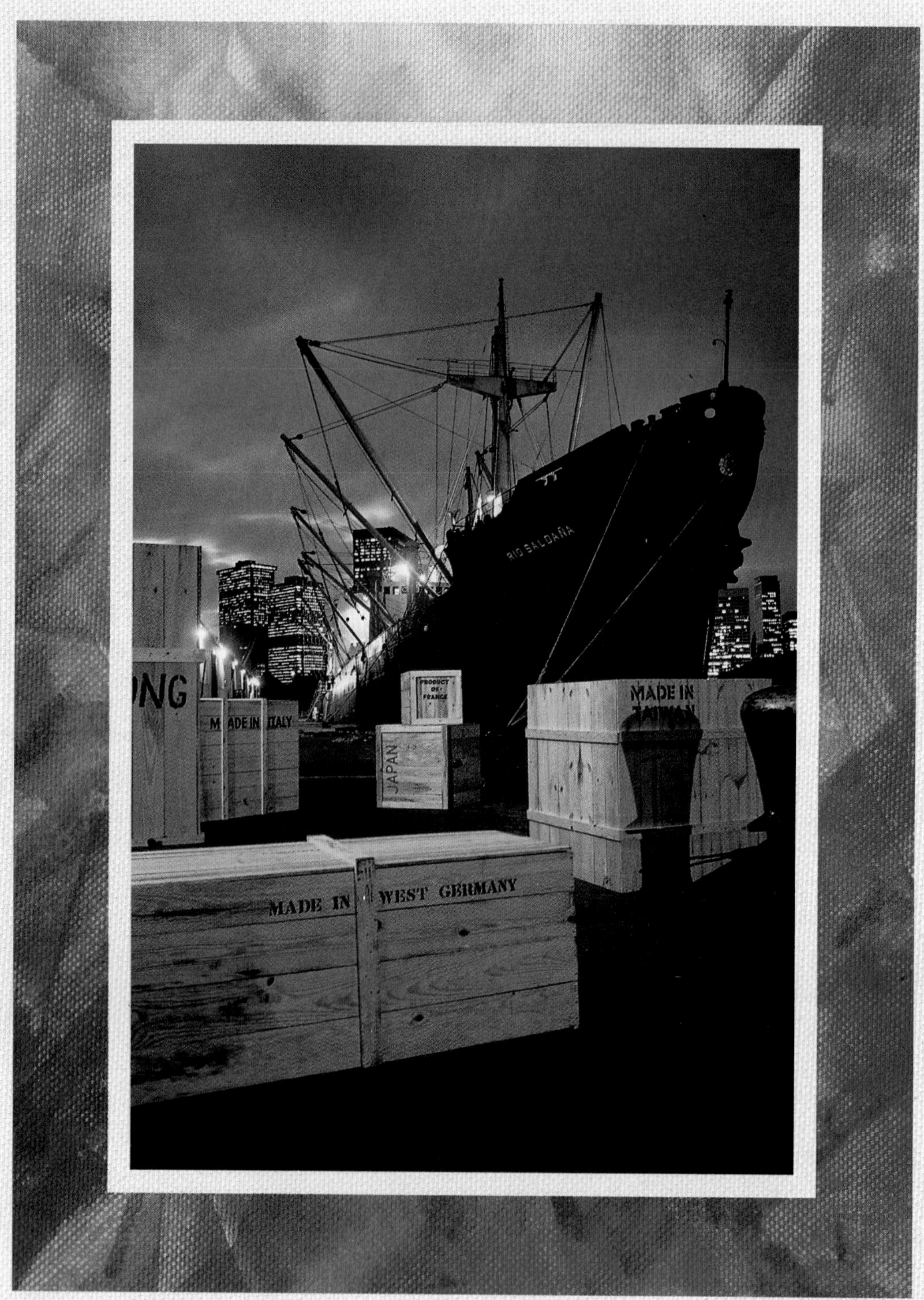

MADE IN ITALY
PRODUCT OF FRANCE
JAPAN
MADE IN
MADE IN WEST GERMANY

23

International Marketing: A Global Approach

Learning Objectives

Upon completing this chapter, you will be able to do the following:

DEFINE
International marketing and *multinational company*.

UNDERSTAND
the similarities and differences between domestic and international marketing.

EXPLAIN
why the European Common Market believes that in 1992 the New Europe will become a major force in the global market place.

IDENTIFY
the economic, cultural, and political/legal forces which must be understood if one is to engage successfully in international marketing.

DISCUSS
the local versus the standardization view of international marketing.

DESCRIBE
what is meant by the term global competition.

MARKETING PROFILE

Staffing the Global Marketing Team

The managers and employees a company hires to staff its overseas operations or travel internationally for the firm are on the front lines of the company's international marketing effort. How successful they are at functioning in a foreign culture and understanding the social, economic, and business conditions of the host country will have a big impact on the overall success of the company's international marketing program. The firm may offer advanced technology or appealing consumer goods, but if it doesn't have a staff that can read cross-cultural signals, it may still fail to gain a foothold in the foreign market.

Unfortunately, the competitive vulnerability of the U.S. seems to include the employees U.S. companies send abroad. According to researchers, approximately 25 percent of U.S. firms' employees sent to work overseas return to the U.S. prematurely. They usually return because they are not performing well, either because of unhappiness or an inability to adjust to work demands. Furthermore, many more employees complete their overseas assignments (usually last no more than two years) but with only marginal effectiveness.

What can be done to improve the competitive edge of U.S. companies by insuring that their international staffs are well chosen? Allen L. Hixon, an assistant director of The Business Council for International Understanding at American University, has some suggestions:

1. *Be careful about hiring from within.* Many companies have a policy of selecting only from within the company when staffing internationally; familiarity with the company's business is prized over cross-cultural experience. As a result, many potentially effective managers are disregarded in favor of employees who have a track record—usually domestic—with the company. But they might not have what it takes to succeed overseas. According to Hixon, "The hard-driving aggressive top sales manager from Cincinnati may be a disaster when dealing with the subtle and harmonious Japanese."

2. *Benefit from experience.* Employees who have already served overseas probably know better than any homebound personnel director what it takes to be successful in a foreign country. These employees' ideas should be considered during the expatriate selection process. If these employees' opinions were heeded, perhaps the syndrome of expatriate divorce and domestic unhappiness would subside, and other problems could also be avoided.

3. *Don't be swayed by office politics.* Overseas assignments are sometimes decided on the basis of friendships or animosities. For example, if the boss doesn't like you, you might find yourself with a long stint in one of the company's more out-of-the-way locations.

4. *Be careful in evaluating expatriate performance.* In certain countries, a company's success is hard to interpret. For example, in less developed or highly bureaucratic countries, developing business may be a slow process with little evidence of progress. Also, in some cultures with very different value systems and rules of etiquette, "yes" may mean "no" and "no" may mean "yes." Companies must develop culturally specific evaluation systems to see how overseas managers are doing—they may actually be doing better (or worse) than domestic standards of success would indicate.

5. *Take time to make a good decision.* Afraid of lacking representation overseas, companies may make precipitous, ill-considered personnel decisions. The harm done by an ineffective or unqualified employee may well exceed the harm associated with leaving a post empty for an additional few weeks or months.

6. *Invest in cross-cultural training.* Even with good personnel selection, the company should still give the new expatriate employee some training in the culture, history, business practices, and, ideally, the language of the foreign country. Despite the obvious importance of language proficiency in helping an employee function smoothly in a foreign country, perhaps as few as 20 percent of U.S. multinational companies require expatriates to know the language of the country they are working in.

If management is willing to follow this advice when selecting and training expatriate personnel, the result should be better company performance in international markets.

SOURCE: Rosalie L. Tung, "Career Issues In International Assignments," *Academy of Management Executive*, August 1988, pp. 241–44, Jeffrey A. Sonnenfeld and Maury A. Peiperl, "Staffing Policy As a Strategic Response: A Typology of Career Systems," *Academy of Management Review*, October 1988, pp. 588–600, James C. Baker, "Foreign Language and Predeparture Training in U.S. Multinational Firms," *Personnel Administrator*, July 1984, pp. 68–72, Allen L. Hixon, "Why Corporations Make Haphazard Overseas Staffing Decisions," *Personnel Administrator*, March 1986, pp. 91–4.

Since the end of World War II, the importance of international marketing has been generally accepted. American corporations, in large numbers, have moved across geographical boundaries and distributed American-made products in the Far East, Europe, Africa, and South America. Similarly, many products from other countries, such as Hondas (Japan), baseballs (Haiti), Nestlé's chocolate (Switzerland), and Norelco electric razors (the Netherlands), have been imported to American markets. International marketing is a two-way street. The expansion of foreign markets for American products has paralleled the expansion of the American market, especially for Canada, Japan, and the countries of the European Economic Community—Belgium, France, Italy, Luxembourg, the Netherlands, West Germany, Great Britain, Ireland, Denmark, Spain, Greece, and Portugal.

In this chapter we will focus on the role American firms play in what is now correctly referred to as the *global marketplace.* We will examine the unique features of global marketing in light of current and predicted events. Procedures for entering global markets and barriers to them will be discussed, as well as marketing mix decisions. And we will briefly discuss organizing for efficient and profitable global operations.

Research and discussion in international marketing has resulted in two opposing views. The first views marketing as a local issue, emphasizing differences across countries in customers, distribution systems, and marketing techniques, and advocating tailoring a marketing program for each country.[1] The opposing view considers marketing as know-how that can be transferred across borders. This view proposes that benefits accrue from standardization.

The either/or type of debate misses the main issue. A totally localized approach yields no competitive advantage in economies of scale, brand recognition, or market growth to a multinational. On the other hand, a standardized approach is not practical because of the differences in behaviors, customers, needs, marketing systems, and laws. The choice between local and standardized marketing will not help marketing managers develop a competitive strategy. Consideration of local issues and needs and using standardization to the degree possible must occur simultaneously. The *Marketing in Action* on the Global Market explores both sides of the debate, pointing out that some marketeers have been modifying the strictly local approach.

Scope of Global Marketing

In 1958, an important international agreement led to the creation of the European Economic Community (E.C.), also known as the **Common Market.** This agreement laid out a plan for a common antitrust law, removal of restrictions on the movement of capital and labor, and the imposition of uniform tariffs on imports from nonmembers.

Today, the General Agreement on Tariffs and Trade (GATT) is the principal multilateral agreement covering world trade. Its purpose is to encourage unrestricted multilateral trade by binding participating nations to negotiating trade rules and by mandating penalties for any deviation. There are 94 nations who are contracting parties to GATT, which is administered from Geneva.[2]

In 1992, a program known as the *New Europe* will become official. It attempts to sweep away the remaining obstacles to free movement of people, goods, services, and capital within the twelve countries of the E.C. The result of concern about economic and technological stagnation, the 1992 project is intended to give new impetus to European integration. A truly unified common market is the objective.[3] This would mean one marketplace of 320 million consumers. It will increase the overall gross

MARKETING IN ACTION

Is the World Ready for Truly Global Marketing?

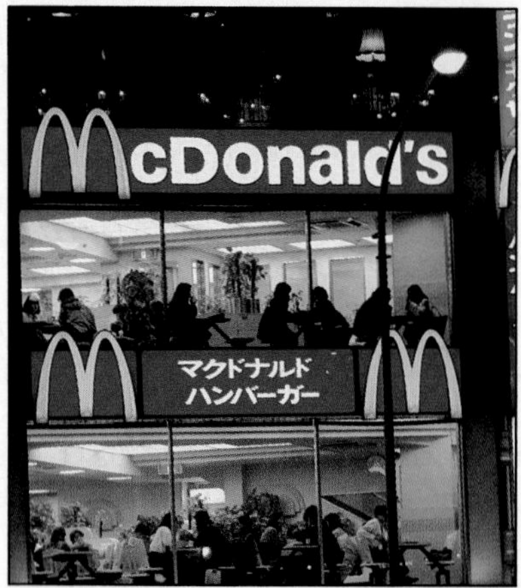

As the 21st century approaches, marketers have to adjust to a whole new world of global competitiveness and burgeoning international trade, but this doesn't mean that the world of the 1990s will be a global village with one culture and set of values. Although global economic modernization is making similar consumer goods and fashions available to more and more people around the world, smart business people must be able to develop marketing programs attuned to individual national markets.

Given the richness and variety of human culture, marketers should tailor advertising, and even products, to national tastes. Nevertheless, this idea has been stiffly challenged by those enamored of "global marketing." They believe that communications and travel have so shrunk the globe that cultural differences have been rendered insignificant.

Actual experience, however, seems to dispute the contentions of global marketers. For example, the Kellogg Company has been in the Brazilian market since 1962 trying to sell its cereals. Since many Brazilians traditionally do not eat breakfast and may eat cereal only as a dry snack, Kellogg has had to develop advertising that teaches consumers the "proper" way to eat cereal—with milk as a breakfast food. Only recently have Brazilian sales of Kellogg's corn flakes begun to pick up, although sales remain low compared with those in other countries. For Kellogg, an advertising campaign geared to American habits might have cost the company the small toehold it now enjoys in Brazil.

The move back to more nationalized marketing campaigns has been prompted by some dismal experiments in "global marketing." For example, in 1984 the Parker Pen Company attempted to market its products worldwide with a "one world, one voice" marketing program. The campaign ignored national differences and marketing suggestions from local managers and subsequently failed.

For those firms that want to retain some of the economies of scale associated with global marketing, there is still room to bring distinct national touches to a worldwide advertising program. For instance, the Coca-Cola Company, long a practioner of global marketing, added "local flavor" to its recent "General Assembly" campaign by using a close-up of a child from each of its different marketing areas to make 21 slightly different versions of the same basic commercial. Kodak and Phillip Morris have also used advertising tailored to local markets to varying degrees.

Advertising differences by themselves are sometimes not enough to spell marketing success. In some cases, the product itself must be changed. For example, McDonald's has adapted the recipe for its popular burgers to suit the Japanese palate. It also offers beer in its German restaurants and tropical-flavored shakes in its Hong Kong outlets. Similarly, General Foods offers a sweeter version of Tang and Kool-Aid in South American markets.

As communications improve and the world's less-developed countries gradually modernize, global marketing may be more widely and effectively used. As long as the human race retains any of its cultural diversity, however, there will still be a place for marketers who understand the distinct needs and tastes of different nations, regions, and cultural groups.

SOURCE: Julie Skur Hill and Joseph M. Winski, "Goodbye Global Ads," *Advertising Age*, Nov. 16, 1987. p. 22.

---

national product as much as 7 percent, or $285 billion, while creating five million jobs and vast economies of scale.

The 1992 E.C. arrangement is also intended to reduce red tape, help keep prices lower, and facilitate movement across borders. For example, University diplomas, apprenticeship courses, and vocational training acquired in a member country will be accepted throughout the E.C.[4]

Although some Europeans are skeptical about whether a true common market will emerge, others like the idea of keeping pace in economic growth and techno-

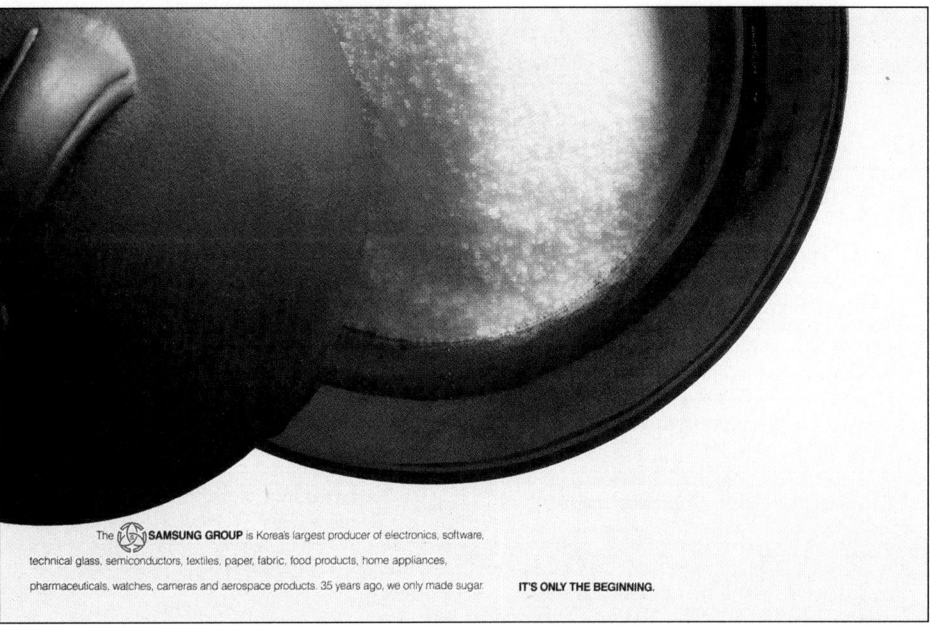

The SAMSUNG GROUP is Korea's largest producer of electronics, software,
technical glass, semiconductors, textiles, paper, fabric, food products, home appliances,
pharmaceuticals, watches, cameras and aerospace products. 35 years ago, we only made sugar.
IT'S ONLY THE BEGINNING.

Korea's Samsung Group has grown into a large international corporation.

logical innovation with the United States, Japan, and Asia's little dragons (Hong Kong, Taiwan, South Korea, and Singapore). A television commercial sponsored by the French government opens with a skinny French boxer squaring off to fight a giant American football player and a large Japanese Sumo wrestler. Suddenly, eleven friends arrive (his E.C. partners), and the opponents turn and quickly leave the ring.

A strong E.C. will contribute to a healthy and robust world economic and trading system. The United States can gain from the 1992 partnership because of close U.S.–E.C. political, historic, and economic ties. In 1987 U.S.–E.C. trade amounted to $146 billion, U.S. investment in Europe was $127 billion, and E.C. investment in the U.S. was $158 billion.[5] United States exporters will find that they are selling to a single market with a general set of standards, directives, and certification procedures.[6]

American companies such as Ford, IBM, and Colgate-Palmolive have always treated Europe like a major single market. First-timers will have to learn to do likewise. This will permit American companies to take advantage of the free trade across borders, easy access to labor pools, and standardization.

The GATT, Common Market, and other international agreements have led to increased interest in and concern about **international marketing,** which is simply marketing across national boundaries.[7] The realities of a world united by vast networks of international marketing activities are illustrated by the following facts:

- Korea's Samsung has replaced Japanese competitors in the U.S. market and is now the number one seller of microwave ovens.
- The world's fifty biggest industrial corporations employ 8.8 million people, more than the population of Sweden.
- Of the top fifty international industrial firms, twenty are American, twenty are European, and nine are Asian (eight Japanese and one Korean). By the way, one, Petrobra's, is Brazilian.

Table 23–1 A Comparison of Local and International Issues

Local (United States)	International (Non-United States)
Primarily one language, customers, history	Multilingual, Multicultural
Homogeneous needs, but with growing ethnic needs: Hispanics, Orientals, Blacks	Fragmented
Distribution system is understood	Different modes of distribution
Advertisement (e.g. television), some legal restrictions on liquor ads	Commercial spots may be available, time slots sold on bid system in some countries
Minimal government involvement	Government involvement differs across countries
One currency, world impact on value	Currencies differ, world impact on value of some currencies
Employees producing products may be unionized. Unions not a major political force	Unions in some nations are major political force

- The Golden Arches of McDonald's are found in Andorra, Kuala Lumpur, Budapest, and Belgrade. In the whole world, more people eat at McDonald's every day than live in Australia and New Zealand.
- Kao Corporation, a $4 billion a year detergent, diapers, and toothpaste company of Japan, bought Andrew Jergens, a Cincinnati manufacturer of beauty lotion and hard soap. They then opened a U.S. office close to the headquarters of Procter & Gamble.

Engaging in global marketing activities is different from marketing products or services in a domestic market (see Table 23–1). More specific differences will be discussed later in the chapter. It is important to recognize that such differences exist, for they must be carefully considered when one devises global marketing strategy and marketing mix.

The growing interest in the global marketplace can be explained by changing competitive structures, coupled with shifts in demand characteristics in markets around the world.[8] Many American firms are meeting competition, not only from domestic companies (Ford vs. Pontiac) but also from global ones (Honda, Nissan, Toyota). Nestlé's candy (Switzerland), Audi cars (Germany), Beck's beer (Germany), Perrier water (France), and Baskin-Robbins ice cream (Great Britain) are providing stiff competition for American products.

Nations have been trading for centuries, and international trade has been a popular topic for researchers to study for decades. The new interest in international competition has occurred because trade among nations has exploded since the late 1950s. Countries are now, more than ever, inextricably tied to each other. The United States President's Commission on Industrial Competitiveness has defined **competitiveness** as *the degree to which a nation, under free and fair market conditions, produces goods and services that meet the test of international markets while simultaneously maintaining and expanding the real incomes of its citizens.*[9]

Table 23–2 Leading American Exporters, 1988

Rank	Company	Export Sales $ Millions	Export Sales % Change 1987–88	Total Sales $ Millions	Total Sales Fortune 500 Rank	Exports as Percent of Sales: Percent	Exports as Percent of Sales: Rank
1	General Motors	9,392.0	7.6	121,085.4	1	7.8	41
2	Ford Motor	8,822.0	15.9	92,445.6	2	9.5	35
3	Boeing	7,849.0	24.9	16,962.0	19	46.3	1
4	General Electric	5,744.0	19.0	49,414.0	5	11.6	29
5	Int'l Business Machines	4,951.0	24.0	59,681.0	4	8.3	39
6	Chrysler	4,343.9	42.3	35,472.7	7	12.2	28
7	E. I. DuPont de Nemours	4,196.0	19.0	32,514.0	9	12.9	26
8	McDonnell Douglas	3,471.0	7.0	15,072.0	25	23.0	5
9	Caterpillar	2,930.0	33.8	10,435.0	35	28.1	4
10	United Technologies	2,848.1	37.5	18,087.8	16	15.8	20

SOURCE: "America's 50 Biggest Exporters," *Fortune*, July 17, 1989, p. 51.

In 1988, the United States trade deficit was approximately $137 billion. Although U.S. exports are about $322 billion, they still only amount to approximately 8 percent of the GNP, compared with 10 percent for Japan and about 20 percent for West Germany.[10] As Table 23–2 suggests, some major American companies are competing well in the global marketplace. Boeing exports account for about 41 percent of their total sales.

REVIEW YOUR MARKETING KNOWLEDGE

- What will the United States have to do to reduce its trade deficit?
- Explain the General Agreement on Tariffs and Trade Act.
- What potential problems do you foresee in the creation of the New Europe (E.C.) in 1992?

The Multinational Corporation

There is no generally accepted description of what constitutes a multinational corporation. Some define it as a company whose foreign sales make up at least 10 percent of its total sales. Others claim that it is a company that has a global products division, rather than simply an international unit. Still others define it in terms of the nationality mix of managers and top executive officers. Four senior executives who view their firms as multinational corporations describe them as follows:

Company A:

We are a multinational firm. We distribute our products in about a hundred countries. We manufacture in over seventeen countries and do research and development in three countries.

Figure 23–1 The Multinational Corporate Orientation

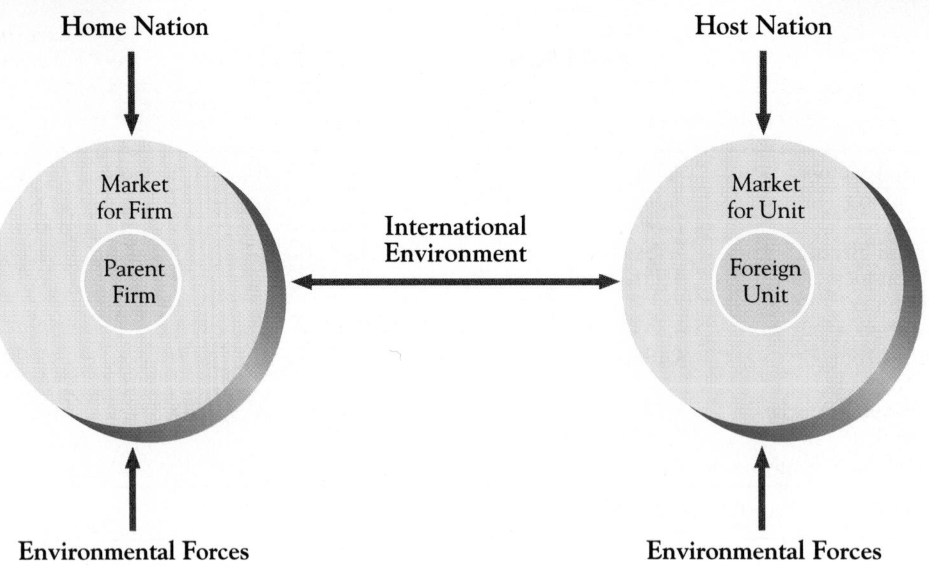

SOURCE: Hans B. Thorelli, *International Marketing Strategy* (Penguin, 1973), p. 330.

Company B:

We are a multinational firm. Only 1 percent of the personnel in our foreign office are nonnationals. . . . In all major markets, the affiliate's managing director is of the local nationality.

Company C:

We are a multinational firm. Our product-division executives have worldwide profit responsibility. As our organizational chart shows, the United States is just one region, on a par with Europe, Latin America, and Africa in each product division.

Company D:

We are a multinational firm. We have at least eighteen nationalities represented at our headquarters. Most senior executives speak at least two languages. About 30 percent of our staff at headquarters are foreigners.[11]

As these descriptions suggest, a **multinational company** is one that has a global orientation. It pursues global marketing objectives by relating world resources (human and raw materials) to world market opportunities.

The difference between *international* and *multinational* is subtle.[12] An international company is a national firm that operates in foreign markets; a firm engaged in multinational marketing not only does business in many different countries, but conducts research, development, manufacturing, and human resource management activities in those countries and employs a multinational work force. Multinational corporations must cross national boundaries with their products, prices, and advertising messages. Thus, multinational marketing is a complex form of international marketing that involves multinational corporations. Figure 23–1 illustrates the environment in which multinational marketing occurs.

Table 23–3 The Ten Largest American Multinationals

Rank	Company	Foreign Revenue (millions)	Total Revenue (millions)	Foreign-Percent of Total	Foreign Operating Profit* (millions)	Total Operating Profit* (millions)	Foreign-Percent of Total	Foreign Assets (millions)	Total Assets (millions)	Foreign-Percent of Total
1	Exxon	$69,386	$97,173	71.4%	$2,208	$4,343	50.8%	$29,914	$62,289	48.0%
2	Mobile	37,778[1]	60,969[1]	62.0	880[2]	1,380[2]	63.8	18,802	36,439	51.6
3	Texaco	31,118	46,986	66.2	833[2]	1,281[2]	65.0	12,956	27,114	47.8
4	Standard Oil Calif.	16,957	34,362	49.3	404[2]	1,377[2]	29.3	8,861	23,465	37.8
5	Phibro-Salomon	16,600	26,703	62.2	218[2]	337[2]	64.7	4,600	39,669	11.6
6	Ford Motor	16,526	37,067	44.6	460[2]	−658[2]	P/D	14,327	21,956	65.3
7	IBM	15,338	34,364	44.6	1,646[2]	4,409[2]	37.3	14,122	32,541	43.4
8	General Motors	14,376	60,026	23.9	−107[2]	963[2]	D/P	12,288	41,363	29.7
9	Gulf Oil	11,513	28,427	40.5	300[2]	900[2]	33.3	7,625	20,436	37.3
10	E.I. du Pont de Nemours	11,057	33,223	33.3	488[3]	1,491[3]	32.7	5,911	24,343	24.3

*Unless otherwise indicated: [1]Includes other income. [2]Net income. [3]Profit before interest and after taxes. P/D: Profit over deficit. D/P: Deficit over profit.
SOURCE: "Hard Times in Any Language, " *Forbes*, July 4, 1983.

Our definition of a multinational company is rather general. Thus, it is difficult to state accurately how many firms are really multinational. The Office of Foreign Direct Investment lists over 4,200 American companies as multinational. There are 30,000 exporting manufacturers, 25,000 companies with overseas branches and affiliates, and 40,000 firms operating abroad on an ad hoc basis.[13] *Fortune's* lists of the 500 largest American corporations and the 200 largest foreign corporations include the most important multinational corporations, but multinational firms come in all sizes. Small multinational firms are growing faster than many of their larger counterparts. The ten largest American multinational corporations, listed in Table 23–3, are familiar names to most Americans. On the other hand, the ten largest non-American multinational corporations are not so well known. Table 23–4 presents some data on these large firms.

Table 23–4 Ten Largest Non-American Multinational Corporations

Company	Country	Sales	Assets	Employees	Industry
Royal Dutch/Shell Group	Britain/Neth.	78,381.1	85,681.3	134,000	Petroleum
Toyota Motor	Japan	50,789.9	40,817.6	86,082	Motor Vehicles and Parts
British Petroleum	Britain	46,174.0	53,030.6	125,950	Petroleum
IRI	Italy	45,521.5	N.A.	417,826	Metals
Daimler-Benz	W. Germany	41,817.9	29,281.6	338,749	Motor Vehicles and Parts
Hitachi	Japan	41,330.7	49,862.4	263,996	Electronics
Siemens	W. Germany	34,129.4	31,829.8	353,000	Electronics
Fiat	Italy	34,039.3	40,424.3	277,353	Motor Vehicles and Parts
Matsushita Electronic Industrial	Japan	33,922.5	39,011.4	134,186	Electronics
Volkswagen	W. Germany	33,696.2	28,358.8	252,066	Motor Vehicles and Parts

SOURCE: "The Foreign 500," *Fortune*, July 31, 1989, p. 291.

Figure 23–2 Decisions in International Marketing

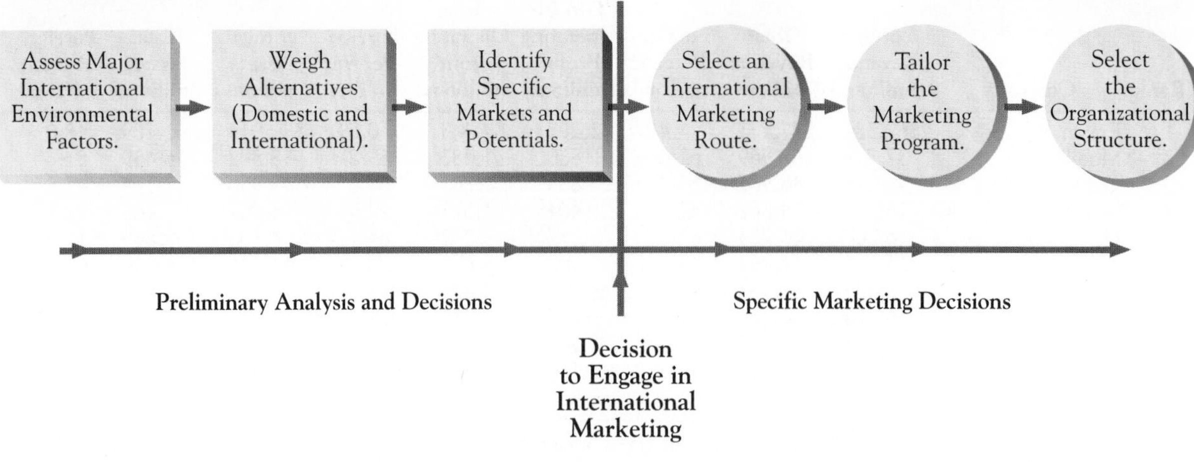
Assess Major International Environmental Factors.
Weigh Alternatives (Domestic and International).
Identify Specific Markets and Potentials.
Select an International Marketing Route.
Tailor the Marketing Program.
Select the Organizational Structure.
Preliminary Analysis and Decisions
Specific Marketing Decisions
Decision to Engage in International Marketing

Many people are surprised to learn that the world's biggest food company is not American but Swiss. Nestlé's, with sales of $23.6 billion a year, is well ahead of the American food giants: Beatrice, General Foods, and General Mills. The bulk of Nestlé's business is in prepared foods—canned and powdered milk, ice cream, infant formula, fruit juices, and bottled water. It operates 309 factories in 53 countries. In the United States there are 37 Nestlé's factories with 27,500 employees. Sales of its products in the United States alone are $2.4 billion, which would put it 160th on the Fortune 500 list, on a par with Quaker Oats. Nestlé's does 96 percent of its business outside of Switzerland.[14]

Another little-known characteristic of multinational firms in the United States is that many of the more publicized are foreign owned. That is, they have operations throughout the United States but are owned by foreign multinational corporations. Try to guess which of the following firms are foreign owned:

- Glidden Paints
- Carnation
- Shell Oil of Houston
- Baskin-Robbins
- Standard Oil of Cleveland
- Gimbel's Department Store
- A&P Supermarkets
- One-a-Day Vitamins
- Saks Fifth Avenue
- Alpo
- Travel Lodge
- Spiegel
- Keebler
- Alka-Seltzer
- Peoples Drug Store

In fact, all these firms are.

American-owned and foreign-owned multinational corporations make many kinds of decisions when they develop international marketing programs (see Figure 23–2). These decisions will form the framework for the remainder of this chapter.[15]

Assessing Environmental Conditions

The first decision in developing an international marketing plan is to choose which environmental dimensions to evaluate. Environmental forces were discussed at length in Chapter 3. Three major environmental forces—economic, cultural, and political/legal—play crucial roles in international marketing and have changed significantly over the past four decades. Some of the more recent changes include the following:

- the rapid increase in international trade and foreign investment around the world;
- the increased purchasing power of countries such as Korea, Taiwan, Malaysia, and Singapore
- the growing economic power, stability, and technological advances in the European economic community, Canada, and Australia
- the emergence of new market opportunities in Latin America, the Soviet Union, the Middle East, and Africa
- the changing value of the American dollar in world markets.

Economic Conditions

Today there are about 5.2 billion people in the world, of whom only 246 million live in the United States. Population growth around the world is about 3.5 percent a year, while the United States is growing at less than 1 percent a year. These data suggest that more new and profitable markets exist abroad.[16]

There are over two hundred sovereign nations in the world, each with marketing opportunities and problems. Several methods have been used to group nations according to economic development. According to one method, *developed* nations include most of western Europe, the United States, Canada, and Japan.[17] These nations have mixed economies dominated by private enterprise and a distinct consumer orientation, but they also have large and growing public sectors. They represent promising markets and investment opportunities.

The *developing* countries are moving from economies based on agriculture or raw material production to industrial economies. There are two groups of developing nations. In the first group are nations such as Australia, New Zealand, South Africa, Israel, Argentina, and Venezuela that enjoy a fairly high standard of living and are likely candidates for increased economic growth. The second group is still in the first phase of development. One-third of the world's population lives in such preindustrial countries, which have a very low standard of living and little purchasing power. They desperately need the products and services of industrial nations, but have difficulty paying for them. International marketing has not been an important consideration in such countries as Pakistan, Chad, Peru, Colombia, Sri Lanka, Tanzania, and Senegal.

A fourth economy, which is not exploited much in terms of American-based international marketing, is the *communist* world. Countries in this group account for another third of the world's population. While political/legal difficulties are associated with doing business with these nations, many of their citizens want the goods and services marketed by organizations in the Western world and Japan, such as Levi jeans, radios, and Western music. Eastern Europe, the Soviet Union, China, and Cuba are vast markets that have barely begun to be tapped. Mainland China is becoming a favorite international market for many American firms, among them Pullman-Kellogg, Hughes Tool, Fluor Engineering, and Coca-Cola.[18] Products that are household names around the world are appearing in China. Kentucky Fried Chicken opened a 500-seat restaurant in Beijing's Tiananmen Square. Pepsi-Cola and Coca-Cola and Nescafe and Maxwell House are waging all-out campaigns to gain market share.[19] The United States Commerce Department reports that the value of American goods flowing to the Soviet Union totaled $2.8 billion in 1988.[20]

Despite political difficulties, communist countries such as China provide a large and virtually untapped market for Western goods.

Distinguishing among nations on the bases of economy, market potential, size, and **per capita income** (a nation's gross national product divided by its population) is important for international marketing decision making. The per capita income in the United States in 1987 was approximately $18,200, while it was only $600 in Bangladesh.[21] Each of these factors must be considered; the consideration of only one may result in poor marketing decisions.

Besides the economy, marketing potential, size, and per capita income, marketers must carefully examine a nation's **economic infrastructure,**[22] the internal facilities, such as communication and transportation services, banks, and distribution organizations, that are available for conducting marketing activities. If, and when, the economic infrastructure of China is developed and the political situation stabilized, the marketing opportunities in that nation of 1.1 billion people should be excellent.

Table 23–5 summarizes the type of marketing functions that are appropriate in countries at various stages of economic development. What is appropriate in developed nations like the United States, Canada, West Germany, and Japan is not at all appropriate in underdeveloped nations such as Ethiopia and Bangladesh.

Cultural Conditions

The manner in which people consume, the priority of their needs, their wants, and the ways they satisfy those needs and wants are functions of a country's culture. One's culture tempers and molds one's style of living. **Culture** is the sum total of a society's beliefs, art forms, morals, laws, and customs acquired by individual members of that society. It is culture that gives people a sense of who they are, of belonging, of what they should be doing.[23]

For the inexperienced marketer, various features of a culture can create an illusion of similarity.[24] For example, a common language does not guarantee similar inter-

Table 23–5 Functions Performed at Different Stages of Economic Development

Orientation	Functions	Stage of Economic Development
Traditional	Barter trade; exchange of goods; central markets prevalent; no specialization; no marketing activity; very rare trading in some form in most societies; for example, ancient Africa's salt trade	Undeveloped country (Bangladesh)
Self-Sufficient	Degree of specialization; small-scale cottage industry; limited entrepreneurial activity; firms are labor intensive; producer is marketer	Less-developed country (Turkey)
Local Markets	Specialization; industry is transitional but with some market orientation; separation of production and marketing; sellers' market conditions prevalent; limited marketing activities	Developing country (Mexico)
Regional, National, and International Markets	Total specialization in production and marketing activities; complete market orientation; national, regional, and export markets tapped; mass distribution practiced	Developed country (United States)

SOURCES: Kaynak Erdener, *Marketing in the Third World* (New York: Praeger, 1982), p. 29.

pretations of a word or advertising message. In advertising, the correct interpretation of a message is extremely important. In England the hope is that a furniture wax "will not tread off" rather than "not wear off," and a shopper purchases "tins" of a grocery product instead of "cans."[25] Failure to take into account language, values, and other cultural differences can lead to marketing problems.

Language. The importance of recognizing language differences must not be underestimated. The literal translation of American advertising messages or brand names may result in ridicule or rejection of products.

- Coca-Cola, when it first entered China, provided local shopkeepers with signs printed in English. The Chinese translated the signs in their own calligraphy, pronouncing the product "ke kou ke la," which translated as "bit the wax tadpole."
- Herculon carpets become "the carpeting with the big derriere" when translated into Spanish.
- Chevrolet's brand name *Nova* in Spanish means "It doesn't go."
- In Japan General Motor's slogan "Body by Fisher" translates as "Corpse by Fisher," and 3M's slogan that its Scotch tape "sticks like crazy" comes out "sticks foolishly."

Language becomes a more serious concern when marketers are selling in multilingual countries such as Canada. Labels in Quebec, Canada, must be in both English and French. The language problems are multiplied tenfold when products are marketed in India, where 203 dialects are spoken.[26]

Color. Colors have different meanings in different cultures. Blue, which is considered a warm color in Holland, is seen as cold in Sweden. White is the color of death and mourning in China and Korea, and purple is an unacceptable color in many Spanish-speaking countries because of its association with death. In France yellow flowers suggest infidelity, while in Mexico they are a sign of death.[27] In Malaysia green is associated with disease. Red is a popular color in China, but it is not well received in Africa.

Customs. The following examples show how customs can influence international marketing programs.

- In Italy it is common to give a child a bar of chocolate between two slices of bread, but a German mother wouldn't think of giving such a snack.
- The average Frenchman uses almost twice as many beauty aids as his wife.
- Germans prefer salad dressing in a tube.
- The elderly are revered in Chinese families, and their opinions are sought out by the young.
- Oatmeal and cornflakes are desserts in northeastern Netherlands, northern Germany, and Scandinavia.

Values. A person's values reflect his or her moral or religious beliefs and are learned through experiences in a culture. These values affect an individual's decisions to purchase certain products. For example, fast-food restaurants like McDonald's, Burger King, and Wendy's would have major difficulties in India, where the Hindu religion forbids eating beef. In Italy a salesman should not call on a woman if her husband is not home. This would certainly cramp the procedures used by pots-and-pans and vacuum-cleaner salespeople.

Political/Legal Conditions

Over the past decade, American multinational corporations have discovered one supposedly rich market after another, only to have the rug pulled out from under them by unexpected political upheavals or changes in restrictions by foreign governments. The lessons were driven home particularly hard by the revolution in Iran. Many American companies lost money, equipment, and good will by moving into Iran without considering the uncertain political/legal environment. Marketing moves into mainland China seem to be following the same pattern. As of yet, no detailed analysis of China markets has been conducted. Figure 23–3 shows the scope of government ownership in selected industries and countries as of 1985.

In recent years, government laws and regulations to boost home country firms or to prohibit outsiders from doing business in home countries have seemingly appeared everywhere. This move toward nationalism has resulted in requirements for minimum local ownership or local product assembly or manufacture, preference of local suppliers for government contracts, limitations on the number and types of foreign employees, increased protectionism, expropriation or confiscation, and using the "French" solution in takeovers: the French company rather than a foreign one takes over a French firm. Foreign regulations are sometimes frustrating to Americans. For example, foreigners are forbidden to take rubles out of the Soviet Union. A business partner usually pays in products rather than cash. PepsiCo, Inc. has been taking Stolichnaya vodka for Pepsi since 1974. In exchange for the 840 million 12-ounce bottles of Pepsi sold in 1987 by 20 Soviet Union bottling plants, PepsiCo imported and sold in the United States 1 million cases of vodka.

Violence, terrorism, kidnapping, and instability are all possibilities in international business. American executives note cases of damaged properties, kidnapped employees, and even assassination. Interestingly, foreign marketers in the United

Figure 23–3 The Scope of State Ownership in 1985

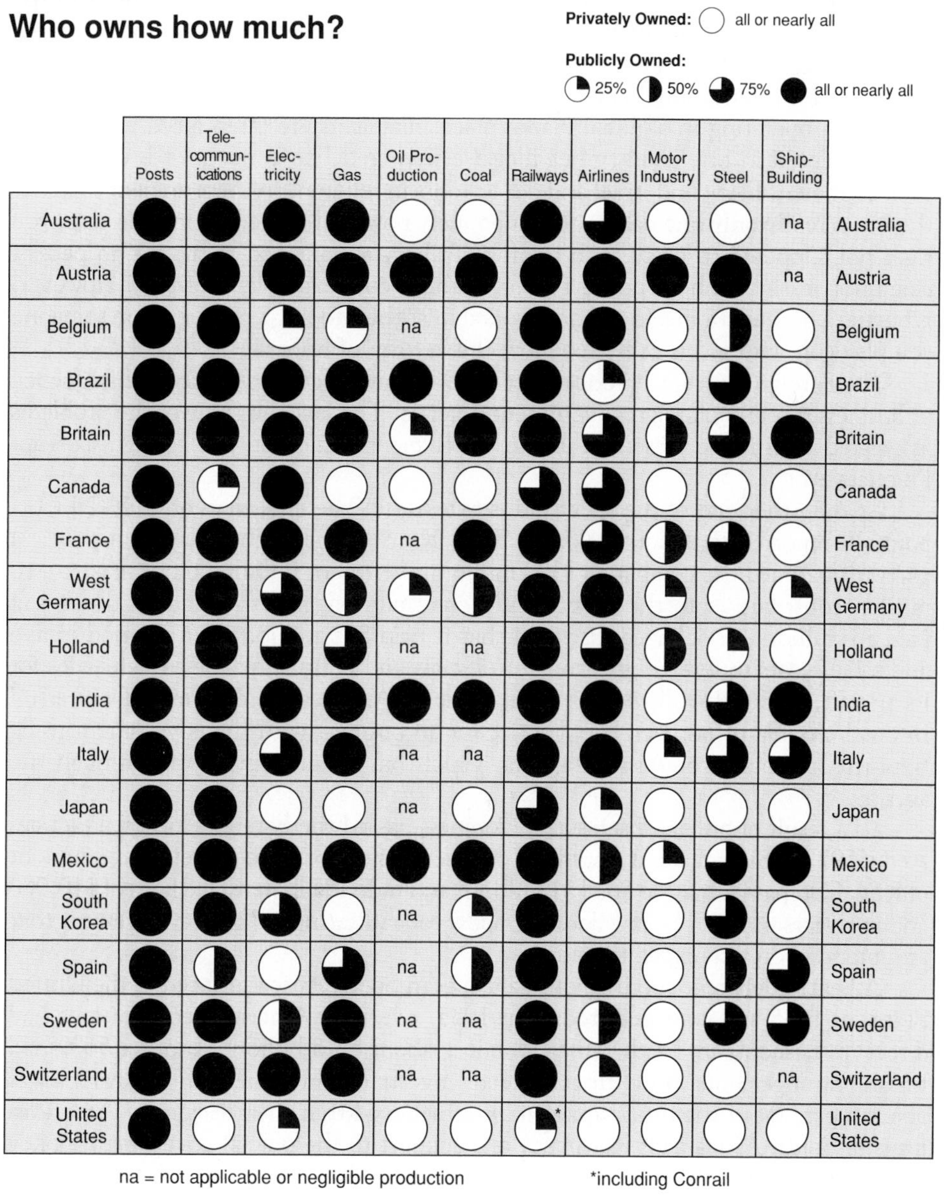

Who owns how much?

Privately Owned: ○ all or nearly all

Publicly Owned: ◔ 25% ◑ 50% ◕ 75% ● all or nearly all

	Posts	Tele-communications	Electricity	Gas	Oil Production	Coal	Railways	Airlines	Motor Industry	Steel	Ship-Building	
Australia	●	●	●	●	○	○	●	◕	○	○	na	Australia
Austria	●	●	●	●	●	●	●	●	●	●	na	Austria
Belgium	●	●	◔	◔	na	○	●	●	○	◑	○	Belgium
Brazil	●	●	●	●	●	●	●	◔	○	◕	○	Brazil
Britain	●	●	●	●	◔	●	●	◕	◑	◕	●	Britain
Canada	●	◔	●	○	○	○	◕	◕	○	○	○	Canada
France	●	●	●	●	na	●	●	◕	◑	◕	○	France
West Germany	●	●	◕	◑	◔	◑	●	●	◔	○	◔	West Germany
Holland	●	●	◕	◕	na	na	●	◕	◑	◔	○	Holland
India	●	●	●	●	●	●	●	●	○	◕	●	India
Italy	●	●	◕	●	na	na	●	●	◔	◕	◕	Italy
Japan	●	●	○	○	na	○	◕	◔	○	○	○	Japan
Mexico	●	●	●	●	●	●	●	◑	◔	◕	●	Mexico
South Korea	●	●	◕	○	na	◔	●	○	○	◕	○	South Korea
Spain	●	◑	○	◕	na	◑	●	●	○	◑	◕	Spain
Sweden	●	●	◑	●	na	na	●	◑	○	◕	◕	Sweden
Switzerland	●	●	●	●	na	na	●	◔	○	○	na	Switzerland
United States	●	○	◔	○	○	○	◔*	○	○	○	○	United States

na = not applicable or negligible production *including Conrail

SOURCE: *Economist*, December 21, 1985.

States can say the same about the U.S., where there are five times more homicides, ten times more rapes, and seventeen times more robberies than in Japan. American business hired in a recent five-year period over 602,000 security officers, an expense that must be added to the price of goods.[28]

Whichever method of assessing the political/legal environment is used, specific knowledge about the legal restrictions in a nation is required. Consider the example of Caterpillar Tractor. For political reasons, the laws of the United States forbid the sale of tractors to North Korea, Libya, and Vietnam. Also, the profits earned by Caterpillar in investments in foreign nations are taxed when brought back to the United States. Caterpillar is subject to American antitrust laws if it acquires a company in Mexico that competes with it in the United States. It is also subject to the laws of the countries in which it is doing business.[29] Even though the international marketer may not be a lawyer, he or she must know how marketing is affected by domestic and international laws.

When operating in a global marketplace, managers are often faced with a situation accepted in one country but illegal elsewhere. The concept of bribery dates back to ancient Egypt and Israel and has its roots in religion. In these ancient societies there was really only one person, the supremely powerful judge hearing the case, you were not supposed to go to with a gift.[30] Bribery is complex; there are no perfect examples of it.[31] Cash for doing a favor is a hard-core example of bribery. However, is buying a product from a friend or encouraging others to buy a product from someone you play golf with at his or her country club a form of bribery?

The Foreign Corrupt Practices Act of 1971 was enacted to reduce the frequency of businesses bribing foreign government officials. The law and some of the problems associated with it are presented in the *Marketing in Action* on the Foreign Corrupt Practices Act.

At the other end of the spectrum is extortion. The chairman of Gulf Oil Corporation reported that South Korea's S. K. Kim, financial chairman of a political party, threatened the company's $300 million investment if Gulf did not make a $10 million contribution to the party. Gulf's chairman haggled the amount down and paid $3 million.[32] Lockheed disclosed that it paid $22 million over a period of five and a half years to foreign government officials and political parties to win sales for its aircraft, a practice followed for a long time by American aircraft manufacturers.[33] In Saudi Arabia it has been the practice for all business with the government to be transacted through commission agents, which has resulted in payoffs through the agents.

As a result of bribery disclosures, Congress passed the Foreign Corrupt Practices Act of 1977, which makes it a criminal offense to offer a bribe to a foreign government official. Companies may be fined $1 million, and individuals may face fines of $10,000 and five years in jail. The law does not apply to facilitating or "grease" payments that are intended only to expedite business.

A heated debate involving political issues in South Africa surfaced in the United States in 1985 and continues today. In 1985, over 400 American corporations had direct investments in South Africa, totaling about $2.6 billion. Another 5600 had trading arrangements. Total direct foreign investment by American companies was about 6 percent of the total capital. Critics believed that the presence of American firms in South Africa adds legitimacy and support to the official government policy of apartheid (*living apart*), discriminatory laws passed in 1913.[34]

Review Your Marketing Knowledge

- Why is it difficult to assess international markets?
- How would a marketing manager use a nation's per capita income in making pricing decisions?
- Why is understanding a nation's culture so important in developing a marketing strategy for a product or product line?

MARKETING IN ACTION

The Foreign Corrupt Practices Act

The U.S. Foreign Corrupt Practices Act (FCPA), enacted in 1977, is a curious fruit of the 1973 Watergate investigations. During the investigations, disclosures were made about U.S. corporations' bribes and questionable payments abroad to further.their business. Subsequently, in the post-Watergate era of morality and accountability, Congress passed legislation prohibiting U.S. business entities from bribing foreign government officials in order to obtain business. The result was the vague and widely unpopular FCPA.

Many people involved in international business dislike the law because they feel a certain amount of petty bribery is unavoidable in business—especially in less developed or communist countries. Although the law supposedly applies only to bribing government officials, this condition can apply very broadly in countries, particularly communist or socialist ones, where many if not most businesses are run by the state. The FCPA's definition (which defines a foreign official as any person who "acts in an official capacity for or on behalf of a foreign government or any department, agency, or instrumentality thereof"), almost any manager in a State enterprise could qualify as a "foreign official." Thus, the FCPA allows payments to employees of foreign governments "whose duties are essentially ministerial or clerical." A key problem in interpreting the FCPA is how to draw the line between officialdom and clerical employees.

While Congress tries to hammer out new trade legislation, American businesspeople must live with the vague wording of the current law. However, Thomas Peele, an attorney with the international law firm of Baker & McKenzie, offers some guidelines for interpreting the current law:

1. *To whom does the law apply?* The law is applicable to all "domestic concerns." This term includes any person who is a citizen, national, or resident of the U.S. who is working on behalf of a firm—American or foreign-owned—whose principal place of business is in the U.S. Foreign subsidiaries of U.S. firms are not included.

2. *When does the FCPA apply?* It applies to those "transactions in which the mails or wire services or other means of interstate commerce have been used in furtherance of a foreign bribe." Importantly, the FCPA does not state that a payment has to be sent through the mail in order to be governed by this statute. If a telex or phone call were made in connection with approving or transmitting the bribe, the FCPA would still be violated.

3. *What payments does the law govern?* The FCPA "prohibits both payments and offers to pay" and may prohibit offering nonmonetary items or "things of value," such as business promises, etc.

4. *What is the liability of the company?* Companies are liable for the actions of their employees and agents if the company "knew or had reason to know" about the employees' intentions to make an illegal payment or offer. Some companies have tried to protect themselves by making contracts with their agents which explicitly prohibit them from making payments prohibited by the FCPA.

Although the FCPA prohibits only those payments made "corruptly"—that is, with "evil" intent, according to U.S. legal definition—the interpretation of corruption is still quite vague. U.S. firms may be liable for bribes that occurred through carelessness or lack of tight supervisory control, as well as those carefully premeditated. In any case, U.S. marketers must be mindful of the FCPA in all international dealings. Although the FCPA is frustrating to many U.S. businesspeople, they should be heartened by the room the current law allows to accommodate gift-giving and other traditional customs that are part of business in many parts of the world.

SOURCE: Thomas Peele, "The U.S. Foreign Corrupt Practices Act," *China Business Review*, January–February 1988, pp. 31–33.

Identifying Specific Markets and Evaluating Market Potential

A company often becomes involved in international marketing in one of two ways.[35] First, an exporter of goods, foreign importer, or government may request that a company market its products or services in the country. Second, after examining its own growth, profit margins, and market opportunities, a company may conclude that international markets look promising.

As with companies moving into a domestic market, those planning to enter international marketing must establish marketing objectives. Reasonable and challenging objectives provide the targets for international business transactions. The targets to achieve include satisfactory profits, long-term investments in plants, future growth goals, or maintenance of a competitive advantage.

Once the objectives are established, the company must decide whether to market in one country or region or in many countries and regions. This decision is based on assessments of the market potentials for various countries or regions.

Finally, a decision on the type of country to include in the marketing plan (underdeveloped, less-developed, developing, or developed) will be made in conjunction with the international marketing objectives already established and the decision to enter one or more foreign markets. In addition, the company should review economic, cultural, and political/legal environmental forces that will affect its choice.

Once attractive international markets are located, it is necessary to identify specific markets for products and services. Placing a potential monetary value on specific markets relies heavily on estimates and forecasts. Certainly forecasts and estimates are subject to error, but they must be made to provide some picture of foreign market opportunities.[36]

Five types of estimates and forecasts are useful:

1. *Estimates of market potential.* This marketing research task uses published data and data gathered through surveys by the organization itself. Sometimes the data are sketchy because marketing research is not well developed in many countries.
2. *Forecasts of future market potential.* To do this with any accuracy, the market analyst must examine environmental conditions thoroughly, considering economic, cultural, and political/legal factors.
3. *Forecasts of sales potential.* This step involves forecasting the company's probable market share. In a foreign market forecasting problems are compounded because the foreign company (for example, an American firm in Brazil) is competing with home country firms and possibly other foreign firms.[37]
4. *Forecasts of costs and profits.* Costs depend on how the company does business in the marketplace (is it exporting, involved in a joint venture, or directly investing).
5. *Estimates of rate of return on investment.* The forecast income stream must be related to the investment stream to derive an estimated rate of return on investment. The estimated rate of return should cover the firm's normal targeted rate of return on such investments and the risks of doing business in that country.[38]

Operating in the International Arena

Once a decision is made to go international, a firm must decide on the type of arrangement needed to enter the foreign market. There are four major alternatives: exporting, licensing, joint ventures, and direct investments.[39] Usually the selection depends on the amount of control a company wishes to maintain over its international marketing activities. Figure 23–4 indicates the degree of control that each option has. Exporting offers the least control and direct investment the most.

Exporting

Exporting is a method of entering a foreign market without investing in overseas plants and equipment. In 1988 American companies exported goods to foreign mar-

Figure 23–4 International Marketing Choices and Degrees of Control

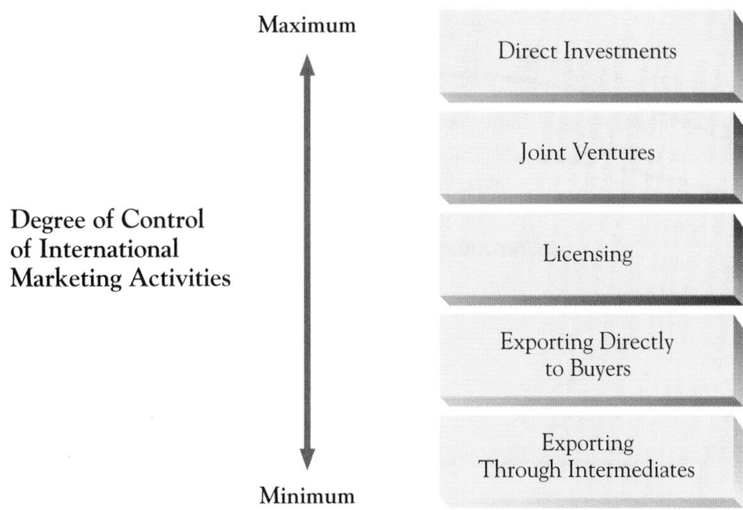

kets worth approximately $322 billion. In the past decade, exports have increased to represent 8 percent of the $4 trillion gross national product. In comparison, the European Economic Community nations exported goods worth $950 billion (including trade among E.C. members), or about 26 percent of their GNP, while Japan exported about $250 billion in goods (see Figure 23–5).[40] Sales can be made through *buyers for export,* individuals or firms in the United States who are usually treated as domestic customers and are served by the domestic salesforce.

In 1988, the United States imported an estimated $459 billion worth of goods. Thus, there was a $137 billion trade gap. Four reasons are cited for this declining gap: moderate American interest rates, the decreasing strength of the American dollar, improved quality of American products, and better knowledge of how to market products in the global marketplace. A continuing trade deficit means that the United States is paying more for imported merchandise than it earns from profits; a continuing deficit of this kind can destroy profits and jobs.

In 1987, California led the nation in exports with $27.5 billion, followed by Texas at $19.7, and New York at $15.5. Some unexpected places are among the busiest U.S. centers. Rochester, New York, for example, exports over $6 billion worth of products which is more than the totals of thirty states.[41] Worker shortages and more overtime there mean that exporting is important to the area. Eastman Kodak, Xerox, and Bausch & Lomb, Inc., all have major facilities in Rochester, and each is a large exporter.

Any international trade that involves not only the exchange of money but other things is called **countertrade.** Barter is a form of such trade, but countertrade is an umbrella term for a variety of noncash or partial cash international transactions. Countertrade is nothing new. It's been used as a trade mechanism between free-market (the United States) and centrally planned (USSR) economies. For example, Soviet leader Mikhail S. Gorbachev has initiated a system to restructure the Russian economy. His *perestroika* could open up many marketing opportunities in the Soviet

Figure 23–5 1987 Exports of Three Leading World Traders

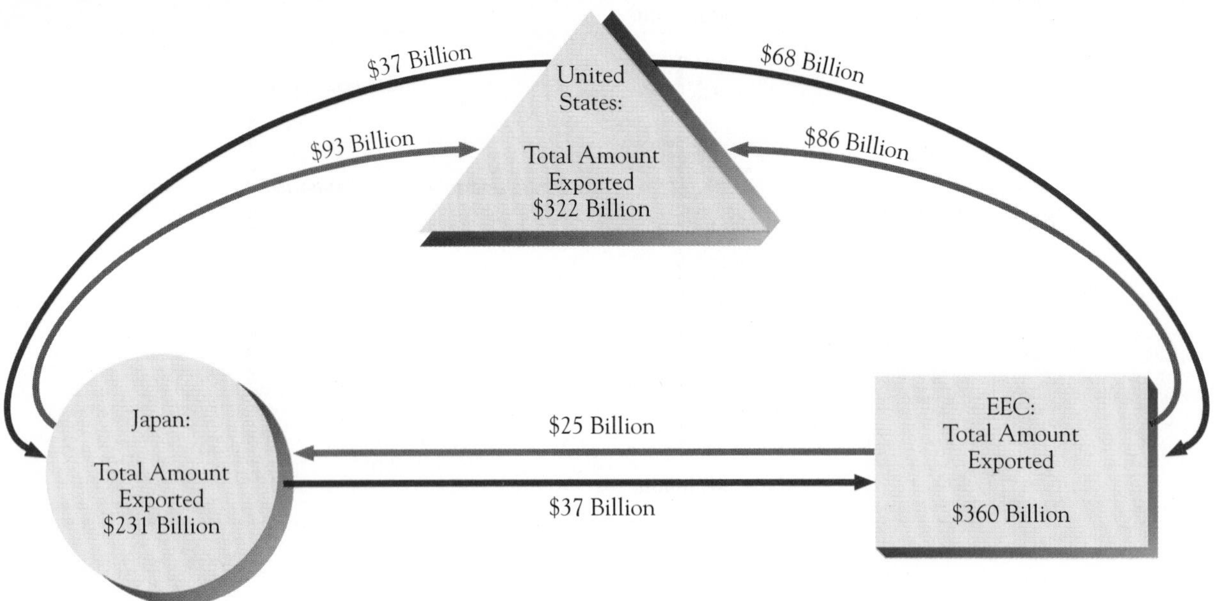

SOURCE: International Financial Statistics, Japan Trade Center, U.S. Department of Commerce, and O.E.C.D. data.

Union. West-Soviet joint ventures and increased trade could lead to a significant increase in efforts to market products to a nation of 284 million people.[42] The Soviet appetite for American, Canadian, E.C., and Japanese products is largely untested. However, the potential markets are being considered by multinationals and even small firms. Mr. Lou Piancone of Piscitaway, New Jersey, has first-hand knowledge of Soviet appetites. He met again and again with Soviet officials and finally, after perestroika became a reality, he is selling pizza in Moscow. On his grand opening day, 3,000 Moscovites lined up in 3 degrees below zero weather at Mr. Piancone's mobile restaurant for pizza.[43]

George Stathakis, President of General Electric Trading Company, estimates that there are now 38 countries that require countertrade by law. Brazil, Mexico, Korea, and Indonesia have all mandated countertrade arrangements; almost all the centrally planned Soviet bloc nations require it in dealings with the West. Countertrade is estimated to be about 30 percent of all trade, or about $600 billion, and it will grow to perhaps 50 percent of trade by the year 2000.[44]

Counterpurchase. This term describes a transaction in which two parties agree to sell other products or services with some balancing of values. Cash, which helps keep the values in balance, does change hands. McDonnell Douglas agreed to offset Canada's $2.4-million, 15-year commitment to purchase jet fighters by buying airframe components from Canadian suppliers and finding buyers for other Canadian goods. Also, General Motors' trading subsidiary, General Motors Trading Co., agreed to buy industrial gloves from China if China used the money to buy GM diesel engines.

Compensation Arrangements. This is a *buyback* arrangement that occurs when a country wants to build a factory or similar large project but can't afford to pay cash. Occidental Petroleum's Armand Hammer negotiated a 20-year, $20-million agreement to build plants in the Soviet Union in exchange for, among other things, ammonia.

Clearing Arrangements. This is an agreement between trading partners in which credits are substituted for cash. For example, if East Germany sells chemicals to Brazil at X value, Brazil credits East Germany's account with X amount of clearing account units. In the future, East Germany can use those units to buy Brazilian coffee. Today Brazil reportedly holds over $1 billion in East European clearing units.

Barter. In its simplest form, *barter* means exchanging goods or services for goods or services. When the goods or services are not exchanged at the same time, there may be some complications.

Since these forms of countertrading are likely to continue, American exporters will have to learn how to conduct themselves. The cruel facts are (1) the United States has a trade deficit; (2) if the deficit is to be reduced there will have to be some amount of countertrading; and (3) countertrading is very unpredictable and requires a commitment by marketing managers to understand and work with the complexities of this type of international trading.[45]

Licensing

A foreign licensee receives specifications for producing products locally, while the licensor receives a fee or a royalty on products sold. A licensing arrangement may offer a foreign firm access to brands, trademarks, trade secrets, or patents. The main attraction of licensing is that the producer risks no capital in granting the license, but gains entry into foreign markets. On the other hand, the producer loses some control in certain situations. For example, General Tire has licensed foreign firms to use its tire technology and others to use its know-how to produce plastic film. They have also made licensing agreements with V-belt, conveyor belt, and battery manufacturers to use their technology in General Tire subsidiary plants.[46]

Joint Ventures

A **joint venture** is a partnership with a foreign firm in which both partners invest money and share ownership and control in proportion to their investment. Xerox Corporation and Siemans AG agreed that the West German company would market Xerox office equipment in Europe.[47] This joint agreement provided Xerox with a new distribution network outside its overseas units. Kentucky Fried Chicken went into a joint venture with Mitsubishi Corporation of Japan. Each firm contributed 50 percent of the capital to start the venture; Kentucky Fried Chicken supplied marketing expertise, and Mitsubishi provided the chickens, cooking equipment, and real estate for store sites.[48]

An important factor in joint ventures is selecting the best foreign company and then maintaining effective communications. The foreign firm's objectives, understanding of the product, and marketing programs and images are important. Government restrictions also influence joint venture arrangements. For example, in Mexico, Japan, and India, foreigners cannot have majority ownership of any joint venture. Without majority ownership there is little control of the marketing decision-making process.

Direct Investment

Direct investments in foreign-based manufacturing and marketing subsidiaries are other ways of international marketing. The company maintains the most control possible over the production and sales of goods in the foreign country. By the end of 1988, cumulative American direct foreign investments totaled over $240 billion. In contrast, direct cumulative investments by foreign-owned companies in the United States exceeded $1.8 trillion.[49]

American firms used direct foreign investments in the 1970s for a number of reasons. First, real savings were achieved because of cheaper labor, raw materials, and transportation. Second, trade barriers against American-made and -shipped imports were avoided. Third, the host country governments viewed direct investments favorably in terms of company image. Finally, the firms retained control over the investment, which was not possible with other routes to international marketing.

The main disadvantages of direct investments are possible devaluation of currency, declining markets, and expropriation. When governments are unstable, they often seize American investments (plants, equipment, parts). This has happened in Cuba, Nicaragua, and El Salvador.

The increase of foreign-owned property, equipment, and land in the United States has generated concern in Washington, D.C. and on Wall Street. For decades, the U.S. has been the leading proponent of foreign investment. But U.S. military planners are troubled by the possibility that the military may be relying increasingly on hardware and software developed elsewhere.[50] These and other arguments are being heard more frequently, but there is still significant opinion that open borders for investment must exist among nations.

In North and South America, each nation has its own policy on foreign investment. Figure 23–6 highlights some policies of Canada, the United States, Mexico, and Brazil.

Some believe that the imbalance between American investment abroad and foreign investment in the U.S. will continue and has developed because of poor priorities in the United States.[51] The Japanese save about 16.7 percent of GNP and invest 13 percent at home. On the other hand, Americans save about 2 percent and invest about 5.5 percent. How can you invest more than you save? With help from abroad; foreigners have invested significantly in the U.S.

Tailoring the Marketing Program

The decisions made to this point should clearly indicate to marketers the similarities and differences between international marketing and domestic marketing. Furthermore, whichever route is taken to enter international markets, there is a significant need for marketing research. In international as well as domestic markets, the marketer must determine the demographic, sociological, and psychological characteristics of customers. However, procedures for gathering marketing information in international markets are not as sophisticated as those in domestic markets. Experimental studies, surveys, panels, and data banks such as those used to study a Chicago, Houston, or Las Cruces, New Mexico, market are not usually available for markets in Ascoli Piceno, Italy, and Alexandria, Egypt. Such standard demographic information as median age, income, size of household, or number of dependents can be difficult to obtain.

Gathering marketing information in international markets is difficult for the following reasons:

Figure 23–6 Who Helps—and Hampers—Foreign Investment

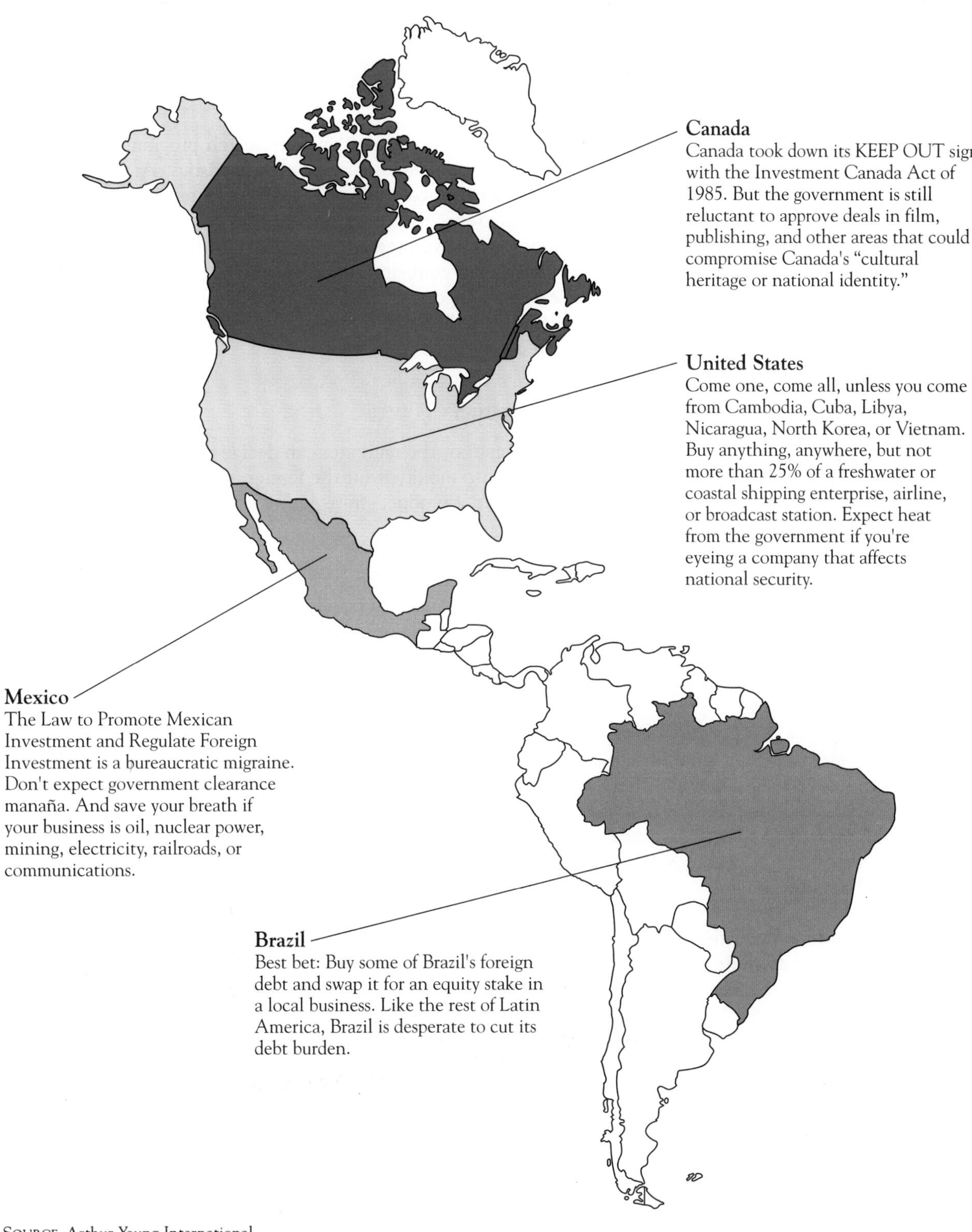

Canada
Canada took down its KEEP OUT sign with the Investment Canada Act of 1985. But the government is still reluctant to approve deals in film, publishing, and other areas that could compromise Canada's "cultural heritage or national identity."
United States
Come one, come all, unless you come from Cambodia, Cuba, Libya, Nicaragua, North Korea, or Vietnam. Buy anything, anywhere, but not more than 25% of a freshwater or coastal shipping enterprise, airline, or broadcast station. Expect heat from the government if you're eyeing a company that affects national security.
Mexico
The Law to Promote Mexican Investment and Regulate Foreign Investment is a bureaucratic migraine. Don't expect government clearance manaña. And save your breath if your business is oil, nuclear power, mining, electricity, railroads, or communications.
Brazil
Best bet: Buy some of Brazil's foreign debt and swap it for an equity stake in a local business. Like the rest of Latin America, Brazil is desperate to cut its debt burden.

SOURCE: Arthur Young International

- Mail surveys are difficult to use in countries with high illiteracy rates.
- Telephone surveys are rarely used, even in industrialized countries such as England and West Germany, because only about one third of all households have telephones. Even when telephones are available, it may take an hour to reach the party being called.
- Long questionnaires are not useful in Hong Kong because people do not want to take the time to complete them.[52]

Despite these problems with developing a sound marketing research program, the firm entering foreign markets must attempt to study market characteristics. Any data, primary or secondary, must be evaluated carefully. The data gathered from government publications, the United Nations, the International Monetary Fund, foreign periodicals, research organizations, and governments of foreign countries should be examined for completeness, reliability, and comparability.

Concern about marketing research is important because product, place, promotion, and price are still controllable ingredients in a firm's program for international marketing. Marketing research can provide guidelines.

Product

With available marketing research information, the marketer can decide whether to sell the same product abroad and at home, to modify it for the foreign market, or to develop an entirely new product. A number of product strategies for adapting to and promoting in foreign markets have been suggested.

Product Extension. The simplest strategy is to offer the same product and message in all markets. Pepsi-Cola, Coca-Cola, Wrigley's, and Levi's follow this strategy, which has worked for them. It did not work for Duncan Hines, which introduced its rich, moist American cakes to England, then found they were too messy for the British to hold while sipping tea. The British also rejected Campbell's tomato soup as too sweet.

Product Adaptation. This strategy involves modifying the product to meet local preferences or conditions. Exxon modifies its gasoline to meet different climates. Nestlé's sells different varieties of coffee to suit local tastes. Mars faced a drop in Bahrain's imports of candy when it was ready to sell M&M's. Marketing researchers determined that the citizens viewed the peanut as a health food. Mars was able to reposition its peanut M&M's, and they were able to sell the idea that, because of the hot Gulf climate, you need a candy that melts in your mouth and not in your hands.[53]

Product Invention. Sometimes a product has to be totally changed to meet a market's needs and preferences. Although the opportunities for inventing new products are great, the response of firms has been small. For example, an estimated 600 million people still scrub their clothes by hand, yet only recently have companies attempted to develop an inexpensive manual washing machine.[54] Colgate-Palmolive has developed an inexpensive, all-plastic, manual machine with the tumbling action of an automatic washer for use in homes without electricity.

Place

To succeed in a foreign market, a firm must have an adequate distribution system. Three major types of intermediaries are used by American manufacturers to penetrate international markets:

1. resident buyers within the foreign nations who work for foreign companies;
2. overseas representatives of foreign firms; and
3. independent intermediaries who either purchase goods and sell them abroad (foreign merchant wholesalers) or arrange to bring buyers and sellers of goods together (foreign agents).

These intermediaries often work for, or sell directly to, wholesalers in foreign countries. Thus, a channel of distribution can be very long. Much has been written about the complexity and length of the Japanese distribution system. Actually, the number of intermediaries used in any nation depends on the product line. For example, the majority of all fresh fish sold in Japan passes through three wholesalers before it reaches the retailer. On the other hand, most shoes pass through only one wholesaler before reaching the retail outlet.[55]

In some foreign markets, American-type retail outlets are not always practical. The supermarket is resisted because of local customs and taboos. Many foods are perishable, since the use of preservatives is uncommon. Thus, packaged goods are resisted because of the fear they contain spoiled food.

Moving a product from a manufacturer to an intermediary to a user is difficult, if not impossible, in some countries. For example, inadequate transportation systems make it necessary for Procter & Gamble to sell soap products door-to-door in the Philippines.

Warehousing and storage facilities are often small, ill equipped, and inadequate. This results in increased costs, delays in shipment, and even lost goods. In general, the effectiveness of distribution can be tied to a nation's level of economic development. For wholesaling, the influence of the foreign import agent declines with economic development. Manufacturer-wholesaler-retailer functions are more distinct in more economically developed nations. In retailing, the more developed a nation is, the more one finds specialty stores and supermarkets (*hypermarches* in France and *Verbrauchermarkte* in West Germany). The number of small stores declines and the size of the average store increases.

Hypermarkets were created by French merchants after World War II because of the need to distribute goods within a country devastated by bombed out roads, bridges, and railroads. Wal-Mart's owner Sam Walton has built two Hypermarket USA stores in the Dallas area. The stores are producing $150 million volume per year, double that of any competing large discount store.[56] By absorbing a lot of business in one location (place) the hypermarket discourages smaller competitors. The average hypermarket is 200,000 square feet, stocks 50,000 items, and has over 50,000 customers who spend an average of $35 each time they shop. An average (large) supermarket is about 40,000 square feet.

Promotion

The ideal promotion message in any country depends on the characteristics of its society. Creativity and versatility are essential in developing an effective international promotion campaign. The creative portion of a promotion message must be based on market analysis, which provides clues about the market.

A marketing advertiser must evaluate each market carefully. Because no completely standardized market exists, promotion and positioning from one country to another must vary. A few examples highlight this need.

- Levi Strauss had difficulty promoting its brand of clothing in Japan. It decided to use the Japanese propensity for hero worship, and Robert Redford and Jane Fonda were used with little success. Then legendary stars

John Wayne, James Dean, and Marilyn Monroe were used. Now Levi Strauss elicits the highest brand awareness scopes in the market.[57]

- General Foods advertises Tang as a breakfast drink in the United States. However, in France, where orange juice is not a breakfast favorite, Tang is promoted as a refreshment.[58]
- Most Americans think of cashmere as being expensive, rich, top of the line. Dawson International, Plc, of Edinburgh, Scotland, which produces 40 percent of the world's cashmere, is trying to change the image. The firm is attempting to "Americanize" the fiber, making it available in a variety of colors, styles, and cuts, and not only in sweaters, but cashmere pants and shirts, targeting the upwardly mobile consumer.[59]

Price

Pricing decisions are made similarly in international and domestic markets. However, cost-plus pricing is generally used more in foreign than in domestic markets. The cost-plus approach, coupled with other international market cost factors (tariffs, shipping costs, and larger margins for intermediaries), can cause major differences in foreign and domestic prices for the same product.

Many American multinational corporations sell their products at lower prices in foreign markets. For example, American drug manufacturers sell penicillin in some foreign markets at lower prices than they charge American customers, because they do not include research and development costs in the foreign prices. This practice is called **dumping.**

Of course, American firms are not the only ones involved in dumping. Many American manufacturers of automobiles, televisions, and appliances have accused Japanese companies of dumping goods on the American market. For example, a 1989 Toyota sold for about $10,475 in Tokyo and $10,150 in Portland, Oregon, in the spring of 1989. The Japanese argue that the additional sales achieved in the United States help lower production costs and the savings are passed on to the American consumer.

Review Your Marketing Knowledge

- Why is exporting so vital to the very existence of Japan?
- Explain countertrade and why it must be used with the Soviet Union.
- What is meant by the term "tailoring a marketing program to a country"?

The Smaller Business and the Global Marketplace

Until now, we have focused our attention on large multinational firms. But we have also presented Lou Piancone and his Moscow pizza parlor. There are numerous opportunities for smaller businesses to find a niche in global markets; quality products and services, patience, persistence, and effective marketing are the keys to success. In fact, recent export expansion in the United States has come from smaller businesses.

The 1988 Omnibus Trade and Competitiveness Act removes some old trade barriers and gives the President authority to take action against trading partners who

MARKETING IN ACTION

Japanese Move into Banking Middle Market

For years, Japanese and other foreign banks have serviced the needs of foreign corporations doing business in the United States. Now a new wave of Japanese banks are targeting small businesses, or the middle market. Concentrated in California, where Japanese banks control 20 percent of the state's banking assets, these middle market banks are targeting accounts too big for the independent banks and not big enough for the large American-owned banks. More than just buying bargain banks, the Japanese are importing long-forgotten concepts in the middle market—strong interpersonal and business relationships and an increased emphasis on service.

Irving Fisher owned a tools and hydraulics distributorship, Fisher Tool Co., that was growing faster than his line of credit. For several years he had a great relationship with his banker at Bank of America. But the bank's policy was that any loan over ten thousand dollars had to be approved by a committee—one that didn't "know Fisher from Adam." So in the end, he was treated as if he had never been the bank's customer in the first place. At California First, a six billion dollar bank owned by Bank of Tokyo, the atmosphere was very different. Not only did they increase his line of credit, they stop by his warehouse every few months to take him out to lunch. It was this consideration that impressed him the most. And the Japanese have been able to assist Fisher Tool Co. in finding suppliers and distributors in Japan, always making sure that on his buying trips he is treated like a V.I.P. This combination of expertise and concern seems to be winning the hearts and business of many California corporations.

Ralph Rittenhouse, a real-estate broker and developer since 1962, had a successful track record when he tried to get financing for a nine-house subdivision in a well-to-do suburb of Los Angeles. However, he was disappointed when Bank of America and other American-owned banks rejected his proposal because developing was his sole source of income. He thought, "Here I am, sitting on $700,000 to $800,000 worth of property where everything is going fast, and they are asking for security." A friend suggested he try Chinese-owned American International's Alhambra branch. Not only did the bank approve the $1.4 million dollar loan, it processed it in 30 days, less than half the time most banks would take.

The service did not stop with promptness. Even before approving the loan, the bank spread the news of the new development, and Rittenhouse's phone rang for weeks with interested customers referred by the bank. Rittenhouse really appreciated bankers who thought of themselves as partners rather than adversaries. Without question, he expects that his next project will be financed by his new Asian associates.

ADAPTED FROM: Joel Kotkin, "A Yen for Lending," *Inc.*, April 1988, pp. 107–110.

---

sometimes have been unfair to smaller businesses. The Act provides all businesses with trade and international market opportunities data.

Smaller businesses in computers, oil field machinery, and medical equipment can continue their involvement within international areas under a law that now makes trade fairer. Smaller firms can capitalize on their ability to develop products quickly and sell them in specific niches in the global marketplace that are not cultivated by large firms. A few examples highlight some small firm successes.[60] Mentor Graphics, from Beaverton, Oregon, buys U.S.-made computers, adds its own software, and packages them in Amsterdam for some of Europe's large high-tech companies: Airbus, Philips, and Siemens. Black Box Corporation, a Pittsburgh company, sells computer communications equipment through mail-order catalogues. They have established a successful joint venture with foreign distributors, and now have a foothold in Europe before the 1992 changes take place.[61]

Three years ago, Bill Rucker was running a small transmission repair business in Fort Worth, Texas, with a local customer base sales of $250,000.[62] Wanting to expand, he considered international sales. He cold-called a parts manager in Australia, who was of course surprised; but a few weeks later, they had worked a deal. Now Bill Rucker's sales are approaching $3 million; his 23 person staff includes employees who speak German, Spanish, and Thai; and 60 percent of his business comes from international markets.

The Japanese and Chinese have stepped into the small business arena in an interesting manner. The *Marketing in Action* on Japanese banking shows how important smaller businesses are to Japanese and Chinese bankers.

Small business could be a major catalyst in developing a major Latin American initiative. The small businesses can move quickly to develop partnerships with Latin American firms. The United States now has 18.9 million Hispanics, accounting for 7.5 percent of the population. Marketing to these Hispanic markets could help American businesses develop strategies and plans for Latin America. American Hispanics are brand conscious and brand loyal.[63]

Another opportunity for small businesses is in the Pacific Rim. If U.S. trade with Asia keeps growing at current rates, by 1995 it will be twice U.S. trade with the European Economic Community. The entrepreneurial spirit of smaller firms is respected by Pacific Rim business leaders.[64] Again, the ability to react, respond, and take action quickly is an advantage of the small firm in the Pacific Rim countries.

Thousands of smaller U.S. businesses now realize the importance of international marketing.[65] And more firms appreciate the potential and profits overseas. International marketing is becoming a top priority.[66] Applying international marketing skills and having high quality products and services available is a strategy that can help reduce the trade deficit, promote better relations between nations, and increase profits.

Personal Computer Exercise

Globalization of marketing and manufacturing functions has increased dramatically in recent years. In this PC exercise, you will be able to evaluate several different international business opportunities. What sources of competitive advantage can globalization of a business create?

KEY POINTS

• Increased competition among nations is healthy if free and fair market conditions exist.

• Discussions about international marketing often center on whether a local or a standardized approach is best. This kind of black or white analysis fails to recognize that most situations and problems are really in the gray area.

• The new era of a free-trading, barrier-free European Economic Community will occur in 1992. There is optimism and some questions of concern about the New Europe.

• A multinational corporation is a firm that does business in many countries, that conducts research, development, manufacturing, and human resource activities in those countries, and that has a work force made up of people from many nations.

• To become involved in international marketing, a firm must first assess environmental conditions. Next, the markets must be scrutinized. Estimating and forecasting market potential, market share, and rate of return are important steps. Decisions must also be made on how to enter the market—through exports, licensing, joint ventures, or direct investments. Finally, the firm needs to conduct marketing research to determine the demographic, sociological, and psychological characteristics of potential customers.

• Marketing programs and mix must be tailored to fit the international situation.

• Product strategies for international markets involve adaptation, extension, and invention.

• Promotional approaches must be tailored to fit the characteristics of a society.

• Many multinational corporations sell their products at lower prices in foreign markets. This is called dumping.

• The potential to be a major player in international marketing exists for quick moving, flexible small businesses. Attractive opportunities for American firms appear to exist in Latin America and the Pacific Rim.

ISSUES FOR DISCUSSION

1. What is the significance of the New Europe to the marketing programs of United States companies?

2. Why would a totally localized marketing approach yield no competitive advantage to a multinational company? What advantages are being referred to here?

3. What are the concerns of critics concerning the dramatic increase in direct foreign investment in the United States?

4. What advantages can smaller businesses employ that large multinationals have trouble using in becoming more deeply involved in international marketing activities and global strategies?

5. The United States does a good job on developing products that people want to purchase. However, turning these products into marketable products is still not done effectively. How can a marketer help a firm commercialize new products in international markets?

6. Why would conducting marketing research be more difficult in Peru than in Canada?

7. Why would a developing nation want to enter into a countertrade agreement with the United States, Canada, or Japan?

8. Do you foresee more joint ventures between American and foreign firms in the next decade? Why?

9. There are some who argue that bribes are such a part of international business that if American firms are to compete they must engage in bribery. What do you think about this viewpoint?

10. What services can American firms continue to export overseas?

GLOSSARY

Common Market: A group of twelve European nations—Belgium, France, Italy, Luxembourg, the Netherlands, West Germany, Great Britain, Ireland, Denmark, Spain, Portugal, and Greece—that have a common antitrust law, no restrictions on movement of capital and labor, and uniform tariffs on imports from nonmembers. In 1992 all trade and movement of people barriers among the 12 countries will be removed.

Culture: The sum total of a society's beliefs, art forms, morals, laws, and customs acquired by individual members of society.

Dumping: Selling a product at a lower price overseas than at home.

Economic infrastructure: Internal facilities that are available for conducting marketing activities.

Exporting: Entering a foreign market without investing in overseas plants and equipment.

Industrial Competitiveness: The degree to which a nation, under free and fair market conditions, produces goods and services that meet the test of international markets while simultaneously maintaining and expanding the real income of its citizens.

International marketing: Marketing across national boundaries.

Joint venture: A partnership between two firms from different countries. The partners share ownership and control in proportion to the investment they have made.

Multinational company: A firm that pursues global marketing objectives by relating world resources to world market opportunities.

Per capita income: A nation's gross national product divided by its population size.

Product extension: The offering of similar products and messages in all areas.

Values: A person's moral or religious beliefs as learned through experiences in the culture.

NOTES

1. Hirotaka Takeuchi and Michael E. Porter, "Three Roles of International Marketing in Global Strategy," in Michael E. Porter (ed.) *Competition in Global Industries* (Boston: Harvard University Press, 1987), pp. 111–46.

2. Pat Choate and Juyne Linger, "Tailored Trade: Dealing with the World as It Is," *Harvard Business Review*, January-February 1988, pp 86–93.

3. Michael Bartholomew, "Profit Now from Europe's 1992 Opening," *The Wall Street Journal*, July 25, 1988, p. 12.

4. "Europe Without Borders: Answers to Some Questions," *Europe*, October 1988, pp. 14–17 and Cees Bruynes, "Europe in 1992 and Beyond: Philips Looks to the Future," *Europe*, October 1988, pp. 18–19.

5. Richard I. Kirkland, Jr., "Outsiders Guide to Europe in 1992," *Fortune*, October 24, 1988, pp. 12–127.

6. Frank J. Comes, Jonathan Kapstein, John Templeton, and Elizabeth Weiner, "Reshaping Europe: 1992 and Beyond," *Business Week*, December 12, 1988, pp. 48–51.

7. Vern Terpstra, *International Marketing* (Dryden Press, 1983), p. 4.

8. C. K. Prakalad and Yves L. Doz, *The Multinational Mission* (New York: Free Press, 1987), p. 39.

9. Laura D'Andrea Tynson, "Competitiveness: An Analysis of the Problem and a Perspective on Future Policy," in Martin K. Starr (ed.), *Global Competitiveness* (New York: Norton, 1988), p. 97.

10. Richard Lawrence, "Little Improvement Seen in Trade Data," *Houston Chronicle*, February 18, 1989, p. 1B.

11. From Howard V. Perlmutter, "The Tortuous Evolution of the Multinational Corporation," *Columbia Journal of World Business*, January-February 1969, pp. 9–10.

12. Warren J. Keegan, *Multinational Marketing Management* (Prentice-Hall, 1984), p.5.

13. Edward C. Barg, "50 Leading U.S. Exporters," *Fortune*, July 18, 1988, p. 70.

14. "The International 500," *Fortune*, August 1, 1988, pp. D7–D8.

15. The notion of a sequential program for reaching international marketing decisions was adapted from Philip Kotler and Gary Armstrong, *Principles of Marketing* (Prentice-Hall, 1989), Figure 21–1, p. 552.

16. Carl Haub, "That Sound Is the Global Population Bomb Ticking," *Houston Chronicle*, August 14, 1988, p. 50.

17. Felix Rohatyn, "America's Economic Dependence," *America and the World 1988/1989* (New York: Council on Foreign Relations, 1989) pp. 53–65.

18. "Empress of the China Trade," *Profiles, Inc.*, May 1988, pp. 29–48.

19. "Laying the Foundation for the Great Mall of China," *Business Week*, January 25, 1988, pp. 68–69.

20. U.S. Department of Commerce, *United States Trade in 1988*, June 1989, p. 18.

21. "The 1990s and Beyond: The U.S. Stands to Retain Its Global Leadership," *The Wall Street Journal*, January 23, 1989, pp. 1 and 6.

22. David N. Hyman, *Economics* (Irwin, 1989), pp. 871–76.

23. Philip R. Harris and Robert T. Moran, *Managing Cultural Differences* (Houston: Gulf Publishing Co., 1987), p. 12.

24. Philip R. Cateora and John M. Hess, *International Marketing*, (Irwin, 1987), p. 110.

25. Arthur O. Fisher, "Advertising of New Products in Foreign Markets," in S. Watson Dunn, ed., *International Handbook of Advertising* (McGraw-Hill, 1964), p. 102.

26. David J. Rachman and Elaine Romano, *Modern Marketing* (Dryden Press, 1980), p. 552.

27. James C. Simmons, "A Matter of Interpretation," *American Way*, April 1983, pp. 106–11.

28. Richard D. Lamm, "Crisis: The Uncompetitive Society," in Martin K. Starr (ed.) *Global Competitiveness* (New York: Norton, 1987), pp. 12–42.

29. Vern Terpstra, "The Antitrusters Aim Overseas," *Business Week*, March 14, 1977, pp. 100–102.

30. Andrew Kepfer, "How to Be a Global Manager," *Fortune*, March 14, 1988, pp. 52–58.

31. George A. Steiner and John F. Steiner, *Business, Government, and Society* (Random House, 1985), p. 612.

32. Steiner and Steiner, *Business, Government, and Society*, p. 614.

33. "State Regulators Rush in Where Washington No Longer Treads," *Business Week*, September 19, 1983, p. 16.

34. Max Obuszewski, "The South African Face Lift," *The Corporate Examiner*, Spring 1983, pp. 1–10.

35. Suggested by Kotler, *Principles of Marketing*, pp. 578–79.

36. Omnibus Trade and Competitiveness Act of 1988, (102 Statute 1107), Public Law 100–418 [HR4848], August 23, 1988.

37. Peter Morici, *Reassessing American Competitiveness*, (Washington, DC: National Planning Association, 1988).

38. Dietmar Keller, "The International Competitiveness of Europe, The U.S.A., and Japan," *Intereconomics,* March–April 1985, pp. 59–64.

39. Earl H. Fry, "Is the United States a Declining Economic Power?" *Business in the Contemporary World,* Summer 1989, pp. 38–47.

40. "The 1990s and Beyond," *The Wall Street Journal,* January 23, 1989.

41. "Rochester Hit Hard by the Exporting Craze," *Marketing News,* October 10, 1988, p. 13.

42. "When the Kremlin Calls, Capitalists Lend More Than an Ear," *Business Week,* August 15, 1988, pp. 56–57.

43. Mark Memmott, "USA Firms Cut Soviet Red Tape," *USA Today,* May 31, 1988, pp. 1B and 2B.

44. Michael Doan, "As Barter Deals Spread, So Does U.S. Concern," *U.S. News & World Report,* January 16, 1984, p. 48.

45. Donald A. Ball and Wendell H. McCullock, Jr., *International Business,* (Plano, TX: Business Publications, Inc., 1988), p. 61.

46. Alex Taylor III, "The U.S. in Fighting Shape," *Fortune,* April 24, 1989, pp. 42–48.

47. "Siemens AG to Market Xerox Corp. Products for Automated Office," *The Wall Street Journal,* February 26, 1982, p. 6.

48. "Will Big Mac Meet Its Match in the Land of the Rising Sun?" *Forbes,* May 15, 1978, p. 118; Martin Tolchin and Susan Tolchin, *Buying into America,* (New York: Times Books, 1988).

49. Jaclyn Fierman, "The Selling of America (Cont'd)," *Fortune,* May 23, 1988, p. 54.

50. Raymond Vernon, "Foreign-Owned Enterprise in the United States: Threat of Opportunity?" *Business in the Contemporary World,* October 1988, pp. 27–36.

51. Fierman, 1988, p. 54.

52. Charles S. Mayer, "The Lessons of Multinational Marketing Research," *Business Horizons,* December 1978, pp. 7–13.

53. "Consumer Nondurables," *Business International,* June 16, 1986, p. 190.

54. Keegan, *Multinational Marketing Management,* p. 321.

55. Joel Dreyfuss, "How to Deal with Japan," *Fortune,* June 6, 1988, pp. 107–118; and Shinya Nakata, "Retailing: Variety of Means and the Conglo-Merchants," *Japan Update,* Summer 1988, pp. 18–20.

56. Bill Saporito, "Retailers Fly into Hyperspace," *Fortune,* October 24, 1988, pp. 147–52.

57. Dorothy Cohen, *Advertising* (Scott, Foresman, 1988), p. 527.

58. Cohen, *Advertising,* p. 530.

59. "Cashmere Supplier Targets U.S. with 'Americanized' Product," *Advertising Age,* October 24, 1988, p. 6.

60. "Made In The U.S.A.," *Business Week,* February 29, 1988, pp. 60–66.

61. George V. Privolos, "Small Business Can Benefit from European Economic Changes If They Take Precautions," *Marketing News,* September 26, 1988, p. 6.

62. Preston Lerner, "Dallas, the World Is Your Market," *Sprit,* December 1988, pp. 89–94.

63. "Fast Times on Avenida Madison," *Business Week,* June 6, 1988, pp. 62–67.

64. Joel Kotkin and Yoriko Kishimoto, "Winning in the Asian Era," *Inc.,* September 1988, pp. 71–76. Also see Joel Kotkin and Yoriko Kishimoto, *The Third Century: America's Resurgence in the Asian Era* (New York: Crown), 1988.

65. Stephen Barbas, "Bush Gets Bad News on U.S. Trade Deficit," *Marketing News,* December 5, 1988, pp. 1–2.

66. François-Xavier Oritoli, *France Magazine,* Fall 1988, pp. 8–9.

CASE APPLICATION 23–1

McDonnell Douglas Corporation

Businesspeople who look to international markets only for export sales are ignoring the vast potential of those markets. Whether because of government fiat or competitive self-interest, many foreign companies are now interested less in purchasing final products than in acquiring technical know-how. As a result, types of cooperation such as licensing agreements and joint ventures have become very popular. Certainly, the successful experience of Japan—which vaulted to its current economic and technical position in large part because of an intensive program of technology transfer in the 1950s and '60s—serves as a model of how to modernize a country. Thus, countries from Brazil to Bangladesh, and also such giants as China and the U.S.S.R., are all eager to modernize their own industries.

The process of technology transfer is highly complex and requires patience and commitment on both sides in order to succeed. McDonnell Douglas Corporation's (MDC) massive transfer of aircraft technology to China is a good example.

MDC's huge technology transfer project began long before any contracts were signed. John Brizendine, president of Douglas Aircraft Company (a subsidiary of MDC), made the first proposal for a technology transfer project in a 1975 letter to the Chinese Ministry of Aeronautics. It was a full ten years, however, before the agreement to license production of the MD–82 was finally signed. During the intervening years, lengthy negotiations were held, a deal to purchase landing gear doors from one of the future technology transfer partners was signed, and progress on the project was slowed by economic and political fluctuations in China. In March 1985, however, a 500-page, 12-year agreement between MDC, the Shanghai Aviation Industrial Corporation (SAIC), and the China Aviation Supply Corporation was signed. The agreement covered licensing the production of 25 MD–82 aircraft (with an option for 15 more), "product support, the establishment of a flight crew maintenance and training center, associated countertrade, future technology cooperation, and technical and management assistance."

The complexity of the project has also been aggravated by the fact that McDonnell Douglas is not an equity partner. As a result, McDonnell Douglas personnel are supposed to act only as technical and management advisers; they may offer opinions, but final decisions are in the hands of the Chinese. MDC advisers must accept the decisions of the Chinese managers or else find diplomatic or persuasive means to change their minds.

The way details of the project are handled would not matter so much if SAIC's main customer, the Civil Aviation Administration of China (CAAC), did not require that all MD–82's be certified by the U.S. Federal Aviation Administration. The production processes at the Shanghai plant must meet the same tough FAA standards as at the MDC plant in Long Beach, California. There is also little room for failure or delays in implementing the project, given the delivery schedule SAIC has with CAAC. According to the agreement between them, two aircraft were scheduled for delivery in 1987, four in 1988, seven in 1989, eight in 1990, and, finally, four in 1991.

In order to meet the project's ambitious schedule, the parties to the agreement established a 20-member joint executive management board that meets monthly and oversees all aspects of the program. One of its concerns has been manager training. It has encompassed both forming effective teams of Chinese and U.S. managers to share technical expertise and do project-related work and training Chinese managers in modern management theory. Approximately 150 SAIC employees went to Long Beach for several months soon after the agreement was signed to learn more about managerial practices and work procedures. One of the key challenges of the project has been to break down the Chinese tendency to polite evasiveness when faced with conflict. At the outset, many U.S. managers were stymied by the indirectness and lack of responsiveness of their Chinese counterparts when dealing with areas of disagreement. Finally, though, in the course of an impassioned 4-day joint seminar, the Chinese overcame their reluctance to air their concerns and criticisms. The result has been a better understanding between Chinese and U.S. management and smoother progress on the project.

One of the great logistical problems has been the language barrier. To combat this problem, the Shanghai factory employs approximately 300 people just to translate the vast number of production manuals and quality control documents associated with the project. The factory also employs at least 80 interpreters; in addition, many MDC employees have their own full-time interpreters. U.S. and Chinese employees are also given the opportunity to improve their foreign language skills through regular English classes or Chinese tutorial sessions.

MDC has also had some trouble motivating local employees. For years, the Chinese communist government embraced an egalitarian wage system in which remuneration had little to do with output. Although the system has changed—a portion of one's pay is now directly related to productivity—layoffs and firings are still rare. In response, MDC has instituted a special system of quarterly bonuses, in addition to standard productivity incentives, which are awarded to shops that exceed certain quality and production standards. MDC has also instituted an overtime pay system to offer employees an incentive for working additional hours. In this way, MDC has been able to make up for costly delays, often the bugaboo of other projects in China.

Despite the daunting complexity of the MD–82 project in Shanghai—which is the largest Sino-American technology transfer to date—the first coproduced aircraft received its airworthiness certificate in July 1987 and went into domestic service the following month. So far the factory has been able to keep to its original production schedule, and hopes are high that it will continue to do so.

Although the coproduction project has undoubtedly been frustrating at times for all the partners, MDC evidently feels encouraged enough by its experience to want to further this kind of cooperation with China. McDonnell Douglas is planning to submit a competitive proposal for the development and manufacture of 150 commercial passenger jets to the Ministry of Aeronautics.

In contrast with MDC, those firms that follow an export orientation may feel clever for having avoided the difficulties of a massive technology transfer project or losing future income by selling proprietary technology. Indeed, there are certain advantages associated with an export strategy. Nevertheless, as more countries try to curb foreign exchange outflow and get more long-term benefits from their investment, companies must be prepared to include technology transfer, joint ventures, countertrade and other forms of cooperation in their portfolio of global marketing strategies. Flexible companies will have more business opportunities open to them. In the world of the future it is likely that all companies in international markets—even the most timid or conservative—will face opportunities where the "new" forms of cooperation are the best, or only, way to go.

SOURCE: From "McDonnell Douglas: The Management Challenge" by Madelyn C. Ross. This article first appeared in the September-October 1987 issue of *The China Business Review*, and has been reprinted with permission of the US-China Business Council.

Questions

1. Why would McDonnell Douglas be interested in participating in a technology transfer with China?

2. What are the most serious problems MDC has encountered in its project with the Chinese?

3. Do you think that MDC is unwise to license proprietary technology in such a potentially large market?

4. Should a company try to maintain an export strategy for as long as possible, in order to protect its proprietary technology and competitive advantage?

CASE APPLICATION 23–2

Procter & Gamble International Makes a Comeback

Despite Procter & Gamble's (P&G) reputation as the premier U.S. consumer goods manufacturer, the company's international division has often had a difficult struggle to make its brands successful in foreign markets. The marketing environment in other countries is often very different from the environment P&G has mastered so well in the U.S. For example, in Europe—one of P&G's important target markets—the company has encountered a lot of competition since firms within the European Economic Community can trade freely across national boundaries. In addition, some of P&G's key international rivals, such as Unilever, apparently have lower requirements for return on investment. As a result, such companies are able to compete vigorously on price. A tendency toward excess manufacturing capacity in consumer products has also made the European market very price sensitive. Besides being hampered by savvy local competition, P&G has also been hamstrung by limited access to commercial TV time, since most networks in European nations are state-run. Finally, P&G has sometimes failed to take into account the unique needs of foreign consumers. After decades of involvement in international markets, however, P&G has altered its traditional strategy and has thus begun to see some positive results in the global arena.

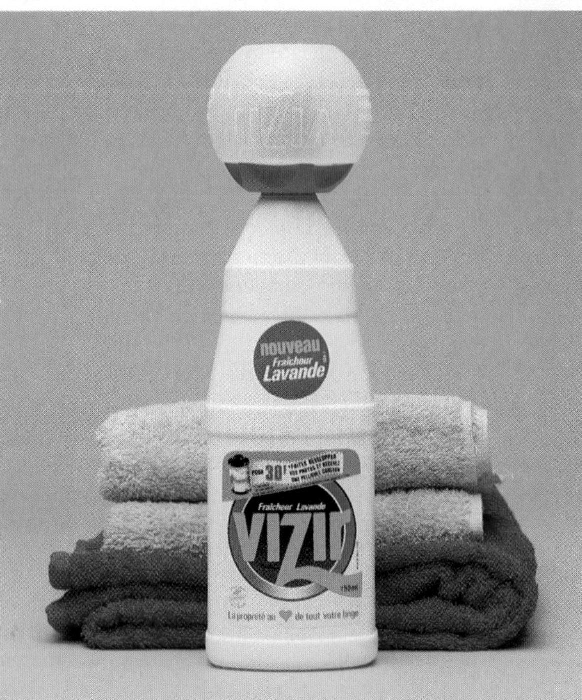

In the past, P&G moved slowly and very cautiously into foreign markets. Only those products proven successful over a period of time in the U.S. were exported. P&G then carefully nurtured demand for those products in foreign markets until the level of demand merited the establishment of a foreign manufacturing unit, a process that often would take years. As a manufacturer in a foreign country, P&G attempted to keep ahead of would-be competitors primarily through technological advantages. But its scrupulous approach to international marketing often gave competitors the chance to overcome P&G's original advantage. For instance, P&G often unwittingly tipped off competitors as to the company's future international marketing strategy through its actions in the domestic market. Likewise, the lengthy process of test marketing and nurturing demand often gave competitors time to improve on P&G offerings. The opportunity for competitors to beat out P&G's Pampers in Japan was in part afforded by the strategy and pace of P&G's product introduction.

Besides suffering from excessive cautiousness and slowness, P&G has also suffered from cultural and organizational rigidity, originally holding that the company's U.S. marketing formula was equally suitable for all foreign markets. Walter Lingle, P&G's first vice president in charge of overseas operations, articulated the company's policy many years ago: "We have decided that the best way to succeed in other countries is to build in each one an exact replica of the U.S. Procter & Gamble organization. . . .

"We believe that exactly the same policies and procedures which have given our company success in the U.S. will be equally successful overseas."

Although this policy may have helped streamline product introductions, the resulting marketing programs were sometimes sorely out of tune with conditions in the foreign markets. For example, in its most notable international marketing failure, P&G rolled out Vizir (a liquid detergent based on the same technology as Liquid Tide) in Europe in the early 1980s. Most European washing machines at the time were not equipped to accept liquid detergents. Using Vizir in powder dispensers wasted about 20 percent of the product. Although P&G persuaded washing machine manufacturers in Europe to design liquid dispensers for their machines, P&G realized that it also needed to find a more immediate solution to its problem, since the average life of washing machines in Europe is about 15 years. The company then decided to offer "retrofit" systems, free to consumers, for simple insertion in the powder dispensers of their machines. But the model number of each machine was needed to get the device right, and most European washers are bolted to the wall—making finding the model number on the back of the machine difficult. P&G was again stymied. Finally, it invented a reusable dispensing ball called the "Vizirette," which is helping Vizir recover in several European markets.

What has P&G done to try to insure against making similar international marketing mistakes? First, the company is attempting to make its international subsidiaries more responsive to local conditions. Although P&G is still committed to a broad global marketing strategy, the company now realizes the importance of encouraging local initiative in the execution of that strategy. In line with this goal, P&G's European organization now includes country "core" teams to suggest ways to tailor the global marketing program to the characteristics of a particular country and a new Asia/Pacific division to help fine-tune the company's marketing strategy to the countries in that area.

Second, P&G has altered its traditional strategy of product introduction. Rather than waiting to see if a product will "fly" in the domestic market before making international plans, new products are now launched with global distribution in mind. Whereas P&G took 15 years to get Pampers into 70 countries, it now aims to get products into world markets in five years or less. Products which P&G feels may be especially competitive or technologically superior may even be introduced in some major foreign markets within months of the U.S. introduction.

Third, the company has relaxed its policy regarding joint ventures. Formerly, the company was only willing to establish wholly owned subsidiaries in foreign countries. Such a policy, however, precluded establishing manufacturing facilities in countries such as Mexico and Malaysia, which restrict foreign ownership. Now P&G is willing to consider various forms of cooperation and ownership.

Finally, P&G made an important strategic acquisition with the purchase of Richardson-Vicks (R-V) in 1985, adding a number of high margin products—such as over-the-counter cold remedies and skin creams—to its product list. Given its unimpressive international profits (despite generally good sales), P&G was eager to acquire some more profitable items. Just as important, however, was P&G's strategy of improving its marketing network and expertise in the developing countries, where it has traditionally been weak. R-V has a strong presence in such countries as Australia, India, Indonesia, and Thailand, as well as in Latin America. P&G should benefit from R-V's distribution networks and management talent. In fact, R-V executives were given a dominant role in P&G's new Asia/Pacific division. In addition, P&G and R-V will directly combine their marketing efforts in smaller markets such as Hong Kong.

P&G's organizational modifications and overhaul of its international marketing strategy have begun to yield profitable results. For example, the company finally began to show a profit in Japan in 1987. Japan may not be the only market in the world, but as one of the toughest foreign markets to crack, it seems to be a symbol of the recent changes in P&G International and the company's resolve to be a more formidable challenger in consumer products across the globe.

SOURCE: Dennis Chase, "A Global Comeback," *Advertising Age,* August 20, 1987, pp. 142–46, 212–14.

Questions

1. Which feature of the international marketing environment discussed in Paragraph 1 seems to pose the greatest challenge to P&G International's success? Why?

2. P&G used to wait until products had become established domestically before marketing them abroad. What are the positive aspects of this strategy? Negative aspects?

3. What are some problems associated with trying to translate P&G's domestic marketing program directly into foreign markets? In which foreign markets would such a strategy be most feasible? Least feasible?

4. Do you think it was wise for P&G to loosen its restrictions on setting up joint ventures? What problems might be associated with using joint ventures as part of an international marketing strategy?

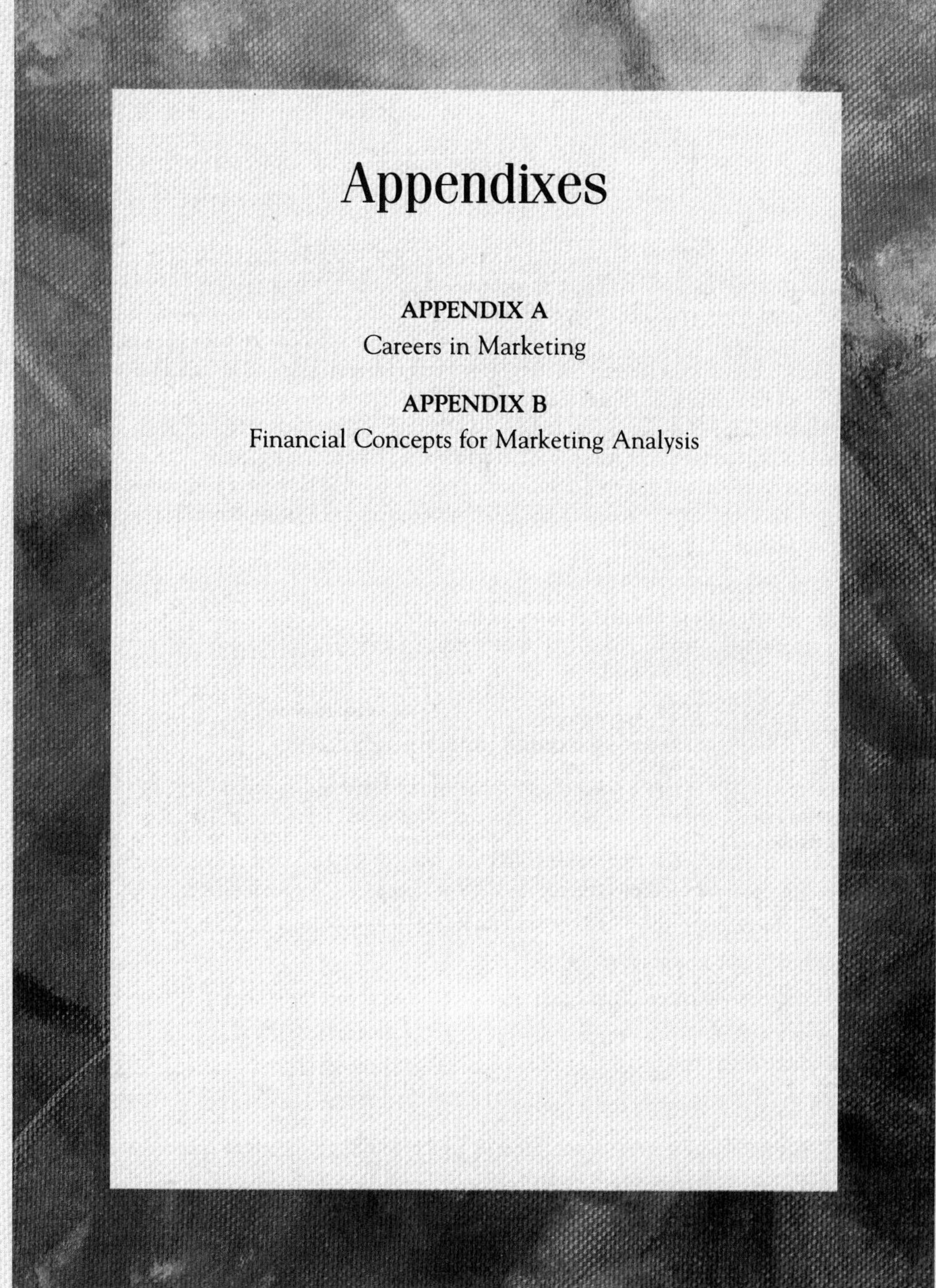

Appendixes

A

Careers in Marketing

Career planning is an individualized process. Each of us has a unique set of values, interests, and work and personal experiences. Understanding how this set of factors blends is an important part of career planning; it is also necessary to understand the requirements of various careers so that your personality and intellectual abilities can be matched to the job. Career decisions will shape your life style.

Marketing is a very broad area of business and, as a result, it employs a variety of people. College students interested in marketing careers have to find out how they fit into the spectrum of career choices available. It should be noted that most people promoted to chief executive officers have marketing backgrounds. The purpose of this appendix is to provide:

1. a few career basics and hints on self-assessment;
2. a description of the major jobs in marketing; and
3. information on the mechanics of getting a job.

Career Basics and Self-Analysis

First, before thinking about specific career areas, sit back and spend some time mulling over those things that you want from a career. Here are a few questions to consider:

- Do you want a job or a career? Do you want it to be personally satisfying, or are the financial rewards enough? How important is career advancement?
- Are the status and prestige associated with a career important to you?
- What about financial rewards?
- Do you have geographical preferences? What about large or small cities?
- What size employer would you prefer to work for? Might this preference change later on?

Now, think about yourself for a minute.

- What education, experience, and skills do you have to offer?
- Are you quantitatively (thing) oriented or qualitatively (people) oriented, or do you enjoy both? There is a place for both types in marketing.
- What are your weak and strong points? How will they relate to your performance on the job?
- What kind of work is interesting?

- What kind of work do you like?
- What kind of work do you do well?
- What kind of work will make you feel worthwhile?

A personal evaluation of these and similar questions is a worthwhile exercise. These questions may help you develop a job or career identity.

Professional Help for Self-Assessment

Professional counselors can help you decide which career path to take. Most high schools and colleges provide free counseling services, where trained professionals help people assess their skills realistically.

Vocational tests are often used to verify one's self-analysis and to reveal any hidden personal characteristics. No one test or battery of tests can make a career choice for you, but tests can supplement the information you're reviewing as you mull over career opportunities and personal characteristics. Your college placement office has counselors who can recommend which tests are most appropriate for the areas you're considering.

In addition, the counselor can help you with your self-assessment by providing publications discussing career opportunities. Some widely publicized and frequently used publications include:

- *College Placement Annual,* College Placement Council, Inc., P.O. Box 2263, Bethlehem, Pa. 18001—published annually. This publication provides information on current job openings in companies. It also provides suggestions for preparing effective résumés and strategies of interviewing for jobs.
- *Occupational Outlook Handbook,* U.S. Department of Labor, Government Printing Office, Washington, D.C.—published annually. This handbook lists all major occupations, with a brief description of job requirements, opportunities available, and future job prospects.

Self-assessment, help from a professional counselor, and career publications can provide the necessary background information to properly plan your career. But in the final analysis, you alone must make the career decision and seek appropriate job opportunities.

Jobs in Marketing

In this section we describe the major marketing positions open to new employees with little or no experience. Read on and see what interests you!

Marketing Research

Marketing researchers provide a great deal of the information businesses need to make sound decisions about the marketing of their products. This involves analyzing data on products and sales, making surveys, conducting interviews, preparing forecasts, and making recommendations on product design, advertising, pricing, and distribution.

Entry-level opportunities in marketing research are fewer than in most other marketing areas. However, as demand for new products and services grows, the need for information and identification of potential buyers increases.

Most marketing research positions are available with either "in-house" research staffs of manufacturing and marketing firms, marketing research consulting firms, or advertising agencies. Government agencies and university research centers are two other possible employers.

You are more likely to be involved with the actual mechanics of research if you join a research consulting firm, but no matter whom you work for, marketing research involves problem-solving.

Trainees generally start as research assistants or junior analysts. At first, this may involve performing clerical tasks such as copying data from published sources, editing and coding questionnaires, and tabulating survey returns. Trainees may learn to conduct interviews and write reports on survey findings. With experience, they may assume responsibility for specific marketing research projects or advance to managerial positions. A capable person may become marketing research director.

What do you need to undertake a career in marketing research? Quantitative and behavioral science skills are important. You must be comfortable with numbers, and you must have an understanding of people's attitudes, tastes, and behaviors. Good communication skills are essential in information-gathering and in presenting recommendations to management. If you are inquisitive, analytical, objective, and rational, you may find yourself challenged and rewarded by the field of marketing research. Good interpersonal skills are also important, since the analyst often deals with managers in the firm and with outside research specialists.

Brand or Product Management

Brand managers, or, as they are sometimes called, product managers, are responsible for planning and directing the entire marketing program for a given product or group of products. In a way, it is like running your own business. A brand manager is involved in new product ideas and research, advertising, sales promotion, packaging decisions, pricing, inventory levels, sales, and the legal aspects of marketing a product. Companies such as Procter & Gamble, General Mills, and DuPont use product managers.

The entry-level position is generally as a brand assistant. You will be given both individual and team projects within your brand group pertaining to all marketing decisions of your particular brand. If you perform well in this capacity, after about a year, you will be promoted to assistant brand manager, often in a different brand group. Your responsibilities will increase, and you will help train the brand assistants below you. After several years of high performance as an assistant brand manager, you may be promoted to brand manager, giving you total responsibility for the marketing effort and performance of your product. From brand manager, a logical promotion progression might be to group brand manager, in charge of several brand groups, and then general manager or vice president of marketing.

In all of these positions, the hours can be long and the work can be frustrating. While you have responsibility for a product's performance, you do not have commensurate authority to see that your directives and plans are put into effect. In brand management, you generally have no authority over anyone except your own small staff. This means that your work must be accomplished through dealing with other departments such as sales, marketing research, and production on a personal basis. Sometimes this can evolve into a political and competitive activity.

An MBA is often a desirable credential for a brand manager, but some firms do hire at the undergraduate level. Other personal characteristics are of greater importance. One is the ability to identify and develop creativity—if not in yourself, then

MARKETING MANAGER

Brand Management in Lodging

If you are currently in a marketing position with a leading packaged goods or services company, you may qualify for an exciting marketing position with **Courtyard by Marriott.** Courtyard is the Marriott Corporation's rapid growth, moderately-priced lodging product and sister division to Marriott Hotels and Resorts.

Reporting to the Director of Advertising and Public Relations, the selected candidate will have the opportunity to become a director within one year. This position will assist the Director in the development of short and longer term marketing strategy and implementation of advertising, direct response, promotion and public relations programs. Responsibilities will also include serving as the liaison with regional marketing departments and the division's ad and PR Agencies of Record, as well as analyzing the product's marketing performance vs. competition. Marketing is integral to the Courtyard Division's goal of at least tripling in size by the mid-1990's.

Qualified candidates should have an MBA, preferably in Marketing, at least three years product marketing experience, with an emphasis on developing and implementing national and regional advertising and PR programs.

Courtyard by Marriott offers an extraordinary opportunity for professional growth and recognition, as well as a competitive salary and benefits package designed to attract leaders who desire a situation that rewards individual contribution and results. For immediate confidential consideration, send a resume with salary history to: **Courtyard by Marriott, Department 935.50CTYD, Marriott Drive, Washington, DC 20058.**

EOE m/f/d/v

Consumer Research Project Manager

Wendy's International, Inc. is an internationally recognized leader in the restaurant industry, with over 3700 restaurants and systemwide sales approaching $3 billion. Our continued commitment to professional marketing support has created this dynamic opportunity.

Key responsibilities of this challenging position include:

- The design, implementation, and evaluation of market research programs; including consumer tracking, product development, and sales promotion programs
- Develop and manage consumer database systems to identify and monitor consumer and business opportunities

Qualified candidates should possess:

- Strong background in market research techniques and applications
- MBA with at least 3 years experience in consumer research, preferably in a restaurant environment
- Excellent communication and interpersonal skills
- PC literate with an aptitude for financial analysis

This is a unique opportunity to make a significant contribution to a vital segment of our business. Individuals must bring a professional, enthusiastic and results-oriented approach to the Consumer Research function. We offer a highly competitive salary and comprehensive benefit package. For consideration, forward your resume in confidence, including salary history to: **WENDY'S INTERNATIONAL, INC., Dept. 432-CR, P.O. Box 256, Dublin, OH 43017.** No third party or phone inquiries, please. An equal opportunity employer, m/f/h.

LADIES PROFESSIONAL GOLF ASSOCIATION

DIRECTOR OF SALES & MARKETING

The Ladies Professional Golf Association (LPGA) is the premier women's sports organization in the world. The LPGA's objectives are to: promote worldwide interest in the game of golf; establish and maintain high standards in promotion, development and conduct of women's professional golf activities; provide vocational opportunities in teaching, tournament play, merchandising and golf promotion for women golf professionals, and protect and further the mutual interests of the LPGA and its members.

The Director of Sales and Marketing will be responsible for developing new LPGA Tour-wide sponsors, promotions, licensing, and special events. He/she will participate in marketing the LPGA to corporate sponsors, the advertising community, and sports marketing agencies. The Director will report to the Vice President, Business Affairs.

The ideal candidate should have a degree in business administration, communications or liberal arts. The candidate selected must have a stable employment history with no less than four years of successful sales and marketing experience in a major corporation, marketing consulting firm, public relations firm, advertising firm, or sports related organization. He/she should have demonstrated skills in sales, television advertising, marketing, negotiating and working with public relations personnel. Further the candidate must fully understand, play, and appreciate the game of golf.

The LPGA will offer a competitive compensation and benefit package. The total amount is dependent upon the background and the qualifications of the person selected. The LPGA is currently in the process of relocating its national headquarters from Houston, Texas.

Send confidential resumes, three letters of recommendation, and salary history by May 15, 1989 to:

Gregg Shimanski
Vice President, Business Affairs
LADIES PROFESSIONAL GOLF ASSOCIATION
4675 Sweetwater Blvd.
Sugar Land, Texas 77479

PRODUCT MANAGER

Borden, Inc., a Fortune 60 consumer products manufacturer, is seeking a highly capable individual to be principal business manager in one of today's fast-growing food product markets. You will be responsible for planning, organizing and controlling marketing activities related to assigned brands. We are looking for a leader who will be strongly oriented to achieving short and long term volume and income goals. You will have close involvement with all phases of strategic and tactical business plans and will coordinate internal and external support groups.

To qualify, you must be a take-charge, goal-directed Marketing professional having at least three years of proven marketing/sales experience with a major consumer packaged goods company. A strong financial orientation, coupled with good communication skills, is essential. A Bachelor's degree is required, an MBA preferred.

We offer an attractive salary commensurate with your qualifications and an outstanding benefits package that includes a matching savings plan and a unique cash accumulation retirement plan. For consideration, send resume with salary history/requirements to: **Professional Staffing, Dept. AA522.**

BORDEN, INC.
180 East Broad Street
Columbus, OH 43215

An Equal Opportunity Employer M/F/H/V

TM

in those around you. An inquisitive personality, the ability to think like a consumer, political savvy, and passion for your work are qualities that will help you become a successful brand manager.

Retailing

In the past, retailers just tended to hope, rather than plan, that the public would buy their merchandise. Now, since the retail industry has more than tripled in size over the past thirty years, and since some major failures have occurred (W. T. Grant, for example), careful study goes into determining customers' wants and needs. Marketing, as well as other business functions, is growing in importance in retailing, and, thus, in demanding better educated and trained managers. Business-school graduates are being placed into more and more management roles, and management salaries can be high despite the notorious reputation retailing has for paying its employees poorly.

Retailing offers a variety of positions, including sales, buying, distribution, and staff functions such as advertising and marketing research. Entry-level jobs may involve some sales work, depending on the store and whether you have any background in retailing. The next positions may be those of assistant buyer and then buyer. In these, the job is like that of running your own ministore within a store, as the buyer often has control over types of merchandise displayed, nature of promotions, and even price levels. The competition among retailers is stiff; to be successful, you need guts, foresight, and creativity.

Another route up the retail ladder is to first manage a department, then gradually work your way up to store manager, and finally move to upper-level management. Probably the best way to get into retailing is through one of the training programs offered by major department store chains such as Macy's, Lord & Taylor, Bloomingdale's, May Stores, and Filene's. These programs give you exposure to a broad view of retailing and substantial responsibility early in your career.

Many retailers say that you either love retailing or you hate it; there is very little middle ground. Work schedules vary with the season, but six-day work weeks are common during the fall and into Christmas. Also, some students have little preparation for a career in retailing except through summer job or intern experience.

In the past, retailing has not been attractive to college graduates, but now that stores have seen the need for business-oriented managers, the opportunities are growing. Entry-level salaries are about average (below average for sales jobs, though) and can go quite high since advancement and responsibility come fast.

Retailing is a special kind of business, with special demands. If it interests you, be aware that you need to start your job search early. You may have to go out and find retailers because they will probably not come and find you.

Advertising

Advertising has traditionally been called a glamorous profession. Those that are in it will tell you that it is also pressure filled and analytical, yet rewarding in its own way. In advertising, the product is communication, and advertising professionals must master its concepts and techniques.

Many ad agencies prefer to hire undergraduates over MBAs for several reasons. First of all, they can pay undergraduates less and then give them a chance to prove themselves before raising their salaries. Second, since most graduate business schools lack emphasis and course work in advertising, MBAs know little more about advertising than undergraduates, but they do have a broader background in business and, perhaps, more maturity.

Several entry-level positions exist in advertising. One can begin as a media buyer, copywriter, or, less often, as a junior or assistant account executive. The media buyer chooses the media that will carry the client's ad and arranges for buying the time and space. Those who write the words for ads or the script for commercials are called copywriters. After a year or two in one of these positions—or sometimes in a position in the agency's marketing research department—you may become a junior or assistant executive. You will do some analytical work and have moderate contact with clients, usually with just one account. From this point on, the responsibility increases and the workload is heavy. Strategic thinking and planning, as well as implementation in a highly competitive, fast-paced environment, become very important. The next promotions are to full account executive, account supervisor, management supervisor, and then into various agency principal positions.

Some agencies offer formal training programs, while others use on-the-job training. While entry-level salaries are low, increases come quickly, and the fringe benefits and bonuses are often very good.

Many executives find that students come to agencies with distorted impressions of advertising. They stress the need for spending some time finding out the realities of the trade. A good way to do this is through the summer programs that many agencies offer. Also, be sure to examine not only the management of an agency, but also its client roster and the quality of the work done for its clients.

Public Relations

Although public relations is a part of the marketing function, the background for positions in this area is often in communications or journalism. Because the public relations department is the link between the organization and its various publics, effective communication skills are of vital importance.

Members of the public relations department must be kept fully advised of internal changes in marketing strategy, advertising, and new products. They must, at the same time, share this and information about products, labor policies, community activities, and social programs with the public. They must also deal directly with the news media and are often responsible for internal communications, including employee and management newsletters.

The entry-level position is usually as a public relations trainee, which could involve preparing press releases or working on company publications. People often specialize in certain areas within the public relations department and/or work their way up to vice president or director of public relations.

Entry-level jobs in public relations are not highly paid, and the compensation for top jobs in public relations depends largely on the firm and its industry. In the past, industrial firms have tended to pay better than consumer marketers. Working toward the goal of projecting the desired company image to the public is an important and difficult task, but a creative and rewarding one.

Sales

There are more job opportunities, especially entry-level positions, in personal selling than in any other area. A college degree used to be unnecessary for selling, but that is becoming less true. Company sales forces are benefiting more and more from the business and technical skills of their salespeople.

Selling positions are found in a wide variety of organizations, both consumer and industrial, and they cover a variety of activities. These positions could involve calling on a number of customers each day, putting up and maintaining displays, checking inventory levels, or taking orders for stock. Problem-solving for customers is increasingly becoming part of the sales job.

There are generally two career paths you can follow in sales. First, a salesperson may make sales a career and become a specialist in dealing with jobbers, chains, or vendors, or in selling to specialized target groups such as independent grocers and hospitals. The person may even specialize in selling particular types of products. The second path is to become sales manager of a region or district, supervising sales representatives and managers under you. This could ultimately lead to becoming national sales manager, vice president of sales, or perhaps even president. Sales is a common route to the top.

Personal selling does have its hardships, though. It often involves a good deal of traveling, nights spent away from home, dealing with hostile or indifferent people, and work that may occasionally seem tedious and unglamorous. It can be lonely, but, at the same time, you are so free of the constraints of an office job that it is almost like being your own boss. It can be very rewarding to know that you represent the company to your customers and have the chance to develop personal resourcefulness as well as product and customer knowledge. Some companies—IBM and Eastman Kodak, for example—view this period in the field as a necessary prerequisite to higher level management positions, and offer sales training programs for a solid introduction to personal selling.

The remuneration for a sales position can be very high, depending on your effort and the compensation plan. In fact, many people, once in sales, spend their entire careers there, choosing the freedom and earning potential over the restrictions and often lower salaries of office management positions.

What do you need to be successful in personal selling? Most firms look for an outgoing personality, a competitive spirit, sensitivity in dealing with people, a foundation in marketing, and the ability to understand one's clients.

Selling is hard work, but it also provides highly visible results, and the potential rewards, both personal and financial, are great. No other job is more important to an organization's success.

Marketing Training Programs

Marketing development or training programs are offered by such firms as the Bell System, Dow Chemical, General Electric, and International Harvester. The details of these programs vary, but, generally, they begin with an introduction to the firm, its products, and its basic marketing functions. In some companies, this involves some time spent in sales. After a good working knowledge of the firm has been developed, you are moved to a more specific area of marketing where you want to gain some experience. This could be one of the marketing support functions such as marketing research, distribution, planning, or product management. There is usually a good deal of freedom allowed in switching back and forth between these areas. Management keeps a close eye on your development and performance in each of these areas.

Firms with these types of programs give you heavy responsibility from the beginning because they are interested in making an effective manager out of you. Thus, the pressures can be great, and the opportunities for rapid advancement can be very attractive.

Figure A–1 Possible Career Paths and Salary Ranges: 1989*

	Entry Level						Advanced Levels
Marketing Research (MR)	Research Trainee → $20–26,000	Senior Analyst → $28–49,000	Director or VP, MR $60–150,000+				
Brand/ Product Manage-ment	Brand Asst. $22–30,000 →	Asst. Brand Manager → $40–48,000	Brand Manager → $48–80,000	Brand Group Manager → $80–90,000	General Manager → $110–180,000	VP, Marketing $200,000+	
Retailing	Asst. Buyer $16–20,000 →	Buyer $25–40,000 →	Merchan-dise Manager → $30–60,000	Store Manager → $30–60,000	Store VP $50–90,000 →	Corporate VP $130,000+	
Advertis-ing	Media Buyer $15–35,000	Copywriter $20–35,000	Jr. Account Executive → $20–45,000	Account Executive → $45–70,000	Account Supervisor → $45–95,000	Manage-ment Supervisor → $45–90,000	Director of Adver-tising $90,000+
Public Relations (PR)	PR Trainee $15–20,000 →	PR Special-ist → $20–$45,000	Director, PR $40–80,000+				
Sales	Sales Rep. $16–60,000 →	District Sales Manager → $30–65,000	Regional Sales Manager → $40–75,000	National Sales Manager → $50–95,000	VP Sales or Marketing $85–500,000+		

* These pay ranges change as conditions like inflation, supply, and demand change; dollar amounts exclude bonuses, and are averages.

Other Marketing Positions

Other marketing positions can be found in a number of areas. Although there are fewer positions available, the opportunities for advancement, challenge, and good salaries are equal to those in the more popular segments of marketing. Some of these, which will not be covered in this appendix, but which you are encouraged to research if they are of interest, are wholesaling, physical distribution, warehousing, consumer affairs, customer relations, sales promotion, credit management, pricing, international marketing, and professorships in marketing.

Figure A–1 lists possible career paths and their average salary ranges. We should also note some upper-end marketing compensation levels. The total remuneration for the marketing vice president for selected companies follows:[1]

Gannett, communications	$525,000
Apple Computers, computers	475,000
Wal-Mart Stores, retailing	400,000
Navistar, trucks and engines	371,000
Tyson Foods, poultry	308,977
William Wrigley, Jr., confections	268,723
Trans World Airlines, airline	201,098
Cummins Engine, diesel engines	196,331
Murray Ohio, bicycles	169,869

The Job Search: A Plan

In school you prepare for examinations by organizing your notes and planning. In searching for a job, you also need to organize and plan. The first job after college can affect your entire career, so a plan is a must. Without it, you will lose valuable time and experience unnecessary frustration. There is no single best job-search plan, but there are some basic principles. Because your time is limited, you must use some systematic procedure to narrow the number of job possibilities.

When evaluating any particular marketing career there are some specific issues that you should consider. Examine the broad career options in marketing described in the previous section with the following questions in mind:

- What are the qualifications for the job? Will you need more education, more experience?
- What is the financial situation? Is the salary reasonable? How are the benefits? What salary is likely in three to five years? Is there going to be a conflict between the value you place on money and your returns from this job?
- What are the opportunities for advancement? Does this appear to jibe with your aspirations?
- What is the present supply-and-demand status for this field and what might it be in the future?
- Will the job involve much travel? Is that desirable or undesirable? How mobile are you?
- What is the atmosphere associated with the job? Is it pressure filled, demanding, cooperative, tranquil, or creative?
- Is this job something that you will be proud of? Does it fit your self-image?
- Is it work that you will enjoy? Is it in line with your goals and ethics? Will you be happy?

Within any given marketing career choice, one faces a number of prospective employers. Each company offers different conditions, opportunities, and rewards to its employees. Here are some important questions to ask about the firms you are considering:

- Does the company have opportunities for a person with my skills, aptitudes, and goals?
- What are the promotion opportunities in the company?
- Does the company usually promote from within?
- What type of professional development is available for new employees?
- What kind of working environment exists within the company?
- What is the future growth potential for the company and the industry?

Answers to these kinds of questions will enable you to narrow the available job opportunities. Answers can be found in such sources as company annual reports, *Standard and Poor's Corporation Records*, and *Dun and Bradstreet's Reference Book of Manufacturers*. Another source is the company's employees. If you know some employees, ask them for first-hand information.

Most companies furnish brochures on career opportunities. These sources are impressive, but they often give a totally positive picture of the company. Consult your school's placement officer to learn more about each company and to determine the accuracy of the brochures.

There are two other sources you should consult—newspapers and professional magazines. The classified ads, especially in the Sunday or weekend editions, provide a lot of job information. These advertisements usually provide information about job vacancies, the type of people the company is looking for, and the person or post office box to contact if you are interested. An outstanding listing of job opportunities appears in *The Wall Street Journal.* It lists jobs at the highest level as well as openings at the supervisory level.

Professional magazines, such as the *Personnel Journal, Training and Industry,* and *Nation's Business,* often list vacancies. These advertisements are for recent graduates or people with work experience. If you are interested in a particular occupation, consulting the professional magazines in that functional area can be helpful. Specialized trade journals are also good sources for job leads. Examples are *Advertising Age, Marketing News,* and *Sales and Marketing Management Magazine.* Even the yellow pages in phone directories are a helpful guide to companies operating in a particular area. Talk to family, friends, faculty members, and others who may know of job leads or people with pertinent information.

Personalizing Through a Résumé

After personal and professional self-assessments and a job search via newspapers, professional magazines, and employment agencies, the next step is to personalize your campaign. This means that you must communicate who you are to others. The basic devices used to communicate are résumés, letters, the telephone, and personal interviews.

A résumé is a written summary of who you are. It is a concise picture of you and your credentials for a job. A résumé should highlight your qualifications, achievements, and career objectives and should present you as an attractive candidate.

There is no generally accepted format for a résumé. Its purpose is to introduce you to the employer and to get you an interview. Few, if any, employers hire college graduates solely on the contents of a résumé. In most cases, you can attract attention with a one-page résumé. Longer résumés are for people who have had extensive professional experience.

Employers like résumés that read well and look good. Résumés read well if they are concise and easy to follow; they look good if they are reproduced on an offset press and are on high-quality paper. There are companies that prepare professional résumés for a fee. The yellow pages of the telephone directory can provide names of firms that sell this service.

Other elements found in good résumés are job objectives, educational background, college activities, work experiences, and references. The arrangement of these elements is a personal decision. But keep the résumés uncluttered and neatly blocked, to create an attractive and informative résumé with eye appeal. Figure A–2 presents an example of an effective résumé.

It may be necessary to prepare a different résumé for each employer, so that your credentials can be slanted for the job openings. Whether you think a different résumé for each company can do the job is a decision that only you can make.

Just as important as the points to include are some points to avoid in preparing your résumé. DON'T

- state what salary you want;
- send a résumé with false information;

Figure A–2 Sample Résumé

JILL M. MURPHY
4896 Creling Drive
New York, NY 10011
(555) 431–0019

OBJECTIVE	A challenging position in marketing, utilizing analytical and problem-solving skills.
EDUCATION	NEW YORK UNIVERSITY
Sept. 1986– May 1990	School of Business Administration Major: Marketing and Finance G.P.A. 3.9; Dean's List; NYU Tuition scholarship School of Social Sciences G.P.A. 3.9; Dean's List; concentration in mathematics and psychology.
Sept. 1982– June 1986	NOTRE DAME HIGH SCHOOL G.P.A. 3.9 Class Honors; Phi Beta Kappa; National Honor Society; State Champion, Women's Extemporaneous Speaking, 1983, Major Delegation Award at National Model United Nations in Washington, D.C., 1985, 1986
EXPERIENCE	**Assistant Marketing Manager,** PepsiCo.
May, 1988– Present	Responsibilities included the coordination of planning, implementing, and evaluating the Pepsi Challenge Program in New York City. This required close liaison with PepsiCo's marketing and sales activities as well as its advertising agency and the media. Achieved increase of over 100 percent in program participants, totaling over 60,000 people. Planned and implemented a Mountain Dew sampling program. On own initiative, developed a Coordinator's Handbook which PepsiCo plans to distribute nationwide.
Sept. 1989– May 1990	**Vice President,** Alpha Kappa Gamma Sorority Responsible for housing policies, personnel relations, and discipline.
Sept. 1988– Sept. 1989	**Assistant Treasurer,** Alpha Kappa Gamma Sorority Responsible for funds to finance all sorority events. Included collection, recording, and billing for sixty-five individual accounts.
Summer 1989	**Salesperson,** Revlon, Inc.
Summer 1988	**Information Manager,** Summer Concert Series at New York University.
ACTIVITIES	**Project Director,** Marketing Club at New York University; Seminar for Republican Campaign Coordinators, Washington, D.C.; New York University Campus Orchestra; NYC Symphony Youth Orchestra.
REFERENCES	Available on request.

- send a résumé that is sloppy and contains typographical errors;
- clutter your résumé with unnecessary information;
- inform employers that you will accept only a certain kind of position; or
- use fancy colors or gimmicks to sell yourself.

A cover letter should accompany the résumé. Its objective is to introduce you and encourage the employer to read your résumé and meet with you. The cover letter should not duplicate the more detailed résumé. Instead, it should add to what is presented and show that you are really interested in working for the company. The cover letter also reveals how well you can communicate. This clue is often used by employers to put prospective employees into one of two categories: a good communicator or a poor communicator.

Employers receive cover letters and résumés from many more job applicants than they can ever hire or even interview. Therefore, they screen whatever letters and résumés they receive. Screening is often accomplished rather quickly, so it is better to present your story and objective concisely and neatly.

The number of letters and résumés you send depends on your strategy. Some people narrow down their list of organizations to the ones they really would like to work for and prepare a personal cover letter to accompany the résumé. Other candidates use a "shotgun" approach. They mail numerous letters and résumés to any company with an opening in a particular area of interest. The newspapers, professional magazines, listings in the placement office, telephone directories, directories of organizations, and tips from friends are used to develop a potential list. Then perhaps as many as 200 letters and résumés are sent out.

The Interview Strategy

An outstanding cover letter, résumé, and job search strategy are still not enough to get you the job you want. You must also perform well at the interview, an oral presentation with a representative of a company. A good recruiter is interested in how a job candidate expresses himself or herself. The interviewer is both an information source and an information prober. As an information source, the interviewer provides you with knowledge about careers in the organization and the company in general. As a prober, the interviewer wants to determine what makes you tick and what kind of person you are.

An Interview Plan

In searching for job openings, it is necessary to have a plan. This is also the case in having a successful interview. In order to do a good job at the interview, you must be thoroughly prepared. Of course, you must know yourself and what type of career you want. The interviewer will probe into the areas you covered in your self-assessment and in developing a career objective. During the interview, you must make it clear why a person with your strengths and objectives should be hired by the company.

The preparation for answering the question "why you" involves some homework. You should gather facts about the employer. Annual reports, opinions from employees of the firm, brochures, up-to-date financial data from *The Wall Street Journal,* and recent newspaper articles can be used. Table A–1 identifies some of the information that can be used to prepare for the interview. Your school library will have this information. Whether the initial interview is on the campus or in the office of the president of the company, prior preparation will impress the interviewer. This preparedness will allow you to explore other areas about the company that you don't know about. It will also allow the interviewer to probe into such areas as your grades, motivation, maturity, ability to communicate, and work experience. This informa-

Table A–1 Homework Information for the Interview

Location of headquarters, offices, plants
Officers of the organization
Future growth plans of the company
Product lines
Sales, profit, and dividend picture
Price of stock (if available)
Competitors of the company
Organizational structure
Kind of entry-level positions available
Career paths followed by graduates
Union situation
Type of programs available for employees (stock option, medical, educational)

tion is important for the company in making a decision whether to have you visit for a second, more in-depth interview.

Interview preparation also involves your personal appearance and motivational state. There isn't enough space here to focus extensively on dress, hair, and value codes. The next best advice is to be yourself and to come prepared to meet with a representative of the organization. If you are to work as an accountant for some firm, then you must comply with standards of performance as well as dress and appearance codes. Use your own judgment, but be realistic: employers don't like shoulder-length hair on a salesman or barefooted production supervisors. These biases will not be corrected in an interview, so don't be a crusader for a cause. The interview is not the best place to project a personal distaste for, or discomfort with, dress or hair-length standards.

Interviewing makes most people slightly nervous, but if you are well prepared and really motivated to talk to the representative, the interview will probably go well. Consider the interview as a challenge you can meet because you are interested in succeeding. An alert candidate with modest confidence has a good chance of impressing the interviewer.

The Actual Interview

The interview has been called *a conversation with a purpose.* During the interview, the company representative and the candidate both attempt to determine if a match exists. Are you the right person for the job? The attempt to match person and job follows a question-and-answer routine. The ability to answer questions quickly, honestly, and intelligently is important. The best way to provide a good set of answers is to be prepared.

Table A–2 provides a list of some commonly asked questions. The way you answer these and similar questions is what the interviewer evaluates. Remember that the interviewer is trying to get to know you better by watching your actions and listening to your replies.

One effective way to prepare for the interview session is to practice answering the questions in Table A–2 before attending the actual interview. This does not mean

Table A–2 Some Questions Frequently Asked by Interviewers

Why do you want to work for our company?
What kind of career do you have planned?
What have you learned in school to prepare you for a career?
What are some of the things you are looking for in a company?
How has your previous job experience prepared you for a career?
What are your strengths? Weaknesses?
Why did you attend this school?
What do you consider to be a worthwhile achievement of yours?
Are you a leader? Explain.
How do you plan to continue developing yourself?
Why did you select your major?
What can I tell you about my company?

to develop "pat" or formal answers, but to be ready to respond intelligently. The sincerity of the response and the intelligent organization of an answer must come through in the interview.

Most interviewers eventually get around to asking about your career plans. The purpose of asking these kinds of questions is to determine your reasonableness, maturity, motivation, and goals. The important point is to illustrate, by your response, that you have given serious thought to your career plans. An unrealistic, disorganized, or unprepared career plan is one way to fail in the interview. Interviewers consider a candidate immature if he or she seems to be still searching and basically confused.

At various points in the interview, it may be appropriate to ask questions. These questions should be important and should not be asked just to appear intelligent. If something is important in evaluating the company, ask the question. It is also valuable if you can ask a question that displays meaningfulness. But don't ask so many questions that the interviewer is answering one after the other. Some frequently asked questions are summarized in Table A–3.

Most interviews last between twenty and thirty minutes. It is best to close on a positive and concise note. Summarize your interests and express whether you are still interested in the company. Interviewers will close by stating that you will hear from the company. You may want to ask if he or she can give you an approximate idea of how long it will be before you hear from them. Typically, an organization will contact a candidate within four or five weeks after the interview.

One valuable practice to follow after the actual interview is to write down some of the points covered. List the interviewer's name, when the company will contact you, and your overall impression of the company. These notes can be useful if you are called for a later interview. Any person talking to ten or more companies usually has some trouble recalling the conversation if no notes are available.

One issue that may or may not come up during the interview is salary. Most companies pay a competitive starting wage. Therefore, it is really not that important to ask what your starting salary will be. Individuals with similar education, experience, and background are normally paid the same. Instead of asking about salary in the initial interview, do some checking in the placement office at your school or with friends working in similar jobs.

Table A–3 Some Questions Frequently Asked by Job Candidates

How is performance evaluated?
How much transfer from one location to another is there?
What is the company's promotion policy?
Does the company have development programs?
How much responsibility is a new employee given? Can you provide me with some examples?
What preferences are given to applicants with graduate degrees?
What type of image does the company have in the community?
What schools provide the bulk of managerial talent in the company?
What are the company's policies for paying for graduate study?
What social obligations would I have?
What community service obligations would I have?

Should you send a thank-you letter after the interview? This seems to be a good way to refresh the interviewer's memory. The follow-up letter should be short. Expressing your appreciation for the interview shows sincerity. It also provides an opportunity to state that you are still interested in the company.

Interviewers are important processors of information for the company, so it is important to impress them. Unfortunately, not every candidate can win (winning means that the candidate will be asked to visit the company or to undergo further interviewing). Why was I rejected? is a question everyone has to ask at some point. Table A–4 lists some of the reasons why candidates are not successful in an interview. It should also be noted that many times the candidate is not at fault at all. Bad luck or company circumstances may prevent the offer being made.

Visiting the Company and the Job Offer

If you are fortunate enough to be invited for a company visit, consider yourself successful. The letter of invitation or telephone message will specify some available dates. If you are still interested in the company, you must send a formal acceptance. Even if you are not interested in visiting, a short note thanking the company displays your courtesy.

In some cases, your visit will be coordinated by the interviewer you already met. However, it may be the personnel department or management development officer who handles the details. The important point is really not who will be coordinating, but that you must again prepare for a series of interviews. During this series, you should be asking specific questions about job duties, performance expectations, salary, fringe benefits, and career paths. It is at this phase of the career and employment decision process that you need specific information.

One of the main reasons for inviting candidates to visit the company is to introduce them to managers and the organization. These introductions will be brief, but they are important. It is reasonable to expect to meet five or more individuals during the company visit. In some cases, you will be given a tour of the plant, office, or laboratory. A wide array of people will be asked to comment on your employability

Table A–4 Some Reasons for Not Winning

Disorganized and not prepared
Sloppy appearance
Abrasive and overbearing
Unrealistic goals or image of oneself
Inability to communicate effectively
No interest shown in the type of company interviewed
Not alert
Poor grades
Only interested in money
Provided contradictory answers to questions

after you leave, so consider every interview important, and remember to act alert, organized, and interested. Many questions are repeated by different managers, but remember that sincerity and interest are variables that these managers will each be asked to comment on.

During the company visit, you will probably not be given a job offer. In most situations, a week or two weeks may pass before the company contacts you. If you are successful, you will receive a formal job offer. After receiving the offer, make an immediate acknowledgment. Thank the employer and indicate an approximate date when you will furnish a decision.

A Concluding Note

This Career Appendix has focused on planning. Self-assessment, awareness of marketing careers, seeking professional help, the job search, personalizing your job campaign, interviewing, and visiting companies all involve prior planning. The person who plans his or her campaign to find a worthwhile and satisfying job will be more successful than the disorganized person. Thus the most important principle in finding the best job for you is to work hard at planning each stage. Good luck.

Additional References on Business Careers

General Career Information

Career Development for the College Student, by Philip W. Dumphy (Carroll Press, 1981).

Careers in Marketing, by David W. Rosenthal and Michael A. Powell (Prentice-Hall, 1984).

Executive Résumé Handbook, by Harold W. Dickhut (Prentice-Hall, 1987).

What Color Is Your Parachute? A Practical Manual for Job Hunters and Career Changers, by Richard N. Bolles (Ten Speed Press, 1987).

Marketing

American Advertising Federation
1400 K St. N.W., Suite 1000
Washington, DC 20005

American Association of Advertising Agencies
200 Park Avenue
New York, NY 10017

American Marketing Association
250 S. Wacker Dr., Suite 200
Chicago, IL 60606

American Society of Transportation and Logistics
P.O. Box 33095
Louisville, KY 40232

Association of Industrial Advertisers
41 E. 42nd Street
New York, NY 10017

Bank Marketing Association
309 W. Washington St.
Chicago, IL 60606

Business/Professional Advertising Association
205 E. 42nd St.
New York, NY 10017

Direct Mail Advertising Association
230 Park Avenue
New York, NY 10017

Direct Marketing Association
6 E. 43rd St.
New York, NY 10017

Industrial Marketing Associates
520 Pleasant Street
St. Joseph, MI 49085

Marketing Research Association, Inc.
P.O. Box 1415
Grand Central Station
New York, NY 10017

National Association of Wholesalers Distributors
1725 K Street, N.W.
Washington, DC 20006

National Consumer Finance Association
1000 16th St., N.W.
Washington, DC 20036

National Retail Merchants Association
100 West 31st Street
New York, NY 10001

Sales and Marketing Executives
International Student Education Division
630 Third Avenue
New York, NY 10017

Women in Advertising and Marketing
4200 Wisconsin Ave., N.W., Suite 106–238
Washington, DC 20016

NOTES

1. From "S&MM Annual Survey of Executive Compensation—Part 2," *Sales & Marketing Management,* November 1988, pp. 46–54.

B

Financial Concepts for Marketing Analysis

This appendix explains some financial concepts and methods that are of special importance in analyzing marketing problems. It covers three topics: cost analysis for evaluating specific projects or expenditures, including so-called "break-even" analysis; operating statements; and analytical ratios based on financial statements.

Cost Analysis

Costs or expenses may be classified in many ways, as Chapter 18 shows. For analytical purposes, costs are customarily distinguished along the following lines: (1) total costs and unit costs and (2) variable, fixed, and discretionary costs.

Total Costs and Unit Costs

Total costs are all the costs associated with an activity. The total cost of manufacturing 1000 widgets is, say, $480. It is divided into the following cost categories:

Direct material	$180
Direct labor	210
Factory overhead	90
Total	$480

The *unit cost* of producing these 1000 widgets is $480 ÷ 1000, or 48 cents per unit. The direct-labor cost per unit is 21 cents, or $210 ÷ 1000.

Unit cost is often a convenient and more meaningful way of expressing costs. The total cost of a family reunion picnic may have been $150. But if it was attended by 100 people, it was only $1.50 per person (unit).

Variable, Fixed, and Discretionary Costs

Fixed costs (FC) are costs where the total amount remains unchanged during a given period of time or over a specified or relevant range of output. A store's annual rental payments of, say, $100 per month, are a fixed cost. If the store's sales in January are 100 units, and in February are 50, its rent is fixed at $100 in each of these months, although its rent per unit of sales rose from $1 in January to $2 in February.

Figure B–1 Fixed Costs and Relevant Range

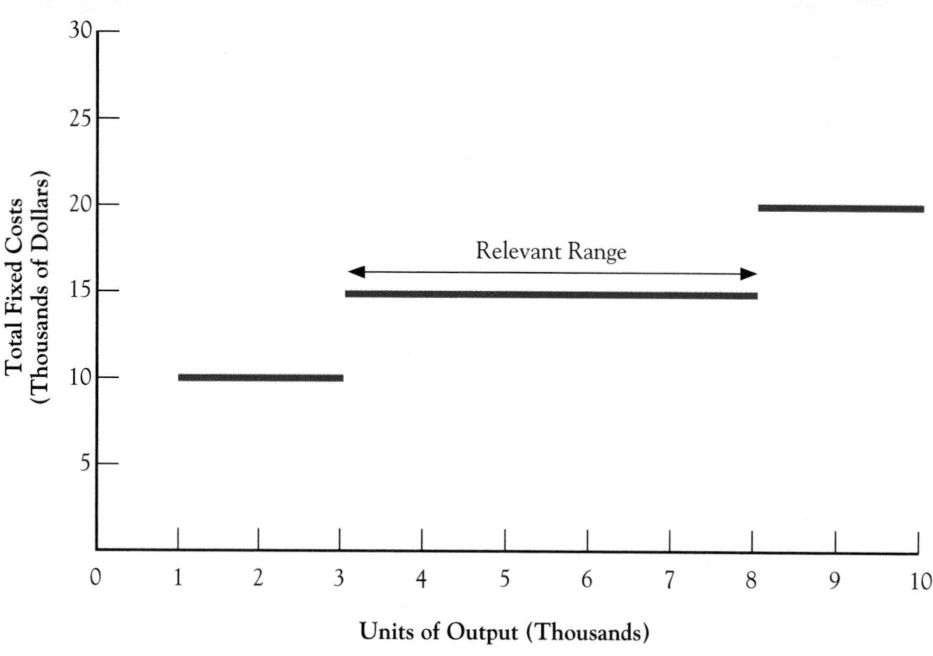

For a manufacturing plant, fixed costs generally include the depreciation and amortization of investment in machinery, most of the cost of a maintenance crew, most of the management and supervisory payroll, real estate taxes, depreciation on the building, and similar expenses. These are costs which remain unchanged over a fairly wide range of plant output and over a given period of time. This range of output is generally called the *relevant range.* In Figure B–1, fixed costs are $10,000 between 1000 and 2999 units of output, $15,000 between 3000 and 7999, and $25,000 between 8000 and 9999. The relevant range is between 3000 and 7999 if that is the output range within which the firm will most commonly operate. Although *total* fixed manufacturing costs may be low under 3000 units, *unit* fixed costs are relatively high in this range. Thus at 2999 output, unit fixed costs are $10,000 ÷ 2999 = $3.333. The lowest fixed costs per unit are at 7999 output: $15,000 ÷ 7999 = $1.885.

Variable costs (VC) are fixed *per unit* of output but vary in total amount directly with output. Suppose a toothpaste packager buys his empty tubes and bulk dentifrice at a total cost of 10 cents per tube. If he fills 10,000 tubes per day, his total materials costs will be $1000, or 10 cents per tube filled. If he produces 100,000, it will be $10,000, also 10 cents per unit. Thus a variable cost is generally uniform (or fixed) per unit, but fluctuates in total in direct proportion to change in total business. Figure B–2 shows this relationship.

Discretionary costs (DC) are costs which, unlike fixed or variable costs, arise mostly at the discretion of the management. Variable costs are caused by changes in output. Fixed costs are caused because a company has decided to go into business, but discretionary costs are different. Advertising expenditures are discretionary costs;

Figure B–2 Variable Cost Chart

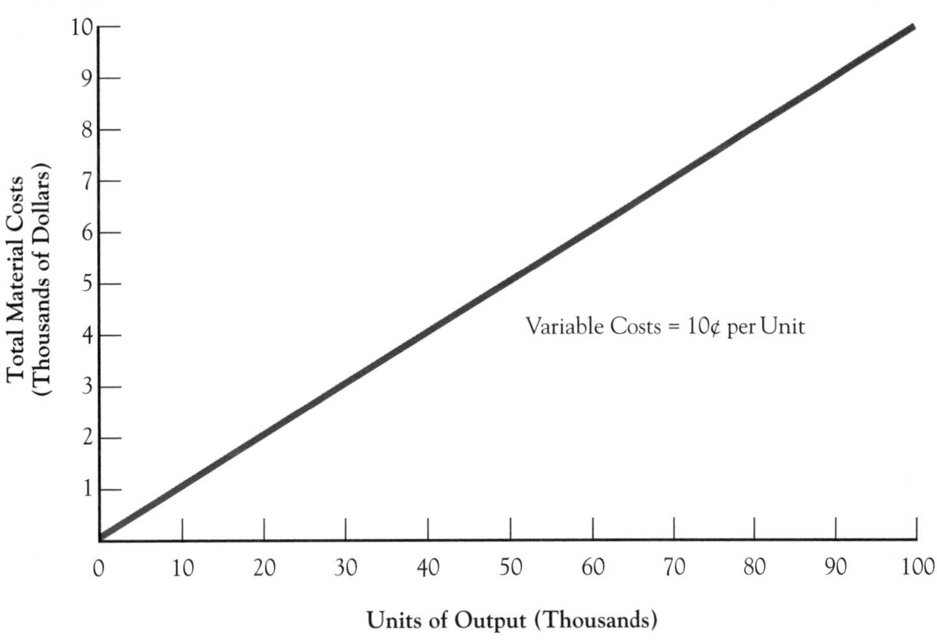

research and development expenditures are discretionary costs. They are distinguished by the fact that management *wants* to incur them. Instead of being caused by changes in production and sales volume, their object is to *cause* changes in sales volume. A company advertises more in order to sell more. Hence, although successful advertising expenditures may *seem* to be like variable costs in that they vary with output and sales, they are different in that they are causes of volume changes, not caused by volume changes.

Break-Even Analysis

Break-even analysis attempts to determine the volume of sales necessary (at various prices) for the manufacturer or merchant to cover his or her costs or to break even between revenue and costs. Break-even analysis is useful in a variety of ways: to help set prices, estimate profit or loss potentials, and to help determine the discretionary costs that should be incurred.

Our toothpaste packager had direct material costs of 10 cents per unit. Suppose that its other variable costs are 5 cents. Its total variable costs, therefore, would be 15 cents. Suppose that it had annual fixed costs of $50,000 and intended to sell the toothpaste to wholesalers for 20 cents. How many tubes must be sold to break even—that is, just exactly to cover all costs? The questions can be answered simply by using the following formula:

$$\text{Break-even units} = \frac{\text{fixed costs}}{\text{unit contribution}}$$

Figure B–3 Variable Cost

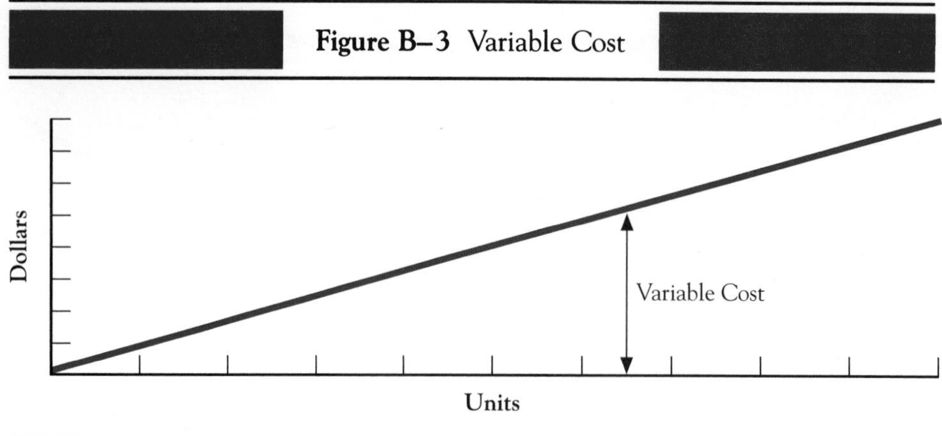

Unit contribution is the difference between unit selling price and unit variable cost:

$$\underset{(\$0.20)}{\text{Unit selling price}} - \underset{(\$0.15)}{\text{variable cost}} = \underset{(\$0.05)}{\text{unit contributions}}$$

The word *contribution* refers to what this difference (5 cents) contributes toward covering fixed costs and producing profits.

The break-even formula yields the following:

$$\text{Break-even units} = \frac{\$50{,}000}{\$0.05} = 1{,}000{,}000 \text{ tubes}$$

In other words, the toothpaste manufacturer must produce and sell 1 million tubes to break even.

This relationship between fixed costs, variable costs, revenues, and the break-even point can be shown graphically. Figure B–3 is a plot of total variable costs against units of output.

Figure B–4 plots total fixed costs against units of output. It is the relevant range cost segment of Figure B–1 stretched out to cover the full range of possible outputs. Thus, for the purposes of this illustration, we assume that fixed costs are constant over the whole range of possible outputs.

Figure B–4 Fixed Cost

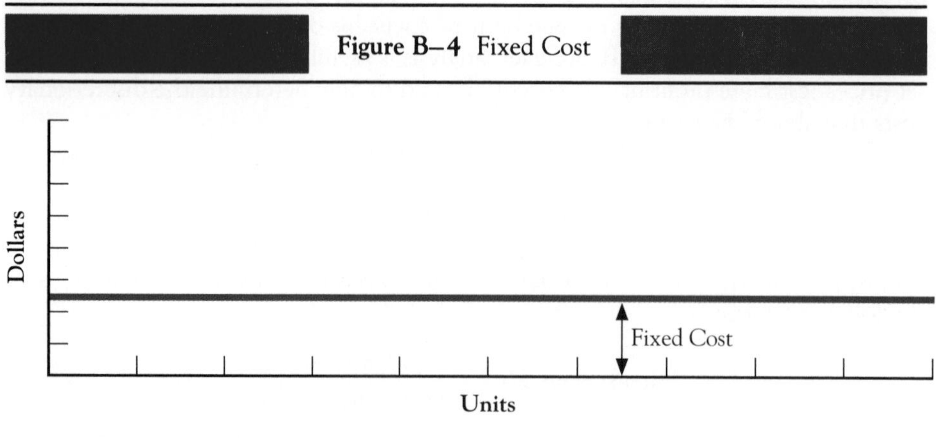

Figure B–5 Total Cost

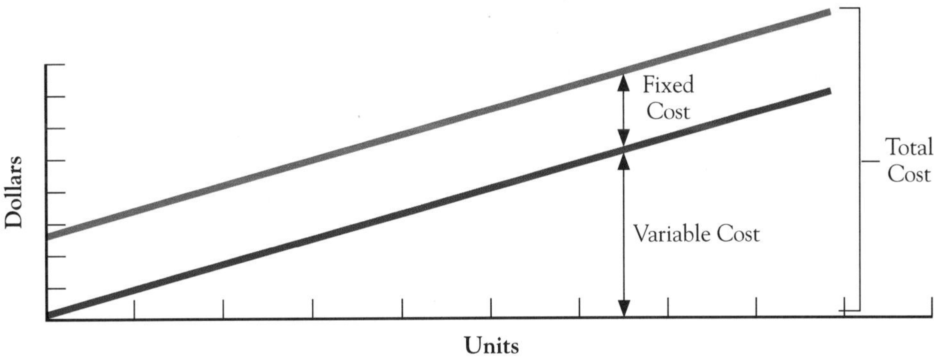

Figure B–5 above is merely the fixed cost of Figure B–4 added to the variable cost of Figure B–3. This gives a combined graph of total cost at various levels of output. (Discretionary costs are ignored for the moment.)

It is important to recognize that the break-even volume is strictly an arithmetic concept. It assumes that this volume is both produced *and sold.* In Figure B–6, if 1,300,000 units are produced, but only 900,000 are sold, the firm does not break even because no revenue has been received for the 400,000 unsold units for which production costs have been incurred. The total cost curve will lie above the total revenue curve.

The break-even logic can also be used to determine the volume of sales needed to yield a specific profit objective. Thus, the question might be, "At present prices (20 cents wholesale), what volume of sales is needed to earn a net profit of $30,000?"

Figure B–6 A Break-Even Chart

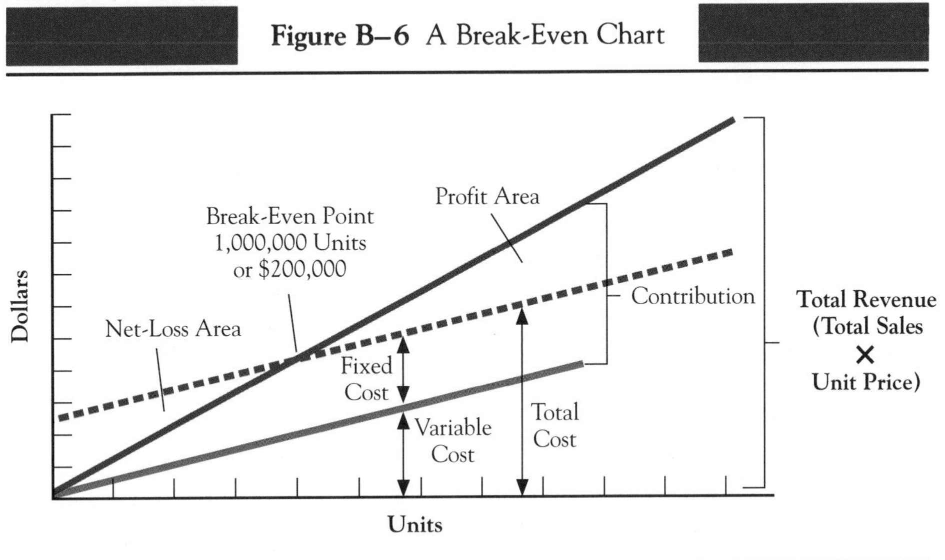

Using the break-even formula as a basis for answering this question, we get:

$$\text{Break-even units} = \frac{\text{fixed costs} + \$30{,}000}{\text{unit contribution}}$$

$$= \frac{\$80{,}000}{\$0.05}$$

$$= 1{,}600{,}000 \text{ units}$$

Proof: $1{,}600{,}000 \times \$0.20$	$= \$320{,}000$
$VC = 1{,}600{,}000 \times \$0.15 =$	$240{,}000$
Difference	$= \$\ 80{,}000$
FC	$= \ \ 50{,}000$
Net profit	$= \$\ 30{,}000$

Suppose that the question is, "What volume of sales do I need to yield a 10-percent profit; that is, a 10-percent profit on sales?" Using the break-even approach again, we get:

$$\text{Break-even units} = \frac{\text{fixed costs} + 10 \text{ percent } (\$0.20 \times \text{break-even units})}{\text{unit contribution}}$$

$$= \frac{\$50{,}000 + 0.10\,(\$0.20\ BE)}{\$0.05}$$

$$= \frac{\$50{,}000 + \$0.02\ BE}{\$0.05}$$

$$\$0.05\ BE = \$50{,}000 + \$0.02\ BE$$

$$\$0.03\ BE = \$50{,}000$$

$$BE = 1{,}666{,}666 \text{ units}$$

Proof: $1{,}666{,}666 \times \$0.20$	$= \$333{,}333$
$VC = 1{,}666{,}666 \times \$0.15 =$	$249{,}999$
Difference	$= \$\ 83{,}334$
FC	$= \ \ 50{,}000$
Net profit	$= \$\ 33{,}334$
$\frac{\$33{,}334}{\$333{,}333}$	$=$ 10-percent profit

The break-even formula is also useful in answering a variety of other questions, such as the following:

1. If fixed costs rise by x dollars and the price remains the same, how much sales increase is needed to break even?
2. If fixed costs rise by x dollars and unit sales remain the same, how much of a price increase is needed to break even?
3. With an expected variable cost increase of y cents per unit, how much of a sales increase is needed at the present price to yield an operating profit of $40,000?

With products that the seller believes may respond favorably to advertising and other promotional efforts, he or she may try to achieve sales expansion via advertising expenditures. Thus in Figure B–7 he or she adds discretionary advertising expendi-

Figure B–7 A Break-Even Chart Showing the Addition of a Discretionary Expenditure

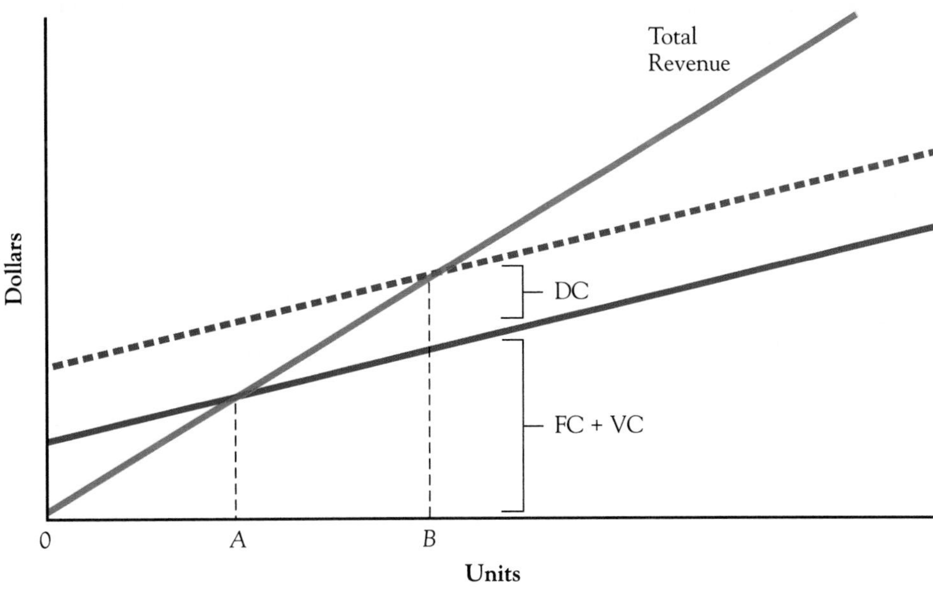

tures (DC) to the present total cost (FC + VC). With total costs now higher, he or she must either sell more to break even (raising sales from *OA* to *OB*) or raise his or her prices at the present volume. The advertising expenditure was made in the expectation that sales would rise in response to that expenditure. Examination of Figure B–7 shows *how much* sales must increase to justify the increased expenditure, and permits the analyst to estimate the profit consequences of different changes in sales volume that might follow from the advertising effort. It does not, of course, say anything about what sales result it would be reasonable to expect.

Costs and Marketing Strategy

It was pointed out earlier that fixed costs are actually not fixed over the entire range of output, but variable costs are also seldom as stable and linear as shown in the break-even chart. For example, if a recession occurs, management is likely to tighten controls and cut variable costs. During good times it may be indulgent and careless and allow variable costs to rise. When competitive activity is severe and sales are endangered, advertising and selling expenditures might be raised to stem the downturn and recoup sales losses, although, in practice, the reverse is frequently done in order to "conserve cash." When the latter is done, management's assumption is obviously that sales will not adequately respond to advertising.

The bigger the unit contribution, the more likely marketing management is to spend more on sales-building promotions. This is not only because it is more likely to have the resources to spend this way, but also because high unit contributions will produce large total profits if sales are high.

The relative sizes of fixed and variable costs are also important in their other effects on marketing strategy. A high variable-cost ratio, and, therefore, a low fixed-cost ratio, makes getting into an industry (that is, *entry*) relatively easier than when the ratios are reversed. This produces extremely competitive conditions in the industry. Good examples are the garment manufacturing industry and the restaurant business. Because the variable-cost ratio is high, nobody is likely to "win" the competition (that is, destroy the competitors) because of the willingness to charge substantially lower prices. The reason is that a high variable-cost ratio generally means that there are few economies of scale; that is, there is little or no high-volume, low-cost productivity that is facilitated by mass technology or mass selling. Higher volume sales do not produce proportionately lower unit costs with which to out-compete the competition. Prices will tend to be low, and where they are substantially above variable costs, they reflect the seller's other advantages such as, in the garment industry, good styling or workmanship, and, in the restaurant business, quality food, service, and entertainment.

A relatively high initial fixed-cost ratio will not only tend to limit the number of producers who will enter the industry but may offer an enormous profit potential. Thus our toothpaste packager, whose equipment could fill thousands of tubes an hour, broke even at 1,000,000 units of output. At 1,600,000 the packager had net profits of $30,000, but at 2,000,000 units, with only a 25-percent increase in output, profits would rise to $50,000 or 67 percent. This is one reason why the packager is more willing to spend money for advertising. It is also the reason why machine-produced consumer goods are more heavily advertised than handicrafted consumer goods. A rising volume of output is spread over fixed costs, and this reduces the average total cost per unit. The higher the fixed-cost ratio, the greater the benefits of full utilization of productive capacity.

Operating (or Profit and Loss) Statement

An operating, or profit and loss, statement is a financial summary of business operations during a period of time. It shows how the various elements of the operation contributed to the final outcome. Like cost analysis, it is one measure of the effectiveness of the firm.

A retailer's operating statement is composed of the following major elements:

$$\text{Sales} - \text{Cost of Goods Sold} = \text{Gross Margin}$$

$$\text{Gross Margin} - \text{Expenses} = \text{Profit}$$

Each element of the operating statement can be expressed as a ratio of sales, and these ratios can be compared with those of other retail outlets of like size and product line to appraise the relative effectiveness of a retailer. Various trade associations and trade publications regularly publish detailed operating statistics and ratios of department and specialty stores, retail food chains, and other types of retail and wholesale firms.

A retail operating statement is much more detailed than the above example. Table B–1 is typical. Since accounting statements are governed by conventions that tend to reflect the peculiarities of the industries or business functions they portray, such a statement requires some explanation.

1. *Gross sales* represent the total value of sales made during the period.
2. *Returns* are the value of credit or cash given to customers for merchandise purchased but subsequently returned. (This may be resold and the revenue of that sale then appears a second time under gross sales.)

Table B–1 Retail Operating Statement

Gross sales		$7,580,340
Returns and allowances		745,325
Net sales		$6,835,015
Beginning inventory	$ 810,055	
Purchases	4,225,017	
Inward transportation costs	55,013	
Gross cost of goods handled	$5,090,085	
Ending inventory	907,153	
Gross cost of goods sold	$4,182,932	
Cash discounts earned	251,192	
Cost of goods sold		3,931,740
Gross margin		$2,903,275
Expenses:		
Payroll	$ 998,765	
Supplies	83,073	
Repairs and maintenance	55,073	
Advertising	184,111	
Delivery	33,582	
Interest	43,700	
Pensions and insurance	129,709	
Depreciation	37,853	
Losses and bad debts	6,211	
Real estate costs	191,403	
Utilities	11,382	
Taxes (other than income taxes)	53,052	
Services purchased	58,491	
Miscellaneous	4,011	1,890,416
Operating profit		$1,012,859
Other income		61,511
Net profit before income taxes		$1,074,370

3. *Allowances* are the value of price adjustments that are given customers who have brought back defective or other merchandise. The adjustments generally keep the items from becoming returns.
4. *Net sales* are gross sales less returns and allowances. This represents the merchant's real volume of business out of which all expenses must be met.
5. *Cost of goods sold* is the cost to the merchant of the goods sold during the period. The merchant who has been in business before the year of the current statement will have started the year of the current statement with a carryover of last year's stock, that is, its *beginning inventory.*

When the cost of goods purchased during the year is added to the cost of transporting them into the establishment, the sum is gross cost of goods handled. Subtracting *ending* inventory at the close of the accounting period, the remainder is gross cost of goods sold.

The final net cost of goods sold is obtained by subtracting cash discounts earned from gross cost of goods sold. A cash discount is a reduction in the price of merchandise offered by a supplier for prompt payment. The reason for stating cash discounts earned separately as a subtraction from gross cost of goods rather than merely stating purchases at a lower figure is for control and analysis purposes. It shows how well the firm's financial management is capitalizing on a particular kind of profit or money-saving opportunity.

There is some difference among businesses about the treatment of these discounts—as merchandise discounts and, therefore, subtracted from gross cost of goods sold, or as *other income earned* and, therefore, added to operating profit. Most retail merchants use the former treatment.

While the net profit outcome is identical, treating it as *other income* results in a higher *cost of goods sold* and, therefore, a lower operating profit. Thus, in Table B–1, what would happen to *cost of goods sold* and *operating profit* if *cash discounts earned* were treated differently?

Variety in Operating Statements

Although the purposes, format, and analytical approaches of operating statements are broadly the same regardless of the type of business, there are some differences among those of retailers, wholesalers, and manufacturers, and differences among types of each of these. The statement in Table B–1 is typical of a medium-sized department store.

Analytical Ratios

A firm is interested not only in how much it sells and how much profit it makes but also in how efficiently various aspects of its operations are being managed compared with some previous time period or with other firms of a similar type and size. Such comparisons are facilitated by looking at various operating ratios or analytical ratios—that is, by stating certain elements of the operating statements as percentages of net sales. Commonly used analytical ratios are gross margin percentage, expense ratio, profit ratio, and markup.

In nearly all cases such ratios use *net sales* as the base. Thus in the operating statement of Table B–1:

$$\text{Gross margin} = \frac{\$2{,}903{,}275}{\$6{,}835{,}015} = 42.5 \text{ percent}$$

$$\text{Expense ratio} = \frac{\$1{,}890{,}416}{\$6{,}835{,}015} = 27.7 \text{ percent}$$

$$\text{Returns and allowances} = \frac{\$745{,}325}{\$6{,}835{,}015} = 10.9 \text{ percent}$$

Markup Computation

Markup is the amount by which the selling price of an item exceeds its cost to the seller. Thus an item which the merchant buys for 60 cents and sells for $1 has a markup (or markon) of 40 cents. For a manufacturer, markup is the difference between its fully allocated cost of producing the product and its selling price.

As pointed out earlier, operating or analytical ratios are generally expressed as percentages of net sales. In the preceding example, the markup percentage is $0.40/$1.00 = 40 percent. It is *not* $0.40/$0.60 = 66⅔ percent.

In ordinary business parlance the term *markup percentage* is generally shortened simply to markup. Hence the answer to the question "What is the markup on that $1 item?" is "40 percent." If there are no returns, allowances, or markdowns on the sale of that item, and no inward transportation costs, we would also say that its gross margin is 40 percent.

Many retailers use markup formulas in deciding how to price an item. Thus, in view of their expenses and profit objectives, retailers may have a standard practice of using a 50 percent markup for certain classes of furniture, 40 percent for men's suits, and 33⅓ percent for linens.

Suppose that the retailer buys a suit for $100 and uses a 40 percent markup formula. What will be the selling price? Not $140. Since the markup percentage is based on *selling* price, the retailer must price the suit such that the difference between that price and the cost is 40 percent. Therefore, to find the selling price of a $100 suit with a 40 percent markup, the merchant makes the following calculation:

Let

$$\begin{aligned} X &= \text{selling price} \\ \$100 &= \text{cost} \\ 40 \text{ percent} &= \text{markup} \end{aligned}$$

Therefore,

$$\begin{aligned} X &= \$100 + 0.4X \\ X - 0.4X &= \$100 \\ 0.6X &= \$100 \\ X &= 100 \div 0.6 \\ &= \$166.67 = \text{selling price} \end{aligned}$$

since

$$\text{Selling price} = \text{cost} + \text{markup}$$

and

$$\begin{aligned} \text{Markup} &= 40 \text{ percent of selling price} \\ \text{Cost} &= 60 \text{ percent of selling price} \end{aligned}$$

Hence given a desired markup, merchants find the selling price by dividing the dollar cost by the percentage cost—that is, the difference between 100 percent and the desired percentage markup. Therefore,

$$\begin{aligned} \text{Selling price} &= \frac{\text{cost}}{(100 \text{ percent} - \text{markup percent})} = \frac{\text{cost in \$}}{\text{cost in percent}} \\ &= \frac{\$100}{0.6} \\ &= \$166.67 \end{aligned}$$

Proof that $166.67 is a 40 percent markup:

$$\begin{aligned} \$166.67 &= \text{price} \\ -\ 100.00 &= \text{cost} \\ \hline \$\ 66.67 &= \text{margin} \\ \frac{\$\ 66.67}{\$166.67} &= 40 \text{ percent} \end{aligned}$$

If merchants know their selling price and markup and want to recall what their costs were, the reverse formula holds:

$$\begin{aligned} \text{Cost} &= \text{selling price} \times \text{cost percent} \\ &= \$166.67 \times 0.6 \\ &= \$100.00 \end{aligned}$$

To convert a markup expressed as a percentage of selling price into one expressed as a percentage of cost, the following formula applies:

$$\begin{aligned} \text{Markup percent on cost} &= \frac{\text{markup percent on price}}{\text{cost percent on price}} \\ &= \frac{40 \text{ percent}}{60 \text{ percent}} \\ &= 66^2/_3 \text{ percent} \end{aligned}$$

To convert a markup expressed as a percentage of cost into one expressed as a percentage of selling price, the following formula applies:

$$\begin{aligned} \text{Markup percent on price} &= \frac{\text{markup percent on cost}}{100 \text{ percent} + \text{markup percent on cost}} \\ &= \frac{66^2/_3 \text{ percent}}{166^2/_3 \text{ percent}} \\ &= 40 \text{ percent} \end{aligned}$$

Hence a 40 percent markup on selling price is equivalent to a 66⅔ percent markup on cost. A 33⅓ percent markup on selling price is equivalent to a 50 percent markup on cost.

Markdown Computation

A markdown is the amount by which a merchant reduces the original selling price of merchandise in order to sell it more easily. Clearance sales, for example, generally involve heavy markdowns.

Just as markup is computed on net selling price, so is markdown. If a merchant buys an item for 60 cents and prices it at $1, the markup is 40 percent. If the merchant subsequently reduces the price to 90 cents, there has been a 10-cent markdown. The percentage markdown is based on the *net* sales price, or 90 cents. Hence the markdown percent is $0.10/$.90 = 11.11 percent.

Markdowns do not appear on the operating statement, except for that portion which represents allowances made to customers who have already bought the item.

While regular markdowns do not appear on the operating statement, they are a significant measure of retail efficiency. All retailers *expect* to incur markdowns. The reason is that they must keep a relatively large inventory and assortment of all classes of goods, even toward the end of a regular buying season (say winter clothes during February), or run the risk of alienating and losing customers to stores that have a good selection at such times. At the end of February and early March, however, many people begin shopping for spring clothes. Hence, at some point the winter supply must be cleared out to make room for the spring supply. Markdown prices are one way to encourage people to buy this end-of-season stock.

Although markdowns are an expected part of retail life, maintaining the proper balance between adequate end-of-season stock and the markdown percentage is a sign of good management. Both high and low markdown percentages suggest some possible management shortcoming.

Most progressive merchants keep separate markdown records, broken down by departments. This is not only for control and evaluation purposes but also for pricing. The fact that markdowns must be incurred requires that this be taken into consideration in the original pricing of the product. Therefore, the amount of typical markdown usually has some effect on the size of the original markup. Hence, the initial markup generally exceeds the expected rate of gross margin.

The markdown percentage of a store or a store department is computed on total net sales of the store or department, not just on the marked-down goods themselves. Thus, if a department buys 50 dresses for $10 each and prices them to yield a markup of 33⅓ percent, its selling price will be $15. If it sells 40 at $15 and marks the remaining 10 down to $12 each and sells these, its gross sales will be

$$
\begin{aligned}
40 \times \$15 &= \$600 \\
10 \times \$12 &= 120 \\
\text{Gross sales} &= \$720
\end{aligned}
$$

If one of the $15 dresses is returned and then resold for $12, the final calculation will be

$$
\begin{aligned}
40 \times \$15 &= \$600 \\
11 \times \$12 &= \underline{132} \\
\text{Gross sales} &= \$732 \\
\text{Returns and allowances} &= \underline{15} \\
\text{Net sales} &= \$717 \\
\text{Markdown} = 11 \times (\$15 - \$12) &= 11 \times \$3 = \$33 \\
\text{Markdown percent} = \frac{\text{markdown, \$}}{\text{net sales, \$}} &= \frac{\$33}{\$717} = 4.6 \text{ percent}
\end{aligned}
$$

Stockturn

Stockturn refers to the number of times a store's average inventory is sold during a given period, generally a year. A common synonym of stockturn is *turnover.*

The stockturn rate may be computed in several ways:

1. by dividing the cost of goods sold by the average inventory at cost;
2. by dividing the net sales by the average inventory at selling price; or
3. by dividing the net sales in physical units by the average inventory in physical units.

Average inventory is computed as follows, using consistently throughout the calculation either cost, selling price, or physical units:

$$
\text{Average inventory} = \frac{\text{beginning inventory} + \text{ending inventory}}{2}
$$

Table B–2 Average Annual Stockturns

Line of Retail Trade	Average Number of Stockturns
Bakeries	18.7
Small Department Stores (under $250,000 annual volume)	2.5
Drugstores	3.9
Dry Goods and General Merchandising	2.4
Furniture Stores ($200,000–$300,000 annual volume)	2.5
Gasoline Service Stations	21.3
Grocery and Meat Stores	17.2
Meat Markets	53.3
Restaurants	35.5
Women's Ready-to-wear	4.1

What a "proper" stockturn rate is depends not only on the industry but also on the strategy of the company in question and on the particular department in the company. Thus, in a supermarket, the meat department's stockturn may be low at 30 times a year, but the canned food department's stockturn may be high at 15 times a year. A Dun and Bradstreet, Inc., study of average annual stockturns is shown in Table B–2.

Acknowledgments

Literary Credits

13 From "Curtis' Salon Selectives Shakes Haircare Market" by Laurie Freeman in *Advertising Age,* March 23, 1987. Copyright © 1987 by Crain Communications, Inc. All rights reserved. Reprinted by permission.
17 From "Dallas Readies Anti-Crime Ads." Reprinted with permission from the December 23, 1974 issue of *Advertising Age.* Copyright © 1974 by Crain Communications, Inc.
26–27 From "How Borden Milks Packaged Goods" by Bill Saporito in *Fortune,* December 21, 1987. Copyright © 1987 by Time Inc. Magazine Company. All rights reserved. Reprinted by permission.
56–57 From "The Yankee Samurai" by Geoffrey N. Smith in FORBES, July 14, 1986. Copyright © 1986 by Forbes Inc. Reprinted by permission.
73 "If Inflation Keeps Soaring" from *U.S. News & World Report,* October 15, 1979. Copyright © 1979 by U.S. News & World Report. Reprinted by permission.
104 "Who Buys New Cars?" from "New Car Buyers" by Jim Schwartz and Jim Stone in *American Demographics,* April 1987. Reprinted by permission.
110 "Aging Trends." Reprinted by permission of *American Demographics.*
114 From "An Analysis of Moviegoers by Life-Style Segments" by Glen Homan, Robert Cecil, and William Wells in *Advances in Consumer Research,* Vol. 2, 1975. Reprinted by permission.
114 From William D. Wells and George Gubar, "Life Cycle Concept in Marketing Research," *Journal of Marketing Research,* November 1966, p. 362. Reprinted by permission of the American Marketing Association.
121 From Joseph Plummer, "The Concept and Application of Life-Style Segmentation," *Journal of Marketing,* January 1974, pp. 33–37. Reprinted by permission of the American Marketing Association.
129 From "Ramada launches marketing program for older travelers," *Nation's Restaurant News,* November 23, 1983. Reprinted by permission.
130–131 From "Goya Crosses All the Borders" by Ellen Schultz in *Marketing and Media Decisions,* September 1986. Copyright © 1986 by C. C. Publishing. Reprinted by permission.
139 From "Shopping for Appliances: Consumers' Strategies and Patterns of Information Search" by William Wilkie and Peter R. Dickinson in *Marketing Science Institute Report,* November 1985. Reprinted by permission.
146 Adapted from *Consumer Behavior: Concepts and Applications* by David Loudon and Albert Della Bitta, p. 306. Copyright © 1979 McGraw-Hill Book Company. Reprinted by permission.
148 From "Trying to Make Beef Appetizing Again" by Edward C. Baig in *Fortune,* November 25, 1985. Copyright © 1985 by Time Inc. Magazine Company. All rights reserved. Reprinted by permission.
152 From "The Birth of U.S. Air" by Harry T. Chandis, *Marketing Communications,* April 1980, pp. 30–32. Reprinted by permission.
162–163 From "The Road Warriors" by Rebecca Fannin in *Marketing and Media Decisions,* March 1987. Copyright © 1987 by C. C. Publishing. Reprinted by permission.
174 "The 'Typical' U.S. Business" from *Sales and Marketing Management,* April 25, 1988. Copyright © 1988 by Bill Communications Inc. Reprinted by permission of Sales and Marketing Management.
175 From Thomas V. Bonoma and Robert Garda, *Marketing Manager's Handbook,* Second Revised Edition (Dartnell Corporation, 1983), p. 838. Reprinted by permission.
178 From "The Buying Center: Structure and Interaction Pattern" by Wesley Johnston and Thomas Bonoma, *Journal of Marketing* (Summer 1981), p. 147. Reprinted by permission of the American Marketing Association.
183 From "Profile of the Purchasing Pro: 1987" by Somberby Dowst in *Purchasing,* October 22, 1987. Reprinted by permission.
184 From "Purchasing Agents' Perceptions of Industrial Buying Center Influence: A Situational Approach" by Donald W. Jackson, Jr., Janet Keith, and Richard Burdick, *Journal of Marketing* (Fall 1984), p. 79. Reprinted by permission of the American Marketing Association.
190–191 From "How to Sell Airplanes, Boeing-Style" by Bill Kelley in *Sales and Marketing Management,* December 9, 1985. Copyright © 1985 by Bill Communications Inc. Reprinted by permission of Sales and Marketing Management.
192–193 From "Federal Express Faces Challenges to Its Grip on Overnight Delivery" by Larry Reibstein in *The Wall Street Journal,* January 8, 1988. Copyright © 1988 by Dow Jones & Company. Reprinted by permission of The Wall Street Journal. All rights reserved worldwide.
203 From "1988 Survey of Marketing Research" by Thomas C. Kinnear and Ann R. Root. Reprinted by permission of the American Marketing Association.
254 From "Marketing Seen as a Factor in Kid Drinking" by Diane Schneidman and "Senator Raps Spuds MacKenzie Promotion" from *Marketing News,* December 4, 1987. Reprinted by permission.
258–259 From "Sears Has Everything, Including a Messy Fight Over Ads in New York" by Robert Johnson and John Koten in *The Wall Street Journal,* June 28, 1988. Copyright © 1988 by Dow Jones & Company, Inc. Reprinted by permission of the Wall Street Journal. All rights reserved worldwide.
266 From "Electrifying" by Steve Weiner in *Forbes,* November 30, 1987. Copyright © 1987 by Forbes Inc. Adapted by permission.
278 "Name That Brand" by Edward C. Baig in *Fortune,* July 4, 1988. Copyright © 1988 by Time Inc. Magazine Company. All rights reserved. Reprinted by permission.
279 From "Brand Name Selection for Consumer Products" by J. McNeal and L. Zeren in *MSU Business Topics,* Spring 1981. Reprinted by permission.

286 "Betty Crocker: New and Improved" by Cathleen Toomey in *Public Relations Journal*, December 1986. Copyright © 1986 by the Public Relations Society of America. Reprinted by permission.
313 From *A Telling Look at the 25 Most Frequently Used Test Markets*, Vol. IV. Copyright © 1987 by Times Publishing Company. Reprinted by permission.
313 "Results of Simulated Test Markets" from "Buyouts Continue at Record Pace" by Jack Honomichl in *Advertising Age*, July 18, 1988. Copyright © 1988 by Crain Communications, Inc. All rights reserved. Reprinted by permission.
317 From "Museum Houses Shattered Dreams" by Sandra Salmans as appeared in *Chicago Tribune*, March 10, 1985. Reprinted by permission of the author.
351 From "Retailer Strategy and the Classification of Consumer Goods" by Louis P. Bucklin, *Journal of Marketing*, January 1983. Reprinted by permission of the American Marketing Association.
376 From "We Sell Service, Not Products" by Ruth Simon in *Forbes*, March 7, 1988. Copyright © 1988 by Forbes Inc. Adapted by permission.
399 From *Retailing Principles and Applications*, 2nd ed., by Dale M. Lewison and M. Wayne DeLozier. Copyright © 1986 by Merrill Publishing Company, Columbus, Ohio. Reprinted by permission.
402 From "Coping with Rapid Retail Evolutions" by Sylvia Kaufman in *Journal of Consumer Marketing*, Winter 1985. Reprinted by permission.
403 From "Marketing vs. Merchandising Mentalities in Retailing Management." Ronald W. Stampfl in *Proceedings of the American Marketing Association 1986*, edited by Joseph Guiltinan and Dale Achabal. Copyright © 1986 by the American Marketing Association. Reprinted by permission.
406 "The Ten Largest Retailers: 1988" from *Fortune*, June 5, 1989. Copyright © 1989 by Time Inc. Magazine Company. All rights reserved. Reprinted by permission.
409 From "Designs Expands Single-Vendor Concept" from *Chain Store Age Executive*, January, 1988. Copyright © 1988 by Lebhar-Friedman, Inc., 425 Park Ave., NY, NY 10022. Reprinted by permission.
414 From "Picking Power Center Tenant Mix" by Jane E. Primo in *Marketing News*, December 5, 1988. Reprinted by permission.
418 From "Mrs. Fields Automates the Way the Cookie Sells" from *Chain Store Age Executive*, April 1988. Copyright © 1988 by Lebhar-Friedman, Inc., 425 Park Ave., NY, NY 10022. Reprinted by permission.
419 From "How to Improve Your Information System" by A. Neal Gelter in *Cornell Hotel and Restaurant Administration Quarterly*, August 1985. Reprinted by permission.
452–453 From "Lotus 1-2-3: This Basic Software Isn't Just for Number Crunching Anymore" by Walter Weart in *Distribution*, February 1988. Copyright © 1988 by Chilton Publishing Company. Reprinted by permission.
454 From "How Top Companies View the Role of Computers" by Jack W. Farrell in Traffic Management, May 1988. Reprinted by permission.
459 From "Atlanta Goes International" by E. J. Muller in *Distribution*, May 1988. Copyright © 1988 by Chilton Publishing Company. Reprinted by permission.
468, 489 From *Promotional Strategy*, 6th ed., by James F. Engel, Martin R. Warshaw and Thomas C. Kinnear. Reprinted by permission of Richard D. Irwin.
491 From "Shift Gets Airborne Out of Holding Pattern" by Kurt Hoffman in *Advertising Age*, May 18, 1987. Copyright © 1987 by Crain Communications, Inc. All rights reserved. Reprinted by permission.
494 From "Carriers Vie for Corporate Segment's Numbers" by Richard Laermer in Advertising Age, March 23, 1987. Copyright © 1987 by Crain Communications, Inc. All rights reserved. Reprinted by permission.
495 From "Out of Sight—Yet Top-of-Mind" by George deLucenay Leon, *Marketing and Media Decisions*, Business to Business Special 1984. Reprinted by permission.
498 From "Underwear: Inspector 12 Takes on the Fruits" by Rebecca Fanin in *Marketing and Media Decisions*, April 1988. Copyright © 1988 by C. C. Publishing. Reprinted by permission.
499 "Advertising Expenditures: 1987" from *Advertising Age*, June 13, 1988. Copyright © 1988 by Crain Communications, Inc. All rights reserved. Reprinted by permission.
500 "The Top Ten National Advertisers: 1988" from *Advertising Age*, September 26, 1988. Copyright © 1988 by Crain Communications, Inc. All rights reserved. Reprinted by permission.
501 "Advertising to Sales Ratios for Selected Advertisers: 1987" from *Advertising Age*, September 28, 1988. Copyright © 1988 by Crain Communications, Inc. All rights reserved. Reprinted by permission.
502 "Advertising Budgets of Selected Brands: 1987" from *Marketing and Media Decisions*, July 1988. Copyright © 1988 by C. C. Publishing. Reprinted by permission.
521 "The Top Ten Advertising Agencies in World Billings and Income: 1987" from *Advertising Age*, March 30, 1988. Copyright © 1988 by Crain Communications, Inc. All rights reserved. Reprinted by permission.
530–533 From "Freezer Burn: Brand Report No. 155, Frozen Entrees" by Paula Schnorbus in *Marketing and Media Decisions*, September 1988. Copyright © 1988 by C. C. Publishing. Reprinted by permission.
551 From "A User's Guide to the Survey of Selling Costs" in *Sales and Marketing Management*, February 20, 1989. Copyright © 1989 by Bill Communications Inc. Reprinted by permission of Sales and Marketing Management.
554 From "Be Concerned with Quality, Not Quantity, of Sales Leads" by Christopher Stockwell in *Marketing News*, March 14, 1988. Reprinted by permission.
561 From *Sales Force Compensation—Dartnell's 24th Biennial Survey*. Copyright © 1988 by The Dartnell Corporation. Reprinted by permission.
608 From "Pumping Up for the Great California Gasoline War" by Liz Murphy in *Sales and Marketing Management*, April 2, 1984. Copyright © 1984 by Bill Communications Inc. Reprinted by permission of Sales and Marketing Management.
628 From "Value-Based Strategies for Industrial Products" by John L. Forbis and Nitin T. Mehta, *Business Horizons*, May 1981, p. 33. Reprinted by permission.
687 From "How to Design a Service" by G. Lynn Shostack in *European Journal of Marketing*, Vol. 16, No. 1, 1982. Reprinted by permission of MCB University Press Limited.
702 From "A Conceptual Model of Service Quality and Its Implications for Future Research" by A. Parasuraman, V. Zeithaml and L. Berry in *Journal of Marketing*, Fall 1985. Copyright © 1985 by American Marketing Association. Reprinted by permission.
706–707 Excerpted from "A New Day That Dawned for Days Inns" by L. Eric Elie in *The Atlanta Constitution*, February 7, 1989. Reprinted by permission.
716 From "Message Factors Finds Its Niche in the Music" by Mary Welch in *Atlanta Business Chronicle*, February 29, 1988. Reprinted by permission.
720 From "When the 'Client' is Human Life Itself" by Richard K. Manoff. Reprinted with permission from the August 22, 1983 issue of *Advertising Age*. Copyright © 1983 by Crain Communications, Inc.
726–727 From "Partners for Life" by Cecelia Reed in *Advertising Age*, November 9, 1988. Copyright © 1988 by Crain Communications, Inc. All rights reserved. Reprinted by permission.
728–729 From "Learning to Deploy a Strategic Weapon" by Janet Meyers in *Advertising Age*, November 9, 1988. Copyright © 1988 by Crain Communications, Inc. All rights reserved. Reprinted by permission.
737 "Top Ten Leading American Exporters, 1988" from "America's 50 Biggest Exporters" in *Fortune*, July 17, 1989. Copyright © 1989 The Time Inc. Magazine

Company. All rights reserved. Reprinted by permission.
739 "The Ten Largest American Multinationals" from "Hard Times in Any Language" in *Forbes,* July 4, 1983. Excerpted by permission.
739 "Ten Largest Non-American Multinational Corporations" from "The Foreign 500" in *Fortune,* July 31, 1989. Copyright © 1989 by Time Inc. Magazine Company. All rights reserved. Reprinted by permission.
753 From "The Selling of America" by Jaclyn Fierman in *Fortune,* May 23, 1988. Copyright © 1988 by Time Inc. Magazine Company. All rights reserved. Reprinted by permission.

Photo Credits

Unless otherwise acknowledged, all photos are the property of Scott, Foresman and Company. Page positions are as follows: (T)top, (C)center, (B)bottom, (L)left, (R)right, (INS)inset.

COVER
Cover illustration by Earl Gee, © Mark Anderson Design. Reprinted with permission of Mark Anderson Design and U.S. Sprint Communication Corporation.

xi Bob Daemmrich
xiii Milt & Joan Mann/Cameramann International, Ltd.
xv David Luttrell
xvii Steve Dunwell
xix Mike Mazzaschi/Stock Boston
xxi Deville/Photo News/Gamma-Liaison
xxiii Les Moore/Uniphoto
2 Steve Dunwell
14 Courtesy, Helene Curtis, Inc.
18 Courtesy, Michigan Travel and Tourism Bureaus, Lansing, Mi.
24 Courtesy, Anheuser-Busch, Inc., DDB Needham Worldwide Inc., Chicago
28 Chris Springman/PhotoFile
30 Courtesy, Merck & Co., Inc.
34 John Blaustein/Woodfin Camp & Associates
37 Mitch Kezar
40 Courtesy, Hewlett-Packard Company
43 Courtesy, BIC Corporation
50 Rob Kinmouth/©/Sports Illustrated for Kids
51 Courtesy, Pepperidge Farm® Inc.
56 Courtesy, CADEC Systems, Inc., Subsidiary of Cummins Engine Company
58 Courtesy, General Electric Corp.
60 Bob Daemmrich
62 NASA
74 Library of Congress
78 Hank Morgan/Rainbow
80 Kakokurita/Gamma-Liaison
88 © 1988, Courtesy Citicorp Citibank, N.A., a subsidiary of Citicorp.
93 Oscar Abolafia/Gamma-Liaison
94 © Frito-Lay, Inc. Printed with permission.
98 Leverett Bradley/After-Image
100 Courtesy, Campbell Soup Company
102L Courtesy, Canon, U.S.A., Inc., Consumer Products Division
102R Courtesy, Canon, U.S.A., Inc.
108 Maps from *The Clustering of America* by Michael J. Weiss. Copyright © 1988 by Michael Weiss. Reprinted by permission of Harper & Row Publishers, Inc., New York
116 Vic Huber/ALLSTOCK
117L Toyota Motor Sales U.S.A. Inc.
117R Courtesy, Lustrasilk Corporation of America
118 Courtesy, JC Penney
123 Gordon's Jewelers
130 Courtesy, Goya® Foods, Inc.
132 Milt & Joan Mann/Cameramann International, Ltd.
134 Ken Kerbs
137 Courtesy, © 1988 Sears Roebuck and Co.
140 Courtesy, © The Procter & Gamble Company
143L Countess Mara
143R Courtesy, Ford Motor Company
148 Courtesy, © 1988 Beef Industry Council and Beef Board
150 Michelin
152 Courtesy, US Air
155L Insight Magazine
155R Dr. Scholl's
162 Courtesy, Ford Motor Company
164 Steve Dunwell
168 Courtesy, Dictaphone Corporation, A Pitney Bowes Company
171 Courtesy, Mack Truck
174 Billy E. Barnes/Stock Boston
183 Courtesy, Dow Chemical Company
187 John Blaustein/McKesson Corporation
190 David R. Frazier Photolibrary
196 Courtesy, Colgate-Palmolive
209 Courtesy, Information Resources, Inc.
220 Courtesy, Beecham Products USA
226 Milt & Joan Mann/Cameramann International, Ltd.
228 © 1985, Schorr. Reprinted by permission, Los Angeles Times Syndicate.
230 Starlight/Roger Ressmeyer
232 Michael J. Pettypool/Uniphoto
260 Rob Nelson/Stock Boston
264 David Luttrell
266 Courtesy, Rayovac Corporation
273 © 1988 Sony Corporation of America, Courtesy, Geltzer Company, Inc.
274ALL Courtesy, The Procter & Gamble Company. Reprinted with permission.
281 Courtesy, LaMaur, Inc.
284 Courtesy, Ralston Purina Company
286 Jim Whitmer
292 Courtesy, FireKing International Incorporated.
294 Chip Carroon/ALLSTOCK
298 Courtesy, TYCO Toys, Inc., Moorestown, N.J.
303 Equipment shown in Honda advertisement are products of American Honda Motor Co., Inc. Advertising created by Dailey & Associates, Los Angeles, Ca.
304 Courtesy, Maytag Company
317 Bob Mahoney/Picture Group
328 Courtesy, Ford Motor Company
330 Mitch Kezar
334 Mitch Kezar
336 Swan Technologies
344 Courtesy, Home Shopping Club, Clearwater, Florida
347 Larry Lefever/Grant Heilman Photography
348 Gerd Ludwig/Woodfin Camp & Associates
350 Courtesy, Brown & Jenkins Trading Company
357 Courtesy, Target Stores
362 Milt & Joan Mann/Cameramann International, Ltd.
368 Mitch Kezar
369 Ken Kerbs
372 Lawrence Migdale
374 James Knowles/Stock Boston
380 Courtesy, Cub Foods
385 Cary Wolinsky/Stock Boston
392 Courtesy, Bergen Brunswig Drug Company
394 Louis Bencze/ALLSTOCK
396 Peter Turnley/Black Star
400 The Dallas Galleria, a Project of Gerald D. Hines Interests
409 © 1989 Designs, Inc. Reprinted with permission of Designs, Inc.
410 Benno Friedman
418 P. Casey Daley
422 Mike Abramson/Woodfin Camp & Associates
426 Courtesy, Fiesta Mart, Inc., Houston, Texas
428 Courtesy, Lands' End, Inc. Reprinted with permission.
430 Steve Dunwell
432 Mark Snyder/PhotoFile
449 Courtesy, Burlington Northern Railroad
451 Milt & Joan Mann/Cameramann International, Ltd.
458 Courtesy, SYSCD Corporation
459 Courtesy, Atlanta Tradeport Associates, A Joint Venture—Wilma Southeast, Inc., Mitsui & Co., U.S.A. Inc.
462 Mike Mazzaschi/Stock Boston
464 Courtesy, Black & Decker
473 Mystery® Guild
474 Courtesy BIC Corporation
479 Courtesy, Dow Corning Corporation, Original Sand Painting by John Kleber
487 McGraw-Hill Magazines
491 Courtesy, Airborne Express

494 Courtesy AT&T, Young & Rubicam New York
495 Courtesy, Barksdale Controls Division IMD Industries, Inc.
496 Wesley Frank/Woodfin Camp & Associates
503L Courtesy, American Dairy Association
503R Courtesy, American Cancer Society
511ALL Courtesy, General Motors Corporation, Oldsmobile Division
514 Courtesy, Pepperidge Farm, Inc.
515 Reprinted Courtesy of Eastman Kodak Company
516 Courtesy, Corning Glass Works
517 Qantas
518 Rolex Watch U.S.A., Inc.
523 Lawrence Migdale/Stock Boston
530 David R. Frazier Photolibrary
534 © Jacques Lowe
536 Steve Dunwell
538 Henley & Savage/The Stock Market
541 Courtesy, Boston Beer Company
543 Courtesy, The Fuller Brush Company
544 Courtesy, Best Kosher Sausage/Milt & Joan Mann/Cameramann International, Ltd. Company
561 Copyright 1988. Compiled from Sales Force Compensation—Dartnell's 24th Biennial Survey: The Dartnell Corporation 1988.
567 Milt & Joan Mann/Cameramann International, Ltd.
568 Courtesy, Hoffman Homes—Builder, Jess Smith—Photographer.
572 Deville/Photo News/Gamma-Liaison
574 Milt & Joan Mann/Cameramann International, Ltd.
577 Focus On Sports
579 © Wolfgang Kaehler
580 ISUZU
582 Courtesy, Lever Brothers Company
603 Courtesy, The Upjohn Company
604 Courtesy, General Motors Corporation, Buick Division
617 Courtesy, RCA, Thomson Consumer Electronics, Inc.
626 Eric Kroll/Taurus Photos, Inc.
643 Courtesy, Computer Vision/Milt & Joan Mann/Cameramann International, Ltd.
644 David R. Frazier Photolibrary
648 Les Moore/Uniphoto
650 DPI
652 Courtesy, KYTV
656 Courtesy, Ballard Medical Products
672 Stacy Pick/Uniphoto
684 Courtesy, Chick-fil-A, Inc.
686 John S. Abbott
688 The Portman
696 David R. Frazier Photolibrary
706 Courtesy, Days Inns of America, Inc.
708 Copyrighted, Chicago Tribune Company, all rights reserved, used with permission. Photo by John Bartley.
710 Courtesy, Harvey Mudd College
716 Courtesy, Jacksonville Symphony Orchestra
717 Courtesy, U.S. Postal Service
720 David Austen/Stock Boston
728 U.S. Army Photo
730 Al Satterwhite/The Image Bank
732 James Willis/TSW/Click Chicago
734 Donald Dietz/Stock Boston
735 Samsung Group
742 Forrest Anderson/Gamma-Liaison
757 David Forbert/Superstock/Shostal
762 Courtesy, McDonnell Douglas Corporation

Additional Credits

134 From "Advertisers Put Consumers on the Couch" by Ronald Alsop in *The Wall Street Journal,* May 13, 1988. Copyright © 1988 by Dow Jones & Company, Inc. Reprinted by permission of The Wall Street Journal. All rights reserved worldwide.
161 "A Baby Bell Gets Some Gray Hairs as Older-People Buyers' Guide Flops" by Mary L. Carnevale in *The Wall Street Journal,* May 16, 1989. Copyright © 1989 by Dow Jones & Company, Inc. Reprinted by permission of The Wall Street Journal. All rights reserved worldwide.
179, 180 From *Industrial Buying and Creative Marketing* by Patrick Robinson, Charles Faris, and Yoram Wind. Copyright © 1967 by Allyn and Bacon, Inc. Reprinted by permission of Jerry Wind.
296 From "A Look at Hasbro's 'Moondreamer' Dolls Shows Creating a Toy Isn't Child's Play" by Linda M. Watkins in *The Wall Street Journal,* December 29, 1986. Copyright © 1986 by Dow Jones & Company, Inc. Reprinted by permission of The Wall Street Journal. All rights reserved worldwide.
299 From "Car Makers Use 'Image' Map as Tool to Position Products" by John Koten in *The Wall Street Journal,* March 22, 1984. Copyright © 1984 by Dow Jones & Company, Inc. Reprinted by permission of The Wall Street Journal. All rights reserved worldwide.
700 "More Lawyers Reluctantly Adopt Strange New Practice—Marketing" by Patricia Bellew Gray in *The Wall Street Journal,* January 30, 1987. Copyright © 1987 by Dow Jones & Company, Inc. Reprinted by permission of The Wall Street Journal. All rights reserved worldwide.
718–719 "College Learns to Use Fine Art of Marketing" by Lawrence Ingrassia in *The Wall Street Journal,* February 23, 1981. Copyright © 1981 by Dow Jones & Company, Inc. Reprinted by permission of The Wall Street Journal. All rights reserved worldwide.

Name/Subject Index

Product/Company Index